Frommer's®

India

4th Edition

by Pippa de Bruyn, Dr. Keith Bain,
David Allardice & Shonar Joshi

WILEY

Wiley Publishing, Inc.

Published by:

WILEY PUBLISHING, INC.

111 River St.
Hoboken, NJ 07030-5774

ISBN 978-0-470-55610-8

Editor: Stephen Bassman
Production Editor: Jana M. Stefanciosa
Cartographer: Tim Lohnes
Photo Editor: Richard Fox
Production by Wiley Indianapolis Composition Services
Front cover photo: Women in conversation in Rajasthan, Mandawa ©Luciano Mortula / Alamy Images
Back cover photo: The Temple elephant gives a blessing at the Arunachaleswara Temple in Tiruvannamalai, Tamil Nadu ©David Pearson / Alamy Images

For information on our other products and services or to obtain technical support, please contact our Customer Care Department within the U.S. at 877/762-2974, outside the U.S. at 317/572-3993 or fax 317/572-4002.

Wiley also publishes its books in a variety of electronic formats. Some content that appears in print may not be available in electronic formats.

Manufactured in the United States of America

5   4   3   2   1

CONTENTS

INDIA

CONTENTS

8 TAMIL NADU: THE TEMPLE TOUR 313

9 KARNATAKA & HYDERABAD: KINGDOMS OF THE SOUTH 364

10 THE HEART OF INDIA: DELHI, THE TAJ, UTTAR PRADESH & MADHYA PRADESH 410

11 RAJASTHAN: LAND OF PRINCES 506

12 GUJARAT: INDIA'S ECLECTIC WILD WEST 593

13 HIGHER ALTITUDES, HIGHER POWERS: AMRITSAR, HIMACHAL PRADESH & LADAKH 603

14 UTTARAKHAND: SACRED SOURCE OF THE GANGES 666

15 KOLKATA (CALCUTTA) & EAST INDIA 689

16 FAST FACTS 735

INDEX 741

LIST OF MAPS

ACKNOWLEDGMENTS

Sincerest thanks to several individuals who assisted and contributed to updating sections of this book; they are: **Abhishek Madhukar** (Kerala, Rajasthan, and Varanasi), **Munira Rampurawala** (Mumbai, Goa, and Kumaon), **Jayati Vora** (dining and nightlife in Mumbai), **Yasmin Menon** (Chennai and Bangalore), and **André Morris** (Amritsar and Dharamsala); we'd also like to give a special mention to **Abishek Madhukar** and **John Thomas.**

HOW TO CONTACT US

In researching this book, we discovered many wonderful places—hotels, restaurants, shops, and more. We're sure you'll find others. Please tell us about them, so we can share the information with your fellow travelers in upcoming editions. If you were disappointed with a recommendation, we'd love to know that, too. Please write to:

Frommer's India, 4th Edition
Wiley Publishing, Inc. • 111 River St. • Hoboken, NJ 07030-5774

AN ADDITIONAL NOTE

Please be advised that travel information is subject to change at any time—and this is especially true of prices. We therefore suggest that you write or call ahead for confirmation when making your travel plans. The authors, editors, and publisher cannot be held responsible for the experiences of readers while traveling. Your safety is important to us, however, so we encourage you to stay alert and be aware of your surroundings. Keep a close eye on cameras, purses, and wallets, all favorite targets of thieves and pickpockets.

ABOUT THE AUTHORS

Pippa de Bruyn is an award-winning journalist, travel writer (author of *Frommer's South Africa*), and freelance editor.

Dr. Keith Bain has a doctoral degree in cinema. When he's not traveling the world in search of fantastic experiences, he spends his time writing and lecturing about film, media, theater, and contemporary culture.

David Allardice is a lawyer with a degree in History as well as a freelance writer and editor. He was born in Durban, South Africa, and also contributes to *Frommer's South Africa*. When he's not backpacking through Asia, he lives in Cape Town.

Shonar Joshi is a writer by profession and explorer by heart. She has dabbled with environmental television reporting, filmmaking, script writing, farming, and traveling—mostly in India, Nepal, and Sri Lanka. Her book *Of Past Dawns and Future Noons* is a testament to the passion with which she regards India and its rich ancient past, present, and future.

FROMMER'S STAR RATINGS, ICONS & ABBREVIATIONS

Every hotel, restaurant, and attraction listing in this guide has been ranked for quality, value, service, amenities, and special features using a **star-rating system.** In country, state, and regional guides, we also rate towns and regions to help you narrow down your choices and budget your time accordingly. Hotels and restaurants are rated on a scale of zero (recommended) to three stars (exceptional). Attractions, shopping, nightlife, towns, and regions are rated according to the following scale: zero stars (recommended), one star (highly recommended), two stars (very highly recommended), and three stars (must-see).

In addition to the star-rating system, we also use **eight feature icons** that point you to the great deals, in-the-know advice, and unique experiences that separate travelers from tourists. Throughout the book, look for:

Finds	Special finds—those places only insiders know about
Fun Facts	Fun facts—details that make travelers more informed and their trips more fun
Kids	Best bets for kids and advice for the whole family
Moments	Special moments—those experiences that memories are made of
Overrated	Places or experiences not worth your time or money
Tips	Insider tips—great ways to save time and money
Value	Great values—where to get the best deals
Warning!	Warning—traveler's advisories are usually in effect

The following **abbreviations** are used for credit cards:

AE American Express	**DISC** Discover	**V** Visa	
DC Diners Club	**MC** MasterCard		

TRAVEL RESOURCES AT FROMMERS.COM

Frommer's travel resources don't end with this guide. Frommer's website, **www.frommers. com**, has travel information on more than 4,000 destinations. We update features regularly, giving you access to the most current trip-planning information and the best airfare, lodging, and car-rental bargains. You can also listen to podcasts, connect with other Frommers.com members through our active-reader forums, share your travel photos, read blogs from guidebook editors and fellow travelers, and much more.

The Best of India

India will humble, awe, frustrate, amaze, inspire, and intimidate you—all on the same day. Home to some of the world's most spectacular medieval structures and largest slums; sacred rivers and filth-strewn streets; deeply religious ritual and endless traffic jams; aristocratic tigers and low-caste untouchables; jewel-encrusted tombs and pavement-bound beggars; ancient traditions and modern-day scams—there is so much to take in. Whether you're here to soak up India's spirituality, chill out on the beaches, or live like a king in the land of princes, this chapter will help you experience the very best India has to offer.

1 EXPERIENCING SPIRITUAL INDIA

Visiting temples that pulsate with devotion will evoke a sense of the sacred, but in India, where religion is such an integral part of daily life, spiritual experiences occur when you least expect them.

- **See Things as They Really Are** (Vipassana Centers throughout India): Maintaining a strict code of silence with no sensory stimulation for 10 days may sound like a self-induced hell, but after attending a 10-day Vipassana meditation course, most people claim transformation and find the mental training invaluable. And it costs nothing. See chapter 3.

- **Witness the Miracle of Hope** (Mumbai): Set to become the world's most populous city within the next few years, India's economic capital is a heady, seething megalopolis, loved and loathed in equal measure. It's also a beacon of hope and promises of a better life for millions of people. Some achieve god-like status as Bollywood superstars, but the vast majority struggle by, ever-hopeful of achieving the type of miraculous success that's seldom seen in real life. You'll see the poor and dispossessed everywhere in India, but in Mumbai, a tour through Dharavi, Asia's largest shantytown and setting for Oscar-winning *Slumdog Millionaire,* will show you a culture of dogged hope and aspiration that will melt even the coldest heart. See chapter 5.

- **Become the Buddha That You Already Are** (Osho International Meditation Resort, Pune, Maharashtra): Attracting controversy for most of his life, the radical, capricious 20th-century mystic Bhagwan Rajneesh—aka Osho—rejected religion, opposed existing social order, and spoke out strongly in favor of independent action that, with disciplined and rigorous meditation, would lead to enlightenment. His teachings form the basis of programs at numerous Osho centers around the world, but his original commune in Pune (not far from Mumbai) has been transformed not into an ashram, but into a campus of beautiful gardens, pyramidal meditation halls, and elegant spaces that include an ultra-Zen guesthouse, cafes, and a huge swimming pool. You'll understand immediately why Osho was known as the rich man's guru, and given enough time here—cloaked in a maroon robe and attending meditational gatherings that many outsiders have labeled as secretive, cultlike, and mysterious, you'll soon discover your inner Buddha. See "Pune and the Osho International Meditation Resort" in chapter 5.

- **Hop on a Motorbike and Head for the Drumbeat** (Goa): Once capital of the global beach party, Goa may be past its prime, but when rumors start that an event is in the making at a to-be-announced venue, keep your ear to the ground. Why? Because only in some deserted clearing near a golden Goan beach can you trance out with the nationals of the world, and find solace in the serenity of a rural villager's smile as she hands over cups of soothing *chai* for the duration of the party. See chapter 6.

- **Leave Your World Behind as You Cleanse Body and Soul** (Kalari Kovilakom, Kerala): Ayurvedic philosophy preaches that your body is a temple and at Kalari Kovilakom, a palace-turned-Ayurvedic hospital that miraculously combines five-star heritage accommodations with the ambience and discipline of an ashram, you'll be compelled to devote all your time and energy towards rejuvenating your physical being and recharging your spiritual energies. Established by India's leading eco-conscious hotel group, CGH Earth, this is the most upmarket health retreat in the country, with daily consultations and treatments by dedicated, highly qualified Ayurvedic doctors, regular yoga classes, meditation sessions, individualized healthful diets, and a regime of personal disciplines designed to help you align body and mind. See chapter 7.

- **Worship the Sunrise as It Touches the Southernmost Tip** (Kanyakumari, Tamil Nadu): You can't help but be moved by a sense of the miraculous when a simple daily occurrence is venerated by thousands of pilgrims who plunge themselves into the turbulent swell, believing that the tri-oceanic waters at India's southernmost tip are holy, while others delight in the glorious spectacle as if it's a Bollywood (the nickname for India's booming film industry) premiere. See chapter 8.

- **Lose All Sense of Reality in the City of Light** (Varanasi, Uttar Pradesh): Drifting at dawn on a boat on the Ganges along Varanasi's bathing *ghats* (steps leading down to the river), against a backdrop of 18th- and 19th-century temples and palaces, you will witness surreal sights—hundreds of pilgrims waist-deep in the Ganges cleansing their souls in its holy waters, while others pound laundry, meditate by staring into the sun, or limber up to wrestle. All the while, bodies burn on the sacred banks, thereby achieving *moksha*—liberation from the eternal cycle of rebirth. See chapter 10.

- **Reach a Spiritual High on Top of the Holiest Jain Mountain at Shatrunjaya** (Palitana, Gujarat). As you puff your way up the seemingly infinite steps winding their way up into the misty, lush forest, you may feel as though you'll never make it down again—or, if you do, it'll be as a different person. The holy Jain mount of Shatrunjaya has over 900 beautiful temples (most in mint condition), coupled with sweeping views of the surrounding countryside, the Gulf of Cambay, and the Shatrunjaya mountains and river flowing through the verdant hills behind. Even if you're a firm non-believer, your heart will be won over. See chapter 12.

- **Make a Wish at the Tomb of a Sufi Saint** (Ajmer, Rajasthan): The great Sufi saint Khwaja Moin-ud-Din Chisti was known as "the protector of the poor," and his tomb is said to possess the power to grant the wishes of all those who visit. His Dargah Sharif is the most sacred Islamic shrine in India, second in importance only to Mecca but frequented by

Hindus and Muslims alike. The atmosphere of pure devotion is both ancient and surreal; some pray fervently, and others tie threads onto the latticework while supplicating the saint to fulfill their wish, while throughout these activities, the *qawwali* singers seated in front of the tomb repeat the same beautiful, haunting melodies that have been sung for centuries. See chapter 11.

- **Carry the Holy *Granth Sahib* to Its Evening Resting Place** (Amritsar, Punjab): In Sikh temples, the *Granth Sahib*—Holy Book of the Sikhs—is an object of devotion in its own right, and nowhere is this more evocative than at the Golden Temple, the most tangibly spiritual destination in the country. In the evenings men line up to carry the precious *Granth Sahib* from its golden sanctuary at the center of the Amrit Sarovar (Pool of Nectar), crossing **Guru's Bridge,** which symbolizes the journey of the soul after death, to **Akal Takht,** where the Holy Book rests for the night. Men can take part in this ceremony by joining the line that forms behind and ahead of the heavy palanquin. Being part of this ancient tradition is a deeply moving experience and indicative of the embracing atmosphere you'll find in Sikh temples throughout India. See chapter 13.

- **Look into the Eyes of the Dalai Lama** (Dharamsala, Himachal Pradesh): There's a good chance you'll meet the Dalai Lama in person if you visit Dharamsala, home to the exiled Tibetan government, which fled its homeland in 1959. Arranging a private audience isn't easy (unless you're Richard Gere), but if you attend one of his public appearances, you will—like everyone else in the audience—receive a personal blessing. And whatever your convictions, when you look into the eyes of His Holiness, you know you are in the presence of pure love. See chapter 13.

- **Witness a Thousand Prayers Take Flight on the Wind** (Leh, Ladakh): Take the overland journey from Manali to Leh and enter the stark world of the Trans-Himalayas—a breathtakingly beautiful yet desolate lunarlike landscape, with arid peaks and ancient Buddhist monasteries perched on rocky crags. Here prayer flags flutter against an impossibly blue sky, sending their silent prayers to the heavens. See chapter 13.

- **Clapping Along during Evening *Aarti* as the Faithful Give Thanks to the Ganges** (Rishikesh, Uttarakhand): By day, Rishikesh is a spiritual Disneyland, where the commercial excesses of packaged meditation and two-for-one tantric yoga hang heavily about the concrete ashrams, bedecked with gaudy statues of Vishnu and Shiva. But at night, to the accompaniment of hypnotic prayers and harmonious singing, the town undergoes a magical transformation. Head for the Parmarth Niketan Ashram Ghat and feel yourself seduced by the divine rhythms during **Ganga Aarti,** when devotees gather to sing their praises at the edge of the Ganges River. See chapter 14.

2 THE BEST TEMPLES, MONUMENTS & LOST CITIES

- **Cave Temples at Ajanta & Ellora** (near Aurangabad, Maharashtra): Fashioned out of rock by little more than simple hand-held tools, the cave temples at Ajanta (created by Buddhist monks btw. the 2nd and 7th c.) and Ellora (a marriage of Buddhist, Hindu, and Jain temples, created btw. the 4th and 9th c.) are the finest examples of rock-cut architecture in India, and deserving of their World Heritage status. The zenith is **Kailashnath Temple,** effectively a mountain whittled down to a free-standing temple. See "Aurangabad & the Ellora and Ajanta Caves" in chapter 5.

- **Lord Gomateswara Monolith** (Sravanabelagola, Karnataka): One of the oldest (ca. A.D. 918) and most important Jain pilgrimage sites, this 18m (59-ft.) statue of the naked Lord Gomateswara—a representation of Bahubali, son of the first Jain *tirthankara,* said to have sought enlightenment by standing naked and motionless for an entire year—is the tallest monolithic statue on earth. See "Exploring the Hoysala Heartland: Belur, Halebid & Sravanabelagola" in chapter 9.

- **Hampi** (Karnataka): Scattered among the Henri Moore–like boulders in the heart of Karnataka's rural interior, Hampi was once the royal seat of the powerful Vijayanagar kingdom, its size and wealth drawing comparisons with imperial Rome. Today, the city has crumbled away to a few starkly beautiful leftovers, but the remote setting couldn't be more romantic. See "Hampi & the Ruined City of Vijayanagar" in chapter 9.

- **Shri Meenakshi-Sundareshwarar Temple** (Madurai, Tamil Nadu): Alive with prayers, processions, garland-makers, and joyous devotees who celebrate the mythological romance between the beautiful three-breasted goddess and her mighty Lord Shiva, this colorful and lively complex of shrines, halls, and market stalls is almost Disneyesque, marked as it is by numerous entrance towers tangled with colorful stucco gods, demons, beasts, and mythological heroes. It truly embodies the spirit of Tamil Nadu's deeply embedded temple culture. See "Madurai" in chapter 8.

- **Taj Mahal** (Agra, Uttar Pradesh): Nothing can prepare you for the beauty of the Taj. The perfect symmetry, the ethereal luminescence, the wonderful proportions, the sheer scale—virtually impossible to imagine from staring at its oft-reproduced image—and the exquisite detailing make this bejeweled monument to love a justifiable wonder of the world. See p. 456.

- **Fatehpur Sikri** (near Agra, Uttar Pradesh): From the intricacy of the glittering white marble screens that surround the *dargah* (tomb) of Salim Chisti, to Parcheesi Court, where the emperor played a ludolike game using the ladies of his harem as live pieces, this magnificent ghost city—built almost entirely from red sandstone in 1571 and deserted only 14 years later—is a testament to the secular vision of Akbar, one of the great players in India's most dynamic dynasty. See p. 459.

- **The Temples of Khajuraho** (Khajuraho, Madhya Pradesh): Built between the 10th and 12th centuries by the Chandela Rajputs, these World Heritage Site monuments are most famous for the erotic sculptures that writhe across the interiors and exteriors. But even the temple designs—their soaring *shikharas* (spires) serving as metaphoric "stairways to heaven"—are striking, and are considered the apotheosis of medieval Hindu architecture. See "Khajuraho" in chapter 10.

- **Mehrangarh Fort** (Jodhpur, Rajasthan): The impenetrable walls of this 15th-century edifice to Rajput valor rise seamlessly from the rocky outcrop on which they were built, literally dwarfing the labyrinthine city at its base; from its crenelated ramparts you enjoy postcard views of the "Blue City" below. In the distance is the grand silhouette of Umaid Bhawan Palace, heritage hotel and residence of the current maharaja.

Within the fort is one of the best palace museums in India. See p. 577.

- **Jain Temples of Rajasthan** (Ranakpur and Mount Abu, near Udaipur, Rajasthan): The Jains put all their devotional passion (and not inconsiderable wealth) into the creation of the most ornate marble temples; with exquisitely detailed relief carvings covering every inch, they are all jaw-droppingly beautiful. Make sure you visit at least one while you're in India, preferably either Ranakpur Temple or Dilwara Temple in Rajasthan. See p. 563.

- **Kumbhalgarh Fort** (near Udaipur, Aravalli Hills, Rajasthan): Protected by impenetrable bastions and a towering perimeter wall which is the second most visible object from space, this 15th-century rambling hilltop fort was only besieged once by Akbar when he poisoned the water supply. Steeped in history and well preserved, march to the top and survey the beautiful Aravalli countryside and the Kumbhalgarh Wildlife Sanctuary that surrounds you. See p. 563.

- **Golden Temple** (Amritsar, Punjab): Arguably the greatest spiritual monument in India. The name derives from the central gold plated Hari Mandir—the inner sanctuary featuring gold-plated copper cupolas and white marble walls inlaid with precious stones—which sits at the center of the "Pool of Nectar."

Every day thousands of disciplined devotees pay their respects, touching their heads to the glistening marble floor while singing devotional songs continuously—a wonderful, welcoming, and humbling experience. See "Amritsar & the Golden Temple" in p. 607.

- **Tabo** (Spiti Valley, Himachal Pradesh): This 1,005-year-old Buddhist complex houses magnificent frescoes and brilliant stucco and relief figures that recount ancient myths and celebrate the deities and demons that make up the Buddhist pantheon. You'll need a flashlight to adequately explore the dark, smoldering halls and shrines lit only by thin shafts of natural light, and brought to life by the resonant chants and ringing of bells by the monks and nuns who populate this sacred center of Tibetan Buddhism. See "Exploring Kinnaur & Spiti" in chapter 13.

- **The Sun Temple at Konark** (near Bhubaneswar, Orissa): An enormous war chariot carved from a massive chunk of rock during the 13th century, this masterpiece of Indian temple art is covered with detailed sculpted scenes, from the erotic to the mythological. Guarded by stone elephants and lions, the immense structure is seen as the gigantic chariot of the sun god emerging from the ocean, not far from Orissa's 500km (310-mile) beach. See "Orissa's Golden Temple Triangle" in p. 718.

3 UNIQUE PLACES TO STAY

Not surprisingly, most of these are in Rajasthan, which has almost 80 heritage properties—castles, palaces, forts, and ornate *havelis* (traditional mansions), now hotels offering varying degrees of comfort.

- **Taj Mahal Palace** (Mumbai): George Bernard Shaw famously claimed that after staying here, he no longer had any need to visit the real Taj Mahal in Agra. Built just over a century ago by an Indian industrialist after he was treated abominably by the colonial snobs at the city's then leading hotel (since demolished), the Taj Mahal Palace was recently reopened after a year of renovations following the 2008 terrorist attacks in Mumbai—it continues to host the world's rich and famous, and remains the most celebrated address in Mumbai. See p. 135.

- **Boutique Getaways in Goa:** Parisian fashion stylist Claudia Derain and her husband, Hari Ajwani, came to Goa on vacation and—like so many—never left. Together with Goan architect Dean D'Cruz, they've created an *Arabian Nights* fantasy in **Nilaya Hermitage,** with only 12 "cosmic-themed" guest suites and gorgeously informal public spaces overlooking paddy fields and coconut-palm groves. Derain and Ajwani are also responsible for the superbly located, beautifully renovated **Fort Tiracol,** a seven-room "hotel" that locates you at the northernmost tip of Goa with only a small, undiscovered village and spectacular views for company. But if you'd prefer the atmosphere of a homey, intimate, and delightfully designed guesthouse set in a village not too far from a gorgeous beach, then head south and kick back at Simon Haywood's **Vivenda dos Palhaços** ("House of Clowns") in Majorda—a place of simple-yet-sumptuous enchantment where you set the rhythm. See chapter 6.

- **Fabulous Beachfront Villas in Goa:** As Goa catches a wake-up call and rediscovers that the neo-hippies are arriving in an altogether more sophisticated avatar, the recent trend has been towards creating wonderful self-sufficient hideaways where you call the shots and there's no chance of fellow guests disturbing the peace or gate crashing your party—which, of course, you're welcome to throw. There are a few special villas to choose from but amongst our favorites are the ultra-luxurious **Aashyana Lakhanpal;** the back-to-basics toes-in-the-sand **Elsewhere…;** and **The Hobbit,** a fashionably quirky rustic chic "house" built into the rocks

and furnished with most modern conveniences. See p. 202, 202, and 203.

- **Adrift aboard *Discovery*** (Kerala): The best way to experience Kerala's backwaters is floating along on a traditional *kettuvallam* (houseboat), but the stylish Malabar Group has upped the ante with *Discovery,* a funky modern interpretation of the Keralan houseboat concept. Accommodations comprise a comfortable and stylish bedroom with well-plumbed en-suite bathroom, separate lounge (can double as a second bedroom), and a rooftop deck (furnished with dining table and loungers) where you can while away the day, looked after by a dedicated staff of three, including a private chef. The packages can include a night at the aptly named **Privacy,** our favorite backwaters villa. See p. 269.

- **Gracious Keralan Homestays** (Olavipe, Backwaters): Experience life on a working plantation, then dine on exquisite home-cooked meals at the family dining table, personally hosted by urbane, charming owners—that's what the best homestays are all about. It's like finding yourself at a private house party, where you are the guest of honor. Our top pick is **Olavipe,** a stately home on an island in the backwaters, where Anthony and Rema provide the warmest welcome this side of Fort Kochi, ensuring that you leave replenished and heartsick to leave. See p. 272.

- **Green Lagoon** (Backwaters, Kerala): Not only do you get a reconstructed Keralite villa all to yourself, but an entire island, complete with a superb pool, full-time butler, and a sense of being in the midst of an entirely different reality. This is the ultimate escape for the well-heeled individualist. See p. 267.

- **Dune Eco-Village** (near Pondicherry, Tamil Nadu): This is the coolest, most individualistic lodging option in Tamil Nadu: An ever-evolving seaside "village" with totally unique cottages, from eco-designed traditional thatched single-room units on stilts right on the beach, to luxury walled L-shaped villas with private plunge pools set amidst sprawling grounds. Under the expert hands-on guidance of director Sunil Varghese, service and cuisine are now superb and Dune has developed into a destination in its own right, yet a hop from the gorgeous seaside town of Pondi, our favorite shopping destination in the south. See chapter 8.

- **Mahua Kothi, Banjaar Tola, and Pashan Garh** (Bandhavgarh, Kanha, and Panna, Madhya Pradesh): Ultra-luxurious safari lodges from India's Taj hotel group and South Africa's &Beyond, each one is not only eye-catchingly pretty and filled with whimsically stylish details, but the sumptuous guest villas or tents are an idyllic retreat after a day of tiger-spotting with the best-trained naturalists in the country. See p. 492.

- **Amarvilās** (Agra, Uttar Pradesh): If you've always dreamed of seeing the Taj Mahal, this is the place to celebrate that achievement. Built within the green belt that surrounds the monument, you can literally see the Taj from your bed, but you'll probably spend just as much time gazing at your immediate surroundings. With its huge reflecting pools, colonnaded courts, terraced lawns, inlaid murals, and pillowed pavilions, this palatial hotel is worth every cent. See p. 460.

- **Rajvilās** (near Jaipur, Rajasthan): The first of the Oberoi's flagship Vilas properties, built like a traditional fortified Rajasthani palace, Rajvilās may not have the history of an authentic heritage hotel, but it offers a level of comfort, luxury, and service other properties cannot match, enabling even the most

world-weary guest to "live in the princely style of Rajasthan." See p. 524.

- **Aman-i-Khás** (Ranthambhore, Rajasthan): Located a stone's throw from India's most famous tiger sanctuary, the superb accommodations—huge temperature-controlled Mughal-style royal tents stylishly divided by cool white drapes—and impeccable service are distinctly Aman. At night, lanterns light your way to the giant flaming *uruli* (large metal vessel) around which guests gather to enjoy the night sky and the ethereal calm, broken only by the occasional call from the wilds. See p. 540.

- **Mihir Garh** (Rohet, near Jodhpur, Rajasthan): Gallop up to this brand-new property on a Marwari stallion to see the silhouette of your dreams appear out of the horizon against the setting sun. Recently established by the same clan responsible for Rohet Garh (a reputable heritage property), this stunning, intimate nine-suite desert sand castle will capture your heart and fuel your imagination, filling your stay with wonderful memories. With a plunge pool or Jacuzzi in every suite, and sweeping views of the surrounding desert and farmland, it's sure to leave a lasting impression. See p. 581.

- **Rawla Narlai** (Rural Rajasthan): Rawla Narlai, the 17th-century hunting retreat of the Maharajah of Jodhpur, is another rural gem that will have you feeling like a royal guest—and it's the ideal stopover if you're traveling between Udaipur and Jodhpur. Surrounded by the rocky granite outcrops deep in the Aravalli Hills, with a pretty medieval village to explore, a gorgeous pool to cool off in, and a stiff climb to reach the summit of a miraculous rock, it's more than a mere stopover—you'll stay for 1 night and wish you'd planned for three. See p. 574.

- **Lake Palace Hotel** (Udaipur, Rajasthan): Built on an island by the maharana in 1740 as a cool summer retreat

THE BEST OF INDIA

1

UNIQUE PLACES TO STAY

(swimming distance from his palace), this is perhaps the most romantic—certainly the most photographed—hotel in India. Whizzing across the waters to your private palace, you'll feel you've finally arrived—and if you've booked one of the heritage suites, you have. Floating like a beautiful white ship on the waters of Lake Pichola, the hotel offers excellent service, a spa-on-water and spectacular rooftop dinners overlooking the City Palace. All with picture-perfect 360-degree views. See p. 567.

- **Shahpura Bagh** (Shahpura, Bhilwara, halfway between Jaipur and Udaipur, Rajasthan): Located in a lush 18-hectare (45-acre) wooded estate with a sense of peace and homeliness not found in any chain hotel, yet also without the sometimes cloying claustrophobia of a heritage property, Shahpura Bagh is a destination location, even with the kids. A family run affair and with excellent food, service, and perhaps the best pool in Rajasthan, this is at least a 2-day visit and the beginning of a lifelong affair. See p. 542.

- **Devi Garh** (near Udaipur, Rajasthan): If you're a modern-design enthusiast, this hotel will blow you away. The formidable exterior of this 18th-century Rajput palace-fort, towering over the tiny village at its base, remains unchanged. But step inside and you'll find a totally reinvented minimalist interior, with 14 floors transformed into 49 chic suites that have clearly utilized the talents of the best young Indian designers—all of whom laid to rest the perception that design here reached its apotheosis with the Mughals. It's an unparalleled modern Indian masterpiece, and a destination in its own right. See p. 571.

- **Umaid Bhawan Palace** (Jodhpur, Rajasthan): Splurge on one of the sumptuous Deco heritage suites in this glorious, monumental palace (still partially inhabited by Jodhpur's royal family),

with the city and its populace somewhere far below. It stands on the summit of a hill, with the staggering Mehrangarh Fort across the way. Guests here are treated like royalty, with access to a private cinema, fabulous lounges, a squadron of butlers, and two pools—one an indoor Deco masterpiece and another at the edge of the beautiful, lush gardens where Liz Hurley married her Indian beau. See p. 578.

- **Amanbagh** (Ajabgarh, Rajasthan): Fringed by date palms and mango and jamun trees, Aman's shimmering pink-sandstone resort is the oasis you have always wanted to stumble upon while traversing the Thar Desert. Begin your day sipping ruby-red pomegranate juice on your private porch, then hike to ancient Somsagar Lake or explore the haunted ruins at Bhangarh. Or go nowhere but your private villa pool on the edge of the palm-lined canal and listen to the joyful twittering of birds. See p. 512.

- **Hotel Eagle's Nest** (Dharamkot, Dharamsala, Himachal Pradesh): High above the bustling cosmopolitan town of McLeod Ganj, this guesthouse offers one of the most charming stays in all of India. Set in a marvelously restored old mission station surrounded by a forest, each of the spacious guestrooms is imaginatively turned out, and the best afford jaw-dropping views of the Dhauladar mountain range. You'll be happy to just loll about all day taking in the fresh, clean air and staring across at splendid vistas. But your hosts—self-proclaimed refugees from London's fast-paced music industry—will be on hand to pamper you, whether it's with their excellent advice for exploring the region or putting together a special meal in the homey kitchen. And when you absolutely must purge your sins, the Dalai Lama's temple is a therapeutic half-hour downhill walk away. See p. 645.

- **Gangeshwari Suite at the Glasshouse on the Ganges** (Garhwal, Uttarakhand): It's the location—just steps away from the raging Ganges River—more than anything that gives this room its special appeal. The simply laid-out sleeping area has a four-poster canopy bed and antique furniture, while the bathroom features a tub carved into the rock, with greenery spilling down the walls. You can relax on your private balcony and watch India's holiest river gushing by, or dive in for a refreshing dip knowing that you're far away from the pollution that enters the river much farther downstream. See p. 675.

- **Shakti Homestays** (Ladakh): In the time-forgotten villages of Ladakh's mesmeric moonscape, you will discover a way of life that's little changed over the centuries. Thanks to an innovative upgrade on the average homestay experience, you can now enjoy the comfort of luxurious linens and fire-fueled heating throughout the night as you bed down in a converted space above a traditional family home. By day you'll explore the region with a knowledgeable guide and driver who will take you to spectacular Buddhist temples, journeying through lunar landscapes and snow-tipped mountains that will leave you awestruck. At night you'll dine with the families whose homes you'll

share, getting to understand a distinctive culture that's a far cry from the increasingly touristy experience of the crowds who flock to Leh, the Ladakhi capital, the moment summer makes access to this remote Himalayan region possible. See p. 658.

- **Glenburn Tea Estate** (Darjeeling): Centered around the 100-year-old Burra Bungalow, which offers just four magnificent rooms, this tea plantation is by far the best place to stay in the "Land of the Celestial Thunderbolt," with great decor, delectable cuisine, and superb views of the Kanchenjunga. You can spend a night at Glenburn Lodge by the river without giving up your room at the Bungalow—the two rooms here are charming, especially at night when bathed in the orange glow of hurricane lamps (no electricity) with only the burbling of the river for music. Picnics (anywhere on the estate) will be served by liveried bearers on portable tables complete with a tablecloth, delicate crockery, and a vase of fresh flowers—all that's missing is a chandelier. See p. 725.

- **360° Leti** (Uttarakhand): If you want to feel top of the world, look no further than this stylish four-cottage paradise perched on a mountain, with panoramic views, fantastic walks and excellent whiskey to come back to. See p. 682.

---

4 MOST MEMORABLE MOMENTS

- **Sharing a Cup of *Chai* with a Perfect Stranger:** You will typically be asked to sit and share a cup of *chai* (tea) a dozen times a day, usually by merchants keen to keep you browsing. Although you may at first be nervous of what this may entail, don't hesitate to accept when you're feeling more comfortable, for while sipping the milky sweet brew

(often flavored with ginger and cardamom), conversation will flow, and you might find yourself discussing anything from women's rights in India to the individualism that mars Western society.

- **Helping Lord Venkatesware Repay His Debt to the God of Wealth** (Tirupati, Andhra Pradesh): Tirupati, the richest temple in India, is the most active religious pilgrimage destination on earth, drawing more than 10 million devoted pilgrims every year (more than either Jerusalem or Rome!) who line up for hours, even days, to see the diamond-decorated black stone idol Lord Venkateshwara (aka Vishnu) for just a few seconds. Afterward, you stare in disbelief as vast piles of cash and other contributions are counted by scores of clerks behind a wall of glass. See chapter 8.

- **Watching the Moon Rise from Pushkar Palace during the Pushkar *Mela*** (Pushkar, Rajasthan): The sunset is a spectacular sight on any given evening, but on the evening of the full moon during the Pushkar *mela*, hundreds of Hindu pilgrims, accompanied by temple bells and drums, wade into a sacred lake—believed to miraculously cleanse the soul—before lighting clay lamps and setting them afloat on its holy waters, the twinkling lights a surreal reflection of the desert night sky. If you're lucky enough to have bagged a room at Pushkar Palace, you can watch this ancient ritual from a deck chair on the terrace on the banks of the lake. See chapter 11.

- **Gawking and Being Gawked At** (Dungarpur, near Udaipur, Rajasthan): As a foreigner, you may attract uncomfortably long stares (particularly on public transport), but there are a few moments that you will recall with a wry smile, like the gimlet eye of the toothless old royal retainer as he watches your reaction to the explicit *Kama Sutra* paintings he will reveal hidden in a cupboard of Dungarpur's 13th-century Juna Mahal—one of the Rajasthan's undiscovered gems. See chapter 11.

- **Playing Chicken with a Tata Truck:** The rules of the road (which is almost always single-laned, potholed, and unmarked) are hard to understand, but it would seem that (after the cow, which is of course sacred) Tata trucks, all with HORN ON PLEASE written on their bumpers, rule the road, an assumption your hired driver is likely to test—and you will, more than once, find yourself involuntarily closing your eyes as destiny appears to race toward you, blaring its horn.

- **Meeting a Maharaja** (Rajasthan): India must be the only place in the world where you can, armed with a credit card, find yourself sleeping in a king's bed, having dined with the aristocrat whose forebears built, and quite often died for, the castle or palace walls that surround it. While most heritage properties are still owned by India's oldest monarchies, many of whom live there, only some (like Mandawa Castle and Deogarh Mahal in Rajasthan, and Nilambagh Palace in Gujarat) are personally managed by these urbane aristocrats. See chapter 11.

- **Unraveling the Intricacies of Hinduism** (Master Guest House, Delhi): Staying here is not only the best-value deal in town, but the sophisticated, charming, and extremely knowledgeable Avnish Puri will take you on a "Hidden Delhi" tour, showing you a world not seen by many outsiders, during which he will unravel Hinduism's spiritual tenets in a profoundly logical way—no mean feat! See p. 438.

- **Being Blessed by an Elephant** (Madurai, Tamil Nadu): While you may expect to see an elephant in a national park, it's always a wonderful surprise when you see one ambling down a crowded street in urban Mumbai or Delhi—these days, though, as authorities work at instilling a modern approach, you're unlikely to see such large beasts in any India city. But outside Thirupparankundram Temple, near Madurai, the resident temple elephant waits patiently to bestow blessings on those willing to donate a rupee. See p. 359

- **Exchanging Printed Paper for a Handmade Kutchi Rabari Woven Masterpiece** (Kutch, Gujarat): Bargaining for unique textiles is a common practice in the bazaars throughout India, but when you stare into the eyes of a seminomadic Rabari woman from Kutch who has spent perhaps over 5 years crafting a particular piece, you understand that this is no mere transaction. You'll be exchanging money for an item that was made over a substantial portion of her life, and is laden with the narrative of her culture.

- **Rocking to the Gentle Rhythm of Lake Pichola under a Firm Hand** (Udaipur, Rajasthan): Taj Lake Palace Hotel's spa boat, moored in the middle of Lake Pichola, is an expeditious vehicle of enlightenment. Book a late-afternoon treatment and emerge from your private sandalwood cabin to see the sun set over the Aravalli Hills and the City Palace lights wink at your newfound sense of peace. It's about not only the destination but how you get there. See p. 560.

5 EXPLORING NATURAL INDIA

- **Watch Cows Sunbathing with Tourists on the Beach** (Goa): While there's plenty of marijuana doing the rounds in Goa, you don't have to smoke a thing to be amused by the mellow cows that wander onto the beach and chill out among the tanning tourists and hawkers. Chewing their cud while seemingly gazing out to sea, these cows really take the Goan motto, *"Sossegade"* ("Take it easy"), to heart. See chapter 6.

- **Ply the Backwaters on a *Kettuvallam*** (Alleppey and Kumarakom, Kerala): Aboard your private houseboat, you aimlessly drift past villages, temples, and churches, watching as village children, unperturbed by your drifting presence, play at the water's edge, and elephants and water buffalo wade at will. Though the facilities might strike the well-heeled as basic, you're looked after by a private team (guide, cook, and pilot) who manage to be both discreetly invisible and at your beck and call. See chapter 7.

- **Quench Your Thirst with Fresh Coconut Water on a Tropical Island** (Lakshadweep): One of India's best-kept secrets, the 36 atolls and coral reefs that make up the remote union territory of

Lakshadweep are rated among the best diving destinations in Asia. Only 10 of the islands are populated, almost exclusively by Malayalam-speaking Muslims who make their living from fishing and harvesting coconuts. These relaxed islanders are supremely welcoming, happily climbing a towering coconut tree to help you quench your thirst. See chapter 7.

- **Wake to Hear a Herd of Elephants Approaching** (Periyar Wildlife Sanctuary, Kerala): The best way to experience this park—famous for its herds of wild elephants—is on a trek with the privately run Periyar Tiger Trail. Accompanied by a naturalist and a game ranger armed with a rifle, you are taken farther into the tourist zone than any other operator is allowed to penetrate. What's more, you are looked after by a team of reformed poachers, who skillfully track and spot animals, carry all the gear, strike camp, cook, clean, and —most important—stand sentinel throughout the night when the danger of being trampled by elephants becomes a serious risk. See chapter 7.

- **Immortalize a Wild Tiger from the Back of an Elephant** (Bandhavgarh and Kanha National Parks, Madhya Pradesh): With the densest population of tigers of any park in India, you are practically guaranteed a sighting at this relatively low-key, remote part of Madhya Pradesh. But it's the approach that's so exciting—elephant *mahouts* set off at dawn to track the royal cats. As soon as they've spotted one, you rendezvous with your pachyderm, which then takes you within striking distance of this most royal of cats. The tiger—unperturbed by the presence of an elephant—will then strike a pose of utter indifference for your camera. See chapter 10.

- **Pick a Picture-Perfect Beach** (Goa, Karnataka, and Kerala): India has some of the world's best beaches, most of them on the Konkan and Malabar coasts which make up India's western shore. Easily accessed, **Asvem** (northern Goa) is an idyllic haven, while just south of here, **Morjim** has been drawing Olive Ridley turtles to its shores for centuries. Both beaches were once well off the well-beaten tourist track, but now, like beautiful crescent-shaped **Palolem** in southern Goa, these lovely stretches have been well and truly discovered. If you're looking for solitude in Goa, check out less-visited spots such as **Agonda** (just 7km/4½ miles north of Palolem) and **Galgibaga**—another designated turtle breeding beach—a little further south. If you're collecting special beach memories, you should head over the border to the sublime and, many believe, mystical **Om Beach**

(Gokarna, Karnataka). In Kerala, the competition is equally stiff, but we award the picture-perfect prize to the seemingly endless virgin beach that stretches off for miles in either direction right in front of the pretty new **Neeleshwar Hermitage** in the still-undiscovered far north. But the absolute stunner, if you can get that far, is at **Bangaram,** one of the paradisiacal hideaways that comprise the truly unforgettable islands of Lakshadweep. See chapters 6 and 7.

- **Find Divinity in *Devbhumi*, "Land of the Gods"** (Kinnaur to Spiti, Himachal Pradesh): The stark, rust-colored, snow-capped slopes in the Indo-Tibetan regions of Kinnaur, Spiti, and Lahaul are the stuff adventurers' dreams are made of, offering sublime mountainscapes, flower-filled valleys, terrifying roads, atmospheric Tibetan Buddhist *gompas* (monasteries), and high-altitude villages that seem to cling to the mountainsides. The region is one of the most profoundly beautiful in the world, but the drive is not for the fainthearted. See chapter 13.

- **Get a Rush While Rafting Down the Zanskar** (Ladakh): White-water rafting on the Zanskar is not only exhilarating and challenging, but you pass through the most incredibly desolate, scenic gorges and stupendous cliffs. A full river journey takes at least 12 days roundtrip from Leh, so this is only for the truly committed—though there are slightly tamer options closer to Leh. See chapter 13.

6 THE BEST EATING & DRINKING EXPERIENCES

- **Street-snacking** (Mumbai): You need to be cautious about where you stop to indulge your curiosity and sample the overwhelming variety of street snacks

available just about anywhere in India. In Mumbai—surely one of the world's great cities for street food—there are numerous casual eateries where you can sample mouth-watering, totally addictive *pani puri* (a crisp, deep-fried flour ball, hollowed-out and filled with taste-bud-tingling morsels) made with filtered water, and *vada pav* (a bun stuffed with spiced fried potato). And if dining street side is beyond you, you can always head to the Taj Mahal Palace's **Sea Lounge** for high tea, when traditional street snacks form part of the formidable buffet. See chapter 5.

- **Bumping into a Bollywood Idol** (Mumbai): Nowhere in India is dining more rewarding than in Mumbai, where the streets are filled with literally thousands of restaurants representing every kind of Indian cuisine. But if it's star-gazing you're after, head for places like the **Olive Bar and Kitchen** restaurant in Bandra or **Enigma** nightclub in Juhu. Alternatively, hang out at **Leopold Café;** casting agents looking for foreigners to work as extras frequently scan the clientele at this favored travelers' hangout. See chapter 5.

- **Eating Alphonso Mangoes in Mumbai:** You may have eaten mangoes in Mexico, Thailand, or even in other parts of India, but until you've had an Alphonso from Ratnagiri in rural Maharashtra, you'll be missing a sensory experience like no other. The king of mangoes has a succulent bright orange pulp, bewitching scent, and divine flavor. See chapter 5.

- **Eating with Your Hands:** Though it may initially go against the grain, there's something immensely rewarding about digging into a delicious meal with your hands. Indians generally do, and—at least once—you should follow suit. Note that ideally you only use your right hand, and

in the north, where the food is "drier," you are traditionally not supposed to dirty more than the first two digits; in the south you may use the whole hand. See chapter 2, "India in Depth."

- **Sipping a Sweet Lassi:** A delicious drink of liquefied sweetened yogurt, this is almost a meal in a glass and should definitely be sampled (some of the best we've tried were in Amritsar, Goa, and Jaipur). Do, however, make sure that no water has been added (including ice), and beware the *bhang* lassi—spiced with marijuana; it can make the usually dreamlike scenes of India a little too out of this world.

- **Dining Alfresco on the Rooftop Terrace of the Taj Lake Palace** (Taj Lake Palace Hotel, Udaipur): There's something very surreal about a romantic candlit dinner on the roof of the Lake Palace Hotel. It's as if you're watching television at the same time: the History Channel in an IMAX theater, staring directly across the water at the uplit 16th-century City Palace whilst sipping champagne and eating organic, free range lal maas. Be sure to press "record." See p. 567.

- **Sampling Bod-Jha, Tibetan Butter Tea, with a Buddhist Monk** (Leh, Ladakh): Many people gag at the taste of butter tea, made with salt and—you guessed it—a good dollop of the clarified butter known as ghee. It's an acquired taste, but if you get the hang of it, sipping the buttery concoction with a friendly Buddhist monk when you visit one of the many monasteries tucked in the lunar landscapes around Leh is a truly memorable experience. See chapter 13.

7 THE BEST AYURVEDIC PAMPERING

For the ultimate Ayurvedic treatment—not so much pampering as a full-on rejuvenation experience that emulates the philosophy of health as a way of life espoused in ancient Indian texts—there's nothing that comes close to **Kalari Kovilakom.** The health programs offered there are so special, in fact, that we've included them amongst India's best spiritual experiences, earlier in this chapter.

- **The Marari Beach** (Alleppey, Kerala): Ayurveda is taken very seriously at this attractive beach resort in South India, not far from Kerala's tantalizing backwaters. The well-stocked Ayurvedic center is run by two physicians, who dispense sound medical advice as well as treatments, and your program is backed up with special Ayurvedic meals at the resort's restaurant. Or forgo the rules and just head for the beach, cocktail in hand. See p. 275.

- **Kumarakom Lake Resort** (Kumarakom, Kerala): The swankiest of Kumarakom's retreats, this has an extensive Ayurvedic spa—one of Kerala's most sophisticated, catering primarily to the well-heeled globetrotter—but there's more besides, like the exquisite, traditionally styled teak-and-rosewood houses with open-air garden bathrooms, a fabulous restaurant, and superslick service. See p. 267.

- **Somatheeram** (Southern Kerala): This shabby-chic center, carved out of red sandy soil and perched on a terraced cliff overlooking a beach, is more hospital than hotel, but it has been inundated with awards for "Best Ayurvedic Center" (mostly from Kerala's Tourism Department). Ayurvedic therapy is the primary reason to book here, joining the many European "patients" who shuffle around in pastel dressing gowns, serene expressions on their tanned faces. See p. 293.

- **Shalimar Spice Garden Resort** (Kerala): Not far from Periyar Tiger Reserve, this lovely inland resort occupies a 2.4-hectare (6-acre) plantation scented by exotic spices. Over and above the enchanting Euro-chic accommodations designed by Italian architect Maria

Angela Fernhof is an intimate Ayurvedic center drawing a regular European clientele. Built according to traditional specifications, with a stone floor, handmade brick walls, and an open fire for heating the medicated oils, the small space is always filled with the aroma of coconut oil. See p. 300.

- **SwaSwara** (Om Beach, Gokarna, Karnataka): With meditation sessions in a gorgeous blue-domed building alongside the pool, and regular yoga classes that encompass a wide range of techniques presented by a skilled master, guests at this top-notch retreat are offered every imaginable type of Ayurvedic treatment, combined with a specialized, individually designed diet, with lectures and art classes to aid in your discovery of self. Set in a superb location just a few minutes' walk from the much-venerated Om Beach, this inspiring resort features wonderful indoor-outdoor suites, designed a bit like traditional Karnataka homes, with open-to-the-elements bathrooms and air-conditioned sleeping quarters. See p. 370.

- **Wildflower Hall, Mashobra** (near Shimla, Himachal Pradesh): The *pièce de résistance* at what once was the mountain retreat of Lord Kitchener and is today the most beautiful resort in the Himalayas is the spa—not only because the highly trained therapists offer the ultimate rubdown (Balinese, Thai, Swedish, Ayurvedic—and that's just for starters), but because it takes place while you stare out blissfully at snow-capped peaks and a magnificent deodar valley, swirling with mists. See p. 621.

- **Ananda-in-the-Himalayas** (near Rishikesh, Uttarakhand): The 1,951-sq.-m (21,000-sq.-ft.) Wellness Center at this destination spa resort, located high above the Ganges, is rated one of the best in the world. This reputation is well earned—thanks not only to its ultraefficient team of therapists, masseuses, and yoga instructors, but also because you are totally pampered from the moment you wake (to a steaming cup of honey, lemon, and ginger) until you retire to a bath (where a candle heats fragrant essential oils) and a bed (warmed by a hot-water bottle). See p. 674.

- **Shreyas** (Bengaluru, Karnataka): Simplicity is the catchword, but attention to detail is never compromised. Relaxed, minus any ostentatious predictability attached to most spas, Shreyas believes in detoxifying the spirit as much as the body. This is as perfect as it can get. See p. 374.

8 THE BEST SAVVY TRAVELER TIPS

- **"You pay what you like"**: This rather annoying response from guides, drivers, and rickshaw-*wallas* to the question "How much will it cost?" will no doubt end with at least one of you feeling very disappointed. Try to find out how much something should cost *before* you enter into this dialogue (we've tried to advise this wherever possible), and always negotiate the fare or rate upfront. (Note that "I come later" is another irritating response, this time after you decline service, and you will need to remain firm or prepare to go through the entire experience again.)
- **"Just look, no buy"**: You will be urged to enter shops from all corners in both explicit and less obvious ways—your driver, guide, even the seemingly innocent bystander offering assistance, are almost all operating on the ubiquitous commission system, and whatever they make on the deal is added to the quoted price. Note that to avoid this kind of hassle, look for the fixed-rate shops or those that mark their wares with prices. But as is the case everywhere, do beware of closely named imitations of fixed-rate shops with good reputations—for example, Cottage Industries Exposition shops, often marked CIE, are seriously overpriced outlets that cash in on the fame (and closely related name) of the government-owned Central Cottage Industries Emporiums. The latter may not be the cheapest, but it offers good value, and you really can "just look, no buy."

- **"We look; we look"**: This response from a rickshaw-*walla* or driver usually means that the person either doesn't know where you've asked him to take you, or you'll end up somewhere with a similar name but nothing else to recommend it (Hotel *Chandra,* for example, rather than Hotel *Chand*). Prebook your accommodations whenever you can, so that you don't have to deal with touts and hawkers when you arrive. And be aware that a hotel or guesthouse that is successful will often have a rival opening within the year with a confusingly similar name.
- **"So where are you from, good gentleman?"** (or more commonly, "Coming from?"): You will be asked this often, so prepare yourself. One of the possible reasons Indians kick-start conversations this way is that where you come from may in the past have indicated caste or social position; whatever the reason, engage in the opener—it's far preferable to living in a five-star hotel cocoon.
- **"Hashish, taxi, guide, young girls?"**: In the well-traveled parts of India, you will be inundated with offers of assistance; again, the best response is to doggedly desist in what is essentially a game of endurance, and certainly ignore those unsolicited offers that are illicit—these can carry a hefty penalty, including a lengthy jail sentence.
- **"Cof-fay, chai; cof-fay, chai; cof-fay, chai?"**: This incessant call given by the

chai-walla wandering the corridors of your train will put to rest any romantic notions about the relaxation of train travel. Note that you will be most comfortable aboard the overnight **Rajdhanis,** which connect all the major cities, while the best daytime trains are the **Shatabdis** (book Chair Class). Time allowing, you should definitely book a "toy train" to the hill stations of Shimla or Darjeeling—the latter approach is so spectacular it has been named a World Heritage Site.

- **"Yes, madam"; "Yes, sir":** You will hear this everywhere, usually from hawkers wanting to draw your attention and con artists wanting to strike up a conversation. Unfortunately, the only way to get rid of these irritants is to completely ignore them. In places like Varanasi, even saying no is perceived as a willingness to interact, and your pursuer will then continue to try to draw you into conversation. Just pretend you can't be bothered, and hopefully, in a little while, you won't.

- **"You wait, no problem":** Finally, we can't emphasize enough how important it is to simply relax and accept whatever's going on around you. Many Indians subscribe to the philosophy that life is destiny, and getting uptight or flying into a rage usually won't solve much. You'll have a far better vacation if you simply give in to the moment and enjoy the experience; after all, the only aspect you have control over is your response.

2

India in Depth

A great triangle of land thrusting out of Asia, past the Bay of Bengal and the Arabian Sea, and deep into the Indian Ocean, India is a vast country (similar in size to Europe) and home to an ancient culture with a host of historic and architectural treasures unparalleled in the world. But more than anything else, it is India's enigmatic "otherness" that so fascinates the first-time visitor, for perhaps no other country on earth can offer so much contrast—traveling within the subcontinent feels at times like traveling through time. From the snowy peaks of the Himalayas, where prayer flags flutter against an impossibly blue sky, to the golden deserts of Rajasthan and Gujarat, where women wear saris saturated with fuchsia and saffron; from the vast plains of Madhya Pradesh, dotted with ruins and tiger parks, to the lush tropical mountains and paradisiacal beaches off the Malabar Coast, the spectrum of images and experiences is stupendous. Perhaps one of the most heterogeneous cultures in the world, with a mosaic of languages, dialects, religions, races, customs, and cuisines, India and its people cannot be defined, labeled, or pigeonholed—only experienced. Whether you're planning your trip to do a spiritual pilgrimage, view (or shop for) its myriad treasures, live like royalty in medieval palaces, unwind on unspoiled beaches, or simply indulge in the most holistic spa therapies known to man, India will leave an indelible impression on you. The following essays are merely a backdrop; to come to grips with the strange and fascinating world that is India, you will need to immerse yourself in some of the reading suggested at the end of this chapter. And travel to India again. And again. And again.

1 INDIA TODAY

by Frommer's authors and Anita Pratap

Pratap is a former CNN bureau chief for South Asia, author, journalist, and columnist for *Outlook*, India's weekly newsmagazine

Whatever your understanding of India today, the exact opposite is probably equally true. Life has changed dramatically since India began to liberalize its economy in the 1990s, and yet it remains a land where several centuries exist simultaneously. If you visit one of its scientific centers, you could well believe you are at NASA, but walk to a village that still has no connection to a drivable road (and there are thousands of them), and you will find people living exactly as they did 2,000 years ago (albeit, perhaps, with a cellphone pressed against an ear or a satellite dish poking out of the roof of a mud house). More than 25% of the world's software engineers are Indian, but another 25% of the Indian population goes to bed hungry every night. Women like Pratibha Patil, the female president of India elected in July 2007, have risen to top positions of power and authority in both the political and corporate world, yet in some regions, girls are still awaiting access to primary school education. Millions more across the country struggle without the most basic human rights.

India has the world's highest number of malnourished children, yet obesity in urban children is a new and menacing problem. The country has armed itself with nuclear weapons, but has difficulty providing drinking water to millions of its citizens. It ranks low in the United Nations' Human Development Index, which measures quality of life, trailing even Sri Lanka and the Maldives in meeting targets set in the U.N. Millennium Development Goals Report, but in terms of purchasing parity, India is the third-biggest economy in the world after the United States and China. During the call center boom time, the country saw the rapid emergence of a large new class of young urbanites keen to flash their disposable incomes, and as a result a luxury market in India exploded, with every international brand from Louis Vuitton to Greubel Forsey vying for their slice of this burgeoning market. Yet, with its shackled judicial system and excessive regulation, India struggles with a reputation as a "mostly unfree" economy coming in at 123 in the 2009 Index of Economic Freedom, trailing even Gabon.

Meanwhile, agrarian crises continue to brew in rural India, with droughts and floods, paradoxically, always major impediments to the earning and survival strategies of millions of people across the nation. In 2009, a much-delayed monsoon once again severely hampered crop production. And to compound natural disaster, India struggles with a massive, often overburdened, infrastructure and bloated bureaucracy. In 2008, the country fell behind China in the Global Corruption Perception Index, and many people on the ground harbor suspicion and some sort of resentment against the government, no matter who's in charge; studies reveal that Rs 9,000 million is paid in bribes by 30% of the population (which lives below the official poverty line) just to coerce public servants into doing jobs they're already paid to do. In mid-July 2009, the issue of corruption came into the limelight in a big way when a bridge under construction for the Delhi Metro collapsed and killed six people; reports revealed that the accident was a direct result of cuts to the safety budget on the project, supposedly to save on construction costs, but in actuality a selfish scheme to put more money into the pockets of fewer contractors than was appropriate.

All of this doesn't exactly enhance India's marketability. It ranks low when it comes to attracting foreign visitors; in comparative studies of India's Travel and Tourism Competitiveness, it comes in lower (relatively tiny places like Panama and Puerto Rico rate higher), and that's in the wake of the most intensive national branding and marketing campaign— "Incredible India!"—the country has yet seen; there are more hotels and tourism products than ever before, and the international imagination has surely been touched by films such as *Slumdog Millionaire* and the success of the book *Shantaram*. Yet acts and threats of terror, perceptions of crime and poverty, and fear of illness, scams, and hostility continue to plague India, keeping many travelers away. No wonder India is confusing, confounding, incomprehensible. How can you make sense of this land? It's like emptying an ocean with a spoon.

All through the 1970s and even 1980s, Western diplomats and journalists predicted the "Balkanization" of India. It didn't happen, but in 1991 India's foreign exchange reserves plunged to a catastrophic $1 billion, barely sufficient to service 2 weeks of imports. India was forced to embark on its radical liberalization program. Since then, India's economy has grown at a rate rivaled only by neighbor China: 2007–08 saw India's thousand-billion dollar economy grow by a staggering 9.8%, the fastest in 20 years; and even with the world economic slump, the nation's GDP grew by 6.7% in 2008–

2009, while the stock market has continued soaring to unheard-of numbers (on May 18, 2009, in fact, the Bombay Stock Exchange rose by 17.3%, the highest single-day percentage gain of any exchange across the world, ever). But this growth has also spurred inflation (which peaked at a whopping 12% in Aug 2008) and a rise in interest rates, not to mention the obvious fact that India will no doubt experience the knock-on effect of the world's economic winter.

Statistics show that the overall standard of living has improved drastically, but the truth is that the benefits of a booming economy have not reached a vast percentage of the population, and India still has the world's largest concentration of poor. Nearly 300 million people live without the basic necessities of life: water, food, roads, education, medical care, and jobs. These are the Indians living on the outer edges of the nation's consciousness, far away in remote tribal areas, barren wastelands, and dirty slums, totally outside the market economy.

With a billion voters, every national election here is the biggest spectacle of fair and peaceful democracy that humankind has ever witnessed. And yet increasingly democracy is often a masquerade for a modern version of feudalism. Clan loyalties propel electoral victories. The victor rules his or her province like a medieval tribal chieftain, often showing scant respect for merit or rule of law. Cronies are hand-picked for jobs, rivals are attacked or harassed, public funds are misused to promote personal agendas. Modern-day versions of Marie Antoinette abound in Indian democracy—while the poor were dying of cold in January 2003 in Uttar Pradesh, India's most populous state, its chief minister, Mayawati, was strutting around in diamonds and celebrating her birthday with a cake the size of a minibus. Later that year, having been indicted by the Supreme Court in a case of alleged corruption, Mayawati resigned only to return to power with a resounding victory. Proof that real choices are limited? Perhaps, but many low-caste people, whose cause Mayawati (herself of low-caste origin) supposedly champions, support her fiery attitude and are inspired that she too can celebrate like India's rich.

In fact, according to a seminal paper presented by Dheeraj Sinha in 2007, the mindset of India as a nation is changing – gone (or fading) are the priestly Brahminical values of knowledge, adjustment, simplicity, and restraint, and "in" are the warriorlike Kshatriya values of success, winning, glory, and heroism. Whereas Indians traditionally took refuge in the idea of karma and fate (see "Hinduism," below), the emerging mindset believes that karma is shaped by one's actions—that it is possible to achieve a life that one desires rather than one that's destined.

This represents a huge shift, and is both the result and the driver of the economic engine that is powering India. But there is one growth industry guaranteed to stymie, if not wreck, genuine progress: the feud between Muslim and Hindu fundamentalists. At the heart of the latter ideology—most acutely represented by the RSS and Bajrang Dal—is the belief that today's Muslims should be punished for historical wrongs perpetrated by medieval Muslim conquerors. It's a belief that is fired by modern-day resentments (such as the concern that Muslims have, proportionally, the highest birth rate in India) and fears that *madrasas* are creating hotbeds of Muslim fundamentalism. The worst Hindu-Muslim rioting and looting happened in the western state of Gujarat in 2002, but bomb blasts still occur almost annually and are proof that sectarian trouble is simply on slow-brew.

Nationalism also takes its toll in the Kashmir dispute that bedevils relations between the nuclear-capable neighbors India and Pakistan. The two countries have fought two of their three wars over Kashmir, engaged in another low-level conflict in 1998, and came to the brink of another in 2002. Driven by popular enthusiasm and political initiatives on either side, there has been a thawing in India-Pakistan relations since then, and the peace process has enjoyed a visible momentum with issues such as visa issuance significantly improved. That said, there is still a lack of progress in resolving many bilateral problems, and any further improvements are unlikely given the recent spike in terrorist incidences (most notably the devastation that occurred in Mumbai in Nov 2008 when terrorists who trained in Pakistan wreaked havoc in various key locations in the southern part of the city).

The problems of nationalism are exacerbated by politicians who try to pit Hindus, who constitute 80% of the population, against the 150-million Muslim minority before elections in order to garner votes—this happened again in 2006 and 2007 in the UP elections, when the BJP released a highly inflammatory CD featuring Muslims slaughtering cows and kidnapping Hindu women.

Yet, recent elections have proved that change is definitely on the horizon. The 2004 polls hinted that the masses cannot be won over for long through this diabolical strategy of dividing communities, and in some subconscious way there seems to be a recognition that if divisive politics win, India will lose. When the nation went to the polls on May 18, 2009, some 420 million voters turned up and effectively took part in the biggest single democratic event in human history. That the voters, a hugely disparate group separated by geographic distance, culture, economic situation, caste, religious belief, and access to the social infrastructure, managed to vote, in Fareed Zakaria's words, "with remarkable intelligence" by rewarding the incumbent ruling Congress for bringing economic growth to the nation, is a momentous feat. Indeed, at the polls, it seemed evident that India's voters had given precedent to economic reform, and within days local stock market indicators went orbital. As India's reform-minded government allocated ministerial portfolios and people on the ground celebrated, media headlines emphatically declared nothing short of a virtual new order. *The Times of India* eagerly reported that "with the Left decimated and the Congress no longer dependent on coercive allies, a stable government would be able to push reforms." In many ways, the election result symbolized the emergence of "a new age for India on the world stage," and the next leg in the evolution of the country's independence—people power had finally usurped state power. And, to preserve the sense of order established by the Congress's first term in power, its leader, Sonia Gandhi, again declined the post of prime minister, retaining Manmohan Singh—highly respected for the role he played in the liberalization of India's economy in the '90s—for the post.

Bill Clinton once said: "India remains a battleground for every single conflict the world has to win." Certainly India copes with huge problems—massive corruption, joblessness, judicial bottlenecks with few convictions and delays of up to 20 years for delivering justice, AIDS, acute water shortages, poverty, disease, environmental degradation, unbearable overcrowding in metropolitan cities, crises of governance, sectarian violence, and terrorism. India adds one Australia to itself every year—*18 million people.* The rural poor (who form the majority) see children as an economic resource, the only security net for old age, and high child-mortality rates necessitate the need for more than one, or two. Apart from India's huge natural growth rate, an estimated two million poor Bangladeshis slip into India every year in search of work.

Impressions

Who is an authentic Indian and who isn't? Is India Indian? Does it matter? Let's just say we're an ancient people learning to live in a recent nation...

—Arundhati Roy, *The Algebra of Injustice*

But this is a country of remarkable stamina. As Manmohan Singh has stated, "Our real strength has always been our willingness to live and let live." Home to scores of languages, cuisines, landscapes, and cultures, India is a giant. But she will move at her own pace. She is not an Asian tiger. She is more like a stately Indian elephant. No one can whip or crack her into a run. If you try, the stubborn elephant will dig in her heels and refuse to budge.

No power on earth can then force her to move. But equally so, she cannot be stopped once she's on the move. And with the slow but fundamental shift from silent acceptance of karma to the belief that one can—and should—give shape to destiny, she is most certainly on the move. There is no point arguing whether this is good or bad. It is good and bad. And it is many things in between.

After all, this is India.

---

2 INDIA PAST TO PRESENT

by Nigel Worden

History professor specializing in the Indian Ocean region

No visitor to India can fail to be overwhelmed by the combination of a bustling, modernizing nation and an ancient but omnipresent past. India's history is everywhere, in its temples and mosques, forts and palaces, tombs and monuments, but it has only recently become a single country, which makes its history a complex one. Successions of kingdoms and empires have controlled parts of the subcontinent, but none unified the whole—even the British Raj's "Jewel in the Crown of the Empire" excluded large swaths of territory ruled by independent princes. Thus the accounts of history vary, and competing versions have often been the cause of bitter conflict. Given the tensions between Hindus and Muslims in South Asia, it is hardly surprising that the Islamic era in particular is highly controversial. Were the Muslims invaders and pillagers of an ancient Indian tradition, as Hindu

nationalist historians claim? Or were they Indians who created a distinctive culture of architecture, painting, and literature by blending indigenous forms with Islamic influences? Is the Taj Mahal a uniquely Indian masterpiece, or a symbol of the Islamic oppressor? As is usually the case with history, it all depends on where you are, and to whom you're talking.

ANCIENT INDIA Historical accounts of India usually begin with the **Harappan civilization** of the Indus Valley, a sophisticated agricultural and urban society that flourished from 3000 to 1700 B.C. (about the same time as the earliest Egyptian civilization); although many of its sites are now located in latter-day Pakistan, you can view Harappan artifacts in places like the National Museum in New Delhi. Not much is known about the people, not least because their writing system has yet to be deciphered, but their active trade with the civilizations of the Euphrates (contemporary Iran and Iraq) show that northern India had links from very early on with the rest of Asia.

A more recognizably and distinctive "Indian" culture developed from around 1500 B.C. in the northern part of the subcontinent, spreading steadily eastward in the 1st millennium B.C., although never penetrating to the far south. This is usually referred to as the **Vedic period.** The ancient written *Vedas* provide a rich record of this era, led by a Sanskrit-speaking elite, which embedded into India Hinduism the caste system (led by a Brahmin priesthood), and the dichotomy between a rural farming majority and an urbanized merchant class, all ruled by local kings and princes. A series of Vedic kingdoms rose and fell, each centered on a city, of which Varanasi is today the oldest-living and best-known example. Much controversy surrounds the interpretation of the "Aryans," as the Vedic culture is known—some claim that they originated as invaders from the north who conquered and subjugated the local population, while Hindu nationalists today see them as the archetypal indigenous Indian—a controversy that makes Indian archaeology a tempestuous field of study. Whichever interpretation you buy into, the influence of the Vedic era is all-pervasive in modern Indian life,

and the historical focus of a modern Hindu identity.

From the 6th century B.C., the Aryan states were themselves subject to invasions from the north, in a cycle of incursion and subsequent local adaptation that was to dominate much of India's history. Even Alexander the Great, hearing of the wealth and fertility of the area, tried to invade, but his army apparently refused to cross the Indus River and instead made their way back to Macedonia. Other invaders (or settlers, depending on your preference) of Greek, Persian, and central Asian origin moved in, challenging some of the indigenous states, such as Shakas of western India and the Magadha state of the northeast. In time, all of these newcomers were absorbed into the local population. It was during this period that Siddhartha Gautama (Buddha) was born in latter-day Nepal; he later moved to India, where he sought—and found—enlightenment at Bodghaya, and starting teaching at Sarnath, just outside Varanasi.

The first large state to emerge in this region was under the **Mauryan rulers** (322–185 B.C.), who incorporated much of northern India, including the region west of the Indus; at its largest, it even reached south to Karnataka. The most famous of these rulers was **Asoka,** who converted to Buddhism after a particularly murderous episode of conquest pricked his conscience; he spread the Buddha's

---

DATELINE

- **Circa 3000–1700** B.C. Harappan civilization of the Indus Valley marks earliest farming communities in the region.
- **1500–600** B.C. Vedic states in the north establish the basis of Hinduism and the *Indic system.*
- **326** B.C. Alexander the Great's army halts at the Indus.

- **322–185** B.C. Mauryan state in North India; conversions to Buddhism under Asoka (reigned 272–232 B.C.).
- A.D. **319–540** Gupta empire reunites northern India.
- **300–900** Pallava empire in Dravidian southern India.
- **900–1300** Chola empire in southern India.
- **1206–1400s** Islamic Delhi *sultanates* established in north.

- **1510** Portuguese establish first European coastal settlement in India.
- **1526** Mughal conquest of Delhi (returned permanently in 1555).
- **1556–1605** Akbar extends Mughal power.
- **1600** Founding of British East India Company.
- **1658–1707** Aurangzeb conquers south for Mughal empire.

teachings throughout northern India, particularly at Sarnath and Sanchi, where you can still view the *stupas* (commemorative cairns) he built. Asoka's decrees, which were inscribed onto rock (literally), carved his reputation throughout the region, while his emblem of four back-to-back lion heads (which you can also view at Sarnath) has been adopted as the modern symbol of India.

Asoka's empire barely survived his death in 232 B.C., however, and in the subsequent centuries local states rose and fell in the north with alacrity. The **Gupta empire** emerged from A.D. 319 to 540 under Sumadra Gupta, who conquered the small kingdoms of much of northern India and Bengal, while his son extended its range to the west. This loose confederacy was marked by a reinvigoration of Hinduism and the power of the Brahmins, which reduced the influence of Buddhism in the subcontinent (though it had taken strong root in Sri Lanka and Southeast Asia). But Hun invasions from the north in turn destroyed Gupta power, and northern India was again split into numerous small kingdoms.

It should be noted that the southern part of India remained unaffected by these developments. With the exception of Asoka's Mauryan empire, none of the northern states extended their influence beyond the central plains, and South India developed its own economic systems, trading with Southeast Asia and across the western Indian Ocean as far afield as the Roman Empire. Dravidian kingdoms emerged, some of which established sizable empires such as the **Pallava** (A.D. 300–900) and **Chola** (A.D. 900–1300). Hinduism flourished, evident in the rich legacy of Dravidian temple architecture (notably at Thanjavur).

THE ISLAMIC ERA   Even Indian historians refer to the period from the 10th to the 16th centuries as "medieval," but a more accurate characterization of it relates to the impact of Islam. Muslim influence from the northwest was evident in northern India from at least A.D. 1000, but it was only with the arrival of Islamic forces from the 13th century onward that its presence became dominant. A succession of fragmented and unstable Moslem states emerged around new centers such as Lahore (Pakistan), Delhi, and Agra, collectively known as the Delhi Sultanates. Conversions to Islam were made among the local population, mainly from the lower castes or where Hinduism was weaker, as in Bengal, but the majority of the population remained Hindu. In most areas the Muslim rulers and their administrators were but a thin layer, ruling societies that followed earlier traditions and practices.

In the south, Muslims made much less impact. Muslim raids in the 14th century

- **1739** Persian sacking of Delhi and removal of the Peacock Throne accelerates Mughal decline.
- **1757** Clive defeats *Nawab* of Bengal at Battle of Plassey, establishing British rule in Bengal.
- **1790s–1820s** British extend power in southern, western, and central India.
- **1856–57** Indian "Mutiny": uprising against British.

- British sacking of Delhi and expulsion of Mughals.
- **1858** Dissolution of East India Company; India to be ruled directly from London.
- **1877** Queen Victoria declared Queen-Empress of India.
- **1885** Foundation of the Indian National Congress.
- **1890s** Bengal famine and plague epidemics.

- **1903** British capital moved from Calcutta to Delhi.
- **1905** Division of Bengal provokes boycott campaigns against British.
- **1906** Muslim League founded.
- **1915** Gandhi returns to India.
- **1919** Amritsar massacre galvanizes Indian nationalist opposition to British.

continues

instead led to unified Hindu resistance by the Vijayanagar empire centered in Hampi, which flourished in the south as one of the strongest Hindu states in Indian history, surviving until the 16th century.

By this stage a more vigorous wave of Islamization had emerged in the form of the **Mughals,** a dynasty that originated in the Persian borderlands (and was possibly driven south by the opposing might of Genghis Khan in central Asia). The Mughals established themselves initially in Kabul, then the Punjab, and in 1555 they finally conquered Delhi, which became their capital. Under **Akbar** (1556–1605) and **Aurangzeb** (1658–1707), the Mughals extended their empire south into the Deccan and, after defeating the Vijayanagar state, deep into the south, although their ambitions to conquer the entire subcontinent were stymied by the opposition of the Hindu Maratha states in the southwest.

Rulers such as Aurangzeb were not slow to show merciless terror against those who opposed them, but previous images of the Mughal empire's ruthless despotism have now been challenged by many historians, who point out that, other than Aurangzeb, the Mughal emperors were happy to allow local rulers to continue in power, provided they regularly sent tribute to Delhi and provided troops and cavalry when needed. Close to Delhi, the fiercely independent Hindu princes of Rajasthan retained their

authority as long as they did not openly flout Mughal rule. Taxes were levied on landowners, but the levels were in general no higher than before. Trade and local textile production flourished in many regions, notably in Bengal and Gujarat. Muslim law, Persian language, and administrative structures were introduced, although in many outlying parts of the empire, local customs continued.

But by the 18th century, the Mughal empire was in decline. Some of this was the result of direct opposition, especially from the Marathas, who were consolidating their power in the southwest, but in other respects, decline might have been a product of the Mughal empire's own prosperity. Local regions such as Bengal, Oudh, and the Punjab began to benefit from economic growth and to assert their independence. When Delhi was attacked by yet more incursions from the north, culminating in the sacking of the city by Persians in 1739 and the hauling off of the fabulously valuable Peacock Throne, symbol of Mughal power, local regions went their own way. In Bengal, the local ruler made an agreement with foreign merchants who had appeared along the coast in the 17th century, allowing them to built a small settlement at the mouth of the Hooghly River (later to become Calcutta) and to trade in cotton and cloth in return for tribute. These foreign merchants were

- **1930** Gandhi leads salt march to protest British taxation policies.
- **1935** Government of India Act gives measure of local self-government to India, but retains British power at the center.
- **1939–45** World War II: India threatened by Japanese advance in Southeast Asia.
- **1942** Gandhi announces "Quit India" campaign and is imprisoned.

- **1946** Labor government in Britain announces future independence for India, with Mountbatten as new viceroy.
- **1947** British leave India. Partitioning into separate states of India and Pakistan. Massacres of refugees across new frontiers. Nehru becomes independent India's first prime minister.
- **1948** Gandhi assassinated by a Hindu fundamentalist.

- **1964** Death of Nehru.
- **1966** Nehru's daughter, Indira Gandhi, becomes prime minister.
- **1975** Indira Gandhi declares State of Emergency but is ousted from power in the 1977 elections.
- **1980** Indira Gandhi regains power.
- **1984** Indian army besieges Sikh temple at Amritsar. Indira Gandhi assassinated

members of the British East India Company, formed in 1600, which had failed to establish a niche in the more lucrative spice trade of Southeast Asia, and was thus forced to settle for less plum pickings along the Indian coastline: They obtained permission from locals to set up stations at Surat and what were to become the cities of Madras and Bombay. They were not the only Europeans to settle in India; the Portuguese had first established a base in Goa in 1510, and in the 17th century the Dutch made similar agreements with local rulers in Bengal, Nagapatnam, and the Malabar coast, while the French set up shop in Pondicherry. Even the Belgians, Danes, and Swedes formed trading companies, but unlike the others, they had little impact on the indigenous culture.

As was the case elsewhere, it was the British who moved from trade to empire in India. In part this was the outcome of inter-European rivalries: The English grabbed French ships and produce in India (along with French Canada) in the **Seven Years' War** (1756–63), then moved on Dutch posts in India and Sri Lanka after the Napoleonic wars. But the main impetus came from their dealings with Indian rulers. In Bengal, English traders were making a killing, often marrying local women and living the high life. Frustrated by their continued and unwelcome presence, the local *Nawab* attacked the

English settlement at Calcutta in 1756, imprisoning a number of people in a cramped cell, where some suffocated. The "Black Hole of Calcutta" martyrs became a rallying cry to justify further incursions by the British: Troops were shipped to Calcutta, which defeated the *Nawab* at Plassey the following year and again in 1764. The British East India Company filled the local power vacuum—and although nominal vassals of the Mughals still lived in the Red Fort in Delhi, the East India Company was effectively the local government.

In the course of the late 18th and early 19th centuries, the company's area of influence grew apace. Presenting itself as the "defenders of Bengal," it forged alliances and provided military support for local rulers in areas such as Bihar and the northwestern regions, then moved in when they defaulted on repayments. By the mid–19th century, English armies (staffed overwhelmingly by Indian troops) overran Oudh and the Punjab. In the south the company moved inland from Madras to the Carnatic and across to Malabar. It inherited the Mughals' rivalry with the Marathas (the region around latter-day Mumbai), which erupted into open warfare in 1810 and led to the company's conquest of the western coast and its hinterland.

by Sikh bodyguards in revenge.
- **1984–89** Indira Gandhi's son Rajiv is prime minister.
- **1991** Assassination of Rajiv Gandhi by a Tamil separatist. Liberalization of the economy by reducing government controls, privatizing, and drastically reducing import tariffs and taxes.

- **1992** BJP-led attack on mosque at Ayodhya.
- **1996** BJP Hindu fundamentalist party wins electoral majority and forms coalition government.
- **2002** Threat of nuclear war with Pakistan over Kashmir averted by international mediation. Gujarat sees tensions between Hindu and

Muslim nationalists inflamed.
- **2004** National elections held; In an unforeseen victory, the Congress-led alliance wins and forms the UPA (United Progressive Alliance) government. Manmohan Singh becomes the new prime minister of India.

continues

While extending their power base, the East India Company still claimed allegiance to the Mughals, whose emperor retained nominal control in Delhi. But this, too, was to end. In 1856 and 1857, following decades of resentment against British policies and their impact, an army mutiny (caused by the use of animal fat on bullet cartridges, which affronted the Hindus) triggered uprisings against the British across northern and central India. Despite claims by later nationalist historians that this was a united revolt against the foreign oppressor, most of the violence in the "Indian Mutiny" of 1856 to 1857 was by Indians against other Indians, in which old scores of class, religious, or regional rivalries were festering. Nonetheless, epic stories abounded of Indian valor or British heroism and martyrdom (depending, again, on which side told them). The British, taken by surprise, only regained control by the skin of their teeth—and by ruthless retaliation. Some of the resisters had appealed to the Mughal emperor to reassert control over India, which in an unwise moment he had agreed to do. The British army sacked Delhi, forced the emperor into exile, and declared the end of the Mughal empire. But London was unimpressed by the chaos that the East India Company rule and policies had brought, and moved to abolish the company's charter, effectively establishing direct rule from London. The pretence was over. India was now to be ruled by a new foreign power.

THE RAJ The East India Company was replaced by a new system of government. The British Crown was represented in India by a viceroy sent out from London who presided over a professional class of British-born and (mainly) Oxbridge-educated administrators appointed through the Indian Civil Service. Most Indians never saw this relatively small body of men (never exceeding 5,000 at any one time), and they in turn were dependent on the military (still primarily composed of Indian troops, or *sepoys,* lorded over by a British officer class) and on another army of Indian lesser-ranking administrators, lawyers, and civil servants, who were prevented by race from rising to the upper ranks. For India, unlike British Africa and Australasia, was not to be a settler colony. The British initially played on the fiction that they were the legitimate successors to the Mughals, mounting spectacular *durbars* (receptions) to demonstrate their power and the loyalty of India's princes— in 1877 the occasion was used to declare an absent Victoria "Queen-Empress of India"; it was only in 1911 that the reigning British monarch finally attended a *durbar.* The British built a set of administrative buildings in "New Delhi," declared

- **2005** India's $575-billion economy grows by a whopping 8.2%.
- **2008** Mumbai is rocked by a multi-pronged terrorist attack which focuses on high-profile tourist locations. Terrorists, who have trained in Pakistan under Lashkar-e-Taiba (LeT) operatives, kill 166 innocent people from India, the U.K., U.S., Israel, and other countries, and cause extensive damage to the landmark Taj Mahal Palace and Oberoi hotels.
- **2009** In the largest election turnout in human history, the Congress Party is given the go-ahead to continue its program of reforms and governance along nonpartisan lines. Manmohan Singh is retained as prime minister and in the days after election results are announced, India's stock exchange becomes the best performing in the world.

the capital in 1903, that today are considered the finest architectural achievements of the empire.

In many ways, British rule was a new experience for India. For one thing, the entire subcontinent was viewed as a single whole, despite the continuation of nominally independent princely states in many of its central regions. With a mania characteristic of the Victorian, the British mapped the landscape; surveyed the diverse systems of landholding; separated inhabitants by race, language, and caste (for census purposes); and built the huge railway network that connects the country today. Much of this had the practical purpose of raising revenues from trade and taxation, since the British were determined that the Raj should be self-financing. But it also created a body of knowledge that was to shape many of their political and social policies, and to solidify categories of race and caste that had earlier been somewhat more permeable.

The Indian economy in the era of the Raj became closely dependent on British and other imperial markets, with promotion of the export of raw materials rather than internal industrialization, although by the early-20th century, parts of Bengal and the region around Bombay were starting to manufacture for local purchasers. It was from the "new" Indian administrative and mercantile classes that the first stirrings of opposition to British rule came. The local modernizers demanded equal access to economic and political opportunities, rather than a return to India's precolonial past. Thus the first **Indian National Congress (INC)** was formed in 1885, with members primarily from Bengal, Bombay Presidency, and Madras. The INC carried out its proceedings in English, and called for access to the higher ranks of the civil service (with examinations for entry held in India, not in Britain) and for relief of the heavy levies on Indian-produced local textiles. By the turn

of the 20th century, after the disastrous famine and plague epidemic that broke out in Bengal in the 1890s, more extremist members of the INC were demanding *swaraj*, or "self-rule," although what they had in mind was a degree of self-government akin to the British dominions in Canada, Australia, or South Africa, rather than total independence. An unpopular administrative division of Bengal in 1905 led to a boycott of British imports, and some Bengali intellectuals began to evoke Hindu notions of a free Indian nation. The British conceded limited electoral reform, granting a local franchise to a tiny percentage of the propertied, but they ominously listed voters in separate voter rolls according to whether they were Muslim or Hindu; a separate **Muslim League (ML)** was formed in 1906.

World War I, in which large numbers of Indian troops served the British cause, dampened anti-British protests and saw a pact between the ML and the INC, not least because of vague British promises of meaningful change once the war was won. But in 1919, British General Dwyer opened fire on a demonstration held in the enclosed space of the Jallianwala Bagh in Amritsar, killing and wounding over 2,000. This gave Indian nationalism its first clear martyrs, and the callousness with which Dwyer's actions were applauded by the British general public inflamed matters further.

The period between the two World Wars saw a seismic transformation of Indian nationalism, growing from the protests of a small elite to a mass-based movement that overwhelmed the British. The figure with whom Indian nationalism is most associated is **Mohandas Karamchand Gandhi,** the "Mahatma." After an early career in law, he developed his concepts of *satyagraha* (nonviolent protest) and passive resistance in defending Indian interests in colonial South Africa before he returned to his native India in 1915. Gandhi persuaded the

INC to embrace a concept of a united India that belonged to all Indians, irrespective of religion or caste. Mass support for Congress campaigns of noncooperation with the colonial state was ensured by well-publicized and symbolic campaigns such as the 1930 march from Ahmedabad to the Gujarat coast to defy a salt tax by making salt from sea water. Membership of the INC soared to over two million. But not all of Gandhi's ideas were triumphs—he was much criticized by some for his failure to support the socialist leanings of Bombay factory workers, while others took little interest in his appeal for religious tolerance or equal acceptance of the outcast *dalits*. The British granted a degree of self-government to India in 1935, although only at the provincial level. Another group that did not accept INC's call for unity was the Muslim League. Fearing Hindu domination in a united India (revealed by the 1935 elections), they began, under their leader Mohammed Ali Jinnah, to call for a separatist Islamic state named "Pakistan" (after the initials of areas they claimed: Punjab, the Afghan states, Kashmir, and Sind). At first, few took this seriously, although Gandhi was alarmed at the divisive trends.

World War II was to change everything. Gandhi and INC leaders called in 1942 for the British to "quit India" and were imprisoned. Although many Indian regiments in the British army supported the Allies, a number of other Indians joined the Japanese-trained Indian National Army under the INC leader Subhas Chandra Bose. After 1945, Muslim and Hindu violence broke out, with each side claiming power. The new Labor government in Britain was now anxious to divest itself of its troublesome Raj and sent Lord Mountbatten as a new viceroy to oversee the process. Mountbatten's decision that the British should cut their losses as quickly as possible by leaving in August 1947 took everyone by surprise. More seriously, he agreed to partition the country to appease

Jinnah and the Muslim League rather than risk continuing civil war in the new state. In a frenzy of activity, "Partition" became official, and the boundaries of the new Pakistan were summarily drawn across the map, splitting the Punjab into two and dividing communities. Millions of refugees spent Independence Day desperately trying to get to the "right" side of the border, amid murderous attacks in which well over a million lost their lives. The trauma of these months still casts a deep shadow over the subcontinent. While the British Raj in India lasted less than 100 years, the processes that led the British to divide the country into two states, India and Pakistan, have fundamentally shaped the modern nation state.

INDEPENDENT INDIA For almost 4 decades, independent India was to be governed by the INC, initially under its leader Jawaharlal Nehru, who had led Congress in the negotiations of 1946 and 1947. Gandhi was bitterly disillusioned by Partition, even proposing at one stage that Jinnah be made prime minister of India to restore unity. This was enough to alienate him from some Hindu nationalists, one of whom assassinated Mahatma in 1948. Such rival visions of the Indian nation were to plague the new country.

The most pressing political issues centered around India's relations with Pakistan. The Indian government was (rightly) accused of fomenting dissent in East Pakistan in the late 1960s, leading to war in 1971. Continued conflict has centered around Kashmir, an independent princely state with a predominantly Muslim population but whose Hindu ruler, under threat from Muslim forces from Pakistan, placed it under Indian rule in 1948. Pakistani and Indian troops have tensely faced each other in the territory ever since. With the development of nuclear weapons by both states, and a militant Kashmiri independence movement, the area is a potential powder keg of international concern.

Under Nehru, internal stability was obtained, remarkable considering the circumstances of India's independence, and until his death in 1964, he established India as the world's leading postcolonial democracy, a key player (along with Sukarno's Indonesia) in the nonalignment movement that avoided Cold War conflicts. Communal rivalries were downplayed by a focus on India's secular status. Regional separatism continued to threaten unity, especially Tamil opposition to Hindi linguistic domination from Delhi, but this was resolved by a reorganization of local states along linguistic lines.

Nonetheless, Congress never obtained more than 45% of the national vote and only held power because of the division of its political opponents. After Nehru's death, its attraction weakened. In an attempt to restore its popularity, his daughter, Indira Gandhi (no relation to Mahatma), became prime minister in 1966. From 1969, she implemented a more populist program of social change, including land reform and a planned economy—a program that was to alienate some of the richer landowners and regional party leaders. Economic restructuring led to strikes and civil opposition in the cities, and in 1975, a state of emergency was declared that lasted 2 years. Believing that she had reasserted control, Indira Gandhi held elections in 1977. The result was the first defeat for Congress, although no party was able to form a united government to replace it, and by 1980 Gandhi was back in power.

The INC never regained its previous level of control, however. Resentment by Sikhs at their failure to secure autonomy in the Punjab culminated in 1984 with the Indian army's siege and capture of the main Sikh temple at Amritsar with thousands of casualties, and Indira Gandhi was assassinated by her Sikh bodyguards. Her son, Rajiv Gandhi, succeeded her, and instituted new programs of economic liberalization,

but he also embroiled India unsuccessfully in the ongoing civil war in Sri Lanka, leading to his assassination in 1991 by a Tamil activist. Although his widow, the Italian-born Sonia Gandhi, inherited leadership of Congress, the era of the Nehru family's domination of Indian politics (which has been compared to the Kennedy family's political impact in the U.S.) was thought by many to be over.

In 1989, Congress was again defeated at the polls, this time led by the Hindu nationalist **Bharatiya Janata Party (BJP)**. Although the BJP initially failed to hold together a coalition government, its strength grew. It accused Congress of allowing India to be dominated by outside interests, including globalized economic forces, but more specifically by Indian Muslims who it considered to be unduly tolerated under Congress's secular state policies. In 1992, a BJP-led campaign led to the destruction of the mosque at Ayodhya, believed to be the birthplace of the Hindu god Ram.

In the 1996 elections the BJP defeated a Congress government plagued by accusations of corruption and emerged as the leading group in the coalition governments that have ruled India since. Under the BJP Prime Minister Atal Behari Vajpayee, tensions with Muslim Pakistan increased, with both sides testing and threatening the use of nuclear weapons, especially in conflicts over Kashmir. Fortunately, 2003 saw a welcome cooling. In 2004 the confident BJP government called for early elections, hoping to cash in on a booming economy and developments in the India-Pakistan peace process. Contrary to all expectations, however, the BJP did not win. Instead the Congress, which had been the opposition party for 8 years, took much of the vote, as did the Left (which unexpectedly won more than 60 seats in the 543-member house). Together with other parties, they formed a ruling coalition, the UPA (United Progressive Alliance).

The next surprise came soon after, when the victorious Sonia Gandhi, leader of the Congress, declined to take on the job of prime minister, appointing instead Manmohan Singh, a former Indian finance minister, to the chair.

By mid-2005, the Congress had been in power for just 1 year; the opposition BJP was in disarray, its political plans to disrupt the functioning of the Congress-led government a mess, and its own dirty linen being washed in public view almost daily. Simultaneously, the normally tenuous relations between India and Pakistan had reached a new high—despite obstacles like unresolved disputes and cross-border terrorism—a strategic factor in the development of the region as a whole. When the next general election rolled around in 2009, voters turned up in larger-than-ever numbers and reaffirmed support for Congress's secular, reformist policies. With Sonia's son, Rahul Gandhi (whom many believe is on course to become the next Gandhi to lead India), impressing crowds and analysts, the party trumped its earlier victory and was able to form a government without forming allegiances with parties likely to compromise its position. Ms Gandhi again appointed Manmohan Singh prime minister, and the media celebrated what felt like the start of a new era in the country's development.

3 THE LAY OF THE LAND

India is a vast country, roughly divided—for the purposes of this book—into North, East, and |South.

The south (again, for the purposes of this book), accessed most conveniently via **Mumbai** (state capital of **Maharashtra**), refers to **Goa, Karnataka** (with an excursion to **Hyderabad,** capital of **Andhra Pradesh**), **Kerala,** and **Tamil Nadu.**

The north refers to **Rajasthan,** its southern neighbor **Gujarat,** and to the west of these states, the nation's capital, **Delhi,** and the sprawling states of **Uttar Pradesh** and **Madhya Pradesh,** which lies in the very heart of the country. Northeast of Delhi lie the largely unvisited states of **Haryana** and **Punjab** (the big exception being the Golden Temple at **Amritsar,** one of India's most wonderful attractions), and—moving directly north of Delhi—**Uttarakhand, Himachal Pradesh** and **Ladakh** (one province in the state of otherwise-unsafe Jammu and Kashmir) in the Himalayas.

The east refers to **Jharkhand** (not a tourist destination), **West Bengal** (centered around **Kolkata,** or Calcutta), **Orissa** (with top attraction Konark), and, moving north into the Himalayas again, the mountain state of **Sikkim** and the tea-growing hill station of **Darjeeling.** Seven more states lie farther east (north and east of Bangladesh); their infrastructure is virtually nonexistent. Because travel in these areas is considered less than safe, they are not covered here, with the exception of two outstanding wildlife reserves in **Assam.**

The largest differences lie between the northern and southern regions. The former offers predominantly a plethora of medieval Mughal and Rajput architecture, ancient cities, deserts, camel safaris, heritage accommodations, tiger parks, Buddhism, and the snowcapped peaks of the Himalayas. The latter is rich with beautiful beaches, Ayurvedic spas, ancient Dravidian/Hindu temples, cosmopolitan colonial coastal towns, and a generally more laid-back atmosphere. We suggest that rather than try to cover both the north and the south, concentrate your energies on one. If you do decide to combine the two, stick to two states, or you'll find yourself exhausted at the end of your vacation.

MUMBAI (BOMBAY) & MAHARASHTRA

Teetering on the edge of the Arabian Sea, its heaving population barely contained by palm-fringed beaches, India's sexiest city is a vibrant, confident metropolis that's tangibly high on energy. The state capital of Maharashtra, this is home to many of the subcontinent's best restaurants and great hotels. It's also the ideal starting point for a tour south along the Konkan railway to **Goa** and beyond. Whichever you choose, do plan for an eastward jaunt to the ancient rock-cut caves of **Ajanta** and **Ellora,** Maharashtra's startling World Heritage Sites, and—if you have any interest in the esoteric or want to immerse yourself in meditation—schedule some time in **Pune,** where the **Osho International Meditation Resort** is the country's most upmarket spiritual center.

GOA

Nirvana for flower children since the late 1960s, Goa still attracts a cosmopolitan mix of youngsters who cruise from beach to beach, looking for action. But Goa is more than a party in paradise. A Portuguese colonial heritage has left an indelible mark on this tiny enclave (India's smallest state), from cuisine to architecture, with plenty to see. And if the crowded beaches and vibrant markets leave you gasping for solitude, you can still find the original Goan paradise on far-flung beaches or in quiet boutique hotels, reviewed in detail in this book.

KARNATAKA & KERALA

Traveling south along India's west coast, you will pass through untouched Karnataka; it's possible you'll overnight in the hip city of **Bangalore.** From there you can head to **Hyderabad,** the 400-year-old capital of Andhra Pradesh, as famous for its food and minarets as for its burgeoning software industry; or south to **Mysore,** "City of Incense"; or to the coast, where you can indulge in yoga and Ayurvedic rejuvenation at **Om Beach.**

Whatever you do, set aside time to explore the lost city of **Hampi,** arguably Karnataka's most evocative attraction, or to join the Jain pilgrimage to anoint the giant feet of **Lord Gomateswara,** said to be the largest monolith in the world. There's more besides, but who can tarry long when **Kerala,** "God's own country," awaits? South India's top destination, particularly for the well-heeled traveler in search of pampering and relaxation, Kerala offers ancient backwaters plied by houseboats, herds of wild elephant, coconut-lined beaches, and, of course, the ancient healing art of Ayurveda.

TAMIL NADU

Occupying a long stretch of the eastern Indian Ocean coastline, India's southernmost state seems little touched by the foreign influences that contributed to the cultural developments in the north. This is where you'll find India's most superb Dravidian temples, from **Mamallapuram** (7th c. A.D.) to the **Madurai temple complex** (16th c. A.D.). When you're all templed out, there's always **Pondicherry,** the former French coastal town where traditional Indian snack joints feature signs proclaiming MEALS READY—BIEN VENUE and loincloth-clad locals converse in flawless French.

DELHI, MADHYA PRADESH & UTTAR PRADESH

Entered through Delhi, capital of the largest democracy in the world, the central states of Madhya Pradesh and Uttar Pradesh are the real heart of India, where great rulers battled for power over vast swaths of India, and where you'll find arguably the densest concentration of top attractions on the subcontinent. From the "seven cities" of Delhi, it's a short train or road journey to **Agra,** home to the Taj Mahal and other superb examples of medieval Mughal architecture. From there you can either head west to Rajasthan, or east—via the erotic temples of **Khajuraho,** considered the pinnacle of Hindu medieval architecture—to the ancient city of **Varanasi,** India's holiest pilgrimage site,

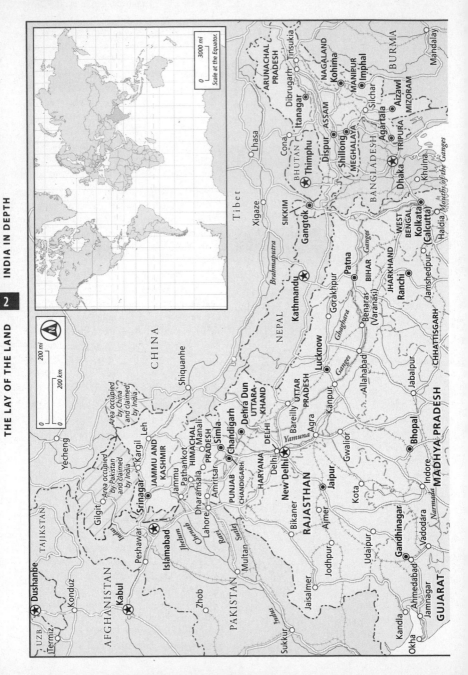

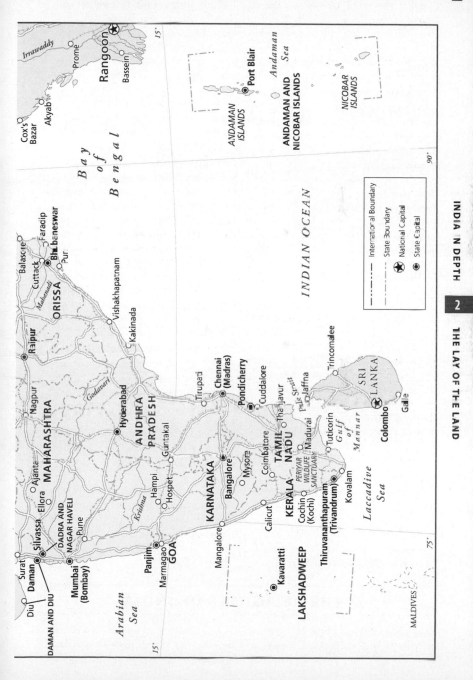

where the faithful come to die on the banks of the sacred Ganges to achieve *moksha*—liberation from earthly life. To escape the well-beaten tourist track, head south to the vast plains of Madhya Pradesh, to **Bandhavgarh National Park,** one of the best places to see tigers in Asia.

RAJASTHAN & GUJARAT With crenelated forts and impregnable palaces that rise like giant fairy-tale sets above dusty sun-scorched plains and shimmering lakes, Rajasthan—literally "land of princes"—epitomizes the romance of India. Whether you choose to linger in the untainted medieval atmosphere of little towns like **Bundi** and **Shahpura,** browse the bumper-to-bumper shops in **Jaipur,** track tigers in **Ranthambhore,** overnight on the lake in the beautiful city of **Udaipur,** or explore the world's oldest living fort in **Jaisalmer,** you will want to see it all. Meanwhile, Gujurat, immediately south of Rajasthan, is where you can explore a number of intriguing ancient sights in and around the capital city of **Ahmedabad,** including the magnificent Modhera Sun Temple and the 900 beautiful Jain temples atop the holy mount of Shatrunjaya. And you can venture into the remote, arid, barren, bleak and beautiful province of **Kutch,** a part of Gujarat where you'll encounter several distinctive ethnic tribes, including the nomadic Rabari people who are known for their intricate embroidery and ornamental adornments.

HIMACHAL PRADESH & LADAKH Bordered by Tibet to the east, Himachal Pradesh incorporates great topographic diversity, from vast, bleak tracts of the rust-colored high-altitude Trans-Himalayan desert to dense green deodar forests, apple orchards, and cultivated terraces. Together with **Ladakh** (known as "Little Tibet"), this is also where you'll find India's largest concentration of Buddhists, their atmospheric *gompas* (monastic temples, including **Tabo,** the World Heritage Site in **Spiti**) a total contrast to the pageantry of Hindu temples. An easy—and highly recommended—detour from the region is to Amritsar to view the **Golden Temple,** arguably the most spiritually satisfying destination in India.

UTTARAKHAND Comprising the pre-Vedic territories of Garhwal and Kumaon, the mountains of the central Himalayan state of Uttarakhand are riven with ancient Hindu pilgrimage routes, and offer wonderful trekking routes. Nonhikers come here to practice yoga at **Rishikesh** on the banks of the holy river Ganges, or to take a road trip through the less-traveled parts of **Kumaon,** possibly ending their sojourn looking for tigers in **Corbett National Park,** which vies with Ranthambhore for accessibility from Delhi.

KOLKATA (CALCUTTA) & THE EAST Kolkata, the much-maligned capital of West Bengal, never fails to surprise the visitor with its beautiful albeit crumbling colonial architecture, sophisticated Bengali culture, and wonderful restaurants and hotels. From here you can either head north to the cooling breezes of West Bengal's hill station, **Darjeeling,** famous for its tea, and on to the Buddhist state of **Sikkim** (in many ways even more remote than Himachal Pradesh); or head south to Orissa to visit the monolithic **Sun Temple** at Konark, yet another of India's awesome array of World Heritage Sites.

---

4 THE RELIGIONS OF INDIA

The diversity of religious belief and practice in India is both unique and somewhat confounding. What follows is a very brief introduction to the religions that took root in India; this will hopefully provide some insight into the patterns and diversity that exist. Tribal religions, ostensibly pagan, often mixed with elements and practices of mainstream religions, still exist in isolated pockets, but are declining rapidly and are not covered here.

HINDUISM To begin the unending journey of studying India, you need to take the first step toward understanding Hinduism, the religion of some 80% of India's population. It can only be a "first step," for like India itself, Hinduism defies attempts to clearly define or categorize, and what may be described as universal Hindu religious practice in one place may very well be contradicted by others elsewhere.

Hinduism has no ecclesiastical order, nor is there a central religious book. (While many religious texts like the ancient *Upanishads* and *Bhagavad-Gita* exist, they are not the "word of God" as the Bible or the Koran.) It is not possible to convert to Hinduism; you are born Hindu, usually into one of the four main hierarchical castes (Brahmin, or "priest"; Kshatriya, or "warrior"; Vaisya, or "merchant"; Sudra, or "peasant") or—at the very bottom of the social order—you are born Dalit, better known as the "untouchables." Unlike organized religions such as Christianity or Islam where truth is specified, categorical, linear, and one-dimensional, truth in Hinduism is in fact extremely multidimensional—contradictions are not bad, but inevitable. Unlike Christianity and Islam, which say there is one true path that leads to one God, Hinduism says there are many paths that lead to many gods (some say—probably hyperbolically 330 million gods, who epitomize a host of human qualities, from gluttony to vengefulness). This intrinsic Hindu acceptance of diversity and multiplicity has defined India's history, allowing it to successfully adapt by absorbing the beliefs of successive invaders. Even today it is not difficult for Hindus to look upon Allah or Jesus as deities worthy of veneration—more than half the devotees who

flock to pray at the famous Muslim shrine in Ajmer in North India or at the fabled Velankanni Church in South India are Hindus.

Rather than a formal religion, Hinduism is considered a way of life, or *Sanatan Dharma* (an eternal path), in which the universe is part of an endless cycle of creation, preservation, and dissolution. The human soul is also part of this cycle, endlessly reincarnated, and seeking freedom. According to Hindu philosophy, we determine our destiny by our actions. *Karma* is the law of cause and effect through which individuals create their own destiny by virtuous thoughts, words, and deeds. Each of us can control the nature and experiences of the next life *(karma)* by "living right" or *dharma*—through *dharma* (a righteous pattern of conduct), individuals determine their *karma*. By resolving all *karmas*, the soul can finally attain *moksha*, an escape from the cycle of life.

There are many sects and denominations within Hinduism, and priests, *sadhus* (holy men), and other spiritually enlightened individuals are important parts of the religious process: *Bhakti* is devotion to and communication with the gods, which devotees express in the performance of *puja* (religious ritual-like prayer), *bhajan* (devotional singing), and meditation. *Puja* may be performed at home or in a temple in front of an idol(s) of god(s). It involves some kind of offering to the gods (flowers being the most common) and is an essential part of the practice of Hindu faith. For Hindus the physical symbol or idol of God is the material form through which God appears in this world. Hindu devotees may worship Shiva, Kali, Ganesha, or any one of thousands of gods and manifestations of gods in the Hindu pantheon, and may believe in a supreme being who is either their chosen deity or some unnamed force even higher than the gods. Hinduism believes in the existence of three worlds: The material universe we live in, the astral plane where angels and spirits live and, finally, the spiritual world of the gods.

BUDDHISM Though Buddhism originated in India around 500 B.C., when the Indian prince Siddhartha Gautama attained enlightenment and became the Buddha (Enlightened One) at Bodhgaya, only some eight million still practice the belief in India, the majority of them from Tibet or Nepal or converted during the mass conversion of lower castes by the anticaste leader Dr. Ambedkar in 1956. (The Buddhist following is, of course, far higher outside India, particularly in the rest of Asia; even in the West, Buddhism appears to be on the rise.)

Unlike any other religion, Buddhism does not advocate belief in a godhead; it instead expects the individual to seek truth within his own experience and control his dharma and karma without relying on divine intervention. Buddhist philosophy is based on the idea that life is riddled with conflict and pain caused by desire (or craving) and ignorance, and to escape from this suffering you need to follow the Eight-Fold Path to gain enlightenment, or *nirvana*. The Eight-Fold Path advocates right understanding, right thought, right speech, right action, right mode of living, right endeavor, right mindfulness, and right concentration. As is the case in Hinduism, each of us carries our karma through a cycle of rebirths until the attainment of nirvana. Meditation, chanting, counting beads, and lighting lamps are some of the ways in which Buddhists pursue their spiritual goal of enlightenment.

JAINISM This began as a reform movement and became a religion under the 24th Jain *trithankara* (prophet) Vardhaman, later called Mahavira (incidentally, a contemporary of Buddha), in the 6th century B.C. Though it never spread beyond India, today some four million Jains live here, predominantly in Maharashtra and Gujarat. The principles of Jainism include strict vegetarianism and extreme reverence

for all forms of life—even insects and plants are believed to have *jives,* or souls. Jains believe in reincarnation and salvation (or *moksha*), which can be achieved through respect for and consideration of all forms of life, and living a life of asceticism, meditation, fasting, and pilgrimage to holy places. According to Jain philosophy, the soul journeys through 14 stages before the final burning up of all karma and freedom from bondage.

There are two sects of Jains—Svetambara and Digambara. Svetambara followers vow to avoid intentional injury to others and to lead a life of honesty and detachment from worldly passions. The Digambaras are even more strict in their beliefs and practices—as a symbol of their complete detachment from material possessions, the highest monks of this sect wear no clothes. In addition, unlike Svetamabaras, Digambaras believe women cannot achieve *moksha.* Their temples are among the finest in India: Karnataka's famous Sravanbelagola Temple is a Digambara temple, while the celebrated Dilwara (Mount Abu, Rajasthan) and Shatrunjaya (Palitana, Gujarat) temples are important Svetambara places of pilgrimage.

SIKHISM This religion emerged in the 15th century out of a rejection of caste distinctions and idolatry under the founder, Guru Nanak, who wanted to bring together the best of Hinduism and Islam. Nine gurus, all of whom are equally revered by Sikhs, followed him, and today there are over 19 million Sikhs in India, mostly in Punjab. Like Hinduism, Sikhism accepts the doctrine of reincarnation, but worship is based on meditation and not ritual or asceticism. Like Muslims, Sikhs believe in one omnipresent universal God; worship takes place in *gurdwaras,* and the holy book is the *Granth Sahib.* The 16th-century Golden Temple at Amritsar is the holiest Sikh place of worship (and has a truly sacred atmosphere).

Charity is an important aspect of the religion, and the *gurdwaras* always run community kitchens where anyone can eat free. Sikhs are expected to never cut their hair—which makes Sikh men, who wind their long hair under large turbans and sport large beards, one of the most easily recognized male communities in India.

OTHER RELIGIONS Zoroastrianism, **Judaism, Islam,** and **Christianity** did not originate in India, but are all represented, with Islam and Christianity (which, incidentally, originated within 600 years of each other) the second- and third-largest religious groups, respectively, in India. Muslims comprise about 13% of the population, while Christians form just 2%. Every major Christian and Muslim sect and denomination is represented, and the beliefs and practices of each group vary accordingly, some with indigenous nuances. But overall they tend to follow the main tenets of these religions as practiced worldwide. It is estimated that only some 5,000 Jews still live in India, mostly in Mumbai, and these numbers continue to dwindle. Zoroastrianism, one of the world's oldest religions, dating from the 7th or 6th century B.C., arrived in India in the 10th century A.D. with refugees fleeing religious persecution in Persia (latter-day Iran). Though numerically they are a tiny religious minority (70,000), the descendants of these refugees (called **Parsis**) have made a distinctive mark as a social and economic group in India. Followers believe in a single God, Ahura Mazda, whose prophet Zarathustra is their guide, and fire is considered sacred and symbolic of God. Parsis therefore worship in a Fire Temple (closed to non-Parsis), and Zoroastrian philosophy regards life as an eternal battle between the forces of good and evil. Again, the path to overcome evil is through good thoughts, words, and deeds. Where possible, their dead are placed in dry wells at a Tower of Silence to be consumed by vultures. This practice is based on the belief that since dead matter pollutes, cremation and burial would pollute the respective elements. Today's Parsis regard this unique method of disposing of the dead as being useful to the cycle of life even after death.

---

5 INDIAN CUISINE

by Niloufer Venkatraman
Anthropologist, writer, and dedicated foodie

Indian cooking is one of the great cuisines of the world. Like the country itself, however, it varies greatly from region to region, and you'll discover a great deal more to savor than the ubiquitous *kormas* and *tikka* masalas (known to the naive simply as "curry") with which most Westerners are familiar. Not only does each Indian community and ethnic and regional group have a distinct cuisine, but there is a great deal of fusion within the country—subtle variations and combinations you're only likely to pick up once you are familiar with the basics. A good way to sample a variety of dishes in a particular region is to order a *thali* (multicourse meal), in which an assortment of items is served. Basic staples that tend to be served with every meal throughout the subcontinent are rice, *dal* (lentils), and/or some form of *roti* (bread). The following is a brief summary of regional variations and general dining tips.

SOUTHERN STATES Food from the coastal areas of India almost always contains a generous quantity of coconut—besides using it in cooking, most Maharashtrian homes offer grated coconut as a garnish to every dish. Rice also dominates the food of southern India, as do their "breads," which are more like pancakes and made of a rice (and/or *dal*) batter—these *appams, idiapams,* and *dosas* are found throughout the south. *Dosas* are in fact a South Indian "breakfast" favorite (consumed anytime), as are *idlis* and *vadas,* all of which have become part of mainstream cooking in many parts of India. *Idli* is a steamed rice and lentil dumpling, *dosa* a pancake (similar batter), and *vada* a deep-fried doughnut-shaped snack. All should be eaten fresh and hot with a coconut chutney and *sambar,* which is a specially seasoned *dal* (lentils), also eaten with steamed rice. In Tamil Nadu a large number of people are vegetarian, but in Kerala, Goa, and Mumbai, you must sample the fresh fish! Delicious kebabs and slow-cooked meals are what you'll find in Hyderabadi cuisine; inspired by the courts of the *nawabs* (nobles), it's similar to Mughlai cooking, but stronger in flavor.

NORTHERN STATES India's great meat-eating tradition comes from the Mughals and Kashmiris, whose *rogan josh* and creamy *korma* dishes, along with kebabs and *biryanis,* have become the backbone of Indian restaurants overseas. The most popular tradition—tandoor (clay oven) cooking—is part of India's Mughal gastronomic heritage. Tandoor dishes are effectively "barbecued" vegetables, *paneer* (Indian cheese), or meat that has been marinated and tenderized in spiced yogurt, cooked over coals, and then served either "dry" as a kebab or in a rich spiced gravy like the *korma.* Recently revived is the tradition of *dum pukht,* enjoyed by the erstwhile *nawabs* of Awadh in Lucknow and the surrounding area. All the ingredients are sealed and slow-cooked in a pot, around which coals are placed. Nothing escapes the sealed pot, preserving the flavors.

NORTHWEST (PUNJAB) SPECIALS Besides trying the various tandoor dishes, you should order *parathas:* A Punjabi specialty, this thick version of the traditional chapati is stuffed with potatoes, cabbage, radish, or a variety of other fillings. Be aware that many North Indians love their ghee (clarified butter); sensitive stomachs (or those watching their weight) should simply specify that they would prefer their *paratha* without ghee. *A general note of caution when dining in North India:* If the menu specifies a choice between oil and ghee as a cooking method, you should probably specify the former. And keep in mind that if you exclusively eat oily, highly pungent, so-called Punjabi fare, you are bound to feel ill, so make sure you vary your meals by dining at South Indian restaurants, which combine a healthy balance of carbohydrate and protein (rice and *dal*); in northern states you will find *rotis* (breads) combined with *rajma* (kidney beans), *puris* (bread) with *chole* (chickpeas), and so on.

EASTERN STATES Freshwater fish (such as *hilsa, bekti,* and *rohu*) take pride of place at the Bengali table, which incidentally considers itself to be the apotheosis of Indian cooking. In Bengal, mustard oil (which has its own powerful flavor) is the preferred cooking oil. Sweets are another Bengali gift to the world; these are made from milk that has been converted to *paneer* (Indian cheese) and that has names like *rosogolla* (or *rasgulla*) and *sandesh.*

SPICES Literally hundreds of spices (masalas) and spice combinations form the culinary backdrop to India, but a few are used so often that they are considered indispensable. Turmeric *(haldi)*—in its common form a yellow powder with a slightly bitter flavor—is the foremost, not least for its antiseptic properties. Mustard seeds are also very important, particularly in the south. Cumin seeds and coriander seeds and their powders are widely used in different forms—whether you powder, roast, or fry a spice, and how you do so, makes a big difference in determining the flavors of a dish. Chili powder is another common ingredient, available in umpteen different varieties and potencies. Then there are the vital "sweet" spices—cardamom *(elaichi)*, clove *(lavang)*, cinnamon *(dalchini)*—which, along with black pepper *(kali miri)*, make up the key ingredients of the spice combination known as *garam masala*. Though tolerance to spicy food is extremely subjective, let your preference be known by asking whether the item is spicy-hot *(tikha hai?)* and indicating no-chili, medium-spicy, and so on. "Curry powder" as it is merchandised in the West is rarely found or used in India. "Curry" more or less defines the complex and very diverse combination of spices freshly ground together, often to create a spicy saucelike liquid that comes in varying degrees of pungency and varies in texture and consistency, from thin and smooth to thick and grainy, ideally accompanied by rice or breads.

STAPLES & ACCOMPANIMENTS All over the country, Indian food is served with either the staple of rice or bread, or both—the most popular being unleavened (pan-roasted) breads (called *rotis*); tandoor-baked breads; deep-fried breads *(puris* and *bhaturas)* or pancake-style ones. Chapatis, thin whole-wheat breads roasted in a flat iron pan *(tava)*, are the most common bread eaten in Indian homes, though these are not as widely available as restaurant breads. The thicker version of chapatis are called *parathas*, which can be stuffed with an assortment of vegetables or even ground meat. Tandoor-roasted breads are made with a more refined flour and include *naans*, tandoori *rotis*, and the super-thin *roomali* (handkerchief) *rotis*. Tandoor breads turn a little leathery when cold and are best eaten fresh.

Dal, made of lentils (any of a huge variety) and seasoned with mustard, cumin, chilies, and/or other spices, is another Indian staple eaten throughout the country. *Khichdi,* a mixture of rice, lentils, and spices, is a great meal by itself and considered comfort food. In some parts it's served with *kadhi*—a savory sour yogurt–based stew to which chickpea flour dumplings may be added. You'll usually be served accompaniments in the form of onion and lime, chutneys, pickles, relishes, and a variety of yogurt-based salads called *raita. Papads* (roasted or fried lentil flour discs) are another favorite food accompaniment that arrives with your meal in a variety of shapes, sizes, and flavors.

MEAT A large number of Indians are vegetarian for religious reasons, with entire towns serving only vegetarian meals, but these are so delicious that meat lovers are unlikely to feel put out. Elsewhere, meat lovers should probably (unless you're dining in a top-end big-city restaurant) opt for the chicken and fish dishes—not only are these usually very tender and succulent, but the "mutton" or "lamb" promised on the menu is more often than not goat, while "beef" (seldom on the menu—beef is taboo for most Hindus, and the ban on cow slaughter continues to be a raging national debate) is usually water buffalo. Again, there are regional differences, as in "Portuguese" Goa, where pork is common.

SWEETS Indians love sweets (called *mithais, mishtaan,* or "sweet meats"), and they love them very sweet. In fact, Western palates often find Indian sweets *too* sweet; if this is the case, sample the dry-fruit-based sweets. Any occasion for celebration necessitates a round of sweets as a symbol of spreading sweetness (happiness). Every region of the country has a variety of specialty sweets made from an array of ingredients, but they are largely milk-based. This includes *pedas* and *laddus* (soft, circular), *barfis* (brownielike), *halwas* (sticky or wet), *kheer* (rice pudding–like), and so on. Whatever you do, don't miss the Indian *kulfi,* a creamy, rich ice cream flavored with saffron, nuts, or seasonal fruit.

FRUITS If the spiciness of the meals unsettles your stomach, try living on fruit for a day. You'll get a whole range of delicious tropical varieties (with any luck, in a basket in your hotel room) ranging from guavas and jackfruit to litchi and the most coveted fruit of them all, the mango. More than 200 varieties of mangoes are grown in India, but the most popular ones (Alphonso or *aphoos*) come from Maharashtra (Mar–June); try to taste one when you're in Mumbai.

BEVERAGES *Chai* (tea) is India's national drink. Normally served in small quantities, it is hot, made with milk usually flavored with ginger and/or cardamom, and rather sweet unless you request otherwise. Instant coffee is widely available (and may be mixed in your five-star hotel's "filter coffee" pot), but in South India you'll get excellent fresh brews. Another drink worth trying is *lassi*, liquefied sweetened yogurt. *Note:* The yogurt is sometimes thinned with water, so you're only safe consuming lassis in places where they can assure you no water was added at all, or where they will make it with bottled water (that you purchase separately). Lassi's close companion is *chaas*, a savory version that is very thin and served with Gujarati/Rajasthani meals. With southern food, it is served with a flavorful assortment of herbs and spices. In general, you should avoid ice in any beverage unless you are satisfied that it is made from boiled water.

EATING ETIQUETTE Eating with your hands: Indians generally eat with their hands, and although many don't do so in five-star Westernized restaurants, the majority will in most other places. Even the simplest restaurant will be able to provide a spoon as cutlery, but if you really want to experience your meal in an authentic manner, follow suit. Note that you should ideally only use your right hand (though in places where tourists go, people are unlikely to be offended if you use your left). In the north, where the food is "drier," you are traditionally not supposed to dirty more than the first two digits of your fingers. In the south, where

the food is much "wetter," you may use the whole hand to eat.

Sharing your food: It is typically Indian to share food or drinks, even if you don't really want to. On long train journeys, you're likely to meet Indian families carrying a lot of food, which they will invite you to share—do sample some, if only to get a taste of home cooking. In return, you can buy them a round of tea or cold drinks when the vendors come by.

Sharing food at a restaurant is another Indian norm; menus are set up to cater to this style of dining. So, for example, if two or more of you go to a Mughlai restaurant, you would order perhaps two kinds of kebabs, two kinds of meat/vegetable entrees, one rice, and several breads *(rotis)*. It's a good way to try a range of items.

The hygiene of *jootha*: While sharing is good manners, *jootha* is considered offensive in many parts. This refers to drinking from the same glass, eating with the same spoon, taking a bite out of someone's sandwich, or "double dipping." To share a bread or snack, break off a piece; when sharing a bottle of water, don't put your mouth to it but tilt your head back and pour. Although there are no definite rules about what is permissible or not, just make sure that you use common courtesy when sharing a meal with others.

SALADS The practice of eating Western-style salads (except raw onion) is not very common, but most restaurants do have them on the menu. Beware that it is only advisable to eat these in top-end restaurants, and make sure that the vegetables have been freshly cut and washed in boiled water.

STREET FOOD Even in smaller cities like Indore and Jaipur, street food has a fantastic tradition and following. *Samosas, vadas, bhelpuri, sev, bhajias,* and a host of deep-fried foods are all delicious, and you should try them on your trip. It's not easy for the first-time visitor to figure out which street foods are safe to eat, however—best to look for an outlet where loads of people are lined up; this means that neither the food nor the oil have been around long. Alternatively, ask your hotel for suggestions.

6 READING INDIA

by Jerry Pinto
Author, journalist, and poet

More than almost any other destination, India demands that you immerse yourself in the local culture to make sense of all you see and experience. And wherever you're headed in India, there's probably a novel you can read to explore the ways people are shaped by the landscape and history around them

LITERATURE The late R. K. Narayan, one of the grand old men of Indian letters, offers a panoramic view of village life in India. He focuses on a gentle prelapsarian village in *Malgudi Days* (Penguin), a good introduction to his work. For a more politicized investigation of the caste system, you might want to read U. R. Ananthamurthy's *Samskara* (Oxford University Press, translated from Kannada), which deals with a dilemma that convulses a village after the death of an unclean Brahmin; or Raja Rao's *Kanthapura* (New Directions), set in a village in South India that has to face the storms of Mahatma Gandhi's civil disobedience movement.

Small-town India is well represented in Arundhati Roy's Booker Prize–winning novel, *The God of Small Things* (HarperCollins), which will make you want to travel the waterways of Kerala to see the village life she describes so vividly. And then there's Bhalchandra Nemade's *Cocoon* (National Book Trust), often referred to as India's *Catcher in the Rye.*

Each of the big cities has at least one big novel. Mumbai's industrial past is presented in a charming story of two boys who grow up in a tenement in Kiran Nagarkar's *Raavan and Eddie* (Penguin

India), but if you're looking for a page-turner, one of the most compelling books you're likely to read this year is the thrilling and enlightening *Shantaram* (Abacus; St. Martin's Griffin), written by Australian Gregory David Roberts and set in a Mumbai that really comes alive. Roberts potently describes the pulsating rhythm of one of the world's headiest cities, penetrating its nefarious underground crime syndicates and getting deep inside the soul of the city's shantytowns. The book has not only taken the world by storm, but is phenomenally popular in Mumbai itself, particularly as the city anxiously awaits its turn as the central location for a big-budget movie based on the book with Johnny Depp in the titular role. Equally captivating, and also an international bestseller, is Vikram Chandra's *Sacred Games* (Harper Collins), a beautifully narrated and utterly gripping account of Mumbai's criminal underworld, seen through the eyes of its most wanted gangster and down-to-earth detective. You might also want to whip through *Q&A* (Simon & Schuster), the totally absorbing novel by Vikas Swarup; the book, incidentally, presents some controversial details of the hero's life that are omitted from *Slumdog Millionaire,* the Oscar-winning film based on the book.

Mumbai is also where Salman Rushdie grew up, and the city is one of the backdrops of his Booker prize-winning (and Booker of Bookers-winning), *Midnight's Children* (Vintage), which tells of two babies swapped at birth, one Hindu and one Muslim, one rich and one poor, both born on the stroke of midnight at India's independence. Mumbai is also the backdrop for his more notorious *The Satanic Verses* (Viking). Rushdie's style of magic realism laced with Mumbai's street lingo was anticipated in G. V. Dessani's single brilliant novel, *All About H Hatterr* (Penguin India).

Kolkata has inspired a plethora of books, including Amit Chaudhuri's plangent tale of growing up in *A Strange and Sublime Address* (Vintage) and Amitav Ghosh's *The Hungry Tide* (Houghton Mifflin), which takes off from the 300-year-old city and stirs up sediment of language and memory in the distributaries of the Ganga, in the Sundarbans. Delhi has an eponymous novel, *Delhi* (Viking India), by one of India's most widely read writers, Khushwant Singh; the book deftly mixes history with contemporary life. (Singh's *Train to Pakistan* [Penguin India] should be read alongside Bhisham Sahni's *Tamas* [Penguin India] to understand the complicated ambivalence of India's relationship with its Islamic neighbor, Pakistan.) But if you're looking for a light, highly readable introduction to India's myriad religious and spiritual paths, pick up a copy of the wholly delightful *Holy Cow* (Bantam Books), written by another Australian, Sarah Macdonald. It's a witty autobiographical account of the author's life as an expat living in Delhi and traveling around the subcontinent in various hysterical attempts to get to grips with a very different culture. Chennai has been well-captured in C. S. Lakshmi's collection of short stories, *A Purple Sea* (University of Nebraska Press).

Another novel to sample is Vikram Seth's compendious look at arranged marriage, *A Suitable Boy* (HarperCollins). This enjoyable novel is set in several cities. If you drive from Varanasi to Agra, you will pass by the scene, described by Seth, of a disaster that befell pilgrims there in the 1980s. (You may also find yourself

incorporating the phrase "a tight slap" into your speech; don't ask—just read.) Other novels of repute include Rohinton Mistry's charming stories of the minuscule Parsi community in *Such a Long Journey* (Random House) and *A Fine Balance* (Faber & Faber), with its unforgettable characters, set during 1975's State of Emergency; I. Allan Sealey's fictionalization of the life of the adventurer Claude Martin in *The Trotternama;* and Anita Desai's *Baumgartner's Bombay,* which takes a compassionate but clear-eyed look at German Jews, refugees from the Holocaust, who stayed on after the British left.

NONFICTION A good way to start a hot debate (as if an excuse were needed) is to be seen reading V. S. Naipaul's *India: A Million Mutinies Now* (Vintage). Many Western readers respond to the mixture of fear and fascination with which Naipaul considers the subcontinent. A far more contemporary and intriguing account of the nation-state that has remained a democracy for most of its 50-year history is offered by Sunil Khilnani's *The Idea of India* (Farrar, Straus & Giroux).

Don't pass up William Dalrymple's wonderful journalistic prose in either *The Age of Kali* or *City of Djinns.* The former looks at some of the pressingly negative issues that affect the people of India. The latter gives a refreshing account of life in modern Delhi while touching on poignant moments in the city's fascinating history.

Journalist P. Sainath's *Everybody Loves a Good Drought* (Penguin India) has won 13 international awards at last count for his account of the country's poorest districts and the ways in which development schemes almost never help the ostensible beneficiaries. Suketu Mehta's *Maximum City* (Viking) captures the frenetic mood of living in Mumbai when the author moves back here, and offers a fascinating scrutiny of the city's underbelly. Read it in association with *Bombay, Meri Jaan* (Penguin India; edited by Jerry Pinto and

Naresh Fernandes), an anthology of writings about the city that includes names as varied as Andre Gidé and Duke Ellington. Gita Mehta's *Karma Cola* (Vintage) is an acerbic and witty investigation into the way in which unscrupulous gurus marketed Indian spirituality to credulous Westerners in search of "enlightenment."

Those interested in Indian spirituality will uncover a wealth of material. Besides picking up the lighthearted *Holy Cow* (above), you should find a copy of Kamala Subramaniam's *The Mahabharata* (Bharatiya Vidya Bhavan), the great epic tale of the war between two clans related by the ties of kinship. *The Mahabharata* also contains the *Bhagavad Gita* or "The Celestial Song," which is often seen as the core of Hindu beliefs. *The Ramayana* (Penguin) by R. K. Narayan offers a good introduction to the epic of Rama, who is exiled and whose wife, Sita, is abducted by the demon king Ravana. Penguin India also does a compact series that includes *The Book of Krishna* by Pavan K. Varma, *The Book of the Buddha* by Arundhathi

Subramaniam, and *The Book of the Devi* by Bulbul Sharma.

For a more academic approach to Indian history, try the somewhat pedantic *Modern South Asia: History, Culture, Political Economy,* by Sugata Bose and Ayesha Jalal (Routledge); *A History of India,* by Peter Robb (Palgrave); or *A Concise History of India* by Barbara Metcalf and Thomas Metcalf (Cambridge University Press). And to learn more about the man at the heart of 20th-century India, take a look at *The Life of Mahatma Gandhi* by Louis Fischer (Easton Press).

Finally, if you're looking for a light read that gives some insight into India today, pick up a copy of Shobhaa Dé's *Superstar India—From Incredible to Unstoppable* (Penguin) in which the author discusses her very personal views on the highs and lows of her country's social, economic, and cultural values.

This is just a start. But be warned—the writing on India is as seductive as the place it describes. Once hooked, you'll want more.

7 BOLLYWOOD & BEYOND: INDIA ON THE BIG SCREEN

by Jerry Pinto & Keith Bain

Mumbai's Hindi film industry, popularly known as Bollywood, is the biggest producer of films in the world, churning out hundreds of movies annually, all of which feature superkitschy images of buxom, bee-stung-lipped heroines gyrating to high-pitched melodies while strapping studs thrust their groins in time to lip-synched banal-and-breezy lyrics. These are wonderful, predictable melodramas in which the hero is always valiant and virile, the woman always voluptuous and virtuous. The battle between good and evil (a bankable hero and a recognizably nasty

villain) must be intense, long-winded, and ultimately unsurprising—audiences do not pay good money to be challenged, but to be entertained.

Before you choose to spend a hot subtropical afternoon watching a Hindi film, know that these films are long, averaging about 3 hours. This is because they are constructed more like Elizabethan plays or old operas. Their audiences do not come for tragedies or for comedies but for full-scale performances that give them everything: the chance to laugh and cry, to bemoan the violence done unto the hero, and the opportunity to cheer as justice is done. These films are also made in defiance of the Aristotelian requirements of unity in time and space, and require from you a willing suspension of disbelief. And though the genre film has just begun—a few historicals such as *Devdas* (nine different versions) and *Parineeta* (The Espoused; 2005); some horror films like *Kaal* (Time; 2005) and *Darna Mana Hai* (Fear is Forbidden; 2003); some war films, including *Lakshya* (Goal; 2004) and *Mission Kashmir* (2000); thrillers, such as *Jism* (Body; 2003); and even political dramas like the post-9/11 *New York* (2009)—most Hindi films still work on this principle.

The top-bracket Bollywood stars, including Amitabh Bachchan (who is nearing 70), the 40-something Shah Rukh Khan (aka SRK, "King of Bollywood," and "King Khan"), heartthrob Aamir Khan, Salman Khan, and relative newcomer, former model John Abraham, are paid incredible sums by Indian standards, earning close to $1 million for a film simply because they are the names that will bring in the audiences. As it is all over the world, women get paid much less, often half of what the male stars are paid, but stars like Rani Mukherjee, Preity Zinta, and former Miss World Aishwarya Rai have their devoted followings.

Increasingly, the influence of Hollywood production values and obsession with consumer culture is becoming evident in major Bollywood releases; to keep the MTV generation (and yes, India has its very own MTV) interested, you can expect to see younger stars with an ever more visible sex appeal engaged in plots that echo some of the preoccupations of the Western silver screen. Bigger bangs, more powerful explosions, and longer chase scenes combine with racier moments, tighter outfits, and about enough attitude to put even the most self-indulgent posers to shame. But it's not all bad. In fact, some

wonderful experiments in storytelling have produced screenplays that pack a punch and wow with the twists and turns invented to keep more world-wise audiences on their toes. Also, collaborative efforts between Bollywood studios and the West are making for enterprising transnational story lines; perhaps the most interesting of these is the intricately crafted *Salaam-E-Ishq: A Tribute to Love* (2007), which travels between continents and across genres and generations to provide a fantasy romance that innovatively blends narrative techniques borrowed from a broad pedigree. It's the type of cinema that cannot fail to steal your heart. Another development is the appearance of films that attempt to somehow deconstruct the Bollywood formula while still playing to the masses. *Dev.D* (2009), for example, is a contemporary, youth-culture oriented reworking of *Devdas,* the classic novel by Sarat Chandra Chattopadhyay, which had already spawned nine film versions. The film is a good chance to get some insight into a very modern understanding of India.

Because India produces more than 700 films a year, it is in fact impossible to be monolithic about all products and speak of only a certain kind of film. Until recently, the government financed arthouse cinema, and there are signs of a growing "indie" movement in which young directors scrape together the finances and make the kind of films they want as opposed to the formulaic catch-all colorful song-and-dance extravaganzas that financiers are comfortable backing. There are also some very serious and hardhitting dramas, and one worth seeing— particularly if you're visiting Mumbai—is *Mumbai Meri Jaan* (2008), which takes a poignant look at the impact of the 2006 train bombings that took 209 lives and left over 700 more injured.

These are probably more likely to be the types of films that provide insight into what India looks and feels like—as does, paradoxically, the British film *Slumdog Millionaire* (2008), directed by Danny Boyle and codirected in India by Loveleen Tandan. If you want a deep, hard look at the social consciousness of the country, look to the wonderful works of Mira Nair, who has crafted fantastic entertainments that tug at the heartstrings and probe many issues without stooping to cheap preachy politicking (the notable exception being her recent work, *The Namesake,* 2007). You would be amiss not to see her *Salaam Bombay!* (1988), about the life of a group of Mumbai street urchins, and *Monsoon Wedding* (2001), a beautiful and poignant romantic comedy about a well-to-do Delhiite family dealing with generational conflicts that complicate traditional marriage arrangements. Work on the much-vaunted film version of *Shantaram,* which Nair is directing, came to a grinding halt in 2007 due to a Writer's Guild strike, but there is talk of production commencing in 2010; based on the riveting best-selling novel (see above), the Johnny Depp–headliner is destined to take the world by storm—if it ever gets made.

Another top-rated woman director to look for is Deepa Mehta, whose trilogy *Fire* (1996), *Earth* (1998), and *Water* (2005) are superbly moving works of high-grade cinema—and certainly preferable to her slightly irritating and kitschy *Bollywood/Hollywood* (2002), set in Canada.

Art listings aside, playing in a theater near you in any city in India will be a film in which the rich hero meets the poor heroine and falls almost instantly in love. He will declare this in song, and the scene will change to New Zealand, Switzerland, or Southeast Asia, depending on which country is most eager to attract the new beneficiaries of India's globalization. The couple will find obstacles put in their path, some by their parents and others by the villain, who will at some point have cast his lecherous eyes on the heroine. Fairly standardized violence will follow—after this comes a misunderstanding that paves the way for another song expressing the grief of betrayal or the pain of parting or that sets up what the industry calls an "item number" (which may have derived from Mumbai slang for a pretty young thing, or an "item") in which a young dancer performs the equivalent of a pole dance for the audience. When the air is cleared, justice and peace have returned to the world, the good have been rewarded, and the villains are dead or rounded up. At the film's end, you will either be floored by the extravagant color, ravished by floods of emotion, and converted to another way of telling stories; or you will be repulsed by excess and sickened by melodrama and the way in which Caucasian extras are used to represent the decadent sexualized Other. But you will not be unmoved.

3

Planning Your Trip to India

Once the playing fields of only die-hard budget New Age travelers, India has in the past decade come into its own for top-end travelers who want to be pampered and rejuvenated as well as spiritually and culturally challenged. Given its vast size, the majority of India's top attractions are remarkably easy to get to, using a clever combination of internal flights or long-haul train journeys and chauffeur-driven cars (no sane traveler would self-drive). With your own car and driver, it's also simple (and increasingly recommended) to get off the beaten track, to avoid the crowds, and perhaps discover India as it was just a few years ago. Hotels, particularly in the heritage category, offer excellent value-for-money in Western terms, and every variety of accommodation, from long-term house rentals to houseboats and homestays, is available in a range of price categories. You will dine, or rather feast, on unique and exceptional flavors, and find yourself overwhelmed by the enormous variety of cuisines; vegetarians will rejoice and carnivores might find themselves rediscovering the pleasures of "pure veg" dining. Despite a number of potential health concerns, sensible travelers will enjoy their sojourn with little more than a brief tummy upset (although you'd do well to heed our warnings about hygiene and water consumption on p. 66-67); arm yourself against mosquitoes and make sure you've had all the necessary shots before setting off. It is, however, very important to plot out your itinerary and make reservations well in advance. Finally, you'll find almost everything you need here, particularly if you're armed with a credit card and *Frommer's India, 4th Edition,* of course.

For additional help in planning your trip and for more on-the-ground resources in India, please turn to "Fast Facts," on p. 735.

1 WHEN TO GO

Your choice of where and when to go will be determined primarily by the weather. India's vastness means that the climate varies greatly from region to region, and sometimes even from day to night, as in the desert regions. The Indian year features six seasons: spring, summer, the rainy season, early and late autumn, and winter, but effectively there are but three—summer, winter, and monsoon.

You'll be better off visiting during the **high-season winter** months (Nov–Mar), when most of the country experiences pleasant, moderate temperatures (still hot enough to luxuriate in the pool), though cities in the north get chillier days as snow falls in the Himalayas. As a rule, always be prepared for warm to hot days, with the possibility of cooler weather at night. (If this has you worrying about how to pack, remember that you can pick up the most wonderful throwaway cotton garments for next to nothing and a real Pashmina scarf in every color to ward off an unexpected chill.) As with all season-driven destinations, there is a downside to traveling during peak months: From December to January, for example, Goa swells to bursting point with foreigners and city folk who arrive for the sensational beaches and parties. Lodging rates soar during these periods, so you may want to wait until the **shoulder season** (Sept–Oct, Mar–Apr), when there are fewer people and rates are very negotiable.

Summer (generally Apr–June) sees little traffic, and for good reason—the daytime heat, particularly in India's north-central regions, is debilitating, even for the locals. This is the time to plan your trip to the Himalayas instead, particularly to high altitude provinces such as Himachal Pradesh and Ladakh in Jammu and Kashmir. Ladakh, a magical region in the far north of the country, can only be visited June through September—the rest of the year it remains a destination that's strictly for hard-core adventurers looking to trek through ultraextreme cold conditions.

The **monsoon** drenches much of the country between June and September, usually starting its season in Kerala. Tamil Nadu and parts of Andhra Pradesh don't get too much rain during this period; instead they get more rainfall from a second monsoon that hits just this region around mid-October and runs through December. In Rajasthan, central India, and the northern plains, the rains typically arrive by July and fall until early September. Some of the regions are at their most beautiful during the monsoon, but it can be difficult to move around, and there is a higher risk of exposure to diseases like malaria. Flooding, power failures, and natural destruction are also not uncommon. We have noticed, however, that the monsoon has become increasing fallible and locals will tell you that global warming has had a devastating impact on the rains. These days, it's possible to spend most of June in Kerala and see only a few days of intense showers.

INDIA'S WEATHER MONTH BY MONTH

The following charts indicate the average maximum and minimum temperatures for each month of the year, as well as the average rainfall, in major tourist-destination cities and towns.

THE HIMALAYAS
Shimla, Himachal Pradesh

	Jan	Feb	Mar	Apr	May	June	July	Aug	Sept	Oct	Nov	Dec
Temp (°F)	48/35	49/36	57/44	66/51	73/58	75/60	71/59	68/59	68/56	64/54	58/44	51/39
Temp (°C)	8/1	9/2	13/6	18/10	22/14	23/15	21/15	20/15	20/13	17/12	14/6	10/3
Average rainfall (mm)	60	60	60	50	60	170	420	430	160	30	10	2

MAHARASHTRA
Mumbai

	Jan	Feb	Mar	Apr	May	June	July	Aug	Sept	Oct	Nov	Dec
Temp (°F)	85/65	86/67	89/72	90/77	91/81	88/81	85/79	84/78	86/77	90/76	90/72	87/68
Temp (°C)	21/18	30/19	31/22	32/25	32/27	31/27	29/26	28/25	30/25	32/24	32/22	30/20
Average rainfall (mm)	0	0	0	0	10	560	650	480	350	80	0	0

SOUTH INDIA
Panjim, Goa

	Jan	Feb	Mar	Apr	May	June	July	Aug	Sept	Oct	Nov	Dec
Temp (°F)	88/70	90/63	90/68	91/75	91/81	88/75	84/73	84/75	84/75	88/75	91/73	91/70
Temp (°C)	31/21	32/17	32/20	33/24	33/27	31/24	29/23	29/24	29/24	31/24	33/23	33/21
Average rainfall (mm)	2	0	0	8	59	825	891	486	246	116	34	8

Cochin, Kerala

	Jan	Feb	Mar	Apr	May	June	July	Aug	Sept	Oct	Nov	Dec
Temp (°F)	87/75	88/77	89/79	89/80	88/80	84/77	83/76	83/76	84/77	85/77	86/77	87/75
Temp (°C)	30/23	31/25	31/26	31/26	31/26	28/25	28/24	28/24	28/25	29/25	30/25	30/23
Average rainfall (mm)	20	20	40	120	310	560	520	340	240	310	160	40

Chennai, Tamil Nadu

	Jan	Feb	Mar	Apr	May	June	July	Aug	Sept	Oct	Nov	Dec
Temp (°F)	82/70	86/72	90/76	94/80	98/83	97/82	93/80	92/79	91/79	88/77	84/74	82/72
Temp (°C)	27/21	30/22	32/24	34/26	36/28	36/27	33/26	33/26	32/26	31/25	28/23	27/22
Average rainfall (mm)	30	10	10	10	40	50	90	120	120	280	330	130

Bengaluru, Karnataka

	Jan	Feb	Mar	Apr	May	June	July	Aug	Sept	Oct	Nov	Dec
Temp (°F)	79/62	84/65	89/69	91/73	89/72	82/69	80/68	79/68	81/68	80/68	78/65	77/63
Temp (°C)	26/16	28/18	31/20	32/22	31/22	27/20	26/20	26/20	27/20	26/20	25/18	25/17
Average rainfall (mm)	0	0	10	30	110	70	100	130	170	150	60	10

DELHI, RAJASTHAN & CENTRAL INDIA
Delhi

	Jan	Feb	Mar	Apr	May	June	July	Aug	Sept	Oct	Nov	Dec
Temp (°F)	68/48	73/53	83/62	95/72	100/80	101/83	93/81	91/80	92/78	90/68	81/57	71/49
Temp (°C)	20/8	22/11	28/16	35/22	38/26	38/28	33/27	32/26	33/25	32/20	27/13	21/9
Average rainfall (mm)	20	20	10	10	10	60	200	200	120	10	0	10

Agra

	Jan	Feb	Mar	Apr	May	June	July	Aug	Sept	Oct	Nov	Dec
Temp (°F)	73/43	78/46	89/55	100/67	107/77	105/83	95/80	92/78	93/75	94/62	85/49	76/44
Temp (°C)	22/6	25/7	31/12	38/19	41/25	40/28	35/26	33/25	33/23	34/16	29/9	24/6
Average rainfall (mm)	10	10	0	0	0	60	210	200	110	10	0	0

Jaipur

	Jan	Feb	Mar	Apr	May	June	July	Aug	Sept	Oct	Nov	Dec
Temp (°F)	71/49	76/54	87/63	97/74	103/80	101/83	91/79	89/77	92/75	91/69	82/59	73/51
Temp (°C)	21/9	24/12	30/17	36/23	39/26	38/28	32/26	31/25	33/23	32/20	27/15	22/10
Average rainfall (mm)	10	0	0	0	10	50	190	200	80	10	0	0

EAST INDIA
Kolkata

	Jan	Feb	Mar	Apr	May	June	July	Aug	Sept	Oct	Nov	Dec
Temp (°F)	77/57	83/63	91/71	95/77	94/79	91/80	89/80	88/80	88/79	88/76	84/67	78/58
Temp (°C)	25/13	28/17	32/21	35/25	34/26	32/26	31/26	31/26	31/26	31/24	28/19	25/14
Average rainfall (mm)	0	20	30	50	110	300	330	260	290	110	30	10

CALENDAR OF EVENTS

For an exhaustive list of events beyond those listed here, check http://events.frommers.com, where you'll find a searchable, up-to-the-minute roster of what's happening in cities all over the world.

Indians love to celebrate, and there is no end to the list of festivals that are held in honor of the gods, gurus, and historical figures that make this such a spiritually saturated and colorful destination. Festivals usually coincide with the lunar calendar, with dates published only a year in advance, so check with the local tourism office about exact dates (some may move into another month). India has relatively few national holidays when attractions, government offices, and banks are closed: Republic Day, January 26; Independence Day, August 15; Gandhi's Birthday, October 2; and Christmas.

JANUARY/FEBRUARY

Basant Festival, countrywide. The onset of spring *(basant)* is marked by various celebrations. Citrus-colored clothes are worn, and there is a profusion of dancing and singing coupled with great dinner spreads and feasts to mark the season of agricultural plenty.

Carnival, Goa. It may not be on quite the same level as celebrations in Rio, but the riot of colorful costumes and processions, as well as the exuberant dancing and music, make this an especially fun time to visit the tiny state and its beautiful beaches.

Desert Festival, Rajasthan. With camel races, camel polo, a Mr. Desert competition, and even prizes for the best-looking camel, this festival is a highlight in the Jaisalmer social calendar.

Muharram. Best experienced in the city of Lucknow, the 10-day Shiite festival commemorates the martyrdom of the grandson of the Prophet Mohammed; during a parade of religious fervor,

penitents scourge themselves with whips—often with nails or blades attached.

MARCH

Ellora Festival of Classical Dance and Music, Maharashtran interior. This festival draws some of the country's top artists to the ancient caves at this World Heritage Site.

Holi, northern India. Celebrated predominantly in the north, this joyous Hindu festival is held during the full moon—expect to be bombarded with colored water and powder.

International Yoga Festival, Rishikesh. Spiritually inclined visitors head here to take classes with *Yogacharyas* from all over the world teaching a variety of yogic disciplines.

Khajuraho Dance Festival, Madhya Pradesh. Get a glimpse of all of India's great classical dance forms.

JUNE/JULY

Rath Yatra, Puri. In Orissa's seaside temple town of Puri, this is one of the largest annual gatherings of humanity; thousands of devotees come together to help pull the Lord of the Universe and his two siblings through the streets on massive cars.

Hemis Tsechu, Ladakh. Although it's become overly-commercial in recent years, this remains the region's most spectacular monastic celebration, scheduled for June 21 and 22, 2010, when the birthday of the founder of Tibetan Buddhism is celebrated with lamaistic masked dances *(chaams)*, chanting, and music at Hemis Monastery. If you'd prefer to catch a Buddhist festival without the flea market atmosphere and touristy vibe, consider disappearing off the beaten track and joining the locals at the smaller, but far more authentic festivals at monasteries such as Lamayuru, where the **Yuru Kabgyat** attracts mostly villagers who arrive on foot, having traveled for miles to join in the spiritual celebrations (June 10–11, 2010; and June 28–29, 2011).

Ladakh Confluence, Choglamsar, Ladakh. Ladakh's new entertainment festival launched in 2009, and promises to be returning annually between June and August (check www.theconfluence. in for this year's dates). It's all about music, culture, and environment, and seems set to join the ranks of India's burgeoning party circuit; excellent world music acts, workshops, and slightly offbeat competitions (including a momo-eating event) will form part of this laid-back version of Glastonbury in the Himalayas.

August

Nehru Cup Snake Boat Races, Alleppey. Kerala's backwaters come alive with these renowned snake boat races. Second Saturday of August.

Independence Day, countrywide. Indians unite to celebrate independence. August 15.

September/October

Ganesh Chhaturthi, countrywide. This 10-day celebration of Ganesha, the elephant-headed god, is popular across India, but Mumbai is arguably the best place to experience this vibrant event, celebrated with huge processions, fireworks, and the construction of special shrines. At the end of the festival, clay images of the god are immersed in the sea.

Kullu Dussehra. Head for the Kullu Valley in Himachal Pradesh, where you can join the crowds when idols of

Hindu deities from around the region are brought together in a colorful Festival of the Gods. Similarly ecstatic revelry occurs in Mysore (Karnataka).

October/November

Diwali (Festival of Lights; also **Deepavali**), countrywide. This huge celebration among Hindu Indians is best experienced on the lawns of Umaid Bhawan Palace in Jodhpur, at a wonderful party hosted by the Maharajah (which hotel guests are invited to attend). Note, however, that just as Christmas has been exploited commercially in the West, Diwali has become a time of excessive noise, increased alcohol consumption, and all-night fireworks.

Pushkar *Mela,* Rajasthan. The annual cattle fair in the tiny temple-and-hippie town of Pushkar, is the biggest of its kind in Asia. Traders, pilgrims, and tourists from all over the world transform this budget tourist mecca into a huge tented city, with camel races, cattle auctions, huge bonfires, traditional dances, and the like.

December/January

Christmas, New Year, countrywide. Prepare for increased hotel prices as wealthy Indians celebrate both Christmas and New Year, often by taking the entire family on an extravagant vacation. New Year, in particular, may be marked by compulsory hidden extras such as special entertainment and celebratory meals. Christmas is celebrated with much fervor, if not more, as it is in the West. City hotels take great advantage of the situation, while in certain areas, such as Goa, midnight Mass and other traditions are observed. **Sunburn,** Goa. Party till you drop, then pick yourself up and carry on dancing. India's party capital is full to bursting over the festival period, but fans of the contemporary electronic music scene won't want to miss this 3 day DJ-mediated extravaganza, reportedly Asia's biggest music festival (www.sunburn-festival.com), Find yourself a small, quiet guesthouse to rest up at between bouts on the dance floor and you'll come away with a New Year's celebration well worth remembering. That's if you can remember anything at all . . .

2 ENTRY REQUIREMENTS

PASSPORTS

Anyone entering India will require a passport. For information on how to get one, see chapter 16, "Fast Facts." The websites listed there provide downloadable passport applications as well as the current fees for processing passport applications. For an up-to-date country-by-country listing of passport requirements around the world, go to the "International Travel" section of the U.S. State Department's Bureau of Consular Affairs website at **http://travel.state.gov**.

VISAS

Travelers to India—unless carrying an Indian, Nepalese, or Bhutanese passport—should apply for a tourist visa from their nearest Indian Consulate or High Commission. This is valid for multiple entries for a prestipulated period of time from the date of issue (this will depend on your travel dates and the country in which you are applying). Given the nature of India's bureaucracy, the rules and fees for application change regularly, so it's best to check with your travel agent or with the relevant authority for the latest visa information. Accurately completed visa application forms must be accompanied by two passport-size photographs (on a light background) and the appropriate processing fee; apply well in advance to avoid unforeseeable delays. You won't be admitted to India unless your passport is valid for at least 6 months after your entry, and it should typically also be valid for at least 3 months beyond the period of your intended stay. Check for fee structure and more details at www.indianembassy.org,

but note that a number of Indian embassies and consulates now outsource the visa procurement process, meaning that you need to go through a third-party that specializes in dealing with entry visas. In the U.S., the Indian Embassy is at 2107 Massachusetts Ave., Washington, DC 20008 (© 202/939-7000); and there are consulates in Houston, New York, San Francisco, and Chicago—but the visa agency you'll be dealing with is **Travisa** (http://india-visa.travisaoutsourcing.com). In Canada, visa applications can be made through http://in.vfsglobal.ca; there are consulate generals in a number of cities across the country. In the U.K., India House is in Aldwych, London WC2B 4NA (© 020/7632-3149; www.hcilondon.net); for visa fees and procurement in the U.K., visit http://in.vfsglobal.co.uk. In Australia, the Consulate General in Sydney (Level 27, 25 Bligh St.; © 02/9223-9500; www.indianconsulatesydney.org) outsources visa applications to **VFS Australia** (www.vfs-in-au.net; © 1900-960-960).

If you're applying for a visa in a country where India does not have a representative, you are advised to make inquiries at the nearest British authority.

A special permit is required for foreigners wishing to visit the Lakshadweep Islands, as well as sensitive border areas including Sikkim, parts of Ladakh, and certain roads in eastern Himachal Pradesh. For Lakshadweep, your permit will be arranged when your accommodations are reserved. Permits for the other restricted regions can be obtained in India, sometimes within a few frustrating hours;

specific details are given in the appropriate chapters. Carry a number of passport-size photographs and copies of the personal particulars and Indian visa pages of your passport to apply for these permits.

CUSTOMS
What You Can Bring into India

You can bring as much foreign currency into India as you like; if you have over $10,000 in cash or traveler's checks, however, you should complete a declaration form. You may not import Indian currency into India. In addition to your personal effects, you are allowed 2 liters of alcohol, and 200 cigarettes or 50 cigars. (Know that foreign liquors and imported cigarettes are very heavily taxed and in some areas difficult to come by.) You may carry a cellphone, camera, and pair of binoculars, but officially you may have only five rolls of film. You must complete a special Tourist Baggage Re-Export Form if you are carrying valuables such as a laptop computer, major video equipment, special camera gear, or high-value jewelry. Although there is a strong possibility that you may encounter difficulties upon leaving if these forms are not completed, you'll discover a general malaise among Customs officials, who seldom hassle foreign visitors on international flights. Also, much of the bureaucratic heavy-handedness has eased in recent years, and there is less suspicion of foreign travelers. In fact, arrival in India is incredibly straightforward and generally hassle-free.

What You Can Take Home from India

You may not export Indian currency. Exchange all notes at the airport before you depart. Note that airport money-changers frequently run out of certain currencies, so you might want to complete any exchange before you go to the airport. There is a restriction on the exportation of anything over 100 years old, particularly works of art and items of cultural significance. It is illegal to export animal or snake skins, ivory, *shatoosh* wool, or anything that has been produced using these materials. Generally, jewelry valued under Rs 10,000 may be exported, while gold jewelry valued up to Rs 2,000 is allowed.

For information on what you're allowed to bring home, contact one of the following agencies:

U.S. Citizens: U.S. Customs & Border Protection (CBP), 1300 Pennsylvania Ave., NW, Washington, DC 20229 (© **877/287-8667;** www.cbp.gov).

Canadian Citizens: Canada Border Services Agency (© **800/461-9999** in Canada, or 204/983-3500; www.cbsa-asfc.gc.ca).

U.K. Citizens: HM Customs & Excise at © **0845/010-9000** (from outside the U.K., 020/8929-0152), or consult their website at **www.hmce.gov.uk**.

Australian Citizens: Australian Customs Service at © **1300/363-263,** or log on to **www.customs.gov.au**.

New Zealand Citizens: New Zealand Customs, The Customhouse, 17–21 Whitmore St., Box 2218, Wellington (© **04/473-6099** or 0800/428-786; **www.customs.govt.nz**).

MEDICAL REQUIREMENTS
For information on medical requirements and recommendations, see "Health," p. 64.

---

3 GETTING THERE & GETTING AROUND

GETTING TO INDIA
By Plane
India's list of international airports is constantly expanding: **Mumbai** (BOM), **Delhi** (DEL), **Hyderabad** (HYD), **Goa** (GOI), **Kolkata** (**Calcutta,** CCU), **Chennai** (MAA), **Trivandrum** (TRV), **Ahmedabad** (AMD), **Bengaluru** (aka **Bangalore,**

BLR), **Amritsar** (ATQ), and **Kochi** (aka **Cochin,** COK) all receive traffic from abroad, and a number of hitherto tiny airports—particularly in Rajasthan—have been expanded to accommodate international arrivals. Modernization at all these facilities, particularly in Delhi and Mumbai, is a priority, but there are many problems—not least of which is that the rate of expansion simply cannot keep up with the exponential increase in traffic. Consequently, the first-time traveler to India may easily be unnerved by the sheer apparent chaos and disorganization of it all. Mumbai receives the greatest amount of international traffic and is the best point of arrival for onward travel to Goa and South India. Be warned, however, that in spite of a recent overhaul, Mumbai airport facilities are poor, and there are plans to shift terminals while new ones are under construction. Most flights arrive in India late at night, in order to leave their Western destinations during daylight hours, so booking an "immediate" onward domestic flight invariably requires some wait at the airport. Delhi's international airport—the principal starting point for journeys throughout North India, including the Himalayan regions and Rajasthan as well as east India—is substantially better. Only fly in to Kolkata (Calcutta) if you plan to explore east India exclusively. If you want to avoid spending too much time at the airport, note that Kingfisher, Jet Airways, British Airways, Virgin, and Air India all have flights with daytime arrival into India.

Most major airline carriers have flights to India; the country's top airlines are **Kingfisher, Jet Airways,** and state-owned **Air India.** All three have direct, nonstop flights from London, but you can fly in from just about anywhere in the world. The majority of flights originating in Europe or the U.S. will touch down either in Mumbai or in Delhi; it is possible to fly direct to many other cities around the country, although that may entail a routing through the Middle East. Both Mumbai's **Chhatrapati Shivaji International Airport** (www.csia.in) and Delhi's **Indira Gandhi International Airport** (www.delhiairport.com) are busy and increasingly so, with dramatic changes to infrastructure in recent years. Delhi's airport has been gearing up for when the city hosts the Commonwealth Games in 2010, while Mumbai's status as the subcontinent's economic capital means that inbound business is always booming. Mumbai, in particular, is geared up for **transit passengers,** with some of the biggest and glitziest hotels in the city in the immediate vicinity of both the domestic and the international terminals—the ins and outs of both these airports (situated some distance apart) are discussed in detail in chapter 10. Delhi's airport terminals have expanded and modernized considerably recently, and most people touching down here spend at least a day or two exploring the historic sights before heading off to see the Taj Mahal in Agra. From Mumbai or Delhi, you can fly to just about any corner of the country.

It's a good idea to shop around for fares on the Internet, through online travel agencies like Travelocity.com, Expedia.com, Mobissimo.com, and Orbitz.com, or through airline websites. Or make use of a consolidator, which hunts for the cheapest available seats on your travel dates.

From North America Count on spending between 13 and 22 hours traveling and most flights require you to touch down at least once in Europe, the Gulf, or an Asian destination. However, your best (from a traveling and a comfort and an environmental point of view) is with either **Air India** or **Continental Airlines,** which both have 13½- to 15-hour nonstop flights from New York's JFK or Newark airports to both Mumbai and Delhi. **Jet Airways** has flights from Newark to Mumbai via Brussels.

From the U.K. Many reasonably priced direct flights are available, or you can take a connecting flight in continental Europe or the Middle East; the latter option hardly seems worth considering since the excellent Indian-owned **Kingfisher Airlines** began it's daily services to Mumbai (with connections to Delhi), and **Air India** offers such affordable fares on this sector and on its nonstop flights between London and Delhi. Of course, you can also fly in with a host of other (pricier) airlines. **Jet Airways** has two daily nonstop flights between London and Mumbai and one a day to Delhi. Jet and Air India are both a lot more affordable than the other two airlines with nonstop flights: **British Airways** has two daily direct flights to both Delhi and Mumbai, daily flights to Bangalore, and occasional direct flights to Kolkata and Chennai; **Virgin Atlantic** operates nonstop flights to Mumbai and Delhi; and there are many more airlines that get you there with a change of planes in their respective hubs.

From Australia & New Zealand You can fly directly to India from Australia. From New Zealand you will more than likely be offered a flight package that incorporates more than one airline. The majority of touchdowns and changeovers are in Malaysia, Thailand, Hong Kong, and Singapore.

From South Africa **South African Airways** flies nonstop to Mumbai several times a week from Johannesburg. Or you can fly via Dubai to Delhi/Mumbai/Cochin on **Emirates.**

FLYING FOR LESS: TIPS FOR GETTING THE BEST AIRFARE

- First, search the Internet for cheap fares. In the U.K., go to **Travelsupermarket** (✆ 0845/345-5708; www.travelsupermarket.com), a flight search engine that offers flight comparisons for the budget airlines whose seats often end up in bucket-shop sales. Other websites for booking airline tickets online include **Cheapflights.com, SmarterTravel.com, Priceline.com,** and **Opodo** (www.opodo.co.uk). Meta search sites (which find and then direct you to airline and hotel websites for booking) include **Sidestep.com** and **Kayak.com**—the latter includes fares for budget carriers like Jet Blue and Spirit as well as the major airlines. In addition, most airlines offer online-only fares that even their phone agents know nothing about.
- Consolidators, also known as bucket shops, are wholesale brokers in the airline-ticket game. Consolidators buy deeply discounted tickets ("distressed" inventories of unsold seats) from airlines and sell them to online ticket agencies, travel agents, tour operators, corporations, and, to a lesser degree, the general public. Consolidators advertise in Sunday newspaper travel sections (often in small ads with tiny type), both in the U.S. and the U.K. They can be great sources for cheap international tickets. On the down side, bucket shop tickets are often rigged with restrictions, such as stiff cancellation penalties (as high as 50%–75% of the ticket price). And keep in mind that most of what you see advertised is of limited availability. Several reliable consolidators are worldwide and available online. **Flights.com** has excellent fares worldwide, particularly to Europe. They also have "local" websites in 12 countries. **Air Tickets Direct** (✆ 888/858-8884; www.airticketsdirect.com) is based in Montreal and leverages the currently weak Canadian dollar for low fares; they also book trips to places that U.S. travel agents won't touch, such as Cuba.

Note: Before you leave home, know what you can carry on and what you can't. For the latest updates on items you are prohibited to bring in carry-on luggage, go to **www.tsa.gov/travelers/airtravel**.

GETTING AROUND

You can research prices and deals on travel and hotels at reliable online travel companies based in India. Try www.makemytrip.com, www.yatra.com, www.cleartrip.com, www.tcindia.com, or www.travelmart india.com. Note that Indian travel sites are not able to accept foreign credit cards, due to intensive antifraud card verification systems.

By Plane

Because train travel is time consuming, and roads generally appalling, the best way to cover huge distances is by air. A handful of very active low-cost airlines means that you have a wide choice at bargain prices; no need to scour all the websites, though, if you're looking for the lowest price—simply log on to www.travelocity.co.in or www.yatra.com, two excellent sites. **Jet Airways** (www.jetairways.com), with its fleet of new planes, First-World service, and good connections, is still a very good airline, but **Kingfisher Airlines** (© 1800/180-0101; www.flykingfisher.com) is definitely our favorite: Aircrafts are brand-new, cabin crew are efficient and superfriendly, and service is exemplary—in the last 2 years Kingfisher has expanded its network to include even niche market destinations such at Agatti in the Lakshadweep islands. They frequently offer a better deal than their competitors, and online booking is painless. National carrier **Air India** (which has completely merged with and absorbed Indian) may be having financial troubles, but services have improved dramatically—in fact, when we've most recently flown with them, they compared favorably against Jet. Another contender for the domestic

crown is **Paramount Airways** (© 800/180-1234; www.paramountairways.com); predominantly based in South India but steadily expanding, it offers full business-class cabins and service at less than economy-class fares. Basically, opt for Kingfisher or Paramount if the price is comparable, but don't hesitate to fly Jet or Air India if the price is right.

Best of the low-budget airlines (and clean, reliable, relatively cheap) is **SpiceJet** (© 800/180-3333; www.spicejet.com). Also worth comparing prices with are **Go Air** (© 800/222-111 or 09223/222-111; www.goair.in) and **IndiGo** (© 099-1038-3838 or 800/180-3838; www.goindigo.in). If price is important, you can usually save money with one of these airlines—but don't expect top-notch service (often no meals or beverages served), and worst of all, you may have lengthy delays. Note that erstwhile Airline Deccan has been completely absorbed by Kingfisher, which has launched a semibudget brand, **Kingfisher Red**, although it's not yet fully understood how this service differs from its full-fare flights. Similarly, **Jet Lite** is Jet's lower-priced wing, accessed via a separate website, www.jetlite.com.

India's **domestic and international check-in and preboarding procedure** may be one of the most rigorous in the world. Technically, check-in will start 180 minutes prior to international departure, and you need to produce a ticket before being allowed access to the airport building (airlines generally have ticketing windows for collection of e-tickets purchased online, or if you need to buy a ticket at the airport; alternatively, speak to a security officer, who will escort you to the appropriate ticket counter). Arriving less than 60 minutes prior to domestic departure is *definitely* not recommended. Your checked baggage must be scanned and sealed before you report to the check-in counter. The list of dangerous items not permitted in your carry-on bags is fairly extensive, but these days no more so than at airports around the world (and because the security is so tight, they tend to be less paranoid about what you can or cannot carry). In any case, India's screening procedures genuinely enhance your sense of security—there are no half-hearted measures, and personnel are generally very pleasant in their attitude, even as you're being frisked by a uniformed army officer. Check-in closes 30 minutes prior to departure. After check-in, you should immediately head for the first security check, which will involve a body pat-down and a scan of your carry-on luggage. Boarding gates close 15 minutes prior to scheduled departure (although delays are fairly frequent), and there may be second body and carry-on checks before you are permitted to board the plane. In some instances, you will be asked to identify your checked luggage on the tarmac. While frequent travelers may be irritated by these ungainly, time-consuming methods, others find the process provides peace of mind.

Tip: Always have your concierge (or yourself to be sure) reconfirm your flight at least 72 hours before departure to save yourself the frustration of arriving at the airport only to find that your name has been deleted from the computer.

By Car

India's roads are statistically the most dangerous in the world—according to *The Times of India,* August 2009, India reported the highest road fatalities in the world with 13 people dying every hour. Self-driven rental cars are simply not available (with the exception of unauthorized operators in Goa) and if they were, renting your own car and attempting to traverse the chaos that passes for traffic is simply suicidal. That said, having your own vehicle—and a driver who knows the roads, can read road signs when they're present, and can communicate with locals—is in

many ways the best way to get around. You can set your own pace, without having to worry about making public-transport connections (a major headache taken care of), and you can see the sights and experience many of the attractions without feeling anxious (your driver will be a huge help in providing advice on customs and pricing—not to mention helping with mundane everyday needs such as topping up your local airtime), as well as experience off-the-beaten-track towns and rural scenes that give you the only sense of real India. And by American and European standards, the luxury of being chauffeured around the country—not necessarily in a high-end luxury vehicle, keep in mind—is ridiculously cheap. Certainly this is the way to go to concentrate on certain parts of India, such as Rajasthan, but it's not advisable as a way to cover long-distance journeys—aim to spend no more than 3 to 4 hours a day in the car (there will be, of course, exceptions). *Note:* Whatever you do, make sure your plan does not include traveling at night.

If you plan to tour North India by car, setting off from Delhi, contact Khaver Ali Khan (khaver@kamalan-travels.com) who will put you in touch with one of his travel experts at **Kamalan Travels** ★★★, and you can create a custom tour within any budget (✆ **011-257-30256,** -33652, or 97-1100-8521; www.kamalan-travels. com). In South India, we wouldn't travel with anyone other than **Kerala Adventures** ★★★ (www.keralaadventure.com) where Babu John in Kochi (✆ **0484/231-3744** or 0484/324-2021; comvoyge@ vsnl.net) and his brother John Thomas in Trivandrum (✆ 0471/243-3398 or 0471/231-9548; touch@keralaadventure. com) provide excellent drivers, interesting itineraries, and a formidable understanding of what it is that a foreign traveler wants to get out of their time in India.

What kind of car? Standard cars are sometimes antique-looking and very romantic Ambassadors, tough cars despite their appearance, but sometimes unpredictable; don't rely on them for long out-of-town journeys—better perhaps to opt for a modern vehicle like the compact Indica. A vehicle with off-road capabilities is essential in some of the more remote and hilly regions, including eastern Himachal Pradesh, Ladakh, Sikkim, and parts of Uttarakhand; it is also recommended for some of the awful road conditions in Madhya Pradesh and Karnataka, for example, where there may be more potholes than patches of tarmac. Air-conditioned vehicles cost more but are always recommended because you may want to keep windows closed in order to shut out the endless traffic noise and pollution.

How much will it cost? Charges for this sort of car hire vary considerably; see our guidelines below. If you use a hotel rental service, you usually have to fork out exorbitant fees—although the vehicle and quality of service will generally be top-notch. At the other end of the scale, you can walk up to a driver in the street, negotiate an excellent deal, and spend the rest of your vacation watching the tires being changed. It's often a good idea to start by contacting the Tourist Development Corporation in whatever state you wish to hire a car (contact details are in individual chapters). Their rates are usually reasonable and fixed; you'll be spared the battle of the haggle; and you won't have to live with the misery of being overcharged. We provide price indications in individual chapters, but a good way to estimate how much a vehicle should cost for a multiday run is to calculate three things: a) the approximate distance you will travel multiplied by the per-kilometer rate (usually between Rs 10 and Rs 20 depending on the car); b) an overnight charge of Rs 150 to Rs 350 per night, plus state taxes, tolls, and across-state permits and fees; and c) the mileage for the car to return to its place of origin, even if it returns empty.

Each chapter lists travel agencies that can assist you with car rental, many with their own fleet of vehicles and drivers; if the price doesn't seem right, shop around. Finally, when it comes to tipping your driver, a fair amount is Rs 200 to Rs 300 for each day he's been with you. If you feel you got exemplary service and want to give him more, however, by all means give him what you feel he deserves. If, on the other hand, you've had to tolerate a surly, uncooperative, and inefficient chauffeur, make sure you let the agency know, and reflect it in the tip as you see fit. *Tip:* Your car driver may sometimes drive you around for an hour in a new city rather than do the sensible thing and ask for directions. Remember, in most cities the best people to ask for directions are usually auto-rickshaw or taxi drivers. If you are on foot, however, more often than not if you ask a rickshaw or cab driver for directions, he'll probably tell you your destination is "too far" and that you need to hire his services.

Warning: If you are involved in an accident, it's best to get out of your vehicle and away from the scene without delay, inform your rental agency or hotel immediately, and have them inform local authorities. An accident involving the injury or death of a cow or person may result in a mob assault on all occupants of the offending vehicle as well as its incineration.

Taxis & Auto-rickshaws These modes of transport are the ways to go within your chosen city or town. Auto-rickshaws are best for short journeys only, being slow, bumpy, and open-air—in other words, open to pollution. Always, always negotiate the rate upfront, having established the average going rate (unless the driver is using a "meter reading chart," in which case check it carefully, and make sure he is not using the night 11pm–5am chart, when charges are higher). We have tried to indicate these rates throughout, but given the potential escalation in fuel costs, it's best to ask about the going rate (your hotel

(Tips) Booking Your Train Ticket at the Station: The Nitty-Gritty

Even though you will be told that there are no special lines or windows for foreigners who want to book train tickets, we assure you that this is not the case. More important, most trains have a quota of seats specifically for foreigners. This means that even if a train is completely booked up, as a foreigner you may be able to get a seat, unless other foreigners booking through the same service have already filled the seat quota. This is valuable information to keep in mind, because an agent cannot book a seat for you on this quota, nor can this be booked from the regular booking window; you must go personally to a **Foreign Tourist Rail Reservation Counter** (sometimes called Foreign Tourist Bureaus) with your passport, and pay either in foreign currency (cash or credit card) or show a currency encashment certificate or ATM receipt. The ticket costs exactly the same as the regular ticket (except for credit card surcharges). Train stations at the following Indian cities have a Foreign Tourist Rail Reservation Counter: Agra-Cantonment, Ahmedabad, Aurangabad, Bangalore, Chennai, New Delhi, Jaipur, Jodhpur, Kolkata, Mumbai, Secunderabad, Vadodara, Varanasi, and Vasco-Da-Gama (Goa). There's also a counter at the Delhi Tourism & Transport Development Corporation office at Indira Gandhi International Airport in the Arrivals lounge. In Mumbai, this office is tucked away next to the Government Tourist Office, on the first floor of the Western Railway Building, opposite Churchgate Station.

or host should know) and figure out a fixed price for a given journey. To get from the station or airport to your hotel, use the prepaid taxi booths; remember to hand over your receipt only *after* reaching your destination. Be aware that in some cities it's a toss-up between forcing the driver to use his meter, only to be taken for a city-wide spin, and agreeing to a slightly higher than normal price and being taken from A to B.

Remember: Carry your passport at all times—many of the borders between states have checkpoints where passports may be checked. Also always have with you at least one photocopy of your passport and visa and four to five passport-size photographs; you will need them for permits and other unforeseen bureaucratic paperwork, like getting a prepaid SIM card for a cellphone.

By Train

India's rail network is the second largest in the world, and you can pretty much get

anywhere in the country by train. That said, train journeys between major destinations can consume massive amounts of time (often more than car travel); and the network, tiers (one of the A/C, or air-conditioned classes may, for instance, be better than non-A/C first class), and connections can be confusing. It's best to determine well in advance whether or not your destination is accessible from your point of origin and which tier is the most comfortable, and then factor in delays; some slow trains stop at every two-hut village along the way, and this can extend traveling time by hours. Generally, you should only consider long-distance train travel if you are assured of exotic scenery (like the **Konkan Railway,** which connects Mumbai with Goa, Karnataka, and Kerala, running along the Konkan coast); or if the journey is overnight (like Delhi to Varanasi) and you have reserved a **first-class air-conditioned sleeper** or **second-class air-conditioned sleeper** berth, preferably the two-tier variety. (Never book regular **second class,** which can be torturous, claustrophobic, and distressing if you are at all intimidated by crowds.) You will be particularly comfortable aboard the overnight **Rajdhani**—the superfast train connects Delhi to Mumbai for Rs 2,145 or to Kolkata (Howrah) for Rs 2,180 in the two-tier A/C (air-conditioned) class; it also connects Delhi with Chennai, Bangalore, Bhubaneswar, Thiruvananthapuram, Abu Road, Ahmedabad, and Ajmer. The best daytime travel train is the **Shatabdi;** these intercity trains have several routes between important tourist destinations (Delhi to Amritsar: Rs 665; Mumbai to Madgaon [Goa]: Rs 700; Delhi to Jaipur: Rs 485). Book a seat in the air-conditioned **Chair Car** class; small meals, tea, coffee, and bottled water are included in the ticket price, seats are comfortable and clean, and toilets are usually usable, but not great.

For extensive railway information, you can log on to **www.indianrail.gov.in**, which shows routes, availability, and prices for all Indian trains, but you cannot book online from overseas. For tips on how to maneuver this rather unwieldy website to get the information you need, see the box below. Better still, visit **www.seat61.com**, the online authority for train travel across the globe with a detailed, dedicated page devoted to train travel in India. Amongst many other issues, it explains in great detail how to purchase a train ticket from outside India using the government-sponsored ticketing website **www.irctc.co.in**. Do note that you can also purchase tickets for train journeys in India using the relatively painless **www.cleartrip.com** website which charges a Rs 100 booking fee per ticket, but allows you to buy your ticket using a credit card.

Purchasing tickets usually requires some advance planning, and it's a good idea to

---

(Tips) Booking Online: Understanding the Indian Railway Website

Using the Indian Railway website can be an exercise in frustration; here are some tips on how to master it with ease. After you log on to **indianrail.gov.in,** click on "Train/Fare Accommodation" on the bottom menu (third choice from the left). Next fill in where you want to depart from (source station name) and your destination, but (and here's the key), only type the first three letters of the name of the place (mum for Mumbai, ban for Bengaluru—because it's name only recently changed from *Ban*galoree—and del for Delhi, and so on). Then fill in the class of service you're interested in (safest to pick "All"). Enter your date of travel (or a fictitious date) and click "get it." This will take you to another window where you narrow your choice of source and destination from a pull-down menu (all places beginning with mum and ban and del). For Bengaluru you may get several choices—and this is another tricky part—you have to pick one (usually the first "Bangalore" choice on the list). You will get a list of all the trains, with times, that run between the two cities. Now pick the train you want by clicking on the white circle to the left of the train's name to highlight it green, then choose your class of service (on the right). At this stage you can change the date if you like, and then get availability or fares. The availability is sometimes not online between 10pm to 6am Indian time, so if you don't get what you want, try again later. The availability chart basically tells you how many seats are still available in the class of service you've chosen.

make all-important **ticket reservations** (particularly for overnight travel) before you leave for India, especially if you're coming during peak holiday season. You can make ticket reservations through your hotel or an agent (usually for a relatively small fee), or you can brave the possibility of long lines and silly form-filling at the train station; that said, check out "Booking Your Train Ticket at the Station," below, to see if the station you're heading

to has a counter set up especially for foreigners. Not only is this an easy way to book your seat, it may be the only way to secure tickets when trains are completely full and agents can do nothing to assist.

Indian Railways Indrail Pass is a "discount" ticket for unlimited travel over a specific number of days (for example, air-conditioned chair car/first and second class: 7 days $135), but these still require reservations and are only likely to benefit

The Romance of Rail: India's Special Train Journeys

India's most famous luxury train, **Palace on Wheels,** currently operates in Rajasthan, and has 14 opulently furnished en-suite saloons, a bar, and two restaurants (℃ **888/INDIA-99** [46342-99] in the U.S. and Canada, 011/2332-5939 or 011/2335-3155 in India; www.palaceonwheels.net or www.thepalaceonwheels. com). Over 7 days, the train travels from Delhi to Jaipur, Jaisalmer, Jodhpur, Sawai Madhopur (Ranthambhore), Chittaurgarh, Udaipur, Bharatpur, and Agra; and finishes its trip back in Delhi. The "Week in Wonderland" trip costs $5,250 to $7,700 double, including all travel, accommodations, sightseeing, and meals, but not taxes. And, if you like the sound of that, you might want to take a look at the similar service (and routing) offered by the very chic **Royal Rajasthan on Wheels** (℃ **877/INDIA-99** [46342-99] in the U.S. and Canada; www.royalpalaceon wheels.com or www.heritageonwheels.com; $8,310–$12,670 double for 7 nights). Other luxury trains in India include: Maharasthra's **Deccan Odyssey** (see chapter 5); **Golden Chariot** (see chapter 9) which makes traveling through Karnataka less tedious; **Fairy Queen,** the oldest operating steam locomotive in the world, dating from 1855, which takes an overnight trip from Delhi to Alwar, Rajasthan (with a visit to the Sariska wildlife sanctuary) and back.

For a truly exclusive train journey board the private **The Viceroy of India**—aka The Darjeeling Mail Tour—which runs just one or two 15-day trips a year from Mumbai to Calcutta via Jaipur, Delhi, Varanasi, and Darjeeling, and is priced at $22,790 (Viceroy class) or $34,390 (Maharaja suite) double (www. gwtravel.co.uk).

Getting to the hill stations of Shimla (Himachal Pradesh), Darjeeling (West Bengal), Matheran (Maharashtra), or Ooty (Tamil Nadu) can be a scenic novelty if you don't mind spending long hours traveling in the atmospheric **"toy trains"** that chug their ways along narrow-gauge tracks to high altitudes by way of an endless series of hairpin loops—fabulous views are guaranteed. And then, of course, there is the **Konkan Railway,** which runs along the Malabar coast and has truly wonderful scenery almost every click-clack of the way.

travelers who expect to make two or more long-distance journeys in a short time.

In every chapter we have included telephone numbers for railway stations, but don't expect too much information from these, if indeed you are even able to get through.

Tip: To avoid unnecessary stress while traveling by train (particularly on overnight journeys), use a chain and padlock to secure your luggage and fasten it to some part of your berth or cabin. Be sensible, and don't leave valuables lying around while you sleep.

By Bus

Unless you are on a serious budget and traveling in India for months, we recommend you avoid all forms of bus travel. Often crammed full of commuters, state-operated buses are driven at bloodcurdling speeds along dangerous and punishing roads. Numerous so-called deluxe or luxury buses, operated by private companies, often ply similarly dangerous routes overnight. You may be tempted to save time and money with this option, but be aware that safety is rarely a priority, and sleeping is almost impossible thanks to generally uncomfortable seating and/or noise. Regular stops at roadside truck stops along the way will have you arriving at your destination bleary-eyed and exhausted, wondering why you've opted for a vacation in hell; on one of our most recent trips we were horrified to witness a "luxury" bus windshield shatter midjourney, and the driver simply continued on (through the night) till he reached his destination. On some routes (such as Delhi-Jaipur or Kochi-Bengaluru), the exception is the comfortable "Volvo" bus with good suspension and skilled drivers. Another exception is the Manali-to-Leh route, where the Trans-Himalayan scenery is jaw-droppingly awesome, and an overnight stop in tents is part of the deal (p. 652). If you do decide to take a bus, a good place to search for deluxe (or "luxury") private services and book them online is **www.ticketvala.com**.

Note: Buses in India do not have onboard toilets (thankfully, given the state of so many of these on trains), so stops are usually at grimy roadside *dhabas* (local diners) or just along the side of the road.

4 MONEY & COSTS

The Value of the Indian Rupee (Rs) vs. Other Popular Currencies

Rs	US$	Can$	UK£	Euro (€)	Aus$	NZ$
1	$0.02	C$0.02	£0.01	€0.01	A$0.02	NZ$0.03

Frommer's lists exact prices in the local currency. The currency conversions quoted above were correct at press time. However, exchange rates fluctuate dramatically. At press time, US$1 bought you around Rs 49, and 1 euro equaled almost Rs 70, while £1 was worth around Rs 80. Bear in mind that in spite of the falling dollar/euro, a few dollars, pounds, or euros go a long way in India. For up-to-the-minute **currency conversions,** log on to **www. xe.com/ucc** or **www.oanda.com/convert/ classic** to check the latest rates.

You cannot obtain Indian currency anywhere outside India, and you may not carry rupees beyond India's borders. You may have to exchange at least some money at the airport upon your arrival; change

India is one destination where it is really worthwhile to arrange an airport transfer with your hotel so that you can avoid waiting in long lines at the airport money-changer, dealing with prepaid booths, or negotiating fees with drivers and touts. After a good night's rest, head to the nearest bank or ATM for a cash infusion.

PLANNING YOUR TRIP TO INDIA

3

MONEY & COSTS

just enough to cover airport incidentals and transportation to your hotel, since the rate will be quite unfavorable.

It's always advisable to bring money in a variety of forms on a vacation: a mix of cash, credit cards, and traveler's checks—although the latter can really prove to be a nuisance and should really only be used as a backup. Be sure to bring more than one kind of credit card since certain cards may not work in smaller towns or at certain ATMs.

In many international destinations, ATMs offer the best exchange rates. Avoid exchanging money at commercial exchange bureaus and hotels, which often have the highest transaction fees.

CURRENCY

Indian currency cannot be obtained before you enter India. The Indian rupee (Rs) is available in denominations of Rs 1,000, Rs 500, Rs 100, Rs 50, Rs 20, Rs 10, and Rs 5 notes. You will occasionally come across Rs 1 or Rs 2 notes—treat them as souvenirs. Minted coins come in denominations of Rs 5, Rs 2, and Rs 1, as well as 50 and 25 paise (rarely seen now). There are 100 paise in a rupee.

Note: Badly damaged or torn rupee notes (of which there are many) may be refused, particularly in larger cities, but less fuss is made over them in small towns. Check the change you are given and avoid accepting these.

Banks offer good exchange rates, but they tend to be inefficient and the staff

lethargic about tending to foreigners' needs. You run the risk of being ripped off by using **unauthorized money-changers;** the most convenient option is to use ATMs while you're in the big cities. Always ask for an encashment receipt when you change cash—you will need this when you use local currency to pay for major expenses (such as lodging and transport, though you should use a credit card wherever possible). You will also be asked to produce this receipt when you re-exchange your rupees before you leave India.

ATMS (AUTOMATED TELLER MACHINES)

Getting cash from your checking account (or cash advances on your credit card) at an ATM is by far the easiest way to get money. These 24-hour machines are readily available in all Indian cities and larger towns and at large commercial banks such as Citibank, Standard Chartered, ABN Amro, and Hong Kong & Shanghai Bank; in fact, these days, there are ATMs even in relatively small towns, although some of them may run out of cash or have limits on the amount that can be withdrawn at any one time. **Cirrus** (© **800/424-7747;** www.mastercard.com) and **PLUS** (© **800/ 843-7587;** www.visa.com) networks span the globe; call or check online for ATM locations at your destination. Be sure to find out your daily withdrawal limit before you depart. You should have no problem withdrawing Rs 10,000 at a time from an ATM (which goes a long way in India),

What Things Cost in India

This is a sampling of *average* prices you're likely to pay in India. Bear in mind that big cities generally have much higher prices than smaller towns, and that any place that attracts tourists inevitably attracts rip-off artists.

	Rupees
Luxury hotel room	Rs 5,000–Rs 36,000
Budget to moderate hotel room	Rs 250–Rs 8,000
Cup of tea from a stall	Rs 4–Rs 10
Cup of tea at a hotel	Rs 10–Rs 250
Newspaper	Rs 2–Rs 5
Weekly magazine	Rs 15–Rs 70
Taxi for the day	Rs 600–Rs 4,000
1km by auto-rickshaw	Rs 9–Rs 15
Meal at a local diner *(dhaba)*	Rs 35–Rs 250
Main course in a luxury restaurant	Rs 150–Rs 1,200

although some ATMs may have slightly lower limits.

Also keep in mind that many banks impose a fee every time a card is used at a different bank's ATM, and that fee can be higher for international transactions (up to $5 or more).

CREDIT CARDS

Credit cards are another safe way to carry money. They also provide a convenient record of all your expenses, and they generally offer relatively good exchange rates. You can withdraw cash advances from your credit cards at banks or ATMs, but high fees make credit card cash advances a pricey way to get cash. Keep in mind that you'll pay interest from the moment of your withdrawal, even if you pay your monthly bills on time. Also, note that many banks now assess a 1% to 3% "transaction fee" on all charges you incur abroad (whether you're using the local currency or your native currency).

MasterCard and Visa are commonly accepted throughout India. American Express is accepted by most major hotels and restaurants; Diners Club has a much smaller following.

TRAVELER'S CHECKS

You can buy traveler's checks at most banks. They are offered in denominations of $20, $50, $100, $500, and sometimes $1,000. Generally, you'll pay a service charge ranging from 1% to 4%

The most popular traveler's checks are offered by **American Express** (✆ 800/807-6233, or 800/221-7282 for card holders—this number accepts collect calls, offers service in several foreign languages, and exempts Amex gold and platinum cardholders from the 1% fee); **Visa** (✆ 800/732-1322)—AAA members can obtain Visa checks for a $9.95 fee (for checks up to $1,500) at most AAA offices or by calling ✆ 866/339-3378; and **MasterCard** (✆ 800/223-9920).

Be sure to keep a record of the traveler's checks serial numbers separate from your checks in the event that they are stolen or lost. You'll get a refund faster if you know the numbers.

(Tips) The Battle of the Haggle

Sure, things are cheap to begin with and you may feel silly haggling over a few rupees, but keep in mind that if you're given a verbal quote for an unmarked item, it's probably (but not always) twice the realistic asking price. Use discretion though, because items that are priced ridiculously low to begin with are hardly worth reducing further—either you're being conned or you're being cruel. To haggle effectively, make a counteroffer under half price, and don't get emotional. Protests and adamant assertions ("This is less than it cost me to buy!") will follow. Stick to your guns and see what transpires; stop once you've reached a price you can live with. Remember that once the haggle is on, a challenge has been initiated, and it's fun to regard your opponent's act of salesmanship as an artistic endeavor. Let your guard slip, and he will empty your wallet. Take into account the disposition and situation of the merchant; you don't want to haggle a genuinely poor man into deeper poverty! And if you've been taken (and we all have), see it as a small contribution to a family that lives on a great deal less than you do.

Traveler's checks are useful in that, unlike cash, they can be replaced if lost or stolen, but they are far less popular now that most cities have 24-hour ATMs that allow you to withdraw small amounts of cash as needed.

5 HEALTH

STAYING HEALTHY

Consult your doctor or local travel clinic concerning precautions against diseases that are prevalent in India. The following cautionary list may have you wondering whether travel is advisable at all. However, don't be alarmed: Millions of travelers leave India having suffered nothing more than an upset stomach—even this small inconvenience should settle within a few days, your system the stronger for it.

General Availability of Health Care

Contact the **International Association for Medical Assistance to Travelers** (**IAMAT;** ⊘ **716/754-4883,** or 416/652-0137 in Canada; www.iamat.org) for tips on travel and health concerns in the countries you're visiting. The United States

Centers for Disease Control and Prevention (⊘ **800/232-4636;** www.cdc.gov) provides up-to-date information on health hazards by region or country and offers tips on food safety. **Travel Health Online** (www.tripprep.com), sponsored by a consortium of travel medicine practitioners, also offers helpful advice on traveling abroad.

VACCINATIONS You will almost certainly be advised to be vaccinated against **hepatitis A, cholera, tetanus,** and **typhoid;** also make sure your polio immunization is up to date. Longer-stay visitors should consider getting the hepatitis B and meningitis vaccinations as well. Note that travelers arriving from yellow fever–infected areas must have a yellow fever vaccination certificate.

When you change money, ask for some small bills (a wad of Rs 10s and Rs 20s) for tipping or *baksheesh* (see "Tipping" in chapter 16, "Fast Facts: India"). At smaller outlets and vendors, you'll also frequently be told that there is no change for your Rs 500 note. Keep your smaller bills separate from the larger ones, so that they're readily accessible.

PACKING A FIRST-AID KIT Besides antidiarrheal medication, of which the most important are rehydration salts (available all over India as ORS—oral rehydration salts), it may be worthwhile to carry a course of antibiotics (such as Ciprofloxacin, which is widely available in India at a fraction of what you'll pay back home) for **stomach-related illnesses**. It's also worthwhile to take an antiseptic cream, and possibly an antibacterial soap (though the type of soap used matters less than vigilance: Wash your hands regularly, particularly before eating). Pack **prescription medications** in your carry-on luggage in their original containers with pharmacy labels, so they'll make it through airport security. Also bring along copies of your prescriptions in case you lose your pills or run out (include the generic name; local pharmacists will be unfamiliar with brand names). Don't forget an extra pair of contact lenses or prescription glasses or an extra inhaler.

COMMON AILMENTS

TROPICAL ILLNESSES Besides malaria, India's mosquitoes are also responsible for spreading untreatable dengue fever and virulent Japanese encephalitis. Again, the best advice is to avoid getting bitten in the first place. (See the tips below.)

MALARIA Most doctors will advise you to take a course of antimalarial tablets, but as is the case elsewhere, the best prevention is not to get bitten. Malaria is a parasitic infection borne by the female Anopheles mosquito, and risks are greater in warm, wet areas (particularly during monsoon) and at night, when mosquitoes are at their most active. Cover all exposed skin with antimosquito creams (many effective creams are available in India) or sprays as evening approaches, and use repellent coils or electric plug-in mosquito repellents as a preventive measure at night, particularly in hotel rooms without air-conditioning. Note that some plug-in repellents can cause a mild throat irritation, in which case stick with creams. Wear loose, floppy clothes that cover as much skin as possible, but remember that mosquitoes sometimes do bite through thin clothing, so you may need to apply repellent on your clothes as well. Note that many travelers on antimalarial tablets suffer side effects including nausea, vomiting, abdominal pain, and even mild forms of psychosis and depression; ask your doctor to suggest an alternative antimalarial that you can take if you end up having serious side effects (but bear in mind that chloroquine is not an effective antimalarial for India).

SEXUALLY TRANSMITTED DISEASES & BLOOD INFECTIONS Keep in mind that HIV and hepatitis B are transmitted not only through sexual contact, but by infected blood. This means that any procedure involving a used needle or a blade can be hazardous. Avoid getting tattoos or piercings, and steer clear of roadside barbers offering shaves (although we've noticed that many barbers do in fact use fresh, unused blades). For haircuts and

> ⓘ **Tips**   **If You Lose Your Plastic**
>
> Be sure to contact your credit card companies the minute you discover that your wallet has been lost or stolen. Also file a report at the nearest police precinct, because your credit card company or insurer may require a police report number. Most credit card companies have an emergency number to call if your card is lost or stolen. They may be able to wire you a cash advance immediately or deliver an emergency credit card in a day or two. **Visa**'s U.S. emergency number is ⓒ **866/670-0955. American Express** cardholders and traveler's check holders should call ⓒ **905/474-0870. MasterCard** holders should call ⓒ **636/722-7111.** If you need emergency cash over the weekend, when all banks and American Express offices are closed, you can have money wired to you via **Western Union** (in India call ⓒ **1-800/44-1851** or 1-800/111-911, or go to www.moneyintime.com; in the U.S. call ⓒ **800/435-2226;** www.westernunion.com). You can **call all these numbers collect by using the access code 000-117.**

procedures such as manicures and pedicures, stick to salons in upmarket hotels. Take the usual precautions if you are about to engage in any sexual activities—AIDS numbers are not well publicized, since the disease is widely associated with taboo and "anti-Indian behaviors," but this is a huge and growing problem, and some doctors and NGO workers we have consulted suggest that India is on track to becoming the world's worst-afflicted AIDS region.

DIETARY RED FLAGS & TUMMY TROUBLES   Many visitors to India fall victim to the ubiquitous "Delhi belly," an unfortunate reaction to unfamiliar rich and spicy foodstuffs that can overwhelm the system and cause symptoms ranging from slight discomfort and "the runs" to extreme cases of nausea, fever, and delirium. To avoid this, simply be sensible. Adjust slowly; move on to spicy foods in small doses. You should also be on your guard about *where* you eat; if you have any fears at all, stick to the upmarket restaurants, usually those in five-star hotels—but do venture out to those recommended in this guide. Remember that uncooked vegetables or fruit can be hazardous if washed in water that has not been boiled,

so peel all your own fresh fruit and avoid salads. Unless you're in an upmarket hotel, don't eat fruit that has already been cut—any water on the knife or on the skin of the fruit is likely to seep into the flesh. Be wary of undercooked meats—they may harbor intestinal worms—and stay away from pork unless you're in a five-star hotel.

The first thing to bear in mind when diarrhea or nausea strikes is that your body is trying to cleanse itself, so only use an antidiarrhea medication (like Imodium) if you are desperate—about to embark on a long train journey, for example. Ideally, you should plan a few days of rest and cut back on all food except plain basics (a diet of boiled rice and bananas is ideal), and drink plenty of boiled water (or black tea) or bottled water with rehydration salts. If your tummy trouble doesn't clear up after 3 to 4 days, consult a physician—you may be suffering from something more serious: a protozoa (amoeba or giardia) or a viral or bacterial infection.

WATER CONCERNS   More than anything else in India, the water is likely to make you ill. For this reason, you should not only avoid untreated drinking water, but be on your guard against any food product that is washed with water or has had water added to it. When buying tea (or *chai*) on the streets, for example, check that the cup is washed with hot water and even ask to dry it yourself—carry a small cloth or napkins so that you can remove any water from anything that is going to go into your mouth; alternatively, carry your own stainless steel cup everywhere you go. Use bottled water when you brush your teeth, and do not open your mouth in the shower. Do not have ice added to your drink unless you've been assured that it's purified (as is typical of upmarket hotels and restaurants). Do be aware that in summer it is not uncommon for vendors selling *lassi* (a deliciously refreshing yogurt drink) to mix ice into their concoctions, and be exceptionally wary of enticing marketplace drinks such as freshly squeezed sugar-cane juice, which will be mixed with untreated water. If you purchase bottled water from roadside stalls, dodgy-looking shops, or small towns, check the seal on the cap and investigate the bottle for any signs of tampering. Also try to determine the age of the packaged water, if it looks like it's been sitting on the shelf for too long, avoid it. The only exception to the bottled water rule may be if you are 100% sure the water has been boiled for 20 minutes, or if you have been assured that the water has been filtered or treated with reverse osmosis or some similarly effective process. Generally, where water is placed in your room in a jug or some such container it has indeed been treated and is drinkable. If you are in the slightest doubt, simply ask. The same goes for street food stalls in larger cities where there is awareness around the dangers of drinking untreated water—simply ask if the water is filtered or not. Remember not to clean wounds, cuts, or sores with tap water. Instead, douse and cleanse any open wound with antiseptic solution, cover it with an adhesive bandage, and consult a doctor if it doesn't heal soon. *Note:* A large

number of restaurants and hotels have begun to take the issue of plastic bottles and their impact on the environment very seriously. We all know and understand that water bottled in plastic is cause for environmental concern. We strongly suggest that you make an effort to cut down on the number of plastic bottles that make their way to India's landfills (or rivers or valleys) by encouraging the use of treated water wherever possible—and give your support to businesses that do so.

BUGS, BITES & OTHER WILDLIFE CONCERNS
Remote areas are alive with insects and creepy-crawlies, but the greatest risk is malaria (see above). Wear shoes when trekking or in wet areas; you can be contaminated from worm-infested soil or mud, which can also be a source of microbial, bacterial, or hookworm infection. Leeches are a common problem in the rainforest regions. Do not try to pull them off your skin; dousing with salt does the trick. It's possible to prevent this nasty experience by wearing special antileech "socks" and dousing your shoes with lime powder. You're more likely to be bitten by a rabid dog or monkey than by a snake, spider, centipede, or sea creature, but it does occur: Wear thick trousers and boots when hiking, tread carefully, keep your eyes peeled, and in the unlikely event that you are bitten, try to get a good look at the animal so that medical staff knows what antivenin to use. And yes, get to a doctor or hospital as soon as possible. Animals are seldom treated as pets in India—as a general rule, steer clear of them, and should you be bitten, use antiseptic and consult a physician immediately.

Animal lovers beware: India will horrify you if you have a real soft spot for animals. You will feel particularly sickened by the "dancing bears" in North India—sloth bears cruelly tethered and forced to perform for tourists—as well as severely malnourished dogs, feral cats, diseased pigs, and even cows, considered sacred, looking emaciated and chewing on plastic bags and cardboard for sustenance. If you can see someone to rant at, do, but for the most part you have to bear it.

RESPIRATORY ILLNESSES The Indian health authorities have taken a relatively firm stance against illnesses such as H1-N1, but despite mandatory form-filling and cursory checks at airports, swine flu victims did turn up in various locations around the country. Authorities have implemented national campaigns to educate people around basic hygiene and preventative health measures to try to prevent the spread of mucus- and airborne bacteria and viruses, but it can be something of a losing battle in a country where throat clearing (often for phlegm) and spitting in public places can sometimes seems to be a national pastime. If you find yourself in enclosed spaces with groups of people, consider covering your mouth and nose with a cloth or handkerchief and wash your hands after making contact with any kind of surface, including someone else's hands.

HIGH-ALTITUDE HAZARDS We have flagged high-altitude concerns in the relevant chapters; if you are going into mountainous regions (particularly in the Himalayan regions like Ladakh and Spiti), be sure to acclimatize adequately (usually over 2 full days) and monitor your body for signs of illness (nausea, faintness of breath, dizziness, headaches). Avoid overexerting yourself and be cautious when consuming alcohol which tends to make a bigger impact at higher altitudes. Be sure to drink plenty of water as dehydration is anther symptom of high altitude sickness. Be aware that cooler temperatures at higher altitudes can make you oblivious to the heightened impact of the sun—take adequate precautions against sunburn (see below).

SUN/ELEMENTS/EXTREME WEATHER EXPOSURE Carry high-SPF sunscreen and use it liberally. It's also advisable to wear a hat or cap during the day, and try to avoid midday sun wherever possible. In the cities, pollution often cloaks the high-level exposure, so keep that hat on. Remember that in the high-altitude Himalayan regions, you can experience cold weather and chilly winds while being burnt to a cinder. During the monsoons, certain regions can become impossible to traverse because of flooding. Orissa, Tamil Nadu, and Andhra Pradesh are prone to cyclones in November and December. Keep abreast of conditions by following weather reports.

POLLUTION Air pollution levels in many Indian cities are very high and contain high levels of suspended particulate matter. This is mostly from vehicles, but in places like Varanasi it is compounded by the use of diesel generators. The best thing to do is to always carry a cotton handkerchief with you to hold over your mouth and nose as a mask to breathe through until you are past the offending area. India is also plagued by noise pollution, and most visitors are usually shocked at how often drivers blare their horns. There's really nothing you can do other than accept that honking is usually a necessary precaution to avoid smashing into people, stray dogs, cattle, and all kinds of other obstacles (including cars).

WHAT TO DO IF YOU GET SICK AWAY FROM HOME

Don't panic. Medicines are widely and easily available in India. You can even describe your problem to your hotel concierge or receptionist and he or she will arrange for the necessary medication to be dropped off, doing away with possible translation problems. Pharmacies and pharmacists hand out pills and antibacterial medication upon request—even those that would require a prescription back home. (This is not always a good thing; if possible, consult a physician before resorting to over-the-counter drugs. Also beware of being given incomplete courses of antibiotics.)

There are hospital listings for major cities in each chapter, but it's best to consult your hotel concierge regarding the best medical attention in town, particularly if you're in a more remote area. In fact, *do not solicit the assistance of anyone who is unknown to your hotel.* Well-documented scams operating in certain tourist destinations involve prolonging your illness in order to attract large payouts from your insurance company. If you or someone you are traveling with needs hospitalization, shell out for a well-known private one, and if you're able to travel, head for the nearest big city. Advise your consulate and your medical insurance company as soon as possible.

It's likely you'll have to pay all medical costs upfront and be reimbursed later.

Medicare and Medicaid do not provide coverage for medical costs outside the U.S. Before leaving home, find out what medical services your health insurance covers. To protect yourself, consider buying medical travel insurance (see "Insurance" in chapter 16).

We list **hospitals** and **emergency numbers** under "Fast Facts" in the individual chapters.

Pack **prescription medications** in your carry-on luggage, and carry them in their original containers, with pharmacy labels—otherwise they won't make it through airport security. Carry the generic name of prescription medicines, in case a local pharmacist is unfamiliar with the brand name.

6 SAFETY

Considering its poverty and population size, India enjoys an amazingly low incidence of violent crime, and the vast majority of visits to India tend to be trouble-free. That said, the usual rules apply—no wandering around back alleys at night, for example, no flashing of valuables or wads of cash. Foreign visitors may be targeted by corrupt cops looking to get a handsome bribe or payoff, so you'd best steer clear of any suspicious behavior such as purchasing illegal drugs. If you're caught, even with marijuana, there is a good chance that you could be thrown in prison. If you're involved in a car accident, have your hotel manager report the incident immediately. Avoid provocative debates and arguments where alcohol may be involved. Exercise caution during festivals and religious processions, where crowds are usually overwhelming and can become unruly.

TERRORISM & CIVIL UNREST The ugly multipronged assault by Pakistani-trained gunmen on Mumbai in November 2008 (known in India as 26/11) devastated not only two of the city's most celebrated luxury hotels, but also targeted several other key tourist spots, including the historic Victoria Terminus train station. Indian authorities have taken these attacks—and earlier incidents, such as the bombing of Mumbai commuter trains on July 2006, and the bombing of the Indian Parliament in December 2001—to heart, and security has been visibly beefed up not only in Mumbai but in key centers around the country. This has meant that India is in fact a great deal safer than before. The exception to this is the northernmost state of Jammu and Kashmir, where the terrorist organization Harakat Ul Mujahideen has issued a ban on Westerners, including tourists. With the exception of the eastern district of Ladakh, avoid travel in this volatile and unsafe war-torn region, no matter what tour operators and tourist offices have to say; regular terrorist attacks continue to occur in Kashmir, and civilians are often targets. Travelers should also exercise extreme caution when undertaking treks

(Warning!) Surviving Scams & Con Artists

In India, scamming is an art form—and you, the tourist, are a prime target. Although it's okay to have a heart, don't fall into the costly pit of naiveté. **Politeness is likely to be your enemy.** If someone tells you upfront that he's not interested in your money, the warning bells should begin to sound; 9 times out of 10, a casual conversation or unintentional tour will end with a request for payment. Remember: **Don't pay for services you have not requested.** And when you do ask for help, ask if there's going to be a demand for money at the end, and **decide on a help fee upfront.** Rude as it seems, often the only way to get rid of a persistent tout, beggar, or con artist is to **ignore him and keep walking without pause.** Here then is a guide to India's most common scams:

- **Street touts** Touts operate under guises of initial friendship, wanting to practice their English or making promises of cheap accommodations or shopping. Often (but not always), the initial kindness turns sour when you don't comply with a suggestion that you buy something or check in at a crummy hotel. When browsing a street or market, you will be accosted by what appears to be the owner of the shop but is in fact one of a host of men to whom shopkeepers pay a commission to bring you inside—"to look, no buy, madam." Since scam artists know that foreigners rely on hired transport, you also need to be particularly wary when considering car hire, taxis, guides, sightseeing tours, or travel agents. The rule is: *Never jump into a deal.*

- **"Official" unofficial operators** Even more annoying than the slippery-tongued con artists of the street are those who operate under the guise of perceived legitimacy by calling themselves "travel agents" or "tour operators"—and a sign saying "government-approved" often means anything but. Before purchasing anything, you need to know in advance what the going rate is, and preferably deal with someone who comes recommended by this book or a reputable operator recommended by your hotel. Time allowing, shop around.

- **Dealing with drivers** Taxi drivers are notorious for telling passengers that their hotel does not exist or has closed for some reason. Never allow yourself to be taken to a hotel or restaurant *unless it is the one you've asked to be taken to* (specified by *exact* name and address). Note that any successful establishment will soon have competition opening with a similar or almost identical name. Drivers also moonlight as restaurant and shop touts and receive a commission for getting you through the door. If a taxi driver is very persuasive about taking you to a particular shop, this is a sure sign that *you're about to be taken for a ride.* Taxi drivers often have meters that have been tampered with, or refuse to use fare-conversion charts issued by the city authority. Whenever you're suspicious about a driver's conduct, ask to be let out of the vehicle immediately, or seek the assistance of your hotel manager before paying the cab fare. When arriving at major airports and train stations, make use of **prepaid taxis** (the booths are clearly marked) whenever possible. Whenever you hire a local taxi, make sure that no one but the driver is riding with you. Even if you are just one person in the back seat, do not under any circumstances agree to allow the driver's friend to ride along. Get out and take another cab if necessary.

- **Bargains** *Beware of unmarked wares*—this means the goods are priced according to the salesperson's projection of your ability to pay. Also beware of the ultimate "bargain." Any deal that seems too good to be true, is. If this all sounds too tedious, head for the government shops, where goods are sold at fixed prices that are *not* a rip-off despite sometimes higher prices (see "The Battle of the Haggle," earlier in this chapter). But again, beware of imitations, such as Cottage Industries Exposition, often only marked "CIE," which are seriously overpriced outlets that cash in on the fame of the good-value government-owned Central Cottage Industries Emporiums.
- **Credit card fraud** Beware of unscrupulous traders who run off extra dockets, then forge your signature. Never let your credit card out of sight.
- **Creating needs** Sometimes a trickster will create your need for certain goods or services. One common Delhi scam is run by shoeshine boys who suddenly appear with their polishing equipment and point to your shoes which, when you look down, suddenly have poop on them. Of course he'll offer to clean it off for you, which you should refuse; the source of the poop is almost certainly the little guy himself or his accomplice.
- **Noting your notes** Recognizing the insecurity that comes with dealing with an unfamiliar currency, swindlers will switch your Rs 500 note with a Rs 100 note and then claim that that's what you gave them. When handing out a fare or paying for a purchase, preferably give the whole amount together rather than handing over each note as you dig it up from your purse or pocket. Also, when you hand over a Rs 500 or Rs 1,000 note, state aloud how much it is.
- **Getting the goods on precious goods** If you're shopping for **silk carpets,** ask the salesman to razor a small sample and light it with a match. Unlike wool, silk does not burn, it smolders. Tricksters will mix silk and wool—which is why you'll need to ask for a sample across the whole color range. And don't fall for anyone who tries to persuade you to purchase **precious stones** on the premise that you can resell them at a profit to a company they supposedly know back home (a Jaipur scam). Note that **gold** is imported and therefore hugely overpriced, so cheap gold jewelry is exactly that.
- **Drugged foods and scam doctors** Be wary when offered food or drink by a stranger. There have been isolated incidences of travelers being drugged or poisoned in order to rob them. Worse still, there are well-documented (though again isolated) accounts of these scammers who then recommend a fraudulent doctor, who will contact your medical insurance company and keep you ill while running up a substantial medical bill.

and travel to remote parts of Ladakh, where solo travelers are not permitted and can potentially be targeted by terrorist factions; in isolated cases, unaccompanied trekkers have been kidnapped or simply disappeared. Travelers to Goa and Himachal Pradesh should stay clear of any drug-related activity—the trade has begun to attract nasty criminal elements. Travel to the northeastern states of Assam, Manipur, Nagaland, Tripura, and Meghalaya remains risky due to sporadic incidents of ethnic insurgent violence. These areas—and Kashmir—have not been included in this guide.

Almost anywhere in India, communal violence can occur without advance warning, but such incidents rarely involve foreigners, and thus far there have been no attacks by Indians directed against Americans or other foreigners. That said, the threat here—as anywhere in the world—should not be ignored completely: Exercise vigilance and caution if you find yourself near any government installations or tourist attractions that might be regarded as potential terrorist targets; avoid political demonstrations, read the local papers, heeding any relevant reports and travel advisories. Access up-to-the-minute travel warnings at **www.travel.state.gov**. U.S. citizens can also contact the U.S. Embassy or the nearest U.S. Consulate for more information about the current situation in areas you plan to visit.

CRIME   India is one of the safest destinations in the world when it comes to violent assault or threat, but petty crime, like pick-pocketing, can be a problem. Apply common sense at all times. Don't carry wallets prominently; and keep a firm hand on purses (women have reported having their purse straps cut or purse bottoms slit). Don't wear flashy jewelry or carry around other valuables. Most hotels have in-room electronic safes where you should stash valuables, including passports and most of your cash. Be discreet about your money, and never take out large wads of cash in public; exercise modesty at all times. Solo travelers are at greater risk of becoming victims of crime; unless you're relatively streetwise, touring India alone may be more pain than pleasure. But know that it is as a victim of a scam that you are most at risk, which at least hurts nothing but your pocket and your pride; see "Surviving Scams & Con Artists," below.

DISCRIMINATION

Africans, African Americans, and other black travelers may sometimes face discrimination, particularly in smaller towns or nightclubs in larger cities, though this is not widespread. Some blacks and travelers from other Asian countries have also faced racist name-calling in India, usually from groups of young men in the street, completely ignorant of difference, and who are best ignored. Single female travelers do need to be careful (see section on "Women Travelers," below.)

---

7 SPECIALIZED TRAVEL RESOURCES

In addition to the destination-specific resources listed below, please visit Frommers.com for additional specialized travel resources.

GAY & LESBIAN TRAVELERS

Homosexuality remains frowned upon in India despite the fact that in July 2009 a Supreme Court ruling finally overturned a discriminatory piece of legislation that had, since colonial times, prohibited so-called "unnatural" sexual relations, criminalizing consensual sex between men. In the aftermath of this acknowledgment of constitutional freedom, the media celebrated widely with endless discussions, debates and relatively newsworthy stories about everything and anything gay, proud, and out. On the other hand, there are religious and political leaders hell-bent on reversing the legislative decision and many who actively promote antigay thinking, qualifying their hatred with the bizarre sentiment that homosexuality is un-Indian. A range of high-profile cases have brought the issue of gay and lesbian rights into the social and political sphere, and there is increased awareness in this regard across all social spheres, not least as a result of gay storylines and subplots creeping into mainstream Bollywood movies, and the rags plump with gossip about which star is in or out of the closet this week. The times certainly are a-changing, but the change is slower for some than for others, so you're likely to encounter a wide range of reactions to homosexuality (even when it's simply a topic in conversation)—from those who clearly covet their gay friends as social accessories to those with overt hostility to those displaying utter indifference.

Finally, don't confuse social norms with sexual behavior. Indian men, for example, are a great deal more affectionate with one another than they are with women in public, and you'll frequently see men walking hand-in-hand, arm-in-arm, and embracing, though this is said to be an act of "brotherliness" without any sexual connotation. Nevertheless, discretion is probably best observed outside your hotel room (note that no one questions same-sex travelers sharing a room).

For more information and gay- and lesbian-friendly contacts nationwide, check out **Indian Dost** (www.indiandost. com); for a more personal perspective, filled with substance and insights read some of the posts on the **Queer India** blog (http://queerindia.blogspot.com). Gay support groups include the **Gay Info Centre** (P.O. Box 1662 Secunderabad HPO 500 003, Andhra Pradesh), **Humsafar Trust** (www.humsafar.org), and to a lesser

extent, **Gay Bombay** (www.gaybombay. org), which mainly offers information on gay venues in Mumbai.

The International Gay and Lesbian Travel Association (IGLTA; © **800/448-8550** or 954/776-2626; www.iglta.org) is the trade association for the gay and lesbian travel industry, and offers an online directory of gay- and lesbian-friendly travel businesses and tour operators; at press time, however, there were just five Indian tour operators listed.

The Canadian website **Gay Traveler** (**www.gaytraveler.ca**) offers ideas and advice for gay travel all over the world.

TRAVELERS WITH DISABILITIES

Most disabilities shouldn't stop anyone from traveling. There are more options and resources out there than ever before. However, it must be noted that India—despite the fact that it has such a high population of people with disabilities— is not well geared for travelers with disabilities. Destinations are far from wheelchair friendly, and it is hard enough for an able-bodied person to negotiate the crowded, filth-strewn, and potholed streets, where cars, animals, and rickshaws drive at will. Access to historical monuments is also difficult (though you will have the small reward of free access). Certainly you would need to be accompanied by a traveler familiar with the destination, and you must carefully sift through the accommodations options, only a handful of which have facilities specifically geared to travelers with disabilities.

Organizations that offer a range of resources and assistance to disabled travelers include **MossRehab** (© **800/CALL-MOSS** [2255-6677]; www.mossresource net.org); the **American Foundation for the Blind (AFB;** © **800/232-5463;** www. afb.org); and **SATH** (Society for Accessible Travel & Hospitality; © **212/447-7284;** www.sath.org).

3

WOMEN TRAVELERS

Foreign women will almost certainly experience India as sexist, but if you are confident, relaxed, and assertive, you are unlikely to experience any serious hassles. However, traveling solo is only for the very brave and thick-skinned, unless of course you're traveling in comfort (using the accommodations selected in this book) and have hired a car and driver for the duration (you are at your most vulnerable when using public transport). At best, you will experience being stared at intensely for an unbearable length of time; at worst you may be groped—some men are convinced that all Western women are loose and slutty. To a great extent, Western cinema and fashion trends have helped fuel the legend that women from abroad welcome this attention, and you'd do well to take precautions, like wearing appropriate (modest) attire. On trains, buses, and in other public places, you are best off ignoring advances or questions from suspicious-looking men. Another strategy that often helps single women travelers ward off unwanted male attention is to wear a ring and invent a husband; if you're approached, say that you are meeting your "husband" at the next station/destination. You should have little difficulty determining when a line of questioning is likely to lead to problems. In particular, steer clear of men who have been drinking alcohol. "Eve-teasing" (the word denoting unwanted attention and public harassment by men) is an offense in certain parts of India, and you are within your rights to report inappropriate advances or remarks to the police—the easiest response, however, is to loudly tell the offender off, and even strike him—you will almost certainly be supported by those around you. You may want to ask whether or not your hotel offers a special room for solo women travelers; these are now offered in a few upmarket hotels in the larger cities, and include special privacy/security features.

Note that women are excluded from entering certain religious sites and attractions (which we have pointed out wherever relevant), but this is unlikely to impact too strongly on your plans. Menstruating women are, technically, not entitled to enter Jain temples or mosques.

A few Indian travel outfits specialize in women-only itineraries. Travel writer Sumitra Senapaty's **Women on Wanderlust** (www.wowsumitra.com) is aimed primarily at Indian women, and includes tours to non-Indian destinations; however there are a few excursions, including treks and river-rafting expeditions, that you may wish to consider. Adventure specialists **18 Days** (www.18days.in; see "Adventure & Wellness Trips," below) also offer several trips that are exclusively for women.

For general travel resources for women, go to www.frommers.com/planning.

MULTICULTURAL TRAVELERS

African Americans and other travelers of African descent will face as much curiosity as someone with blond hair and blue eyes, but also some degree of discrimination, though this is neither widespread nor specific to a particular region. Mostly this takes the form of travelers being told a hotel or nightclub is full when it really isn't. Senior Travel

India is not for the fainthearted, and this is definitely the one place senior travelers should use the services of a reliable agency and organization that targets the 50-plus market.

Members of **AARP**, 601 E St. NW, Washington, DC 20049 (© **888/687-2277;** www.aarp.org), get discounts on hotels, airfares, and car rentals. AARP offers members a wide range of benefits, including *AARP The Magazine* and a monthly newsletter. Anyone over 50 can join.

Many reliable agencies and organizations target the 50-plus market. **Elderhostel**

(© 800/454-5768; www.elderhostel.org) arranges worldwide study programs for those aged 55 and over. **ElderTreks** (© 800/741-7956, or 416/558-5000

outside North America; www.eldertreks. com) offers small-group tours to off-the-beaten-path or adventure-travel locations, restricted to travelers 50 and older.

8 SUSTAINABLE & RESPONSIBLE TOURISM

CUSTOMS & ETIQUETTE
As a rule of thumb, pay attention to what local people are doing, and try to blend in as much as possible.

APPROPRIATE ATTIRE In India, your attire will often signal your status, and casual dress will make it more difficult for you to elicit respect. Women should wear loose, cool clothing that covers up as much as possible. Exposed flesh suggests that you're too poor to dress properly, or that you're shameless about flaunting your body. Transparent and tight clothes are also considered shameless; the more you can disguise your shape, the better. Men should avoid short shorts, which are considered bizarre outside large cities or beaches. Women visiting public beaches should be as discreet as possible and avoid sunbathing on empty beaches. In mosques and Sikh *gurudwaras* you need to make sure your head is covered—a worthwhile purchase is a scarf you can keep in your bag at all times. In certain Hindu temples—particularly in South India—a man may be required to wear a *lungi* (a long piece of cloth worn like a kilt) and remove his shirt. Always check what others are wearing before venturing in, and approach slowly so that someone can intervene before you offend the sanctity of the holy sanctuary.

SHOES Shoes are never worn in places of worship—you are even required to remove your shoes when entering certain churches. It makes good sense to wear a pair of comfortable, cool, and cheap sandals, like flip-flops—they're easy to remove and unlikely to be stolen; leaving a pair of

expensive shoes outside a temple or mosque is not a good idea. However, you can leave your footwear with an attendant outside for a tiny tip (Rs 2–Rs 10)—and you will almost certainly get them back. Some museums and historical monuments may also require you to remove your shoes, and you should extend a similar courtesy when entering someone's home. In Sikh *gurudwaras* you are expected to wash your feet after removing your shoes.

TOUCHING Public physical contact between men and women is far less acceptable in India than in other parts of the world. Some Indians—particularly those who live in the larger cities and have traveled—understand that Western men and women may shake hands (or even kiss) as expressions of social friendship, but you should be cautious of casually touching an Indian woman in small towns and villages. Even the slightest touch can have a sexual connotation. Remember that it is not unusual to encounter someone who has never seen a foreign face; attempting to shake hands with such a person may prove overwhelming to him or her. When in doubt, fold your hands in front of you, bow your head slightly, and simply say *"Namaste"* (pronounced nah-mah-*stay*). Traditionally, Indian people use the left hand as part of their toilet routine. Consequently, the left hand is considered unclean, and you should only offer your right hand when greeting someone. Don't touch a religious object with your feet or left hand. People generally use the right hand for handing over or receiving cash as the left is considered inauspicious. If you wish to put your feet up in a train or other form of public transport, take your shoes off first. If you are booked on a higher berth and don't want to leave your expensive shoes at floor level, put them in a plastic bag and take them up to your berth with you. If you inadvertently touch/kick someone with your foot, it's customary to extend an apology. In fact you will notice that in some parts of India, if an Indian accidentally touches you with his foot, he will immediately follow that up with a hand gesture that first lightly brushes you with the tips of the fingers and then brings that hand up towards his chest or forehead. Even if nothing is said, this constitutes an apology.

AVOIDING OFFENSE Indians love to discuss all manner of subjects, and more educated individuals will readily get into wonderfully heated debates—which may be among your most memorable moments in India. Do exercise discretion, however, when trying to understand the enigma of India's overwhelming poverty and the caste system. Don't harshly judge or criticize things you don't understand fully; Indians can be quite passionate about their nation and will defend it unequivocally. Words are seldom enough to offend an Indian, but avoid strong swear words in the context of an argument or insult. And always be considerate and humble when entering a place of worship.

EATING & DRINKING When eating at someone's home, remember that it is not unusual for the woman to cook and spend the entire evening serving. Don't interfere with this custom, and don't venture into the kitchen—especially if you're a man. Foreign women will generally be treated as "honorary men" and should dine at the table unless an alternative suggestion is made. Note that the above rules apply more in orthodox homes and to a much lesser degree in modern city homes, where in fact it is polite to offer help, even if the answer is negative. Use only your right hand when eating (unless knives and forks are used), and follow the lead of your host when you're unsure. Don't be afraid to ask about the food, but you must be quite firm about not drinking water (unless it's bottled) and being mindful of salads and cut fruit (see above). Consider bringing your own bottled water with you.

MIND YOUR TEMPER When confronted with bureaucracy and IST (Indian "Stretchable" Time), maintain your cool. Schedules are bound to go awry and government offices are notoriously inefficient, so there's simply no point in losing your temper. You'd be well advised to adopt a similar attitude with wealthy and "important" Indian men who, as a matter of course, cut into line. Rather than fly into a rage, point out the lack of consideration firmly and earnestly or, better still, smile beatifically and practice a meditation technique.

PHOTOGRAPHY Photography at airports or military installations is strictly forbidden, as it is at all burning *ghats* (crematorium sites) in Varanasi. Note that carrying a camera to attractions throughout India will add significantly to your entry fee. In touristy areas don't be surprised if people offer to be photographed and then demand payment.

SAYING YES EVEN WHEN THE ANSWER IS NO When you ask for directions, people will often send you in the wrong direction rather than admit they don't know the way. Try not to ask questions that require a yes or no answer, because you will almost always only hear yes. In other words, rather than ask, "Is this the way to the Gateway of India?" try, "Can you tell me the way to the Gateway of India?" If the person seems hesitant when giving you directions, verify that you are going the right way by asking someone else a few minutes down the road.

General Resources for Green Travel

In addition to the resources for India listed above, the following websites provide valuable wide-ranging information on sustainable travel. For a list of even more sustainable resources, as well as tips and explanations on how to travel greener, visit www.frommers.com/planning.

- **Responsible Travel** (www.responsibletravel.com) is a great source of sustainable travel ideas; essentially a travel agency that focuses on sustainable vacation planning, it's run by a spokesperson for ethical tourism in the travel industry. **Sustainable Travel International** (www.sustainabletravelinternational.org) promotes ethical tourism practices, and manages an extensive directory of sustainable properties and tour operators around the world.
- In the U.K., outspoken **Tourism Concern** (www.tourismconcern.org.uk) works to reduce social and environmental problems connected to tourism. The **Association of Independent Tour Operators** (AITO; www.aito.co.uk) is a group of specialist operators leading the field in making vacations sustainable; click on their "Responsible Tourism" section for links to responsible tour operators.
- **Green Living** (www.greenlivingonline.com) is a Canadian enterprise with extensive content on sustainable living, including travel and transport ideas.
- In Australia, the national body that sets guidelines and standards for ecotourism is **Ecotourism Australia** (www.ecotourism.org.au); it's largely focused on tourism within Australia but will give you ideas for your India trip. **The Green Directory** (www.thegreendirectory.com.au), **Green Pages** (www.thegreenpages.com.au), and **Eco Directory** (www.ecodirectory.com.au) offer sustainable travel tips and links to green businesses that will help you better understand the possibilities for more responsible living.
- **Greenhotels** (www.greenhotels.com) recommends green-rated member hotels around the world that fulfill the company's stringent environmental requirements. **Environmentally Friendly Hotels** (www.environmentallyfriendlyhotels.com) offers more green accommodation ratings.
- For information on responsible outdoor recreation activities throughout the world, visit **Tread Lightly** (www.treadlightly.org).

9 SPECIAL-INTEREST TRIPS & ESCORTED TOURS

ACADEMIC TRIPS & LANGUAGE CLASSES

Ekno Experience ★★ (www.eknoexperience.com) is based in the Himalayan region of northern India and has a number of learning packages for travelers interested in spirituality, Buddhism, Tibetan culture, and more esoteric activities such as reiki, tarot card reading, meditation, and yoga

ADVENTURE & WELLNESS TRIPS

With huge swaths of Himalayan mountains; a massive coastline; an age-old traditional health system that has massage as one of its keys components; a wealth of spiritual and mystical knowledge systems; wildlife reserves sheltering tigers, elephant and unbelievable birdlife; and an ever-expanding market for daring and adventurous fun, India is a formidable destination for anyone looking to combine their vacation with a more rigorous and intense experience. Whether you're looking to sweat from exertion or rejuvenate mind, body, and soul, you'll find your fix somewhere in this diverse destination.

Innovative U.K.-based travel agency **Black Tomato** ★★★ (www.blacktomato.co.uk) will put together just about any sort of trip you care to imagine, and they're always up for a challenge. They do off-the-beaten-track tours quite well, and are good at combining luxury with adventure activities and more daring travel experiences. Their website is a good place to start if you're looking for ways of injecting your trip with some added adrenaline: Their 10-day "India + Extreme Thrills" itinerary, for example, includes hot-air ballooning, zip-lining over an ancient fortress city, tiger tracking on elephant back, and an Enfield motorbike safari.

HIKING & ADVENTURE Start off by looking at what **Shakti** (www.shaktihimalaya.com) is offering, especially for its admirable approach to responsible tourism. If none of its programs suit you, try **Mountain Kingdoms** (www.mountainkingdoms.com) or **TransIndus** (www.transindus.co.uk), although the latter's itineraries are not limited to outdoor excursions. **Steppes East Ltd.** (www.steppeseast.co.uk) is another reputable option; it lets you conveniently create your personal itinerary online. Other Himalayan trekking outfits are **Aquaterra Adventures** (www.treknraft.com), **Mountain Travel/Sobek**

(www.mtsobek.com), and **Adventure Center** (www.adventurecenter.com); the latter two also have general adventure expeditions. Another interesting home-grown Indian adventure specialist company is **18 Days** (www.18days.in), which organizes a variety of treks (some of which are for women only) and river adventures, most of which happen in the Himalayas; all their trips typically last 18 days, but they offer shorter versions for those with less time.

CYCLING TOURS Kerala Adventures ★★★ (www.keralaadventure.com) arranges bicycle tours in South India, designed to enable you to get under the skin of the local culture; besides traveling along back roads and country byways, you'll mingle and interact with local people, have the opportunity to stay in regular homes (or in tented camps), and dine at family tables.

ON HORSE, ELEPHANT, OR CAMEL BACK **Wilderness Travel** (www.wildernesstravel.com) specializes in Rajasthan camel safaris and elephant expeditions. **Equine Adventures** organizes riding vacations in Rajasthan (www.equineadventures.co.uk). In the Himalayas, Nitin Gupta of **Dusty Trail Adventures** ★★ (http://dustytrail.in) designs superb high-altitude horseback trails.

WILDLIFE, BIRDING & BUTTERFLY VACATIONS Wildlife enthusiasts can check on the numerous options for group bird- and wildlife-watching trips from **Naturetrek** ★★ (www.naturetrek.co.uk). For small, high-end, exotic bird-watching tours of India, look no further than **Victor Emanuel Nature Tours** ★★★ (www.ventbird.com), based in Austin, Texas; the tours are usually sold out as soon as they come online. Victor often includes the "Palace on Wheels," a weeklong journey through Rajasthan (including Agra) in a luxury train (for standard Palace on Wheels tours, see "Getting Around," earlier in this chapter), and there are wildlife trips to more exotic corners of India, such as Assam. In South India, highly recommended tour and travel operator **Kerala Adventures** ★★★ (www.keralaadventure. com) organizes all kinds of specialist vacations with naturalists and guides specially trained to take wildlife, birding, and butterfly enthusiasts' interests into account. In fact, Kerala Adventures is the operator that many specialist operators use to create their itineraries, merely adding their commission to what Kerala Adventures quotes. So dealing directly with Kerala Adventures will save you money. You can enjoy a trip dedicated purely to nature, or combine a wildlife/birding tour with other kinds of activities and general sightseeing.

DIVING For diving adventures in Lakshadweep, take a look at the packages offered at www.diveworldwide.com.

HERITAGE & WEDDING TOURS Travel writer **Dagmar von Harryegg** is based in Australia but is passionate about India, particularly the desert states of Rajasthan and Gujarat, where she has developed an extensive network of contacts and friends, from elephant *mahouts* to reclusive princes. She offers personally tailored special-interest trips (anything from yoga or bird-watching to Bollywood and/or classical dance lessons) for a maximum of eight travelers—preferably friends, thereby ensuring a flexible timetable "cruising in wonderfully old-fashioned Ambassador limousines with overnight stays in off-the-beaten-track destinations." She also arranges large Hindi-style traditional weddings for couples looking for a really memorable nuptial celebration. Most trips take off in Delhi and can include a visit to the Taj Mahal. For information, contact Dagmar at dagmarvh@tpg.com.au.

MOTORBIKE SAFARIS Motorbike safaris are increasingly popular; if you can handle the fabulous Enfield motorbike, get in touch with **Shepherds Realms Camps & Adventures** ★ (C-8/8115, Shepherd's House, Vasant Kunj, New Delhi; ⓒ 011/2649-2849 or 98-1871-2970; www.asiasafari.com), operated by ex-army captain, Raj Kumar; he's not the suave sort, but provides an excellent service for his bike tours into the Himalayas. Also specializing in motorcycle tours is **Blazing Trails** ★ (www.blazingtrailstours. com), which, in addition to the Himalayas, also heads south and into Rajasthan.

SPA VACATIONS & WELLNESS RETREATS Ayurvedic getaways—particularly in the south Indian state of Kerala—have long been a major draw among European vacationers looking for the type of rejuvenation and healing that falls outside the scope of Western medicine. Ayurveda inevitably involves plenty of massage, which translates as a deeply pampering form of medicine. Ayurvedic spas and hospitals are now available practically anywhere in India. The best intensive Ayurvedic retreat in the country is **Kalari Kovilakom** ★★★ (p. 258), which offers a variety of extremely upmarket and authentic rejuvenation, healing, weight loss, and antiage packages. Kovilakom was conceived by CGH Earth (www.cghearth.com), an eco-conscious Kerala-based hotel group which also runs **SwaSwara** ★★★ another swish Ayurveda and yoga resort, this time on the coast of Karnataka. Both places are highly recommended, as are the Ayurvedic centers at all CGH Earth properties.

Among the specialist tours offered by **On the Go** (www.onthegotours.com) there are spa breaks in the Himalayas and Ayurvedic breaks in Kerala.

For more ideas about places in India to cleanse mind and body, see "Discovering Spiritual India," below.

FOOD & WINE TRIPS

COOKING Those looking for a cooking vacation can get their aprons and bathing suits out and head to Goa, where **On the**

Go organizes a variety of special-interest trips (www.onthegotours.com).

For authentic, down-to-earth tours that endeavor to get under the skin of local culture, take a look at what's offered from **Insider Tours ★★** (www.insider-tours. com). They don't specialize only in India, but do offer several trips in the north and south of the country, and have specialist birding and food tours; the latter include exposure to a variety of cuisine types and an introduction to various aspects of food and culinary culture, predominantly in the south Indian state of Kerala.

Most kitchens in South India welcome inquisitive visitors, with chefs proud to share the culinary secrets that make this cuisine so addictive—Paradisa Plantation Retreat (www.paradisaretreat.com) in particular worth highlighting here, as are the CGH Earth properties (www.cghearth. com), many of which run regular cooking demonstrations—but for a more formal approach to tuition it's worth signing up for one of the cooking classes offered at many of the homestays in Kerala where you're trained up in a number of specific dishes: Vanilla County (http://vanillacounty.in) and The Pimenta (www.harithafarms.com) are two such places where lessons take place in the family kitchen of a home on a spice plantation in the foothills of Kerala's Western Ghats (an easy drive from Fort Kochi). After preparing a number of traditional vegetarian dishes, you sit down and dine with the family, and spend time touring local cultural sights.

VOLUNTEER & WORKING TRIPS

Contributing your time, energy, skills and knowledge while traveling in a foreign country can be a life-changing experience. In India, it often means working for the upliftment of the poor and inevitably puts you in direct contact with people living a reality you might never even have imagined possible. Please don't expect to change

the world, but rather go into any volunteer situation with an open mind and an open heart; don't condescend and assume you have all the answers—you don't, and you've signed up to contribute your services, not dictate to the very people you've come to help. We've noted a few agencies you can contact to find out about volunteer positions, but before embarking on this somewhat courageous mission, you might want to check out **Volunteer International** (www.volunteerinternational.org), which has a list of questions to help you determine the intentions and the nature of a volunteer program. For general info on volunteer travel, visit **www.volunteer abroad.org** and **www.idealist.org**.

Projects Abroad (www.projects-abroad.co.uk) is a U.K.-based organization with volunteer placements and internships in developing nations around the globe. Their projects are aimed primarily at gap year travelers, students looking for summer placement, or anyone looking for a career break. Volunteers will be based in Sivakasi near the city of Madurai in the southern Indian state of Tamil Nadu. Volunteers can choose from a wide range of services, including journalism, medicine and healthcare, teaching, and sports work; a 2-week volunteering position costs around $1,995 (a full month costs $2,445), which covers transfers, insurance, food, and lodging. Accommodations are basic (either with local families or in hostels), but with an emphasis on allowing you to experience an authentic, local way of life.

ATMA Mumbai ★ (Atma Education Trust, 794/1, 1st floor, Satguru Shopping Centre, 3rd Rd., nr Khar Station, Khar West, Mumbai; ② 022/26059810; www. atmamumbai.org) is an educational development NGO with a focus on providing assistance to other NGOs and on improving the lot of children. They work with several schools in Mumbai, and provide non-paid opportunities for volunteers willing to teach or giving administrative support. You'll be required to commit yourself to a project for a minimum of 3 months and there is no financial support of any sort, although they will assist you in finding local accommodation and will pick you up from the airport and provide a basic orientation tour of the city.

Reality Tours and Travel ★★★ (1/26, Akber House, Nowroji Fardonji Rd., opp. Laxmi Vilas Hotel, Colaba, Mumbai; ℂ 98-2082-2253 or 022/2283-3872; www.realitytoursandtravel.com) is an innovative local tour company that runs walking tours through Mumbai's Dharavi slum. They have also started their own kindergarten and community center in Dharavi, and are in the process of launching an NGO called Reality Cares. They can help you find a suitable volunteer position within Mumbai, working either with ATMA (above) or other NGO and volunteer organizations. If you are unsure about how you'd like to contribute your time and energy, Krishna, one of the young, dynamic founders of Reality Tours, will help you understand the city dynamic and its needs.

Ekno Experience ★★ (www.eknoexperience.com) has a number of placements for volunteers willing to work, predominantly as teaching or child care givers, but there are also positions for health care givers and special needs care givers. The organization can put together packages that combine volunteering programs with unique travel experiences.

Rogpa Charitable Trust ★★ (Kapoor House, near Tibetan Ashoka Guest House, Jogiwara Rd., McLeod Ganj, Dharamsala; ℂ 98-1665-9549; www.rogpa.com) focuses on Tibetan refugees in Dharamsala, and runs a **Baby Care Centre,** which has places for up to 10 international volunteers who are invited to work with the children for a minimum of 15 days. Volunteers work alongside a full-time staff of seven caregivers of Tibetan origin and are expected to provide love and care for around 35 children all under 3 years of age; duties include storytelling, sleep supervision, hosting play time, feeding, cleaning, and diaper changing. Past volunteers have reported that the job is exhausting but extremely fulfilling. You'll find images of the experience on Facebook.

One more organization to consider if you're interested in working with Tibetan refugees, is **LHA Charitable Trust** ★★ (ℂ 01892/22-0992; www.lhasocialwork.org), which provides opportunities for foreigners in various fields, from health care and education to building maintenance and computer technology. The trust also offers services to foreigners, including Tibetan language and cooking classes, yoga and meditation workshops, and various therapeutic treatments such as massage and reiki.

ESCORTED GENERAL-INTEREST TOURS

Escorted tours are structured group tours with a group leader The price usually includes everything from airfare to hotels, meals, tours, admission costs, and local transportation.

Despite the fact that escorted tours require big deposits and predetermine hotels, restaurants, and itineraries, many people derive security and peace of mind from the structure they offer. Escorted tours—whether they're navigated by bus, motorcoach, train, or boat—let travelers sit back and enjoy the trip without having to drive or worry about details. They take you to the maximum number of sights in the minimum amount of time with the least amount of hassle. They're particularly convenient for people with limited mobility and they can be a great way to make new friends.

On the downside, you'll have little opportunity for serendipitous interactions with locals. The tours can be jam-packed with activities, leaving little room for individual sightseeing, whim, or adventure—plus they often focus on the heavily touristed sites, so you miss out on many a lesser-known gem.

For midrange and budget tours, U.K.-based **Imaginative Traveller** ★★ is popular for its midrange-priced escorted tours (www.imaginative-traveller.com), and includes a tour of the remote northeastern states of Assam, Meghalaya, and Nagaland, which aren't covered in this book.

San Francisco–based **Geographic Expeditions** ★★★ (1008 General Kennedy Ave., San Francisco, CA 94129-0902; ℂ 800/777-8183 or 415/922-0448; www.geoex.com) is rated among the world's best tour organizers, with innovative, well-structured trips that combine off-the-well-trodden-path experiences with must-see sights. Their portfolio currently includes village tours of Ladakh and Rajasthan, journeys through the south, and trips that focus on festivals in certain regions. Most of their tours last between 12 and 18 days; while they have a schedule of planned departure dates, they are also able to tailor any departure to suit you and your party, irrespective of size. Geographic Expeditions also offers the possibility of completely personalized 100% customized trips, offering all the services you'd expect on a group tour.

One of India's foremost tourism operators, **Sita World Travel** (called **SOTC** in some places) is represented throughout the length and breadth of India. Sita offers a wide range of tours to cover a range of budgets and interests. These include sightseeing trips and excursions to India's top attractions, as well as soft-adventure and special-interest tours that can really get you off the beaten track (www.e-holidaysindia.com).

Note that many of the recommended individual and adventure operators listed above offer escorted group tours.

For more information on escorted general-interest tours, including questions to ask before booking your trip, see www.frommers.com/planning.

10 DISCOVERING SPIRITUAL INDIA

However you choose to spend your time in India, you are unlikely to return home unaffected by your sojourn here. Indeed, you are likely to find a moment of enlightenment in the most unexpected places, whether you're engaged in conversation with a shopkeeper over a cup of *chai* or people-watching on a suffocatingly crowded city street. But for generations visitors have come to India specifically seeking some sort of spiritual transformation, and the increasing plethora of first-rate accommodations and Western-style food options are making it easier than ever—and in some ways more difficult, by cocooning travelers from unvarnished India.

Basic **yoga** classes are conducted in many places all over the country, as are the various techniques and methods of meditation. But the best way to experience and improve your skills in either or both of these disciplines—and possibly find true bliss or meaning in life through a spiritual leader—is to spend time at an **ashram,** where philosophical (or religious, depending on where you go) discourse accompanies a meditation and/or yoga program. There are innumerable ashrams all over the country, some the domain of a dynamic *guru* (the teacher whose role it is to assist the spiritual awakening of devotees); while others (like the Vipassana centers; see below) are not driven by a single personality. In the following paragraphs we discuss where you can go to study and practice classic spiritual disciplines during your trip to India.

MEDITATION The most upmarket meditation center in India is the **Osho International Meditation Resort** in the city of Pune (near Mumbai; www.osho. com; see chapter 5). It's aimed at those who aren't concerned with giving up the real world while they search for enlightenment. Here, you're surrounded by 20 hectares (50 acres) of lush greenery (styled on the Japanese water garden), and the campus consists of marvelous pyramidal meditation halls, with a stylish Zen-styled guesthouse, cafes, the esoteric "Multiversity," magnificent swimming pool, and recreation facilities. For Rs 550 per day (excluding accommodation), you can fill your day with a variety of inward-looking activities, ranging from the intensive early morning "Dynamic Meditation" to the slightly surreal "Evening Meeting of the Brotherhood of the White Robe," during which you get to focus on Osho's voice, recorded during his time on earth. There's another Osho retreat near Dharamsala in Himachal Pradesh, but it's less welcoming of people who aren't already familiar with Osho's teachings (p. 175).

One of India's most ancient meditation techniques is **Vipassana,** which translates as "seeing things as they really are." Taught at 10-day residential courses at many centers around the country, this program is not for the fickle—during the course of the program you must adhere to a strict code of conduct, such as consuming nothing after midday. For many, however, the hardest part of the course is the rule of absolute silence, in which you're not allowed to speak (or read) a word for the first 9 days. The lack of any form of entertainment or sensory stimulation as well is meant to assist true inner awakening. This is certainly one of the most authentic meditation programs you will find anywhere, and one not based on devotion to a single guru or charismatic personality. The course is also *absolutely free* with no charges

for food and board. Check out **www. dhamma.org** for more details.

For meditation in the Tibetan Mahayana Buddhist tradition, **Tushita Meditation Centre** (www.tushita.info), a few miles north of Mcleodganj, offers short- and long-term programs for beginners as well as the experienced. Unlike Vipassana courses, which are more or less secular and nonsectarian, Tushita courses include teaching of Buddhist philosophy and religion as well as different meditation techniques.

If all this sounds too committed, *Sudarshan Kriya,* the revered Sri Sri Ravi Shankar's highly acclaimed breathing and meditation technique, can be learned through courses conducted by **The Art of Living Foundation** throughout India. For details, see the sidebar "Learn the 'Art of Living' with India's Hot New Age Guru" on p. 372 or visit **www.artofliving.org**.

YOGA For seriously dedicated yoga students willing to make a commitment of at least a month, the country has several well-known centers. Be aware, however, that at most of these places, room facilities are rather basic. The **Bihar School of Yoga** has an ashram on the banks of the Ganga in Munger, Bihar, where students come from around the world, usually for at least 4 months (www.yogavision.net). Requiring at least 1 month of dedicated practice is the hugely popular (and highly regarded) **Shri K. Pattabhi Jois Ashtanga Yoga Institute** in Mysore, where the fee of Rs 27,530 for the first month (Rs 17,416 for each subsequent month) is heftier than most, and does not include room and board (see www.kpjayi.org); note, however, that the venerated yoga master who founded the institute (or *shala*), Krishna Pattabhi Jois (aka Guruji), passed away in May 2009. For yoga in the tradition of that most famous of Indian yoga gurus, **BKS Iyengar,** you can contact the regional center in Mumbai. The courses at the Pune headquarters are only for long-term yoga experts and are booked up to 2 years in advance (www.bksiyengar.com). Less intensive, and more flexible for the traveler, is the **Himalayan Iyengar Yoga Centre** (www.hiyogacentre.com). This visitor-friendly organization has retreats in two locations: in Goa right on the sand dunes at Arambol Beach, and in Dharamkot (an hour's drive from Dharamsala, in Himachal Pradesh).

ASHRAMS For those travelers intent on working on their dharma and karma, destinations such as Varanasi (Uttar Pradesh), Bodhgaya (Bihar), Rishikesh, and Haridwar (both in Uttarakhand) have numerous centers, each providing some direction to an individuals' spiritual quest. In Rishikesh, **The Divine Life Society** welcomes daily visitors to its ashram on the banks of the Ganga; it professes to embrace the essential truth found in all the religions of the world. Chanting continues 24 hours a day (check the website www. sivanandaonline.org for details). In Bodhgaya, the **Root Institute** (www.rootinstitute.com) runs 6- to 12-day courses and retreats in Buddhist philosophy and spiritual awakening meant to bring peace and happiness to daily life. You can also attend 1-day workshops and take short courses on topics such as how to meditate, peaceful living and dying, and transforming problems into happiness. Accommodations are available at the institute.

You can also find programs offered by more well-known groups, such as **ISKCON** (Hare Krishna; www.iskcon. com), **Ramakrishna Mission** (www. sriramakrishna.org), and **Aurobindo Ashram** (www.sriaurobindoashram.org) in Puducherry (Pondicherry), as well as gurus with large, worldwide followings such as Sri Mata Amritanansamayi Devi—better know to the world as **Amma** (or "The Mother" or "The Hugging Guru")—who has her ashram in Amritapuri in Kerala (www.amritapuri.org).

For a deeper, more authentic experience—spiritually and culturally—**Arunachala,** the ashram dedicated to the teachings of the late Bhagavan Sri Ramana Maharshi, is 3 hours west of Chennai, in Tiruvannamalai, Tamil Nadu (www. arunachala-ramana.org). Rooms are small, basic, and cheap, but you will have to book 1 month in advance.

Finally, another fairly upmarket ashram, one with a strong following among Westerners, is run by the **Siddha Yoga** foundation at Ganeshpuri, also near Mumbai (www.siddhayoga.org). Note that this ashram does not encourage casual tourists dropping in; you have to be in touch with their programs to be allowed onto the beautiful walled estate.

A note of caution: Although all the yoga and meditation centers listed here are legitimate, care should be taken before embarking on any spiritual journey in India. (If you don't believe us, read Gita Mehta's *Karma Cola* [Vintage Books], an acerbic and witty investigation into the way in which unscrupulous gurus market Indian spirituality to credulous Westerners in search of something more "enlightened.") There are some who feel that spiritual teaching should come free, while others argue that spiritualism is being packaged for Westerners in a way they can relate to, and performs basically the same function as a psychotherapist might in the West. Most important: Be aware that literally thousands of gurus and ashrams, "pseudo" or "real," are spread all over the country, some of whose principal aim is to part you from your money or, in worst-case scenarios, to sexually exploit you. Principally, be suspicious of two things: gurus who claim to have supernatural or magical "powers" or are "miracle workers," and those who ask for hefty donations. Check credentials and make your choice wisely.

11 TIPS ON ACCOMMODATIONS

One of the best developments in the past decade has been the increase in **luxury boutique-type options** offering international standards of service and comfort and flavored with Indian accents—like beautiful craftsmanship and ancient traditions (we're talking Ayurvedic masseurs on tap) —which means that the subcontinent is now a very desirable destination for the visitor wanting relaxation and pampering. To find the most unusual independent hotels, guesthouses, and homestays, an excellent resource for those who don't want the classic resort or chain hotel experience is Alastair Sawday's *Special Places to Stay: India* (www.sawdays.co.uk), at press time about to go into its third edition. Though the properties listed pay to be in the book, they are all, almost without exception, special in some way; the best are included in this book (plus many more that cannot afford or choose not to pay for publicity).

Capitalizing on the desire for totally individual boutique-style lodgings, CGH Earth (www.cghearth.com; our favorite chain in South India), has been purchasing, building and/or skillfully renovating heritage properties throughout the south, and staffing it with locals usually with one of their highly trained managers at the helm. Their properties are so unique, and their standards generally so high, that— should your entire South India itinerary comprise only their properties—you will return home delighted.

Of course we all knew India had "arrived" when the ultraluxe **Amanresorts** entered the fray with **Amanbagh,** arguably the finest resort-style property in India, but the pace was first set by the **Vilās** properties, owned by India's very own, very fabulous **Oberoi** chain. Besides the Vilās properties (the best of which is **Amarvilās** in Agra, though many rate

Udaivilās in Udaipur as their top choice), Oberoi runs some of the very best city hotels, as well as several spa resorts in key tourist destinations and a luxury backwater cruiser in Kerala. As with the three Aman properties in India (including their exceptional new hotel in Delhi—probably our favorite city hotel in the country), Oberoi hotels and resorts attract top dollar, but you can generally count on superb service and attention to detail. Best of all, you can often get great discounts on room rates by reserving in advance over the Internet (**www.oberoihotels.com**). Note that Oberoi also operates a tier of smaller, less opulent hotels under the **Trident** banner; aimed principally at business or family travelers; trained to Oberoi standards, service in these hotels is excellent and they usually offer very good value.

India's other famous hotel chain is the **Taj** (www.tajhotels.com), with an enormous inventory of properties, particularly in South India, where Oberoi is largely absent. Quality varies somewhat (and service does not match that of the Oberoi group), but comfort is generally guaranteed, particularly in big cities and resort destinations—the best properties are the **Taj Mahal Palace** in Mumbai (less so the adjoining Tower wing), **Rambagh Palace** in Jaipur, **Lake Palace Hotel** in Udaipur, and **Umaid Bhawan Palace** in Jodhpur. They also offer comparatively excellent service and facilities at their hotels in smaller cities such as Aurangabad and Chandigarh. At press time, the Taj group is rolling out an extensive rebranding campaign, and has introduced several new identities (often used for existing properties); these include **The Gateway** (usually middling, unexceptional hotels) and **Vivanta by Taj** (very exclusive business hotels). Taj also operates a budget chain,

Ginger (see City Hotels below for more on this).

Safari experiences have changed dramatically since the Taj group launched **Taj Safaris,** teaming up with acclaimed South African conservation group **&Beyond** (formerly CC Africa). Their first luxury safari lodge, **Mahua Kothi,** at the Bandavgarh tiger reserve in Madhya Pradesh, is a sublime, sexy property with some of the country's best guides. They already have three more lodges in Madhya Pradesh—at Kanha, Panna and Pench—and are planning more in the next few years. Meanwhile, Amanresorts' tented lodge at Ranthambhore, **Amani-Khás,** remains superlative.

Don't think that India's high-end hotel sector is anywhere near saturated. The **Four Seasons** opened its first hotel in Mumbai in 2008, and it is among our favorite city hotels in the country (with an interesting location, brilliant concierge desk, and good community development programs). And two fairly low-key local chains have emerged: **Ista Hotels** (now in Amritsar, Bengaluru, and Hyderabad) and **O Hotels** (currently in Pune and Goa) both offer pretty good homegrown luxury, and are likely to expand their portfolios in the next few years. One Indian chain that is aiming to compete with Oberoi and Taj is **The Leela,** which has teamed up with Kempinski and, having sorted out its service standards, is scheduled to open many large, luxurious, environmentally conscious hotels in the next few years.

HOMESTAYS All over Kerala (and a few other places), people are converting rooms of their homes into guest rooms for tourists to rent, at incredibly reasonable prices. Guests share the public spaces with the family, which lives in the home, and often dine with them. Many of these homestays are gorgeous heritage homes and their owners extremely hospitable. It's a good way to interact with an Indian family and get a taste of local culture and cuisine (www.homestaykerala.com, for instance, has an extensive list of such properties). But don't expect room service and the kinds of amenities you get at a full-service hotel. If you are looking for a dash of luxury with your homestay experience, look into the tours through Ladakh offered by Shakti (see above).

HERITAGE HOTELS Staying in a medieval palace or fort is a unique and wonderful option among India's accommodations (particularly in Rajasthan), especially when your host is the aristocrat whose forebears built the palace or fort in which you're overnighting; the best are discussed in detail in relevant sections throughout this guide. Many were built centuries ago, so it's not surprising that heritage hotels are seldom the most luxurious option, with the possibilities of many stairs, dodgy plumbing, low ceilings, strange room layouts, and other eccentricities. Acting principally as marketing agencies for privately owned palaces, forts, and *havelis* (Indian mansions), as well as a number of small resorts around the country (primarily North India), it's worth checking out **www.heritagehotels.com** as well as the portfolio of properties that are bookable through **WelcomHeritage** (www.welcom heritagehotels.com).

Most heritage properties are individually owned, but a group that enjoys an excellent reputation for selecting and renovating these is **Neemrana;** check out **www. neemranahotels.com** to view their select collection of really lovely boutique heritage hotels, often located in off-the-beaten-track destinations; rates generally represent excellent value for these atmospheric gems, and some of their most recent renovations (such as the awesome Le Colonial in Fort Kochi) are absolute masterpieces. As mentioned earlier, CGH are similarly investing in heritage properties, such as the gorgeous Maison Perumal in Pondicherry and Visalam in Tamil Nadu's Chettiar district.

Tip: Be aware that any hovel will attach "palace" to its name in the hopes of attracting more customers. This is often amusing if you're walking past, but can be disastrous if you're checking in.

CITY HOTELS The biggest problem in big cities and popular tourist areas is that the good hotels are often priced way out of reach, while moderate options are thin on the ground. **Midrange hotels** are substandard by Western standards, though considerably cheaper. Wherever possible, we've provided budget options that are scrupulously clean and moderately comfortable. A chain of budget hotels we recommend is **Ginger** (© **800/22-0022** or 022/66014-634; www.gingerhotels.com). Launched by Indian Hotels (owners of the Taj group) and catering specially to the middling business market, these 101-room "Smart Basics" hotels offer accommodations priced at under Rs 1,500 for a double. They won't have any of the opulence of the Taj hotels; in fact, rooms are small and rather plain in design, albeit comfortable and with all the amenities, including an ATM in the hotel. At press time, Ginger had just opened its 20th hotel, with several more imminent openings planned. Another budget chain worth looking into is **Lemon Tree.** This relative newcomer offers comfortable hotel accommodations and facilities at a price that its competitors are finding impossible to beat. It's by no means luxurious, with that slightly stark pared-down atmosphere typical of any budget hotel, but everything is gleaming new and service is pretty slick.

Most of the top-of-the-range city hotels are operated by major international chains—specifically those discussed earlier in this section.

THE RATING SYSTEM India's hotel rating system refers to size and facilities on offer, not the potential quality of your stay. Often the best hotels have no rating because they are heritage properties and—despite their overwhelming loveliness—don't conform to the norms laid down by India's tourism department.

Warning: As a general rule of thumb, government-run properties are best avoided throughout the country.

BARGAINING In India, even hotel rates are up for a bit of hard-core bargaining. If you're thin-skinned, bargain online (many hotels offer Internet-only discounts); alternatively, show up and stay tough—when you hear the rate quoted, brazenly pretend to walk out; there's no shame in India in turning back and accepting the rate. You'll also be surprised to find that luxury hotels in cities can often be had at midrange prices, simply because room occupancy is low. Always ask about daily specials, and call and check prices: In this book we generally provide the published (official) "rack" rate for accommodations, but most business and large luxury hotels have now gone over to the "rate of the day" or "best available rate" system which means that you should always investigate actual prices of places that have taken your fancy—even if they appear beyond your reach, the actual rate may be substantially lower.

In remote areas, small towns, and villages, and many places in Goa and the Himalayan foothills, you can find good (basic but clean) budget accommodations at unbelievable prices. The same cannot generally be said of the major cities, where a cheap, dingy hotel may expose you to bedbugs and despair; stick to the budget recommendations in this book.

Note: Prices in a number of the hotel listings throughout the book are stated in U.S. dollars or, increasingly, in euros—this is, in fact, the way hotels targeting foreign markets quote their rates.

Tip: All over India, floors are marked and understood differently from many in the U.S. First floor is the floor above the ground level, second floor is the floor above that, and so on. The ground floor or lobby level is just that.

Of Hotels & Taxes

Almost every hotel in India will quote a rate to which an additional luxury tax is added; this varies from state to state. This tax applies to all luxury hotels, or the moment the room price goes above a certain level (which depends on the state, and sometimes the city). Restaurant and hotel bills get a different tax, and alcohol and other luxuries get a different set of taxes all together. Some states such as Tamil Nadu add an astronomical 73.5% tax to imported liquor; as a rule, locally produced alcohol is taxed less than foreign imports. *Always* check whether the tax has been included in the rate you've been quoted and, if it hasn't, exactly how much it is.

SURFING FOR HOTELS

In addition to the online travel booking sites **Travelocity, Expedia, Orbitz, Priceline,** and **Hotwire,** you can book hotels through **Hotels.com; Quikbook** (www.quikbook.com); and **Travelaxe** (www.travelaxe.com).

Many budget and moderate hotel websites (where indeed they do have them) are poorly maintained, which means you may come across tariffs and information dating as far back as the previous decade. Smaller hotels change e-mail service providers almost as often as they change sheets. For basic information on about 3,000 listed hotels in India, the website for the **Federation of Hotel and Restaurant Associations of India** (www.fhrai.com) can be a useful if undiscriminating resource.

You'll also come up against a plethora of accommodations booking services that presume to be direct representatives of the hotel you're searching for, but that actually hike up the lowest available tariff considerably, which may leave you feeling ripped off before you even bed down. Always compare the website rate with the cheapest rate offered directly by the hotel before making a reservation. On the upside, several hotel networks offer unbelievable Internet discounts that simply can't be ignored.

For access to some truly wonderful "Hip Hideaways and Boutique Hotels," check out the offerings at **i-escape.com ★★★,** which gives detailed reviews (and booking facilities) for many of India's most stylish hotels, retreats, and villas.

LANDING THE BEST ROOM

Somebody has to get the best room in the house; it might as well be you. First, make sure your room has air-conditioning (unless you're in the cool mountain regions where it isn't needed). Ask for a room with split air-conditioning (an air-conditioner with a separate indoor and outdoor unit); it's far less noisy—and ugly—than a window air-conditioner. If there's no air-conditioning, ask whether there is a ceiling fan or a water-cooling system. Be sure to request your choice of twin, queen- or king-size beds. Ask for rooms with views (many hotel staff don't understand this concept in India, so it's best to look around on arrival), and specify if you prefer a shower or tub (tubs in medium or budget category are usually old and stained, so don't shy away from shower-only options—which are far more environmentally friendly anyway). Ask for one of the most recently renovated or redecorated rooms—bathrooms in particular seem to suffer heavy wear and tear in India.

Tip: Indians often use the term "hotel" to refer to a restaurant or eating place, so don't be surprised if someone suggests you eat at a hotel down the road, and you arrive there to find a five-table shack.

4

Suggested India Itineraries

India is such a vast country and has so much to see that visitors are tempted to pack in as much as possible. Begin any trip to India with the knowledge that no matter how long your vacation, it will not be long enough. Knowing this can help you make the best of your time here and prevent you from planning a punishing schedule that will leave you not only thoroughly overwhelmed, but with an uncomfortable feeling that you've rushed through most of what you did see.

Despite greatly improved accommodations and transportation options, India is still a challenging destination, and you should always be prepared to take in stride a delayed flight, slow check-in, or upset tummy on, say, a long-distance train. Set aside time to acclimatize and simply unwind—this is, after all, a vacation.

Ideally, you should use this book's "Best Of" chapter to work out a route that covers those experiences or sights that really appeal to you, as the range of possible itineraries is endless; what we've suggested below are three rather full programs covering either North or South India over a **2-week period.** If possible, extend your trip—2 weeks is not enough time to come to grips with India—and set aside more time for those destinations that sound most appealing to you. The fourth itinerary is for those who want to experience India at a languid, easy pace while still taking in key attractions—and there is no better place to do this than in southern India.

You could, of course, combine a trip to both the north and the south, but then you really should stick to one state (even one hotel!) in each area. For instance, you can arrive in Delhi, travel through Agra and then Jaipur, Bundi, and Udaipur, covering this region in 8 days, and then head south to Kerala. In Kerala, you can cover Cochin and Kumarakom (cruising the backwaters) and finish off with a couple of days south of Kovalam (or, better still, in the less-discovered far north of Kerala), before flying out of Bengaluru or Mumbai.

None of the itineraries below include a trip into any of the fabulous Himalayan regions covered in this book. If you do in fact extend your time in India, make your way from Delhi to the Golden Temple in Amritsar, and then explore the remote valleys of Kinnaur, Lahaul, and Spiti before heading into surreal Ladakh; alternatively, you can take a road trip from Delhi through the picturesque Kumaon in Uttarakhand, or take off from Kolkata to Darjeeling (book the famous toy train there) and Buddhist Sikkim.

Whatever you decide to do, we highly recommend that you end your trip in one of India's natural paradises, at least to recover from the sensual assault you'll experience exploring the crowded and often polluted urban areas. These oases include the beaches on the Malabar coast and Goa, the backwaters of Kerala, the lunar landscapes and wooded hills of the Himalayas, and the wonderful hotels and resorts in Rajasthan.

Important: Should limited time force you to include only the most obvious stops in your itinerary, you will invariably only make contact with those locals who depend on you for a living, which regrettably could leave you with a frustrated sense that many of India's inhabitants are grasping, manipulative, or downright pushy. This is why it's so important to get off the beaten tourist track, and book at least one homestay in order to experience firsthand the warmth, hospitality, and generosity of the Indian people and their culture, which celebrates an ancient philosophy of the guest as god.

1 NORTH INDIA HIGHLIGHTS IN 16 DAYS

Stunning Mughal architecture, heritage hotels, old palaces, forts, and colorful markets make North India an exciting experience that imparts a heady, sensory feeling in any visitor. No 2-week trip can exhaustively cover all the main sights, but this itinerary covers many of the most popular tourist attractions of northern India. It's a hectic schedule, so keep in mind that relaxation is required between sights, if only to catch your breath and dwell on what you've seen before leaping forward to the next equally striking sight.

Days ❶–❸: Delhi

You'll most likely arrive in Delhi in the wee hours of the morning. As a general rule, take it easy on Day 1 in India—the country takes serious acclimation. There's no better way to ease into your trip than to start your vacation at Delhi's finest hotel, **Aman,** a brand-new city property from one of the finest nonhotel "chains" on earth. Allow yourself a late morning on Day 2, and hire a car and driver for the day if you want to wander out for some slow-paced sightseeing. Take in central New Delhi's imperial architecture—beginning at **India Gate,** built to commemorate those who died in World War I. From there, set off on foot along **Rajpath** to the beautifully ornate gates of **Rashtrapati Bhavan,** official residence of the president of India. Then drive south to visit the 12th-century **Qutb Minar.** For a break, escape to **Lodi Gardens,** where lawns and golfing greens are studded with the crumbling 15th-century tombs of once-powerful dynasties. A short drive west brings you to the splendid medieval buildings of **Humayun's Tomb** (which your suite at Aman will overlook) and **Hazrat Nizamuddin Aulia.** Finally, stop off at **Dilli Haat** and check out the range of handicrafts and handmade goods sold by artisans from around India, before you seek out one of Delhi's superb restaurants, such as **Spice Route** at another contender for the title of Delhi's best hotel, The Imperial.

On Day 3, explore **Old Delhi (Shahjahanabad).** Must-sees include **Lal Qila (Red Fort)** and **Jama Masjid,** both built by Shah Jahan, the most prolific architect of the Mughal empire. You can also stop off at vibrant **Gauri Shankar Temple,** which has an 800-year-old lingam (a phallic symbol used in the worship of the Hindu god Shiva); **Sisganj Gurudwara,** an unassuming but atmospheric and welcoming Sikh temple that marks the spot where Guru Tegh Bahadur, the ninth Sikh guru, was beheaded by Aurangzeb; and **Sunehri** and **Fatehpuri masjids.** If you can handle the massive crowds, wander around **Chandni Chowk, Khari Baoli** (reputed to be Asia's biggest spice market), and jam-packed **Kinari Bazaar**—but keep a close watch on your belongings at all times.

Days ❹ & ❺: Varanasi & Khajuraho

Fly into Varanasi, a crumbling maze of a city that rises from the *ghats* (steps) on the western banks of the Ganges River. Varanasi is in many ways quintessential India—it is one of the holiest of Indian pilgrimage sites, home of Shiva, where the devout come to wash away their sins. Many come here to die with the hope that they may achieve *moksha,* salvation of the soul from the cycle of birth, death, and rebirth. Take

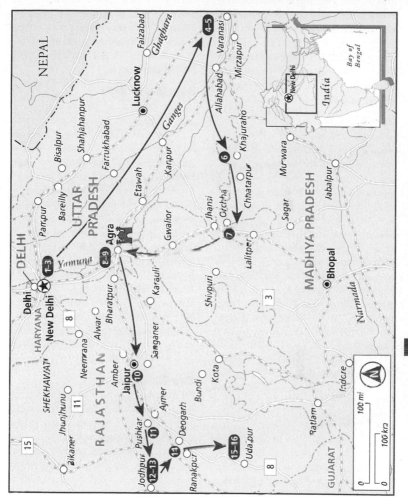

a **boat cruise** past the *ghats* at dawn; you can repeat this at sunset or, better still, head for **Dasashwamedh Ghat** to watch the **Ganga Fire Arti.** For 45 minutes, young Brahmin priests perform age-old prayer rituals with conch shells and burning braziers, accompanied by drummers, while children hawk candles for you to light and set adrift. Aside from these must-sees, you should set aside some time to wander the ancient lanes of the **Old City,** particularly those around **Kashi Vishwanath Temple.** When you feel the need for peace and solitude, hire a car and visit **Sarnath,** where Buddha first revealed his Eightfold Path to Nirvana; spend a few hours exploring the archaeological ruins and the modern Buddhist temple and monasteries. Overnight at **Ganges View Guesthouse** in Varanasi, a lovely, comfortable colonial lodge at the edge of the river or you could move away from the bustle and opt for the classy atmosphere at the newly opened **Nadesar Palace.** On the afternoon of Day 5, take a flight to Khajuraho. After you check in at your hotel (preferably **The Grand Temple View**), head off immediately to either the Eastern or Southern Group of temples, with Samson George as your guide.

Day ⑥: Khajuraho

Khajuraho is known the world over for its beautiful, taboo-breaking erotic sculptures, images that are almost as intimately associated with India as the Taj. But the temples also represent an outstanding synthesis of advanced architecture and refined sculpture. Try to enter as soon as the **Western Group** of temples opens (sunrise), not only for the light's quality, but to avoid the busloads of tourists who will arrive later. Take your time admiring the beautifully rendered friezes of gods, nymphs, animals, and energetically twisting bodies locked together in acts of hotblooded passion. Cover the Western, Eastern, and Southern Group (unless you visited them the day before), ending your day at the 50-minute **sound-and-light show** held at 6:30pm, which provides a fascinating history of Khajuraho.

Day ⑦: Orchha

From Khajuraho, drive to Orchha, the deserted royal citadel of Raja Rudra Pratap, on a rocky island on the Betwa River. This is one of India's most fabulous Mughal heritage sites and a wonderfully relaxing stop sandwiched between the intense huckster-heavy destinations of Varanasi/Khajuraho and Agra. Orchha, founded in 1531, was the capital of the Bundela kings until 1738. Today the weathered temples, palaces, and cenotaphs are the royal quarters of emerald parakeets and black-faced langurs, while traditional whitewashed, flat-roofed structures house the laid-back villagers. Besides the **palace complex,** three beautiful temples are

worth seeking out, as well as 14 graceful *chhatris* (cenotaphs) commemorating the Orchha rulers, built upstream along the riverbank. Though all these can be covered in a day, get the most out of this surreally tranquil haven by spending the night at the **Orchha Resort.**

Days ⑧ & ⑨: Agra

Drive to Jhansi, and take an express train to Agra, home of the **Taj Mahal.** Besides the exquisite Taj, visit the city of **Fatehpur Sikri** and the tombs of **Itmad-ud-Daulah** and **Akbar,** as well as well-preserved **Agra Fort.** If you can afford it (and this one is worth saving up for), overnight at the Oberoi's luxurious **Amarvilās,** where your room will have a view of the Taj Mahal. Ideally, visit the Taj at dawn and spend the whole morning there. Built by Shah Jahan as an eternal symbol of his love for his favorite wife, Mumtaz Mahal, the Taj has immortalized him as one of the great architectural patrons of the world. Not only does the Taj have perfect symmetry, ethereal luminescence, and wonderful proportions, but every inch of marble is covered in exquisite detail.

Day ⑩: Jaipur

Drive to Jaipur, where you can explore the **City Palace** and **Amber Fort** in a day; you'll need a little more time if you want to go to **Samode Palace,** an hour's drive away. However, no amount of time is enough for the shopping; Jaipur is a **bargain-hunter's** haven, where you will find gorgeous Rajasthani crafts for sale that are hard to resist. In Jaipur, overnight at **Taj Rambagh Palace** (if you prefer an authentic historical experience close to the heart of the city), or **Rajvilās** (if you enjoy the illusion of being far away from everything, combined with absolute luxury). Alternatively, stay at Samode Haveli, easily the best heritage property in the Old City, or simply refer to any of the heritage properties reviewed, which cover a range of budgets.

Day ⑪: Pushkar

Late in the afternoon, drive from Jaipur to the temple town of **Pushkar,** stopping en route to view **Dargah Sharif,** the top attraction of **Ajmer** along the way. Get your "Pushkar Passport" as early as possible, which will then free you from further harassment by priests. Spend the night on the shores of Pushkar Lake, preferably at **Pushkar Palace.**

Note: If Pushkar lake is dry (which it has been of late) you might want to consider skipping Pushkar, pausing instead at the small and remote village of Shahpura, where family-owned Shahpura Bagh is one of our favorite places to stay in Rajasthan and the mild-mannered village makes a great alternative to the pushy, rather ugly town of Pushkar.

Days ⑫ & ⑬: Pushkar & Jodhpur

Start out early to explore Pushkar, a charming (if very filthy, touristy) town surrounding a sacred lake on the eastern edge of the Thar Desert, and an important pilgrimage site for Hindus. Browse the **street bazaar,** where you can pick up the most gorgeous throwaway gear, great secondhand books, and CDs at bargain prices. Pushkar can be explored entirely on foot— it will take you about 45 minutes to walk around the holy lake and its 52 *ghats* (stairs). From Pushkar, move on to **Jodhpur,** where you must set aside half a day to visit fabulous **Mehrangarh Fort and Museum,** arguably Rajasthan's most impressive and cleanest fort, with sheer clifflike walls that soar above the city. Situated on another raised outcrop, with sprawling grounds creating a majestic ambience, is **Umaid Bhawan Palace,** built by Maharaja Umaid Singh as a poverty-relief exercise to aid his drought-stricken subjects. Designed by Henry Lanchester, a great admirer of Lutyens (the man who designed New Delhi), it was started in 1929, took 3,000 laborers 13 years to

complete, and remains one of the best examples of Indo-Saracenic Art Deco style. If you don't mind the splurge, try to spend the night at the Palace (preferably in one of the beautiful Deco-styled historical suites), and catch the setting sun from the edge of the lovely outdoor pool. Breakfast at **The Pillars** restaurant, where you can enjoy a spellbinding view of the fort in the distance. Move on to the new, sexy Mihir Garh and go for a sunset gallop into the Thar Desert, or relax at the endearing **Rawla Narlai** or even (if you don't mind a lengthy detour) **Fort Seengh Sagar** to overnight.

Days ⑭ & ⑮: Udaipur

Enjoy the morning at Migir Garh or Rawla Narlai, then head to Udaipur, stopping at the **Ranakpur temples** (and, if you've left early enough, Kumbhalgarh, overnighting at Aodi) en route. In Udaipur overnight at the fabulous, fabled **Lake Palace** or any of the recommended accommodations that have a lake view. Time allowing, take a sunset cruise on the lake or enjoy a muscle-tingling treatment in the Taj's spa boat. The following day, visit the **City Palace and Museum** in Udaipur. Prime attractions worth pursuing and doable in the time available are the temples at **Nathdwara** and **Eklingji.** Or spend the rest of the day lounging around the pool under the shade of its 263-year-old mango tree. If you wish to squeeze in an extra day, do so at **Devi Garh,** 45 minutes outside Udaipur.

Day ⑯: Udaipur & Delhi

Enjoy a leisurely morning roaming Udaipur's lovely bazaars, or relax at the Devi Garh pool, before taking an afternoon flight back to Delhi. If you have space left in your baggage (fat chance!), stop for last-minute souvenirs and gifts before you board your flight home.

2 THE GOLDEN TRIANGLE & RAJASTHAN HIGHLIGHTS

Though this itinerary includes Delhi, Agra, and Jaipur (the "Golden Triangle") and captures many of the essential Rajasthan sights, it does not include **Jaisalmer,** one of Rajasthan's most wonderful destinations, primarily because it's not very easy to get to. In a 2-week vacation that also takes in Delhi and Agra, it would be hard (but not impossible) to include Jaisalmer. Best to extend your stay in India by a few days if you want to cover this oldest "living" fortified city in Rajasthan. Located in the heart of the Thar Desert on India's far western border, Jaisalmer has breathtakingly beautiful, crumbling sandstone mansions, though its main attraction, **Sonar Killa (Golden Fort),** is reason enough to travel this far west, not least because it may not exist in a few years time. Though not as impressive as Jodhpur's Mehrangarh Fort, Jaisalmer has its unique charm as an inhabited medieval fort. So if you do come to Jaisalmer, plan to spend 2 nights, not least because it takes so long to get here.

Days ❶–❸: Delhi

After your long flight and no doubt middle-of-the-night arrival, have a car waiting for you and check in at Delhi's finest hotel, **Aman,** at one of the city's superb midrange guesthouses, **Amarya Haveli** or **Amarya Gardens,** or at the best budget accommodations in town, the stylish **Master Guest House,** which will also arrange an airport transfer (book well in advance). When you feel you're ready to face the world, take in a few New Delhi sights, including **India Gate,** built to commemorate those who died in World War I. Walk from **Rajpath** to **Rashtrapati Bhavan,** where the president of India lives. After you cover the 12th-century **Qutb Minar** complex in South Delhi, grab a table at **Park Balluchi** before browsing the shops in Hauz Khas. After lunch, visit the garden tombs of **Humayun** and of **Hazrat Nizamuddin Aulia** (the saint Sheikh Nizamuddin Aulia), one of the holiest Muslim sites in India. Time allowing, stop off at **Rajghat,** the place where Gandhi was cremated in 1948. Of course if you're here to shop or want to browse, scrap these and head for **Dilli Haat,** a great place to check out the range of handicrafts you'll find on your travels through India. Pick one of Delhi's excellent restaurants for dinner (consider booking a table at the gorgeously designed **Véda,** or check if **Olive Bar and Kitchen** has reopened).

Prepare yourself for the chaos of the crowded streets of 17th-century **Shahjahanabad,** or Old Delhi—just a few kilometers from Connaught Place, it feels a hundred years away, and the pungent smells from the ancient streets are a heady reminder that you are far from home. Still surrounded by crumbling city walls and three surviving gates, the vibrant, bustling Shahjahanabad, built over a period of 10 years by Emperor Shah Jahan, is very much a separate city—predominantly a labyrinth of tiny lanes crowded with rickshaws and lined with *havelis* (Indian "mansions"), their balustrades broken and once-ornate facades defaced with rusted signs and sprouting satellite dishes. Start with imposing **Lal Qila (Red Fort)** and **Jama Masjid,** India's largest mosque. If the crowds haven't left you exhausted, visit **Gauri Shankar Temple, Sisganj Gurudwara,** and **Sunehri** and **Fatehpuri masjids.** The city's lanes and back lanes are exciting to wander through, especially **Chandni Chowk, Khari Baoli** (the spice market), and **Kinari Bazaar**—but do hold on tightly to your belongings.

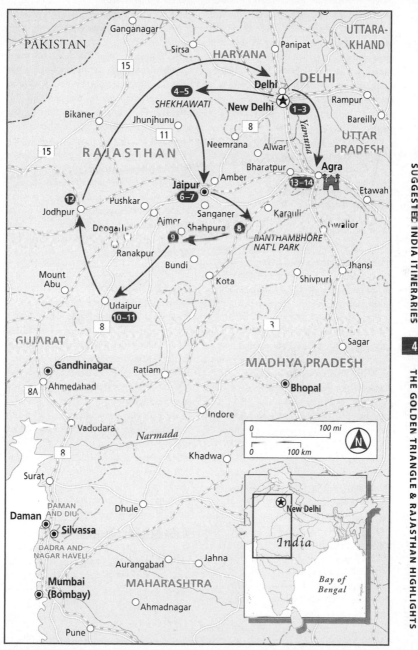

Days ❹ & ❺: Shekhawati

Make an early start and drive to the Shekhawati region, the open-air art gallery of Rajasthan. Today there are some 30 "painted towns" in the region, but the most essential to include in a first-time itinerary are **Ramgarh, Nawalgarh, Fatehpur,** and **Mandawa.** Mandawa is a quaint town with a number of beautifully painted buildings; it is also centrally located and has the best accommodations in the area. Overnight at Desert Resort as your first choice and then opt for the gracious **Castle Mandawa.**

Days ❻ & ❼: Jaipur & Ranthambhore

Drive to the "Pink City" of Jaipur. If possible, book into the wonderful **Rajvilās** (more resort than hotel), though Jaipur is one city that has a host of pleasant heritage options to suit every budget. If you prefer the authenticity of a real heritage hotel, book a room in the opulent and well-located **Rambagh Palace** or the more low-key **Samode Haveli** inside the Old City. Explore the **City Palace,** including a visit to Hawa Mahal and Jantar Mantar, and then focus on sites farther afield: **Amber Fort,** first royal residence of the Maharajas of Kachchwaha, lies 11km (6¾ miles) north, while popular **Samode Palace** is an hour's drive away. Jaipur, famous for gems and jewelry, enamel and brassware, blue pottery, embroidered leather footwear, rugs, tie-and-dye cotton fabrics, hand-blocked prints, fine *Kota doria* saris, and ready-made linens and home furnishings, is a **shopper's paradise.** You could spend days bargain-hunting through the region's wonderful crafts, so be prepared to extend your stay by at least a day. If this is not possible, set off on the evening of Day 7 to **Ranthambhore National Park,** and overnight at **Aman-i-Khás,** for the finest "tenting" experience in India.

Day ❽: Ranthambhore

Take an early morning or afternoon game drive into the park. Set aside a few hours to visit **Ranthambhore Fort,** whose high, jagged escarpment has towered over the park's forests for nearly a thousand years. Go **tiger tracking;** the highlight of a trip here is spotting a tiger. Even if you don't see a tiger (and do be prepared for this eventuality), the physical beauty of the park is worth experiencing. Other species to watch for include *caracal* (a wildcat), crocodile, *nilgai* (large antelope resembling cattle), *chital* (spotted deer), black buck (delicate buck with spiraling horns), *chinkara* (a dainty gazelle), and sambar. The park also holds leopards, wild boars, sloth bears, and rich birdlife. At night, unwind around a campfire and swap stories with other travelers, or discuss the fate of the highly endangered tiger.

Day ❾: Shahpura

Drive to the expansive wooded estate of family-run **Shahpura Bagh,** where you've got quaint, off-the-beaten-track Shahpura—one of the more unspoiled villages in Rajasthan—right on your doorstep. When you're not relaxing by the pool, explore Shahpura⊠s narrow streets, with photo opportunities everywhere: old men beating copper pots into perfect shape; tailors working with beautiful fabrics on ancient Singers and ironing with coal-heated irons; huge mounds of orange, red, and yellow spices offset by fresh, colorful local vegetables; rickshaws carting women adorned in color-saturated saris; ancient step wells and temples blaring live music.

Days ❿ & ⓫: Udaipur

Visit Udaipur's lovely bazaars and towering **City Palace and Museum.** Take a boat ride on Lake Pichola and overnight at either **Lake Palace** or one of the other accommodations with a lake view. Or spend the night at elegant **Devi Garh** just

26km (16 miles) from Udaipur. If the lake is dry, tarry no longer than a day, moving on the next day to one of the excursions outside Udaipur. Begin with the temples at **Nathdwara, Nagda,** and **Eklingji;** then move on to the awesome Jain temples at **Ranakpur, Kumbhalgarh Wildlife Sanctuary,** and magnificent **Kumbhalgarh Fort.** Alternatively, consider another long, full-day trip to **Chittaurgarh,** site of the most legendary Mewar battles. Overnight on Day 11 at **Rawla Narlai** or **Deogarh Mahal,** from where you can head northwest for Jodhpur.

Day ⑫: Jodhpur & Delhi

Make an early start to drive to "the Blue City" of Jodhpur and explore fabulous **Mehrangarh Fort and Museum.** For many, this looming, 15th-century edifice to Rajput valor is still Rajasthan's most impressive fort, with walls that soar like sheer cliffs 122m (400 ft.) high—literally dwarfing the city at its base—and a proud history of never having fallen to its many invaders. Don't miss **Umaid Bhawan**

Palace, once the largest private residence in the world—a vivid reminder of the decadence the Rajput rulers enjoyed during the British Raj (if you have an extra day, consider staying at the Palace, now a superb luxury hotel). Catch a flight to Delhi, where you can relax after a long day.

Days ⑬ & ⑭: Agra

From Delhi, drive to Agra to visit the jewel of India, the **Taj Mahal,** stopping en route at **Fatehpur Sikri.** Visit **Itmad-ud-Daulah's tomb** and **Agra Fort.** If you have the time, see beautiful **Jama Masjid,** built in 1648 by Jahanara Begum, Shah Jahan's favorite daughter. Overnight at the Oberoi's **Amarvilas,** a worthwhile splurge for your last night in India. Ideally, you can visit the Taj at dawn on Day 14 and spend as much time as you like there before you head back to Delhi for your flight out. If you get into Delhi before nightfall, you'll still have time to do last-minute shopping, as most shops are open till at least 7pm.

3 SOUTH INDIA: TEMPLES & TEA, BEACHES & BACKWATERS

South India is where the great Dravidian kingdoms were established, and anyone interested in ancient history and grand temples must visit Tamil Nadu or Karnataka. Here we've included only a few temples, but if you crave more, you'll find an exhaustive variety of exquisitely carved temples to explore. For natural beauty and rejuvenation, there are few places in India like Kerala, India's most verdant state, where we recommend you end your trip. This itinerary also takes you through its tea estates, backwaters, wildlife parks, and rainforests.

Days ❶ & ❷: Bengaluru or Mumbai

Fly straight into Bengaluru or Mumbai. You'll probably arrive in the middle of the night, so spend the day relaxing or wandering through Karnataka's capital city. If you're in Bengaluru, at some point take in **Bull Temple** on Bugle Hill. Built by the city's original architect, Kempe Gowda, this 16th-century black-granite statue of

Nandi (Shiva's sacred bull "vehicle") literally dwarfs its "master," and is kept glistening by regular applications of coconut oil. Stay at either the ultramodern **Park.hotel** or the **Taj West End** for old-world charm. If you're on a budget, book a room at lovely **Villa Pottipati.** If you arrive in Mumbai instead, you can spend the day relaxing at one of the city's numerous luxury hotels (preferably in a

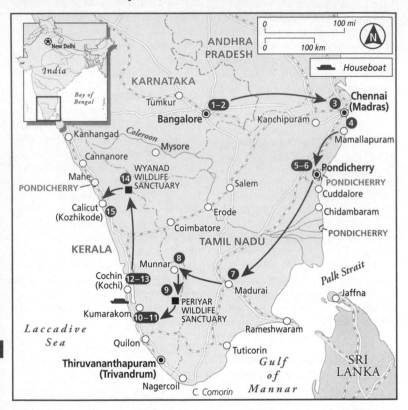

heritage suite at the **Taj Mahal Palace** or on the top floor of the **Four Seasons**) or at a good-value option like **Ascot.** Set aside a few hours to wander around and acclimate yourself to India's most bustling megalopolis.

Day ❸: Chennai & Mamallapuram

From Bengaluru (or Mumbai), fly to Chennai (or take the train). You can either head straight down the coast to **Fisherman's Cove** resort (1 hr.) or take a detour to **Kanchipuram** 80km (50 miles) southwest of Chennai to visit the temples there before heading to Fisherman's Cove. If you prefer to be closer to Mamallapuram, book a room at **Temple Bay** resort instead. En route, stop along the scenic East Coast Highway at the cultural centers of **Cholamandalam** and

Dakshina Chitra for local arts and crafts. **Dakshina Chitra** is a heritage center showcasing different living styles from India's four southern states: Karnataka, Tamil Nadu, Kerala, and Andhra Pradesh.

Day ❹: Mamallapuram

Set out early and take in Mamallapuram's monolithic shrines and rock-cut cave temples, which lie scattered over a landscape heaped with boulders and rocky hillocks. Among these, the excellent **Shore Temple,** built to Lord Shiva, and the **Five Rathas,** a cluster of temples named for the five Pandava brothers of *Mahabharata* fame, are definitely worth seeking out. The celebrated **Arjuna's Penance** is the largest relief-carving on earth. When you've finished your tour, you can enjoy a great seafood meal at one of the numerous beach shacks or restaurants before continuing down the coast to the French colonial town of Puducherry (aka Pondicherry). Overnight at nearby **Dune Eco-Village,** or in Pondi at **Miason Perumal** or **Hotel de l'Orient.**

Days ❺ & ❻: Puducherry (Pondicherry) & Trichy/Thanjavur

Besides hanging out in your antiques-filled colonial hotel or sauntering around the oceanfront **French Quarter,** you can visit **Auroville,** an interesting experiment in alternative living, also optimistically known as the City of Dawn (if you plan ahead you can enter the sci-fi Matrimandir, well worth the extra effort it takes to book); or you can join New Age travelers and earnest pilgrims and visit the atmospheric ashram of **Sri Aurobindo.** While wandering the Quarter, you may want to take a look at the **Sacred Heart of Jesus (Eglise de Sacre Coeur de Jésus),** an 18th-century neo-Gothic Catholic church on South Boulevard; and at the **Church of Immaculate Conception** on Mission Street. At twilight, stroll to **Goubert Salai** (Beach Rd.), where you'll see the colonial **Hôtel de Ville** (now the Municipal Offices building) and a statue of Gandhi standing at the pier. On Day 6, drive southwest, to Trichy, to see the sacred temple town of **Srirangam,** then overnight at **Ideal River Resort** near Thanjavur.

Day ❼ & ❽: Thanjavur & Chettinad Region & Madurai

After viewing the **Brihadeshvara Temple** in Thanjavur at dawn, head into the rural delights of the **Chettiar district,** where you can admire the peeling facades of mansions that line the dusty streets of **Kanadukathan,** just outside Karaikkudi, before retiring to your very own mansion, the gorgeous **Visalam.** From the Chettinad area, Madurai is a 2-hour drive southwest; once there, choose between the gracious **Taj Gateway**

Pasumalai Madurai or the chic new boutique hotel, **Heritance Madurai.**

Day ❾: Madurai

Early in the morning, visit **Shri Meen-akshi-Sundareshwarar Temple,** one of South India's biggest, busiest pilgrimage sites. Garish stucco gods, demons, beasts, and heroes smother the various towers in a writhing, fascinating mass of symbolism, vividly painted a riot of bright colors. Near the inner gate, a temple elephant, daubed with eye shadow and blusher, earns her keep by accepting a few rupees in exchange for a blessing—bestowed with a light tap of her dexterous trunk. From here you can wander at will, finding your way at some stage to the **Thousand Pillar Museum,** housed in the impressive 16th-century Hall of a Thousand Pillars. This hall has 985 elegantly sculpted columns, including a set of "musical pillars" that produce the seven Carnatic musical notes when tapped. All around the complex of shrines and effigies, various *pujas* (prayers) and rituals are conducted. Once you're done exploring the site and have spent an hour or so wandering the lanes adjacent to the temple, either retire to your hotel and return to witness the evening ceremony, or push on and drive to Munnar, sometimes referred to as Kerala's Scottish highlands. Overnight at **Windermere Estate** or one of the planter's bungalows at **Tea Sanctuary.**

Day ❿: Munnar

Munnar is a collection of vast green tea estates first established by a Scotsman in the late–19th century. Besides enjoying the rolling mists and endless greenery, you can arrange a **tea factory visit** and a stopover at the **Tea Museum.** To get up close to some of the world's last Nilgiri tahr (a variety of mountain goat or ibex), visit nearby **Eravikulam National Park.** Existing only in the mountain grasslands of the Western *ghats* at altitudes above 2,000m (6,560 ft.), the tahr is as endangered as the tiger.

Day ⑪: Periyar

Drive to **Periyar Tiger Reserve,** originally the hunting grounds of the Maharajah of Travancore. The park covers 777 sq. km (303 sq. miles) and is divided into core, buffer, and tourist zones. Although this is a tiger reserve, tiger sightings are rare, particularly in the tourist zone, but the reserve is also home to the elephant, sloth bear, sambar, Indian bison or gaur, wild dog, leopard, spotted deer, Malabar flying squirrel, barking deer, and Nilgiri tahr, as well as some 260 species of birds. More than 2,000 species of flowering plants grow here, including at least 150 different kinds of orchids. Organize a **private boat launch** ride from where you can view animals coming to drink at the water's edge. You can also take one of the 3-hour **daily walks,** which give you the opportunity to admire the area's stunning flora. To ensure you have a close-up encounter with an elephant, go on a 30-minute **elephant ride** in the park. Overnight at **Shalimar Spice Garden** or **Spice Village.**

Day ⑫: Kumarakom

Drive to the heart of Kerala's backwaters region to Kumarakom, which has by far the best accommodations. Idle away the hours on a backwaters cruise, indulge in Ayurvedic therapies, and laze under the tropical sun— that's about as busy as your day is likely to get. Overnight at the **Kumarakom Lake Resort** or **Coconut Lagoon** (or **Green Lagoon** if you don't mind shelling out for absolute exclusivity)—or head for the beach resorts at Mararikulam.

Day ⑬: Houseboat

Reset your watch to a rhythm of life that has remained relatively unchanged for centuries: Board a *kettuvallam,* one of the long, beautifully crafted cargo boats that ply the waterways. The houseboat experience allows you to aimlessly drift past villages, temples, and churches and be thoroughly exposed to the rural lifestyle of the backwaters. As you drift along, you

can watch women, unperturbed by your presence, wash their long ebony tresses or pound away at laundry, while children play at the water's edge, men dive for mussels, and elephants and water buffalo wade at will. Although the onboard facilities might strike some as rather basic, you'll be spoiled rotten by your private team—a guide, a cook, and a pilot—who work hard to make your experience unique and exceptional.

Days ⑭ & ⑮: Kochi (Cochin)

Travel north to Kochi and settle into a hotel in **Fort Kochi** (we recommend the Old Harbour Hotel or Le Colonial), then explore Fort Kochi on foot. Start your tour at the harbor near Vasco da Gama Square, where you can watch the **Chinese fishing nets,** then visit **St. Francis Church** and **Santa Cruz Cathedral.** Stop to admire the facade of **Koder House**—built in 1808 by Jewish patriarch Samuel Koder, it's a good example of the hybrid Indo-European style that developed in Cochin. Also nearby is the **Pierce Leslie Bungalow,** a charming 19th-century mansion reflecting Portuguese and Dutch influences on local architecture. Take an auto-rickshaw to Mattancherry, where you should visit the **Dutch (Mattancherry) Palace** and **Paradesi Synagogue** before discovering the fragrant scents of Kerala's **spice warehouses.** Make time to visit a few of the antiques warehouses, where some real treasures are to be found. A **sunset cruise** around the harbor is another must; it's the best way to enjoy the most-photographed of Cochin's historic sights, the Chinese fishing nets that form wonderful silhouettes against a red- and orange-hued sky.

Day ⑯: Wyanad

From Cochin, take the early Cannanore Express train to Calicut, from where you can catch a taxi for the 2-hour journey to Sulthan Bathery in Wyanad. Without a doubt the best accommodations, **Tranquil Resorts** is a wonderful opportunity to stay in one of two luxury "treehouses" on a 162-hectare (400-acre) coffee and vanilla plantation at the edge of Wyanad National Park. Visit tea, pepper, cardamom, coffee, banana, and coconut plantations, or take one of the many splendid walks on this scenic estate; alternatively, take a trip into the park or to Edakkal Caves. Either way, the hospitality of Victor and Ranjini Dey at this gorgeous planter's bungalow makes for an excellent end-of-trip sojourn.

Day ⑰ & ⑱: Wyanad & Neeleshwar & Home

From the Wyanad Hills, head for the unexplored far-northern coast of Kerala, where you can laze on the beach right in front of the exceptional new Neeleshwar Hermitage (near Kanhangad), visiting nearby Bekal Fort and stopping by Anandashram, one of the intriguing, totally tranquil ashrams in the vicinity. And, for an evening of lively entertainment, ensure that your hosts have organized for you to witness a ritual *theyyam* performance. Hearts heavy with regret, you must now make your way back to Mangalore (or Calicut) to fly to either Mumbai or Bengaluru to connect to your flight home. If you arrive in Mumbai, you will need to transfer from the domestic to the international airport. En route, you can stop off for dinner at one of the superb restaurants near the airport (Peshawri at ITC The Maratha; or Celini, the Italian restaurant at the Grand Hyatt, if you'd prefer a less spice-intense meal), before you catch the late-night flight home.

---

4 A LEISURELY SOUTHERN SOJOURN

South India is perfect for a slow-paced 2-week vacation that's more unhurried escape than hectic vacation filled with must-see sights. This itinerary does explore a few tourist sites, but mostly it's about relaxing and enjoying a few beautiful and varied environments. Kerala is the ideal place to unwind and indulge; this is, after all, where succumbing to therapeutic Ayurvedic massages and treatments is as mandatory as idling away an afternoon aboard a slowly drifting *kettuvallam,* or sipping coconut water under a tropical sun.

Days ❶ & ❷: Mumbai

Though Mumbai is India's busiest city, it's also a perfect place to begin an unhurried vacation. From the airport, head either to the Taj Mahal Palace & Tower (only a Heritage Wing room will do), The Oberoi, or the Four Seasons; enjoy the warm weather on a sun-bed by the pool, or make your way to the hotel spa for the pampering you deserve after that long journey. Alternatively, stay at the more affordable Ascot, Colaba's best-value hotel. Mumbai doesn't have a wealth of historical attractions; it's a city you *experience* rather than sightsee, and sampling the restaurants' fare should be high on your must-do list. From your hotel you can also explore on foot the Marine Drive/ Chowpatty Beach area, and if you're at all inspired by Gothic Victorian architecture, plan a jaunt through Mumbai's older districts. Stop off at the Gateway of India, from where it's a 15-minute walk north to Fort, passing the Prince of Wales Museum as well as a host of Raj-era Gothic architectural highlights. From the museum, continue to Flora Fountain and beyond to Victoria Terminus Station. Wander back to the Fountain, taking in the impressive High Court building and the Rajabai Clock Tower, which overlooks the Bombay University complex. Some of the best restaurants in Mumbai are in this general neighborhood, so take your pick. If you want to sample the coastal seafood for which Mumbai is famous, go no farther than **Mahesh Lunch Home** in Fort.

Days ❸ & ❹: Goa

Fly to Goa, old Portuguese colony and beach paradise. Take your pick of accommodations, from sprawling beachfront five-star hotels to small boutique hotels. If pampering is part of your plan, book into the **Nilaya Hermitage,** a gorgeous getaway with a splendid spa, or head south to the quirkily stylish **Vivenda dos Palhaços,** where your Anglo-India host Simon Haywood and his lovely crew will arrange just about anything for you. If you can drag yourself away from the beach and poolside, explore Old Goa; most sights are clustered together, so it can be covered in a few hours. These include **Arch of the Viceroys,** built in 1597 in commemoration of the arrival of Vasco da Gama in India; **Church of St. Cajetan,** modeled after St. Peter's in Rome; and **Adil Shah's Gate,** a simple lintel supported by two black basalt columns. Southwest of St. Cajetan's are the highlights of Old Goa: splendid **Sé Cathedral,** said to be larger than any church in Portugal; and the **Basilica of Bom Jesus (Cathedral of the Good Jesus).** Nearby is the **Convent and Church of St. Francis of Assisi,** while up the hill are the ruins of the **Church of St. Augustine;** below are the **Church and Convent of Santa Monica** and the **Chapel of the Weeping Cross.**

Days ❺ & ❻: Hampi

Take the biweekly train from Goa to Hampi, endure an overnight bus ride, or fly to Bengaluru the previous evening, from where you can get a convenient overnight train to Hospet. Check in at **Hampi's Boulders.** Spend your time leisurely exploring the ancient city, whose isolated ruins are scattered among impossibly balanced wind-smoothed boulders and immense stretches of verdant landscape. Highlights are fabulous **Virupaksha Temple**

and **Vitthala Temple,** dedicated to an incarnation of Vishnu and one of the most spectacular of Hampi's monuments; also make sure to see the **royal enclosure,** which incorporates the ruined palaces where the Vijayanagara kings would have lived and held court. Not much survives, but you can still visit **Hazara Rama Temple** (where the royals went to worship), a small **stepped tank,** and **Mahanavami Dibba** (a platform where performances and entertainment were held). On the outskirts of the royal complex, you will see the *zenana* enclosure, marked by the two-story Indo-Saracenic pavilion, **Kamala (Lotus) Mahal,** and, just outside the enclosure, the awesome **Elephant Stables.**

Days ❼ & ❽: Kochi (Cochin)

Take the train to Bengaluru and from there fly to Kochi, where you should get a room in Fort Kochi (at either the **Old Harbour Hotel, Le Colonial** or **Secret Garden**). Fort Kochi can be explored on foot. Visit **St. Francis Church** and **Santa Cruz Cathedral;** stop to gaze at the famous **Chinese fishing nets.** Drive to **Mattancherry Palace (Dutch Palace)** and **Paradesi Synagogue** before following your nose to the **spice warehouses.** Antiques lovers will be bowled over by Kochi's antiques warehouses full of real treasures. Take a **sunset cruise** around the harbor at dusk and then dine on a seafood platter at one of Kochi's wonderful restaurants.

Days ❾ & ❿: Kumarakom

Drive towards Alleppey to experience Kerala's backwaters. Spend 2 nights at one of the wonderful homestays in the region (**Olavipe** is the ultimate) or on a **houseboat;** alternatively, book into **Green Lagoon, Coconut Lagoon,** or **Kumarakom Lake Resort.** If you opt for the houseboat experience, you bed aboard a *kettuvallam,* one of the long, beautifully crafted cargo boats that ply the waterways—a wonderful way to experience the

rural lifestyle of the backwaters as you aimlessly drift past villages, temples, and churches. If the facilities strike you as too basic, and if you're not interested in a homestay either, spend the night at the intimate **Philipkutty's Farm** and take a sunset backwaters cruise instead.

Days ⑪–⑬: Kovalam & Beyond

Drive to **Trivandrum** and continue beyond it to immerse yourself in the simple beach life at **Karikkathi Beach House** or the famous (and, sadly, recently expanded) **Surya Samudra.** Spread over 8 hectares (20 acres) amid terraced gardens, Surya has such a glorious setting that as soon as you arrive you will wonder why

you didn't come straight here in the first place. Accommodations are in the centuries-old carved wooden cottages transplanted from villages around Kerala. Much of your time here is best spent lazing by the infinity pool carved out of the rock bed or on one of the two beaches. Spend the rest of your time here enjoying Ayurvedic treatments and massages. At Karikkathi, on the other hand, there's no pool, no other guests, and a dazzling beach pretty much all to yourself. If you can bear to tear yourself away, take an early morning excursion to sacred **Kanyakumari,** the southernmost tip of India, where three oceans meet and crowds worship the sunrise; or to **Padmanabhapuram Palace,** for several centuries the traditional home of Kerala's Travancore royal family.

Day ⑫: Trivandrum & Home

Completely relaxed and rejuvenated, make your way back to Trivandrum, and from there fly to Mumbai or Bengaluru for your international flight back home. If you arrive in Mumbai, where you will have many hours before your flight, enjoy dinner at one of the marvelous restaurants in Mumbai's suburbs or at one of the hotels near the airport where many Mumbaikers regularly go for upmarket entertainment and spoiling service.

City of Dreamers: Mumbai & Maharashtra Side Trips

On track to becoming the world's largest city within the next decade, Mumbai will do no less than bowl you over. It is a mind-boggling megalopolis—for some, a fantastic whirlwind of chaotic, exuberant energies; for others, a disorderly mess, frightening in the way of some biblical Gomorrah. There's no doubt about it—Mumbai will not leave you unaffected.

Teetering on the edge of the Arabian Sea, its heaving population barely contained by palm-fringed beaches, India's commercial capital, formerly known as Bombay, is a vibrant, confident metropolis that's tangibly high in energy.

Originally home to Koli fisherfolk, the seven swampy islands that today comprise Mumbai originally commanded little significance. The largest of the islands was part of a dowry given by Portugal to England, which promptly took control of the six remaining islands and then leased the lot to the East India Company for a paltry £10. Massive land-reclamation projects followed, and by the 19th century all seven islands had been fused to form one narrow promontory and India's principal port.

Today the city continues to draw fortune-seekers from across the subcontinent. Thousands of newcomers squeeze their way in every day, adding to the coffers of greedy slumlords and placing the city, which already has a human density four times greater than New York City's, on target for a population of 22 million by 2015. As India's economy booms, Mumbai's real estate prices have soared through the roof as investors continue to scour every acre for viable new projects, rapidly transforming the city into an incredible futurescape of remarkable high-rises. And in the midst of it all sprawls Asia's largest slum, a relatively flat and sodden terrain that is home to a million poor—yet extremely industrious—souls. In a bid to show the world how Mumbai's vivacious spirit exists in even the most trying circumstances, there are now a few riveting tours that take you under the belly of the city, into the vast shantytown that shook the world with vivid scenes in *Slumdog Millionaire* and *Shantaram*. A city with a dual identity, Mumbai is as flamboyantly materialistic as it is downright choked by squalor and social drudgery. The citizens of Mumbai pay almost 40% of India's taxes, yet half of its 18 million people are slum dwellers. While the moneyed groovers and label-conscious shakers retire in luxury behind the security gates of their million-dollar Malabar Hill apartments, emaciated survivors stumble home to cardboard shacks in congested shantytowns or onto tiny patches of open pavement. At every intersection these destitute hopefuls stand, framed against a backdrop of Bollywood vanity boards and massive billboards selling supersexy underwear and sleek mobile-phone technology. Feeding into this social schizophrenia are the one-dollar whores, half-naked fakirs, underworld gunmen, bearded *sadhus*, globe-trotting DJs, and, of course, movie moguls and wannabe starlets.

Many believe that is the city's unputdownable prosperity that has made it a target for such tragic incidents as the 2008 attacks in which the main train terminus

(Fun Facts   **You Say Mumbai, I Say Bombay**

In 1995, Bombay, the name the British bestowed upon the city, was renamed in honor of the local incarnation of the Hindu goddess Parvati, "Mumba Devi." The city's name change (along with a host of others that harked back to its colonial past) was enforced by the ruling Shiv Sena, a Hindu fundamentalist party that eschews the presence of any other than the Marathi people, a glaring irony given that this is a city of immigrants—a cocktail influenced as much by the grand Gothic monuments left by the British as by the many cultures who've set up shop here. Although it's difficult to understand how goodwill can prevail in a city led by politicians bred on xenophobia, Mumbai's well-intentioned optimism and its social cosmopolitanism prevail, and many of Mumbai's English-speaking inhabitants still refer to it as Bombay.

as well as two of the city's finest hotels—the Taj Mahal Palace and The Oberoi—were besieged by terrorists. True to its spirit, however, following this and other violent assaults, Mumbaikers have always bounced back with spectacular vigor. The city is once again pumping with energy, and while there's a noticeable security presence, spirits are definitely on the up. Even as the world recoils in economically uncertain times—and some of Mumbai's myriad building projects did seem to pause for a while—there seems to be no stopping the pace of development. Touch down here and you'll discover a metropolis that's comfortably on the move.

It's not just the economic disparities that are bewildering: Looking down from the Hanging Gardens on Malabar Hill, you see the assertively modern metropolis of Nariman Point—but just a little farther south, on Malabar Hill, is the Banganga Tank, one of the city's holiest sites, where apartment blocks overlook pilgrims who come to cleanse their souls by bathing in its mossy waters. Twenty-first-century Mumbai is brassy and vital, yet it can also transport you to another epoch. It is, in this sense, a quintessentially Indian city, encapsulating the raw paradoxes of the entire subcontinent.

Your plane will almost certainly touch down in Mumbai—it's the most common point of arrival for visitors, and well connected to the rest of the country (including the magnificent **Ajanta and Ellora Caves,** located in northern Maharashtra, and described later in this chapter). If you're looking for peace and quiet in meditative surroundings, you should definitely consider heading to the nearby city of **Pune** where the **Osho International Meditation Resort** (also discussed in this chapter) is a major draw for global citizens on the search for New Age enlightenment packaged in its most upmarket avatar. If Mumbai is to be purely a transit hub, there are more than enough connections—by plane, train or road—for you to move on as fast as jet lag and arrival times dictate. But if you want to experience modern India at its vibrant best, and dine at what are arguably some of the finest restaurants in the country, tarry for at least 2 days. You may arrive appalled by the pitiful faces of the poor, shocked by the paradox of such wealth and poverty, and overcome by the heavy, heady stench and toxic pollution. But give India's dream factory a little time, and you'll discover it has a sexy, smoldering soul, and a head-spinning groove worth getting hip to.

1 ARRIVAL & ORIENTATION

WHEN TO GO

Mumbai's humidity—even in the small hours of the morning—is felt instantly, and the sun shines year-round, except in the monsoon months. You always seem drenched in warm sweat, and the heat can be terribly cruel, making sightseeing far less agreeable than a tour of the city's wonderful restaurants and drinking holes. Winter (Nov–Feb) is still hot, although not so entirely unpleasant; the sultry sea air sets the tone for an adventure in exotic dining and an intoxicating jaunt through lively, Victorian-era streets that are constantly crammed with people. The only real relief from the heat comes for brief periods in December and January, and midyear, when the annual monsoon drenches the city with heavy, nonstop tropical rains. Although the monsoon can be a difficult time to explore the city (and has in the past brought life-threatening floods), it can also be beautiful to watch the downpour from the safety of a well-located terrace or from under a sturdy umbrella.

ARRIVING

BY PLANE Mumbai's sprawling **Chhatrapati Shivaji International Airport** (www. csia.in) is looking a whole lot better than it did just a few years ago, and continues to undergo renovation; things may not seem world class just yet, but they're definitely getting there (there's even a Disney-themed children's corner designed to stave off boredom during long waits between flights). The **International Terminal** (2A and 2C; ✆ 022/2681-3000) is located in Sahar, 29km (18 miles) north of Colaba, the touristy enclave in the city's far south. Flights typically arrive and depart between midnight and dawn which can make finding your feet difficult; catch the evening flight on **Kingfisher Airlines** (www.kingfisher.com) from London, however, and you'll land midmorning (after a spectacularly comfortable flight, by the way). A **Government of India Tourist Office** (✆ 022/2682-9248) at the airport should be open 24 hours but—as is the case in most of India's tourist offices—it's certainly not the best place to obtain advice; you'll find the contents of this book far more useful.

Although there is now at least one ATM at arrivals, it's usually run out of money, so if you intend catching a taxi from the airport, arrive with some cash in order to buy local currency from one of the fast and friendly foreign exchange booths located near the exit. However, if you're new to the city, it's advisable to arrange an **airport transfer** to meet you—primarily because you will be accosted by a loud, expectant mass of touts and taxi drivers the minute you exit the terminal doors; it can be a bit overwhelming for first-time visitors and some of these characters need to be treated with a degree of caution. If you are expecting a pickup, don't get sidetracked or deterred from boarding the correct hotel shuttle—ignore strangers offering help.

Hiring a taxi on the spot needn't be too much of a chore. Simply make use of the convenient (if overpriced) **prepaid taxi service** (✆ 022/2682-9922) located in terminal 2A (accessible by foot from 2C); a trip to a Colaba hotel should cost in the region of Rs 400 to Rs 480, plus an additional Rs 10 per luggage item; a trip in a superior Cool Cab will be Rs 150 more (although there have been reports that these taxis aren't as clean as they should be), and you might just get a better deal on a metered taxi (although finding one here has become near-impossible). Expect to pay well over double these rates for a hotel airport transfer, but you'll also get a much better vehicle to travel in; the Four

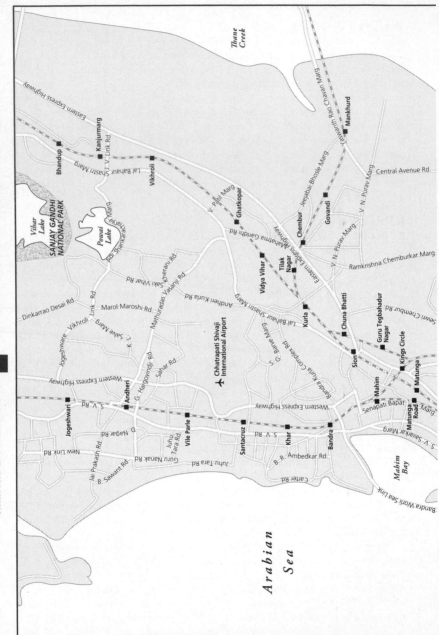

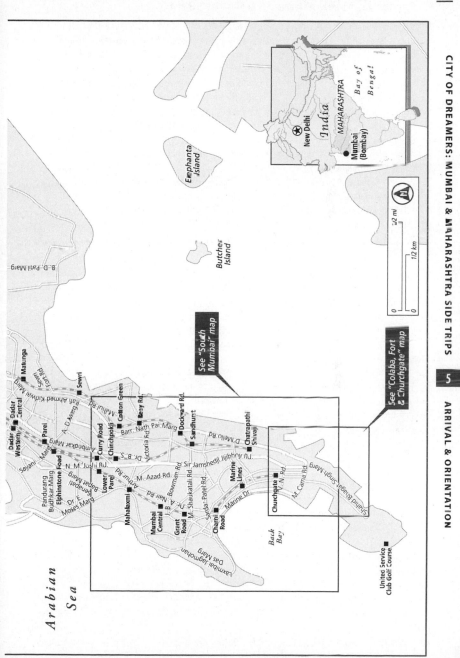

Exploring Maharashtra on a Moving Palace

Western India's version of the famous Palace on Wheels train is a lavish 21-car luxury train called **The Deccan Odyssey,** which traverses Maharashtra's stunning coast. The 7-day journey begins in Mumbai and wanders down the coast to Goa via gorgeous beaches untouched by commercialization. It then stops in the historic city of Pune (p. 172) before moving on to Aurangabad (where you can visit the Ajanta and Ellora caves; p. 182), and finally returns to Mumbai. You'll travel by night and sightsee during the day, all the while getting the royal treatment, with luxurious cabins and high-end service (included are a personal valet, on-board gym, and Ayurvedic spa)—food is outstanding. If you intend seeing Maharashtra in style, there really is no better way to go; contact **Deccan Odyssey:** in the U.S. call 🕐 **888/INDIA-99** [46342-99]; in the U.K. call toll-free 0125/8580-600; in India call 011/2332-5939 or 011/2335-3155; www.thedeccanodyssey.com, www.the palaceonwheels.com, or www.deccan-odyssey-india.com; a deluxe cabin costs $320 to $390 per person sharing per night and includes everything except service tax; discounts are sometimes available.

Seasons sends a luxurious BMW for around Rs 3,200, and the Taj Mahal Palace now even has two Jaguars in its fleet. Because many international flights arrive late at night, traffic delays are usually not a problem, and you should be at your hotel within an hour even if you're staying downtown. If you arrive by daylight, don't expect to get anywhere quickly (unless you're staying at one of the hotels near the airport).

If you are flying direct from Mumbai's international airport on to the next destination, note that you will have to transfer (there is a free bus every 15 min.; make sure you get on it) to the **Domestic Terminal** (1A and 1B; 🕐 **022/2626-4000** or -4001) located in Santa Cruz some 4km (2½ miles) from the international terminal and 26km (16 miles) north of the city. If you have a long wait before your flight, you will have to spend it in a very uncomfortable airport seat—another good reason to rather spend some time in Mumbai itself. If you have arrived at the Santa Cruz terminal from another part of the country and plan to spend some time in Mumbai, you can either use the prepaid service (Rs 330 to Colaba, plus Rs 10 per luggage item), or use the phone hot line to get a metered Meru cab and pay only Rs 270 (the outlandish markup on the prepaid service a result of serious union politics, and metered taxis being denied parking space at the airport—go figure!). Since domestic flights are likely to arrive during the day, be prepared for a long, congested, frustrating journey into Mumbai. There's also a tourist office at the domestic airport (🕐 **022/2615-6920;** daily 7am–11pm), but there's little need to dally here.

Note: **Auto-rickshaws** are banned from the city's center, so don't rely on these for trips originating from either of the airports unless your hotel is located in their immediate vicinity. Technically, you could use a rickshaw to get to the hotels in Juhu (the city's favorite beach precinct), but the trip is a long one and you'll inhale noxious traffic fumes along the way. Besides, unless you're traveling extremely light, there won't be much space for you to stow your luggage

BY TRAIN   Good railway connections link Mumbai to all parts of the country, although journeys are long and, unless you opt for one of the smoother semiluxury services, likely to be extremely grueling. Since the terrorist attacks at Chhatrapati Shivaji Termi-nus, or CST (otherwise known as "VT," Victoria Station), in late 2008, most of the smarter trains that once terminated there now curtail their journeys at stations farther north. This inevitably affects trains arriving from Central, South, or East India, which may terminate at Dadar (pretty much in central Mumbai) or the Lokmanya Tilak Ter-minus at Kurla (more north). From the north, you'll arrive at either Mumbai Central Station (most southerly), Dadar, or Bandra; check with your hotel to determine the best disembarkation point. After an inevitably lengthy train ride, you'll probably want to grab a taxi to your hotel; see "Getting Around," later in this chapter, and perhaps check first with your hotel to hear what the taxi fare *should* be.

CITY LAYOUT

Mumbai city lies on the western coast of India, on a thin peninsula that extends south-ward almost parallel to the mainland. At the southern end of this peninsula are Colaba and the adjoining Fort area, on the east of which lies Mumbai's deep, natural harbor and India's busiest port. West of Fort, hugging the Arabian Sea, is the popular promenade Marine Drive, which begins at the business district of Nariman Point and terminates at Chowpatty Beach and Malabar Hill. These are the focal nodes for tourists who, unlike the locals, often refer to the area as downtown. In fact, locals say they are going "into town," by which they mean they are going toward South Mumbai, the area stretching south from Mahim Creek to Colaba. South Mumbai is where most tourists base them-selves—it's especially convenient if you'd like to explore the historic heart of the city on foot. Here you'll find attractions like the Gateway of India and the Chhatrapati Shivaji Maharaj Vastu Sangrahalaya (aka Prince of Wales Museum), and the thickest concentra-tion of restaurants and accommodations that are geared for foreigners. The South Mum-bai neighborhoods are described in detail below. There are, however, many enticing reasons to stay in less overtly tourist-centric areas like Worli, Bandra and Juhu—for one, you'll get to see where many Mumbaikars (or Bombayites) live (whereas south Mumbai is pretty much a business zone that quiets down considerably after dark)—Bandra is a particularly upbeat area plumb with homes belonging to jet-set Bollywood stars and a real magnet for some of the trendiest crowds in town. Even if you don't stay here (or along the hip beachfront strip at Juhu, slightly north of Bandra), it'd be a real shame not to take at least one trip into the suburbs, even if your sole mission is to shop till you drop (in which case, definitely put Worli on your itinerary, too). Bandra and Juhu are also close enough to the airport (without being flush up against the runways) to make them convenient for making a relatively quick getaway when your departure rolls around.

NEIGHBORHOODS IN BRIEF

COLABA & NARIMAN POINT

Because of its proximity to most of Mumbai's landmarks and colonial build-ings, this, the southern tip of Mumbai, is the real tourist hub. In many ways its location has contributed to Colaba's slightly seedy side, though certain areas have recently been rejuvenated. Many of the city's budget accommodations are

situated along roads leading off **Colaba Causeway,** punctuated by (at the north-ernmost end) the **Taj Mahal Hotel,** Mumbai's most famous hotel, which is located opposite the **Gateway of India,** its most famous landmark, across from which you can see the oil rigs of Bombay High. The area around the Gateway of India is called **Apollo Bunder,** though the easiest way to get there is to ask for directions to the Taj. Southwest of this is **Cuffe Parade,** an upmarket residential neighborhood, and farther south, the restricted navy Cantonment.

If you travel west from Colaba to the other end of the narrow peninsula until you hit the sea, you'll arrive at **Nariman Point,** starting point of Marine Drive. This was once Mumbai's most bustling business district; although many airline offices and several foreign embassies are still situated here and there are many businesses that refuse to give up the prestige of being based here, Nariman Point is facing massive competition from the burgeoning purpose-built business zones farther north.

FORT

North from Colaba is the business neighborhood called Fort. By day the area comprising **Fort, Fountain, Ballard Estate,** and **CST** (or **VT**) **Station** is an extremely busy commercial district, but at night the neighborhood is rather forlorn, with many of the large parks *(maidans)* empty. A little beyond CST Station is **Crawford Market,** which leads to the heart of Mumbai's congested markets.

Just west of the Fort area is **Churchgate Station. Veer Nariman Road,** the street leading from Churchgate Station to Marine Drive, is lined with restaurants.

MARINE DRIVE TO MALABAR HILL

Prestigious **Marine Drive** (aka Netaji Subhash Chandra Bose Marg) stretches from Nariman Point in the south to Malabar Hill in the north. Edged by a broad, well-maintained promenade that follows the curve of the seafront, this is a very popular place to take a morning or evening walk. At night the streetlights along this drive accentuate the dramatic arch of the bay, giving it the name **Queen's Necklace,** though obviously

this term is less frequently used these days—still, images of this sweep of prime waterfront real estate (with the world's second highest concentration of Deco architecture after Miami) tend to feature on anything promoting Mumbai as a travel (or investment) destination; if you want a room with a view, you'll probably choose a hotel along this strip. On a more prosaic level, Marine Drive is a long, often traffic-clogged, arterial road that runs along the curve of Back Bay and ends at **Chowpatty Beach,** from where roads climb toward the upmarket neighborhood of Malabar Hill. **Malabar Hill** connects to Napean Sea Road and beyond to **Breach Candy, Kemps Corner,** and **Peddar Road**—all upmarket residential areas.

CENTRAL MUMBAI

Central Mumbai extends beyond Crawford Market through **Mohammedali Road** and **Kalbadevi** to **Mumbai Central Station** and the fast-growing commercial areas of **Lower Parel** and prime seafront district of **Worli** which, thanks to the arrival of the new Four Seasons Hotel, has become one of the best places to be based for a thorough exploration of Mumbai (access to either the north or the south of the city is about an hour either way, and the new Bandra-Worli Sea Link dramatically cuts down travel time to Bandra). The greatest developments are occurring around **Phoenix Mills,** where some of the erstwhile mill buildings have been converted into shopping complexes, restaurants, and gaming and entertainment spots. West from Mumbai Central Station are **Tardeo** and **Haji Ali,** where a mausoleum located on a tiny causeway-linked offshore island enshrines an important Muslim holy man. The popular shrine is reachable only during low tide, but serves as an exotic-looking landmark in yet another of Mumbai's bays.

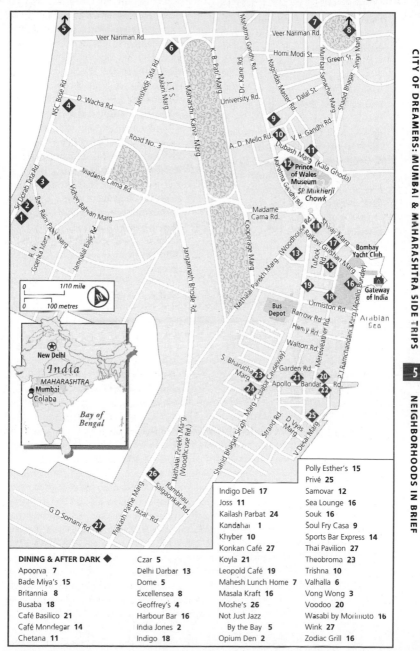

Polly Esther's **15**
Privé **25**
Samovar **12**
Sea Lounge **16**
Souk **16**
Soul Fry Casa **9**
Sports Bar Express **14**
Thai Pavilion **27**
Theobroma **23**
Trishna **10**
Valhalla **6**
Vong Wong **3**
Voodoo **20**
Wasabi by Morimoto **16**
Wink **27**
Zodiac Grill **16**

Indigo Deli **17**
Joss **11**
Kailash Parbat **24**
Kandahar **1**
Khyber **10**
Konkan Café **27**
Koyla **21**
Leopold Café **19**
Mahesh Lunch Home **7**
Masala Kraft **16**
Moshe's **4**
Not Just Jazz
  By the Bay **5**
Opium Den **2**

Czar **5**
Delhi Darbar **13**
Dome **5**
Excellensea **8**
Geoffrey's **4**
Harbour Bar **16**
India Jones **2**
Indigo **18**

DINING & AFTER DARK ◆
Apoorva **7**
Bade Miya's **15**
Britannia **8**
Busaba **18**
Café Basilico **21**
Café Mondegar **14**
Chetana **11**

North of Mahim Creek extend Mumbai's vast suburbs, from where millions commute daily. First up, just across the creek, is **Bandra** which, along with Juhu and Andheri (West), just north of it, is where Bollywood stars live and hang out. Although it's not really on the tourist circuit, Bandra, being home to a sizable portion of the city's elite, is packed with lively restaurants, steamy clubs, trendy bars, and countless shops. At night young people gather, especially along **Carter Road** and Turner Road to drink, smoke (cigarettes or dope), and chill out before making their way to favored clubs. The area around **Juhu Beach** is where many of the city's middle classes escape; crowded with a host of vendors flogging popular eats, ice cream, coconuts, and fresh fruit juice, it's worth a visit to soak up Mumbai's carnivalesque atmosphere rather than contemplate sunbathing on the beach, which is filthy, or venturing into the even dirtier seawater. It does, however, have some fine hotels, restaurants, and nightclubs—Enigma at Juhu's JW Marriott Hotel is one of Mumbai's most happening spots.

Just east of Juhu lie the city's two airports and a host of upmarket hotels. The area of **Andheri (East)** around the international airport has become a crowded (and rather polluted) commercial and residential neighborhood. Yet many business visitors prefer to stay in this part of town if their business lies here, to avoid the stressful commute. Farther north in the suburbs is **Goregaon,** home to Film City, where many Bollywood movies are shot; past that is **Borivali,** from where Mumbai's most popular theme park, EsselWorld, is accessible. Beyond, the city goes on (and on), with little to tempt the visitor.

VISITOR INFORMATION

For the best listings of the city's current events and what's hip and happening, look no further than the twice-monthly magazine *Time Out,* widely available. You could try the **Maharashtra Tourism Development Corporation** (Madame Cama Rd., Nariman Point; ✆ **022/2202-4627** or -7762; www.maharashtratourism.gov.in; Mon–Fri 10am–5:30pm and Sat 10am–3pm), or the main **Government of India Tourist Office** (123 Maharishi Karve Rd., Churchgate; ✆ **022/2203-3144,** 022/2207-4333 or -4334; Mon–Fri 8:30am–6pm, Sat 8:30am–2pm), both of which should be able to assist with general tourist-related information. However, if you're staying at one of the city's better hotels, your concierge will be a better source of information on sightseeing, performances, events, and activities (although you may need to negotiate hard to get the lowdown on truly local restaurants and more offbeat attractions—our prize for the best concierge advice in the city goes to the folks at the Four Seasons). Another excellent source of information—as well as assistance with just about any kind of query, problem or emergency—is **Reality Tours & Travel** (✆ **022/2283-3872;** 24-hour line ✆ **98-2082-2253;** www.realitytoursandtravel.com). Krishna, one of the founders of this community-oriented tour company, knows the city inside out and is particularly astute at interpreting it for outsiders. His team will go so far as to source magazines, clothing and other essentials for you if you end up in the hospital, so can definitely also answer more mundane questions; for more information on their sightseeing and slum tours, see p. 120.

(Fast Facts) Mumbai

Ambulance In case of accidents or medical emergencies, dial ℭ **102** or **1298**, or call ℭ **105** for a cardiac ambulance. You can also contact **Bacha's Nursing Home** (La Citadelle, New Marine Lines; ℭ **022/2203-2977** or 022/2200-0963) or **Bombay Hospital** (Bombay Hospital Rd., New Marine Lines; ℭ **022/2206-7676**; www.bombayhospital.com). Or try **Swati Ambulance** (ℭ **022/2387-1215**), which has 24-hour service.

American Express The office is near the Jehangir Art Gallery at Kala Ghoda (Trade Wings Ltd., 30 K Dubash Marg, Kala Ghoda; ℭ **022/6634-4334**). Hours are Monday to Saturday 10:30am to 6pm.

Area Code The area code for Mumbai is **022**.

ATMs Undoubtedly the most convenient way to get local currency, ATMs are to be found throughout the city, most of them with 24 hour security guards. Your best bet for a quick transaction is to head for an ATM belonging to either HDFC, HSBC, ICICI, SBI, or Standard Chartered.

Bookstores **Crossword Bookstore** (Mohammedbhai Mansion, Kemps Corner, below flyover; ℭ **022/2384-2001** through -2004) has a Western ambience and Mumbai's largest selection of books. Alternatively, stop at **Shankar's Book Stall** ((ℭ **92-2411-1790**), a tiny stall just outside Café Mondegar, Colaba Causeway; or at **Strand Book Stall** (Sir PM Rd., Fort; ℭ **022/2266-1994** or -1719), which offers books at great discounts. Inside the Taj Mahal Hotel is **Nalanda** (ℭ **022/2287-1306**), a good spot to shop for coffee-table books and travel-related selections

Car Hires See "Getting Around," below.

Consulates **U.S.:** Lincoln House, 78 Bhulabhai Desai Rd., Breach Candy (ℭ **022/2363-3611** through -3618; Mon–Fri 8:30am–1pm and 1:45–5pm; closed second and last Fri of the month and on Indian and American national holidays). **U.K.:** Second Floor, Maker Chambers IV, 222 Jamnalal Bajaj Rd., Nariman Point ((ℭ **022/6650-2222;** Mon–Thurs 8am–4pm and Fri 8am–1pm). **Australia:** 36 Maker Chambers VI, 220 Nariman Point ((ℭ **022/6669-2000;** Mon–Fri 9am–5pm). **Canada:** Sixth Floor, Fort House, 221 D.N. Rd., Fort (ℭ **022/6749-4444;** Mon–Thurs 9am–5.30pm; Fri 9am–3pm). **South Africa:** Gandhi Mansion, 20 Altamount Rd., Cumbala Hill, near Kemp's Corner (ℭ **022/2351-3725/6;** Mon–Fri 8:30am–5pm).

Currency Exchange **Thomas Cook India** is located in the Thomas Cook Building, Dr. D. Naoroji Road, Fort (ℭ **022/2204-8556**), and is open Mon–Sat 9:30am–6pm. Or head to the American Express Office (details above).

Directory Assistance The main directory information number is ℭ **197** (if you can get through). For talking Yellow Pages service or any other useful information, call the much more helpful **Just Dial Services** at ℭ **022/2888-8888, Times Infoline** at ℭ **022/6700-5555,** or **DNA Infoline** at ℭ **022/2666-6666.**

Drugstores Most hotels will happily source any medication you require, but drugstores (called pharmacies or chemists) are plentiful and readily hand over prescription drugs (even without a prescription). In South Mumbai, **Bombay Hospital Pharmacy** (ℭ **022/2206-7676**) at the hospital in New Marine Lines is open 24 hours, as is nearby **Dava Bazaar** (32 Kakad Arcade; ℭ **022/6665-9079**).

If you're in the north, **Empire Chemists** (© **022/2671-8970**), near Juhu, is a reliable option.

Emergencies See "Police," below.

Hospitals **Breach Candy Hospital,** 60 Warden Rd., Breach Candy (© **022/2367-1888** or -2888; emergency © **022/2364-3309**), is open 24 hours and is one of the most advanced and reliable hospitals in Mumbai. **Bombay Hospital,** Bombay Hospital Rd., New Marine Lines (© **022/2206-7676;** www.bombayhospital.com), is more centrally located and has a 24-hour ambulance service. In Bandra (W), **Lilavati Hospital & Research Centre** (© **022/2642-1111,** 022/2643-8281, or 022/2655-2222) is a modern facility.

Internet Access There's hardly a hotel in town without Wi-Fi; access is seldom free, however, so you may end up looking for an Internet cafe. For a cheap (around Rs 30 per hr.), reliable connection, pop into **LSM PCO Service,** Shop no. 7B Abubakar Mansion, Mahakavi Bhushan Rd., Colaba (© **022/2202-2452**). Open daily 9am to 11pm, it's just around the corner from Café Mondegar. For better broadband speeds, try **Amrut Cyberworld Cybercafé** near Churchgate Station (8 Prem Court, behind Samrat Hotel; © **022/2284-0174**).

Maps The *Eicher City Map* is the most definitive, accurate and helpful tool you could hope for (pick it up from bookstores noted above)—but we doubt you're ever going to actually use it!

Newspapers & Magazines For the scoop on day-to-day city news, buy a copy of the local rag *Mid Day,* sold on street corners and at intersections from early in the morning. *The Times of India* and *Hindustan Times* are both good national dailies that provide the lowdown on current and social events; most hotels deliver a copy of at least one paper to your room. *Time Out Mumbai* is a twice-monthly magazine that has the best listings of events and happenings, as well as interesting city features.

Police Call © **100** for a general police emergency. Local numbers are: Colaba © **022/2285-6817;** Cuffe Parade © **022/2218-8009;** Juhu © **022/2618-4308;** Khar © **022/2649-6030;** Malabar Hill © **022/2363-7571;** Andheri © **022/2683-1562.**

Post Office The **General Post Office** is right near Chhatrapati Shivaji Terminus on St. George Rd., off Nagar Chowk (© **022/2262-0956**); it's open Monday to Saturday from 9am to 8pm. However, unless you're genuinely interested in checking out the building for its superb architecture, you'll save considerable time and energy by asking your hotel concierge to handle any postal items.

Restrooms Make full use of your bathroom facilities *before* you head out for a day of sightseeing. Use only restrooms in hotels and upmarket restaurants.

Taxis See "Getting Around," below.

Travel Agencies Contact IATA-affiliated **NAC Travels Pvt. Ltd.,** 412 Raheja Centre, Nariman Point (© **022/2202-8810**), or the dependable **Travel Corporation of India (TCI)** in the Chandermukhi Building (first floor), also at Nariman Point (© **022/2202-1881** or -7120). On Colaba Causeway, near Café Mondegar, is **Uniglobe Venture Travel Services** (Metro House, Colaba Causeway; © **022/2287-6666**), which offers reliable ticketing and other travel-related services. Most travel agents will arrange to deliver tickets to your hotel.

Mumbai is a city on the go—but don't expect to get anywhere fast, because traffic is lousy at the best of times. Around a million vehicles crowd the streets, and each week another 1,400 scooters and cars join the congestion caused by battered black-and-yellow taxis, Marutis, Indicas, expensive sedans and SUVs, copies of leftover red double-decker Routemaster buses, and the occasional bullock-cart. You will certainly need to take a taxi to get around (or, if you're arriving from the airport, arrange a transfer with your hotel; see "Arriving," earlier in this chapter). If you're staying in the Colaba-Fort area, you will, for the most part, be able to explore the area on foot.

PUBLIC TRANSPORTATION

BY TAXI **Metered taxis** (in which you don't bargain but pay a rate dependent on mileage predetermined by a structured fare card) are available everywhere (flag them down when you see the meter flag up), but note that you'll be riding in rather battered Fiats from the 1960s (which can be an adventure in its own right). That said, Mumbai is one of the few places in India where using the meter is the norm—in fact, no local would go anywhere without a taxi driver using his meter. Typically, the taxi meters in Mumbai are mounted on the vehicle hoods, and taxi drivers are required to carry a conversion chart that tells passengers how much they owe, based on the original fare displayed on the ludicrously old-fashioned meters. Do not start the journey before checking to see if the driver is carrying the correct chart; these are sometimes tampered with, so vital information is missing—for example, the part of the chart informing you that the rates quoted are for nighttime travel, which are higher. We've also traveled with unscrupulous drivers who perform such obvious deceptions as obscuring the meter display and faking the reset action at the beginning of the journey in order to inflate the fare charge; in other incidents, drivers have tried multiplying the meter reading by some ludicrous amount (like 100) and calling your bluff with an over-the-top charge. Don't panic—immediately ask to see the chart and set the would be con artist straight. He'll inevitably apologize. If you're in any doubt, ask a policeman or your hotel doorman to decipher the fare for you; fares are Rs 13 for the first mile (1⅔km) and Rs 8.50 for each subsequent kilometer, but in essence you can calculate how much you have to pay by multiplying what's on the meter by approximately Rs 13; add on 25% if you are traveling between midnight and 5am, and Rs 5 to Rs 7 per piece of sizable luggage. Nothing more, except a fair tip if the driver hasn't tried to cheat you.

You will also see more modern-looking taxis with digital meters plying the streets. These generally cannot be flagged down in the same way as the yellow tops; they're referred to as call cabs, and you'll almost certainly need to book one in advance or through your hotel. One of the better call cab outfits is **Meru Cabs,** recognizable as green Esteem cars with large advertising banners and a white light on top (available) or red (engaged); they're equipped with GPS, digital tamper-proof meters and printers (for a receipt), radio, and A/C, and tend to have better-trained drivers (although some of the traditional Mumbai taxi drivers are quite knowledgeable). They're a definite step up from the beaten-up black-and-yellow taxis typical of Mumbai. The downside is that even though you can hail one curbside, you rarely see a vacant Meru cab, and the phone service (© 022/4422-4422; open 24/7) requires at least 4 hours' advance notice. If you want to book one several days in advance you can do so on their website (www.merucabs.com) and receive an e-mail confirmation, or SMS "MERU" to 57575. **Gold Cabs** (© 022/3244-3333) also runs a smaller fleet of

(Tips) Dealing with Beggars

When long-time BBC India Bureau Chief Mark Tully was asked: "How do you cope with the poverty of India?" he responded, "I don't have to; *they* do." As a first-time visitor, you will no doubt be struck first by the seemingly endless ordeal of the impoverished masses. Families of beggars will twist and weave their way around the cars at traffic lights, hopping and even crawling to your window with displays of open wounds, diseased sores, crushed limbs, and starving babies, their hollow eyes imploring you for a few lifesaving rupees. Locals will tell you that these poverty performances are Mafia-style rackets, with protection money going to gangs, and sickly babies being passed around to gain more sympathy for their "parents." In the worst of these tales of horror, children are maimed to up the ante by making them appear more pathetic (a reality, you will recall, that is dealt with on quite a visceral level in the Oscar-winning film *Slumdog Millionaire*). Begging is now officially outlawed in Mumbai, and for anyone returning to the city there are noticeably fewer taps at taxi windows—sadly, though, nearly all begging that happens at traffic lights involves children. Many of the kids who might otherwise be outright begging for money are now selling low-priced literary paperbacks at intersections; surely you can spare a few dollars for a good book? But, if it's just a hollow-eyed face staring through the glass, the choice is stark: Either lower the window and risk having a sea of unwelcome faces descend on you, or stare ahead and ignore them. To salve your conscience, tip generously those who have made it onto the first rung of employment.

yellow cabs in various car models; again you'll have to book a few hours ahead. Fares for both are higher than regular cabs (from Rs 15 per kilometer); the meter starts only after you sit in the cab (unless you call and keep it waiting more than 10 min.).

If you're looking for a vehicle for the day, you can strike a deal with a private taxi driver directly, but here you should negotiate the deal upfront—you should pay around Rs 700 to Rs 800, plus a tip, for an 8-hour (or 80km/50-mile) stint. Note that it's worth shelling out extra for an air-conditioned cab—you're likely to spend long stretches waiting in traffic jams at overcrowded intersections. To rent an air-conditioned car and an English-speaking driver privately (which will cost a bit more but may remove the hassle of haggling), the following operators are recommended: **Cool Cabs** (Worli ✆ 022/2492-7006; or in Andheri ✆ 022/2822-7006, or 022/2824-6216); **Ashtapura Travel World** (907 Arcadia, N.C.P.A. Marg, Nariman Point; ✆ 022/2283-4689; http://carhirers.com); **Euro Cars** (Suburban Service Station, 261 S.V. Rd., Bandra W.; ✆ 022/2655-2424; www.eurocars-india.com); and **Ketan Travels Pvt. Ltd.** (R.T. Bldg., P.M. Rd., Vile Parle E.; ✆ 022/2614-0554; www.ketancars.com). **Carzonrent** (✆ 860/500-1212; www.carzonrent.com) offers chauffeur-driven cars throughout the subcontinent.

Hiring a taxi through your hotel can get very pricey, but the fleet of cars maintained by some of the upmarket hotels is unlikely to be matched in quality by anyone in the city (if you choose your hotel by the quality of its vehicles and chauffeurs, be sure to stay at the Four Seasons, which offers silky-smooth BMWs), and it may be convenient to have transport charges added to your hotel bill. Do, however, remember to tip your driver directly.

BY TRAIN Train travel in the city is strictly for the adventurous, but then again, a ride on a train in the afternoon (or on Sun) gives you the opportunity to see how the other half lives, as the tracks wend their way through some of the city's most squalid slums. Extending northward of Churchgate is the Western Railway local train line, and moving north of Victoria Terminus (or CST; see below) is the Central Railway network. Together, these two suburban train systems transport over six million commuters each day. A first-class return ticket from Chhatrapati Shivaji Terminus (aka Victoria Terminus or VT) to the suburb of Thane costs about Rs 210. Travel only during off-peak (noon–3pm is best) times and leave luggage and valuables in your hotel room. I don't advise this, but if you really want to get a feel for the way of life experienced by the millions of people who commute into the city each day, you could probably survive the 30- to 40-minute ride from VT to Bandra during the after-work rush hour (although some don't, literally—it's rare, but people have been crushed to death in the sardine-packed compartments)); the cheapest tickets are around Rs 8.

ORGANIZED TOURS & TRIPS

You will be offered tours of various descriptions by at least half the people you meet on the streets of Mumbai; everyone from your taxi driver to the man who asks you for the time will have a contact in the tourism industry who'll be more than happy to take you "sightseeing." Use your discretion, watch your wallet, and remember that Mumbai's traffic makes it impossible to see everything in 1 day.

To arrange a legitimate tour of the city, set it up through your hotel, which should have access to the best guides (meaning those with the best English and best knowledge); better still, check out some of our favorite tours and specialist guides discussed in the "Into the Belly of the Beast: Getting Beneath Mumbai's Skin" box on p. 120).

---

3 WHAT TO SEE & DO

Mumbai doesn't have the wealth of historical attractions of, say, Kolkata or Delhi. Rather, it is a city that revolves around its commerce, its manic pace, and the head-spinning energy exuded by the millions of diverse people who have settled here. This is a city you *experience* rather than sightsee, and sampling from the fantastic restaurants (and trying a few recommended street food stalls) described later in the chapter should be highest on your must-do list. Mumbai does have some one-of-kind attractions you should make time for; and be sure to set aside time to explore at least part of the **Colaba-Fort area,** described below, on foot—do this at the beginning of the day before the heat becomes suffocating. Another good area to explore on foot is the **Marine Drive/Chowpatty Beach stretch,** possibly after a boat trip to **Elephanta Island.** You may also wish to visit **Malabar Hill,** also in the South Mumbai area and home to two top attractions (see below), as well as the **Hanging Gardens** (also known as Ferozeshah Mehta Gardens). Laid out in the early 1880s, the terraced park at the top of Malabar Hill covers (or "hangs over") the city's main water reservoir, but unfortunately it fails to live up to its spectacular-sounding name. The best reason to visit here is to wander over to **Kamala Nehru Park** (across the road from the Hanging Gardens), from where you have a great view of Nariman Point's skyscrapers and the sumptuous curve of Marine Drive.

For a time trip experience, and a taste of a much-older Mumbai, head towards the center of the city and check out the **Worli fishing village,** populated by descendants of

(Moments) Into the Belly of the Beast: Getting Beneath Mumbai's Skin

For all its chaos and controversy, Mumbai's diversity, along with its fascinating history as a cultural melting pot, makes it an incredibly nuanced destination, well worth investing a little time getting to know beyond the obvious and touristy confines of the Colaba-Fort precinct; these days, it's also possible to venture into Dharavi—the largest slum in Asia, colorfully documented and dramatized in the hugely popular *Slumdog Millionaire*—where you discover, instead of misery, an extremely industrious and vibrant community. Several exceptionally enthusiastic people offer an assortment of escorted tours, and we highly recommend that you sign up for at least one such outing. While most companies do offer standard sightseeing excursions, the best trips tend to be specialist tours themed around a specific aspect of Mumbai's dynamic personality; you can also ask most of these companies to design a tailor-made tour based on any specific interests.

The most in-depth **slum tour** offered in Mumbai is by good-value, community-oriented **Reality Tours & Travel** ★★★ (1/26 Akber House, Nowroji Fardoni Rd., Colaba; ℂ **022/2283-3872** or 98-2082-2253; www.realitytoursandtravel.com). After stopping at the famous **Mahalaxmi dhobi ghat** (apparently the world's largest open-air laundry) and driving through the city's **red-light district** (where you'll hear harrowing stories about some of the girls who find themselves imprisoned here), you arrive at the edge of the slum and set off on foot to meet some of the people who live and work there. You'll see a plastic recycling operation, visit inside a tiny, one-room family home, explore a variety of neighborhoods, and see one or two schools run by charitable trusts (including a kindergarten started by Reality Tours). It's one of the most riveting tours we've been on anywhere in the world—you can either join a group (never more than five people; Rs 800) or opt for a private tour (Rs 3,200). Try to specify that you want Krishna, one of the cofounders of the organization, as your guide—he's utterly charming, filled with insights, and has a magnificent rapport with the people in the slum. Krishna also arranges **market tours, village tours,** and more traditional **sightseeing tours.**

Doing it in style and offering a very wide array of well-packaged and impeccably delivered tours (from sightseeing walks through historic Fort to tours of the bazaars, and visits to Worli fishing village) is **Mumbai Magic** ★★★ (ℂ **98-6670-7414;** www.mumbaimagic.com), a true labor of love from the multitalented, super-sophisticated Deepa Krishnan. She aims to single-handedly transform the face of tourism in India—city by city, she's launching her own brand of high-grade guiding services throughout the country. Not only that, but she's probably the single biggest authority on what's hip, happening, and worthwhile in this, her home city, with delicious opinions and well-researched knowledge on just about everything that's going on here—she's even serves as TripAdvisor's resident expert on Mumbai. Using only expert "Deepa-certified" guides (all women), she puts together **highly specialized escorted sightseeing trips,** many of them themed in unusual and interesting ways, such as her **Jewish heritage tour.** Deepa offers a **Spirit of Dharavi** tour, but it is not a walking tour through the slum, but rather a chance to see Dharavi in its wider context as a part of the rapidly evolving city—for example, you'll see a gold market in the slum and compare this to a nearby middle-class South Indian market in Matunga. If you have time for just one of Deepa's experiences, though, make it the **Mumbai Local ★★★**, an ingenious tour where you spend 4 hours with a couple of English-speaking youngsters who take you around the city using standard-issue public transport—a red double-decker bus, a black and yellow taxi, and a local train—explaining how it all works, and the city is experienced by ordinary citizens. It's a marvelous day out, and a far cry from any typical sightseeing excursion. Deepa's prices start at Rs 1,500 per person for a 2-hour walking tour, and from around Rs 4,000 per person for a personalized tour in a car. The Mumbai Local tour is Rs 2,000, including tea, snacks, and lunch.

If you fancy dipping into the city from a literary point of view, or want to understand its art in more depth, contact Shriti Tyagi of **Beyond Bombay ★★★** (© **98-6776-4409;** beyondbombay@gmail.com). She's put together clever concept-driven tours that, in the case of her lively **bookworming tours,** evolve out of the plots and characters from popular books set in Mumbai—her *Shantaram* tour is very popular, but she also brings to life relevant episodes from Suketu Metha's *Maximum City*, and will happily research other pertinent books and prepare an exclusive tour for you based on that. Also available are other ingeniously themed tours—***thali* tripping** for foodies, **Bollywood tours** for film buffs, and ***rasta* shopping excursions** for shopaholics. Shriti is the former editor of a prominent Indian art journal, so she's probably the best person in the city with whom to discover its art; she'll enlist a textile designer to accompany you on a market tour, and perhaps a journalist to take you through some social history. A typical 3-hour walking tour costs around Rs 3,000, and driving tours run Rs 5,000, with no more than six people on a tour.

Shriti's landmark-oriented tours are good for getting a sense of the city, but if you like building design, a group of young architects conducts **Bombay Heritage Walks** ((© **022/2369-0992;** www.bombayheritagewalks.com), usually on Sundays mid-September to early May, with special monsoon walks June to September. If you have any interest in architecture, they're quite a gripping way to take in various fascinating parts of the city.

Finally, you could see the city on one of the invigorating full-morning **South Mumbai Cycle Tours** that happen every Sunday (Sept–June), when the streets are relatively free of traffic. The tour starts at 7am from Eros Theatre opposite Churchgate Station, and culminates with lunch at Café Mondegar in Colaba. You'll take in Marine Drive's Art Deco buildings, and check out the diversity of Classical, Gothic, Neo-Gothic, and Indo-Saracenic buildings and landmarks in both well-known and undiscovered parts of south Mumbai; there's some commentary on the history, too. The tour costs Rs 1,250 per person for a minimum of six participants, and includes the cycle, guide, breakfast, and lunch; check out www.odati.com for more information.

the original Koli community that inhabited these islands when they really were still islands; they still eek out an existence in much the same way as they've been doing for centuries. Well, almost. Ironically, this idiosyncratic peasant colony—often abuzz with foul-mouthed, hot-tempered fishwives—occupies the northern tip of Worli Sea Face, a stretch of prime real estate and part of one of Mumbai's hottest emerging neighborhoods. At the southern end of Worli, the strikingly designed **Nehru Centre** houses the city's unexceptional **Planetarium,** as well as an exhibition covering the entire history of the nation in fairly absorbing detail (even if its displays are very old fashioned). Not far from here is **Mahalaxmi Race Course,** an alternative place to hobnob with certain kinds of Mumbai socialites; it's in close proximity to the Mahalaxmi **dhobi ghat,** the world's biggest open-air laundry, and one of the city's most fascinating scenes—you can watch the laundrymen for hours from the bridge above the railways of Mahalaxmi Railway Station.

Finally, although not necessarily for the squeamish, it must be said that perhaps the most eye-opening insights into Mumbai life are to be garnered from a tour of **Dharavi,** recognized as Asia's largest slum, and likely to change your way of looking at the world forever (see the box below for details on slum tours).

EXPLORING COLABA & FORT

If you're at all inspired by Gothic Victorian architecture, then a jaunt through Mumbai's older districts is essential. Most tours kick off at the **Gateway of India** (see below), but a more authentic place to start, given Mumbai's origins, is **Sassoon Docks ★★** (aka the Fisherman's Market; daily 4am–noon except in the monsoon when weather dictates whether trawlers go out or not), which lies just south of the Gateway, off Shahid Bhagat Singh Marg (near Colaba Bus Station). Most of the delicious seafood dishes in the city's finest establishments start out here, where Koli women in rainbow-colored saris whip the shells off prawns while others gut and sort fish. Get here early (5am), when the boats return with their first catch, for the vibrant, communal spirit as baskets full of fish are moved around the dock through various stages of processing. It makes for absorbing viewing.

From here, walk back (or catch a cab) to the Gateway, possibly stopping for a refresher at the Taj Mahal Palace's **Sea Lounge,** situated directly opposite (see box below). From here it's a 15-minute walk north to Fort, Mumbai's cultural center, where you will find the superb **Prince of Wales Museum** (see later), nearby **Jehangir Art Gallery,** and the **National Gallery of Modern Art,** as well as a host of Raj-era Gothic architectural highlights. From the museum you can either head north along M. Gandhi Road to Flora Fountain, hub of downtown Mumbai, or travel southwest down the famous Colaba Causeway.

Surrounded by colonial buildings that testify to the solid architecture of a bygone era, **Flora Fountain** has, since 1960, had to compete for attention with a **Martyrs' Memorial** that honors those who died in the creation of the state of Maharashtra. As you head toward the fountain, take in the impressive **High Court** building (which overlooks the **Oval Maidan** [also called The Oval], where aspiring cricketers practice their paces), the neoclassical **Army & Navy Building,** and the 78m (256-ft.) **Rajabai Clock Tower,** which towers over the **Mumbai University** complex. East of the fountain lies **Horniman Circle,** where you will find the **Town Hall,** a regal colonnaded building with original parquet wood floors, wrought-iron loggias, spiral staircases, and marble statues of leaders associated with Mumbai's history. The major draw here is the **Asiatic Society Library,** which has a collection of around 800,000 valuable texts. You can join the seniors and students who fill the library's popular reading room to peruse local newspapers and check

(Moments) Mumbai's Ultimate Afternoon Escape

One of Mumbai's quintessential must-do experiences is high tea at the Taj Mahal Palace's gorgeous **Sea Lounge** ★★★ (© **022/6665-3366;** daily 10am–midnight), a popular haunt of the city's socialites who famously gather here to exchange gossip and tie up arrangements for family weddings. In fact, you won't only be watching boats floating by in the harbor behind the Gateway of India (seen here through gigantic picture windows), but inevitably witnessing couples in the throes of courtship while their mums and aunties get to know each other over cucumber sandwiches and cups of the finest Assam and Darjeeling teas. Along with an update of its design that's added a few contemporary colors and exquisite fabrics to the posh-but-cozy interior, the Sea Lounge now also serves traditional street snacks and *chaat* from a metal cart parked near the cake and sandwich buffet. For a mere Rs 850, you can stuff yourself silly, washing down the *pani puri* and *vada pao* with as much coffee and tea as you can manage. Take your time and lose yourself in the spectacular juxtaposition of the glamorous world you're in against the lively scene down by the harbor wall, always brimming with camera-clicking vacationers immortalizing themselves in front of one of India's most celebrated monuments.

out the public book collection, but you'll need special permission if you're interested in viewing the priceless treasures.

Also facing Horniman Circle is the late-19th-century Gothic Venetian **Elphinstone Building** and, opposite it, on Veer Nariman Road, **St. Thomas's Cathedral,** thought to be the oldest colonial structure in Mumbai. (Note that if you head west along Veer Nariman Rd., lined with restaurants, you will come to Marine Dr.) St. Thomas's Cathedral is a stark contrast to the pink and blue neoclassical **Kenneth Eliyahoo Synagogue,** Mumbai's oldest and loveliest Sephardic synagogue, located off K. Dubash Marg, on Forbes Street. North of Flora Fountain, up Dr. Dadabhai Naoroji Road, is the Art Deco–style Parsi fire temple, **Watcha Agiary.** Built in 1881, it features carvings in a distinctly Assyrian style.

If you prefer shopping (albeit of a tourist-trap nature) to architecture, opt for the famous **Causeway** (now officially renamed **Shahid Bhagat Singh Marg,** though, thankfully, no one refers to it as such). Budget travelers have long been drawn to this vibrant street, but in recent years Colaba and its side streets have begun to slip into an increasingly urbane and upmarket second skin. Hip bars, swinging clubs, and tasteful restaurants are drawing the smart crowd. Anything and everything seems to be available from the hawkers on Colaba's sidewalks and back alleys, whether it's fruit, cheap cigarettes, currency, or hashish. Shop in exclusive boutiques or rummage through heaps of cheap trinkets sold on the sidewalks, where you can bargain for everything from imitation perfume to piles of cheap, tasteless T-shirts, all the while avoiding the advances of streetwise beggars and con artists sporting half-moon smiles and incongruous American accents.

Beyond the southernmost end of the Causeway (that's if you manage to get this far south before grabbing a taxi and heading for the peace of your hotel room!), in the restricted Navy Nagar area, you will see the neo-Gothic **Afghan Memorial Church of**

St. John the Evangelist. Dating from 1858, it memorializes those who fell in the First Afghan War—proof yet again of Mumbai's mosaic past.

TOP ATTRACTIONS

Banganga Tank ★★ Here the paradox of traditional life coexisting with unbridled modernization is all too vivid. Near the edge of the Arabian Sea at the southern tip of Malabar Hill, several small, crumbling, stone-turreted temples and flower-garlanded shrines surround a rectangular pool of holy water in an area of looming modern-day skyscrapers and encroaching urbanization. Ritual bathers who come here believe the mossy waters have healing powers and originated from a natural spring created by an arrow shot by Rama (the hero of the *Ramayana*), who rested here while on a mission to rescue his beloved Sita from the demon king's abode in Lanka. The source of the spring is said to be an underground offshoot of the Ganga, and the waters are considered just as sacred as those of the great river itself. In the shadow of one of present-day Mumbai's most prosperous neighborhoods, Banganga continues to function as an out-of-time devotional hub, its tolling bells and mantra-chanting *pujaris* drawing devotees to worship the divine. If you're here in December, scour local newspapers for news of the open-air concerts held at the Banganga Festival.

Walkeshwar Rd., Malabar Hill.

Dharavi ★★★ (Moments) More than half of Mumbai's population are slum-dwellers, most of them—and they include hotel workers, engineers, waiters, taxi drivers, most of the city's police force, teachers, tour guides, you name it—existing with their entire (sometimes extended) families in tiny tenements smaller than a typical hotel bedroom. Although it's not an attraction in the traditional sense of the word, interest in Dharavi, Asia's largest shantytown, has grown exponentially in the wake of the *Shantaram* phenomenon and Oscar-winning *Slumdog Millionaire,* in which life in Mumbai's poorest neighborhoods is given more than a cursory or condescending glance. Hemmed in by Sion in the east and Mahim in the west, this particular "slum" is spread over 175 hectares (482 acres) and is home to around one million people; 72% of these people are forced to use communal bathing facilities—or worse still, face the stress of performing personal toilet functions in the open, often along the train tracks. Visit here on any given day, and you'll find it brimming with life and held together by an overwhelming industriousness; around $650 million is generated from goods exported from here each year—among the major industries here, are leather, recycling, and heavy machinery. A visit to Dharavi (on an escorted guided tour, of course) will not only prove tremendously enlightening, but will also touch you deeply, pulling into perspective just about every experience you have anywhere in this city and for that matter, in India.

For details of tour companies that visit Dharavi, see "Into the Belly of the Beast: Getting Beneath Mumbai's Skin" on p. 120.

Elephanta Island Caves ★★★ For a taste of Mumbai's early history and an opportunity to view the city's skyline from the water (not to mention escape from the tumult of the streets), grab a ferry and head out to Elephanta Island, declared a UNESCO World Heritage Site in 1987. The hour-long trip also provides a good introduction to Hinduism; the guides on board describe the religious significance of what you're about to see, though the origins of the Shiva temple caves—thought to date from the revivalist Hindu movement between A.D. 450 and 750—remain obscure.

Entry is via the main northern entrance to a massive hall supported by large pillars, where the enormous Trimurti statue is housed. At 6⅓m (21 ft.), the remarkable sculpture depicts Shiva in his three-headed aspect: as Creator (Vamadeva, facing right), Protector (Maheshmurti, the crowned face at the center), and Destroyer (Bhairadeva, facing left, with serpents for hair). Left of the Trimurti is Shiva as both male and female: Ardhanar-ishvara, an aspect suggesting the unity of all opposites. Other sculptures refer to specific actions of the god and events in Hindu mythology, but many were damaged or destroyed by the Portuguese, who apparently used the Hindu gods for target practice. It's practical to bring along a local guide (free) even though they rarely speak very good English. Watch listings for music and dance performances. *Tip:* Plan your trip so that you can witness sunset over the Mumbai skyline on your return journey, then pop into the Taj Mahal Hotel for a postculture cocktail. Note that music and dance festival performances are held here every year in February.

9km (5½ miles) from Mumbai. Admission Rs 250. Ferry tickets sold at booths near the Gateway of India. Ferry ticket Rs 120 return. Boats depart from the Gateway of India every half-hour Tues–Sun 9am–2:30pm; last ferry from Elephanta departs 5pm—do not miss it.

Gateway of India & Taj Mahal Palace ★★★

Easily the most recognizable remnant of the British Raj, the Gateway was designed by George Wittet (also responsible for the Prince of Wales Museum). The Gujarati-inspired yellow basalt structure was supposed to commemorate the visit of King George V and Queen Mary, who arrived in 1911 to find a fake cardboard structure instead; the Gateway was eventually completed in 1924 and was the final departure point for the British when they left Indian soil in 1947. It is the most obvious starting point for any tour of Mumbai (and is where the boats to Elephanta are launched), and to this end it draws large numbers of visitors as well as hordes of locals keen to take money off unsuspecting foreigners. The area makes for a quick-fix introduction to Mumbai tout dynamics; expect to be offered everything from photographs of yourself posing here to hashish to young girls. Opposite the Gateway is an equestrian statue of Chhatrapati Shivaji, the Maratha hero who gives his name to several renamed Mumbai institutions.

More impressive—in beauty and size—is the hotel behind the Gateway, which in many ways symbolizes Mumbaikars' determined and enterprising attitudes. Inspired by its namesake in Agra, the **Taj Mahal Palace** (see "Where to Stay," later) was built just over a century ago by an ambitious industrialist named Jamshedji Tata—according to legend, because he wanted to avenge the whites-only policy of Watson's, then the city's poshest hotel. Designed by a European architect who mailed the plans to India, it has been said that the hotel was mistakenly constructed back-to-front, so what was meant to be a fantastic sea-facing facade actually overlooks a side street. Of course that modern myth is patently untrue: The hotel was designed to receive guests arriving by land and was built to shelter the entrance from offshore winds. So, although the original front facade now faces the swimming pool, it was certainly never intended to face the sea. What cannot be refuted is how much it dominates Colaba's waterfront, its six-story domed structure best viewed from an offshore boat. (We cannot, however, account for the unwieldy, terribly vulgar modern tower wing attached to the original "palace.") In fact, it is the hotel's image as a symbol of the city's prestige (and popular hangout for Western visitors and businessmen) that made it a target during the awful attacks that rocked Mumbai in 2008. Here, along with other sites around the city, armed gunmen besieged guests and staff and many long hours of gruesome battle transpired, leaving among others, the family of the general manager dead. It was a serious blow at the very heart of the city, but as countenance of Mumbai's indomitable spirit, the hotel reopened on December 21, 2008, albeit not in its entirety, and with intense new security procedures that have left the building looking cordoned off to the outside world.

Don't let the security cordon prevent you from taking a look inside the Taj Mahal Palace, however. The best way to experience both the Taj and the Gateway is to head inside the hotel and make for the **Sea Lounge** for high tea (see "Mumbai's Ultimate Afternoon Escape" box on p. 123); you'll enjoy sublime views of the Gateway while getting a taste of one of the city's foremost social institutions, not to mention inhabiting a space that's played host to a veritable who's who of international politics and celebrity (everyone, from Gandhi to Nehru to Mick Jagger to Madonna, has stayed here).

Chhatrapati Shivaji Maharaj Marg. Gateway information: ☏ 022/2202-3585 or -6364.

Jain Temple ★★ This is arguably the prettiest temple in Mumbai (indeed, Jain temples are generally the prettiest in India). If your itinerary does not include a visit to one elsewhere (the most famous being in Rajasthan), do make the time to visit Mumbai's. Members of the Jain community are known to be exceptionally adept in the world of business, and although they believe in self-restraint and aestheticism (orthodox Jains will not tread on an ant, and at their most extreme wear masks to avoid breathing in even tiny insects), they pour large sums into the construction and maintenance of their places of worship. Officially called **Babu Amichand Panalal Adishwarji Jain Temple,** this beautifully decorated and adorned temple has an entrance flanked by two stone elephants. The downstairs area houses an array of deities and saints, including an image of Ganesh that recalls historical links between Jainism and Hinduism.

Ridge Rd., Walkeshwar (Malabar Hill). ☏ 022/2369-2727. Daily 5am–9pm.

Mahalaxmi Dhobi Ghat ★★★ It's a fascinating spectacle, looking down on row upon row of open-air concrete wash pens, each fitted with its own flogging stone, while Mumbai's *dhobis* (around 200 *dhobi* families work together here) relentlessly pound the dirt from the city's garments in a timeless tradition. Known as the world's largest outdoor laundry, the municipal Dhobi Ghat in Mahalaxmi is where Mumbai's traditional washerfolk—or *dhobis*—provide a wonderful service, collecting dirty laundry, washing it, and returning it neatly pressed, all for a very small fee. Stubborn stains are removed by soaking garments in a boiling vat of caustic soda; drying takes place on long, brightly colored lines; and heavy wood-burning irons are used for pressing. At the very least, it's a great photo opportunity, though most locals think it rather amusing that their everyday work arouses such curiosity. (Note that there is another Dhobi Ghat off Capt. Prakash Petha Marg, Colaba, which may be more accessible.)

Dr. E. Moses Rd. (near Mahalakshmi Station).

Mani Bhavan Gandhi Museum ★★ Mahatma Gandhi lived in this quaint Gujarati-style house from 1917 to 1934, and it was here in November 1921 that he conducted a 4-day fast in order to restore peace to the city. This quiet three-story home on a beautiful laburnum tree–lined avenue now preserves the spirit of the man who selflessly put his nation before himself. There's a library of Gandhi-related works, as well as displays of photographs, posters, slogans, and other items that document and explain Gandhi's legendary life; dioramas depicting major events and turning points in his fight for the nation's freedom draw particular attention to his devotion to the poor. You can see Gandhi's old *charkha* (spinning wheel), which in many ways symbolized the struggle for independence, as it represented a return to roots and to sustainable home industry, where anyone can weave his or her own cloth. A visit to this tranquil spot makes a welcome change from the continuous hubbub of life in Mumbai—go up to the roof to really appreciate the relative stillness of the surrounding neighborhood.

19 Laburnam Rd., near Malabar Hill. © 022/2380-5864. www.gandhi-manibhavan.org. Admission Rs 10; donations appreciated. Daily 9:30am–5:30pm.

Marine Drive & Chowpatty Beach ★★★ Marine Drive (renamed Netaji Subhash Chandra Marg) follows the sweeping curve of sea that stretches north from Nariman Point's high-rise buildings to infamous Chowpatty Beach, located at the foot of Malabar Hill. It's the ultimate seaside promenade, where Mumbaikars come to escape the claustrophobia of central Mumbai, gratefully eyeing an endless horizon while strolling or jogging along the broad windswept promenade. In the evenings, casual, single-item snack stalls are set up for brisk trade; a stroll along here also takes in the world's second-largest stretch of Art Deco buildings (in future years, there'll be heritage plaques identifying the most significant of these). Having undergone an extensive refurbishment and general neatening-up in recent years, there's another huge beautification project on the back-burner (apparently buried under a deluge of bureaucratic mismanagement) that will, among other things, include open-air galleries and improved walkways, and at Nariman Point, a breakwater promontory will extend 280m (918½ ft.) into the sea, culminating in a stepped amphitheater. Even before all that happens, this is the city's ultimate sunset spot, when—having watched the orange globe sink into the Arabian Sea—you can witness the street lights transform Marine Drive into the aptly named Queen's Necklace, a choker-length of twinkling jewels adorning Back Bay. The scene is perhaps best enjoyed with cocktail in hand at one of the Drive's classier establishments—the InterContinental's rooftop lounge and restaurant, **Dome**, is where you should be.

Once the sun has set, catch a ride (or walk) north along Marine Drive to Chowpatty, Mumbai's oldest seafront. Chowpatty is no longer the filth-ridden extravaganza its long-acquired reputation suggests (though it's still not in any state for sunbathing or swimming), and at night it assumes the demeanor of a colorful fair. Children of all ages flock to ride the ancient Ferris wheels and tacky merry-go-rounds, and fly-by-night astrologers, self-styled contortionists, snake charmers, and trained monkeys provide the flavor of the bazaar—and bizarre—especially on weekends. This is where locals love to consume the city's famous street snacks, especially *bhelpuri:* crisp puffed rice, vegetables, and fried lentil-flour noodles doused in pungent chutneys of chili, mint, and tamarind, then scooped up with a tiny, flat *puri* (puffy deep-fried bread). Chowpatty *bhelpuri* is renowned throughout India, sold here by the eponymous *bhelwallas,* who now ply their trade in Bhel Plaza, where other traditional treats like *kulfi* are on offer at dirt-cheap prices.

Note: It's inadvisable to eat here—unfortunately, flavor, not hygiene, enjoys top priority. However, after you've watched the multitudes gorging vast quantities of assorted snack foods, cross the street and get your own *chaat* (as *bhelpuri* and similar snacks are called) at **Cream Centre** ★★ (25 Fulchand Niwas, Chowpatty Beach; © 022/2367-9222 or -9333; noon–midnight). For close to 50 years, this vegetarian snack place has been serving up delicious food—so good, in fact, that whenever you pass Chowpatty Beach in the evening, you'll see a queue of people waiting to get in. Alternatively, make a meal of the signature *channa bhatura* (spiced chickpeas and a large *puri*), a typical Punjabi dish that is made everywhere but rarely so well as here. When you're done, step out of the restaurant, turn left, and walk down to the end of the pavement to a hole-in-the-wall (but very hygienic) juice shop called **Bachelorr's** (yes, with two r's) for deliciously refreshing seasonal fresh fruit

(Moments) Touching God

There were still hundreds of people streaming onto Chowpatty Beach for the finale on Monday, when idols of Ganpati are immersed in the sea. I had expected to see the shore where it normally is, but today it extended another quarter-mile—thousands of people were already in the water! Trucks with 6m-high (20-ft.) Ganesh idols lined up on the sand, awaiting their turn alongside families wanting to drop their small, lap-sized idols into the sea. Engulfed by teeming masses and deafened by the sound of singing devotees and driving drumbeats, Vanessa and I locked hands so that we wouldn't lose each other. As we navigated the crowds, one of the large Ganesh idols rocked forward off its flatbed, prompting a small stampede as people standing nearby tried to escape. Luckily, the men holding the ropes managed to steady and pull the giant idol upright. Hundreds of volunteers and security officials worked to maintain order, many thankfully eager to help two conspicuously foreign women—one official even held an entire line of men at bay. As he ushered us to a less crowded space, a giant Ganesh adorned with plastic grass and flowers passed en route to the shore. The security guard watched the two of us admiring the decorations and asked, "Would you like to touch God?" "Sure!" I exclaimed. As I reached over to touch Ganesh's feet, I wondered why every Monday couldn't include an intimate moment with the divine.

—Megan Neumeister, Indophile

ice creams and juices—but do make sure you ask for your juice without ice, water, or masala.

To experience Mumbai at its most exuberant, head to Chowpatty Beach for the culmination of **Ganesh Chaturthi** ★★★, the city's biggest and most explosive celebration. Held in honor of the much-loved elephant-headed god (here called Ganpati), the 10-day festival culminates on the last day, when a jubilant procession is held and thousands of huge Ganpati idols are immersed in the sea. Ganesh Chaturthi is held in September; for exact dates contact the Government of India Tourist Office, and to whet your appetite, read "Touching God," above).

Marine Drive's pedestrian promenade flanks Mumbai's western seaboard, stretching from Nariman Point in the south to Chowpatty Beach some 3km (2 miles) north.

Prince of Wales Museum ★★★   Renamed Chhatrapati Shivaji Maharaj Vastu Sangrahalaya, but thankfully also known just as "museum," this is Mumbai's top museum and arguably the best in India, providing an extensive and accessible introduction to Indian history and culture. The Indo-Saracenic building itself is lovely, but it is the collection that is outstanding, not least because it is well laid out (unlike the collections of most museums throughout the subcontinent) and aided by a useful audioguide highlighting "Curator's Choice" exhibits. The central hall features a "précis" of the collection, but don't stop there—from sculptures of Hindu deities to beautiful temple art, Buddhist *thangkas* from Nepal and Tibet to gruesome Maratha weaponry, there is much to see. Highlights are found on the first floor: Among them, the spectacular collection of more than 2,000 miniature paintings representing India's various schools of art (look for the portrait of Shah Jahan, creator of the Taj Mahal), and the exhibit relating to the Indus

My Bombay/Mumbai

All of Mumbai's contrasts and paradoxes are characterized for me on a trip to the Banganga Tank at Walkeshwar. There's a ring of old temples, and right by them are the homes of people whose families have served as priests for these temples for generations. Residents still perform priestly rituals early in the morning, go off to their computer jobs, returning in the evening to be priests once again. Standing on the steps of the Banganga Tank, I look up and see skyscrapers that represent some of the most expensive real estate in the world, and alongside them, shanties. For me, this encapsulates the Bombay story.

I also like to walk around The Oval (*maidan*, in downtown Mumbai) for another kind of contrast. On one side you have beautiful neo-Gothic buildings that look as if they've been transplanted from another continent, albeit with typically Indian flourishes and intricate carvings. Walk over to the other side of this huge field and you see Art Deco buildings from the 1930s and '40s with nautical and tropical motifs, again embodying a distinctive Bombay quality. Only Miami has something close to this. The northern end of the field has a cricket training academy but on Sundays, the maidan is overrun by dozens of impromptu cricket games, and in the middle of the chaos, a group of Nigerians can often by found playing football. Another great place I like to wander is Chor Bazaar and the adjoining Mohammedali Road. A flea market, Chor Bazaar is filled with a jumble of interesting things, and you can snag some good vintage finds—furniture, posters, coins, records—or just window shop and laugh at some of the ridiculously naïve copies of old objects and artifacts."

—Naresh Fernandes, Editor, *Time Out Mumbai.*

Valley Civilization (which is remarkably civilized considering that it dates from 3500 B.C.). Least impressive is the natural history section with its collection of stuffed animals.

Note: Art lovers may wish to include a visit to **Jehangir Art Gallery** (© **022/2284-3989**), located a little farther along M. Gandhi Road, and open daily from 11am to 7pm, free of charge. You can probably give the main exhibition halls on the ground floor a miss—the exhibits there are fairly mediocre. Instead, head upstairs to **Gallery Chemould** (© **022/2284-4356;** Mon–Sat 11am–6pm), a tiny, history-filled gallery that often features some of India's best contemporary artists. For reviews of current art exhibitions, consult *Time Out Mumbai* or "The Hot List," the entertainment supplement in the local rag *Mid Day.*

159/160 Mahatma Gandhi Rd., Fort. © **022/2284-4519.** www.bombaymuseum.org. powm@vsnl.com. Rs 300 including audioguide. Tues–Sun 10:15am–6pm.

Victoria Terminus ★★★ Rechristened **Chhatrapati Shivaji Terminus** as part of Mumbai's nationalist-inspired anti-Raj campaign, this baroque, cathedral-like train station—still known to everyone as "VT"—must rank as Mumbai's most marvelous Raj-era monument. India's very first steam engine left this station when it was completed in 1887; today at least a thousand trains leave every day, carrying some 2½ million commuters in and out of the city. Targeted in 2008 as part of a wider attack on the city by a group

Need a Fortifying Break in Fort?

Stadium (📞 **022/2204-6819**) is a cheap, unpretentious Irani restaurant outside Churchgate Station where you can sip *chai* or a cold drink while you contemplate your next move. Across the street (though you will have to walk all around to get there) is **Gaylord** (Mayfair, Veer Nariman Rd., Churchgate; 📞 **022/2204-4693**) an old fashioned cafe with a terrace and an all-day bakery selling fresh breads, croissants, and assorted bites—great to recover your strength after a day of pounding the sidewalks or idling in traffic.

of terrorists, the station has been undergoing some renovation, and attempts to beef up security mean that there are now armed guards around all the entrances. Don't let that put you off, though—and don't be alarmed by the sheer number of commuters should you happen to turn up during peak hours. With its vaulted roofs, arches, Gothic spires, flying buttresses, gables crowned by neoclassical sculptures, stone carvings, and exquisite friezes, the terminus is an architectural gem, worth entering to see the massive ribbed Central Dome (topped by a statue of the torch-wielding "Progress") that caps an octagonal tower featuring beautiful stained-glass windows with colorful images of trains and floral patterns. But come, too, for the spectacle of the disparate people, from sari-clad beauties to half-naked fakirs, who make up Mumbai. Get here just before lunch to watch the famous *dabba-wallas* stream out into the city: A vast network of *dabba-wallas* transfer some 200,000 cooked lunches, prepared by housewives for their office-bound husbands, and kept warm in identical *dabbas* (metal lunch containers), through a unique sorting and multiple-relay distribution system; later in the afternoon these empty *dabbas* are returned to their home of origin. The success of this system (no one gets the wrong lunch) is proof of how well India works, despite its reputation for obstructive bureaucracy. In fact, following a study of this network, U.S. business magazine *Forbes* gave it a Six Sigma (99.99% accuracy) performance rating, which means that just one error occurs in six million transactions.

Dr. Dadabhai Naoroji Rd., Fort.

MARKETS

Mumbai has more than 70 markets, and it's worthwhile to spend a couple of hours exploring at least one, not so much for the shopping (for that, see "Shopping," later in this chapter) as for the human spectacle of it all. Flowers are an intrinsic part of Indian culture, and **Bhuleshwar Wholesale Flower Market** ★★ (CP Tank Circle; dawn–noon) is the best place in the city to witness the Indian romance with color and fragrance. Note that according to Hindu beliefs, if you touch or sniff the flowers, you'll ruin them—so don't. The name **Chor Bazaar (Thieves' Market)** ★★ (Mutton St., off Sardar Vallabhbhai Patel Rd.; Sat–Thurs 11am–7pm) conjures up *Arabian Nights'* cloak-and-dagger intrigue and visions of precious rings sold with the finger of the former owner still attached, but in reality this is a fun place to rummage through an extravagant assortment of antiques, fakes, and junk and get into the rhythm of that favorite Indian pastime: bargaining. It's also highly likely that—unless you're an expert on antiques—you'll end up buying something that might look a few hundred years old, but which was churned

> ## (Moments) Bewitched by Alphonso
>
> Along with the unbearable heat, summer brings forth crops of beauteous mangoes, dozens of varieties of which are available only in India. King of them all is unquestionably the Alphonso. You may have eaten mangoes in Mexico, Thailand, or even other parts of India, but until you've sucked on the succulent bright orange pulp of the Alphonso, with its bewitching scent and unimaginably divine flavor, you'll miss a sensory experience like no other. The best Alphonsos originate from Ratnagiri in rural Maharashtra. To make sure you're getting the real thing, ask your hotel to find you one, or—better still—explore the fruit section at Mumbai's **Crawford Market.** Prices start at Rs 1,500 a dozen in March and go down to Rs 120 a dozen when the season peaks in May; the mangoes often need to be kept a day or two to ripen before eating.

out by a talented craftsman just this morning. In short, it's a good idea to browse here, but you'd better be on your toes if you have any plans to leave with a valuable antique.

If you visit only one market, make it **Crawford Market** ★★★ (Lokmanya Tilak Marg and Dr. Dadabhai Naoroji Rd., Mon–Sat 11:30am–8pm), Mumbai's quintessential fresh-produce shopping experience, now officially known as **Mahatma Jyotiba Phule Market.** Dating from the 1860s, it combines the traditional Indian bazaar experience with both Norman and Flemish architecture; pay attention to the bas-relief frieze above the main entrance—it was designed by Rudyard Kipling's father. Admire the colorful pyramids of heavenly mangoes (see "Bewitched by Alphonso," box above) and ripe bananas, but steer clear of the disturbing pet stalls.

Clothing is one of Mumbai's major exports, and at **Fashion Street** ★ (Mahatma Gandhi Rd., across the road from Bombay Gymkhana), a motley collection of shops and stalls, you will pay a fraction of the prices asked in foreign stores. Much of what is here is surplus stock; other garments have been rejected by quality controllers. Start your haggling at under half the quoted price.

Taxi drivers get nervous when you tell them you want to visit **Zaveri Bazaar** (jewelry market) ★★ (Sheik Memon St.; Mon–Sat 11am–7pm). You'll soon discover why. Shoppers and space-fillers shuffle and push their ways endlessly through narrow gaps in this cluttered, heaving market, and it's often impossible to inch forward by car—or even on foot. Behind the street stalls and milling masses, glittering jewels are sold from family shops. If the glitzy accessories don't fascinate you, perhaps you'll be drawn to packed **Mumbadevi Temple,** where the city's namesake deity is housed. Activity around the temple is chaotic, with devotees splurging to prove their devotion to the powerful goddess.

Less familiar to tourists, is **Null Bazaar** (20 SV Patel Rd.; © 022/2346-1008), where you can browse the **Bombay Lungi Market** for namesake lungies (sarongs made for men, more typically worn in South India) crafted from Madras cotton.

CRICKET

Although hockey is India's official national sport, cricket is by far the best-loved game, and even watching a group of schoolboys practicing in a field is an experience unto itself. Mumbaikars play the game with an enthusiasm that's quite intoxicating—almost as if it provides some measure of relief from the hardships of daily life. In cricket-crazy India, the stars of the game are worshiped as keenly as film stars and gods, and Indian spectators

(Moments) Catch a Bollywood Blockbuster

You can't say you've properly done the biggest film-producing city on earth if you haven't gone to the cinema to catch a blockbuster. Listings are found in daily newspapers, where you can also determine quality and even figure out the story-line by reading reviews written by contenders for the world's bitchiest critic; alternatively, ask your hotel concierge for recommendations. Of course, you can always get completely into the swing of things by picking up a copy of one of Bollywood's gossip magazines. *Filmfare* and *Stardust* not only fill you in on what's hot or what's not, but are crammed with glossy, airbrushed close-ups of silver-screen idols. Even though the growth of multiplexes has killed virtually all the old cinema houses, some still offer historic Art Deco appeal. Get tickets to watch a film at the once wonderful but now run-down **Eros Cinema** (opposite Churchgate Station; (C) **022/2282-2335**) or lovely **Liberty Cinema ★★** ((C) **022/ 2203-1196,** a short walk from Eros, near Bombay Hospital), where upper-stall (at Liberty) or dress-circle (at Eros) tickets (the best in the house) still cost under Rs 100. Besides the Bollywood melodrama, you get to admire the wonderful Art Deco interiors, with majestic high ceilings, white cedar and teak paneling, '60s-style soda fountain, magnificent huge etched mirrors on the stairwells, mock fountains, and old movie posters. It's possible to get a little more involved in the Bollywood scene, either by joining a personalized tour led by a working assistant director (with Beyond Bombay; see p. 121), or by getting yourself landed a part as an extra in a movie (scouts often trawl Leopold Café, p. 154, looking for foreigners to add to the scenery of forthcoming blockbusters).

at international games have the ability to transform even the blandest match into an exciting event.

During the season (Oct–Mar), several matches are held each week at **Wankhede Stadium** (Churchgate), which is where Mumbai's big national and international games are hosted. Tickets are sold by the **Mumbai Cricket Association** ((C) **022/2281-9910** or -2714), but it's worth asking your concierge to arrange good seats for you at a decent price (top-tier tickets can go for as much as $100 officially, and up to $300 on the black market). There's no doubt that watching a cricket match in an Indian stadium with tens of thousands of fans is one of the more fascinating experiences to be had in India, but if crowds make you nervous, watch the World Cup, Sharjah Cup, or any major cricketing event live at a local bar or lounge, with a few dozen cricket-crazy Indians to provide the spectacle.

4 WHERE TO STAY

With greater supply than demand for rooms in Mumbai over the last few years, and the emergence of numerous five-star properties in the suburbs, rooms in downtown Mumbai can often be booked at good rates. Don't always go by a hotel's published tariff; ask about seasonal or daily discounts and cruise the Internet for bargains. It's not uncommon to find ridiculously cheap deals for rooms in hotels like the Taj President, available even

(Moments) Giggling Is Good for You

Mumbai is many things, including the hometown of Dr. Madan Kataria, the infectiously joyous man who spread **Laughter Yoga** to the whole world. Today there are nearly 90 laughter clubs in Mumbai alone, and over 5,000 around the globe. Dr. Kataria says that you don't even need a sense of humor to take part in these vibrant and wonderfully relaxing, stress-relieving, life-changing sessions where you focus on breathing, body relaxation through stretching, and fun exercises that include different kinds of laughter-inducing techniques. It's one sort of therapy you really should try out while you're here—you can track down a club while you're in Mumbai, or even start one back in your home town. Sessions in Mumbai happen early each morning throughout the city—a good choice is the club that meets at the Worli Sea Face, organized by Mohit Kapoor ((℃) 022/2422-8895 or 98-2006-5119). The website of **Dr. Kataria's School of Laughter Yoga** has all the details, as well as contacts for clubs around the world ((℃) 022/2631-6426; www. laughteryoga.org), and explains how you can initiate your own laughter groups.

during the popular winter season. That said, budget travelers should be prepared to spend more on lodging in Mumbai than in any other city on the subcontinent; standards at the low end can be difficult to stomach, so you're better off forking out a little more for a decent place to stay.

Marine Drive is a great option if you want a prime view of the Arabian Sea, but it's pricey. With a variety of options to suit every budget (top choice obviously being the Taj Mahal Palace & Tower, reviewed below), Colaba-Fort is where most tourists end up, but these days there's as much fun (although not as many historic attractions) to be had in areas like Worli, Bandra and Juhu, all of which offer great shopping, dining and nightlife options. If you are literally overnighting and have no desire to spend time in Mumbai, a number of options are located close to the international airport, but there are very few bargains here. A good compromise is Juhu, which has cheaper choices and a great nighttime atmosphere, and is only a 30-minute drive from the airport.

MARINE DRIVE

Within walking distance of the city's commercial center, Marine Drive is a great place to base yourself, not least for the sea views and sense of space these provide—offering a relief from the hustling, bustling streets that lie east. Expect to pay for the privilege, however, since prices for real estate along this famed strip are as breathtaking as the views.

Very Expensive

InterContinental Marine Drive ★★★ The great location goes without saying, but the sense of intimacy, and the sumptuousness of its enormously proportioned accommodations really make this a stand-out among the other expensive business hotels along Marine Drive. Amid all the great design (with a modernized tribal arts theme throughout) and (we'll say it again) very impressive size of the rooms (there's lots of focus on ensuring you get a good night's sleep). You're offered a free 20-minute in-room massage, and the ultra-plush beds are complemented by an extensive "Pillow and Quilt Menu." A Bose music system delivers perfect sound throughout the room, and bathrooms are lusciously laid-out, too. Most rooms offer some view of the sea, but the pricier "deluxe seafront" units are best. It's all very lovely, but service can feel a bit curt, and when we were last here we overheard guests complaining of bogus telephone charges, so definitely worth checking your bill before handing over your credit card

135 Marine Dr., Mumbai 400 020. ℂ **022/3987-9999.** Fax 022/3987-9600. www.mumbai.intercontinental. com. 58 units. Rs 19,500 deluxe double; Rs 21,500 deluxe bay view double; Rs 23,500 deluxe sea front double; Rs 28,500 deluxe bay view suite; Rs 33,000 deluxe corner suite; Rs 50,000 luxury suite; Rs 75,000 presidential suite. Rates exclude 10% tax. Children under 12 stay free if sharing without extra bed. AE, DC, MC, V. **Amenities:** 2 restaurants, lounge, 2 bars, including Dome (see "Mumbai After Dark," p. 165); airport transfers (Rs 2,900 plus tax); concierge; free DVD & CD library; health club; room service. *In room:* A/C, TV/ DVD, fax (in most), hair dryer, minibar, music system, Wi-Fi (Rs 350/hr.; Rs 1,200/day).

The Oberoi ★★★　The best hotel on Marine Drive will emerge by 2010 after year-long renovation. It's particularly from a service point of view that The Oberoi wins hands-down; touches like being met at the terminal gate, your luggage dealt with for you, right through to the personal butler on each floor summoned by the touch of an "Ask Jeeves" button, and genuflecting staff members who go out of their way to make you feel revered, are typical Oberoi, and worth every dollar. If Mumbai is your first port of call, you'll find the genteel atmosphere a relief—tranquil and sophisticated, yet very relaxed, this is where you want to retreat after spending a few hours out on the crowded streets. All accommodations are spacious, with tasteful decor, but the best rooms are the luxury sea-view rooms, with stunning sea views and gorgeous sunsets turning the whole room a pale pink before the Queen's Necklace starts to sparkle—a dazzling predinner spectacle. *And*, these rooms include airport transfers. *Note:* If the rates here are a tad stiff, overnight in the adjoining **Trident Nariman Point** (reviewed below), where you'll enjoy a taste of the Oberoi's famous service (albeit shared with many more guests) and you'll have your pick of both sets of facilities.

Nariman Point, Marine Dr., Mumbai 400 021. ℂ **022/5632-5757,** or -6887 reservations. Fax 022/5632-4142. www.oberoihotels.com. 333 units. At press time, The Oberoi is closed for extensive renovations, and scheduled to reopen by 2010. Rates are currently unavailable. AE, DC, MC, V. **Amenities:** 3 restaurants; lounge; bar; airport transfers (free for certain room categories); butler (on each floor); concierge; health club and spa; large outdoor pool; room service. *In room:* A/C, TV/DVD, CD (deluxe rooms & suites), fax, hair dryer, minibar, Wi-Fi (chargeable).

Expensive

Hotel Marine Plaza ★★　Any address along Marine Drive is highly sought after, and the former Bombay International is no exception, though it's not in the same class as The Oberoi, InterContinental, or the Trident. Like the hotel, the Deco-styled marble lobby is small, its main stairway concealing a lounge from where you stare up at people in the glass-bottom pool five floors up. Besides taking a dip, the pool deck is where you'll get wonderful views over Back Bay and the entire Queen's Necklace strip. Most of the accommodations are suites, some of which are relatively well-priced but require neck-straining to get a look at the view; make sure to specify a room with a direct sea view. Ironically, the cheapest ("superior") rooms (there are just four) all face the sea full-on; they're slick and smart, albeit in an old-fashioned sort of way (carpets, old sofas, old TVs, and very low furniture). Note, too, that if it matters, you should specify if you require a king-size bed.

29 Marlne Dr., Mumbai 400 020. ℂ **022/2285-1212.** Fax 022/2282-8585. www.hotelmarineplaza.com. hmp@sarovarhotels.com. 68 units. Rs 16,000 superior double; Rs 18,000 executive suite double; Rs 24,000 deluxe suite double; Rs 28,000 special suite double. Rates include breakfast; 10% tax extra. AE, DC, MC, V. **Amenities:** 2 restaurants; pastry shop; bar; airport transfers (Rs 1,800–Rs 1,860); health club; rooftop pool; room service. *In room:* A/C, TV, hair dryer, minibar, Wi-Fi (Rs 450/hr.; Rs 1,860/day).

Trident Nariman Point ★★★ Often regarded as the mass-market sibling of the attached Oberoi, this is one of Mumbai's slickest, smartest, and friendliest business hotels, and enjoys an enviable position with excellent views across Back Bay and the entire Marine Drive strip. While accommodations are sumptuous (sleek and light-filled, with plenty of modern-looking blonde wood, big back-supporting beds with silky white linens, and extensive amenities for demanding business travelers), it's primarily in the area of service that this colossal hotel trumps competitors down the road (neither the InterContinental nor the Marine Plaza come close). On top of the excellent in-house dining options (a smart-casual dress code is in place—no shorts) and a luscious new spa, you can also rely on the concierge desk to achieve near-miracles, and—should you take our advice and book a Taj Club room (with a sea view, of course)—you'll enjoy the services of a butler, making your stay feel extraspecial.

Marine Dr., Nariman Point, Mumbai 400 021 (ℂ **022/6632 4343.** Fax 022/6632-5000. www.tridenthotels. com. 540 units. Rs 10,250 superior double; Rs 11,750 deluxe sea view double; Rs 13,250 premiere double; Rs 14,750 premiere sea view double; Rs 16,750 Trident Club double; Rs 18,000–Rs 74,000 suite. Club and suite rates include breakfast and airport transfers; all rates exclude 10% tax. AE, DC, MC, V. **Amenities:** 2 restaurants; including India Jones (see review, p. 148); lounge, bar; airport transfers (Rs 2,647); babysitting; butler service (Club floors and suites); Club floors with executive privileges; concierge; health club and spa; large outdoor ocean-facing pool; room service. In room: A/C, TV/DVD, hair dryer, minibar, Wi-Fi (Rs 800/day)

Inexpensive

If your budget can't stretch to pay for the suggestions above, check out **Sea Green Hotel** (ℂ **022/6633 6525** or 022/2282-2294; www.seagreenhotel.com) at 145 Marine Dr. Together with the adjoining **Sea Green South Hotel** (www.seagreensouth.com), this is the best (if not the only) budget option on Marine Drive, where relatively large guest rooms with French doors (and flaking paint) open onto balconies overlooking Back Bay. It has a slightly seedy air, and furnishings are way out of date (some would say awful), but the attached shower-toilets are large and clean, and each room comes with TV, metal wardrobe, vinyl-covered desk and table, and a small fridge; and there's Wi-Fi, too (Rs 100/hr.; Rs 700/day). Aside from a small lounge in the lobby, there are no other facilities, making this a bare-basics, functional budget hotel, where you'll be investing as little as Rs 3,600 (inclusive of taxes and a 10% service charge, but no breakfast) for an air-conditioned double. *Tip:* Try to book room 504, one of the few rooms with a glassed-in shower; it even has a sideways sea view from the balcony.

COLABA

Generally considered the city's tourist hub, this enclave at the far southern end of the city enjoys the city's densest concentration of sights, hotels, and restaurants (of which the best are reviewed below); Colaba and Fort are ideal if you like to step out of your hotel and walk around as opposed to jumping into a chauffeur-driven vehicle and being whisked off to your next port of call. While some of the city's premiere hotels—such as the Taj Mahal Palace and the excellent-value Ascot—are here, this area is also known for having a large number of budget dives and while this is more or less true, it's clear that most of these places have put effort into smartening up in recent years, so it's increasingly possible to find a relatively good deal (at least by Mumbai standards) without roughing it too much.

Very Expensive

The Taj Mahal Palace & Tower ★★★ George Bernard Shaw declared that after staying here, he no longer needed to visit the Taj Mahal in Agra. As the crowning glory of the city's hotel scene, The Taj Mahal Palace may well double as the nerve center for moneyed mischief, but it remains a great blend of old-world charm and modern conveniences. Nothing can compare to the sublime historic ambience of the rooms and suites in the Palace, all of which are being extensively overhauled (smartened up with more modern amenities and slicker finishes, but retaining their substantially old-world ambience, carefully chosen antiques and vintage artworks, and indisputable authenticity) following damage done to the property during the tragedy that befell the city in 2008. The Taj has long been in the process of reinventing itself to keep its crown as *the* most celebrated address in Mumbai, and despite many a la mode additions (the plush **Jiva** spa, modern world-class restaurants, jazzy infusions of color against a regal architectural background, and souped-up airtight security), the hotel still recalls an era of superb elegance. While we highly recommend the sea-facing rooms and exceptional suites in the historic Palace wing (all of which are scheduled to be relaunched by 2010), we still feel that accommodations in the hotel's looming business-oriented Tower Wing are a bit of a letdown (with small, bland bathrooms).

Apollo Bunder, Mumbai 400 001. © **022/6665-3366.** Fax 022/6665-0300. www.tajhotels.com. At press time only the Tower Wing, comprising 268 of 565 units, are operational; the Palace is scheduled to reopen by 2010. Tower Wing: Rs 19,750 superior city-view double, Rs 21,250 superior sea-view double, Rs 22,750 deluxe city-view double, Rs 24,250 deluxe sea-view double, Rs 28,750 Taj Club city-view double, Rs 30,750 Taj Club sea-view double, Rs 75,000 executive suite, Rs 95,000 luxury suite. Palace Wing rates unavailable at press time. Rates exclude 10% tax. Rates for Taj Club rooms and suites include airport transfers, butler service, breakfast, high tea, and cocktails. AE, DC, MC, V. **Amenities:** 6 restaurants, including Wasabi (see review, p. 148), Souk (see review, p. 150), and Masala Kraft (see review, p. 150); legendary pastry shop; 2 lounges; including Sea Lounge (see box on p. 123); 2 bars, including Harbour Bar, the oldest bar in the city (p. 167); airport transfers (Rs 3,140); babysitting; concierge; health club and spa; large outdoor pool; room service; yacht. *In room:* A/C, TV/DVD, fax (on request; free), hair dryer, minibar, Wi-Fi (Rs 150/¹/₂ hr.; Rs 650/day).

Expensive

The Gordon House Hotel ★   Set among a rash of rather ordinary old-fashioned hotels, Colaba's most exuberantly styled hotel is perfect for those raring to have a good time. Unfortunately, it's no longer the good deal it was when it opened, and a stay here means you'd better be prepared to put up with a lot of noise until very late at night. On the other hand, the themed guest rooms can be kind of fun: Best are the no-nonsense Scandinavian rooms (smart, contemporary units with parquet floors and sleek Ikea-style furniture, timber blinds, and black-and-white photographs). Mediterranean rooms are less severe (with bright blues and yellows, tiled floors, cane chairs, and cool aqua-toned bathrooms). But the feminine Country Floor is strictly for fans of pastels, floral, and patchwork designs. Be warned, too, that accommodations are small (if well proportioned), and bathrooms tiny. Trouble is, the nonstop thumping from the in-house nightclub tends to prevent you from getting a proper night's sleep.

5 Battery St., Apollo Bunder, Colaba, Mumbai 400 039. © **022/2289-4400.** Fax 022/2289-4444. www.gh hotel.com. 29 units. $325 double; $525 Versailles Suite; $50 extra bed. Rates include breakfast. AE, DC, MC, V. **Amenities:** Restaurant; bar; nightclub; airport transfers (Rs 2,000); free CD and DVD library; concierge; health club privileges; room service. *In room:* A/C, TV/DVD, CD, hair dryer, minibar, Wi-Fi (Rs 140/hr.; Rs 600/day).

Taj President ★★   A far-reaching overhaul of just about the entire hotel has rendered many of the rooms at this fine business hotel among the smartest in the city. Coupled with a range of features designed to make your stay that much more comfortable and ergonomic (from the lobby's island-style check-in desk, to the sleek room layout), it may have been built for corporate types, but the great dining venues, superb Wink bar (see "Mumbai

After Dark," p. 165), and an especially beautiful spa, mean that you can also have fun, relax and really kick back here. Besides which, the redesign of the deluxe premium rooms has rendered them among the most inspired-looking spaces in the city—fabulously cosseting rooms with beautiful parquet floors, textured wallpaper, raw silk blinds, rough granite bathrooms, and clever detailing, complemented by all-modern features, including a fab surround sound system; step into these rooms and you feel like you're in a space that was created especially for you.

90 Cuffe Parade, Mumbai 400 005. ℂ **022/6665-0808.** Fax 022/6665-0365. www.tajhotels.com. president. mumbai@tajhotels.com. 292 units. Rs 16,000 executive double; Rs 18,000 deluxe double; Rs 20,000 deluxe premium; Rs 23,000 executive suite; Rs 27,000 deluxe suite; Rs 30,000 deluxe premium suite. Deluxe rooms and executive suites include breakfast. Rates exclude 10% tax. AE, DC, MC, V. **Amenities:** 3 restaurants including Thai Pavilion (see review, p. 150) and Konkan Café (see review, p. 149); pastry shop; bar; airport transfers (Rs 2,500); babysitting; concierge; health club and spa; large outdoor pool; room service. *In room:* A/C, TV/DVD, fax (on request), hair dryer, minibar, MP3-compatible surround sound system (deluxe premium rooms), Wi-Fi (Rs 150/¹/₂ hr.; Rs 650/day).

Moderate

Ascot Hotel ★★ (Value) Extensive refurbishment has transformed this vintage hotel (on a road lined with decaying vintage facades) into one of Mumbai's best deals. Rooms here are not just comfortable and sleek, but far more spacious than you'll find elsewhere in this part of town—even at twice the price. Styled in neutral shades with lots of blonde wood (bordering on that insipid Scandinavian look), rooms have gleaming marble floors, large comfy beds, and good granite showers; definitely worth the extra $10 are the deluxe units, which are positively huge *and* they have wonderful bay windows from where you get to watch the scene below (although these rooms also get a bit more noise) the higher up you go, the more of the neighborhood you see. Don't get too excited—there's no pool, and the receptionists can be a bit ditsy (or rude, depending on their mood)— but the location and the relative luxury compared to the sucky dregs down the road (we're referring to the Godwin and Garden, chief offenders hereabouts), make this a winner; it's also a better bet than overpriced Gordon House.

38 Garden Rd., Colaba, Mumbai 400 039. ℂ **022/6638-5566.** Fax 022/6638-5555. www.ascothotel.com. 25 units. Rs 6,000 superior double, Rs 6,500 deluxe double; Rs 8,000 suite. Rates include breakfast; 10% tax extra. AE, MC, V. **Amenities:** Restaurant; airport transfers (Rs 900); room service. *In room:* A/C, TV/DVD, fridge, hair dryer, Wi-Fi (free).

Inexpensive

If you can't get a room at Suba Palace (reviewed below), and you really want to be in Colaba, you may want to consider one more incredibly cheap, decent option worth noting is **Bentley's Hotel** (17 Oliver Rd., Colaba; ℂ **022/2284-1474** or -1733; www.bentleys hotel.com; bentleyshotel@hotmail.com), which has old, threadbare accommodations with enough character and antique furniture to make them livable. You can get a room with wooden floors, a balcony, air-conditioning, and an attached bathroom for Rs 2,360; be warned that at least several days' advance reservation might be necessary.

Hotel Suba Palace ★ (Value) What a difference good management can make. Here's an example of a small, excellent value place that's really improved over the years, steadily enhancing the quality of the rooms and the services offered—without disproportionately hiking its prices. Despite being a rather nondescript hotel with a side-street location and total absence of views, it's close to all the Colaba action, and very close to the Gateway of India and Taj Mahal palace hotel. Rooms are neat as a pin, and have undergone a refreshing makeover leaving them looking very smart and businesslike (gleaming floors, thick mattresses, plasma TVs, and a fresh coat of paint), despite being quite compact; they also benefit from double-glazed windows. It may not offer character, but this is a top choice for the astute budget-conscious traveler—there's even free Wi-Fi, and you can hire a laptop if you didn't bring your own. A great little secret.

Near Gateway of India, Apollo Bunder, Mumbai 400 039. © **022/2202-0636** or 022/2288-5444. Fax 022/ 2202-0812. www.hotelsubapalace.com. info@hotelsubapalace.com. 49 units. Rs 3,700 double; Rs 600 extra person. Rates include breakfast; 10% tax and 10% service charge extra. AE, DC, MC, V. **Amenities:** Restaurant; airport transfers (Rs 1,000); room service. *In room:* A/C, TV, hair dryer (on request), minibar (with soft drinks), Wi-Fi (free).

CHURCHGATE

Technically incorporating the southern portion of Marine Drive, Churchgate is a narrow stretch of prime real estate stretching between the vast Oval and Cross maidans (parklands) and Back Bay. Found here are several cricket stadia, including world famous Wankhede, and the southernmost terminal of the Western Railway, Churchgate station.

Moderate

Just a few minutes' drive from both Colaba and Marine Drive is **West End Hotel** ★ Ⓥalue (45 New Marine Lines, next to Bombay Hospital; © **022/2203-9121;** www.westend hotelmumbai.com; Rs 4,300 double), a good midrange option with a retro '70s ambience that's entirely unironic (in fact, the hotel is much older than you'd think). Most of the rooms (which are large and spotlessly clean) have renovated bathrooms, and it's the old-fashioned furniture and decor that makes this such a quaint, charming place to stay. It doesn't hurt, either, that the staff can be so very obliging. If you don't mind the sometimes hectic daytime noise drifting up from bustling New Marine Lines, ask for a room at the front—these have balconies from where you survey the scene before venturing out to explore the city.

Less successful when it comes to service standards and ambience is the neat, clean and highly functional (if soulless) **Astoria Hotel** (4 Jamshedji Tata Rd., Churchgate; © **022/ 6654-1234**), which unfortunately suffers from a misguided superiority complex. Sure, the lobby has the smooth look of a modern business hotel, but the bedrooms don't really evoke the same sense of recent refurbishment. They have everything you need, but are very ordinary and, given their price (Rs 4,000–Rs 6,000 double), look a bit tacked together, with tiny, boxy bathrooms.

Inexpensive

Chateau Windsor Hotel Ⓥalue   With clean, very basic rooms on the first to fifth floors of an apartment block (not always easy to spot—it's next to the disheveled-looking Ambassador hotel), this is one of Mumbai's hidden gems. Sure, it's unspectacular, but it's cheap—perhaps the best option in its price bracket—and well managed. Do specify that you want a superior or deluxe room; these units have small balconies, stone tile floors, and foam mattresses with clean white sheets and towels. The simple, inelegant furnishings include an armless "sofa," a linoleum-topped table, and a small, narrow cupboard (What more do you need? Now go out and explore!). Although there is no restaurant, you can sit in the terrace garden and nosh, or get room service (light snacks only); you'll have few reasons to do this, however, given the neighborhood's selection of excellent restaurants. Morning tea is on the house, and the kitchen is available for you to do your own cooking—as long as it's vegetarian.

86 Veer Nariman Rd., Churchgate, Mumbai 400 020. ℂ **022/2204-4455.** Fax 022/2202-6459. www. chateauwindsor.com. info@cwh.in. 60 units. Rs 2,400 standard double with shared bathroom; Rs 3,000 medium standard double; Rs 3,900 superior double; Rs 4,500 deluxe double; Rs 400 extra person. Children under 12 free. Rates exclude 10% tax. AE, MC, V. **Amenities:** Airport transfers (Rs 1,100); room service. *In room:* A/C and fan, TV, fridge (in deluxe and superior rooms), Wi-Fi (Rs 100/hr.; Rs 500/day).

CENTRAL MUMBAI: WORLI, BANDRA & JUHU

Mumbai's upscale seaside suburbs don't have a tourist center, but they are studded with new restaurants, bars, endless shopping, and a vibrant nightlife, sans Colaba's seedy edge. Worli is just a short drive from Colaba and Nariman Point and features some of the less-touted attractions, including Mahalaxmi Racecourse, the Nehru Centre (with the city's planetarium), Worli fishing village, the dhobi ghat, and a long stretch of seafront, known as the Worli Sea Face. Worli is now connected to Bandra by a 4½km (2¾-mile) *setu* (sea bridge) that will hopefully cut down commuting time considerably as soon as people know how to use it efficiently. The sea link means that the heavily touristed downtown area is now much closer to both vibrant Bandra and the adjacent "beach holiday" suburb of Juhu; the latter attracts a predominantly local, moneyed crowd, and as such affords in many ways a genuine introduction to Mumbai as a leisure destination rather than an overblown business capital. Juhu's relative proximity to the airport (it's a 30-min. drive) makes it the ideal stopover if you have no strong desire to engage with the historical side of the city, or if you need to recover from jet lag before moving on. Most of Bollywood's film stars live and hang out in this part of Mumbai, so it's definitely where you should stay if you have an interest in bumping into them (and it really does happen) or simply want to spend time in trendy bars and restaurants. The best accommodations—the slick and vibey **Four Seasons** in Worli, the superbly-positioned **Taj Lands End** in Bandra, and to a lesser extent, the **JW Marriott** in Juhu—are reviewed below, along with a handful of more affordable options, all in Juhu.

Very Expensive

Four Seasons Hotel Mumbai ★★★   It starts with the city's slickest airport pickup—a silky smooth BMW ride (wildly pricey, but worthwhile) that takes you across the brand new Bandra-Worli Sea Link—and is sustained by seamless service and crisp attention to detail that perfectly bridges the gap between business and leisure. With its manageable room count, snappy staff (all with model good looks and big, friendly smiles), and just the right amount of intimacy and warmth, this strikes us as the best of Mumbai's upmarket hotels. And while the architecture (contemporary, slim, and heavenward-thrusting) hints at bland modernism, there's much to elevate your stay above the ordinary—whether it's the bird's-eye views from the pool deck, planning an offbeat itinerary with the excellent concierge team, or the impeccable rooms. You'll sleep on the fattest mattresses in town, next to the bed are copies of *Maximum City* and *Shantaram* (the author of which is a regular guest), and huge windows frame the city (ask for a room on the top floor). An apprenticeship program for disadvantaged young people suggests a willingness to give back and the hotel is involved in other community outreach programs, too. Simply put: This is our favorite.

114 Dr. E. Moses Rd., Worli, Mumbai 400 018. ℂ **022/2481-8000.** Fax 022/2481-8001. www.fourseasons.com/ mumbai. 202 units. Rs 17,650 superior double, Rs 19,650 deluxe double, Rs 21,650 deluxe sea view double, Rs 24,650 premiere double; Rs 30,000–Rs 201,700 suite. **Amenities:** 3 restaurants, including San Qi (see review on p. 157), and 1 rooftop restaurant that will be up and running by 2010), bar; airport transfers (Rs 3,000 in a BMW); ATM; babysitting; concierge; cultural talks and workshops; DVD library; health club and spa with Indian and Western treatments, and yoga, meditation, and aerobic studios; members'

> **(Fun Facts) Business As Usual in the Eye of the Bureaucratic Storm**
>
> Nobody said doing business in Mumbai was easy, and *starting* a business can be a nightmarish process of endlessly cutting red tape. Before opening, the new Four Seasons Hotel, over and above the usual paperwork rigmarole was forced to procure an epic 165 government permits, including (can you believe it?) a special license for the vegetable weighing scale in the kitchen, as well as one for each of the bathroom scales in the guest rooms. Fortunately big money goes a long way towards speeding up any process where politicians and government officials are involved, but we can fully appreciate just why so much of Mumbai's business happens underground. Mercifully, at least for guests at the Four Seasons, not only do the bathroom scales work (we even used them to check our luggage weight before an international flight!), but as a tax incentive, newly constructed hotels are exempt from charging room tax for the first 15 years of operation. Yet another good reason to stay in rapidly growing Worli.

club with exclusive meeting rooms, lounges, and library; large outdoor rooftop pool; room service; yoga. *In room:* A/C, TV/DVD, hair dryer, minibar, MP3-docking station/radio, Wi-Fi (Rs 980 per day).

JW Marriott Hotel ★   The opulent JW remains Juhu's most luxurious hotel, and continues to be a favored hangout for Bollywood stars, members of Mumbai's distinguished air-kissing crowd, and, of course, the voyeurs who come to witness this ongoing soap opera. Although you may get a good view of the beach, the hotel itself is disconnected from the shore (literally, due to security reasons) and the aim seems to be on focusing your attention inwards, towards the many dining and recreational facilities located within what is ultimately a vast hangout for wealthy locals who use this as their lounge (and also their nightclub; see "Mumbai After Dark," p. 165). Certainly, it's not a place where you'll feel as if you're coming home when you walk through the front door. Set over five floors, the guest rooms are comfortable, with modern, albeit rather predictable, decor and amenities; each has some kind of sea view, though most are side views. Things would be a whole lot better if the staff were more welcoming, or at least bothered to change the repetitive, hypnotically dull lobby soundtrack.

Juhu Tara Rd., Juhu Beach, Mumbai 400 099. (℃) **022/6693-3000.** Fax 022/6693-3100. 355 units. The hotel operates a "Rate of the Day" policy, so the following ranges are indicative: Rs 16,500–Rs 23,500 deluxe double; Rs 16,500–Rs 25,000 executive ocean double; Rs 18,000–Rs 30,000 executive premium double; Rs 24,000–Rs 90,000 suites. Executive room and suite rates include breakfast, transfers, and executive lounge access. AE, DC, MC, V. **Amenities:** 4 restaurants, cafe, bar, nightclub; free airport transfers (for executive rooms and suites); babysitting; concierge; executive level floors; heath club and spa; outdoor pool and children's pool; room service. *In room:* A/C, TV, hair dryer, Internet (Rs 500/hr.; Rs 1,000/day), minibar.

Taj Lands End ★★★   When it comes to location, the name says it all—far away from predictably tourist-centered Colaba, this hotel enjoys a lovely seaside setting at the southern tip of one of Mumbai's hippest suburbs where some of Bollywood's biggest names reside and thousands of cool young things come out to play on weekends and after dark. Each and every guest room (all handsomely renovated and supplied with such useful amenities as mobile phones, with air time) affords views of the Arabian Sea through a haze of palm trees—choose one facing the new Bandra-Worli sea link bridge. If you don't mind the extra expense, opt for one on the smart new upper-level Club floor rooms, definitely the best in the house, with extra-swish services. While the vast lobby is often buzzing with business deals going down, a short uphill walk takes you to one of the city's three "miracle hotspots"—Mount Mary church, especially enchanting after dark.

Land's End, Bandstand, Bandra (West), Mumbai 400 050. ✆ **022/6668-1234.** Fax 022/6699-4488. www. tajhotels.com. landsend.mumbai@tajhotels.com. 493 units. Rs 22,500 deluxe sea view double; Rs 24,500 luxury sea view double; Rs 26,500 Taj Club; Rs 50,000 executive suite; Rs 75,000 luxury suite; Rs 135,000 grand luxury suite; Rs 250,000 presidential suite. Club rates include breakfast, cocktail hour, high tea, and one-way airport transfer. Daily discounts available. AE, DC, MC, V. **Amenities:** 4 restaurants, lounge bar, pool bar; airport transfers (Rs 1,000); Club floors with butler service, private lounge, and express check-in and -out; concierge; health club and spa; outdoor pool and children's pool; room service. *In room:* A/C, TV, hair dryer, minibar, Wi-Fi (Rs 300/hr.; Rs 600/day).

Moderate

For more midrange options, try the newly expanded **Hotel Sea Princess** (Juhu Tara Rd.; ✆ **022/2661-1111** or 020/2646-9500; www.seaprincess.com), where you should request a sea-facing deluxe luxury room (book online for the best rates); they've been recently overhauled, but the views through the bay windows (although you may need to first move the armchairs out the way) are still the prime attraction. Also recommended (and on Juhu beach) is **Citizen Hotel** (✆ **022/6693-2525;** www.citizenhotelmumbai. com), which has small rooms (with tiled floors and fresh, if over-the-top, decor) and closet-size bathrooms, but the deluxe sea-facing units (Rs 8,500 double) have great views from large windows overlooking the Arabian Sea.

Juhu Residency Boutique Hotel ★ (Value) From the outside it looks a bit like a sealed-off bunker (dark glass prevents you from seeing in), but once inside you discover a sweet little hotel (with a faintly Egyptian theme), welcoming staff, and very slick rooms (with a great big bed, pair of armchairs, plasma TV, and a modern look with local accents). All that's lacking (besides a pool) is the possibility of sea views—it's set 1 block back from the beach—which may defeat the very purpose of staying in Juhu. Still, you can enjoy the breeze while chilling at the rooftop bar and restaurant, from where you look out over a fascinating urban jungle, studded with huge palm trees and alive with horn-honking motorists. Things here are relaxed, and the comfortable rooms come with such thoughtful touches as having a copy of the latest *Time Out Mumbai* next to your bed.

148B Juhu Tara Rd., Juhu, Mumbai 400049. ✆ **022/6783-4949.** Fax 022/6783-4950. www.juhuresidency. com. reservations@juhuresidency.com. 18 units, all with shower only. Rs 5,000 executive double; Rs 7,500 premium double. Rs 1,200 extra bed. Rates include breakfast. AE, DC, MC, V. **Amenities:** 2 restaurant; 2 bars; free airport transfers; room service. *In room:* A/C, TV, hair dryer, minibar (in premium rooms), Wi-Fi (free).

Novotel Juhu Beach Mumbai ★★ (Value) At press time this was arguably the best-value hotel in Mumbai, but you'll need to act quick, because the good rates are part of the introductory offer following its July 2009 launch. The decaying former Holiday Inn has been transformed beyond recognition into a bright, modern leisure complex with direct beach access—greatly enhanced by the resort-style arrangement of pool, terrace loungers, restaurants, and one swinging bar (with live jazz and substantially lower mark-ups on drinks than other hotels)—that makes it feel a lot more like a vacation spot than the snobbish Marriott, and with far superior service to the annoying Sun-n-Sand. Rooms are plush, with carpets and a sleek modern look that's nevertheless restrained (with a single piece of art), so you're not going to end up wasting too much time in here; they

also all have some kind of sea view (you'll need to choose an "Ocean Room"—currently at no extra cost—or a suite for a direct sea view). Breakfast is a great buffet spread that includes Maharashtrian sparkling wine.

Balraj Sahani Marg, Juhu Beach, Mumbai 400 049. ✆ **022/6693-4444.** Fax 022/66934455. www.novotel. com. h6926-re@accor.com. 203 units, all with shower only. Rs 7,500 standard double; Rs 8,500 premium double; Rs 18,000–Rs 25,000 suite. Rates include breakfast and airport transfers; 10% tax extra. AE, DC MC, V. **Amenities:** 4 restaurants, lounge, bar; free airport transfers; children's play area; concierge; health club and spa; large outdoor pool; room service. *In room:* A/C, TV with media hub, hair dryer, minibar, MP3-docking station (in premium rooms), Wi-Fi (free in premium rooms; otherwise Rs 400/hr.).

Inexpensive

Without suggesting a major lifestyle change, an excellent choice for bargain-hunters is Juhu's **ISKCON Ashram** (Hare Krishna Land, Juhu; ✆ **022/2620-6860;** www.iskcon mumbai.com; guesthouse.mumbai@pamho.net), which has simple, clean rooms in the guesthouse attached to the very popular Hare Krishna temple. It's definitely the cheap (Rs 2,995 for an air-conditioned double, including tax) and cheerful (rooms are spacious, clean, and have balconies) nonhotel alternative for visitors open to a bit of a cultural experience (although you won't be asked to join the Krisna Consciousness movement, you can watch the crowds thronging to the temple), and you have the added incentive of laying claim to the fabulous vegetarian meals served at the adjoining restaurant, Govinda's (see review on p. 158).

NEAR THE AIRPORTS

The reasons for staying here are obvious, but it seems a pity to hole up in these cocoons when The Taj Mahal Palace, Four Seasons, and Oberoi beckon from the south.

Expensive

The Gordon House Suites ★★   This quirky (and in many respects, gimmicky and kitsch) hotel near the international airport will come as a shock to anyone expecting straight-laced business-geared luxury. Here, the designer was clearly given free reign to play and experiment; so, like the original Gordon House in Colaba, rooms are themed and there's substantial drama in just about every choice of color, texture, furniture and fitting—they're far and away the most fun rooms in Mumbai. The most exciting units are probably the red "Fire" rooms, which evoke warmth and passion, the ice-cool "Glacier" rooms, and the "Marine" rooms with their aquamarine ceilings and white marble floors—other units suffer from baroque overkill. Apart from the loud colors in some units, rooms are quiet, and very comfortable, with fat mattresses and gorgeous white linens; we love the glass-wall showers, too. Although at press time there are still encroaching slums (which apparently are being cleared to make way for more high-rise luxury), the hotel itself features landscaped gardens with fountains, waterfalls and pools. At least you won't be bored while you recover from your flight.

Off International Airport Approach Rd., Marol, Andheri (E), Mumbai 400 059. ✆ **022/4090-6633.** Fax 022/4090-6632. www.ghhotel.com. 102 units. Rs 18,000 double; Rs 29,000 suite; Rs 1,500 extra person. Rates include breakfast; 10% tax extra. AE, DC, MC, V. **Amenities:** 3 restaurants, lounge, bar; free airport transfers; concierge; country club and spa with gym, outdoor Jacuzzi, Olympic-size pool, sauna, and tennis courts (club access Rs 2,000 per room); DVD library; room service. *In room:* A/C, TV/DVD, hair dryer, heated towel rack, minibar, Wi-Fi (Rs 150/hr.; Rs 600/day).

Grand Hyatt Mumbai ★★★ ⓥalue   This happens to be one of Mumbai's vibiest accommodation choices, practically always abuzz with a diverse crowd. Somehow, though, the enormously scaled interiors mean that you never feel overwhelmed by guest numbers, and the high staff-to-guest ratio means that there's just about always someone taking care of you. We especially appreciate the smiling faces in the fabulous Celini restaurant where breakfast is served. Guestrooms are smart, sleek, utterly comfortable, and the entire hotel is done out like a Modern art gallery—plenty of quirky and appealing pieces by contemporary Indian artists, and staff even conduct tours of the exhibition. Finally, because it's so close to the city's main arterial highway, access to the city (or the suburbs) is not nearly as cumbersome as it is if you're based right at the international airport; when first built a few years back, it was thought that the hotel stood in the middle of nowhere—now the area is transforming into an important, planned business hub, with this very grand hotel at its heart.

Off Western Express Hwy., Santa Cruz (East), Mumbai 400 055. © **022/6676-1234.** Fax 022/6676-1235. www.mumbai.grand.hyatt.com. Rs 14,000 Grand double; Rs 15,500 Club double; Rs 18,500–Rs 80,000 suite. Rates include breakfast; no extra taxes. **Amenities:** 4 restaurants, bar, poolside bar (seasonal), gourmet store, lounge; airport transfers (Rs 1,200–Rs 1,500); art tours (of in-house collection and changing exhibitions); ATM; concierge; executive level floors with butler service; health club and spa with jogging track, 2 pools, basketball, beach volleyball, yoga, tennis court, whirlpool bath, and saunas; room service; spa. *In room:* A/C, TV, hair dryer, Internet (broadband; Rs 500/hr.; Rs 1,100/day), minibar.

Hyatt Regency ★★★ (**Value** As is the case with most any airport hotel, the only reason to book here is as a transit passenger, and as such the Hyatt comes up trumps. You will be picked up from the airport, and swept away for the 5-minute drive to the hotel. You arrive to a huge space almost always abuzz with arriving and departing travelers, including scores of airline staff. The sleek (and most important, silent) guest rooms deliver every comfort, with a judicious use of space, imaginative lighting, and smart fittings. One entire wall is a mirror, floors are Malaysian teakwood, desks are swivel-top slabs of glass, and the televisions are flatscreen. White-marble bathrooms offer a choice between large rain showers or separate step-down bathtubs—a welcome treat after a long plane journey. The **Club Prana spa** is a popular pre- and postflight venue.

Sahar Airport Rd., Mumbai 400 099. © **022/5696-1234.** Fax 022/5696-1235. www.hyatt.com. 401 units. The hotel operates a rate of the day pricing policy; the following are indicative: Rs 7,500 Hyatt room double; Rs 10,500 Regency Club double; Rs 14,500 junior suite; Rs 17,500. Regency Club and suite rates include breakfast, airport transfers, and Internet access. AE, DC, MC, V. **Amenities:** 3 restaurants, lounge, pastry shop, bar and wine cellar; airport transfers (free for Regency Club rooms and suites, otherwise Rs 1,000); health club and spa; large outdoor pool; room service; squash courts; lighted tennis courts. *In room:* A/C, TV, hair dryer, minibar, Wi-Fi (free for Regency Club rooms and suites, otherwise Rs 550/2 hr.; Rs 1,100/day).

The Leela Kempinski ★ After driving up a long, tree-lined driveway, you enter a vast incense-filled marble lobby—there's flowing water, stone-carved dancing goddesses, and live musicians whipping up tunes on tabla and sitar. Despite being a very serious-minded business hotel (and a little old-fashioned), you'll be very well looked after here, and take comfort in knowing it's one of the most environmentally conscious places to stay. It's also where the Dalai Lama stays when he's in town. Built on reclaimed swampland, The Leela now brims with tropical greenery and the lushest gardens in town. Competition from newer, more innovative hotels has prompted an upgrade of all facilities, including the plush modern rooms—although we still think the large amoeboid pool, set next to cascading fountains and lotus ponds, is the best place to be (you'll hardly believe you're just 5 minutes from the airport in one of the world's largest cities). To take full advantage, reserve a Royal Club room, which comes with excellent perks (and rooms offering the slickest, most cosseting luxury).

Sahar, Mumbai 400 059. ⓒ **022/6691-1234.** Fax 022/6691-1212. www.theleela.com. 390 units. Rs 18,000–Rs 19,000 premier double; Rs 22,500 Royal Club double; Rs 26,000 Royal Club parlor; Rs 26,000–Rs 150,000 suite. Royal club rates include breakfast; rates exclude 10% tax. AE, DC, MC, V. **Amenities:** 4 restaurants, bar; airport transfers (free for Royal Club guests; Rs 800 international, Rs 1,200 domestic); health club and spa; pool; room service; Wi-Fi (Rs 562/hr.; Rs 899/day). *In room* A/C, TV, hair dryer, Jacuzzi (in suite), minibar,f Wi-Fi (free in suites; Rs 562/hr.; Rs 899/day).

Moderate

The best value in the vicinity of the airports is offered by the slick, no-nonsense **Hotel Suba Galaxy** ★ (N.S. Phadke Rd., off Western Express Highway, Andheri [E], Mumbai 400 069; ⓒ **022/2682-1188;** www.hotelsubagalaxy.com; Rs 5,500 double including tax and breakfast), which offers a trouble-free stay in well-maintained rooms at a much better rate than you'll find at the large luxury places (although if you score a very good deal at either of the Hyatts, definitely stay there). Rooms are modern and stripped back, but have everything you'll need for a comfortable overnight stay—you'll need to ask if you want a large bed, though, as most rooms are singles and twins.

Note: If you only need a room for daytime use between flights, this hotel also has a special "Day" rate of Rs 3,500 for rooms used between 9am and 6pm only.

5 WHERE TO DINE

Nowhere in India is dining more rewarding than in Mumbai. The city literally holds thousands of restaurants, and being a city of migrants, every kind of Indian cuisine is represented—though Konkan, or coastal food, is considered the local specialty. You can mingle with the city's crème de la crème at fine-dining or hip venues, or choose from a vast array of inexpensive eating places. And while traditional restaurant-type experiences are varied and plentiful, we urge you to get down with the locals from time to time and sample traditional street food—like *vada pav* and *pani puri*—from one or two of the recommended outlets (see "The Skinny on Street Food" box, p. 152); we can't guarantee hygiene at places we don't mention, but your concierge should be able to tell you where you can try delicious local specialties without doing yourself an injury. Also on your must-do list should be a visit to an Udipi (or south Indian fast food) restaurant, and a meal at one of Mumbai's classic Irani restaurants serving fresh inexpensive breads and *chai*. Not surprisingly, vegetarians are particularly well catered to in just about all Mumbai restaurants. *Note:* Bear in mind that Mumbaikars usually venture out to eat late, around 9pm, so if you're intent on eating at a popular fine-dining restaurant and don't have a reservation, you may be able to score a table if you show up by 7:30pm.

SOUTH MUMBAI: COLABA, FORT, CHURCHGATE & MARINE DRIVE

Very Expensive

If you really want to dine among the crème de la crème and don't mind shelling out top dollar for the experience, then by all means book a night at **The Zodiac Grill** ★★★, one of the fine dining establishments at the Taj Mahal Palace & Tower. The quality of the French cuisine—served in an atmosphere of restrained opulence—has made it a legend among the city's well heeled, many of whom no doubt come here to be completely cushioned from mainstream society. Main courses start at Rs 1,950, and a degustation menu runs Rs 5,500 to Rs 6,500

Old School Seafood Thrillers

Anyone with a penchant for seafood will love dining in Mumbai—whether it's Coastal, Konkani, Mangalorean, or Malvani cuisine, you are in for a treat. Besides **Mahesh Lunch Home** (p. 154), **Konkan Café** (p. 149), and **Trishna** (p. 151), there are plenty of old-fashioned places where you can find truly excellent fish and seafood, usually without denting your wallet much at all. Two hugely popular local favorites are right near the tourist hubs of South Mumbai: Do make an effort to check out **Apoorva** ★ (Vasta House, S.A. Brelvi Marg, near Horniman Circle, Fort; ✆ 022/2287-0335 or 022/2288-1457; daily 11:30am–4pm and 6pm–midnight), which has not only wonderfully authentic Manglorean fare (including delicious prawn *koliwada*), but a massive range of crabs, oysters, lobster, pomfret, and other thrillingly fishy fare, some of which is especially tempered for foreign tastes (read: nonspicy). In a similar league is **Excellensea** ★ (Bharat House, 317 Shahid Bhagat Singh Rd.; ✆ 022/2261-8991) where the obvious choice is prawn *qassi*, rich with sauce that demands mopping up with some fresh Indian breads (like *idlis*, *appams*, and *neer dosas*). Note that if you are in any of these Konkan restaurants, you may want to try the *sol kadi*, a slightly pungent coconut milk drink—it takes some getting used to, but is a great appetizer. Farther north, in Bandra, you'll get real value for money and atmosphere at the friendly **Soul Fry** ★ (Pali Mala Rd, across from Pali Market; ✆ 022/2604-6892), serving home-style Goan dishes. Try the flaky stuffed grilled *rawas* (a local fish). Monday is karaoke night, and even if you can't sing to save your life, it's a great experience to watch extremely talented locals unabashedly take the mic and have the whole place rocking well past midnight. If you'd rather not head all the way to the suburbs, there's a newer branch, called **Soul Fry Casa** ★★ (Currimjee Bldg., MG Rd.; ✆ 022/2267-1421; daily 7pm–midnight), opposite Mumbai University in Fort and promises the best of the original Soul Fry (and often even better food), plus lots of live music and action around the bar to accompany the delicious seafood.

Indigo ★★★ FUSION/INTERNATIONAL Restaurateur-chef Rahul Akerkar has created a restaurant that tops every food critic's A-list and is widely heralded as one of the world's best. Angelina Jolie and Brad Pitt, Liz Hurley, the Clintons, and every other international celebrity passing through Mumbai seems to stop here. Indigo's chic ambience is enhanced by the clientele: By 9:30pm the entire bar section is heaving with the city's Beautiful People. Most important, though: Local devotees rave about the food. The excellent risotto with black olive tapenade is one constant on a menu that changes once a year—make it your first choice, but don't be afraid to sample many more of the outstanding dishes. Their tuna loin (spiced with fenugreek and a Shiraz and clove reduction) is scrumptious, and vegetarians will be blown away by the many choices for them. End with the chocolate fondant with jalapeño peppers or, if available, the dreamy lemon soufflé. Indigo's Sunday brunch with accompanying jazz band and free-flowing Indian liquor is legendary; if you'd like to stuff yourself silly while rubbing shoulders with Mumbai socialites, book in advance.

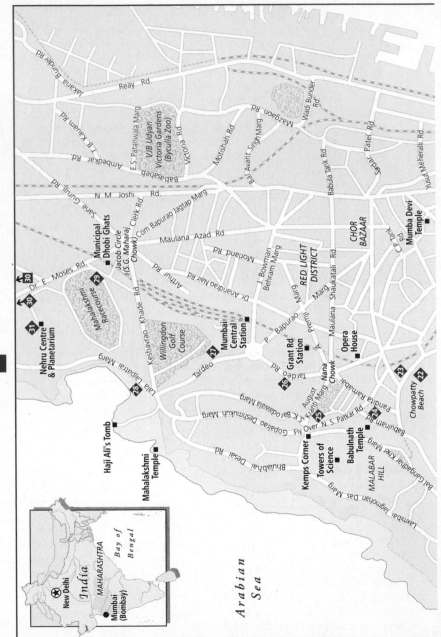

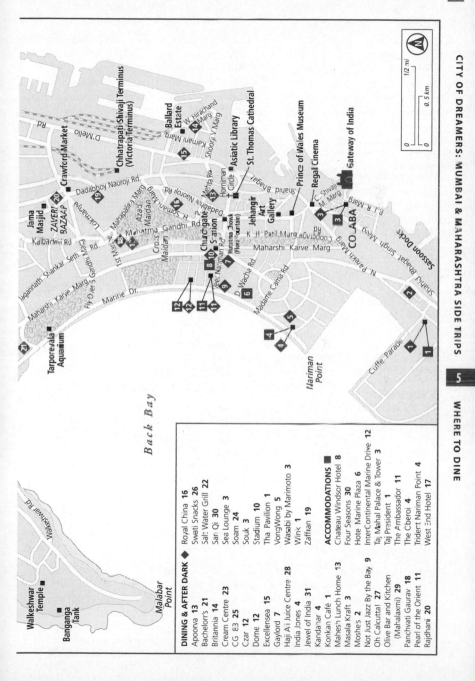

0   1/2 mi
0   0.5 km

DINING & AFTER DARK ◆
Apoorva **13**
Bachelor's **21**
Britannia **14**
Cream Centre **23**
CG 83 **25**
Czar **12**
Dome **12**
Excellensea **15**
Gaylord **7**
Haji Ali Juice Centre **28**
India Jones **4**
Jewel of India **31**
Kandahar **4**
Konkan Café **1**
Mahesh Lunch Home **13**
Masala Kraft **3**
Moshe's **2**
Not Just Jazz By the Bay **9**
Oh Calcutta! **27**
Olive Bar and Kitchen
  (Mahalaxmi) **29**
Panchvati Gaurav **18**
Pearl of the Orient **11**
Rajdhani **20**
Royal China **16**
Swati Snacks **26**
Salt Water Grill **22**
San Qi **30**
Sea Lounge **3**
Soam **24**
Souk **3**
Stadium **10**
Tha Pavilion **1**
VongWong **5**
Wasabi by Marimoto **3**
Winx **1**
Zaffran **19**

ACCOMMODATIONS ■
Chateau Windsor Hotel **8**
Four Seasons **30**
Hotel Marine Plaza **6**
InterContinental Marine Drive **12**
Taj Mahal Palace & Tower **3**
Taj President **1**
The Ambassador **11**
The Oberoi **4**
Tridert Nariman Point **4**
West End Hotel **17**

4 Mandlik House, Colaba. ℂ **022/6636-8999** or -8980. www.foodindigo.com. Reservations essential. Main courses Rs 485–Rs 1,850; Sun brunch Rs 1,744. AE, DC, MC, V. Daily noon–2:45pm and 7:30–11:45pm.

Kandahar ★★ NORTHWEST FRONTIER This has long been one of our favorite Mumbai dining establishments and a great place to sample the traditionally rich cuisine of the Northwest Frontier as well as enjoying some lighter, home-style dishes. At the time of writing, however, Kandahar remains closed while The Oberoi hotel undergoes extensive renovations and refurbishment following the tragic events that transpired in Mumbai in late 2008. When the hotel emerges from its slumber (definitely by 2010), expect Kandahar to once again be at the top of its game.

The Oberoi, Marine Dr., Nariman Point. ℂ **022/6632-5757.** Reservations essential. Average meal Rs 1,500. AE, DC, MC, V. Daily 12:30–2:45pm and 7:30–11:30pm.

Wasabi by Morimoto ★★★ JAPANESE Rated as one of the world's top 100 eateries, this is by far Mumbai's top Japanese restaurant—hallowed ground for anyone who worships at the alter of celebrity chef Masaharu Morimoto, aka "Iron Chef." Seafood is flown in from around the world for the extensive sushi and sashimi menu (which features sea urchin, flying fish roe, sweet shrimp, jackfish, and fatty tunny—stay away if you're concerned about the carbon footprint), and there's an extensive vegetarian selection (try the crispy "Oroshi Ankake" tofu, or Kinoko mushroom curry), not usually available in Japanese restaurants. For a bit of drama at the table, order the *ishi yaki "buri bop"*—a yellowtail dish prepared on a hot stone right in front of you. Also interesting are the miso marinated black cod, and the Chilean sea bass in black bean sauce, ginger and shaved scallion. Don't leave before trying the wasabi crème brûlée, and when you come back, try the tofu cheesecake.

Taj Mahal Palace & Tower, Apollo Blunder, Colaba. ℂ **022/6665-3366.** Reservations essential for dinner. Sushi/sashimi Rs 325–Rs 500 per piece, Rs 2,050–Rs 3,945 assorted; sushi rolls Rs 500–Rs 750; main courses Rs 825–Rs 1,575; teppanyaki Rs 875–Rs 1,550. AE, DC, MC, V. Daily 12:30–2:45pm and 7–11:45pm.

Expensive

CG 83 ★★ CHINESE This upmarket Oriental restaurant is highly regarded among the city's elite—well-attired diners blend in perfectly with the slick and sumptuous decor. Despite its considerable good looks, though, this reinvention of the erstwhile China Garden is actually best appreciated for the quality of its creative cuisine. The menu here is dreamt up by Nelson Wang, the food hero who invented India's nationally famous Manchurian chicken, and he continues to experiment by adapting Chinese dishes through subtle variations influenced by different parts of the Orient. There's nothing on the menu that isn't exceptional, but the prawns—either wrapped in bacon, or marinated with chilies and pepper—are a real highlight.

Om Chambers, 123 A.K. Marg, Kemps Corner. ℂ **020/2363-0842.** Main courses Rs 280–Rs 390. AE, MC, V. Daily 12:30–3pm and 7–11:30pm.

India Jones ★★★ PAN-ASIAN The menu is a treasure trove of exciting Asian dishes. If you'd rather not spend time wading through the menu, settle on the humungous two-person Grand Platter, which will take you on a veritable culinary odyssey, starting with soups and appetizers and culminating in a platter of green chicken curry, wok-fried prawns, stir-fried sea bass with celery, barbecued pork with honey, wok-fried mixed vegetables in black-peppercorn sauce—and the list goes on. For the not-so-ravenous, there's plenty to choose from: superb silken tofu, wok platters, live seafood (try the grouper, filleted and steamed with Vietnamese mint), and a separate *teppanyaki* counter (extremely popular, so book your seat). Wait staff are also adept at making spot-on recommendations, so no need to panic about the voluminous menu. Finally, it's a big tossup between India Jones's legendary *tab tim krob* (jellied water chestnut and sago in chilled coconut milk) and the sublime green tea and wasabi ripple ice cream. Our only complaint? The cheap wooden chopsticks.

Trident Nariman Point, Nariman Point. ℰ **022/6632-4343.** Main courses Rs 450–Rs 1,500, Grand Platter Rs 1,750 per person; unlimited dim sum lunch Rs 1,250. AE, DC, MC, V. Daily 12:30–2:45pm and 7:30–11:45pm.

Joss ★★ PAN-ASIAN   Since opening in 2004, this has grown into one of Mumbai's best places for modern Asian cuisine. Chef Farrokh Khambata has carved quite a name for himself catering to the city's discerning foodies; he specializes in Japanese, Malaysian, Balinese, Chinese, and Indonesian fare, tending to invigorate known favorites with a bit of personal flair. Above all else, it's what he does with fish that impresses—his Japanese sea bass with shoyu and ginger is superb, as is the miso-encrusted Chilean sea bass. But then how about Mekong whisky flambéed prawns, crab cappuccino soup, or the Oriental crab bisque? He also makes silken tofu steaks that virtually melt on the tongue, and there's an excellent Balinese curry cooked in the clay pot. Khambata's sushi has quite a following, and there are Japanese set menus for those of us who can't make up our minds. Expect exquisite desserts, too, like the hot Kahlúa soufflé and chocolate cigars with prune and Armagnac ice cream. This is one chef who loves to give diners something to talk about.

K. Dubash Marg, Kala Ghoda. ℰ **022/6635-6908.** www.jossrestaurant.com. Main courses Rs 340–Rs 1,000. Japanese set menu Rs 1,100–Rs 1,800. AE, MC, V. Daily 12:30–3:30pm and 7:30–11:30pm.

Khyber ★★ NORTH INDIAN   Khyber has been going strong for decades now, and its classic Mughlai cuisine and tender kebabs remain outstanding, although not quite up to earlier standards. Start with *kali mirch rawas* (fish seasoned in black pepper), firm yet meltingly good; or chicken *badami* (in rich almond sauce) and *paneer shashlik* (grilled Indian cottage cheese, spices, and vegetables). Follow these with Khyber *raan* (lamb) or mutton *chaap* Mughlai and piping-hot *naan* bread. To cleanse the palate (Mughlai cuisine is very rich), order the fresh seasonal fruit or the *ras malai*. Besides the great food, Khyber is an experience in royal dining: The opulent decor includes original paintings by some of India's most famous artists (the likes of M. F. Hussain and Anjolie Ela Menon). Not much changes at this Mumbai institution, and service is sometimes slow.

145 MG Rd., Kala Ghoda. ℰ **022/2267-3227** through -3229. Reservations required but are only guaranteed for seating before 8:30pm or after 10:15pm. Main courses Rs 250–Rs 695; average meal Rs 1,350. AE, DC, MC, V. Daily 12:30–3:30pm and 7:30–11:30pm.

Konkan Café ★★ COASTAL   After walking through the vast marble lobby of the refurbished Taj President, stepping inside this recreated Mangalorean village comes as a bit of a surprise—the mood is laid back and summery, although not quite beach shack. It's here that Chef Ananda Solomon has earned his reputation (and quite a following) for his heavenly dishes from up and down the Konkan coast. It's a region that stretches from Karnataka, through Goa, and right up to Maharashtra, which means there's quite a variety and a range of tastes, tied together by Solomon's love of pounding his masalas by hand and then biding his time to ensure he gets just the right tastes. Although the menu is constantly reinvented, look for specialties like the *meen pollichathu, rawas* cooked in a spicy tomato-onion sauce and baked in a banana leaf; and the heavenly *sukha* mutton. You can also sample specialties like *kori kachpu,* a yellow chicken curry, or fish *moilee,* pomfret rubbed with turmeric and lime and cooked in fragrant coconut milk. If you're left with any doubts, get the consistently good seafood *thali*. And, of course, no coastal meal would seem right without a quick nip of *feni*, the prodigiously famous Goan liquor distilled from coconuts or cashews.

Taj President Hotel, 90 Cuffe Parade ℭ **022/6665-0808.** Main courses Rs 395–Rs 695. AE, DC, MC, V. Daily 12:30–2:45pm and 7–11:45pm.

Masala Kraft ★★★ CONTEMPORARY INDIAN   Now famous as *the* place Hillary Clinton chose to dine when she visited Mumbai mid-2009, this is one of the city's finest dining experiences, made memorable by the many unique and special dishes. Uncomplicated decor helps focus your attention on the task at hand—to choose from a tantalizing selection of dishes that take the best of Indian cuisine and bring them up to date for a more international palate. To savor a range of tastes, ask for a Mumbai lunch featuring various local specialties, served in stacked metal lunchbox containers—you'll get an assortment of tastes and flavors (prawns, chicken curry, Malwani fish curry and minced lamb *keema*, all with rice and *roti*) that echo a typical home-style meal (a vegetarian version is also available). If you'd prefer to choose from the a la carte menu, you'd best ask your waiter for assistance: the *galouti kebab* (minced lamb) is divine; so too the water chestnut and pea curry; *sarson ke phool* (broccoli florets in mustard and pickled spices); newspaper fish *(paper walli machi);* and an absolutely perfect dal makhani (black gram and red kidney beans simmered overnight and finished off with butter and homemade cream). Finish off with a masala chai *kulfi,* and then ask for some *paan.*

Taj Mahal Palace & Tower, Apollo Blunder, Colaba. ℭ **022/6665-3366.** Reservations essential for dinner. 5-course meal Rs 1,550–Rs 2,100. AE, DC, MC, V. Daily 12:30–2:45pm and 7–11:45pm.

Souk ★★ MEDITERRANEAN/MIDDLE EASTERN   Plenty of light, flavorful dishes accompany the full-on, close-up views of the Gateway of India. At lunch, be sure to reserve a table at the window, and prepare for a long, languid experience in the company of society women trading gossip. At night, the venue is predictably romantic. The menu carefully showcases an array of flavors, from traditional Lebanese *sharvarma,* Turkish *kebab istanbuli,* and Athenian-style grilled lamb chops, to Casablancan lamb shank *(lahm barkook),* Moroccan prawns *chermoula,* and Greek chicken stew *(dijaj stifatho).* Kick off with a selection of hot and cold mezzes: Syrian *kibbe, cigara boregi* from Damascus, Egyptian *fattir,* and *sambusek* from Beirut—the combinations are endless. There's also a popular mezze buffet offering the usual suspects (hummus, salads, baba ghanouj, tabbouleh, falafel, and assorted olives), together with meat- or seafood-based salads and delicious, hot pita bread. And between morsels, you can sit back and take in the views, and contemplate the mains. We'd opt for a tagine—lamb for meat-eaters, and green beans, artichoke and *fassulia* for vegetarians. There's also an interesting variation of Moroccan *b'stilla,* made with asparagus. Finish with rose petal ice cream and a cup of Moroccan mint tea.

Taj Mahal Palace & Tower, Apollo Blunder, Colaba. ℭ **022/6665-3366.** Reservations highly recommended. Mezzes Rs 475–Rs 625, mezze samplers Rs 950–Rs 1,050; main courses Rs 695–Rs 1,550. AE, DC, MC, V, Daily 12:30–2:45pm and 7–11:45pm.

Thai Pavilion ★★★ THAI   This beautifully designed, sophisticated restaurant at the Taj President in far south Mumbai was the city's first Thai restaurant and still its best. Although it's over 15 years old, a design update has injected a dose of cool, too, so you can stare at the stunning textured walls (made from hundreds of panels of sculpted wood collected from across the country) or you can hop onto a barstool around the big, busy open kitchen and watch as chefs churn out dish after delectable dish. It's hard to know where to start, so order a maparoo mojito while you decide between *miang kham phak* (wonderfully creamy tofu wrapped with betel leaf, served with plum sauce), stir-fried morning glory flavored with yellow bean paste, stir-fried sea asparagus with raw mango, or soft-shell crabs with pomelo. The grilled lamb comes with a lovely mint and cucumber sauce, and the steamed John Dory is perfectly flavored with lemon and garlic. Save room for *fok thong sankaya* (steamed custard served in a baby pumpkin) or, just as delicious, spiced crème brûlée with sun-dried rose petals. If you want a table on a weekend night, you'd better book—you'll be among the city's flashest foodies.

Taj President, 90 Cuffe Parade. © **022/6665-0808.** Reservations highly recommended. Main courses Rs 550–Rs 760. AE, DC, MC, V. Daily 12:30–2:45pm and 7–11:45pm.

Trishna ★★★ SEAFOOD Another restaurant frequented by the who's who of Mumbai, Trishna is considered one of the best in the world (although many Mumbaikers prefer better-priced Mahesh Lunch Home, reviewed below). Butter pepper garlic king crab is Trishna's signature dish, but you'll also find jumbo pomfrets and tiger prawns (done in any style) cooked to perfection. Despite its reputation as a somewhat snobbish restaurant, Trishna isn't about ambience (it's a very ordinary white interior with old-fashioned banquets)—everyone is here for the food. Recommended dishes include pomfret Hyderabadi—barbecued with black pepper, it's a true masterpiece; pomfret *hariyali* enveloped in green masala and baked in a tandoor; fish *sholay* kebab; Kolhapuri prawns (spicy, so steel yourself with a drink); or squid expertly prepared with butter, pepper, and garlic. Service borders on snooty, and if you ask for suggestions you're sure to be recommended the most expensive items on the menu. Don't expect to get in any night without a reservation, unless you're willing to arrive by 7pm and be out by 8pm; getting in at lunch (when you'll probably overhear air-kissing housewives scandalizing loudly at the adjacent table) may be easier.

Birla Mansion, Sai Baba Marg (next to Commerce House), Kala Ghoda, Fort. © **022/2270-3213** up to -3215. Reservations essential for dinner. Main courses Rs 150–Rs 620; fish sold by weight; crab/lobster/ prawns Rs 550–Rs 2,500. AE, DC, MC, V. Mon–Sat noon–3:30pm and 6:30pm–midnight; Sun noon–3:30pm and 7:30pm–midnight

VongWong ★★ THAI/CHINESE A scented elevator couriers you up to yet another visually appealing Oriental restaurant in Nariman Point. It's the love child of the eponymous chefs Vong and Wong, one Chinese and one Thai—both masters—and together they've put together over 300 dinnertime items (and a fine dim sum selection at lunch) on a menu that'll more than likely overwhelm you. Try steamed red snapper, grilled Chilean sea bass, chicken *sui mai*, or for something different, the fragrant egg curry. Dishes are masterfully flavored (although some say too subtly spiced) and inevitably excellent. VongWong is a seriously pretty, very stylish venue, and has made a big impression on a certain crowd, but you might have issues with the size of the portions—they're in inverse proportion to the size of the menu.

Express Towers, First Floor, Nariman Point. © **022/2287-5633** through -5635. Main courses Rs 450–Rs 1,200. AE, MC, V. Daily 12:30–3pm and 7:30pm–12:30am.

Moderate & Inexpensive

A survivor since 1973, **Delhi Darbar** (Holland House, Colaba Causeway; © **022/2202-0235;** daily 11:30am–12:30am) is a Mumbai institution serving rather standard (and oily) Mughlai and Punjabi food. It has several branches in Mumbai, but we recommend only the one at Colaba. No one comes here for the ambience or service—most come for

(Moments) The Skinny on Street Food

Mumbai is probably the world capital of street food. Thousands upon thousands of workers commuting through this vast megalopolis each day need to stave off their hunger before dealing with crushing public transport, and you'll see an endless, thrilling array of places to snack on everything from *bhel puri* to *vada pav* (pronounced "pao"), which is the ultimate Mumbai street snack—basically a bun *(pav)* sliced open and packed with a fried mash potato ball and a spicy concoction of chili and garlic. Street food is something you should be careful about experimenting with anywhere in India. The spots we recommend are not on the street; they serve sanitized (yet authentic) versions of what is available on the street. One place where you can safely try street food—and it's one of our absolute favorite spots to snack—is **Kailash Parbat** ★★ (Sheela Mahal, 1st Pasta Lane, Colaba; ℂ 022/2281-2112), which serves authentic Sindhi food brought to Bombay by the Mulchandani family when they moved here from Karachi following Partition. Pay first, and then approach the relevant counter with your receipt. Ask for a portion of *pani puri* (you'll get six for Rs 25) which are like little mouthful-size explosions of flavor. The *puri* is a round hollow pocket of deep-fried flour; the *puri wallah* pokes a hole in it with his thumb and stuffs it full of chickpeas, sprouted *mung* beans, and mashed potato. Then he dips it in a vat of tamarind chutney to add a hint of sweet, and then into cold *pani* (water), flavored with mint and chilies. He'll plop it on your plate and you pop the entire thing in your mouth—it'll be the start of an addictive relationship. After you've had your fill, march back to the cash register and order a *kesar pista lassi*. It takes awhile to prepare—elegantly topped off with a layer of thick curd and a sprinkle of saffron—but your patience will be suitably rewarded with one of the most delicious drinks you've ever tasted.

You get to eat real Mumbai-style street food under very sanitary (if busy and noisy) conditions at **Swati Snacks** ★★, in Tardeo (248 Karai Estate, Tardeo Rd.;

the tandoori dishes or the mutton or chicken *biryani*. Ignore the Chinese menu, and don't expect any alcohol to be served. No booze at **Koyla** ★ either; a popular rooftop hangout above the Gulf Hotel (Apollo Bunder Rd; ℂ 022/6636-9999; www.koyla ethniccuisine.com; Tues–Sun 7:30pm–12:30am), it's recommended for its leisurely ambience and setting: a candlelit, canopied terrace with Arabian music playing in the background. The most popular item on the menu is not food, but the *sheesha* (hookah or pipe), with fruity flavors like green apple and strawberry. The food is mediocre, but order some kebabs just to enjoy the cool evening breeze, or come after dinner to relax, sit back, and linger over a "mocktail." The atmosphere is laid-back and no one will hustle you out—but service can be painfully slow. Reservations are recommended; even then, expect a wait. The cover charge will be redeemed against your bill.

Britannia ★★ (Moments) IRANI   This no-nonsense, no-frills, 90-year-old Irani (Persian) restaurant is the last of a dying breed of establishments once found on every corner of South Mumbai. The environment is simple and functional, with little room for extras

$©$ **022/6580-8406** or 022/2352-4994; daily 11am–11pm), where there's inevitably a (fast-moving) queue for the restaurant, but you're also able to buy from the take-away window. They too have excellent *pani puri*, but are famous for *panki chatni*, thin pancakes steamed in banana leaf, and superb *peru nu shak* (spiced guava eaten with Indian bread). Locals come here more for the traditional Gujarati dishes not found anywhere else. You can also sip a soothing glass of hygienic sugar cane juice and round out your meal with homemade fruit-flavored ice creams.

You can enjoy fare similar to Swati's without the potentially long wait and in a quieter, more composed, setting at **Soam** ★ (Sadguru Sadan, opposite Babulnath temple, Chowpatty; $©$ **022/2369-8080**; noon–11pm), a vegetarian joint with a bright, contemporary ambience and some dedicated healthier options on its menu.

Bandra's famous hygienic street-food stop is **Elco Pani Puri Centre** ★★ at Elco Arcade on Hill Road ($©$ **022/2645-7677**), once a street stall that famously operated illegally, but has since expanded to include an air-conditioned restaurant that, like Kailash Parbat, uses filtered water to prepare its snacks. You can venture inside for a more staid experience, but we still prefer the spontaneous people-watching that happens outside where you stand at the efficient *pani puri* counter (buy your coupon at the nearby cash register first) where the delicious mouth-size morsels are handed over one by one. Afterwards, order a glass of fresh watermelon juice, and grab a plastic stool so you can tuck into a plate of *bhel puri*—crushed *puris* mixed with *sev* (tiny noodles made from chickpea flour), puffed rice, chopped boiled potato, onion, coriander, chili, and a couple of sweet and tangy chutneys.

like presentation and ambience. Most people come here to consume one or more of three excellent dishes: Berry *pulao* (a version of the Iranian *zereshk polow*) is the outstanding signature dish, made with succulent spiced boneless mutton (or chicken), fragrant long-grain basmati rice, and tart barberries imported from Iran. *Patra ni machchi* is pomfret fish coated in chutney made with cilantro, coconut, and assorted spices; wrapped in a banana leaf; and steamed—always moist and flaky with flavors all the way down to the bone. The mutton *dhansak* is a combination of fragrant brown rice and thick *dal* in which the meat has been cooked—a dense, hearty meal that tastes a million times better than it looks. (Vegetarians, though catered to, should give this restaurant a miss.)

Ram Gulam Rd., opposite New Customs House, Ballard Estate, Fort. $©$ **022/2261-5264.** Main courses Rs 70–Rs 240. No credit cards. Mon–Sat 11:30am–4pm.

Indigo Deli ★★★ ECLECTIC/INTERNATIONAL   This fabulous upmarket-yet-buzzing eatery is very much in the image of a New York delicatessen. Offering such down-to-earth fare as pastas and burgers, but also catering to the health conscious and

Feeling Peckish?

Towards the southern end of Colaba Causeway is one food treat spot you shouldn't pass by. **Theobroma** (Cusrow Baug, Shop no. 24, Colaba Causeway; © **022/6529-2929**) is a small, quite marvelous bakery run by Kainaz Messman and her mother, Kamal, who make you feel immediately at home. You can sit at one of the few tables and nibble on their famous brownies (there are 10 varieties to choose from) or one of the other innumerable rich desserts and pastries. If you're not the sweet tooth type, you can choose from various gourmet-quality sandwiches (try the chicken pesto), or freshly baked breads, the best of which is the light, flavorful focaccia.

more refined palate, the space-deprived venue packs in a lively, devoted crowd—they arrive for the Western breakfasts (served all day long), and keep going until after midnight. Besides daily specials and a la carte dishes, you can choose from a variety of imported cheeses, cold meats, and fresh breads—all of exceptional quality—that can be transformed into sandwiches of your choice; check the counter for scrumptiously fresh salads, too. There's comfort food galore: pizzas (yes, the proper, crispy kind), near-perfect risotto, and on a hot day their tomato gazpacho really hits the spot. Prices are steep—and you'll pay through your nose if you want a glass of wine—but the ambience is so on the pulse of Mumbai that just about anyone you talk to will mention this among their favorites in a city that's plump with great choices.

Ground Floor, Pheroza Bldg., Chhatrapati Shivaji Maharishi Marg, Apollo Bunder. © **022/6655-1010.** Sandwiches average Rs 350; main courses Rs 450–Rs 750. AE, DC, MC, V. Daily 9am–12:30am.

Leopold Café ★ ⓂMoments ECLECTIC   Okay, so this is pretty much *the* quintessential tourist eatery, these days known as much for the buzzy atmosphere as it is as the first choice for fans of the David Gregory Roberts novel, *Shantaram*. This is where wannabe literary types come in hopes of scoping their hero or perhaps catching a moment when some of the underworld activity written about in the book actually comes to life. In reality, this is simply a very overhyped dining institution, but one you'd do well to experience (if only once, and briefly) while in Colaba. Why it's such a hit with foreigners is a mystery, since the food is good but not exceptional, the atmosphere can be noisy and rather smoky, and bills are often wrong. If you're keen to get the inside scoop on how Bollywood films are made, hang out here; casting agents looking for foreigners to work as extras on current productions frequently scan the clientele for able bodies at this favored travelers' hangout.

Colaba Causeway. © **022/2287-3362.** Main courses Rs 95–Rs 140. AE, DC, MC, V. Daily 7am–midnight.

Mahesh Lunch Home ★★★ COASTAL/SEAFOOD   The ceiling may be too low and the tables too close together, but this seafood restaurant should not be missed if you love fish—it's one of Mumbai's best restaurants, consistently dishing out exceptional specialties. Everything is incredibly fresh, but favorites include *surmai* fry, pomfret curry, and tandoori pomfret—all outstanding. The latter (listed as a starter, but available as a main) is served flawlessly moist; eaten with butter *naan*, it provides a heavenly gastronomic experience. Also try the scrumptious prawns *Koliwada*, crab tandoori, pomfret in green masala, or any of the fish curries or *gassis*, all first-rate. (Note that *gassi* refers to the

What's Up with Udipi?

Restaurants serving South Indian fast food (also called Udipi restaurants) can be found on just about every street, and a meal at one is an essential Mumbai experience. The Udipi phenomenon arrived in Mumbai in 1935 when Rama Nayak, a Kannadiga (migrant from Karnataka) entrepreneur started the legendary Udipi Boarding House in Fort. Serving traditional, nourishing, pure vegetarian meals, it was named after the town near his home village, and after he later opened two more restaurants with Udipi in the name and other migrants from western Karnataka cottoned onto the same business idea, "Udipi" became the generic moniker used by Mumbaikers when referring to South Indian eateries. There are plenty of places to choose from—in fact, one official statistic states that Kannadigas own 70% of the city's 11,000 or so officially licensed restaurants—but if you sample only one and are willing to go the extra mile, make it one of our two favorites in the South Indian hub of **Matunga**. At the compact **Café Madras** ★★ (King's Circle; ✆ **022/2401-4419;** Tues-Sun 7am-2:30pm and 4-11pm) it's Tamilian-style *dosas* that reign supreme, and it's worth sampling a few different varieties (check the chalkboard for the day's specials) to see what a difference the type of flour makes. For an authentic South Indian *thali,* you've simply got to try **A. Ramanayak Udipi Shri Krishna Boarding ★★** (Lal Bahadur Shastri Market Bldg., first floor, near Matunga Railway Station; ✆ **022/2414-2422;** Tues–Sun 10:30am–2:30pm and 7–10pm), now run by Rama Nayak's son. Purchase a coupon for either a limited or unlimited *thali,* and grab a seat; you can expect a no-frills experience where food— *chapattis* or *puris,* vegetables, *dal,* curd, and rice—is served on a banana leaf, and you eat with your hands You'll also get a cup of buttermilk, and, when you're just about done, a sweet dessert.

thick, spicy, coconut-based Manglorean curry, while the "curries" on the menu are a thinner version of the same.) Mahesh also serves meat, chicken, and Chinese dishes, but only the misguided would come here for any of that.

8D Cawasji Patel St., off Pherozeshah Mehta Rd., Fort. ✆ **022/2287-0938** or 022/2202-3965. Most main seafood dishes Rs 110–Rs 270; jumbo pomfret/crab/lobster Rs 400–Rs 1,700. AE, DC, MC, V. Daily 11:30am–4pm and 6–11:30pm.

Moshe's ★★ MEDITERRANEAN/LIGHT FARE This upmarket cafe showcases the culinary talents and business acumen of Moshe Shek. A Mumbaiker who honed his skills abroad before returning home to etch out his own bit of celebrity, he's made swift work of turning this tightly packed space into a hugely successful miniempire—there are now several branches around the city, and he has a near-compulsive loyal (and sometimes very loud) following. You too should definitely turn up to sample his adventurous Middle Eastern fusion food, or even just to try out his sandwiches, snacks, or impressive breakfasts (the smoothies and health drinks are brilliant). Inspired by his time in Israel (Shek is Jewish), he turns out some very tasty specialty dishes like Turkish *turlu turlu* (roasted vegetables), chicken stuffed with couscous and pine nuts, and tagines from Morocco. And despite going slightly commercial, he also likes to experiment—the coffee bean–infused chicken is quite something. Evenings can get a bit crazy in here as the crowds inevitably turn up—but that might be half the fun, and certainly a clue as to this place's enduring popularity.

7 Minoo Manor, Cuffe Parade, Colaba. © **022/2216-1226.** Main courses Rs 250–Rs 575, breakfast Rs 50–Rs 200, sandwiches Rs 170–Rs 200. AE, MC, V. Daily 7:30am–midnight.

Samovar ★★ INDIAN/LIGHT FARE   This long, narrow restaurant inside Jehangir Art Gallery is another South Mumbai institution that has retained its charm and low prices in spite of its popularity. With quick, efficient service and a policy of not hurrying diners even if others are waiting, this is the perfect stopover after a day roaming the Prince of Wales museum and other local landmarks. Start with a delicious seasonal fruit juice—the guava juice is the best when it's in season. *Boti* rolls (spiced meat wrapped in chapatis) rival with *parathas* (fried breads with a great assortment of stuffings) to satiate the taste buds along with the yummy bean-sprout salad. A stop here is a must: This is as close to home cooking as you are likely to get on a short visit to Mumbai. At press time, there was some talk of Samovar closing down, so call ahead to check.

Jehangir Art Gallery, Kala Ghoda, Fort. © **022/2284-8000.** Main courses Rs 50–Rs 160. No credit cards. Mon–Sat 11am–7pm.

CENTRAL MUMBAI: WORLI, TARDEO & CHOWPATTY BEACH

Among the most famous eateries in this central part of town, is **Jewel of India** (© **020/2494-9435;** daily 12:30–3pm and 6:30–11:30pm) at the Nehru Centre, although we often find ourselves completely absorbed at the bar, or checking out what the many Mumbai families who frequent this place are getting up to (Sunday afternoon is best for social voyeurism). It's a large, elegant, old-fashioned kind of place, and the menu looks more like a shopping list than an aid to decision-making—there are literally dozens of Indian dishes; your best bet is to call Agneto Fernandes, the maitre d', over to your table and ask him what's what. He'd like nothing better than to help you choose wisely.

Copper Chimney ★★★ KEBABS/MUGHLAI   For more than a quarter of a century, Copper Chimney has delighted those looking for the perfect kebabs. To this end, two pages of the menu are dedicated to kebabs, from the popular *reshmi* kebab (chicken) to the *jhinga nisha* (tandoori prawn kebabs). These tender, creamy, smoky-flavored, melt-in-your-mouth kebabs can be followed by traditional Dum Pukht specialties such as chicken *makhani* (butter chicken) or the even more exquisite Peshawari lamb. No matter what you pick, you will leave satisfied. There's also a daily buffet lunch, but don't be swayed by the variety—some of the best items on the menu (such as the unfailingly wonderful butter chicken) are not offered at the buffet. Note that while Copper Chimney branches are found all over the city, this is the one to patronize (don't confuse it with the bland mall version on the other side of Worli).

12-A Lotus Court, Dr. Annie Besant Rd., Worli. © **022/2492-0505** or -5353. Main courses Rs 210–Rs 400; tiger prawns Rs 725. AE, DC, MC, V. Daily 12:30–3:30pm and 7:30pm–12:30am.

Oh Calcutta! ★★ BENGALI   The famous hand-pulled rickshaw of Kolkata stands outside this singular eatery at Tardeo, not far from the Haji Ali mosque. The restaurant's specialty is its freshwater fish, flown in especially from Kolkata. For starters, *kakra chingri bhapa,* or prawn and crabmeat cake spiced and steamed in banana leaves, is superb, but so is everything else; even the simple fish fry is outstanding. Close your eyes and order either the *daab chingri* or the *chingri malai* curry, both coconut-milk-based prawn curries, both different and gently flavorful, with steamed rice. For more robust flavors, try *illish machher patur, hilsa* fish marinated with mustard and green chili paste and steamed in banana leaf. As a Bengali restaurant, fish dominates the menu, but vegetarians are well catered to and can order a number of dishes, including the classic banana flower and potato dish *mochar ghonto.*

Hotel Rosewood, Tulsiwadi Lane, Tardeo. (©️ **022/2496-3114** or 022/6680-6216. Reservations recommended on weekend nights. Main courses Rs 225–Rs 550. AE, MC, V. Daily noon–3pm and 7pm–midnight.

Olive Bar and Kitchen ★★ (Moments) MEDITERRANEAN   Despite its reputation as one of the city's singularly popular Bollywood stargazing venues (not to mention being a big hit with singles of all persuasions looking to score), this glittering übertrendy establishment also happens to serve very good Mediterranean meals (studiously prepared by Olive's award-winning chef, Max Massimilianto Orlati—yes, a true Italian). The menu is fairly predictable, and you'll probably want to stick to the lighter Italian dishes—you wouldn't want to be too distracted from the scene around you by a large plate of food. Arrive early and sit in the lovely open-air space outside, always buzzing with Beautiful People; it's a perfect spot for lingering over multiple drinks—and who knows which hot star you might bump into. *Note:* There is now a branch of Olive at the Mahalaxmi Race Course, where lunch is served daily. Mahalaxmi Branch is at Amateur Riders Club, Mahalaxmi Race Course, Mahalaxmi (©️ **022/4085-9595** or -9596); open daily 12:30–4:30pm.

Tourist Hotel, 14 Union Park, Pali Hill, Khar (W), Bandra. (©️ **022/2605-8228** or -8229. www.olivebarand kitchen.com. Reservations highly recommended. Main courses Rs 250–Rs 865; prix-fixe lunch menu Rs 399. AE, DC, MC, V. Mon–Sat 7:30pm–1:30am, Sun 12:30–4.30pm and 7:30pm–1:30am.

San Qi ★★★   ASIAN   You'll be stumped for choice at this two-level fine dining establishment at the Four Seasons—it's really three eateries seamlessly joined at the hip. Three top chefs—imported from their respective native lands and armed with a desire to create culinary adventure while satisfying traditional tastes. Chef Kato's *chawanmushi* custard with foie gras is a legend in the making, but you'll probably want to join the crowd at the teppanyaki counter, or investigate the enticing robatayaki offerings. Mumbai's fresh seafood works well in Chef Then Kok Leong's kitchen; the wok-fried prawns are done simply with garlic, and he prepares a sublime marinade for his crisp pomfret fillet. But you really should check out Chef Shahid Latif's fresh take on traditional Indian (mostly Lucknowi) dishes. His kebabs (worth ordering just to see what comes out of those impressive-looking state-of-the-art traditional ovens) are amazing, but there are contemporary India offerings from the tandoor, such as smoked honey mustard sea bass with sautéed greens, fennel, and cumin—talk about giving Indian cuisine an international edge!

Four Seasons Hotel, 114 Dr. E Moses Rd., Worli. (©️ **022/2481-8000.** Reservations recommended. Japanese main courses Rs 600–Rs 2,100; sushi and sashimi Rs 300–Rs 650; teppanyaki main courses Rs 1,200–Rs 2,400; *robatayaki* Rs 350–Rs 1,200; Cantonese main courses Rs 700–Rs 1,300; Indian main courses Rs 500–Rs 1,200; set menus Rs 1,300–Rs 1,900. AE, DC, MC, V. Daily 11:30am—3pm and 7pm—midnight.

THE NORTHERN SUBURBS: BANDRA & JUHU

If you don't mind stepping inside the globalized interior of yet another of Mumbai's many Western chain hotels, then we don't mind drawing your attention to the quality Italian on offer at **Mezzo Mezzo** ★ (©️ 022/6693-3220) in Juhu's JW Marriott. Popular with well-to-do Mumbaikers, this is one hotel eatery that's worth venturing out of tourist Colaba for (and even more enjoyable if you get a table by the window). Another lavish hotel haunt is **Vista** ★★ at the Taj Lands End (©️ 022/6668-1234); it's extremely popular for decadent, long-winded Sunday brunches and languid, lazy knock-out breakfasts. It's open round-the-clock, so is also the perfect place to satisfy a crazy hunger after a long, hard night on the town—and when the sun comes up, there are great views over the ocean.

At the other end of the spectrum is **Govinda's** (© **022/2620-0337**), at the Hare Krishna Temple in Juhu (see below).

Aurus ★★ (Moments MODERN EUROPEAN   Okay, we admit it's not going to be picking up too many awards for its food—it's decadent-sounding and occasionally quite good, but certainly not memorable—but when it comes to atmosphere and glamour (models and air-kissing movie stars are virtually part of the decor), there are few places that can hold a candle to it. Candles, in fact, set just the right mood out on the deck that edges onto the beach (reserve a table); indoors, the atmosphere steers more towards sophistication. Many hip Mumbaikers see this more as a place to spend all night sipping cocktails created by a team of studious mixologists, and you'll probably end up agreeing with them—do give the food a chance, though. The Chilean sea bass (with saffron cream) is usually spot-on, the lamb chops perfectly grilled, and jalapeño chicken just delicious. A word of caution, though—this place is booming on weekends (Fri especially) and you may find the mix of music and rowdy scenesters at the bar a bit too overwhelming—another reason to book an outdoor table.

Ground Floor, Nichani Kutir, Juhu Tara Rd., Juhu. © **022/6710-6666**. Reservations highly recommended. Main courses Rs 500–Rs 1,250. AE, MC, V. Daily 7:30pm–12:30am.

Govinda's ★ (Value VEGETARIAN/NORTH INDIAN   A sign above the entrance reads "WELCOME TO HARE KRISHNA LAND," and you're encouraged to "spiritualize your eating," but the food is tasty, excellent value, and perfectly hygienic. At the large, clean marble-floored dining hall of the ISKCON temple (not too far from Juhu's beachfront), you can gorge from a massive all-vegetarian buffet (no onions or garlic, either) happy in the knowledge that your food has already been tasted by the gods, and is therefore blessed. Between mealtimes, there's a snack and a la carte menu—try Govinda's Special Dosa, stuffed with vegetables, cheese, and cottage cheese, and wash it down with a spicy special thandai, a milk drink made with fruit, sweet syrup, and masala spices; it's refreshing and delicious. Sidestepping all promises that this is "cuisine with philosophy," you can now order pasta, pizzas, and even mocktails here, but we'd suggest you stick to the traditional Indian dishes, which are excellent, if often cooked in pure ghee (clarified butter), which can make the meal quite heavy.

ISKCON, Hare Krishna Mandir, Juhu Tara Rd., Juhu. © **022/2620-0337**. Buffet Rs 270; Sun buffet Rs 320; snack time and a la carte menu dishes Rs 30–Rs 120. MC, V. Daily 7:30–11am, 12:30–3:30pm, 4–6pm and 7:30–10:30pm.

Out of the Blue ★★ EUROPEAN/INTERNATIONAL   Part nonstop festival, part restaurant, this vibey Bandra hangout attracts a savvy crowd out for a bit of entertainment as accompaniment to some fairly decent dishes. There are art exhibitions, tarot readers, musicians, magicians—plus there's room for many other improvised events and happenings likely to raise an eyebrow and keep you smiling. It's strictly European on the food front, but with hints of local influence (how about the masala mafia pasta, or *desi* fondue?) to keep things interesting. We love the seafood—prawns marinated in chili and lime, and deliciously spiced grilled fish. Plus there's a spa menu for anyone watching his or her figure.

Hotel Pali Hills, 14 Union Park, off Carter Rd., Khar (W). © **022/2605-8227**. Main courses Rs 175–Rs 400. AE, DC, MC, V. Daily noon–3:30pm and 7pm–midnight.

The Thali: A Meal Unto Itself

You can't leave this city without consuming at least one *thali,* the meal that really tests the size of your appetite! It works like this: Sit down, and in less than a minute you're expected to declare which *thali* you want—ordinary, special, and so on. Seconds later, a large, stainless-steel (or silver) plate *(thali)* arrives along with six to eight small bowls *(katoris)* resting on it. The waiters then fill every one of the multiple *katoris* as well as the rest of the plate with a large assortment of steaming-hot spiced vegetables, savories, *dals,* beans, *rotis, puris,* and potentially much more. To wash it down, you're served water (best avoided unless you're certain it's been purified) and a glass of delicious, superthin, cumin-flavored buttermilk *(chaas).* As you eat, your *katoris* will be topped up, so indicate what you want for seconds, thirds, fourths—a veritable onslaught that won't stop until you say so (although some waistline-minded restaurateurs have started serving "limited *thalis*"). Then it's a round of rice or *khichdi* (a mixture of rice and *dal*) and, in some restaurants, dessert. Not only are *thalis* a great value (you pay Rs 50–Rs 250), but they come pretty close to the home cooking of the country's Gujarati (or Rajasthani) population (and there are *thalis* from most other parts of the country, too). There are so many good *thali* places to choose from, but **Panchvati Gaurav** ★★ (Vithaldas Thackersay Marg, across from Bombay Hospital, Marine Lines; ✆ **022/2208-4877;** Tues–Sun 11am–3pm and 7–10:30pm; Mon lunch only) definitely stands out—especially at lunchtime, when office workers flock here. It's dedicated to producing Gujarati *thalis* that are world-class, excellent value, and served with a bit of a flourish (they even have a nonspicy *thali*). Another local favorite, and the ideal place to end a visit to nearby Crawford Market, is **Rajdhani** ★ (361 Sheik Memom St.; ✆ **022/2342-6919;** daily noon–4pm, Mon–Sat 7–10:30pm), which also specializes in Gujarati meals (with Rajasthani *thalis* once a week)—the space is tiny, but the tastes are exceptional. If you're looking for a *thali* joint closer to Colaba, **Chetana** ★ (34 K. Dubash Marg, Kala Ghoda; ✆ **022/2284-4968;** www.chetana.com) is a highly recommended, strictly vegetarian place with many delicious options, including a Maharashtrian *thali,* and one aimed at health-conscious foodies. Attached to the cafe is a very handy bookstore that's especially good for books on spirituality and Indian philosophy, history, and culture.

Penne ★★ (Value) ITALIAN   Like a bright, modern trattoria, this snazzy, unpretentious Juhu restaurant offers authentic pasta, risotto and 13-inch Neapolitan-style pizzas, and is a good place for a reasonably priced steak. Start with gamberi Portofino—fresh prawns sautéed with lemon, chili peppers, garlic, and herbs, and served on a bed of pasta with creamy white wine sauce—and then order the New Zealand rack of lamb, which is oven-grilled, scented with lavender, and hugely successful. Lighter dishes, like the vodka-flamed penne pasta, and the lobster risotto with Jura whiskey are also highlights, as is the delectable grilled John Dory, served with a sublime lemon butter mustard. However, if you want to join the regulars for a massive full-fledged feast, you'll have to turn up for the massively popular weekly barbecue buffet that happens every Sunday between noon and 4:30pm—come very hungry.

14 Silver Beach, AB Nair Rd., Juhu. ✆ **022/2625-5706.** Main courses Rs 330–Rs 1,450; pizza Rs 400–Rs 525. MC, V. Daily noon–12:30am.

Prithvi Café ★★ LIGHT FARE Another prime people-watching spot, this pleasant, unpretentious café is where many of Mumbai's up-and-coming and struggling *artistes* come to nosh and discuss their art. The cafe serves great fresh *parathas* and a variety of teas and coffees over which you can linger undisturbed—the nonalcoholic Irish coffee is legendary. The menu is a literal tour de force of Mumbai's best-loved dishes and snacks, borrowed from the eating houses that made them famous. It's an ideal place to sample traditional *chaat,* yummy samosas, good old *vada pao,* and excellent kebabs, without having to wonder through the city.

Prithvi Theatre, Janki Kutir Society, Juhu Tara Rd., Juhu. ✆ **022/2617-4118.** Main courses Rs 50–Rs 275. No credit cards. Mon 3–11:30pm; Tues–Sun 12:30–11:30pm.

6 SHOPPING

From internationally renowned haute couture to dirt-cheap one-season wonders, intricate jewelry and unique antiques to tawdry gifts and fabulous textiles, Mumbai is known as a shopper's paradise, and you'll find pretty much everything the country has to offer here. If you're shopping on the street or in the markets (see "Markets," earlier in this chapter), take your time, sift and sort, establish authenticity, and, if necessary, don't be afraid to bargain hard. Bear in mind that (as elsewhere in India) a "bargain," particularly when it comes to jewelry and antiques, is probably a cheap bauble or reproduction—fakes are a dime a dozen, as are the con men who sell them. By and large, you can steer clear of the kitschy outlets that line Colaba Causeway and the surrounding area, but be on the lookout for little gems that may be hiding down a side street (we've mentioned quite a few below). Besides the areas described here, you will find that the suburb of Bandra has become a local shopping haven, with Linking Road, Hill Road, and several other streets overflowing with shops and street stalls selling clothes, shoes, and everything else under the sun. In addition, Western-style multistory department stores are filled with all kinds of garments and fashions, and the trend towards a fully-fledged mall culture is definitely in full gear—sadly (for some), most of the shops are Western franchises, meaning you need to hunt a bit to discover underrepresented local outlets. You'll find several shopping complexes in the converted mill compounds of Lower Parel (right next to Worli, in central Mumbai)—the Phoenix Mills area is a shopper's dream. Note, too, that most major stores described below have a parallel store in either Bandra or Juhu, so if you're based in north Mumbai, call and check before making a trip downtown. If you don't mind a potentially massive capital outlay, it's worth knowing that the in-house shops at the Taj Mahal Palace & Tower are stocked with sought-after Indian (and international) brands and products (particularly Pashmina shawls, from simple water Pashminas at around Rs 2,000 to high-end quality ones for Rs 10,000), though obviously you pay a price for the convenience of location, and the shopping experience is relatively sterile. The same holds true for the shopping arcade at the **Trident Nariman Point.**

(Moments) Shopping Beneath the Grandstand

If you choose to make an event out of just one shopping venue, we urge you to head for **Bungalow 8 ★★★**, a fabulously eclectic store stashed into an elegantly converted space beneath the benches of world-famous Wankhede cricket stadium. Beautifully laid out, with vintage furniture as a backdrop, and stocked with all kinds of curious, beautiful, wearable, and collectible objects—from jewelry and clothing to chandeliers—Maitthili Ahluwalia's gorgeous store is a destination in its own right. The shop is located under the stadium's north stand (Vinoo Mankad Rd.), in block E-F; your cab driver will get you to the stadium, but call ℂ **022/2281-9880** if you need help finding the exact spot—you wouldn't want to end up in the home team's dressing room, would you? Check it out at www.bungaloweight.com.

INDIAN HANDICRAFTS & TRADITONAL SOUVENIRS

Central Cottage Industries Emporium (behind Regal Cinema; ℂ **022/2202-6564** or -7537; daily 10am–7pm) is the large, government-owned, fixed-price shop aimed at tourists, with a reputation for carrying well-crafted items that offer relatively good value (not the cheapest stuff out there but you won't get ripped off). Established during the late 1940s in an attempt to sustain traditional handicrafts, the massive showroom is crammed full of everything and anything that's likely to remind you of India. We're not recommending it, but at the very least, a visit here will give you an idea of what items should more or less cost. A far superior shopping experience, with a more up-to-date look and contemporary service standards, is **The Bombay Store** (Sir P.M. Rd., Fort; ℂ **022/2288 5048**, -5049, or -5052; Mon–Sat 10:30am–7:30pm, Sun 10:30am–6:30pm), where you'll find every imaginable Indian handicraft and design, from bed linens and crockery to incense and aromatherapy oils (not to mention some very touristy souvenirs bearing the store's own logo). An alternative branch that we like is in the High Street Phoenix Mills complex in Lower Parel (it's in a tucked away section of the mall; ℂ **022/2497-1024**); among the usual stock of sandalwood Buddha statues, candle stands, leather accessories, and homewares, they sell a range of handsomely packaged "Chai-time" teas (ideal gifts), as well as vintage photographs of the city. Directly opposite, is an even more fascinating store, **Omved ★** (ℂ **022/4004-8218**), selling mostly organic products, including textiles made from organic cottons (from which they fashion luxurious bed linens and T-shirts), organic spices, massage oils and toiletries (for men and women), and 100% natural, Ayurvedically treated baby products. If you want to give something back (and don't mind getting something lovely in return), visit **WIT** (Women's India Trust) **★★** (23 Bombay Market, Tardeo; ℂ **022/2351-1753;** www.wit.org.in) where a wide range of handcrafted items—from soft toys to unique artworks—are produced by a charitable organization that trains women from underprivileged backgrounds, providing skills and opportunities to many people who might otherwise be destitute. Shoppers who care should also visit **Shrujan—Threads of Life ★★★** (Saagar Villa, 38 Bhulabahi Desai Rd., Breach Candy; ℂ **022/2352-1693;** www.shrujan.org) where you can pick up homewards and ethnic designer wear embroidered by a women's collective from the drought- and earthquake-affected region of Kutch (in Gujarat); they produce truly stunning one-off pieces, so this is well worth a visit. Finally, **Dhoop ★★** (101 Khar

Sheetal Apartments, Dr. Ambedkar Rd., Unio Park, Khar ★; ✆ **022/2649-8646;** www. dhoopcrafts.com) is a brilliant assemblage of craft products from across India, produced and sourced in conjunction with charitable organizations—everything here is handmade and your patronage helps sustain a traditional skill.

HOMEWARE & BEAUTIFUL OBJECTS

Easily one of our favorite stores in the country, **Good Earth** ★★★ (www.goodearth india.com) has several branches across India, and even one in Singapore. There are three beautiful outlets in Mumbai: The one across the road from the Marriott in Juhu (R/154 Juhu Tara Rd.; ✆ **022/2611-2481**) specializes in fabulous textiles and fabrics—not to mention everything in between, including glassware, candles, and especially popular dinnerware. Look out for coasters, lampshades and gorgeously fun cushion covers by Krsna Mehta and Sangita Jindal (under the "Bombay Project" label)—their offbeat designs cleverly rework classic Mumbai icons and images to create hip reminders of your stay here. You can also pick up copies of Fiona Caulfield's brilliant *Love Mumbai* guidebook— it's packed with tips on the best shops in the city. Good Earth's branch at Raghuvanshi Mill (Senapati Bapat Marg, Lower Parel; ✆ **022/2495-1954**) has a huge showroom as well as a fairly decent cafe with some scrumptious salads (but slow service). With less down to earth prices, but specializing in the finest quality, **Ravissant** ★★ (New India Bldg., Madame Cama Rd., Colaba; ✆ **022/2287-3405**) has a selection of sterling-silver teapots, vases, photo frames, and assorted stylish collectibles that sport clean modern lines and hark back to the Deco period. Yet, among all the restrained minimalism, you'll also encounter fabulous waist-high silver Ganesh statues—apparently they sell like hotcakes.

Contemporary Arts and Crafts, in the residential neighborhood of Napean Sea Road (near Kemps Corner; ✆ **022/2363-1979;** Mon–Sat 10am–8pm, Sun 10am–7pm), has tasteful and sometimes uncommon gifts from all over India. If you're shopping in Bandra, make time to visit the very upmarket **Frazer and Haws** store (Landmark Bldg., Pali Naka, Bandra; ✆ **022/6675-0200**), which carries eclectic and funky silver objets d'art, including sleek idols of Indian gods and goddesses like Ganesha and Lakshmi.

FASHION & FABRICS

Bombay's fortunes were built on its cotton mills so you'd be right in assuming this is a great city to shop for fabrics, whether for you to wear or have fashioned into something later—and there are plenty of tailors who'll whip you up something fabulous in just a few hours. While you'll be overwhelmed with choice when it comes to global labels, you really should seek out the edgy, memorable wardrobe pieces by local designers.

Having created garments for Hillary Clinton, Demi Moore, and Liza Minnelli, and earned the accolades "Crystal King" and "Czar of Embroidery," Azeem Khan is one of Mumbai's best-known designers. To find your very own slice of Indian haute couture, visit **Azeem Khan Couture** ★★ in Colaba (1 Usha Sadan Bldg.; ✆ **022/2215-1028;** www.azeemkhan.com). **Ensemble** (Great Western Bldg., 130/132 Colaba Causeway; ✆ **022/2284-3227**) is another upmarket boutique, owned by designer Tarun Tahiliani, where you will find the greatest variety of East-meets-West evening wear; besides his own creations, prominent designers to look for here include Rajesh Pratap, Monisha Jaisingh, Tarana Rajpal, Abhishek Gupta, Sunita Shankar, and Sabyasachi. If you're after an even more glamorous, exclusive experience, visit **Tarun Tahiliani Boutique** (Villar Ville, Ramchandani Marg, Apollo Bunder; ✆ **022/2287-0895;** www.taruntahiliani.com), where you can choose from some of the finest saris, suits and bridal garments you can imagine.

Bridging the gap between outrageously exclusive and boho cheap, is **Bombay Electric** ★★★ (1 Reay House, BEST Marg, Colaba; ℭ 022/2287-6276; www.bombay electric.com), which carries simple, pretty accessories, as well as a stellar designer collection by Indian and international designers. Depak and Priya Kishore, who started the store, also have their own range of delectable, stylish clothing lines under the label, Ghee Butter. And there are less elaborate, more affordable T-shirts and collectibles that make great gifts, too.

At the far end of Colaba (away from the Taj) is the **Courtyard** ★★ (Minoo Desai Marg, Apollo Bunder), where chic boutiques are filled with goods from a range of Indian designers (such as Manish Arora)—recommended stores include the very chic **Hot Pink** (ℭ 022/6638-5482); **Abraham and Thakore** (ℭ 022/6638-5486), where you'll find fantastic shirts for men; **Rabani & Rakha** (ℭ 022/6638-5476) for saris; and **Manish Arora** (ℭ 022/6638-5464; www.manisharora.ws) for modish women's wear and accessories. If you want to pick your way through some of the best in Indian designs, but don't fancy moving from shop to shop, head for **Kimaya** ★★ (2 Asha Colony, Juhu Tara Rd.; ℭ 022/2660-6154) in Juhu (it's opposite the Sea Princess Hotel), where owners Pradeep and Neha Hirani seem to have gathered all the finest Indian brand ladies fashion under one roof. They also have a store for men—**Ayamik** (Shop no, 1, Sea Palace, Juhu Tara Rd.), as well as an alternative branch in Kemps Corner (ℭ 022/2386-2432).

For cheap, casual, well-cut cottons, **Cotton World,** near Indigo restaurant, is the perfect stop. At **Indian Textiles** (Taj Mahal Palace; ℭ 022/2202-8783 or 022/2204-9278), you'll find some of the best Benarasi woven silks and brocades in the country, sold by the yard, as well as authentic Pashmina shawls. Also look for hand-dyed silk stoles by **Jamnadas Khatri** (ℭ 022/2242-5711 or -2277). Hand-loomed products are found in abundance at fabulous **Fab India** (Jeroo Bldg., 137 M.G, Rd, Kala Ghoda; ℭ 022/2262-6539; other outlets in Bandra). **Amara** (Hughes Rd.; ℭ 022/2387-9687 or -2530) in Kemp's Corner is a good place to check out the work of different designers—all top end—with the option to pause between fittings for a bite to eat or a quick spa treatment. To view (and hopefully take home) the work of less-established designers, head for **Aza** ★ (21 Siffy Apartments, Altamount Rd.; ℭ 022/2351-7616), just off Pedder Road. After checking out the work of tomorrow's fashion gods, you can explore the decidedly fashionable neighborhood—a preserve of the ultrawealthy.

If you've loved the furnishings at many of the Taj hotels around the country, make your way to **Zeba** in Colaba or Worli (Bhaveshwar, 148–B, Dr. Annie Besant Rd., Worli Naka, ℭ 022/2495-3711; also at Royal Terrace, 58 Wodehouse Rd., Colaba, ℭ 022/2218-8797) for extensive collections of highly desirable home textiles, accessories, carpets, and *dhurries* in great original styles. Zeba is owned by the flamboyant Krsna Mehta, whose outfit creates in-house designs for its textiles in cotton, silk, jute, and a range of graceful fabrics, using both earthy and vibrant colors. Zeba will custom-design any living space. **Yamini** (President House, Wodehouse Rd., Colaba; ℭ 022/2218-4143 or -4145; also in Bandra, ℭ 022/2646-3645) stocks designer linen, tablecloths, bolsters, curtains, bed covers, napkins, and even lampshades. Also at Colaba (near Indigo restaurant) is **Maspar** (Sunny Bldg., Mandlik Rd.; ℭ 022/2287-5619) a new store with quality home furnishings in contemporary designs and beautiful colors.

If you're fascinated by saris but don't know where to begin, make your way to **Kala Niketan** ★★ (ℭ 022/2200-5001 or -4952) at Marine Lines, where you will be bowled over by the stunning variety, colors, and over-the-top service. Salesmen not only assist you with your purchase, but can help you get a blouse stitched and offer serious tips on how to drape that gorgeous fabric.

Famous Indian designer **Ritu Kumar** ★★★ has several outlets specializing in silk and cotton designer-ethnic wear, much of it a blend of Western and Indian influences—all showstoppingly elegant. Head for her boutique at Phoenix Mills Annexe (462 Senapati Bapat Marg, Lower Parel; ℂ **022/6666-9901**), or either of the branches on Warden Road (ℂ **022/2367-8593** or -2947) or at Trident Nariman Point.

Another boutique that is a must-see for fashionistas is **Mélange** ★ (Raj Mahal Bldg., 33 Altamount Rd., Kemps Corner; ℂ **022/2353-4492** or -9628; www.melangeworld. com), known for its ultrafeminine designer dresses made from delicate chiffon. If you don't plan to visit Jaipur, stop at the Mumbai branch of **Anokhi** (Rasik Nivas, Metro Motors Lane, off Hughes Rd.; ℂ **022/2368-5761**), for its East-meets-West garments, accessories, and housewares. Nearby is the turquoise-walled **Neemrana** store (Opera House; ℂ **022/2361-4436**), with its gorgeous ethnic designs.

India's most famous *dhurrie* designer is **Shyam Ahuja** (78 India House, Kemps Corner; ℂ **022/2386-7372**), known for outstanding and expensive hand-woven products. Besides gorgeous home furnishings, table linen, bathrobes, and towels, you can purchase authentic Pashmina shawls here.

JEWELRY

Tribhovandas Bhimji Zaveri (241/43 Zaveri Bazaar; ℂ **022/2342-5001** or -5002), stretching over five separate floors, has a reputation for exceptional gold and diamond jewelry that dates back to 1865. It's very popular with Mumbai's wealthier crowd, so don't expect exceptionally good prices. Considered one of the country's finest places for designer contemporary jewelry, **D. Popli & Sons** ★★ is a family owned operation going strong since 1928; it's conveniently located, too, behind the Regal Cinema in Colaba (Ready Money Building, Battery St., ℂ **022/2202-1694** or 022/2204-2055). **Gazdar** (Taj Mahal Palace & Tower shopping arcade; ℂ **022/2202-3666**) has been selling Indian, Western, antique, and contemporary jewelry since 1933; again, the prices go with the territory. Serious buyers looking for one-of-a-kind pieces should consider contacting **Paulomi Sanghavi** (Hughes Rd.; ℂ **022/2367-6114** or 022/6634-7475; personal meetings by appointment only) or you can browse her unique ready-made designs in the store. Alternatively, walk into any one of the numerous jewelry stores along Hughes Road, such as **U. T. Zaveri** (Dharam Palace; ℂ **022/2367-9575**), where the designs are unusual and the salespeople extremely helpful.

ART, ANTIQUES & FURNITURE

For a startling array of antique finds and colonial furniture, there's no place like **Mutton Street** in the Chor Bazaar (see "Markets," earlier in this chapter; closed Fri), which is a wonderful place at which to browse and discover hidden treasures. You'll spot plenty of imitation antiques and faux products here, but these are usually pretty easy to identify. Store owners will often (but not always) tell you which are genuine items and which are reproductions. If, however, walking through dirty streets and sifting through dusty shops is not your cup of tea, head straight for the more established antiques stores in the city, some of the best of which are downtown in the Colaba-Fort area. **Natesan's Antiqarts** (ℂ **022/2285-2700**), conveniently located at Jehangir Art Gallery, deals principally in stone, wood, and bronze items. Whether you pick up an ornate teak and sandalwood carving, a bronze piece created using the 4,500-year-old lost-wax process, or a refurbished antique, Natesan's will arrange shipment. Nearby **Phillips Antiques** (opposite the

Regal Cinema in Colaba's museum quarter; © 022/2202-0564; www.phillipsantiques. com) offers a similar service; besides four-poster beds, armchairs, writing tables, and hat stands, you'll find gorgeous porcelain and pottery, brass and silverware, and a range of marble items for the home, not to mention ornamental pieces, antiquarian maps, lithographs, engravings, old photographs, and lovely lamps. Filled with beautiful objects, **Heeramaneck** (below Hotel Suba Palace, Battery St., Colaba; © 022/2202-1778 or 022/2285-6340) is another essential pit stop for antiques lovers. It has an especially good collection of Victorian and Indian silverware, including tea sets, candle stands, and sometimes cutlery as well. Two more places where you can track down exciting antiques, include **Artquest** (1, Dsaulat Bldg., Colaba; © 022/2215-0220; bijlani@bom2.vsnl.net. in), and **Tribal Route** (18/19 Aram Nagar 2, J.P. Rd., Machlimaar, Versova; © 99-6705-8847; tribalroute@gmail.com).

Finally, if you're keen to furnish your home with superb Indian furniture, then the best place in the city has got to be **Pinakin** ★★★ (second floor, Raghuvanshi Mills Compound, Senapati Bapat Marg, Lower Parel; © 022/6600-2400; www.pinakin.in), the sophisticated showroom of interior designer and architect Pinakin Patel. Even just visiting here will be a talking point back home.

---

7 MUMBAI AFTER DARK

Mumbai is hectic financial capital by day, but at night it's all about fun, delirious mayhem, and a good dollop of managed mischief—it's most definitely a city that never sleeps, with some of its defining adventures happening after sunset. The best way to figure out what's going on in the city is to pick up a copy of *Time Out Mumbai*, the twice-monthly magazine that has the most comprehensive Mumbai listings, including the lowdown on the best bars and clubs and a choice selection of all kinds of entertainment events. "The Hot List" supplement in the daily tabloid *Mid Day* also carries extensive listings of live music events, stage productions, and film screenings. *The Times of India* features an extensive "Bombay Times" section that lists and advertises cultural activities, entertainment happenings, and movies.

THEATER & LIVE MUSIC

Mumbai has numerous performance spaces, including its premier **National Centre for the Performing Arts** (Nariman Point; © 022/2283-3737; www.ncpamumbai.com). The NCPA houses several stages, including the city's "first opera theater," Jamshed Bhabha Theatre, which saw its first operatic production in 2003. English dramas and lavish musical concerts are held in the Tata Theatre; the aptly named Little Theatre features work of a more intimate scale. For offbeat drama, student work, and small-scale music and dance, the black-box Experimental Theatre, with its audience proximity, is the place to go.

Both Indian and Western theater and music performances are staged in the main auditorium of **Nehru Centre** (E. Moses Rd., near Mahalaxmi Race Course, Worli; © 022/2493-2667). There's also a smaller stage for experimental work.

Not far from Juhu Beach is Mumbai's best-loved venue for serious entertainment— **Prithvi Theatre** ★★ (Janki-Kutir, Juhu-Church Rd.; © 022/2614-9546; www.prithvi theatre.org). Owned by Bollywood's founding family, the Kapoors, Prithvi has a small, intimate performance space with great acoustics, and the aisles and steps are often crammed with enthusiasts. India's top productions are staged here during an annual drama festival (Nov–Dec), and the garden café (see p. 160) outside is popular with the city's culturati. Over the first weekend of every month (except June–Sept), free play readings and other performances are held in the gardens at **Horniman Circle** in the Fort area; contact Prithvi for details.

Definitely the top venue in the city for live music, the brilliant **Blue Frog** ★★★ (Todi & Co., Mathuradas Mill Compound, Senapati Bapat Marg, Lower Parel; ✆ 022/4033-2300) also has our vote as one of the most excellent nights out in Mumbai, if not the country. It's also considered Mumbai's dreamiest-looking nighttime venue, with eye-catching design that imaginatively synthesizes contemporary and old-world styles. Check the newspaper entertainment listings or visit the website (www.bluefrog.co.in) to find out what's showing—but even if there's nothing on the lineup that blows your hair back, it'd be worth your while to stop by for a few hours just to soak up the sensational atmosphere, admire the acoustics, find yourself dazzled by the lighting, and watch Mumbai's social set at its most playful and unhinged. Blue Frog is open daily from 7pm, and there's a Rs 300 cover charge.

On a more prosaic level, and something of a leftover from another era, is **Not Just Jazz By the Bay** (143 Marine Dr.; ✆ 022/2285-1876). With live acts churning out rock, blues and country (and, jazz, too) from Wednesday to Saturday, it's not a place of cultural innovation, but you may get a kick out of the studenty karaoke sessions held Sunday through Tuesday.

BARS, LOUNGES & OTHER WATERING HOLES

Fortunately, there's more to Mumbai's sophisticated social scene than the beer-quaffing tourist scene at **Leopold Café,** where the majority of the faces you see turn out to be foreigners (or Bollywood agents looking to co-opt foreigners as background scenery for their latest movies). By all means stop by Leopold's (see full dining review, p. 154), which has become even more legendary since it featured so heavily in David Gregory Roberts' *Shantaram,* but please don't assume this to be a place that's in any way synonymous with modern-day Mumbai. The city, as you'd imagine, has a great deal more to offer.

South Mumbai

Wink ★★★ (✆ 022/6665-0808) is the classy, ravishingly handsome watering hole at the Taj President in Nariman Point. What was once the more staid and serious (and single-mindedly business-oriented) Library Bar, Wink has become known as a seriously spunky gathering point for playful socializing, complete with cool beats from a former club land DJ, and a special range of drinks—the "winktinis" are reason enough to spend a couple of hours here. If the high-energy excitement around the main bar gets too much, you can sink into plush sofas in the lower-octane adjoining lounge where state-of-the-art sound cushioning means you don't have to leave the premises to engage in normal conversation. They even do a selection of detox cocktails, such as the unique and yummy "ancient cure."

Also gorgeously designed and aiming to attract a similar crowd, is **Valhalla** ★★ (✆ 022/6735-3535; www.valhalla.co.in), a sexy new all-day business lounge and nighttime tapas bar in the Eros Theatre Building in Churchgate. The subtly-marked entrance is around the left hand side of the Eros front entrance; head upstairs and the hostess will lead you into a vast room presided over by a hand-carved throne upholstered in pink—try one of their yaquitinis (a fresh grape martini) and sample the *albondigas* (meatballs) as you tap your toes to chilled DJ-spun electronic tracks. If your holy grail is a chic, exclusive lounge bar, nothing beats **Opium Den** at the Trident Nariman Point (© 022/ 6632-6320), which attracts well-heeled 30-something locals, expats, and hotel guests. Not far away, **Geoffrey's** (© 022/2285-1212) is the cozy bar (with overdone English-pub decor) at the Hotel Marine Plaza; it's often packed with an after-office crowd.

But for an unabashed übertrendy night out, there's nothing to touch **Indigo** ★★ (4 Mandlik Rd.; © 022/6636-8999 or -8983; see "Where to Dine," earlier in this chapter), still considered Colaba's hippest joint, and *the* place to see and be seen; low tables with flickering candles light up the who's who of Mumbai as they sip expensive wines and decadent cocktails against a ravishingly sexy backdrop of glamour and social voyeurism. At Indigo, you'll need to dress the part or end up feeling like the punch line in a cruel joke. However, there's a lot less air-kissing and pretense at next door **Busaba** ★★★ (© 022/2204-3779), where by all accounts you'll be served better-mixed cocktails (superb fig mojitos, by the way) at prices less likely to attract a second mortgage.

Also geared for a trendy night out, but this time packaged together with one of the finest views in the city—on the top floor of the InterContinental Marine Drive—is **Dome** ★★★ (© 022/3987-9999), an open-air, candlelit venue that's conceived to take full advantage of both the night sky and the glittering Queen's Necklace. With the dark blue horizon just beyond the terrace's glass railing and a star-studded sky above, Dome commands perhaps the best vista in the city. Sink into the inviting off-white sofas and overstuffed armchairs that surround scented candles and order a Caipiroska or a Mojito, or even a Long Island Iced Tea. You need to get here before sunset (it's open from 5:30pm), though, to best experience one of the city's defining moments. The Japanese food is unexceptional (and pricey), but there are few more appropriate places from which to watch the sun dip behind the horizon. Once you're done with views, or the weather's bad, you could try **Czar** ★, also at the InterContinental, which is the city's only vodka bar. Sporting baroque chandeliers and a chic neo-Society feel, it's a sophisticated (overtly bling) place to lose a few hours—there's a DJ on Saturdays, when you pay Rs 1,000 (per person or per couple) to get in, and occasionally even a bit of impromptu dancing.

Finally, if you really are in the mood for a more traditional/laid-back/old-fashioned night out, Mumbai has hundreds of places where you can nurse your beer, accompanied by just about any ambience you care to imagine. Of course, the oldest official bar in the city—with a license to prove it—is **Harbour Bar** (© 022/6665-3366) at the Taj Mahal Palace. A decent enough place for a quiet drink, the view of the Gateway of India is probably its best feature. Up the road from Leopold's, another Colaba institution is the cheerfully old school **Café Mondegar** ★★ (near the Regal Cinema; © 022/2202-0591), "Mondy's" to regulars, where you're as likely to rub shoulders with local punters as thirsty tourists. Under the gaze of caricatures by Mario Miranda, you'll soon find yourself slipping back to the '70s and '80s, aided by the decidedly Western jukebox selection. Nearby is the **Sports Bar Express** (© 022/6639-6681), perfect for beer-quaffers who can get a 1½-liter pitcher of beer for around Rs 300; you can also play pool or shoot hoops.

Central Mumbai, Bandra & Juhu

Many Mumbaikers will tell you that to find the city's most happening nightlife you need to head north. If you're serious about socializing, we recommend you throw caution (and your budget) to the wind, and make a beeline to the impeccably beautiful (perhaps slightly over-the-top) **Shiro** ★★★ (Bombay Dyeing Mills Compound, Pandurang Budhkar Marg, Worli; © 022/2438-3008), which, in design, pays tribute to the Far East, drawing a jet-setting clientele. With flickering candles and edgy lighting, boldly

Gay Bombay

Mumbai is considered the most accepting and cosmopolitan of India's cities, with openly gay Bollywood and TV stars, and plenty of socially connected people with armloads of gay friends. Much of that has to do with the fact that, as a big, bustling city on the move, Mumbai has always been less fussy about the private lives of its citizens—and it's only the gossip columns that waste too much time speculating about who's sleeping with whom. Still, the public gay scene is a remarkably small one, restricted to weekly club nights, private gatherings, and a few organizations furthering the human rights cause. There are no dedicated gay clubs or bars (not officially anyway), and most gay circles tend towards private get-togethers; with homosexuality unbanned as recently as mid-2009, there hasn't before been much scope to transform the scene into anything substantial—and there are still enough people here living in the shadow of strict family traditions and religious piety (at least in public). Now that India is finally out of the closet, and homosexuality no longer outlawed, there's likely to be a bit more of a scene happening in Mumbai. For the time being, there are only a small handful of places where you can expect any regular gay parties. In Colaba, **Voodoo** (Arthur Bunder Rd., off Colaba Causeway; ✆ **020/2284-1959**) has a weekly gay night on Saturdays (Rs 250), but it's terribly seedy, far too cramped, and frequented by many of the wrong kinds of people, not to mention prostitutes. Then again, some find this sort of sleaze works just fine (but keep well away from the toilets). A much better option is to check out what's been lined up by the city's two main LGBT organizations. **Salvation Star** (www.salvationstar.com) is the more interesting (and fresher) group that caters to a discernibly with-it crowd and ensures a steady supply of up-to-date beats spun at parties held in a regular club venue. **Gaybombay** (www.gaybombay.org) has been around for long enough to have established a fairly loyal following; the parties are quite well subscribed, and music treads a fine balance between decent Bollywood tracks and pure cheese. Still, that's what draws the crowds, and both gay men and lesbians do show up, so put on your saffron-colored tutu and your dancing shoes and go join them. A warning, though: Don't fall for scamsters who make a trade out of hustling gay men and then threatening to expose or blackmail them.

colored walls, high ceilings, and a plethora of Buddha statues making no effort to curb expenditure or hedonism, this place gets the balance between opulence and good taste just right. And, boy, do they mix a mean cocktail—for a price, of course. If Shiro proves too overwhelmingly Zen-tastic, you could always pop in the nearby **Hard Rock Café** (✆ **022/2438-2888**), which is extremely popular with a broad cross-section of Mumbaikers who usually help create an atmosphere that's quite distinct from your Hard Rock back home.

While Shiro only opens at night, another highly recommended Worli establishment—this time a laid-back, no frills, all-day wine bar—is Ivy ★★ (Indage House, Annie Besant Rd.; ✆ 022/6654-7939). It's salubrious and welcoming, and you needn't fuss too much about what you wear; neither will you need to contact your bank manager before visiting—a glass of wine starts at under Rs 50. Ivy kicks off at 11am.

If you're looking to stand cheek by jowl with the city's most beautiful men and women, then make sure you set aside at least one night for drinks and mischief at Bandra's superhip **Olive Bar & Kitchen** ★★ (Pali Hill Tourist Hotel, 14 Union Park, Khar [West]; ✆ **022/2605-8228**), where the acknowledged pastime seems to be distinguishing the models from the celebrities. Also in Bandra, **Seijo and the Soul Dish** ★★ (second floor, Krystal, Waterfield Rd.; ✆ **022/2640-5555**) has a trendy New York look (which is increasingly ubiquitous throughout urban India) with Japanese touches, regular live music and bartenders who know their business.

Farther north, **Vie Lounge & Deck** ★★ (102 Juhu Tara Rd.; ✆ **022/2660-3003;** www.vie.co.in)—perched at the edge of Juhu Beach—is a shimmering venue with an open-air lounge overlooking the Arabian Sea. Come here for the sea breeze and laid-back ambience. It's the perfect place for a wind-down martini after a long day, or—if you prefer to get wound up before an exhilarating night on the town—take advantage of their 4 to 7pm happy hour. Also in Juhu, and unquestionably the best reason to travel this far north after dark, is **Aurus** ★★★ (Nichani Kutir, Juhu Tara Rd.; ✆ **020/6710-6666**), a sublime venue affording sensational views of the sea, kissed by twinkling lights. Aurus isn't all that easy to spot from the road, so make sure your cab driver or chauffer knows where it is before you head off, or you'll waste time searching. Aurus only opens at 8:30pm, so you may want to start at Vie and then make your way here once the sun sinks.

If you disapprove of the swing towards social trendiness, don't panic—the suburbs have their share of old school haunts as well. If you miss the intimacy of your hometown local, head out towards Haji Ali and stop in at **The Ghetto** ★ (30B Bhulabhai Desai Rd., Breach Candy; ✆ **022/2353-8418**), a small, popular, and totally unpretentious hangout near the Mahalaxmi Temple. While it's no dive, the place in some respects lives up to its name—a slightly dingy entrance, graffiti on the walls, and a complete lack of dress code—which is probably why the regulars (collegians and after-workers rub shoulders with graying hippies, all of whom still salute Bob Marley and Jim Morrison) are so uncompromisingly devoted to this place. That, and the fact that the music remains strictly "rock 'n' reggae" (there's a band from time to time, too; entry free). You can even dance if you want to. For a similar vibe—and a more varied, sometimes hard-core soundtrack—in Bandra, consider paying tribute to the ever-popular **Toto's Garage** (30 Lourdes Heaven, Pali Junction; ✆ **022/2600-5494**), where the main attraction, apart from the music, is the shell of a car hanging from the ceiling over patrons' heads.

NIGHTCLUBS

While you could spend your entire stay in Mumbai partying in a different club each night and recovering the following day in your hotel room—this is one Indian city that loves to party—be aware that the nightclub scene is not concentrated on a single street, and most clubs close earlier than in the West. Mumbai's partying has also been tempered by the government's early closing rule. Although Western music is popular and has the buff and the gorgeous strutting their stuff every night of the week, Mumbaikars (thankfully) have a deep passion for contemporary Hindi songs as well, and it's not unusual to spot young studs demonstrating the choreographed rhythms of *MTV India*'s latest Bollywood video, much to the delight of their female companions. There are literally dozens of nightspots in the city, the most attractive (as far as decor goes) being in the five-star hotels. The nightclub scene has largely shifted to the suburbs of Bandra and Juhu, so

> **(Tips) Before You Queue in Club Land**
>
> Club entry fees differ depending on the night, and prices are typically per (heterosexual) couple; you'll usually get the price of admission back in coupons that can be exchanged for overpriced drinks at the bar. Many nightclubs charge extra for males entering alone, while most don't allow "stag" entry at all, though foreigners may sometimes sidestep this rule (and your concierge—if you're staying at the *right* kind of establishment—should be able to arrange a seamless passage through the front door). Closing times vary each night; there are "official" (currently 1:30am) and unofficial hours—which essentially means that clubs may stay open later than the time stipulated by law. The popularity of a club is sustained only if it can keep the cops out and stay open into the wee hours of the morning (five-star clubs can remain open until 3am, since they are inside private hotels). If you're traveling on a budget, you may want to take a page out of a hard-partying Mumbaikar's book and tank up at one of the city's watering holes before heading to a nightclub, where drink prices are usually exorbitant. In general, fun-loving locals hit more than one nightclub/bar/lounge per evening throughout this island city; if you hook up with a group, you may want to join them—although you should be extremely wary of getting in a car driven by someone who is drinking.

much so that even affluent South Mumbaikars who wouldn't normally venture to the 'burbs make a beeline for the happening clubs there. For the most up-to-date news on what's hot and what's not, get a copy of *Time Out* and talk to your concierge, because the nightclub scene changes rapidly. In particular, check whether the club recommended to you is popular with underage kids, as some clubs are, in which case you'd better avoid them.

Bling ★★   For late-night celebrity spotting, this is probably your very best bet, and hot-to-trot Mumbaikers are happy to travel this far north—to The Leela Kempinski hotel near the airports to rub shoulders with the hippest of the hip. Owned by well-known DJ Akin, you can expect a fair mix of house, commercial, and Bollywood tracks spun to satisfy an appreciative crowd. Open Wednesday to Saturday, 10pm to 3am; Rs 1,000 per couple. The Leela Kempinski, Sahar, Andheri (W). © 022/6691-1338.

Enigma ★★   Some call it sleazy—packed with pot-bellied Bollywood producers and would-be starlets dressed to seduce them—but this is nevertheless one of Mumbai's hottest nightspots. Although we think of it more as a study in the anthropology of excess and the cult of celebrity, you're welcome to join the bright shining stars on the large dance-floor (DJs play a mix of commercial tracks from the West and up-to-date Bollywood favorites), or at least watch the heady, intoxicating scene from the relative safety of the circular central bar (be warned—drinks ain't cheap). Marriot hotel guests (and silver screen superstars) get to jump the invariably long queue outside. Open Wednesday to Saturday; entrance is Rs 1,000 to Rs 2,500 per couple, with coupons redeemable for drinks. JW Marriott, Juhu Tara Rd., Juhu Beach. © 022/6693-3000.

Play ★★   In the heart of the gentrified Phoenix Mills Compound, Play is the updated incarnation of Ra, but still plays the latest rage in loud music, from hip-hop to Hindi

Late-Night Munchies?

And finally, if it's well past midnight and you're hungry, there are a couple of popular late-night feeding grounds in South Mumbai, both of which are real institutions among the party crowd. **Zaffran** (B Block, Sitaram Bldg., Dr. D.N. Rd., near Crawford Market; ⓒ **022/2344-2690**) has good Indian food (the murgh zaffrani tikka is delicious) and service going till 4am. A real late-night Mumbai institution in Colaba is **Bade Miya's** ★★ (Tulloch St., Apollo Bunder; ⓒ **022/2284-8038;** daily 7pm–4am), a down-to-earth hangout for anyone looking to satisfy a hunger; there are kebabs, and *naan* stuffed with egg and minced chicken or lamb (forget about what that sounds like—try it!), and very spicy chicken livers— cooked on an open grill and served in slightly shoddy surrounds (bear in mind that you're here for the food, nothing else).

remixes—but it is undeniably obsessed with all things Bollywood, so definitely the place to come if you want to learn some silver screen dance moves. The bar **(Voyeur)** is separate from the dance areas, but both attract an extremely upbeat (and rather young) crowd on weekends. Open Wednesday to Saturday 9pm to 1:30am; entry costs R1,500 per couple. Phoenix Mills Complex, 462 Senapati Bapat Marg, Lower Parel. ⓒ **022/6661-4343.**

Poison ★★ For Mumbaikers who really like to strut their stuff to the hottest beats (especially when the decks are manned by international DJs who are flown in from time to time), this is probably the hippest club in Mumbai. With a decent-size dance floor and a trendy international look. If you go on a Saturday night, you'll be one of at least a thousand guests! But don't worry: The club has 930 sq. m (10,000 sq. ft.) of space, and the air-conditioning still manages to work with that many bodies around. Bouncers at the door enforce a strict dress code: no shorts, sandals, saris, *salwar* suits, and (sorry, guys) no stags. Open Tuesday to Saturday 9:30pm to 1:30am; entry is Rs 1,000 to Rs 1,500 per couple. Basement, Krystal, 206 Waterfield Rd., Bandra (W). ⓒ **022/2642-3006.**

Polly Esther's Although we think this überpopular Colaba nightclub is way past its prime, it continues to attract a heady crowd—from teenyboppers to 40-somethings— with its mix of predictable mix of Bollywood, pop, and '80s music. The retro theme is echoed in posters of Michael Jackson and Madonna, while a roving Polaroid man takes your picture for Rs 100. There's plenty of space so things never feel cramped and crowded, but it's never going to be considered sexy or swanky, either. Open Tuesday to Sunday 9pm to 3am; entry from Rs 1,000 per couple. Gordon House Hotel, Apollo Bunder, Colaba. ⓒ **022/2287-1122.**

Privé ★★ Privé, behind Radio Club in Colaba, is so nauseatingly exclusive that members of the "general" public are only welcome on Wednesday nights. As a foreign visitor, however, you'll surely squeeze past the bouncers—just make sure your concierge arranges this in advance, and dress like it's your last night on earth. On the other hand, if you're a card-carrying celebrity or in with the Bollywood aristocrats, you might just stand a chance on your own. Incidentally, we think it's incredibly snooty. It's open Wednesday through Saturday from 9:30pm to 1:30am, and may go on later. 41/44 Mon repos, Ground Floor, Minoo Desai Rd., Colaba. ⓒ **022/2202-8700.**

Zenzi Mills ★★ For voyeurs there's plenty to see as you tap your feet to mostly excellent electronic tracks in a venue that's refreshingly uncommercial. Sun Mills Compound, Senapati Bapat Marg, Lower Parel. (C) **022/4345-5455.**

8 PUNE & THE OSHO INTERNATIONAL MEDITATION RESORT

Pune is around 125km (77¹/₂ miles) SE of Mumbai

Pune is Maharashtra's second major city and known to seekers of spiritual enlightenment the world over as the place where the dynamic New Age guru, Bhagwan Rajneesh—known to his devotees and enemies as Osho—established his controversial commune back in the 1970s. Today, Osho's vision for an appropriately modern environment where people from around the world can come to unlock the meaning of his discourses on spiritual enlightenment is realized in the form of a "Meditation Resort." Neither an ashram nor a cult headquarters (as many naysayers would have you believe), Osho's landscaped New Age campus (the grounds are exquisite enough to be an attraction in themselves) is a magnet for all sorts of people looking to find a different sort of meaning in their lives. They're not the only visitors to the city, though, since Pune has become a major industrial hub, attracting many foreigners who come to work and strike deals. Above all else, Pune looks and feels like a city that—like Mumbai—is on the move, expanding and modernizing at an incredible rate. While the spirit of upward mobility is evident, the city is also brimming with references to its past, particularly to that most venerated Maratha freedom fighter Chhatrapati Shivaji, who fought bitterly here against the Mughals who sought to conquer Maharashtra—you will, however, need to visit Pune's slightly cluttered **old quarter** to get a feel for the past; in particular, look out for symbols of Pune's immense love for the elephant-headed god, Ganesh, venerated here with gay abandon during the annual Ganesh Chaturthi. The area is easy enough to explore, even if only to check out the beautifully decaying *havelis* that line the streets, visit its colorful fruit and vegetable market, and check out the exhibits at one of the country's best-stocked museums. Besides being a university town with plenty of diversions for a younger crowd, Pune's altitude of around 600m (1,968 ft.) means that it stays relatively cool, and doesn't suffer from any of Mumbai's incessant humidity. For now the city also remains comparatively uncongested, although it's increasingly a magnet for people who are not prepared (or able) to put up with overpopulated Mumbai's soaring real estate costs

ESSENTIALS

GETTING THERE You can fly from **Mumbai** to Pune (both **Kingfisher** and **Jet Airways** have daily flights). However, while the flight from Mumbai lasts a mere 45 minutes, you'll spend so much time getting to the airport and then waiting for your plane, that we strongly suggest you consider taking a train, which takes 3 to 5 hours. If you're coming from **Delhi,** definitely fly; **Kingfisher** has daily flights departing at 3pm and 9:10pm, while in the morning there are two economy service flights on **Kingfisher Red.** Flights from Delhi take 2 hours. **Rail connections** between Mumbai and Pune are plentiful (and average 4 hr.), but you should endeavor to book your seat at least a few days in advance. For a good-value, fast journey, book an air-conditioned chair car seat on either the **Pragati Express** or the **Deccan Queen;** you'll be in Pune within 3½ hours. Another train

(Fun Facts) What's in a Name?

Many called him a cult leader and he's been branded everything from false prophet to criminal. Ever wondered how a 20th-century mystic came to be known as **Osho?** He explained that the name, which he adopted in the late 1980s just before his death, is derived from the William James word "oceanic," which is meant to mean "dissolving into the ocean." "Oceanic describes the experience," he said, "but what about the experiencer? For that we use the word 'Osho.'" Triumphantly for him, "Osho" also has historical roots in the Far East, where it also means "The Blessed One, on whom the sky showers flowers." That hasn't stopped many people from somewhat disparagingly referring to him as both a "sex guru" (he was vehemently against all forms of social and personal repression) and "the rich man's guru" (he famously owned 99 Rolls Royces—all of which were gifted to him by wealthy devotees), worse still, many of his followers refer to him as a god-man, whereas Osho shunned all religion. He is, in every possible sense, a true enigma.

you can try is the **Sahyadri Express.** It's also worth noting that the Mumbai-Pune Highway is vaunted as the most modern and efficient in the country, so road trips are not only exceptionally smooth by India standards, but also the scenery as you pass through the Western Ghats (lush, rolling mountains that separate the western coastal belt from the Indian interior); hire a car for the journey, or—for a fraction of the price—get a seat on one of the many "luxury" buses that ply the route from morning to night.

VISITOR INFORMATION & TRAVEL AGENCIES The fascinating Osho website (www.osho.com) offers all you need to know about the Meditation Resort. If you're curious about the Meditation Resort but unsure about whether or not to sign up, you can join one of two daily "silence tours," which take you around the campus and provide useful information about what to expect; the brief tours kick off at 9am and 2pm and cost just Rs 10 (this is the only way to see the resort without taking an AIDS test). If your interest is in the city itself, you could approach the **Maharashtra Tourism Development Corporation** (© 020/2612-6867), which has satellite counters at the airport and railway station; they're not a whole heap of help, however, so rather speak to locals, staff at the resort, or your hotel concierge. **K.K. Travels** (© 020/2436-3399 or -0099; www.kktravels.com) has a counter at the Osho Resort and can handle arrangements for airport pickups (Rs 600), local sightseeing, and any onward travel (a shared taxi to or from Mumbai airport costs Rs 650 either way). Another agency you can approach is **TC Travel & Services** (210/211 Metro House, Mangaldas Rd.; © 020/6400-8216).

GETTING AROUND If you're based at the Osho Resort, you'll probably be happy to stay in the vicinity of the meditation compound, and there's plenty to do within walking distance of the resort. Auto-rickshaws congregate near the resort entrance and are ubiquitous throughout the city; most will use their meters without having to be asked, others will happily offer you an "as you like" fare deal (in which you pay what you feel the driver's time, effort, and fuel have been worth; be fair). Pune Municipal Transport runs daily **sightseeing tours,** which you can book at the Pune Railway Station (© 020/3293-0008); they're unspectacular, but a mere Rs 152 gets you a seat on the A/C bus.

5

With the city's rapid expansion as a major industrial hub, many visitors (including large numbers of foreign businesspeople) tend not to venture far from the green, upmarket suburb of Koregaon Park. Situated around 30 minutes northwest of Pune's historic heart, this is also where hundreds of Osho devotees congregate around the Westernized cafes and restaurants in the immediate vicinity of the meditation resort they've come to experience. While the Osho Resort is surely the central reason for visiting, the historic Old City is architecturally and culturally fascinating enough to hold your attention for a while, and it's also where you'll discover one of India's most intriguing museums. You can take in the best of the city's "other" sights in one morning, and finish off with lunch in a traditional Maharashtrian diner (see "Where to Dine," later), before heading back to the resort for more earnest introspection. While here, do drop by the colorful **Mahatma Phule Market ★★** where orderly rows of fruit and vegetable stalls operate in a Victorian-era warehouse. You may also want to explore some of the streets and laneways around the market—many of the haveli-style buildings are architecturally intriguing, and a total contrast to the lavish modernism in Koregaon Park.

En route to the market, you'll probably pass the looming walls of **Shaniwarwada Palace** (Rs 100; Wed–Mon 8am–6pm) established here by the Peshwa rulers in the eighteenth century; no need to stop, though, since the palace itself has long been in complete ruin—the highlight being the views from the ramparts. If you are interested in learning more about the history of the city and the palace, you can check out the **sound and light show** that's staged here most evening (Rs 25; Wed–Mon 8–9pm) and gives some insight into the impact that Maharashtrian hero Shivaji had on the region. The palace is just a short distance from one of Pune's most beloved religious icons, a statue of Ganesha, the popular elephant-headed god. The basic little temple, no more than a roof over the venerated deity idol, is known as **Shrimant Dagdu Sheth Halwai Ganpati Mandir ★★** (Budhwar Peth), considered one of the most important temples in India, despite being a fairly recent construction. Ganesh, who is believed to be the god who can make wishes come true (believers whisper their desires into the ear of the rat upon which Ganesha rides), gets especially intense attention during the annual Ganesh festival, and each night a lovely *arti* ceremony is held here, attended by many devotees.

A short rickshaw ride from the market brings you to the intriguing **Raja Dinkar Kelkar Museum** (see below), which is one museum you shouldn't miss. Afterwards, you can visit one of Pune's prettiest buildings, the delicate-looking **Shinde Chhatri ★★** (© 020/2685-2141; Rs 2; daily 9am–6pm), located south of the race course in Wanowrie. This gorgeous cenotaph inters the *samadhi* (memorial) of the great Maratha warrior, Mahadji Shinde, whose descendants, the Scindias, are the royal family of Gwalior (p. 496). The vessels at the feet of the warrior's silver likeness are used in a daily *puja* ceremony, performed in the morning. If, after your city visit, you're keen on a bit more culture, stop off at the **Tribal Museum ★** (28 Queens Garden), which curates objects, icons and handicrafts associated with Maharashtra's tribal communities; photographic displays provide some anthropological insight into their lives.

Serious yoga enthusiasts might want to take a look at the website of the **Ramamani Iyengar Memorial Yoga Institute** (© 020/2565-6134; www.bksiyengar.com), where the founder of the global Iyengar Yoga movement still holds court. However, you need to be a veteran of the form with many years of practice if you intend joining one of his advanced courses. Beginners will have to dedicate themselves to one of the monthly induction programs that requires month-long participation.

Raja Dinkar Kelkar Museum ★★★   One of the most fascinating museums in the
country, this massive collection of objects spans the banal and the extraordinary, showcasing the arts and crafts of every possible corner of the country, starting with magnificent
Yali ("evil-crusher") sculptures at the entrance, five-headed *marutis,* and an elaborate
carved zodiac wheel. Assembled by the eponymous Dr. Kelkar, an optician and poet, the
museum grew out of Kelkar's penchant for historical poetry, which he famously wrote
under the alias Adnyatwasi. He yearned—obsessively, it would seem—to possess items
that would evoke the spirit of the history he was writing about, so he made a lifelong
career of collecting (over 20,000 items were amassed in 60 years). Today, only 12% of
the entire collection is on display, mainly due to space limitations. The museum demonstrates that there is a little bit of art in every creation, no matter how functional the
object. Yet, alongside the dazzling array of combs (in wood, ivory, horn, and metal), the
coconut graters, safes, noodle-makers, chairs, and kitchen utensils, there are giant Rajasthani carvings of mounted elephants, 12th-century stone dancers from Halebid, antique
manuscripts, examples of tribal art, and crocodile-skin body armor that would make
Giorgio Armani cry. Some of the more unusual exhibits include a selection of erotic
nutcrackers (not exactly what you think), more types of guitarlike instruments than you
ever imagined existed, and a South Indian suit of armor made from fish scales. Set aside
at least an hour (even two) to do this place justice. *Note:* There are plans to relocate the
museum to much larger, purpose-built premises, some 2 hours outside Pune. When this
is eventually built, it's hoped that the entire collection will be curated; but that's in the
distant future.

"Kamal-Kunj," Natu Baug, 1377–78 Shukrawar Peth. ✆ **020/2448-2101.** www.rajakelkarmuseum.com. Rs
200. Mon–Sun 9:30am–5:30pm

THE OSHO INTERNATIONAL MEDITATION RESORT

His name is synonymous with meditation and New Age catchphrases like "totality,"
"awareness," and "conscious living." Osho—once known as Bhagwan Rajneesh—is probably the most famous guru the modern world has known, and his teachings a compelling
upgrade on the work and spiritual systems of countless mystics who came before. A
philosopher and academic, Osho was groundbreaking, sensational, hugely popular,
and—for politicians and religious leaders—a massive headache. He drew thousands of
followers to communes around the world, and managed to raise hackles everywhere he
went, infuriating the American government (he was arrested in the U.S., and allegedly
poisoned while in prison) and getting himself barred from a long list of countries. Even
now, 20 years after his death, his legacy causes suspicion among many Pune residents and
naysayers everywhere.

  Whatever you might have heard, the very best of Osho's teachings on enlightened living
and meditation continue to inspire thousands who come to the **Osho International
Meditation Resort** ★★★ each year, most of them looking to reconnect with themselves
or find motivation for their quest towards leading a more meaningful life. The resort is the
same commune—now much expanded and elegantly prettified—that grew around Osho
in the 1970s when he gave almost daily discourses in Hindi and English covering his
insights into all the major spiritual paths, including yoga, Zen, Taoism, tantra, and Sufism,
and talking in detail about Gautama Buddha, Jesus, Laotzu, and other important mystics.
In the early 1980s, he developed a degenerative back disease and traveled to the U.S. in
anticipation of surgery. He ended up on a ranch in Oregon where a devotional community
that became known as Rajneeshpuram (the largest spiritual community ever started in the
U.S.) grew around him and quickly attracted suspicion from all quarters; Osho's arrest,

imprisonment, and deportation followed—all under varyingly mysterious circumstances—after he was charged with immigration fraud and tax evasion. Following several years spent traveling the world in search of asylum, and being denied visas, entry, or support in a string of countries, many of them under political pressure from Reagan's government, Osho finally returned to his Pune ashram in 1987. For the next 3 years he developed some of his most innovative meditation techniques and initiated the compulsory evening darshan known as the Evening Meeting of the Osho White Robe Brotherhood—to this day, the "meeting" is the culmination of all daily meditations and workshops held at the resort. In 1989, he gave up his name in favor of Osho, and a few months later, in January 1990, died from complications believed to have arisen from being poisoned while in prison in the U.S.

The commune that Osho left behind may have changed somewhat and adapted with the times to some extent, but the focus here is still overwhelmingly on meditation. According to Osho, meditation is the only path to enlightenment and is essential if you are to "become the Buddha that you already are"—the resort strives to be a place where you can work on achieving just that. While at the resort (don't come here expecting to find an ashram—aside from a few rules regarding dress, general decorum, and attitude, there's nothing of the monastic lifestyle that you might associate with ashram life—and there's a huge pool, relaxation facilities, cafes, and health club), you're encouraged (but certainly not compelled) to attend as many meditation sessions as you can cram into a day. Each session is markedly different from the next, so you get to experience a range of personal insights. From well-known approaches such as Tibetan humming, silent sitting, and meditative breathing, to Osho's own techniques that include dancing ("there is nothing more miraculous for meditation than dancing," he said), gibberish, "letting go," and the grueling, invigorating "dynamic meditation" held every day at 6am—one of the triumphs of the resort is that you have a chance to discover methods that work for you.

On top of the timetabled regime of meditations, there are talks and lectures, and you can sign up for one of the programs at the **Multiversity,** where seriously "alternative" courses, designed to pave the way to a smoother existence (without the strictures of the social world), are offered at extra cost. Taught by practitioners from a range of disciplines and backgrounds (and from all over the world), these workshops may sound ethereal—with titles such as "Dehypnosis, Self-hypnosis and Meditation" or "The Beauty of Darkness"—but they're mostly practical and, at the very least, will help you see the world from a different perspective. You can also go in for various healing treatments, therapies, and massages, or reiki.

All this happens in a very relaxing, soothing environment—the campus of modern buildings spreads around a variety of gorgeous gardens with rock pools, waterfalls, and gleaming courtyards, while various pyramidal structures (including the massive Osho Auditorium, where most meditations take place) lend a real sense of dignified otherworldliness to the place. A small boutique, **Osho Galleria,** sells robes (plain maroon ones are worn throughout the day, while white ones are worn for the main evening meditation; Rs 480 each), meditation chairs, mats, eye-masks, and other meditation paraphernalia, and there's a bookstore packed with Osho readings. Whatever you do, don't miss at least one meditation session in the sensationally beautiful mirrored **Chuang Tzu Auditorium,** the meditation room in the house where Osho lived—as you traipse in for your meditation (wearing white socks to protect the untreated marble floors), you pass thousands of books that fill Osho's private library, and file into an exquisite, mirrored room that seems like something out of a futuristic sci-fi movie. There's also a very smart guesthouse (right next to the main auditorium)—your best accommodation choice if you're serious about your time here (see "Where to Stay," below).

Declaring him to be one of "1,000 Makers of the Twentieth Century," the U.K.'s *Sunday Times* wrote that Osho's "teachings are uncompromisingly radical, antirational, and capricious. They invite the individual to free him- or herself from all the social conditioning: The only commitment is to be open and honest, to enjoy life, love oneself." Indeed, any time spent at the resort will clue you in to Osho's crusade against social conditioning. A basic tenet of Osho's philosophy is that social norms, regulations, strictures, and rules need to be broken down completely and that an entirely new way of life needs to be forged—the resort is about "deprogramming" and old hands here will tell you that it is we who carry the "asylum" of the socialized world around with us. These are unsettling concepts if you're in any way nervous about looking beyond the conventional, but there's really nothing much to fear, and there are no unreasonable demands placed on anyone who attends. If nothing else, you're likely to have a good time, meet interesting people from all walks of life, and discover at least a hint of inner peace.

By all accounts, if you speak to some of the devotees who work at the resort and who knew him before he left his body, Osho thrived on controversy and went out of his way to challenge convention—worth knowing if you're expecting to find religion, or some goodie-two-shoes, happy clappy hippie colony (although some devotees do tend to smile a lot, hug one another, and break into spontaneous dancing). It'd also be worth your while to read some of Osho's discourses before committing to time at the resort—he delivers compelling evidence of his desire to change the very essence of human thinking. At every turn he encouraged humanity to become more human—a profound challenge, but one that we all have a stake in. At this Meditation Resort, you may just have an opportunity to face that challenge. It might well be the start of a personal revolution.

Note: During the quieter summer and monsoon months, the resort runs a 2- night, 3-day "Amazing Weekends" package (Rs 14,600 double, including accommodation, meals, robes, HIV test, and your daily meditation pass)—it's an excellent deal, and great value if your time is limited or you need to test the waters before committing to a longer stay. However, it's worth noting that 2 days is really just enough time to find your feet—if you want to experience a profound shift, you'd do well to make a longer commitment. 17 Koregaon Park. (✆ **020/6601-9999.** www.osho.com. Daily meditation pass Rs 550. Entry to the resort is dependent on obtaining a negative result on an HIV test conducted at the Resort's Visitor Centre during the registration process.

WHERE TO STAY

Pune has a vast selection of hotels, including several newly built upscale properties aimed at the burgeoning business market. Many of these are very conveniently located within walking distance of the Osho Resort, which also has its own very efficient, very Zen, guesthouse (reviewed below)

Expensive

In addition to the better-located hotels reviewed below, another interesting choice is Pune's very own version of **The Gordon House Hotel** ★ (132A University Rd., Ganeshkind; ✆ **022/6604-4100/4;** www.ghhotel.com) where, as with the two sister hotels in Mumbai, rooms are characterized by a theme. You can go for the clean-lined Ikea look of the Scandinavian rooms or the overly dainty apple green and floral ensemble in the Country rooms—but we definitely think you'll have more fun in either the macho "Don's Den" or minimalist "Zen & Now" suites. The hotel has a lovely light-filled

A Home Away from Home in Pune

Pune's packed with accommodations, but most of these cater to the city's multitudinous business travelers—so if you want anonymity and kid-glove service you'll find it easily enough. The perfect antidote for anyone who's grown weary of hotel blandness is **Casa Nava** ★★★ (℃ **98-2316-9507;** www.casanava.com), a string of individually designed apartments (from studios to three-bedroom units) that can be rented for a day, a week, or as long as you want. Each flat is personally furnished and decorated by Nava Sanders, an Israeli interior designer who arrived in Pune 15 years ago and fell in love with the place. Today, she braves the traffic on her little scooter, keeping an eye on nearly 30 different places in and around the tree-filled lanes of Koregaon Park, and all convenient for the Meditation Resort. Each chic little unit has its own character—decor is a mix of effervescent European design, traditional Indian art, hand-picked fabrics (and curtains made from recycled saris), and bold colors or cheerful motifs that tie everything together. Each bright, light-filled, slightly boho property is tended by a housekeeper and there's a handyman to deal with any potential problems. It's like being a full-on resident, but without the hassle. Besides which, Nava herself is always on hand to assist—she recommends restaurants, gyms, spas, and salons, helps with travel arrangements, and lets you in on the best shopping secrets. Top picks include the Zen-simple White House apartment, with a rooftop balcony poised above the neighborhood park, and the "Studio Flat" at Casa Shanti—an enormous space with a river view, statues of Hindu gods, and a wonderful, partially covered terrace. Each unit has a full kitchen with enough bits and pieces to make it feel just like home—Nava will show you where to shop for groceries. All this, and the price is just perfect, too—from Rs 1,500 to Rs 3,000 per night for a one-bedroom apartment, to Rs 4,500 to Rs 5,000 for a two-bedroom unit; there are larger places, too. Your laundry gets done for Rs 200 per week, and most electricity (within reason) is included in the price.

lounge, a restaurant with live music, a spa, and access to a five-screen multiplex and shopping mall, all of which is only going to prove distracting if you're trying to get in touch with the inner you through daily meditation.

The O Hotel ★★ This glitzy, fresh hotel is all about good looks, kinky design-centric novelties, and high-level pampering; ultimately, it's quite a bit of fun, too. Everywhere you look there's a quirky feature, whether it's the huge variety of unusual light fittings, the dreamy use of colors and patterns, the starlight effects in the elevators, or great views from the rooftop pool (where you can dine at tables parked in the water). Rooms are sleek, slick, ultramodern spaces with bathrooms divided from the living area by a curtain that can be pulled back to allow you to watch TV while lying in the tub. Aside from a pillow menu featuring, among others, a mustard pillow, there are thick, firm mattresses with lusciously soft linens, and very cushy leather armchairs. The spa features a set of open-air rooftop cabanas—beautiful massage spaces with views over Koregaon Park; lying here, you can see Osho's main auditorium, probably before drifting off into a beautiful reverie.

North Main Rd., Koregaon Park, Pune 411 001. *℃* **020/4001-1000.** Fax 020/4001-1009. www.ohotelsindia.
com. 112 units. Rs 11,500 deluxe double; Rs 13,500 Club double; Rs 17,500 suite. Rates include breakfast
and airport transfers; 10% tax extra. AE, DC, MC, V. **Amenities:** 3 restaurant; including Addah (see "Where
to Dine," below), outdoor hookah lounge, 2 bars; free airport transfers; health club and spa; large outdoor
rooftop pool; room service; Wi-Fi (in lobby; Rs 400/hr.). *In room:* A/C, TV w/video on demand, hair dryer,
Internet (broadband; Rs 393/hr.; Rs 770/day), minibar.

St. Laurn ★★   Panels of primary colors add a dash of fun to the steel and glass facade
of this smart, contemporary hotel that opened in 2007. Step inside and it feels as though
you've entered a compact version of a modern airport—in fact, even the staff uniforms
resemble airline outfits. Lots of mirrors and massive windows help create an illusion of
space; swaths of marble and straight, unfussy lines keep things looking slick and impeccably professional. The rooms are thoroughly modern, yet—thanks to a designer's
touch—rather handsome, with wood flooring, smart rugs, leather headboards, and glass
walls separating the bathroom from the sleeping area. There's a rooftop pool with
360-degree views of the city and leafy Koregaon Park; you can also get a good view from
your room if you book an odd-numbered unit on floors five, six, or seven.

15A, Koregoan Rd., Pune 411 001. *℃* **020/1000-8000.** Fax 020/1000 8099. wwww.stlaurnhotels.com. 63
units. Rs 12,000 executive double; Rs 13,000 superior double; Rs 14,000 deluxe double; Rs 1,000 extra
bed. Rates include breakfast, airport transfers, and daily suit pressing. AE, DC, MC, V. **Amenities:** 2 restaurant; lounge, bar; free airport transfers; tiny health club; rooftop pool; room service. *In room:* A/C, TV/DVD,
hair dryer, minibar, Wi-Fi (free)

Taj Blue Diamond ★★   At press time, Pune's oldest five-star hotel was getting a
well-deserved face-lift, especially in its public areas. Don't despair at the grotty exterior,
built before this was a Taj property—once you step inside, it's a calm, elegant environment with genteel service and up-to-date accommodations geared towards high-powered
business travelers (who comprise around 99% of the guests). Rooms have a more classic
look than those at either St. Laurn or The O, with cream-colored walls, plenty of gleaming marble, and great big glassed-in showers (only the suites have tubs)—no tricksy color
schemes or crazy lighting, but rather good views over Koregaon Park, especially from the
upper floors. The North Indian specialty restaurant is one of the few upmarket places
where you can try traditional Maharashtrian recipes.

11 Koregaon Rd., Pune 411 001. *℃* **022/6602-5555.** Fax 022/6602-7755. www.tajhotels.com. bluediamond.
pune@tajhotels.com. 111 units. Rs 16,500 deluxe double; Rs 19,000 deluxe premium double; Rs 25,000
deluxe suite; Rs 30,000 presidential suite; Rs 500 extra bed. Rates (except deluxe rooms) include breakfast
and one-way airport transfer. AE, DC, MC, V. **Amenities:** 3 restaurants, including Mystic Masala (see
"Where to Dine," below), bar; airport transfers (Rs 560; one way free except for deluxe rooms); health club
and massage facility; pool; room service. *In room:* A/C, TV/DVD w/media hub, hair dryer, minibar, steam-
shower (in suites), Wi-Fi (Rs 224/hr.; Rs 673/day).

Moderate/Inexpensive

Hotel Sunderban   You'll need to book well ahead if you intend staying at this old-
fashioned budget hotel right next door to the Osho resort. The air-conditioned rooms,
especially, fill up fast, and the midyear discounted rates (with more than 50% off some
rooms) make this a popular choice with devotees checking in for prolonged periods. In
its favor, the hotel retains much of that mellow charm that comes with age—there's a
large lawn (onto which the rooms and verandas face) and decor is an unusual mix of Art
Deco, Pop Art, and functional Modernism. To really confuse matters, the most expensive, refurbished "studio" rooms in the newer wing are trying pretty hard to look contemporary (proper mattresses, marble floors, bright orange walls, and plasma TV) While

feeling a bit run-down, there's real vintage atmosphere here, and totally bearable if you can put up with stuck-in-a-groove staff, flaking paint, flayed fabric, and occasionally, strange odors, too.

19, Koregaon Park, next to Osho International Meditation Resort, Pune 411 001. © **020/2612-4949** or 020/2612-8388. www.tghotels.com. Rs 700–Rs 800 economy double; Rs 1,000 standard double; Rs 2,000 A/C executive double; Rs 3,000 deluxe double; Rs 3,500 A/C deluxe double; Rs 4,000 A/C super deluxe double; Rs 4,000 Osho suite; Rs 7,500 A/C studio; Rs 500–Rs 1,000 extra person. Rates include breakfast; 10% tax extra. Off-season discounts apply Apr–Sept. MC, V. **Amenities:** Lounge; airport transfers (Rs 350); room service. In room: A/C (some), TV, fridge, Wi-Fi (free).

The Osho Guesthouse ★★ (Value) This must be the Rolls Royce of Zen-styled lodgings—simple, elegant, and free of distractions (like phones and TVs) likely to interfere with your reason for being here. Beyond a 24-hour reception, a small lobby lounge, and laundry service, most activities (besides sleeping and showering) happen in various other parts of the campus (although lunch is taken in the efficient canteen-style cafe right next door to the guesthouse). Staying here makes it that much easier to participate in life at the resort, particularly when it comes to attending the strenuous 6am Dynamic Meditation session (a core ingredient of your Osho experience), without wasting time rushing back and forth to your hotel. Bedrooms are compact, with a functional modern design, and a sense of impeccable order prevails from the moment you're greeted at the front desk.

17 Koregaon Park, Pune 411 001. © **020/6601-9900.** Fax 020/6601-9910. www.osho.com. guesthouse@ osho.com. 60 units (all with shower only). Dec–Feb Rs 5,000 double; Mar–Nov Rs 3,500 double. Rates exclude 10% tax. MC, V. **Amenities:** The guesthouse is part of the Osho International Meditation Resort, incorporating 2 cafes, evening snack and beverage bar, a variety of meditation spaces; health club; Internet (in dedicated cybercafe; Rs 1/min.); medical center; large outdoor pool; tennis court; travel agency. In room: A/C, no phone.

The Samrat Hotel (Value) It's a characterless business hotel in an unfetching location (opposite the railway station) and accommodations are very ordinary-looking. Rooms feel like converted offices, with marble floors, low beds, and that dreary modular look that afflicts so many midrange places. But here, the room quality is more than made up for by the pleasant disposition of the staff and the exceptionally good rates. Everything is spotless and the restaurant is a real haunt for the local office crowd. Besides, it's only 1½km (1 mile) from the Osho resort, and that's where you're likely to spend most of your time anyway.

17, Wilson Garden, Pune 411 001. © **020/2613-7964.** Fax 020/2605-5460. thesamrathotel@vsnl.net. 51 units (tubs in suites only). Rs 2,200 executive double; Rs 2,900 A/C executive double; Rs 3,600 suite; Rs 400 extra person. Rates include breakfast; 10% tax extra. DC, MC, V. **Amenities:** Restaurant; bar; free airport transfer; room service. In room: A/C (some) and fan, TV, fridge (in suites), Wi-Fi (Rs 113/hr.; Rs 338/day).

WHERE TO DINE

Over and above the healthy fare served at the Osho resort (strictly accessible to card-carrying Oshoites who've signed up for a meditation pass), there's no lack of quality eating spots in this rapidly evolving city; the real trick is to find one of the original eating houses where locals go for their daily lunchtime feast. The best of these don't even have English signboards, nor do they look very much like restaurants from the outside anyway. If you're exploring the Old City, one of the most authentic places to stop for a good typical Maharashtrian vegetarian *thali* (platter), is **Badshahi** on Tilak Road. None of the upmarket hotels will have a clue what you're talking about if you ask about it, but an auto-rickshaw driver should be able to get you there. Don't expect any of the staff to speak any English, but when they see you arrive and hear you ask "*Thali?*" you'll be greeted with enough gestures to let you understand that you need to pay first (around Rs 50) and then wait a few moments until one of the tiny tables (mostly taken by single men on their lunch break) becomes free. The whole experience is a trip back to another era, with a totally absorbing ambience, cluttered with many years of history. As a foreigner, you'll feel like an unexpected VIP—excuse the stares and polite smiles—and staff go out of their way to feed you to the brim. The meal consists of limitless *chapatti,* which you use to mop up an assortment of vegetables and spicy, currylike dips (see "The *Thali*: A Meal Unto Itself," on p. 159 for more details). As you'll see from your fellow diners, there's no set pattern dictating *how* you feast—use your fingers, experiment, but don't drink the water—and the servers will continue ladling more of whatever you desire onto your metal dish. If only they made them like this back home . . .

For an upmarket version of honest Maharashtrian cuisine, there's no beating **Mystic Masala** at the Taj Blue Diamond (see below), which gets more interesting later at night when the business crowds leave and the Puneite families file in. Another hotel eatery that has the in-crowd flocking is **Addah** ★ (① 020/4001-1000), the poolside brasserie on the rooftop of the spiffy new O (see "Where to Stay," above). The main attraction is undoubtedly the setting—you feast under the stars, ordering from a variety of Indian dishes cooked on open coals in the live kitchen—so if the menu doesn't grab you, settle in at Addah's outrageously a la mode bar, **Minus** ★★★, which has been an instant hit with Pune's chichi crowd (so it's probably not compatible with a more meditational mood you're likely to pick up at the Osho resort).

There's more North Indian cuisine at **The Great Punjab** (5 Jewel Tower, Lane 5, Koregaon Park; ① 020/2614-5060), which serves good portions of authentic, rich, and delicious Punjabi favorites, as well as a few items you don't find just anywhere—do try the mince meat and ribs *(kheema champ),* which you can slop up with a couple of fresh *parathas.* For a cheap, quick meal, hit legendary **Prem's** (28/2 Koregaon Park; ① 020/2613-0985), which caters unashamedly to the international crowd from the Osho resort (which means there's a selection of European dishes alongside the very good Indian options).

Throughout the day, you'll find Oshoites gathered around the tables at Koregaon Park's **German Bakery** ★ (291 Vaswani Nagar; ① 020/2613-6532) which is pleasant enough (despite rather rude service) and serves incredibly good healthful breakfasts, delicious baked goods, and decent coffee. Try not to be put off by the persistent auto-rickshaw-cum-drug *wallahs* who hang around outside the cafe—they're irritating, but harmless. Another all-day hangout, but where the vibe is definitely better at night, are the string of casual eateries at **ABC Farm** (2 Moledina Rd., Pune Camp; ① 020/2613-8275), where you can browse around for a menu and ambience that suites your mood; currently, the rustic-trendy Shisha Café is incredibly popular (although we've found the service slow enough to send us packing). Far better, and a little more grown up, though, is **Kiva The Lounge** ★ (Range Hills Rd.; ① 020/2553-8339), which is probably more suitable as a hangout for drinking and lounging as it is a place for its casual dining; do be warned that it gets extremely noisy in here, usually a result of uproarious support for its music. Finally, the top choice in town for Pan-Asian cuisine is **Malaka Spice** (see below), which definitely takes the prize as the most unique of Pune's smarter restaurants.

Malaka Spice ★★ PAN-ASIAN   The look is minimalist, spiced up with good-looking art on the walls that double as a gallery for contemporary Pune artists. Adding a different kind of spice is an on-site caricaturist who hops from table to table producing quirky keepsakes by which to remember your evening here. The food, too, is quite memorable, and owners Praful and Cheeru pride themselves on using ingredients that are grown on farms around Pune especially for them; all their herbs are organic, and what isn't available locally is specially imported—no tins, canned or powdered, or preserved ingredients, either, apparently. Start with the duck *momos* (Tibetan dumplings), and then follow up with one of their famous curries: Vietnamese Topaz curry, or flavorsome Penang curry with cinnamon, cloves, coconut milk, galangal, onion, and lemon. They do wonderful things with prawns (try the lemony steamed tigers); and the wild ginger mutton is divine. Proceed with caution if you're not a spice person—the food has gotten at least one report involving an upset tummy. Finish with mango or watermelon sorbet.

Lane 5, across from Oxford Properties, Koregaon Park. ⓒ 020/2615-6293, -2008, or 98-2306-4050. www. malakaspice.com. Main courses Rs 165–Rs 250. MC, V. Daily 10am–11pm.

Mystic Masala ★★The devoted chef has put great effort into researching village recipes and come up with versions of traditional dishes that work well for an international palate. A few unique dishes worth trying include *aloo chi wadi* (potato leaf stuffed with gram flour, then steamed and fried), *bharleli vangi* (brinjal stuffed with masala and peanut paste, and then cooked), and the utterly delicious and simple *pitla* (seasoned gram flour that arrives looking like yellowish mashed potato). The traditional country chicken *(kombdi kolhapuri)* is highly recommended, as is the slightly dry, unspiced lamb dish, *sukka muttana.* Order *jawaraachi bhakri* (whole millet bread) as an accompaniment and to mop up any sauces, and finish off with a bowl of the delicious *paan* ice cream. At lunchtime, you can order a Maharashtrian *thali,* but you'll miss out on the elegant Indian classical music that's performed here live every night.

Taj Blue Diamond, 11 Koregaon Rd. ⓒ 022/6602-5555. Main courses Rs 255–Rs 705, leg of lamb Rs 1,255. AE, DC, MC, V. Daily 11:30am–3pm and 7–11:30pm

9 AURANGABAD & THE ELLORA & AJANTA CAVES

Aurangabad is 388km (240 miles) NE of Mumbai

The ancient cave temples at Ellora and Ajanta are among the finest historical sites India has to offer, and a detour to this far-flung region of Maharashtra to view these World Heritage Sites is well worth the effort. You can cover both Ellora and Ajanta comfortably in 2 days, but for those who are truly pressed for time, it is possible to see both sets of caves in a single (long, tiring) day. To do this, you'll need a packed lunch from your hotel, and plenty of bottled water. Set out for Ajanta at about 7am, reaching the ticket office as it opens (recommended for the tranquillity of the experience, even if you're not trying to cover both in a day). Spend no more than 3 hours exploring Ajanta, before heading for Ellora; your driver should be aware of the detour along the Ajanta-Aurangabad road that will get you there much faster. The caves at Ellora are spread out, so don't drag your heels, and be sure not to miss the ultimate jaw-dropper, known as "Cave 16": the Kailashnath temple complex is more carved mountain than cave. The world's largest monolithic structure, it is twice the size of the Parthenon. Note that Ajanta is closed on Monday and Ellora on Tuesday.

ESSENTIALS

GETTING THERE   The quickest way to get here is to fly; Aurangabad's airport is just 10km (6¼ miles) from the city center; **Kingfisher** (℃ **022/6649-9393** in Mumbai, or 1-800/233-3131 anywhere in the country; www.flykingfisher.com) flies from Mumbai each night at 8:30pm (landing an hour later), and there's a 2-hour flight from Udaipur at 11:15am. **Jet Airways** (℃ **022/3989-3333** or 1-800/225-522 in Mumbai, 0240/244-1392 in Aurangabad) and **Air India** (℃ **022/2202-3031** or 1-800/180-1407) also flies here. For a cheaper, fairly comfortable, but much longer journey, book an air-conditioned chair car seat on the **Tapovan Express** for an early morning departure from Mumbai, arriving in Aurangabad nearly 7½ hours later. If you'd rather not waste half a day traveling, an alternative is the overnight **Deogiri Express,** although you'll be pulling in at an inconvenient time very early in the morning.

VISITOR INFORMATION   You'll find a tourist information booth at the airport arrivals hall, where you can pick up brochures on Aurangabad, Ajanta, and Ellora. The **India Tourism Development Corporation (ITDC) office** at Krishna Villa, on Station Road (℃ **0240/233-1217** or 0240/236-4999; Mon–Fri 8:30am–6pm, Sat 8:30am–2pm), is where you can get tourism-related information and book a **private guide** for the caves, although it's cheaper to pick one up at the caves themselves. The state tourist office at the **MTDC Holiday Resort** (Station Rd., Aurangabad; ℃ **0240/233-4259;** www.maharashtra tourism.gov.in; daily 7am–1pm and 3–8pm) operates tourist buses to Ajanta (Rs 300) and Ellora (Rs 200).

GETTING AROUND   Taxis and **auto-rickshaws** are widely available in Aurangabad, and you'll be approached at the airport by the usual touts offering you a "good deal." Though the scamsters and touts here are far less aggressive or annoying than those you encounter farther north, always arrange the fare upfront; a taxi from the airport into the city should cost about Rs 250. **Classic Travel Services** (at the MTDC Holiday Resort; see above; ℃ **0240/233-7788** or -5598, or 93-2521-2444; www.classictours.info; contact@ classicservices.in) will arrange just about any type of transport for travel within Aurangabad and environs (count on around Rs 2,000 for a full day with a car and driver, less if you're only going to Ellora); if you're in any way unsure, ask to speak to Anil Kumar (℃ **93-2600-3533**). All hotels have travel desks that will organize a car with a guide for any of the sights in the area; the best guides for the caves can be organized through Kishoor at the travel desk at the Taj Residency (see "Where to Stay," later).

AURANGABAD

Aurangabad takes its name from the last of the great Moghul emperors, the hard-edged Aurangzeb, who enacted an almost Shakespearean drama in the 17th century when he took control of the empire by murdering his siblings and imprisoning his father, Shah Jahan (p. 424), before leaving Delhi in 1693 to make this city his base. Today the sprawling city is one of the fastest-growing industrial centers in India, and while it's the most convenient base from which to visit two of India's most exquisite historic attractions, the cave temples at Ellora and Ajanta, it's not really a destination in its own right. However, time allowing, it has a few attractions worth noting. Best known is **Bibi-ka-Maqbara—** also known as the "Black Taj Mahal"—a mausoleum built for Aurangzeb's empress by his son, Azam Shah, and a supposed replica of the more famous mausoleum built by his grandfather in Agra. Set amid large landscaped gardens and surrounded by high walls, it's primarily interesting from a historical point of view, lacking as it does the fine detail and white marble of its inspiration (the builders were forced to complete the project in stone

The Finest of Fabrics

Aurangabad is the only place in the world where Himroo art and Paithani weaving is still practiced, a millennia-old brocade-weaving craft that combines silk and cotton yarn into an almost satinlike fabric. Weavers spend around 2 to 3 months working on a single Paithani sari, even longer on more intricate and detailed designs. A custom-woven Paithani sari with gold-plated thread, featuring a design based on one of the Ajanta murals takes a year to produce and cost up to Rs 200,000. A beautiful Himroo shawl can cost anywhere from Rs 1,000 to Rs 25,000, depending on the workmanship. Pay a visit to the **Aurangabad Himroo Art & Paithani Weaving & Training Centre** (Jaffar Gate, Mondha Rd., Aurangabad) to shop or see weavers at work, or stop at **Paithani Silk Weaving Centre,** 54 P1 Town Center, behind Indian Booking Office, opposite M.G.M. College (© **0240/248-2811;** daily 11am–8pm).

and plaster because of financial constraints). Although you can't enter the tomb itself, an amble through the grounds (admission Rs 100; daily sunrise–9pm) affords you the opportunity to compare this project with the original Agra masterpiece. If you follow the dirt road that leads past Bibi-ka-Maqbara up into the hills for some 2km (1¼ miles)—a stiff climb—you will come across the **Aurangabad Caves** (Rs 100; sunrise–sunset), a series of nine man-made Buddhist caves dating from the 6th to 8th centuries. Similar to the Buddhist Caves at Ajanta (but not in the same class), they feature original painting fragments and offer spectacular views of the city and the landscape beyond.

On the way to Ellora is **Daulatabad Fort ★★★** (Rs 100; sunrise–sunset), a spectacular medieval hill fortress that makes for thrilling exploration (you'll need at least 2 hours to do it justice—it's a vast complex of labyrinthine passages, multiple storied buildings, and precipices, with a number of stiff climbs to get to the best views). Built by the Yadavas in the 12th century, it comprises an elaborate system of mazelike tunnels that served as an ingenious defense system: Once intruders were holed up deep within the tunnels, guards would welcome them with flaming torches, hot oil, or burning coals, effectively grilling them alive.

A place largely untouched by tourism is **Lonar Crater**—created some 50,000 years ago when a meteorite careered into the basalt rock. It has a diameter of 1,800m (5,904 ft.), making it the largest crater in the world. Filling the bottom of the crater is water in which Ram and Sita are believed to have bathed while they were exiled from Ayodhya; temple ruins lie at the water's edge. Tranquil and remote, the crater is about 150km (93 miles) east of Aurangabad.

THE BUDDHIST CAVES OF AJANTA ★★★

106km (66 miles) NE of Aurangabad

During the 2nd century B.C., a long, curving swath of rock at a sharp hairpin bend in the Waghora River was chosen as the site for one of the most significant chapters in the creative history of Buddhism. Buddhist monks spent the next 700 years carving out prayer halls for worship (*chaitya grihas*) and monasteries (*viharas*) using little more than simple hand-held tools, natural pigments, and oil lamps and natural light reflected off bits of metal or pools of water. They decorated the caves with sculptures and magnificent murals that depict the life of the Buddha as well as everyday life.

The caves were abandoned rather abruptly after almost 9 centuries of activity and were only rediscovered in 1819 (by a British cavalryman out terrorizing wild boars). Time has taken its toll on many of the murals, and modern-day restoration projects have even contributed to the near-ruin of some of the work. Despite this, the paintings continue to enthrall, and it's hard to imagine the patience and profound sense of spiritual duty and devotion that led to the creation of this, arguably the best Buddhist site in India.

It takes some time to explore all 29 caves (which are numbered from east to west), and the sensory overload can prove exhausting; try at least to see the eight described below. It's a good idea to make your way to the last cave, then view the caves in reverse numerical order—in this way you won't be running with the masses, and you won't have a long walk back to the exit when you're done.

Richly decorated with carved Buddha figures, **Cave 26** is a *chaitya* hall featuring a *stupa* (dome-shaped shrine) on which an image of the Master seated in a pavilion appears. In the left-hand wall is a huge carved figure of the reclining Buddha—a depiction of the *Mahaparinirvana*, his final salvation from the cycle of life and death. Beneath him, his disciples mourn his passing; above, celestial beings rejoice. Featuring the greatest profusion of well-preserved paintings is **Cave 17,** where maidens float overhead, accompanied by celestial musicians, and the doorway is adorned with Buddhas, female guardians, river goddesses, lotus petals, and scrollwork. One celebrated mural here depicts Prince Simhala's encounter with the man-eating ogresses of Ceylon, where he'd been shipwrecked.

Cave 16 has a lovely painting of Princess Sundari fainting upon hearing that her husband—the Buddha's half-brother, Nanda—has decided to become a monk. **Cave 10** is thought to be the oldest Ajanta temple, dating from around the 2nd century B.C. Dating from the 1st century B.C., **Cave 9** is one of the earliest *chaitya grihas*, and is renowned for the elegant arched windows carved into the façade that allow soft diffused light into the atmospheric prayer hall. A large stupa is found at the back of the prayer hall.

Cave 4 is incomplete, but its grandiose design makes it the largest of the Ajanta monasteries. Take a quick look, then head for **Cave 2.** The facade features images of Naga kings and their entourage. Inside the sanctum, a glorious mandala dominates the ceiling amid a profusion of beautiful floral designs, concentric circles, and abstract geometric designs with fantastic arrangements of flying figures, beasts, birds, flowers, and fruits. On the walls, well-preserved panels relate the birth of the Buddha.

Cave 1 is one of the finest and most popular of the *viharas* at Ajanta, especially renowned for the fantastic murals of two bodhisattvas (saintly beings destined to become the Buddha) that flank the doorway of the antechamber. To the right, holding a thunderbolt, is Avalokitesvara (or Vajrapani), the most significant bodhisattva in Mahayana Buddhism. To the left is bejeweled Padmapani, his eyes cast humbly downward, a water lily in his hand. Within the antechamber is a huge seated Buddha with the Wheel of Dharma (or life) beneath his throne—his hands are in the *Dharmachakra pravartana mudra,* the gesture that initiates the motion of the wheel. On the wall to the right of the Buddha is an image of the dark princess being offered lotuses by another damsel.

Last but not least, for a magnificent view of the entire Ajanta site and an idea of just why this particular spot was chosen, visit the viewing platforms on the opposite side of the river; the natural beauty of this horseshoe-shaped cliff is the perfect setting for a

ⓘ Tips Ajanta Travel Advisory

The drive from Aurangabad to Ajanta takes between 2 and 3 hours, so you're advised to set off early in the day to avoid as much of the midday heat as possible. There are two ways of getting to the caves. Generally, visitors are dropped off in the public parking lot, several miles from the caves themselves; here you'll find stalls selling awful souvenirs, snacks, and tourist paraphernalia, and "guides" flogging their services. You'll also find green, eco-friendly buses that are the only vehicles allowed in the vicinity of the caves. Purchase a ticket (Rs 30) and hop aboard for the short drive from the Fardapur T-junction to the Ajanta ticket office. A far more rigorous but rewarding alternative is to have your driver drop you at the "Viewpoint," reached via a turnoff some distance before the official parking facility. From here you can take in a panoramic view of the site across the river, then make your way down the rather difficult pathway (don't attempt this route if you're unsteady on your feet) and eventually to a footbridge that spans the Waghora River. Make for the ticket booth and proceed to the caves. Be sure to arrange to have your driver collect you from the parking lot when you're done.

project so singularly inspired by spiritual fervor. It may even be the ideal starting point for your exploration.

Note: You will be required to remove your shoes before entering many of the caves, so take comfortable (and cheap) footwear that slips on and off easily.

Rs 250. Tues–Sun 8am–6pm. No flash photography.

THE BUDDHIST, HINDU & JAIN CAVES OF ELLORA ★★★

30km (19 miles) NW of Aurangabad

Ellora's 34 rock-sculpted temples, created sometime between the 4th and 9th centuries, were chiseled out of the hillside by Buddhists, Hindus, and Jains. A visit here allows for an excellent comparison of the stylistic features and narrative concerns of three distinct but compatible spiritual streams.

Of the 12 Buddhist cave-temples, carved between the 6th and 8th centuries, the largest is **Cave 5.** The "cave of the celestial carpenter, Vishwakarma" **(Cave 10),** is acknowledged to be most beautiful of the Buddhist group. A large ribbed, vaulted chamber, it houses a big figure of the Teaching Buddha, while smaller figures look down from panels above. The atmosphere here is chilling, a place for the suspension of worldly realities and for complete focus on things divine. In the three-story *vihara* (monks' domicile) of **Cave 12,** note the monks' beds and pillows carved out of rock. **Cave 13** marks the first of those carved by the Hindus which, when viewed in combination, offer a wealth of dynamic, exuberant representations of the colorful Hindu pantheon: Shiva as Natraj performs the dance of creation in **Cave 14** (where he is also seen playing dice with his wife Parvati and piercing the blind demon Andhaka with a spear); and in **Cave 15,** the manifold avatars of Vishnu tell numerous tales while Shiva rides the divine chariot and prepares to destroy the palaces of the demons.

Created over 150 years by 800 artisans, **Kailashnath Temple (Cave 16)** ★★★ is the zenith of rock-cut Deccan architecture, and Ellora's star attraction—widely considered

---

| Tips   Ellora Travel Advisory

These caves are only 30km (19 miles) from Aurangabad, but you should rent a car and driver for the day for transfers between certain caves. Starting at **Cave 1,** visit as many of the principal caves (don't miss **Cave 10**) as you have time for, until you reach **Cave 16,** where you should arrange for your driver to pick you up and then drive you to **Cave 21,** which is worth investigating. Having seen this cave, again have your driver take you to **Cave 29,** located alongside a waterfall, reachable via a rather dangerous pathway. Another short drive will take you to the **Jain Group** of temples, of which **Cave 32** is the best example.

Be warned that Ellora is enormously popular—especially during weekends and school vacations. Time your visit accordingly, or get here as soon as it opens, preferably not on a weekend. Ellora can be explored independently or with a guide—best to hire someone legit through your hotel, or through Anil Kumar at Classic Travel (see "Getting Around," earlier).

India's finest work of art—also known simply as **Kailasa.** A dazzling visualization of Mount Kailash, the mythical sacred abode of Shiva in the Tibetan Himalayas, it is unlike the other caves at Ellora, which were excavated into the hillside—it is effectively a mountain that has been whittled down to a free-standing temple, measuring 1,700 sq. m (18,299 sq. ft.). The intricacy of detail is remarkable; the temple basement, for example, consists of a row of mythical elephants carrying lotuses in their trunks as they appear to support the entire structure on their backs. Sculpted detail abounds in the temple and its excavated courtyard, with hardly an inch of wall space left unadorned—demons, dwarfs, deities, humans, celestial *asparas,* and animals occur in abundance. In the Nandi Pavilion facing the entrance is a beautiful carving of Lakshmi surrounded by adoring figures; seated in a pond, she is being bathed by attendant elephants carrying pots in their trunks. Also be on the lookout for *mithunas* —male and female figures in erotic situations.

The five Jain caves form a distinct cluster some distance north of the Hindu caves. Of these, **Cave 30 (Chhota Kailasa)** is the largest and the first to be excavated—it's a smaller, incomplete replica of the Hindu Kailasa cave, decorated with Jain saints and goddesses; within the sanctuary is an image of the founder of Jainism, Mahavira, who sits on a lion throne. Finest of the Jain caves is **Indra Sabha (Cave 32).** Here, an open court is adorned on each of its sides with carvings of elephants, lions and *Tirthankaras* (teachers worshipped by the Jains), and features a monolithic shrine in the center. Of special interest is the sculpture of the mother goddess, Ambika, recognizable from the child resting in her lap; beneath her is a lion, while a tree towers above. There are also ceiling paintings here depicting heavenly maidens and couples flying among the clouds.

The final cave, **no. 34** is a small Jain sanctuary with a seated Mahavira at its center.

Ellora Caves free. Entry to Kailashnath Temple Rs 250, free for children under 15. No flash photography. Wed–Mon 9am–5:30pm.

WHERE TO STAY

The palatial **Taj Residency** (reviewed below) is in many respects light-years ahead of the competition—thanks to a new wing and a full-blown decision to upgrade the entire hotel, it's made most other hotels in town look positively old-fashioned. One exception is the **Lemon Tree** (reviewed below)—part of a midrange chain that is steadily closing the gap between luxury and budget digs in key locations around the country—that was carefully crafted from the old bones of the former President Park. A further option you may wish to consider—and one which has long tried to match the Taj—is the **Rama International ★** (www.welcomhotelrama.com). Attractive interiors and perky modern rooms (starting at Rs 4,900 double) are the stand out feature here, but service and facilities don't quite match those at its main rival. Particularly disappointing is the pool: It's too darn small.

If you want ultracheap and functional and intend to eat out, then by all means endure a night or two at the government-run **MTDC Holiday Resort** (Station Rd., Aurangabad 431 001; ✆ 0240/233-1513), which offers relatively clean rooms in a central location (near restaurants, the taxi hub, and travel agencies) but little else (and you'll need to check out at 9am). Insist on an air-conditioned unit that costs Rs 1,100 double; family rooms are Rs 1,200. You may also wish to ask about rooms at the MTDC's hotel at **Fardapur** (✆ 02438/24-4230), some 5km (3 miles) from the Ajanta Caves; deluxe air-conditioned doubles go for Rs 900, but there are no restaurants to escape to, so you'll have to put up with the dull in-house option.

Amarpreet (Value) It ain't pretty, nor is it aiming at five-star status, but this is a serviceable budget hotel with neat, clean bedrooms, a pair of respected restaurants, and an obliging staff. Considering that Aurangabad is pretty much just a place to rest between trips out to the caves, we see no reason why you won't be perfectly comfortable here. Staff will happily arrange cars and guides, and are practically falling over themselves to come to your aid. If you fancy a special view, ask for a room facing the Bibi ka Muqbara; these rooms (at the back) are also less prone to traffic noise. Club rooms are altogether better than the slightly tacky deluxe units (which are carpeted, have very old furniture, and don't have tubs). At press time, the hotel was undergoing massive expansion (they're even getting a pool), so if you're concerned about the potential impact of construction noise, check ahead to see what the current status is.

Jalna Rd., Aurangabad 431 001. ✆/Fax **0240/662-1133,** 0240/233-2521, -2522, or -2523. www.amarpreet hotel.com. 30 units, with plans for 100 after extensive renovations. Rs 3,100 deluxe double; Rs 3,800 Club double; Rs 5,500 executive deluxe suite double; Rs 750–Rs 900 extra person. Rates exclude 10% tax; high season surcharge may apply. MC, V. **Amenities:** 2 restaurant; bar; airport transfers (Rs 250); children's play park; Internet (broadband in business center; Rs 50/hr.); room service. *In room:* A/C and fans, TV.

The Ambassador Ajanta ★　Set amid lovely lawns with fountains and well-maintained flower beds, this rapidly aging hotel offers good facilities and relative comfort—fine for relaxing after a hectic day of cave exploration, but in no way up to date with modern standards. Moghul artworks, statues, and objets d'art decorate the public areas, presumably recalling the creative spirit of Ellora and Ajanta, but bedrooms could do with a smartening up. Strangely, the cheaper executive rooms (on the fourth floor) feel altogether more comfortable—they have more dated (slightly vintage) furniture and finishes, but the ambience is better, with plush carpets, improved mattresses and (should you look carefully) erotic handles on the bedside drawers. The best rooms overlook the pool. Sadly, service is remarkably sluggish—so many people standing around observing.

Jalna Rd., CIDCO, Aurangabad 431 003. ✆ **0240/248-5211** through -5214. Fax 0240/248-4367. www. ambassadorindia.com. 92 units. Rs 5,000 executive double; Rs 6,000 superior double; Rs 6,000 executive suite; Rs 7,000 deluxe suite; Rs 9,500 Ajanta suite; Rs 12,000 presidential suite; Rs 800 extra bed. Children under 12 stay free if sharing without extra bed. Rates exclude 10% tax. AE, DC, MC, V. **Amenities:** Restaurant; bar; free airport transfers; babysitting (on request); badminton court; health club and basic spa; jogging track; large outdoor pool; room service; squash court; tennis court. *In room:* A/C, TV, DVD (on request), hair dryer, minibar, Wi-Fi (Rs 140/hr.; Rs 340/day).

Lemon Tree ★★ (Value) Close to the airport (10 min.) and the train station (20 min.), this smart, good-value hotel is a welcome addition to Aurangabad's hotel scene; light-filled public areas and fresh-looking rooms that are modern and sleek with wooden floors, large beds (and orthopedic mattresses), and plenty of bright, cheerful enhancements (modern artworks and colorful fabrics) to spruce things up. The best ones face the garden pool—a fine place to rejuvenate after visiting the caves—and there are a host of amenities (including a spa) to keep you occupied should you be looking for distractions while in Aurangabad. They've added thoughtful touches, too, like having PlayStation in the hip little lounge, along with board games and a pool table. The best feature, though, must be the stellar service; staff seems genuinely concerned about your well-being.

R-7/2 Chikalthana, Airport Rd., Aurangabad 431 210. © **0240/660-3030.** www.lemontreehotels.com. 102 units. Rs 5,000 superior double; Rs 6,000 deluxe double; Rs 7,000 executive double; Rs 10,000 suite; Rs 1,000 extra bed. Rates include breakfast; taxes extra. MC, V. **Amenities:** Restaurant; bar; airport transfers (Rs 200); health club and spa; large outdoor pool; room service. *In room:* A/C and fans, TV, hair dryer, minibar, Wi-Fi (Rs 160/hr.).

The Meadows (Kids) Surrounded by 5.2 hectares (13 acres) of pleasant greenery, this small resort is great if you'd rather stay out of town. Accommodations are in a variety of simple cottages, the size and level of privacy varying according to price. Deluxe units are quite basic, so opt for the superior category (ask for G1), with white marble flooring, stiff cane chairs, and tiled bathrooms with drench showers. Save for the striped drapes, there's not a lot of decoration, but the plain white rooms are fine when contrasted with the lush garden surroundings. There's plenty here to keep young children occupied (including rabbits) while you relax in a quiet corner after sightseeing under the Maharashtrian sun (albeit with highway traffic noise now a constant presence). Breakfast is served poolside, under large, umbrella-like canopies; exotic birds, wild parrots, and butterflies provide the entertainment, and while staff aren't all adept at English, everyone puts in a good enough effort. *Note:* Apparently, a major revamp and upgrade is scheduled, and with this might come a big jump in prices; call ahead to check.

Gat no. 135 and 136, Village Mitmita, Aurangabad-Mumbai Hwy., Aurangabad 431 002. © **0240/267-7412** through -7421. Fax 0240/267-7416. www.themeadowsresort.com. Reservations (Mumbai): © **022/6654-8361** or -8362. Fax 022/2203 3622. reservations@themeadowsresort.com 48 units. Rs 4,950 deluxe double; Rs 6,050 superior double; Rs 9,900 1-bedroom suite; Rs 13,200 2-bedroom suite; Rs 1,320 extra bed. Rates include breakfast. AE, MC, V. **Amenities:** 2 restaurant; bar; adventure sports on request; free airport and train station transfers; children's playground; health club and spa; small library (books, music, and movies); large outdoor pool and children's pool; room service; skating rink. *In room:* A/C, TV, DVD (in some), hair dryer, minibar (in suites), Wi-Fi (Rs 50/hr.; Rs 960/day).

Taj Residency ★★★ This is far and away the best hotel in town, and built with plenty of architectural references to a Mughal palace; the management of this lovely hotel is aiming very high. Not only the look, but also the service, has undergone dramatic improvement, providing elegant digs for both business travelers and vacationing cave-explorers. The deluxe rooms in the newer wing (which seamlessly fuses with the original building) are the most fashionable accommodations—plush and superbly fitted, they all have views over the pool and surrounding garden. But more recent refurbishment has transformed many of the original, more dated rooms into smart executive units with wooden floors and a sleek modern ambience; they're smaller than the deluxe rooms, but aimed at business travelers, but are the best value here. The hotel gives practical training to students of the hotel management school next door, which often means getting better-than-average service from wide-eyed, very enthusiastic youngsters. *Note:* Plans are afoot to augment services to the deluxe rooms and suites by adding dedicated butlers.

8-N-12 CIDCO, Rauza Bagh, Aurangabad 431 003. © **0240/661-3737.** Fax 0240/661-3939. www.tajhotels. com. residency.aurangabad@tajhotels.com. 66 units. Rs 6,500 superior double; Rs 7,500 deluxe double; Rs 9,500 luxury double; Rs 17,000 junior suite; Rs 22,000 luxury suite. Suite rates include breakfast. Rates exclude 10% tax. AE, DC, MC, V. **Amenities:** 2 restaurants, outdoor barbecue cafe, bar; airport transfers (Rs 323); babysitting; badminton court; concierge; croquet; health club (spa to be added by 2010); minigolf; large outdoor pool; room service. In room: A/C, TV, hair dryer, minibar, Wi-Fi (Rs 240/hr.; Rs 600/day).

WHERE TO DINE

The classiest place to eat is at the **Taj Residency** (© **0240/661-3939**), where there's currently a very good round-the-clock cafe-style restaurant with an eclectic menu. We recommend you ask the obliging chef to prepare something Mahatrashtrian—the Malwani fish curry is a good bet, as is their home-style lamb in tomato-onion gravy (muttonacha pandhra rassa), but the kitchen can make good suggestions based on your preferences. (Note that there's also a new Thai and Oriental specialty restaurant scheduled to open at the Taj by 2010.) Another smart choice (at least in terms of the quality of its food), is the pair of side-by-side restaurants at Hotel Amarpreet: they're called **China Town** and **India Street,** both do delicious, satisfying dishes at very affordable prices, and the attached old-fashioned bar is a real trip down nostalgia lane. Another spot worth trying is **Angeethi** (opposite Nupur Theatre, Jalna Rd.; © **0240/244-1988**), one of Aurangabad's most popular restaurants, particularly with the business set. Try the Afghani chicken masala (pieces of boneless chicken cooked in a cashew-nut gravy), or the popular—and spicy—tandoori chicken masala. For something authentically Maharashtrian, order chicken kolhapuri (not on the menu, but ask for it anyway), a spicy-hot chicken dish with a sharp chili, onion, and garlic base; if you can handle the sting, it's delicious.

Perhaps slightly overrated, we still fancy **Tandoor** ★★ (Shyam Chambers, Station Rd.; © **0240/232-8481;** daily 11am–3pm and 6:30–11pm) as the best restaurant in town. It's a very slick multicuisine place that's been a hot favorite since 1988—although it's a bit far from the main hotels. You can spend ages pondering the extensive menu, or you can ask the welcoming manager, Mr. Hussain, for his choices. Okra (bhindi) is not on the menu but can sometimes be made to order. The house specialty is definitely the kebabs; get a mixed tandoori sizzler with a selection of chicken kebabs or the fenugreek-leaves-flavored kasturi kebab (chicken) and kabuli tandoori chicken (marinated in creamy yogurt and flavored with ginger, garlic, turmeric, and white pepper), all outstanding. If you're looking for a mild curry that's been delicately prepared to bring out the most subtle flavors, ask for chicken korma—the sauce is made from cashew nuts, poppy seeds, sweet-melon seeds, and white sesame seeds. Those craving a break from all things spicy can get the baked vegetables on a bed of spinach.

But if it's real authenticity you're looking for, head to the no-frills **Thaliwala's Bhoj** (Kamgar Bhavan, Bhau Phatak Smruti Rd., opposite Hotel Kartiki; © **0240/235-9438**) and order a thali for a mere Rs 70 (to find out what to expect, see "The Thali: A Meal Unto Itself," on p. 159). Waiters (who generally don't speak a syllable of English) will fill your platter with wonderful concoctions—mop it all up with savory, freshly prepared chapatti, and you're sure to be a convert. Finally, for a pleasant lunch on the way back from Ellora, try **Ambience,** which belongs to the same group that owns the excellent Tandoor restaurant in Aurangabad (see above). It's set in pleasant gardens 12km (7½ miles) outside the city, in the vicinity of Daulatabad Fort. The place is also a lovely, atmospheric venue for dinner. Contact the manager (© **0240/261-5995;** daily 9am–midnight), or inquire at Tandoor.

6

Goa: Party in Paradise

Nirvana for dropouts, flower children, and New Age travelers since the late 1960s, Goa peaked as a hippie haven in the '70s, when Anjuna Beach became a rocking venue for party demons and naturalists who would sell their last piece of clothing at the local flea market for just enough cash to buy more dope and extend their stay. For many, Goa still conjures up images of all-night parties and tripping, naked hippies sauntering along sun-soaked beaches. But there is more to this tiny western state than sea and sand, dropouts, and hedonists. Goa's history alone has ensured that its persona, a rich amalgam of Portuguese and Indian influences, is unlike any other in India.

Arriving in 1498, the Portuguese christened it as the "Pearl of the Orient" and stayed for almost 500 years (forced to leave, finally, in 1961—the last Europeans to withdraw from the subcontinent), leaving an indelible impression on the local population and landscape. Goans still take a siesta every afternoon; many are Catholic, and you'll meet Portuguese-speaking Mirandas, D'Souzas, and Braganzas, their ancestors renamed by the colonial priests who converted them, often by force. Garden Hindu shrines stand cheek-by-jowl with holy crosses, and the local *vindaloo* (curry) is made with pork. Dotted among the palm groves and rice fields are dainty villas bearing European coats of arms and imposing mansions with wrought-iron gates—built not only for European gentry but for the Brahmins who, by converting, earned the right to own land.

Over the past decade Goa has become more hip than hippie, with well-heeled Indians frequenting the new rash of flashy international-style restaurants and design-conscious furniture and lifestyle stores at which they shop in order to adorn their ostentatious Goa mansions. Joining them every winter are the white-skinned package tourists, who come to indulge in the commercialized trance culture, and Indian youngsters who cruise from beach to beach, legs wrapped around cheap motorbikes and credit cards tucked into their Diesel jeans.

Goa is a more laid-back, "anything goes" version of India, a cosmopolitan tourist-oriented place of five-star resorts, boutique guesthouses, and ever more enchanting villas remodeled for international travelers. In many ways Goa is the perfect introduction to a country that, elsewhere, can be very challenging. Of course, when the crowds arrive, particularly over New Year, Goa's beaches and markets are anything but tranquil. Sun beds and shacks line the most commercial beaches, and hawkers haggle ceaselessly with droves of Europeans here to sample paradise at bargain prices while Mumbai and Bangalore puppies crowd the shoreline bars and restaurants. If it's action you're after, there are endless opportunities for all-night partying and reckless abandon. But Goa's true pleasures are found away from the crowds, on the more remote beaches to the far north and south, on the semiprivate beaches adjoining luxury resorts, or in the charming guesthouses farther inland. Come for at least 3 days, and you may end up staying for a lifetime—as a number of very content expats from around the world will attest to. However you decide to play it, live the local motto, "Sossegade": "Take it easy."

Tips   Mayhem in Paradise: When Not to Get Your Goa Groove On

Every year from December 23 to January 7, tens of thousands of tourists, both domestic and foreign, descend on Goa, so if you plan to spend Christmas or New Year's here, expect to negotiate crowds everywhere, particularly along the bursting-to-the-seams Baga-Candolim stretch. You can avoid the crowds to some extent by confining yourself to your hotel or guesthouse, but all the popular bars and restaurants will be filled to capacity, with queues so long they can cause traffic jams. Besides, everything—particularly accommodations—will be extremely expensive at this time (room and villa rates virtually double up on the already extravagant high season rate that runs from Nov through mid-Mar); many places also tack on an additional surcharge for the in-house "festive party" (even if you don't plan to attend). If loud and raucous merriment (accompanied by a definite sense of being ripped off) is not your style, avoid Goa during this time; your money will go twice the distance here once the sardine-format revelers have departed. On the other hand, the best-value period is the summer and postmonsoon season (mid–Mar through May and Oct), when prices are reasonable, crowds thinner, and the whole vibe a damn sight more mellow; you may find yourself at a loose end if you're looking to get your party shoes on, though.

1 ARRIVAL & ORIENTATION

ESSENTIALS

GETTING THERE   By Air   The state capital is Panjim (also called Panaji), which is pretty much centrally located; **Dabolim Airport** lies 29km (18 miles) south. It's possible to fly directly to Goa from Europe, as many travelers arriving on charter flights from the U.K., Germany, Holland, Switzerland, and Scandinavia do. A more likely scenario is that you'll be capping off your wider India trip by letting your hair down here; for that you can fly in from Mumbai (a mere 40 min.) or Delhi, as well as from Kolkata, Chennai, Kochi, Hyderabad, Bangalore, and Ahmedabad. If you really cannot wait to sink your toes into the Goan sea sand, your best bet is to book a direct flight from London with **Kingfisher** (www.flykingfisher.com); there's a short stopover in Mumbai before you hop on a connecting plane and commence your holiday immediately. See p. 55 for details on alternate airlines offering the best and/or cheapest service for domestic flights in and out of Goa. There's a helpful government **tourist desk** (✆ 0832/251-2644) in the baggage-claim hall. A few hotels offer complimentary airport transfers, but more often than not, you'll be charged for the service; you can either arrange this in advance (when making your reservation), or make use of the **prepaid taxi** counter, which eliminates the need for any bargaining and haggling over price. The trip to Panjim should cost Rs 490; for destinations in north Goa you're looking at between Rs 650 and Rs 1,250; slightly less for the resorts along the central coast; and a little pricier if you go all the way to Palolem. Given Goa's popularity with both international and domestic tourists, prebooking your accommodations here is essential, and don't fall for a tout's offer of "discount" lodgings—chances are the rooms will look like they fell off the back of a bus.

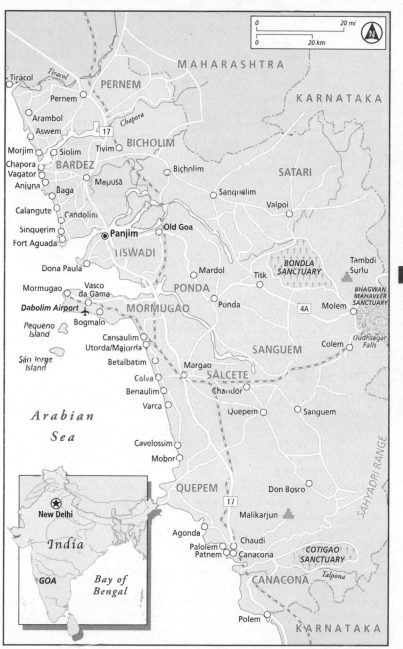

By Train Goa's three main jumping-off points are **Thivim** in the north (20km/12 miles inland from Vagator), **Karmali** (12km/7½ miles from Panjim), and **Madgaon** (also known as Margao) for the resort-intensive central coastal stretch. If you're going straight to Palolem, or any of the gorgeous beaches in the far south, jump off at **Canacona,** also known as Chaudi. Several trains travel daily from Mumbai to Goa along the **Konkan Railway;** most of these take a good 10 to 13 hours, so it's best to book the overnight **Konkan Kanya Express,** which leaves Mumbai at 11pm and gets into Madgaon at 10:45am. For a slightly quicker option, you'll need to get up real early for the 5:10am **Mumbai-Madgaon Jan Shatabdi** (from Victoria Station; Thurs–Tues), which (theoretically) reaches Madgaon by 1:55pm. If you're traveling from the south, catch the 11am **Matsyaganda Express** from Mangalore to Madgaon (6½ hr.); the trip offers mesmerizing views along the Konkan coast. Note that it's worthwhile to book your seat in your home country (www.irctc.co.in or www.konkanrailway.com), especially if you plan to head to Goa soon after your arrival in India or in peak season when trains between Mumbai and Goa are often fully booked; you may also ask your Mumbai hotel concierge to take care of it. For railway inquiries, call **Madgaon** (② 0832/271-2790; reservations ② 0832/271-2940). Taxis and auto-rickshaws are readily available at all the stations waiting to zip you off to your hotel.

By Bus If you want to travel to Goa but all trains and flights are full, or if you want to save on airfare, your next-best option is a bus from Mumbai, Pune, Hyderabad, Bangalore, or Mangalore. Numerous overnight buses leave from Mumbai (near Metro Cinema–Fashion St.) every day at 7pm; book an air-conditioned bus and bring a blanket (although some companies supply these). Preferably, this should be a sleeper (around Rs 1,000). If you're traveling alone, note that you will sleep beside a stranger; if this makes you nervous, buy two tickets. Another option is to go for a semisleeper or "slumberette," a comfy 135-degree reclining seat which is slightly cheaper. **Paulo Travels** (Goa: ② 0832/663-7777 or 0832/243-8531 through -8537; Mumbai: ② 022/2643-3023; www.paulo travels.com) is a reliable private operator with an efficient online booking system; bookings can also be made at the small ticket booths near St. Xavier's College, Mumbai. If you are booking through other agents, make sure you ask for a Volvo bus (better suspension, more spacious seating) and that you get a confirmed ticket with your seat number. For the north Goa beaches, jump off at Mapusa; for the south, at Panjim, Margao, or Canacona (best to ask the conductor where the best stop for your destination is). *Note:* A single woman can request to have another woman seated beside her, though this may not always happen. Seats in the first few rows have more leg room.

VISITOR INFORMATION You don't need to waste your time in Goa shuffling around looking for a tourist office; speak to the owner or concierge where you're staying, and you'll get everything you need to know. For general information on the state, visit **www. goatourism.org**. Goa's tourism department releases a twice-monthly magazine called *What's On* (② 0832/222-4132; www.goa-tourism.com), which gives a comprehensive listing of the events and parties scheduled in all corners of Goa. Many of the upmarket hotels also stock various advertising brochures, maps and booklets that may have *some* useful information or list upcoming events.

GETTING AROUND Note that it shouldn't take much longer than 4 hours to cruise the entire coastline, so everything in this chapter is within easy reach. For quick reference, here are distances between major destinations from Panjim: Margaon 33km (21 miles);

Mapusa 13km (8 miles); Old Goa 10km (6¼ miles); Calangute 16km (10 miles); Vagator 22km (14 miles); Ponda 30km (19 miles).

By Motorbike   Motorbikes are *très* cool in Goa, and you'll encounter an endless barrage of young backpackers and old hippies zipping around Goa's roads on two-wheelers—sans helmets (potentially a little frightening). You can rent a bike for around Rs 200 to Rs 300 a day with a private license plate as opposed to Rs 250 to Rs 500 a day for a government-approved bike (these are identified by their yellow license plates); note that if you are stopped by the traffic cops, you will be fined for renting a private vehicle. Have your international two-wheeler driver's license handy, and check the bike thoroughly before handing over any cash (if you don't have a license, a gearless bike is easy to use even if you've never ridden them before). Note that if you hire a two-wheeler without insurance, you must pay for the repairs. You can find motorbikes practically everywhere, but we really recommend that you do this only through your hotel or guesthouse, or through the aforementioned **Paulo Travels.** If you don't have a license, there are plenty of **motor-cycle pilots** in Goa—which is a more cost-effective way of getting around than by taxi. When someone stops to ask if you need a lift (and they will), negotiate a price in advance. And if you don't like the pace or style of driving, say something immediately. All approved pilots will have yellow license plates—which does not necessarily mean they will have helmets; be warned that motorcyclists are killed on these roads every year.

By Taxi & Auto-Rickshaw   Negotiate privately with one of the many taxi drivers found around tourist areas—including those near your hotel entranceway (you can get one through your hotel, of course, but at a five-star lodging the cost will almost double—in fact, if you *look* like you're staying at one of the upmarket places, chances are you'll be quoted accordingly). Figure on spending Rs 1,000 to Rs 1,500 for about 80km (50 miles) or 8 hours of sightseeing, but specify which locations you hope to cover. Remember that if you need a one-way lift to a more remote region, you'll be asked to pay for the return journey. In fact, many drivers now charge twice the distance no matter how near or far the drop-off. If you plan to take a day trip to a far-off beach, you're better off fixing a price for the day (Rs 1,400 for a trip to Palolem from Anjuna—substantially more if you require an air-conditioned vehicle). An additional Rs 50 to Rs 100 is usually charged after 9pm. Auto-rickshaws are cheaper than taxis, but a great deal more uncomfortable. **Dalesh** is a reliable taxi driver ((C) **98-2210-2964**) who can be booked for the whole day or for a pickup or drop-off. South of Panjim, you can contact **Wilson Fernandes** ((C) **98-2384-2587**), who is based in Colva; he charges Rs 1,000 to Rs 1,200 for a trip from Palolem to the airport, and around Rs 3,000 for a return trip from the south to Fort Tiracol in the north. *Note:* All rates vary according to demand, season, and vehicle type. If you're counting rupees, you might want to ask the rates from a couple of taxi drivers before settling on a ride.

By Car   Goa is also perhaps the only place in India where you can hire self-drive cars, but given the driving culture (and complete lack of adequate road signage), we wouldn't recommend doing so; like many of the motorbike rental services, most of the car rental outfits aren't registered or licensed to commercially rent out vehicles. Consequently, you may not be properly insured—you hire at your own risk; if you have an accident, you pay for the repairs. For better, fully insured cars with or without a chauffeur, call Dominic of **Vailankanni Auto Hires** ((C) **0832/248-9568,** 0832/329-0584, or 98-2210-1598; www.goacabs.com), based in Candolim.

Staying Active Above & Below the Water

Barracuda Diving India (Sun Village Resort, Baga-Arpora; ℂ **0832/227-9409** through -9414, or 98-2218-2402; www.barracudadiving.com; barracuda@vsnl. com) is a PADI–recognized dive center where you can rent equipment or take diving courses and get certified (from beginner to advanced levels). Venkatesh Charloo and Karen Gregory, both master diver-trainers, offer a wide range of dive safaris across the entire south Indian coast, including Karnataka, where visibility can reach up to 30m (100 ft.). In south Goa you can not only escape the crowds, but start a new hobby: **catamaran sailing.** Consistent weather conditions makes Goa an idea spot to sail. Based on beautiful, still-secluded Patnem Beach, **Goa Sailing & Water Sports** (ℂ **98-5045-8865;** www.goasailing.com) is a highly recommended operation. You can hire a catamaran with or without an instructor (Rs 2,000/Rs 3,000 per half-day; Rs 3,000/Rs 4,500 full day), and even take a short course during which you'll learn to sail. With enough time, you can learn to sail, or take a water-borne trip to other remote pockets of paradise—like Agonda, Honeymoon and Butterfly beaches. **Atlantis Water Sports** (ℂ **98-9004-7272;** www.goa-cruise.com) operates an Indian dhow built in 1924; on offer are a range of regular cruises, including breakfast with the dolphins and a sunset cruise, and you can hire the boat on a private basis, too. Most of the upmarket resorts offer a range of watersports facilities, and you'll find jet-skiing, parasailing, windsurfing, wakeboarding, scuba diving, and other ocean-going pastimes available from various makeshift structures on the beaches, particularly along the beach between Baga and Aguada (look at the foot of Vila Goesa Rd., Cobra Vaddo, Calangute). **Goan Bananas** (ℂ **0832/227-6362** or -6739, near the Silver Sands Beach Shack, Baga Beach) organizes jet-skiing (Rs 1,300) and parasailing (Rs 800–Rs 1,000). Offering similar services on Sinquerim Beach, is **Thunder Wave Water Sports** (ℂ **0832/247-9779**), based near the Taj Aguada resort complex.

By Bus Buses ply their way up and down the state, stopping in a rather chaotic fashion whenever someone needs to get on or off. If you're in a hurry, try to catch an express bus; otherwise you could be in for an endless series of stop-starts—it is, however, the cheapest way of getting around (less than $1 from one end to the other) and a fun way of getting acquainted with local folk (and Goan music)! Most buses stop after 7:30pm.

By Boat Betty's Place (ℂ 0832/287-1038; www.bettygoa.com), a beach shack near The Leela Kempinski resort on Mobor Beach in south Goa, offers a variety of boat trips, including customized cruises—these need to be booked quite well in advance. At Kenilworth Beach Resort, also in south Goa, **Sea Adventure** (Utorda; ℂ 98-2216-1712) organizes bird-watching and a backwater cruise that takes in basking river crocodiles. There are countless early morning **dolphin-spotting cruises** up and down the coast, but unfortunately there are so many boats and water scooters gunning for the poor dolphins that the sustainability (and pleasure) of this activity has been diminished in recent years; until tourism authorities wake up and bring some order we would urge you not to add to the harassment.

MGM International Travels has offices in Panjim (Navelcar Trade Centre, opposite Azad Maidan; ℂ **0832/222-0972** or 0832/242-1865; wwwmgmtravels.com), Calangute (Simplex Chambers, Umtavaddo; ℂ **0832/227-6073**) and Anjuna (Cabin Disco, Soranto Vaddo; ℂ **0832/227-4317**). Other reliable travel agents include **Trade Wings** (1st floor, Naik Building, opposite Don Bosco School, Panjim; ℂ **0832/243-2430**) and **Footprints Tours & Travels,** run by Angeline Lobo (Shelter Guest House, Vaddi Candolim; ℂ **98-5047-1639** or 0832/309-0594; www.goafootprints.com). The **Goa Tourism Development Corporation** (Trionara Apartments, Dr. Alvares Costa Rd., Panjim; ℂ **0832/242-7972** or -0779; www.goacom.com/goatourism; daily 9:30am–5:30pm) has full-day tours of the north and the south aimed primarily at domestic tourists.

ⓕ *Fast Facts*   Goa

Airlines Even the smallest hotels are able to make air travel arrangements for you and usually charge a small fee to process tickets, which saves you the hassle of having to travel all the way to Panjim. Alternatively, book your seats online; both **Kingfisher** (ℂ **0832/254-2020**) and **Jet** (ℂ **0832/243-8792**) have very user-friendly websites, or you can try www.travelocity.co.in for the best deals and sometimes discounted fares. Jet is open Monday to Saturday 9am to 6pm (Patto Plaza, near the Patto Tourist Hotel and the bus stand, Panjim; ℂ **0832/243-8790**). An assortment of budget airlines (p. 55) offers cheaper airfares.

Ambulance Dial ℂ **102** or 108, or you can call the **Panjim Ambulance and Welfare Trust** (Panjim; ℂ **0832/222-4824**). Also in Panjim, call the 24 hour **Vintage Ambulance Service** (ℂ **98-2305-9948**). In Margao, call the local **Ambulance Trust** (ℂ **0832/273-1759**). In Mapusa, call ℂ **0832/226 2372**.

American Express Call **American Express** (ℂ **1600/1801-242** or 1800/1801-245).

Area Code The area code for **Goa** is ℂ **0832**.

ATMs While some of the smaller villages may not have ATM facilities, for the most part you won't have to search hard to find one. Ask your hotel for the nearest machine with credit card facilities, and—unless you're staying somewhere remote (like Fort Tiracol)—you shouldn't need to travel far to draw money. Taxi and auto-rickshaw drivers can also usually take you to one without much bother (preferably during the day). In Panjim, there's an ICICI ATM at the Sindur Business Centre on Swami Vivekananda Road.

Banks & Currency Exchange For the best rates, you can exchange cash and traveler's checks at **Thomas Cook** In Panjim (8 Alcon Chambers, D. B. Marg; ℂ **0832/222-1312;** Mon–Sat 9:30am–7pm). Another location is between Baga and Calangute, at the State Bank of India, in the Hotel Ofrill Building (ℂ **0832/227-5693**).

Car Rentals Try **Sita World Travel** (101 Rizvi Chamber, Caetano Albuquerque Rd., Panjim; ℂ **0832/222-0476**, -0477, -3134, -6477, or 0832/242-3552).

Drugstores Go to **Farmacia Universal** in Panjim (Behind People High School; ℂ **0832/222-3740;** 24 hr.). **Walson and Walson Chemist** can be found on Calangute (ℂ **0832/227-6366;** daily 9am–9pm).

Emergencies In Panjim, dial ℂ **102** for an ambulance, and ℂ **101** in case of fire. See "Police," below.

Helpline Call ℂ **0832/241-2121** for all kinds of information, including changed phone numbers.

Hospitals **Dr. Bhandari Hospital** (ℂ **0832/222-4966** or -5602) is in Panjim's Fontainhas area. For hospital emergencies (and preventative treatments) in Margao, the **Apollo Victor Hospital** (ℂ **0832/272-8888**; emergency hot line: ℂ **0832/ 272-6272**) is recommended, and there's an evenings-only branch in Panjim, too (First Floor, Velho Bldg.; ℂ **0832/564-7400;** open 5–8pm). In Mapusa, **Vrundavan Hospital** (ℂ **0832/225-0022** or -0033) is reputed to be the best.

Internet Access High numbers of backpackers mean plenty of Internet facilities (Rs 25–Rs 90 per hr.), particularly in tourist areas. Wherever you are, ask or look out for **Sify iway** cybercafes (or use the locator menu on their website to find a nearby location; www.iway.com).

Police Dial ℂ **100. Panjim Police Headquarters** (ℂ **0832/242-8400** or -3400) is on Malaca Road, at the western edge of Azad Maidan.

Post Office Panjim's **General Post Office** is at Patto Bridge and is open Monday to Friday 9:30am to 5:30pm.

GOA'S BEST BEACHES

Goa's reputation for having some of the world's best beaches is well-deserved, but inevitable commercialization has taken its toll, with the infamous **Baga-to-Candolim** area (north of Panjim) now part of a tourist-infested strip of sun loungers, backed by over-commercialized beach shacks serving beer, cocktails, and what could once be relied upon to be fresh seafood (now increasingly dubious)—the sort of packaged beach experience best avoided. You can find pockets of paradise here, though, and if you stick to our recommended accommodations in this area, they'll definitely point you in the right direction. A little north of Baga, **Anjuna** comes alive with parties and trance music during the winter, when all kinds of revelers gather to find out where the real underground action is happening. It also has what was once a fabulous Wednesday Market, a tad too predictable and monotonous now—not to mention crowded to bursting—with almost every vendor selling the same wares. Just north of Anjuna is lovely **Vagator** ★, with stark red cliffs and the disheveled remains of Chapora Fort looming overhead. But things do improve the farther away from the mainstream crowds you manage to get. **Asvem** ★★ is still a pretty awesome beach, and although still comparatively unencumbered by the masses, regulars complain that it's not quite as pristine as it was just a few years back, and of late large numbers of Russians have begun to settle on this stretch, buying land and starting private enterprises, much of it rumored to be the wrong side of the law. A little north of Asvem, **Arambol** ★★★, seductively far away from the package-tour masses, is one of the last refuges of hard-core hippies.

Though there are no private beaches in Goa, some of the best-kept stretches of sand in the southern part of the state (which usually means south of Panjim) are maintained for the near-exclusive use of guests staying at the five-star resorts fronting them. As long as you don't try to use hotel loungers, there's nothing stopping you from making use of "their" beach space. The long, long stretch of beach from **Bogmalo to Mobor** is well worth investigating if you're looking for a more private spot, and it's relatively close to both the capital and to north Goa, so don't hesitate to explore the region. In the far south, gorgeous **Palolem** ★★★ has just one large resort close by (the tired and badly-managed InterContinental Lalit, a few miles south), and is perhaps the prettiest beach in Goa—a title which is, during the season, sadly threatened by overcrowding. In just a few years, it's become home to a sizable neohippie community (or, as one discerning Goan hotelier calls them, "the great unwashed"), as well as ever-increasing development. Once on the beach, you just need to walk far from the crowds, and you should find a slice of tranquillity, and Palolem has, mercifully, yet to be overwhelmed by day-trippers. Just 7km (4 miles) north of Palolem, **Agonda** ★★★ is even more isolated and peaceful (again, not quite as much as it once was), while to the south, **Galgibaga** ★★★ is another remote haven with eucalyptus trees and empty stretches of sand. This time, the beauty is forever protected because the beach is a designated Olive Ridley breeding area. And then, of course, there's **Om** ★★★ beach, south of the border, an hour or two into the neighboring state of Karnataka, considered by many to be the best beach in India. Om is still comparatively untouched save for a few seasonal shacks, and the extremely tranquil, very special yoga and Ayurvedic retreat, SwaSwara, where you're ensconced in a gorgeous setting on a vast acreage with pathways leading directly from your beautiful villa to the beach (see "Discover the Universe within at Om Beach" box, on p. 370 in the Karnataka chapter for the lowdown on one of the most special hideaways in India).

2 NORTH GOA

Goa's reputation as a hangout for hippies during the '60s and '70s was made on the northern beaches of **Calangute, Baga,** and **Anjuna.** Along with the relaxed lifestyle and good times came busloads of Indian men keen to observe free-spirited foreigners and, finally, a crackdown by local government. This forced fun-loving hippies to head to more remote tracts of coastline, leaving the door open for backpackers and package tourists. Thus were the north's most famous beaches transformed into tanning lots for the masses—even Anjuna has become an Ibiza-like experience—and today no card-carrying hippie would deign to set foot on the beach that stretches between Calangute and Baga (defined by resort-centered **Sinquerim** in the south to **Vagator** in the north). That said, you can't deny the beauty of the beaches (in south Vagator, **Ozran Beach** is peaceful and beautiful, with relaxed swimming in a bay at its southernmost end)—certainly this is where you'll want to be if you're here to party during the season. Baga is the smaller, slightly less-developed area of activity. Beach shacks-turned-establishment hangouts like **Britto's** (Baga) and **Fisherman's Paradise** (Calangute) are crowded with beer-quaffing visitors recovering from the previous night's adventure at the legendary bar-cum-nightclub, **Tito's,** now a veritable strip-mall of entertainment outlets. Still, beach shacks are very much a part of Goan culture, and if you can track down those that haven't gone commercial (a la sponsorship by major drinks conglomerates), you may just sample some of the old life.

For a sense of Goa's hippie origins, head for **Arambol,** Goa's most northerly "discovered" beach (36km/22 miles northwest of Mapusa), before you hit the utterly remote and untouched beach at **Keri.** Arambol is no longer the undiscovered paradise it was just a few years back, but it offers better bodysurfing that Anjuna or Vagator—the water's a little more turbulent. It draws quite a crowd during the season (you arrive through a lane

Mind-Altering Yogurt Drinks

Be warned that the "special lassis" served at some Goan beach shacks may dramatically increase your amusement at the cows ambling along the shore or apparently sunbathing alongside the snow-white tourists on Baga Beach. The "special" component is *bang,* or marijuana.

crammed with stalls selling CDs and T-shirts, and laid-back restaurants playing competing brands of music), but the setting is nevertheless lovely, with a hill looming over a small freshwater lake fed by a spring. The farther north you walk, the more solitude you enjoy. Besides looking at beautiful bodies, you can spend hours watching the surf glide. Another option is to head a little farther south from Arambol for **Asvem** Beach; while the Russians may have set up camp here it's still a great beach, and is where you'll fall in love with a beautiful restaurant called **La Plage** (see review on p. 215)—one the best in the state—disguised as a simple beach shack offering sustenance and style that's not all that easy to come by among the hoi polloi magnets of Baga-Calangute. Immediately south, secluded and largely undeveloped **Mandrem** is a peaceful fishing village and beach separating Asvem from the dark sands of **Morjim,** popular with the Olive Ridley turtles that have been coming here for centuries and, more recently, Russian tour groups and expats keen to carve out their own place in paradise.

If you're taking a break from the beaches and lust for a bit of culture but don't have time to tour any of the heritage homes recommended in the southern part of Goa, drop in at the **Calizz museum** ★ (Bammon Vaddo, Candolim; (✆ **0832/325-0000;** www.calizz.com; daily 10am–9:30pm). Curators here have made an impressive attempt to trace the evolution of local architecture and re-create traditional Goan homes. Each house is filled with intriguing artifacts and antiques, kitchen utensils, maps, paintings, medical paraphernalia, spectacle frames, jars, bottles, and so on—some of it several hundred years old, and painstakingly collected over the years by Laxmikant Kudchadkar. You can also see the differences in Goan-Portuguese and Hindu styles of architecture and enjoy a taste of traditional cuisine. The guided tour ends with a bizarre 3-D display of Hindu gods and mythologies—perhaps the only sore point in this grand affair.

WHERE TO STAY

North Goa offers a wide range of accommodations, but we've handpicked those that afford a sense of exclusivity and are more likely to satisfy any craving for tranquillity or an experience other than the mass-market humdrum defined by package tourism. Perhaps the finest place in all-Goa is **Nilaya Hermitage,** where aesthetic splendor wrestles with a sublime, untouched location for poll position as its top selling point. At Goa's very northernmost point is the rather remote enclave of Tiracol, where the owners of Nilaya Hermitage have restored seven rooms in the old headland fort. If you're design conscious, want to be relatively close to the beach and in the heart of the tourist zone—yet keen on a boutique "nonhotel" experience, another top option is **Pousada Tauma** (reviewed below). If you're looking for something more midrange, head for **Siolim House** or **Panchavatti** (reviewed below), or one of the **Casa** properties, a small chain of boutique hotels. But if you're here to be left alone to simply enjoy the beach with as few intrusions as possible, you'll definitely want to check out the selection of top villa-style stay in our round-up on p. 202.

(Moments) **Shopping the Global Village Markets**

Anjuna is the site of Goa's **Wednesday market,** where a nonstop trance soundtrack sets the scene and 1,000 stalls sell everything from futuristic rave gear to hammocks that you can string up between two palm trees on the nearby beach. It's a wonderful place to meet people from all over the world as well as Rajasthanis, Gujaratis, Tibetans—even drought-impoverished Karnataka farmers with "fortune-telling" cows. It's a bit like London's Camden, but everyone's tanned and the weather's almost always wonderful. Come the weekend, Goa's global residents have traditionally headed for either of the two **Saturday Night Bazaars—Ingo's** or **Mackie's**—where most of the spending has always seemed to involve liquor and food. In Arpora, Ingo's is on a larger scale—but, according to rumors, no longer run by Ingo himself, but by the owner of the grounds upon which the market was established—and both dole out essentially the same ingredients of live music, eclectic cuisine, and shops galore selling semi-precious stones, paintings, books, clothes, music, and handicrafts churned out by long-term international visitors. There have long been disputes between locals and the organizers of these markets, however, so they frequently close down or relocate; best to ask someone local for the latest gossip. In any case, the more interesting markets are the local ones. Once a week, folk from villages all across Goa breeze into Mapusa for the **Friday Market** ★★, where they set up large tables groaning under the weight of extraordinarily large-size vegetables, strings of homemade pork sausages, basketfuls of *kokum*, pickles like *chepnim* and *miscut* made out of tender mangoes, prawn *balchao* and Bombay duck pickles, a freshly baked assortment of Goan breads, all kinds of confectionary goodies like *bebinca* and *dodol*, guava cheese, and wines. Of course, the market is just as packed with mundane items ranging from knockoff designer underwear to masonry bits and cheap plastic slippers. If you have space to take home a souvenir, look for the red rooster water jug—you'll find one in every Goan home, ostensibly to chase away evil spirits. When you're pooped from shopping, drop into **Café Xaviers** (opposite the banana section), which sells refreshingly cold coffee shakes and delicious Goan sausage with *poee* (flat Goan bread). Another reason to come is the interesting **Other India Bookstore** (next to New Mapusa Clinic; (C) **0832/226-3306;** www.otherindiabookstore.com), which stocks up on academic books related to issues like the environment, agriculture, and spirituality. On Thursdays, there's a lively market in **Pernem,** in the far north of Goa—it's pretty much undiscovered by tourists, so an altogether enchanting experience.

Very Expensive

Situated on the short peninsula where the Portuguese built their defensive Aguada Fortress, is **Taj Fort Aguada** ★★ (Kids) ((C) **0832/664-5858;** www.tajhotels.com), a resort complex comprising three different properties (the Beach Resort, Hermitage, and Holiday Village) clustered together around one of the most spectacular locations in all of Goa.

Villas, Goan-Style

Goa's reemergence as a more fashionable, suddenly trendy Arabian Sea hangout has much to do with the launch of world-class villas such as Ajai Lakhanpal's awesome **Aashyana Lakhanpal ★★★** (Escrivao Vaddo, Candolim; © **0832/ 248-9225** or -9276. www.aashyanalakhanpal.com; Rs 199,500–Rs 622,650 per week), a haven of impeccable style and sophistication that attracts utterly savvy world travelers, aristocrats, and their favorite dinnertime companions. Ajai one of a few savvy beach lovers who's turned a piece of prime Goan real estate into a luxurious hideaway, providing the ultimate getaway for the fortunate few. The gorgeous five-bedroom villa has every imaginable luxury—beautiful pool, romantic sleeping quarters, elegant furnishings, and decor that's a careful mix of antique and modern—all in a setting that is both tropical idyll and luxurious mansion. Rates include breakfast, airport transfers, and a private staff. Ajai also has two more villas: **Aashyana Casinhas,** which consists of three cottages, each with two bedrooms (Rs 45,500–Rs 144,500 per week), and **Villa Venus,** a three-bedroom villa (Rs 174,300–Rs 249,900 per week).

If you'd rather forgo the sophistication, and don't really need all that space anyway, preferring to leave your friends at home, then you need to head farther up the coast to the extreme north, between Asvem and Arambol, where you'll find tranquillity on the beach at **Elsewhere ... ★★★**, a simple, paradisiacal kind of place that's right on the sand, far from the touristy throng, and shot through with a lovely sense of the past. Fashion photographer Denzil Sequeira considers his ancestral property the biggest secret in Goa, but given how long you need to book in advance, word is definitely out. Away from the crowds, it has an absolutely stunning beach, several lovely, simple houses to stay in, and great food. It's one of the most idyllic boutique properties in Goa, found at the end of a road and reached by crossing a bamboo footbridge through thick green groves—like all good hideaways, finding it nigh impossible, and once there you'll seldom have the urge or inclination to leave. You won't find chic interiors or heavy themed designs here: The two- and three-bedroom villas are filled with relics from the past—original tiles, collections of old altars, antique furniture, and planter's chairs and deck beds on verandas and porches overlooking a distinctly tropical beach scene. In place of the obligatory pool you have the entire Arabian Sea to swim in, al fresco showers, and hammocks strung between the trees. Two of the villas, the Piggery and the Bakery, are air-conditioned, while the Priest's House (where Denzil's uncle once lived), and 125-year-old Captain's House (where Brad Pitt and Angelina recently stayed) are more about the breeze. Coming here has a definite purpose—to

From up here, you get picture-postcard views of the beach, which stretches all the way to Baga, 8km (5 miles) north. Behind the main **Beach Resort** block are 42 cottages tucked almost invisibly among groves of lantana, cashew, and bougainvillea bush; these are the best places to stay at the Beach Resort (from Rs 18,250) although you don't get a clear view of the sea from all. Alternatively, for absolute privacy (ideal for groups or families), take lazing about to new dimensions. Don't expect to find shacks, vendors, or shops; but your hosts will help you with trips to the markets, restaurants, and party zones, if you desire. Come between October and February, and you may spot Olive Ridley and rare loggerhead turtles, since the beach out front is a protected nesting zone. The food is terrific, even though it tends to take forever to get it, and the staff is unobtrusive and ever helpful. And if you want to party, you can probably find something 15 to 20 minutes away. You'll need to reserve well ahead; do it online at www.aseascape.com, or contact gaze@aseascape.com (© **93-2602-0701** for last-minute bookings or emergencies only). You can expect to pay $1,477 to $2,404 per week; much more during the festive season.

Finally, if you don't mind being quite close to some of the regular action, the former hippie headquarter village of Anjuna shelters one of the ultimate Goan hideaway "villas," a rustic chic place named **The Hobbit** ★★★ (© **0832/227-4629** or 98-2005-5053; www.thehobbitgoa.com). Fashioned in and around a rock, this was once (minus windows, doors, and ceilings) the psychedelic digs of Anjuna's famed '70s hippies, and you're likely to walk right past the boundary hedge before finding it. Refurbished by the extremely chilled-out Chinmayi and her husband, rally driver Farad Bathena, the Hobbit took birth in 2006, and comprises three boho-sexy rooms on two different levels, done up simply but tastefully (all with air-conditioning and private bathrooms); a sitting and dining room, meditation alcove, and kitchenette; and plenty of porches, a roof terrace, a tiny plunge pool, and semi-open bathrooms around exposed rock with sweeping views of the beach and the neighboring cliff. Even though you are right near the action (2 min. walking distance from the beach), the Hobbit remains secluded, there are unlikely to be any intrusions, but you do have TV, DVD, and Internet should you wish to maintain contact with the outside world. For meals, you can use the services of two nearby shacks—**Curly's** (seafood) and **Shiva's** (Israeli), which are more than happy to "home" deliver via your very own house attendants who go out of their way to make your stay comfortable. The Wednesday Flea Market is a stone's throw away, and parties are fairly common in this area but (fortunately) not held on a nightly basis. Ask Chinmayi for the details if you want to make sure you're at the right place at the right time—or far away from it. Rates are almost embarrassingly fair—Rs 9,900 to Rs 14,400 per night for the entire villa (six adults), including a one-way airport transfer, and housekeeping services, although substantially higher over Christmas and New Years; children under 12 stay free, and you're responsible for your own meals. The Hobbit, like most villas in Goa, is closed during the monsoon (June–Sept).

consider one of the more exclusive **Hermitage** cottages (Rs 18,250–Rs 38,300 for a one-bedroom villa), built as a retreat for delegates during the 1983 meeting of the Commonwealth heads of government. The cottages are set amid terraced gardens of exotic orchids, bougainvilleas, cashew trees, jasmine, and Krishna ficus. Each villa has a separate living room; a dining area; one, two, or three bedrooms; two bathrooms; a *balcao* (balcony);

and a private garden. Interiors are luxurious and include all modern amenities; request a villa near Sunset Point, where cocktails are served while the sun descends over the Arabian Sea. It's quite a stiff climb between the cottages and the hotel lobby (shared with the Beach Resort) and if you're feeling lazy, there are courtesy vehicles for the short transfer. Sharing the facilities is the more informal **Taj Holiday Village** (from Rs 13,250), fronted by Sinquerim Beach, with cottages and villas in reds, pinks, blues, and yellows scattered among towering coconut trees and lush vegetation. Accommodations at this resort vary considerably, ranging from lavish sea-facing villas to less desirable suites in clusters or duplex cottages. Although its facilities make it immensely popular with families, it wouldn't be your first choice if you're looking for peace and quiet. Facilities, as you can well imagine, are extensive, with every imaginable watersport and distraction laid on, including a spa and some of the finest restaurants in Goa; the head chef, Urbano de Rego, is widely acknowledged as the world's greatest Goan chef, having created the restaurant versions of many classic local dishes.

If you prefer a resort with a fresher look, do investigate the brand-new **O Hotel** (opening in late-2009), aiming to provide some modern-era competition to the Taj from its location at Dando on Candolim Beach (✆ **0832/304-7000;** www.ohotelsindia.com); for some idea of what to expect (albeit in a city context), read our review of the O Hotel in Pune (p. 178). There will be 75 rooms and, if the Pune version is anything to go by, a truly luxurious, state-of-the-art spa, not to mention a frenzy of unbridled designer-crafted fun throughout.

Nilaya Hermitage ★★★　Ex-Parisian fashion stylist Claudia Derain and her Indian husband, Hari Ajwani, started this exclusive hillside resort when they fell in love with Goa during a vacation from Europe. Together with Goan architect Dean D'Cruz, they have created something out of *Arabian Nights*, with 12 cosmic-themed guest suites featuring vibrant colors, terrazzo flooring, and minimalist decor. Giant mosquito nets hang from high-beamed ceilings, and sweeping archways lead off to open-plan bathrooms with views of the tropical garden. Like a chic harem, the split-level, saffron-colored "Music Room" is where guests unwind on sprawling mattresses or meditate while soothing music plays beneath a high, blue-domed ceiling. Overlooking paddy fields and coconut palm groves, the setting is romantic and classy, and although not on the beachfront, Nilaya is Goa's most celebrated getaway, as its extensive celebrity guest list (Kate Moss, Peter Lindbergh, Philippe Starck) indicates.

Arpora Bhati, Goa 403 518. ✆ **0832/227-6793,** -6794, -5187, or -5188. Fax 0832/227-6792. www.nilaya. com. 11 units. Oct–Dec 19 and Jan 11–Apr: 320€ double; Dec 20–Jan 10: 490€ double; May and Aug–Sept rates may be discounted. Rates include breakfast, dinner, taxes, and airport transfers. AE, MC, V. Closed June–July. **Amenities:** Restaurant; breakfast area; lounge; bar; free airport transfers; Ayurvedic center; cultural performances; fitness room; large outdoor pool; room service; spa; tennis court; yoga pavilion and meditation room. *In room:* A/C, TV/DVD (on request), hair dryer, Wi-Fi (planned for 2010).

Pousada Tauma ★★★　Of the upmarket boutique resorts in north Goa, this one stands out for its distinctive local character, thanks in no small part to the fastidious attentions of Neville Proenca, the charming owner-manager, who worked with award-winning architect Dean D'Cruz to create his magical retreat. Even though it's located in the heart of a bustling tourist center (a 10-min. walk from overpopulated Calangute Beach), it is sheltered from the high-season madness by thick, verdant vegetation and feels like a beautiful fortress against the outside world. Fashioned entirely out of Goan laterite stone and set around a beautiful pool with cascading water, each suite is uniquely styled and themed with eccentric Goan antiques (a cradle-turned-table; dentist-chair-turned-recliner); each has its

own balcony, overlooking either the garden or pool, and simple bathrooms done in shattered tile mosaics. Pousada is the perfect getaway for artists and sophisticated socialites.
Neville has quietly been developing an additional 3,000 sq. m (32,291 sq. ft.) of gardens
alongside the original property, where yoga and meditation sessions are held; and he's renovating a gorgeous old beach house for guests to use not too far from here, in Candolim.

Porba Vaddo, Calangute, Bardez 403 519. ☎ **0832/227-9061.** Fax 0832/227-9064. www.pousada-tauma.
com. 12 units. Oct and Mar–Apr: 210€ standard suite, 235€ superior suite, 320€ deluxe suite; Nov–Dec 19
and Jan 11–Feb: 225€ standard, 250€ superior, 340€ deluxe; Dec 20–Jan 10: 250€ standard, 275€ superior,
350€ deluxe; May–Sept: 140€–155€ standard, 150€–180€ superior, 180€–260€ deluxe; 80€ extra bed.
Rates include breakfast and lunch or dinner; 10% tax extra. MC, V. No children. **Amenities:** Restaurant
(Copper Bowl; reviewed on p. 214), bar; airport transfers (Rs 1,000–Rs 1,200); fitness room; Internet (free);
large outdoor pool; room service. *In room:* A/C, TV, hair dryer on request, minibar.

Expensive

Fort Tiracol Heritage Hotel ★★★ (Moments) You need to catch a public ferry to
get there, but once you do you'll feel like you've reached a sanctuary that's untouchable.
Restored by the same talent-filled couple responsible for Nilaya Hermitage (reviewed
above), it may not have all the luxuries and distractions of a resort, but it does have an
epic location, spectacular views of the sea, and a sense of charm and style that are really
hard to beat. Seven rooms are built into the fortress rampart (choose Friday, the loveliest
suite, with a large balcony)—windows and Mediterranean-style terraces open towards the
water, with views along Goa's coast—and in the courtyard the old Portuguese church is
still used by the villagers. Rooms are beautiful, decorated in saffron and ocher, gold and
black, with expansive open-design bathrooms, and a chic minimalism with strategic use
of period furniture, large wrought-iron designer beds, uniquely patterned linens, and
pared-down ornamentation recognizing the fort's historical origins, built by a maharajah
to protect this enclave from the Portuguese. Although the views are outstanding and the
food superb, you may find life a little dull (no pool, and the beach is a 3-min. ferry away)
and isolated (90 min. from Baga). However, it's hard to beat if you want to *really* get away
from it all, and you can rent a speedboat for dolphin-watching, take a cruise on the
wooden dhow, or mingle with members of Tiracol's tiny village community.

Tiracol, Pernem 403 524. ☎ **02366/22-7631** or 0832/652-9653. www.forttiracol.com. 7 units. Sept–Mar
Rs 7,600 double, Rs 9,600 suite; Apr–May Rs 6,080 double, Rs 7,680 suite; June–Aug Rs 5,320 double, Rs
6,720 suite; Dec 20–Jan 10 Rs 9,500 double, Rs 13,500 suite. Rates include breakfast and dinner; 10% tax
extra. AE, MC, V **Amenities:** Restaurant; bar; lounge with CD; airport transfers (Rs 2,000–Rs 3,000); dhow;
Internet (in office; for e-mail only); massage center. *In room:* Fans, TV/DVD (in suites; also on request, Rs
300/day).

Panchavatti ★★★ (Finds) If you're looking for a little peace and quiet in a soul-
stirring setting and don't care too much for phones, air conditioners, bathtubs, and the
like, then Isla (Loulou) Van Damme's place is the ultimate refuge from the frenzy of
India. Most people come to Goa for the beaches, but Loulou's guesthouse (also her
home), with its stunning location on a hill on Corjuem Island, is where you come to put
your feet up and relax, take a dip or yoga instruction, or contemplate life. Meals are to
die for, served on the large open colonnaded balcony that overlooks the valley. In Loulou's inimitable style, there are no latches or locks on any of the doors and bathrooms are
curtained off from the bedrooms by thin cotton saris. Book one of the four rooms that
open onto the large balcony (the rest overlook a central courtyard and garden). The pool
is fabulously placed—on the edge of a hill. When you want to experience the beach,

---

> **(Tips) Take It Easy, Take It Slow**
>
> It's hardly worth the effort warning you of potentially slow service in many of Goa's small hotels and restaurants. It's the Goan way to take things easy, and waiting a few extra minutes for your meal really isn't going to spoil your vacation. You'll do far better to simply ease into the mellower way of life and savor the chef's efforts when they finally reach you. As they say in these parts: *Sossegud*— Take it easy!

---

however, you'll have to hire a taxi for the 30-minute schlep there. Or use the bicycles to explore the island.

Collomuddi, Corjuem Island, Aldonna, Bardez, Goa 403 508. *©* **98-2258-0632** or 0832/395-2946. http:// islaingoa.com. info@islaingoa.com. 7 units. Dec–Jan Rs 9,000 double; Mid-Oct–Nov and Feb–May Rs 8,000 double. Rates include all meals and soft drinks. No credit cards. Closed June to mid-Oct except for yoga workshops. **Amenities:** Dining area, music room with library; Ayurvedic massage; babysitting; bicycles; outdoor pool; limited room service; yoga and meditation. *In room:* Fan, hair dryer on request.

Moderate

There are quite a number of soulless places in the midrange category; many cater specifically to package tourists who fly in to bronze their neon-white skin and overindulge on cheap liquor. We assume you've got other plans, so the places we've reviewed below generally have a bit of character. Of these, **Siolim House** is the most authentic option, set in a beautifully restored Portuguese villa that once belonged to the Governor of Macau; and **Wilderness** is an inland eco-resort that offers a complete alternative to the beach holiday most people associate with Goa. In addition to these, you can also go in for the totally intimate and very private atmosphere of the two rooms attached to the seasonal restaurant, **Ku ★** (*©* **93-2612-3570;** ku.morjim@rediffmail.com; $110–$175 double), run by a European couple, but decorated in a Balinese-cum-Japanese style that works amazingly well when surrounded by rice paddies and a lovely water garden. The slick design cleverly blurs the line between outdoor and indoor living—perfect for Goa's sultry, tropical atmosphere. If you like the sound of **Casa Vagator** and **Casa Britona** (both reviewed below), then you might also appreciate the classy styling of **Casa Colvale ★★** (*©* **93-7308-1973;** www.casaboutiquehotels.com), a snazzy 12-room contemporary hotel with a pretty setting on the Chapora River. It's several kilometers inland from Anjuna, so not the first choice if the beach and hippie vibe is important to you, but it has a fabulous infinity pool and superb deck straddling the water's edge; there's also a speedboat on hand to get you where you need to go. The intimate spa here is also a big highlight. Doubles run Rs 6,000 to Rs 9,000; much higher during the Christmas/New Year period, and lower during the monsoon. This is likely to be a hip place to meet savvy, sophisticated vacationers from Mumbai, Delhi, and Bengaluru

Casa Anjuna ★★ A very slick little operation in the center of Anjuna village, but tucked away from the crowds in a quiet neighborhood, this is a lovely old Portuguese bungalow with annexes, plenty of greenery, comfortably decorated rooms, a lovely garden for candlelit dinners, and a rooftop restaurant for lazy morning breakfasts. It offers atmosphere, style (albeit with reproduction antiques mixed in with originals), and good cuisine, although the service is a little slow. Upstairs units are more private—choose one of the luxury rooms (no. 11 or 10) up here for a bigger space furnished with a magnificently carved bed and antique armoire, a fabulous built-in shower area, and real "lord of the manor" views. For a completely different feel, the penthouse has a modern, chic aesthetic with plasma TV, awesome mosaic shower and cushy seating nook. Although the setting feels almost as if you're in a tree-filled grove in the middle of nowhere, staff do occasionally crank up the music flooding the pool area with reggae beats.

D'Mello Waddo, Anjuna, Bardez 403 509. (C) **0832/227-4125.** www.casaboutiquehotelsgoa.com. 21 units. Oct Dec 15 and Apr–May Rs 6,000 deluxe double, Rs 7,000 luxury double, Rs 9,000 suite, Rs 12,000 penthouse; Dec 16–Dec 26 and Jan 6–Mar Rs 7,000 deluxe double, Rs 8,000 luxury double, Rs 10,000 suite, Rs 13,000 penthouse; June–Sept Rs 3,500 deluxe double, Rs 4,500 luxury double, Rs 5,000 suite, Rs 8,000 penthouse; Dec 27–Jan 5 Rs 12,000 deluxe double, Rs 14,000 luxury double, Rs 15,000 suite, Rs 18,000 penthouse; Rs 1,000 extra bed for child under 12. Rates include breakfast; 10% tax extra. MC, V. **Amenities:** Restaurant; lounge; poolside bar; airport transfers (Rs 800 Rs 1,000); Internet (free for e-mails; small charge for browsing) large outdoor pool; pool table; room service; small spa with massage. *In room:* A/C, TV, hair dryer on request, kitchenette (in penthouse).

Casa Britona ★   Far away from the crowds, this 17th-century Customs warehouse, located on the riverside in the fishing village of Charmanos, has been converted into a colonial-style boutique hotel by Goan architect-hero, Dean D'Cruz. With just 10 individually furnished rooms, you are ensured privacy, though sound travels fairly easily between rooms. Ask for a room on the first floor; these share a long veranda (with planter's chairs) overlooking the pool. Almost 40 minutes from the shore, this may not be the ideal location for beach lovers (for that, book Casa Vagator, a thoroughly modern hotel by the same owner), but you are assured of peace, excellent service, and a multitude of chirping birds as backdrop while you unwind on the lounge deck by the pool or on the wooden boardwalk on the Mandovi River. On the boardwalk are tables where you can be served a lovely dinner by candlelight.

Charmanos, Badem, Salvador-do-Mundo, Bardez 403 101. (C) **0832/241-0962** or 98 5055-7665. Fax 0832/ 241-3389. www.casaboutiquehotelsgoa.com. 10 units. Oct–Dec 15 and Apr–May Rs 4,000 deluxe double, Rs 6,000 luxury double; Dec 16–Dec 26 and Jan 6–Mar Rs 7,000 deluxe double, Rs 8,000 luxury double; June–Sept Rs 2,500 deluxe double, Rs 3,500 luxury double; Dec 27–Jan 5 Rs 12,000 deluxe double, Rs 13,000 luxury double; Rs 1,000 extra bed for child under 12. Rates include breakfast; 10% tax extra. MC, V. **Amenities:** Restaurant; TV lounge; Internet by request (Rs 100/hr.); outdoor pool; room service. *In room:* A/C, hair dryer on request.

Casa Vagator ★   A popular seaside miniresort, this is the best place to stay in Vagator—it's got high design ambitions, direct beach access, and many fine views (especially from the beautiful penthouse suite). There's nothing old-fashioned or heritage-themed here. The designers have gone for a bold contemporary look with sleek furniture, modern artworks, lamps and fittings, geometric fabric designs, and emphasis on creating flow through the different spaces. It's a bit like having a slick city pad transported to the seaside, with interesting split-level rooms. Don't think twice about booking a luxury room (larger spaces with good-size bathrooms and a little patio), or—better still—the superb penthouse suite with its breezy design, billowing curtains, multiple balconies and sea view from the shower. Towards the end of the day, plunk yourself on the hilltop deck overlooking Vagator Beach, toast the setting sun, and then ask for dinner to be served here. There's a chichi indoor restaurant and bar with an attached fan-cooled open-air rooftop lounge, but it's approached via a bland stairway area that makes you feel as if you're suddenly in an apartment block.

House no. 594/4, Ozran, Vagator 403 507. (C) **0832/652-9841.** www.casaboutiquehotels.com. 12 units (some with shower only). Oct–Dec 15 and Apr–May Rs 6,000 deluxe double, Rs 7,000 luxury double, Rs 12,000 penthouse; Dec 16–Dec 26 and Jan 6–Mar Rs 7,000 deluxe double, Rs 8,000 luxury double, Rs

14,000 penthouse; June–Sept Rs 3,500 deluxe double, Rs 4,500 luxury double; Dec 27–Jan 5 Rs 16,000 deluxe double, Rs 17,000 luxury double, Rs 24,000 penthouse; Rs 1,000 extra bed for child under 12. Rates include breakfast; 10% tax extra. MC, V. **Amenities:** Restaurant; lounge; bar; airport transfers (free during monsoon season; otherwise Rs 1,000–Rs 1,500); Internet (Rs 100/hr.); room service; small spa with massage. *In room:* A/C, TV, DVD (in luxury rooms and penthouse suite), Jacuzzi (in penthouse suite).

Laguna Anjuna ★

Tucked away in a quiet area amid paddy fields, this place is languid, rustic, and mellow. It's a resort of sorts, but perfect if you want the best of both worlds—you're close enough to Anjuna Beach to enjoy the vibe, yet far enough away to be undisturbed by any potential party atmosphere, not to mention the crowds that turn up for the flea market. A large amoeboid pool flanked by dense foliage gets all the attention here, with assorted laterite rooms and cottages clustered together at the back with domes and sloping tiled roofs, each entirely unique, and linked by pebble pathways. The spacious rooms are the most astounding shapes, forming their own contours between palms, and are provided with mirrors, chests, local crafts, and wrought-iron beds covered in cool green and yellow linen. Dean D'Cruz designed the laterite cottages, but they're looking a little tired these days, sorely in need of maintenance, but if you're not too fussed, they're just fine for a tropical holiday. With a piano and pool table inside and dining outside, the restaurant-bar is extremely casual, with an eclectic mix of music playing (sometimes blasting) right through the day.

Soranto Vado, Anjuna 403 509. ✆ **0832/227-4305** or -3248. ✆/fax 0832/227-4305. www.lagunaanjuna. com. info@lagunaanjuna.com. 23 units. Oct–Dec 19 and Jan 11–Mar 15 Rs 5,500 double, Rs 7,500 2-bedroom suite; Dec 20–Jan 10 Rs 9,200 double, Rs 14,000 2-bedroom suite; Mar 16–Apr Rs 4,000 double, Rs 5,500 2-bedroom suite; May–Sept Rs 3,200 double, Rs 5,500 2-bedroom suite; Rs 1,200 extra bed. Rates include breakfast and taxes. AE, MC, V. **Amenities:** Restaurant; bar; airport transfers (Rs 800–Rs 1,200); large outdoor pool; pool table; room service; spa. *In room:* A/C, TV, minibar, Wi-Fi (free).

Mykonos Blu ★ (Kids)

The name of this sleek, smart, brand-new small hotel directly across the road from Baga Creek clues you in to the look the designers were going for. It's been fashioned to resemble a tiny, compact Mediterranean resort, all whitewashed and sun reflective, with bold blue accents; in a low-rise block overlooking the blue mosaic pool, the attractive rooms all have little sitting areas, fat mattresses on big beds built into arched laterite alcoves, and balconies. The duplex room, with a spectacular vaulted brick ceiling and a view of the creek, is excellent value, with a loft bedroom for children. The suite, with no privacy between the two bedrooms, is good if you literally want to keep an eye on the kids. It's away from the raucousness of Baga Beach, and although it doesn't have a seafront location, it's quite conveniently located for trips all over the north Goan coast, as well as some very good restaurants.

Bagawada (next to Lila Café), Arpora, Bardez 403 516. ✆ **0832/227-7891** through -7896. www.mykonos blu.co.in or www.milestonehotels.in. Reservations ✆ **022/6741-3337.** mumsales@milestonehotels.in. 20 units. Rs 6,000 double, Rs 7,000 duplex (sleeps 4), Rs 8,000 suite (sleeps 4). Rates include breakfast; 10% tax extra. MC, V. **Amenities:** Restaurant; bar; airport transfers (free for stays of 3 nights or more; otherwise Rs 1,400); boat; rooftop health club and spa (planned for 2010); outdoor pool; room service. *In room:* A/C and fans, TV, mini bar, Wi-Fi (planned for 2010).

Siolim House ★★

It doesn't get more authentic than this—a chance to sample historic architecture in a 300-year-old Portuguese mansion and experience the ebb and flow of genuine village life. Accommodations are atmospheric and lovely, and retain so much of their original character, thanks to savvy, sensitive restoration by the owner, Varun Sood, a with-it and debonair raconteur, businessman, and charmer; chat with him and he'll shares his insider views on Goa. The entire house recalls a bygone age and is filled with original antiques, wrought-iron four-poster beds, and lots of dark wood to set off the white walls. If possible, avoid the rooms around the courtyard, though, as these pick up some noise from the public areas. Besides, the upstairs superior rooms are even more appealing (Macassar being our personal favorite); they're massive, with high ceilings and loads of windows (but no A/C) that fill the interior with magnificent light and a welcome breeze. He's also created a lovely garden and poolside environment, and the intimate restaurant serves great fresh fish. You can rent scooters and Bullet motorcycles, and staff arrange tours up and down the coast, and you can attend Sunday mass at Siolim village's beautiful church, just down the road.

Waddi, Siolim, Bardez 403 517. © **0832/227-2138** or 98-2258-4560. Fax 0832/227-2941. www.siolimhouse. com. 7 units. Oct–Dec 19 and Jan 11–Apr Rs 6,600 double, Rs 8,300 superior double; Dec 20–Jan 10 Rs 11,025 double, Rs 13,000 superior double; Rs May–Sept Rs 4,000 double, Rs 5,000 superior double. Rs 1,500 children over 12, Rs 750 children 5–12. Rates include breakfast; 10% tax extra MC, V. **Amenities:** Restaurant; common room with lounge, TV, DVD, Wii gaming console, and library; airport transfers (Rs 1,000); large outdoor pool; table tennis; Wi-Fi (in restaurant; free). *In room:* A/C (in some) and fans.

Wildernest ★★★ Finds

Miles away from the clichéd Goan image of sun and sand, this wilderness retreat is considered one of the world's top eco-resorts. Sandwiched between two wildlife sanctuaries near the Maharashtrian border, some 800m (2,624 ft.) above sea level, this is the "love-child" of a group of villagers, eco-crusaders, and three forest departments that saved 180 hectares (450 acres) from becoming a timber and mining wasteland. Having resurrected the land, the team stuck fast to its natural-material-only rule. The result is delightful; ingenuity has left its stamp everywhere: on walls, lights, even signposts, culminating in the most awesomely located infinity pool, surrounded by forested hills, with waterfalls cascading in the distance and fed by natural spring water. Cottages are simple, but come with extraordinary views of either the forest or the valley. Cuisine features a delectable mix of recipes from Goa, Maharashtra, and Karnataka, and is served in earthen pots. Wildernest is a haven for trekkers and birders alike: You're likely to spot paradise flycatchers, Malabar grey hornbills, and long-billed vultures. And, as you head off on early morning forest trails, you'll spot telltale signs left by bears and leopards.

Swapnagandha, off Sankhali, Chorla Ghats 403 708. © **93-4111-2721** or 0831/420 7954 or -1662. Fax 0831/ 243 1762. www.wildernest-goa.com. 18 units. Nov–Apr 14 Rs 6,000 forest view double, Rs 7,000 valley view double, Rs 10,000 family cottage (4 people); Apr 15–Oct Rs 3,200 Forest View double, Rs 4,200 Valley View double, Rs 6,000 Family Cottage. 1 child under 10 can stay free in forest and valley view cottages. Rates include all meals, evening tea, most activities, and taxes. Rates are much higher Dec 25–Jan 2. No credit cards. **Amenities:** Restaurant; bar; airport transfers (free for stays of 2 nights; otherwise Rs 1,800); bicycles; bird-watching; nature walks and treks; large outdoor pool. *In room:* Fans.

Yab Yum Resort ★★ Kids

With stone and thatch dome "pods" dreamt up by the owner after watching a futuristic TV series in the 1970s, this turns out to be one of the most authentic and lovely places to stay in Goa—*The Independent* called it the "quintessential tropical retreat." Set behind the dunes on the edge of Aswem village amid coconut groves and banana trees, with the beach just a few paces away, the cluster of pods resembles a cute rustic village—steps lead up to the front door of your palm-frond-thatched igloo-shaped hut that rests on a solid plinth made from locally excavated lava rock. They're a far cry from the dark, sweaty, often-gloomy backpacker digs that saturate Goa's beachfront locations. Each one has a large stone bed, handmade mattress, cotton linens, cane and mango wood furniture, hanging space, cotton rugs and floor loungers, mosquito nets and incense, and reading lamps. The best, with sea views, are the pods set atop the dunes. There are also four whitewashed cottages in the traditional Indo-Portuguese style. You can order meals and drinks, delivered to you at your room, or on the beach or wherever, and organic breakfasts are brought to you each morning. Children are especially well taken care of—there's a special tent for them and an on-site governess when you need respite.

Ashvem Beach, Mandrem. © **0832/651-0392.** www.yabyumresorts.com. info@yabyumresorts.com 17 units (all shower only). Dec 15–Feb Rs 4,400 standard dome/cottage double, Rs 5,000–Rs 5,500 family dome/twin cottage/Honey Pod, Rs 11,000 double suite pod; Mar–Apr 14 and Oct–Dec 14 Rs 3,300 standard dome/cottage double, Rs 4,000–Rs 4,400 family dome/twin cottage/Honey Pod, Rs 8,800 double suite pod. Rates include breakfast and taxes. MC, V. Closed Apr 15–Oct. **Amenities:** Light meals and bar service; airport transfers (Rs 1,200); babysitting and children's activity tent; Internet (in the office, for e-mails; free); outdoor dipping pool and children's pool; tailor; yoga and massage center. *In room:* Fans, Wi-Fi (Rs 200/day), no phone.

Inexpensive

Occupying the same infinitely peaceful location (and with the same excellent staff and restaurant) as Elsewhere (one of our favorite collection of "villas;" see p. 202), are the rustic-luxury **Otter Creek Tents** ★★ (© **0832/224-7616;** www.aseascape.com). Bargain hunters should really consider one of these three tents ($407–$663 double per week; $1,126 over Christmas and New Years), which overlook the freshwater creek; these are furnished with four-poster beds and have en-suite bathrooms with hot showers and personal lounges on a bamboo jetty. And there's a great sense of exclusivity, to boot.

Another decent budget-oriented option (and one which you needn't take for an entire week) would be to bag one of the two suites at **Hotel Bougainvillea** (© **0832/227-3270** or -3271; www.granpasinn.com) in Anjuna, some distance from the beach. Built by owner Betina Faria's grandfather, it's also fondly referred to as Granpa's Inn and is a well-regarded hangout for backpackers looking for something a little more substantial and characterful than the shacks and impromptu guesthouses nearer the beach. Actually, the fact that Bougainvillea is a couple of miles away from the beach may be a bit of a letdown for some—for others, the distance from the flea market and endless vendors of Anjuna may be its saving grace. There's a convoluted list of room categories, with standard (basic) doubles from Rs 850 to Rs 2,150; but those prized suites cost Rs 1,250 to Rs 2,450. Try to book the one with its own garden. The small accommodations are quiet and cool; there's a lovely garden, swimming pool, and old pool table. Both short and long sessions of Brahmani yoga are held on the premises.

Presa di Goa ★★ Value Luxembourg native Edouard Spaeck and his adopted Goan son Judas (with wife, Cynthia) have turned this country house in Nagoa into a cool retreat, offering unbelievable value; each room has a small balcony with a table and cane chairs where your breakfast is served. Rooms, each named after a flower (we recommend Crossandra), are furnished with well-restored colonial antiques, including ultrafirm four-poster beds (although those in the deluxe rooms are a little small), sofas, desks, and wardrobes or chests of drawers, handsome Indian artifacts, and cool cotton gowns. Although the closest beach is overrun Calangute, what you wake up to here is a chorus of birds and the shrill hum of what appears to be a lively forest—although you're actually in the quaint, off-the-beaten-track village of Nagoa. Should you happen to be there on a Friday, hop into the car and go shopping with the cook to the Mapusa weekly market. At press time, seven new suites were scheduled to open in the Portuguese colonial mansion on the adjacent property.

353/1 Arais Wado, Nagoa, Calangute, Bardez 403 517. © **0832/240-9067** through -9069 Fax 0832/240-9070. www.presadigoa.com. reservation@presadigoa.com. 7 units (most with tubs). Jan 3–Apr 15 56€–57€ double, 67€–82€ junior suite, 97€–107€ special junior suite, 17€–20€ extra bed; Apr 16–Dec 17

40€–48€ double, 48€–70€ junior suite, 73€–90€ special junior suite, 8.50€–17€ extra bed; Dec 18–Jan 2 75€ double, 100€–125€ junior suite, 150€ special junior suite, 25€ extra bed. Children 2–6 pay 50% with extra bed. Rates include breakfast and beach transfers; 10% tax extra. MC, V. Closed June. **Amenities:** Restaurant, bar; airport transfers (Rs 900); outdoor pool; room service. *In room:* A/C, TV, hair dryer on request, Wi-Fi (free).

WHERE TO DINE

Beach-shack dining is one of the essential Goa experiences—sipping *feni* while you feast on grilled tiger prawns or masala shark at unbelievable prices is a must. With at least 200 licensed seasonal shacks between Candolim and Baga, you certainly won't go hungry, but with names like Lover's Corner, Fawlty Towers, and Goan Waves, don't expect culinary magic. Best to stick to the following recommendations, or ask around for this seasons hot picks, since shacks come and go, and some of the good chefs make a habit of relocating.

At Calangute, **Souza Lobo** enjoys a legendary reputation for seafood—and deservedly so. Reserve a table on the beachfront patio and order the tandoor kingfish and crab-stuffed *papad*, or the expensive but excellent grilled lobster or tiger prawns (⌀ **0832/ 228-1234** or 0832/227-6463; daily 11am–11pm; reservations taken before 8pm; after that, wait in line). While in Baga, check out **Casa Portuguesa** (Baga Beach, ⌀ **0832/ 227-7024;** closed Mon and May–Oct), set in an old bungalow near the beach; the chicken *cafreal* is highly recommended. If you have a sweet tooth, **Chocolatti** (409A Fort Aguada Rd., Candolim; ⌀ **93-2610-3522**) is simply irresistible when it comes to home-made chocolates and brownies.

A number of good restaurants can also be found along the stretch of road between Arpora Hill and Baga Creek, leading inland from Baga Beach. When Indian spices begin to take their toll, **Lila Café ★★** (near Baga River, Arpora-Baga; ⌀ **0832/227-9843;** Wed–Mon 9am–6pm, closed May–Sept), a great breakfast and lunch cafe (and apparently where Gregory Peck, David Niven, and Roger Moore hung out when filming *Sea of Wolves*), is the perfect spot (with views of paddy fields and coconut groves) to enjoy a proper coffee as you unwind with a mixed crowd. A selection of breads (including great pumpernickel sandwiches) and croissants is served with a variety of toppings; the salads are fresh and crunchy, and there's well prepared catch of the day. Also on Baga Creek, is famous **J&A's Little Italy ★★** (⌀ **0832/228-2364** or 98-2313-9488; daily 6pm–midnight, closed end of Apr to Sept), where Jamshed and Ayesha Madon serve fantastic pastas, wood-fired pizzas, and organic salads in a great alfresco setting. During peak season there's always a long wait (well worth it), so do make reservations. The *regalo di mare* (prawns and squid in a tomato vinaigrette dressing served with pesto crostini) and *crespelle coi gamberi* (crepes stuffed with seafood) are personal favorites. Or try the delicious steaks or the perfect al dente pastas tossed in heavenly sauces.

Arguably one of the hottest (and most expensive) places this side of Panjim is **A Reverie** (next to Hotel Goan Heritage; ⌀ **98-2317-4927**), an extremely fancy (and quite beautiful) restaurant with extravagant modern European cuisine—reports are up and down, however, with many people (even those who've loved the food in the past) complaining about fallen standards. In nearby Dando, between Aquada and Calangute, **Shiro ★** (Sinquerim Beach, Candolim; ⌀ **0832/665-3366**) is Goa's first real Japanese restaurant (although there are a few dishes from other Far Eastern nations as well). Besides sushi—with a strong seafood bias—there are fusion items, too, but the sashimi platters are certainly what should draw you here. Shiro is housed in a vast beachside premises, with contemporary minimalist décor that helps with the venue's transition into a club later at night.

A Bluffers Guide to the Unique Flavors of Goa

If you don't know your *xacuti* from your *baboti,* here's a short guide: Spicy chicken *cafreal* is marinated in green herbs, ginger, cinnamon, pepper, chili, mace, fresh coriander, and garlic, and then fried. *Vindaloo* is a curry usually made with pork and marinated in vinegar, garlic, chilies, and assorted spices. Prawn *Balchao* is a sweetish shrimp preserve made with spices and coconut *feni. Ambo-tik* is a hot curry made with onion, cumin seeds, pepper, and garlic, and soured with *kokum* berries—it's usually made with baby shark (although other fish can be used). The state's favorite fish, kingfish *(isvon),* is best sampled *"recheado"*— stuffed with chilies and spices blended in vinegar; not recommended if you're unfamiliar with spicy food. *Xacuti* is a coconut-based masala prepared with Goan spices; *baboti* is a sweet and spicy ground-beef dish. *Sorpotel*—not for the faint-hearted—is traditionally a spicy concoction of pork, offal (mostly liver), *feni,* vinegar, red chilies, and spices. Another unusual dish is the Portuguese *cabidela,* prepared by cooking rice with chicken and rabbit blood and meat; *caldeirada* is a typical Portuguese seafood stew. *Uned* are the small round rolls that feature on the Goan breakfast table and are traditionally delivered fresh from the bakery each morning (if you're staying in Panjim's Latin quarter, Fountainhas, you might hear the delivery man on his bicycle doing the rounds). *Bebinca* is the traditional layered dessert made with lots of eggs and coconut milk. *Dodol* is made with jaggery (sugar) and should always be accompanied with vanilla ice cream; *doce* is a sweet rice pudding from Portugal. Goa is famous for its cashew nuts available in many forms; get the roasted salted variety (great with any drink) from Zantye's or Kajuwala in Panjim. *Kokum* (fruit of a plant by the same name), served as a syrupy juice, is a delightful thirst quencher; when mixed with coconut milk, garlic, and salt, it becomes a digestive aid called *sol kadi.* Speaking of drinks, *feni* is the deceptively light alcoholic spirit distilled from the cashew fruit (or coconut); try it, but be wary.

Heading north, to Anjuna, **Sublime** (near the football field; © **98-2248-4051**) offers fusion food and presentational styles that are quite difficult to classify, even for American owner Christopher (for example, he uses a French recipe for fish, which is accompanied by traditional Indian green lentils and an Italian sauce!). A reasonable, well-established alternative is **Xavier's** (near the flea market, Praia de San Miguel; © **0832/227-3402;** daily 9am–11pm)—it has a lovely ambience (with additional seating in the garden), and the seafood is always fresh and the lamb chops excellent. But perhaps the most reliable place in Anjuna, this time good for delicious pizza, is **Basilico** (D'mello Vaddo, near Casa Anjuna; © **0832/227-3721;** daily 11am–midnight). It's run by an Italian, which explains the authenticity and subtleties in flavor so often lacking in the many knockoff Italian joints.

After Seven—The Restaurant ★★★ EUROPEAN   It's definitely worth tracking down this difficult-to-find restaurant (located between Calangute and Candolim near the Sarkar ice factory), as it's one of Goa's best dinner venues. Owned by the gracious ex-Taj hotel duo, Leo D'Souza and superchef Soumyen Chakraborty, it's a really pleasant alfresco place set on the lawns of Leo's house. You can watch your meal being cooked in the glass-fronted kitchen, and discuss how you liked it afterward, when Soumyen visits every table. Begin with the near-legendary Camembert soufflé, and move on to the delectable "Ocean's Fantasy" seafood platter. This is also one spot in Goa where you can happily indulge your lust for a juicy steak—order the chargrilled filet with blue cheese sauce. And do prepare yourself for either the chocolate mousse with orange Curaçao or the unbelievably light and delicious orange soufflé.

1/274B, Chapel Lane, off the Calangute-Candolim main road, Gaura Vaddo, Calangute, Bardez. © **0832/ 227-9757** or 92-2618-8288. Reservations essential. Main courses Rs 300–Rs 1,000. AE, MC, V. Daily 7pm–midnight. Closed May–Sept.

Bean Me Up ★ (Kids) ORGANIC/VEGETARIAN   An American with roots in Italy and Germany, Lisa Camps started this ultra-wholesome, all-organic restaurant as an alternative to the nonvegetarian food that dominates Goan menus. Meat-lovers won't miss anything once they sample Lisa's tofu lasagna or one of the daily house specials. But most delicious are the huge salads Lisa promises are the "safest in Goa." Expect soy in almost everything at this "Soya Station," including tofu ice cream and tofu cheesecake. If all this sounds too over-the-top healthy and New Age for you, there's always wood-fired pizza; or simply come to sip on one of the healthy cocktail-style drinks and catch a dance performance or live Spanish band on Sundays. Children are well taken care of in the kids' corner, with its comfy floor mattresses and cushions, reading and coloring books, and—yes, 'fraid so—a TV playing Cartoon Network.

House no. 1639 Deul Vaddo, Anjuna-Vagator, near Vagator Petrol Pump. © **0832/227-3479.** Reservations suggested for dinner during peak season. Main courses Rs 80–Rs 250. MC, V. Daily 8am–4pm and 7–11pm; call about slightly different Sat hours.

Bomra's ★ (Value) BURMESE   With Goa bursting at its seams with every conceivable kind of restaurant, a little Burmese hangout could get entirely lost or, as is the case with Bomra's (named after the owner-chef), really stand out. With only the basic accoutrements needed to make a place pleasing to the eye—low cane chairs and paper lamp-shades—the main emphasis here is on the food, which is absolutely top-notch. Start with the homemade fried Shan tofu (made from gram flour) with tamarind soy sauce, or the excellent spicy rare beef salad with basil, mint, coriander, and sprouts. For a main course, try mussel curry with coconut milk and lemon grass or any of the specials—pork belly with cashew-nut crust, or steamed snapper lemon grass with chili fish sauce and jaggery (unrefined sugar) served atop a banana leaf on a wooden platter. Round off your meal with chocolate fondant and homemade vanilla ice cream.

Souza Vaddo, opposite Kamal Retreat, Fort Aguada Rd., Candolim. © **98221-06236.** Reservations highly recommended during high season. Main courses Rs 90–Rs 250. No credit cards. Daily 7:30–11:30pm.

Britto's ★ (Moments) GOAN   This is a bit of a local institution; an archetypal Goan beach shack at one end, and extremely popular restaurant at the other, where owner-chef Cajetan Britto has been dishing out his crowd-pulling specialties for years. Acquaint yourself with the local flavors by tucking in to the pork *vindaloo* or prawn curry, and come back later for chicken *xacuti*, fish *caldeen*, or the superb crab curry. There are less spicy options for tamer tastes, too, including a formidable seafood platter and even steak. There's always action aplenty here—whether live music, super-smooth celebs hanging out on the beach, or simply a festive crowd ordering round after round of chilled beer. You'll find this Goan favorite towards the northern end of Baga beach.

Baga Beach, Santo Vaddo, Calangute. © **0832/227-7331** or -7629. Main courses Rs 80–Rs 270. MC. Daily 9am–11:30pm. Closed June 20–Aug 7.

Copper Bowl ★★★ GOAN/SEAFOOD   It's not just the sensational seafood that makes dining here so pleasurable, it's the wonderful setting—intimate and lush and seemingly hidden from the world in a peaceable garden kingdom. Served from copper pots, the Goan curry dishes are exquisite; try coconut-based chicken *xacuti* (pronounced cha-*coo*-ty) or fragrant prawn *balchao,* a mouthwatering combination of crispy prawns, aromatic spices, chili, onion, and prawn powder. If your taste leans more toward non-spicy, try the seafood in coconut-milk soup, followed by the "Seafood Treasure"—baby lobster, prawns, and two kinds of fish served in a banana leaf. There's a formidable menu, but nothing will be served unless it's fresh.

Pousada Tauma, Porba Vaddo, Calangute. ℭ **0832/227-9061.** Reservations essential for nonresidents. Main courses Rs 300–Rs 700, lobster/tiger prawns Rs 1,000–Rs 1,400. MC, V. Daily 7:30am–10:15pm.

Fiesta ★ ITALIAN   A bit of an oasis off Baga-Calangute's bar-lined main drag, this is one of Goa's more romantic restaurants, set in a lovely beachfront garden and run by an energetic couple named Yellow and Maneck Contractor. It's worth coming even if just for the magical ambience (and excellent thin-crust pizzas, fresh pastas, but slow service) or a pick from their legendary dessert menu.

7/35 Saunta Vaddo, Tito's Lane, Baga. ℭ **0832/227-9894** or 0832/228-1440. www.fiestagoa.com. Main courses Rs 150–Rs 450. MC, V. Daily 7pm–midnight. Closed May–Sept.

Florentines ★ ⓥⓐⓛⓤⓔ GOAN   The great thing about this place, despite the plastic chairs and typically thrown-together ambience, is that you get to dine with locals, apparently untrammeled by tourism. For more than 25 years, Florence da Costa's heaving chicken joint has been pulling in a crowd. Here, far from the well-trodden tourist beat (although, if you look foreign—or, better still, if you book a table—you seem to get preferential treatment), you'll witness well-to-do Goan families fighting over who gets to pay the bill, while dozens more wait expectantly for a table. The chicken is legendary. It's prepared in a variety of ways—the chicken *cafreal* is popular, but you can go for chicken *xacuti* or chicken *vindaloo,* too. Tables inside benefit from overhead fans, but the covered terrace outside is a better bet; expect zero frills, no music (just the progressively louder din from scores of happy diners), and food to be slumped onto the table. The chicken is served with soft Portuguese-style rolls and comes with a knife and fork, but you really should follow the example of fellow guests and use your fingers. Everyone here looks like they're drinking soft drinks, but look carefully and you'll see that those are mixers for generous measures of *feni,* the potent locally brewed liquor.

Chogm Rd., Saligao, Bardez. ℭ **0832/227-8122** or -8249. Main courses Rs 40–Rs 80. No credit cards. Tues–Sun 11:30am–3pm and 6:30–10:45pm.

Ku ★★ PAN-ASIAN   Owned and run by Marie and Chris, a Spanish-French couple, this Zen-themed place focuses on sushi and Vietnamese dishes. There is no menu—rather listen to the brief list of daily offerings suggested by lovely Maria; she'll be working with whatever she's managed to source from the market today. If you're lucky, you'll get to sample her sugar-cane prawns, delicious spring rolls, and the Thai soups are lovely too. It's a two-level restaurant made from wood and bamboo—there's a water fountain stocked with fish and some plants, but the pleasure here is being surrounded by green open space (which you can appreciate since the place is open for lunch only). *Note:* Like many of the better eateries in Goa, Ku is very difficult to find and there aren't any signs to speak of, so ask, and carry a mobile phone so you can call if you really get stuck.

Gaude Vaddo, Aswem, Morjim. ℭ **93-2612-3570.** ku.morjim@rediffmail.com. Main courses Rs 220–Rs 380. Cash only. Daily 11:30am–3pm. Closed May–Sept.

La Plage ★★★ FRENCH/FUSION   This charming slice of Gaul is the wave-mak-
ing venue established by the owners of erstwhile Le Restaurant Francais (always one of
our Goan favorites). Now the fun-loving accidental restaurateurs Morgan, Florence, and
Serge have transplanted the elegant yet laid-back atmosphere brought with them from
the Continent to a lovely location on Asvem Beach. Occupying a cluster of shacks amid
tall palm trees with thatched roofs and, for walls, sheer blue and yellow curtains billowing
in the breeze, you sit on deck chairs at simple white tables and are serenaded by mellow
tunes. The ambience might be relaxed, but the menu is a promise of a luxurious, memorable meal, and Chef Morgan certainly delivers. Tender fillets of tuna, served rare and
encrusted with sesame seeds and drizzled with a sweet-tangy soy sauce; or calamari
stuffed with ratatouille; and another stand-out favorite has got to be sardine filets with
wasabi cream. The menu features innovative dishes concocted by Morgan, who likes to
"escape" (read: "experiment"), so menus change regularly. More must-tries include tiger
prawn carpaccio with fresh vanilla oil, and filet of sardines on phyllo pastry with mint
coulis. Be sure to leave space for the addictive chocolate cake, whose recipe Morgan once
used as *baksheesh* at airport Customs.

Asvem Beach, near Papa Jolly Hotel, Aswem, Morjim. ⟨℡⟩ 98-2212-1712. frenchfoodindia@hotmail.com.
Main courses Rs 260–Rs 690. No credit cards. Daily 9:30am–9:30pm. Closed May to mid-Nov

SHOPPING

Besides the vibrant markets (see "Shopping the Global Village Markets" box on p. 201),
north Goa has several stores worth checking out. **Casa Goa** ★★ is a stylish boutique
featuring luxuriously comfortable fashion items by celebrated Goan designers Wendell
Rodricks, Rajesh Pratap Singh, and Brigitte Singh as well as local artwork, silk drapes,
restored furniture, a variety of antiques, and prints of Mario Miranda's cartoons (Cobra
Vaddo, Calangute-Baga Rd.; ⟨℡⟩ 0832/228-1048). Then take a look at **Leela Art Palace**
nearby; with any luck, proprietor Ravi will be in. You might find yourself agreeing to
accompany him on an exotic journey into some of the country's remotest regions, where
he regularly treks to source tribal art. Also in Calangute, **Subodh Kerkar Art Gallery,**
run by Goa's well-known watercolorist, showcases contemporary Indian art including
ceramics, hand-painted chests, and Rajasthani sculptures (Gauro Vaddo; ⟨℡⟩ 0832/227-
6017). Each Tuesday, an interesting classical dance and music performance is held at the
gallery (6:45–8pm; Rs 300).

Located in a 200-year-old Portuguese mansion, **Sangolda** ★★★ is the lifestyle boutique venture by Claudia and Hari Ajwani, the dynamic duo behind the beautiful Nilaya
Hermitage and Fort Tiracol hotels; here you can shop for unusual home accessories and
furniture sourced from all over India—from Keralan rattan loungers to Rajasthani chests.
Attached is a gallery-cum-coffee-shop (E2–6 Chogm Rd., Sangolda; ⟨℡⟩ 0832/240-9310).
Design junkies should also definitely make an effort to visit **Monsoon Heritage** ★★★, a
contemporary studio created by internationally renowned designers Yahel Chirinian and
Doris Zacheres (selected as one of the 23 most happening designers in the world by
UrbanO magazine), who pair huge discarded tropical trees with mirrors and glass to cre-
ate exclusive design pieces for the (very) rich and famous. You'll find their showrooms in
Paris and Santa Monica, but their main base (and inspiration) is right here (601 Fernand
Wado, Porvorim, Bardez; ⟨℡⟩ 0832/651-5298; www.monsoonheritage.com). Another
unique duo is Sonja Weder and Thomas Schnider, who use eco-friendly materials as
much as possible and create some very striking articles ranging from furniture to lotus-
leaf lazy Susans and a whole range of wall objects and gorgeous lamp shades—all of it

(Moments) **Psychedelic Journeys: What Next for the Late, Great Goan Party?**

Rave parties are now almost as synonymous with Goa as hippie culture, but there's been much recent hullabaloo about the death of Goa's hardcore party scene—many bemoan the fact that they missed what all the hype was about, while generally locals can finally breathe a sigh of collective relief for the end of the noise, the drugs, the mischief-making, and the (in some minds, scandalous) reputation Goa has always had as an alternative hippie enclave. And, sure, the party scene has definitely calmed down a bit, but it has by no means come to an abrupt and grinding halt, even if the late night noise ban has quelled a lot of the mania. It's probably safe to say that the parties have gone deeper underground—and, in an entirely wrong spirit, moved into city-style clubs. If you end up partying the night away in a club, you're probably missing the point, since the Goan trance scene has always been about dancing under the stars or outdoors through the day, surrounded by Goa's considerable beauty and energized by music, nature and good vibes. Times are, of course, a-changing...

If you want to attend one of the winter gatherings, once known as full moon parties (but now as likely to happen by day in a remote location), you'll probably have to ask around at the shacks (at Vagator, Anjuna, Arambol, or Palolem). Location is often kept secret until late in the evening to avoid harassment from cops and generally disclosed only a few hours before the party starts. These underground dance and music parties start around 11pm and go till at least 8am. Various intoxicants are freely available and consumed (but they're very much illegal), and local women set up stalls outside selling *chai* and snacks. DJs play psychedelic trance music (the "Goan trance" that has become a global genre); ravers often dress up in old-fashioned costumes and wear rave belts and colorful clothes, all part of setting the mood for their psychedelic journey, which inevitably entails a lot of good-hearted mischief. Regulars insist that these are not just massive techno freak-outs where everybody is "tripping," but a mystical, devotional experience akin to a spiritual encounter.

In south Goa, the scene is compact enough to make finding the party quite straightforward, but in the north, you're going to need to put in some effort. A few obvious spots for picking up the scent of out-of-the-way parties are the **Saturday Night Bazaar** in Arpora, Anjuna's **Wednesday Market,** or the ever-popular **Shore Bar.** The latter is a party institution right on Anjuna beach; it really picks up on Wednesdays, when the market crowd redeploys here to continue the revelry, and the sunset scene is a virtual tourist cliché (albeit with a pretty cool crowd). Even cooler, though, is the other "institution:" **Nine Bar** ★★, on top of a hill overlooking Ozran beach at Vagator. As the sun sinks to provide

available at **Soto Décor** ★★ (Sotohaus, 1266/f, Anna Vaddo, Candolim; © 98-2298-3321; www.sotodecor.com). Nearby is a fun boutique called **Happily Unmarried** (© 93-2512-2150), where you can pick humorous knickknacks—strictly for singles. Janota is another classic moment, the DJs up the volume and furiously belt out deafening trance and psychedelic music—a haven for trippers and a nightmare for the rest of the world, but only till around 10pm, when things shut down and it's time to move on. Aside from the obvious locations in north Goa, there are also good vibes (and a better crowd) in and around Palolem in the far south. Palolem is also where India's first so-called **silent parties ★★★** have really taken off—you pick up a set of headphones and dance to the music, but the outside world doesn't have to hear a thing. Launched in 2008, the **Silent Noise Headphone Parties** (📞 **97-3093-5334;** www.silentnoise.in) are a revolutionary answer to Goa's 10pm music ban. The parties happen Wednesday ("Retronica") and Saturday at **Neptune's Point;** revelers are provided with advanced wireless headsets that allow you to switch between each of the 3 DJs playing that night; founder Justin Mason (a DJ himself since the '80s) procures outstanding international as well as Indian DJs (look out for Ma Faizel, an icon of the hip Indian electro scene), and you're able to switch between house, trance, hip hop or even rock tunes, spun simultaneously by different DJs. The venue comes with all the frills of the modern party era, including massage chairs and impeccable lighting. And, should you wish to tune out and engage in meaningful conversation for a moment, all you need to do is whip the headset off—no need to scream at the top of your lungs to ask for a drink.

The most happening clubs competing to attract the who's who with great let-your-hair-down ambience, fabulous music, and terrific cuisine include **Club Cubana** (Arpora Hill; 📞 **98-2337-2910**)—beautifully located atop a cliff with a swimming pool open at night and the focus on hip-hop and R&B music—and legendary **Tito's** (📞 **98-2276-5002;** www.titos.in). This local expire has been going for years and attracts anyone and everyone who's up for a party in a range of different-but-the-same venues (definitely nothing groundbreaking here); a good choice here is **Mambo's,** an open-air pub that's part of the Tito's franchise, where DJs spin 1980s rock music (but no trance). For a less rocking atmosphere accompanied by fairly good food, check out **Kamaki** ((📞 **98-2327-6520;** 6am–6pm recorded music, 6pm–6am DJ), a lounge bar up the road from Tito's that's open 24 hours. For an upmarket buzz, join the vibey, sexy-smart crowd at **Shiro ★★** (📞 **0832/645-1718**), the Candolim sibling of the ultrahip Mumbai restaurant-bar (p. 167) with a spectacular beachfront setting. Finally, although you should be cautious about planning a vacation here around New Years, since 2007, Goa has hosted the biggest music festival in Asia, **Sunburn ★★★** (www.sunburn-festival.com), for 3 days at the end of the year; check the website, though for specific dates, lineup, and venue.

the label for the unconventional footwear of **Edward Pinto ★★★** (Janota, Adleia Aurino, Povorim; 📞 **0832/241-2129;** www.janotagoa.com). He and his designer wife, Angela, have a seasonal store called "The Haystack" in Arpora (10am–8pm), while their studio is at Aldeia Aurino (near Damian de Goa, Porvorim, Bardez; © 0832/241-2129; 9am–7pm). They also have a stall at Ingo's Saturday Nite Bazaar. If you love shoes, make every effort to pick up a pair of Pinto's.

Eco-crusaders should make every effort to visit Earthworm ★★ (264/79, First Floor, Green Valley, Alto Porvorim; © 0832/241-0871; earthwormgoa@gmail.com), conceived by a pair of nature-loving Goan entrepreneurs looking to put the hype around sustainable lifestyles into action. Their green store sells environment-friendly products (read: low impact, organic, recycled) and local crafts, and disseminates ideas on sustainable living and conservation

Finally, for bibliophiles, **Literati** ★★★ (E/1-282, Gaura Vaddo, Calangute; © 0832/ 227-7740; www.literati-goa.com) is the best bookstore in the state, with tons of atmosphere, too. You can sit for hours in the terrific book cafe and read or browse or buy secondhand as well as newly published works, while at the same time enjoying a delicious brownie or a tall glass of chilled *kokum* (fruit drink). Ask owner Divya Kapur about any upcoming events like poetry or book readings and writing workshops.

---

3 PANJIM & OLD GOA

Panjim is 600km (372 miles) S of Mumbai

Located at the mouth of the Mandovi River, the state capital (also known as Panaji) relocated here from Old Goa in 1759, when bubonic plague finally wiped out the once-spectacular trade city. Panjim is today a breezy, laid-back town that lends itself to easy exploration. The chief attraction is the wonderful colonial Portuguese architecture, particularly in the eastern neighborhoods of **Fontainhas** and **Sao Tome,** where the atmospheric cobbled streets are lined with old mansions and churches dating as far back as the mid-1700s—look for Fontainhas's **Chapel of St. Sebastian,** where the crucifix from Old Goa's "Palace of the Inquisition" is now kept. With head upright and eyes wide open, the figure of Christ on the crucifix here is quite unlike the usual figures, which feature lowered head and eyes.

Dominating Panjim's town center is the imposing **Church of the Immaculate Conception,** built in the Portuguese baroque style in 1541. Nearer the water's edge is the **Secretariat;** an old palace of Adil Shah of Bijapur, this became the Portuguese viceroy's residence when the colonial administration moved here.

Wandering around Panjim on foot shouldn't take more than a few hours, but do spare some time for the **Municipal Market**—outside the smell will let you know when you're near the fish sellers, while inside, the orderly layout of vendors pushing the mountains of fruit, vegetables, and myriad other kitchen consumables will have you reaching for your camera. If you're pushed for time, confine your Panjim exploration to Fontainhas and hop onto an auto-rickshaw or on the back of a bike to **Old Goa** (30 min. from Panjim; reviewed in detail below). In its heyday reputedly larger than the city of London and one of Asia's great trade centers, today it's only Old Goa's monumental churches that hint at the former splendor which earned it the nickname "Rome of the East." From Old Goa, it's a short trip (and a great contrast) to view the popular Hindu temples that lie north of the dull town of Ponda, on National Highway 4. Very few Hindu temples dating from earlier than the 19th century still exist—affronted by the Hindus' "pagan" practices, the Portuguese tore them down—but Ponda became a repository for a large number of idols smuggled from the coast during the violent years of the 16th-century Inquisition.

| **Moments**   **Lights! Camera! Carnival!**

Each year in February, during the festivities leading up to Lent (a 40-day period of fasting that's carefully observed by Goa's large Catholic community), the people of Goa get down for 3 days and nights of hedonistic revelry as King Momo commands them to party hard. **Carnival,** Goa's most famous festival, is a Latin-inspired extravaganza of drinking and dancing that traces its roots from ancient Roman and Grecian ritual feasts. Cities and towns come under the spell of colorful parades, dances, floats, balls, and bands, concluding with the red-and-black dance at Panjim's Club National. Celebrations of a different sort happen much later in the year when filmmakers and stars congregate for the annual **International Film Festival of India** (http://iffi.nic.in), held in Panjim, for 10 great days of film-frenzied action. The 40th annual festival happened in 2009 from late November through early December. And if you are in Goa over the hectic New Year period, you might want to at least check out some part of **Sunburn,** the massive music festival that started here in 2007 and keeps revelers supplied with 3 days of international standard dance music (www.sunburn-festival.com).

Particularly noteworthy in this regard is **Sri Mangueshi Temple,** built specifically as a refuge for these refugee deities. A path lined with palm trees leads to a colorful entranceway, behind which the tiled, steep-roofed temple exemplifies a fusion of Hindu and Christian architectural styles, hardly surprising considering that it was constructed by Goan craftsmen weaned on 200 years of Portuguese church-building. Walking distance from here (15 min. south) is the slightly less commercial (no temple "guides") **Sri Mahalsa Temple.** Another half-hour from Old Goa is **Sahakari Spice Plantation** (Curti, Ponda; ✆ 0832/231-2394; www.sahakarifarms.com)—if you're not heading down to Kerala you might want to take a tour here. It's quite a commercial venture, but the tours provide an interesting insight into Indian spices, along with plenty of quizzing by the well-informed guides about basic facts related to your food.

EXPLORING OLD GOA ★★

The once-bustling Goan capital is said to have been the richest and most splendid city in Asia during the late 16th and early 17th centuries, before a spate of cholera and malaria epidemics forced a move in 1759. Today, this World Heritage Site is tepid testament to the splendor it once enjoyed. The tranquility behind this well-preserved tourist site (barring the grubby stands selling refreshments and tacky souvenirs) belies the fact that it was built on plunder and forced conversions, though you'll see little evidence (like the basalt architraves) of the mass destruction of the Hindu temples initiated by fervent colonialists. Besides, it's remarkable to witness the scores of Catholic Indians who turn up to worship in some of the country's most venerated cathedrals.

The entire area can easily be explored on foot because the most interesting buildings are clustered together. To the northwest is the **Arch of the Viceroys,** built in 1597 in commemoration of the arrival of Vasco da Gama in India. Nearby, the Corinthian-styled **Church of St. Cajetan** (daily 9am–5:30pm) was built in 1651 by Italian friars of the Theatine order, who modeled it after St. Peter's in Rome. Under the church is a crypt in which embalmed Portuguese governors were kept before being shipped back to Lisbon—in 1992,

Fun Facts **Hindu Christians**

In 1623 the pope agreed to tolerate converted Brahmin Catholics, who were then allowed to wear the marks of their Hindu caste. This extraordinary concession played its part in allowing Goa to ultimately adopt a practice of syncretism that embraced Hindus and Christians alike, though it drew its fair share of criticism from the more narrow-minded: The British adventurer Sir Richard Burton once noted that the "good" Hindus converted to Catholicism by the Portuguese were simply "bad" Christians.

three forgotten cadavers were removed. St. Cajetan's is a short walk down the road from **Adil Shah's Gate,** a simple lintel supported by two black basalt columns.

Southwest of St. Cajetan's are the highlights of Old Goa: splendid, behemoth **Sé Cathedral ★** (Mon–Sat 9am–6:30pm; Sun 11:30am–6:30pm), which took nearly 80 years to build (in local laterite stone) and is said to be larger than any church in Portugal; and the **Basilica of Bom Jesus** (see below). The so-called Miraculous Cross, housed in a box in a chapel behind a decorative screen, was brought here from a Goan village after a vision of Christ was seen on it—apparently a single touch (there is a hole in the glass for just this purpose) will cure the sick. The surviving tower of the Sé's whitewashed Tuscan exterior houses the Golden Bell, whose tolling indicated commencement of the *auto da fés,* brutal public spectacles in which suspected heretics were tortured and burnt at the stake. Nearby, the **Convent and Church of St. Francis of Assisi** (now an **archaeological museum:** Rs 5; Sat–Thurs 10am–5pm) has a floor of gravestones and coats of arms; notice that the images of Mary and Christ are unusually dark-skinned.

Basilica of Bom Jesus (Cathedral of the Good Jesus) ★   Opposite the Sé, the Basilica of Bom was built between 1594 and 1605 as a resting place for the remains of the patron saint of Goa, Francis Xavier (one of the original seven founders of the Jesuit order and responsible for most of the 16th-c. conversions). The withered body of the venerated saint lies in a silver casket to the right of the altar, his corpse surprisingly well preserved (although one arm is on display in Rome and a missing toe is believed to have been bitten off in 1634 by an overzealous devotee looking to take home her very own relic, during the first exposition of the body—now a decennial event; the next St. Francis Festival is incidentally in 2017).

Up the hill from the Basilica are the splendid ruins of the once awe-inspiring **Church of St. Augustine;** below is the **Church and Convent of Santa Monica and Chapel of the Weeping Cross,** where a miraculous image of the crucified Christ is said to have once regularly bled, spoken, and opened its eyes.

Mon–Sat 6am–6:30pm; Sun 11:30am–6:30pm.

WHERE TO STAY

To sample authentic neighborhood life, it's worthwhile spending a night in the heritage quarter that's developed in Panjim's oldest area, Fontainhas—here there's a resolutely faded Portuguese atmosphere, and if you stay at one of the smaller guesthouses reviewed below, you'll get a feel for the way people—many of them unaffected by tourism—live in the Goan capital. There's also the option of forgoing the heritage properties that we prefer and heading for the **Goa Marriott Resort** (www.goamarriottresort.com), an upmarket waterfront hotel situated on the outskirts of the city. Staying here, however, slightly misses the point of being in Panjim, and there are better resorts north and south of here. The clutch of guesthouses and small family run hotels situated in the heart of the Fontainhas neighborhood, not only have more character, but will immerse you in the spirit of the place far better than the luxurious resortlike places tucked behind the security booms. Also in the city, but a bit of a walk from the historic neighborhoods, is the brand new **Vivanta by Taj** (www.tajhotels.com), definitely the classiest place in town, even if not exactly brimming with local flavor. It's more a business hotel than anything else, with sleek contemporary rooms behind a facade from a different 20th-century era; ask for a room with a balcony or porch so you can at least catch a glimpse of the outside world while you're here.

Panjim People's ★ Situated in Panjim's historic Fontainhas district, this is a four-room heritage hotel (formerly a prominent local school) with huge bedrooms (rooms A and B are especially enormous) and modern bathrooms reached via a long, steep stairway; each features an antique rosewood four-poster bed, *almirah*, planters, chairs, and lace curtains. Open the many windows to let in the light and the breeze and park yourself in front of your *balcão*—you'll feel yourself spirited back in time as the neighborhood sounds seep in. This is our first choice among the three distinct, very authentic Goan guesthouses owned and managed by retired engineer Ajit Sukhija ("his first love is furniture; his second, old buildings") and his son Jack (who, incidentally, is a whizz on local history and culture, and gives a tour of the neighborhood if you ask).

31 January Rd., Fontainhas, opposite Panjim Inn 403 001. www.panjimpeoples.com. **Reception:** Panjim Inn, E-212, 31st January Rd., Fontainhas. ② **0832/222-8136**, -6523, -1122, or -6523. Fax 0832/243-5220. www.panjiminn.com. 4 units. Oct–Apr 15 Rs 7,200 superior double, Rs 1,000 extra person, Rs 500 child; Apr 16–Sept Rs 5,400 superior double, Rs 900 extra person, Rs 350 child; Dec 24–Jan 2 Rs 9,000 superior double, Rs 1,500 extra person, Rs 750 child. Rates include breakfast; 10% tax extra. MC, V. **Amenities:** Restaurant and bar (at Panjim Inn, across the road); airport transfers (Rs 500–Rs 600); Internet (in the gallery; ½ hr. free). *In room:* A/C, TV, fridge, no phone.

Pousada Panjim ★ (Value) This is a restored colonial-era Hindu-design house in a predominantly Catholic neighborhood. There's nothing particularly luxurious about this atmospheric guesthouse, but it offers a fairly authentic taste of Panjim's 19th-century upper-class lifestyle (along with hot water and "proper" plumbing). The simple rooms are furnished with antiques (including four-poster beds) arranged around an empty, courtyard—or *tulus*—where women traditionally prayed and performed the morning *arti*. Windows and balconies look onto the back streets and backyards of Panjim's old "Latin Quarter." The better-looking rooms are on the first floor, so book one of these. As with the nearby Panjim People's (see above), guests at the Pousada have breakfast at the older, Catholic-built, sister hotel, **Panjim Inn,** where there's a good restaurant and more space to unwind with a beer or a book. The inn offers budget rooms in an old family property dating from 1880, and there's a newer wing offering smart, antique-styled rooms with chunky hand-carved rosewood beds—the best have big French doors that open on to a small private terrace overlooking the main road and the river.

House no. 156, Circle no. 5, Cunha Gonsalves Rd., Fontainhas. Reception at **Panjim Inn,** E-212, 31st January Rd., Fontainhas 403 001. ② **0832/222-8136** or -6523. Fax 0832/222-8136 or -6523. www.panjiminn. com. 9 units (with shower only). Oct–Apr 15 Rs 1,980–Rs 2,070 double, Rs 2,700–Rs 2,750 deluxe double, Rs 3,600 superior/suite; Apr 16–Sept Rs 1,620 double, Rs 1,800 deluxe double, Rs 2,340 superior/suite; Rs 600 extra person; Rs 300 child. Panjim Inn has 24 units with the same rates. Rates include breakfast; 5%–8% tax extra. Rates slightly higher Dec 24–Jan 2. MC, V. **Amenities:** Restaurant, lounge, bar (all at

Panjim Inn); airport transfers (Rs 500–Rs 600); Internet (in the gallery; $^1/_2$ hr. free). *In room:* A/C, TV, fridge, no phone.

WHERE TO DINE

While you can eat heartily and comfortably at **Panjim Inn,** it would be a shame not to sample the produce of a few other kitchens in Fontainhas. Besides **Viva Panjim** and **Horseshoe** (both reviewed below), you can enjoy an atmospheric evening at Luiz D'Souza's **Hospedaria Venite** ★ (31st January Rd., Fontainhas; ✆ **0832/242-5537;** daily 8:30am–10:30pm), a tiny upstairs restaurant in a 200-year-old building where you can sit on the balcony and order wonderful Goan specialties (or try the delicious shrimp salsa and stuffed crab). The restaurant, which has been going for over 50 years now, features a floor made from wood salvaged from a wrecked Portuguese ship, and in one room the walls are thickly covered with decades of graffiti, amateur artworks and assorted paraphernalia, making this feel like a seriously boho hangout. You can also head across the Mandovi Bridge to Povorim where **O'Coquiero's** (near Water Tank; ✆ **0832/241-7271**) has been churning out traditional Goan food for decades (try the squid masala or chicken *cafreal*). For more on Goan food, see "A Bluffers Guide to the Unique Flavors of Goa," on p. 212.

Down the road from the Goa Marriott Resort (which, incidentally, has a very decent seafood restaurant, **Simply Fish,** overlooking the bay) is **Mum's Kitchen** (Martin's Building, D. B. Marg, Miramar; ✆ **98-2217-5559**). It has a laid-back Mediterranean atmosphere (some call it middle class) and does wonderful crab *xec-xec* (cooked in thick, spicy coconut gravy), prawn curry with bimley, Bombay duck, and pomfret *recheado* (fish stuffed with hot spices and pan-fried); the fried cauliflower is especially good. The owner, Rony Martins, not only invites you to examine his kitchen for standards of hygiene and his fish for freshness, he is on a mission to revive authentic Goan cuisine. He sources and adopts old "grandma" recipes and has started "A Cry of Goa": an exercise to save Goan cuisine. Definitely avoid the fries, though.

To sample traditional Goan sweets while wandering Fontainhas, pop into **Confeitaria 31 de Janueiro,** one of the oldest bakeries in the state (31 January Rd.; ✆ **0832/222-5791**).

Horseshoe ★★ GOAN/PORTUGUESE   If you're looking for that one special place to enjoy a truly authentic Portuguese or Goan meal, make this it. Owner Vasco Silveira was born in another former Portuguese colony, Angola, but settled here years ago—his fine little restaurant celebrates 3 decades in 2010. Here, the lack of atmosphere is compensated for by excellent food and a more professional approach than you'll find at most other places in town, including Viva Panjim (below). Besides stocking expensive Portuguese wines and offering many exotic-sounding specialties, Vasco also boasts that his is the only place in India where codfish (*bacalhau cozido com grâo*—very pricey) is served. Try one of the pork dishes, like *feijoada,* a hot mix of meat, beans, and spicy sausages with red chilies and plentiful spices; less spicy is the *leitâo assado,* roast piglet in wine sauce. You can also sample Goan-style clams—*sukhem tissero*—prepared with coconut and spices, and quite unique. There's plenty more to choose from, but be sure to finish off with bebinca, a traditional Goan dessert.

E-245, Rua de Ourem, Fontainhas. ✆ **0832/243-1788.** Main courses Rs 145–Rs 725. MC, V. Oct–May Tues–Sat 12:30–2:30pm, Mon–Sat 7–10:30pm.

Viva Panjim ★ ⓥ**alue** GOAN   Tucked down a narrow alley in Panjim's Latin Quarter (a short walk from Panjim Inn), this is a very popular (and slightly cramped) restaurant with tables that spill out into the cobbled road and nearby courtyard. Something of a culinary celebrity, Linda De Souza churns out very tasty Goan dishes, including huge portions of spicy fish curry (try kingfish *xacuti*). Prices are dirt-cheap and Linda comes out to check on you after she's prepared your meal. The only drawbacks here tend to be the slightly disheveled appearance of the outside tables (some of them squashed up against the plumbing)—which can be okay from an atmosphere point of view, but isn't particularly comfortable—and the waiters (wearing waistcoats and bow ties in the searing heat) are well meaning but ultimately slack.

House no.178, 31st January Rd., behind Mary Immaculate High School, Fontainhas. © **0832/242-2405.** Main courses Rs 80 Rs 140. MC, V. Daily 11:30am–3:30pm and 7–10pm.

SHOPPING

For authentic Goan souvenirs, proceed to **Velha Goa Galleria** (© 0832/242 6628) in Fountainhas, Panjim, for *azulejos*, attractive Portuguese-style hand-painted tiles and ceramics. They are happy to pack these delicate items carefully so that they survive the journey home.

Fashion junkies will love the **Wendell Rodricks Design Space ★★★** (158 Campal, near Luis Gomes Garden; © 0832/223 8177; www.wendellrodricks.com). Wendell believes in affordable designer wear, and his store has everything from evening gowns to casual wear. What makes his collection stand out is the emphasis on organic fabrics—his cottons are naturally dyed, too, using vinegar, onion, turmeric, indigo, and guava leaves, and everything is preshrunk. Then there's **Sôsa's ★★★** (E-245 Rua de Ourem; © 0832/222-8063; Mon–Sat 10am–7:15pm), a trendy fashion store stocking couture by Goan designer Savio Jon (who makes relaxed, pretty, summery cotton dresses and very elegant men's shirts as well as other young and rising designers. **Barefoot—The Home Store** (31st January Rd.; © 0832/243 6815) stocks some beautiful and very affordable glassware, including some lovely vases in extraordinary shapes; they also carry homeware, handicrafts, and clothing for men and women. You can browse quality homeware, textiles and furniture at **Fusionaccess** (Dias House, 13/32 Rua de Ormuz; © 0832/665-0342; www.fusionaccess.com), located in a building opposite the Ferry Wharf. There are framed vintage posters and photos, cushion covers, wonderful textiles for curtains, and rather unusual mesh tower and mesh ball candles worth asking about. **Broadway** (1st Floor, Ashirvada Bldg., 18 June Rd.; © 0832/664-7038; www.bbcbooks.net) is Goa's largest bookstore with a far-reaching range. And, if by the end of your stay you're sufficiently hooked on Portuguese-Goan music, head for **Rock & Raga** (June Rd., in Rizvi Tower; © 0832/564-3320), which has a good selection of local bands.

4 THE CENTRAL COAST

Compared with the beach playgrounds of north Goa, the beaches south of Panjim are more about solitude and stretches of virgin sand (with the north only a short ride away). For the most part, you'll be sunning yourself on whatever beach is slap-bang in front of your resort hotel—each with its own idyllic setting, these stretches of largely untouched beaches are paradise. Nearest of the beach resorts to the airport, and one of the quietest of south Goa's more popular beaches, Bogmalo has quaint shacks (as well as a number of ugly concrete buildings), fishing boats, and a view of two small islands some distance out to sea—ask about trips to the islands at the **Watersports Goa** shack, which also has equipment for activities like windsurfing and water-skiing. As you move down the coast, you'll discover that you're on a seemingly endless stretch of beach until you reach the headland at **Mobor;** with the exception of development-mutilated **Colva,** much of this is pristine, practically untouched by the sort of commercial mayhem that has besieged Baga-Calangute in the north. You can unfurl your beach towel and cozy up to a friendly beach shack almost anywhere here—just be sure to check that you only swim in areas where lifeguards are stationed, or ask about the local swimming conditions at your hotel.

Alternatively, consider a meandering trip via the Goan interior, traveling past Ponda to the Bhagwan Mahaveer Sanctuary to view Goa's oldest Hindu temple, **Mahadeva Temple** in Tambdi Surla, and the 600m-high (190-ft.) **Dudhsagar (Sea of Milk) Falls.** Constructed from slabs of black basalt, the 11th-century Mahadeva Temple is one of the few to have survived the Portuguese, thanks largely to its distance from the coast (some 75km/46 miles from Panjim). To reach the falls, you will need a jeep, so either set off with one from the outset (see "Arrival & Orientation," earlier in this chapter), or hire one in nearby Collem. Take lunch (look out for greedy monkeys) and a bathing suit for a swim in the deep, icy pool surrounded by rocks and wild greenery; be cautious at the falls, however, as each year a number of careless visitors drown because they underestimate the depth of the water, or bash their head on the rocks after diving in. There is little reason to spend much time in Goa's second city, **Madgaon (Margao),** which has little more to offer than a stroll through the sprawling spice-scented town market—a maze of covered stalls selling everything from garlands of flowers and peeled prawns to sacks bursting with turmeric, chilies, and tamarind. The town does boast some gorgeous crumbling colonial architecture, and two particularly worthwhile house museums are in the nearby villages of **Loutolim** and **Chandor** respectively (see "A Trip Down Goa's Architectural Memory Lane," below); or you can visit **Quepem** to combine a heritage visit with an authentic Goan meal (see "Feasts with a Nostalgic Twist," on p. 229).

WHERE TO STAY

The stretch of coastline from Panjim to Mobor has more five-star resorts (the big, sprawling kind with countless activities laid on) than north Goa, and the number is added to annually (raising the hackles of eco-watchdogs). Most of these resorts are characterless but very child-friendly, often with separate pools and activities, and babysitters are always available. If you're looking for the best of these, the **Leela** (p. 226) is off the charts. However, our first choice for a wonderful and inspiring stay is **Vivenda dos Palhaços** (p. 226)—it's not a beach resort at all, but a boutique guesthouse offering all the comforts of a real home, coupled with great style, a welcoming atmosphere, and a charmed location.

Bogmalo

Close to both Panjim and Margao (the main market town in the south), and 5 minutes from the airport, Bogmalo offers a swimmable beach and plenty of water sport options but without the intense overcrowding of Baga-Calangute. It is not, however, as secluded as the beaches you'll find if you travel farther south; nor—thanks to visible concrete developments—is it quite so beautiful. The only decent accommodation here is **Coconut Creek** (✆ **0832/253-8090;** coconutcreek@dataone.in; Rs 5,250–Rs 10,000 A/C double, depending on the season), which is generally full with long-term charter groups and offers the basic requisites—pool, cottages, greenery, and beach at walking distance. Owned by the same family is the simple and stylish **Joets ★** (Bogmalo Beach; ✆ **0832/ 253-8036**), a fishing cottage turned guesthouse, right on the beach; upstairs bedrooms each have balconies and private sitting areas (Rs 2,900–Rs 6,000 double). More important,

A Trip Down Goa's Architectural Memory Lane

Goa's unique architecture has to some extent been well preserved, so much so that—away from the coastal belt, toward the interiors as well as in Panjim, Mapusa, and Margao—you'll find entire lanes and villages of beautiful old houses, some crumbling, others restored but all offering great insights into the original inhabitants and their status in society. To prove that Goa isn't just about lounging on beaches and stomping on the dance floor, there are a couple of ways to get a close-up look at some colonial-era architecture. If you're interested in decoding buildings, or in exploring some of Goa's historic neighborhoods and villages, contact Heta Pandit of **The Heritage Network** (© **98-2212-8022;** www.heritagenetworkindia.com) or pick up a copy of *Walking in Goa* (Eminence Designs Pvt. Ltd.) or *Houses of Goa* (Architecture Autonomous). The network also organizes events in historic homes, including festive dinners with traditional entertainment. In **Loutolim** (10km/6¼ miles north of Margao), you can tour the Araujo Alvares family home **Casa Araujo Alvares** (www.casaaraujoalvares.com; arrangements through Loutolim's Ancestral Goa Museum; © **0832/277-7034;** Tues–Sun 9am–1pm and 2–6pm), while 13km (8 miles) west lies the old Portuguese village of Chandor and the impressive **Casa de Braganza** ★, Goa's largest residence. The two-story facade of this Indo-Portuguese mansion—which practically takes up an entire street—features 28 balconies fronted by a lush, narrow garden. The land-owning Braganzas rose to prominence during the 17th century and today are divided into two clans, the Pereira-Braganzas and the Menezes-Braganzas, who occupy separate wings of the house. The large, high-ceilinged rooms (including a 250-year-old library) are filled with original antiques, rosewood four-poster beds, mosaic floors, and Belgian glass chandeliers. Sun-lit galleries and parlors are filled with bric-a-brac, and French windows open onto an interior garden. You can arrange to have a private tour conducted by Mrs. Braganza (© **0832/278-4201;** Rs 100 per visitor); concentrate on the west wing, which is in the best condition

Joets has a "happening" restaurant with live music on Friday—make reservations and ask for a corner table by the sea.

Cansaulim, Utorda & Majorda

With locals for neighbors, rather than the resorts and concrete developments found in the more built-up areas along the coast, the best place to stay, anywhere in Goa south of Panjim, is **Vivenda dos Palhaços** (reviewed below). Nearby, boasting the biggest pool in the country, not to mention handsome rooms, manicured grounds, and snappy service, is the **Park Hyatt Goa Resort and Spa** ★★ (© 0832/272-1234; www.goa.park.hyatt. com)—spread over 18 hectares (45 acres) on the virgin beach of Arossim, it's a massive piece of Cansaulim real estate, with 250 slick rooms and plenty of distractions (from parasailing and jet-skiing to yoga and Ayurvedic massage) if you're not satisfied just lazing on the beach. Although it's utterly modern, architects styled the resort like a sprawling Indo-Goan pousada; tropical plants and mother of pearl chandeliers help the concept along, accommodations are elegant, fresh and light-filled, and you can dine in a different venue just about every night of the week. The best rates are available online several months in advance; a standard double starts at Rs 9,900—but you'd do well to invest in a sea-view room (Rs 14,400–Rs 15,500 double). Not too far away, in Utorda, is the older, much smaller **Kenilworth Beach Resort** ★ (✆ **0832/275-4180;** www.kenilworthhotels. com), which has always struck us as a perfectly lovely place with friendly service and good facilities. It's a better value than the Hyatt (even if rooms are slightly older fashioned), and although you won't necessarily have the same extensive menu of services (or high-end dining options), you'll be right on the beach, with some lovely beach shacks in easy striking distance.

Vivenda dos Palhaços ★★★ (Finds) Simon Haywood's sumptuous, homey village hideaway epitomizes how a classy Goan boutique hotel should look and feel. Simon, who grew up in Calcutta, was schooled in England, and has lived in New Zealand and Mumbai, has done a fine job of restoring and then beautifully decorating this enchanting house tucked away amongst the trees and bushes. Detailed and personal, each room is blessed with antiques, and studious color schemes offset by carefully sourced bric-a-brac and *objets*—Madras has a partially open-to-the-elements bathroom; all-white Ooty boasts a magnificent shattered mirror mosaic shower; and the Master Suite is just plain enormous, with an equally vast bathroom (and tub). The Chummery, set in the garden, has two private porches and a vast library of its own—you could spend weeks just soaking up the tranquil vibe. Designed like the back of a truck, the fabulous open kitchen is where you can order drinks, ask for assistance with *anything,* or simply chat with the staff. Well-shaded grounds shelter a pretty pool, and there are myriad comfy sitting areas, an impressive library, and good art on the walls—even the guest toilet is done out with a sense of fun and nostalgia. This is a perfectly peaceable kingdom, albeit with many of the authentic sounds from your surrounds—pigs and chickens forage on neighboring plots, and young boys yell excitedly during afternoon football. Vivenda dos Palhaços—the "House of Clowns"—may be a mouthful, but get your tongue around it because we cannot recommend the place highly enough.

Costa Vaddo, Majorda, Salcette, 403713 Goa. ✆ **0832/322-1119.** www.vivendagoa.com. 7 units (most with shower only), including 1 seasonal luxury tent. High season Rs 5,250–Rs 9,350 double; summer and monsoon Rs 3,500–Rs 5,750 double; festive season R 8,360–Rs 11,950; Rs 1,500 extra bed. Children under 14 pay Rs 100 per year of age. Rates include breakfast and taxes. MC, V. **Amenities:** Dining room, lounge, bar; airport transfers (Rs 400–Rs 850); art gallery, babysitting; beach drop-off/pickup (Rs 50); bicycles (Rs 200 per day); library. *In room* A/C and fans, hair dryer (on request), library (in one), no phone, Wi-Fi (Rs 80/¹/₂ hr.)

Benaulim, Varca & Cavelossim

Midway down the south coast, once you get beyond the uglified beach at Colva (completely ruined by hapless development) are some of the prettiest, uncrowded, and pristine stretches in all of Goa. There are several very good, well-serviced resorts here, including the **Taj Exotica** (reviewed below), on Benaulim beach; but the **Radisson White Sands** (✆ **0832/272-7272;** www.radisson.com/goain) at nearby Varca isn't too shabby either, with all the requisite resort amenities, a vibey beach bar, and bland, predictable, sleek rooms. However, the top full-blown resort in Goa, **The Leela,** is a good deal farther down the coast, neatly cut off from most other developments, with its own stretch of beach *and* riverside location on the lovely Mobor headland.

The Leela Kempinski ★★★ (Kids) Widely considered India's top beach resort (and one of the few with a stringent eco-policy), there's no denying the appeal and beauty of this extravagant resort set at the edge of a fairly vast stretch of near-unspoiled coast. Adding to the natural pull of the paradisiacal beach and rhythmically crashing waves of the

Arabian Sea, is the design of the resort itself, centered on a man-made lagoon that mean-
ders and curls among the lush vegetation, neatly scattered accommodation wings, and
12-hole golf course. Even the lobby manages to set the right mood, echoing (in design
and decor at least) a Vijayanagar temple, complete with elaborate carvings and impressive
statuary and *objets*. There's a swath of room categories to choose from—the trust fund–
level Club villas are far and away the best, with enhanced privacy (separate pool, dining
areas, and wonderful proximity to a dense neighboring forest), a number of included
extras (such as airport transfers), and the best looking accommodations. It's extremely
expensive, but there are always excellent deals and packages available in the low season
(especially during monsoon).

Cavelossim, Mobor, Goa 403 731. ℂ **0832/287-1234.** Fax 0832/287-1352. www.theleela.com. 186 units.
High season Rs 23,000, pavilion double, Rs 27,000 conservatory premiere double, Rs 40,000 lagoon suite,
Rs 45,000 lagoon deluxe suite, Rs 53,000 Club suite, Rs 65,000 Club pool suite, Rs 100,000 Royal Villa, Rs
135,000 presidential suite; low season Rs 11,000 Pavilion double, Rs 14,000 conservatory premiere double, Rs 20,000 lagoon suite, Rs 25,000 lagoon deluxe suite, Rs 30,000 Club suite, Rs 40,000 Club pool suite,
Rs 50,000 Royal Villa, Rs 100,000 presidential suite. Rates include breakfast, airport transfer by coach; 10%
tax extra. Club, Royal Villa and presidential suite rates include butler service, laundry, airport transfers,
minibar, and in-room high tea. Rates much higher Dec 28–Jan 3. AE, DC, MC, V **Amenities:** 4 restaurants,
including Susegado (see review on p. 229), 2 bars, nightclub, lounge, free airport transfers (by coach;
otherwise Rs 4,200); babysitting; bicycles; boating; casino; children's activity center; club wing w/private
restaurant, pool, and beach restaurant-bar; croquet; 12-hole golf course; health club and spa; large outdoor swimming pool and children's pool; room service; 3 floodlit tennis courts; watersports; yoga and
meditation. *In room:* A/C, TV/DVD, CD (in most), hair dryer, minibar, Wi-Fi (Rs 150/hr.; Rs 900/day)

Taj Exotica Goa ★★   This resort features lovely surroundings (23 hectares/56 acres
of landscaped gardens with 36 varieties of hibiscus trees), nicely appointed accommodations, warm service, and a kick-ass beach that might just as well be private. Even the
cheapest "deluxe" guest rooms are spacious, with large picture windows and private patios
or balconies. Ask for one on the ground floor—these are accessed via their own garden
areas. The private villas are ideal if you don't want to be in the main block, which looks
something like a large Portuguese hacienda—specify a sea-facing room for a decent view
(cheaper villas look onto the garden). The gorgeous sunset pool villas have private plunge
pools—plus, the main pool is large and inviting.

Calwaddo, Benaulim, Salcete, Goa 403 716. ℂ **0832/277-1234.** Fax 0832/277-1515. www.tajhotels.com.
exotica.goa@tajhotels.com. 140 units. Rs 18,500–Rs 35,500 garden villa room double, Rs 20,500–Rs
37,500 deluxe sea view double, Rs 24,700–Rs 40,500 sea view villa, Rs 25,700–Rs 42,500 luxury double, Rs
28,400–Rs 50,500 pool villas, Rs 44,600–Rs 67,500 luxury suite, Rs 113,000–Rs 144,500 presidential villa.
Christmas and New Year stays attract compulsory additional costs for special meals. AE, MC, V. **Amenities:** 5 restaurants; lounge; bar; free airport transfers; archery; babysitting; badminton; beach volleyball;
bicycles; children's activity center; clay pigeon shooting; concierge; 9-hole golf course (pitch and putt);
health club and Ayurvedic spa w/yoga and aerobics; helipad; jogging track; large outdoor pool w/Jacuzzi
and children's pool; pool tables; room service; 2 tennis courts; table tennis; watersports. *In room:* A/C, TV,
DVD (in some), hair dryer, minibar, Wi-Fi (Rs 224/hr.; Rs 673/day).

WHERE TO DINE

Another downside of staying at the resorts—besides being totally cut off from the world
you've come to visit—is that you'll invariably be dining in-house. Not necessarily a bad
thing, only you'll miss some of the alternative culinary diversions on offer. So, if you are
holed up at one of the big luxury pads, make a point of leaving the compound at least
once in order to savor a meal that's more down-home, perhaps, but more than likely a
better match for authenticity.

A little south of Majorda is the tiny stretch of sand known colloquially as "Sunset Beach," but officially called Betalbatim. The little village is probably best known for its famous beachside restaurant, **Martin's Corner** ★ (Binvado, Betalbatim; ℭ **0832/288-0061** or -0413; daily 11am–3:30pm and 6:30–11pm), where Martin Pereira's widow, Carafina, runs the kitchen with an iron fist. She began cooking wonderful dishes for this family restaurant back in 1994, when it opened with only two tables. Now Martin's sons operate a successful and extremely popular courtyard establishment, surrounded by mango, coconut, and jackfruit groves. Order snapper *recheado,* butter-garlic prawns, or pomfret *caldin* made with a coconut milk curry. Carafina makes a mean homemade masala, prepared according to a secret family recipe with fresh Goan spices. After dark, things can hot up as popular bands really liven things up.

Zeebop by the Sea ★★ (Moments) GOAN/SEAFOOD   Midway between the Hyatt and Kenilworth resorts, and an easy bicycle ride from Vivenda do Palhaços, this is perhaps the best beach shack-style restaurant in Goa, although there's no shack, and the crowd tends to be a good mix of savvy locals and tourists. White wooden tables are set among dugout canoes and huge cart wheels scattered across a large patch of flat sandy dune overlooking the water, a short distance away. Waiters in orange tropical shirts and black slacks scamper between the tables, serving up locally caught seafood like rock fish, zebra shark steak (try this grilled with garlic butter), silver pomfret, sea bass, red snapper, or whatever the fishermen have landed today. If you want to add a little zing to your fish, ask for it to be prepared with *recheado* spices. Lobster, peri-peri prawns, and a blow-out seafood platter are also available. The food doesn't look like much on the plate, but somehow the chef coaxes very special flavors out of the meat and every morsel is melt-in-the-mouth succulent. As with any beach venue in Goa, get here before sunset and feast your eyes on the horizon, best accompanied by a supply of ice-cold beers. Avoid the "coffee."

Near Kenilworth Beach Resort, Utorda. ℭ **0832/275-5333** or 982-215-4541. Main courses Rs 90–Rs 180. MC, V. Daily 9am–11pm. Closed late May to Aug.

Benaulim, Varca & Cavelossim

You can probably forgive yourself for choosing to sample at least one of the near-legendary eateries at the Taj Exotica. **Alegria** ★★ (daily 12:30–2:30pm and 7:30–10:30pm) is where the most delicious home-cooked Goan, Portuguese, and Hindu Goan Saraswat meals are prepared. Mainstay dishes include *arroz de chorizo* (traditional Goan *pulao* of locally made spice pork sausages), *sungtache koddi* (prawns in a fragrant gravy of coconut milk and mild spices), *sungtache peri-peri* (pan-fried farm-fresh prawn marinated with red chili and toddy vinegar), and *kombdiche xacutti* (succulent chicken morsels simmered in a blend of roasted spices with coconut). Upstairs, **Miguel Arcanjo** ★★ (same hours) makes some of the best pizzas in Goa. And that's not all—for starters try the shrimp glazed with honey and garlic or the Lebanese *mezze* accompanied by *horiatiki* salad, followed by delicious double lamb chops or duck roasted with dry cherry sauce. Even the oven-baked snapper is irresistible. Finally, but most atmospherically, **Lobster Shack** ★★ (daily 7:30–11pm; dismantled during off season) enjoys a rather romantic setting by the sea, right on Benaulim Beach, where the venue does a good-spirited job of emulating a typical Goan beach shack, albeit with an upmarket buzz. With the crash of waves and polite band setting the ambience, choose your fish from the display and watch as it's prepared in the open kitchen. Even better than Lobster Shack, though, is The Leela's superb **Susegado,** reviewed below.

ⓂMoments Feasts with a Nostalgic Twist

In the village of Raia, is possibly Goa's finest restaurant, lorded over by celebrity-status chef Fernando de Costa, who has converted part of his own home into the warm and traditional **Nostalgia** ★★★ (ⓒ **0832/277-7054** or -7098 or 982-210-3467 or 982-215-1296; daily 11am–3pm and 7–11pm). The name is in part to do with the decor—filled with antiques and carefully sourced *objets*—but also refers to the revival of Goan dishes that are quite forgotten in other parts. Expect to pay no more than Rs 700 for two people getting stuffed on delicious, authentic Goan dishes, prepared according to two different traditional Goan styles, either Saraswat or Catholic. Good Goan bands belt out vibey, soul-stirring tunes, and the atmosphere is quite smart. Besides many of the signature Goan curries, it's well worth sparing a thought for the desserts, many of which are seldom prepared elsewhere. For an even more intimate and personal experience, call ahead to **Palácio Do Deão** ★★★ (across from Holy Cross Church, Quepem; ⓒ **0832/266-4029** or 98-2317-5639; www.palaciododeao.com; daily 10am–6pm) and ask if the hostess, Celia Vasco da Gama, will prepare a meal for you—served in a belvedere behind the beautiful renovated heritage house owned by herself and her husband, Ruben. A charming couple, the Vasco da Gamas serve delicious, home-style versions of traditional Goan favorites—*fofos do queijo* (cheese balls) and *peixe com molho* (whole fish filled with green masala) among many more—polished off with authentic-tasting bebinca. Lunch here costs Rs 400 per person.

Just outside the entrance to the Radisson in Varca, **Pereira's** (ⓒ **0832/277-2413,** 0832/277-2603, or 989-071-1363; closed June–Sept) is the more authentic (and good-value—although by no means cheap) option, where Goans and tourists (including guests of the Radisson) are catered to with one of those ridiculously eclectic and far-reaching menus—stick to the Goan seafood.

Susegado ★★★ GOAN/SEAFOOD With the constant roar of the ocean mediated by cool Indian tunes, this lavish version of the traditional Goan beach shack is an excellent choice for a special night out. Set on a stone plinth on the beach at the edge of The Leela's manicured lawns, you sit at properly laid tables, on comfy, soft-covered cane chairs, and are treated like gold by friendly waiters who make informed recommendations (as opposed to telling you that "it depends on your taste," which is a standard response in Goa's beach restaurants). It's the seafood that you absolutely *must* go for—ask what's fresh and interesting today, or choose the best-looking specimen from the display. Sea bass is special to this part of Goa, and red snapper is always a good choice (it's featured on the Fisherman's Catch platter, along with Tiger prawns and squid). The fish is sold by weight (quite reasonably) and is best accompanied by perfectly crispy french fries. For dessert, there's a selection of Movenpick ice creams, or a decadent chocoholic platter (with chocolate brownie, chocolate ice-cream, and chocolate cheesecake).

The Leela Kempinki, Cavelosim, Mobor. ⓒ **0832/287-1234.** Reservations for nonguests essential. Main courses Rs 395–Rs 3,995. AE, DC, MC, V. Daily 12:30–3:30pm and 7–10:30pm; closed June–Sept.

Palolem is 40km (25 miles) S of Madgaon

If you're on a tighter budget and looking for a party atmosphere that's a little more reminiscent of the scene in north Goa (yet without the same commercial intensity), head farther south to the picturesque stretch of coast that stretches south from **Agonda** ★★ to the protected Olive Ridley turtle breeding beach of **Galgibaga** ★★★, another remote haven with eucalyptus trees and empty stretches of sand. The most famous beach—unfortunately now also increasingly overstocked with tourists and day-trippers—is **Palolem** ★★. Until just a few years back, this was a thoroughly remote and tranquil hideaway; thankfully, though, despite the intrusion of shacks, trinket-peddlers, and human traffic, it remains one of India's most beautiful stretches of coastline, a gorgeous sandy crescent cove lined with coconut palms and manned by fishermen with their outrigger boats that line the northern end of the beach. It remains relatively free of day-trippers, but if you find the crowds too much, simply walk until you find a quieter spot, even if you need to end up on neighboring **Patnem** ★★. Accommodations in Palolem and Patnem, as well as still-lovely Agonda (just 7km/4½ miles north of Palolem) were once limited to thatched tree houses or wooden houses on stilts, but now there are even semismart guesthouses available—some with hot water. At sunset, Palolem becomes a natural meditation spot; the sun disappearing slowly behind the beach's northernmost promontory casts a shadow over local fishing boats, swimmers, joggers, cavorting dogs, and pockets of befuddled-looking cows, as the bars and restaurants come to life with pleasant lounge music. Palolem is also the birthplace of Goa's enterprising new "silent party" scene (see box on p. 216).

WHERE TO STAY

In the southernmost reaches of the state, there is only one large resort, and quite frankly it's a huge disappointment, particularly since it commandeers such a gorgeous stretch of beach—Raj Baga. You could subject yourself to the substandard service and atrocious architecture at **The InterContinental Lalit Goa Resort,** which is overrated, but that would be doing yourself an immense disservice, not to mention locating yourself just a little too far (around 3km/2 miles) from the action; frankly, this is probably the least appealing of the five-star resorts in Goa—if you *must* stay in a large resort, choose one of those along the central part of the coast (see above).

In Palolem you'll have to venture back to nature at one of a handful of budget-chic options (such as the wonderful **Bhakti Kutir** eco-resort, reviewed below), or try **The Village Guesthouse** (reviewed below), which brings a touch of style to a traditionally rustic and earthy lodging scene. There are plenty more down-home options hereabouts, but if you fancy a bit of honest-to-goodness glamour thrown in with your beachfront idyll, look no further than the **Turtle Lounge** (see below) in Agonda. On the other side of Palolem, Patnem is a peaceful and lovely beach with very few hassles; the best place to stay is **Home** ★ (© **0832/264-3916;** www.homeispatnem.com; $30–$47 double), operated by a laid-back Swiss couple. Accommodations all have attached bathrooms and are scrupulously clean, if quite basic; the restaurant is also Patnem's best.

Bhakti Kutir ★ (Value) Described by some as "hippie-chic," this is by far Palolem's most atmospheric and eco-friendly option, though don't expect any real luxury. It's the brainchild of Panta Ferrao, a Goan lawyer who (aided by his German wife, Ute) dropped

out to start an ecologically sensitive resort that would empower local people with skills
and provide relatively comfortable accommodations. The mud-plastered bamboo "cottages" are made entirely from natural materials, with en-suite toilet facilities—squat toilets (organic, of course) and bucket showers. Try to book room no. 6, which is built on different levels; no. 8, a double-story unit with an upstairs balcony; or the "stone house" (built with Panta's German in-laws in mind) with more traditionally Western facilities (like a toilet). Come prepared for mosquitoes, dark pathways, and plenty of back-to-nature experiences. Workshops and cooking classes are held for those wishing to extend their knowledge of local culture; so too an assortment of esoteric activities like Ayurvedic treatments, yoga, and meditation. They've added an alternative school to keep the kids happy and busy.

296, Colomb, Palolem, Canacona 403 702. (©) **0832/264-3469** or -3472. Fax 0832/264-5211. www.bhakti kutir.com. 22 units. Oct Rs 600–Rs 2,000; Nov and Mar Rs 1,200–Rs 2,500; Dec–Feb Rs 1,800–Rs 4,000. Rates exclude taxes. Rates are flexible in the low season and much higher Dec 15–Jan 15. No credit cards. **Amenities:** Restaurant; amphitheater; bar; airport transfers (Rs 1,200); Ayurvedic and healing center w/ massage, yoga, meditation, mud baths, cooling baths; babysitting; children's playschool; small library; pool table; tailor. *In room:* No phone.

Turtle Lounge ★★ (Finds)

A wonderful discovery on still-unspoiled Agonda Beach, Turtle Lounge consists of just two to-die-for split-level wooden bungalows set on the edge of the beach next to a gorgeous little restaurant-bar of the same name. Owned and designed by Bernd Slotta, a German fashion photographer and stylist, they're immaculate and spacious, really putting the rest of the beach hut scene to shame. Bernd has imbued both spaces with real style: beautiful fabrics, rich colors, and clever use of light to create a romantic atmosphere. There are no frills or hotel-like accoutrements; nor are there any in-room amenities (including hot water or mosquito nets), but the glossy design (with very sexy bathrooms), ultracomfy beds, and perfect setting more than make up for this. Leave the door of your upstairs bedroom open at night and fall asleep with the moon-kissed sea in full view, the dull slosh of waves an ever-present soundtrack. The equally stylish little restaurant has a limited but good menu, and the bar—with a chandelier dangling from the palm tree—is sociable without being overwhelming. Service is, if anything, overzealous.

Agonda Beach, Canacona 403 702. (©) **94-2125-7165** or -7164. www.turtle-lounge.com. 2 units (shower only). Rs 5,000–Rs 8,000 double. No credit cards. Open mid-Nov (weather permitting) through mid-May. **Amenities:** Restaurant; bar; airport transfers (Rs 1,200); room service. *In room:* No phone.

The Village Guesthouse ★ (Value)

It's not on the beach, but it's the only place in Palolem with actual style, not to mention fabulous, modern bathrooms, and healthful breakfasts (real coffee, good tea, homemade muesli). The guesthouse occupies an unlikely looking property (and a very kitsch-looking double-story house) in Palolem village, leased from a local family and operated by a lovely Anglo-Irish couple who've spent years chilling out in Palolem, and finally decided to bring some dignity to the lodging scene. Inside, the atmosphere and decor is Zen-minimalist—there's ample space, assorted Buddha statuary, framed black and white photographs, and fresh, modern, all-white rooms with frame-style poster beds brightened by a single colorful throw atop quality linens. There's plenty of solar-heated hot water, and as we've hinted already, exceptional showers.

House no. 196, nr. Govt. Middle School, Palolem, Canacona 403 702. (©) **0832/264-5767.** www.village guesthousegoa.com. 7 units. High season Rs 2,000 standard double, Rs 3,000 large double; summer Rs 1,500 standard double, Rs 2,000 large double; festive season Rs 2,500 standard double, Rs 3,500 large double. Rates include breakfast. MC, V (credit card payment incurs a fee). *In room:* A/C and fan, TV, Wi-Fi (free).

Although it's only open in the season, Agonda's **Turtle Lounge** (see above) is surprisingly stylish and hip. It's also probably the best place to dine this far south. If you're spending the day on Palolem's increasingly crowded beach, it's worth diverting your attention at lunchtime for some peace and quiet at Bhakti Kutir's unpretentious little health food restaurant, **Aahar,** where you're served inexpensive, delicious local and organic meals under a giant cloth draped from the surrounding trees—try the *dal* and red spinach, served with organic rice, coconut chutney, and fresh, nutty hummus; or sunflower seed and *moong* (mung) bean-sprout salad with steamed spinach, toasted nuts and seeds, and tofu, served with homemade whole-wheat rice-bread. The fish curry, served as part of a thali, and the only nonvegetarian meal here, is light and not too spicy, made with coconut gravy—wipe up the juice with the millet *chapatti* provided. Wine is available and you're able to sample tribal liquors here. Elsewhere in Palolem, you'd do well to stick to whichever beachfront restaurants are pulling a crowd this season—standards are generally up and down. However, we've never had a really bad meal at **Droopadi** ★ (*©* **98-2268-5138;** daily 8am–10pm, closed June–July) where you sit on cushioned cane armchairs at tables in the sand; there's recommendable fresh seafood (the day's catch is chalked up on the board), and even the pasty is fairly tasty; best of all, though, is the nonstop action on the beach, and it's a fine place to take in the sunset. On Agonda Beach, look no further than the slick **Turtle Lounge** (see "Where to Stay," above).

God's Own Country: Kerala & Lakshadweep

Sailors once swore that a blind man could steer a ship to the Malabar coast, guided by nothing more that off-shore winds heavy with the scent of Kerala's fragrant spices. This is a coastal idyll that once lured endless flotillas for its black gold and now draws travelers to indulge in some of the subcontinent's most restful, laid-back pleasures. India's most verdant state—rated by *National Geographic Traveler* as one of the world's 50 must-see destinations and also one of "ten earthly paradises"—is a seamless landscape of palm-lined beaches rising to meet steamy jungles and plantation-covered hills, watered by no less than 44 tropical rivers. Once thronged by merchants clambering to trade for spices, today the coast is often bustling with visitors who come here primarily to unwind and indulge. This is, after all, where succumbing to a therapeutic Ayurvedic massage is as mandatory as idling away an afternoon aboard a slowly drifting *kettuvallam,* or sipping coconut water under a tropical sun before taking in a ritualized Kathakali dance. Eastward, the spice-scented **Cardamom Hills** and wild elephants of **Periyar** beckon, while a short flight west takes you to the little-known but sublime tropical reefs of the **Lakshadweep** islands. All of which make Kerala not just a must-see on your southern India itinerary, but a major destination in its own right.

A thin strip on the southwest coastline, sandwiched between the Lakshadweep Sea and the forested Western Ghats that define its border with Tamil Nadu to the east, Kerala covers a mere 1.3% of the country's total land area, yet its rich resources have long attracted visitors from across the oceans—it is in fact here that the first seafarers set foot on Indian soil. Legend has it that King Solomon's ships traded off the Malabar coast between 972 and 932 B.C., followed by the Phoenicians, Romans, Chinese, Portuguese, and Arabs, all of whom came to stock up on Malabar's monkeys, tigers, parrots, timber, and, of course, the abundance of spices that were literally worth their weight in gold. Seafarers not only brought trade but built synagogues and churches in the emerging port cities, while an entirely Muslim population set up shop on the islands of Lakshadweep. Despite its religious cosmopolitanism (many locals will tell you they subscribe to both Hinduism and Christianity), Kerala's Hindu tradition is deeply engrained in daily life. Most Kerala temples do not permit non-Hindus to enter, but the months of February to May bring magnificent temple processions through the streets—the most jaw-dropping being the April/May Thrissur Pooram—involving thousands of chanting devotees and squadrons of elephants adorned in flamboyant caparisons (ornamental coverings).

Contemporary Kerala was created in 1956 from the former princely states of Travancore, Kochi, and Malabar. Largely ruled by benevolent maharajas who introduced social reforms emphasizing the provision of education and basic services, Kerala remains one of the most progressive, literate, and prosperous states in post-independence India—and at the same time retains an untouched charm. In 1957, it became the first place in the world to democratically elect a Communist government, and the

Ayurveda: Kerala's Healing Balm

Drawing on some 5,000 years of Vedic culture, Ayurveda is the subcontinent's traditional science of "life, vitality, health, and longevity" or, to tap into a more contemporary catchphrase, "the science of well-being," and where better to experience it than Kerala, where the tradition originated. Renowned for its curative and rejuvenating powers (and a gift said to be from no other than Lord Brahma), Ayurveda works on your physical, mental, and emotional well-being by rectifying any imbalances in the five eternal elements: space (ether), air, earth, water, and fire. These elements manifest themselves in three subtle energies or humors known as the *tridoshas—vata, pitta,* and *kapha*—when perfectly balanced, you have a healthy human constitution; if not, the imbalance translates into various ailments. Ayurveda is most often enjoyed by foreigners as a way to rejuvenate cells or boost the immune system, but it has a proven track record in treating a wide range of specific ailments, from obesity to osteoarthritis. For these more therapeutic procedures you will need to stay a minimum of 3 days (even better: 2–3 weeks) and follow a dietary regimen that is prescribed and managed by an Ayurvedic doctor and attendant staff.

It takes $5^{1}/_{2}$ years of training to qualify as an Ayurvedic doctor, who is then able to prescribe the herbal remedies and related therapies. While much of what is practiced in Ayurvedic medicine has similarities to Western medical practice (the first 3 years of training in anatomy are basically the same), the most significant difference lies in the area of pharmacology, since Ayurvedic medicines are all natural. Some may scoff, but no one can deny the sheer pleasure of the primary form of treatment: deep, thorough massage with herbal-infused oils. Which is why Ayurveda suits those skeptics who simply seek the ultimate in pampering, whether you opt for a soothing facial treatment, in which the face is massaged and steamed with herbal oils, or for an energizing full-body massage performed with hands and feet (and often by several masseuses simultaneously); your skin will glow and your mind will feel clear. True skeptics take note: To truly experience the strange bliss and resultant high of

first Indian state to introduce a family planning program. Despite Kerala's high population density, Keralites have the country's highest life expectancy and lowest infant mortality rates. Kerala is also considered one of the most peaceful parts of India, a claim substantiated by its prosperity—the state remains a major source of India's bananas, rubber, coconuts, cashews, and ginger, and now, tourism.

The downside of all this prosperity? A highly educated and comfortable popula-

tion has meant that many are unwilling to do menial jobs, and service standards are low given that tourism is for many the primary source of income. Others cash in on the tourism boom with no long-term thought for the future, and for the first time pollution is becoming a problem in paradise. Still others head for the Gulf to seek their fortunes, returning with sufficient cash to tear down the traditional carved wood dwellings that so greatly characterize the region and replace them

Ayurveda, book a *sirodhara* treatment, wherein 5 to 6 liters of warm herbal oil (selected according to the body constitution) are poured steadily onto your "third eye" (the forehead) for the better part of an hour while (or after which) you are massaged—said to retard the aging process (by arresting the degeneration of cells), it certainly relieves the body of stress (some compare it to taking a tranquilizer), and is likely to turn you into a complete convert.

No matter which balm you choose, you'll find that the well-practiced masseuses of Kerala will treat your body like a temple; for them, the massage or treatment is almost a spiritual exercise. Of course, it helps to know that your body is being worshiped when you're lying there in your birthday suit (note that in strict accordance with Indian piety, you will be assigned a same-sex therapist). Whatever its purported virtues and pleasures, Ayurveda lures thousands of Westerners to Kerala, which in turn sustains a thriving industry that puts food on the table for many people. The downside of this has been an unprecedented mushrooming of quick-fix Ayurvedic "centers" throughout the state. Almost every hotel in the country now offers Ayurvedic "treatments," many staffed with therapists back from a short training stint in Kerala and having insufficient knowledge of technique (reusing oils that should be discarded, for example). To ensure that you get the real deal, look for the top-of-the-range "Green Leaf" certification issued by the Department of Tourism, or the equally trustworthy (for nontherapeutic programs) "Olive Leaf" centers. These certifications are based on strict criteria covering the quality of the physicians, programs, medicines, and facilities offered. We review the best resorts with this accreditation in this chapter, but if you really want to experience the ultimate in Ayurvedic discipline and undertake an experience that will not only recharge your batteries but inevitably change your life, turn to p. 258 and read about **Kalari Kovilakom**. This sensational retreat is undoubtedly one of the world's foremost facilities for engaging with the more spiritual side of India's increasingly global science of life.

with "modern" status symbols. Of course, many of these traditional homes have been bought and reassembled at top-notch resorts like Coconut Lagoon and Surya Samudra, a practice vilified as exploitative by Kerala native Arundhati Roy in her Booker Prize–winning *The God of Small Things*. For visitors, however, a stay in these *tharavadu* cottages is one of the most charming aspects of a trip to Kerala, along with its tropical beaches and backwater cruises; and lounging in a hammock at one of the region's top resorts can make you forget you're in India.

If you're interested in a more authentic experience of the subcontinent, combine your trip with a few days in neighboring Tamil Nadu, the spiritual heartland of southern India (p. 313). But if all you're looking for is rejuvenation, head straight to the backwaters, then wash up on some of the world's most beautiful beaches. "God's Own Country" is one tourist slogan that really does deliver.

1 KOCHI (COCHIN) ★★★

1,080km (670 miles) S of Mumbai

Kochi is not the capital of Kerala, but it is a great deal more charming than Trivandrum, and, blessed with a good airport and infrastructure, is for many the ideal gateway to the state. In fact, this has been the case since 1341, the year nature carved out Kochi's harbor with a massive flood, and the city became the first port of call for Arabs, Chinese, and, finally, European sea merchants, who sailed for barter into what came to be known as the "Queen of the Arabian Sea."

Lured by the promise of pepper, the Portuguese under Vasco da Gama arrived in 1500, and the Franciscan friars who accompanied the explorer Pedro Alvarez Cabral established a church and set about converting the locals. By 1553, the Maharaja of Kochi had granted permission for the construction of the first European fort in India, and what had been an obscure fishing hamlet became India's first European settlement. In 1663, Kochi fell to the Dutch, and 132 years later, to the British. Each of these foreign influences left their mark, resulting in a distinctly Indo-European culture, most evident in the architecture.

Today, Kochi (or Cochin, as it was formerly known) comprises three distinct areas. **Old Kochi,** comprising the down-at-heel but wonderfully atmospheric Mattancherry and its more pristine neighbor, Fort Kochi, lie on one of two peninsular arms that shield the Kochi harbor, and hold the most historical interest. Opposite it, on the mainland that creates the eastern peninsula, lies modern **Ernakulam.** Between the two are islands, now well connected by bridges, including **Willingdon Island.**

Fort Kochi, the oldest European settlement in India, retains an old-world charm. Although it has now largely been given over to tourism, the town's heritage buildings and broad, peaceful streets make this the preferred place to overnight. Its battlements no longer stand, but the combination of Portuguese, Dutch, Jewish, British, and local influences is evident in the tiled, steep-roofed bungalows that line its quaint streets, and it's home to the oldest synagogue in the Commonwealth. From here Mattancherry, with its wonderful warehouses filled with antiques and trinkets, is a short rickshaw drive away. Plan to spend 2 nights in Kochi, enjoying its charming atmosphere and low-key sights at a lazy, relaxed pace. Take in a Kathakali performance, dig into the delectable seafood, enjoy a romantic sunset cruise around the harbor, and, if you're at all interested in bargain-priced antiques, get ready to wade through stores packed with unexpected curiosities.

ESSENTIALS

VISITOR INFORMATION Kerala (www.keralatourism.org) has the best tourism organization in India, starting with a helpful **Airport Information Counter** (✆ **0484/261-0115**), usually open for all arrivals.

GETTING THERE & AWAY **By Air** **Cochin International Airport** (✆ **0484/261-0115**) is one of India's best. It's located alongside National Highway 47, in Nedumbassery, which is 42km (26 miles) from the historic heart of Fort Kochi. There are flights to and from most major centers in India; international flights are mostly from the Middle East, including Dubai, Singapore, and Sri Lanka

A prepaid taxi service into the city is available at the airport; transfers to Fort Kochi should cost Rs 695. A better plan is to e-mail or call **Kerala Adventures** (✆ **94-4703-5627** or 0484/231-3744; touch@keralaadventure.com) with your flight details a few days in

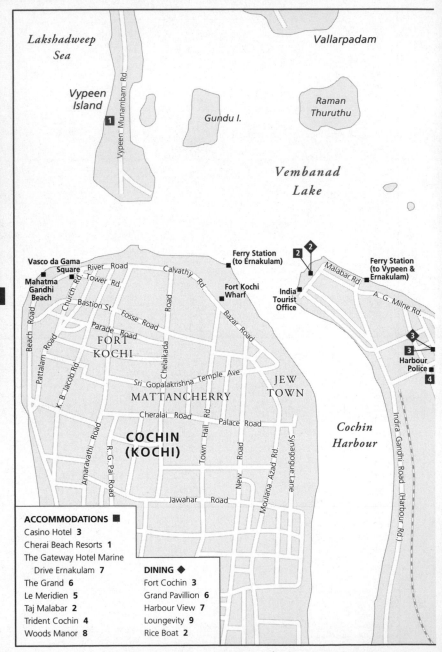

Lakshadweep Sea

Vypeen Island

Vallarpadam

Raman Thuruthu

Gundu I.

Vembanad Lake

Vasco da Gama Square
River Road
Calvathy Rd.
Ferry Station (to Ernakulam)

Ferry Station (to Vypeen & Ernakulam)

Malabar Rd.

Mahatma Gandhi Beach

Vypeen-Munambam Rd.

Church Rd.
Tower Rd.
Bastion St.
Fosse Road
Parade Road
FORT KOCHI
Fort Kochi Wharf
India Tourist Office

A. G. Milne Rd.

Beach Road
Pattalam Road
K. B. Jacob Rd.
Chelakada Road
Bazar Road
Chelaikada

Harbour Police

Sri Gopalakrishna Temple Ave.
MATTANCHERRY
JEW TOWN

Cheralai Road
Palace Road
Town Hall Rd.

COCHIN (KOCHI)

Amaravathi Road
R. G. Pai Road
New Road
Moulana Azad Rd.
Synagogue Lane

Cochin Harbour

Jawahar Road

Indira Gandhi Road (Harbour Rd.)

ACCOMMODATIONS ■
Casino Hotel **3**
Cherai Beach Resorts **1**
The Gateway Hotel Marine
  Drive Ernakulam **7**
The Grand **6**
Le Meridien **5**
Taj Malabar **2**
Trident Cochin **4**
Woods Manor **8**

DINING ◆
Fort Cochin **3**
Grand Pavillion **6**
Harbour View **7**
Loungevity **9**
Rice Boat **2**

advance, and have a driver waiting for you on arrival; price for a non-A/C car is Rs 725; with A/C Rs 1,010.

By Train   Kochi is well connected by rail to almost every part of India. Some of the journeys can be long and grueling, however, so check on times, or opt for train travel only within Kerala. Departing from Delhi, the biweekly (Tues and Sat) **Trivandrum Rajdhani** makes its way to Kozhikode, Kochi, and Trivandrum; this is one of the best connections in Kerala—some of the journey is very scenic but it's a punishing 48 hours if you start from Delhi. For schedules, see www.indianrail.gov.in. Again, with prior notice, **Kerala Adventures** (see above) will pick you up from the station.

Kochi has two principal commuter railway stations: **Ernakulam Town Station** (© 0484/ 239-0920 or -5198) and **Ernakulam Junction** (© 0484/237-5429 or -5131). The **computerized reservations office** is at the Junction Railway Station (Mon–Sat 8am– 2pm and 2:15–8pm; Sun 8am–2pm). For reservations, call © **132;** for status of current reservations, call © **1316.**

By Road   Traveling around Kerala with a rented car and driver can be wonderful and exhilarating; there's plenty of natural beauty worth taking in, and Kerala's main roads are in relatively good shape; see "Guided Tours & Travel Agents," below, for our top recommendation here. North of Kochi, coast-hugging National Highway 17 passes through Kozhikode and runs all the way to Mangalore and Mysore in Karnataka, and on to Mumbai. Traveling south between Kochi and the capital Trivandrum (6 hr.), National Highway 47 has been resurfaced in recent years, and the highway really spreads out for the popular segment between Kochi and the backwater towns of Alleppey and Kottayam. For journeys between Kochi and Madurai, you can expect long but beautiful stretches along National Highway 49, which traverses hairpin mountain passes, or you can detour via Periyar for equally scenic views. Private and state buses connect Kochi with many cities and towns throughout South India; these provide something bordering on a theme-park experience, however, and have a reputation for thrill-ride speeds. For long-distance private bus schedules (much more comfortable and punctual) to (and from) Ernakulam, contact **Kerala SRTC Office** (© 0484/237-2033); alternatively the **Karnataka SRTC** (© 0484/236-0229) and **Tamil Nadu** (© 0484/237-2616).

GETTING AROUND   **By Taxi & Auto-Rickshaw**   Speak to your hotel management about the most up-to-date rates. For the most part, it's best to negotiate a mutually agreeable fare before starting off; expect to pay Rs 7 per kilometer, with a Rs 10 minimum charge; alternatively, you can offer a small-but-generous Rs 50 for an hour's sightseeing within Fort Kochi and Mattancherry. After 10pm the rate is one and a half or double. Taxicabs are reasonable (1 hr. around Rs 150) but really only useful if traveling farther afield: A one-way trip between Fort Kochi and Ernakulam shouldn't cost more than Rs 350. If you're hiring a car and driver for travel around Kerala, you should be charged no more than Rs 1,400 per day (up to 200km), plus Rs 150 per overnight halt.

Note that the bridges connecting the mainland and Fort Kochi with the islands usually charge a toll, which you will be expected to pay.

By Ferry   The ferry is a cheap way to get to and from any of Kochi's main areas; the journey between Fort Kochi/Mattancherry and the mainland takes around 30 minutes and departs every half-hour; Willingdon lies around 15 minutes away. Ernakulam's most important jetty is the **Main Boat Jetty** (off Fore Press Club Rd.) for services to Willingdon Island, Fort Kochi, and Cherrai Beach; at Fort Kochi the main jetty is next to Brunton Boat Yard. **High Court Jetty** off Shanmugham Road, from where you can get to Bolgatty Island, is less regular since the construction of the bridge between Bolgatty and the mainland. Ferry services begin at 6am and continue until 9:30pm; fares are nominal.

GUIDED TOURS & TRAVEL AGENTS **Kerala Adventures** (Vysagam Apartments, Kasthurba Nagar, Kadavanthara, Cochin; © **0484/231-3744** or 0484/324-2021; www.keralaadventure.com; comvoyge@vsnl.net) is an excellent local agency with a fleet of reliable vehicles and drivers; it's headed by the inimitable Babu John (comvoyge@vsnl.net; 24-hr. emergency number © **94-4703-5627**), who is extremely knowledgeable about the best places to stay in Kerala (and Tamil Nadu), and will go to extraordinary lengths to show you the best the state has to offer. Babu John (along with his brother John Thomas, in Trivandrum; see p. 278) specializes in customizing itineraries according to budget, time, and preferences; he's well-versed in the needs of foreign clients, with all services provided at excellent rates. For example, a 7-day package covering Kerala (including all fuel, taxes, parking, toll fees, and your own chauffer) will cost you around Rs 9,450 to Rs 10,850 for a non–A/C car, and around Rs 11,550 to Rs 14,000 for an A/C vehicle—hard to beat. If you're the kind who doesn't plan ahead, you can even arrange for Babu to pick you up at the airport, and ask to be shown a few hotels in your preferred price range before deciding where to stay. Don't feel, either, that you need to head into Cochin in order to avail yourself of his services—he'll gladly dispatch a vehicle and driver to any part of South India, so your Kerala adventure can begin even before you arrive.

Not a travel agency as such, but worth investigating if you haven't planned anything in advance but would like to arrange a day trip, rent a bike, or book a backwater cruise, is **Traveller's Paradise** (K.L. Bernard Master Road in Fort Cochin (© **0484/221-8633;** www.bloominthenaturalway.com), a charitable initiative where all profits go towards supporting the development of local villages, helping to provide education, health benefits, and general social upliftment.

WHEN TO GO In terms of climate, the best time to visit Kerala is between October and March. December and January are peak-season months, and many resorts charge accordingly, some even tripling their rates; if you plan to visit during this time, book well in advance. Note, however, that August is when boat races are held, and September can be really pleasant—not too muggy, with the lakes filled with monsoon water and prices low. Rates are also favorable in April, which is temple festival time (though the heat is a little more intense, you're catching the tail end of the season, when most resorts start routine maintenance). In fact, from February to May, caparisoned elephants often take to the streets to participate in spectacular temple festivals; by far the biggest and most colorful is the **Thrissur Pooram Temple Festival,** which takes place at the end of April/early May, 74km (46 miles) north of Kochi. With two rival temple groups, each armed with 15 elephants and gorgeously heisted parasols, vying with each other to make their procession and fireworks display grander than preceding years, this is a photographer's dream and well worth planning a trip around. Bear in mind, however, that most hotels in Thrissur will be booked for many months in advance, so plan well ahead, and ask Babu John (see "Guided Tours & Travel Agents," above) for assistance—given enough warning, he can even arrange for you to witness the festival (which sees thousands of ecstatic devotees crushed into the streets around the temples—potentially as frightening as it is thrilling) from a hotel rooftop. Thrissur is (58km/36 miles) from Kochi airport.

7

(*Fast Facts*) Kochi

Airlines For the Kingfisher city office, call (©) 0484/235-1144; for their airport counter, call (©) 0484/261-0055. For Jet Airways, call (©) 0484/235-8879 (airport (©) 0484/261-0037); Spicejet ((©) 0484/261-1750); Indian/Air India ((©) 0484/261-0040; domestic (©) 0484/261-0041; international (©) 0484/261-0011); Paramount ((©) 0484/261-0404); Emirates ((©) 0484/261-1195); Qatar ((©) 0484/261-1304); Etihad ((©) 0484/261-1770).

Ambulance Dial (©) **102.**

Area Code The area code for Kochi is (©) **0484.**

ATMs Kochi has hundreds of ATMs; ask your driver or host for the nearest.

Banks There are more than 50 banks in Kochi. Hours are Monday to Friday 10am to 3pm (some 9am–1pm); Saturday 10am to 1pm (some 12:30pm). Some have evening counters and a few open Sunday. See "Currency Exchange," below.

Bookstores Both branches of **Idiom Books** are wonderful for a wide variety of books on India, its culture, and its literature. In Fort Kochi, the store is at the corner of Bastion and Quirose streets ((©) **0484/221-7075;** Mon–Sat 9am–9pm, Sun 10am–6pm). In Mattancherry, it's opposite the Boat Jetty on Jew Street ((©) **0484/222-5604**).

Car Hires & Taxis On average, you can expect to pay Rs 150 per hour or Rs 8 per kilometer for a taxi. The **Government of India Tourist Office** (near Taj Malabar Hotel, Willingdon Island; (©) **0484/266-8352;** Mon–Fri 9am–5:30pm, Sat 9am–1pm) has a fleet of Ambassadors. Also try **Sita World Travel** (Tharakan Bldg., M.G. Rd., Ernakulam; (©) **0484/237-4122**) or **Kerala Adventures** (see "Guided Tours & Travel Agents," above).

Currency Exchange You can exchange currency and traveler's checks at any of the many banks in Kochi, like **Canara Bank** in Fort Kochi (Kunnumpuram Junction, Amaravathy Rd.; (©) **0484/221-5467;** Mon–Fri 10am–2pm and 2:30–3:30pm, Sat 10am–noon) or **Standard Chartered** (M.G. Rd., Ernakulam; (©) **0484/235-9462;** Mon–Fri 9:30am–4:30pm, Sat till 1pm). **Thomas Cook** is also on M.G. Rd. ((©) **0484/236-9729;** Mon–Sat 9:30am–6pm) and has a branch at the airport ((©) 0484/261-0052 or -0032). Note that credit cards outside of big hotels are not the norm (and some of these accept only MasterCard and Visa), so always carry some cash.

Drugstores Medilab (Doraiswamy Iyer Rd., Ernakulam; (©) 0484/236-8963) is open around the clock, as is Ernakulam Medical Centre on the NH Bypass ((©) 0484/280-7101).

Emergencies For **police emergencies**, dial (©) **100;** to report a crime, call (©) 1090. For fires and other emergencies, including medical services, call (©) 101.

Hospitals There are more than 500 hospitals and clinics in Kochi, some specializing in particular ailments, and a number of them highly respected. If you have a medical emergency, your hotel should be able to organize the best medical match; alternatively, call **Medical Trust Hospital** ((©) **0484/235-8001**) or **General Hospital** ((©) **0484/236-1251**).

Internet Access Just about all the hotels offer some kind of Internet access. Fort Kochi also has plenty of Internet "cafes" (back rooms behind shops). These generally charge more than any of the options in Ernakulam. **Call'n'Fax/Shop'n'Save** (Princess St.; © **0484/221-5438;** Mon–Sat 8am–10pm, Sun 9am–10pm) charges Rs 40 per hour.

Post Office Use the **General Post Office** in Mattancherry (© **0484/236-0668**) or the Kochi Head Post Office in Fort Kochi (behind St. Francis Church).

WHAT TO SEE & DO

Lazy and laid-back, **Fort Kochi** offers a tranquillity that is in complete contrast to the heaving city experience of Ernakulam. Along with **Mattancherry** and **Jew Town,** Fort Kochi forms the historic heart (also known as **Old Kochi**) of the city—it is, after all, a town where 14 different languages are spoken, and tumbled-down mansions line narrow ancient lanes. Near the water's edge, old warehouses (or *godowns*) are filled with the state's treasured cash crops—pepper, tea, Ayurvedic herbs, whole ginger, and betel nuts—being dried, sorted, and prepared for direct sale or auction. The area is wonderful for historic walks, particularly into Jew Town, which hosts the remains of a community that dates back to the 1st century A.D., augmented during the 16th century when the Inquisition brought a fresh wave of Jewish immigrants here. Today only a small handful of aging "white Jewish" families remain in Kochi, but their residential quarter retains a charming ambience, with cobbled streets and fascinating antiques shops and spice markets.

Man-made **Willingdon Island,** a short ferry ride or bridge journey away, was created in the 20th century by large-scale dredging. There is a good hotel here, but the island is primarily concerned with naval and commercial port activity and is not worth visiting unless you're based here. **Bolgatty Island,** reached by ferry, is of no interest other than the rather lovely heritage "palace" on its shores, which has been converted into a poorly managed state government hotel.

Exploring Old Kochi

Start your 2-hour walking tour at the harbor near Vasco da Gama Square, where you can watch fishermen hoisting their catch from the cantilevered **Chinese fishing nets** that line the shore, then head along Church Road to **St. Francis Church** (see below). Keep going toward Parade Road (where you'll see the Malabar House Residency; see "Where to Stay," below). Turn right into Parade Road then left along Dutch Cemetery Road, passing **Thakur House** and the **cemetery** on your right, as well as the remains of the 16th-century **Fort Immanuel.** Just after this you will turn north (left) up Elephinstone Road, making a left onto Ridsdale Road. After popping into Cinnamon (see "Shopping," later) and perhaps watching the boys and men playing cricket on the **Parade Ground** park opposite the store, turn right into Bastion Street and drift in the direction of **Santa Cruz Basilica** (see below). If you're ready to take a break, turn right before this into **Peter Celli Street,** where you can't miss the lovely **Tea Pot** (see "Where to Dine," later); service is excruciatingly slow but the ambience is lovely. Or take the next street left into Burgher and stop at **Kashi Art Café** (see later), where the contemporary art and vibrant atmosphere provide a contrast to the historic surroundings.

When you're ready, head toward Tower Road, where you will find the lovely red-brick **Koder House,** not far from where you started your tour. Built in 1808 by Jewish patriarch

Samuel Koder, Koder House is a good example of the hybrid Indo-European style that developed in Cochin. It's also an example of an overpriced guesthouse (see "Where to Stay," below), so if you want to appreciate the interiors, ask to see a room—they're quite popular, however, so you may have to settle on taking a drink in the lovely upstairs lounge (while there, snoop a bit and see if you can spot the overhead bridge that links this hotel to the one behind—this was formerly one large property). Next door to Koder House, the **Old Harbour Hotel** has made a more successful, dynamic transition to hospitality (see "Where to Stay," below), and you'd do well to book dinner at the in-house restaurant, **1788** (see "Where to Dine," later), where you should pause immediately for a cooling glass of organic carrot and gooseberry juice. Beyond is the **Pierce Leslie Bungalow,** a charming 19th-century mansion reflecting both Portuguese and Dutch influences.

While in the vicinity of the fishing nets, you might want to wander along the harbor's edge for a while (this stretch is very popular at sunset), watching fishermen sell their catch. When you've had enough, catch an auto-rickshaw to Mattancherry, where you should visit the **Mattancherry (Dutch) Palace** and **Paradesi Synagogue** (see below) before discovering the fragrant scents of Kerala's **spice warehouses.** Make time to visit a few of the antiques warehouses, and don't be put off by the layers of dust—there are some real treasures to be found. End your day full circle with a **sunset cruise** ★★ around the harbor; this is the best way to enjoy the most-photographed of Kochi's historic sights: the Chinese fishing nets that form wonderful silhouettes against a red- and orange-hued sky.

The Top Attractions

Chinese Fishing Nets ★★ Said to have been introduced by traders from the court of Kublai Khan, these cantilevered nets, set up on teak and bamboo poles, are physical remnants of Fort Kochi's ancient trade with the Far East. Fishermen work the nets all day long, lowering them into the water and then hauling them up using a remarkably efficient pulley system. The best place to watch them at work is from **Vasco da Gama Square** or from a boat at sunset. Nearby, the Indo-European **Bastion Bungalow** (now the official residence of the Sub Collector) dates back to 1667; built on the site of the old Dutch Fort's Stromberg Bastion, it is believed to stand above a network of secret tunnels.

Vasco da Gama Sq. is on the water's edge along River Rd.

Mattancherry Palace ★★ Also known as the Dutch Palace, this large two-story 16th-century building was actually built by the Portuguese, who gave it to the Raja of Kochi as thanks for trading rights and favors granted to them. When the Dutch claimed Kochi in 1663, they took control of the palace and gave it a makeover. The large two-story building with its sloping roofs and pale walls is now a shadow of what it must have once been. Part of it is open to visitors, and displays include a collection of coronation robes, palanquins, and royal family portraits, but the real reason to visit is to view the bedroom chamber, where vibrant murals, executed in vivid red, green, and yellow ocher, are truly exquisite. Particularly notable are erotic scenes of the divine lover, Krishna, surrounded by enraptured female figures. Vishnu, Shiva, and various Hindu deities fill the large walls, their eyes wide and bodies full. These are among the first examples of a school of painting specific to Kerala.

Palace Rd., Mattancherry. Admission Rs 5. No photography. Sat–Thurs 10am–5pm.

Paradesi Synagogue ★★★ Kochi's first Jewish settlers arrived from Yemen and Babylon as early as A.D. 52; this—the oldest synagogue in the Commonwealth—was originally built 1,500 years later. Set in a corner of Jew Town and rather hemmed in by

Black Gold

In Kerala, pepper is still sometimes referred to as *karuthu ponnu*, or "black gold," and represents the backbone of the state's international spice trade. Although the furious trade around spices has subsided considerably these days, the sorting houses, warehouses, and auction houses from which these valuable products find their way to the rest of the world still operate in much the same way they have for centuries (though given the current crises surrounding many of the traditional cash crops, there is a possibility that these side-street sights will not be around forever). Ask your guide or auto-rickshaw driver to take you to the ginger, black pepper, betel nut, and Ayurvedic medicine warehouses, reminiscent of Salman Rushdie's *The Moor's Last Sigh;* or head for the **Kochi International Pepper Exchange** on Jew Town Rd., Mattancherry (✆ **0484/222-4263**), where until recently you could see Kerala's black gold being furiously sold off to the highest bidder; sadly, this is now done electronically.

other buildings, with only the 18th-century clock tower visible from the outside, it must be entered before you can view its most interesting feature: the beautiful blue-and-white Cantonese ceramic floor tiles—each individual tile hand-painted, so no two are alike. Above, glorious Belgian chandeliers dangle from the ceiling. At one end of the hall, old Torah scrolls are kept behind the gilded doors of the holy tabernacle.

Only a handful of Jews remain in Kochi (around five or six), though they uphold the traditions of their ancestors, and the synagogue is moving testament to the effects of the Diaspora. The number remaining are not enough to form a *minyan* (the number of men needed to sustain a synagogue), so Jews from outlying areas travel to Kochi to worship in this historic Judaic monument; they also rely on Jewish visitors to help make up numbers for ceremonies, so definitely make your presence known if you qualify. The synagogue elders are understandably concerned about tourist numbers, and numerous signs warn that no one is allowed upstairs, no one is allowed inside the pulpit, and no one is allowed to touch anything. You are also expected to be demurely attired.

Jew Town Rd., Mattancherry. Admission Rs 2. Sun–Thurs 10am–noon and 3–5pm; closed for Jewish holidays.

St. Francis Church ★   India's earliest European church was originally constructed in wood, but this was replaced by a stone structure in 1546. It was also originally Roman Catholic, but under the British it became Anglican. Vasco da Gama was originally buried here when he died in Kochi on Christmas Eve, 1524; although his body was later moved to Lisbon, he is still memorialized here with a tombstone. Having passed through the hands of Franciscan friars, Dutch Protestants, and Anglicans, the presiding Church of South India continues to hold its services here every morning at 8am. As at Hindu temples and Muslim mosques, you are required to remove your shoes before entering; note the large *pankahs*—air-conditioning of old—still hanging over the pews, alongside the ancient ceiling fans.

Church St., Fort Kochi. Mon–Sat 9:30am–5pm.

Santa Cruz Basilica ★   Pope Paul IV elevated this Portuguese church to a cathedral in 1558, but the original building was destroyed by the British in 1795. A new building was commissioned on the same site in 1887; it was declared a basilica in 1984 by Pope

John Paul II. The basilica's interiors are worth a look, especially the caryatids and exquisite stained glass.

Parade Rd. and K. B. Jacob Rd., near Bastion St., Fort Kochi. www.santacruzbasilica.org. Mon–Sat 9am–1pm and 3–5pm; Sun morning Mass only.

WHERE TO STAY

Fort Cochin is the area with the most historic charm and, compared with most Indian cities, a thoroughly laid-back vibe; best here are **Le Colonial** (utterly sumptuous interiors), **Brunton Boatyard** (waterfront location), **Malabar House** (chichi decor), and **Old Harbour Hotel** (best value and a wonderful atmosphere). In fact, this small enclave has the highest density of heritage accommodations in the country, so it's hard to be disappointed here. Alternatively, if you demand a large, full-amenity hotel, opt for Willingdon Island, a 10-minute ferry ride away, and useful if you really want to be far away from the crowds—it's hassle-free, although also a little empty on atmosphere.

If you don't mind being far from the ambience of Fort Kochi and the harbor, there's one relaxing out-of-town option worth considering Far more satisfying, however, and Kochi's best opportunity for a beach experience, is the thoroughly laid-back **Cherai Beach Resorts,** some 30km (19 miles, or 40 min.) north of Kochi by road, or 15km (9⅓ miles) from the Vypeen jetty. Savvy locals swear by the place, both as a chance for respite from the daily grind, and for its dining, so don't turn your nose up just because it's pretty basic. Ask for a heritage cottage with an open-air bathroom and patio on stilts overlooking the backwaters; although the newer rooms are sleeker, they lack the charm of these. Service and amenities may be obvious shortfalls, but the location at the edge of one of Kerala's most scintillating (and relatively undiscovered) beaches will definitely make up for this; besides, the Ayurvedic rejuvenation massages are a treat, and the Keralite meals superb. *And* it's a very good value at Rs 2,000 to Rs 5,500 (© **0484/248-1818** or 0484/241-6949; www.cheraibeachresorts.com).

Fort Kochi
Very Expensive
Brunton Boatyard ★★★   Situated at the water's edge on the site of a bustling boatyard, this is the best located hotel in Fort Cochin, and the space gives it the edge on Malabar House, particularly if you're traveling with kids. A smart, whitewashed colonial warehouse-style building with sloping tiled roofs, deep verandas, and spacious high-ceilinged rooms, the designers have successfully captured the gracious ambience of a bygone era, but with all the comforts of modern living. Each room has its own balcony from which to enjoy views of the fishing boats and ferries that cruise between the islands. Original and reproduction antiques include typical Kerala four-poster beds, high enough off the ground to make the footstools a necessity. Suites include a personal butler and kitchenette. The free sunset cruise from the hotel's own jetty is a great way to kick off the evening, and cooking demos on the rooftop make you feel part of a BBC food program. The only possible drawback to staying here is the hotel's proximity to the active and noisy waterways, but on the other hand, the low-level soundtrack lends an air of authenticity.

Near Aspinwall, Calvathy, Fort Cochin 682 001. © **0484/221-5461** through -65. Fax 0484/221-5562. bruntonboatyard@cghearth.com. Reservations: CGH Earth, Casino Bldg., Willingdon Island, Cochin 682 003. © **0484/266-8211** or 0484/301-1568. www.cghearth.com. 26 units. Nov–Apr 335€–360€ standard double, 445€–505€ deluxe suite double, 45€ extra person; May–Oct Rs 7,590 standard double, Rs 10,925 deluxe suite double; Rs 2,000 extra person. Rates include breakfast and taxes. All-inclusive rates also available. AE, DC, MC, V. **Amenities:** 3 restaurants, including The History & Terrace Grill (see review,

p. 255), tea lounge, bar; airport transfers (Rs 1,300–Rs 2,000); bicycles; Ayurvedic center; cooking demonstrations; Internet (in business center; Rs 100/hr.) library; large outdoor pool; room service; sunset cruise (free); guided walking tour, yoga and meditation. *In room:* A/C, TV, hair dryer, minibar.

Koder House ★ It's not as polished as any of the better-priced places in the vicinity (and service is tentative at best), but its main selling point has got to be its authenticity (little has changed since it was built in 1808 and it's stuffed with antiques) and the sheer enormousness of its rooms. Frankly, though, we're not sure what you're going to do with all that space, and there's some odd arrangement of furniture and appliances that makes us wonder just how serious these people are about running a hotel. Sure, there's a small pool (with hardly a jot of space around it) and a restaurant (that serves Jewish specialty dishes), but if you peer into the premises of the Old Harbour next door, you'll probably want to relocate there immediately. Still, the location is convenient and there's a pair of pretty lounges to inhabit when you get bored exploring your suite.

Tower Rd., Fort Cochin 682 001. ℓ **0484/221-8485.** Fax: 0484/221-7988. www.koderhouse.com. koderhouse@ gmail.com. 6 units. Oct–Mar Rs 10,400–Rs 13,023 junior suite double, Rs 13,000–Rs 15,600 deluxe suite double, Rs 3,000 extra bed; Apr–Sept Rs 5,000 double, Rs 2,217 extra bed. Rates include breakfast; 15% tax extra. AE, MC, V. **Amenities:** Restaurant, 2 lounges; airport transfers (Rs 1,000); Jacuzzi; small outdoor pool; spa. *In room* A/C, TV, Wi-Fi (free).

The Malabar House ★★★ Step inside this chunky white 18th-century colonial British bungalow at the edge of the Parade Maidan, and you're immediately cooled by rooms in vibrant colors, a lush courtyard, and the sound of trickling water. This tiny, very contemporary boutique hotel has a tropical inner courtyard (trees, potted shrubs, and stone pathways) with a lovely plunge pool, wooden foldaway chairs, a small open-air theater area, and a covered restaurant. Rooms (some of which are quite small; suites, however, are palatial) feature waxed black Kadapa stone floors offset by bright red, turquoise, or yellow walls; each features a selection of paintings, sculptures, and period furniture reflecting the cultural heritage of Kerala, while the narrowish beds, solid in every sense, are made from carved teak and rosewood. Not only good-looking, this was also the first operation in India to be certified by Green Globe, the global environmental certification program for travel and tourism.

1/268, 269 Parade Rd., Fort Cochin 682 001. ℓ **0484/221-6666.** Fax 0484/221-7777. www.malabar house.com. reservations@malabarhouse.com. 17 units. Oct–Dec 19 and Jan 11–Apr 220€ deluxe double, 300€–360€ suite; Dec 20–Jan 10 285€ deluxe double, 380€–460€ suite; May–Sept 150€ deluxe double, 200€–250€ suite; 35€ extra bed. Rates include breakfast; 15% tax extra. AE, MC, V. **Amenities:** Restaurant, wine and tapas lounge; airport transfers (Rs 1,100); babysitting (with prior notice); bicycles; outdoor pool; room service; Ayurvedic spa; tailor. *In room:* A/C and fans, TV, DVD (in Malabar Suite) hair dryer, minibar, Wi-Fi (free).

Expensive

Le Colonial ★★★ This wins the prize for Kerala's most elegantly interiored hotel, and it's surely among the most beautiful in the country. Although the grounds are small (but with room for a decent pool and sun loungers), there's so much to look at on the inside, that you just might forget to explore Kochi. This is apparently the oldest colonial-era building in Kochi, and supposedly where St. Francis himself once stayed, and where Vasco da Gama died. A transformed—and perfectly renovated—16th-century tea bungalow, the architects and designers have injected this posh-yet-homey boutique hotel with painstaking attention to detail, imbuing it with great personality and filling it with exquisite antiques, impeccably restored furniture, and eye-catching artworks. All the rooms are sumptuous and very comfortable, but the price you pay determines the amount of personal space and type of bathroom you end up with. This is among the most glamorous pieces of heritage design you'll see anywhere in India—if you don't have the money to stay here (yes, it's pricey), it's certainly worth splurging on a meal here.

1/315 Church St., Vasco da Gama Sq., Fort Cochin 682 001. ℂ **0484/221-7181** through -7184. Reservations: Neemrana Hotels, A-20/B, Feroze Gandhi Marg, New Delhi 110 024. ℂ **011/4666-1666.** Fax 011/ 4666-1600. www.neemrana.com. sales@neemrana.com. 8 units. Midseason Rs 11,500–Rs 17,500 double, Rs 6,500 small double; low season Rs 7,000–Rs 10,000 double, Rs 4,500 small double; peak season Rs 17,000–Rs 24,000 double, Rs 11,000 small double. Rates include breakfast plus one other meal, soft drinks, tea, coffee, and laundry; 15% tax extra. AE, MC, V. **Amenities:** Restaurant (Mountbatten; see "Where to Dine," p. 252); airport transfers (Rs 900–Rs 1,800); medium-size outdoor pool; room service. *In room* A/C, TV, Wi-Fi (free).

Old Harbour Hotel ★★★ (Value)

This 1808 bungalow was until recently the residence of an old tea-broking family, and renovation has been very sensitive; even the entry-level superior rooms retain a sense of history and space. Owner Edgar Pinto is an avid collector of excellent modern Indian art; a Swiss architect breathed life back into the dilapidated structure and then styled it with a sexy integration of locally sourced antiques and contemporary color—a big triumph is the sense of space and tranquillity thanks to a generous garden and pretty pool. Garden-view rooms are a little more generous size-wise (choose "Tower"), but the garden "cottages" are the best value, with lovely outdoor bathrooms. Usually suites are not worth the money (unless you're traveling with kids), but the huge Princess and Palace suites, both with a harbor view, are bargains and simply palatial. It's not positioned right on the waterfront like Brunton (but pretty darn close), but it's got atmosphere and class and offers excellent value; and the rooms are more spacious than those at Malabar House. Book immediately.

1/328 Tower Rd., Fort Cochin 682 001. ℂ **0484/221-8006.** www.oldharbourhotel.com. 13 units, most with shower only. High season Rs 7,500 superior double, Rs 9,300 garden view double, Rs 10,600 garden cottage double; Rs 14,200 suite; low season Rs 5,250 superior double, Rs 6,510 garden view double, Rs 7,420 garden cottage double, Rs 9,940 suite. Rates include breakfast and taxes. AE, DC, MC, V. **Amenities:** Restaurant (1788, reviewed on p. 255), lounge; airport transfers (Rs 1,200); small Ayurvedic center; large outdoor pool; rooftop yoga (free). *In room:* A/C and fan, TV on request, fridge, hair dryer, Wi-Fi (Rs 200 for entire stay).

Tea Bungalow ★

Still in its infancy (opened in early 2009), this guesthouse-sized hotel occupies a restored bungalow built in 1912; it's yet another decent newcomer to Kochi's heritage scene, yet (unwittingly) looking very contemporary. While it's antique on the outside, once you step inside there's not much in terms of historic ambience. Instead, it offers bright, attractive rooms and a fresh, welcoming atmosphere, and while the rates skyrocketed at press time you'll definitely be able to bargain them down. The spacious interiors have marble floors and boldly colored walls and the smart, upbeat rooms (there's hardly an antique in sight) are named and themed after different Indian Ocean ports (personal favorites are Goa, Zanzibar and Mauritius)—the best are in the main house and have large doors connecting the bathrooms with private gardens, so you can enjoy a virtual open air shower. While the dining area is a trifle bland, lively barbeques are held around the pool. A decent alternative if the more authentic places are full.

1/1901 Kunnumpuram, Fort Kochi 682 001. ℂ **0484/301-9200.** www.teabungalow.in. info@teabungalow. in. 10 units. Oct–Mar $300–$340 double; Apr–Sept $215 double. Rates include breakfast; 15% tax extra. AE, MC, V. **Amenities:** Restaurant, poolside barbecue lounge, library-lounge with TV, bar; airport transfers (Rs 900–Rs 1,200); outdoor pool; room service. *In room:* A/C, TV, hair dryer, Wi-Fi (free).

Trinity ★★

The stone entranceway is engraved with the date 1740 and the initials of the Dutch East India Company (VOC), which had its offices here. It's another labor of love by the Malabar House team, and for some time now, this has been a really chic little hidden away guesthouse appealing to those after utter privacy. Although the name will likely change once five new rooms are added (a brand-new block is being built), currently the three lovely suites share a lounge and guests avail of facilities at The Malabar House, just a short stroll away. The emphasis here is on good looks and the rooms are decorated with lovely artworks and dramatic photographs—in the Red Suite are lithographs by MF Husain, an important (and highly controversial) Indian artist; the collection also runs to tribal art and other historic artifacts. Of the pretty outdoor bathrooms, most coveted is the Red Suite with its fine chill out area. Trinity (or whatever it will be called) will soon have a spa and restaurant.

1/658 Ridsdale Rd., Parade Ground, Fort Cochin 682 001. Reservations: ☎ **0484/221-6666.** Fax 0484/221-7777. www.malabarhouse.com. 3 units, all with shower only. Oct–Apr 220€ Blue deluxe double, 300€ Yellow suite, 360€ Red suite; May–Sept 150€ Blue deluxe double, 200€ Yellow suite, 250€ Red suite; 35€ extra bed. Rates include breakfast; 15% tax extra. AE, DC, MC, V. **Amenities:** Breakfast room and lounge; guests may use pool, restaurant, and bar at The Malabar House (reviewed above). *In room* A/C and fan, TV/DVD.

Moderate

Secret Garden ★★★ Ⓥalue This 2-year-old guesthouse tucked away down the backstreets not far from the Dutch Cemetery is one of the most alluring options in Kochi. Your host, Thora, is an Icelandic architect who, together with a team of Kerala craftsmen, breathed new life into this sturdy old building, transforming it into a really cozy sanctuary that feels a million miles from the tourist hordes. There are currently just four rooms (two of them triples), and even once Thora has completed work on three more, this'll still be a haven of tranquillity. The elegant rooms feature a mix of colonial and Kerala style furniture, and are fine-tuned for a hassle free stay. Get up early for yoga under the mango tree before sitting down to a healthful breakfast at a table laden with homemade bread, organic jams, fruits, yogurt, and proper coffee. After a day of exploring (by bike, if you wish) and rummaging through antiques, you'll be skipping home, longing for a dip in the luscious little pool—it'll feel so much like your very own magical hideaway.

11/745 Bishop's Garden Lane, Fort Kochi 682 001. ☎ **0484/221-6685,** 99-4747-4050, or 98-9558-1489. www.secretgarden.in. 4 units (3 more planned). Oct–Mar Rs 5,500 double; Apr–Sept Rs 4,125 double. Rates include breakfast and taxes. MC, V. **Amenities:** Breakfast room, library-lounge with TV, CD library and computer; airport transfers (Rs 800–Rs 1,400); bicycles; small outdoor pool; morning yoga. *In room* A/C, hair dryer on request, no phone, Wi-Fi (free).

Tower House ★★ Ⓥalue Yet another new hotel (since 2009), this is a successful conversion by India's prolific heritage-oriented Neemrana group—authentic digs and a boutique hotel experience at bargain rates. The sumptuous old two-level building (part of the old lighthouse tower) is a warren of scrupulously restored spaces, so it's an adventure just getting to your room as you move through grand reception rooms and prissy-looking parlors, all the time enticing you to peek into the different rooms along the way. With a huge collection of carefully sourced antiques and rooms in a variety of shapes, sizes, and configurations, the ideal stay would commence with a tour of each one. Even the smallest doubles are spacious and elegantly furnished. While the rooms are excellent value, beware that some of the enormous suites (with a third bed included in the price) are beautiful but without windows. Service is well meaning (although not on par with Neemrana's slicker Le Coloniale), and given how mediocre the competition is, you'd be crazy to stay anywhere else in this price category.

I/320 and 321 Tower St., Fort Cochin 682 001. ⓒ **0484/221-6960** through -6962. Fax: 0484/221-6963. Reservations: Neemrana Hotels, A-20/B, Feroze Gandhi Marg, New Delhi 110 024. ⓒ **011/4666-1666.** Fax 011/4666-1600. www.neemranahotels.com. sales@neemranahotels.com. 14 units, most with shower only, some with tub and shower. Oct–Apr Rs 3,750–Rs 5,000 double, Rs 4,500–Rs 6,000 grand double, Rs 6,000–Rs 8,000 luxury suite; May–Sept Rs 2,500 double, Rs 3,000 grand double, Rs 4,000 luxury suite. AE, MC, V. **Amenities:** Restaurant, 2 lounges, bar; airport transfers (Rs 900); Internet (broadband in the office; free for e-mail checking); outdoor pool (by 2010). *In room* A/C and fans.

Inexpensive

If you're on a tight budget, make an advance booking (do make sure that it's one of three that has a balcony) at the seven-room **Raintree Lodge** (1/618 Petercelli St.; www.nivalink.com/raintreelodge; raintree@fortcochin.com; Rs 2,000–Rs 2,300 double plus 15% tax). It's located in the heart of the old town; guest rooms are no-frills, but clean and decorated with antiques and *objets,* and the beds are comfortable; tubs look worse for wear but overhead showers mean you don't have to lie in them. Because it's so small (although some rooms are disproportionately large) with no public amenities (bar a rooftop with a relatively nice view), it feels rather like renting a tiny flat, although you can rent bikes, arrange transfers and get guides through the friendly check-in clerk.

If you're looking for a genuine homestay experience, there's no beating **Delight** (reviewed below)—particularly if staying with warm and hospitable people is of any significance (what other reason would you have for choosing a homestay?). Alternatively, if you value comfort over personality, have a look at slightly more expensive **Bernard Bungalow** (1/297 Parade Rd.; ⓒ **0984/742-7999,** 0484/221-6162 or -6160; www.bernardbungalow.com; Rs 1,500–Rs 3,500 double, depending on room and season), run with an iron hand by Coral Bernard. She's a bit of a battleaxe but her rooms are so clean you could practically eat off the floor. Pick a room upstairs and you'll feel very much a part of the home she's lived in for the past 30 years, without actually encroaching on her space (don't bother with the rooms on the ground floor). Pick room 105 and you get to overlook The Malabar House next door; at press time, Coral was adding one or two new rooms, but its safe to say that she is retaining her homestay roots despite a more guesthouselike presentation—after all, she and husband, Bernard, lived here 32 years before opening up for guests. Also recommended is **Walton's Home Stay** (Princess St.; ⓒ **0484/221-5309;** www.waltonshomestay. com), which has recently had a face-lift that has greatly improved its nine rooms (they all have private verandas and are air-conditioned; Rs 1,200–Rs 2,600 double); and the even better-value **Noah's Ark Homestay** (see below).

Delight ★ ⓥ**alue** It's the people—a lovely, warmhearted family—that makes this 300-year-old Portuguese house worth considering. Accommodations may be slightly rudimentary, but they're well-thought out, with personally designed fittings, furniture, and decor. Owner David Lawrence, who grew up in this house, even created false ceilings in the rooms to mimic the ambience of a traditional Keralite house: "We had no architect, no designer—it's all done to our thinking. We think it's good for ordinary people," he says. In fact, the rooms are pretty cute, with a few inoffensive kitschy elements thrown in; showers are open plan, but there's always hot water thanks to solar heating, and clean towels and linens. David's wife, Flowery, gives cooking lessons, and you'll chew the fat around the breakfast table for hours. This ain't luxury, but it's authentic, and nowhere else will you find keener insights into life in a Roman Catholic Fort Kochi household. Besides, David is like a one-man travel agency, and he really knows local history.

Parade Ground, Post Office Rd., Fort Kochi 682 001. ⓒ/fax **0484/221-7658** or 0484/221-6301. www. delightfulhomestay.com. 6 units, all with shower only. High season Rs 2,500 A/C double, Rs 1,600 (non-A/C double; low season Rs 1,200 A/C double, Rs 800 non-A/C double. Rates include breakfast and taxes. MC, V. **Amenities:** Family dining room, TV lounge; airport transfers (Rs 650–Rs 695); cooking classes. *In room:* A/C (in some) and fan.

Hotel Fort House ★ (Value)

The best feature of this budget "hotel" is undoubtedly its location right on the waterfront—it even has a private jetty (though no rooms overlook the water as such). Two wings of simple, unfussy rooms opening on to shared verandas run along either side of a leafy open courtyard, with the harbor at one end, and the main road on the other. Rooms in the newer wing are shabbily elegant, and clean with no frills—just a few cane chairs, a simple bed made up white sheets, and a large spherical light dangling above. Request a room close to the water and you'll have less road noise (although harbor traffic never lets up). As is often the case at such budget lodges, the whole place buzzes with travelers—it's great for lazing on the porch with a book, or simply staring out at the endlessly coming and going ships. Local guides and sightseeing can be arranged, and an in-house tailor can whip up casual clothing in a matter of hours. There is also a brand-new Ayurvedic center, but still no pool.

2/6A Calvathy Rd., Fort Cochin 682 001. (℃) **0484/221-7103** or 938-748-6150. www.hotelforthouse.com. fort_hs@yahoo.com. 16 units, all with shower only. High season Rs 3,800 standard double, Rs 2,500 smaller double; low season Rs 2,660 standard double, Rs 1,750 small double. Rates include breakfast; 15% tax extra. MC, V. **Amenities:** Restaurant; airport transfers (Rs 750–Rs 850); Internet (broadband near reception; Rs 50/hr.); tailor. *In room:* A/C, no phone.

Noah's Ark Homestay (Value)

Run by a warm and welcoming family that loves meeting you as much as you'll enjoy spending time in their home, this is one of Fort Kochi's best homestays, and very conveniently located if you want to be right up close to all the action. The large family home is in the Modernist style—lots of concrete, twisting stairways, straight lines and sharp angles, but with wonderful natural light and generous balconies. Interiors have a touch of the '70s to them and they're immaculately clean, with ample space and decent furniture. The real reason you're here, though, is to experience a family's warm hospitality, getting beyond the usual tourist jibe. That's possible, but your hosts will just as easily put together excursions and cruises and a night at the theater—or set you up with a good Ayurvedic treatment.

1/508, Fortkochi Hospital Rd., Fort Kochi 682 001. (℃) **0484/221-5481** or 97-4536-5260. www.noahsark cochin.com or www.noahsarkhomestay.com. 6 units, all with shower only. Oct–Mar Rs 1,500 standard double, Rs 2,000 deluxe double, Rs 2,500 deluxe double with balcony; Apr–Sept Rs 1,200 standard double, Rs 1,800–Rs 2,000 deluxe double. Rates include breakfast. No credit cards. **Amenities:** Dining room; airport transfers (Rs 750–Rs 850); Wi-Fi (free). *In room:* A/C (in some).

Willingdon Island

Besides the two very smart options here, there's also one very well run, good-value option in the form of old-fashioned **Casino Hotel** ((℃) **0484/266-8211** or 0484/301-1568; www.cghearth.com), the eponymous headquarters of high-end eco-conscious chain, CGH Earth. Like the Trident (reviewed below), it's a little far from the historic sights and without any sort of view (watery or otherwise), but it offers all the comforts and amenities you'll need (including a superb seafood restaurant, **Fort Cochin,** reviewed on p. 254), and service is just lovely. High-season rates start at 115€ double (breakfast and taxes included).

Taj Malabar ★

It may have hit the list of 100 Best Hotels in Asia, according to *Travel + Leisure* in 2007, but this stalwart of Kochi's luxury hotel scene really seems to be treading water these days. Willingdon's only waterfront hotel, it's certainly an elegant property, but feels increasingly geared towards business travelers. After the decadent public areas and superb water's edge location, though, rooms are a real drawback. They're divided between those in the slightly more generously proportioned one-floor Heritage Wing (where, compared with the boutique hotels in Fort Kochi, there's not much character these days), and the more compact rooms in the Tower Wing (think ship's cabin), a modern construction with a smart look, but cubbyhole bathrooms. The only real reason to choose a room here would be to admire the sunset from one of the corner Tower rooms (710 is our pick), but personally we'd rather be enjoying a cruise, cocktail in hand, or watching the scene from the edge of the gorgeous infinity pool.

Willingdon Island, Cochin 682 009. (✆ **0484/266-6811** or -8010. Fax 0484/266-8297. www.tajhotels.com. malabar.cochin@tajhotels.com. 96 units. Rs 14,300 superior double; Rs 15,400 superior sea-view double; Rs 16,500 deluxe sunset-view double; Rs 18,700 heritage wing sea-view double; Rs 22,000–Rs 24,200 suite. Rates exclude 15% tax. Up to 50% discount in low season; rate of the day applicable throughout the year. AE, MC, V. **Amenities:** 4 restaurants, lounge, bar; airport transfers (Rs 1,848–Rs 2,317); Ayurvedic spa; babysitting; boat cruises and yacht hire; health club; large outdoor pool with Jacuzzi; room service. In room: A/C, TV/DVD, hair dryer, minibar, Wi-Fi (Rs 160/¹/₂hr.; Rs 751/day).

Trident Cochin ★ (**Value**) This dignified business hotel is quiet, tasteful, and replete with modern conveniences plus Kochi's most polished service. Accommodations surround a pleasant courtyard where you can swim in the pool and dine alfresco. An effort has been made to personalize the public spaces with traditional artifacts and ornaments, and the entrance is dominated by a giant *uruli* cooking pot mounted on old black-and-gold snake-boat prows. Rooms are sleek with lots of blond timber and elegantly compact bathrooms. These are also probably the quietest bedrooms in Kochi—double glazed for the convenience of airline crews that bed down here. All in all, it's a very slick, professional place, and were it not for its location (neither in the heritage area nor on the waterfront), it would be a top pick. But then the rates—which offer much better value compared to the nearby Taj—would not be so enticing.

Bristow Rd., Willingdon Island, Kochi 682 003, Kerala. (✆ **0484/266-9595.** Fax 0484/266-9393. www.trident hotels.com. 85 units. Rs 9,200 superior double; Rs 11,700 deluxe double; Rs 15,600 suite. Rates exclude 15% tax. Ask about special deals, or book online for better rates. AE, DC, MC, V. **Amenities:** 2 restaurants, bar, lounge; airport transfers (Rs 1,800); Ayurveda center; babysitting; concierge; currency exchange; gym; pool; room service. In room: A/C, TV/DVD, clock radio/MP3 docking station, hair dryer, minibar, Wi-Fi (Rs 125/hr.; Rs 960/day).

WHERE TO DINE

Seafood, always fresh, should be at least one course. Seerfish, a large, meaty white-fleshed fish, is by far the most reliable, as are prawns. And Perhaps the most acclaimed of the seafood joints is **Fort Cochin** (reviewed below), one place that's definitely worth making a special trip for (in this case, to Willingdon Island). If you'd prefer a more fine-dining atmosphere, the **Rice Boat** ★ (✆ **0484/266-6811;** 12:30–2:45pm and 7:30–10:45pm) is the small-but-gorgeous seafood restaurant at the Taj Malabar—floor-to-ceiling glass walls and a curved cane ceiling make the best of its position right on the water's edge. It's an excellent place to indulge in some fusion dishes, like rice hoppers (traditional rice "pasta cakes") served with smoked salmon, tropical fruit, and coconut chutney, or cubes of seerfish cooked with ground coconut and raw mango, and served with *idlyappams*. It's not cheap by Kerala standards, and seafood is not really in league with the more simple fare served at Fort Cochin, but it's still darn good!

Wine is a relatively new phenomenon among India's elite, and Kochi now has its own wine lounge and tapas bar, **Divine** ★, above the restaurant at The Malabar House

(✆ **0484/221-6666;** 11am–11pm). Here where you can sample 12 top Indian vintages and perhaps settle in for a long night with a few bottles of the highly quaffable cabernet sauvignon or the oak-aged Chantilli chardonnay, accompanied by delicious, decadent-sounding bites; try the tiger prawn samosas, or jalapeños stuffed with creamy mushroom. It's small, but with a *très* trendy look if you prefer designer glamour to harbor views (of which, of course, there are none). As with Malabar House's own **Malabar Junction** (reviewed below), Kochi's best eating establishments are for the most part still located in hotels, but there are notable exceptions, including the very unpretentious **Dal Roti** (1/263 Lilly St.; ✆ **0484/221-7655** or 97-4645-9244; dhal.roti@gmail.com), which is perfect if you're bored with seafood and South Indian spicing. Owners Ramesh and Kalpana serve delicious North Indian fare in a lovely, casual atmosphere: whitewashed walls and simple pine benches and tables arranged around a terra-cotta Nandi (a sacred Hindu bull). Its simple "village"-style cooking is very good, and wonderful value: sample the delicious *murg mussalam* (whole stuffed chicken) or a meal-size *thali* (platter) and mop up the juices with *alu paratas* (unleavened whole-wheat bread stuffed with potato). If, on the other hand, you *do* want to try traditional Keralite cooking, and combine the experience with a dazzling location on the edge of the water (literally, when the weather's good, the tables are set up on the jetty), the restaurant at **Hotel Fort House ★** (✆ **0484/221-7103**) has a rock-solid reputation. That's largely thanks to owner Nova Thomas's Portuguese-influenced dishes (her great-grandmother being of Portuguese descent) like pork *vindaloo*—though we'd definitely opt for the Kerala-style grilled tuna, or the highly recommended seerfish *pollichathu*, wrapped in banana leaf and grilled.

If you're wanting an exceptionally romantic night out, you should reserve a space at Le Coloniale's in-house restaurant, **Mountbatten ★★★** (noon–3pm and 7–10:30pm), where there isn't really a menu, but you can order just about whatever you want—chef Raju is good with Indian (north or south), Italian, French, and Keralite dishes, but it's best to chat with him first to decide what you'd like. The seafood is excellent, and you can rely on Raju to come up with a sumptuous set menu, too. If you want to sample something out of the ordinary, ask about his pineapple and grape curry, made in a coconut gravy. Everything, including the breads and ice cream, is prepared in-house. You can bring your own wine, or ask in advance for something to be purchased on your behalf; you really must book, though, and definitely ask to sit under the staff at a table near the pool.

For pit stops during the day while wandering around Fort Kochi, there are now a handful of good options: **Kashi Art Café ★** (Burgher St.; ✆ **0484/221-5769;** http://kashiartcafe.com), located in a restored Dutch heritage house, is a novel cafe-cum-art-gallery with tables and benches made out of coconut trunks. It serves hot and cold beverages with cakes or sandwiches (with *real,* hearty bread). Kashi's owners have also started a tiny eatery in their own home—the clever concept has neighborhood housewives preparing their personal specialties, so there are just a handful of items offered. The place is called **Shala ★★** and it's only open for dinner (5:30–9:30pm); because it's so small we suggest you call ahead to book a table and to hear what's on today's menu (✆ **0484/221-6036**).

Another pretty little cafe-style venue is **Tea Pot** (Peter Celli St.; ✆ **0484/221-8035;** tpleaz@hotmail.com), run by Sanjai, a laid-back hippie type. Order the *appam* with vegetable stew (chopped vegetables in a very mild coconut base; Rs 100) and a ginger lime soda (or one of more than 30 teas), then settle down with a good book or a garrulous partner—the food takes awhile to get there, but it's almost always worth the wait. Also joining the lineup of cafes, is the quiet, compact little back veranda and tree-shaded garden at CGH Earth's new contemporary art gallery, **David Hall ★★**, where you can

Traditional Keralite Feasts

If you're invited, don't pass up the opportunity to enjoy a traditional *sadhya* feast while in Kerala. In truth, even the simplest breakfast meal is a feast in Kerala, so forgo the eggs and toast and order whatever's going. The most well-known feast food is of course the *dosa,* a crispy thin pancake, or the *idly* (also spelled *iddly* or *idli*), a small compressed rice and lentil wedge—both are served with *sambar* (a vegetable and lentil gravy) and various chutneys (coconut, mint, peanut, tomato, and chili). The famous *"masala dosa"* is when the pancake is stuffed with a spicy potato dish. Also delicious is *puttu,* a fine rice powder and grated coconut "cylinder," which is often served with baked banana and mildly spicy chickpea stew. Or there's the steamed rice pancake known as *appam,* served with vegetable "stew" (chopped vegetables and cashews in coconut milk). At traditional feasts, expect rice and ghee (clarified butter), served with various stews and curries like *sambar, rasam, kootu, pacchadi, appalam,* and *payasam,* all of which will be heaped endlessly upon your *ela* (leaf). Seafood in Kerala is exquisite and plentiful. A popular dish is *meen moilee,* a delicate fish curry tempered with fresh coconut milk (*chemeen,* incidentally, means "prawns"). Coconut is a staple used in many dishes: *Avial* is a mixed-vegetable "dry" curry prepared with coconut, cumin, and turmeric; and *aadu olathiyathu* is a coconut-based curry made with cubes of fried mutton.

order light Indian meals, sandwiches, salads, and morish cakes and cookies; you'll find it opposite the Parade Ground, near St. Francis Church (Church Rd., Fort Kochi; ✆ 98-470-6325; www.davidhall.in; daily 11am–7pm).

Fort Cochin ★★★ SEAFOOD   Considered one of Kerala's best seafood restaurants, this casual catch-of-the-day semi-alfresco pad—located in the low-key Casino Hotel—is something of a Kerala institution. The atmosphere is rustic: Tables are set around a huge banyan tree and the menu is scrawled on a blackboard. Choose from a range of freshly caught seafood displayed on a cart that makes its way from table to table, and decide how you would like it prepared—grilled whole with heaps of spices, or delicately sliced with subtle herbs; the obliging maitre d' will help you make up your mind and then your choice will be prepared at an open grill in full view of the curious Chinese carp that have been swimming in the nearby fish tank since before we first ate here.

Casino Hotel, K.P.K. Menon Rd., Willingdon Island. ✆ **0484/266-8221** or -8421. Prices determined on the day and by weight. Mixed-seafood platter Rs 875. AE, DC, MC, V. Daily 7pm–midnight.

The Grand Pavilion ★★★ INDIAN   Okay, this may not be grand in the decor sense, but the Keralite and Indian food is delicious. And cheap. Which is why the place is always jam-packed with locals, and apparently has been since the '60s when The Grand really was. Seafood is superb, with the signature *karimeen pollichathu* a definite must-have. If you're not feeling that hungry, start with a plate of *chemeen ularthiyathu* (tiny prawns; ask that they not be too spicy), then follow with vegetable stew to be mopped up with the most delectable crisp-edged, soft-centered *appams,* and a plate of tender *malai* chicken, prepared in the tandoor, and served with mint sauce. All that food, and still the bill won't top Rs 700 for two. A huge dining hall, filled to the brim with a loyal

Indian clientele, and faultless food makes this 20-minute trip from Fort Kochi most definitely worth it. Make sure you book ahead.

M.G. Rd., Ernakulam. ℂ **0484/238-2061.** www.grandhotelkerala.com. Main courses Rs 75–Rs 150. MC, V. Daily 12:30–4pm and 7–11:30pm.

The History & Terrace Grill ★★★ KERALITE   Two restaurants in one, more or less. The Terrace Grill (closed during the monsoon) has a great location overlooking busy Vypin boat jetty and the waterfront, and you can spend hours watching the passing parade while you feast on the superb signature seafood platters, filled with lobster, tiger prawns, scampi, squid (a little tough), and the catch of the day. Order a combination of "Mattancherry Spiced," for some local flavor, and the more subtle lemon garlic butter. If the mosquitoes become bothersome, you may decide to move inside to The History where you can continue your meal to the accompaniment of live traditional classical music. The History feels like a large, elegant old-world dining hall, and has a much more varied menu (although you can't *order* the Terrace Grill's seafood platter here), with most of the recipes borrowed from the kitchens of Kochi families. New chef Ajeeth Janardmanan has spent much of 2009 visiting local Kochi families to unearth recipes that might otherwise end up lost to the world—if you're at all interested, call him over and find out about his discoveries, and then let your taste buds decide.

Brunton Boatyard, 1/498 Fort Kochi. ℂ **0484/221-5461** through -5465. Main courses Rs 300–Rs 750; seafood platter Rs 1,200–1,400. AE, DC, MC, V. Daily 7:30–10:30pm.

Malabar Junction ★★ MEDITERRANEAN FUSION   Along with **Rice Boat** (Taj Malabar's pretty restaurant), this is Kochi's answer to fine dining, though here it is alfresco, with guests seated in the small, lush courtyard area, watching (at night) a performance on the adjacent stage, the hotel and plants lit up to great effect. The atmosphere is very romantic, and if you can't decide between Indian, Keralite, or European food, this is the place to be—there's good variety, from the decadent Fisherman's Dream (a plate of tiger prawns and red snapper) to the gourmet Malabar burger (prime beef with green pepper and chili sauce, served with okra and ginger-flavored tomato sorbet). Chef Biju also likes to show off his diverse talents with a couple of degustation menus; we'd opt for the six-course classical version, which includes a wonderful tiger prawn curry. Top the evening off with homemade ginger and pepper ice-cream, and then slink upstairs to **Divine,** the hot new wine lounge (see "Kochi After Dark," below).

The Malabar House, 1/268–269 Parade Rd., Fort Kochi. ℂ **0484/221-6666.** Main courses Rs 380–Rs 600, seafood platter Rs 1,500, degustation menu Rs 1,100–Rs 2,000. AE, DC, MC, V. Daily 7am–midnight.

1788 ★★★ KERALITE/FUSION   This breezy inside-outside restaurant at Old Harbour Hotel has the most intriguing menu in Kochi; the chef hails from Puducherry and clearly has a profound love of experimenting with local traditions, gearing them up for a fine dining experience by giving them an international spin. You might be tempted to dive head first into the seafood platter (you can even preorder a specific fish and hope it's caught the day you dine), but it would be a shame not to taste crab *ularthiyathu,* cooked in an earthenware urn with a spicy masala (so not really for delicate palates), or the Cochin shrimp curry, or home-reared Kerala duck curry, or the coconut fish. If you're keeping away from the spices and curries, then there's a marvelous crab risotto, or pumpkin *olan,* which is typically Keralite, made with semiripe pumpkin and lentils. Finish off with chocolate soup, made with homemade ice cream and nuts and flavored with cardamom and ask for a table near the lotus pond—on most nights in season you'll be serenaded by flute and tabla players.

Old Harbour Hotel, 1/328 Tower Rd., Fort Kochi. ℂ **0484/221-8006.** Reservations essential Dec and Jan. Main courses Rs 330–Rs 550, tiger prawns Rs 660, jumbo prawns Rs 770, mixed platter Rs 1,050, seafood platter Rs 1,350. MC, V. Daily 7:30–10:30am, noon–3pm, and 7:30–10:30pm.

SHOPPING

With the exception of Cinnamon (see below), where Bangalore-based buyers show off their exceptional eye for modern Indian design, and a small branch of the ever-popular **Fabindia** (1/279 Napier St.; ℂ **0484/221-7077;** www.fabindia.com), Fort Kochi itself caters primarily to mass tourist tastes. The goods for sale are neither cheap nor exceptional. You'll have far more fun exploring the antiques dealerships in neighboring Mattancherry, most of which are jam-packed with weird, wonderful, and genuine pieces from Kerala's multifangled past; catch a rickshaw to Crafters (see below), then wander around this area. The biggest outfit in the area, Crafters is less likely to offer discounts, but dig around the dark corners of the little shops tucked around this legendary antiques shop, and bargain hard: Try offering half of the quoted price, and settle halfway between the two. If you'd like to do your shopping in slightly more salubrious environs, then definitely set aside some time for **Ethnic Passage** (see below). Also in Jew Town and worth popping into is **Galleria Synagogue Art Gallery** (ℂ **0484/222-2544**), where local artists are well represented; art and antiques lovers should also check out **Lawrence Art Gallery** in Synagogue Lane (ℂ **0484/222-3657**). Finally, do stop off at **Traveller's Paradise** (see below)—you may go in only to support a worthy cause, but you'll probably emerge with bulging eco-friendly bags.

Cinnamon ★★★   A branch of Bangalore's trendy store, this is Kochi's most fashionable outlet. With a cool gallerylike ambience, Cinnamon sells modern *objets*, shoes, and fashions that are entirely homegrown and produced by some of the best designers in India (ask about garments by Abraham & Thakore, Vivek Narang, Sonum Dubal, Priyadarshini Rao, and Jason Anshu). Find fishing nets made into pillowcases, coconuts fashioned into purses, vintage prints of Hindu deities, silk caftans, and cotton dresses and tunics ideal for the Indian heat. Open Monday to Saturday 10am to 7pm. 1/658 Ridsdale Rd., Parade Ground, Fort Kochi. ℂ **0484/221-7124.**

Crafters   In the heart of historic Mattanchery's Jew Town, Crafters is an antiques fetishist's dream come true. A huge selection of unique antiques and handicrafts, ranging from religious curiosities to that perfect doorway, are displayed in five different stores, and piled up high in a massive warehouse style, with so much to take home you'll find it hard to leave empty-handed; staff members are dab hands at arranging for purchases to be shipped abroad. Before you purchase anything, though, do look around the other antiques shops in Jew Town; Crafters has the best selection, and prices are fair, but you won't find real bargains here. VI/141, Jew Town. ℂ **0484/222-3346,** -7652, or 93-8860-5069.

Ethnic Passage ★★   It's been a long time coming, but Kochi finally has what looks and feels like a smart retail arcade. Linking Jew Town's main bazaar with the synagogue, this chic little center was still partially vacant at the time of research, but with at least one quality bookstore (stocking tomes on India and esoterica) and an antique outlet up and running, and pretty handicrafts and jewelry for sale (and talk of Fabindia setting up shop here, too), it looks set to be *the* one-stop shopping destination in Old Kochi. Best of all, if you're exhausted from all that hard bargaining, you can rest up at **Café Jew Town,** imbibing the atmosphere along with a thick cake wedge. Jew Town. ℂ **0484/222-5601.**

Niraamaya ★   If you're in any way curious about the healing power of Ayurveda, pay a visit to this small *"Ayur vastra"* boutique, which sells organic cotton products that are

Kathakali & Kalaripayattu: Kerala's Ancient Art Forms

A stay in Kochi affords you the opportunity to sample Kerala's best-known classical art form—Kathakali, a performance style that delves into the world of demons, deities, soldiers, sages, and satyrs, taken from Indian epics such as the *Mahabharata*. Combining various theatrical and performance elements, it is said to have developed during the 16th century under the auspices of the Raja of Kottaraka, and today the best Kathakali school is in Kalamandalam, founded by a poet named Vallathol Narayan Menon in 1930. Here, students undergo a rigorous training program that lasts 6 years and includes massage techniques, extensive makeup training, and knowledge of the precise and subtle finger, body, and eye movements that constitute the language and grand emotions of Kathakali. There is also a host of instruments that may be mastered, as no performance is without musical accompaniment. So striking are the costumes, makeup, and jewelry associated with this form of dance-theater that the image of the elaborately adorned, heavily made-up, and almost masklike face of the Kathakali performer has become the state's most recognizable icon. Performers employ exaggerated facial expressions (only enhanced by the makeup— bright paint applied thickly to the face) and a highly technical set of symbolic hand gestures (known as *mudras*). Vocalists and musicians help set the mood, utilizing the *chengila* (gong), *elathalam* (small cymbals), and *chenda* and *maddalam* (drums). Traditionally, Kathakali performances are held for entire nights, often as part of festival events. In Kochi, however, a number of Kathakali groups stage short extracts of the longer pieces specifically for tourist consumption. Kerala is also renowned for its unique martial arts form: the supremely acrobatic Kalaripayattu, believed to be the oldest defense-combat system in the world. Apparently discovered in ancient times by traveling Buddhist monks who needed to protect themselves against marauding bandits, Kalaripayattu is believed to predate more recognizable forms, like kung-fu, that emerged farther east. For demonstrations of Kathakali and Kalaripayattu, see recommendations below.

apparently infused with Ayurvedic medicines. They stock a lovely range of men's shirts (from Rs 900) and women's tops (from Rs 500)—hand woven and dyed in subtle shades and natural colors, they're incredibly light and ideal for the hot Kerala climate. But the producers claim that the material on your body will also contribute to improved health. They also sell shawls, bed linen (apparently good for back pain), and yoga mats infused with similarly healthful potions. 1/622, Quiros St., Fort Kochi. (C) **0484/326-3465** or 93-4901-3173. www.ayurvastraonline.com.

Traveller's Paradise ★★★　 Under supervision of a French stylist, this community-oriented boutique carries a range of beautiful goods—from stylish linens and fabrics to handmade village crafts—with profits going to needy villages. Local women are employed, and the charitable organization based here arranges excursions (including backwater cruises and village tours) that benefit local communities and emphasize eco-friendly principles. K.L. Bernard Master Rd., Fort Kochi. (C) **0484/221-8633.** www.bloominthe naturalway.com.

(Moments) Ultimate Detox: Change Your Life & Recharge Your Soul at Kalari Kovilakom

Upon arriving at India's most intensive—and beautiful—Ayurvedic center, your shoes are removed, you're handed white cotton kurta pajamas, and as you're led to your suite, you pass a sign reminding you to "LEAVE YOUR WORLD BEHIND." Indeed, your time at **Kalari Kovilakom** ★★★—among the finest places in the world to experience no-nonsense mind-body realignment—will reshape your attitude to life, and prepare you to take on the world with renewed vigor (and a healthier body). That will only be after a period of at least 2 weeks, when you finally emerge from your intensive Ayurveda program. Forget about spas and quick-fix diets. Whether you're here to detox, shed pounds, or *finally* deal with a recurring ache, pain, nervous complaint, or heart condition, this is a hard-core system of getting the balance right through Ayurvedic treatments (with plenty of massage), yoga, meditation, and ancient dietary rules (strictly vegetarian, no refined oil, nothing artificial). You're also encouraged to get into a routine of flushing out your suppressed mental and emotional issues—painting, talking, and even praying are encouraged as ways of getting the subconscious a little more out in the open.

As much as this all sounds like we're describing the restrictive lifestyle of an ashram, you are in fact staying in a full-blown Keralite palace. Stepping over the threshold is like stepping into a beautiful film set, only all the big, splendidly decorated and authentically furnished rooms are real—and they come with modern luxuries (including air-conditioning, and handsome modern bathrooms). Kalari Kovilakom was built in the traditional Keralite style by the Rani (queen) of Kollengode in 1810. Attached to the main palace, where the royal family lived, is a Victorian-style guesthouse designed to accommodate Western guests (who, because they were deemed to be larger, were thought to require more space). Today, you can choose between the sumptuous Kovalikom suites, or the even more spectacular (and costlier) Venganad suites, not that it matters too much since just about everywhere you turn there's something beautiful to look at, be it a fantastic statue or a delicately decorated column.

The minimum stay here is 14 days, and because there are so few distractions (no TV, no shops, no bars—and you're encouraged to switch off your mobile phone) you start to feel and understand the passage of time; these will feel like

KOCHI AFTER DARK

When the sun starts to sink, you should be watching it turn the harbor waters pale pink, either on a harbor cruise or, a cocktail in hand, from the **Harbour View** bar at The Gateway Hotel Marine Drive in Ernakulam (see above). Once the sun has set, head down M.G. Road to the Avenue Regent hotel and grab a sofa at **Loungevity,** a cool white minimalist lounge bar, and watch the city of Kochi network at the trendiest nightspot in the untouristy part of the city (© **0484/237 7977;** www.avenuehotels.in). Alternatively, if you want to stay in Fort Kochi, a Kathakali or Kalaripayattu demonstration (see below) the most precious and meaningful 2 weeks of your life. This is a program sought after by high-profile businesspeople and world leaders in need of the ultimate detox, destress, and rewiring. From the time you arrive, you're on a strict program of Ayurvedic treatments—starting with deep cleansing treatments that involve taking medicated ghee that purges toxins from your body, not to mention bringing all kinds of emotions to the fore. Meals are individually prescribed by your Ayurvedic physician—and there's none of the muck that might slip into the daily diet, even by accident, in the outside world. At mealtimes—after your hands are ceremoniously washed—each dish is explained to you, and you're encouraged to maintain silence as you dine, helping you focus on the food, the nourishment it provides, and the energetic properties contained within. On top of that, you'll be drinking nothing but medicated or ginger-infused water—for some junkies, giving up caffeine may be the first step in a string of achievements here, but the effects are quickly visible, which does encourage you to push through. It's comforting, too, knowing that fellow guests have also given up the outside world.

This is not an ashram, but neither is it a place for any run of-the-mill lazy vacation—there is plenty of hard work and even some unpleasant moments (especially during the initial phase when your body is sloughing off the worst of what your normal life has done to it). Getting the balance right can be a very difficult adjustment for anyone grown too attached to everyday life (and that means all of us). But if you have the will and the money and feel the time is right to change your world forever, then this could well be the most rewarding time you ever spent away from home. The minimum 2-week *manashanthy* (stress relief) program costs 5,000€ to 6,800€ for a single person (7,450€–9,200€ double; rates depend on the type of suite you occupy), while the *pancha karma* (rejuvenation) and *sthanlyakina chikitsa* (weight reduction) programs start at 6,900€ per person, or 10,550€ double, for 21 days. Various other packages, including the 28-day antiaging *(rasayam chikitsa)*, are available, or you can have the doctors design a completely individual set of treatments for you. Rates include everything from airport transfers to daily Ayurvedic treatments, and you have the attention of your Ayurvedic doctor and yoga instructor throughout your stay.

can easily fill the gap before a fine seafood dinner. Or simply spend the evening sampling glass after glass of India's top vintages at The Malabar House's tiny wine lounge, **Divine** (see "Where to Dine, above).

Cultural Performances

In Fort Kochi, the **Kerala Kathakali Centre ★★★** (Kathakali Mandapam, K.B. Jacob Rd.; © **0484/221-5827** or -7552; www.kathakalicentre.com) near Santa Cruz Basilica hosts the best Kathakali demonstration in the city (see "Kathakali & Kalaripayattu:

Kerala's Ancient Art Forms," above). Kathakali performances (Rs 200) are held daily from 6 to 7:30pm, with makeup demonstrations starting at 5pm. Afterwards, the center also hosts hour-long Indian classical music performances, starting at 8pm; on Saturdays, another classical dance form is performed instead of the music concert. Martial arts demo shows are held in the afternoon at 4pm. If you're interested in attending a proper all-night Kathakali performance at a temple, speak to one of the organizers at Kerala Kathakali; some of their top performers are often involved in authentic rituals.

If you want to cram as much variety into the evening as you possibly can, then catch the kaleidoscopic look at Kerala's traditional dance forms at the strictly-for-tourists **Greenix Village,** opposite Fort House hotel, just down the road from the Brunton Boatyard. The nightly showcase is a bit heavy-handed, with a thundering narration explaining each of the dances, but at least you get to see forms other than Kathakali, including a short *theyyam* piece (not quite so riveting when it's out of context), and a sampling of *koodiyattam,* the oldest surviving Sanskrit theater form. Tickets are Rs 300, and in season it's probably a good idea to book in advance (Kalvathy Rd., Fort Kochi; ✆ **0484/221-7000;** www.greenix.in). The theater has a permanent exhibition on all of Kerala's dance forms, which you can walk through prior to the show, and there's a good little bookstore to peruse afterwards. Shows start at 6:30pm (with makeup from 5:30pm) and last an hour. Kalaripayattu sessions happen 8 to 9am and 3 to 4pm.

The other, more famous Kathakali venue, featured on a number of television programs, is inconveniently located in Ernakulam, near the Junction Railway station—the **See India Foundation** (Kalathi Parambil Lane; ✆ **0484/237-6471**) hosts nightly performances, introduced to the audience by P. K. Devan—he reveals the religious roots and philosophy behind the *katha* (story) and *kali* (play). Performances are held between 6:45 and 8pm; makeup starts at 6pm.

While there are a number of dedicated training schools *(kalaris)* where Kerala's traditional martial arts form, Kalaripayattu, is taught for its intended purpose, it is usually performed in a staged environment for tourists. **Shiva Shakti Kalari Kshetram** (Kaloor, Ernakulam; ✆ **98-9529-0635**) holds daily demonstrations of Kalaripayattu from 5 to 6pm; the institute also provides training and Ayurvedic massage based on principles derived from the art of Kalari. Another option is **Dakshina Bharatha Kalari** (✆ **0484/221-8776**), with daily shows at 7pm.

2 LAKSHADWEEP ★★★

Between 200km (124 miles) and 450km (279 miles) W of Kerala's coast

Ask any globe-trotting island-hopper if the world still holds any undiscovered gems, and Lakshadweep will be among the first names to crop up. One of India's best-kept secrets, the 36 atolls and coral reefs making up the remote Union Territory of Lakshadweep are an extension of the better-known Maldives island group. Only three Lakshadweep islands—Agatti, Kadmat, and Bangaram—are open to foreign tourists, and the Indian government employs a strictly enforced entry-permit system. All the islands are "owned" by the indigenous people, and land is unavailable for purchase by nonnatives—even a man marrying a local woman may not buy land here.

Ten islands in the archipelago are populated, almost exclusively by Malayalam-speaking Sunni Muslims who make their living from fishing and harvesting coconuts. Only

Minicoy Island, which is closest to the nearby Maldives, shares aspects of its neighbor's culture, including a Maldivian dialect known as Mahl.

Being Muslim, the islands are officially dry, and alcohol is only available on Bangaram, which is technically uninhabited by locals; avoid carrying any liquor with you. You are strongly advised to bring insect repellent since the mosquitoes become alarmingly active once the sun descends.

ESSENTIALS

PERMITS   Foreigners can only visit the islands with prebooked accommodations and an entry permit. Visitors intending to stay at the Bangaram Island Resort (the best of the two options available to foreign travelers) can have all permit arrangements made through the **CGH Earth central reservations** (Casino Building, Willingdon Island, Cochin 682 003; ✆ **0484/301-1711;** fax 0484/266-8001; www.cghearth.com). Foreigners must supply their name and address, as well as nationality, place and date of birth, passport number, place and date of issue, and expiration date, and also give their Indian visa number and expiration date. Permits usually take 2 full working days to be processed; they cost Rs 200 for adults over 18, and Rs 100 for children. The CGH Group will also book your flight to and from Kochi (or Bangalore) for you.

To make your own permit arrangements (a laborious process; best avoided), contact the **Society for Nature, Tourism and Sports (SPORTS)** run by Lakshadweep Tourism (✆ **0484/266-8387**) in Kochi. Or contact their Delhi office (✆ **011/2338-6807**).

VISITOR INFORMATION   See "Permits," above. For details about Lakshadweep, contact the Assistant Manager, SPORTS, Lakshadweep Administrative Office, Willingdon Island, Kochi (✆ **0484/266-8387;** 10am–1pm and 2–5pm; closed Sun and second Sat of the month).

GETTING THERE   Unless you fancy a time-munching trip from Kochi by ship (14–20 hr.), you'll have to get to Bangaram by air: Kingfisher (www.flykingfisher.com) flies daily from Cochin (and Bengaluru) to the tiny airfield on Agatti (Agathi) Island; the private airline usually offers a better deal than state-owned Indian Airlines, but do check for deals. You can also leave all the travel arrangements in the hands of CGH Earth when you book your accommodation; at press time they were getting return tickets for Rs 12,000. At Agatti you'll be met by a resort representative who'll usher you to a waiting boat anchored near the shore not far from the airport for a memorable 90-minute journey to nearby Bangaram Island (Rs 1,400). Alternatively, you could shell out for a transfer via helicopter (Rs 6,000), which is the only way of transferring if you visit during the monsoon season (mid-May through mid-Sept).

DIVING THE REEFS

Experienced divers rank the reefs of Lakshadweep among the best diving destinations in Asia, particularly the coral islands of Bangaram, Tinakara, Pirelli 1, and Pirelli 2. Bangaram Island Resort hosts **Lacadives,** a small dive center that was the first CMAS (an international underwater-sports federation) dive organization in India, with its headquarters on the island of Kadmat. Bangaram is known in particular for unique dives to spots such as Manta Point, where manta rays are a seasonal attraction; the Grand Canyon around the isle itself offers magical underwater viewing, as does Perumal Par, a submerged bank with world class diving (Rs 3,000 per dive, excluding equipment hire). Lacadives offers diving courses, rents out equipment, and conducts up to three dives a day, as well as night diving. If you're not a qualified diver, you can rent a mask and go on one of the resort's snorkeling trips to a nearby wreck where an assortment of marine fauna will have you begging for more; alternatively, bring a doctor's certificate indicating that you're fit to dive and you can have your first scuba experience here (Rs 24,000 for a 4-day course, including four open-water dives; Rs 7,500 for the 1-day resort course). For details, contact the **Lacadives Diving Centre** (at Bangaram: ✆ **93-8861-9494;** in Mumbai: E-20, Everest Bldg., Tardeo Rd.; ✆ **022/6662-7381** or -7382; www.lacadives.com; lacadives@gmail.com). Note that there is no diving during the monsoons (mid-May through Sept).

WHERE TO STAY

Bangaram Island Resort ★★★   Eco-consciously designed to all but disappear into the surroundings, the modest resort remains quite basic, with emphasis on the captivating setting rather than fussy luxuries—the result is pure heaven. Up against the biggest hoteliers of the day, CGH (now CGH Earth) won the rights to host visitors here based on their commitment to ecological principles long before they were fashionable. Today, this peaceful 50-hectare (123-acre) island is still nothing but untouched beaches and towering coconut palms—no newspapers, television, minibars, or even air-conditioning get in the way of experiencing the island's beauty. Guest cottages—thatch-covered huts, really—are arranged in a row a short distance back from the beach, and are spartan and clean: simple cane furniture, mesh screen windows, and private porches. The atmosphere here is so removed from workaday worries (and you don't need to worry about snakes, scorpions, or monkeys either—although there are plenty of insects) that you'll find no excuses not to recline in your hammock and stare into the magnificent cobalt waters, or discover a new addiction to diving, which is a major draw. On foot (take shoes for coral-covered stretches), you can skirt the entire island in about an hour; en route you will discover a host of stunning milky-white beaches to call your own. There's an Ayurvedic massage center for those days when sunbathing gets too stressful, and early risers can salute the rising sun with yoga on the helipad at 6:30am. It's the stuff of an old-fashioned dream vacation.

Bangaram Island, Lakshadweep. Reservations: CGH Earth, Casino Bldg., Willingdon Island, Cochin 682 003. ✆ **0484/301-1711.** Fax 0484/266-8001. www.cghearth.com. crs@cghearth.com. 24 cottages, all with shower only. Nov–Apr 300€–360€ standard hut double, 550€–600€ 2-bedroom deluxe hut (sleeps 4), 125€ extra person; May–Oct Rs 8,500 2-bedroom deluxe hut (sleeps 4), Rs 2,860 extra person. Rates include all meals and taxes. Discounts for stays of 7 nights or more in high season. AE, DC, MC, V. **Amenities:** Restaurant, bar; airport transfers by boat (Rs 1,400 return, Sept 15–May 15 only) or by helicopter (Rs 3,200; May 16–Sept 14); Ayurvedic center; beach volley ball; boating, kayaking and sailing; dive center; fishing; snorkeling; telephone; yoga and meditation. In room: No phone.

---

3 THE BACKWATERS ★★★

Alappuzha is 85km (53 miles) S of Kochi; Kumarakom is 95km (59 miles) S of Kochi

Kerala's backwaters comprise a web of waterways that forms a natural inland transport network stretching from **Kochi,** the northern gateway, to **Kollam** (or **Quilon,** as it's been renamed), the backwaters' southernmost town. At its heart is Vembanad Lake, on the eastern shores of which lie the top-notch resorts of **Kumarakom** and its Bird Sanctuary, and on its south bank, the little town of **Alappuzha,** the unofficial capital of the backwaters. Inland, just 12km (7½ miles) east of Kumarakom, is **Kottayam,** the bustling town described by Arundhati Roy in her Booker Prize–winning *The God of Small Things.*

(Moments) Snake Boat Races

Every year Kerala's backwater canals host the world's largest team sport, when scores of streamlined 30m (100-ft.) chundanvalloms—commonly known as snake boats because their prow looks like the raised hood of a snake—are propelled across the waters at impressive speeds, cheered on by an exuberant audience. Typically, snake boats are manned by four helmsmen, 25 singers, and up to 100 oarsmen rowing in unison to the terrific rhythm of the *vanchipattu,* or "song of the boatman." The oldest and most popular event is the **Champakulam Moolam Boat Race,** held in monsoon-soaked July, but the most famous water battle is undoubtedly the **Nehru Trophy Boat Race,** held on the second Saturday of August on the Punnamada backwaters of Alleppey in conjunction with Kerala's important *Onam* harvest festival. Tickets for the event, which features at least 16 competing *chundanvalloms* and attracts thousands of excited supporters, are available from the **District Tourism Promotion Council office** (see "Visitor Information," below), but best to ask your hotel or houseboat operator to arrange these. If you're not visiting during the rainy season, you'll be glad to hear that a rerun of the event— organized with the tourist season in mind, so be warned— happens in February.

Located at the foot of the Western Ghats, it has two historically significant (but ultimately missable) early Syrian Christian churches. But, then again, you're hardly here to visit monuments and attractions—you're here to lap up a blissfully melancholic way of life, and witness daily bucolic dramas played out upon the waterways and among the coconut groves.

Kumarakom has the most luxury accommodations, all strung along the shores of Vembanad Lake, but unless you're a dedicated birder, there's not a great deal to do here. Indulge in Ayurvedic therapies, and laze under the tropical sun—that's about as busy as your day is likely to get; then board a houseboat cruise, where the passing scenery and languid pace (and, should you be paying for luxury, discreet service) is enough to lull you into a comfortable coma. Between November and March, the local **Bird Sanctuary** becomes home to numerous migratory flocks, many of which fly in from Siberia. Regularly seen here are little cormorants, darters (or snake birds), night herons, golden-backed woodpeckers, tree pies, and crow pheasants. Given its exclusivity and sublime setting, Kumarakom does not offer accommodations for budget-oriented travelers; for that you'll need to look farther south to **Alappuzha** (pronounced Ala-*pur[d]*-ha, or Alleppey if you can't be bothered), also the focal point of backwater cruise operators, and the only backwater town worth spending a few hours indulging in a bit of retail therapy.

The entire backwaters region is a tranquil paradise and sustains a delightfully laid-back way of life that has endured for centuries—perfect for sultry, idle, do-nothing houseboat adventures that take you into the heart of Kerala country life. Despite the massive increase in traffic from the tourist boom, floating along these waters will be the highlight of your sojourn in south India (see "Hiring the Best Houseboat," below).

ESSENTIALS

VISITOR INFORMATION   The official authority responsible for dishing out information to visitors is the **District Tourism Promotion Council,** which has various offices in the different backwaters towns. The main office is in **Alappuzha,** near the Boat Jetty (℃ **0477/225-3308;** www.dtpcalappuzha.com; daily 9am–5:30pm). If your main interest is getting information on houseboats, see "Hiring the Best Houseboat," below.

GETTING THERE   By Road   Taxis are easily available in all major towns and cities. From Kochi a taxi should cost at most Rs 1,200 and get you to Kottayam in about 1½ hours; farther south, Alappuzha is better connected (better road) and should take around 1 hour. It is a 5-hour journey from Idukki/Periyar, the same from Munnar. Trivandrum lies 4 hours away.

By Air   For the northern backwater towns, the nearest airport is at Kochi; around 76km (47 miles) by road by car to Kottayam/Kumarakom, or 85km (53 miles) to Alappuzha.

By Train   Though there are railheads in Kottayam (15 min. from the Kumarakom resorts), Alappuzha, and Kollam, your best bet is to get to Trivandrum or Kochi and then head out by road; all resorts offer transfers.

GETTING AROUND   By Water-Taxi & Ferry   Kottayam, Alappuzha, and Kollam are all connected by ferries that ply the route, with six departures to Kottayam daily. State Water Transport Department ferries between Alappuzha and Kottayam (a 3-hr. round-trip) depart from the tourist boat jetty near the bus station. Ferries between Alappuzha and Kollam take 8 hours, departing from both the Alleppey and Kollam boat jetties at 10:30am and arriving in Kollam/Alappuzha around 6:30pm (cost is Rs 300); after this you can catch a road taxi back. Be warned, though, that although you'll spot Chinese fishing nets and typical Kerala houses along the way (not to mention all kinds of non-routine activity, you need real stamina and patience to "enjoy" the entire day-long trip. If you're in a hurry you can ask about speedboats (Rs 700 per hour; maximum four passengers), which more than halve the journey time (but are more injurious to the environment).

GUIDED TOURS, CRUISES & PACKAGED TRIPS   Alappuzha's well-meaning **District Tourism Promotion Council** (near Boat Jetty, Alappuzha; ℃ **0477/225-3308**) organizes tickets for the daily backwater ferry between Kollam, Kottayam, and Alappuzha (see above). DTPC also offers private cruises costing upwards of Rs 200 per hour on a motorboat, and around Rs 150 per hour on a "country boat"; an overnight trip (22 hr.) on a *kettuvallam* houseboat will run you Rs 3,500. See "Hiring the Best Houseboat," below, for recommended guided overnight trips. Alternatively, any of the accommodations listed below can organize backwaters cruises—for many it's part of the package, though this is definitely not the same as having a houseboat to call your own. Finally, if you don't feel like planning any of this, but don't mind entrusting yourself to a classy, top-notch organization, take one of the all-inclusive deals offered by **Malabar Escapes** (the owners of The Malabar House in Kochi; www.malabarescapes.com); not only do they have one of the best backwater properties in Kerala, **Privacy,** and a super houseboat (see "Hiring the Best Houseboat," below), but they can line all these options up to give you a truly upmarket sojourn, taking in the best southern Kerala has to offer.

CRUISING THE BACKWATERS

Reset your watch to a rhythm of life that has gone unchanged for centuries by boarding a *kettuvallam,* the long, beautifully crafted cargo boats that ply the waterways with cargo (if you don't mind being referred to as such). An engineering feat, a *kettuvallam* is made from lengths of ironwood, *anjili,* or jackwood, and not a single nail is used in the construction—it's joined with thick coir (from the outer shell of a coconut) ropes, and sealed with fish oil and a black caustic resin produced by boiling cashew kernels.

Cruising Kerala on the World's Smallest Luxury Liner

Leave it to Oberoi to take the traditional backwater cruise to new heights with the **MV Vrinda**—not exactly a liner, but the ultimate in luxury on Kerala's backwaters, and very Agatha Christie. After all, only on board the MV *Vrinda* can you find yourself watching life along the river from a comfy rattan chair on the breezy upper-deck lounge, or from your plush settee in the air-conditioned dining room while staff keeps a watchful eye out for a raised finger. On the first night, after a scenic 4-hour cruise on Vembanad Lake, you dock at a jetty for dinner (a thoroughly elegant affair accompanied by Kathakali dancers), then bed down in one of only eight smart cabins, each decked out with luxuries like TV and DVD, en-suite showers, and lovely king-size beds. The following day, the boat makes its way to Lake Pamba, where you can climb aboard a small rice boat to explore the narrower backwaters; the following day another rice boat excursion takes you to see an 18th-century church and century-old Hindu temple at Nedumudy, with a qualified guide. Three nights later you wend your way back by road to Kochi. Typical of the Oberoi, food is outstanding (there's an a la carte menu but you can pretty much get what you want) and you are treated like royalty—perfect if you prefer to travel in a somewhat sanitized manner, ensconced in a luxurious cocoon. The 3-night package runs from October to April and costs Rs 95,000 for two, including all meals, excursions, and Kochi airport transfer. To reserve your berth, contact Oberoi Hotels & Resorts at © **800-11-2030** or 011/2389-0606 (www.oberoihotels.com); children under 12 are not permitted.

The houseboat experience allows you to aimlessly drift past villages, temples, and churches and be thoroughly exposed to the rural lifestyle of the backwaters. As if you're on the very large set of a reality TV show (with a huge dollop of the Discovery Channel thrown in), you can watch as women, unperturbed by your drifting presence, wash their long ebony tresses or pound away at laundry; children play at the water's edge and men dive for mussels; and elephants and water buffalo wade at will. Fishermen suavely holding umbrellas above their heads suddenly drift by, while floating vendors using single-log canoes and other modest craft deliver commodities such as rice and coir fiber. On the shore, toddy tappers whisk up palm trees (note that you can ask to stop at a village to buy unforeseen necessities like beer or coconut toddy); see "Scrambling for Their Tipple," below. And when the sun sets, the sky lights up in magnificent shades of orange and red. Gliding past the rural communities that cling to the banks is without a doubt one of the most relaxing and romantic ways to witness a timeless lifestyle, where people rely on impossibly tiny tracts of land to cultivate subsistence crops and keep a few animals, using slender jackfruit wood canoes to get around, deliver goods, and do a spot of fishing. And of course it is always rather marvelous to be waited on hand and foot by three servants.

The original concept of turning cargo boats into tourist cruise vessels was the brainchild of Babu Varghese of TourIndia (an outfit that incidentally fell into temporary disarray since Varghese employed a hit man to punish his partner—high business drama,

> ## (Fun Facts) Scrambling for Their Tipple
>
> For generations, agile young village men have been clambering up coconut palms to tap into the sweet sap known as toddy, or *kallu,* which is collected from the flower pod. Like their fathers and their fathers' fathers, these "toddy tappers" have made a good living over the years harvesting the sap to drink right away (sweet and refreshing, but definitely an acquired taste) or to ferment into an alcoholic drink. The morning's toddy is already a heady tipple by evening—by the next day, it's prodigiously potent.

India-style). Varghese transformed the *kettuvallam* into a livable houseboat by expanding the original size to include two or three rooms, a flush toilet, a shower, and a small viewing or sunbathing platform. With designs that owe some allegiance to the Chinese junk but that more closely resemble a small Sydney Opera House, these beautiful crafts were initially propelled by pole but now more usually by a small (and it is hoped quiet) motor. In 2007 the state government finally started taking action against those engines that pollute, and not a minute too soon: 8 years back there were perhaps 15 houseboats operating out of Alappuzha; today the figure is in excess of 650—all the more reason to be careful with whom you book, and to seriously consider coming in the off-season.

While the general idea is to wind your way aimlessly through the waterways, one of the most popular stop-off points for visitors is **Champakulam,** where 500-year-old **St. Mary's Church** shows definite traces of Hindu influence—from the small statue of Christ assuming a pose typical of Krishna, to the custom of leaving one's footwear outside. Another stop worth scheduling is at the **Amritapuri Ashram** (© **0476/289-6179** or -6278; www.amritapuri.org), home of the world's most famous female guru, **Amma,** who is endearingly known as the "Hugging Mother." The Mother is today a global phenomenon—some call her a living god—and is said to believe in physically manifesting her love and compassion for humanity—she has embraced thousands of devotees, literally; if she's not on tour, this is exactly what she will do to you! If this sounds a little too touchy-feely, visit just to wander the ashram grounds and have lunch with those residing there; the Raheem Residency (see "Where to Stay," below) organizes visits here from Alleppey (2 hr. away by speedboat).

Note: Two more stops worth considering (reached this time by vehicle) are the **Elephant Orphanage,** where you can get up close and personal with the elephants (usually including at least one baby) that are cared for here, as well as **Mannar** and **Aranmula,** towns famous for their metal icons and mirrors respectively.

WHERE TO STAY

Ideally you will combine a night or two at one of the resorts or guesthouses recommended below with at least two more on a houseboat. Most of the top luxury resorts are strung along the eastern shores of Lake Vembanad; the exceptions are the top-rated **Privacy, Olavipe,** and **Green Lagoon** (all reviewed below), all of which lie on backwaters on the northern end of the lake. You can reach most of them by car, but many prefer to pick you up from a prearranged jetty, which heightens the sense of escape. Some, like **Coconut Lagoon, Philipkutty's Farm,** and **Green Lagoon,** can in fact only be reached by water. In short, this is one area you should plan and book in advance regardless of season, so that the necessary transfer arrangements can be made. Alleppey is the only town worth exploring at any length, and perhaps a better contrast to a lakeside resort; there is also a good guesthouse here—Raheem Residency (reviewed later). *Note:* Taxes usually run 15%; do check whether it's included when asking for rate quotes. From May to September, rates are generally half those of the peak season, which is December and January (also when the influx of tourists really undermines the experience of being here in the first place); September is a particularly good month to visit for houseboat excursions. Unless you're staying at one of the smaller places, don't even think about coming here between Christmas and early January—prices skyrocket and the atmosphere will be anything but relaxing.

Lake Vembanad & Surroundings

A stay on the backwaters has become an essential stop on any Kerala itinerary, small wonder then that there has been a surge in development on the eastern shores of Vembanad Lake, with its spectacular sunset views to the west. In fact, there's a daunting array of options hereabouts—spanning the gamut from bustling resorts to splendidly intimate, well-run homestays. In truth, there's something to satisfy all tastes and budgets, and there are small, relatively untouristy spots far from the maelstrom, too.

Very Expensive

Green Lagoon Resort ★★★ Why have a room to yourself when you can have an island? If there's one Backwater spot where you'll feel the urge to totally bliss out, this is it. Initially a retirement project, Green Lagoon is a collection of beautiful reconstituted Kerala wooden houses on several small islands, all now linked with footbridges. Each luxury villa has its own large pool, a butler, and dizzyingly good food, most of it home-grown, fresh out of the water, or delivered by boat. Should you so desire, your only interaction with the outside world will be through your butler or at mealtimes—and as you watch villagers catching crabs and fish by hand in the water just beyond your large private garden. On the other hand, there's a stylish private gallery (of art and traditional artifacts from the owner's private collection) on one island, and a boat to whiz you off to the city or to explore nearby villages on other islands. At dusk, temple music drifts across the water and you can make out all kinds of domestic activity on nearby islands. It's not exactly cheap, but if you can afford it, the Green Lagoon is the best deal on the backwaters—a unique combination of sultry-chic styling and immersion in an otherworldly waterscape.

Island House, Vettila Thuruthu, Eramalloor P.O. 688 537. © **98-4605-1630,** 98-4601-4911, or 0478/645-1811. www.green-lagoon.com. 4 units. Nov–Dec 23 and Mar–Apr 360€–400€ double; Dec 24–Jan 5 600€–640€ double; Jan 6–Feb 480€–520€; May–July 120€–160€; Aug–Oct 180€–220€; 10% more per each extra person. Rates include breakfast, driver's accommodation, Internet, and mobile phone use; 15% tax extra. AE, MC, V. **Amenities:** Multiple dining venues; dedicated butler; gallery; 1 outdoor pool per villa. *In room:* A/C, TV/DVD w/movies, CD with discs, fridge, hair dryer, Wi-Fi (free).

Kumarakom Lake Resort ★★★ (Kids) Like so many of its predecessors, this large award-winning resort comprises exquisite *tharavadu*-style carved teak and rosewood houses with curved terra-cotta tiled roofs, many of them reassembled originals salvaged from Kerala villages. The interiors are decidedly more luxurious than those of their neighbors, however, with rooms furnished to a very high standard; some feature expensive antiques and lovely examples of temple mural art. Each room (except the eight pavilion rooms in the new, characterless block at the back) has a tiny garden into which open granite-floored drench showers and basins have been installed. The main pool is at

Hiring the Best Houseboat

Take this cruise at the right time, and it will possibly be the highlight of your holiday in Kerala, so book during shoulder season, and make sure you hire a good boat. *Kettuvallam* houseboats are available at various levels of luxury, and may be rented for day trips or for sleep-in journeys of several days; we recommend that you spend 2 nights on board, since it takes one to realize how relaxing the process is, and the major attractions are watching the setting sun turn the lake orange before settling down in the middle of the lake for the night (all boats must be moored or anchored by 6pm for the fishermen to cast their night nets), and witnessing the activities of households on the smaller backwaters at dawn and dusk (only possible on the second day). Most houseboats feature solar-panel power and heating, biotoilets, and an average cruising speed of 8 to 10kmph (5–6 mph). Although the facilities might strike some as rather basic, you'll be spoiled rotten by your private team—minimum of two, a cook and pilot—who work hard to make your experience unique and exceptional (and discreetly manage to leave you to experience the backwaters in peace). Meals are authentic Kerala fare—if you're curious about Kerala cuisine, you're welcome to observe proceedings in the tiny kitchen at the rear end of the boat. With the huge increase of traffic on the backwaters, don't expect exclusivity—try to avoid booking over the peak season. September is to our mind the best month, when the water is high, harvest is due, races are scheduled, and tourist numbers are relatively low.

One of the simplest and most sensitive conversions of the *kettuvallam* has been done by **Spice Coast Cruises** ★★ (House Boats, Puthenangadi, Alleppey; ✆ **0484/266-8221** or 0478/258-2615; spicecoastcruise@cghearth.com), who have cleverly increased the number of "awnings" (for views as well as breeze) and created a comfortable sun deck "bed" with white bolster cushions on the elevated section of the boat up front—perfect for lounging around with a book (though the "captain" steers from the front, you soon forget his presence); just behind is your coir-carpeted dining room, furnished with unpretentious antiques. The tiny bedroom comes with A/C (running at night only), and in our experience staff struck just the right balance between attentiveness and discretion. Rates are 290€ to 380€ double during high season (Rs 7,730 in the off-season), all meals included; while a two-bedroom (sleeping four) costs 475€ to 535€, or Rs 10,825 per night in low season.

Three more reputable companies, each with huge and reliable fleets, are **Lakes & Lagoons** (✆ **098-4705-1566;** lakes_lagoon@satyam.net.in), **Rainbow Cruises** (✆ **0477/224-1375;** www.backwaterkerala.com; reservations@rainbowcruises.in), and **Soma Houseboats.** The latter specialize in boats with a separate elevated viewing platform; for this luxury make sure you book one

the water's edge with a bar adjacent—perfect for sundowners—while in another section a second meandering pool snakes its way past the "pool villa" cottages, which means you can swim around the property directly from your back door. The best of these is no. 144, of its "Upper Deck" houseboats (© **0471/226-8101;** www.somahouseboats. com); prices vary according to season, number of bedrooms, and the length of your cruise, but you should be able to get a basic, air-conditioned one-bedroom houseboat for as little as Rs 9,250 during the season (much less if you chose a quieter period). Both Rainbow and Soma have earned Gold Star classification from the state government and are considered the top of their class.

If you prefer to go with sentiment, you can also investigate **TourIndia** (© 98-9560-5243; www.tourindiakerala.com), the company that pioneered the houseboat concept and were then imitated by countless others. They've stuck to their guns, though, and now operate 12 boats.

But if you don't mind forgoing the traditional *kettavallam* design, the best houseboat experience is aboard ***Discovery*** ★★★ (© 0484/221-6666; www. malabarescapes.com). Launched in late-2006 by Malabar Escapes (Kerala's much-lauded boutique hotel chain, responsible for The Malabar House in Fort Cochin), this is a gorgeous modern interpretation of the houseboat concept, with a large upper deck where you dine and sunbathe (furnished with dining table and loungers), a comfortable and stylish bedroom (though no reading lamps), large shower room and dressing area, and a separate, spacious lounge—all A/C. The team works hard to create routes where you won't come across other houseboats, but the likelihood is slim these days, and you will probably dock your final night at Privacy (see below), one of our favorite backwaters villas, from where you start and end your journey. The only drawback, besides the hefty price tag (350€–450€ per night, including all meals), is the early morning "check-out"—you're required to be off the boat by 10am—no doubt another great reason to top and tail your houseboat tour at Privacy. You can also opt for a 3-night package on board the boat, with 2½ full days spent getting a better understanding of backwaters life; you'll visit a market, dine in an authentic village home (one of the best meals you'll have), and watch kathakali in it's spiritual context in a temple. *Discovery* has an edge of modernity and style that makes it our personal pick as far as houseboats go.

Another top option if money is no object is the small fleet of well-equipped houseboats belonging to **Kumarakom Lake Resort** (p. 267)—they're among the most luxurious on the lake, and highly recommended. They are also slightly cheaper than Discovery; Rs 15,000 to Rs 22,500 one-bedroom, Rs 25,000 to Rs 35,000 two-bedroom, Rs 2,000 extra person. In addition to all meals and taxes, these rates include access to the facilities at the Resort, too.

But for 100% luxury and genuflecting service from India's best-trained hoteliers, the top-of-the-range choice is of course the ***Vrinda;*** see "Cruising Kerala on the World's Smallest Luxury Liner," above.

which is right on the edge of the lake, with fabulous views. Altogether more private are the heritage villas, which now all have large plunge pools alongside the outdoor bathroom; slightly more expensive villas also have lake views.

Kumarakom North P.O., Kottayam 686 566. © **0481/252-4900** or -4501. Fax 0481/252-4987. www.the paul.in. klresort@vsnl.com. 59 units, 3 houseboats. Mar–Nov Rs 14,000–Rs 17,000 luxury pavilion double and meandering pool villa double, Rs 17,000–Rs 24,500 heritage villa, Rs 42,000–Rs 62,000 presidential suite; Rs 3,000 extra bed; Dec–-Feb Rs 22,000–Rs 30,000 luxury pavilion double and meandering pool villa double, Rs 30,500–Rs 42,500 heritage villa, Rs 72,000–Rs 85,000 presidential suite, from Rs 6,000 extra person. Rates include breakfast and local transfers; presidential suite rates include airport transfers; 15% tax extra. Minimum 2-night stay. Houseboats: Rs 15,000–Rs 22,500 1-bedroom, Rs 25,000–Rs 35,000 2-bedroom, Rs 2,000 extra person. Houseboat rates include all meals and access to resort facilities; 15% tax extra. AE, DC, MC, V. **Amenities:** 2 restaurants, bar; free local railway station or boat jetty transfers; airport transfers (Rs 4,500); babysitting; bicycles; billiards; boat rides; children's play area; cultural program; fishing; health club and Ayurvedic massage center; 2 large outdoor pools and Jacuzzi; room service; table tennis; Wi-Fi (in public areas and business center; free); yoga. *In room:* A/C, TV, hair dryer, minibar, Wi-Fi (in heritage villas; free).

The Zuri Kumarakom (Overrated)

Gleaming black lacquer-coated gods dot the fringes of a vast, overmanicured lawn; reception desks are miniature reproduction boats; golf carts zip guests between their rooms and the restaurants—it's soon clear why staff at this, the former Radisson Plaza Resort, wears beige uniforms. It's a resort that could be just about anywhere and, in fact, the design really pulls your attention away from the backwater action you came to witness. Sadly, unless you book one of the extremely pricey lake-view pool villas—which are indeed lovely, positioned as they are right on the shore of the lake, each very private and with its own generously sized plunge pool and a magical lake vista—you are paying a lot of money for a nice new room with a view of another nice new room. For some reason the architects saw fit to design the entire resort around a man-made "lagoon," so most rooms circle what is really just a big pond. In its defense, The Zuri offers everything you'd expect from a five-star resort, with the exception of equitable service—some of the people working here are borderline hostile and, if you prefer the resort lifestyle, it's hard to see why you wouldn't rather opt for Kumarakom Lake Resort, where the architecture at least evokes some kind of local atmosphere.

Karottukayal, Kumarakom, Kottayam 686 563. © **0481/252-7272.** Fax 0481/252-7282. www.thezurihotels. com. reservations.kumarakom@thezurihotels.com. 72 units. Rs 17,000–Rs 18,000 Zuri double, Rs 18,500–Rs 22,000 deluxe double, Rs 23,000–Rs 30,000 cottage double, Rs 50,000–Rs 75,000 presidential pool villa. Rates include breakfast; tax extra. AE, MC, V. **Amenities:** 2 restaurants, lounge, 2 bars, cigar bar; airport transfers (Rs 3,500); amphitheater for cultural performances; bicycles; billiards; fishing; health club and spa; large outdoor pool w/Jacuzzi; room service; yoga and meditation. *In room* A/C, TV, butler (in pool villas), hair dryer, minibar.

Expensive

Coconut Lagoon ★★★ (Kids) If private alfresco showers and hammocks rather than room service and television are your idea of bliss, then this is your kind of lakeside idyll. Some of the reassembled wooden *tharavads* here date from the early 1700s, and each has been reassembled according to ancient carpentry rules known as *thachu shashtra*. The emphasis here is on providing an authentic Kerala feel and having as little impact as possible on the natural environment. Indeed, much of the resort's rustic charm lies in its simplicity (this was the first place to even think about the impact of tourism on the environment, and they've taken huge strides to try and counter the negative effects). The best values are the "standard" heritage bungalows numbered 219 to 221, 223, and 225 to 228—these face the Kavanar River yet cost no more than those clustered around pathways. Not as fancy as Kumarakom, but with a wonderfully warm and laid-back atmosphere, great sunset cruises with live Indian musicians to serenade the setting sun, and a host of incredible body-curing Ayurvedic treatments at reasonable prices.

Kumarakom, Kottayam 686 563. (© **0481/252-5834** through -5836. Fax 0481/252-4495. www.cghearth. com. coconutlagoon@cghearth.com. Reservations: c/o CGH Earth, Casino Building, Willingdon Island, Cochin 682 003. (© **0484/301-1711.** Fax 0484/266-8001. 50 units. Nov–Apr 304€–334€ heritage bungalow double bungalow, 364€–389€ mansion double, 509€–579€ deluxe pool villa double, 82€ extra person; May–Oct Rs 10,690 heritage bungalow and mansion double, Rs 15,525 deluxe pool villa double, Rs 2,860 extra bed. Rates include all meals and taxes. Breakfast-only rates also available. AE, DC, MC, V. **Amenities:** 2 restaurants, bar; airport transfers (Rs 3,000), free boat transfers; excellent Ayurvedic center; cooking demonstrations; cultural performances; houseboats; Internet (at reception; Rs 200/hr.); large outdoor pool; sunset cruise; yoga. *In room:* A/C, minibar.

Privacy ★★★ If you're more of a "villa" person, crave solitude and hate the impersonal resort vibe, this is a great option: two secluded traditional bungalows situated at the edge of Vembanad Lake. The waterfront "Privacy Suite" is exactly that, with lake views from your bed, while the "Heritage Cottage" is set slightly farther back, behind the pool and deck, with its own, more traditional charm (and friendlier rates). The location and atmosphere certainly live up to its name, with a maximum of only two parties present and even then set quite far apart from each other, meeting only for meals (if you choose) and at the pool. Besides the fabulous location, interiors are in a class of their own, designed by talented owner Joerg Drechsel (of superstylish Malabar House). Privacy may make you feel a million miles from anywhere, but it's only 45km (28 miles) from Kochi and 15km (9½ miles) from the backwater-access town of Alleppey.

Kannankara PO, Alleppey 688 527. (© **0478/258-2794.** Reservations: The Malabar House, 1/268, 269 Parade Rd., Fort Cochin 682 001. (© **0484/221-6666.** Fax 0484/221-7777. www.malabarescapes.com. 2 units. High season Oct–Apr 220€ Heritage Cottage, 360€ Privacy Suite; May–Sept 150€ Heritage Cottage, 250€ Privacy Suite. 35€ extra bed. Rates include breakfast; 15% taxes extra. Cottage rented to 1 party at a time. MC, V. **Amenities:** Electric country boat; kitchenette; mountain bikes; outdoor pool. *In room:* TV, fax.

Moderate

Far less luxurious than the resorts reviewed above, but offering lake-facing rooms at a fraction of the price, is **Whispering Palms,** where a lake-facing cottage (make sure you specify "lake," not "lagoon") costs only Rs 8,500 double with all meals included (© **0484/238-1122;** www.abadhotels.com; 15% tax extra). The downside is less-than-riveting accommodations. Better-looking, but situated near Alappuzha (on Vembanad Lake but without the sunset views), **Punnamada Serena Spa Resort ★** (www.punnamada. com) offers a handful of lake-view rooms that are charmingly decorated with four-poster beds, straw curtains, and massive picture windows framing the lake, and a real bargain at Rs 10,500 to Rs 15,000 double in high season. Make sure you specifically bag one of these rooms, since other accommodations suffer from some crazy design flaws (in fact there are odd, distracting touches throughout the resort). There's a large pool, a round-the-clock Ayurvedic center, and now a brand-new spa (open since Oct 2009), which has prompted a name change (this was formerly more plainly called Punnamada Backwaters Resort). Clearly they are aiming very high indeed; they have their own houseboat, too, with well-priced packages that combine a night on the water with another on shore.

But neither of these resorts has the intimacy of the Backwaters' increasing number of well-run homestays, including a few that feel just like classy little guesthouses. One such place is the very attractive **Anthraper Gardens Home Stay ★** (© **0478/281-3211;** www. anthrapergardens.com) in Chertala (40 min. from alleppey and 90 min. from Cochin). This historic family home is perched just a few steps from the water's edge and set amidst 557 sq. m (6,000 sq. ft.) of landscaped gardens (some might find them a bit too cultivated compared with the jungle-style wilds normally associated with the Backwaters). With wraparound verandas, large rooms, high ceilings, and period furniture, the home affords some gracious living, together with most modern conveniences (there's even a TV lounge, if you really can't help yourself). Bedrooms (the best of which even have air-conditioning; Rs 5,850–Rs 8,100) are attractively renovated and great natural light. While you get to interact with your helpful hosts and feast on authentic Keralite food, there is some sense that this is first and foremost a business (you're charged for cooking demonstrations and yoga and even access to the pools at nearby resorts, and there's a large banquet room where lunches are laid on for coach loads of tourists), so it doesn't quite compete with the warmth and personality (or personalities) that you'll find at a thoroughly humbling homestay like **Olavipe** (reviewed below).

Casa del Fauno ★★★   This is not—as the new owners would have you believe—a homestay; it's actually a very enchanting guesthouse built by the talented and creative Italian architect who established Shalimar Spice Garden (reviewed on p. 300). Here, again, she cleverly combined local and European elements to create a unique fusion style that feels elegant, sumptuous, playful and beautiful all at once. And, in a way, it does feel a bit like a home—albeit one made for spoiling and that could easily be interpreted as a resort-in-miniature, with a pretty garden stretching to the edge of Vembanad Lake. Rooms are impeccable, minimalist spaces with a few baroque touches, either built-in or four-poster beds, and huge bathrooms with sunken tubs. Rooms are imaginatively styled, with more than a hint of bohemian flair: Bits of colored glass, a section of lintel, or simple pieces of crockery are used to decorative effect. The house is run with dignified calm by the always-serene, Vinod Joseph, a most sensitive manager; he can arrange Ayurveda and yoga sessions for you, and will conjure up country boats and local sightseeing (or restaurant) trips at short notice.

Muhamma P.O. Aleppey District 688 525. ℂ **0478/286-0862** or 98-4776-5451. www.casadelfauno.com. Reservations: Sebastian Rd., Kaloor, Cochin 682 017. ℂ **98-9576-6444.** info@casadelfauno.in. 6 units. Oct–Mar Rs 8,500–Rs 9,000 elegant double, Rs 9,000–Rs 9,500 elegant cottage, Rs 9,500–Rs 10,000 deluxe suite; Apr–Sep Rs 6,600 elegant double, Rs 7,600 elegant cottage, Rs 8,600 deluxe suite; Rs 3,000 extra bed (adult), Rs 1,500 extra bed (child aged 6–12). Children under 6 free. Rates include breakfast. No credit cards. **Amenities:** Dining room, lounge, TV lounge, bar service; airport transfers (Rs 1,200); babysitting; concierge; Internet (Rs 50/hr.); large outdoor pool. *In room:* A/C, fan, no phone.

Olavipe ★★★ ⓥalue   Our favorite homestay in India comes complete with a stately and authentic house dating from 1851, a sophisticated family with an illustrious and long history, a working farm (entertaining guests is just a sideline, pursued because the family is gregarious), a superb family cook, and very comfortable accommodations. The fourth-generation Tharakans are clearly very proud of their ancestral home and roots, and the house feels rather like a private museum, with old farm records and implements and photographs and paintings charting events from their great-grandfather's time. There isn't much to do in the sense of hotel-type amenities (this is a family home, after all), nor is there a pool, but if all you want to do is experience the rhythm of farm life (you'll be the only foreigners in the nearby village) and sit down to meals with an intellectually stimulating and charming family, prepared by the talented chef (now in his mid-70s), then you will feel blessed at Olavipe indeed. Besides, Kochi is less than an hour away (25km/16 miles), and Antony (who worked for Rajiv Gandhi) and his sophisticated wife, Rema (an award-winning broadcaster), will arm you with the best shopping tips—that's if you can tear yourself away from their soothing conversations.

Thekkanatt Parayil, Olavipe 688 526. ℂ **0484/252-2255** or 094-4714-2410. www.olavipe.com. homestay@ olavipe.com. 6 units. Rs 8,500 double. Rates include all meals, tea, coffee, in-house activities and taxes. No credit cards. **Amenities:** Dining room; bicycles; canoes; Internet access (free); extensive library. *In room:* Fans.

Philipkutty's Farm ★★ (Kids) You arrive on the island by poled boat and then experience firsthand the hospitality of a local farming family, albeit in the privacy of your very own waterfront cottage, surrounded by banana, nutmeg, coconut, and pepper plantations. Accommodations are in breezy cottages on either side of the family home; they are a wonderful synthesis of Keralite design—open-plan living, carved wooden doors, antique furnishings, and verandas—with modern convenience (big bathrooms with glassed-in showers) and amazing natural light. Owner Anu Mathew, sophisticated and sweet in equal measure, treats her guests as part of the family yet provides privacy and time to soak up the tranquillity; in fact, she runs this place with the efficiency of a small hotel. Anu and her mother-in-law are also the kitchen genies, preparing three marvelous feasts a day, and you're welcome to watch them cooking in the kitchen. The only real drawback is that there's no pool, but some guests cool off as locals do, by venturing into the waters of Vembanad Lake.

Pallivathukal, Ambika Market P.O., Vechoor, Kottayam 688 582. © **04829/27-6529**, -6530, or 98950-75130 www.philipkuttysfarm.com. 5 units, all with shower only. Oct–May Rs 9,900- Rs 12,000 double, Rs 19,800–Rs 24,000 2-bedroom villa; June–Sept Rs 7,000 double, Rs 14,000 2-bedroom Villa; Rs 3,000 extra person. Children under 6 stay free, Rs 2,000 children 6-12. Rates include all meals, tea, coffee, sunset cruise on country boat, and farm excursions. No credit cards at present, plan to accept MC and V soon. **Amenities:** Dining pavilion; airport transfers (Rs 1,800); country boat; Internet (broadband; free or for a nominal fee), library. *In room:* Fans, fridge.

Inexpensive

Emerald Isle ★ Far from the resort crowd, this 150-year-old heritage villa, located on a 3-hectare (7½-acre) plantation, will suit travelers looking for an authentic Kerala backwater homestay experience. The adventure begins when a boatman picks you up in a dugout canoe and rows you to the Job family home. There you are welcomed with filter coffee, tea, coconut water, or toddy. The home is sparklingly clean and old-world charm abounds—wicker chairs on the verandah, period furniture, and all-round quaint rusticity. The en-suite guest rooms are simply furnished; ask for one with an open-air bathroom. Freshly prepared meals are eaten with the family, but you can pick what's on the menu: Choose among chicken curry and *appams* (lace pancakes), *karimeen pollichathu* (pearl spot fish), *avoli* fry, *neimeen* curry, egg roasts, or catch of the day. The Jobs—truly genuine, honest workaday folk—will organize boat cruises, backwater trips, fishing, walks through paddy and coconut plantations, and village tours; they even have their own houseboat.

Kanjooparambil-Manimalathara, Chathurthyakary P.O, Alleppuzha 688 511. © **0477/270-3899**, 0477/329-0577, or 94-4707-7555. www.emeraldislekerala.com. info@emeraldislekerala.com. 4 units. Rs 5,000–Rs 5,500 double; Rs 5,800–Rs 6,300 A/C double. Children 5–10 Rs 350; under 5 free. Rates include boat transfers and all meals. No credit cards. **Amenities:** Dining room, small lounge; Ayurvedic massage; bicycles; boat cruises; cooking classes; fishing. *In room:* A/C (some), fans.

Our Land ★ (Value) This place gets a star for remoteness and laid-back simplicity—if you need luxury, modern trimmings, or loads of facilities, look elsewhere. Set among mango, gooseberry, cashew, guava, banana and coconut trees on a 2.4-hectare (6-acre) island that's accessible only by boat, it's a rough-and-ready sort of place that's a favorite with birders who come for the solitude and chance to spot 61 species. Accommodations have a slightly old-world, functional feel (despite the modern, dull furnishings), with red oxide floors, large showers in tiled bathrooms, and wooden beds simply, neatly made up; each room has a private porch with chairs and a bed for daytime schmoozing—all of these face directly onto the waterway. Book the honeymoon room, raised up on wooden

> ## (Fun Facts   Kerala's Floating Supermarket
>
> Don't be alarmed if, while scanning the Backwaters, you suddenly set eyes upon a garish red-and-white checkered miniature ship cruising through the waterways. In fact, you might even want to find a way to get a look at what's happening on board. It's India's first waterborne supermarket, known as the **Floating Triveni,** and was launched on June 7, 2009, as a way of bringing the convenience of everyday retail shopping to the island-bound villagers who live in Alappuzha district's Kuttanad backwaters. Covering 53 locations and catering to over a million people, the floating minimall carries everything from toiletries to home appliances (which must be ordered in advance, of course) at below-market prices. It's 16m (53 ft.) long with a staff of eight, and the state cooperative which owns it plans to get it recognized by the Guinness Book of World Records. Meanwhile, there are plans for two more island-hopping supermarkets in the Kochi and Kollam backwaters.

stilts and with a porch out front providing great vantage over the water. Learn to use the traditional Ottali net to fish, and enjoy regular interactions with the local villagers; this is a good place to learn about paddy cultivation. At press time, the owners are building a houseboat, after which they plan to commence with a much-needed pool (although building here takes awhile, since access is only by boat).

Near Pallathuruthy Bridge, Alappuzha-Changanassery. (€) **94-4779-8108** or 98-4777-1229. www.our land.in. bookourland@gmail.com. 6 units. Nov–Mar Rs 4,500–Rs 5,000 double; Apr–Oct Rs 4,300. Rates include all meals and activities. No credit cards. **Amenities:** Restaurant; bicycles; bird-watching; boating and backwater cruises; fishing; guided hikes. *In room:* A/C and fans.

Mararikulam: Top Beachfront Options

The best beachfront options are found in an area known as Mararikulam, and provide an excellent alternative to being directly on the backwaters, while you always have access to them. Of the places we've reviewed, **Marari Beach Resort** offers the most by way of facilities, and comes with excellent, warm service—it's also relatively large (although well spread out, so perhaps not the best choice if you're looking to get away from it all. To do that, look no father than **A Beach Symphony** (also reviewed below), which is the absolutely fabulous reworking of a series of fishing cottages set back from the beach, and luxuriously remodeled for leisure-loving vacationers like yourself. Consider these, particularly if you like a vacation that moves at your own pace.

A Beach Symphony ★★★   If the whole resort experience leaves you cold, rent one of these fishermen's cottages located right on the beach—you all but wake up with the sand between your toes. You can prebook your most-desired cottage, but that hikes the price by Rs 1,500 per night, and frankly, they're all gorgeous. Violin (an entirely new building—the others are renovated; three more are planned) has a private plunge pool in its own garden, and Como is closest to the beach. The design is fresh and appealing, a blend of traditional art and craft with a slick modern sensibility, and some of the best-looking bathrooms (all open air, with huge showers) in Kerala. No restaurants or soulless buffet spreads here: meals are served on your balcony—lovely light lunches (grilled fish,

It's a Homestay, But That's Not All . . .

Visitors to **Motty's Homestay Villas** ★★ tend to fall in love with their hosts, Motty and Lali, and many return time and again to experience the warmth and authentic Keralite welcome to their Syrian Christian heritage home in Alleppey. There are four spacious wood-floor rooms, with family heirlooms (Motty is a collector), antique beds (although mattresses and pillows could be better), and private veranda (Rs 6,000 double with breakfast and dinner). Lali is a guru in the kitchen, preparing awesome Keralite feasts and sharing her recipes with you before you leave; Lali will even show women how to don a sari so they can look the part. This couple seems to genuinely love having you around, and Motty regularly bundles guests into the car for a short orientation of the town. Children are well looked after and treated as part of the family. Besides the Alleppey homestay which is just 4km (2½ miles) from the beach, Motty also has a stake in **A Beach Symphony,** four wonderfully renovated fisherman's cottages at right on Marari beach— perfect if you're looking for a more independent, escapist vibe (reviewed on p. 274). Then, for the complete Kerala Backwater's experience, you can top off your visit with a night aboard Motty's **houseboat,** manned by a duo that also cooks up a storm (Rs 5,500 double, including all meals; A/C extra). Although at press time his website was still a bit of a muddle, you can check it all out at www.alleppeybeach.com— click on "Stay with Host," for the homestay—or call Motty at ✆ **0477/224-3535** or 98-4703-2836.

chicken, or fresh sardines, with salads and homemade dressings) and dinners prepared to order (there's no menu as such, so you consult with the chef). Stationed here you really do feel as if you've been washed ashore on some exotic, luxurious beach idyll, but if you like to keep busy and explore, Belgian owner-managers Jan and Christel go out of their way to help; they'll arrange anything from tuk-tuk trips to ayurvedic massages at the local hospital.

Marari Beach, Mararikulam, Alleppey. tel] **97-4429-7123.** www.abeachsymphony.com. 4 units, all with shower only. Nov–Mar Rs 10,000–Rs 12,500 double, Apr–Oct Rs 7,500 double. Rates include breakfast; 15% tax extra. MC, V. **Amenities:** In-house dining; airport transfers (Rs 1,700–Rs 2,500); bicycles; large outdoor pool; room service; yoga. *In room* A/C and fans, hair dryer (on request), no phone.

Marari Beach ★★★ (Kids) This is a truly great eco-friendly resort, with easy, direct access to a 25km (16-mile) beach shared only with fellow guests, local fishermen, and the resort's vigilant lifeguards. Spread over 15 hectares (36 acres) of lawns and pathways enveloped by coconut groves, it has a big-resort vibe, with 62 comfortable and very spacious stand-alone thatched cottages, designed like fisherman's houses—interiors are pretty simple and unfettered and with partially alfresco showers. For environmental reasons, everything is set very far back from the beach; you can hardly see the sea, even from the best rooms (which happen to be nos. 18–20, located along the beach-facing front, and conveniently located near the bar, restaurants, and pool), although the dull roar of the ocean is ever-present. But the sea is just one of Marari's many laid-back charms, from great tours to Kochi, Alleppey, and further afield to slick cooking demonstrations. The extensive Ayurvedic center (Green Leaf) is also considered one of Kerala's

(Tips) Shopping in Venice of the East

If you are a serious shopper, you'll definitely want to consider a stay at Raheem Residency. Bibi, the Irish owner, is full of great advice on retail therapy. Don't miss a trip to the famous **Bhima Jewellers** (established here in 1925, with only certified gold on sale, and branches now throughout India) located on Mullackal, the main shopping street in Alleppey, as well as the **Maheshwari Fabric Showroom** and the wooden handicrafts near the DTPC boat jetty—all within easy striking distance of the Residency; ask for a map.

best, serviced by excellent doctors and therapists who offer wonderful pampering at really reasonable rates.

Mararikulam, Alleppey 688 549, Kerala. (C) **0478/286-3801** through -3809. Fax 0478/286-3810. www.cghearth.com. 62 units. Nov–Apr 329€–349€ garden villa double, 509€–579€ garden pool villa double, 579€–649€ deluxe pool villa double, 82€ extra person; May–Oct Rs 9,210 garden villa double, Rs 12,545 garden pool villa double, Rs 14,385 deluxe pool villa double, Rs 2,860 extra person. Rates include all meals and taxes. Breakfast-only rates available. Discounts for stays of 7 nights or more in high season. AE, DC, MC, V. **Amenities:** 2 restaurants, TV lounge w/DVD library, 2 bars; airport transfers (Rs 2,000–Rs 3,200); Ayurvedic center; badminton; beach volleyball; bicycles; cooking demonstrations; cultural workshops; library; huge outdoor pool; recreation room; 2 tennis courts; Wi-Fi (in recreation room; Rs 100/hr.); yoga. *In room:* A/C, hair dryer, minibar.

In Alleppey

Raheem Residency ★★ A great little guesthouse, located opposite the main Alappuzha beach, with a very organized travel desk to arrange all your sightseeing, be it shopping for temple umbrellas in town, arranging a four-stop temple walking tour, riding an elephant, or booking a short- or long-term houseboat cruise. The bungalow, built in 1868 by Gujurati traders, was skillfully renovated in 2003 to create seven gracious bedrooms catering to guests looking for low-key boutique-style digs. The highlight of your stay is likely to be dinner, taken early on the covered rooftop and the perfect theater seat from which to watch locals thronging to the beach at sunset (particularly on a Sun) or, on the other end, spy on young adults receiving their first driving lessons, carefully avoiding the boys playing cricket in the dusty park. By no means a five-star hotel, but with attentive and helpful staff, the only drawback can sometimes be noise from revelers on the street—ask for one of the newer superior deluxe rooms around the internal courtyard to avoid any such disturbance.

Beach Rd., Alleppey 688 012. (C)/fax **0477/223-9767** or -0767. www.raheemresidency.com. 10 units, most with tub. Oct–Apr 140€–170€ deluxe double, 170€–210€ superior deluxe double; May–Sept 90€ deluxe double, 110€ superior deluxe double; 30€ extra bed. Rates include breakfast; 15% tax extra. 2-night minimum stay Dec 15–Jan 15; no children under 15 Oct–Apr. MC, V. **Amenities:** Restaurant, library lounge; airport transfers (Rs. 1,700); Ayurvedic center; babysitting; bicycles; Internet (broadband; free); outdoor pool; room service; yoga. *In room:* A/C and fans, TV (in Begum's Nook only), hair dryer.

Kollam

The official southern end of Kerala's backwaters (1,220km/756 miles south of Mumbai) is focused on lovely Ashtamudi Lake, lined with Chinese fishing nets and coconut groves. Far less touristed than either Alleppey or Lake Vembanad, the area spreading around Kollam is often bypassed altogether. Which, right now, may be the area's strongest selling point—this part of the backwaters may offer the chance for real tranquillity and escape, even during high season. For too long there has been a lack of quality accommodations, though with new projects in the works, there is no doubt that this area—still delightfully undiscovered—is worth keeping an eye on. We suggest you keep checking with **Malabar Escapes** (www.malabarhouse.com) on any new developments with their upcoming property here; when it opens, it will be far and away the finest place to stay (you have our word on it).

You'll find a contemporary, upbeat outlook at **Club Mahindra Backwater Retreat, Ashtamudi** ★ (© 0476/288-2357; www.clubmahindra.com), the result of a far-reaching overhaul of another resort. Accommodations are in double-level whitewashed cottages arranged along the edge of Ashtamudi Lake, and the entire resort is altogether more neat and presentable than Aquasserene. Here, interiors have been fashioned to resemble modern holiday homes, so they have up-to-date appliances and comfy furnishings, without resembling the standard bland hotel look too much. Since Club Mahindra is first and foremost a destination for its members, it can get completely packed with vacationing Indian families—that could mean you'll battle to get a room.

---

4 TRIVANDRUM & VARKALA

1,200km (744 miles) S of Mumbai

Thiruvananthapuram ("City of the Sacred Serpent") is the mouthful of a name given to Kerala's seaside state capital, but thankfully almost everyone calls it Trivandrum (if you want to impress locals, though, try saying it slowly: Tiru-vanan-tha-poo-ram). Although the city has some interesting museums and a temple that's of great significance to Hindus (and off-limits to non-Hindus), the main reason you'll find yourself here is to utilize the city's excellent transportation connections and head for the beautiful beaches that surround it. North lies Varkala, which has been a popular seaside vacation spot since the early 20th century—no doubt because of its proximity to Trivandrum (a mere 10- to 20-min. drive south)—and as a result has become overcommercialized and saturated with tourist-hungry businesses. If you're looking for Kerala's most stunning, upmarket seaside options, many with more-or-less private beaches, you'll have to travel farther south of Kovalam (see "Kovalam & Kerala's Southernmost Coast," later in this chapter).

ESSENTIALS

VISITOR INFORMATION   As the state capital, Trivandrum has plenty of outlets for tourist information, most of which (if not more) can be accessed on the state's comprehensive website, **www.keralatourism.org**. There are two **tourist information counters** at the **airport;** one caters to international arrivals (© 0471/250-2298) and the other to domestic flights (© 0471/250-1085; daily 10am–5pm, closed a flexible hour for lunch). There are also information counters at the **Central Bus Station** in Thampanoor (© 0471/232-7224) and at the **Railway Station** (© 0471/233-4470), both of which are open daily from 8am to 8pm. Kerala's **Department of Tourism** operates a 24-hour toll-free information line (© 1600/425-4747). Also providing tourist information is the Department of Tourism's **Tourist Facilitation Centre** (Park View, Museum Rd., opposite the museum complex; © 0471/232-1132; daily 10am–5pm). For local tour information and bookings, go to the **Kerala Tourism Development Corporation** or KTDC, either at Hotel Chaithram, adjacent to Central Bus Station in Thampanoor (© 0471/233-0031; daily 6:30am–9:30pm), or at Hotel Mascot (© 0471/231-6736).

GETTING THERE & AWAY   By Road   As mentioned earlier, Kerala is ideal for exploration with a hired car and driver; roads are relatively good, the countryside is spectacular, and Trivandrum is connected by principal roads and highways with all parts of the country. For car/driver hire recommendations, see "Guided Tours," below. Super Deluxe bus services are operated by the **Kerala State Road Transport Corporation;** long-distance buses operate from the Central Bus Station in Thampanoor (© 0471/232-3886), while shorter journeys start and finish at the City Bus Stand in East Fort (© 0471/246-3029). Private operators run so-called deluxe coaches to more distant towns and cities in South India, usually overnight, but remember that most night buses make regular pit stops, making sleep impossible. If you're budgeting your time and money, however, by all means go by bus—just make sure you've booked a nonstop (Volvo) bus. Though the journey is long, it's relatively comfortable and cheap (an overnight bus from Bangalore to Kochi for instance, takes 10 to 11 hours and costs less than Rs 1,000; buses are air-conditioned, have reclining seats, usually provide blankets, and stop only two or three times for toilet/food breaks. Before setting off, try to determine precisely where you need to get off; these buses usually stop at several points in the destination city, with the conductor screaming wildly in a language you don't understand—try to make sure he lets you know specifically when it's time for you to get off.

By Air   Trivandrum is connected by air to Delhi, Mumbai, Kochi, Chennai, Bangalore, Hyderabad, and Tiruchirapali. **Trivandrum International Airport** (© 0471/250-1424 for international flight information; www.trivandrumairport.com) is served by all the Indian airlines including **Kingfisher, Jet Airways, Paramount,** and **Spice Jet** (airlines rated the most reliable, with the best service standards). There are also international flights from various Asian cities, Middle Eastern hubs (including Dubai and Abu Dhabi, both convenient for connections from Europe), and nearby Malé in the Maldives. The airport is 6km (3¾ miles) from the city center, and you can pick up a set-fee prepaid taxi for the journey into town inside the terminal, or shell out a little more and arrange with John Thomas (**Kerala Adventures;** touch@keralaadventure.com) for one of his charming drivers to pick you up (Rs 495–Rs 695 to Kovalam beach, depending on whether or not you need A/C; Rs 1,045–Rs 1,465 to Chowara or Poovar).

By Train   There are regular trains between Trivandrum and other important destinations in Kerala, including Kochi (under 4 hr.), Alleppey (3½ hr.), Kollam (1½ hr.), and Varkala (1 hr.). If you're coming from Chennai in Tamil Nadu, the overnight **Trivandrum Mail** is convenient. Trains also reach India's southernmost point, Kanyakumari; the journey takes around 2½ hours.

   Thiruvananthapuram Central Railway Station is just east of M.G. Road, on Station Road; for general railway inquiries, call © **131.** For reservations, call © **132** or 0471/232-3066, or you can access the **Interactive Voice Response** service by calling © **1361.**

GETTING AROUND   By Taxi & Auto-Rickshaw   In this region you will probably need a taxi from the airport (or your hired car and driver if you've been traveling around the state) to take you to your Kovalam resort; after this you're unlikely to need transport, with the exception of a possible brief foray to a nearby market. For this you're best off using a rickshaw; these officially charge Rs 10 for the first 1½ km, plus around Rs 5 per additional kilometer, although you might want to settle on a fair price before setting off. To hire a car and driver, see "Guided Tours," below.

By Motorcycle & Scooter   You can rent an Enfield or Honda on a daily basis from Kerala Adventures (𝄢 0471/243-3398) in Trivandrum.

GUIDED TOURS & TRAVEL AGENTS   To make the most of your time, we strongly recommend hiring a private car and driver, and set off on a personalized trip from Trivandrum. Our personal preference would be to use the top-notch local outfit **Kerala Adventures** (House No. 101 Geeth, Golflinks Rd., Sasthamangalam, Trivandrum; 𝄢 0471/243-3398 or 0471/231-9548; www.keralaadventure.com; touch@keralaadventure.com); proprietor John Thomas (24-hr. emergency contact 𝄢 98-4706-5548 or 99-9507-6829) provides a seamless service and has never let us down no matter how convoluted our schedule. He is also adept at putting customized itineraries together—he's not afraid to take you well off the beaten track if you like adventure, and arranges all sorts of specialized trips (for birders, cycling enthusiasts, and even ardent campers, for example). Shopping around? Then you could also get a quote from **Sita World Travel** (𝄢 0471/247-0921 or 0471/246-0173; trv@sitaindia.com) or try **Tourindia** (𝄢 0471/232-8070 or 0471/233-1507), which has been involved in several innovative alternative tourism projects in Kerala. **KTDC** (Hotel Chaithram, adjacent Central Bus Station, Thampanoor; 𝄢 0471/233-0031; Mon–Sat 6:30am–9.30pm) runs conducted sightseeing tours in and around the city. Aimed primarily at domestic tourists, they are not recommended, but are a cheap way of taking in as many of the sights as possible.

(*Fast Facts*)   Trivandrum

Airlines The airlines with the most useful services to and from Trivandrum are **Kingfisher Airlines** (𝄢 1800-2333-131 or 0471/250 8822) and **Jet Airways** (𝄢 0471/272-1018 or -8864); you can also contact Jet at the airport (𝄢 0471/250-0710 0860).

Area Code The area code for **Trivandrum** is **0471**.

ATMs Numerous ATMs in Trivandrum accept Visa and MasterCard (and also American Express); note that there are far fewer facilities south of the capital, so best to draw cash for incidentals in the city.

Banks You can exchange currency and traveler's checks at any bank; a conveniently located bank is **Canara Bank** at Spencer Junction, M.G. Road (𝄢 0471/233-1536; Mon–Fri 10am–2pm and 2:30–3:30pm, Sat 10am–noon). Alternatively use one of the many ATMs throughout the city.

Car Hire See "Guided Tours," above.

Currency Exchange See "Banks," above. Thomas Cook is also located on M.G. Road (𝄢 0471/233-8140 or -8141).

Drugstores City Medical Service (Statue; 𝄢 0471/246-1770) or Central Medical Stores (Statue; 𝄢 0471/246-0923).

Emergencies For fires and other emergencies, including medical services, call 𝄢 101.

Hospitals Medical tourism is becoming quite a trend in Kerala; here are a few reputable options in Trivandrum: **Kerala Institute of Medical Sciences,** P.B. No.1, Anayara (𝄢 1800/425-4748; www.kimskerala.com); **Sree Uthradom Thirunal Hospital,** Pattom (𝄢 0471/244-7566; www.suthospital.com); **Sree Chitirathirunal**

Medical Institute, Medical College (© **0471/244-3152**); **Cosmopolitan Hospital,** Pahaya Rd., Kumarapuram, Pattom; © **0471/244-8182; 24**-hr. ambulance © **94-4794-7321;** www.cosmopolitanhospitals.in); and the **Regional Cancer Centre,** Medical College; © **0471/244-2541;** www.rcctvm.org.

Internet Access Hotels nowadays all provide access—most have Wi-Fi. If you're stuck, though, look for the signs for **Sify iway** or **Reliance Webworld**—these Internet centers usually provide faster connections than most.

Police Dial © **100.** Thampanoor Police Station (© **0471/233-1843**) is on Station Road. For road accidents, call the police **help line** at © **98-4610-0100.**

Post Office The **General Post Office** (© **0471/247-3071;** Mon–Sat 8am–7pm, Sun 10am–4pm) is along M.G. Road.

WHAT TO SEE & DO IN TRIVANDRUM

With palm-lined beaches beckoning, Trivandrum is unlikely to detain you longer than it takes to arrange your transfer out of there, but it has a number of interesting buildings, including the stately **Secretariat and Legislative Assembly,** situated along Mahatma Gandhi Road, which is the main boulevard and center of activity through town. M.G. Road runs more or less north to south and links the two most significant areas of tourist interest: the **Museum Complex,** to the north of the city; and the Fort area, which houses **Padmanabhaswamy Temple** and **Puthenmalika Palace Museum,** to the south. It is possible to walk from one area to the other (about 45 min.), and there are numerous shops en route. Alternatively, auto-rickshaws continuously buzz along the road's length, and you will have no trouble catching a ride from one area to the other. It's worth wandering M.G. just to shop; if this is all you feel like doing, don't bother with the sights and make a beeline for **Natesan's** (© **0471/233-1594;** www.natesansantiqarts.com), the city's largest and most reputable antiques and art dealer, with original bronze, silver, teak, sandalwood, stone, and wood carvings as well as manufacturer's replicas. **Hastakala** (Gandhariamman Kovil Rd.; © **0484/233-1627**) specializes in Kashmiri goods including hand-woven carpets, quality Pashminas, and Tibetan and tribal jewelry. For a uniquely Keralite souvenir, go to the **SMSM Institute** (off M.G. Rd., behind the Secretariat, near the British Library; © **0471/233-0298**) and pick up an Aranmula metal mirror (produced by combining herbs with molten metal to produce a dazzlingly reflective surface), or browse the **Gram Sree Craft Centre.** Book lovers could spend a day in **DC Books,** the biggest in Kerala (www.dcbooks.com); there are four branches in the city, but your best bet is to head to the one in Karimpanal Statue Avenue. And if you're looking for clothing for all ages, **Aiyappas,** opposite the SL Theatre Complex (© **0484/233-1627;** www.aiyappas.com), is a good place to start, while **Karalkada** (© **0471/247-4520;** www.karalkada.com) has the most superb hand-woven cotton fabrics, saris, *kavanis, kurthas,* and dhotis, and is *the* place locals come to shop when looking to buy something special for an imminent wedding or religious ceremony.

Museum Complex ★   Many of Trivandrum's cultural sites are clustered in a huge formal public garden at the northern end of the city. **Napier Museum** occupies an early Indo-Saracenic building, created in 1880 in honor of the then-governor of Madras, Lord Napier. This priceless collection includes excellent 12th-century Chola bronzes, wood carvings, stone idols, and fascinating musical instruments, while more unique pieces include a temple chariot, a 400-year-old clock, and a royal cot made from herbal wood. Fine-art enthusiasts should visit **Sri Chitra Art Gallery,** which holds an assortment of miniature paintings from the Rajput, Moghul, and Tanjore schools, as well as more exotic works from Japan, China, Bali, and Tibet. One of the country's foremost artists, Raja Ravi Varma (1848–1905), whose well-known oil paintings explore Hindu mythological themes, is represented here. **K.C.S. Paniker Gallery** is a wholly unnecessary diversion, as is the **Natural History Museum** (unless you want to see stuffed animals and dolls in traditional costumes)—the anthropological exhibit at Kolkata's Indian Museum is far superior. And stay away from the **zoo,** particularly if you're an animal lover—like most zoos in India, it lacks the funding to build bigger, more humane habitats for its animals.

Museum Rd. Napier Museum ✆ **0471/231-8294.** Sri Chitra Art Gallery ✆ **0471/247-3952.** Purchase tickets for all museums at the ticket booth. Admission to Museum and Art Gallery Rs 10. Thurs–Sun and Tues 10am–4:45pm; Wed 1:30–4:45pm.

Padmanabhaswamy Temple ★ This Dravidian-style Vishnu temple, said to be the largest in Kerala, may be off-limits to non-Hindus, but the "temple guides" manage to target foreigners with great ease, leading them to the obligatory spots from which to photograph the seven-story-high entrance tower, or *goparum,* which is pretty much all that can be viewed from the outside. The temple—one of 108 sacred Vishnu temples in India—is believed to have come into existence on the first day of the Kaliyuga era (3102 B.C.). Legend has it that the temple "materialized" after a sage prayed to Vishnu asking him to appear in a form that he could comprehend with his limited human vision—but the greater part of the complex was built during the 18th century. The temple is fronted by a massive tank, where devotees take ritual dips. Alongside a promenade are stalls selling ritual items, religious souvenirs, and flowers for use inside the temple.

Fort, Trivandrum. ✆ **0471/245-0233.** Closed to non-Hindus. 4am–noon and 5–7:30pm.

Puthenmalika (Kuthiramalika) Palace Museum ★★ A secret, private passage is believed to connect Padmanabhaswamy Temple with this Travancore-style palace, built in the early 18th century by the social reformer Maharajah Swathi Thirunal Balarama Varma, a poet and distinguished musician. Known as the Horse Palace because of the 122 carved horse brackets that buttress the exterior walls, the buildings include elaborate carvings, among them two extravagant thrones—one made from 25 elephant tusks, another made entirely from Bohemian crystal. Visitors are also allowed into the maharaja's music room, from where you get the same view of the temple that was apparently a source of inspiration to the erstwhile ruler. Despite the value of much of the collection, the buildings are in need of renovation; the beauty of the carved teakwood ceilings and collected objets d'art are sometimes masked by insufficient lighting and neglectful curatorship. You'll be taken around by an "official" guide—obviously he'll require a small tip.

100m (328 ft.) from the temple, Fort. ✆ **0471/247-3952.** Entrance Rs 20 adult, Rs 10 children. Tues–Sun 8:30am–1pm and 3–5:30pm.

ARTS & ENTERTAINMENT

Shree Karthika Thirunal Theatre (alongside Lucia Continental Hotel; ✆ **0471/247-1335**), in Trivandrum's Fort district, holds regular classical dance-theater performances (mostly Karnatic, but also Hindustani) throughout the year. The theater has its own company but hosts outside groups showcasing various genres, including Kathakali, Mohiniattam, and Bharatanatyam.

You can observe **Kalaripayattu** martial arts classes, and even arrange special performances or lecture demonstrations, through **C.V.N. Kalari** (East Fort, Trivandrum; ✆ **0471/ 247-4182;** www.cvnkalarikerala.com). Established in 1956, this institution has represented India at numerous international festivals.

WHERE TO STAY & DINE

Walk up the spiraling incline of **Maveli Coffee House** (btw. the Tourist Reception Centre and KSRTC bus stand; daily 7:30am–10pm), if only to be able to say afterward that you've dined in one of the world's oddest restaurants, which somewhat resembles a squat, ocher-colored version of Pisa's leaning tower. Located diagonally opposite the railway station, this unique coffeehouse was designed by Laurie Baker, the renowned English architect who pioneered environmentally sustainable architecture and worked on hundreds of projects in southern India before passing away in Trivandrum, his adopted home, in 2007. It's a favorite hangout for the locals and an interesting spot in which to spend some time rubbing shoulders with the groundlings and businesspeople who come here for their *idlis, dosas,* and *chai* or coffee.

If you're exploring the Secretariat, head across the road to **Arul Jyothi** (Mahatma Gandhi Rd.; daily 6:30am–10pm). The capital's civil servants pile in here at lunchtime, when there's much ordering of *thalis* (the ubiquitous platter featuring Indian breads and various curries and chutneys) and wonderful *masala dosas.* If you're keen to browse newspapers from back home, stop at the British Library nearby; it has a good collection of magazines and international dailies (just show your passport to enter). Alternatively, **Kadaleevanam** (Prakrithi Bhojanasala Hotel Mas Annexe, near the SL Theatre, Chettikulangara; ✆ **0471/247-2780;** daily 8am–9:30pm; no credit cards), where the owners pride themselves on the fact that they have no fridges or freezers (all food, cooked on wood fires, is served within 3 hr. or not offered to customers) and use only organically grown vegetables and whole grains, apparently prepared according to the principles of naturopathy. The set meal will run you a mere Rs 100.

For more salubrious surrounds, the smart **Tiffany's** at the Muthoot Plaza is rated by locals as the best restaurant in town (Punnen Rd.; ✆ **0471/233-7733;** daily 12:30–3pm and 7:30–10:30pm), although the smart crowd is slowly warming up to the dining offered at **The 5th Element,** an all-day venue at the Taj Residency hotel on C.V. Raman Pillai Road, Thycaud (✆ **0471/661-2345**).

There is little reason not to head south before nightfall, but if you really must stay in the city, **Muthoot Plaza** (reviewed below) remains (in our opinion, anyway) Trivandrum's best hotel—it's more intimate and has a classier ambience than even the brand new **Taj Residency** ★ (C.V. Raman Pillai Road, Thycaud; ✆ **0471/661-2345**), which has sleek modern rooms and a host of business facilities (and big halls to host weddings for the city's biggest and brightest families). Rooms facing the large, underutilized pool cost Rs 8,500 double, but the cheaper city-facing rooms (Rs 7,500) actually give you something more interesting to stare out at. An altogether more engaging option, and within walking distance of the Muthoot (should you feel the urge to rush off for an air-conditioned meal) is **Varikatt Heritage** ★, a green oasis off bustling Puynnen Road. This is the best homestay in town, filled with quality antique furniture and presided over by the welcoming Colonel Roy Kuncheria, who enjoys playing the gracious host to a handful of guests. Each of the Colonel's three advertised rooms open onto the front veranda, so make sure you get one of these; there's also another room facing the courtyard, which is less appealing (✆ **0471/233-6057** or 98-9523-9055; www.varikattheritage.com; roy@ varikatt.com; Rs 3,000 double, Rs 3,500–Rs 4,500 suite). Budget travelers just looking

Snack Food, Kerala-Style

Although tourists are normally advised to stay off street food, there's one kind of street snack you can sample without a problem in Trivandrum. Banana chips are a Keralite's favorite snack, and you'll see *thattu kadas*, temporary food carts (particularly at night), with men slicing and frying bananas in coconut oil right on the street, almost all over Kerala. Buy them piping-hot and lightly salted—they're even more scrumptious than potato chips. Good spots to buy these fresh are near the British Library, or at a small shop in Kaithamukku (about 3km/2 miles west of the central train station), where A. Kannan has been frying some of the best banana chips in Kerala for close to 15 years. Note that banana chips come in myriad flavors depending on the variety of banana used. Those made with ripe bananas are slightly sweet, but we suggest you go for the thinly sliced variety. Be warned, however: They are seriously addictive.

for a decent en-suite room for the night should head for **Ariya Nivaas Hotel** (© 0471/233-0789; www.hotelskerala.com/ariyanivaas), an office-block-style hotel that offers good, clean air-conditioned lodging conveniently located near the Central Railway Station for under Rs 1,000. Staff is friendly and can help with travel arrangements. The hotel has a decent restaurant and a useful 24-hour checkout policy. It's often full, so book in advance.

Muthoot Plaza ★★ (**Value** The city's chicest little hotel looks a bit like a seven-story steel and glass mall, and it's traditionally a hangout for businesspeople who come to the state capital to pay *baksheesh* to various government representatives, but once inside you discover a plush, compact oasis of tranquillity and rather good taste. Rooms are very well-appointed and extremely comfortable and despite the lack of views (and matchbox-size bathrooms), have more character than the new Taj (and it's nearer all the more interesting built heritage, including the University). With good service (starting with the sharp, on-the-ball elegantly attired receptionist to a concierge who can put together personalized tours of the region), a convenient location, plans for a new pool (should be up and running by 2010), and very reasonable rates, this feels like the perfect small city hotel, especially after a hard day of bargain hunting.

Punnen Rd., Thiruvananthapuram 695 039. © **0471/233-7733.** www.themuthootplaza.com. 57 units. Rs 3,500–Rs 6,700 Plaza double, Rs 7,500–Rs 9,500 deluxe suite, Rs 13,000–Rs 18,000 presidential suite, Rs 1,000 extra bed. Rates include breakfast, deluxe suite rate includes lunch or dinner, presidential suite rate includes all meals; 15% tax extra. AE, DC, MC, V. **Amenities:** 2 restaurants, bar; airport transfers (Rs 600); concierge; room service. *In room* A/C, TV, floor butler, hair dryer, minibar, Wi-Fi (free).

NORTH OF TRIVANDRUM: THE RED CLIFFS OF VARKALA

A 55km (34-mile) drive north of Trivandrum (1 hr. by train), the seaside resort of Varkala draws numerous Hindu pilgrims who come to worship in the 2,000-year-old **Sri Janardhana Swami Temple** and ritualistically cleanse themselves in the mineral spring waters that gush from Varkala's ruby-red laterite cliffs. The cliffs overlook the aptly named "Beach of Redemption." Varkala attracts scores of backpackers searching for an untouched beach paradise—and a decade ago, they might have found just that. Over the years, hawkers and shack-dwellers have drifted in and set up shop along the tops of the cliffs; the coconut palms have been replaced by cheap guesthouses and open-air cafes; and children flog cheap jewelry, yards of cloth, and back-to-nature hippie gear.

Nonetheless, being a holy beach, the sand at the base of the cliffs stays relatively free of human pollution—it's neither a convenient public toilet facility nor a waste-dumping ground. Instead, devotees of Vishnu attend to earnest *puja* sessions, offering banana leaves piled with boiled rice and brightly colored marigolds to be carried away by the ocean. Usually, the sand is soft and lovely, and you can find a quiet cove for sunbathing without the crowds that are inescapable in Kovalam. In fact, you can find relative peace and calm if you restrict your beach activities to the morning; by lunchtime the gawkers (female bathers are advised to be discreet), hawkers, and dreadlocked Europeans start to file in, and it's time to venture back to the hotel or guesthouse.

Other activities for visitors here include Kathakali demonstrations, elephant rides, village tours, and backwater trips. You can also take a pleasant evening walk (or auto-rickshaw ride) to the cliffs to visit Sunset Point. If you don't want to walk back, keep the rickshaw for your return trip (round-trip around Rs 50–Rs 60; more if you want to go farther up the cliff).

Where to Stay & Dine

Varkala has plenty of accommodation choices, virtually all below par, with the predominant market clearly more the backpacker or budget end of the spectrum. Bucking this trend is the classy **Villa Jacaranda** (reviewed below).

If you prefer hotels, your best bet is the **Hindustan Beach Retreat** (✆ 0470/260-4254/5; www.hindustanbeachretreat.com), which looms hideously over the southern end of Varkala beach. An unattractive five-story hotel it may be, and certainly the stuff of any eco-enthusiast's nightmares, it affords the best proximity to the beach, *and* has a pool (albeit one that's likely to be inundated with shrieking kids). Rooms, all with views of the Arabian Sea (not to mention *puja* being performed on the shore), are comfortable and bathrooms spick-and-span, but it's all a bit sterile; on the other hand this is the closest you get to the beach, lined with casual restaurant-shacks and flaunting a wannbe-hippie vibe, so you could spend the day with your toes in the sand pretending to be a beach bum and then retreat to your middle-class box. Standard doubles go for Rs 3,000 to Rs 4,000, depending on season, and rates include one meal; executive rooms cost Rs 500 more.

The two best places to eat in Varkala, with clean kitchens, good food, decent atmosphere, and great views, are **Clafoutis** (Clafouti Heritage Beach Resort, above Papasham Beach, North Cliff; ✆ 0470/260-1414) and **Café Delmar** (Hill View Beach Resort, North Cliff; ✆ 0470/645-1566). Both serve good fresh fish and seafood. Café Delmar offers a hodgepodge of Indian, Italian, and even Mexican cuisines—and they do real espresso (from an extensive coffee menu), *jaffles* (toasted sandwiches), and pizzas. The chicken tikka biriyani is considered a top choice, and we definitely recommend the *lassi* here—simply excellent. If you're unsure about what's what, the Indian menu items at least come with fairly meaningful descriptions. Clafoutis also has a bafflingly extensive menu with Indian, Thai, Italian, and Chinese options, and a huge list of mixed drinks. The real reason to come, though, is for the sunset view from the upstairs deck; it's probably the most mesmeric scene in Varkala—with the waves crashing somewhere far below, you almost feel yourself adrift over the ocean. Sink back into your seat and, cocktail in hand, meditate on the sinking sun.

Villa Jacaranda ★★ ⓥalue   By far the best option in Varkala—not so much for amenities (of which there are few) or luxury (it's no-frills), but for a sense of intimacy. This is a genteel guesthouse on South Cliff, with tasteful rooms put together with an eye for detail—and lots of personal space. Rooms are simple and minimalist, but the whole look vibes perfectly in the context of such a moody, atmospheric beach resort. Located between the village and the southern end of the beach, it's ideal for exploring both, and an entirely manageable walk to North Cliff and back. At night you'll return to your candle-lit veranda; book room no. 2 or 4 and you'll have the additional pleasure of sea views—the perfect accompaniment to breakfast served right outside your door (no. 4 is the large upstairs unit and a stand-out choice). The only drawback? No pool. And, for families, no kids.

Temple Rd. West, Varkala 695141, Varkala. ⓒ **0470/261-0296.** www.villa-jacaranda.biz. Nov–Feb Rs 3,300–Rs 5,000 double; Mar–Oct Rs 3,300–Rs 4,400. Rates include breakfast; 15% tax extra. No credit cards. No children under 8. **Amenities:** Airport transfers (Rs 1,500); Internet (broadband; free); yoga. *In room:* Fan.

---

5 KOVALAM & KERALA'S SOUTHERNMOST COAST

Kovalam is 1,216km (754 miles) S of Mumbai

A mere 16km (10 miles) south of Trivandrum, Kovalam has been a haunt for beach tourism since the 1930s, but its fame as a coastal idyll has wrought the inevitable. Discovered by hippies and then by charter tour groups, it is now home to a virtually unbroken string of holiday resorts, its once-virgin charm plundered by low-rise concrete hotels. Even so, Kovalam's three crescent-shaped sandy beaches, flanked by rocky promontories and coconut palm groves, remain quite impressive. You can watch fishermen ply the waters in so-called catamarans (derived from the local word *kattu-maram,* these are simply a few timbers lashed together) as they have for centuries, at night assisted by the red-and-white lighthouse that beams from Kovalam's southernmost beach.

Lighthouse Beach is, in fact, a guiding light to the charter types, and where you'll find the bulk of cheap (mostly unashamedly ugly) hotels, restaurants, and bars, with fishing-net-strewn Hawa Beach and less-crowded Samudra Beach lying to the north. After the rigors of India's crowded cities and comfort-free public transport, budget travelers are lured by the easy, comfortable (and high) life offered here, often staying until money (or good weather) runs out. You can rent umbrellas and watersports equipment along the beach, or hop aboard a fishing boat for a cruise out to sea. Stalls sell colorful fabrics, pseudo-ethnic hippie trinkets, and fresh fruit, fish, and coconut water; music wafts from shack-style cafes, and unofficial bars survive strict liquor laws by serving beer in ceramic mugs and teapots. (***Party animals note:*** The vibe at Kovalam is far, far tamer than Goa's.)

Immediately south of Kovalam is **Vizhinjam Beach,** the site of the erstwhile capital of southern Kerala's first dynastic rulers and, between the 8th and 13th centuries, a major natural port for local kingdoms. Now a poor fishing hamlet of thatched huts overlooked by a pink mosque, Vizhinjam is an interesting contrast to the tourist hubbub of Kovalam; swimming here, however, is dangerous, no doubt the reason for its relatively untouched atmosphere. A number of shrines are found in Vizhinjam, including a rock-cut cave enclosing a shrine with a sculpture of Dakshinamurthy; the outer wall of the cave includes a half-complete relief depicting Lord Shiva and his consort, Parvati.

(Moments) India's Ultimate Sunrise Gathering

Just 87km (54 miles) southeast of Trivandrum, across the border with Tamil Nadu, **Kanyakumari** (also known as Cape Comorin) is not only India's southernmost tip but the much-venerated confluence of the Arabian Sea, the Bay of Bengal, and the Indian Ocean. **Watching the sun rise from the subcontinent's southernmost point ★★** is an age-old ritual that attracts thousands of Indian pilgrims each morning. They plunge themselves into the turbulent swell, believing that the tri-oceanic waters are holy. Others revel in the glorious spectacle as though it were a major Bollywood premiere. Nature's daily show here becomes something akin to a miniature festival, with excited pilgrims besieged by *chai-*, coffee-, and souvenir-*wallas* selling everything from kitschy crafts (how else to describe conch shells with plastic flower bouquets glued to the top?) to ancient postcards and outdated booklets. But it's all part of the experience, which is quite wonderful; you can't help but be moved by the mass of people who gaze on a natural daily occurrence with such childlike wonder, effectively bestowing upon the event the spiritual significance that draws the crowds in the first place.

To get here, you need to arrange for an early morning wake-up call and have your hotel schedule a taxi. You should reach Kanyakumari at least half an hour before sunrise in order to take in the mounting excitement as the crowds prepare to greet the new day. Once the sun is up, you'll have a good view of two rock islands not too far offshore. One of these is the site of the **Swami Vivekananda Rock Memorial** (Rs 15 daily *darshan* or viewing of a deity; 8am–4pm), reached by the half-hourly ferry. The memorial commemorates a Hindu guru and social reformer's meditative sojourn on the island in 1892. Several bookstores selling spiritual tomes are found on the island, but the best experience is to be had in the **Dhyana Mandapam,** a room where absolute silence is maintained so that pilgrims can meditate before a golden *om* symbol. A set of

Farther south, the Ayurvedic resorts that can still lay claim to the beach idyll that put Kovalam on the map dot the coast (see "Where to Stay & Dine," below). Visitors staying at any of these should seriously consider a day trip that takes in **Padmanabhapuram Palace** (see review below), on the way to **Kanyakumari,** India's southernmost tip, where you can enjoy one of the most interesting cultural experiences on the subcontinent (see "India's Ultimate Sunrise gathering," below).

Note: For details on finding visitor information points and contacting suitable travel agencies, see "Essentials" under the Trivandrum and Varkala section, earlier. In **Kovalam,** visit the **Tourist Facilitation Centre** (℃ **0471/248-0085;** Mon–Sat 10am–1pm and 1:30–5pm) near the entrance to the Leela resort (it's just beyond the security check post). Besides giving information, the center assists with tour bookings, car hires, boat rides, and lodging—enthusiasm is not their strongpoint, however. *Note:* Consider any recommendations for government-owned accommodations very carefully—they tend to be poorly managed and often run-down.

Parvati's footprints is enshrined in a temple built for it on the island. On the adjacent rocky island, a massive sculpture of the celebrated ancient Tamil poet-savant **Thiruvalluvar** stands 40m (131 ft.) high, punctuating the horizon like some bizarre homage to New York's Statue of Liberty.

The only attraction in the town itself is famous **Kumari Amman Temple** ★ (daily 4:30am–noon and 4:30–8:30pm), dedicated to Kanyakumari, a virgin goddess. Devotees enter the temple through the north gate, making their way around various corridors and bridges before viewing the deity, here depicted as a young girl doing penance with a rosary in her right hand. It's said that her sparkling nose jewel—seen glowing from some distance away—was installed by Parasurama (Lord Rama, an avatar of Vishnu) himself. Non-Hindus wishing to enter the temple must remove shoes, and men must remove shirts and wear a dhoti (although a *lungi* passes; purchase one before you leave Kovalam). A willing temple priest will lead you on a very brisk (queue-jumping) tour of the temple, ending with the obligatory suggestion that a donation would be quite acceptable.

En route back towards Kerala, you can buy cheap, delicious palm fruits from children on the roadside and visit the fantastic palace in the town of **Padmanabhapuram,** capital of Travancore until 1790 (see review below). If, for some reason, you get trapped in this ramshackle, pilgrim-choked town, head for **Hotel Maadhini** (East Car St.; ⊘ **04652/24 6857** or 6787; www.hotelmaadhini.in; Rs 900–Rs 1,900 double), where you will be woken predawn with tea and an urgent suggestion to watch the rising sun from your balcony. (**Note: Kanyakumari sunsets,** which are obviously more convenient to reach, also draw a crowd but are only visible mid-Oct to mid-Mar and are not quite as atmospheric, except perhaps for *chaitra purnima,* the full-moon evening in Apr when the sunset and moonrise can be viewed simultaneously along the horizon.)

Padmanabhapuram Palace ★★★   Although technically in Tamil Nadu (but a mere 55km/34 miles south of Trivandrum), this gorgeous palace—one of the finest examples of secular architecture in India—was for several centuries the traditional home of Kerala's Travancore royal family. It's still well-maintained, and a meditation room features two lamps that have burned since its construction, tended by two dutiful women. Built over a number of generations during the 17th and 18th centuries, the palace exemplifies the aesthetic and functional appeal of Kerala's distinctive architectural style: sloping tiled roofs; elaborate slatted balconies; cool, polished floors; and slanting walls and wooden shutters—all effectively designed to counter the intense sunlight and heat. The private living quarters of the royal family are a maze of open corridors and pillared verandas; outside, small garden areas feature open courtyards where the sunlight can be enjoyed. Note that the king's chamber is furnished with a bed made from 64 different types of medicated wood and has its own beautifully decorated prayer room.

Padmanabhapuram is 55km (34 miles) south of Trivandrum. Admission Rs 10. Tues–Sun 9am–4pm. Ticket office closed 1–2pm. Visitors must be accompanied by a guide and must remove footwear.

WHERE TO STAY & DINE

Backpackers head for the budget hotels on the fringes of Kovalam's beaches, which, during peak season (Dec–Jan), are completely overrun by tourists and relentless hawkers. With the notable exception of The Leela, most lodging in Kovalam is less pleasant than cheap, and you're likely to be at the constant mercy of blaring music from the beach and its sprawl of cafes. Note that these cafes are fine for a snack, but each should be judged according to the number of customers. The rule of thumb is: If it's empty, the food has been standing around too long.

The resorts reviewed below have been chosen because they are situated away from mainstream Kovalam and offer peace, tranquillity, and charm, as well as some of the world's most pristine stretches of coastline. The prize for top location still goes to Surya Samudra; if you haven't opted to stay here (see below), it's definitely worthwhile taking a drive out to dine at **Surya Samudra's open air restaurant ★** (© 0471/226-7333). The semicircular terrace is perched high above the ocean and palm-fringed beach and cooled by the fresh sea breezes. Presuming the menu hasn't changed too dramatically by the time it reopens, you can assume that seafood will be the order of the day: Don't miss the superb grilled tiger prawns or the fish curry (succulent pieces of white fish in a spicy red sauce; order with chappatis). Vegetarians can opt for the vegetable *theeyal* (spicy gravy), this time with Kerala *paratha* (flatbread). And for the truly unadventurous, there is a selection of Western dishes.

Another very pleasant dining venue is The Leela's loungy beachside restaurant, **Tides ★★** (© 0471/248-0101; noon–3pm and 7–10:30 or 11pm), which does a feisty selection of Malaysian, Vietnamese, Chinese, and Thai dishes, best appreciated under the stars in the alfresco section (there's a covered option during the monsoon); in winter there's also a great barbeque where you can choose from a selection of freshly caught seafood (fish Rs 1,500/kg, tiger prawns and lobster Rs 3,000/kg) dusted with mouthwatering organic lemon-butter; Rs 1,600 gets you a feast-sized seafood platter served with *naan* bread. Top it all off with chocolate samosas, or water chestnuts in coconut cream.

Note: During the season, there's entertainment most nights—try avoiding the live bands cranking out Western covers, but some nights there are Kerala martial arts displays or, better still, Indian classical music.

In & Around Kovalam Beach

Not as great on location as the Leela, but worth a mention is the **Taj Green Cove Resort ★** (© 0471/248-7733; www.tajhotels.com), offering 59 rooms in a number of blocks set amid 4 hectares (10 acres) of tropically landscaped gardens on the Kovalam Cliffside (some 300m/984 ft. from the beach). Cottages have traditional Kerala-style thatched roofs and are hidden among palm trees—maintaining privacy from the outside, but still offering good views. Rooms aren't as beautiful as the handsome open-plan lobby-lounge area promises, but they have large picture windows framing either the sea or garden views. Make sure to ask for a sea-view room—at Rs 14,000 a mere Rs 2,000 more than a standard garden view unit (but both much more expensive during the hectic period between Christmas and mid-Jan). Both of the Taj's restaurants, **Jasmine Bay,** an alfresco space at the edge of the hotel's popular infinity pool, and **Curries,** serve good food, but the place to dine (in season) will be at the new seafood restaurant on the beach. The resort also has a great-looking non-Ayurvedic Jiva spa, but it's not nearly in the same league as the fabulous spa at The Leela Kempinski (reviewed below), nor as personal as the "light" Ayurvedic treatments on offer at Lagoona Davina (also below)

Lagoona Davina ★★   Described as "barefoot chic," this small, lagoon-facing property was converted into a laid-back boutique sanctuary by adventurer Davina Taylor Phillips over a decade ago. While the tourism boom has spawned encroaching development, the views of the lagoon and beach—where fishermen pull in nets every morning in a kind of synchronized dance—are still splendid. Rooms are small and bathrooms very basic, but there are lovely touches throughout, like hand-loomed linens, silk tented ceilings, a personally selected assortment of toiletries, and the caftans and camisoles Davina has made for you to live in while you're here. Guests in the main "guest house" (a low-slung, single-story rectangular building facing the lagoon) and more spacious Maharaja rooms also enjoy the services of a personal room attendant; also available are the services of a tailor, and special floating dinners for two. It's a place for yoga and meditative calm, although there's now a "business suite" with a computer for anyone who finds it too scary to take a real break from the office. There's also one fully tented room. *Note:* Although the beach is close by, it's not good for swimming. Also, it's eco-friendly, so no air-conditioning. And relaxation-friendly, so no children.

Pachalloor, Trivandrum 695 027. (✆ **0471/238-0049** or -4857. Fax 0471/246-2935. www.lagoonadavina. com. 18 units, all with shower only. Nov–Apr Rs 4,300 Rajasthan tents and cottage rooms, Rs 4,500 business suite, Rs 5,000–Rs 5,900 sea view double and Maharaja double; May–Oct Rs 2,500 Rajasthan tents and cottage rooms and business suites, Rs 2,800–Rs 3,200 sea view double and Maharaja double. Rates exclude 15% tax. MC, V. Surcharge on credit card payments. No children under 16. **Amenities:** Restaurant, small library w/indoor games; Ayurvedic massage; boating; cultural programs (seasonal); meditation; outdoor pool; tailor; yoga. *In room:* Internet (USB modem provided; 3 hr./day free).

The Leela Kempinski Kovalam Beach ★★★   If you're looking for five-star resort-style amenities and snappy service, along with stunning views over the Lakshadweep Sea, this is the place to be. Like most Kovalam beach resorts, it is built into a cliff face, but to Leela's advantage, the resort is well connected with the well-maintained beach, thanks to elevators and golf carts that traverse the hill between reception and sea (well suited to the infirm and lazy). The original hotel rooms—the "Beach View" category—are a little too like living in a large hotel, with low-ceilinged rooms ranged along corridors; also hotel like, but sumptuously so, are the much more luxuriously appointed rooms in the Sea View Club wing—views here are simply sensational, with little balconies perched virtually above the crashing water. We've always preferred the freestanding "Pavilion" bungalows right next to the beach; these are slated to be transformed into two-bedroom private pool villas—until then, they're the best value. *Note:* The Leela's Divya spa is arguably the best and most spectacularly situated spa in India—sign up for a muscle-tingling Kalari Massage, performed in an open-air room with ocean for a soundtrack, and ask for the version with two therapists.

Kovalam Beach, Thiruvananthapuram 695 527. (✆ **0471/248-0101.** Fax 0471/248-1522. www.theleela. com. reservations.kovalam@theleela.com. 182 units. Oct–Apr 15 Rs 13,000 garden view pavilion double, Rs 15,000 beach view superior double, Rs 17,000 beach view deluxe double, Rs 24,000 Club double, Rs 35,000–Rs 65,000 suite; Apr 16–Sept Rs 11,000 garden view pavilion double, Rs 13,000 beach view superior double, Rs 15,000 beach view deluxe double, Rs 22,000 Club double, Rs 30,000–Rs 55,000 suite. Rates exclude 15% tax. Rates much higher Dec 23–Jan 3 when a 5-night minimum is enforced and extremely expensive gala dinners are compulsory. AE, MC, V. **Amenities:** 3 restaurants, various lounges, 2 bars; airport transfers (Rs 1,200); badminton; bikes; children's activities; club wing; concierge; cooking classes; cultural performances; golf (at Trivandrum Golf Club); 2 health clubs; jogging track; library; 3 pools; room service; snooker; Ayurvedic and wellness spa; table tennis; tennis court; yoga. *In room:* A/C, TV, hair dryer, minibar, Wi-Fi (Rs 150/hr.; Rs 750/12 hr.); butler service in club wing.

7

When Klaus Schleusener, a German professor who was based in Chennai in the '70s and '80s, first laid eyes on these aptly named beaches (Chandra means "moon," for the moonrise; Surya means "sun," above where it sets), he knew he had to own the cliff promontory that divided them. Naming the property Surya Samudra, Klaus built the original octagonal "Sea Front Deluxe" unit as his personal getaway. Alarmed at how centuries-old carved wooden cottages from villages around Kerala were being torn down to make way for modern homes—he came up with the inspired idea to transplant them, and so created a trend that helped set Kerala's huge tourism industry in motion. Today he's moved on (his enchanting new **Green Lagoon** in the Backwaters, is reviewed on p. 267), but the resort he created survives, albeit now under differently minded businessfolk who, according to some, are intent on diminishing its appeal (see review below).

Located on the other side of Surya Samudra, on Chandra beach, is the very basic **Bethsaida Hermitage** resort (✆ 0471/248-1554; fax 0471/248-1554; www.bethsaida hermitage.com). This collection of thatched bamboo and stone beach cottages was begun by a local priest who wanted to start an eco-friendly endeavor that could be used to aid a local orphanage. It's looking a little run-down at present and not worth booking unless you can reserve one of the most recently built "sea-view" rooms (60€–90€) behind the pool. These rooms are spotless, spacious, and close to the beach. Hot water is at the mercy of an occasionally moody electrical system, and you need to bring your own toiletries. Don't arrive expecting luxury and you'll feel good knowing that your room's rate (slightly overpriced, considering) contributes to the welfare of some 2,500 children. We have had reports from regular guests of the generally wonderful staff getting drunk on the job and then taking a few days to recover—the result being absolutely no service whatsoever for the next few days—rather a daunting prospect. That incident happened over the Christmas–New Year period, however, but we'd strongly advise that you investigate fully the current status of management before booking here.

Out of sight, but not far from here, is **Coconut Bay Beach Resort** (✆ 0471/248-0566; www.coconutbay.com), one of the most efficiently run resorts on the coast, with an unpretentious and low-key atmosphere and a very serious focus on Ayurveda. It's small (only 27 units), but—as is the norm hereabouts—accommodations (which are pretty ordinary, with ugly furnishings) are in a variety of categories, scattered around a hodgepodge of lawns and coco palms strung with hammocks. In its favor, it's right up against the beach, with a truly mellow atmosphere. If you're a solo traveler, the best units are one of only five non-air-conditioned beach rooms (✆ 098-4706-9654; 46€–71€ single, depending on season, including all meals), which are off to one side and right above the beach; book room 301 and you have a semiprivate veranda area with the best view at the resort. Great views, too, from deluxe beach villas 203, 205 and 206 (109€–153€ double with all meals) and superior deluxe villa 201 (152€–190€ double with all meals). As with all the Ayurvedic resorts (and this one, too, is Green Leaf accredited), the specialty here is on long-stay treatment packages, so check the website for the lowdown on all the deals.

Karikkathi Beach House ★★   The tranquillity of its location—right on Surya Beach, but 400m (1,312 ft.) from the nearest vehicle access point—will leave you breathless. Though it's not nearly as elevated at Surya Samudra (and you may miss the pool), the advantage here is the immediacy of the seafront. For this is a beach resort in the true sense—a set of two pretty bungalows that compel you to spend time dawdling across the sand and frolicking in the waves (you need to be a fairly strong swimmer). No resort

activities and no meal times—you set your own rules. Each cottage has two en suite
double bedrooms linked by a lounge. They're exquisitely decorated—not too modern,
and sufficiently rustic that you still feel yourself at the edge of the beach; very romantic.
There's no TV or air-conditioning, but plenty of natural ventilation (and fans) instead.
We can hardly imagine a finer place to do nothing but imbibe the simpler things—fishing boats bobbing on the water, the moon glimmering off its surface, and a private staff
to take care of you; meals are served in your cottage or on the verandah. Power outages
are inevitable, but unlikely to spoil your mood.

Cliff Beach Garden, Mulloor Thottam (south of Kovalam, north of Chowara, via Nagar Bhagavathi Temple)
Pulinkudi, Thiruvananthapuram 695 521. ℂ **098-4706-9654** or 0471/240-0956. www.karikkathibeach
house.com. karikkathi@yahoo.co.in. 2 cottages rented on an exclusive basis; rooms can also be rented
individually. May–Oct 199€ per cottage, 99€ double room; Dec–Feb 390€ per cottage, 195 double room;
extra bed 30% of double room rate. Prices vary other months. Rates include all meals and taxes. 7½%
discount for 7-night stays, 15% discount for 14-night stays. Ayurvedic packages available on weekly basis.
MC, V. **Amenities:** Airport transfers (12€). *In room:* Fans.

Surya Samudra ★★★   This is Kerala's most famous resort, and deservedly so. When
we were researching this edition, an all-out renovation was underway, and neither the
security guard nor builders would let us have a peek at what was going on. Surya traditionally accommodated a maximum of 44 guests, all in traditional-style cottages perched
high on a terraced hillside overlooking the sea and two pretty beaches—and it has always
been this setting, amid gardens of hibiscus trees, banyans, and coconut palms interspersed with rustic pathways and statues, that lent it immeasurable charm. Surya was
never as slick as a five-star hotel, but the atmosphere was romantic and the setting totally
glorious. They've added quite a few new cottages and have gone to town in terms of
luxury, but we're hoping the extensive upgrade of facilities won't detract from the original
charm and that it'll emerge better than before, with a more attentive staff (which has
traditionally been quite lazy) and many small details (like loose toilet seats) sorted out.
But with the way development has been going along this stretch of Kerala, the recent
expansion may, sadly, compromise the ambience completely.

Pulinkudi, Mullar P.O. Thiruvananthapuram 695 521. ℂ **0471/226-7333.** Fax 0471/226-7124. www.
suryasamudra.com. 32 units. Oct–Apr 15 225€–250€ rock garden double, 300€–400€ heritage double,
1,100€ Banyan Tree Bungalow; Apr 16–Sept 140€–150€ rock garden double, 175€–225€ heritage double,
600€ Banyan Tree Bungalow; add 15% for extra bed. Massive hike in rates Dec 22–Jan 8 when a 4-night
minimum stay is enforced. Rates include breakfast; 15% tax extra. MC, V. **Amenities:** Restaurant, poolside
bar; airport transfers (chargeable); Ayurvedic spa; babysitting (with prior booking); boating; small library;
large outdoor pool; room service; yoga. *In room:* A/C, minibar.

Chowara Beach

Located below the small village of Chowara, within verdant cliffs towering along it, this
long stretch of powdery white sand is located 12km (7½ miles) south of Trivandrum and
30 to 40 minutes from the airport. Chowara Beach is not only very pretty (the same
cannot be said of most of the accommodations here), but the sea here is usually rather
tame—hardly surprising then that it has several resorts strung along it, some would say
too many resorts, in fact. However, you're unlikely to end up staying here unless you've
come for a fairly stringent Ayurvedic program (which is the raison d'être for most of these
places anyway). The exception is Travancore Heritage, which—despite having the most
sophisticated-looking Ayurvedic center—has a slightly more leisurely approach; trouble
is their best accommodations are a bit of a slog from the beach. Besides the places we've
reviewed below, one other option is well-priced **Nikki's Nest** (Azhimala Shiva Temple

Rd., Pulinkudi, Chowara; ⓒ **0471/226-8821,** -8822, or 0471/226-7822; www.nikkis
nest.com; 90€–125€ double with air-conditioning, including breakfast, 15% tax extra),
which unfortunately suffers from interminable early morning temple noise that kicks off
each day at 5am. If you can endure the unexpected wake-up or are an early riser, it's not
too bad a choice, with a fairly welcoming staff and on-hand owners to make your stay feel
quite comfortable. Accommodations are in slightly dark thatch-roofed cottages (rooms
203 and 204 are closest to the beach) or in restored traditional wooden Kerala houses (202
is the one to book here; alternatively, 201; 105€–125€ double); half are air-conditioned,
and they're neat and tidy but (like Coconut Lagoon; reviewed above) ultimately rather
kitsch and with rather unhandsome finishes (bathrooms are really quite hideous, with
massive frosted glass sliding shower doors). Again, the reason you're here is for the
Ayurvedic treatments; like Somatheeram, this place has Green Leaf accreditation, and
after your massage you can trundle down to the beach or spend hours daydreaming at the
restaurant, which has equally spectacular views and heavenly fresh fruit juices.

Note: All of these "resorts" offer a wide variety of packages that include specified or
personalized treatments and therapies, often based on stays of between 2 weeks and 1
month—this is their big draw. In fact, these resorts exist more as centers for Ayurvedic
patients than as vacation retreats. If you're not interested in Ayurveda—or perhaps
yoga—the best options here are Thapovan and Travancore Heritage, which are less congested by robe-wearing guests wandering through the grounds in a post-treatment daze.

Dr. Franklin's Panchakarma Institute & Research Centre ⟨Value⟩

It's not pretty,
but if you're serious about Ayurveda and don't intend wiping out your savings, this is a
good budget option, offering perhaps the most focused Ayurvedic experiences in south
Kerala (as the name suggests). Dr. Varghese Franklin has more than 50 years' worth of
experience as a practitioner (he started Somatheeram's Ayurvedic center), and offers a
host of therapeutic programs, longevity treatments, and specialized slimming programs,
as well as practical training workshops (such as "You and Your Spine"). Massage, yoga,
and Ayurvedic cooking courses are also conducted here. There are no suites or fancy
rooms—the basic bedrooms have doubles beds with mosquito nets, tiled floors, and neat
attached bathrooms (shower only); deluxe units have private patios where you can sip
herbal tea between treatments. For mega-budgeteers, there are a few simple mud huts,
each with twin beds and attached bathrooms—useful if you're planning on hanging
around for longer courses. The grounds are comfortable enough, but this isn't a resort, so
you'll probably want to take full advantage of the free shuttle to the beach (although the
10-min. walk isn't too bad).

Chowara P.O., Thiruvananthapuram 695 501. ⓒ **0471/248-0870** or 0471/226-7974. Fax: 0471/226-8071.
www.drfranklin.com. franklin@dr-franklin.com. 25 units, some with shower only. Aug–Mar 38€–45€
deluxe double, 48€–55€ A/C deluxe double, 28€–32€ special room double, 18€–20€ Panchakarma hut
double; Apr–July 28€ deluxe double, 38€ A/C deluxe double, 20€ special room double, 15€ Panchakarma
hut double. Extra bed 20% of rate. Rates include breakfast; taxes extra. MC, V. **Amenities:** Restaurant;
airport transfers (free w/Ayurveda packages); cooking courses; cultural performances; Wi-Fi (in restaurant; free); yoga. *In room* A/C (in some) and fans, TV (except in huts), no phone in huts.

Manaltheeram Ayurveda Beach Village ★

With Green Leaf accreditation for its
Ayurvedic center, a great location right on the beach (not to mention a well-positioned
sea-view pool and open-air restaurant from where you can see where the beach disappears
into the horizon), and relatively flat terrain (meaning there's far less hiking up and down
stairs than at nearby Somatheeram; reviewed below), Manaltheeram is still a contender
as one of the better "treatment resorts" in southern Kerala. Most accommodations are in

"Ordinary" and "Special" (read: sea-view) cottages: These are standard thatched round villas. Book Special cottages 525 to 530 for the most privacy—they're better value than the so-called "Kerala houses," although there's a 5% surcharge for preselecting your choice of digs (although you can probably bargain this away). As with any of these Ayurveda retreats, the best deals are on packages that last at least 2 weeks.

Chowara P.O., Thiruvananthapuram 695 501. (℗ **0471/226-6222.** Fax 0471/226-7611. www.manaltheeram. com. mail@manaltheeram.com. 57 units. Nov–Apr 80€–92€ standard double, 92€–106€ garden cottage double, 116€–134€ special cottage double, 158€–180€ standard Kerala House double, 210€–242€ A/C Kerala House double; May–Oct 56€ standard double, 64€ garden cottage double, 86€ special cottage double, 120€ standard Kerala House double, 148€ A/C Kerala House double. 20% extra per person sharing; children under 12 free if sharing. AE, MC, V. **Amenities:** Restaurant; airport transfers (Rs 675; free for most Ayurveda packages); Ayurvedic center; cultural performances; Internet (broadband); Rs 2/min.); outdoor pool; room service; tailor; yoga and meditation. *In room:* A/C (in some) and fans, fridge (in deluxe units).

Somatheeram Ayurvedic Health Resort ★★   As much beachfront hospital as vacation destination, this resort has been inundated with awards for "Best Ayurvedic Centre"—they're state-issued, however, by people with no knowledge of what a vacation is about. The primary reason to book here is for a Somatheeram package: Massages and treatments are provided in a hygienic environment by a team of experienced, professional staff (12 doctors and more than 50 therapists) who offer serious Ayurvedic rejuvenation and therapeutic packages (average stay here is 2 weeks) rather than just luxurious pampering. The most interesting accommodations are in traditional wooden Kerala houses, which have the standard shaded verandas and hand-carved pillars and are usually the most comfortable rooms; some (like 109 and 110) have open air bathrooms. Better value is to opt for an ordinary *nalukettu* room in one of these four-bedroom cottages—the best by far (for the fabulous sea views) are nos. 102 and 101.

Tip: Don't confuse this place (the one with the slick, contemporary S-design branding) with neighboring **Somatheeram Ayurvedic Beach Resort** (℗ **0471/226-8101;** www.somatheeram.in), which is the result of a split in the family business. The "Health Resort" has the more convenient location for the beach and better accommodations, extensively renovated in 2009. The "Beach Resort" is owned by the same brother who owns nearby **Manaltheeram Ayurvedic Beach Resort** (reviewed above); all three offer equitable Ayurvedic packages.

Chowara P.O. 695 501. (℗ **0471/226-6501.** Fax 0471/226-6505. www.somatheeram.org. info@somatheeram. org. 66 units. Nov–Apr 80€–92€ standard double, 116€–134€ special cottage double, 158€–180€ Kerala standard double, 210€–242€ Kerala deluxe double, 260€–300€ Sidhartha suite double; May–Oct 56€ standard double, 86€ special cottage double, 120€ Kerala standard double, 148€ Kerala deluxe double, 180€ Sidhartha suite double. 20% extra per person sharing. MC, V. **Amenities:** Restaurant; airport transfers (Rs 675; free for certain Ayurveda packages); Ayurvedic center; cultural performances; Internet (near reception; Rs 2/min.); library; large outdoor pool; room service; tailor; yoga & meditation. *In room* A/C (in some) and fans, fridge (in deluxe units).

Thapovan Heritage Home ★ ⓥalue   Divided into two distinct properties—one up the hill and one quite close to the edge of the beach—this is a good budget choice with a more salubrious atmosphere, and better looking (if very basic) accommodations, than are found at Nikki's Nest. It's also more intimate in terms of room numbers and spread over a good swath of land. The two big drawbacks are likely to be the absence of airconditioning (but if you've come for a rejuvenating vacation with Ayurvedic treatments, then you'll know that chilled air is ultimately incompatible with good health); fortunately, the sea is near enough for you to cool off there (a good reason to choose the seaside property). So turn on the fans and open all the windows—or find a spot in the garden where you can relax with the dull roar of the ocean not too far off. Beachfront rooms (in a series of sea-facing cottages, two rooms per cottage) have direct beach access (201–204 and 401–404 are best)—a boon for anyone who gets frustrated at being able to see but not touch. Rooms are a little boxy, with basic furnishings and finishes, but very clean and have cane chairs, yoga mats, and a shared porch. This is a relatively well-kept secret, and one of the better values hereabouts.

Nellikunnu, Mulloor P.O., Thiruvananthapuram 695 521. © **0471/248-0453**, -2430, or 93-4975-2072. www.thapovan.com. thapovan@gmail.com. Beach Property: 18 units (shower only). 36€ Eagles Nest double, 55€ beach cottage and beach house double, Rs 750 extra bed. Hillock Property: 13 units (shower only). 36€ old house double, 45€ hideout double, 55€ teakwood house and hillock cottage double, Rs 750 extra bed. Rates exclude 15% tax. Wide range of Ayurvedic packages available. MC, V. **Amenities:** 2 restaurants; airport transfers (Rs 600); Internet (broadband; Rs 60/hr.); library; yoga. *In room:* Fans.

Travancore Heritage ★★   This is considered to be at the top end of the Kovalam lodging spectrum, with 5¼ hectares (13 acres) of seafront real estate with a mix of hotel-style wings and a sprinkling of Kerala-style cottages set in a vast garden of tamarind and jackfruit trees and coconut palms. The best rooms are the heritage "premiums" (which have sea views); these are for the most part furnished with high, wood-frame beds, old wicker-backed planter's chairs, and blinds made from gilded white *lungi* material. If you want to be near the beach, you'll need to book a room in the bland Beach Grove wing, reached—mercifully—by elevator, and with its own pool. Avoid the Premium "Mansion," which is a similarly bland wing, with no freestanding units; it's more expensive than the heritage homes and hard to tell why. The Ayurvedic center here may not have the years of history associated with Somatheeram, but facilities look a heck of a lot better, with 45 therapists and none of that depressing rural hospital ambience.

Chowara P.O., Trivandrum 695 501. © **0471/226-7828** through -7831. Fax 0471/226-7201. www.the travancoreheritage.com. frontoffice@thetravancoreheritage.com. 90 units. Oct–Mar Rs 5,700–Rs 6,800 Beach Grove double, Rs 7,000–Rs 8,300 Heritage Home double, Rs 7,800–Rs 9,000 Premium Mansion double, Rs 7,800–Rs 9,800 Heritage Premium double, Rs 9,300–Rs 11,800 premium suite double; Rs 14,800–Rs 18,100 pool mansion double, Rs 1,100–Rs 1,500 extra person; Apr–Sept Rs 3,100 Beach Grove double, Rs 3,700 Heritage Home double, Rs 4,400 Premium Mansion double, Rs 5,400 Heritage Premium double, Rs 6,200 premium suite double; Rs 10,000 pool mansion double, Rs 900–Rs 1,500 extra person. Rates include breakfast; 15% tax extra AE, MC, V. **Amenities:** 3 restaurants w/bar service; airport transfers (Rs 1,000–Rs 1,200); Ayurvedic center; cultural performances; health club; Jacuzzi; library; 2 pools; room service. *In room:* A/C and fans, TV, minibar, Wi-Fi (free).

Poovar Island

Kerala's southernmost resort destination (40 min. from Trivandrum), at the border between Kerala and Tamil Nadu on a remote stretch of river lagoon, provides a taste of the backwaters, with palm-fringed rivers, together with the ocean views of a beach resort. The sea here is rough, so it's not a great place for ocean swimming, and with the proliferation of resorts in a relatively small area in the past 7 years, its tranquillity has been compromised. Before the building frenzy began, Poovar Island Resort was the pace to be, but don't be fooled by the glossy brochures and designs, which fail to mention the ongoing sewage problems of their romantic "floating cottages." Best of the five biggish resorts here is **Isola Di Cocco** (© **0471/221-0008;** www.isoladicocco.com; standard doubles from Rs 5,500 in high season, breakfast included), mostly due to the fact that it takes its Ayurvedic treatments and packages very seriously at very good value. Not only that, but there's some semblance of a style that's fitting with the whole lagoon-cum-beach vibe of the area. Accommodation is perfectly comfortable if a little unimaginative, with no personal touches or design forethought (or, more tellingly, sea views), but everything is spotless and spacious, and there've been some extensive refurbishments as recently as **295** 2009. If you choose to stay here, opt for one of the 10 lake-view rooms (16, 17, and 53–60), which fall in the Heritage Category (Rs 4,000–Rs 7,000 double with breakfast, depending on season). Service is friendly, and the Indian food is good.

Right next door to Isola, with more of a concrete hotel resort atmosphere and extensive facilities, is **Estuary Island** (© 0471/221-4355; www.estuaryisland.com), which does afford views towards the sea (although, as with all the Poovar resorts, you don't see the ocean but rather a lovely beach that divides the lagoon from the ocean). While the rooms are exceptionally bland, they're well stocked with amenities, and if you don't mind forgoing the estuary view from the cheaper standard units (Rs 4,000–Rs 9,000 double), you can get a much larger and more private Estuary Premium cottage (Rs 6,000–Rs 10,000 double, including boat transfers) in a secluded section behind the main block. There's plenty here to keep children busy (including a kids' pool and park), and the beer parlor built over the water is a good place to sit with a pair of binoculars and see what the fishermen are up to. Green Leaf–accredited Ayurvedic treatments are available, and there's a fleet of assorted boats (with or without motor).

However, if you really have the spirit of adventure in you, there's only one place you want to be.

Friday's Place ★ (**Moments** If you scream at the sight of a frog and have an abiding hatred of insects, you'd better look elsewhere. This tiny lodge tucked deep inside a jungle just off the lagoon is where you can reconnect with your eco-warrior. It comprises only four wooden cottages (two high on stilts) in the wilderness extending straight out into the Neyyar backwaters, so environmental impact is negligible. Designed by owners Mark and Sujeewa Reynolds (who personally run the retreat), the cottages are solar-powered and sport an eco-friendly sewage system—two rooms share a common bathroom. Newly added is the chic two-level Tsunami House, a solid stone cottage like nothing you've ever laid eye on; it's minimalist but comfy, with a large downstairs bathroom. Rates may seem a little steep, but you're paying for the pleasure of a true Robinson Crusoe–style adventure, complete with a bevy of Man Fridays tending to basic needs or preparing fresh, wholesome meals. Note that the retreat has no road access, is only open mid-October through April, and serves vegetarian meals only. Bring books, iPod, and a willingness to get back to basics.

Poovar Island, Attupuram, Uchakada P.O., Thiruvananthapuram 695 506. © **0471/213-3292.** www.fridays place.biz. 5 units, 2 with attached bathroom, all with shower only. £105 cottage double, £150 Tsunami House double. Rates include all meals. Minimum stay 3 nights. No credit cards. **Amenities:** Dining area/ lounge; airport transfers (£10); country boat. *In room:* No phone, Wi-Fi.

6 THE CARDAMOM HILLS & PERIYAR TIGER RESERVE

Thekkady (Periyar) is 190km (118 miles) from Kochi and 145km (90 miles) from Madurai

Each year, around half a million travelers make their way up into the Cardamom Hills, where the crisp, cool air is redolent with the scents of spices, and soaring mountains give way to tea plantations and dense jungle. Most people intent on seeing the best of Kerala head from the backwaters to the village of Thekkady, gateway to **Periyar Tiger Reserve,** the stomping grounds for large herds of wild elephants and apparently where as many as

22 to 40 tigers avoid being spotted. Although it's true that Periyar is one of India's largest and most popular elephant reserves, this is not a wilderness experience in the true sense. Unless you opt for an overnight trek or one of the full-day hikes, the popular boat trip on the lake feels much like being processed like sheep by regimented nature rangers, and the intense tourist activity around the roads leading to the gates is quite disheartening.

However, with a couple of lovely places to stay, it is well worth overnighting here if you are traveling by car from Kerala to Tamil Nadu (or vice versa), though the most direct route (if you're driving between Madurai and Kochi) is via **Munnar,** which lies 4 hours due north of Thekkady. At a much greater altitude than Periyar, Munnar is a collection of vast green-tea estates first established by a Scotsman in the late 19th century—it's hardly surprising, then, that the area is sometimes referred to as Kerala's Scottish highlands. In the days of the Raj, it became a popular "hill station"—a place to escape from the summer heat in the plains. Today the landscape—for the most part—retains a classic hill station atmosphere. Watched over by Mount Anamudi, South India's highest peak (2,695m/8,840 ft.), Munnar's primary attractions are its gorgeous views of rolling hills covered with tea and cardamom plantations, and the cool climate—great, if you intend to stay more than 1 night, for leisurely walks and cycle-tours (not to mention a close encounter with the endangered Nilgiri tahr, a variety of mountain goat).

ESSENTIALS

VISITOR INFORMATION   All Periyar Tiger Reserve inquiries should be made through the **Divisional Forest Office,** Thekkady (© **04869/22-2027;** Mon–Sat 10am–5pm, closed second Sat of the month). Note that entry to the park costs Rs 300 and is only open between 6am and 6pm. Easiest by far is to ask your hotel to make arrangements; all the resorts will book and transfer you to the KTDC-arranged excursions (see "Periyar Tiger Reserve," below).

In Munnar, the **Tourist Information Centre** (© **04865/23-1516;** www.munnar. com; Mon–Sat 9am–7pm) in Old Munnar is relatively helpful.

GETTING THERE   From Kochi   Periyar/Thekaddy is a 4-hour drive east of Kochi, a long but (once you're beyond the city limits) enjoyable drive that traverses mountain roads ascending 900m (2,952 ft.) above sea level. Munnar is about 5 hours from Kochi (and a 2- to 3-hr. drive north of Periyar), and another beautiful drive; you'll pass tea plantations and spice-growing embankments and drive through lovely sections of forest. Do the drive in the monsoon season and you'll witness some spectacular waterfalls, too.

From Madurai, Tamil Nadu   Both Munnar and Thekkady lie around 4 hours away from Madurai; if you're really in a hurry, Munnar will shave a few minutes off.

Note: Traveling by bus is arduous and time consuming, at worst hair-raising, but if you want to save money, this is the way to go.

GETTING AROUND   You can pick up a ride on a auto-rickshaw or taxi almost anywhere in the **Periyar** area, with hordes of vehicles waiting at the bus stand. Overcharging foreigners is common; try to ascertain from your hotel what the going rate for a particular route is, and bargain upfront. Taxicabs and auto-rickshaws are readily available in and around **Munnar,** or you can arrange a car and driver through your hotel.

WHERE TO STAY EN ROUTE TO KERALA'S HIGHLANDS

With 4 to 6 hours of endlessly enchanting scenery between Kerala's coast and the Western Ghats which form a natural border with Tamil Nadu, there's nothing to stop you from simply racing to your destination at the entrance to the Periyar Reserve or in the

Finding Serenity Between the Backwaters & the Hills

If you're traveling between Kochi (or the backwaters) and Periyar, another great spot to stop off for a few days is the aptly named **Serenity ★★** (Payikad, Kanam PO, Vazhoor; ℂ **0481/245-6353**), which is an excellent place to remove yourself entirely from the beaten track and get a look at Kerala-style country life in a setting that really does feel far away from the tourist bandwagon. Like both Vanilla County and Paradisa, it's a gorgeous destination in its own right, and definitely worth investigating if you're taking a more leisurely approach to travel, and prefer to get off the beaten path a bit. A converted 1920s bungalow in the heart of a rubber plantation, Kanam Estate, it offers six guest rooms, high wood-beam ceilings, polished floors, cane chairs, four-poster beds, traditional masks mounted on display stands, and a gorgeously located pool. You can arrange for Lakshmi, the tame 30-year-old in-house elephant, to come in and play for the day—it costs a whopping 100€ and you only get about 4 full hours of interaction (which includes riding, feeding, and even washing her), but she's a great hit with kids (and grown-ups, too). Make sure it's not ceremony or harvest season, when elephants throughout the state are in huge demand and kept busy. If she's not available, you'll need to settle for one of the other diversions available here—there are bikes for an independent tour of the nearby villages; guided plantation tours; bullock cart rides (50€); cooking classes; and revitalizing Ayurvedic treatments. And while it's a great place for families to spend time together, Serenity, as the name suggests, is also a superbly romantic hideaway, or one where you can simply put your feet up and forget about the rest of the world. Reservations are made through **The Malabar House** (ℂ **0484/221-6666;** www.malabar escapes.com; doubles 150€–220€ in Kochi.

highlands tea country around Munnar. But that would be a complete shame, since there are a handful of utterly captivating places to bed down along the way—more than that, these are may very well be the highlight of your trip, and very relaxing spots, indeed.

Paradisa Plantation Retreat ★★★   We wouldn't dream of coming to Kerala without spending a night here: About 90 minutes from Periyar's entrance, with stupendous views of the reserve's forested hills from its elevated position on an old spice plantation, this is as peaceful as it gets. Equally uplifting is the cuisine—there is no menu per se but plate after plate is carried into the open-air dining area where, with luck, the charming and urbane owner Simon Paulose will be holding court. There's always more than you can possibly eat, but eat you will, because you will never taste this exact combination of exquisite home-cooked flavors again, more's the pity (though guests are welcome to spend time in the kitchen, learning how to reconstruct the retreat's delicious meals, and a recipe book may be forthcoming). Accommodation is just what you'd expect from a retreat: gorgeous, and very, very private—salvaged traditional Keralan teak houses, all making the most of the unobstructed views of the rolling green hillsides.

Murinjapuzha P.O. Idukki District, Kerala 685 532. ℂ **04869/288-119** or 0944/7088-119. Reservations: ℂ **0469/270-1311** or 0469/260-2828. www.paradisaretreat.com. info@paradisaretreat.com. 12 units. Rs 10,500 double deluxe cottage. Rs 18,500 Cardamom cottage; extra bed add 20%. Rates include breakfast; taxes extra. Christmas and New Year's Eve supplement. Meals Rs 950. MC, V. **Amenities:** Dining;

Ayurvedic treatments arranged at nearby medical center; outdoor pool; room service; walks and excursions to tea plantations (free); Wi-Fi (unreliable connection; free).

Vanilla County ★★★ ⓥalue   Deep in plantation country, this is an absolutely authentic homestay in a 60-year-old bungalow, and a place to experience true, down-to-earth Kerala family life with all the added drama of a naturally awesome setting. Like Paradisa (above), it's quite far from Periyar (2 hr.; same distance from the Backwaters), so consider it a destination in its own right, where you get beyond the ordinary tourist experience. Bedrooms are spacious, comfortable, and spotless—owners Baby Mathew and Rani (and two children) take great pride in their home and they warmly share it with you. You'll get to know the ins and outs of their daily lives, learning from them (in the kitchen and the rubber and spice gardens) and exploring local sites with an excellent guide. Head off on hikes where you'll meet beautifully friendly people, then return to the cooling waters of the estate's two gorgeous rock pools, or slip into a hammock in the garden, and prepare for one of Rani's astonishing feasts. Do not forget to sample her unique banana jam at breakfast.

Vagamon Rd., Mavady Estate, Teekoy 686 580. ⓒ **04822/28-1225** or 04822/32-5397. http://vanilla county.in. 6 units. Rs 7,000 double; Rs 3,000 extra person. Children under 5 free. Rates include all meals, activities, and local transportation. MC, V. **Amenities:** Dining room, lounge; airport transfers (Rs 10/km.); cooking classes (Apr–Sept; Rs 500/dish); Internet (in lounge; free); 2 natural rock pools; yoga (packages available). *In room:* Fans, no phone.

THE PERIYAR TIGER RESERVE

Originally the hunting grounds of the Maharajah of Travancore, Periyar Tiger Reserve was declared a wildlife reserve (previously called the Periyar Wildlife Sanctuary) in 1933. In 1979 it became a Project Tiger Reserve—India's homegrown initiative to protect the big cats' dwindling numbers. Today Periyar covers 777 sq. km (2,012 sq. miles), and is divided into core, buffer, and tourist zones. Although tiger sightings are very rare, particularly in the tourist zone (although there was a sighting reported on Dec 26, 2008), the reserve is home to elephants, sloth bears, sambar, gaur (a relative of the water buffalo), dhole (a wild dog), leopards, spotted deer, Malabar giant squirrels (a sighting is likely to be a highlight—they're huge), barking deer, Nilgiri tahr, and over 300 species of birds. It contains around 1,700 species of flowering plants, including at least 145 different kinds of orchid.

The best way to experience Periyar is with a Periyar Tiger Trail (see "Back to Nature on the Tiger Trail" box below); other than this, all access to the park is cheap, making excursions popular with exuberant domestic tourists who tend to be noisy, which somewhat inhibits one's enjoyment of natural scenery. Most opt for the 2-hour **boat cruise** on Periyar Lake, from where—if you're lucky—you can view animals coming to drink at the water's edge. Unfortunately, you're more likely to experience nonstop din from children (and their parents) who refuse to obey pleas for silence, preferring to rove around the boat and video each other. There are five boat departures a day, and you'd do well not to be on any of them. Less subscribed are the daily **nature walks** and **green walks;** these 3-hour treks depart at 7am, 10am, and 2pm and cost Rs 100 (maximum five in a group), and provide you with the opportunity to admire some of the stunning flora of the region; better still are the **bamboo rafting** trips in which a maximum of 10 people are taken on a full day's worth of rafting combined with some trekking (Rs 1,000 per person; 8am–5pm). Check **www.periyartigerreserve.org** for details on these and other adventures such as **jungle patrol** (a nighttime hike; Rs 500), and the **bullock cart discovery,** where you ride through the countryside exploring traditional villages. However you choose to

(Moments) Back to Nature on the Tiger Trail

By far the most exciting and tranquil way to experience the park is a 2- or 3-day **Periyar Tiger Trail ★★**. Armed with antileech footwear and a sleeping bag (supplied), and accompanied by two forest officials and five guides, you are taken farther into the tourist zone than any other operator is allowed to penetrate. What's more, you are being led and looked after by a team of reformed poachers (sandalwood, cinnamon bark, and bison being their loot of choice) who know the terrain and the wildlife better than anyone. They skillfully track and spot animals, carry all the gear, strike camp, cook, clean, and—most important—stand sentinel throughout the night when the danger of being trampled by elephants becomes a serious risk. They also now play an essential role in catching poachers who remain active in the reserve.

You need to be moderately fit for the trail; you'll walk between 20km and 35km (12–22 miles), and there are (this being the great outdoors) no luxuries or conveniences along the way. The chances of spotting a tiger are slim at best, but you'll almost certainly come across elephants, wild pigs, sambar, black monkeys, wild dogs, and bison, and when you're not trekking to your next campsite, you'll be relaxing under forest cover or alongside a lake tributary. Meals are wholesome, authentic Kerala vegetarian fare: sweet *chai* and pleasant snack lunches served on silver trays with the grass for a tablecloth and a beetle symphony as background. Toilet functions are performed in the great outdoors. Each trail is limited to five visitors, with very limited departures each week, so reserve well in advance, particularly in peak (winter) season, when it is often booked a year in advance. The trek starts between 8 and 9am, so you'll have to stay near the park the previous night—your last taste of luxury before hitting the great outdoors. At press time the 1-night trail is Rs 3,000 per person (Rs 5,000 if you happen to be the only person on the trail), and the 2-night trail is Rs 5,000 (or Rs 7,500 if you're alone). For bookings or information, contact tourism@periyartigerreserve.org or call ⓒ **04869/22-4571** or visit www.periyar tigerreserve.org

Note: All trails are run by the park, so while there are tour operators offering Periyar Trails excursions, all you essentially get by booking through them is an additional middleman fee (though you might think the $30-odd additional charge worth it if you're struggling to contact the park or get confirmation on your booking). If you prefer to go this way, contact Trivandrum-based **TourIndia** (ⓒ **0471/232-8070** or 0471/233-1507; www.tourindiakerala.com; tourindia@vsnl.com), which charges $170 per person for the 2-night trail, subject to a two-person minimum. If you have any special interests, such as ornithology, TourIndia will make arrangements to have a specialist guide you.

explore the park, remember that temperatures can be freezing from November through February, so pack warm layers.

Note: Whatever activities you have in mind, you're better off making all your arrangements through your hotel. Avoid any unsolicited offers from "guides" promising to take you on walks or tours into the reserve; this will only waste your time and test your patience.

Where to Stay & Dine

With the exception of the atmospheric KTDC Lake Palace, which is inside the park, visitors to Periyar are limited to accommodations that lie within a few minutes of each other along Thekkady Road (which links nearby Kumily with the park gate). Of these, we like the more intimate, unkempt, and jungly atmosphere of **Shalimar Spice Garden** (see below), but the eco-pioneering chain, CGH Earth, has done fantastic things with **Spice Village** (also reviewed below), and is a great option if you prefer things superneat and tidy, efficient service, and an array of facilities. If you're just passing through and looking for a cheap, excellent Indian meal, the restaurant at Hotel Ambadi (www. hotelambadi.com) is the place. Packed to capacity with domestic tourists, it offers superb value (the most expensive items are half a chicken for around Rs 100 and prawns for Rs 125), delicious (very spicy) food, and surly service. Alternatively, if you just want to snack on croissants and tea or coffee, make your way to the pleasant little cafe at Wildernest (see below), where breakfast should cost you around Rs 100.

KTDC Lake Palace ★

The sense of escaping the hustling around Thekkady (Periyar's commercialized entrance) kicks in as soon as you take the 15-minute boat ride across Periyar Lake to reach a forested peninsula, inhabited only by a handful of staff, fellow guests, and assorted wildlife. Occupying its own promontory, this is by no means a palace but a lovely low-slung stone, wood, and tile-roofed bungalow—the former game lodge of the Maharajah of Travancore. The best reason to book is for the sense of exclusivity (it takes a maximum of 12 guests and is very popular, so book well in advance) and the remote setting, best enjoyed from the wraparound veranda; you're likely to spot a variety of game and plenty of birds. The six "deluxe" guest suites are spotlessly clean and wonderfully old-fashioned, with a few pieces of antique teak furniture, including four-poster twin or double beds. Don't expect luxury or high levels of service, but do look forward to peace and tranquillity; bring books, and arrange a predawn wakeup call and guide to take you into the forest on foot.

Within Periyar Tiger Reserve Sanctuary. Reservations: Aranya Nivas and Lake Palace, Thekkady 685 536. © **04869/22-2024.** Fax 04869/22-2282. www.ktdc.com. aranyanivas@sancharnet.in. 6 units. Oct–Nov, Mar–June 14 and Aug–Sept Rs 16,000–Rs 20,000 double; Dec–Feb Rs 20,000–Rs 25,000 double; June 15–July Rs 10,000–Rs 15,000 double. Rates include all meals and boating. AE, DC, MC, V. **Amenities:** Restaurant; boat cruises; room service. *In room:* TV.

Shalimar Spice Garden ★★★

This laid-back resort, situated on a 2.4-hectare (6-acre) plantation, offers the most enchanting accommodations in the Periyar area. Scattered over a landscaped terraced hillock behind the chic lobby (a converted 300-year-old traditional *pathayam,* or granary), granite and pebble pathways lead to the thatch-roofed cottages with cool interiors—very basically furnished, but with polished terraces from where you can listen to the rustling forest sounds; outside and in, the scents of plantation spices and fruit fill the air. Cottage interiors feature whitewashed walls—there's no art, but terra-cotta tile floors, unusual lamps and lots of dark wood offset by beautifully colored fabric keep things interesting; a few have stained glass and breezy loggias. There was a strong commitment to the environment during construction, and today rainwater is harvested and water recycled, and the kitchen uses only organic farm produce—bathroom amenities and laundry products are also organic. And, thanks to a new chef, service

> **Tips** **Alternatives to Spotting Elephants in Periyar**
>
> You can pick up a range of spices from a massive number of shops lining the streets of Kumily, the nearest town to Periyar, but the best option is to head straight for **Kerala Spices Centre** (Thekkady Rd.; ℰ **0486/92-2201**), where the gregarious owner offers an informal tourist bureau. He also sells nuts and delicious cardamom tea, and has created a spick-and-span room for a homestay experience (around Rs 6,000 a night), with an emphasis on cooking—not only are you invited into the kitchen to watch his talented wife prepare her delicious meals, but you will accompany her to the local markets. A stone's throw from here is the **Mudra Kathakali Centre** (Thekkady Rd.; ℰ **94-4715-7636;** http://mudrakathakali.com; Rs 125). The 1-hour shows feature graduates of the Kala-mandalam school. Show times (usually at 4:30pm and 7pm, but get there 30 min. early to watch the performers put on their elaborate makeup) change with the seasons, so call ahead. And, if only to experience one of the most unlikely attractions in Kerala, you could always visit the **wax museum** next door. The most appealing place to shop hereabouts—at least in terms of visuals—is **Red Frog** (Lake Rd.; ℰ **04869/22-4560** or 94-4703-2276; www.galleryredfrog.com), which sells organic spices and clothing made from natural fibers in a gleaming white space; there are pretty objects resembling antiques, too, and a few decent books.

has improved, but if it's still slow, grin and bear it—the location is so lovely that you simply have to adapt to the pace and enjoy it.

Murikkady P.O., Kumily, Idukki 685 535. ℰ **04869/22-2132** or -3232. Fax 04869/22-3022. www.shalimar kerala.net. shalimar_resort@vsnl.com. 18 units, some with tubs. Oct 15–Mar Rs 7,500–Rs 10,000 elegant room double, Rs 10,000–Rs 12,500 Kerala cottage double, Rs 12,500–Rs 15,000 elegant cottage double, Rs 15,000–Rs 17,500 Honeymoon cottage double, Rs 3,750 extra adult, Rs 2,500 per child; Apr–Oct 14 Rs 6,000 elegant room double, Rs 7,000 Kerala cottage double, Rs 8,000 elegant cottage double, Rs 10,000 Honeymoon cottage double, Rs 1,500 extra adult, Rs 750 per child. Children under 6 free without extra bed. Rates include breakfast; 15% tax extra. MC, V. **Amenities:** Restaurant, lounge, reading room w/small library and TV, bar service; airport transfers (Rs 3,500–Rs 4,000); Ayurvedic center; large outdoor pool; yoga. *In room:* Heater, Wi-Fi (Rs 150/hr.).

Spice Village ★★ **Kids**   Alive with the fragrance of lemon grass, this huge "rustic village" resort is the most professionally run in the area, with groomed grounds, well-maintained bungalows, and the best staff-to-guest ratio in Thekaddy. Spread over a huge area around a network of pathways and intersections, the whitewashed cottages are very pretty, each one topped with thatch—a swell of thick elephant grass propped up by slim timber poles. Interiors are spacious but simply furnished (no need to shell out for the "deluxe" units unless you want more privacy and a bathtub). From the moment you arrive, staff is eager to please: They arrange guided plantation tours, Periyar excursions, excellent Ayurvedic spa, and various cultural and wildlife activities, including the services of qualified naturalists. With an organic farm, vermi composting site, and paper-making center, you know you're supporting eco-friendly policies—you can also help by frequenting the carbon-neutral restaurant.

Thekkady-Kumily Rd., Thekkady 685 536. ℰ **04869/22-2314** through -2316. Reservations: c/o CGH Earth, Casino Bldg., Willingdon Island, Cochin 682 003, ℰ **0484/301-1711.** Fax 0484/266-8001. www.cghearth.com. 52 units, some with tubs. Nov–Apr 294€–329€ standard villa double, 414€–444€ deluxe villa double, 82€ extra person; May–Oct Rs 9,210 standard villa double, Rs 13,225 deluxe villa double, Rs 2,860 extra person. Rates include all meals and taxes. Breakfast-only rates available. AE, DC, MC, V. **Amenities:** 2 restaurant, bar w/billiards table; Ayurvedic center; badminton court; basketball court; cooking demonstrations; cultural performances; nature center and 3 naturalists; pool; room service; tennis court, Wi-Fi (in restaurant and nature center; free); yoga and meditation. *In room:* A/C and fan, fridge, hair dryer.

Wildernest ★ Ⓥ**alue** An unwieldy-looking stone and brick construction, designed around a jackfruit tree, this budget boutique hotel stands on a small plot beside the main road leading to the reserve entrance. Accommodations are huge, high-ceiling, spotless rooms with homey, unfussy furnishing, wildlife watercolor prints, and tidy finishes— what more could you want? Well, folks at Wildernest throw in a brilliant breakfast and offer well-meaning assistance throughout your stay, including all arrangements for the reserve. Choose a Terraced Room if you want an upstairs patio (from where you spot fruit bats nesting in the bamboo trees across the road), or a Secret Garden room if you prefer a secluded private garden. This place offers incredible value, and is well managed; the only letdown is the relatively simple (though not uncomfortable) beds.

Thekkady Rd., Thekkady 685 536. Ⓒ **04869/22-4030** or 04869/21-1471. www.wildernest-kerala.com. 10 units, all with shower only. Rs 2,750–Rs 3,250 double; 20% less Apr–Sept; Rs 750 extra bed; children aged 5–12 pay Rs 500 if sharing. Rates include breakfast; 15% tax extra. MC, V. **Amenities:** Cafe; small library. *In room:* Fans, TV.

MUNNAR: HOME OF TEA & TAHRS

Munnar town itself is rather unpleasant and increasingly clogged by impulsive development; thankfully, the region's real attractions lie on its outskirts where it is still possible to find solitude in hidden away spots that have so far withstood the onslaught of tourist exploitation—especially if you pick a small, quiet place to lodge.

With tea-covered slopes spread out as far as the eye can see, watching the mists creep over the valleys and come to rest like a blanket on the jade-colored hills is almost as refreshing as luxuriating in the cool climate—a welcome relief before you descend to the tropical Kerala coast or to sultry Madurai in neighboring Tamil Nadu. There are moments when the region draws comparisons with the Scottish Highlands, dotted with enormous boulder outcrops and souring rocky peaks.

Almost all the plantations are owned by the powerful Tata company, the same mighty conglomerate that produces India's buses, Sumo four-by-fours, the world's most affordable car (launched 2009), and the Taj hotel chain. **Tea factory visits** can be arranged either through your hotel or by contacting Tata's regional office (Ⓒ **04865/23-0561** through -0565), through which you can also visit the **Tea Museum** and the tea factory's processing unit (Tues–Sun 10am–4pm). To get up close to some of the world's last Nilgiri tahr (a variety of mountain goat or ibex), arrange a visit to nearby **Eravikulam National Park.** Existing only in the mountain grasslands of the Western Ghats at altitudes above 2,000m (6,560 ft.), the tahr is as endangered as the tiger, with fewer than 2,000 left. The park has been a great success, with dedicated tea planters, once the primary hunters of the tahr, now doubling as voluntary wildlife wardens. The 2007 census shows a healthy population of 800, almost double what it was 30 years ago. Note that you can participate in the annual census, which will ensure up-close encounters with both the tahr and the planters and rangers who protect it. It is held for a week in April; for more information call the park office (see contact information below). Of course, sighting what is basically a goat, no matter how rare, may not be as exhilarating as spotting a tiger, but your chances are far higher—in fact the tahrs have grown so used to visitors that you can get within a few yards of them. Enter the park at the Rajamala

Once in a Blue Bloom

Visitors to India's southern highlands in 2006 were lucky enough to witness the blooming of the rare and exotic **Neelakurunji plant.** Its violet blossoms transform the hillsides around Munnar for 1 month—but only every 12 years. A pleasant 34km (21-mile) trip from Munnar, Top Station (the highest point on the Munnar-Kodaikanal road, from where you enjoy panoramic views of the surrounding plains and hills) is the place to witness this natural spectacle, but it won't happen again until 2018.

entrance, 15km (9⅓ miles) from Munnar, where you can buy tickets at the park office (© 04865/23-1587; entry Rs 50, light vehicles Rs 10; daily 8am–5pm). Avoid the usual noisy crowds by arriving early.

Where to Stay & Dine

If you can't get in to **Windermere** or **Casa Montagna** (both reviewed below), you might want to look at **The Siena Village.** With 28 units and a long list of facilities (including a conference hall), it's very much a resort with a dull ambience, but the location, a lovely half-hour drive from Munnar in what feels like genuine hill country (although the area is feeling the steady encroachment of neighboring properties), is really lovely. Accommodations are comfortable enough but without any flair (a single framed print, hung too high, is the only wall decoration) and despite being spread around a wide expanse of neatly trimmed lawns and a central open air pavilion can feel a little cluttered. Our biggest objection is that views from many of the rooms are obscured; ask for one with an upstairs bedroom (© 04060/24-9261; www.thesienavillage.com; Rs 4,600 deluxe double, including breakfast). Before booking with a resort that isn't recommended here, it's worth knowing that the Kerala authorities are taking a very hard line against resorts erected illegally on reserve land, so when developers take chances, authorities respond by razing the offending properties to the ground—it can mean that your choice will be nothing but a pile of rubble by the time you get here (although the places below are all legit).

Casa Montagna ★ (Finds) Marketed as a "Boutique Homestay on the Hills," this is a truly tranquil spot and one where it's possible to feel a million miles away from civilization with nothing by misty views across a near-mystical horizon. Set on a 40-hectare (100-acre) spice and cardamom plantation that feels much like a huge, lush overgrown forest, there's been plenty of home carpentry to create large and airy accommodations with great showers and plenty of windows allowing for great natural light, not to mention awesome views over the mist-laden valley that seems to drop away from the edge of the neatly trimmed lawn. Bag the so-called honeymoon cottage, and you'll enjoy maximum privacy, lulled to sleep each night by the stream that runs nearby. Although things are pretty personal, a homestay this is not; for the most part you'll be well looked after by the lovely staff that prepares meals to your taste, places flowers in your room, and takes you for walks through the thick, jungly plantation-forest, pointing out unusual trees and different spices. Note that electricity is all self-generated, and is usually only turned on when necessary (in the morning and at night).

Peak Gardens, Chinnakanal PO, Muttukadu, Munnar 685 618. © 04868/20-3050. www.casadelfauno.in. Reservations: Sebastian Rd., Kaloor, Cochin 682 017. © 98-9576-6444. info@casadelfauno.in. 6 units.

It's a Planter's Life

For a time trip back to the days when lily-white Raj-era plantation bosses would gather to discuss the grade of their latest tea leaf harvest, and extol upon the virtues of life in the hills, stop by the old-world-style **High Range Club** (www.high rangeclubmunnar.com)—founded in 1905 as The Gymkhana Club. Do so if only to see where retired planters have literally hung up their hats (in the Men's Lounge), or to shoot the breeze (or a few rounds of snooker) with the gentrified folk who still drift through these sanctified, but now slightly worn, rooms straight out of another era. You could even end up staying the night—there are decent rooms and cottages (built in 1935 and modified back in the '70s with enclosed verandas, glazed windows, and mosaic tiles) for Rs 1,000 to Rs 2,000 per night, and meals are very well priced, too.

However, if you really want to get out and stay amid the verdant tea-covered hills, nothing could be more authentic than a night in one of the five former planter's bungalows constituting **The Tea Sanctuary** ★★. With panoramic views of the vast tea and eucalyptus plantations, these sturdy (and, for a change, rather intelligently restored) cottages don't offer a heck of a lot to do indoors (except lounge by the fireplace) but you have access to a sprawling terrain, with tennis, golf, fishing, sightseeing, and trekking easily arranged. A private staff of two (including a personal chef) do much to make your stay pleasurable, and because they're owned by one of the major tea companies hereabouts—Kanan Devan Hills Plantations (KDHP House, Munnar; ✆ **04865/23-0141;** www.theteasanctuary. com; tourism.munnar@kdhptea.co.in)—you'll have hassle-free access to huge areas of tea country. Count on spending Rs 4,000 to Rs 5,500 double, with breakfast and dinner and all taxes included.

Oct–Mar Rs 7,000 elegant double, Rs 9,000 deluxe double; Apr–Sept Rs 6,000 elegant double, Rs 7,000 deluxe double; Rs 3,500 extra bed (adult), Rs 2,000 extra bed (child aged 6–12). Children 5 and under free. Rates include all meals. No credit cards. **Amenities:** Dining area, cigar room, library-lounge w/TV/DVD; bicycles; concierge; Internet (free); plantation walks. *In room:* Fan, heater.

The Tall Trees   Located 8km (5 miles) outside of scruffy Munnar town, this aptly named miniresort consists of pale-gray clapboard-style bungalows, many of them on stilts and arranged so that none of the 561 trees in the 26-hectare (66-acre) woodlands had to be felled. Of the three cottage categories, the standard—spacious, with a balcony—should suffice; the two-bedroom luxury cottages will suit families. Interiors, with bland, minimal furnishings (some badly frayed), lack the character promised by the scintillating setting, but this needn't detract too seriously from the peaceful environment, with great bird-watching from your veranda (although some of the architectural design hampers the view). It can be a long walk uphill to the restaurant, so request a cottage close by if you're not that fit. Then again, the food isn't great, and service is patchy, so if you're inclined to be demanding, you're in for a bit of a struggle. Steel your nerves by preparing for claustrophobic bathrooms and ask for extra blankets when you check in.

Bison Valley Rd., Munnar 685 618. ✆ **04865/23-0641** or -0331. www.ttr.in. 19 units. Rs 8,000–Rs 10,500 standard cottage; Rs 12,000–Rs 14,500 deluxe cottage; Rs 20,000–Rs 22,500 2-bedroom luxury cottage; Rs 2,500 extra bed. Rates include all meals; 15% tax extra. 2-night minimum stay in peak season. MC, V.

Amenities: 2 restaurants; Ayurvedic spa; bicycles; children's park; Internet (broadband in shop; Rs 50/hr.); mountaineering; recreation center; golf and aquatic pursuits by prior arrangement.

Windermere Estate ★★   Also located just outside Munnar, on a 24-hectare (60-acre) cardamom estate, this is one of the finest places to stay in the region. Accommodations are bright and clean, with wooden ceilings and floors and dark cane furniture. Best value are the simple valley-view rooms with stunning vistas of the surrounding tea-clad hills and forests; if you're staying more than 1 night and like your space, there are six very spacious "cottages" (big enough to take another person), and the spanking new 93 sq. m (1,000-square-ft.) Planter's Villas, which offer relative luxury in addition to dazzling views from perfectly positioned private balconies. Warm, discreet service is designed to make you feel as if you're lord of your very own plantation estate. The surrounding landscape is exceptionally good for early-morning walks, organized daily, and you can try your luck fishing in one of several nearby streams. Food is fresh family cuisine, with everything sourced from local farms; like so many homestay-type experiences, it far surpasses the buffets you get at the five-star resorts.

P.O. Box 21, Pothamedu, Munnar 685 612 (© **04865/23-0512.** Fax 04865/23-0978. Reservations: c/o Mr. Shamnaaz or Ms. Divya Raj, Windermere House, Seaport Airport Rd., Trikkakara, Kochi 682 021. (© **0484/242-5237.** Fax 0484/242-7575. www.windermeremunnar.com. info@windermeremunnar.com. 18 units. Rs 5,150–Rs 6,850 valley view double; Rs 7,850–Rs 10,250 cottage double; Rs 11,750–Rs 14,250 Planter's Villa double; add 25% per extra person. Rates include breakfast; 15% tax extra. MC, V. **Amenities:** Dining room, library-lounge, tearoom; basketball; fishing; Internet (currently only broadband; Rs 100/hr.); trekking; Wi-Fi (planned; $^{1}/_{2hr.}$ free, thereafter Rs 100/hr.). *In room* TV (in cottages and Planter's Villas), fridge (in cottages and Planter's Villas), hair dryer.

7 / NORTHERN KERALA

Kozhikode is 146km (91 miles) NW of Kochi; Kannur is 92km (57 miles) NW of Kozhikode

Even though northern Kerala's history as a major spice-trade destination is well documented, it remains relatively untouched by tourism. This is largely because of the 8-hour drive it takes to get here from Kerala's better-favored (and more rigorously developed) beaches and backwaters in the south. Nevertheless, this can be a wonderful region to explore if you are looking to get away from the tourist crowds, and have time to spare. Certainly if you're traveling overland from Mysore, Karnataka, to Kerala, it makes excellent sense to spend a day or two exploring this relatively untouched part of the subcontinent, particularly the **Wyanad Hills,** which remains one of India's last true wilderness areas. Malabar's far northern coastal region, stretching from **Kannur** all the way up to **Bekal,** just before the state's border with Karnartaka, has also begun to undergo its evolution into a tourist destination, albeit one for a more laid-back and crowd-free experience. The area now boasts one of the loveliest places to stay in all Kerala, and the beaches here are virgin territory. A warning, though: While this remains an excellent place for travelers keen to escape the predictable tourist hot spots, the area is gearing up to see a big increase in visitors

ESSENTIALS

VISITOR INFORMATION   In Kozhikode (formerly Calicut), a **Kerala Tourism information booth** (© **0495/270-2606;** daily 10am–1pm and 2–5pm) is located at the railway station. In Kannur, inquire at the **Kannur District Tourism Promotion Council**

(Taluka Office Campus; © **0497/270-6336;** Mon–Sat 10am–5pm, closed Sun and second Sat of the month).

GETTING THERE   By Air   There are daily flight connections to **Karipur Airport** (© **0495/271-2630** or -1314)—located 25km (16 miles) south of Kozhikode—with Mumbai, Chennai, Kochi, Trivandrum, Goa, Mangalore and Coimbatore. International flights from Dubai and Doha also land here regularly, making direct connections from Europe possible. Note, though, that the nearest airport for destinations in the far north of Kerala is actually **Mangalore,** over the border in Karnataka. An airport is currently being planned for Kannur.

By Road   Kozhikode, Kannur, Thallassery, Kanhangad and Bekal are all on National Highway 17, which gets tricky in places as you head farther north. To get from Kozhikode to Vythiri in the Wyanad mountain ranges, you'll need to take the Kozhikode-Bengaluru highway; best to hire a car and driver (see "Getting Around," under Kochi). If you have more time (and less money), look into bus connections which are ultimately available from just about anywhere; call the local KSRTC Office in Kozhikode on © **0495/2723-796.**

By Train   Kozhikode and Kannur are both important jumping-off points for trains running up and down the coast of Kerala, so it's not difficult finding a berth from either Kochi or Trivandrum if you're heading north, or from Mangalore (and other, more northern, hubs) if you're heading into Kerala. Be warned that these trips are incredibly lengthy and arduous. Daytime journeys are wonderful if you're keen on watching the fabulous passing scenery, but you'll need stamina and patience. Dial © **133** or 0495/270-1234 for inquiries at the **Kozhikode Railway Station,** or © **0495/270-3822** for reservations. If you're treating yourself to time at Neeleshwar Hermitage (see "Where to Stay," below), in the northernmost reaches of the state, then you'll hop off at nearby **Kanhangad** (a name that doesn't roll so easily off the tongue, so be sure to write it down when buying your ticket)—let them know which train you're arriving on and someone will fetch you from the station.

GETTING AROUND   Auto-rickshaws are fine for short trips in Kozhikode and Kannur, but for longer journeys you will have to hire a car and driver, or hop on a train (see above).

KOZHIKODE & THE WYANAD RAINFOREST

Archaeological evidence suggests that civilizations inhabited the fertile forests of the Wyanad around 3 millennia ago. Today pockets of tribal populations still practice time-old rituals and eke out a simple existence in harmony with nature, but the wonderfully temperate climate and almost permanently sodden soil has also meant that the region supports a sprawling network of coffee, cardamom, betel nut, pepper, and rubber plantations, stretching over the undulating hills in every direction. And between the cultivated hills, there's a dense rainforest, studded with splendid rocky outcrops and easily accessible Neolithic caves.

Malabar trade, which is still largely focused on spices and textiles, once centered on the teeming coastal town of **Kozhikode,** the unofficial capital of the North. Until recently known as Calicut—incidentally where the term *calico* (or white, unbleached cotton) originated—this is where Vasco da Gama was first welcomed in 1498; at the nearby village of Kappad, a commemorative plaque memorializes the spot where the Portuguese explorer is said to have landed. Still famed for its old spice market, Kozhikode

Not Quite Kung-Fu Fighting

While in Kozhikode you can watch students perform Kerala's spectacularly acrobatic, high-flying martial art form, Kalaripayattu (see the sidebar "Kathakali & Kalaripayattu: Kerala's Ancient Art Forms," earlier in this chapter) at **C.V.N. Kalari Nadakkavu** (E. Nadakkavu, Nadakkavu P.O., Kozhikode 673 011; ℰ **0495/276-9114** or -8214; www.cvnkalarikerala.com; cvnkalari@sify.com). The school holds open classes 6 to 8:30am and 4 to 6:30pm—with prior notice, foreigners with some martial arts training are allowed to join these. Ayurvedic treatments are given during the day.

can be an interesting, if offbeat, place to explore between Ayurvedic treatments (available at the Harivihar Heritage Home, reviewed below) and shopping for textiles or gold and silver. To most, however, the city is more of a go-between point for journeys farther south or north, or inland to Kerala's highest rainfall region, the **Wyanad Hills** ★★★. One of India's last true wildernesses, the hills are home to some truly soothing get-away-from-it-all accommodations, including **Tranquil,** where you can bed down in a luxurious treehouse surrounded by a 160-hectare (400-acre) working coffee plantation (see below).

Where to Stay
Please don't think of the Wyanad Hills as a day trip. If you head out that way, be sure to book a place to stay; chances are you won't want to leave.

In Kozhikode
Kozhikode may not be packed with options, but it does have one of the finest little guesthouses in the state—the handsome **Harivihar** is reviewed below. As far as hotels go, your best bet is **The Gateway Hotel Beach Road Calicut** ★ (ℰ **0495/661-3000;** www.tajhotels.com; doubles from Rs 4,500), the only five-star hotel in town, aimed at the luxury business-oriented traveler. In terms of facilities (with two restaurants and a decent pool), it's the best place in town, with smart, clean, neat and forgettable guest rooms. There's also a good Ayurvedic rejuvenation program that's been greatly enhanced over the years; you can be assured of professional service, and all treatments are made in consultation with the resident doctor. It's also just minutes from the spice market. This is a good hotel for an overnight stop, but in no way a place you should choose to tarry; for that you'd be better off at Harivihar. But, if you're sold on the anonymity of hotels, and looking for a cheaper alternative to The Gateway, take a look at the **Fortune Hotel Calicut** (ℰ **0495/276-8888;** www.fortunehotels.in). It's not great, but it's functional, and bedrooms are a perfectly acceptable mix of modern convenience and floral decor; standard doubles go for just Rs 2,900, including breakfast and taxes.

Harivihar Heritage Home ★★ (Value) In the heart of Kozhikode, but a million miles from the hustle and bustle of the city, this is the gracious family home of Neethi Srikumar and her husband, both doctors and humble hosts who've crafted a beautiful guesthouse from their 170-year-old royal homestead. Visitors from across the globe come to learn about (and experience) the healing art of Ayurveda (it's Kerala's only Green Leaf–certified homestead) or immerse themselves in Indian culture and philosophy—there's an important Kalari center nearby, and you can even ask for a session with an astrologer. Or head out on a tour of the best gold, silver and textile shops, before visiting

---

Tips **Getting the Most out of Kozhikode**

Since tourism in Kozhikode has never been a major industry, it takes local smarts to get the lowdown on the city, learn about its historically significant places and know how to bargain properly in its best markets and shops. The best local guide is **Mr. Mohan,** and you'll need to book him in advance to accompany you as you explore by car (which you must arrange); he'll charge around Rs 500 for half a day; call him at ✆ **94-4607-8996,** or have the folks at Harivihar make all the arrangements.

---

the centuries-old spice market. Accommodations—like the entire house—are elegantly minimalist; antiques set off the original features of the house with a faint nod to contemporary flair. You'll leave this haven rejuvenated, restored, and ready to tackle anything. Be prepared, though: no alcohol, and no meat is served here.

Bilathikulam, Calicut 673 006. ✆ **0495/276-5865.** www.harivihar.com. admin@harivihar.com. 7 units, all with shower only. 104€ double. Rates include all meals and taxes. No credit cards. **Amenities:** Dining room; airport transfers (Rs 500–Rs 800; free for stays of 6 nights or more); astrology sessions; Ayurvedic center; bathing pond (pool with untreated water); cultural performances (on request); Internet (for e-mail checks only); small library; shopping trips; yoga. In room: A/C (in 2 rooms).

In the Wyanad

It takes about 2 hours to drive the 90km (56 miles) from the coastal city of Kozhikode to **Vythiri,** the nearest village to many of Wyanad's resorts, the best of which is **Tranquil** (reviewed below). Note that the owners of Green Magic Nature Resort—once considered "the best tree-house experience in Asia," but which received some bad press in recent years—have recently launched a sequel to their first project. **Green Magic Nature Resort 2** offers an altogether more rustic treetop stay than you'll get at Tranquil, but if you choose to investigate further, start at www.tourindiakerala.com. Besides Tranquil, which is a marvelous place to discover plantation life while chilling out (and eating well) in a veritable rainforest, you may want to check out the 36-unit **Vythiri Resort** ★ (✆ **04936/ 25-5366** or -5367; www.vythiriresort.com), not least for its excellent Serena spa with Ayurvedic facilities. If it's not too crowded, the atmosphere can be enchanting (if totally resortlike), with monkeys playing in the trees, and a rope bridge over the fast-moving stream leading to the restaurant and pool. Doubles cost around Rs 6,500 but for an extra Rs 1,000 you can stay in a suite; all meals are included, as is morning yoga and meditation. There's also a chance to stay in one of their ingenious treehouses, smartly decorated and taking full advantage of their setting right in the midst of the forest; Rs 12,500 gets you a memorable night high above the forest floor, with matchless morning views into the thick, slowly clearing mist. *One drawback:* This resort is extremely popular with large family and tour groups, especially in the summer, so if you're looking for a little more peace and quiet, head instead to **Edakkal Hermitage** (reviewed below), which really puts you far off the beaten track and in the lap of mesmerizing scenery just 12km (7½ miles) from the town of Sultan's Battery. Another good choice that's wonderfully intimate is **Fringe Ford** ★ (Cherrakarra P.O., Talapoya Post, Mananthavadi; ✆ **98-4544-2224**), a colonial bungalow situated on a 400-hectare (1,000-acre) estate that's fabulously cut off from the world, but doesn't hold back on home comforts and excellent scenery. Built by a British settler almost a century ago, Fringe Ford was initially cultivated for pepper, cardamom, and coffee but the current owner has let the jungle reclaim most of that—now, once again, elephants, leopards, and giant Malabar squirrels call the rain-soaked hills home. Doubles run Rs 4,000 to Rs 5,700, including all meals, tea, and snack, and a pickup from Thalapoya, the nearest village; the rate also includes the services of a guide for treks within the estate.

Edakkal Hermitage ★ ⟨Value⟩ Located near the Edakkal Caves (where Neolithic carvings are a fleeting distraction from natural beauty), this is a rustic hermitage in the true sense. Each of the simple, neat cottages (with wooden floors and basic tiled wash-rooms) is named after a world-famous cave site; most have huge windows affording extraordinary views of the Western Ghats. Although the rooms themselves are nothing special (except perhaps for the giant naturally occurring boulders that burst through the wall), you should book either Lascaux or adjacent Chauvet—the gigantic rocks out front form natural terraces. Or, for better privacy, ask for the hilltop twin cottage, but prepare for a serious climb up. The treehouse is more suitable as a thrilling adventure for young-sters than a place you want to relax in (there's no hot water). Meals are for some the biggest joy here—on your first night, you dine by candlelight in a natural cave; it's an utterly romantic experience. A laid back, battery-recharging kind of place—bring a pile of books and prepare to lose track of time.

Wyanad 673 592. ⟨C⟩ **04936/26-1178.** Reservations: ⟨C⟩ **04936/22-1860,** 04936/26-0123, 98-4700-1491 or 94-4726-2570. www.edakkal.com. 7 units. Rs 3,450–Rs 4,500 double, Rs 1,000 extra person. Rates include all meals and taxes. MC, V. **Amenities:** Restaurant, TV lounge; transfers (Rs 15/km.); Ayurvedic massage center; badminton; table tennis. In room: No phone.

Tranquil ★★ Located at the edge of the Wyanad National Park, this is one of the best ways to experience life on a 160 hectare (400-acre) working coffee plantation, filled with the warm hospitality of Victor Dey and his wife, Ranjini. Standard accommoda-tions are forgettable, but it would be almost unthinkable to pass up the chance to sleep in one of the two **treehouses** ★★★ and fall asleep to the cacophonous chorus of cicadas and myriad other forest sounds that work like a natural orchestra all around you as you float high above the rainforest canopy. There are two options here: you can request the sumptuous "tree villa" 40m (131 ft.) aboveground and spread across three Flame of the Forest trees. It's equipped with the comforts of home (even DVD) and has a private deck with cane furniture. The two fully functioning bathrooms come with flush toilet and shower. The second, more authentic, treehouse is no less comfortable, but more compact, and with entirely different scenery, and a stream gushing directly below you. If you're afraid of heights, opt for the deluxe room in the main house. The Deys, both fine racon-teurs, arrange plantation tours, and there are various walks on the estate, all signposted, taking you through fabulous scenery.

Kuppamudi Coffee Estate, Kolagapara P.O. 673 591, Sultan Bathery, Wyanad. ⟨C⟩ **04936/22-0244.** Fax 04936/22-2358. www.tranquilresort.com. tranquil@satyam.net.in or homestay@vsnl.com. 10 units. Oct–Mar Rs 12,750 standard double, Rs 16,800 treehouse, Rs 17,000 deluxe double/suite, Rs 18,600 tree villa; Apr–Sept Rs 9,250 standard double, Rs 12,000 treehouse, Rs 12,500 deluxe double/suite, Rs 13,500 tree villa. Rates include all meals and plantation tours; 15% tax extra. MC, V (credit cards for room only; other charges cash only). **Amenities:** Dining and lounge areas; airport transfers (Rs 2,750); Internet access (in office, for e-mail only; nominal charge); Ayurvedic treatments; plantation tours; outdoor pool. In room: Fans, TV/DVD, fridge (in treehouse, tree villa, and deluxe units), hair dryer.

KANNUR & KERALA'S NORTHERNMOST COAST

Kannur—previously known as Cannanore—is a pretty coastal town predominantly inhabited by what is locally known as the "Malabar Muslim." Unlike North India, where

Islam was more often than not established through violent conquest, here it arrived initially through trade, and grew through love; Arab sailors coming to Malabar in search of precious spices married local women, establishing the Mappila (or Malabar Muslim) community, which in turn developed its own Arabi-Malayalam songs and poems and the "Mappila Pattu." This oral record of the unique history of the broad-minded Calicut rulers stands in stark contrast, for instance, with that of the intolerant Portuguese tyrants. Immediately south of Kannur, are the harbor towns of **Thalassery** (formerly Tellicherry) and **Mahé;** the latter once a French enclave, now a union territory still legislated from Pondicherry and best known for the availability of cheap fuel, liquor, and other goods unlikely to be of much interest to you.

Tourism in this northerly region of Kerala is only recently coming into its own, which has distinct advantages if you're looking to get away from the crowds. Besides beaches of considerable beauty—where you're more likely to run into fishermen, villagers performing their toilet rituals (not necessarily something you *want* to witness), or nesting Olive Ridley turtles than vendors, restaurant shacks, or signs of tourism—the region is famed for the abundance of its *theyyam* **performances,** compelling socioreligious ritual dramas executed in elaborate costumes and masks and culminating with special blessings bestowed upon the spectators. Kannur is a major center for *theyyam,* but if you'd rather discover a far less commercial guise of the art form, head farther north, where not only does one of the best new hideaways in the state, **Neeleshwar Hermitage,** nestle alongside a virgin beach, but you can also visit soul-stirring ashrams and check out the view from Kerala's largest fort.

If you're traveling into Kerala from Karnataka or other regions farther north, don't be tempted to race through this beautifully untouched part of the state. Nowhere else will you find beaches in such perfect condition, villages as unaffected by tourism, and such unhampered places to visit.

What to See & Do

If you're looking for a safe, practically untouched sunbathing and swimming spot, head for **Muzhapilangad Beach,** 15km (9⅓ miles) south of Kannur, where you'll probably have much of the 4km (2½-mile) sandy stretch all to yourself. Remember though that you need to be a little more modest about your beachwear than you would at home or in Goa—particularly when ambling to and from the beach; women should not wander around in bikinis or, heaven forbid, go topless. Closer to the city, which the Europeans called Cannanore, the Portuguese built imposing **Fort St. Angelo** (free admission; daily 8am–6pm), a monumental laterite edifice from which visitors can view the fishing harbor below.

Around 70km (43 miles) north of Kannur lies **Bekal,** Kerala's largest fort, thought to date from the mid–17th century, though there is no accurate account of its construction. While the structure itself is vast and impressive, it's the views that really take you breath away—looking inland from the top of the watchtower you should be able to see the Western Ghats, while from the fort's ramparts you'll get a good idea why this was considered such a useful spot from which to keep watch over the coast. The fort (© **0467/ 227-2900** or -2007) is open to visitors daily between 9am and 6pm; admission is Rs 100 (ticket sales until 5pm only). The future of the area is reaching a tipping point as developers are in the process of starting up half a dozen hotels in the immediate vicinity of the fort—while this signals much-needed investment, it also means that the time to visit is now. South of Bekal the tiny market town of Nileshwar is where boats are stationed for trips along the Valiyaparamba, northern Kerala's very own **backwaters,** which remain

(Moments) Placating the Gods with Theyyams

Peculiar to the tribal region of northern Malabar, this ritual dance form evolved as a means of placating ancient village gods and ancestors. Combining temple ritual, rustic ballads, and folk art, *theyyams* are essentially representations of the collective consciousness of the village. Heavily made-up men with masks, elaborate costumes, spectacular jewelry, and often 2m-high (6½-ft.) headgear essentially become oracle-like incarnations or manifestations of the godhead or of a valorous ancestor. The ceremony begins with a song of praise, performed in honor of the presiding deity; this is followed by a dance strongly influenced by Kalaripayattu, the traditional Kerala martial art thought to predate the better-known Far Eastern forms like kung fu. *Theyyams* traditionally last an entire night and include a great deal of music, singing, and lighting of torches—oil lamps are ceremoniously brandished as shields and swords, and you may witness hypnotic music, prophetic moments, and even fire-walking. *Theyyams* are usually held between November and April (the sacred season), usually in a specially allocated temple or family compound. If you stay at a place like Neeleshwar Hermitage, staff will always know when and where performances are happening and will happily arrange all the details for a visit. To ensure your chances of seeing a performance, visit **Sri Muthappan Temple** at Parassini Kadavu, 18km (11 miles) north of Kannur, which has early morning and evening performances throughout the year. However, you'll need to be a bit more proactive if you want to track down an authentic *theyyam* that isn't staged for visitors, and if you do attend one, it's a good idea to stay on through the entire all-night ceremony. It's usually only after midnight that the bigger, more elaborate costumes are put on, and the performance becomes increasingly aggressive, building to a heart-stopping crescendo.

uncluttered and totally undiscovered compared with the touristy backwaters of the south (admittedly, there isn't quite so much to see, either). Trips along the river can be arranged through Neeleshwar Hermitage (see "Where to Stay," below).

For an experience that might touch you spiritually, a worthy visit in this part of Kerala is to **Anandashram** ★★, also known as "The Abode of Bliss," a thoroughly tranquil center for meditation and worship in the town of Kanhangad (© **0467/220-3036;** www.anandashram.org; papa@anandashram.org). The ashram was founded in 1931 by Swami Ramdas and Mother Krishnabai (lovingly called Beloved Papa and Pujya Mataji); they've both passed on, but continue to be venerated at the ashram where their teaching—that "to love all is the true Bhakti of God"—is the central tenet of life for thousands of devotees. One of the central activities here is for rows of devotees to wander through the grounds chanting the holy phrase "Ram Nam"—it's an attempt to spread the holy vibrations throughout the ashram in order to help disciples attain a higher state of mind. The ashram has a continuous program of chanting and readings, starting at 5am and going on until 9:30pm each day.

Although more specifically "Hindu," also worth visiting is the nearby **Swami Nithyananda Ashram,** where there are 44 meditational caves created during the first quarter of the last century, this time by another famous guru who spent most of his time in nothing but a loincloth. The caves can be visited between 5:30am and 5:30pm, and afterwards you can take a look at the north Indian-style temple perched on top of the caves. Unlike the majority of Kerala's temples, foreigners aren't banned from entering here.

Where to Stay

By a long stretch, the best place to overnight in the northernmost part of Kerala is **Neeleshwar Hermitage** (reviewed below), nestled on the edge of a spectacularly pristine stretch of seemingly endless beachfront near the lively town of Kanhangad (which is where you'll alight if you're arriving by train). Neeleshwar is not only within easy striking distance of Bekal Fort (some 19km/11¾ miles north), but is also convenient for all the other attractions of this part of Kerala, not least of which is a designated Olive Ridley hatching area (the turtles usually lay their eggs in July and August, but this can be delayed till as late as October). There is also a more old-fashioned homestay-style option, a family run guesthouse in Thalassery, just south of Kannur, called **Ayisha Manzil** (reviewed below).

Ayisha Manzil ★★   Occupying a majestic cliff-top position with a terrace overlooking the sea, this lovely two-story mansion was built by an East India Company tradesman in 1862. Bought by a family of Muslim spice traders in 1900, today it is still run by the Moosas, and combines modern facilities (like a beautiful pool overlooking the ocean) with sumptuous wooden antiques, unique family heirlooms, and ancient plumbing. Traditional Keralite and Malabari dishes are served in the family dining room, and Faiza, the lady of the house offers a course in local Mappila cookery which she's even presented in France. Rooms differ in size and layout, but all have loads of character, with tall four-poster beds, ancient light fittings, high ceilings, and enormous drench showers. Insist on an upstairs sea-facing room, where you'll have more privacy and splendid views across cobalt seas. Outings to Thalassery's fruit markets, temples, and the local martial arts school are arranged, as are tours through the property's original cinnamon plantation, apparently once the largest in Asia.

Court Rd., Thalassery 670 101. ℭ **0490/234-1590**. cpmoosa@rediffmail.com. 6 units. Rs 11,500 double. Rates include all meals, taxes, and beach transfers. No credit cards. Closed Apr 15–July. **Amenities:** Dining room; large outdoor pool. In room: A/C, no phone.

Neeleshwar Hermitage ★★★ (Finds)   Behind a patch of pristine, virgin beach tucked off to the side of a peaceful fishing village this is paradisiacal Kerala still undiscovered by mass tourism. It seems almost a shame to let this secret out of the bag, but it offers a taste of Kerala before it became famous. Accommodations are in idiosyncratic Kerala-style cottages with coco palm thatch roofs that echo the homes of local fishermen—rooms are large, high-ceilinged, and well thought out with great big beds, luscious linens, and chic open-to-the-elements bathrooms built around coconut palms. The beach is a short stroll away from your private porch, but staff organize all kinds of outings, and at night there are visits by cultural performers, including demonstrations of Kalari and various dance forms. It's a well-run, lovely little operation and surely a blueprint for how we wish tourism could run everywhere. *Note:* This is a strictly no-smoking resort, with a no-plastic policy, among other environmental initiatives.

Ozhinhavalappu P.O., Neeleshwar, Dist. Kasaragod 671 314.ℭ **0467/228-7510,** or 0467/228-8876 through -8878. Fax: 0467/228-7500. www.neeleshwarheritage.com. crh@vsnl.net. 16 units. Oct–Mar Rs 14,000 sea view double, Rs 11,500 garden view double, Rs 3,000–Rs 3,400 extra bed; Apr–Sept Rs 10,150 sea view double, Rs 7,950 garden view double, Rs 2,200–Rs 2,600 extra bed. Rates include breakfast; 15% tax extra. MC, V. **Amenities:** 2 restaurants, club house w/TV, bar (planned); airport transfers (from Mangalore; Rs 3,800 A/C, Rs 3,300 non-A/C); Ayurvedic and general massage center; bicycles; cooking classes; cultural activities and lectures; houseboat cruises; library/reading room; large outdoor pool; Wi-Fi (in lobby; free); yoga and meditation classes. In room: A/C and fans, hair dryer, MP3 docking station.

...ecember 26, 2004, that infamous earthquake measuring 9.0 on the Richter ...e struck Indonesia's coast, triggering the tsunami that sped across the Indian ...an, destroying everything in its path. The Andaman Islands and Tamil Nadu ...e the worst-affected Indian states, with an estimated loss of 8,000 lives. In ...il Nadu, the districts of Nagapattinam and Cuddalore suffered most, but the ...omandel Coast's tourist sites emerged more or less undamaged; in fact, a new ...covery was made at Mamallapuram when the wall of water receded (see ...er). The destruction also produced some good initiatives. Besides plans to ...tall an internationally coordinated high-tech tsunami early-warning system, a ...ogram called the Loyola Empowerment and Awareness Programme has offered ...ernative, more secure career paths for hundreds of children on the north coast. ...ked to Chennai's respected educational institutions, the program has offered a ...w generation of kids—once slaves to their destiny as fisherfolk—opportunities ...o pursue careers in diverse new sectors such as catering and publishing.

...nial mansions have been restored as ...els—the kind of "temple" that will ...eal to the lazy hedonist in you. Having ...ght your breath in the wide boulevards ...d air-conditioned shops of Pondicherry, ...u should travel to Tiruchirappalli, to ...plore the holy temple town of **Sriran-** ...m, before moving on to the 11th-cen- ...ry **Brihadeshvara Temple,** situated in ...earby **Thanjavur,** the Chola capital for ...00 years. Or skip Srirangam and head ...via Thanjavur) to the **Chettinad** region, ...where the wealthy Chettiars built palaces ...nd painted mansions to rival the havelis ...constructed by the merchants and aristo- ...crats of Rajasthan, one of which is now a

fine boutique hotel. Either way, your final and most important Tamil Nadu stop will be the temple town of Madurai, to visit the magnificent **Sri Meenakshi-Sundar- eshwar Temple.** A place of intense spiri- tual activity, this temple is where up to 15,000 pilgrims gather daily to celebrate the divine union of the goddess Meen- akshi (an avatar of Parvati) and her eternal lover, Sundareshwar (Shiva)—one of the most evocative experiences in all of India.

Note: **Kanyakumari,** the venerated southernmost tip of Tamil Nadu, and another worthwhile addition but best reached from Kerala, is discussed in chap- ter 7.

1 CHENNAI

Chennai, India's fourth largest city, is neither ancient nor lovely but it is—like Bangalore and Hyderabad—booming. The first British settlement in India, it was established in 1639 by the East India Company on the site of a fishing village called Chennaipatnam. Madras, as the capital of Tamil Nadu was formerly known, is today a teeming, sprawling, bustling industrial metropolis, a manufacturing hub occasionally referred to as the "Detroit of the South," where many of India's IT companies are located. Unless you're here on business, or keen to shop, the city itself is only marginally fascinating—a strange mix of British Raj–era monuments, Portuguese churches, Hindu temples, and ugly 21st-century buildings, massive billboards, and concrete overpasses; even one of the longest

Tamil Nadu: T
Temple Tour

If your idea of India is one of ancient temples thick with incense and chanting masses worshiping dimly lit deities covered with vermilion paste and crushed marigolds, then Tamil Nadu is where your mental images will be replaced by vivid memories. Occupying a long stretch of the Bay of Bengal coastline known as the Coromandel Coast, India's southernmost state is dominated by a rich cultural and religious heritage that touches every aspect of life. For many, this is the Hindu heartland—home to one of India's oldest civilizations, the Dravidians, who pretty much escaped the Mughal influence that permeated so much of the cultural development in the north. Ruled predominantly by the powerful Chola, Pallava, and Pandyan dynasties, Dravidian culture flourished for more than 1,000 years, developing a unique political and social hierarchy, and an architectural temple style that has come to typify the south. In spite of globalization and the political dominance of the north, Tamil Nadu has retained its fervent nationalist sensibility—an almost zealous pride in Tamil language and literature, and in its delicious and varied cuisines. Outside of Chennai and the coastal stretch south to Pondicherry, it is also a state that remains virtually unchanged despite the tourism boom of the past decade, and exploring it provides a far more textured experience than provided by its popular neighbor, Kerala.

Thanks to heavy summer downpours, Tamil Nadu is green and lush—particularly in the Cauvery Delta toward the west, where the great Dravidian kingdoms

were established temples built, and region, with the pretty much a quin experience. By co Madras, as some stil tal established by th century, exudes no s marily of interest as a the region's best attra **Kanchipuram,** one o cities of India, and well and **Sri Venkateshwara** pati, just over the be Pradesh). It is said to temple in the world, w prepared to line up fo days—to hand over an an lion to help Vishnu settle h god of wealth. By contrasu doned temples in the sea **Mamallapuram,** just 2 ho Chennai. Here, right near th the Pallavas built the earliest monumental architecture India during the 5th and 9t From Mamallapuram it's a rel drive farther south to the for coastal colony of **Pondicherry** with its charming colonial eclectic community, and bohem sphere—is perhaps the best shop tination in southern India. Altho French officially left years ago, Po ry's Gallic spirit is still very much traditional Indian snack joints signs proclaiming MEALS READY; VENUE; locals clad in *lungis* (trad Indian clothing) may converse in Fi and gorgeous antiques-filled Indo-F

(Fun Facts) Rule of the Screen Gods

It's not just temple gods who are worshiped here—screen "gods" are adored by the local population, enough to elect them to the highest political office: In fact, the majority of Tamil Nadu's leaders have kick-started their careers on the big screen, and nowhere else is politics quite as colorful (Schwarzenegger, move over). Across the state, you'll still see peeling billboards featuring the swollen face of **Jayalalitha,** the controversial actress-turned-politician who has been in and out of political power for almost 2 decades. Kicked out of office on corruption charges in 2001, she jumped back in to reclaim her position a few years later, tossing her successor in jail in a drama worthy of a high-voltage Bollywood spectacle. Jayalalitha made the headlines again in 2009 when she vowed to support efforts to create a Tamil homeland within the island nation of Sri Lanka. The 30-year Sri Lankan civil war, in which the minority Tamil community was seen to be dominated and discriminated by the Sinhalese majority, was always of importance in Tamil Nadu, but gained international attention during April/May 2009, when the Sri Lankan government finally crushed the Tamil Tigers, a terrorist organization said to have pioneered the use of suicide bombers. Despite her promised strong-arm tactics, Jayalalitha, leader of the AIADMK, was not voted back into power during the 2009 local elections, but posters of the winning DMK leaders (including the actor J. K. Ritheesh) were splashed with milk when the results were announced—an act of reverence usually associated with worshipping deities in Tamil's temples.

urban beaches on earth is not enough to hold the attention for long. Most travelers arrive here simply because it's a transport hub and soon leave, distracted by the attractions that start only a few hours away—among them, **Kanchipuram,** city of "a thousand temples," is a day excursion away, or a day trip en route to the beach resorts near **Mamallapuram,** a World Heritage Site, which lie directly 2 hours south. Even charming **Pondicherry** is only 3 hours away, making Chennai a destination of choice only with businessmen here to catch the coattails of one of India's fastest-growing cities.

ESSENTIALS

GETTING THERE & AWAY **By Air** There are daily flights to Chennai's **International Anna Airport** (Airport Information Centre; © 044/2256-1818) and the **Kamaraj Domestic Airport** (a minute's walk from each other) from all major destinations in India; note that both Madurai and Tiruchirappalli can be reached by flight from here. If you want to utilize the train while here, the Southern Railways computerized ticket reservation counter is just outside the domestic terminal exit. The airports are situated just over 12km (7½ miles) southwest from the center but the ride to downtown Mount Road/Anna Salai can take 30 to 40 minutes; costs start at Rs 350 for a non-A/C taxi. You can also catch the train into town (Park, Egmore, and Beach stops) if you're willing to lug your luggage 500m (1,640 ft.) down the road to Trisulam Station.

By Train Chennai has two major railway stations. **Chennai Central** (in George Town) connects Chennai with most major destinations throughout India, while the second-largest,

(Finds) **Great Guided City Walks** ★★★

Storytrails ((C) **994-004-0215;** www.storytrails.in) conducts a number of interesting walking tours through Chennai—in many ways, this is the best introduction to an Indian city, particularly for newcomers to India. The **Peacock Trail** (Rs 595, including breakfast; 7 or 7:30am–10 or 10:30am, or evenings) covers the ancient temples and heritage of Mylapore, the old heart of modern Chennai, said to predate the city by some 2,000 years. The **Bazaar Trail** (Rs 795; 4:30–7:30pm) takes you through the historic, colorful, chaotic, and vibrant George Town on foot and cycle rickshaw, visiting (among others) flower and vegetable markets, an experience that gets you feeling as close to local as is possible. But perhaps the best (if you're as much as a fan of southern Indian cuisine as we are) is the **Spice Trail** (Rs 1,500, including lunch; 9am–2pm), in which you are taken from narrow streets to fine-dining restaurants to experience the delicious and diverse flavors of South India, with advice on how to re-create some of the recipes provided along the way; come hungry!

Egmore ((C) 131), is usually the point of arrival and departure for trains within Tamil Nadu or Kerala. Some trains from within the state now also pull in at **Tambaram** Station; not ideal as this is an hour from Chennai. You can get recorded train information by dialing the computerized (C) **1361** (remember to have your train number); alternatively call information at (C) **133** for arrivals and departures. Express trains take 6 hours from Chennai to Tiruchirappalli and 7½ hours from Chennai to Madurai; book a seat on an A/C chair car. To plan train travel, we suggest you go online to **www.indianrail. gov.in** or **www.southernrailway.org.** Or book your train at your hotel, at a travel agency (see below), or at the Rajaji Bhavan Complex (ground floor) in Besant Nagar.

By Road You may not realize it by glancing at a map, but Tamil Nadu is a fairly massive chunk of India, and it will take more than 15 hours to drive from Chennai to Kanyakumari in the far southwest of the state. Nevertheless, getting around is best done in the relative comfort of a rented car, with the wonderful rural landscape unfurling mile after mile (keep the window open to smell the freshness of turned earth and roasting cashews), and a driver who knows the way. **Kerala Adventures** ★★★ ((C) **0484/231-3744;** www. keralaadventure.com; comvoyge@vsnl.net) is our top pick in the south; its Chennai office is headed by Sharon Thomas (C) **999-437-7402.** There are set tours offered on their website; alternatively Sharon will prepare a quote based on a personalized itinerary, taking in the best of Tamil Nadu before moving across the mountains into Kerala's Cardamom Hills and west to the coast, or over to Mysore and Karnataka. Kerala Adventures tariff structure is not only transparent (their website includes tariffs for set tours), but offers excellent value, and drivers are excellent. For tours solely within Tamil Nadu, you can use **GRT Tours & Travels** ((C) **044/6550-0000**), but they will try to push you to stay in their hotels and resorts, all of which are comfortable but not necessarily the best in each class. Also reliable, and worth getting alternative quotes from, are: **Sita World Travel** (www.sitaindia.com), **Travel House** (www.travelhouseindia.com), or **Madura Travel Service** (www.maduratravel.com). Regular buses are available for travel to almost any point in the state, as well as Bangalore, and Tirupati; contact the **State Express Transport Corporation Bus Stand** ((C) **044/2479-4707;** daily 7am–9pm). Note that

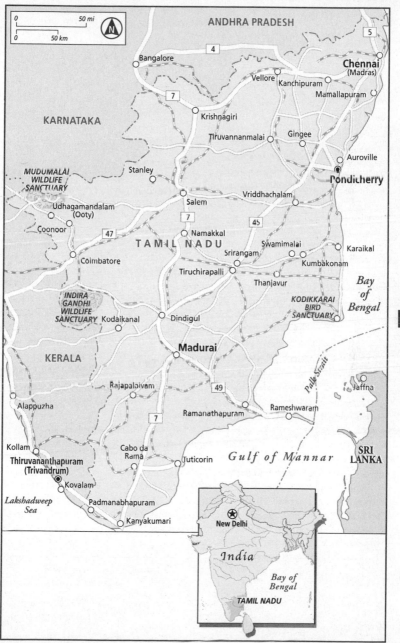

there is a new hop-on, hop-off tour from Chennai to Mamallapuram (four departures in the morning from Chennai starting 9am; four departures from Mamallapuram in the afternoon starting 4.15pm); for more information visit www.tamilnadutourism.org/hopontour.html.

VISITOR INFORMATION   For general tourist information, contact the busy but attentive staff at **Indiatourism** (© **1913;** 154 Anna Salai; © **044/2846-0285** or -1459; indtour@vsnl.com; Mon–Fri 9am–6pm, Sat 9am–1pm), located across the road from Spencer's. *Chennai This Fortnight: Explocity* is a useful bimonthly booklet that recently celebrated it's 20th birthday; it highlights restaurants, nightlife, accommodation and shopping options, and has listings for just about everything, from suggested walks to entertainment events—it's also available online: www.chennai.explocity.com. To get a real feel for the city, purchase a copy of the relatively new glossy magazine *044* (referring to the city's area code).

ORIENTATION & NEIGHBORHOODS   Extending westward from the Bay of Bengal, Chennai is unwieldy to explore, and it's best to concentrate on one area on any given day. Linking the north and south of the city is Anna Salai (also known as Mount Road), which starts out as G.S.T. Road near the airport in the southwest, and terminates at Fort St. George in George Town in the northeast. Two major rivers snake their way through the city—the Cooum River in the north, and the Adyar River several miles south. Between these, the most popular section of Marina Beach stretches between the sea and the city's busy inner districts, where you'll find most of its hotels. George Town lies just north of the Cooum's confluence with the Bay of Bengal. Southwest of George Town (around the Cooum River), Egmore and Triplicane form the heart of the commercial city; Egmore is home to the **Government Museum,** one of Chennai's top sights. Farther south, the neighborhoods of San Thome and Mylapore are the old heart of the city, and where you'll find the city's two other top sights—**San Thome Cathedral** and **Kapaleshvara Temple.**

GETTING AROUND CHENNAI   By Taxi & Auto-Rickshaw   Chennai is a large, sprawling city, and its many sights are spread out and quite impossible to cover on foot. Auto-rickshaw drivers in this city are particularly adept at squeezing impossible fares out of foreign visitors—you would be well warned to always fix a price upfront. Unlike other large cities, Chennai does not have taxis cruising the streets or idling at taxi stands. If you want a taxi, best to phone for one—though for short distances, this is hardly worth the long wait or cost. **Call taxis** run fairly reliable meters that start at a minimum base fare of Rs 50 for 3km (2 miles), with Rs 10 for every additional kilometer. You can also negotiate flat rates. After 9pm, fares are surcharged anything from 25% more to double. For a full listing of taxi companies, or one nearest to your hotel, check out www.chennai taxi.com, or call **Bharati Call Taxi** (© **044/2814-2233;** T. Nagar), **Dial A Car** (© **044/2811-1098;** Mylapore), **Comfort Cool Taxi** (© **044/2538-4455;** Egmore), or **Zig-Zag Call Taxi** (© **044/3245-7788;** Ashok Nagar).

(Fast Facts   Chennai

Airlines   Phone numbers you may need are: **Jet Airways** (© **3987-2222,** or airport 2256-1818); **Spice Jet** (© **1800-180-3333** or 098-7180-3333); **Kingfisher** (© **1800-233-1131** or 1800-1800-101).

Ambulance For an ambulance, dial ℂ **102.** Or dial **Apollo Hospital** (ℂ **1066** or 2829-3333). Apollo Hospital's location on Anna Salai may be the most convenient.

American Express The **American Express** office is at 501 Spencer Plaza, Anna Salai; open Monday to Friday 9:30am to 6:30pm; Saturday 9:30am to 2:30pm.

Area Code The area code for **Chennai** is **044.** For directory inquiries dial 197; time in English 174; change of telephone number in English 1952; 24-hour information service 4444-4444.

ATMs There are numerous ATMs around the city; ask your hotel concierge or driver about a machine near you.

Banks & Currency Exchange There are a large number of foreign exchange dealers; again ask your hotel concierge, host, or driver. Note that most are closed on Sundays.

Bookstores **Higginbothams** (116 Anna Salai; ℂ **044/2256-0586;** daily 9am–7.30pm) has a great selection of books as well as Indian music. **Landmark** (3 Nungambakkam High Rd./M.G. Rd.; ℂ **044/2827-9637** or 044/2823-7438; daily 9am–9pm) is said to be Chennai's largest and most popular bookstore; it also has a selection of music, stationery, and other items, but the loud popular music piped through the speakers can be unnerving.

Car Rentals **Avis** is at 1/24 GST Rd. (ℂ **044/2234-4747**). See "Getting Around Chennai," above.

Drugstore Located on the second floor of Spencer Plaza (769 Anna Salai) is **Health & Glow** (ℂ **044/5205-6013;** Mon–Sat 9am–8pm, Sun 11am–7pm). Alternatively see under hospital below.

Embassies & Consulates **U.K.:** 20 Anderson Rd.; ℂ **044/5219-2151;** Monday to Friday 8:30am to 4pm. **U.S.:** 220 Anna Salai; ℂ **044/2011-2000;** Monday to Friday 8:15am to 5pm. **New Zealand:** "Maithri," 132 Cathedral Rd.; ℂ **044/2811-2473;** Monday to Friday 8am to 12:30pm, Saturday 8 to 11:45am.

Emergencies Police ℂ **100.** Fire ℂ **101.** (See "Ambulance" above.)

Hospital Internationally acclaimed **Apollo Hospital** (21 Greams Lane, off Greams Rd.; ℂ **044/2829-3333** or -0200) offers the city's top medical services; it also has a good round-the-clock pharmacy.

Internet As is the case in other cities, your most reliable bet is to find a **Sify iway** (when in Mylapore, head for the outlet on 59 Dr. Radhakrishnan Rd.; there's also one at 22 College Rd., Nungambakkam) or **Reliance Web World** (outlets in RAPuram, Anna Salai, Alwarpet, and Nungambakkam).

Police For emergencies, dial ℂ **100.** For traffic police, dial ℂ **103.**

Post Office Ask your concierge, host, or receptionist to post small cards and letters (around Rs 15 per stamp). For larger items, use the **General Post Office** on Rajaji Salai, George Town, or the **Head Post Office** on Anna Salai. Better still, call **Fedex** (125 Peters Rd., Royapettah) at ℂ **044/2835-0449.**

Taxis See "Getting Around Chennai," above.

Unfortunately, the city's attractions are very spread out, and getting around can be nightmarish; select a few choice sights in one area or get an air-conditioned taxi for the day.

SOUTH CHENNAI Exploring Marina Beach and the temples and churches of Mylapore, the old heart of Chennai, can be done on foot; to cover the sights further south you're probably best off hiring a car for the better part of the day; be prepared for traffic.

Presuming you've already spent the night in Chennai, get a predawn start by taking in the early morning activities along the 12km (7½-mile) **Marina Beach**—if you're there early enough (around 6am) you can watch the fishing boats being launched. If you'd rather sleep in, save the beach for dusk, when it becomes a colorful pageant of boys playing cricket, families strolling, vendors selling souvenirs, and food carts offering fast-food snacks. Given that it's the world's second-longest city beach you might want to concentrate your energies on the best area: the vicinity of Triplicane, along Kamaraj Road, walking towards South Beach Road.

The 8th-century **Parthasarathy Temple** (off Triplicane High Rd., west of South Beach Rd.; daily 7am–noon and 4–8pm) is very near the main drag of Marina Beach; dedicated to Krishna, it is believed to be Chennai's oldest temple, though extensively renovated by the Vijaynagar kings in the 16th century.

Farther south (this is quite a long walk, but pleasant enough given it's along South Beach Rd. with views of the beach and sea; if it's too hot, catch a rickshaw), near the lighthouse, lies Mylapore's **Basilica of San Thome** (San Thome High Rd., Mylapore; daily 6am–6pm), where the so-called final resting place of Thomas the Apostle has become a neon-lit attraction. Legend has it that St. Thomas, one of Christ's disciples, was martyred at St. Thomas Mount (see below) after spending the final years of his life preaching on a nearby beach. Stained-glass windows recount the slain saint's tale, and wooden panels depict Christ's final days on earth. The interior is also now decked with modern kitsch: bits of tinsel, polystyrene, and a halo of fairy lights.

Near the basilica (1km west) is Chennai's most impressive temple: **Kapaleshvara ★★** (also spelled Kapaleeshwar/Kapaleswarar; off Kutchery Rd. and Chitrukullan N. St., Mylapore; daily 6am–12:30pm and 4–8:30pm) is a classic example of Dravidian architecture, and the thronging devotees will give you an idea of what Tamil Nadu's devout worship is all about. The temple is marked by a 36m (118-ft.) *goparum* (gateway) tower adorned with detailed figures and inscriptions dating from A.D. 1250; if you're destined for the temples of Tamil Nadu this is a fine foretaste (though by the same token, missable if you're pushed for time). A hive of activity at the best of time, the place really comes alive during the Arupathumoovar Festival, held usually around 10 days in March. From here you can walk to **Luz Church** (Luz Church Rd.), built by the Portuguese, and said to be the oldest church in Chennai.

If the congestion and chaos of Chennai has you beat, hop in a cab and visit the peaceful 16th-century **Church of our Lady of Expectations (Senhora da Expectaçáo)**, atop **St. Thomas Mount.** Built in 1523 by the Portuguese, the little church provides fine views over the city and is serenely removed from the city's nonstop commotion. Along the way (or on the way back), spend some time roaming the gardens of the **Theosophical Society ★★**, a sprawling 108 hectares (270 acres) of rambling pathways and shaded by trees including an enormous Banyan tree, said to be 400 years old. The society was founded in 1875 in New York by American Civil War veteran Col. Henry S. Olcott and Russian Madame Helena Petrovna Blavatsky. They based their belief primarily on Hinduism but promoted the equality and truth of all religions. The duo moved it to Chennai

in 1882. The international headquarters of the society is still here, in the 1776 Huddle-
stone mansion, where relief imagery and quotations representing various faiths are on
display, and there is an excellent library, though to gain full use of the latter you need to
register with the society (E. Adyar; ℂ **044/2491-3528**, -7198, or -2904; daily 8:30–
10am and 2–4pm).

CENTRAL CHENNAI At the heart of Chennai, Anna Salai is the city's major business-
lined artery. North of Anna Salai is Egmore, where you will find Chennai's top museum,
and to the west, Nungambakkam, an upmarket residential area that is home to an
increasing number of hotels and businesses, as well as Khader Nawaz Khan Road, where
you will find the densest concentration of Chennai's boutique and high-street stores. Best
to hop onto auto-rickshaws to get around this congested part of the city.

The **Government Museum and National Gallery** ★★ (Pantheon Rd.; ℂ **044/2819-
3238**; admission to Pantheon Complex Rs 250; camera fee extra; Sat–Thurs 9:30am–
5pm) is considered one of the finest receptacles of 10th- and 13th-century bronze
sculpture in the country, including the Chola Nataraj—sculptures of Shiva dancing in a
ring of cosmic fire, these are almost as definitive of India as the Taj Mahal. The museum,
a complex of six buildings and 46 galleries, is a definite stop if you're at all interested in
Indian art as there are also 11th- and 12th-century handicrafts and Rajasthani, Mughal,
and Deccan paintings. One of the buildings in this complex is the beautifully renovated
Museum Theatre, where you can sometimes catch a dance or a music performance.
While in Egmore, pop into **St. Andrew's Kirk** (off Periyar E.V.R. High Rd., northeast
of Egmore Station, Egmore; ℂ **044/2561-2608**; daily 9am–5pm)—inspired by London's St. Martin-in-the-Fields, St. Andrew's steeple rises 50m (164 ft.) into the air; you
can climb this to reach a small balcony for a good city view. Alternatively, head south to
Khader Nawaz Khan Road for some retail therapy.

NORTHERN CHENNAI A tour to admire George Town's grand architectural colonial
heritage—the main reason to venture north can mostly be covered on foot (heat allowing)—best on a Sunday when traffic is at a minimum.

Set aside a few hours to visit **Fort St. George** ★★ (Kamaraj Rd.)—the first bastion
of British power in India, constructed in 1640. The cluster of gray and white colonial
buildings with pillared neoclassical facades now houses the Tamil Nadu State Legislature
and the Secretariat. Visit its **Fort Museum** (ℂ **044/2567-1127**; admission Rs 100;
Sat–Thurs 10am–5pm; still camera without flash allowed with permission from tourist
office; video camera extra fee) to see the collection of portraiture, oil paintings, sketches,
vintage photographs, silverware and etchings that reveal the nature of colonial life in early
Madras. In the compound you will also find Asia's oldest existing Anglican church, **St.
Mary's** (daily 9:30am–5pm), incidentally where Yale University's founder, Gov. Elihu
Yale, was married. The church has numerous 17th- and 18th-century gravestones—look
for the Latin memorial to Mrs. Elizabeth Baker (1652), believed to be the oldest British
inscription in India.

Just north of the fort is the red-sandstone **High Court** (Mon–Sat 10am–5pm), built
in the mid-19th century in the Indo-Saracenic style, and still in use today. Guided tours
of the building take in the various courtrooms, many of which are remarkably decorated.
Busy **George Town,** bounded by Rajaji Salai and N.S.C. Bose Road, was once known as
"Black Town," a racist appellation for a settlement occupied by East India Company
textile workers who came from Andhra Pradesh in the mid-1600s (the name "Chennai,"
incidentally, is derived from the name given to the area by the dyers and weavers who

lived here: Chennapatnam). Today, George Town is a bustling collection of streets that should be explored on foot—but again, not a good idea in the middle of the day.

Tip: Fans of the iconic **Enfield Bullet**, a contemporary classic due to its looks rather than performance, may know that it is manufactured in a Chennai factory (18km/11 miles north of Anna Salai); you can arrange for a 90-minute tour of the factory, a highly recommended experience for motorbike enthusiasts or anyone with a yen for the nostalgic (© **044/4204-3300;** www.royalenfield.com; Rs 500; Mon–Fri 9:30am–5:30pm). Ironically there are no Enfield tours of Tamil Nadu.

DAY TRIP TO THE SACRED CITY OF KANCHIPURAM ★★★

All of Kanchipuram's roads lead to *goparums,* the unmistakable temple gateways that tower over you as you prepare to enter the sacred temples. This 2,000-year-old city of "a thousand temples"—also called Kanchi—is best seen as a day trip out of Chennai, or en route to Mamallapuram, and is (along with Srirangam's temples, and the main temples in Thanjavore and Madurai) the top temple destination in the state. With a rich heritage, it's famous as a seat of both Shaivaite and Vaishnavite devotion as well as for its exquisite silk saris. It was here that the Dravidian style really had its roots, and the sheer profusion of temples makes this an ideal place to get a feel for how South Indian temple architecture has developed over the centuries. The oldest structure in town is **Kailasnath Temple** (Putleri St.; 1.5km/¾ mile out of the town center; daily 6am–12:30pm and 4–8pm), entered via a small gateway. Built by the same Pallava king responsible for Mamallapuram's Shore Temple, Kailasnath shows signs of evolution from its seaside forebear; it's also less overwhelming than many of the more grandiose Tamil temples.

The 57m (187-ft.) whitewashed *goparum* marking the entrance to the 9th-century Shaivite **Ekambareswara Temple** (Puthupalayam St.; 6am–12:30pm and 4–8pm; non-Hindus not allowed in sanctum), Kanchi's largest, was added as late as the 16th century. Through a passageway, visitors enter a courtyard and the "thousand-pillared" hall (though the number of pillars has dwindled significantly over the years). Within the temple, a mango tree believed to be 2,500 years old apparently yields four different

---

A Shrine to Shakti & Silk

In general, Indian visitors are drawn to **Kanchipuram** for two main reasons: its famed Kamakshi Amman temple is one of India's three holiest shrines to Shakthi, Shiva's female form, depicted as his consort, and—with 75% of the population employed in the hand-loom industry—its superb silk. The city is famous for producing the most exquisite hand-loomed silk saris in the world—called *Kanjeevarams,* the bridalwear of choice that become coveted heirlooms. A single *Kanjeevaram* sari costs anything from Rs 2,500 to Rs 100,000 or more, and can—depending on the intricacy of the pattern (often taken from temple carvings) and vividness of the colors (*zari,* gold thread, is often interwoven with the silk)—take from 10 days to a month to weave. Of course, you don't have to wear a sari to covet the silk; plenty of haute couture designers have discovered its beauty, and any fashionista with international aspirations will include an item made from Kanchipuram silk on her ultimate wish list.

(Tips) Tamil Temples: What to Wear & When to Visit

Tamil Nadu's temples teem with devotees, and viewing their carvings and shrines as a non-worshipper is a privilege. Visitors are expected to follow the same dress code as devotees: women must bare neither their shoulders nor their legs—wear long dresses or skirts (or trousers if you must); shirts or T-shirts must have sleeves, or you may cover straps with a loose shawl. Men may not wear shorts (though dotis are allowed). No one may wear shoes of any description inside the temple; leave them outside, or, if there is one, at the depot you'll find at the entrance (have Rs10 handy to tip the man who looks after them). If you're concerned about leaving an expensive pair of sandals in a stranger's hands, purchase a cheaper pair. Note that all temples close during the midday heat—between noon and 12:30pm and reopen at 4pm; time your visit accordingly. It is allowed to take photographs but use your common sense and do not intrude on people who are here to worship—switch your flash off and/or keep it pointed at inanimate objects. Temple elephants may be photographed but usually only if you are donating a rupee and been/being blessed; again, if you use an intrusive flash, restrict yourself to only one photograph.

varieties of the fruit. Legend has it that it was here Shiva and Parvati were married, and that Parvati fashioned a lingam (phallic symbol) of earth, one of the five sacred Hindu elements. As a test of her devotion, Shiva sent a flood through the town that destroyed everything in its path except the lingam, which she protected from the deluge with her body. (*Tip:* Be on the lookout for touts who will aggressively try to get a donation out of you at this temple.)

Dedicated to *Shakti*, which celebrates creation's female aspect, the 14th century **Kamakshi Amman Temple** (Mangadu; daily 6am–12:30pm and 4–8:30pm) was built by the Cholas. Apparently, the tank there is so sacred that demons sent to bathe were cleansed of their malevolent ways and the goddess Kamakshi (a form of Parvati) is thanked for luring and marrying Shiva in Kanchipuram (every Feb or March the lover deities are carried here on massive chariots—a temple festival you will see almost everywhere at certain times of the year). Other worthwhile temples include **Vaikunta Perumal Temple** and **Varadaraja Temple,** both of which are dedicated to Vishnu.

Note that, like elsewhere, Kanchi's temples close from 12:30 until 4pm, which means that you'll need to head out rather early or—better still—arrive in time for evening *puja* (prayer). However, traffic into and out of Chennai can get hellish during peak hours. If you're hot and hungry, head for the air-conditioned room at the **Saravana Bhavan** (there are two outlets, one at 504 Gandhi Rd; the other on Nellukkara Rd near Sri Kusal; both 6am–10:30pm), where you can feast on reasonably priced South Indian *dosas* (savory pancakes) along with delicious vegetarian thalis (multicourse platter).

Kanchipuram is 80km (50 miles) southwest of Chennai, taking 90 minutes to 2 hours to drive. It has no good accommodation options, hence our suggestion that you do this as a day trip from Chennai, or en route to Mamallapuram, leaving early enough to see the temples in the morning and arriving in Mamallapuram in time for a seafood lunch. Ask about guided tours of the temple town at the tourist office, or arrange for a guide along with a driver in Chennai. Otherwise, guides can be picked up around Kailasnath Temple for around Rs 250 to Rs 350; ask to see certification.

WHERE TO STAY

Chennai has a large inventory of business-orientated hotels, providing reliable comfort and standardized service; the option that stands head and shoulders above the rest is the lovely **Taj Connemara,** the only hotel that has an old-world charm along with five-star service and efficiency and offering better value than it's glitzy big brother, Taj Coromandal (though the latter, being the most expensive hotel in town, is good for spotting local celebs). The Courtyard Marriot is also a solid choice, though the lack of pool is a drawback, and Raintree (reviewed below) has the edge in terms of atmosphere and eco-credentials. Those on a budget should look no further than Lemon Tree (reviewed below), or Chennai's first B&B, **Footprint.** If you have no interest in the city and want to immerse yourself directly in a festive vacation atmosphere, you can also head straight down the coast to **Fisherman's Cove,** one of Tamil Nadu's most charming resorts, located right on the beach, and a mere 50 minutes' drive (28km/17 miles) from Chennai airport (and about 20km/12 miles from Mahabalipurum).

Note that if you're just in transit, a few good hotels are located near the airport, the best of which is the low-rise **Trident** (*©* **044/2234-4747;** www.tridenthotels.com). It's 3 minutes away from the airport (airport transfers are free); the CBD is about 20 minutes away. Staffers have all benefited from the Oberoi school of training, so service levels are among the best in the city, with facilities very much aimed at the business traveler. Mindful of their core market, rooms are also soundproofed, with blackout blinds to further cocoon the potentially jet-lagged traveler. The pool area is great; you'd never know you were in a semi-industrial area (until aircrafts take off, of course). If the rates strike you as steep (from Rs 10,500 double), you should see what neighbor **Radisson GRT** (www.radisson.com) is offering; at press time it was pretty identical, but rates for both hotels change daily and can be heavily discounted depending on availability; rooms at Radisson have undergone a makeover and are looking more plush (if a little over-furnished) than the Trident, and it has one of Chennai's most celebrated restaurants (see dining below), but when it comes to service (and pool) the Trident has the edge.

Note: Many of the city's upmarket hotels offer significant discounts on published rates depending on occupancy; so do check online and use the rates below only as guidelines. Note also that there is a luxury tax of 12.5% on all hotel rooms (10.3% on services like Wi-Fi or airport transfers); quoted rates rarely include this.

Footprint ★★ (Finds B&Bs are virtually unheard of in India ("homestay" is the term here, with a potential lack of privacy that that may imply), but hopefully Footprint, tucked away on the second floor of an apartment building behind the ITC Park Sheraton Hotel, is the start of a new trend. Brainchild of Rucha and Ashish Gupta, Footprint is essentially used by travelers transiting through Chennai on their way to or from the Andamans (Ashish is cofounder and director of "Barefoot at Havelocks" in the Andaman Islands, hence the name). It's quiet, private, classy (fresh flowers, Auroville incense, great linens, a choice of pillows), well located (in the south-central posh suburb of Alwarpet, close to shops and restaurants), filled with thoughtful touches and just unbelievable value. Rucha and her small staff (breakfast cook/concierge/chambermaid) is on hand to assist with any queries, from how much to pay your rickshaw driver, to where to eat (or order in) and shop for specifics. (*Note:* no walk-ins, so book in advance.)

Flat 2a and 2b, Gayatri Apts., 16 South St, Sriram Nagar, Alwarpet, Chennai 600 018. ✆ **044/98400-37483** or 3255-7720. Fax 044/2434-2668. www.footprint.in. bookings@footprint.in. 9 units (all en-suite; showers only). Rs 3000 double, including breakfast. Children under 12 Rs 250; extra adult Rs 500. MC, V (100% upfront payment required). **Amenities:** 2 small living areas; dining area; daily newspapers and selection of glossy magazines; small library nook; airport transfers; concierge; Internet (free). *In room:* A/C, TV, Wi-Fi (free)

Lemon Tree ★ ⓥalue This relative newcomer offers comfortable hotel accommodations and facilities at a price that its competitors are finding impossible to beat. It's by no means luxurious, with that slightly stark pared-down atmosphere typical of any budget hotel, but everything is gleaming new and fresh (or was at press time; at these rates the hotel occupancy will remain high and may take it's toll!). It also has a ladies-only floor; excellent-value standard rooms; dedicated smoke-free rooms (worth specifying), and the kind of facilities and generous touches (like free morning newspapers) one associates with more expensive options. Staff is generally also of high caliber. The only drawback is that its location in Guindy means it's a little far from the center—at least 45 minutes to Egmore railway station (25 min. to the airport).

72 Sardar Patel Rd., Guindy, Chennai 600 018. ✆ **044/4423-2323.** Fax 044/4423-2121. www.lemontree hotels.com, hi.cn@lemontreehotels.com. 108 units. Rs 2,900 standard (single occupancy only); Rs 4,400 double superior; Rs 6,500 double executive; Rs 7,500 studio. Rates include breakfast. MC, V. **Amenities:** Restaurant; lounge with pool table, PlayStation, and other games; airport transfers (Rs750); fitness center; outdoor pool; room service. *In room:* A/C, TV, minibar, Wi-Fi (Rs 80/30 min.).

The Park ★★ The Park (not to be confused with the **ITC Park Sheraton and Towers** on TTK Rd.) is the place to mainline straight into Chennai's nightlife. Once the trendiest hotel in town, some of the effects are looking a little dated, and the reception area is showing a little wear and tear (as do bathroom fittings), which is why we prefer Raintree. But there's no doubting its place in the hearts of Chennai movers and groovers, who flock here to dine at the 24-hour eatery off the lobby, **Six-O-One (601),** recommended for its unusual, varied menu (and one of the best *masala dosas* in the city), as well as to the **Leather Bar** and **Pasha,** two of the city's most popular after-hours hangouts (see below). Having covered Chennai's social scene (being a guest here gives you free access), you can retreat to your extremely comfortable "pod," and sleep off events on one very comfortable mattress. The Park's other celebrated feature is its terrific rooftop: a sparkling pool surrounded by *diwans* (Indian recliner sofas), shaded by white cotton drapes that billow in the breeze. The snazzy Ispahani shopping center is within walking distance.

601 Anna Salai, Chennai 600 006. ✆ **044/4214-4000.** Fax 044/4214-4100. www.theparkhotels.com. 214 units. Rs 11,500 deluxe double; Rs 13,500 luxury double; Rs 15,000–Rs 40,000 suites. Extra bed Rs 2,000. AE, DC, MC, V. **Amenities:** 3 restaurants; bar; nightclub; doctor-on-call; fitness center; rooftop pool; room service. *In room:* A/C, TV, hair dryer; minibar, Wi-Fi (Rs TK).

Raintree ★★ South India's first five-star "Ecotel" (an international collection of vaguely environmentally responsible hotels) Raintree is in every respect a classy joint, with elegant rooms, excellent (though relatively pricey) restaurants, a hip bar-lounge, and great city views from the top floors and rooftop pool area (not quite as sexy as The Park's, but views, rooms and atmosphere in the rest of the hotel are better). The deluxe category is small but adequate—do however try to book one on the fifth floor (sixth and seventh floors are reserved for club and suite category); not only for the views but noise (Havana, the basement lounge-bar is a popular party venue). The hotel's location, in quiet, affluent Alwarpet, is also a bonus, with mature trees taking the edge off the concrete surroundings, yet near enough to the throbbing city chaos (just off TTK Road and a block from Chamiers). Personally, we think it's a better bet (and value) than The Park.

120 St. Marys Rd, Alwarpet, Chennai 600 018. ⓒ **044/2815-6363.** Fax 044/2815-6969. www.theresidency.com. restowers@vsnl.net. 105 units. Rs 8,500 double deluxe; Rs 10,500 Club double; Rs 15,000 suite. Rates include breakfast. AE, DC, MC, V. **Amenities:** 3 restaurants; lounge-bar w/dance floor; airport transfer (Rs 1,047 including taxes); doctor-on-call; fitness center and spa; rooftop pool; room service. *In room:* A/C, TV, DVD on request, hair dryer, minibar, Wi-Fi (Rs125/30 min.).

The Residency Towers ★ Ⓥalue This comfortable hotel plays runner-up to Lemontree as the best-value hotel in town; it's a little more pricey, but depending on what you want to do in the city, it's downtown location is convenient (though personally I'd opt for the more personal Footprint B&B). Book a room on the 11th floor (the only non-smoking floor, with standard rooms); book a Residency Club room and they'll throw in a complimentary airport transfer (though you can get a taxi for a great deal less than the additional Rs 1,700 this will run you). Room decor is pretty bland and basic—clean and functional is what you're paying for here. The pool area, surrounded by AstroTurf, is a little drab and unwelcoming but at least it's there. *Tip:* Dining options here are not great; better to eat at the **Copper Point,** the in-house restaurant at neighboring hotel **GRT Grand** (the latter has slightly more luxurious rooms, by the way, with rates running at around Rs 3,000 higher; take a look at www.grtgrand.com); Copper Point offers great Indian fare at a buffet groaning with both South and North Indian dishes, and very good value at around Rs 300 per person. If you're looking for a break from Indian, GRT Grand also has a new Mediterranean restaurant: **Azulia** has been receiving rave reviews and is packed with locals as well as hotel guests.

Sir Thyagaraya Rd., Chennai 600 018. ⓒ **044/2815-6363.** Fax 044/2815-6969. www.theresidency.com. restowers@vsnl.net. 174 units. Rs 5,200 double standard; Rs 6,900 Residency Club double; Rs 8,400–Rs 20,000 suite. Rates include breakfast. MC, V. **Amenities:** 3 restaurants; restaurant-pub; doctor-on-call; health club; outdoor pool; room service. *In room:* A/C, TV, minibar, Wi-Fi (Rs 100/hr.; Rs 500/day).

Taj Connemara ★★★ This is a real city oasis, our favorite Chennai hotel by far, with discreet, efficient service yet radiating an atmosphere of leisure in this otherwise strictly business city. Although the exterior is *very* unprepossessing, enter and you are transported into another era (it's been here since 1891, albeit much changed), with grand, gracious public spaces, wide corridors, and high-ceilinged rooms, all tastefully and luxuriously decorated. Book a room that opens onto the delightful lush courtyard where comfortable loungers are arranged around a large sparkling pool (deluxe rooms 27, 29, 31, 33, 35, 37 or heritage rooms 80, 82, 84 or 86)—this is the perfect place to recover after a bout of shopping at next door Spencer Plaza (or the many other Chennai options; see "Shopping," below). Facilities are top-notch (pillow menus and the like), staff superb and food delicious: a recipe for total comfort.

Binny Rd., Chennai 600 002. ⓒ **044/6600-0000.** Fax 044/6600-0555. www.tajhotels.com. connemara.chennai@tajhotels.com. 150 units. Rs 13,000 superior double; Rs 15,000 deluxe double; Rs 17,000 heritage double; Rs 18,000–Rs 33,000 suites. Extra bed Rs 1,000. AE, DC, MC, V. **Amenities:** 2 restaurants; coffee shop; bar; babysitting; doctor-on-call; fitness center; outdoor pool; room service. *In room:* A/C, TV, hair dryer, minibar, Wi-Fi (Rs 125/30 min.; Rs 200/60 min.; Rs 600/day).

Taj Fisherman's Cove ★★★ Ⓚids This bright, breezy resort—ideal if you have no desire for city pleasures—is set on 8.8 manicured hectares (25 acres) bordering the beach, with a labyrinth of tidy, shrub-lined pathways and, at it's center, a gorgeous pool, replete with swim-up bar. It's a total refuge from the city, yet within the hour you are in bustling Chennai; it's proximity to the city means it is also one of the busiest beach resorts in

India, welcoming corporate jamborees during the week and extended families over week-ends, all reveling in their beachfront escape. Most guest rooms are in the main hotel block, which can be incredibly noisy; better by far to book one of the shell-shaped garden cottages scattered about the cropped lawns—these are delightful, with bamboo-enclosed alfresco showers, bright interiors and breezy patios with Chettinad swings (sea-view cottages C4–C14, right on the beach, are best). Larger luxury sea-facing villas are also available; each with semiprivate garden and palm trees supporting your own hammock. The Cove is simply a great place to catch your breath, with a vast array of activities; the seaside restaurant (reviewed below) is also a treat.

Covelong Beach, Kanchipuram District, Chennai 603 112. ⓒ **044/6741-3333.** Fax 044/6741-3330. www. tajhotels.com. fishcove.Chennai@tajhotels.com. 50 units, 38 cottages. Rs 10,000 standard double room; Rs 11,000 standard sea-view double; Rs 12,500 cottage garden-view double; Rs 15,500 sea-view cottage; Rs 17,500 sea-view villa with private garden. Supplements charged Dec 22–Jan 8. AE, MC, V. **Amenities:** 3 restaurants; 2 bars; beach volleyball; badminton; bicycles; catamaran trips; children's activity center; cycling; ecology tours/walks; fishing excursions; fitness club; Internet (Rs 330/hr.); library; pool; spa; tennis. In room: A/C, TV, hair dryer, minibar, Wi-Fi (Rs 224/1 hr.; Rs 600/day).

WHERE TO DINE

The city has a dearth of independent fine-dining options, with almost all still remaining cloistered in the city's five-star hotels; of these the **Great Kabab Factory ★★★** at the Hotel Radisson draws a very vocal and loyal local following, despite it's inconvenient location near the airport. The 'Factory' offers a fixed menu featuring five melt-in-the-mouth kebabs (two chicken, two mutton, one fish), served with a delicious selection of specialty breads; it's challenging but try to leave space for the dal and choice of biryanis that follow.

Fine dining aside, we'd like to encourage you to experience the delicious and varied flavors of South India surrounded by Chennaites; better still, do so with your hands (see "Eating with Your Hands," below); other than heading for a **Saravana Bavan** outlet, there is the slightly more salubrious **Woodlands Hotel** option, reviewed below—both Chennai institutions. South Indian restaurants in Chennai are usually vegetarian; if you need your protein, opt for a Chettinad restaurant, where meats are coated in intense spices. Aside from the atmospheric Raintree (reviewed below), there's **Karaikudi ★**: the original is at 84 Radhakrishna Salai (ⓒ **044/2491-0900**) but there are now quite a few branches all over the city. It's by no means fine dining (for that Raintree is the ticket) but the food is good. Try the special Chettiar chicken pepper roast with *appams*, the *Kadia* (quail roast), or the *Varuval* (fried pigeon) and unbelievably good value: an average meal here will run you a mere Rs 100 to Rs 150 per person!

If you're bored with South Indian food, you'll also find many of the world's tastes well represented in the city. If you're mood is for the richer sauces of North India, **Dhaba Express ★** on Cenotaph Road in Anna Nagar is one of the best; offering good hearty, reasonably authentic Punjabi food (signature dishes include the sarson-da-saag and makke-di-roti), and an informal atmosphere, with alfresco table seating on "authentic" charpoys (woven beds); prices are better than the other highly rated North Indian restaurant, Copper Chimney, located on Cathedral Road (the benefit of heading to Copper Chimney is it's proximity to Zarra, a Spanish-style tapas bar that is a cool place to have a drink and people-watch before or after dinner). Opposite Dhaba Express is **Cornucopia,** serving a reasonable menu of European/Southeast Asian–style food, but if you're looking for a total break from the East, head for **Bella Ciao ★** (4 Shree Krishna Enclave, off Water Land Dr., Kottivakkam Beach; ⓒ **044/2451-1130**), run by an Italian couple.

(**Moments**) **Eating with Your Hands**

A superb and authentic introduction to South Indian cuisine is a meal at an out-let of **Hotel Saravana Bhavan,** where waiters wander around ladling the con-tents of huge pots onto your banana leaf (the one near the Egmore station may be most convenient, or the one on Khader Nawaz Khan Rd., which many locals rate best). We recommend that you sit in the large hall where the locals eat with their hands (there is usually a small, drab air-conditioned room where "refined" Indians and foreigners eat the same food with cutlery and plates—not nearly as much fun, and pricier to boot). It can be a bit intimidating for first-timers to dig in with fingers for tools, given that many of the dishes are quite liquid, but use the rice as a mop and try a variety of taste combinations—all hugely delicious; remember to use your right hand only, and wash at the clearly visible basins before and after your meal. If you find this daunting, or you're simply not sure how to proceed with the many courses that are piled onto your banana leaf (remember to rinse this with the water that's on the table), ask your driver (assuming you have one) to join you for lunch and follow his lead. Ask what each spoonful is, and by the end of your meal you'll have taken a crash course in South Indian food. It's also incredible value: The special Tamil Nadu thali is an assortment of 23 items for around Rs 100. If that much food seems overwhelm-ing, order a mini lunch (an assortment of tasty items, including the "definitive taste" of Sambar, a gravy that is mopped up with a variety of pancakes) and a tra-ditional South Indian coffee.

It's a great venue—the garden of an old converted house near the beach, with outdoor seating; while it's billed as the best Italian joint in town, this is a very relative recom-mendation. If you're downtown, the new Bella Ciao venue at 140 Nungambakkam High Rd. may suit you better; it's also alfresco (this time on a rooftop), and serves the same menu (© **044/2833-0085**).

The densest concentration of restaurants is on and around TTK Road; of these one of the best is **Lemon Tree ★★**, the elegant Chinese restaurant located in the basement of the Raintree hotel, and serving a superb if pricy menu. Raintree also has a small roof top restaurant, **Above Sea Level ★**, which serves great views of the city along with average but tasty fare.

Finally, Chennai also has several shop-and-unwind stops worth considering as lunch destinations. **Amethyst** (Jeypore Colony, Gopalapuram; © **044/2835-1627**), is set in a delightful old colonial bungalow where you can choose to sit indoors or outdoors under the shade of huge, century-old trees, sipping a decent cappuccino, after browsing for designer clothing in Western designs and Indian fabrics. **Chamiers** (Chamiers Rd./ Muthuramalinga Rd., across from ITC Park Sheraton; © **044/2431-1495**), situated in a charming bungalow, offers food similar to that at Amethyst: juices, and fresh salads and sandwiches served in the shade of an almond tree. It's attached to Anokhi, the leading Jaipur design store (see chapter 11), where you can buy Western-style clothes designed in traditional India hand-block-print fabric. Both Moca Café and Chamiers (and the stores) are open every day of the week.

Bay View Point ★★★ SEAFOOD   There's nothing like eating seafood with your feet in the sand, watching a moonrise creating a glittering crease in the swirling velvet black of the ocean. This is one of the most romantic restaurants in India, the best seafood restaurant in/near Chennai, and reason enough to book into the Taj Fisherman's Cove (or head here for lunch). Seafood, prepared in open-air kitchens, is delicious, and can be as spicy as your taste buds require—ask the chef to hold back, as the delicacy of the seafood can be obscured by a heavy hand with spices.

Covelong Beach, Kanchipuram District. (C) **044/6741-3333.** Reservations essential Main courses Rs 275–Rs 725. AE, DC, MC, V. Daily 12:30–3pm and 7:30pm–midnight.

Krishna @ New Woodlands Hotel ★★ (Value SOUTH INDIAN   Delicious, unpretentious, and cheap, the Krishna Restaurant at the New Woodlands hotel is a Chennai institution, serving excellent South Indian thalis along with dosas, Idli, uthappam, vadas, and so on, to its very loyal locals as well as newcomers to the state. For the latter it's the perfect introduction to South Indian cuisine, with prices so low you can order a ton of stuff and get to know what it is that you really like. You can eat with your hands (everyone else does) but will be supplied with cutlery, so there's no pressure. Most of the staff don't speak English but there is always someone in the dining hall who can explain in halting English some of the ingredients. This is also a good place to sample typical South Indian filter coffee. (*Note:* The hotel offers very cheap rooms, from Rs 900, but unlike the food, not recommended.)

72-75 Radhakrishnan Salai, Mylapore (C) **044/2811-3111.** Main courses Rs 40–Rs 115 AE, DC, MC, V (only for bills above Rs 250). Daily 6am–10:30pm.

Raintree ★★★ CHETTINAD   It was in this atmospheric outdoor restaurant that this unique South Indian cuisine first emerged from the Chettiar family kitchen and into the commercial arena. The rain trees were sadly swept over by a massive storm some years back, but a number of palms still bravely screen off Spencer mall, and the ambience, lit with fairy lights and candles, is very pleasant indeed. Try to book a table in front of the stage, featuring a slick classical dance and music program. Sipping on a wide-brimmed copper goblet of *vasantha neer,* honey-sweetened coconut water, flavored with mint leaves, you can't go wrong with crunchy *Karuveppilai year,* prawns marinated in a spicy curry paste and deep fried, as a starter, along with *Urugai idli vathakkal* (pickle-filled cocktail *idlies*) and *Kuzhi paniaram* (rice and lentil batter tempered with spices and shallow fried on a special griddle). Leave space for mains, of which the *kozhi Chettinad,* tender boneless chicken in an authentic Chettinad gravy, best had with *appams* (rice flour pancakes) and *Meen kozhumbu* (spicy fish curry with shallots, garlic, onion, tamarind pulp, and fresh mango—have this with lemon rice, or soak up with a *dosa*), will blow you away. Even if you don't have a sweet tooth, do not leave without trying the *elaneer paayasam*—tender coconut kernels, coconut milk, and condensed milk—arguably the best dessert in the state.

Taj Connemara, Binny Rd. (C) **044/5500-0000.** Reservations essential in winter season. Main courses Rs 275–Rs 525 (Prawns Rs 725). AE, DC, MC, V. Daily 7:30pm–midnight.

CHENNAI AFTER DARK

Unlike Bangalore, Chennai doesn't have much of a nightlife, thanks to its rather ortho-dox values, and a police force that keeps a strict eye on official closing time: midnight. The only real options are located within upmarket hotels, making access relatively easy for foreign visitors. If all you want is to have a drink, one of the classiest places to do so is still the **Leather Bar** (© **044/4267-6000**), at The Park hotel on Anna Salai. After-wards, saunter over to The Park's nightclub, **Pasha** (© **044/5214-4000;** Wed–Sun), a crowded club that's all about being seen—it warrants a visit even just for a few minutes to watch (easy if you're residing at The Park, which automatically gives you free access). Another groovy watering hole, attracting a slightly older crowd, is **Havana** (© **044/4225-2525**), in the Raintree Hotel—this is more of a lounge-bar, comfortable for peo-ple-watching and particularly entertaining when the (small) disco floor gets productive. The **Bike & Barrel** at The Residency Towers is more faux English pub than disco, and has the awful habit of holding karaoke nights, but on certain nights the place is trans-formed into a more happening spot—look out for evenings when DJs Anto and Vivek spin retro remixes and reedits, or play popular motion picture sound tracks. More high-brow fare is served at **Rhapsody,** the lounge-bar at Courtyard by Marriot—while there's no dance floor it's a great venue, and like Havana attracts a more sophisticated local crowd. Alternatively, head over to **Distil** (© **044/5500-0000**) at the Taj Connemara: With large-screen TVs, it has a bit of a sports-bar feel, but when it's full it has an energetic buzz, and the fresh fruit cocktails are great: try the lychee vodka or the watermelon mar-tini. **Fort St George** (© **044/6600-2827**) at Taj Coromandel serves the most expensive beer in the city, and attracts a suitably well-heeled and glossy clientele.

SHOPPING

Chennai isn't charming, but it does offer good shopping—if you want a one-stop mall destination, head to the labyrinthine **Spencer Plaza,** conveniently located opposite Taj Connemara. Said to be the largest shopping complex in South India, Spencer Plaza was Chennai's first mall, and is still the most popular, but with low ceilings and claustropho-bic corridors, and a generally confusing layout, this is not mall shopping as you know it in the West. It has around 400 shops; if you haven't for instance had a chance to shop at the famous **FabIndia,** where you can pick up cotton garments, *kurtas* (tunics), and ethnic furnishings and linens for next to nothing, you can do so at the small Spencer Plaza outlet. There are however five more outlets in the city, all open daily; if you hate malls, the best (and biggest) FabIndia outlet is in a beautifully renovated heritage home: Ilford House, 3 Woods Rd. (off Anna Salai; © **044/2851-0395** or 044/5202-7015). Spencer Plaza also has an outlet of **Hidesign,** the Pondicherry-based outfit renowned for top-quality leather goods, created by Indian craftsmen and internationally renowned Italian designers. There is also a Hidesign in the **Ispahani Center** (one of the city's smallest, glitziest and most peaceful malls) located on Nungambakkam High Rd.; © **044/2833-2111** or 044/5214-149); here you can also pop into **Casablanca** for men and women's wear (women shouldn't miss a look at particularly the Gecko range). But perhaps the best shopping experience, also in Nungambakkam, is to stroll along **Khader Nawaz Khan Road** ★★★: potholed it may be, but Chennai's retail "golden mile" holds the densest concentration of Indian high-street designer stores in the city (as well as, bizarrely, a Marks & Spencer). If you're not going to Pondicherry, this is where you can browse the goods produced by the community in the City of Dawn at **Naturally Auroville Bou-**

tique (8 Khader Nwaz Rd.; © 044/2833-0517); also pop into **Cotton World** just above, and don't miss **Evoluzione** at #3 (© 044/4213-9800).

If you prefer a more sanitized environment, browse the Taj Coromandel's **Khazana Shop** (37 M.G. Rd.; © 044/5500-2012 or -2827), where you'll find a particularly good selection of top-quality silks, saris, and various objets d'art in an upmarket, luxurious environment (and pay the price). Across the road from the Coromandel, **Central Cottage Industries Emporium** (672 Anna Salai; © 044/2433-0809 or -0898) is the fixed-price government emporium with a virtual monopoly on package tourist shoppers. Farther up the road is **Poompuhar**, the government emporium of Tamil Nadu (818 Anna Salai, near recommended bookstore Higginbothams), which has a better selection of art pieces unique to the state—this is a good place to pick up a Thanjore painting or woodcarving, or bronze figurines. Before you reach Poompuhar you will pass the respected **Victoria Technical Institute** (www.vitichennai.com), also on Anna Salai, which stocks predominantly paintings and carvings.

Cane & Bamboo ★ (21 Marshalls Rd., Egmore; © 044/2852 8672) is another good shop for curios and gifts—trays, bowls, spoons, lamps, and other handicrafts made of different types of wood sourced from all over India—and managed by the knowledgeable Mrs. Thangam Philip, who can tell you about the different artifacts she stocks. But perhaps our favorite Chennai shop is **Amethyst** ★★★ at 14 Padmavathi Rd in Gopalapuram (see "Where to Dine," above): an excellent collection of clothing, furniture, and souvenir handicrafts made with Indian fabrics and a mix of traditional and fab modern Indian design elements (look out for the Avadh collection of contemporary clothes from Lucknow with "retro" accents, and stunning jewelry made by Amrapali) and a great coffee shop where you can relax while pondering just what to purchase. Nearby is **Kalpa Druma** ★ (71 Cathedral Rd., Gopalapuram; opposite Chola Sheraton © 044/2811-7652 or -1695), spread across three buildings, one of them five stories high, for a huge variety of housewares, handicrafts, gifts, and antique furniture across all budgets—hard to believe that Chennai has the only outlet! Like Amethyst, **Chamiers** ★★★ (85 Chamiers Rd, © 24311495; www.chamiersshop.com) offers a holistic shopping experience, with a cafe where you can sip organic coffee or fruit juice. Aside from the variety of gifts, and the well-known international Indo-Western brand Anokhi, there's Lokessh Ahuja, an interesting menswear range. Finally, even if you have absolutely no intention of buying a silk sari, you must visit **Nalli Chinnasami Chetty** ★★★ (9 Nageswaran Rd., T. Nagar, near Panagal Park; © 044/2434-4115; www.nallisilk.com), a Chennai institution, where you can't help but fall in love with the exquisite silks, including the famous Kanchipuram silks. While on the busy shopping mecca of T. Nagar, look out for **Kazaana Jewellery** ★ (the other outlet is on Cathedral Rd., the first shop in India to introduce a "guarantee card" to buy back any item at market rate); aside from quality saris and silks, T Nagar street is one of the best places to look for clothing bargains, while Pantheon Road is the place for cheap but attractive linen. And eco-warriors shouldn't leave town without looking over **Prana: Live Natural** (D6 6th St., near Chintamani, Anna Nagar East; © 044/4217-0077): organic clothing for men and women, all natural or naturally dyed (or "safe-chemical" dyed).

WORLD'S WEALTHIEST TEMPLE: TIRUPATI ★★

Situated on a peak of the Tirumalai Hills, overlooking Tirupati (just across the Tamil Nadu border into Andhra Pradesh), is the second busiest and richest religious center on earth (after the Vatican), drawing more than 10 million devoted pilgrims every year.

8

(Tips) Jumping the Queue

Wealthier pilgrims can now make use of a computerized virtual queue system that streamlines the *darshan* experience. Pilgrims buy an armband imprinted with their *darshan* time, shaving hours—even days—off their wait in line. Foreign visitors should bring their passports and appeal to the Assistant Executive Officer or A.E.O. (ask one of the temple police for directions) for a special **darshan ticket,** which costs anywhere from Rs 200 to Rs 4,000 depending on the kind of speedy access you request (you will also be fingerprinted and photographed at this stage; ask your hotel if you need to book this a day in advance). Paid for at a special counter, it cuts waiting time to around 2 hours. Note that men must wear long pants or *lungis;* women must be conservatively dressed with long skirts and shoulders covered. Prior to entering the queue, you'll be asked to sign allegiance to the god. Avoid taking part if you suffer from claustrophobia, since you'll still have to spend an hour or two within cagelike passages designed to prevent line-jumping. Temple activities commence at 3am with a wake-up call to the idol (*suprabhatham*) and continue until 12:45am the following morning. On Sundays the temple closes.

Certainly the richest temple in the world, the Dravidian-style **Sri Venkateswara Temple** is said to be the heart of Hindu piety, but in many ways it appears to exist expressly for the collection of wealth connected to a legendary loan: Lord Venkateswara, the living form of Vishnu, apparently borrowed an enormous amount of money from the God of Wealth in order to secure a dowry for his bride. Devotees donate generously in order to help their god settle his debt—the loan must be repaid in full, with interest, before the end of this epoch. Annual donations of jewelry, cash, and gold (along with sales of *laddus* or sweets and donated human hair) total around 1.5 billion rupees. Much of this goes to the temple kitchens that prepare meals, free accommodations for pilgrims, and various charitable hospitals and schools.

The inner shrine is presided over by a diamond-ornamented 2m (6½-ft.) black idol that stands at the end of a narrow passage. Pilgrims queue for hours, sometimes days, excitedly preparing for *darshan*—the extraordinarily brief moment when you're all but pushed past the god by guards to ensure that the sanctum doesn't become clogged with devotees, many of whom succumb to the moment by falling to the ground. Waiting amid the mass of anxious, highly charged pilgrims, you'll get a good sense of the religious fervor of the Hindu faith. By the time you reach the moment of *darshan,* thousands of excited, expectant worshipers will be behind you, chanting Vishnu's name. Once out of the inner shrine (one of the few in South India that non-Hindus can enter), you'll make your way past a massive fish-tank-like enclosure, where temple clerks count the day's takings—possibly the most cash you're ever likely to see in one place.

Note: As you're waiting in line, you'll see many shaven heads—it's common practice for believers to have their heads tonsured before going before the deity as a devotional sacrifice. As a result, a lucrative human hair business contributes significantly to the temple coffers—Far East and Italian wig manufacturers are major consumers of world-renowned Tirumalai hair, shorn by a fleet of barbers permanently in the service of the temple.

For information you can log on to **www.ttdsevaonline.com** for tickets, but you'll more than likely find everything sold out—in which case you can try calling the call center (© **0877/223-3333** or 0877/227-7777, ext. 3679). The easiest ways to get here are by plane (the nearest airport, Renigunta, has regular flights from Chennai, Hyderabad, and Bangalore); alternatively travel by train from Chennai (or Hyderabad, Bangalore, or Mumbai). To overnight, prebook a room at the dependable (and popular) **Fortune Kences** (© **0877/225-5855;** www.fortuneparkhotels.in; kences@fortunepark hotels.com; doubles from around Rs 1,900), which is located in the heart of the town, near the temple, and draws the well-heeled devotees. Service is very good, and the hotel is comfortable (but not luxurious).

2 MAHABALIPURAM (MAMALLAPURAM) ★★★

51km (31 miles) S of Chennai

A visit to this once-thriving port city of the Pallavas, a dynasty that ruled much of South India between the 4th and 9th centuries A.D., is an excellent introduction to South Indian temple architecture, and the surrounding resorts offer a much more holiday atmosphere than Chennai. Established by Mamalla, "the Great Wrestler," the tourist town of Mahabalipuram attracts thousands to view the earliest examples of monumental architecture in southern India—incredible rock-cut shrines that celebrate Hinduism's sacred pantheon and legends. Even today, the descendents of these early sculptors continue to create carvings for temples, hotel foyers, and tourists; the sounds of sculptors chipping away at blocks of stone echo through the narrow lanes, an aural reminder of the sort of devoted craftsmanship that must have possessed the original masons who created the World Heritage monuments. It's possible to survey the best monuments in a morning, provided you get an early start (ideally, long before domestic tourists arrive en masse around midmorning). This leaves you time to unwind on the pleasant beach and dine on a plate of simply prepared fresh seafood. You could even overnight, enjoying its charming village-like atmosphere, a million miles from the 21st-century hustle that is Chennai. Alternatively, you can move on to Pondicherry after lunch and be sipping Gallic cocktails before sundown.

Next stop (about halfway mark to Mamallapuram) is **DakshinaChitra ★**, a nonprofit heritage center showcasing different living styles of India's four southern states: Tamil Nadu, Karnataka, Andhra Pradesh, and Kerala. It has relocated or rebuilt real 18th-, 19th-, and 20th-century houses and re-created village streets and workplaces typical of each state, and there are goods for sale as well as artisans (weavers, potters, glassblowers, puppeteers) demonstrating their skills. Informative guided tours of the reconstructed heritage villages are available; alternatively there is a good map given out with the entry fee (Muttukadu, East Coast Rd., 30km/18 miles south of Chennai; © **044/2747-2603;** www.dakshinachitra.net; entry Rs 200; child Rs 20; Wed–Mon 10am–6pm).

DakshinaChitra has plenty of activities for kids but beleaguered parents with overactive kids will find the most successful stop just 15km (9 miles) north of Mahabalipuram, the **Madras Crocodile Bank Trust ★** (www.madrascrocodilebank.org; Rs 30; children under 10, Rs 15; photo with croc or python Rs 50; feeding crocs Rs 30; Tues–Sun 8am–6pm) was set up by the famous New York–born herpetologist Romulus Whitaker in 1976. It is today an extremely successful breeding and research center that sustains around 2,500 crocodiles, including 14 of the world's 26 species, and puts these much

Tips   En Route to Mahabalipuram: The East Coast Road Hop

Travelling between Chennai and Mahabalipuram along the East Coast Highway, you may want to schedule enough time for a number of interesting stops along the way. First up is **Cholamandalam Artists' Village** (Injambakkam, 13km/8 miles south of Chennai; ℭ **044/2449-0092;** daily 9am–7pm), established in the 1960s and home to a community of some 20 artists, with a permanent exhibition of their paintings, sculpture, graphic arts, and batik. Further south is **Kalakshetra** ("Temple of Art"), a celebrated school for traditional music and dance "with the sole purpose of resuscitating in modern India recognition of the priceless artistic traditions of our country and of imparting to the young the true spirit of Art, devoid of vulgarity and commercialism." It was set up in 1936 by the celebrated Rukmini Devi Arundale, who studied ballet under Russia's great ballerina Anna Pavlova; on her return to Chennai she studied *dasi attam* (also known as *Bharat-natyam*), traditionally restricted to temple dancers, and regenerated interest in this classic dance form. Visitors interested in observing day classes are welcome by prior arrangement (the school has produced some of the country's most revered modern-day dancers) and performances are regularly staged in the school's auditorium. Visit **www.kalakshetra.net** for the calendar of events (Thiru-vanmiyur, 29km/18 miles south of Chennai; ℭ **044/2491-1169** or -1836).

maligned creatures in a new light. Did you know for instance that it is not chromosomal configuration but temperature, timing, and incubation duration that determines the sex of crocodile offspring?

ESSENTIALS

GETTING THERE & AWAY   Mahabalipuram is 2 hours south of Chennai, on the East Coast Highway. Buses from Chennai arrive and depart every half-hour from the suburban Koyambedu bus stand (state-owned buses at Mofussil and private buses at Omni stand). Pondicherry is around 40 minutes away by road.

VISITOR INFORMATION   The **Government of Tamil Nadu Tourist Office** (Kovalam Rd.; ℭ **04114/242-232;** Mon–Fri 10am–5:45pm) can supply you with limited information (like a map of Tamil Nadu) and a few booklets on the town. Peak season is December to February; July and August, when the French are on vacation, is also busy.

GETTING AROUND   All of the town's attractions can be reached on foot, or you can catch an auto-rickshaw.

EXPLORING THE SHRINES & TEMPLES

Mahabalipuram's monolithic shrines and rock-cut cave temples lie scattered over a landscape heaped with boulders and rocky hillocks. Among these, the excellent **Shore Temple,** built to Lord Shiva, and the **Five Rathas,** a cluster of temples named for the five Pandava brothers of *Mahabharata* fame, are definitely worth seeking out, so too the celebrated **Arjuna's Penance,** largest relief-carving on earth—try to see these as early in the day as possible, before busloads of noisy vacationers descend. Also try to view **Mahishamardini Mandapa** (give the nearby government-run Sculpture Museum a miss). If you feel the need to visit an active temple, head for **Talasayana Perumal Temple,** dedicated to Vishnu. It stands on the site of an original 9th-century Pallava temple but was rebuilt during the 14th century by the Vijayanagar King Parang Kusan, who feared that the sea would eventually erode Shore Temple. Half-hour *puja* (prayer) sessions are conducted daily at 9am, 11:30am, and 7:30pm. About 4km (2½ miles) north of Mahabalipuram, **Tiger Cave** ★ (Covelong Rd.) is the site of an 8th-century shrine to the tiger-riding goddess Durga. It's thought that the shallow cave, with its sculpted *yalis* (mythical beasts) framing the entrance, might have been used for open-air performances.

Arjuna's Penance ★★★ Opposite Talasayana Perumal Temple, the world's largest bas-relief is commonly referred to as "The Descent of the Ganges," depicting the sacred penance performed by one of the Pandava brothers. Standing on one leg, the meditative Arjuna contemplates Shiva—a painful reparation performed while lively representations of the gods, celestial nymphs, elephants, monkeys, and other creatures look on. A naturally occurring cleft down the rock is said to represent the Ganges, a symbol that comes to life during the rainy season when water flows into a tank below. Just a few feet away, to the left of Arjuna's Penance, is **Krishna Mandapam** ★, another bas-relief, carved in the mid–7th century; this one depicts Krishna using his divine strength to lift a mountain to protect people from imminent floods. The duality of the god's nature is expressed in carvings of him going about more mundane activities, including flirting with his milkmaids. Near Arjuna's Penance, to the north, is the huge spherical boulder known as **Krishna's Butter Ball,** balancing on a hillside.

W. Raja St.

Mahishasuramardini Cave ★★ A lighthouse tops the hill where you'll find a number of superb rock-cut shrines— seek out **Mahishasuramardini Mandapa,** remarkable for the two impressive friezes at each end of its long veranda. In the panel to the right, Durga, the terrifying mother of the universe, is seated astride her lion *vahana* wielding an assortment of weapons. She is in the process of destroying the buffalo-headed demon, Mahisha, who disturbs the delicate balance of life. At the opposite end of the veranda, Vishnu is depicted sleeping peacefully on his serpent bed, the sea of eternity; gathered around him, the gods appeal to him to continue the creation. Also atop the hill, **Adivaraha Mandap** features various sculpted figures and mythical scenes, including one large panel of Vishnu as a gigantic boar.

W. Raja St.

Panch Pandava Rathas ★★★ The initial sight of these five *(panch)* monolithic stone shrines, set in a sandy fenced-off clearing, is dramatic, even though the structures themselves—named for the five brother-heroes of the *Mahabharata* and resembling temple chariots *(rathas)*—are incomplete. The ancient sculpting techniques are astonishing: Carved out of single pieces of rock from the top down, these shrines reveal perfect, precise planning. The dome-shaped *shikhara* (tower finial) found on some of the temples became the template for later South Indian temples, successful experiments that were further refined and enlarged.

E. Raja St., 1km (a half-mile) south of Arjuna's Penance. Tickets available from ASI booth at the entrance. Single ticket for both Five Rathas and Shore Temple costs Rs 250. Daily 6:30am–5pm. Approved guides can be hired at the entrance.

Shore Temple ★★★ Perched at the edge of a sandy beach on the Bay of Bengal, where it has been subjected to centuries of battering by salt water and oceanic winds, this early-8th-century stone temple is considered one of the oldest temples in South India,

Lost City: The Temple Uncovered by the Big Tsunami

When the powerful wall of water began to recede from the shores of Mahabalipuram, it uncovered ancient rock sculptures of lions, elephants, and peacocks—all fairly common motifs used to decorate walls and temples during the Pallava period in the 7th and 8th centuries. Could this be the remains of a once thriving city, submerged below the sea when the shoreline changed? Archaeologists working off the coast after the December 2004 tsunami have already uncovered the remains of a massive collapsed temple, built entirely of granite blocks, renewing speculation that Mahabalipuram was a part of the legendary Seven Pagodas, written of in the diaries of European travelers, and that six temples remain submerged in the ocean.

and a forerunner of the Dravidian style. Its two carved towers inspired a style that spread throughout the region and to more distant Asian shores. Vishnu is found reclining inside one shrine, while two others are dedicated to Shiva. A low boundary wall topped by rock-cut Nandi bulls surrounds the temple, and a veritable pride of lions rear their heads from the base of the pillars.

Northeast of the Panch Pandava Rathas, at the beach. Tickets available from ASI booth at the entrance. A single ticket for entrance to both the Five Rathas and the Shore Temple costs Rs 250. Daily 6:30am–5pm. Approved guides can be hired at the entrance.

WHERE TO STAY & DINE

The GRT is hands down the best place to stay if you want to overnight within walking distance of Mahabalipuram's temples, but if you don't mind foregoing hotel comforts for a night or two, the village itself has a number of small, very basic budget lodgings, most of them located right on the beach, though everything in Mahabalipuram is within walking distance. **Greenwoods Beach Resort** (greenwoods_resort@yahoo.com) is neither on the beach nor a resort but offers reasonable lodgings and facilities for the price: Rs 950 to Rs 1,450 for an en-suite A/C room, and they offer a few hotel-like facilities (like airport transfers from Chennai and in-room massages).

The quality of the lodgings on the beachfront varies from year to year, with the best being the most recently painted or extended—in 2009, **Hotel Daphne** (by no means a "hotel," but rather a small double-story sea-facing apartment block) was the latest addition to the seafront, and therefore offering the neatest, cleanest en-suite rooms at a mere Rs 650; bookings are through Anant, co-owner of **Moonraker's** (© **044/2744-2115** or -2811; http://moonrakersrestaurants.com). Located at 34 Othavadai St (which leads down to the beachfront), Moonraker's is incidentally considered to be Mamallapuram's best seafood restaurant: order your seafood grilled rather than fried, and/or ask for head and bones to be removed. If you prefer your seafood with a sea view, **Santana** (© **094/4429-0832** or 098/4078-9576; babusantana@rediffmail.com), owned by the affable Babu Santana, has a beachfront deck where you can snack on plates of fresh grilled calamari and chips, masala-fried prawns and salad, or vegetable *kuruma* with chapati, while enjoying the view of the Shore Temple with the cooling sea breeze (you can stay here too but rooms are needing a coat of paint). Note that July through August is lobster season; Babu can also arrange outings on the traditional fishing boats that line the beach in front of the restaurant.

After the Great Temple Bay (reviewed below) the so-called **Ideal Beach Resort,** located just a little farther north (3km/2 miles from Mahabalipurum), is your next bet; the older rooms are old-fashioned but with charm; the new wings are unimaginatively designed and horribly decorated, and are wildly overpriced. Opt for a standard cottage at Rs 4,500, and utilize the lovely pool area (© **044/2744-2240;** www.idealresort.com; doubles Rs 2,750–Rs 12,000). (Whatever you do, avoid the **Fortune Chariot Beach Resort**—ill-conceived and badly designed, with few sea views, and depressingly ugly. Not even the pool has a view, but faces the back-end of the presidential suite; given these mistakes, the rates are prohibitive.)

Great Temple Bay ★ (Kids) This is by far the best option within walking distance of the village of Mahabalipuram; a beach resort that's close enough to enjoy a view of the Shore Temple from certain aspects (it doesn't have half the charm of Fisherman's Cove, which lies about an hour north). The resort has undergone a massive investment during the past 2 years, doubling its bed capacity from 72 to 144, and now has the atmosphere of a sprawling golf resort, with units cheek-by-jowl overlooking what is billed as (at 200m/656 ft.) the longest pool in India. While the new pool units clustered along this are sumptuously furnished, you could be anywhere; the best part of the hotel is definitely still the (unrenovated) old part, which has the sea views: ask for a front chalet with unobstructed sea-view, or, first prize, for a "sea-view villa". With so many activities on offer kids have a blast; bring out your inner child by having your feet nibbled by hundreds of fish at the Ayurvedic Spa. (*Note:* service can be slow when full.)

Kovalam Rd, Mammalapuram 603104. © **044/2744-3636.** Fax 044/2744-3838. www.grthotels.com. 144 units. Rs 7,000–Rs 9,000 chalet sea-view/bay room sea-view/pool view; Rs 11,000 villa sea-view; Rs 15,000 suite sea-view. Rates include breakfast. Taxes extra. AE, DC, MC, V. **Amenities:** 2 restaurants; bar; babysitting; doctor-on call; mini golf course; room service; ayurvedic spa. *In room:* A/C, TV, computer (villas and suites only), hair dryer, minibar, Wi-Fi (free).

3 PUDUCHERRY (PONDICHERRY) ★★★

189km (117 miles) S of Chennai

Pondicherry's ancient history dates from the Vedic era; the Romans traded here 2 millennia ago, and the Portuguese arrived in 1521. Dutch and Danish traders followed, but it was the French—who purchased the town in the late 17th century, only relinquishing their hold in 1954—who left by far the most enduring legacy. Now a Union Territory, with its own local government, this seaside colony retains its French élan, tempered by South Indian warmth, making it one of India's most relaxing destinations, with virtually all sights and shops within walking distance. After hanging out in your antiques-filled colonial hotel and sauntering around the broad boulevards of the tranquil **French Quarter** (where you'll see old men in thick-rimmed spectacles under the apparent illusion that they're in a Parisian *arrondissement*), it comes as a pleasant shock to step over the "Grand Canal" into a typical Tamil town, where cracked pavements are jam-packed with people and shops, and wares on offer blend Indian craftsmanship with Western-influenced designs. Even if you're not a keen shopper or particularly interested in French colonial architecture, you can immerse yourself in the spirituality of Puducherry (as it is increasingly referred to) by joining the New Age travelers and Indian pilgrims here to pay their respects at the ashram of **Sri Aurobindo,** their blissful commitment making this a bizarrely authentic spiritual experience. Or you can visit nearby **Auroville,** an interesting experiment in alternative living, also optimistically known as the City of Dawn. Ashramic allure and Aurovillian aura aside, Pondi (as it is affectionately called) is the type of charming seaside town where you arrive for a quick overnighter and will end up wishing you could stay for longer; like Goa, it has a number of expats whizzing around on scooters to prove the strong pull it exerts. And, yes, it's far friendlier than Bordeaux.

ESSENTIALS

GETTING THERE & AWAY At press time Pondicherry's long-awaited airport (which was due to open around Mar 2009) was still many months from completion due to the runway being washed away, but check if you'd prefer to fly; Kingfisher airlines will no doubt service this route. Until then, Pondicherry is best reached by road from Chennai, a 3-hour drive (140km/87 miles from the airport) along a mostly good quality two-lane highway; a taxi from Chennai airport here will run you around Rs 2,000 (Rs 1,800 if you're coming from Pondi). There are also regular buses (Rs 50–Rs 60) connecting Pondi with Chennai. To get here by train from Chennai (or Madurai/Trichy), you must first travel to Villuparam (VM) station, which is located an inconvenient 30 min. drive away from Pondi's beachfront (buses every 10–15 min. in peak time); the journey by rail takes 5 hours from Chennai. See chapter 3 for online rail reservations.

VISITOR INFORMATION Pondicherry's helpful **Tourism Information Centre** (40 Goubert Ave.; ℂ **0413/233-9497;** fax 0413/233-0532; www.tourism.pondicherry.gov. in; daily 9am–5pm) can help you with maps, brochures, and tour bookings. A good locally based travel agent is **Travelmate** (ℂ **0413/420-0525;** www.thetravelmate.com).

GETTING AROUND By Taxi & Auto-Rickshaw Auto-rickshaws prowl the streets in some areas, actively soliciting fares. Overcharging is rife, but if you've got several miles to cover, it may be worthwhile to hire one; the minimum charge is Rs 30 for 6km (3¾ miles). Pondi to Auroville costs around Rs 250 by auto-rickshaw and Rs 350 to Rs 400 by taxi; two recommended taxi operators are Sarvanan (ℂ **94420-68821**) and Mr. Anand from Ganapathy Travels (ℂ **94420-66853**).

By Bicycle Parts of Pondicherry are immaculate and ideal for exploration by bike. You can rent a bike (Rs 35–Rs 40 per day) from the Pondicherry Tourism Information Centre (see above). Ask about hiring the services of a guide who can cycle along with you. Alternatively, pop into **Sri Manonmani Amman Cycle Store** (ℂ **98941-72244**) on Mission street, opposite the South India Bank, for a wide choice of bicycles and scooters.

GUIDED TOURS Guided tours and sightseeing trips can be arranged through Pondicherry Tourism (see above); Rs 250 for full day bus tour (9:45am-5pm) or Rs 150 for half day. Alternatively you can also pick up a very good Heritage Trail map, with two clearly indicated walks (covering The French Quarter and The Tamil Quarter), and explore at your own pace. Alternatively, for heritage walks with a guide, make direct contact with **Indian National Trust for Art & Cultural Heritage** (INTACH, 14 Labourdonnais S.; ℂ **0413/222-5991** or -7324; www.intach.org; ashokpan@yahoo.com).

INTERESTING DATES Proof of its multicultural roots and current inhabitants are found in Pondi's annual calendar of important dates: Pongal, a Tamil harvest festival, is celebrated in January, while Masi Mangam, in which deities from 38 temples are taken to the sea for symbolic immersion, followed by their devotees, takes place during full moon over the Feb to March period. Bastille Day in July is the next big event, followed by Sri Aurobindo's birth anniversary on August 15, and the Fete de Pondicherry August 15 to 17.

The joy of Pondicherry is the fact that you can do it all on foot, experiencing the wonderful contrast between the French and Tamil quarter. Start by wandering through its tree-lined French Quarter, which developed around the beachfront and Bharathi Park, and is today one of India's most prepossessing neighborhoods, with wide boulevards, uncluttered roads, bilingual signs, stately government buildings, and gorgeous classical-influenced colonial villas. Then step into another world by crossing the "Grand Canal" aqueduct, into the area the French used to call "black town"—typically Tamil, with tiny shops lining crowded streets, beeping motorbikes and rickshaws, and—at night—an almost carnival atmosphere. The architecture in the Tamil part is also charming, though less obviously so—typical of the state, these are "talking streets": wall-to-wall intimate and designed for socializing, with interiors usually having several courtyards; the first floor, assuming there is one, tends to show more French colonial influences. Besides strolling the streets and enjoying the peacefulness of the French quarter or the bustling chaos of the Tamil part of town, you could spend a good few days browsing shops for some of the best bargains to be had in such a small town atmosphere, and taking the seaside promenade for evening strolls along with the locals and predominantly French tourists. The only other attractions (and really, this is one place you can feel entirely guilt-free doing nothing!) are the serene and powerful **Aurobindo Ashram,** and a trip to **Auroville** (the "City of Dawn"), the latter a must for anyone who remains a hippie at heart.

It's lovely just aimlessly wandering through the French Quarter, but you may want to make sure your walk takes you past the **Sacred Heart of Jesus (Eglise de Sacre Coeur de Jésus),** an 18th-century neo-Gothic Catholic church on South Boulevard, as well as the facade of the **Church of Immaculate Conception** (Mission St.) which has an air of pageantry enhanced by colorful banners (note also how many Christian devotees remove their shoes before entering). But for a real air of celebration head for **Sri Manakula Vinayagar Temple ★,** off a side street around the corner from the Ashram, and so popular that it's cordoned off during the early evening hours; It is dedicated to Ganesha, the elephant-headed god, and Lakshmi, the temple elephant, marks the entrance (see box).

For a quick glimpse of local historic memorabilia and collectibles, visit the **Pondicherry Museum** (49 Rue St. Louis; © **0413/233-6203;** Tues–Sun 10am–5pm), housed in a 17th-century colonial mansion once occupied by the French administrator. The museum features a collection of carriages and carts, stone sculptures, and a formidable bronze gallery, as well as finds from nearby excavations that show that Romans traded on this coast in the 1st century A.D. Along the same road, which runs along the northern end of a square known as **Government Place,** is **Raj Nivas,** the late-18th-century mansion occupied by Pondicherry's lieutenant governor.

At twilight, head for **Goubert Salai** (Beach Rd.). The most interesting sights along the promenade (aside from the locals enjoying themselves) include the colonial **Hôtel de Ville** (now the Municipal Offices building), the round Douane (Customs) House, and the 4m (13-ft.) statue of Gandhi standing at the pier. If you're here for a few nights, it's also worth looking into the cultural events, art exhibitions, and film screenings conducted regularly by Pondicherry's **Alliance Française** (© **0413/233-8146;** fax 0413/233-4351; afpondy@satyam.net.in; Mon–Fri 8:30am–12:30pm and 2:30–6pm).

Aurobindo Ashram ★★   Located in the French heart of Pondicherry, just off Goubert Ave, Aurobindo Ashram draws a global mix of ardent devotees and ordinary people searching for peace; there are no compulsory meditation or rituals, simply learning to surrender to the divine principle and being open to the divine force. Sri Aurobindo, a

(Moments) Blessed by Lakshmi, the Elephant

Temple elephants, usually beautifully "made-up" and jangling ankle bracelets, will dispense their blessings—a tap on the top of the head with their trunk—in exchange for a rupee, dexterously picked up from the flat palm of the devotee, and immediately handed over to the mahout. It's a charming ritual (and a real delight for kids), never better experienced than at Pondi's Sri Manakula Vinayagar Temple, where pretty Lakshmi bats her eyes and blesses the hundreds of devotees who throng around the temple daily. The fact that she's outdoors is a boon for photographers, and her handlers are also very relaxed, allowing anyone to take photographs of Lakshmi (though the crowds can make for a tricky shot).

politically active British-educated Bengali who sought asylum from the British in this small French enclave, took to meditation and yoga while developing theories of enlightenment that integrated his personal spirituality with the tenets of modern science. He met Mirra Alfassa, a Paris-born artist on a similar spiritual quest, in 1914; she became his soul mate, and her ministrations earned her the appellation "The Mother." Founded as a place to foster evolution to a higher level of spiritual consciousness, the ashram opened in 1926. With a significant following and numerous published titles to his credit, Aurobindo finally left the running of the ashram to Mirra, retreating into solitary confinement for 24 years before finally passing away in 1950; The Mother followed in 1973. Today, those who share their vision of a better world come to pray and meditate aside the memorial chambers *(samadhis)* of Sri Aurobindo and The Mother, which lie in the center of the incredibly peaceful main courtyard. It's a very humble place, not like the huge or ancient temples typical of Tamil, but the atmosphere is sacred. Within the house (where the couple once lived) you will find the wise elders of the ashram, who are available for questions—if you have any burning spiritual issues, this is the place to air them; the answers you will receive will inspire. (Don't forget to visit Lakshmi at nearby Sri Manakula Vinayagar Temple afterwards.)

Rue de la Marine. (C) **0413/223-3649.** www.sriaurobindosociety.org.in Free admission; no children under 3. Daily 6am–noon and 2–6:30pm.

WHERE TO STAY
In Pondicherry

Pondicherry is made for pedestrians, and there seems little point in basing yourself in a hotel in modern Pondi, no matter how popular (thinking of Hotel Atithi here), if it necessitates then having to drive into the French heart of Pondi. As such you'll probably want to base yourself in the more peaceful and very charming French Quarter, from where you can walk anywhere; as such all the recommended options are in the French Quarter, with the exception of the charming **Maison Perumal** (reviewed below), which is located in a beautifully restored Tamil home just below Mission Street (the main shopping drag). Despite having no sea views, this is currently our top pick in Pondi itself (Dune being the best out-of-Pondi choice), primarily because of the exceptional service levels: Part of the highly respected CHGroup, who specialize in unpretentious elegance, Maison Perumal is the latest in a line of boutique properties the group is opening in

The City of Dawn: Sixties Sci-Fi in the 21st Century ★★

Conceived in 1964 by Sri Aurobindo's French-born disciple, Mirra Alfassa ("The Mother"; see "What to See & Do: Aurobindo Ashram"), the experimental "universal town" of **Auroville** (literally "City of Dawn") was founded on a tract of land some 8km (5 miles) north of Pondi. It was based on Mirra's vision of a place that could not be claimed or owned by any nation or creed, where people who aspire to "a higher and truer life" could live freely and in peace, devoted to the practice and discovery of Divine Consciousness—a city that would ultimately become a living embodiment of the essential human unity. Largely designed by French architect Roger Anger, **Auroville** drew a group of citizens from all corners of the globe and was inaugurated in 1968, when soils from around the world (128 nations and Indian states) were symbolically placed as a gesture of Universal Understanding in an urn along with the Auroville Charter. Today it is still home to a suitably diverse population, and understandably somewhat insular; some have been here from its inception, but many more continue to arrive over the years, making this the most interesting, globally representative community in India, and effectively its only privately owned "suburb," built almost entirely on the hippie principles typical of the '60s.

At its spiritual and physical heart is the huge futuristic spherical structure spanning 36m (118 ft.) in diameter and known as **Matrimandir,** or Mother's temple, a symbolic space devoted to the "divine creatrix." Covered in glistening gold discs fixed to the outer surface of the dome, it looks like a faux UFO from a 1960s sci-fi film set. The inner marble chamber houses 12 meditation "petals" (each concerning attitudes towards the Divine and humanity worth striving for, such as sincerity, humility, gratitude, courage, generosity, and peace). At the center is a huge man-made crystal (said to be the largest in the world) that reflects the sun's rays and produces a concentrated light to enhance meditation. Visitors wishing to enter the Matramandir must make an appointment after visiting the Garden and 2 days in advance (© **0413/2622268;** call 2-4pm).

Radiating from the Matrimandir and its gardens, which also have an amphitheater (built with red Agra stone) where the occasional performance is held,

Tamil Nadu, a move that is helping to put Tamil Nadu as firmly on the map as their properties did for Kerala.

Other than those reviewed below, it's also worth looking into the relatively new **Richmond Hotel ★**, which opened in late 2008 in the French Quarter at 12 Labourdannais St., 4 blocks back from the seafront (© **0413-2346363;** www.theresidency.com; Rs 3,500–Rs 4,000 double). A narrow colonial-era building, the Richmond is a small property, with just 14 compact rooms boasting all modern conveniences; we certainly wouldn't mind ending up here if our recommendations reviewed below were full. However, some rooms are a little on the dark side; request a room that overlooks the street or the back of the building, that is, a room with plenty of windows to let in natural light, the city is architecturally conceived along the lines of a galaxy, evolving organically within certain preset parameters. The original design planned accommodations for 50,000 residents; currently there are about 1,500 from 35 countries, all apparently committed to being "willing servitors of the Divine Consciousness." Every year new citizens are accepted into the City of Dawn, based on the needs of the existing population and following a stringent evaluation. Far more than a place for devotion and meditation, Auroville is an experiment in self sufficient living that supposedly takes both nature and culture into account, with all members providing some service to the community. Certainly its architectural innovation and utopian idealism make this a place of interest for anyone with a penchant for the unusual, the ethereal, or the novel, but living here is no doubt a great deal more challenging since the mediating presence of The Mother is no longer there to smooth over the flaws of life among mere mortals. But it is the global residents of Auroville who give Pondicherry its unique flavor, with many running restaurants and retail outlets in the coastal town and beyond.

As a day visitor you will need to stop at the **Tourist Information Centre** (© **0413/262-2239;** www.auroville.org), where you can pick up brochures, shop, snack, and watch a video presentation—a prerequisite before moving on to visit the Matrimandir (Mon–Sat 9:30am–12:30pm and 2–4pm; Sun 9:30am–12:30pm) and surrounding gardens. It is a 10-minute walk to the Matrimandir; a shuttle vehicle is available (ask where to wait when you get your ticket). Note that the cafeteria kitchen prepares delicious, wholesome, extraordinarily cheap vegetarian fare—time your visit for lunch. Given that the Auroville community is predominantly (and predictably) craftsmen and artists, the retail area adjacent to the cafeteria are also worth a look-in (Kalki particularly, though there is more for sale in their Pondicherry outlet on Mission St.). If you're interested in overnighting in Auroville, visit Guest Service, located upstairs at the Solar Kitchen building, or visit www.aurovilleguesthouses.org (see recommendations below).

such as 1210, 1212 or 1202. The hotel has no outside gardens, and the bland mod interiors don't reflect any sense of place. If this is important you may want to take a look at nearby **Hotel de Pondichéry** on 38 Rue Dumas (© **0413-2227409;** www.hotelde pondichery.org; Rs 2,000–Rs 3,200 double). This heritage hotel, a block back from the seaside, in a gorgeous colonial villa with gardens that run into the Le Club group of restaurants (comprising Bistro, Indochine, and Le Club), was undergoing a much-needed renovation at research time—given that this was once one of our favorites before it became increasingly dog-eared, damp and run-down, we are much heartened that steps have been taken to remedy the situation. However, as it was very much in progress, we cannot vouch for the end product as yet (furniture would need a similar investment) so final opinions are tempered (but do write and inform us of yours!). Right next door, at 36 Rue Dumas, is **Dumas Guest House** (𝒞 0413-2225726; www.dumasguesthouse. com) another 17th-century colonial heritage building that has been converted into a simple guest house offering eight clean but spartan rooms, surrounded by nice gardens, and a deal at R 1,500 double. For spotlessly clean budget accommodations right on the sea, look no further than **Sea Side Guest House** (14 Goubert Ave.; 𝒞 0413/233-6494). It's basically a small hostel-like hotel, run by the Aurobindo Society, so service is either benign or indifferent, and there are no real amenities. But the combination of location and price is unbeatable: a double A/C room with sea view costs a mere Rs 775; sea-facing suites cost Rs 975 a day; extra mattress Rs 150. The only possible irritant is the fact that the gates are locked at 11:15pm, and no alcohol is allowed on the premises. It's understandably popular, so book well in advance.

Hotel de l'Orient ★★   More guesthouse than hotel, this slightly run-down but exceptionally characterful 1760s manor house is in the heart of the French Quarter. Each of the guest rooms—set around an inner courtyard shaded by citrus and neem trees—are furnished with French colonial antiques, capturing the period grandeur of a colonial nobleman's mansion, though not all rooms are created equal, and not everyone likes the slightly decaying look. Top favorites are Karikal (a truly "Grand Room" with terrace and veranda, Rs 6,000) and Yanaon (a bargain, given its size, at Rs 4,500). Arcot, which has a patio, is also a great choice, as is Surate (both Rs 3,250), while Cassimbazar is a great twin-bedded room. Service is well meaning but untrained. Most accommodations overlook or are linked to the romantically candlelit courtyard restaurant, **Carte Blanche,** where local "Creole" cuisine, a blend of South Indian and French, is served. *Tip:* Don't miss the attached Neemrana gift shop; it has some wonderful, fair-priced souvenirs sourced from all over India—worth a visit even if you're not overnighting here.

17 Rue Romain Rolland, French Quarter 605 001. 𝒞 **0413/234-3067.** Fax 0413/222-7829. www.neemrana hotels.com. Delhi reservations: Neemrana Hotels Private Ltd., A–58 Nizamuddin E., New Delhi 110 013. 𝒞 **011/2435-6145** or -8962. Fax 011/2435-1112. sales@neemranahotels.com. 14 units plus 2 in annex; avoid these. Rs 3,000–Rs 6,000 double. AE, MC, V. **Amenities:** Restaurant. *In room:* A/C, hair dryer on request, Wi-Fi (free).

Le Dupleix ★★   Owner Dilip Kapur (creator of the internationally renowned leather brand Hidesign) and his glam wife, Jacqueline, restored and modernized this 18th-century French colonial villa, turning it into an urbane, compact guesthouse, Pondi's first true boutique hotel. There's no doubt that it's a looker, but parts (like the outdoor silk coverings) are looking a little faded during our last visit. Sadly staff here—oblivious to the competition gearing up—still tends to look down on the rest of the world. The best rooms are the two luxury penthouses (modern glass and teak boxes of which no. 15 is best; no. 14 is bigger), but I'd rather be at Dune Village for this money; of the deluxe rooms, no. 9 is best. Note that entry-level "superior" rooms (nos. 3 and 4) are really very tiny. Residents of Le Dupleix may use the pool at The Promenade. Food is hit and miss.

5 Rue De La Caserne, French Quarter 605 00. 𝒞 **0413/222-6999.** Fax 0413/233-5278. www.sarovarhotels. com. ledupleix@sarovarhotels.com. 14 units. Rs 5,200 superior double; Rs 7,000 deluxe suite; Rs 8,500 luxury penthouse; Rs 9,200 luxury suite. Extra person Rs 1,500. MC, V. **Amenities:** Restaurant; bar; airport transfers (Rs 3,100); board games; room service. *In room:* A/C, TV, DVD player on demand, hair dryer, minibar, Wi-Fi (free).

Maison Perumal ★★★   This beautifully renovated heritage guesthouse, an oasis of calm located just off bustling Mission street, is in the Tamil side of town and feels therefore more anchored in real, living Pondi. Aside from this, the best reason to book here is the efficient and warm Dinu Ramakrishnan, who, along with his well-trained staff, ensures that this is the best-run guest house in Pondicherry. Service is attentive yet discreet; staff is clearly as delighted to be here as you will be. Rooms are elegant and cool; it's a pity that the bathrooms (shower only) are so tiny but it's a small price to pay for the sense of pampering (and shower pressure excellent). It's an easy walk to the main shopping area, a short rickshaw ride (Rs 30) to the French restaurants on the other side of town. Not that you'll need to dine elsewhere; food, like the rest of the services, is a very high standard. If rooms are still available at Rs 4,500, snap 'em up!

44 Perumal Koil St., Tamil Quarter 605 001. ℂ **0413/222-7519** or 09442127519. Fax 0413/222-7523. www.cghearth.com. maisonperumal@cghearth.com. 10 units. Rs 4,500–Rs 6,000 double. MC, V. **Amenities:** Restaurant; bar; airport transfers (Rs 2,700); room service. In room: A/C, Wi-Fi (free).

The Promenade ★★ A small, purpose-built seaside hotel from the same team that brought us Le Dupleix, trendy Promenade doesn't have quite the charm of its heritage sister, but book a sea-facing room and you'll have the glistening waters of the Bay of Bengal to make up for it, as well as a small pool to cool off in. With a buzzing designer-style bar and new pizzeria, this is also the most happening after hours option in Pondi (which means it can be noisy for residents). Rooms are well designed, with huge leather headboards, raw-silk bed throws, teak-framed doorways and floors and Zen-like low-level beds and floating cupboards; the compact bathrooms are showing signs of age. Staff are not as snooty as Le Dupleix but service is slow, and waiting for your booking to be found or room to be ready can be unforgivably long.

23 Goubert Ave., French Quarter 605 001. ℂ **0413/222-7750.** Fax 0413/222-7141. www.sarovarhotels. com. promenade@sarovarhotels.com. 35 units. Rs 5,700 deluxe non-sea-facing double; Rs 6,900 sea-facing double; Rs 10,500 suite. Extra bed Rs 1,000. Rates include breakfast. MC, V. **Amenities:** 2 restaurants; bar; airport transfers (Rs 3,100); board games; pool; room service. In room: A/C, TV, DVD player on demand, hair dryer, minibar, Wi-Fi (free).

Villa Helena ★ Value Owned by Roselyne Guitry, a perfumer from Burgundy who has lived in Bangkok, Delhi, and now Pondicherry, this guesthouse started out as an annex in which Roselyne could keep her collection of antiques and traditional furniture. A natural decorator, she claims the place was "thrown together," and operates her villa as a nonprofit hobby and an opportunity to meet people from around the world. The communal porch with gracious arches and pillars, where you can relax in planters' chairs, is a plus, while the two deluxe rooms on the ground floor of the heritage building have lovely high ceilings. It's all rather quirky and charming, and really good value, but don't expect doting staff or any real amenities (or even staff that speaks English)—for that you're better off at Hotel de l'Orient. Only four units, so book well in advance.

13 Lal Bahadur Shastri (Bussy St.), French Quarter 605 001. ℂ **0413/222-6789** or 0413/420-0377. Fax 0413/222-7087. villahelena@satyam.net.in. 4 units. Rs 2,200 standard double; Rs 2,800 deluxe. No credit cards. In room: A/C, TV (in deluxe).

Auroville

If you'd like to stay in Auroville (the only way to get to know this fascinating community, and worth it if you wish to meet with the crafters and artists living here), there are more than 30 guesthouses spread throughout the community, rated between A (basic, with shared bathroom) through to C (en-suite with fan or A/C) and D (studios or apartments or cottages with own kitchen or kitchenette)—for the full list along with informal photographs, take a look at www.aurovilleguesthouses.org. Depending on when you go, and the size of your accommodation, you're looking at around Rs 400 to Rs 1,400 per person with the upper reaches charged during high season (usually July–Aug and Dec–Mar).

Depending on your interest, we recommend the following: **Afsanah ★**, a cool, classy, Zen-style guest house with six double rooms and three "Japanese" cottages on the grounds, and an unpretentious focus on pottery, meditation, and horseback riding (*①* **2622048** or **9345400700;** afsanah_gh@auroville.org.in). Those looking for a healing beach retreat would do well to book into one of the 13 double rooms at the aptly named **Quiet Healing Centre,** located within sight and sound of the ocean, and offering various therapies, classes and workshops to enhance well-being (*①* **2622329** or 2622646; quiet@auroville.org).

If you're looking for a thoroughly authentic Auroville experience, and prepared for the minimum 1-week stay, **Verite Guest House** is all about communal living, including shared (vegetarian) meals, organic gardening, sustainable technology and daily group meditation (*①* **2622045;** verite@auroville.org.in). A double room with attached bathroom will cost Rs 960 to Rs1,100 per person per night; a "capsule," a thatch and bamboo hut suspended off the ground on a granite pillar, with common bathroom facilities, will cost Rs 395 to Rs 450 per person per night.

Perhaps the best introduction to Auroville, certainly if you just want to be in the center of things (such as walking distance to the Visitor Centre restaurant and matramandir), is the efficient **Centre Guest House,** oldest and largest (20 double rooms) in Auroville (*①* **2622155;** centerguesthouse@auroville.org.in). Single rates are between Rs 400 and Rs 1,000; double occupancy rates range from Rs 800 to Rs 1,600; this includes three meals, laundry, bicycle, and guest contribution to Auroville.

8 Outskirts of Pondicherry

There are two good beach resorts within easy striking distance, so if you prefer to do nothing but relax around a pool, meditate, practice yoga, and enjoy fabulous Ayurvedic massages and food, with the option of popping into Pondi for short shopping trips, Dune Village (below) is not only our first recommendation, but hands down one of the best beach resorts in all of India. **Kailash Beach Resort** (*①* **04132/619-700;** www.kailashbeachhotel.in; from Rs 3,500 double), a 37-unit retreat situated about 20 minutes south of Pondi, and run by the well-traveled Raj, an ex-publisher, and his French wife, Elisabete, is another possibility. It's billed as a beach resort, but there are no sea views (the beach is a short stroll away), and you're more likely to find yourself by the massive 33m (108-ft.) pool than braving the pounding surf (in fact, the sea along the entire Coromandel coast is usually too rough to swim in, so don't do this alone). The sprawling pink buildings are apparently inspired by Sikkim architecture, with plenty of carved doorways and deep terraces with comfortable seating; rooms are cool and comfortable though positively bland when compared to the Dune Village.

The Dune Village ★★★ (Kids) If you're looking for a real holiday away from it all, either as a family or couple, with just occasional shopping forays into Pondi, and days spent by the pool after healing Ayurvedic treatments, make Dune Village your home for at least 3 nights. Food is of the best you'll get in South India, and the Ayurvedic treatments the best we've had in Tamil Nadu, but it's the design ethos that captivates. We loved this ever-evolving "village"—an apt descriptor given its collection of totally individual cottages set amid sprawling grounds—from the outset, but under the expert hands-on guidance of director Sunil Varghese, service and cuisine have evolved, and Dune is now a superslick destination, regularly featured in glossy magazines. Appealing to anyone with an artistic and/or ecological bent, who'll delight in the highly creative expressions of the people and artists involved in the making of the village, from eco-designed traditional thatched single-room units on stilts right on the beach, to luxury walled L-shaped villas with private plunge pools. *Tip:* Dune Village, a great party venue, is often host to live music concerts from December to February; make sure you book in advance for one of these.

Pudhukuppam Keelputhupet, 605 014 Tamil Nadu ℂ **0413/265-5751.** Fax 0413/265-6351. www.the dunehotel.com. booking@thedune.in or booking@epok.in. 51 units. Nature cooled Rs 5,500 double; A/C cooled Rs 7,950; A/C suite Rs 11,950; A/C luxury Rs 18,250. Rates include breakfast and taxes. Additional person Rs 1,000; child Rs 400. Children under 5 stay free in parent's room. 20% off Apr–June. AE, MC, V. **Amenities:** 2 restaurants; bar; Ayurvedic treatments; beach volleyball; bicycles, children's playground and activities; DVD library (1,500 titles); kites; open-air auditorium; pool; pottery; room service; spa therapies; table games; tennis; volleyball; yoga and meditation (daily). *In room:* A/C (some), DVD player, minibar (some).

WHERE TO DINE

Given the Indian and French influences, it's hardly surprising that Westerner's feel spoiled for choice in Pondicherry, and space constraints are the only reason the following restaurants are not reviewed in full. Almost all of them, incidentally, are walking distance from one another. When night falls and temperatures are balmy, you'll definitely want to dine alfresco: Aristo's rooftop (reviewed below) is a good inexpensive and authentic choice; on the other end of the spectrum is **The Lighthouse Grill,** the rooftop restaurant at The Promenade (see above): a sexy, atmospherically lit evening space, with a slick bar/club-type atmosphere.

For casual restaurant dining, it's a toss-up between two Pondi stalwarts: **Satsanga** (see below) or **The Bistro** (38 Rue Dumas St.; ℂ **0413/222-7409;** www.leclub-raj.com), located in the gardens of what had become (though currently being revamped) the rather run-down heritage Hotel de Pondichéry. Set beneath a thatched roof, with roll-down blinds, cane furniture (green plastic seats for the spillover), and lots of potted plants, The Bistro (aka Indochine) has a lovely, laid-back courtyard garden atmosphere somewhat spoiled by the awful piped Western music, and probably the biggest cocktail menu in Tamil Nadu (this, along with the cheap prices account for its popularity with young backpackers). You could also try **Rendez-vous Café** (30 Rue Suffren; ℂ **0413/233-0238**), where tables laid with checkered cloths give a cheerful continental atmosphere; try the pork *vindaloo;* the seafood platter (huge) is also good. There is A/C available if it's unbearably hot; if not, sit on the rooftop terrace. For a slightly more cosseted old-fashioned romantic atmosphere, head over to the leafy, candlelit courtyard at Hotel de l'Orient (see "Where to Stay" above for address). Local chefs, working with the French executive chef, change the menu at **Carte Blanche** ★ pretty regularly but the concept is to keep fusing French recipes with Indian ingredients (predominantly coconut and curry leaves); there's limited space here so book if you're not staying here.

For a more informal vibe, and very cheap fare, **Sea Gulls,** located on the beach (near Park Guest House) is also a short stroll away. Food is nothing to write home about but portions are huge. Better still, if all you're wanting is a light snack-type meal of salads and whole-grain bread (and with the heat this is often ideal), head upstairs to the shaded roof terrace at **Kasha Ki Aasha** (23 Rue Surcouf; 0413/2222963). It's predominantly a gift shop; while the all-female staff is helpful and kind, be warned: Service is interminable, so take a book and relax.

Finally, if you find the French-influenced cuisine a little pretentious here on the subcontinent and prefer the deadly hot spices of the local Chettinad cuisine, an alternative to Aristo's A/C room (see below) is nearby **Appachi** (8 Rangapillai St.; © 0413/222-0613). It's *very* popular with locals, so get here early or be prepared to wait for a table.

Tip: If you're looking to escape the heat after shopping in Mission Street by stepping into an A/C refrigerator, or simply have a sweet tooth, **Sri Krishna Sweets** (86 Mission St.) is a spotlessly clean multicuisine canteen-style restaurant-cum-sweet shop, with a tempting array of traditional treats behind gleaming glass counters.

Aristo ★ Value CONTINENTAL/INDIAN   If you can take your Indian spicing like a local, and want quick service (a rarity in Pondi), then head for Aristo, a rooftop restaurant overlooking chaotic Nehru Street. Expect little from the decor—plastic seating and plain crockery—but at night the place is breezy, lit with fairy lights, and enthusiastically twittering birds in a cage compete with a background soundtrack of pop songs and the honks and beeps of busy traffic below. Food is very reasonable and for the most part pretty good. Make a beeline for the *biryanis* (prepared for 4 hr.); if you find it's too hot to eat something meaty (often the case) try the *poisson du chef:* Chef Anwar's special fish in mushroom sauce. Or try the Ceylon egg *paratha* (pancakelike bread, stuffed with meat and onions, wrapped in egg, and fried lightly); accompany that with just about anything that strikes your fancy—it's all extremely tasty and excellent value for money.

114 Nehru St. © **0413/233-4524** or 0413/430-8202. Main courses: Rooftop Rs 90–Rs 200; Chettinad restaurant almost everything under Rs 100. MC, V. Daily 11:30am–4:30pm and 6:30–10pm.

Salle A Manger ★★ CONTINENTAL/INDIAN   Located in a new heritage hotel called Calve, yet another upscale hotel to open in the Tamil part of town, this newbie is currently the classiest dining option in Pondicherry. Like Carte Blanche (see above) Salle A Manger serves Franco-Tamil Creole cuisine, but the emphasis here is more firmly on the Indian (best to choose from this menu), and the surroundings more salubrious. It's a great place to come and celebrate a special occasion but at press time had been struggling to make inroads in the local dining community, so if you're not traveling in peak season and you like your restaurants bustling, best call ahead and find out just how busy they expect to be on the night you plan to visit.

36 Vysial St. © **0413/222-3738.** calve@vsnl.net, info@calve.in. Main courses Rs 100–Rs 220. MC, V. Daily 11:30am–4:30pm and 6:30–10pm.

Satsanga ★ FRENCH   This Pondi institution, still owner-run by Pierre Elouard, an expat from the south of France who has been living in Auroville for well over 40 years, is considered the best French restaurant in Pondi. It's certainly a pleasant enough venue, particularly in the evenings when the alfresco courtyard-style restaurant, with deep eaves all round to keep it cool, looks at its most romantic. Furnishings and general maintenance are less stellar during the harsh light of day, and we've heard some complaints about lackadaisical service; not enough to stop the large contingency of French tourists Pondi attracts from dining here however. If you're a carnivore, opt for their legendary green-pepper filet *(filet au poivre vert)* or the fish Provençal; the bouillabaisse is also a signature.

30 Labourdonnais St.; © **0413/222-5867.** Main courses Rs 200–Rs 300. MC, V. Daily 8am–10pm.

SHOPPING

Pondicherry is paradise for shoppers: Not only because of the cosmopolitan and hugely creative effect Auroville has had on the retail market, but just about everything is within walking distance (and there are plenty of eager rickshaws if not), and the goods on offer

are often better value than what is charged in Delhi and Mumbai, where much of the
Auroville and ashram goods are destined.

First stop has to be Mission Street to spend at least an hour at Auroville's best outlet, **Kalki** ★★★ (132 Mission St.; ℂ 0413/233-9166), where you browse for super non-leather footwear, hand-painted silk clothing, perfumed candles, incense, oils, ceramics, jewelry, and handmade paper items to the accompaniment of artsy, esoteric music. It's not that cheap, but the atmosphere and selection is fantastic. If there's anything you want that's not in your size, you can arrange to have it made and couriered to your next destination. Across the road is **Casablanca** (165 Mission St.; ℂ 0413/222-6495 or 0413/233-6495), one of South India's funkiest department stores (owned by the glam couple who created Le Dupleix and The Promenade), with top international brands spread over three floors. If you love linen, head straight upstairs and peruse the gorgeous Gecko stock (gecko@auroville.org.in). There's also plenty of homewear stuff. Casablanca is also a great place to pick out a stylish new leather handbag, belt, briefcase, wallet or suitcase from the **Hidesign** selection on offer, or you can pop around the corner to its seconds outlet in Nehru Street—Hidesign is sold all over the world (last count 2,000 outlets) but never cheaper than here, where leather goods that appear flawless are sold at up to 50% of the original asking price.

Also an easy stroll from Casablanca is the **Titanic Factory Outlet** (33 Aambalathadayar Madam St.; parallel to Nehru St.; ℂ 0413/234-2075), for international brands (Guess, Ralph Lauren, Gap, Tommy Hilfiger, Timberland, and the like) that have for some spurious reason been rejected or are simply surplus, and now sold at unbelievable prices—a great place to dig for clothing bargains, but give yourself plenty of time (and be wary of how the excitement of cheap individual purchases can result in a cumulatively large bill!). Also on Mission Street, next to the Church of Immaculate Conception, **Focus** bookstore (ℂ 0413/234-5513) has hundreds of books on Indian culture and religion, owned and run by the ashram. Heading north down Mission street you will find the new outlet of **Diva**, a new fashion outlet that sells outrageously cheap pretty jewelry as well as modern clothing for Indian women— a Chennai institution, Diva is a great place to pick up some dirt-cheap items that are clearly not Western, and may transform your look (ℂ 0413/222-7468; www.divastyle.in). Nearby, at 44 Aurobindo Street is **Home Trotter Stores**, a great little homewear store (ℂ 0413/222-1600).

Backtracking to Nehru Street, the tiny **Boutique Auroshree** (18 Jawaharlal Nehru St.; ℂ 0413/222-2117) sells clothes and handicrafts from all over India; it has a small selection of silver jewelry, paintings, and handcrafted bronze, brass, and sandalwood items. In the same street **La Boutique d'Auroville** ★★ (36 J.N. St.; ℂ 0413/262-2150) is after Kalki and Csablanca a must-do stop, with plenty more goods from Auroville, including lovely pottery and handmade paper to original garments, and unbelievably well-priced leather items. Deeper into the French quarter, **Curio Centre** (40 Roman Rolland St.; ℂ 0413/222-5676) has a serious selection of objets d'art as well as indigenous and colonial antique furniture. Next door is **Art Colony** (32 Romain Rolland St.; ℂ 0413/233-2395), with mostly antiques (as well as some reproduction furniture), wood carvings, and handicrafts. If you're interested in art, specifically paintings, don't miss **Cottonwood** ★★★ (Rue Nidarajapayer, next door to Touchwood, a great cafe with Internet service), which showcases the work of top local artists—with luck you'll leave with a canvas signed by Dhanasegar or Stridher. Also on this part of town is **Kasha-Ki-Aasha** (23 Rue Surcouf; www.kasha-ki-aasha.com); aside from the clothing downstairs, there's a cafe upstairs, a good place to snack and stop for tea (though service is atrocious).

> ## (Tips) Carting the Shopping Back Home
>
> For many people, India is the number-one place to shop, and Pondicherry is quite possibly our favorite village-style town to do so; problem is, you'll soon run out of luggage space, and the last thing you want is to be weighed down. Here's the plan: Head down to the nearest domestic counter (there are dozens, virtually on every street; try Best Cargo on 71 Aurobindo St.) and courier your shopping to your final destination. It costs no more than around Rs 50 to Rs 60 per kilo and takes around 3 days—worth it given the inflated prices you pay for goods in Mumbai and Delhi.

Finally, if you're looking for a shopping experience to fill your camera (rather than just suitcases), head down **M.G. Road** on Sunday to peruse the market that springs up from 8am to 10pm, with more than 100 stalls creating a carnival atmosphere. Packed with people and stalls, this is exuberant local life at its best and pure Tamil Pondi. Equally so the fish market, held daily (5am–2pm) on M.G. Road: It's pure mayhem (and rather smelly; take a hanky if you have a sensitive nose), but it's the real deal, and a far cry from the land of chichi boutiques.

4 TIRUCHIRAPPALLI (TRICHY), THANJAVUR & CHETTINAD REGION

Trichy: 325km (202 miles) from Chennai; 55km (34 miles) from Thanjavur; 90km (56 miles) from Chettinad

Tiruchirappalli, "City of the Three-Headed Demon," sprawls at the foot of colossal **Rock Fort,** where the Vijayanagar empire built its once-impregnable citadel when they wrested power from the Cholas in the 10th century. During the bitter Carnatic wars, French and British forces battled for control of the city, both keen to establish control of the looming hilltop fortress. Today a number of neo-Gothic Christian monuments remain as evidence of the British influence during the 18th and 19th centuries, when a cantonment was established here and when the present-day city was built, but it is the nearby temple town of Srirangam that draws visitors here. Another legacy of the mighty Vijayanagars, the holy town of **Srirangam** occupies an island in the Cauvery; with outer walls that are more than 3.2km (2 miles) long, is considered one of the most impressive temple towns in South India. It is awkward to include a visit here as a daytrip as the distances are long and you will need to set aside a good few hours to explore Srirangam (and preferably not in the middle of the day when the heat is most intense), so you will likely have to spend the night in unprepossessing Trichy if you intend to include this in your itinerary; alternatively push through in the early evening to Thanjavur (an hour away) and spend the night there, rising the following day to see the **Brihadeshvara Temple,** before heading to the rural delights of Chettinad.

Almost directly east of Tiruchirappalli (or Trichy, as you may refer to it if you can't master the tongue-twister), **Thanjavur** was once the capital of the Chola empire—which included present-day Kerala, Sri Lanka, and parts of Indonesia. Today its 11th-century **Brihadeshvara Temple,** built by the Chola kings, is a World Heritage monument, and is (together with Mahabalipurum, Srirangam, and Madurai) one of the most important stops on Tamil Nadu's temple route. Having visited the Brihadeshvara Temple, plan to overnight in the **Chettinad** region, which lies around 1½ hours south of Thanjavur. Known predominantly for its pungent, spicy cuisine, this little-known area, comprising some 75 villages centered around the town of Karaikudi, is enjoying a slow revival as visitors, keen to explore the palatial mansions built by the wealthy Nattukottai Chettiars, wander dusty lanes to admire the peeling facades and enjoy the peace of semi-deserted streetscapes. The place to stay is **Kanadukathan,** a tiny heritage village sprawled around the Chettinad Palace, with tranquil village scenes that form a wonderful contrast to the bohemian sophistication of Pondi and the chaotic temple towns of Trichy, Thanjavur, and Madurai.

ESSENTIALS

GETTING THERE & AWAY   Trichy is the major hub in the area and you can fly into Trichy airport from major southern cities (including Chennai or Trivandrum and Kozhikode, in Kerala). Trichy airport is 8km (5 miles) from the city. Chennai is 7 hours away by road; slightly quicker by train—several daily trains then also connect Trichy with Madurai. From Pondicherry, the fastest way to get to Trichy is by hired car; it's a good 3-hour drive. Alternatively, you can travel by bus, or via train from Villapuram. Thanjavur lies 50km (31 miles) east of Trichy; either hire a car or travel by separate train for the 1-hour journey.

The Chettinad region is connected by road and train. It lies about 1½ hours from Thanjavore (2 hr. by car from Trichy), and 2 hours from Madurai, making it an ideal overnight stop between Thanjavore and Madurai.

VISITOR INFORMATION   **Government of Tamil Nadu Tourism Department** (1 Williams Rd., Cantonment [Trichy]; © **0431/246-0136;** Mon–Fri 10am–5:45pm) can supply you with information, maps, and brochures. **Thanjavur's tourist office** (Hotel Tamil Nadu Complex Jawan Bhavan; © **04362/230-984;** Mon–Fri 10am–5:45pm) provides good information on local sights and can help you with transport. Your best source of local information in Chettinad region is your host.

GETTING AROUND   This is definitely one area where it is worthwhile to hire a car and driver. If you've arrived in Trichy by train or plane, do this through your hotel or the tourist information center. You can manage to see Srirangam and Brihadeshvara Temple in a single, exhausting day, leaving for Madurai or Chettinad region the following day.

WHAT TO SEE & DO
Tiruchirappalli
While there is nothing much to see beyond generally ugliness in Trichy, you will spend anywhere from a half- to a full day in the atmospheric temple town of **Srirangam,** most of it embraced by the **Sri Ranganathaswamy Temple,** which lies a tedious 40-minute drive through congested traffic north of the city. In the evening, time allowing, you may wish to climb the steps to the summit of **Rock Fort** to witness the sun setting over the city (entrance at China Bazaar; small admission fee and camera fees; daily 6am–8pm). This is also the time you're likely to encounter the greatest number of devotees coming to worship at the Shiva temple (off-limits to non-Hindus) and paying tribute to the elephant-headed god, Ganesh, at his summit shrine; again the sanctum us off-limits to non-Hindus but the views are sublime. Little of the old fortification has survived (though some inscriptions date from the 3rd c. B.C.), but you may be interested to know that at

3,800 million years old, the rock itself is said to be one of the oldest on earth, predating the Himalayan range by around a million years. Alongside Rock Fort is the huge **Teppakulam Tank,** and across from this, **Our Lady of Lourdes Church,** built in 1840. If you can face another temple visit, Sri Jambukeshwara Temple lies further north of

Srirangam and Sri Ranganathaswamy Temple ★★★
Just 7km (4⅓ miles) beyond Trichy, the vibrant, ancient holy town of Srirangam—one of India's biggest temple complexes—is the site of sprawling **Sri Ranganathaswamy Temple,** whose seven concentric boundary walls *(prakarams)* enclose 240 hectares (600 acres). Within the temple walls, a web of lanes lined with houses, shops, and businesses is also enclosed, making for fascinating exploration of what feels like a heaving medieval village. Dedicated to Vishnu (worshipped here as Ranganatha), the town sees almost nonstop feverish and colorful activity, with communal gatherings and festivals held throughout the year. The original 10th-century temple was destroyed by a Delhi sultan, but reconstruction began in the late 14th century. Ongoing expansion by Trichy's successive rulers culminated in the late 20th century, with the elaborately carved and brightly painted **Rajagopuram,** not only the largest of the 21 *goparums* (tower gateways) that surround the immense complex, but said to be the largest in Asia, soaring to a height of 72m (236 ft.). The most important shrines are within the inner four boundary walls, entered via a high gateway where smaller shrines mark the point beyond which lower-caste Hindus could not venture. Within this enclosure, you'll find a temple to the goddess Ranganayaki, as well as the **thousand-pillared hall,** which dates back to the Chola period; non-Hindus may not enter the inner sanctum. Arguably the most impressive of all is nearby **Seshagirirayar Mandapa,** where the pillars are decorated with stone carvings of rearing horses mounted by warriors. For a memorable view of the entire complex, make sure to purchase a ticket (Rs 10) to climb to the rooftop.

7km (4⅓ miles) north of Trichy on an island on the River Cauvery. Free admission. Rs 50 still camera, Rs 150 video camera. Daily 6am–noon and 2 or 4pm–8 or 10pm. No photography allowed inside the sanctum.

Thanjavur
Brihadeshvara Temple ★★★
This granite temple, a World Heritage Site built by the Chola kings 1,000 years ago, stands in a vast courtyard, surrounded by a number of subsidiary shrines. The central temple was built—at great expense—by the Chola Rajaraja I for the worship of Shiva, and non-Hindus may not enter. Pyramidal in shape, the monumental tower or *vimana* over the inner sanctum rises almost 70m (230 ft.) and is visible for miles around. It's capped by an octagonal cupola carved from a single block of granite that was hauled into place along a ramp that is said to have been 6km (3¾ miles) long. Within the sanctum is a 4m (13-ft.) lingam; facing the sanctum, a colossal 25-ton Nandi monolith (Nandi being the vehicle for Shiva), carved from solid granite, dominates the courtyard. Numerous extant inscriptions on the molded plinth describe the enormous wealth of the temple (much of it booty from Rajaraja's successful campaigns), as well as the copious acts of ritual and celebration that took place here. In its heyday, an enormous staff was maintained to attend to the temple's varied activities; these included everything from administration to procuring dancing girls.

West of Thanjavur bus stand. Visitors may be able to make prior arrangements for entry to the sanctum and the upper floors of the temple by contacting the local tourist office. Daily 6am–noon and 3:30–8:30pm.

Thanjavur Palace Complex & Art Gallery ★
Built as the home of the Nayak rulers, the 16th-century **Royal Palace** has fallen into a state of minor ruin and could be struck from your itinerary but for the impressive **Thanjavur Art Gallery ★★** (daily

10am–1pm and 2–5pm; admission Rs 20). The gallery, housed in the Nayak hall of the palace, has an eclectic collection of stone and bronze idols, mostly from the Chola period (8th–9th c.), and the sensuous casts of particularly Parvati are certainly worth admiring. Within the palace, you should also climb the narrow and tricky steps of the **arsenal tower** for views of the complex and the entire city, including Brihadeshvara Temple. Inside 17th-century **Durbar Hall,** built by the Marathas, who ruled after the Nayaks, is a throne canopy decorated in the distinctive mirror-glass Thanjavur style. Next to the art gallery is **Saraswati Mahal Library,** which houses a collection of rare books—including Sanskrit works and 18,623 palm-leaf manuscripts—assembled by the Maratha ruler Serfoji II, who ruled until 1832 and was a great patron of the arts. A small museum inside the library has a few exhibits worth looking at, including a macabre explicitly illustrated 1804 manuscript entitled "Punishments of China."

Tip: Opposite the entrance to the Palace Complex, on East Main Street, are a couple of worthwhile shopping destinations: **Kandiva Heritage** (No. 97; © **04362/231293**) deals in Thanjavore paintings, wooden carvings, and antique and reproduction bronze items, and is well worth a stroll through, but we challenge you to leave empty-handed from **Tanjore Collections** (No. 105; © **04362/234117**; www.cottageartsemporium. com), a two-story emporium stuffed with goods from all over India. Bargain hard.

East Main Rd. (2km/1¼ miles NE of the temple). For information about Thanjavur Art Gallery, contact the Art Gallery Society (© **04362/239-823**). Palace Rs 50. Camera and video more. Art Gallery Rs 20. Daily 9am–1pm and 3–6pm.

Chettinad Region

Known as the Marwadis of the South, the Nattukottai Chettiars were a powerful trading community that rose to prominence during the 19th and 20th centuries, specializing in money lending and wholesale trading with the East. While not particularly ostentatious, the Nattukottai Chettiars gave expression to their immense wealth by building massive fortified mansions and temples in the rural villages that spawned them. Their fortunes waned somewhat after World War II, with the new generation of ambitious Chettiars seeking their own pots of gold in the cities of India and beyond, and the majority of these mansions are now padlocked and empty for much of the year, opened only for the occasional marriage ceremony or Bollywood film shoot. Some of the larger homes are opened for visitors keen to view the teak and stone-pillared courtyards, ornate doorways and ceilings, crystal chandeliers, and dusty portraits of the powerful patriarchs who once ruled these now-empty corridors. If you see only one, make it the **Chettinad Palace,** the family home of Raja Sir Annamalai Chettiar, noted educator and business magnate, who built this most ornate of the mansions at the turn of the 20th century in **Kanadukathan.** The best way to arrange access is through the proprietors of the guesthouses who have opened their homes to paying guests. Equally pleasurable is to simply wander alone through the tiny village of Kanadukathan, watching children fetch water from the central stepwell and wizened old ladies gossiping on front porches that equal them in faded glory; keen shoppers should also set aside a few hours to plunder the antiques shops in nearby **Karaikudi,** unofficial "capital" of the Chettinad region.

WHERE TO STAY & DINE

No matter which way you look at it, if you want to see both the Sri Rangathaswamy and Brihadishwara temples, you'll have to make do with a hotel in either Trichy or Thanjavur—a pity, because neither has exciting accommodations. Of the two, Thanjavur has the better option in the **Ideal River View Resort** (see below). Alternatively, skip one of the temples and head directly to Visalam in Kanadukathan (Chettinad) one of our favorite lodgings and locations in south India. If you need to have lunch in Trichy, the Sangam's **Chembian** (see below) serves an excellent lunchtime South Indian thali for just over Rs 100; in Thanjavur, head for the Ideal Resort.

Tiruchirappalli (Trichy)

Breeze Residency (Value) Having enjoyed a thorough remodel when it was taken over by new management in 2008, this is now our first choice in Trichy, and with rooms starting at Rs 2,700 it should be yours if you're watching your budget. Like nearby Sangam, Breeze Residency (formerly known as Jennys) enjoys a typical downtown location, surrounded by ugly buildings and busy roads within walking distance of the bus and train station. While rooms remain bland motel style they are clean and reasonably neat, with new albeit cheap fittings in bathrooms. The restaurant isn't as good as Sangam's however. Overall an acceptable choice if you have to spend the night in Trichy.

3/14 McDonald's Rd, Trichy 620 001. ℂ **0431/241-4414.** Fax 0431/246-1451. www.breezehotel.com. 123 units. Rs 2,700 double; Rs 3,200–Rs 4,500 suite. Extra person Rs 600. Rates exclude taxes; include breakfast. **Amenities:** Restaurant; bar; airport pickup (Rs 310); pool; room service. *In room:* A/C, TV, minibar, Wi-Fi (Rs 221/12 hr. and Rs 338/day).

Hotel Sangam Tiruchirappalli Long considered the best lodging option in Trichy, Breeze Residency is certainly giving the Sangam in Tiruchirappalli a run for its money. Sangam remains clean and reasonably comfortable but is definitely showing the patina of age; bathrooms in particular need an update, and as such it's a rather depressing place to find yourself on a hard-earned vacation. It has adequate facilities, including one of the best Indian restaurants in town, and while service can be slow it is well meaning. But you'd be far better off—if at all possible—pushing on through to the similarly priced but far better Ideal Resort in Thanjavur or, preferable still, spending your time and (just a little more) money at Visalam in Chettinad region.

Collector's Office Rd, Trichy 620 001. ℂ **0431/241-4700** or 0431/424-4555. Fax 0431/241-5779. www. hotelsangam.com. 54 units. Rs 4,000–Rs 4,750 double; Rs 7,500 suite. Extra person Rs 1,000. Rates exclude taxes; include breakfast. **Amenities:** Restaurant; bar; coffee shop; airport transfer (Rs 300); gym; pool; room service. *In room:* A/C, TV, minibar (soft drinks), Wi-Fi (Rs120/30 min.; Rs 400/day).

Thanjavur

We like Ideal Resort both as a luncheon and overnight stop because of its tranquil rural atmosphere, but if you want to be in the heart of Thanjavur, the best option in town is the 50-room **Hotel Parisutham** (ℂ **0436/223-1801;** www.hotelparisutham.com; around Rs 8,000 double). It's been refurbished from top to bottom and rooms are looking spotless, the pool area is pretty and sparkling clean, and it's a mere 5-minute walk to the temple and another 5 minutes to the bus and train stations. However, we think it's overpriced given that the hotel is essentially an unattractive 70s monstrosity, and amenities offer nothing particularly superior—though it's been spruced up, it's an old-fashioned hotel with no real defining attributes other than a great location. But if you can negotiate a better price, do it. Until such time, the best-value deal in town is found at **Hotel Gnanam** on Anna Salai Rd (www.hotelgnanam.com), which is also walking distance from the temple, bus, and palace. Gnanam is pretty basic but rooms are comfortable and clean, there's free Wi-Fi in the lobby (when working), and the rooftop vegetarian restaurant is a good place to dine at night. Given the accommodation standards, it's a *real* steal at Rs 1,400 double (including breakfast and taxes). Noisy location though, so ask for a room at the back (or shell out for the Ideal Resort).

Ideal River View Resort ★   Located a few miles outside of Thanjavur, Ideal boasts a peaceful rural setting on a lazy riverbank—a welcome relief from the usual big-city chaos. It's a sprawling property, with some charmingly old-fashioned units in the original main building, and the majority in two-story cottages running parallel to the river; the large dining and entertainment terraces have similar bucolic views (a la carte menu when available is incidentally excellent, though you'll wait for it!). Rooms were extensively overhauled in 2008, with great showerheads and thick mattresses just some of the welcome changes. Just about every room has a sit out with garden views, and there are hammocks for you to curl up in; there's also a big pool and plenty of loungers. The free drop off (10am) and pick up (4pm) into Thanjavur (about a 20-min. drive) is useful for those not traveling with their own car and driver.

Vennar River Bank, Palli Agraharam. ⓒ **0436/225-0533.** Fax 0436/225-1113. www.idealresort.com. 30 units. Rs 3,500–Rs 4,500 double. Extra bed Rs 500. Does not include taxes. MC, V. **Amenities:** Restaurant; bar; Ayurvedic center; bicycles for hire; daily town transfer at fixed times (free); games room: Internet Rs 150/60 min.; pool; railway pickup (Rs 200 plus tax); room service. In room: A/C, hair dryer, minibar, Wi Fi (Rs 67/30 min.).

Chettinad Region

We love the peace and tranquility of Kanadukathan ★★★, and with CGH Earth bringing some slick hotel-style standards to this hitherto rough tourism gem it's even more worth a detour—even if only for lunch. The Visalam's (see below) **Chettinad Kitchen** is where lunch is prepared in an open kitchen under the auspices of one of the village dowagers—served on a banana leaf it is always utterly delicious, as are the Indian breakfasts. A less atmospheric venue, but enjoying a legendary reputation for Chettiar cuisine is **The Bangala** in nearby Karaikudi, the bustling center of the entire Chettiar region. If you want to ship home some large antique pieces such as Chettiar pillars and door frames, Karaikudi is the place to forage. **The Bangala** is an extremely friendly and efficiently run guesthouse (hands-on owner Mrs. Meenakshi Meyyappan is a real character; her staff clearly in awe of her) and currently being extended into a 25-room joint, with a new pool being excavated. Accommodations are nowhere near as delightful as that at Visalam (room nos. 3 and no 4 are best; avoid rooms 9 to 12) or authentic as Chettinadu Mansion. If you wish to lunch here as a nonovernight guest (worth it if you have time), contact Mrs. Meyyappan at least a day before (ⓒ **04565/220-221;** www.thebangala.com).

Anandham Swamimalai, Kumbakonam ★   Even though it's not exactly typical of Chettiar in any way, or conveniently located (Thanjavur lies southwest an hour away; Trichy yet another hour farther west), this award-winning eco-heritage resort-retreat, located near the village of Swamimalai—the center for the state's bronze casting—is ideal should you wish to procure or meet the artisans who produce the bronzework Tamil Nadu is famous for. Designed to mimic a typical Indian village, the resort sprawls over 2.4 hectares (6 acres) adjoining the Cauvery River and has tried to create a "nonhotel" atmosphere (deer wandering around; a pool designed like a well; serene, unmanicured gardens) which it pretty much achieves. So-called "deluxe" rooms are pretty spartan, and furnished with a mix of reproduction or authentic Chettinad antiques. The old block has the more atmospheric rooms, while the new block rooms are bigger (if you can, book no. 125, off a delightful courtyard). Vegetarian cuisine is good if overpriced by Indian standards.

Tip: If you plan to include Mysore in your South India itinerary, you could head over from here, scaling the Eastern Ghats to overnight at sister property: the atmospheric **Lake Forest Hotel,** located on Yercaud Lake, a hill station near Salem, before continuing on to Mysore.

6/30B Timmakudi Agiraharam, Baburajapuram PO, Swamimalai (4km/2¹/₂ miles from Kumbakonam) 612 302. © **04352/480-044.** www.indecohotels.com. 27 units. Rs 4,800 deluxe double; Rs 6,700—Rs 7,530 suite double. Excludes taxes. MC, V. **Amenities:** Restaurant; Ayurvedic center; pool; pottery; yoga. *In room:* A/C, TV, minibar (soft drinks only).

Chettinadu Mansion ★ This is the closest you get in southern India to experiencing a night in a Rajasthani heritage hotel, with a semiaristocratic (in nature if not title) host at the helm, and a palace as neighbor. This is the family home of larger-than-life Mr. Chandramouli (cousin of Raja Sir Annamalai Chettiar, owner of the neighboring Palace) and with luck he'll be holding court on the deep *thinnai* beside the arched entrance. The house is a classic Chettinad beauty: black-and-white marble tiles and massive granite pillars from Italy, brilliant blue cast-iron pillars imported from Birmingham, and so on. Upstairs you'll find the most delightful rooms (insist on one of these seven rooms), each painted with *trompe l'oeil* Art Nouveau–style tile patterns and furnished with antique beds and reproduction fittings and furnishings. Bathroom fittings are cheap and showing their age. There's an outdoor terrace from which to enjoy the rooftops of the heritage village as the sun starts to dip, as you sip the best *chai* in Tamil Nadu.

SARM House, behind Raja's Palace, Kanadukathan, Sivaganga Dist, Tamil Nadu 630 103. © **04565/273-080.** www.chettinadumansion.com. chandramoulia@yahoo.com. 11 units. Rs 4,400—Rs 5,500 double. Meals Rs 600. MC, V. **Amenities:** Dining hall; room service; station transfers.

Visalam ★★★ (Value) We wouldn't dream of coming to Tamil Nadu without spending at least one night in this beautifully restored Art Deco home, built by one of the wealthy Chettiars for his eldest daughter Visalakshi. Now owned by Visalakshi's granddaughter, it was restored and skillfully renovated in 2007 by the excellent Kerala-based company CGH Earth. Bedrooms are gorgeous and huge (ask for the room on the top floor) and service is sterling: staff (sourced from the village) are genuinely warm and thoughtful, while CGH manager Johny runs what is the best boutique hotel in the Chola heartland with military precision. The large walled pool garden and generally immaculately maintained grounds are a further boon. Johny will plan plenty of activities to fill your days; we opt to do nothing but relax and wander around the village, and it remains the highlight of every Tamil trip.

Kanadukathan, Sivaganga Dist, Tamil Nadu 630 103. © **04565/273301.** www.cghearth.com. johny peter@cghearth.com. 15 units. Rs 5,625 double, breakfast included. (Rs 9,005 double, full board.) Extra person Rs 2,000. MC, V. **Amenities:** 2 restaurants; room service; station transfers.

5 MADURAI ★★★

498km (309 miles) SW of Chennai; 100km (62 miles) S of Trichy

The holy temple town Madurai—apparently named for the nectar that flowed from Shiva's hair as a blessing for the new city (*madhuram* is the Tamil word for sweetness)—was built by the Pandyan king Kulasekara. The oldest living city in the Indian peninsula, it was the capital of a kingdom that ruled much of South India during the 4th century B.C., and conducted trade as far afield as Greece, Rome and China—one of the earliest written records of its splendors, written by the Greek ambassador Megasthenes, dates from 302 B.C. Along with great wealth, Madurai generated great festivals of poetry and writing—the **Tamil Sangams**—the first of which are said to have been held 2 millennia ago. Throughout its history, various dynasties battled to control the city. The Pandyas made it their capital for 1,000 years, only relinquishing control during the 10th century to the Chola king Parantaka. During the 13th century, after enjoying a brief spell as an independent Sultanate, it joined the Hindu Vijayanagar empire, who ruled from Hampi, leaving the administration to the Nayaks. The Vijayanagars built much of the temple during their reign, which lasted until the 16th century, when the Nayaks wrest control from the Vijayanagar. The Nayaks invested heavily in their city, building it on the pattern of a lotus, until the arrival of the British in 1736.

Today Madurai, Tamil Nadu's second-largest city, is a hodge-podge of chaotic streets and rutted lanes leading into industrial sectors plagued by pollution and traffic jams and other ills characteristic of unchecked development. The heart of it is—the streets a series of concentric squares surrounding the Meenakshi temple, forming a mandala that is believed to be activated by the myriad devotees' clockwise perambulations of the temple—unchanged for almost two thousand years, and atmospherically charged (similar in some ways to Varanasi, India's ancient city in the north). It is a fascinating city, a place of pilgrimage and joy, and in many ways the embodiment of Tamil Nadu's temple culture. Certainly the labyrinthine **Meenakshi Temple**—celebrating the love of the Meenakshi goddess and her groom, Sundareswarai (the "Handsome God"), an avatar of Lord Shiva—is easily our first choice among Tamil Nadu's temple destinations.

ESSENTIALS

GETTING THERE & AWAY There are flights connecting Madurai to Chennai, Tiruchirapalli, Bangalore, and Mumbai. The **airport** is 12km (7½ miles) south of the city center. **Jet Airways, Air Deccan,** and **Kingfisher** offer flights; check www.yutra.com for best deals. Taxis charge around Rs 300. Trains from all over southern India pull in at **Madurai Junction Railway Station** (W. Veli St.; © 0452/274-3131), which has a good Tourism Department information center that is open daily. The train journey from Chennai is 8 hours (via Trichy); from Bangalore, 11 hours. From Pondicherry you'll need to catch a cab to Villipuram (30-min. drive) then travel for 6 hours by train. There are two bus stands. The Central Bus Stand (7km/4⅓ miles from center) is the arrival point from Chennai and other north, south, and eastern districts. If you are arriving from the west, including Kerala, you will disembark at Arapalayam Bus Stand (2km/1¼ miles from railway station). If you're traveling by car, a 10-hour direct journey from Chennai, it's best to overnight along the way, preferably in the Chettinad area. The drive between Madurai and Kochi in Kerala takes 8 hours; best to overnight in Munnar or the Periyar area, or you could head over the Ghats via Elephant Hills in the Kodaikanal area (see box).

VISITOR INFORMATION Staff at the **Government of Tamil Nadu Tourist Office** (W. Veli St., next to the Tamil Nadu Hotel; © 0452/233-4757; Mon–Fri 10am–5:45pm; Sat 10am–1pm) provides maps, advice on government-sponsored hotels and shops, and recommendations on guides. As elsewhere, beware of fake "official guides" you meet on the streets.

GETTING AROUND Auto-rickshaw drivers tend to have a field day with foreign visitors; establish a flat rate before heading off.

FESTIVALS Try to time your visit to coincide with the **Chittrai Festival,** held at the end of April/early May, when Shree Meenakshi's marriage to Lord Sundareswara is celebrated by dragging the divine couple from temple to temple on magnificent chariots, accompanied by elephants and drummers, with revelers reaching fever-pitch radiance. The couple is again heralded during the **Teppam Festival** (aka "Float" Festival), held sometime in January and February (traditionally then the most auspicious time of the year to get married in Madurai), when they are set afloat on a beautifully adorned raft in the tank near the Thirupparankundram Temple. It's supposed to be a romantic interlude for the couple, who consummate their passion later that night in the temple. Another good time is during the **Avanimoola Festival,** held in late August through early September, when temple cars are heaved through the streets by hundreds of devotees.

WHAT TO SEE & DO

The principal reason to visit Madurai—for you as well as for tens of thousands of Hindu pilgrims—is to experience the ecstatic spiritual life of **Meenakshi Temple;** though the numbers of international tourists traipsing about (and the introduction of an entrance fee for foreigners) has unfortunately made the experience a little more commercial, it is still a magnificent temple, particularly at 8:30pm when the evening *"aarti"* takes place (see below).

Legend recalls that Meenakshi began life as a glorious princess, born of fire with three breasts and eyes like a fish. As she grew older, she overpowered all the gods with her impossible beauty until she encountered Shiva, upon which her third breast disappeared, as was foretold, and she immediately proposed to him. Madurai is where the divine couple was married, and where their celestial union is celebrated daily, making Madurai one of the holiest cities in India

While sitting inside the temple itself can provide hours of entertainment and a palpable sense of Tamil Nadu's deep spirituality (as well as a sense of its religious commerce), the streets immediately near the great temple are full of character, and are best experienced by just wandering around. Head down Nethaji Road (exit from the West Gate) and keep your camera handy for the great view back down the narrow stall-lined road, over which the magnificent *goparum* towers.

Not far from the temple, **Tirumalai Nayak Mahal** (Palace Rd.; 1.6km/1 mile north of temple, ✆ **0452/233-2945;** admission Rs 50; daily 9am–1pm and 2–5pm) is a 17th-century Indo-Saracenic palace built by Tirumalai Nayak, much of it dismantled by his grandson, who rebuilt his palace in Tiruchirapalli; the remaining parts were later restored by Madras governor Lord Napier in 1858. Aside from the "Heavenly Pavillion"—a rectangular courtyard with 18m-high (59 ft.) colonnades—not much of the original atmosphere survives, and it's a bit of a letdown after the vibrancy of the temple.

Fans of the Mahatma may be interested to know that it was in Madurai in 1921 that Gandhi historically exchanged his *kurta* and *dhoti* wardrobe for the loincloth, typically worn by the poor. Today the bloodstained *khadi* loincloth he wore when he was assassinated is encased in a glass shrine at **Gandhi Memorial Museum,** which chronicles India's history leading up to independence (Tamukkam, 5km/3 miles east of the city center; ✆ **0452/253-1060;** www.madurai.com/gandhi.htm; free admission; daily 10am–1pm and 2–5:45pm). Avoid the adjacent **Government Museum,** where visitors experience 2 million years of history in 30 seconds as they whiz past a 9th-century Vishnu statue, 12th-century Pandyan works, undated Chola statues, and a stuffed polar bear.

If the Meenakshi Temple doesn't blow you away, and you'd like to experience a truly authentic temple experience as yet untainted by any form of tourism, take a rickshaw to **Thirupparankundram Temple ★★,** 8km (5 miles) from Madurai center, but very much part of the continuous sprawl of the temple town. While it's by no means as decorative as the Meenakshi Temple, this evocative cave temple is older and has a very sacred atmosphere, particularly on Friday, when women with marriage or family troubles place candles or sit on the temple floor and create *rangoli* patterns on the ground, using colored powders, ash, and flowers as offerings to Durga. Take a few rupees along to offer to the

(Finds) Perfume City

While walking through the temple you will come across women selling garlands of jasmine flowers—purchase one for a small donation (Rs 10/Rs 20) and ask the seller to tie the garland in your or your female companion's hair, or simply hang it around your neck and breathe in the sublime perfume of the Madurai jasmine flowers, said to give off a unique fragrance, for which tons are exported all over the world. If you're here for a few days make time to visit the city's bustling 24-hour flower market, located behind the equally compelling fruit and vegetable market (between North Chitrai and North Avani Moola sts.) where vendors deal in masses of the most gorgeous blooms, many of them destined to become temple or wedding garlands.

resident temple elephant, **Owayat,** who shuffles and waits to bestow blessings after gracefully accepting your offering in his cupped trunk. If you make it into the inner sanctum (strictly speaking not allowed, but the friendly priests may turn a blind eye) you will see the ghee-blackened carvings of the gods, carved into the holy mountainside on which the temple has been built.

Last, if you're up for one more temple experience, set aside a day (or preferably two, given the long drive) to visit **Rameshwaram.** An island off the southern tip of India, Rameshwaram has a legendary role in the epic of Lord Rama and is today considered by many to be the second holiest place in India for Hindus (after Varanasi). It's not en route to any other sites, so you will have to return the way you came; it's also a little far for a day trip (350km/217 miles round-trip), though many foreign visitors tend to opt for this, given the lack of pleasant accommodation options on the sacred island. (if you do decide to stay, we recommend the **Hotel Royal Park,** just 2km (1¼ miles) from the temple, with has standard amenities and room facilities; ℂ **04573/221-680;** www.hotelroyalpark.in).

It's also worth being warned that the smell from the nearby waters is, on certain days, appalling. Aside from the temple's incredible pillared courtyard, the key attraction and worth seeing, it is not architecturally on a par with the Meenakshi Temple, but the carnival-like atmosphere—created by domestic pilgrims for whom a visit here is the fulfillment of a spiritual quest to visit the seven holy sites of Varanasi, Rishikesh, Haridwar, Pushkar, Kanchipuram, Madurai, and Rameshwaram—is what a trip to the temple destinations of India is all about.

Shri Meenakshi-Sundareshwarar Temple ★★★ (Moments)

One of South India's biggest, busiest pilgrimage sites, attracting up to 15,000 devotees a day, this sprawling temple, always undergoing renovation and repairs, is a place of intense spiritual activity. A 6m-high (20 ft.) wall surrounds the complex, and 12 looming *goparums* (pyramidal gateways)—the most impressive in south India, with the four highest reaching 46m (151 ft.)—mark the various entrances. Garish stucco gods, demons, beasts, and heroes smother these towers in a writhing, fascinating mass of symbolism, vividly painted in a riot of bright Disneyesque colors—these are repainted every 12 years and currently (painted in 2008) looking absolutely gorgeous. Traditionally, entrance to the complex is through the eastern **Ashta Shakti Mandapa,** a hall of pillars graced by sculptural representations of the goddess Shakti in her many aspects, and devotees then perambulate in

(Fun Facts) **Pulling Out Sin**

You may notice devotees, particularly of Ganesh, standing before their god and tugging their ears—this action is symbolic of pulling out sin!

a clockwise direction but you are welcome to enter through any gate (the northern gate is quieter, and you can see the houses of the priests, some 50 of whom are in the temple's employ, and live communally in the humble lane leading up to the gate), and then wander at will. Adjacent to the mandapa is **Meenakshi Nayaka Mandapa,** where pilgrims purchase all manner of devotional paraphernalia and holy souvenirs. Near the inner gate, a temple elephant earns her keep by accepting a few rupees' donation in exchange for the usual blessing—bestowed with a light tap of her dexterous trunk (note that if you wish to photograph her you would do well to donate a few rupees rather than just take a photograph and irritate her mahout). From here you can wander in any direction, finding your way at some stage to the impressive 16th-century Hall of a Thousand Pillars. This hall (or museum, as it is also called) has 985 elegantly sculpted columns, including a set of "musical pillars" that produce the seven Carnatic musical notes when tapped (a ticket officer will gladly demonstrate in exchange for a tip).

All around the complex of shrines and effigies, various *pujas* (prayers) and rituals are conducted as spontaneous expressions of personal, elated devotion, or under the guiding hand of the bare-chested Brahmin priest (also identified by their shaved foreheads, long hair tied in a knot, three horizontal stripes of ash on their forehead, signifying that they are Shaivite and brass trays with camphor and ash offerings). Layer upon layer of ghee and oil have turned surfaces of many of the statues smooth and black, with daubs of turmeric and vermilion powder sprinkled on by believers seeking blessings and hope.

At the heart of the complex are the **sanctums** of the goddess Meenakshi (Parvati) and of Sundareshvara (Shiva). What often eludes visitors to the heaving temple at Madurai is the city's deeply imbedded cult of fertility; behind the reverence and severity of worship, the Meenakshi Temple is a celebration of the divine union of the eternal lovers, represented symbolically at around 8:30pm (could be earlier or later; ask on the day) when they are ceremoniously carried (a ritual you can observe until they enter the inner sanctum, which is off-limits to non-Hindus) before Shiva is deposited in the Meenakshi's chamber (whose nose ring is even removed so as not to get in the way), retired for an evening of celestial fornication. This is the time to head

for the stairs around the great tank, where devotees gather to chat and relax at the end of the day. Many of the groups of people you see sitting around are in fact arranging their own unions; the temple is a place where men and women of marriageable age are presented to families.

Temple Tips:

- Dress sensibly: Visitors, both male and female, must be discreetly dressed to gain access—no exposed shoulders or bare midriffs or legs.
- Get a guide: For your first visit it is highly recommended that you do so accompanied by a good guide. We recommend you contact and book a visit with the knowledgeable, eloquent **Rishi** ★ before even leaving (mobile © **9843065687** or rishiguide@ yahoo.co.in).

- Temple times: After visiting with a guide, go back just to wander around and enjoy the atmospheric scenes; serious photographers will also get very different photographs at various times of the day. A visit at the end of the day (around 8:30 or 9pm) when the divine couple is put to bed is recommended.
- Photographers take note: The taking of photographs must be discreet. People are here to worship and any form of intrusion by Westerners taking photographs is rude.
- Seeing it from above: Most of the souvenir shops in the vicinity of the temple will invite you to "come see temple view free only looking," and once inside it's quite hard to extricate yourself without purchasing something. The exception to this is **Meenakshi Treasures,** a government-recognized export house, on 30 North Chitrai St. (($\mathcal{C}$ **0452-263-0986**). They also have lovely goods if you wish to browse.

Bounded by N., E., S., and W. Chitrai sts. ($\mathcal{C}$ **0452/234-4360.** www.maduraimeenakshi.org. Admission Rs 50. Daily 5am–1pm and 4–10:30pm. Evening *aarti* 8:30pm. Thousand Pillar Museum: Rs 5. Daily 7am–8pm. No entrance to main sanctum for non-Hindus. Deposit shoes outside entrance.

WHERE TO STAY & DINE

There are plenty of places to stay in Madurai, and the best are reviewed below. Two others you may want to consider, both located north of the river, around 10 minutes' drive from the temple, is the **Fortune Pandiyan Hotel** (www.fortunehotels.in) and **Sangam** (www.hotelsangam.com). Both are large and utterly characterless, and charge similar rates (around Rs 4,000–Rs 4,750 for a room; Rs 500 for an airport transfer); of the two, Sangam is currently preferable thanks to the more recent renovation efforts (2007). But given that you can bag a Club Room at Heritance for Rs 3,500 (see below), I wouldn't think twice before booking one of these, the best-value rooms in town—move fast though, as there are only seven!

If you want to be walking distance to the temple and immersed in the fabulous (albeit noisy) atmosphere of the lanes that radiate from it, Royal Court (reviewed below) has the edge in terms fittings and amenities, but a very good alternative, particularly if you're watching your rupees, is a standard room at **Hotel Park Plaza:** a steal at Rs 2,100 double, including breakfast (avoid suites). The receptionist's shirt may be grubby but the rooms are not—fittings are looking a little worn but are sparkling clean, as are the marble floors and linens.

The most atmospheric place to dine in the city at night (weather permitting) is on a rooftop with a view of the temple goparums. In the city center your two best options are the pleasant **Mogul Rooftop Barbeque Grill House** ★ at Royal Court (see below), where a good meal will never break the bank (note however that no alcohol is served), or the equally good-value vegetarian restaurant **Surya** ★ (where alcohol is served but no meat). Surya, within sight of Mogul, is located on the rooftop of the Hotel Supreme (entrance from West Perumal Masonry St.; exit the temple's West Gate and walk down Town Hall road, then turn right into West Perumal).

For a more fine-dining occasion, look no further than **On Board,** the elevated al fresco terrace at the Taj (not to be confused with The View, where cuisine standards are patchy). There is a very good set menu (predominantly tandoor-style kebabs), and it is only open at night, when the city sparkles at your feet. The menu is priced at Rs 1,500 (plus taxes) but is well worth the splurge for the atmosphere alone.

GRT Regency ★ (**Value**) It's big and it's bland, but this professionally run hotel—part of the small but growing South Indian GRT chain—is the best-value option in its price category. The deluxe rooms, renovated in 2009, are definitely worth the extra Rs 1,000 per room, featuring all the modern touches you'd expect from an upmarket corporate hotel (standard rooms are same size and comfortable, but decor is very dated). It's a slickly managed outfit, with generous touches (free Wi-Fi and daily newspapers) designed to make guests feel at home (the exception being the pool area, which could do with a bit of screening and greening). It's not walking distance to anything, so you have to catch a taxi to get to Madurai's atmospheric streets; if this is important, book Royal Court. Alternatively, if you like your hotels to have character and atmosphere, you'd be better off at the Gateway (assuming you're happy to pay for the privilege).

38 Madakulam Rd., TPK Rd., NH7, Palanganatham Signal Junction, Madurai 625003. ℭ **0452/237-1155.** www.grthotels.com. mail@grtregency.com. Rs 3,750 standard double; Rs 4,750 deluxe double. Rates include breakfast; exclude taxes. AE, DC, MC, V. **Amenities:** Restaurant; bar; airport transfer (Rs 500); Ayurvedic massages; babysitting; gym; pool; room service. *In room:* A/C, TV, hair dryer, minibar, Wi-Fi (free).

Heritance Madurai ★★★ At last, Madurai has a stylish, luxurious boutique hotel to cater for the well heeled; a lush, peaceful oasis (like The Gateway, though with none of The Gateway's glorious views) located around 15 minutes' drive from the Meenakshi Temple. Opened in late 2008 on the sprawling grounds of what used to be the Old Madurai Club, the Heritance is still a work in progress (Wi-Fi is planned but not yet available). But it is clear just how classy the final outcome will be, with the club buildings, once private gathering place for the wealthy textile mill owners, artfully renovated, and new villas built in similar style using local and recycled materials, including honey-colored Nagamali Hills granite, stone slabs from abandoned textile mills, and Chettinad doors and pillars taken from derelict homes. The Luxury Villas are huge, each with separate private plunge pool and gorgeous drench shower rooms; the seven Club Rooms, all opening onto a deep shared stoep (veranda), offer exceptional value, given that they enjoy access to all the same facilities, including the magnificent swimming pool, prettiest in Tamil Nadu.

11, Melakkal Main Rd., Kochada, Madurai 625 004. ℭ **0452/2385455.** Fax 0452/2383001. www. heritancemadurai.com. 35 units. Rs 8,200 double Luxury Villa; Rs 3,500 Club room. Extra person Rs 1,500; child Rs 1,000. Taxes and breakfast extra. AE, DC, MC, V. **Amenities:** Restaurant; bar; airport transfer (Rs 600); babysitting; pool; room service. *In room:* A/C, TV, hair dryer, minibar.

Royal Court ⟨**Value**⟩ This unpretentious, professionally run hotel offers very good value—certainly the standard rooms are the best in this price category—and is certainly the best option if you want to be right in the heart of this bustling temple town (though, if you're on an even tighter budget, the nearby Hotel Park Plaza as mentioned above will do very well). It's literally a stone's throw from (virtually opposite) the station and a 10-minute walk from the Meenakshi Temple (20 min. from the airport). It's not luxurious but very comfortable, with basic hotel rooms aimed at business travelers who require certain standards, including double-glazed windows to ensure that you're cocooned from the chaos below. Another good reason to stay here is the food; the rooftop terrace, **Mogul,** serves great meals and enjoys the same views as the more famous Supreme (you can wave to the Supreme guests across the rooftops), but the surroundings, with plenty of lush plants to soften the edges, are more salubrious. Note that in strict accordance to the beliefs of the owners, no alcohol is served in the hotel. There's also no pool to cool off in.

4 West Veli St., Madurai 625 004. ℭ **0452/435-6666.** Fax 0452/437-3333. www.royalcourtindia.com. 69 units. Rs 3,100 standard double, Rs 4,000 executive double; Rs 6,000 suite. Rs 600 extra bed. Taxes extra. AE, DC, MC, V. **Amenities:** 2 restaurants; airport transfer (free); gym; Internet; room service. *In room:* A/C, TV, Wi-Fi (Rs 100/hr.).

The (Taj) Gateway Hotel, Pasumalai Madurai ★★ Situated on a hillock known as Pasumalai, and blessed with 25 hectares (62 acres) of tree-filled grounds, this colonial-style hotel—offers panoramic views of the sprawling town, including the tall *goparums* of its

(Moments) Tracking Elephants in the Forested Ghats of Tamil Nadu

The Eastern and Western Ghats (mountain ranges) of South India meet in Tamil Nadu and it is here, deep in the cool highlands, that some of India's most popular hill stations are located. As elsewhere, these "stations" were traditionally where the British retreated to during the hottest months, and they are still immensely popular summer destinations, though now predominantly with domestic visitors, who fill the streets of Ooty and Coonor (located in the Nilgiri Hills) and Kodaikanal (in the Palani Hills) to capacity. For the most part these hill stations are truly not worth the time and effort it takes to get to them, with plenty of unchecked development stripping them of their original charm, and huge visitor numbers (500,000 descended on Ooty in Apr 2009 alone). The real gems of the Ghats lie off the beaten path, surrounded by indigenous forests that hide its rich and varied wildlife, including some of India's rarest birds. One such gem is the charmingly rustic **Elephant Valley Farm Hotel,** located some 25km (16 miles) from Kodaikanal (℘ **0454/2230399;** www.elephantvalleyhotel.com; Rs 3,300– Rs 4,700 double including breakfast, additional meals Rs 500 per person) Part of a working organic farm and coffee estate, and seamlessly adjoining a nature reserve, it's a wonderful laid-back nonhotel, with just 12 rustic bungalows— some of them totally secluded and set deep in the forest; warm attentive staff, and the most delicious, nutritious food: just the place to catch your breath before descending into the heat and chaos of Madurai. It is possible to drive to Elephant Valley from Munnar, in Kerala, overnighting for 2 nights (management will e-mail you a driving tour); 2 nights may seem like a long time but you will need at least this to enjoy the pace and peace of life here. It's by no means luxurious accommodations, but then again, luxury is a relative concept. Here a huge bonfire every night takes the place of TV and one of the most memorable moments in India may await: As your steed picks its way through the forest at dawn (the stable has fabulous horses) you hear a loud crack; silhouetted just below the canopy is your first glimpse of that rarest of sights: an Indian elephant in the wilds.

most famous temple. The main building, built in 1891, is decorated with hunting trophies and includes a well-stocked colonial-style bar with deep verandas, wicker chairs, and whirring overhead fans. Accommodations are spread over 5 different blocks (let them know if you're not mobile); the best are the very spacious executive rooms, offering fantastic views of the city and temple from wide bay windows (book room no. 21 or 22) and balconies. Superior rooms are also very comfortable, offering either pool or garden views. It's not nearly as glamorous as Heritance, but the old-style accommodations and warm, attentive service (though it can be slow!) make this still our favorite pick.

40 T.P.K. Rd., Pasumalai, Madurai 625 004. ℘ **0452/237-1601.** Fax 0452/237-1636. www.tajhotels.com. 63 units. Rs 6,500 standard double; Rs 7,600 superior double; Rs 8,200 executive double. Extra bed Rs 1,000. Rates include breakfast. Taxes extra. AE, DC, MC, V. **Amenities:** 2 restaurants; bar; airport transfers (Rs 529); Ayurvedic center; babysitting; badminton court; Internet access; pool; room service; tennis court. In room: A/C, TV, hair dryer, minibar.

9

Karnataka & Hyderabad: Kingdoms of the South

Sixteenth-century visitors to the royal courts of present-day Karnataka returned to Europe with stupendous tales of wealth—cities overflowing with jewels, and streets littered with diamonds. Over the centuries, the lush green state that occupies a vast chunk of India's southwestern seaboard and much of the Deccan plateau saw numerous kingdoms rise and fall, powerful dynasties that left legacies of impressive palaces and monumental cities scattered throughout the interior, some of them well off the beaten track, but worth the effort and time it takes to seek them out.

The postindependence state of Karnataka, unified in 1950 on the basis of common language, is predominantly made up of the once-princely state of Mysore and the Berar territories, which used to be part of the Nizam of Hyderabad's kingdom. Once one of the richest cities in India, Hyderabad is now the vibrant capital of neighboring Andhra Pradesh, and a possible excursion from Bangalore, state capital of Karnataka. **Bangalore** may have been renamed **Bengaluru** in yet another attempt to strip away the legacy of the Raj and assert its Indian identity, but it remains in many ways the country's most "Western" city, famous for its energetic nightlife, sophisticated design sense, and highly evolved computer and technology industries. Although it offers little by way of sightseeing attractions, it's a great place to relax; you can shop by day and explore the bars and clubs at night before taking an overnight train to explore the ancient city of **Hampi.** The great medieval Hindu capital of the south is said to have once rivaled Rome in wealth and, with the ruins of the 14th-century Vijayanagar kingdom set in a boulder-strewn landscape that proves fascinating in its own right, this is deservedly Karnataka's most famous attraction.

Karnataka's other primary destination is **Mysore,** the famous "City of Incense," where vibrant markets are perfumed with the scents of jasmine, musk, sandalwood, and frangipani. Ruled by India's most enlightened maharajas, Mysore is home to some 17 palaces, of which **Amba Vilas** is arguably India's most opulent. Just a few hours south of Mysore is **Rajiv Gandhi National Park,** home to herds of wild elephant and the elusive Bengal tiger. Northward lie the **"Jewel Box" temples** built by the mighty Hoysala warriors in the cities of Belur and Halebid, best reached via Sravanabelgola, home to one of the oldest and most important Jain pilgrimage sites in India: an 18m (60-ft.) statue of the naked **Lord Gomateswara,** said to be the tallest monolithic statue on earth and one of the most spiritually satisfying destinations in India.

1 BENGALURU (BANGALORE)

If you've been in India awhile, the capital of Karnataka will probably feel like a long, soothing break from endless commotion. The first city in India to get electricity, Bengaluru continues to blaze the trail in terms of the country's quest for a modern identity. Once

(Tips) Planning Your Tour

Most travelers head directly for **Bengaluru,** Karnataka's capital, using it as a springboard to fly to **Hyderabad,** capital of Andhra Pradesh (discussed at the end of the chapter), or—more usually—as a base from which to catch an overnight train to and from the "lost city" of **Hampi,** which lies 320km (198 miles) north. (Note that more adventurous travelers, usually backpackers, can also catch a bus from Goa and head straight to Hampi.) Remote and serene, Hampi is good for a few relaxing days—at least 3 days if you intend to explore the undervisited **temples of the Chalukyas,** which lie north of Hampi. The second principal destination in Karnataka is **Mysore,** again usually reached from Bengaluru. If you're traveling to or from Tamil Nadu or Kerala, it's also possible to drive directly to Mysore, passing **Rajiv Gandhi National Park,** or to approach it from the coastal city of **Mangalore,** which is in turn connected to Goa and Kerala via the Konkan railway. Spend at least a day in Mysore before spending the next day or two visiting the beautifully decorated **11th-century temples** at Belur and Halebid, and the nearby **Jain monolithic statue** at Sravanabelgola. Karnataka also has a few stunning **beaches,** just south of the Goan border, but unless you can make do with limited facilities, save your sunbathing for Goa and Kerala. Finally, if the heat and dust of the plains is exhausting, then a quick escape lies just 3 hours from Mysore, in the cool coffee plantations of **Coorg.** And if all this sounds like a mission to plan, simply hop on to the super-luxurious **Golden Chariot** (www.thegoldenchariot.co.in) and chug your way across the state, taking in all the major sights (with Goa thrown in as a bonus) over just 7 days (see "Getting There," below).

known as the Garden City, the country's most pristine city evolved significantly when the high tech revolution arrived and Bengaluru suddenly found itself at the center of the nation's massive computer hardware and software industries, earning it new sobriquets such as Pensioner's Paradise, and Silicon City. Its cosmopolitan spirit, fueled as much by its lively bar and cafe culture as by the influx of international businesspeople, gives India's high-tech hub a high-energy buzz, yet it's tangibly calmer and cleaner than most other places in the country, with far and away the best climate of any Indian city—no doubt one of the reasons the majority of upwardly mobile Indians rank it the number-one city in which to live.

Unless you go in for cafe society or are keen to see India's new moneyed elite flash their bling and wads of cash, you won't find very many attractions in Bengaluru—perhaps a relief in a country that is so saturated with historic must-sees. An excellent option to the standard sightseeing would be to opt for a walking tour (see "Walk the Talk," below). The city's real appeal is its zesty contemporary Indian lifestyle and its usefulness as a base getting to the extraordinary temples and ruins of the Deccan interior and the cities of Hyderabad and Mysore.

ESSENTIALS
GETTING THERE & AWAY   By Air   Bengaluru's airport (35km/22 miles from M.G. Rd.) is the busiest in South India, connected to most of the major cities in India (including,

Fun Facts   Getting "Bangalored"

Thanks to flexible labor laws, cheaper operational costs, excellent linguistic abilities and reliable, sophisticated IT infrastructure, major U.S. companies such as General Electric and American Express shifted their back-office processing operations to Bangalore in the mid-1990s, and many of the world's major corporations followed suit, bringing with them millions of new jobs. In fact, with so many business processing jobs outsourced from the West to Bangalore, the term "getting Bangalored" meant losing your job to someone in Bangalore!

of course, Hyderabad). British Airways and the excellent Kingfisher, India's top private carrier, fly direct to Bengaluru from London daily. Kingfisher Airlines also fly direct from San Francisco, while Jet Air fly via Brussels from New York, London and Toronto. Alternatively there are several international carriers that fly to Bengaluru via Mumbai, Delhi and Chennai. For domestic and international flight availability and reservations try www.yatra.com or www.makemytrip.com. To get to your hotel from the airport, it's best to use a taxi; expect to pay about Rs 600 to Rs 800 from the prepaid counter. (*Note:* City traffic is a nightmare in this city, so consult your hotel for a realistic time frame in trying to reach the airport, depending on where you are and what time of day it is.)

By Train   As a major transport hub, Bengaluru is reached by a significant number of rail connections. Journeys from North Indian cities, however, are extremely time-consuming; the fastest connection with Delhi takes 35 hours, while Mumbai is 24 hours away. From Chennai (capital of Tamil Nadu), take either the evening or the morning 5-hour Shatabdi Express or the overnight Bangalore Mail, which leaves late and gets in early. To get to Mysore from Bengaluru, catch the 2-hour Shatabdi Express (departs Wed–Mon at 11am) or else take an ordinary passenger train (which departs several times a day and takes only 1 hr. more than the Shatabdi) and enjoy the sights and sounds of local commuters, many of whom begin impromptu song competitions in order to pass time. For Hyderabad, catch the comfortable overnight Rajdhani Express (departs four times a week at 8:20pm). Since 2009, Mangalore has been connected by rail to Bengaluru (Mangalore Express), although so far, there is only an overnight option available. Bengaluru City and Bengaluru Cantonment are the two railway stations; the latter is a bit closer to the main downtown area.

By Road   For the greatest amount of freedom, you should hire a car and driver, particularly if you plan to get off the beaten track. To get to Mysore there is a very comfortable and convenient option of air-conditioned KSRTC Volvo buses that run at hourly intervals from the Kempegowda Bus Stand (✆ **080/2287-3377**).

VISITOR INFORMATION   Karnataka State Tourism Development Corporation (KSTDC) information counter is at St. Mark's Rd. (✆ **080/4132-9211;** daily 9:30am–7:30pm). **Karnataka Tourism** (Khanija Bhavan, Race Course Rd.; ✆ **080/2235-2901** through -2903 or 080/2227-5869 or -5883; http://kstdc.net; Mon–Sat 10:30am–5:30pm, closed Sun and second Sat of the month) is reliable for sightseeing information rather than info on accommodations and dining; ask for a copy of *Bangalore This Fortnight* or visit it online at **www.explocity.com**. The **Government of India Tourist Office** is at the KSFC Building, 48 Church St. (✆ **080/2558-5417;** Mon–Fri 9:30am–6:15pm,

Tips **Under the Skin: Must-Reads**

Often a guidebook will provide a great deal more insight into a city than a visit to its tourism bureau. **Ticket Bengaluru** by Roopa Pai (Stark World) and **Love Bengaluru** by Fiona Caulfield (Hardys Bay Publishing) are two such books, dealing respectively with everything that this city offers, from the best *dosa* joints to the ideal pub hop, coolest buys to trendiest hot spots. While Roopa offers something for everyone across the spectrum, Fiona is clearly speaking to big spenders.

Sat 9am–1:30pm), where you can pick up a copy of the free quarterly guide *City Info* (also supplied in most hotels).

GETTING AROUND **By Auto-Rickshaw & Taxi** Insist that auto-rickshaw drivers use their meters. Generally, the first kilometer will cost Rs 14; each kilometer after that costs Rs 7. After 9pm, drivers will make you pay "one and a half," or 50% above the recorded fare. You won't find taxis that you can just hail off the street, but metered **"call taxis"** are available almost all over the city; see our recommendation in "Fast Facts: Bangalore," below, or ask your hotel for a reputable number. Expect to pay minimum fare of Rs 75 for 3km (2½ miles), Rs 12 each additional kilometer, plus extra for waiting and luggage.

With Car & Driver Less than 4 hours will be charged as per the meter rules mentioned above; Rs 650 is the going rate (at press time) for a 4-hour tour, which will include 40km (25 miles) of free mileage (Rs 14 for every extra kilometer). To hire a car and driver, try **Hertz** (© **1800-22-6000** or 099725-02292), which operates around-the-clock, as does **Cel Cabs** (© **080/6060-9090**).

GUIDED TOURS & TRAVEL AGENTS KSTDC (address above; © **080/2235-2901**) conducts sightseeing tours in the city as well as around the state. **Skyway International Travels** (St. Mark's Rd.; © **080/2211-1401**) and **Marco Polo Tours** (2 Janardhan Towers, Residency Rd.; © **080/2221-4438**) are reliable all-arounders. For trekking, get in touch with www.junglelodges.com, Karnataka Mountaineering Association (© **080/2226-9053**) and **Get Off Ur Ass** (© **080/2672-2750;** www.getoffurass.com) for some unusual trips. **Mystery Trails** (www.mysterytrails.com) is a Forest Department initiative specializing in treks within wildlife zones, including Chamarjanagar where the notorious bandit/poacher Veerappan hid for 2 decades. Today it enables local tribal communities to learn and earn at the same time.

Fast Facts **Bengaluru**

Airlines The airport number is © **080/4058-1111.** See chapter 3 for details on more airlines, almost all of which service this busy hub.

Area Code The area code for **Bangalore** is **080.**

ATMs Visit the shop-intensive vicinity of M.G. Road.

Bookstores **Strand Book Stall** is at S113-114 Manipal Centre, Dickenson Road (© **080/2558-0000;** www.strandbookstall.com). **Higginbothams** is at 68 M.G. Rd. (© **080/2558-6574;** www.higginbothams.com). **Sankar's Book Stall** is at 15/2

Museum Rd. (© **080/2558-6867**). The huge **Landmark** bookstore can be found at Forum Mall in Koramangala (© **080/2206-7640;** www.landmarkonthenet.com), far from downtown Bengaluru. **Select Bookshop** (off Brigade Rd. © **080/2558-0770;** www.selectbookshop.net) and **Blossom Bookstore** (Church St. © **080/2532-0400;** www.blossombookhouse.com) are excellent secondhand shops with extensive collections to browse through.

Car Rentals **Gullivers Tours & Travels** is at B2-SPL Habitat, no. 138, Gangadhara Chetty Rd. (© **080/2558-0108** or -3213). Another reliable name is **Srushti Travels** (© **98-4503-2213**).

Currency Exchange Exchange cash or get credit card advances from **Wall Street Finances** (3 House of Lords, St. Mark's Rd.; © **080/2227-8052;** Mon–Sat 9:30am–5.30pm) or from **Standard Chartered** (Raheja Towers, 26 M.G. Rd.; © **080/2559-4043;** Mon–Fri 10.30am–5pm, Sat 10:30am–1:30pm). Alternatively, you can go to **Thomas Cook** (55 M.G. Rd.; © **080/2558-1337** or 080/2559 4168; Mon–Sat 9;30am–6pm).

Directory Assistance The number © **080/2222-2222** operates much like a talking Yellow Pages service, where you get free updated telephone numbers and addresses for various city establishments. Other options are **Just Dial** © **080/2333-3333,** or **Get It** © **080/2235-5555.**

Drugstores Twenty-four-hour pharmacists include **Cash Pharmacy** (© **080/2212-6033**), **Manipal Hospital** (© **080/2526-8901**), and **Mallya Hospital** (Vittal Mallya Rd., south of Cubbon Park; © **080/2227-7979**).

Emergencies Dial © **100** for police emergencies.

Hospital Both **Manipal Hospital** (98 Rustum Bagh, Airport Rd.; © **080/2526-8901** or -6447) and **St. John's Medical College and Hospital** (Sarjapur Rd.; © **080/2553 0724** or -2411) are decent options. For quick **ambulance** services call © **102.**

Internet Access Cybercafes abound in this IT-savvy city. The reliable **Sify i way** is at various locations; call (© **080/2654-6113**) to find out the nearest to where you are; www.iway.com). **Reliance Webworld** on M.G. Road (© **080/3033-6666;** www.relianceinfo.com) is another good option with outlets all over the city.

Police Dial 100 for the Emergency Helpline; to register a complaint dial © **080/2294-3400,** -3399; there is an All Women's Police Station at Ulsoor © **080/2294-2585.**

Post Office As always, your best bet for sending mail is through your hotel. The **GPO** (© **080/2286-6772** or 080/2289-2038; Mon–Sat 10am–6pm, Sun 10:30am–1pm) is, however, architecturally interesting. It's located at the intersection of Raj Bhavan and Ambedkar Road. Dozens of courier options are available—try **FedEx** © **080/2529-3210.** Other reliable and less expensive options are Professional Couriers or Blue Dart; you will find their outlets all across the city and in practically every market.

Railway For inquiries, dial © **139** or 2220-0971.

Taxis Call **Gopinath Radio Call Taxi** (© **080/2360-5555** or 080/2332-0152; 24 hr.); alternatively **Spot City Taxi** (© **080/4110-0000**).

(Moments) **Side Trip to Gokarna: Discovering the Universe within at Om Beach**

Often cited as the top beach in India, **Om Beach** ★★★ lies near Karnataka's important pilgrimage town of Gokarna—about 3 hours south of Goa's Dabolim Airport. Black rocks divide the superb white sand into three interconnected bays that more or less resemble the Sanskrit "om" symbol, the Sanskrit invocation that Hindus believe created the universe. Om is but one of five lovely beaches at Gokarna—other tempting, appropriately named stretches include Half-moon Beach and Paradise Beach. Infrastructure here was practically nonexistent a few years back, but new shacks and small "guesthouses" have been emerging every season. The good news is that this is also the setting for **Swa-Swara** ★★★ (✆ **0838/625-7131** through -7133; www.swaswara.com), one of the loveliest Ayurvedic, yoga and meditation retreats in the country, a slick, luxurious operation by Kerala-based group, CGH Earth. Set atop a cliff above the beach and sea (access to which is a pleasant stroll through lush vegetation), this yoga retreat comprises 24 Konkan-styled indoor-outdoor villas set amid 12 hectares (30 acres) of palm trees and paddy fields. Each cottage has an air-conditioned bedroom, but the open-plan living area, bathroom, and covered upstairs terrace, are open to the elements and even incorporate a small garden. There's a good pool, art studio (where you can take classes), a quiet yoga *shala*, and a spectacular blue-domed hall for meditation sessions (the yoga master is excellent—see if you can stay awake through his ultra-relaxing yoga *nidra* sessions). There are no restrictions or routines to follow, although you can opt for a healing or rejuvenation program that involves a stricter diet and regular consultations or treatments; but that depends on you. It's a special place, where the tranquillity of the setting, the magic of the ocean, and the hands-on support from a dedicated, well-trained staff allows you to reconnect with yourself, ideally resetting your clock to the rhythm of your soul (which is what the Kannada term SwaSwara implies). You're encouraged to stay at least 7 nights; the cost is 900€ per person sharing, with all meals (the food is extraordinary) and certain activities included, and Ayurvedic packages are also available.

If, however, you're not looking to cleanse your body and mind, but simply want to be near the gorgeous beach, take a look at **Om Beach Resort** (Jungle Lodges: ✆ **0802/559-7021** or -7024; www.junglelodges.com), which offers large, comfortable accommodations with all-modern amenities but tasteless finishes. Without the lavishness of SwaSwara or its body-tingling massage regimens, you'll have no excuse not to spend all day on the beach, where, incidentally, you can probably shack up in a simple place for even fewer rupees. Operating under the same banner is the laid-back and rustic **Devbagh Beach Resort** (✆ **0838/222-1603;** www.junglelodges.com) in Karwar, an hour or two (depending on road conditions) north of Gokarna, where guests stay in log cabins on stilts among groves of casuarina trees. Spend your days snorkeling, visiting outlying islands, beachcombing, or lazing in your hammock.

WHAT TO SEE & DO

Although it was ruled by various dynasties, Bengaluru's chief historical sights date back to the 18th-century reign of Hyder Ali and his son Tipu Sultan, "the Lion of Mysore," who put up the most spirited resistance to British imperialism. But more than anything, the temperate climate of Bengaluru is about experiencing an Indian city that brims with bars, restaurants, clubs, and positive energy—a great place for walking, window-shopping (many of the most design-savvy items found in Mumbai and Delhi originate in this city), lounging in al-fresco coffee shops, and letting your hair down—at least till 11:30pm, after which the city more or less shuts down.

If you're an early riser, the one sight that is an absolute must, is a visit to the bustling **City Market ★★**—an absolute riot of colors, sights, smells, and sounds, with mounds of flowers (Bengaluru contributes to 70% of India's floral export) and fresh vegetables. The best time to visit is between 6 and 8am. Next off, set off for Bugle Hill, site of the **Bull Temple** (sanctum timings daily 7:30–11:30am and 4:30–8:30pm). Built by the city's original architect, Kempe Gowda, this 16th century black-granite statue of Nandi (Shiva's sacred bull) literally dwarfs his "master," and is kept glistening by regular application of coconut oil. Nearby is a Ganesha temple (Sri Dodda Ganapathi), which houses an enormous statue of the elephant-headed deity made of 100 kilos (220 lbs.) of rank-smelling butter. Apparently this idol is remade every 4 years, and the butter distributed to devotees as *prasad* (blessed food).

WHERE TO STAY

Bengaluru's popularity as a venue for international and national conferences has made it achieve the highest average room rates and occupancy in India, especially during the week. On the positive side, there are a huge range of excellent top-quality hotels, of which our favorites (all reviewed below) each have a unique personality—we like **The Park.hotel** for its contemporary überslick styling and in-house nightlife, **Taj West End**

Walk the Talk ★★★

When Arun Pai, an IIM/IIT graduate decided to drop out and take to the streets, he breathed new life into a city. Hundreds of years of history, several cultures, astounding foresight—Arun saw that Bengaluru has so much more to offer than just shopping and IT driven agendas. And so the team was born and the stage set: Be it software engineer Savita, who takes you to a cluster of unassuming rocks in the midst of a modern neighborhood from where a young man looked beyond and was inspired to make a city, or engineer-turned journalist Roopa as she takes you down the lifeline of Bengaluru, pointing in all directions to the handprints left by the British, or finally, environmentalist Vijay, a walking, talking encyclopedia, who will surely make you revere trees by the time you emerge from the 250-year-old Lalbagh gardens—the **Bangalore WALKS** are a must! Conducted over the weekend, each of the 3-hour-long walks includes breakfast in places that are themselves institutions. The walks are well designed, articulate, interesting, amusing, and intriguing; from Bengaluru to Bangalore- -walk on (© **098806-71192; www.bangalorewalks.com**).

Learn the "Art of Living" with India's Hot New Age Guru

Sri Sri Ravi Shankar, once a disciple of Maharishi Mahesh Yogi (renowned spiritual guide of the Beatles), is the subcontinent's hottest New Age guru—many consider "The Art of Living," his nonsectarian philosophy of enjoying life for the moment, the perfect spiritual currency for our material times. His main ashram lies on 24 hectares (60 acres) of lush green hillside in south Bengaluru, where every evening thousands of the city's well heeled gather for the evening lecture and *satsang* (devotional singing). The articulate Sri Sri's appeal lies in the fact that he does not emphasize incarnation or abstinence, but encourages his disciples to enjoy the present without guilt while also encouraging them to contribute towards humanitarian and environmental concerns. His adherents—predominantly from India's growing urban elite (including Kingfisher's Vijay Mallya, the "Branson of Bangalore"), but also hugely popular on foreign shores (apparently San Franciscans have a real penchant for his teachings)—can go about their hectic lives and remain relatively apolitical yet feel good about not discarding all sense of religion and tradition.

A philosophy of convenience, some say, but even his fiercest detractors admit the value of *sudarshan kriya*, an ancient breathing technique taught when you attend the "Art of Living" course. The 30-minute-a-day practice is said to encourage the flow of oxygen to the whole body, ostensibly discouraging the storage of toxins and thus helping release anxiety, frustration, depression, and anger, leaving you with a genuine sense of calm and well-being.

To attend an evening session (at times with the guru himself) or an Art of Living course spread over several days, call ahead (21st Km, Kanakapura Main Rd., Udayapura, Bengaluru 560 082; ⓒ 080/2843-2273 or -2274; www.artof living.org).

Hotel for its gorgeous greens and heritage atmosphere, and charming **Villa Pottipati,** as the best-value deal in the city. We also recommend two great out-of-city options—**Our Native Village** and **Shreyas.** However, you may want to compare online rates with the following roundup of the city's best hotels, which offer the same or similar top-end luxury and amenities.

No too far from the where all the action is, **ITC Hotel Windsor Sheraton & Towers** (25 Windsor Sq., Golf Course Rd.; ⓒ **080/2226-9898;** fax 080/2226-4941; www. welcomgroup.com; doubles from Rs 20,000) retains the look and character of a neoclassical English country house. With its old-world charm and obvious Raj hangover, it's popular with Bollywood's elite and high-profile businesspeople and politicians; ask for a room in the Manor Block, which overlooks the deliciously cool garden. Another good reason to stay here would be the top-notch award-winning dining options, each of which are worth at least one visit. The **Oberoi** ★★ (37/39 M.G. Rd.; ⓒ **080/2558-5858;** www.oberoihotels.com; doubles from Rs 21,000) is another excellent hotel, located in the heart of the shopping precinct, with the usual high service standards we have come to rely on from India's best hotel group. It's extremely picturesque, with balconies draped with blossoming creepers and set amid gardens with lovely views over the lawns and the swimming pool. Standard units are not quite as large or as elegant as those at the ITC Windsor Sheraton, but they're spacious enough and luxuriously decorated with floral fabrics and antique finishes; ask for a room on an upper floor for better views. Adjacent is the **Taj Residency** (✆ **080/6660-4250;** www.tajhotels.com; doubles from Rs 16,000), popular as a business hotel (and at press time offered better value than its sibling, Gateway Hotel on Residency Road), and abuzz after its recent makeover; it also has a fabulous new restaurant, Graze (see "Where to Eat")—ask for a lake-facing room. If you're in the mood for really over-the-top opulence, **Leela Palace Kempinski**—judged at the time of its opening in 2001 by *Forbes Magazine* as one of the world's best business hotels and, in more recent times, as the Best Eco Friendly Five Star in India by the Government of India—is the hands-down winner, though it's not as central as Oberoi or Taj. A baroque rendition of contemporary Indo-Saracenic architecture, looming large in pale pink, it offers enormous "conservatory" rooms with private balconies and, along with all the modern conveniences, elegant four-poster beds, rococo gold-gilt lamps, and silk duvet covers. Deluxe rooms are also very spacious and styled in the same manner (23 Airport Rd.; ✆ **080/2521-1234;** www.theleela.com; doubles from Rs 20,000; suites range from Rs 30,000 to a whopping Rs 1,500,000 for the Maharaja suite).

A good 20 minutes away from the city centre but offering good value given the size of your lodgings (one and two-bedroom apartments), the **Royal Orchid** (47/1 Dickenson Rd., ✆ **080/2558-4242;** one-bedroom from Rs 10,000), adjoins the Karnataka Golf Club, which means the views are lovely and green (a claim only the Taj West End and ITC can make). The temperature-controlled rooftop pool is a nice surprise, and free Wi-Fi a boon for those addicted to their laptops. Service is not as slick as you'd expect in a five-star hotel but genuine and well meaning nevertheless. Other than one- and two-bed apartments, they have very affordable suites and executive doubles—be sure to ask for a room with a view. Following international trends, all-suite hotels are in fact becoming increasingly popular: **The Paul** ★★ (✆ **080/4047-7777;** www.thepaul.in; doubles from Rs 9,000), a recent entrant, is the most exclusive option in this category, with 54 luxurious suites measuring between 120 sq m and 375 sq m (400 sq ft. and 1,250 sq ft). If you've visited their sister property, Kumarakom Lake Resort in Kerala, you'll expect the attention to detail and great taste lavished on the otherwise unimaginative hotel architecture so prevalent in the city. Warm teak wood floors and traditional sit-outs, plush rooms done in silks and tweeds, with massive televisions and efficient kitchenettes, fountains in the atrium with live piano in the evenings (except Tues)—the only missing ingredient are good views; the quietest suites are on the eastern side.

Much cheaper and less luxe but perfectly serviceable, **St. Mark's** is a small, neat business hotel (✆ **080/2227-9090;** www.stmarkshotel.com) with doubles from Rs 6,500; at this price it is extremely popular, so book ahead. Alternatively, if you would rather skimp on accommodation and splurge on other things, then **Ramanashree Brunton** (2/1, Brunton Rd.; ✆ **080/3051-9000;** www.ramanashree.com; Rs 4,000–Rs 5,000 double) is another budget option that offers simple but functionally adequate rooms, ideal if all you're looking for is a clean and efficient place to rest your head after shopping at MG Road. Or try Casa Piccola, a pleasant homestay in a quiet neighborhood close to shopping destinations—it caters to all basic needs, even throwing in free Internet and offers an air of relaxed informality which you may even prefer to the anonymity of hotel atmosphere (2, Clapham Rd., Richmond Town, near M.G. Road; ✆ **080/2299-0337;** www. casapiccola.com; doubles from Rs 3,300).

374 Our Native Village ★★★ Although the "Village" won't pamper you in the way a traditional five-star will, it may well be just the pampering your conscience needs. For most hotels, even those who push their eco-credentials, "green" initiatives start and end with a few mandatory changes like light bulbs and less laundry, but here is a place, just 40km (25 miles) from the city, that goes the whole nine yards: rain-harvested water; electricity generated from biogas plants, solar panels and windmills; every scrap of food and animal waste is converted to methane gas; manure is produced in-house for the organic vegetable garden and even the construction was done using clay from the site itself. Even the swimming pool is oxygenated with aquatic plants, so dragonflies give you company. No air-conditioning because the rooms are airy, no TV because you're expected to work hard at getting your bullock-cart driving license. A totally different experience, this is an inspiring stay that will open you to new ways of existence.

Hessarghata P.O. Box 8802, Bengaluru 560 088. ℅ **080/4114-0909.** www.ournativevillage.com. 24 units (all with showers). Rs 10,300 double. Rates include all meals. Taxes extra. Visit the website for specific packages. AE, MC, V. **Amenities:** Dining room; airport transfer (Rs 2,000); doctor-on-call; traditional village games; library; natural pool; spa; steam room.

The Park.hotel ★★ Themed around Bengaluru's reputation as India's information-technology city and its historic connection with silk production, this compact hotel features top-class interiors by Tina Ellis (of London-based Conran). In the lobby—dominated by a gigantic silk curtain—rough, smooth, and suede textures are offset with brushed metal and a row of large white orbs of light, while staff is smartly turned out in pale gray jackets over white T-shirts, an efficient look that is matched by service levels. Guest rooms are on the small side and don't have great views (ask for a pool-facing room), but they are beautifully finished—oak flooring, designer rugs, black-and-white photographs of Bengaluru, and minimalist metal-framed four-poster beds with the softest goose feather pillows and duvets—inadequate soundproofing is perhaps the only flaw. Rooms on the Residence Floor come with a host of additional services.

14/7 M.G. Rd., Bengaluru 560 001. ℅ **080/2559-4666.** Fax 080/2559-4667. www.theparkhotels.com. resv. blr@theparkhotels.com. 109 units. Rs 17,000 deluxe double; Rs 18,000 deluxe balcony double; Rs 19,000 deluxe terrace double; Rs 21,000 luxury double; Rs 22,000 residence floor; Rs 24,000 terrace suite; Rs 28,000 premiere suite; Rs 3,000 extra bed. AE, DC, MC, V. **Amenities:** 3 restaurants; lounge bar; airport transfers (Rs 2,100, free for Residence rooms); babysitting; currency exchange; doctor-on-call; health spa; library; outdoor pool; room service; theater; valet. *In room:* A/C, TV, minibar, Wi-Fi (Rs 150/half hour, Rs 750/full day).

Shreyas ★★★ One of the best Yoga retreats in India, Shreyas is simply addictive. Chanting in a machan, open platform for *yogasana,* gardens for getting your hands dirty, paths for evening walks, Balinese and Thai massage for ultimate relaxation, secreted niches for contemplation—it's all here. One can endlessly explore the spaces and be surprised every turn of the way. We recommend the tented cottages which are a delight with their large windows, bamboo screens, chunky chests and smart *daris;* spacious bathrooms open into a pebbled yard. Evenings are utterly magical with hurricane lamps and paper lanterns and impromptu dining decor. No alcohol/meat/tobacco may seem harsh but it's surprising how easily you will take to fresh pomegranate juice with barbequed tofu and embrace the overall wellness ethic. Limited to just three accommodation choices (a three-room garden cottage, three poolside cottages, and eight tented cottages) set in 10 hectares (25 acres), the atmosphere is discreet and personal, amenities are luxurious and service a living reality of what Shreyas stands for—excellence.

Santoshima Farm, near Golahalli Farm, Nelamangala, Bengaluru 562 123. ℅ **080/2773-7102.** Fax 080/2773-7016. www.shreyasretreat.com. 14 units. $340 single, $460 double; extra bed for up to 8 years

…es include all meals, daily yoga and chanting sessions,
… for specific packages. AE, MC, V. **Amenities:** Dining
…ng machine; doctor-on-call; gym; music/film/book
… *room:* A/C, hair dryer, Internet (complimentary).

… Leading Hotels of the World, West
… Victorian boardinghouse. Today the
… its old-world charm while providing guests
…ly lobby features a central atrium with skylight,
…ing on the walls, lots of plants, plush sofas, and a
… are spread over more than 9 hectares (22 acres) of
…lage—although there is a buggy to whisk you to your room
…ght to walk through the meandering paths under century-old
…e various pitched-roof-veranda blocks and more recent structures
…ar colonial architecture; each has a private balcony overlooking the
…ens. Try to book in the Heritage Wing, which has four-poster beds and
…ed Bengaluru-theme lithographs. Some of the Luxury and Grand Luxury
… are by comparison rather ordinary, but the private balcony with lovely views is a
…nsolation.

Race Course Rd., Bengaluru 560 001. © **080/6660-5660.** Fax 080/6660-5700. www.tajhotels.com. 117
units. Rs 22,500 luxury double; Rs 24,500 luxury grand; Rs 29,500 taj club; Rs 40,000–Rs 2,00,000 suites. Rs
1,500 extra bed. Taj Club rooms and suites include breakfast and airport transfers. AE, DC, MC, V. **Amenities:** 3 restaurants; bar; airport transfer (Rs 2,670); babysitting; currency exchange; doctor-on-call; fitness
center; golf and riding on request; laptop computers for hire; room service; 2 outdoor tennis courts.
In room: A/C, TV, hair dryer, minibar, Wi-Fi (Rs 240/hr, Rs 722/day). Taj Club units: butlers, DVD players, fax
machines on request.

Villa Pottipati ★★★ **Value** Surrounded by fruit and flowering trees, this stately
villa is the most authentic and reasonably priced heritage experience you can have, and
amazingly enough, right in the heart of this city of steel, glass, and concrete. Service is
personal and exceptional, with the kind of attention guests probably enjoyed a century
ago, and furnishings in keeping with the heritage character. Set meals are served indoors,
or outdoors under a canopy of mango trees; everything we tried was delicious. As at all
Neemrana properties, each guest room is different; if you're fussy, ask for a tour of unoc-
cupied others before making your mind up. The Venkatagiri Suite, with a turquoise-blue
Venkatagiri sari covering the bed, offers incredible value, with a living room, a private
dressing area, an area for kids, two large wardrobes, a bathroom with a large bathtub, and
a veranda. The Rajadurga Suite rewards early birds with spectacular sunrise views. The
fabulous Kanchipuram Suite has a private pillared balcony, an anteroom for kids, and an
old-fashioned, lime-green bathroom.

142, 8th Cross, 4th Main Rd., Malleswaram, Bengaluru 560 003. © **080/2336-0777** or 080/4128-0832
through -0834. Fax 080/5128-0835. www.neemranahotels.com. 8 units. Rs 4,000–Rs 6,000 double; Rs 800
extra bed. Rates include morning "bed tea" and evening tea. Taxes extra. AE, MC, V. **Amenities:** Dining
room; bar; airport transfer (Rs 900); concierge; currency exchange; doctor-on-call; outdoor pool. *In room:*
A/C, TV, hair dryer, Wi-Fi (Rs 200/day).

WHERE TO DINE

With Bengaluru's IT boom, the number of professionals with disposable cash keeps rising
exponentially—leading in turn to a perpetual explosion of options on the dining scene.
We've reviewed a combination of upmarket eateries with excellent and very atmospheric
budget alternatives.

As in Tamil Nadu, you can get a good, clean, wholeso[...] meal") all over Bengaluru. Most famous of all is **MTR** (revie[...] good for its Tamil Iyengar food, especially the must-have *puliyog[...]* rice), is **Kadambam** (112 C South Block, Manipal Centre, [...] branches as well). Gold-framed pictures of deities line the wall, the [...] is spotless, the food is cheap and delicious, and the filter coffee—if, th[...] oped a taste for sweetened South Indian filter coffee—extraordinary. V[...] (32, Gandhi Bazaar; ℂ **080/2667-7588**) is where you head for the best [...] town, while for authentic Karnataka cuisine, **Halli Mane** (no. 14, 3rd C[...] Sampige Rd., Malleswaram; ℂ **080/4127-9754**) is Bengaluru's busiest resta[...] ing pure vegetarian, dirt-cheap thalis, or buffet meals (Rs 75). For affordable, n[...] ian coastal Karnataka cuisine, **Unicorn** (94/3 Infantry Rd.; ℂ **080/2559-1670**)[...] The menu changes every week, but expect fish, coconut milk, and lots of flavor—[...] the signature Unicorn Special Prawns. And if you aren't hopping across to Hydera[...] have a taste of excellent Andhra cuisine at **Bheema's** (No. 31 Asha Bldg., Church [...] ℂ **080/2558-7389**)—almost everything is great and super spicy so bring a few tissues[...] There are a couple of rooftop restaurants with eclectic menus that are very popular as[...] well: **Ebony** ★★ (13th Floor, Ivory Tower Hotel, Barton Centre, 84 M.G. Rd.; ℂ **080/2558-9333**) more for its open-air views, and **Paparazzi** (reviewed below) for its innovative cuisine—both have great ambience and music and an excellent bar attached.

The most delicious ice creams and sundaes are available at **Corner House** (44/1 Residency Rd.; ℂ **080/2521-6312**), which, owing to its popularity, is arguably the narrowest space with the biggest vibe in Bengaluru. The Death By Chocolate (Rs 115) is just that—no trip to Bengaluru is complete without at least one shot at surviving it. And given that caffeine runs in the blood here, you'll have no problems getting your fix— great coffee options available with eats at Café Coffee Day, Barrista and Nilgiri Café outlets all over the city. But if you really want the best of the lot, make an effort and head for **Brahmin's Café** ★★ (daily 8am–10pm), a hole-in-he-wall tucked into the crowded lanes of Chamrajpet, close to Ramakrishna Ashram—straightforward and simple, this is the best place to sample south Indian filter coffee. (*Note:* In Karnataka, you may overhear the person sitting next to you order coffee and say "by two"—this seems to be the norm at most budget restaurants or roadside stalls, which means one coffee into two glasses. It's not so much an economic factor that has brought this about as one of sharing—after all, too much caffeine is never a good thing.)

In the big hotels, besides those reviewed below, the following are worth a mention: For North and South Indian cuisine, **Jamavar** at Leela Palace Kempinski (ℂ **080/2521-1234**) is one of Bengaluru's class acts, with arguably the best tandoor dishes in town. For specialty South Indian cuisine, there's no better place than **Dakshin** (ℂ **080/2226-9898**), the upmarket restaurant at the Hotel Windsor Sheraton, with a menu that represents the best of all four southern states. It's hard to know what to order from their extensive menu, so go with the maitre d's recommendation or get a thali (the seafood thali, Rs 1,050, is fab). Staying with Indian, **Masala Klub** (ℂ **080/6660-5660**), with tables set alongside a 100-year-old tamarind tree in the gardens of Taj West End, attempts to prove that Indian cuisine doesn't always mean an overdose of oil and spices—die-hard enthusiasts may disagree, but in this health conscious day and age, the concept certainly seems to be working. The ambience in this stylish indoor-outdoor restaurant is great, especially in the evenings, and other than the extensive wine and food menus, you can do your own grills, marinated in herbs and spices, on imported Matterhorn stones. A recent phenomena, but one which the local hoi polloi haven taken to like the proverbial ducks to water, is the **Sunday Champagne Brunch** which almost all five-star hotels now offer, allowing you an afternoon of conscience-free decadence as you wine, dine and float in refreshing pools—reserve ahead.

If you need to catch your breath while shopping at V.M. Road, nip over to the extremely popular **Sunny's** ★ (Embassy Diamante, Vittal Mallaya Rd.; ℂ 080/2212-0496; www.sunnysbangalore.com), which has a spacious outdoor and indoor seating area and lounge bar. The eclectic menu is a reflection of Bengaluru's growing sophistication and the desserts are to die for. **Shiok,** which means "yummy" in Malay (96, Amar Jyoti Layout, Inner Ring Rd.; ℂ 080/6571-5555; www.shiokfood.com), a fine-dining restaurant-cum-cocktail-lounge run by owner-chef Madhu Menon, who has traveled extensively in the Far East to study different styles of cooking, is another favorite. Thai, Malay, Indonesian, and Singaporean dishes are on offer, with—apparently—more than 60% of the ingredients flown in from overseas, making it rather pricey in terms of "food miles" but worth it. **Olive Beach** ★ (16 Wood St., Ashok Nagar; ℂ 080/4112-8400; www.olivebarandkitchen.com) lives up to its high culinary style and pulls in the city's who's who, just as it does in Mumbai and Delhi. Pebbled paths wind through a heritage bungalow, revealing an atmosphere full of light and laughter, especially as you sip the quintessential Olive margaritas. Book a spot under the cherry tree. Giving i-t.ALIA (reviewed below) a good nudge, both in cuisine and atmosphere, is **Gian Carlos** ★★ (4/1, Walton-Lavelle junction; ℂ 080/4157-1350; www.giancarlosplace.com). Even though the brain behind this very cool restaurant may be sitting in some other part of the world, what he has started is definitely in full throttle with simple, elegant interiors (plus a great rooftop option for the evenings) and some utterly delicious Italian gourmet fare—the wood-fire pizzas are simply delicious as are their innovative Itushis (Italian sushis); the affable Sandeep will be only to happy to guide you through the bewildering choices in hand.

And there's more—driving an hour through Begaluru's evening traffic may not seem the best way to work up an appetite, but it's worth it to reach **Grasshopper** ★★ (45 Kalena Agrahara, Bannerghatta Rd., past the Meenakshi Temple; ℂ 080/2659-3999; meal for two Rs 3,000 without alcohol), an urban warehouse full of surprises—stylish accessories and clothes, theatrical performances and a European fine dining restaurant serving delectable seven course gourmet fare. Fashion designers Sonali and Himanshu decided to expand their creativity from Hidden Harmony, their own line of clothes, to Grasshopper: Emphasis is on subtle flavor and presentation and meals are tailor-made for each table according to preferences—prawns with ginger, sesame and seaweed, veal chops with blue cheese butter and lemongrass ice cream are some of the favorites. Incredibly romantic by night, the outdoor restaurant is open for lunch only on the weekends. Reservations are a must.

Blue Ginger ★★★ VIETNAMESE Lush tropical foliage, a lotus pond, and the scent of frangipani in bloom set the mood for Taj West End's Vietnamese restaurant and open kitchen. The decor is Vietnamese-chic: chairs crafted out of water hyacinth fiber and large stone urns filled with petals; silk lanterns and flaming torches—even the crockery has a Vietnamese military procession running all around it. Start with the asparagus and crab meat soup along with a crunchy raw mango salad, followed by the coconut-based Vietnamese *caris* (curry) served in a clay pot, and accompanied not by rice but a baguette. You could also try scallops in black pepper, garlic and oyster sauce and the scrumptious stir fried prawns in tamarind sauce. End with lemon grass and ginger crème brûlée or the very refreshing rose petal ice cream.

Taj West End. ℂ 080/6660-5660. www.tajhotels.com. Main courses Rs 650–Rs 1,400. AE, DC, MC, V. Daily 12:30–3pm and 7:30–11:45pm.

Swinging in the Hip City of Bengaluru ★★★

The following hip spots are all basically close enough to each other to paint the town red with a number of venues; just call a cab. Start (or end) with Park. hotel's **i-BAR ★★★**, still one of Bengaluru's most happening spots, particularly on frenetic Friday's, which are dedicated to Bollywood. Alternatively, head for **13th Floor ★★** (Ivory Tower Hotel; Barton Centre, M.G. Rd.; ℂ **080/4178-3333;** www.hotelivorytower.com; dress code for men), a sexy 120-seater rooftop cocktail lounge where you get a large dose of the Bengaluru skyline—this is definitely *the* place to be if any day-night cricket matches are going on at the near-by Chinnaswamy Stadium, where everyone downs a few extras with every six hit, irrespective of which side scored—to console or celebrate! Nearby, in a century-old stone building, is what once used to be part of the Blighty Tea Rooms, a popular British hangout, and now the location of the local **Hard Rock Café ★** (St. Mark's Rd.; ℂ **080/4124-2222**) with its "Love All, Serve All" motto, tons of memorabilia and great rock. Aside from i-BAR, a "must-do" is the stunning **Taika ★★** (Church St.; ℂ **080/4151-2828**) with its summery look and totally chilled vibe; skip merrily between the two choices in hand— Club Above, tapping to popular music, and Club Beyond with its special theme every night (single entry charge for both clubs). And of course no visit to Bengaluru would be complete without having a couple at **Shiro ★★** (Third Floor, UB City Mall, VM Road. ℂ **080/4173-8861**)—gigantic Buddha sculptures in an ultra-spacious roof top setting make it a winner visually, and with an 80s pop loop, hip crowd, and amazing fig mojitos, this is currently *the* flavor. **NASA** (1/A Church St.; ℂ **080/2558-6512**) is worth a giggle: Staff is decked out in pilot outfits, and the interior is like the inside of a sci-fi space module; the bar is called the "Fuel Tank" and the loo is known as the "Humanoid Disposal" area. It's good for an afternoon pint, but happy hours draw massive crowds. For mean metal and a crowd that likes to sing along, look no further than **Purple Haze** (M.G. Rd., near Richmond Circle; ℂ **080/2221-3758;** www.purplehaze.co.in). If you don't care much for a pub hop, then zero in to **Kosmo ★★** (off Cunningham

Graze ★★★ FUSION   Bedecked in orange and beige, this simply accoutered award winner (Best Restaurant of the year 2008, Times Food Guide) has an intimate and personal atmosphere (small, cozy, waiters friendly as opposed to obsequious), and fabulous cuisine dished out from an open kitchen. Our personal favorites were seared scallops with fresh corn and Parmesan foam for starters, followed by the delicious rib-eye; pan-seared Waygu beef served with mashed potato and béarnaise sauce; or the roasted halibut, served with steamed lentils, oyster mushrooms, and sherry oxtail sauce. For dessert, look no further than the sinful piping hot chocolate soufflé served with freshly made chocolate ice cream. Mexican chef Oscar, the wizard conjuring this dream meal, is sure to be found advising guests on what to eat or else quietly smiling at the many compliments given by grateful patrons. You can also graze the fantastic collection of the whiskeys and wines.

Taj Residency, 41/3 MG Rd. ℂ **080/6660-4444.** www.tajhotels.com. An average 3-course meal is Rs 2,000—Rs 3,500 with wine and dessert. All credit cards. Daily 12:30–3pm and 7pm–midnight.

Rd.; ℂ **080/41702030**) with its three-in-one choice of seating—the al-fresco Buddha Garden (cafe during the day), two bars and DJ's spinning at Music Lounge, and classy dining at the Terrace to the background of jazz and blues—service however, is not good. At **Fuga** ★★ (No. 1 Castle St., Ashok Nagar; ℂ **080/4147-8625** or 98-4524-7914; www.fuga.co.in), elegantly wasted would be the way to be, if one had to blend in—it's got plush interiors, a mix of hip-hop, house, and club seeing the night through, great food, and a trendy, well-heeled crowd—all at a whopping Rs 1,000 per couple. Not enough time for Goa? No worries—head straight for the terrifically chilled out **Opus** ★★ (Vasanthanagar, ℂ **080/2344-2580**), for its Goan ambience, local live acts in an open amphitheater, and reasonable food; given its proximity to the prime venue for international gigs, it's perfect to pop in for a pre- or postconcert drink. On the other side of the fence, the Oberoi Hotel's smart **Polo Club** combines deep leather sofas with the ubiquitous TV sports entertainment. The last word in exclusivity goes however to Leela's **Library Bar** (ℂ **080/2521-1234**; www.theleela.com), for which you will pay dearly but come away feeling like an English Lord—sink into a leather sofa, order a brandy, light up a cigar and leaf through a collectors item from the library.

It may be a bit muted during the week (which makes for romantic evenings), but come Saturday and Taj West End's **Blue Bar** ★ set amid greens is all set to bring the house down—well, in its own classy way of course. **Liquid** ★★ (Ista Hotel, Swami Vivekanada Rd.; ℂ **080/2555-8888;** www.istahotels.com) is also very popular for its candlelit alfresco bar with live music and indoor lounge for chilly evenings. And while Mumbai's **Geoffrey's** brings its English Pub atmosphere to Bengaluru (Royal Orchid, Airport Rd., ℂ **080/2520-5566**), **Dublin**, the watering hole at the ITC Windsor Sheraton (ℂ **080/2226-9898**), serves—yep, you guessed right—an Irish pub vibe.

(Note: A strict no-smoking law has been put into place in all public areas.)

i-t.ALIA ★★★ ITALIAN/INTERNATIONAL   Rated the best Italian restaurant in Bengaluru by the *Times Food Guide* and Restaurant of the Year by *Taste & Travel Food Guide*, i-t.ALIA is led by the celebrated Mandaar Sukhtankar. The menu may have items that are a mouthful to pronounce, but once you taste them, you will be left speechless. Flavor enjoys top priority here, but for the maestros in the kitchen, creative presentation is equally important. Three kinds of mushrooms, each cooked differently, makes a fabulous starter followed by the hand cut spaghetti with grilled lobster and crab meat or the scallop, anchovy, and late harvest wine risotto. Make sure you have enough space for one of the best desserts in the country—the delicious *Ficchi al forno—specialita dello chef* (baked fresh figs).

The Park.hotel, 14/7 M.G. Rd. ℂ **080/2559-4666.** www.theparkhotels.com. An average 3- to 4-course meal is Rs 2,000–Rs.3,000 with wine and dessert. AE, DC, MC, V. Daily noon–2:45pm and 7–11:45pm.

Karavalli ★★★ SOUTH INDIAN   This indoor-outdoor restaurant has been wowing guests and winning awards for more than a decade now. Sit in the open-air courtyard under the huge canopy of a rain tree on wrought-iron garden chairs, or inside, in what resembles a Mangalorean home, with high ceilings, antique furniture, and walls adorned with old seafarer maps and a grandfather clock. For seafood lovers, Karavalli is a godsend, with Goan baby lobster, Mangalorean black pomfret, and pearlspot caught off the shores of Cochin in Kerala. The west coast also provides fresh *bekti*, shrimp, prawns, scampi, squid, sear, sole, and ladyfish, while the varying cuisines of India's southern coastal regions provide inspiration for dishes originally found in home kitchens. Chef Narain Thimmiah drums up sensational starters like the Chevod Balchao and Coorg fried chicken; if you've any room left for the main course, try the Alleppey fish curry or the Karavalli mutton curry with *appams* (savory rice-batter pancakes) and wash it all down with plenty of *rasam* (excellent drink for digestion, flavored with tamarind and pepper).

Taj Gateway Hotel, 66 Residency Rd. (*C*) **080/6660-4545**. www.tajhotels.com. Main courses Rs 1,500–Rs 2,000; lunch thali Rs 750–Rs 950. AE, DC, MC, V. Daily 12:30–3pm and 7:30–11:30pm.

Koshy's Restaurant and the Jewel Box (Value) INDIAN/CONTINENTAL   Easily the most popular eating and meeting place on M.G. Road, this 50-year-old restaurant has changed little over the years. Food is varied, but it's more or less beside the point; you come here for the energetic buzz. It's a favorite gathering spot and has a distinct local flavor, attracting the coffeehouse intellectual and budding artist alike. You won't be bothered at all if you prefer to linger endlessly over a beer (Rs 100) and your book. Those who would rather steer clear of the action can sit in the quieter, but rather bland, air-conditioned section, the Jewel Box.

39 St. Mark's Rd. (*C*) **080/2221-3793** or -5030. Average meal Rs 350. AE, DC, MC, V. Daily 11:30–3:30pm and 7:30–11pm.

Mavalli Tiffin Rooms (MTR) ★★ (Moments) SOUTH INDIAN VEGETARIAN   Possibly *the* essential Bengaluru eating experience, this is an excellent spot to sample the chaos of a traditional "tiffin" room, where scores of locals rush in for the Indian version of fast food, served since 1924 with attitude and gusto from shiny silver buckets by notoriously surly waiters in white. If you're here during lunch, order a thali and eat with your fingers from a silver tray onto which various authentic South Indian concoctions are heaped and continuously replenished. You can also try the lighter fare, especially the *Bisi Bele Bath*, made out of rice, lentils, tamarind, chilies, ground spices, coconut, and vegetables and, last but not least, topped with calorie-intensive ghee. You sit in rather indecorous surroundings (the current venue was built in 1949 and hasn't changed at all in over 40 years) on brown plastic chairs at marble-top tables with orange steel legs; grab a table upstairs. *Tip:* Adjacent, the **MTR Store** sells a wide range of South Indian treats and delicacies, including popular sweets (like *badam halwa* and *ladu*) and ready-to-eat savories.

14 Lal Bagh Rd. (*C*) **080/2222-1706**. mavallitiffinrooms.com. Typical meal Rs 75; individual items Rs 5–Rs 20. No credit cards. Tues–Sun 6:30am–noon, 12:30–2:30pm, and 7:30–9pm.

Paparazzi ★★ FUSION   The head will surely spin as you enter this fabulous rooftop restaurant with its one of a kind two-story-high bar—enough to make teetotalers do a rethink! High ceilings swathed in fabric, dim lighting, candlelight, great music and the views couldn't get any better—alas, it isn't open during the day but the night lights look magnificent through the large plate-glass windows; the best way to experience the Bengaluru traffic. For those not brave enough to dive headlong into quintessential Indian,

Rejuvenation City: Tiptop Spas

Prompted by the emergence of an overstressed, well-heeled workforce, Bengaluru has a number of well-known luxury and medical spas. SPA.ce (70, Cunningham Rd.; ✆ **4132-7526;** www.spacethespa.com; by appointment only), is a world-class stand-alone spa in the middle of the city that uses signature fragrances created by Ally Mathan. Of the hotel spas we recommend **The Spa** at Leela Palace Kempinski (✆ **080/2521-1234**) and **Jiva** at Taj Residency; for more committed treatment programs, take a look at the following four luxury spas, all located about an hour outside Bengaluru. Aside from **Shreyas** (see "Where to Stay," above), **The Golden Palms Spa** (✆ **080/2371-2222**), owned by Bollywood director Sanjay Khan, is part of an upmarket resort that not only provides routine spa treatments, but is the spot for discreet cosmetic surgery and anti-aging treatments. The attitude toward pampering is more laid-back at the internationally affiliated **Angsana Oasis Spa and Resort** (✆ **080/2846-8893;** www.angsana.com), offering spa packages from $825 for 2 nights (including taxes, meals, airport transfers, and a few treatments). Neither of these spas will restrict your diet or ban smoking or alcohol, and on weekends you can wholeheartedly tuck into their barbeque and grilled cuisine. In contrast, **Soukya International Holistic Health Centre** (in Whitefield, 30 min. from Bengaluru; ✆ **080/2794-5001** through -5004; www.soukya.com) is a medical spa that focuses on therapeutic and complementary therapies. Run by Dr. Isaac Mathai, his nutritionist wife, Suja, and a battery of experts, this is a nonsmoking, alcohol- and meat-free spa where everything is low fat, low salt, low spice, and organic. The focus is on individually created "holistic wellness programs" (from Hawaiian hot stone to specialized Ayurvedic treatments) that strengthen the body's immune system, including those belonging to some rather famous people, like healthy-living guru Andrew Weil, Fergie, Princess of York, and Archbishop Desmond Tutu. *(Note:* If you are planning to continue to Goa from Karnataka, also take a look at **Swaswara**—a yoga retreat on the northern tip of Karnataka's coast, bordering Goa.)

Chef Rana Dominic Gomes comes to the rescue with contemporary fusion food which is not always top class but certainly a welcome break from the "same old same old." For starters go in for the delectable *chicken chanduri* (chicken tossed in peri peri sauce) and then head straight for the terrific *chicken tikka risotto*—our favorite; the *tandoori salmon* and the *chicken roulade makhani* are also good.

Royal Orchid Central, Dickenson Rd. ✆ **080/2558-4242.** www.royalorchidhotels.com. Typical meal Rs 1,500 without wine and dessert. AE, DC, MC, V. Daily 12:30–3pm and 7:30–11;45pm.

SHOPPING

You'll find the city's major shopping centers along and around **M.G. Road, Commercial Street,** and **Brigade Road.** M.G. Road is where you'll find the fixed-price tourist-oriented (no bargains or bargaining) **Cauvery Arts and Crafts Emporium, Central Cottage Industries Emporium,** and **Karnataka State Silk Industries Emporium.** Fabulous silks and home textiles, as well as contemporary silverware from Neemrana and traditional silver jewelry from Amrapali and Jaipur, are some of the highlights available in **Shop Ananya,** located next to the Hotel Sarovar at 9/1 Dhondusa Annexe, Richmond Circle (© 080/2299-8922). **Mysore Saree Udyog** (No. 294, first floor, Kamraj Rd, across from the entrance to Commercial St.; © 080/2558-3255) is also popular with Westerners for fabrics in gorgeous colors and textures. But for the real experience, head for the shops on **Chikpet Main Road,** and let your head swim as you sit on floor mattresses, with salesmen opening sari after sari. And if it's the gorgeous Indian jewelry that beckons, then look no further than the two oldest stores in Bengaluru, both of which were once patronized by the Mysore royalty—**C. Krishnaiah Chetty & Son** (Commercial St.; © 080/2558-8731; www.ckcsons.com) and **Ganjam Nagappa and Sons** (Infantry Rd.; © 080/2226-1233). Little more down to earth is **Srishti** (100 Ft. Rd., Indiranagar; © 080/2521-0176; also at Leela Galleria)—ask for their antique jewelry collection. Speaking of antiques and other collectibles in bronze, stone, teak, and silver, call on **Natesan's Antiqarts** (76 M.G. Rd.; © 080/2558-8344 or -7427). Pick up beautiful ethnic home accessories, rugs, and other gifts at **The Bombay Store** (99 EGK Prestige, M.G. Rd.; © 080/2532-0014 or -0015). With four levels of saris and *salwar kameez* (for women) and *sherwanis* (for men), and a nonstop clientele, you can understand why staff at **Deepam Silk International** insists that there is "nowhere else in the whole world" better to shop for silk garments (67 Bluemoon Complex, M.G. Rd.; © 080/2558-8760). He produces the largest share of beer in India, owns one of the most successful airlines, a Formula One team as well as an IPL cricket team, and now he's built the newest hotspot in town on a road named after his industrialist father—**UB City** on **Vittal Mallya Road,** is Vijay Mallya's latest offering and although still incomplete, lures high-end shoppers to its massive chrome and glass designer stores like Goodearth, Canali, Dunhill London, just to name a few. **Embassy Chambers** and **Embassy Classic** (in the Lavelle and St. Mark's Rd. vicinity) are where you will find all the Indian designers like Rohit Bal, Rajesh Pratap Singh, Neeru Kumar, Manish Arora, Abraham and Thakore and Ffolio. And make sure you drop in at **Cinnamon** (11 Walton Rd., off Lavelle Rd.; © 080/2222-9794), which showcases some of India's best designers in this cool, stylish boutique. Getting its name from an enormous tree in its garden, **Raintree** (4 Sankey Rd., across from ITC Windsor Sheraton), an old colonial bungalow shared by several designers offers all kinds of accessories, clothes and furniture. Away from the hub is **100 Ft. Boutique** (Indirangar; © 080/25277752), with its funky collections of everything from bags and lamps to offbeat furnishings—the attached restaurant is an incentive to go there. It's somewhat of a drag through nightmarish traffic to get there (aside from 100 Ft. Boutique, the above recommendations are all manageable distances from each other) but the **Leela Galleria** (The Leela Palace Hotel, 23 Airport Rd.; © 033/2521-1234; www.theleela.com) boasts some of the hottest and biggest brands both from India and overseas, making window shopping a pleasure with live piano in the background and Barista at hand for a quick fix.

CULTURAL ACTIVITIES

Check the local dailies for information about cultural events. Besides art exhibitions and traditional dance and music performances, Bengaluru draws major international artists, including pop and rock stars.

The violin-shaped auditorium known as **Chowdaiah Memorial Hall** (Gayathri Devi Park Extension, Vyalikaval; © 080/2344-5810) hosts regular classical music performances, as well as film, dance, and drama. Plays are regularly staged at **Rabindra Kalakshetra**

(Jayachamarachendra Rd.; ℂ **080/2222-1271**), where you can also catch occasional art exhibitions. Numerous art galleries around the city host contemporary Indian art and other exhibitions. **Venkatappa Art Gallery,** attached to the Government Museum (Kasturba Rd.; ℂ **080/2286-4483;** Rs 10; Tues–Sun 10am–5pm), displays more than 600 paintings year-round. **Karnataka Chitrakala Parishat** (Art Complex, Kumara Krupa Rd.; ℂ **080/ 2226-1816;** www.chitrakalaparishath.org) has a varied collection of traditional paintings, leather puppets, and artifacts from all over Karnataka. Visit its various art studios and gallery spaces, the open-air theater, and (in particular) the Roerich and Kejriwal galleries. Featuring artists from around the globe, check out a New York based gallery **Streisand Art** (382, 100 Ft. Rd., Indiranagar; ℂ **080/2520-3535;** www.streisand-art.com). While **GallerySKE** (82, St. Mark's Rd.; ℂ **080/2223-8312;** www.galleryske.com) is a good place for alternative art, **One Shanti Road** (1, Shanti Rd., Shantinagar; ℂ **080/2222-0236;** www. 1shanthiroad.com) is a nonprofit artist-led initiative, offering a great space and opportunity for across the globe interaction. Other than the many live acts around the city, the open-to-all **Levis Jam** takes place on the first Sunday of each month—check www.freedomjam. net for details.

Nrityagram Dance Village (along the Bengaluru-Pune Hwy., 35km/22 miles from Bengaluru) is a renowned center for Indian dance training. Performances feature students as well as established artists. Organized tours of the facility include lecture demonstrations designed to introduce you to Indian culture, life philosophy, and both *kathak* and *odissi* dance forms (ℂ **080/2846-6313;** www.nrityagram.org; tours Rs 20 per person; Tues–Sun 10am–5:30pm, dance classes 10:30am–1pm). A through-the-night dance and music festival is held in February; it attracts almost 30,000 spectators, so decent seating is at a premium.

---

2 MYSORE ★★★

140km (87 miles) SW of Bengaluru; 473km (293 miles) N of Chennai; 1,177km (730 miles) SE of Mumbai

A city of palatial buildings and tree-lined boulevards, laid-back Mysore is possessed of a quaint charm, a dignified hangover from the days when it was the capital of a rich princely state, and remains a popular destination for travelers, particularly for its **Maharajah's Palace.** Built over a period of 15 years at the turn of the 20th century, at a cost then of over Rs 4 million, this astonishing Indo-Saracenic palace is testament to the affluence of one of India's greatest ruling dynasties. During the 10-day **Dussehra Festival,** held here during the first half of October, the entire city is dressed up in show-off style; each night **Mysore Palace** is lit up by 80,000 bulbs, and on the final evening of festivities, the maharajah, dressed in royal finery, leads one of the country's most spectacular processions on elephants through the city streets. Mysore is also an ideal base from which to explore the temples known as the **"Jewel Boxes"** of Hoysala architecture, which lie some 3 hours north, as well as the nearby Jain pilgrimage site at **Sravanabelgola.**

ESSENTIALS

GETTING THERE & AWAY   Trains from Bengaluru (3 hr.) and Hassan (for Hoysala heartland; 2–3 hr.) pull in regularly at the **railway station** (ℂ **131** or 0821/242-2103), situated at the intersection of Jhansi Laxmi Bai Road and Irwin Road. Frequent and comfortable AC Volvo buses ply the road between Mysore and Bengaluru (Rs 250) starting from the main bus-stand; journey takes approximately 3 hours. For Rajiv Gandhi

National Park and Coorg, your best option is to hire a car. (*Note:* If traveling by own vehicle, set aside an hour to visit the 400-year-old Banyan tree en route to Mysore, spread over a hectare (4 acres)—plenty of tourists but worth the detour.)

VISITOR INFORMATION   For information, visit the **Karnataka Tourist Office** (Mayura Yatri Niwas, JLB Rd., near railway station; *C* **0821/242-3652;** daily 6:30am–8:30pm).

GETTING AROUND   Negotiate **taxi** prices in advance, or hire a vehicle for the day (recommended if you wish to visit the Keshava Temple; expect to pay Rs 835 for half day and Rs 1,100 for full day). **Auto-rickshaws** are cheap and plentiful; you can either insist that the driver use his meter (Rs 15 at the start) or fix a price upfront; the latter is likely to get you to your destination quicker (see chapter 3). Don't pay for any taxi or vehicle without first checking its condition. You can organize a car through your hotel travel desk, but it's likely to be more expensive (Rs 835–Rs 1,100).

GUIDED TOURS & TRAVEL AGENTS   Operating since 1976, **Seagull Travels** (8 Best Western Ramanashree Hotel Complex, Bengaluru-Niligiri Rd.; *C* **0821/252-9732,** or 0821/426-0054 and -3653; fax 0821/252-0549; www.seagulltravels.net; daily 9:45am–8:45pm) handles a wide range of travel needs, including ticketing, taxi arrangements, and individually packaged tours (although prices can fluctuate arbitrarily). Seagull can also help arrange your trip to the popular government-owned Jungle Lodges and Resorts across Karnataka. Another local travel agent is **Skyway International Travels** (3704/4, Jhansi Laxmibai Rd.; *C* **0821/244-4444;** fax 0821/242-6000; www.skywaytour.com; skyway mys@airtelmail.in).

WHAT TO SEE & DO

Besides Mysore's most famous palace, the Maharajah's Palace, and Keshava Temple, you might want to visit **Jagan Mohan Palace** (west of Mysore Palace, Dewan's Rd.; Rs 10; daily 8:30am–5pm), which once served as the royal auditorium. The building now exhibits South India's oddest assortment of kitsch memorabilia from the massive private collection of the Wodeyars. Southeast of downtown (3km/2 miles away), **Chamundi Hill** is where you can join throngs of huffing-puffing pilgrims, some of who recite or read Hindu verses along the way (going by car is also an option). Stop first at the **Shiva Temple,** where devotees circumambulate the statue in a clockwise direction while a friendly priest dishes out sacred water and dollops of vermilion paste. The summit of the hill is very active with pilgrims come to pay their respects to Durga. You can buy a *dar-shan* ticket from the computerized ticketing booth and join the queue for a peek at the deity inside **Sri Chamundeswari Temple** (3:30–6:30pm); or you can wander around the hilltop exploring smaller temples, many of which serve as bases for bright-robed grinning *sadhus* (holy persons) wanting to sell you a private photo opportunity. Near the Race Course is the **Karinji Lake** (8:30am–5:30pm), a particularly beautiful spot during the early morning and evening when you get to see a large number of birds—it also has a Butterfly Park for which you need a good reserve of patience and luck. Half an hour away from the city center, the **Brindavan Gardens** ★★ (park open from 10am–8pm; light and fountain timings: 7–8pm summer, 6:30–7:30pm winter) are quite a sight—make sure you go in the evening when hundreds of lights make it very magical and get a taste of quintessential Indian joviality when a lone fountain at the end of the gardens breaks into a "dance" set to Indian film songs. You can also stay on at the **Royal Orchid** ★★ (*C* **0823/6257-257;** www.royalorchidhotels.com; Rs 5,000 Queen–Rs 6,000 King doubles): superbly located, overlooking the gardens on one side and the dam with the river Cauvery on the other side. Modern and antiquated simultaneously, it's a nice option if you want to explore the gardens in the morning and enjoy lazing over a book or beer.

Finally, no trip to Mysore is complete without getting lost in the dizzying scents of jasmine, musk, sandalwood, frangipani, and incense as you wander through the city's vibrant **Devraj Market ★★**. Mysore is also famous for its silk and sandalwood oil, and you can witness the production of both by taking a side trip to Vidyaranyapuram, 15 minutes away. For an escorted tour of the **Government Silk Weaving Factory,** call ℂ **0821/248-1803** (visiting hours daily 9–11am and 12:15–3:30pm; shop hours 9:30am–7pm); the **Government Sandal Oil Factory** is right next door (daily 11:30am–4pm). If time is short, you can also hop into **Cauvery Arts and Crafts Emporium** (Sayaji Rao Rd.; 10am–6pm) which is like a one-stop shop for all that Mysore has to offer. Although not open to casual visitors, an absolute eye-opener is the astonishing **Infosys Global Education Centre** (ℂ **0821/240-4101**) on the outskirts of the city—a world class campus spread over 135 hectares (335 acres) for budding IT trainees, it stands as a striking contrast to the stereotype of ramshackle educational institutions across the country. Use all contacts, pull all strings to set foot inside!

Keshava Temple ★★★   Situated 38km (24 miles) from Mysore in the small village of Somnathpur, this is perhaps the best-preserved and most complete Hoysala monument in existence. Also referred to as Chennakeshava Temple, this beautiful religious monument is presided over by Vijayanarayana, one of the 24 incarnations of Vishnu. Built as early as 1268, it is constructed entirely of soapstone and rests on a raised plinth; typical of Hoysala temples, it has a star-shaped ground plan and exquisitely sculpted interiors. It's really worth exploring in detail; you may have to urge or bribe the caretaker to crank up the generator so that you have enough light to properly observe the three shrines in the temple. Somnathpur is serene and remote, and the lawns around the monument are ideal for picnicking—ask your hotel for a packed lunch. The best time to photograph the temple is around 4:30pm, when the sun creates a fantastic play of shadow and light, especially along the row of pillars.

Somnathpur is 38km (24 miles) east of Mysore. Admission Rs 100. Daily 8am–5:30pm.

Maharajah's Palace (Amba Vilas) ★★★   Generally considered *the* palace in South India, this was designed by Henry Irving at the turn of the 20th century; 15 years of nonstop construction produced a fabulous domed, arched, colonnaded, and turreted structure with lavish interiors—teak ceilings, carved marble handrails, gilded pillared halls, ivory deities, rococo lamp stands, Italian crystal chandeliers, stained-glass windows, miles of white marble floors, and ceilings made from stained glass brought all the way from Glasgow. You'll be hard-pressed to find an undecorated section of wall or ceiling; frescoes, paintings, statues, and delicate relief carvings recall religious as well as secular scenes, including glorious state processions. Within the inner courtyards, growling stone felines guard stairways, while elsewhere, elaborately carved rosewood doors mark the entrances of yet more splendid halls and chambers. Paintings by Raja Ravi Varma, golden chariots, gilt-framed mirrors, stately family portraits (including a wax sculpture of the maharajah), and all manner of ornate fantasy objects add to the spectacle of abundant wealth. Overlooking the parade grounds, brought to life during the **Dussehra Festival** (Sept or Oct), a terraced grandstand pavilion is covered by a heavily decorated and frescoed ceiling, while huge, decaying chandeliers dangle precariously over the seating.

Don't bother to purchase an additional ticket for the disappointing **Maharajah's Residential Palace,** where, sadly, a display of items gathers dust.

Ramvilas Rd., Mizra Rd., and Purandara Rd. ℭ **0821/242-2620.** Admission: Amber Vilas Rs 20; Residential Palace Rs 20. Daily 10am–5:30pm.

WHERE TO STAY

Although small, Mysore offers a good variety of hotels, ranging from business hotels, heritage properties, and resorts, to dirt-cheap establishments. If you're interested in the latter category, walk around Gandhi Square and take your pick, although expect nothing more than a bed and roof over your head. Or head for no-frills **Hotel Siddhartha** (Guest House Rd., Nazarbad; ℭ **0821/428-0999** or -0888; siddhartahotel@hotmail.com), situated at a convenient distance from the palace, station, and bus stand. The rooms are small but are clean and functional. The range starts from Rs 860 to Rs 3,250—some rooms have Indian-style bathrooms (the toilet is sunk into the ground), so stipulate Western-style beforehand—203, 201 are the best in size and view. The in-house restaurant **Om Shanthi** has a great local atmosphere and is extremely popular with regulars, who have been coming for 25 years—*rawa dosai, mallige idli* (in Kannada "mallige" means jasmine, and these slightly flattened balls of rice flour are reputedly as soft as the flower itself), and the filter coffee are all top class. Adjacent, **Hotel Sandesh the Prince** is loud and gaudy in appearance but has decent rooms and offers all the basic facilities including a pool and gym (Guest House Rd., Nazarbad; ℭ **0821/243-6777;** doubles from Rs 3,995). **Regaalis** is the best business hotel and combines a fair amount of luxury with value for the money. The poolside barbecue is popular, while **Gardenia,** its multicuisine restaurant, serves the best buffet in town (13-14 Vinoba Rd., Mysore 570005; ℭ **0821/242-6426;** www.ushalexushotels.com; doubles from Rs 4,600–Rs 7,500). **Ginger** (Nazarabad Mohalla ℭ **0821/663-3333;** www.gingerhotels.com; doubles from Rs 1,800), a new budget option available across the country and managed by the Taj group, offers spotless accommodation in its now-familiar orange and blue shaded rooms.

Finally, for those looking to turn over a new leaf in wellness, 20 minutes from the city center is the verdant **Indus Valley Ayurvedic Centre** (Lalithadripura; ℭ **0821/247-3437** or -3263; http://ayurindus.com; ask about programs) offering excellent long-term therapies in peaceful surroundings. The pool is massive and cottages although simple, are more than adequate.

The Green Hotel ★★ Built in the 1920s, this award-winning hotel has lots of character and faded glamour; it's not luxurious but a stay here will have you feeling very good anyway. The hotel is owned by a charity that employs disadvantaged people at good wages and, true to its name, tries to be environmentally conscious. Light filters through stained-glass windows, and the large, open public spaces are swathed in teak and brimming with old-world charm, while interiors are full of a motley assortment of antique furniture and colorful memorabilia. The Palace has only seven rooms (avoid the tiny Rose and Marigold rooms), but the New Wing has plenty more, all garden-facing, although they lack the historical flavor.

Chittaranjan Palace, 2270 Vinoba Rd., Jayalamipuram, Mysore 570 012. ℭ **0821/251-2536** or 0821/425-5000, -5001, and -5002. Fax 0821/251-6139. www.greenhotelindia.com. 31 units. New Wing: Rs 2,750—Rs 3,750 double. Palace Rooms: Rs 5,250 Marigold, Rs 3,250 Writer and Small Bollywood. Palace suites: Rs 6,250 Maharani Suite, Rs 5,750 Princess's Room, Rose, and Large Bollywood. Rs 800 extra bed. Rates include breakfast. MC, V. **Amenities:** Restaurant; bar; doctor-on-call; green auto-rickshaw service; Internet (Rs 130/hr.); library; room service; TV room; volleyball. *In room:* Fan.

Royal Orchid Metropole ★★ In the heritage category, it's a bit of a tossup between The Green Hotel and the 120-year-old Royal Orchid Metropole, built by the Maharaja

of Mysore to entertain his foreign guests. The stately colonial structure is a striking contrast to neighboring Hotel Regaalis (mentioned above) and extremely popular with foreign tourists for its laid-back ambience and good cuisine. The standard rooms are small
but located away from the road, while the bigger royal rooms hear a fair amount of traffic noise—still, these are preferable given the greater charm of antique furniture and
patios or balconies. The bathroom of the only suite in the hotel incidentally features the
first bathtub to be brought to India from England, still functioning today without leaks!
Real silver swings and chairs from Rajasthan adorn the tiny lobby, while a 100-year-old
portrait of Tipu Sultan looms large in **Tiger Trail,** the in-house restaurant that is quite
popular with locals as well.

5 Jhansi Lakshmibai Rd., Mysore 570005; (C) **0821/425-5566.** www.royalorchidhotels.com. 30 units. Rs
5,600 Royal; Rs 6,600 Heritage; Rs 7,500 Maharaja Suite. Rates include breakfast. Taxes extra. **Amenities:**
Restaurant; bar; doctor-on-call; outdoor pool. *In room:* AC, TV, minibar; Wi-Fi (Rs 200/hr., Rs 600/day).

The Windflower Spa and Resort ★★   Situated in the quiet environs of the Mysore

race course (3km/1¾ miles from the city center) and flanked in the distance by the Chamundi Hill, this relative newcomer is located on a 4-hectare (10-acre) property. It is midway between a high-end hotel and boutique resort, and exudes a sense of space from the
moment you walk into its delightful reception area. Cottages line the shallow canal-like
pond with gorgeous giant brass *urlis* (cauldrons) placed at intervals, and plenty of swaying
palms. Almost the entire resort has been designed using furniture from Indonesia —massive
low beds with a wooden step, chunky teak wood coffee tables, sofas with silk covers, and
lots of cane and bamboo everywhere. The **Emerge Spa** offers plenty of treatments and
won't leave your pockets empty. (*Warning:* You will probably be greeted by a snow-white
Australian cockatoo called Rosy, who has a fondness for punching holes in footwear.)

Maharanapratap Rd., Nazarbad, Mysore 570 010. (C) **0821/252-2500.** Fax 0821/252-2400. www.thewind
flower.com. 39 units. Rs 4,500 Executive; Rs 5,400 Deluxe; Rs 7,200 Club Class Suite, Rs 9,900 Royal Presidential Suite. Rs 1,000 extra bed. Rates include breakfast. AE, MC, V. **Amenities:** Restaurant; bar; currency
exchange; doctor-on-call; fitness center; pool; spa. *In room:* AC, TV, DVD player, Wi-Fi (complimentary).

WHERE TO DINE

Visitors with a sweet tooth will get a kick out of the local specialty, Mysore *pak (mysurpa),*
made from gram flour and liters of ghee (clarified butter). You'll find a number of outlets
at Devaraja Market. The best place to try is at **Bombay Tiffany's** ((C) **0821/2427-511**);
the famous and long-established **Guru Sweet Mart** (Sayaji Rao Rd.) or any of the Nandini milk stalls—all equally good. Hotel Dasaprakash's canteenlike restaurant **Akshaya**
(Gandhi Sq.; (C) **0821/244-2444**) serves simple, hygienic vegetarian fare, typical of the
region, and a sumptuous thali that costs just Rs 55!

Le Olive Garden ★★ (Finds) NORTH INDIAN/ECLECTIC   The in-house restau-

rant at Windflower Spa and Resort (reviewed above) offers alfresco dining in a leafy garden
with geese and wind chimes for company. Arranged on landscaped terracing, the dining
area is surrounded by water and reached by tiny bridges. Most of the dishes are Indian,
with a good range of kebabs offered, but you can also order Chinese or choose from a
small selection of Continental dishes. We recommend the *murgh malai kebab* (chicken
grilled with fresh yogurt cream) or the *Peshawari kebab* (pistachio- and almond-flavored
grilled chicken). The owner of the resort is also the proprietor of Joy ice cream, famous in
this part of the country, so it makes perfect sense to end with a bowl of delicious butter-
scotch ice cream or the Olive orange-flavored caramel custard. Incidentally, you won't find
better iced coffee (don't ask for ice cream in it) anywhere else in Karnataka.

VISITING RAJIV GANDHI NATIONAL PARK

Originally the private property of the Maharajah of Mysore, Karnataka's most popular
elephant hangout became a national park in 1955, 3 years after the princely state of
Mysore was absorbed into post-colonial India. Situated 95km (59 miles) southwest of
Mysore, and spread over 511 sq. km (199 sq. miles) filled with teak, rosewood, sandal,
and silver oak trees, Rajiv Gandhi National Park is also generously populated by *dhole*
(wild dogs), *gaur* (Indian bison), antelope, sloth bears, panthers, otters, crocodiles,
cobras, pythons, falcons, eagles, and great Indian horned owls. Keep an eye peeled for
tiny *muntjac* deer; they stand only .6m (2 ft.) tall and are crowned by finger-length ant-
lers. The big draw, of course, are the tigers (btw. 60 and 65 reside here), but sightings are
subject to a great deal of luck—although when Goldie Hawn came here to shoot a
documentary, she apparently spotted several. Ms. Hawn stayed at the popular **Kabini
River Lodge,** the most practical place to be if you want to have access to the park without any organizational fuss. A charmingly rustic retreat some 6 hours by car from Bengaluru (3 hr. from Mysore), Kabini is spread over 22 hectares (55 acres), incorporating
lush forest and largely untamed vegetation, just the way a "jungle resort" should, with
the maharajah's original 18th-century hunting lodge as centerpiece. Accommodations
with the best positions are the river-facing cottages. Expect small bathrooms, dated green
sofas, and lumpy mattresses covered with charming Indian throws. Eyeball the skies for
birds like hoopoes and drongos, try a brief coracle (boat) trip, go for an elephant ride or
tiger spotting, and—of course—partake of the meals and tea laid out for you according
to a precise schedule. The lodge was set up by Col. John Felix Wakefield, who at 92 still
lives on the premises. Book a room at Kabini well in advance, and plan to arrive there at
least an hour before the afternoon safari, which begins at 4:30pm (© **08228/26-4402**
through -4405; head office in Bengaluru © **080/2559-7021,** -7024, or -7025; www.
junglelodges.com; standard package 2 days, 1 night per person, $160; includes all meals,
safaris, park entrance, and elephant and boat rides). For companies that offer the services
of a car and driver for the 3-hour drive, see "Guided Tours & Travel Agents" under
Mysore "Essentials," above.

Resorts have also begun to spring up in this hitherto lesser-known area. Across the
river from Kabini River Lodge, **Orange County Kabini** (www.orangecounty.in; © **080/
4191-1000**) offers two kinds of lodging—private pool huts and Jacuzzi huts, ranging
between $360 and $460. The huts—mud cottages with thatched roofs—are as close to
"spirit of the land" as you'll get, for luxury is the defining word here. All cottages are
tastefully designed and spacious, but the pool huts are best for location, with the river
virtually lapping at the edges. Those coming for an eco-experience or wanting to be more
in the thick of the wildlife will find it a tad commercial—ideal time to visit would be
midweek when the fewest tourists are around. **Cicada Resorts** (© **080/4115-2200;**
www.cicadaresorts.com) is slightly older and less manicured than Orange County, but
their safari vehicles are the best in the area. Standard rooms are bland and overpriced;
suites are nicer (Rs 12,000–Rs 18,000). Spend your days kayaking and evenings gazing
into the bonfire (there's no TV).

OF COORG & COFFEE

Legend has it that in 1670, Baba Budan, a Muslim pilgrim, carried seven coffee beans
from Arabia (where the export of only processed beans was allowed) and planted them

in the Chikmagalur region of Karnataka, thus introducing coffee to India. Today the state is the largest producer of coffee in the country, and a large chunk of it comes from a gorgeous area known as Kodagu, or, as the British called it, Coorg, an elevated region that lies 3 hours southwest of Mysore. With undulating hills, this is a superb trekking destination, and as yet still somewhat of a secret.

Five and a half hours from Bengaluru and 2 hours from Mysore, the capital of Coorg is **Madikeri,** an unexceptional town but a convenient base for treks in the area. If you don't intend to hike, however, you could opt for a quieter, more luxurious getaway in the midst of a coffee plantation at Orange County (run by the same company that operates Orange County Kabini), or an even more authentic stay in the rustic Rainforest Retreat (both reviewed below). As is the case elsewhere, a number of homestay options have emerged in the last few years, but most don't meet our standards of hygiene and ambience. If you plan on staying within the town itself, then **Gowri Nivas** (New Extension, Madikeri; ✆ **094481-93822;** www.gowrinivas.com; doubles at Rs 3,500), is a sweet and clean place, run by the extremely chilled Bopanna and his wife, Muthu. They can also help you get to the top of **Tadiyendamol ★★,** the highest peak in Coorg at 1,750m (5,740 ft). A little lower than Madikeri, a massive planter's bungalow, once the residence of the Diwan to Raja of Coorg, has been taken up by the expert Neemrana Hotels Group and opened to tourists. The Swiss-styled **Green Hills Estate ★** (www.neemranahotels. com; ✆ **011/4666-1666;** doubles from Rs 5,000), is surrounded by coffee plantations, and still very reminiscent of the days when the Chengappa family (now living a stone's throw away) lived in the grand style here. Wooden stairs lead to massive suites, antiques and period furniture are in every corner, with frayed tiger skins on the floors, and a slightly disconcerting dining area uses the once-majestic animals of surrounding forests as wall décor. It's all utterly charming when there are other guests staying there. If the culture of the area intrigues you, ask for Kartik, who has grown up in these environs, but of course the best way of getting acquainted with the Coorgi way of life is to attend a wedding— nonstop fun, and full of interesting rites and ceremonies. Essentially agriculturists, the Coorgis, also known as the Kodavas, are a distinct community, with strict adherence to the code of merry-making, and occasions to celebrate are never wanting. Interestingly, they are said to be descendents of Alexander's army, something that could well be true given that they always carry some form of weapon—thankfully, rarely ever used.

Orange County Coorg ★★

From the moment you arrive at this lovely 16th-century Tudor-style resort, surrounded by a 120-hectare (300-acre) coffee and pepper plantation, and are welcomed with a delicious glass of fresh sugar-cane juice, you know you're in for a treat. Connected by cobbled pathways, the thatched and tiled cottages are divided into clusters and spread out over almost 20 hectares (50 acres). The Private Pool Villas are worth the money, with huge bedrooms and spacious dining and sitting areas that lead out to a decent-size private pool set in the middle of a garden with your very own pepper tree. There are plenty of dining options to choose from and caffeine addicts can get their fix in the lounge, where coffee is free of charge. *Tip:* If too much coffee produces an energy rush, head for **Bylckuppe,** 30km (19 miles) away. The second largest Tibetan settlement outside Tibet, its Golden Monastery is spectacular, featuring three gigantic gold-plated statues and huge wall frescoes. There are plenty of smaller monasteries in town, along with slightly drab carpet-, incense-, and noodle-making units. (You may want to avoid the months of May–June and Dec, when this resort can become unbearably full and noisy.)

Karadigodu Post, Siddapur, Coorg 571253. ℂ **08274/258-481** or -482. Fax 08274/258-485. www.orange county.in. 59 units. $258 County Cottages; $306 Presidential Villa; $428 Pool Villa; $476 King's Court (4-person suite); $53 extra bed. Rates include all meals and taxes. MC, V. **Amenities:** 2 restaurants; bar; coffee lounge; badminton; boating; cycling; doctor-on-call; fishing; gymnasium; health spa; library; 2 outdoor pools; room service; spice tour; transfer (Rs 6,250 from Bengaluru, Rs 2,250 from Mysore). *In room:* A/C, TV.

Rainforest Retreat ★★ (Finds) When a microbiologist and botanist got together and decided to experiment with organic farming and biological pest-control, little did they realize how interested the rest of the world would be. Anurag and Sujata, soon compelled to make a guest room for a regular stream of friends, are today almost always running full, despite having expanded accommodation within their 9 hectares (22 acres). Tents and cottages are scattered amidst banana, orange bamboo and coffee plants (ask for the striking old brook-side deluxe cottage); no-nonsense accommodation is in keeping with the surroundings and ethos of the place. The rustic dining area with stone tables and benches is where simple home-cooked fare is devoured after long walks (guided walks are included in the price) and the evening bonfire, enjoyed with chilled beer (kept in the river on days when the fridge goes bust). With only solar-power for lights and water heated on coal and fire—this is the real green deal.

P.O. Box 101, Coorg 571201. ℂ **08272/265-638.** www.rainforestours.com. 5 units. 2 Deluxe Cottages with 2 bedrooms each Rs 4,000 (double) Rs 2,000 (single); Plantation cottage with 2 independent rooms Rs 3,000 (double) Rs 1,750 (single); 2 Tents Rs 2,000 (double) Rs 1,500 (single). Rates include all meals, hikes and taxes. MC, V. Open Oct–May. **Amenities:** Solar heating in all rooms and tents; transfer (Rs 300 from Madikeri Bus stand/Rs 2,500 from Mysore/Rs 5,000 from Bengaluru); hot water. *In room:* Fireplace in Plantation Cottage.

3 EXPLORING THE HOYSALA HEARTLAND

Halebid is 220km (136 miles) W of Bengaluru; Belur is 14km (9 miles) SW of Halebid; Sravanabelagola is 85km (53 miles) SE of Belur.

The Hoysalas were ferocious warriors who, despite regular military campaigns, found time to allow their love for the arts to flourish. What remains of this once-powerful dynasty are their beautiful temples, usually commissioned to commemorate their victories or successful covenants made with their gods. Situated at the edge of the Western Ghats, the temples of the once-powerful cities of **Belur** and **Halebid** are often referred to as the "Jewel Boxes" of Hoysala architecture, and are comparable with the religious monuments of Khajuraho (in Madhya Pradesh) and Konark (in Orissa). The artists who created these compact, assiduously sculpted temples demonstrated enormous regard for the rules of proportion, and went to extreme lengths to ensure absolute spatial precision. Exterior temple walls are invariably covered in detailed sculpted decoration, while inside you will discover hand-lathe-turned filigreed pillars and figures with moveable jewelry, also carved from stone. The gods paraded at these temples are over 8 centuries old, yet continue to impress with the vigor with which they carry out their superhuman duties, slaying demons and moving mountains, while celestial maidens admire their reflections in eternally reflecting mirrors.

In quite a different vein, the living pilgrimage center at **Sravanabelagola** is where you will find the world's tallest monolithic sculpture. The statue of Gomateswara, a naked ascetic saint, is the object of one of the biggest Jain pilgrimages in the country—lacking any decoration whatsoever, yet awesome in its sheer grandeur.

To see these highlights of Karnataka's religious heritage, you have to veer off the main drag a little. Fortunately, if you're pressed for time, it is possible to cover all three destinations with ease in a single day. Most visitors base their exploration of this region out of the dull and dusty town of Hassan, but the coffee-growing town of Chikmagalur, 25km (16 miles) from Belur, offers far more glowing surroundings, and the pleasant accommodations of the **Taj Gateway Hotel.**

ESSENTIALS

GETTING THERE & AROUND The most convenient way to see the Hoysala sights is to hire a car and driver in Mysore or even Bengaluru. (It is incidentally possible to see all three main attractions in one long day and return to the better accommodations available in Bengaluru, but should you want to take it a little easier you can overnight in either Hassan or Chikmagalur; see below.) If you don't want to drive from Mysore, a more affordable option is to catch a train from Mysore to Hassan (3 hr. away), from where you can pick up a taxi for a full day of sightseeing (approx. Rs 1,500). Hassan can also be reached overland from Mangalore (see "Traveling Via Mangalore," below). If you need to hire a vehicle in Hassan, we recommend **Mr. Altaf** (✆ **94-4825-6479;** or ask the manager at Hotel Southern Star to give him a call), who offers excellent rates.

VISITOR INFORMATION Visit the friendly **Regional Tourist Office** (Vartha Bhavan, B.M. Rd.; ✆ **08172/26-8862;** 10am–5:30pm, closed Sun and second Sat of the month) if you need to stock up on brochures. You can also deepen your knowledge at Hotel Mayura Velapuri's **Belur Tourist Information Centre** (Temple Rd.; ✆ **08177/22-2209;** daily 9:30am–6:30pm). In Halebid, there's a **Tourist Help Desk** (Mon–Sat 10am–5:30pm) at Hoysalesvara Temple. You can pick up ASI-certified **guides** outside each of the two main temples in Belur and Halebid.

BELUR

Now a sleepy hamlet, Belur was the capital of the Hoysala kings at the height of their reign. The magnificent soapstone **Temple of Lord Channakeshava ★★★** (free admission; daily sunrise–sunset), built over a period of 103 years, was commissioned to commemorate the victory of Vishnuvardhana over the Cholas from Tamil Nadu; apparently, it was so admired by Belur's iconoclastic Muslim invaders that they decided to leave it intact.

Built on a star-shaped plan, the temple stands on a raised platform within a courtyard surrounded by an outer wall. After you survey the courtyard, approach the temple by climbing the short flight of steps. Despite its compact scale, the profusion of carved decoration is spectacular, the multicornered shape of the temple allowing maximum space for sculptures of Vishnu and a vast retinue of Hindu images. Covering the flat-roofed building are detailed representations of myriad themes—ranging from erotica to religious mythology, everyday events to episodes from the *Ramayana*—arranged in bands that wrap the entire exterior in delightful compositions. The temple itself is borne by almost 650 stone elephants. Don't miss the various bracket figures, which are considered the highlight of Hoysala workmanship. Use a torch to study the temple interior, at the center of which is a pillar adorned with smaller versions of the temple's 10,000 sculpted images. Belur is a living temple, and a silver-plated image of Vishnu within the inner sanctum is still worshiped; *puja* (prayer) is performed at 9am and 7pm each day, and the inner sanctums are closed between 1 and 3pm and 5 and 6pm.

Once known as Dwara Samudra, "the gateway to the sea," Halebid usurped Belur's position as the Hoysalan capital in the 12th century. Unfortunately, when the Muslim invaders arrived, Halebid failed to escape their wrath. Appropriately, its current name means "old city," as it consists of only a dusty road and some well-crafted temples amid a lush landscape with the Western Ghats as a distant backdrop. Exquisitely sculpted **Hoysalesvara Temple** ★★★ (free admission; shoe-check Rs 10; sunrise–sunset) is the largest of the Hoysala temples. Hoysalesvara actually consists of two distinct temples resting upon a star-shaped platform, both dedicated to Shiva. It has more complex and detailed carvings than those at Belur. You can discover the 20,000-odd sculptures in and around the temple on your own, or enlist the services of a **guide** (who will approach you as you arrive at the monument; expect to pay around Rs 200, but do include a tip). You can visit the on-site **Archaeological Museum** (Rs 2; Sat–Thurs 10am–5pm) to see more stone statues of Hindu gods, gathered from Halebid and its immediate environs. If you want more of the same, without the touristy vibe, head for **Kedareshvara Temple,** 300m (984 ft.) away and marked by its serene location.

Also in Halebid are several **Jain Bastis** that allude to the religious tolerance of the Hoysala kings, who extended patronage to other faiths. Although lacking the immense carved decoration of the Hindu monuments, **Parswanathasamy Temple** (free admission; daily sunrise–sunset) enjoys a lovely lakeside location.

SRAVANABELAGOLA ★★★

For members of the peace-loving, nonviolent Jain faith, this is one of the oldest and most important pilgrimage centers, famous for its colossal 18m (59-ft.) statue of Lord Gomateswara, said to be the tallest monolithic statue on earth, and reached by climbing the 635 steps that lead to the hill's summit. Naked and imposing, the statue is a symbolic representation of worldly renunciation.

Commissioned in A.D. 981, the **Statue of Gomateswara** ★★★ is a representation of Bahubali. Son of the first Jain Tirthankara Adinatha, Bahubali renounced his kingdom and sought enlightenment by standing naked and motionless for an entire year while contemplating the meaning of life. Seen in detail on the legs of the statue, the creepers and plants twisting their way up his body are symbolic of his motionless mission of spiritual discovery. A special celebration (*Mahamastakabhisheka,* or the Great Annointing) is held here every 12 years, when the giant monolith is bathed with bucketfuls of milk and honey. The next ceremony takes place in 2018.

WHERE TO STAY & DINE

Accommodations close to the temples are limited and hardly the stuff of kings. You'll find a number of government-run hotels in both Belur and Halebid; these have restaurants of questionable quality and extremely basic rooms. In Halebid, the tourism department's **Hotel Mayura Shanthala** (Temple Rd.; 🕿 **08177/27-3224;** doubles Rs 260) is within striking distance of a number of temples, but you get what you pay for (very little). Equally so at Belur's **Hotel Mayura Velapuri** (🕿 **08177/222-209;** doubles Rs 432), located just outside the temple entrance. Better to opt for **Hotel Southern Star Hassan** (🕿 **08172/22-51816** or -51817; www.ushalexushotels.com; doubles from Rs 3,000), which offers pleasant service (including sightseeing advice) and safe dining. It's certainly not luxury level, but guest rooms are comfortable and clean. Views from odd-numbered rooms are of a less built-up part of the town.

(Tips) Traveling Via Mangalore

Once a seaport of some significance, Mangalore is an important center for the processing and export of Karnataka's spices, coffee, and cashews, and known as the *bidi* cigarette capital of the world. (The *bidi*, effectively a roll of dried tobacco leaf, is also known as the "pauper's puff." Apparently 90 people die every hour in India from tobacco-related cancer.) Its greatest significance for travelers is that it makes a convenient pit stop on the section of the Konkan Railway that runs between Goa and Kerala, and provides road access to Belur, Halebid, and Sravanabelgola, as well as Mysore. **The Gateway Hotel** (Old Port Rd. ✆ **0824/666-0420;** www.tajhotels.com; doubles from Rs 4,000) is the best hotel in Mangalore. Accommodations are comfortable, if not particularly luxurious. If you're feeling flush, book a suite with a river-cum-ocean facing view (Rs 8,000). Staff will arrange trips to the beach and local temples, as well as tours of a cashew-nut factory or tours to see how Mangalore's famous red-clay roof tiles are made.

The Gateway Hotel, Chikmagalur ★★ Located just outside the small coffee-growing town of Chikmagalur, this hillside retreat—originally built as a government rest house—is comfortable and idyllically remote, with sloping red-tile roofs echoing the style of the local colonial Malnad plantation homes. Reserve one of the cottages; these have high-pitched ceilings, polished floors, two double beds, and large balconies with scenic views. (Reserve no. 119 for an especially large balcony.) The attached bathrooms are spacious but have showers only. Visits to nearby coffee plantations set off Monday to Saturday at 3:30pm. You can also kick back and allow yourself to be stroked into good health at the Ayurvedic massage center.

K.M. Rd., opposite Pavitravana Jyothinagar Post, Chikmagalur 577 102. ✆ **08262/22-0202** or -0404. Fax 08262/22-0222. www.tajhotels.com. 29 units. Rs 5,700 standard garden view double; Rs 5,900 superior pool-view double; Rs 6,600 cottage mountain view. Rs 900 extra bed. AE, DC, MC, V. **Amenities:** Restaurant; bar; currency exchange; cycling; doctor-on-call; Internet (Rs 150/half hr.); pool; pool table; room service; table tennis. *In room:* A/C, TV, minibar, Wi-Fi (Rs 200/hr./ Rs 600/day).

Hoysala Village With clusters of cottages spread over 2 hectares (5 acres) and surrounded by ample greenery, Hoysala Village is ideal for a 1-night stopover if you don't necessarily want to travel all the way to Chikmagalur. It's not exactly posh and the unimaginative interiors leave much to be desired, but it does have a pool, a bar and decent cuisine—ask for a room or suite in the fourth cluster closer to the pool area, which has a nice patch of garden with hammocks. Given the limited options in hand and the large tourist inflow, it's a blessing, but if you care about your accommodation surroundings, try The Gateway in Chikmagalur.

Belur Rd., Hassan. ✆ **08172/256-764,** -793 or 080/25325302. www.trailsindia.com. info@trailsindia.com. 33 units. Rs 4,000 standard rooms; Rs 4,500 suites. Rates include all meals. AE, DC, MC, V. **Amenities:** Restaurant; bar; airport transfer (Rs 3,500); carom, chess; pool; room service. *In room:* A/C, TV.

4 HAMPI & THE RUINED CITY OF VIJAYANAGAR ★★★

Hampi is 460km (285 miles) NW of Bengaluru and 13km (8 miles) E of Hospet

The surreal, boulder-strewn landscape of Karnataka's hinterland is the backdrop to the largest complex of ruins in India. Hampi, capital of one of India's most formidable empires, the powerful Vijayanagara—whose rule stretched from the Arabian Sea to the Indian Ocean—was home to a population of half a million, and protected by more than a million soldiers. Set in a vast valley sprawling from the banks of the Tungabhadra River, the splendid "City of Victory"—where even the king's horses were adorned in jewels—is now a ghost city with numerous temples, fortification ramparts, stables, royal apartments, and palaces, popular with determined sightseers and trance and rave party disciples. Long popular with Bollywood as a shooting location, Hampi is also where scenes from the 2005 Jackie Chan thriller *The Myth* were shot. Hampi may be a little difficult to get to, but this remoteness is to a large extent its charm. You can easily enjoy 2 or 3 days in this serene atmosphere, particularly if you've booked at **Hampi's Boulders** (see "Where to Stay," below), a comfortable resort within striking distance of the ruins.

ESSENTIALS

GETTING THERE   The overnight **Hampi Express** leaves Bengaluru daily at 10:20pm, arriving in unremarkable Hospet, the nearest town, at 7:40am. From Hyderabad, the Rayalseema Express departs at 5:25pm and arrives early the following morning, at 5:10am. Hampi is 15km (9⅓ miles) away. Taxis charge around Rs 600 for the one-way trip; be sure to negotiate. Hampi is also connected to Goa by an overnight bus service. **Kingfisher Airlines** operates flights from Goa and Bengaluru to Vidyanagar airport at Toranagallu (38km/24 miles from Hospet)—check the website (www.flykingfisher.com) for details.

VISITOR INFORMATION   If you reserve lodging at **Hampi's Boulders** (see "Where to Stay," below), you'll have no better source of information than your host, Bobby. In Hampi Bazaar, the unusually helpful staff at the government-run **tourist office** (© 08394/ 241-339; Apr–May daily 8am–1:30pm, June–Mar daily 10am–1:30pm and 2:15– 5:30pm) can provide information and organize coach bookings (not recommended) and English-speaking guides. At Hotel Malligi (see "Where to Stay," below), you can hire an **audioguide** for around Rs 50. In Hampi, you can pick up information and guides (Rs 500 from the **information office;** © 08394/241-339) on Bazaar Street. If you're a stickler for detail and thorough research, pick up *New Light on Hampi* (Marg Publications) by John M. Fritz and George Michell.

GETTING AROUND   By Taxi & Auto-Rickshaw   Hampi's ruins cover 39 sq. km (15 sq. miles), and should be explored on wheels. Bicycles (for rent in Hampi Bazaar) are fine for the energetic, but only in winter. Taxis (Indicas around Rs 1,000 for a full day, without air-conditioning, or Qualis at Rs 1,800) or even auto-rickshaws (count on Rs 400–Rs 500) are better if you'd rather not deal with maps, heat, and dirt tracks. Do, however, get out on foot whenever you can to soak up the atmosphere.

EXPLORING THE RUINED CITY OF VIJAYANAGARA

For anyone with dreams of Indiana Jones–style adventuring, the Hampi ruins provide the perfect setting—an ancient city with isolated ruins scattered among impossibly balanced wind-smoothed boulders and immense stretches of verdant landscape. Listed as a World Cultural Heritage Site, various excavations have uncovered evidence to suggest that Vijayanagara was occupied as long ago as the 3rd-century-B.C. Mauryan era. During early medieval times, armies were regularly dispatched to the Deccan by the Delhi Sultanate as part of its campaign to establish an empire that would encompass the whole of India. During one such campaign in the early 14th century, the invading forces captured Harihara and Bukka, two princes of Warangal, and took them to Delhi, where they fell in with the Sultanate. This allegiance eventually saw Harihara being crowned king of the region that is today known as Hampi. In celebration, Harihara lay the foundations of Vijayanagara, his new capital, on the southern banks of the Tungabhadra. His brother, Bukka, succeeded him 20 years later and ensured widespread support by issuing an edict that granted all religions equal protection. The monarchs who followed extended patronage to all manner of artists, poets, philosophers, and academics, effectively making Vijayanagara a center of learning that, in its grandeur, captivated visitors from as far away as Arabia, Portugal, and Italy.

The kingdom reached its zenith during the reign of Krishna Deva Raya (1509–29), when international trade flourished under progressive commercial practices and foreign trade agreements. Early accounts of the city tell of its massive fortifications, broad boulevards, grand gateways, efficient irrigation systems, and splendid civic amenities. The kingdom of Vijayanagara fell in 1565 when five allied Deccan sultans laid siege to the city, which they then apparently ransacked—their soldiers looting, killing, and destroying at will.

While some of the individual ruins can only be visited upon purchase of a ticket, most of Hampi is a veritable free-for-all, with tame security in the form of a handful of guards at the major monuments. This means that you can mix and match your itinerary as you see fit, moving between the different locations in a taxi or—if you're up for it—on a bicycle. Before you set off, pick up information or engage the services of an official guide from the government tourist office in Hampi. You can see Hampi's highlights in a morning if you set out early enough. However, it's spread over a vast area, and exploring can be quite exhausting, particularly in the midday heat—don't overdo it, or even the most impressive monuments begin to look like more of the same. In fact, with Virthala Temple now illuminated at night and plans afoot to light up more of Hampi's main monuments, it may be worth returning at twilight.

Hampi Bazaar is a broad, dusty boulevard lined with stalls and restaurants. It leads to the entrance of **Virupaksha Temple ★★★**, which predates the Vijayanagara kingdom yet remains a center of living Hindu faith (even though Hindu idols have been removed from the surrounding temples). Virupaksha's towering *goparum* is lavishly sculpted and rises several stories; within its courtyards, monkeys and children careen around ancient pillars, while a sad-faced temple elephant takes tips for much-rehearsed blessings granted with her trunk. In the far right corner of the complex, tucked within a chamber, look for the shadow of the main *goparum,* which falls—miraculously, it would seem—as an inverted image on the temple wall, created by light passing through a small window. South of Virupaksha Temple is a temple housing a massive **Shiva lingam** (phallic symbol) standing in a pool of water. Carved from a single rock, the lingam is adjacent to a fantastic **monolithic statue of Narasimha ★★**, the man-lion avatar of Vishnu. Although partially damaged, the one-piece carving dating to the early 16th century is one of the finest sculptures at Hampi.

9

Some distance from the bazaar, on a high elevation, is the spectacular **Vitthala Temple ★★★**, dedicated to an incarnation of Vishnu, and one of the most fabulous and famous of Hampi's monuments. One of Hinduism's most enduring images, an ornate **stone chariot ★★★**, is found here. With solid stone wheels that can turn on their axles, the chariot faces a shaded dance hall where ancient musical dramas were once played out and from where you can now enjoy panoramic views of Vijayanagara. The pillars of the temple are commonly referred to as "musical pillars," each one producing a different note when tapped.

Nearby, the **King's Balance** was once a scalelike instrument used to measure out grain or even gold against the weight of the king. The weighed item was then given to the priests (or to the poor, depending on your guide's story).

The **royal enclosure ★** incorporates the ruined palaces where the Vijayanagara kings would have lived and held court. Not much survives, but you can still visit **Hazara Rama Temple,** where the royals went to worship, a small stepped tank, and **Mahanavami Dibba,** a platform where performances and entertainments were held. On the outskirts of the royal complex, you need to buy a ticket to see the *zenana* enclosure, where the two-story Indo-Saracenic pavilion known as **Kamala (Lotus) Mahal ★★** features massive pillars, delicately punctuated arches, and fine stucco ornamentation; its unusual design blends elements of Muslim and Hindu architecture. Within the same enclosure are quarters believed to have been used by Hampi's Amazonian female guards, described by several Portuguese travelers. Just outside the enclosure are the superb domed **Elephant Stables ★★★**.

13km (8 miles) east of Hospet, Belary District. Guides can be hired through the government tourist office in Hampi Bazaar for Rs 300 half-day and Rs 500 full day. Entrance to Virupaksha Temple Rs 2; 6am–12:30pm and 2–8pm. Entrance to both Lotus Mahal and Elephant Stables Rs 220; 8am–6pm. The Hampi Festival takes place Nov 3–5.

WHERE TO STAY

You may come across signposts sporting the name Kishkinda Heritage Resort—it is anything but "heritage" and extremely full in high season with children, thanks to the amusement and water park attached to it. However, **Kishkinda Trust** (✆ 08533/26-7777; http://thekishkindatrust.org) does do some interesting work—cross over to **Anegundi** on the other side of the river, where local people both show off their craftwork as well as how they make it—it's a new initiative, but one well worth supporting. KSTDC's **Hotel Mayura Bhuvaneshwari** at Kamalapuram (✆ 08394/241-574; http://kstdc.net; A/C doubles Rs 1,800) is a much cheaper option (in every sense) to Hampi's Boulders (but useful in case it's full). They can also arrange a Hampi tour (Rs 175).

Hampi's Boulders ★★   Set among the enormous natural boulders that define Karnataka's splendid landscape, this is your best bet in Hampi. Private, remote, and immersed in nature, Boulders is 6km (3¾ miles) from Hampi, reached by crossing the river in a coracle (small boat) after a pleasant half-hour walk or a 10-minute drive. Nearby is a 4,800-hectare (12,000-acre) animal sanctuary, home to wolves, panthers, hyenas, foxes, jackals, sloth bears, and crocodiles. Accommodations in the Executive Cottage are top-notch; living rock boulders bulge through the walls, and the entire structure feels like a miniature castle (where, in the huge bathroom, the "throne" allows the occupant to gaze onto the river). Guest cottages are pleasant, with attached bathrooms and private patios; ambience and furniture simple, but they're still far better than anything else near Hampi, and the setting is unmatched. Meals are served in a semiexposed thatched-roof dining area; there's no menu, but a buffet with a predominantly South-Indian selection is served.

Narayanpet, Bandi Harlapur; P.O., Via Munirabad-R-S, Koppal District and TQ 583 234. Ⓒ/fax **08539/234-774,** or information 94-4803-4202 or 92-4264-1551 and security on 94-4818-9939. 13 units (with showers). Rs 3,000 per person or Rs 6,000 per couple standard non-A/C double; Rs 4,000 per person or Rs 8,000 per couple standard A/C double; Rs 5,000 per person or Rs 10,000 per couple executive double. No credit cards. **Amenities:** Restaurant; birding; doctor-on-call; fishing; play area; pool; guided tours and safaris; beach volleyball.

Hotel Malligi Ⓥalue Long-standing base for visitors to Hampi, this huge campus of guest rooms, restaurants, and modest tourist facilities offers a wide range of accommodations, with the only disadvantage of being almost 45 minutes away from the ruins. Guest rooms are generally comfortable—those in the "super luxury" category are clean, with tiled floors, wood-paneled walls, and very '80s fittings and furniture in shades of brown. At just Rs 220 more, executive suites are slightly more attractive, in shades of gray and blue, with large bathrooms with tubs (not in best shape) and private balconies. Bollywood stars shooting films in the area, however, book only the Honeymoon Suite, where a ceiling mirror hovers over the circular bed. Budget rooms are ridiculously cheap, considering the hotel's amenities (including a pool, essential after a grueling day of sightseeing under the pounding sun), though they offer little in the way of comfort or taste. Ask for the informative CD-ROM on Hampi.

10/90 J.N. Rd., P. B. no. 1, Hospet 583 201. Ⓒ **08394/228-101.** Fax 08394/227-038. www.malligihotels.com. 160 units. Rs 450 non-A/C double; Rs 650 non-AC semi-deluxe double; Rs 1,500 standard double; Rs 2,200 luxury single; Rs 2,800 luxury double room; Rs. 4,500 executive suite. AE, MC, V. **Amenities:** 2 restaurants; bar; airport transfer (Rs 1,100); bookshop; currency exchange; Internet (Rs 60/hr., Rs 360/day); play area; pool; pool table; room service. In room: A/C, TV, minibar (in most rooms).

WHERE TO DINE

Other than Mango Tree (reviewed below) which is a sure bet, there is nothing much to choose from, despite the fact that there is no dearth of makeshift shacklike restaurants in Hampi. Most are adequate and in keeping with the backpacker vibe of the place, serving Indianized versions of global cuisines to cater for the myriad tourists who pass through here—ask for **New Shanti** in the main Hampi Bazaar for probably the best wood-fire pizzas.

Mango Tree ★ Ⓜoments VEGETARIAN Although the food here is simple, the rustic setting is undeniably welcoming. A lovely walk through a banana plantation takes you to an unassuming gateway; enter and you sit under an enormous mango tree with a swing, in the backyard of a local family home, surrounded by boulders, acres of greenery, and kingfishers darting through the air. In front of you, the Tungabhadra River glides by. There's no electricity; you dine sitting on the ground on straw mats at low, portable tables set at terraced levels, while the proprietor, Krishna, and his family wait on you. Start with a special *samosa* with a touch of cream cheese on top, stuffed with tangy tomatoes and chopped potato. Follow it up with a Mango Tree special thali or Mango special curry served on a banana leaf; finish with a cup of *chai* or quench your thirst with a banana coconut lassi.

400m (1,312 ft.) downriver from the main Virupaksha temple tank, Hampi. Ⓒ **94-4876-5213** or 08394/241-944. Meals under Rs 150. No credit cards. Daily 7am–9:30pm.

Waves FUSION Generous portions and plenty of cold beer (not freely found in Hampi) make this a popular if anonymous place to get a wholesome meal while you're in the Hampi area. It's on a covered terrace overlooking Hotel Malligi's pool and is open all day—which makes it a convenient spot to grab breakfast before you set out for the ruins. Stick to the Indian dishes, and be prepared for an invasion of mosquitoes once the sun goes down.

Hotel Malligi, 10/90 J. N. Rd., P. B. no. 1, Hospet. ✆ **08394/228-101.** Most main courses Rs 75–Rs 150. AE, MC, V. Daily 6am–midnight.

5 SIDE TRIP TO NORTHERN KARNATAKA ★★★

If you'd like to get off the principal tourist beat and discover the Deccan's architectural treasures in less-chartered territory, definitely set aside a few more days to explore the splendid remains of the erstwhile **Chalukyan Empire** and—tucked within one of the state's northernmost corners—the Muslim city of **Bijapur,** filled with mosques, minarets, mausoleums, and palace ruins.

The easiest way to get to these sites is to rent a car and driver in Hospet (you can arrange one through Hotel Malligi; Rs 2,600 for a return trip (Hospet to Badami is about 4 hr.); drive to Badami, stopping at Aihole and Pattadakal either on your way in or out. It is quite possible to spend a long day traveling from Hospet or Hampi to all three Chalukya sites, including a stop at **Mahakuteshwara** and **Mallikajuna temples** en route. After that you can either proceed to Bijapur, or return to Hampi before nightfall. If you prefer something a little less hectic, however, overnight in Badami, and then continue your journey the following day. The best accommodations choice is **Hotel Badami Court** (✆ 08357/220-230 through -233). It's located 2km (1¼ miles) from the town center and has a pool and decent air-conditioned rooms with TVs and bathtubs (ask for one of the garden-facing rooms, which are quieter) for around Rs 4,200 including breakfast.

BADAMI, AIHOLE & PATTADAKAL

Around 4 hours by car from Hospet, the remote, modest town of **Badami** was established around A.D. 543 when it became the capital of the Chalukyas, one of the most powerful of the Deccan dynasties. Today its most significant attraction is the complex of **cave temples ★★★** (Rs 220; daily sunrise–sunset) carved into the imposing horseshoe-shaped red-sandstone cliff that once formed a natural fortification at the southern end of the town. Enter the pillared interiors and you'll discover elaborate symbolic and mystical carvings of the highest quality (not to mention a few scampering monkeys). It's worth hiring the services of a guide (around Rs 200 for up to 3 hr.) to gain some understanding of the symbolism. Also worth exploring are the **Bhutanatha temples,** built over 4 centuries at a picturesque location at the edge of the Agastyatirtha water tank; and atop the hill, 7th-century **Malegitti Shivalya Temple,** unusually decorated with dwarfs, geese, and various geometric patterns. Time allowing, stop at the **Archaeological Museum** (✆ 08357/22-0157; Rs 2; Sat–Thurs 10am–5pm) to see well-preserved sculpted panels depicting the life of Krishna, and the **Lajja Gauri** sculpture, an extraordinary fertility cult symbol. Less than 30km (19 miles) from Badami, en route to Aihole, is the small settlement of **Pattadakal** and its UNESCO World Heritage–listed **temple complex ★★★** ($10; daily sunrise–sunset), where Chalukyan temple architecture reached its zenith in the 7th and 8th centuries. Some, like Papanatha Temple built around A.D. 680, are in the northern Indo-Aryan style, while others, like the main Virupaksha Temple built 80 years later, are in the South Indian Dravidian architectural style, with tiered pyramidal rather than conical roofs. A dance festival is held at Pattadakal each January. (Note that if you're **399** pressed for time, the Pattadakal stop can be skipped.)

About 17km (11 miles) away, the riverbank village of **Aihole ★★★** is strewn with some 70 abandoned temples, built between A.D. 450 and 650 as architectural experiments by the early Chalukyan kings. Historians theorize that these obsessive rulers had a guild of architects, artists, and artisans working for them, and the variety of styles, including the Gupta (northern), incipient Dravidian, and elements of Buddhist architecture, reflect the various stages in the development of Chalukyan architecture. The chief attraction among these, fashioned along the lines of a Buddhist *chaitya* (prayer hall), is **Durga Temple ★★★**, with its magnificent circular colonnaded veranda studded with stunning sculptures and intricate carving. Contrast this with the Jain **Meguti Temple ★★** situated atop a nearby hill—with an inscription putting its construction at A.D. 634, this was perhaps the last temple to be built in Aihole.

The interiors aren't lighted, so you should carry a flashlight—the detailing is well worth studying. In some temples, you'll discover images of fierce Chalukyan warriors in action, while elsewhere, amorous couples engage in a different sort of action. Admission to the main complex of temples is free; entrance to Durga Temple is Rs 90. Hours are daily sunrise to sunset.

BIJAPUR

The walled city of **Bijapur,** in the far north of Karnataka, is often referred to as the "Agra of the South" because of its profusion of Muslim architecture. First founded during the reign of the Chalukyan dynasty, between the 10th and 11th centuries, Bijapur passed into Muslim rule and later into the hands of the Bahamani kings. When these rulers fell into decline, the city was taken over by its governor, Yusuf Adil Khan, the founder of the Adil Shahi dynasty, who established rule over the Deccan during the 16th and 17th centuries, with Bijapur as their capital. Muslim mausoleums, mosques, palaces, pavilions, and *burkha*-clad women will remind you that this is a city unlike any other in Karnataka. Head to the very helpful local **tourism office** (Station Rd.; ✆ 08352/250-359; daily 10am–5:30pm) to hire a guide and get assistance with sightseeing. Monuments are open from sunrise to sunset and entry is free except where listed. Within the fortified **Citadel** in the city center lie the remains of royal structures, including **Anand Mahal** (Pleasure Palace), and **Saat Manzil.** Outside Saat Manzil is beautiful **Jal Mandir,** or water pavilion, now dry, so you can admire its carvings and porticos. Not far away (near the tourist office) is incomplete **Bara Kaman** ("12 Arches"), the roofless tomb of Ali Adil Shah II—a wonderful piece of architecture comprising 12 arches—surrounded by a garden.

Outside the Citadel's walls, near the edge of the city, is **Ibrahim Rouza ★★★**, the gorgeously proportioned and heavily decorated mausoleum of Ibrahim Adil Shah II and his wife, Taj Sultana (admission Rs 90; daily 6am–6pm; leave shoes outside). Ignore the garbage dump near the entrance and admire what is considered the most beautiful Muslim structure in the Deccan, featuring richly engraved walls and inscribed ornamental stone windows. Move on to **Gol Gumbaz ★★★**, the world's second-largest dome (after St. Peter's in Rome), atop the mausoleum of 17th-century sultan Muhammad Adil Shah (Mahatma Gandhi Rd.; admission Rs 220, video cameras Rs 2,200; leave shoes outside; daily 6am–6pm). Renowned for its remarkable engineering and stereophonic acoustics, the Gol Gumbaz can get noisy as visitors test the echo effect created by the massive dome—multiple distinct echoes are said to be produced for each sound uttered in the whispering gallery upstairs. Most visitors don't bother to whisper, however, which may leave you with an experience akin to an auditory hallucination. As is the case with the

Taj, try to arrive as soon as the gates open for the most atmospheric visit. It's worth scaling the 115 steps to reach the dome's terrace for the excellent views of the formal gardens and tombs.

Jami Masjid (free admission; daily 6am–6pm), close to Gol Gumbaz, is the city's other major attraction. Also incomplete, this is the largest mosque in the region, dating back to A.D. 1576, when Ali Adil Shah I reigned. Consisting of a large dome and gorgeous white arcaded bays, this impressive mosque is spread over some 10,000 sq. m (107,639 sq. ft.).

Where to Stay & Dine in Bijapur

Hotel Madhuvan International   Bijapur's "top" business hotel doesn't offer the luxuries you might expect in cities catering to substantial numbers of Western visitors (hence also the low price). Accommodations are comfortable enough, however, and some rooms have views of Gol Gumbaz. You can organize your sightseeing through the hotel, and take meals in the relaxing garden restaurant (which serves only vegetarian food, by the way).

Station Rd., Bijapur 586 104. © **08352/25-5571** through -5573. Fax 08352/25-6201. www.hotelmadhuvan. com. 36 units. Rs 2,025 non-A/C double; Rs 2,475 A/C double. Taxes extra. MC, V. **Amenities:** Restaurant; doctor-on-call; room service. *In room:* AC, TV.

---

6 HYDERABAD

490km (304 miles) N of Bengaluru

Named after Hyder Mahal, wife of Muhammad Quli, a 16th-century ruler of the Qutb Shahi dynasty, Hyderabad was one of the largest and wealthiest of India's former princely states. The city built its fortune on the trade of pearls, gold, steel, fabric, and, above all, diamonds, which some believe remain hidden beneath the foundations of **Golconda Fort,** precursor to the city some 10km (6¼ miles) away. Once the most famous diamond mining area in the world, Golconda was where the 108-carat Koh-i-Noor diamond (not to mention the Orloff, Regent, and Hope diamonds) was excavated. It was in fact Golconda's legendary wealth that attracted the attention of the voracious Mughal emperor Aurangzeb, and with the aid of an inside agent he captured the fortress in 1687. Aurangzeb's invasion marked the temporary decline of the city, but when the Mughal empire began to fade, the enterprising local viceroy, Asaf Jah I, promptly proclaimed himself *Nizam,* and established independent rule over the Deccan state. Under the notoriously opulent Nizams of the Asaf Jahi dynasty, their power cemented by an alliance forged in 1798 with the British East India Company, Hyderabad again became a major influence, and even contributed to the British military campaigns against the recalcitrant Tipu Sultan of Mysore.

Hyderabad is more than 400 years old, but today the state capital of Andhra Pradesh is as famous for its burgeoning information technology and biotech research industries as it is for its minarets, and it is precisely this stark contrast that makes it such an appealing destination. Like Bengaluru, this is one of India's fastest-growing cities, with a projected population of 7.5 million by 2015, and a substantial part of the city is the almost overnight growth of the vast suburb of **Cyberabad,** where Microsoft and Oracle are but two major players in the development also known as Hi-Tech City, responsible for the city's economic upswing. Yet, despite its newfound attractiveness as a business destination, the city remains steeped in history, and you're just as likely to share the road with camels and bullock carts, and haggle alongside Muslim women covered from head to toe in black *burkhas,* as you are to converse with cellphone-wielding yuppies. There may not be much by way of specific sights to see in Hyderabad, but it has a vibrant culture, excellent-value luxury hotels, and a heavenly cuisine—perhaps the most enduring legacy of the decadent tastes and patronage of the cultured *Nizams* who first put the city on the map.

ESSENTIALS

GETTING THERE & AWAY   Hyderabad is pretty much smack-dab in the middle of very little else, so you're best off flying in. In fact, you might want to kick off your South India trip from here, with British Air flying direct to Hyderabad from Heathrow, and plenty of connecting flights to Hyderabad available through European hubs such as Amsterdam and Frankfurt, and also through Middle Eastern cities such as Dubai and Doha. There are also plenty of domestic flights connecting the city with every major destination in India including a number of daily (2-hr.) flights from and to Delhi as well as Bengaluru, Mumbai, Kolkata, Chennai, and Tirupati (see Tamil Nadu). The **Rajiv Gandhi International Airport** (Shamshabad; www.hyderabad.aero; ℂ 040-66546370 airport; **1407** for Indian Airlines inquiries, **142** for recorded flight information) is 35km (22 miles) north of the city; a taxi into town should cost between Rs 500 and Rs 650. **Trains** to and from Bengaluru, Tirupati, Chennai, and Mumbai take at least 14 hours; book an overnight journey, and make it several days in advance (As a rule, air-conditioned coaches are preferable to the ordinary in terms of cleanliness and food but the latter are far more entertaining, if you can bear the smell). There are two main stations: Nampally (also known as Hyderabad Deccan) and Secunderabad, with most longer-distance trains arriving at the latter. Call ℂ **1345** for specific information about outbound services.

VISITOR INFORMATION   For the lowdown on sights, tours, and events, visit **Andhra Pradesh Travel & Tourism Development Corporation** (ℂ 040/2329-8456; open 24 hr.), on the corner where Secretariat Road becomes Tank Bund. Avoid **Andhra Pradesh Tourism** right next door; the stench that hangs in the air from the fish market nearby competes with the staff's incompetence; you could fare better by calling their 24/7 help line (ℂ 040/2345-0444). The railway stations also have information counters. *Big Hyderabad* (Rs 30) is a monthly booklet listing a wealth of information about the twin cities of Hyderabad and Secunderabad. *CityInfo* (www.hyderabadcityinfo.com) appears every 2 weeks and provides extensive information about hotels, restaurants, and current events, as does *Go Hyderabad* (monthly; Rs 15).

If you want to do some serious reading up on Hyderabad other than the brochures supplied by the Tourism Department, then try two of the bigger and better bookstores in the city—**Walden** (6-3-871 Greenlands Rd., Begumpet; ℂ 040/2341-3434 with a branch at Trendset Towers, Road No. 2, Banjara Hills; ℂ 040/2335-1613; open daily) and **A. A. Husain & Co.** (5-8-551 Abid Rd.; ℂ 040/2320-3724; closed Sun).

Useful numbers: For **24-hour pharmacies,** call **Apollo Hospital** (ℂ 040/2323-1380; www.apollohospitals.com) or **Care Hospital** (ℂ 040/2323-4444; www.carehospitals. com). The local **telephone search engine** (ℂ 040/2444-4444) is extremely helpful in providing phone numbers and addresses of almost everything in the city.

GETTING AROUND   Actually comprising the twin cities of Hyderabad and Secunderabad, Hyderabad is spread over a vast area, and its few sights are scattered, so you're best off renting a car and driver for a half or full day. See **SOTC** (details below) for 24-hour car-hire service; or call **Easy Cabs** (© **040/4343-4343;** www.easycabs.com); a half day tour costs between Rs 700 and Rs 1400, doubling for a full day extension.) Aside from this the Old City is best explored on foot.

GUIDED TOURS & TRAVEL AGENTS The **Andhra Pradesh Travel & Tourism Development Corporation** (see "Visitor information," above) runs full-day guided tours of the city (Rs 270) and 3-day trips to Tirupati (Rs 1,750 including a night's accommodations). There are also daily tours to Nagarjuna Sagar (150km/93 miles away; Rs 450; only on the weekend), where excavations during the construction of a dam revealed an ancient Buddhist site. All the salvaged structures and antiques are now housed in a museum on an island. SOTC (3-5-874 Hyderguda Rd.; © **040/6699-9922;** www.sotc. in Mon–Sat 10am–6pm) can make all your travel, sightseeing, and car-hire arrangements. For alternate quotes, call **Sai Bon Voyage** (© **98-8562-8111** or 040/6684-3333; www.saibonvoyage.com).

WHAT TO SEE & DO

To see Hyderabad in a day, first drive to **Qutb Shahi Tombs** (9:30am–6:30pm; closed Fri), where Hyderabad's dynastic rulers are buried. The tombs, built in grey granite with stucco ornamentation, are an interesting mix of Persian, Pathan, and Hindu styles. Standing at the center of its own garden, Sultan Muhammed Quli Qutb Shah's tomb is considered the most impressive. Built around the same time as his tomb, the mortuary bath **(Hamaam)**—where the dead were washed before being laid to rest—lies at the center of the enclosure. From here, consider walking to **Golconda Fort;** have your driver show you the route, which is about 2km (1¼ miles) and takes you through lively villages where you may even be invited in for a cup of *chai* and a chat. Allow at least an hour to explore the ruins of the historic citadel, arranging for your driver to pick you up at the entrance.

Next, head to **Charminar,** a four-sided archway with soaring minarets. It was laid out by Muhammad Quli Qutb Shah as the centerpiece of a great new city when Golconda's disease epidemics forced him to move his seat to the banks of the Musi River. Explore the Old City quarter on foot, heading westward into **Laad Bazaar ★★★**, where double-story houses with tiny wooden shutters line narrow lanes. Wandering through these perpetually congested narrow lanes, you'll encounter numerous *burkha*-wearing women scanning the stalls for bargains, and you're likely to score a deal on anything from old saris, pearls, *bidi* (surface ornamentation) work, and silver and gold jewelry to paper kites, henna, turmeric, and cheap china. *Lac* bangles, made from shellac encrusted with shiny, colorful stones, are a Hyderabadi specialty that you'll find in huge quantities here. It's also where the people of Hyderabad go to buy traditional bridal wear, or *Khopdia Joda,* consisting of a *kurta* pajama, *choli,* and *ghunghat.*

When you've had your fill of the Old City, the interiors of **Salar Jung Museum** are a cool diversion, filled with an unprecedented assortment of kitschy collectibles and works of art (see below). Also interesting for antiques-lovers is **Purani Haveli,** near the Salar Jung Museum, where several *Nizams* were born and lived. When Nawab Mir Mehboob Ali Khan, the sixth *Nizam,* lived here, he had a 73m-long (240-ft.) wooden chamber built with 150 huge cupboards (probably the world's largest walk-in closet), to stock his extensive collection of fine clothing and shoes (also called Nizam's Museum; Rs 70; Sat–Thurs 10am–6pm). Even better is the **Chowmohalla Palace ★** (daily 10:30am–5pm; Admission Rs 150), located near Charminar. Other than the enlightening photographs and other memorabilia of the Nizams (including vintage cars, amazing collection of weapons and even the original bedroom) spread through four palaces, the complex with its lovely courtyards and fountains is now used increasingly for traditional music soirees in Urdu and Persian. Next up, visit India's second-largest mosque (purportedly the seventh largest in the world): **Mecca Masjid** (Kishan Prasad Rd., near Charminar) is said to have been built with a few bricks brought from Mecca, and attracts thousands of worshipers during *Namaaz,* Friday prayers. It's off-limits to non-Muslims during prayers, but visitors are welcome at other times. Leave your shoes with an attendant before making your way through a long room that houses the tombs of the Nizams of the Asaf Jahi dynasty. Non-Muslims cannot enter the prayer hall but can view proceedings through a screen. In Gulzar Hauz is **Jami Masjid,** Hyderabad's oldest functioning mosque, dating back to 1597.

Round off the day by watching the sun set over Cyberabad from white-marble **Birla Mandir** ★ (Kalabahad Hill; free admission; daily 6am noon and 3–9pm). Commissioned by the Birlas, India's foremost industrial magnates, the main temple is dedicated to Lord Venkateshwara, and is pleasantly free of greedy "guides" and the like. Perched on a hilltop, it looks beautiful when lit at night.

While moving around the city, it is virtually impossible to not cross the main 16th-century **Hussain Sagar** (lake). While portions of it are not so enticing (giving out a sewage-like smell), there are cleaner and more charming areas which have become hotspots for the more trendy and upmarket local crowd. In the middle of the lake is a massive 18-meter-high (60 ft.) monolithic statue of Lord Buddha. Boat rides from different points on the lake-hugging **Necklace Road** take you to the rock on which the statue has been affixed (speedboat Rs 160 for four persons; ferry Rs 30).

If you're here for another day, consider a half-day excursion to the **Ramoji Film City** (Rs 300; be there before 2pm) for an amusing and interesting exposure to the South Indian film industry. It's packed with local star-struck tourists, and you have a good chance of coming face to face with the top actors of the day—one of their song-and-dance sequences may just be the highlight of the trip. (Check to see what's on by calling ✆ **040/2341-2262;** www.ramojifilmcity.com.) If all you want is to find yourself in a green lung, the best option lies in the middle of the city: The semiforested **KBR Park** is a wonderful place for an early morning walk.

Golconda Fort ★★ Sitting at an elevated height on the outskirts of Hyderabad, Golconda—seat of the Qutb Shahis—was once a magnificent citadel and center of the world diamond trade. The fort took 62 years to build, and when it fell to Aurangzeb in 1687, he tore the place apart looking for diamonds and gold. Left to the birds of prey that circle high above the once-daunting battlements, Golconda would have become a tranquil retreat were it not for its popularity with visitors, who noisily explore the ramparts of Hyderabad's most illustrious attraction. That's why it's best if you visit it as soon as it opens, or around twilight (when it's far cooler and the dimming evening sky sheds a mysterious aura over the stone ruins).

Enclosing the graffiti-smeared remains of bazaars, homes, fields, barracks, armories, mosques, camel stables, Turkish baths, and water reservoirs, the battlements incorporate 87 bastions and extend some 5km (3 miles) in circumference. Four of the original eight gates are still in use; present-day visitors enter via the **Bala Hissar gate**—large teakwood doors with metal spikes designed to withstand charging elephants. Guides can assist by demonstrating the tremendous acoustics of the structure—a clap here is heard clearly when you are at the fort's highest point, 1km (½ mile) away; this was once an invaluable security-cum-intercom system. The Royal Palace complex comprises buildings constructed by the Qutb

Tips   Getting a Good Guide

You'll be confronted by many would-be guides at the entrance to the Golconda Fort—ask around for **M. D. Rathmath** or **Shaikh Rajiv,** who both have a good grasp of English. The going rate is around Rs 350 for 2 to 3 hours (you could up this to Rs 450 if the service is really good). At the end of the day, the guides gather on the lawn outside the fort entrance, near the ticket booth; join them if you're interested in learning more about Hyderabad culture.

Shahi kings during different periods. Most are decorated with floral designs, glazed tilework on the walls, and cut-plaster decorations indicative of the Qutb Shahi style. Sadly, where royalty once went about their daily lives, rats, bats, garbage, grime, and tourists have taken over. At the top of the fort is the **Baradari,** reached by three stone stairways. As you make your way up, look along the walls for the remains of limestone pipes once part of a sophisticated plumbing system that used Persian wheels to carry water up the hill, so that it could be piped in for bathing, flushing cistern systems, and keeping the palace cool. The climb to the top is worth it for the excellent views alone.

The fort hosts an extremely popular **sound-and-light show** that recounts the history of Golconda using the illuminated ruins as a backdrop. There are performances in English each night; but be warned that power failures can disrupt the performance—and be sure to take insect repellent.

Situated 6km (3³/₄ miles) west of the city. ℂ **040/2351-2401.** Admission Rs 100. Tues–Sun 10am–7pm. English sound-and-light show: Admission Rs 40. Mar–Oct daily 7–8pm; Nov–Feb daily 6:30–7:30pm. Tickets available 30 min. before the show; line up early.

Salar Jung Museum ★★★   Marketed as the world's largest private collection of art, artifacts, and antiques, this eclectic assortment of more than 30,000 different exhibits was assembled by Salar Jung III, who served as prime minister *(wazir)* to the Nizam of Hyderabad. It's a truly fascinating collection—particularly the textiles and fine art section, which includes a fine collection of Indian miniature paintings demonstrating the evolution of styles and the differences between Rajput, Deccan, Pahari, and Mughal paintings, though the displays are somewhat disorganized. One of the most valuable pieces must be a 9th-century edition of the *Koran,* written in beautiful Kufic script. The weaponry collection includes a diamond-encrusted sword used ceremonially by the Salar Jungs, as well as pieces used by Mughal emperors. There's something to be said for the sheer profusion of design objects, ranging from boxes studded with precious gems and vessels blown from Indo-Persian glass to a chair made of solid ivory, a gift from Louis XV to Tipu Sultan. In one room, large crowds are drawn to a famous musical clock with a toy watchman who emerges from behind a door every hour in time to beat a melodious gong. Give yourself at least 90 minutes to explore.

C. L. Badari, Malakpet. ℂ **040/2452-3211.** www.salarjungmuseum.in. Admission Rs 150. Sat–Thurs 10am–5pm, 4:15pm last entry. There is also a separate entrance to view the famed jewels of the *Nizams* for which the admission is Rs 500, Sat–Thurs 11am–6pm. Cameras not allowed.

WHERE TO STAY

At press time, exquisite **Falaknuma Palace** (Tank Bund Rd.), a work of astonishing architectural opulence that has hosted the likes of King George V, was in the process of being converted into a heritage hotel by the Taj hotel group. This is likely to be the best place to stay in Hyderabad when it opens in 2011; visit www.tajhotels.com for ongoing developments. Other than our recommendations below, you could opt for **Green Park** (Begumpet; ℂ **040/2375-7575;** www.hotelgreenpark.com; doubles from Rs 6,250), which is very good value for its location and excellent service and facilities—all that's missing is a pool.

Aalankrita ★★ (Value) A doctor couple infatuated with antique furniture went on a buying spree almost a decade ago until they found they had no more space to keep their treasured finds, so they bought some land, built one room styled as a typical village house, with antique stairs, frames, and doors—all this multiplied, and today they own a full-blown resort. Lovely antiques, mostly from the Chettinad region in Tamil Nadu, Kerala, and Rajasthan, are in all the rooms (sadly a dearth of art), and there's also an Ayurvedic massage center, beautiful gardens, friendly staff, and good cuisine. Accommodation is available as independent cottages (Gruha) as well as rooms in a main block (Devkrupa). Designed to resemble a village, it's replete with a traditional *mandapam,* where Indian marriages can take place—if you'd rather not become an inadvertent wedding guest, check before confirming your booking.

20 min. from Secunderabad Club, Shameerpet Rd., Thumkunta Village, Shameerpet Mandal, R.R. District 500 078. ℂ **08418-247464/161/162.** Fax 08418-247013/014. www.aalankrita.com. 112 units. Rs 3,000 standard room; Rs 3,500 executive room; Rs 3,750 studio cottage; Rs 4,000 penthouse; Rs 4,500 deluxe cottage; Rs 8,500 crystal suite; Rs 12,000 presidential suite; Rs 1,000 extra bed. Rates include breakfast and taxes. AE, MC, V. **Amenities:** 3 restaurants; lounge bar; airport transfer (Rs 1,250); arts and crafts gallery; Internet (Rs 100/hr.); meditation center; playground; outdoor pool. *In room:* A/C, TV, minibar, Wi-Fi (on request).

Hyderabad Marriott Hotel & Convention Centre ★★ (Value) Yet another bid to appeal to their target—the business traveler—Marriott now boasts the largest convention center in the country. Given its location next to the Hussain Sagar Lake, it's almost

---

Asthmatics Say "Aaah!"

One of the world's largest alternative medicinal gatherings takes place annually at **Nampally Exhibition Grounds** in Hyderabad, usually on June 7 or 8. Just as the monsoon sets in and brings with it all sorts of seasonal respiratory illnesses, hundreds of thousands of asthmatics from all over India flock to the city to receive an unusual cure administered orally by the Bathini Goud brothers. A special herbal medicine, prepared by using water from the family well only, is stuffed into the mouth of a 2- or 3-inch *murrel* (sardine). The fish is then slipped into the patient's mouth, who swallows the slithering creature alive (the Gouds claim that the wriggling fish increases the efficacy of the medicine because it clears the patient's throat; for those who are strict vegetarians or particularly squeamish, a banana acts as a substitute, albeit a poor one). The result: For more than 162 years, countless people have reported relief from a variety of respiratory-type disorders. Said to have been given to an ancestor of the present-day Gouds by a Hindu holy man back in 1845, the secret formula has been passed down through the generations and administered free of charge in accordance with the saint's wishes. Visit **www.bathinifish.com** for details.

a sure shot that most rooms will have a good view. Combine that with plush decor, prompt service, and the recently introduced Revive bed—sink into luxurious comfort bedecked in the finest linen and designer duvets—and you've got a good deal in hand, albeit in an environment repeated everywhere in the world. As the rooms are a little small, you may want to fork out a little extra to stay at the exclusive executive level, with a very beautiful lounge offering all possible amenities to pamper you and spacious rooms done in earthy tones, dark wood and marble.

Opposite Hussain Sagar Lake, Tank Bund Rd., Hyderabad 500 080. © **040/2752-2999.** Fax 040/2752-8888. http://marriott.com. 293 units. Doubles from $212–$273. Rates include breakfast. AE, MC, V. **Amenities:** 2 restaurants; bar; airport transfer (Rs 3,385); doctor-on-call; fitness center; pool; Wi-Fi (Rs 441/hr., Rs 882/day). In room: A/C, TV, hair dryer, Internet broadband connection (Rs 414/hr., Rs 827/day).

Ista ★★   As you drive to this brand-new business hotel, an amazing paradox greets you—massive cranes shape steel-and-chrome giants for the biggest companies in the world, amid century old boulders and shrubbery dotting the landscape—it is by far the most interesting place to stay if you want to be anywhere near what is shaping up to be as the future Hyderabad. Under the flagship of the award winning Ananda in the Himalayas, Ista is spread over 7 hectares (17 acres) of greenery and boulders. It's functional and smart, although a wee bit dull. Rooms are a bit small and need better soundproofing—opt for the luxury category which come with porches, wooden floors, large walk-in closets, stylish lighting, and for once, a terrific office chair at the desk. It may be a good half-hour away from the city but you have the best spa in town to come back to!

Rd. no. 2, I.T. Park, Gachi Bowli Hyderabad 500 019. © **040/4450-9999.** Fax 040/4450-8888. www.ista hotels.com. 160 units. Rs 15,000 premium; Rs 16,000 deluxe; Rs 19,000 luxury; Rs 25,000 deluxe suite; Rs 33,000 luxury suite; taxes extra. All rooms include breakfast; except for premium, others offer complimentary Wi-Fi, transfers, cocktails, and laundry. AE, DC, MC, V. **Amenities:** 2 restaurants; bar; tea lounge; airport transfer (Rs 1,100); concierge; currency exchange; doctor-on-call; health club; heated pool; room service; spa with steam and sauna. In room: A/C, TV, minibar; Wi-Fi (Rs 120/hr., Rs 600/day).

ITC Hotel Kakatiya Sheraton & Towers ★★★   Not as opulently over-the-top as Taj Krishna, this hotel is billed as the best business hotel in town. Public spaces are smartly decorated in a vibrant and culturally evocative assortment of objets d'art typical of the region—decorative silver *bidri* pieces, detailed frescoes, and elegant furniture in rich fabrics. Guest rooms are wonderfully spacious; even the cheapest corporate rooms are large and nicely finished (twins only). The best views are of Hussain Sagar Lake, the city, and the pool (book a room with a number ending in 01, 03, 05, 11, 17, or 19 for the least obstructed view). The atmosphere here is one of down-to-earth sophistication. Staff is friendly and helpful, if not always on the ball.

Begumpet, Hyderabad 500 016. © **040/2340-0132.** Fax 040/2340-1045. www.welcomgroup.com. 188 units. Rs 16,500 executive club double; Rs 23,500 Sheraton Tower; Rs 30,000 ITC One; Rs 26,000–Rs 70,000 suite. Tower rooms and suites include breakfast and happy hour. AE, MC, V. **Amenities:** 3 restaurants; 2 bars; tea pavilion; patisserie; airport transfer (Rs 2,300); concierge; currency exchange; doctor-on-call; health club; pool with Jacuzzi; room service. In room: A/C, TV, minibar, Wi-Fi (Rs 300/hr., Rs 600/day).

Taj Krishna ★★★   Situated in the upmarket suburb of Banjara Hills, Hyderabad's most luxurious hotel has some of the city's most exclusive restaurants (see "Where to Dine," below), its best nightlife option, and proximity to shopping outlets. Fashioned to emulate the opulence and (sometimes high-kitsch) style of an Indian palace with sumptuous arches, *zardozi* (embroidered) panels, cuddapah stone with mother-of-pearl inlaid marble pillars, its lobby is packed full of ornately engraved mirrors, rococo marble statues, Asian vases, an original French gold-encrusted ornamental grandfather clock, and a

(Tips) Best Biryani ★★★

Available practically anywhere, Biryani is best enjoyed with a spicy *mirch ka salan* (chili curry) and yogurt salad; lately, however, most of the restaurants are taking a shortcut and cooking *biryani* in open cauldrons—although tasty, it's not quite the same thing. Try **Azizia,** adjacent the Nampally railway station: It is said to be the home of *biryani,* and its chefs claim to be descended from the *Nizams'* master chefs; alternatively try **Paradise** (Paradise Circle, M.G. Rd.), **Café Bahar** in Himayatnagar, Shadab or **Medina,** in the Old City (we actually preferred the *biryani* in these places more than at the top-end restaurants—and that too at a fraction of the cost!).

fountain spouting water into a dark marble koi pond. Rooms are elegantly appointed with fine linens, old-world paintings, and some with chandeliers. The lake and pool facing suites on the Taj Club floors are the best, with a host of amenities. (*Note:* Bear in mind that the Taj group has a cheaper, less opulent but comfortable brother in town.)

Rd. no. 1, Banjara Hills, Hyderabad 500 034. (C) 040/6666-2323 or 040/2339-2323. Fax 040/6666-1313. www.tajhotels.com. 261 units. $375 deluxe double; $480 Taj Club (includes breakfast and airport pickup); $715 deluxe suite; $900 luxury suite; $1,500 presidential suite. AE, MC, V. **Amenities:** 4 restaurants; bar; tea lounge; nightclub; airport transfer (Rs 1,900); badminton (by arrangement); concierge; currency exchange; doctor-on-call; golf (by arrangement); health club; Internet (Rs 200/hr., Rs 600/day); outdoor pool; room service; squash (by arrangement). *In room:* A/C, TV, minibar, Wi-Fi (Rs 200/hr., Rs 600/day).

WHERE TO DINE

In Hyderabad, food is as important as life itself (a world-view no doubt inherited from the *Nizams,* who reveled in culinary intemperance) and known for its *dum*-style cooking (its origins in Lucknow): the practice of sealing the pot or dish and gently simmering its ingredients over a slow fire, thereby increasing the absorption of aromatic spices. Lavishly decorated in vibrant blues and distinctively Hyderabadi objets d'art, **Dum Pukht ★★★** (ITC Kakatiya Sheraton & Towers; (C) 040/2340-1032; www.welcomgroup.com; Rs 550–Rs 1,500) is the city's most celebrated upmarket restaurant, and known for its *dum*-style dishes. (*Dum Pukht* literally means cooking by locking in steam.) Try the chef's *kareli ki nahari,* mutton shanks cooked in their own juices and marrow, tinged with cardamom and saffron. Melt-in-the-mouth *kakori* kebabs prepared from finely minced mutton, green papaya, cloves, and cinnamon are skewered, chargrilled, and eaten with *sheermal,* saffron-and-milk-infused flaky bread.

One of the best examples of *dum*-style cooking is *biryani,* Hyderabad's most time-honored dish, best made with marinated mutton which, together with basmati rice and spices, is prepared in a sealed pot for an aromatic result—see tip box below/above.

Finish your meal with Hyderabad's famous desserts: *khubani ka meetha* (apricots and cream) or *double ka meetha* (bread pudding with cashews and almonds). Another place that serves authentic *biryani,* this time in an elegant atmosphere, is **Firdaus ★★★** (Taj Krishna, Rd. no. 1, Banjara Hills; (C) 040/6666-2323; www.tajhotels.com; Rs 500–Rs 1,600). Another good meal here is the *raan-e-firdaus:* tender lamb steak marinated in assorted spices and tandoor grilled. But really, all the meals are fit for a *Nizam,* especially enjoyed against a backdrop of live *ghazal* music. Also in Banjara Hills, on Road no. 1, is a three-in-one restaurant: At **Fusion 9** you can select food from nine different parts of

Watering Holes

Some of the hippest bars have been around for several years and seem to be getting better with age, much like the wine they serve. **Touch** (Trendest Towers, Rd. no. 2, Banjara Hills; © **040/2354-2422;** cover Rs 1,000/on Sat; 7pm–midnight) is an absolute knockout, drawing the trendiest crowd and celebs yet keeping the media at bay. **10 Downing Street** is even more popular but less self-conscious; it's a great place even for singles and belts out rock music on most days with karaoke on Thursdays. (My Home Tycoon Bldg., Begumpet; © **040/6662-9323;** cover Rs 700 on Sat; 11am–11pm). Even if you aren't bunking at the Taj Krishna, drop in at **Ahala** (© **040/6666-2323;** cover Rs 1,200 per couple on weekends; Wed Ladies Night/Fri Corporate Night; 6pm–midnight)—a gorgeous lounge for a casual and classy evening, although we have seen it getting quite frenetic, in a fun way!

the world. **Deli 9** is famous for its deliciously rich pastries—after polishing off a few Norwegian pork chops or tenderloin steak, order the must-have Black Magic pastry (© **040/6550-6662**).

If you're keen to sample more regional Andhra cuisine without forever losing your sense of taste (it is intensely fiery), take a table at **Chutney's** (© **040/2335-8484;** Shilpa Arcade Rd. no. 3, Banjara Hills) to sample their *pesarattu* (spiced mung bean flour pancake) eaten with *allam pachadi* (ginger pickle). Better still, make your way to the first floor and take your pick of a huge variety of vegetarian dishes from North and South India at their reasonably priced all-you-can-eat daily buffet spread (Rs 167). Another value-for-money restaurant is **Abhiruchi** on S.D. Road (**040/2789-6565** or -2227). It has superfast service and excellent food for dirt-cheap prices—along with the thali, order the *mutton gongura* as a side dish (a spinachlike leaf that grows in Andhra mixed with goat meat).

One of the best buffets in town is at **Collage** ★ (© **040/4450-8888;** www.istahotels. com), the coffee shop at Ista. With its indoor and outdoor options, lavish spread during lunch (only *a la carte* at night), live-station sushi, kebab and *teppanayaki* grill, European, Italian, Japanese and Indian fare to choose from, it's understandably popular—make reservations for the Sunday special brunch which comes with unlimited sparkling wine and beer (Rs 1,100). Another 24-hour dining option is **Okra** ★★ (© **040/2752-2999;** http://marriott.com), at the new Hyderabad Marriott—with open kitchens, a relaxed atmosphere located by the pool, candlelit in the evening, Okra can be quite charming.

Finjaan (opposite Mughal Residency Apts., Main Rd. Toli Chowki; © **040/2356-1738;** www.finjaan.com), was the first teahouse to open in Hyderabad in 2006. At this tiny and simple establishment, brothers Salman and Mohammed Taiyebi are only too happy to educate on all 37 kinds of tea and the health benefits of your particular cuppa.

SHOPPING

Pearls are a major draw in Hyderabad—it is said that 9 out of 10 pearls in the world travel through Hyderabad for piercing and stringing—the craftsmanship is unsurpassed here. But do be careful: There are a lot of fakes out there. **Kedarnathji Motiwale** (near Bata, Pathergatti; © **040/2456-6667;** www.kedarnathji.com) has been supplying authentic pearls and jewelry since 1908; hardly surprising then that a number of imper- sonators sporting the same name have cropped up—make sure you're in the shop with the photograph of the president of India giving an award to the owners. **Meena Jewellers** (Babukhan Estate; © **040/2329-9509;** http://meenajewellers.com) is also recommended, particularly if you're after exotic-looking pieces typical of Indian bridalwear. Catering to the wealthy is **Krishna Pearls & Jewellers** (www.krishnapearls.com), with branches in several of the upmarket hotels, including Taj Krishna (© **040/2339-5015**), Taj Banjara (© **040/6656-4833**), and the ITC Kakatiya Sheraton & Towers (© **040/ 2340-0811** or 040/5556-4844); the main city showroom is at 22-6-209 Pathergatti Rd. (© **040/2441-7881**). Another well-known and reliable name is **Jagdamba Jewellers** (Gupta Estate, Basheerbagh Circle; **040/2323-6486;** www.jagdamba.com). Besides high-quality Hyderabadi pearls, these jewelers also design and manufacture gold jewelry and various traditional handicrafts.

For high-quality traditional Indian garments, visit **Kalanjali,** a Hyderabadi institution, with four floors of air-conditioned shopping under one roof (opposite Public Gardens, 5-10-194 Hill Fort Rd., Saifabad; © **040/2342-3440;** www.kalanjali.com). And to absorb the scents and colors of one of India's most evocative bazaars, spend some time in **Laad Bazaar ★★** near Charminar (see "What to See & Do," above).

As in any of India's growing and constantly changing cities, Hyderabad too has its share of malls—**Hyderabad Central** (Panjagutta Cross rds.; © **040/6643-0000**) draws the maximum crowd and is a hangout for the young; **Lifestyle** (© **040/2341-0013;** www.lifestylestores.com) and **Shopper's Stop** (© **040/2776-1084;** www.shoppersstop. com), both at Begumpet, are other popular malls with a variety of branded stores. Hyderabad's version of the Dilli Haat in Delhi is called **Shilparamam ★** (© **040/2310-0455;** www.shilparamamhyd.org; entry Rs 20)—artisans and craftsmen from all parts of India gather and demonstrate, create, and sell their craftwork and handlooms here. The annual crafts fair is held here in December.

10

The Heart of India: Delhi, the Taj, Uttar Pradesh & Madhya Pradesh

The capital of India, Delhi, and its neighboring state, Uttar Pradesh, compose the geographical and historical heart of India, with ancient cities and awe-inspiring monuments that make for definite inclusion in the itineraries of most first-time visitors to the subcontinent.

With comfortable accommodations and a host of fascinating sights, Delhi is a good place to acclimatize. But the main reason most visitors touch down here is its proximity to some of North India's most impressive sights, like the **Golden Temple** at Amritsar, one of the most spiritual destinations in India (see chapter 13); **Jaipur,** capital of Rajasthan, "land of princes" (see chapter 11); and nearby **Agra.** The Mughal capital of Agra is famed for the timeless beauty of its monuments, of which the **Taj Mahal** is the most famous, but it is in the city of **Varanasi,** east of both Delhi and Agra, that time has indeed stood still. Believed to be the oldest living city in the world, Varanasi is the holiest destination in Hindu India, where true believers come to die in order to achieve *moksha*—the final liberation of the soul from the continuous rebirth cycle of Hindu life. Rising like a densely populated crust from the banks of the Ganges, the city is saturated with a sense of the sacred, but while the experience is almost mind-altering, the crowds and filth you may encounter in the city's tiny medieval streets are not for the fainthearted. For those who prefer to keep the chaos of India at arm's length, you might want to consider a side trip to **Lucknow,** the state capital, where space and serenity prevail, and where the decadence and good taste of the ruling *Nawabs*—Shiite Muslim rulers or landowners—live on in the rich cuisine and majestic *imambaras,* or tombs.

South of Delhi and Uttar Pradesh sprawls **Madhya Pradesh,** a vast landlocked state that contains some of the loveliest untouched vistas on the subcontinent. The most famous sights here are the deserted palaces of **Orchha** and the erotic shrines of **Khajuraho**—both easily included as side trips between Delhi or Agra and Varanasi. Deeper south, which sees a great deal less tourist traffic, lie **Sanchi,** one of the finest Buddhist *stupa* (commemorative cairn) complexes in Asia, and **Mandu,** an exotic Mughal stronghold. To the east lie **Kanha** and **Bandhavgarh National Parks,** the latter with the densest concentration of tigers in India, and thus a magnet for those in search of the Indian safari experience, particularly since African safari specialists &Beyond have teamed up with the Taj group to prduce luxury lodges to rival those near Ranthambore National Park in Rajasthan. These Madhya Pradesh excursions will suit those keen to escape the hassle of more obviously tourist-orientated destinations, but they take careful planning to reach; details are provided throughout the chapter.

1 DELHI

200km (124 miles) NW of Agra; 261km (162 miles) NE of Jaipur; 604km (375 miles) NE of Jodhpur

The capital of the world's largest democracy has a fascinating history, but with a population of 14 million sprawling over some 1,500 sq. km (585 sq. miles), and plagued by the subcontinent's highest levels of pollution, growth, and poverty, Delhi's delights are not immediately apparent. Even Delhiites, many of whom were born elsewhere, seldom show pride in the city they now call home, bemoaning its drab mix of civil servants, aspiring politicians, and avaricious business folk; the ever-expanding slums and "unauthorized" colonies; the relatively high levels of crime; and the general demise of traditional ways. Yet Delhi is in many ways the essence of modern India, with its vivid paradox of old and new, rich and poor, foreign and familiar.

Today, to the return visitor, what is startlingly noticeable is the unprecedented growth; to some extent, this is a natural, organic expansion, but it's also part of a mapped-out initiative to prepare the city for its highly anticipated role as host of the 2010 Commonwealth Games and as a leading Asian capital. Beyond the "Games City" moniker, there's the somewhat draconian-sounding "Master Plan for Delhi 2021," which aims to thrust the capital—kicking and screaming if need be—into a better, brighter (and, perhaps sadly, thoroughly Westernized) future. It's clearly a role that local government is taking seriously, because the change is palpable. As the city spreads, giving rise to entire new cities like Gurgaon and Noida—devoted almost entirely to economic growth—high rises and malls and residential colonies are mushrooming everywhere. Some residents are left with their jaws hanging in disbelief, but most work furiously at the altar of capitalist expansion. The expanding megalopolis of Delhi really is more "National Capital Region" than mere city.

Some believe the mobilization of capital and resources is responsible for quite positive transformation. Pollution levels are supposedly dropping, and government officials seem to introduce new modernization schemes every week. You're unlikely to see cows roaming the streets of the capital any more; those that dare are rounded up and taken to stray cow facilities, and in May 2007, the traffic department vowed to crack down on all forms of dangerous driving. But there are ill-considered political choices, too. In 2007, street food was officially banned in the capital (although you still find it practically everywhere), and there was fervent talk of outlawing cycle-rickshaws in Old Delhi. Sadly, such decisions often come from wealthy politicos who have never been into the heart of the old city and have little idea how much a part of daily Delhi life roadside food stalls and rickshaws are. Regardless, Delhi is on the move, indifferent to the loss of tradition as it plays an impressive game of catch-up with the West.

Delhi is an excellent starting point for exploring North India, not only because of its ample transport connections and relatively sophisticated infrastructure, but because the history of Delhi, one of the oldest cities in the world, is essentially the history of India (see "A Tale of Seven Cities," below).

The city is littered with crumbling tombs and ruins, most of which are not even on the tourist map. They—like the elephant trundling alongside a traffic-logged road, where handwritten posters for CUSTOM CONFISCATED GOODS SOLD HERE vie with glossy fashion billboards—are just part of the strange fabric of Delhi. It doesn't have the vibrancy of

The Plight of the Delhi Beggars

Some 50,000 people live on Delhi's pavements or squalid open lots. These squatters are predominantly from rural areas, following the illusionary notion that once in the city, their lives will change for the better. Tragically, for many, it is just the opposite and by the time the truth dawns on them, it is too late, caught in a web of debt that restricts them from turning back. Those who can secure jobs are saved, but for the rest, the situation is bleak. An entire Beggar Mafia operates in Delhi (as it does perhaps anywhere where there is acute poverty) and it is only a matter of time before newcomers are picked up, and made to undergo horrific ordeals under the pretext that it will eventually aid them in their new job—begging. This is a job open to all—the young (children as young as 3 years of age), the sick, the old—but sadly, with no reward, as money earned goes virtually directly to the gang leaders, who offer "protection" (usually from themselves) as reward. By law it is now illegal to give money to beggars and while many may consider this heartless, there is good reason for it: Each time you give money, you are actually encouraging beggary and keeping it alive. Reasons apart, the heart may still cry out and so the next best thing to do would be to give food—carry a few packs of cookies or fruit with you; it may bring a smile to many a face, even more than a few rupees would. Alternatively, consider booking a walking tour with **Salaam Baalak Trust City Walk** (✆ **011/2358-4164;** www.salaambaalak trust.com); these take you through the city's hodgepodge of streets and back alleys and are led by street children, who relish the gainful employment this offers (see "Guided Tours," later).

Mumbai or the atmosphere of Kolkata, but in 1 day you can go from marveling at the sheer grace of the soaring **Qutb Minar Tower,** built in 1199 by the Turkish Slave King Qutb-ud-din Aibak to celebrate his victory over the Hindu Rajputs, to gawking at that 1920s British imperialist masterpiece, palatial **Rashtrapati Bhavan.** You can wander through the sculptural **Jantar Mantar,** a huge, open-air astronomy observatory built in 1725 by Jai Singh, creator and ruler of Jaipur, experience the tangibly sacred atmosphere surrounding the **tomb of the 14th-century Sufi saint,** Sheikh Nizamuddin Aulia, or admire the **16th-century garden tomb of Mughal Emperor Humayun,** precursor to the Taj. Or, after the chaos of exploring the crowded streets of 17th-century **Shahjahanabad,** Delhi's oldest living city, you can escape to **Rajghat,** the park where Mahatma Gandhi was cremated in 1948; or to **Lodi Gardens,** where lawns and golfing greens are studded with the crumbling 15th-century tombs of once-powerful dynasties. And still you haven't covered the half of it . . .

But despite its host of attractions, unless you're staying in one of its top hotels (of which colonial-era Imperial and spanking-new Aman are almost destinations in their own right), Delhi is not a very relaxing destination, and it is as famous for its pollution (rated among the top 20 worst-polluted cities in the world for decades) as it is for its sights. Unless you're a history buff or here on business or like to get caught up in the hustle and bustle of a big city, spend as much time as you need to recover from jet lag, choosing to view only a few of its many attractions (the best of which are listed below), and then move on. The rest of India, with its awesome array of experiences and beauty, awaits you.

DELHI, THE TAJ, UTTAR PRADESH & MADHYA PRADESH

5 DELHI

Amritsar

HIMACHAL PRADESH

Simla

1

Chandigarh

PUNJAB

CHANDIGARH

Dehra Dun

UTTARAKHAND

CHINA (TIBET)

10

1

HARYANA

17 Rishikesh

CORBETT NP

Mahendrangar

NEPAL

DELHI

Delhi

New Delhi

Yamuna

Bareilly

RAJASTHAN

UTTAR PRADESH

8

KEOLADEO NP

Taj Mahal

Fatehpur Sikri

Agra

Jaipur

2

Lucknow

Gorakhpur

Kanpur

Ghaghara

RANTHAMBHORE NP

3

Sawai Madhopur

Gwalior

25

Bhognipur

Ganges

Allahabad

Sarnath

Kota

Jhansi

2

Bundi

3

Orchha

Khajuraho

27

7

Varanasi

Panna

26

PANNA NP

MADHYA PRADESH

BANDHAVGARH NP

Sanchi

Bhopal

Narmada

Jabalpur

Umaria

Indore

Mandu

KANHA NP

Bilaspur

CHHATTISGARH

MAHARASHTRA

Nagpur

6

Raipur

43

New Delhi

DELHI

UTTAR PRADESH

MADHYA PRADESH

India

ORISSA

Godavari

Vishakhapatnam

Bay of Bengal

ANDHRA PRADESH

Hyderabad

Kakinada

Bay of Bengal

0   100 mi
0   100 km

N

ACCOMMODATIONS ■
Ahuja Residency **40**
Amarya Gardens **51**
Amarya Haveli **58**
The Ambassador Hotel **39**
Claridges **31**
Delhi Bed and Breakfast **48**
The Hans Hotel **18**
Hyatt Regency **63**
The Imperial **23**
The Manor **48**
Master Paying Residential
  Guest Accomodation **1**
The Oberoi **41**
Oberoi Maidens **10**
The Park **21**
Hotel Palace Heights **34**
Radisson **65**
Shangri-La Hotel **24**
Taj Mahal Hotel **30**
Taj Palace Hotel **2**
ITC Maurya Sheraton
  Hotel & Towers **3**

DINING ◆
19 Oriental Avenue **24**
Basil and Thyme **35**
Baujee ka Dhaba **61**
Bukhara **3**
China Kitchen **63**
Chor Bizarre **12**
Dhaba **31**
Diva **54**
Haldiram's **6**
House of Ming **30**
It's Greek to Me **66**
Karim **13**
Khan Chacha Kebab Corner **38**
Latitude 28 **38**
La Piazza **63**
Masala Art **2**
Naivedyam **61**
Oh! Calcutta **50**
Olive Bar and Kitchen **62**
Orient Express **2**
Oriental Octopus **45**
Park Balluchi **60**
Ploof **46**
Power of Pranthas **7**
Punjabi by Nature **64**
Sagar **53**
Sakura **22**
Sevilla **31**
Shalom **54**
Smokehouse Grill **50**
The Spice Route **23**
Sawgath **52**
Taipan **41**

Threesixtydegrees **41**
TK's Oriental Grill **63**
United Coffee House **19**
Varq **30**
Veda **15**
Wasabi **30**

ATTRACTIONS ●
Akshardam Temple Complex **25**
Aman **47**
Chandni Chowk **4**
The Crafts Museum **26**
Dilli Haat **57**
Gandhi Smriti **32**
Hazrat Nizamuddin Aulia **44**
Hauz Khas **61**
Humayun's Tomb **43**
Jain Temple and Charity
  Birds Hospital **8**
Jama Masjid **14**
Lala Qila (Red Fort) **9**
Lodi Gardens **38**
Lotus Temple **49**
National Gallery of Modern Art **28**
National Museum & Library **29**
Nehru Memorial
  Museum & Library **33**
Purana Qila (Old Fort) **27**
Qutb Minar **59**
Rajghat and Gandhi Museum **11**
Santushsti Shopping Centre **35**
Shanti Home **67**
Sisganj Gurudwara **5**

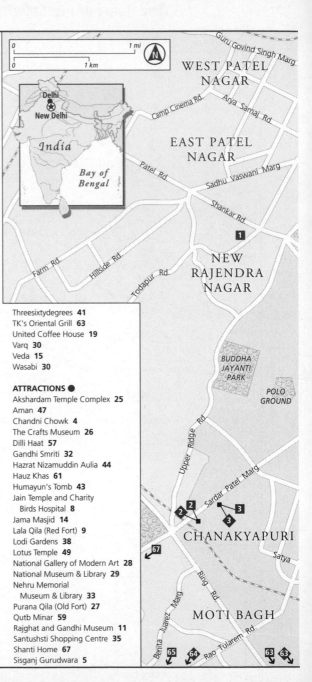

0 ——— 1 mi
0 ——— 1 km

Delhi
New Delhi

India

Bay of
Bengal

WEST PATEL NAGAR
Guru Govind Singh Marg
Camp Cinema Rd.
Arya Samaj Rd.
EAST PATEL NAGAR
Patel Rd.
Sadhu Vaswani Marg
Shankar Rd.
Farm Rd.
Hillside Rd.
Todapur Rd.
NEW RAJENDRA NAGAR
BUDDHA JAYANTI PARK
POLO GROUND
Upper Ridge Rd.
Sardar Patel Marg
CHANAKYAPURI
Satya
Ring Rd.
MOTI BAGH
Benita Juarez Marg
Rao Tularem Rd.

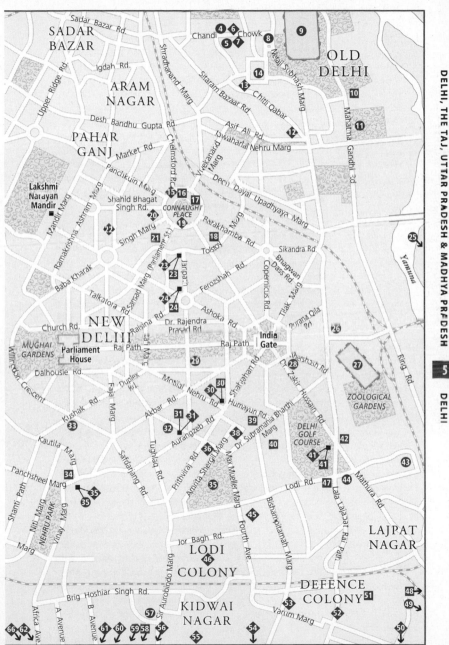

A Tale of Seven Cities

Chosen by the strategically astute invaders who attacked from the north, east, and west, Delhi was not only the gateway to the fertile Gangetic plains and watered by its own Yamuna River, but it enjoyed some protection from the west by the Aravalli Mountains that cross latter-day Rajasthan, and by the Himalayas to the north. Despite this, waves of invaders resulted in the creation—and more often than not destruction—of at least seven distinct cities. The earliest accounts and archaeological finds date from 1000 B.C., when—according to the *Mahabharata* epic, most revered of Hindu religious texts—the Pandavas and their cousins the Kauravas battled for the city of **Indraprastha,** thought to be located under the present ruins of Purana Qila, citadel of the sixth capital. But the earliest existing ruins date from A.D. 736, when the Tomara Rajputs, one of the self-anointed warrior clans to which Rajasthan gave birth, built the fortress **Lal Kot,** around which grew **Qila Rai Pithora,** today known as the first city of Delhi. In 1180 the Tomaras were ousted by the Chauhan Rajputs, who were in turn forced back to Rajasthan by the Slave King Qutb-ud-din Aibak, a Turkish general. He built the **Qutb Complex,** which remains one of the most interesting sights in the city (see "The Top Attractions," later in this section). Aibak served under the Afghani Muhammad Ghori until Ghori's assassination in 1206. Aibak took over the Indian spoils of war, founding the Delhi Sultanate, which was to rule Delhi and the surrounding region for almost 2 centuries. In 1303, the Delhi Sultan Ala-ud-din Khilji built the second city, **Siri,** near present-day Hauz Khas. Then the Tughluqs built **Tughlaqabad,** 8km (5 miles) east of the Qutb Complex, but this was deserted in 1321 and little remains of the third city. After a brief sojourn in latter-day Maharashtra, the Tughluqs moved the city again in 1327, this time between Lal Kot and Siri, and named this fourth city **Jahanpanah.** A mere 27 years later it was moved again, this time some distance north to an eminently sensible position on the Yamuna River. Named **Ferozabad,** this sprawling fifth city was, according to legend, one of the richest in the world. But how the mighty do fall or, according to the Persian prophecy, "Whoever builds a new city in Delhi will lose it." Timur drove the Tughluqs out of Delhi, and while his successors, the Sayyids and Lodis, did not build brand-new cities, their tombs are found scattered in the appropriately named **Lodi Gardens.** Their defeat by the Mughal Babur signaled the end of Sultanate rule and the start of the Mughal empire, one of the world's greatest medieval dynasties, which ruled the region for over 200 years.

It was Babur who first moved the capital to nearby Agra, but his son **Humayun** chose to return to Delhi in 1534, only to be forced into exile by the advancing army of the Afghan Sher Shah, who took possession of **Purana Qila** (literally "old fort") in 1540, rebuilt this sixth city, and renamed the citadel **Shergarh.** Fifteen years later, Humayun finally ousted the Afghan, only to die an ignominious death a year later, falling down his library steps—his tomb, which can be seen from the southern gate of Purana Qila, remains one of Delhi's top attractions.

Humayun's son, Akbar—generally revered for his religious tolerance and diplomacy—again chose to move the capital back to Agra. Only after Akbar's grandson, Shah Jahan, built the Taj Mahal for his wife, did Delhi again become the capital in 1638. Shah Jahan, the greatest architect of the Mughal dynasty, rebuilt an entirely new city, using materials from the ruins of Ferozabad (and, it is said, leaving the corpses of criminals to settle in the foundations). Not known for his humility, he named it **Shahjahanabad.** Shahjahanabad is still very much inhabited, and is today usually referred to as "Old Delhi," home to many of the city's top attractions. After Shah Jahan was viciously deposed by his son, Aurangzeb (see "The Life & Times of the Mughal Emperors," later in this chapter), Mughal power began to wane, and with it the importance of Delhi. It was only with the advent of British power that Delhi again played a pivotal role in the affairs of India. After the "Indian Mutiny" (or "The First War of Independence," depending on who's talking), a direct result of the racist and exploitative policies of the British East India Company, India was annexed by Britain as its colony in 1858, and Delhi was declared the capital of the Raj in 1911. The last (at least for the time being) of Delhi's cities to be built, **New Delhi** took shape between 1911 and 1933. Designed by the British imperialist architects Lutyens and Baker, New Delhi's major buildings have a simple, almost brutal classicism and are considered the finest artifacts of the British Empire, their sheer scale symbolizing its fascist ideals. But again Delhi was lost to her rulers, and in 1947 India's first democratically elected prime minister was sworn into power. The bungalows of New Delhi became home to Indian masters. Ever a city of paradoxes, Delhi's jubilation was tinged with tragedy, for this was also for many the demise of ancient Delhi: With the division ("Partition") of the subcontinent into India and Pakistan, bloody street battles between Hindu and Muslim broke out, leading to the wide-scale immigration of Delhi's urbane Muslim population to Pakistan, and to an even bigger, reverse influx of Punjabis from what is now Pakistan. Primarily farmers, but with a reputation for hard work and business acumen, the Punjabi immigrants effectively doubled the population of Delhi and forever changed its image of itself as a birthplace of civilization. As William Dalrymple describes it in *City of Djinns,* Delhi—"grandest of grand old aristocratic dowagers"—had become "a nouveau-riche heiress: all show and vulgarity and conspicuous consumption." But if one thing is constant, it is Delhi's ability to reconstitute itself. Indeed, with fierce development in the adjunct metropolitan areas of Gurgaon and Noida, a rapidly expanding Metro system, and a stringent plan in place to drastically develop the city's infrastructure ahead of the 2010 Commonwealth Games, there are signs that Delhi's desire is to become a city of the future, molded along capitalist ideals and increasingly in line with Western expectations for a high-yield international hub. And, with pressure from the Supreme Court, local government has been consistently installing an ever-tightening schedule of laws designed to gentrify and unclog the city of cows, beggars, illegal businesses, and pollution-spewing vehicles. One can only hope that Delhi's historic heartbeat will not be lost in the process.

VISITOR INFORMATION   To pick up a free map of Delhi or to get up-to-date information on sights, city tours, and taxi/rickshaw prices, head for the **India Tourism Office** at 88 Janpath (near Connaught Place; ✆ **011/2332-0005** or -0008; www.incredible india.org; Mon–Fri 9am–6pm, Sat 9am–2pm). You will also find Government of India Tourist offices at both airports (open 24 hr.). Do not confuse these with so-called "government authorized" tourist offices, which are not authorized by anyone and are very adept at fleecing the unsuspecting. You will find these fakes particularly along Janpath and at the New Delhi railway station; make sure you seek assistance only at 88 Janpath or from one of the recommended tour operators (see below). If you intend to travel anywhere during your sojourn in India by train, you may choose to make all your reservations in Delhi (though these are just as easily available in other big cities). You can make bookings at the helpful Indian Railways Counter at the airport or any of the reservation counters in the city. Alternatively, for information, visit the **Delhi Tourism and Transport Development Corporation** (**DTTDC**; 18A D.D.A SCO Complex, Defence Colony; ✆ **011/2464-7005** or 011/2336-5358; www.delhitourism.nic.in; Mon–Sat 9:30am–6pm), or see "Getting There: By Train," below.

GETTING THERE   By Air   Most major international airlines operate in what is one of the best-connected cities in south Asia. Delhi has separate domestic and international airports that lie 8km (5 miles) apart; a free hourly shuttle bus runs between them. *Tip:* During high inflow periods the shuttle times may be increased but bear in mind that, should you merely be in transit ie arriving at international terminal and due to connect with a domestic flight somewhere in India, you will have to factor in enough time to wait for this shuttle bus to transfer you. Alternatively, make sure you have enough time to draw money from an ATM and catch a cab between the two terminals; cost is around Rs 250. Also, note that the domestic airport has two terminals, 1A and 1B, also connected by free shuttle bus; check which one you need to be at before leaving. **Indira Gandhi International Airport** (✆ **011/2560-2000;** www.delhiairport.com) lies 20km (12 miles) southwest of Connaught Place (the city center), 40 minutes to an hour away. The cheapest way (but one to be avoided) to get into town is to catch a State Transport bus (Rs 50 plus luggage fee), but if you've just crossed time zones you'll want to opt for a taxi: Choosing, let alone negotiating with, a taxi driver is likely to make your head spin, so we recommend you prebook with **Easycabs** (✆ **011/4343-4343;** www.easycabs.com). You can do this on their website; the driver will wait for you in case of flight delay, though waiting charges are applicable. If you don't want to prebook, find the Easycab counter at the airport where you can pay on pre-paid basis by cash or credit card; rates range from Rs 300 to Rs 600 for rides from the airport to the main hotels in town. If you want to do it for less it's best to book a taxi at the official **prepaid taxi kiosk** (just outside the arrivals hall; ask for directions, and don't be sidelined by those who claim they will take you at the same price). It offers fixed rates, with a small fee for each piece of large luggage, but expect to pay between Rs 200 and Rs 300 (25% more from 11pm–5am); these government-monitored cabs are not in as good condition as the private companies. Note that if you've just arrived in India, it's not worthwhile to hire an auto-rickshaw; they may be cheaper than taxis, but they're very slow and bound to be uncomfortable if you're burdened with luggage—plus, you will almost certainly be pressured into handing over more money even if the price has been discussed upfront. You can of course ask your hotel to arrange the transfer, though this will more than likely double the price (we've included these in reviews of recommended accommodations throughout); some room categories at upmarket chains include chauffeured transfers in the rate. Note that you can change money at the international airport at the State Bank of India or Thomas Cook counters (both 24 hr.).

By Train Of the five stations, most trains arrive at either **New Delhi Station,** a 10-minute walk from Connaught Place, or at **Old Delhi Station** in Shahjahanabad. (Note that if you're traveling on to Agra, you may need to catch the passenger train that leaves from **Nizamuddin Station,** south of Connaught Place.) For rail inquiries and reservations, call © **131** from 8am to 8pm. All stations are well-serviced by taxis and auto-rickshaws. Again, head for the prepaid auto-rickshaw and taxi counters or negotiate the fare upfront—expect to pay Rs 50 to Connaught Place, slightly more to Shahjahanabad/Old Delhi—or insist on using the meter, although there is no guarantee they haven't been rigged (see rates under "Getting Around," below). Note that if you plan to travel elsewhere in India by train, you don't necessarily need to prebook all your train trips in Delhi (see chapter 3 for details on train travel) but you may prefer to get organized here. It's still easiest to do this with a recommended travel agent—while it's become easier to book independently thanks to the Internet, there are complication such as foreigner quotas and not being able to choose your berth, as well as sometime difficulties with credit card payments; unless you're familiar with the system you can save yourself these headaches by using the services of a professional for very little additional money! **Sadhana Travel** (© **011/2646-5312,** 011/4161-8278, or 98-1005-2471; www.sadhana travels.com) offer professional assistance with air travel and tour itineraries; or work with a travel agent attached to your hotel. However, keep in mind that on some trains a small quota of seats is set aside for foreign travelers. A travel agent cannot book these seats; you will need to go to the station to a special counter to book them (again, see chapter 3).

GETTING AROUND The **Delhi Metro** (www.delhimetrorail.com) is increasingly useful, particularly for covering longer distance (like getting to Oberoi Maidens in the north), but as is the case elsewhere, subways also provide no sense of the city layout or passing sights. During peak hours, the tube can also get overcrowded and claustrophobic, and women traveling alone may get unwelcome attention. Ticketing agents are still not very clued in or helpful, either. However, it's a very cheap and effective way of getting around, particularly if your lodgings are near a station, in which case you should definitely purchase a 1-day card (Rs70), or a 3-day (Rs200) if you're staying longer.

There are three lines along which the Delhi Metro operates. To make it easier for you to understand which to opt for, we have clubbed places of interest, restaurants and hotels next to each metro option (**Note:** This refers only to those that lie along the metro routes).

Line 1: Dilshad Garden—Rithala (Rajghat, Akshardham)

Line 2: Jehangirpuri—Central Secretariat (Oberoi Maidens, Master Paying Residential Guest Accommodation, Chor Bizarre, Karim, and Old Delhi sites such as Red Fort, India Gate)

Line 3: Indraprastha—Barakhamba Road—Dwarka (Shangri-La, The Imperial, The Park, Shanti Home, Hans Plaza, Hotel Palace Heights, Veda, Jantar Mantar, National Museum, Pragati Maidan)

The best way to get around while orienting yourself is still in Delhi's **black-and-yellow taxis** or, for short distances, **auto-rickshaws** (run on eco-friendly CNG—compressed natural gas), but be sure to agree on the price upfront. For instance, traveling from Connaught Place to Red Fort shouldn't cost more than Rs 50 by auto-rickshaw, Rs 150 by taxi. Delhi has the most complacent auto-rickshaw drivers in the country; if they don't feel like going where you're asking, they'll simply refuse you service. Often, this is a ploy to press you for more money (official rates are Rs 10 for the first kilometer, and Rs 4.50 for every kilometer thereafter). If you feel you're being overcharged, accuse the driver of cheating and threaten to report him (often simply pretending to dial the police on your mobile phone does the trick); to really complain, dial ✆ 011/2301-0101 or 011/4340-0400 (24 hr.). If the idea of having to haggle like this turns your stomach, **Mega Cab** (✆ 011/4141-4141; www.megacabs.com) is a radio taxi outfit that offers a convenient, marginally more expensive alternative, with a fleet of air-conditioned cars outfitted with working meters (Rs 15 per kilometer) available around-the-clock; their drivers usually keep you abreast of their arrival via cellphone. In case you cant get through, similar outfits like **Delhi Cab** (✆ 011/44-333-222) and the reliable **Meru Cabs** (✆ 011/4422-4422; www.merucabs.com) are also recommended, as are Easycabs (see Arrival above).

If you'd prefer to hire a car and driver for a half- or full day, arrange this through your hotel or, for better rates (and reliable drivers), through **Sunrise Car Rental** (✆ 011/2687-7434) or **Aelpe Services** (✆ 93-1374-1072).

If you plan to tour North India by car, setting off from Delhi, contact the excellent Khaver who will put you in touch with one of his travel experts at **Tushita Travels,** and you can create a custom tour within any budget (✆ 011-2573-0256 or 2573-3652; khaver@tushita-india.com; www.tushita-india.com). Also look into what **Greaves Travels India** (✆ 011/2437-3523 or -3528; www.greavesindia.com) can offer, another reputable operator with good drivers.

Note: It is inadvisable to travel anywhere during rush hour—you will almost certainly find yourself in a traffic jam in one of the most polluted cities in the world.

GUIDED TOURS   You can book an air-conditioned bus tour of New Delhi (daily 9am–2pm) and/or Old Delhi (daily 2:15–5:15pm) through **Delhi Tourism** (see "Visitor Information," above). Tours cost Rs 100 each, or Rs 195 for both; monument admission fees are extra. Also offered are long-distance tours that include trips to Agra, Jaipur, and Rishikesh, but we definitely recommend you opt for a private operator. Two of the most popular are **Go Delhi Luxury Tours** (✆ 98-9988-8207; www.godelhi.net), and **TCI** (✆ 011/2331-5834 or -5838; www.tcindia.com). Their tours are more personal, and the higher tariff (upward of Rs 1,000 per person, excluding monument entry) ensures that you get a decent English-speaking guide and an air-conditioned vehicle. Another reliable option which comes highly recommended is **Le Passage to India** (✆ 011/4165-3100; www.lepassagetoindia.com)—it would be best to check with all three for the best rate available. But if you're tired of predictable presentations of history, we urge you to book a tour with the unusual **Blowhorn Travel** ★★★ (✆ 0124/410-1328; www.blowhorn travel.com) who provide a series of innovative itineraries, keeping the idiosyncrasies of Indian culture in mind, and often studying it through the eyes of interesting personalities such as Lucy Peck, architectural historian and Khushwant Singh, son of a builder; truly a breath of fresh air to tourism gone stale, and catering to one to eight persons max. If Old Delhi (and really, this should be your first port of call) is your focus, we also recommend **Tallis & Company** ✆ 0124/400-4458; www.tallisandco.com) whose services and guides are extremely professional and thorough.

For an excellent introduction to Hinduism, as well as visits to some of the lesser-known sights in Old and New Delhi, book into **Master Paying Residential Guest Accommodation** (see "Where to Stay," later in this section)—the erudite proprietor gives one of the best tours we've had in India, and runs the best-value guesthouse in Delhi, too.

If you'd care to learn more about life on the streets of Delhi, and fancy a walking tour, contact **Salaam Baalak Trust City Walk** (© 011/2358-4164; www.salaambaalaktrust. com), although you'd better be prepared to have your heart broken. The daily walks through the city's hodgepodge of streets and back alleys are led by street children who will share views on life that will possibly change your reality forever, but the initiative is well worth supporting as it makes a real difference to these children's lives to be gainfully employed in this manner (see "The Plight of the Delhi's Beggars" box). Alternatively **INTACH** (The Indian National Trust for Art and Cultural Heritage; 71 Lodhi Estate; © 011/2464-1304; www.intach.org) conducts 2-hour morning walks through Chandni Chowk on Saturdays.

Another company worth highlighting is **Exotic Journeys**—all you need to do is supply proprietor Raj Singh with your budget (as low as $100 per day, including car, driver, and accommodations—or higher, of course), number of days, and area of interest, and he will customize an excellent trip, kicking off with 2 days of sightseeing in Delhi. Contact him at exotic@del2.vsnl.net.in or exoticjourney@vsnl.com, or call © **011/2612-4069.**

(Fast Facts) Delhi

Airlines Most international airline offices are located on Janpath, Connaught Place, and Barakhamba Road. **Jet Airways** is located at Jetair House, 13 Community Centre, Yusuf Sarai; you can get in touch with them on their 24-hour reservation number: © 011/3989-3333. Other useful airline numbers: **Jetlite** (© 011/2567-5879 or 1800-22-3020); **Kingfisher Airlines** (© 1600/180-0101); **Spice Jet** (© 1600/180-3333 or 98-7180-3333). **Indian Airlines** is still the best connected airline, though not our preferred choice, it's located at Safdarjung Airport (© 011/2462-2220) and is open 24 hours; for general inquiries call © 1800/180-1407 from your mobile. You could also contact the **Airport** (© 011/2566-1000 or 2560-2000).

Ambulance For an ambulance call either © **102,** or **East West Rescue** at © 011/2469-9229, -0429, or -3738.

American Express The office is located at A-1 Hamilton House, A-Block Connaught Place (© 011/3988-0030).

Area Code The area code for **Delhi** is **011.**

ATMs There are hundreds of ATMs in the city; ask your hotel which is the closest. Alternatively, head for Connaught Place, where (among others) HSBC, Standard Chartered, and Citibank ATMs offer 24-hour cash machines that take Visa and MasterCard.

Banks Hours are normally Monday to Friday 10am to 2pm, Saturday 10am to noon, though many banks are also open 9am to 5pm. It's quickest to use 24-hour ATMs. See "ATMs," above.

Bookstores The best are in Khan Market—try **Bahri & Sons** (✆ **011/2469-4610;** www.booksatbahri.com), or **Full Circle** (✆ **011/2465-5641;** www.atfullcircle.com). If you're looking for something downtown, **Bookworm** (29 B-Block Connaught Place; ✆ **011/2332-2260**) is excellent, and will often obtain a book you want within 24 hours even if it's not in stock. In Jor Bagh. **Om** bookshop also has a huge collection and many branches in prime locations (E-77 South Ex Part I, ✆ **011/2465-3792;** and 45 Basant Lok, Vasant Vihar, ✆ **011/2614-3530** are the two main outlets).

Car Hires See "Getting Around," above. For upmarket cars and other travel arrangements, the best operator is **Banyan Tours and Travels** (✆ **0124/456-3800;** www.banyantours.com); while their rates may be higher than others, their service is impeccable. Another operator to try is **Tallis & Company** (877 Udyog Vihar, Phase V, Gurgaon; ✆ **0124/400-4458;** www.tallisandco.com).

Currency Exchange The international airport has 24-hour currency exchange but no facilities to let you draw money on your credit cards, so bring foreign notes or traveler's checks if you intend to catch a taxi from here. Thomas Cook is located at the airport (open 24/7) and at The Imperial hotel (Mon–Sat; see "Where to Stay," later in this section). See above for American Express. For cash withdrawals or exchange, see "ATMs" and "Banks," above.

Directory Assistance To get numbers texted to your mobile phone (or e-mailed to you), call **Just Dial** (✆ **011/6999-9999**).

Doctors & Dentists All hotels listed here have doctors on call. The hotels are also your best bet for finding a reputable dentist.

Drugstores There are numerous 24-hour drugstores throughout the city. Best to ask your hotel to arrange a delivery or pickup.

Embassies & Consulates **U.S.:** Shanti Path, Chanakyapuri (✆ **011/2419-8000;** Mon–Fri 8:30am–1pm and 2–5:30pm). **U.K:** Shanti Path, Chanakyapuri (✆ **011/2419-2100;** Mon–Fri 9am–1pm and 2–4pm). **Australia:** 1/50-G Shanti Path, Chanakyapuri (✆ **011/4139-9900;** Mon–Fri 8:30am–1pm and 2–5pm). **Canada:** 7/8 Shanti Path Chanakyapuri (✆ **011/4178-2000**). **New Zealand:** 50-N Nyaya Marg (✆ **011/2688-3170**).

Emergencies For police call ✆ **100;** for local stations ask your hotel or call the Government of India Tourist Office. See "Ambulance," above. For complaints about taxi or auto-rickshaw drivers, dial ✆ **011/2301-0101** or 011/4340-0400. For any tourism-related emergencies, call the **Tourism Hotline** (✆ **011/2336-5358**).

Hospitals **All India Institute of Medicinal Sciences** (✆ **011/2658-8500**), on Ansari Nagar, has a 24-hour trauma unit. Alternatively, head for **Ram Manohar Lohia Hospital** (Baba Khadak Singh Marg; ✆ **011/2336-5933** or -5525) or, farther afield, is **Apollo Hospital** on the Delhi–Mathura Road (✆ **011/2682-5858** or -5801); both have 24-hour emergency service.

Internet Access Numerous outlets are located all over the city and charge Rs 25 to Rs 75 per hour.

Mobile Phones You can buy prepaid cellphone cards almost anywhere in Delhi (see chapter 3); however, the procedure has been severely complicated by various anti-terrorism laws that will require you to supply ID photos and copies of your passport and visa, and possibly proof of residence. Call pricing options also vary considerably according to network and package purchased. Best to ask your hotel about the best (and simplest) rental scheme, or call **Matrix** at © **011/2680-0000** (www.matrix.in); they promise to deliver a phone to you within 2 hours.

Newspapers & Magazines **Indian Express, Hindustan Times,** and *The Times of India* are good national dailies that provide the lowdown on (largely) the political scene. *Outlook* and *India Today* are weekly news magazines that cover a range of issues; of the two, *Outlook* is more populist and interesting to read. *Time Out New Delhi* (Rs 50) is a superb source of (sometimes sycophantic) information about every conceivable activity in town, with good accounts of new establishments and entertainment events; you can access most of it on www.timeoutdelhi. net. It's considerably better than *First City,* a reasonable monthly magazine carrying comprehensive reviews and listings. *Delhi Diary* is a city guide published weekly, and *The Delhi City Complete Guide and Magazine* (Rs 20) is published every 2 weeks; both are available at hotels and tourism offices and include events listings. You can also check out the latter's website at www.thedelhicity.com. A good Web-based source of information on Delhi is www.gocityguides.com for general advice as well as what's on the cards for the month, but reviews are even less critical than *Time Out.* For travel further afield, *Outlook Traveller* (www. outlooktraveller.com) is a top-quality locally produced travel magazine.

Police See "Emergencies," above.

Post Office Try the post office at Parliament Street (© **011/2336-4111**) or the **GPO** at Gol Khana, 5 minutes from Connaught Place. But best to ask your hotel to mail items.

Restrooms Avoid free public restrooms but in emergencies, you can use the Pay & Use facilities (Rs 2) or independently managed Sulabh Shauchalya ("shauchalya" means toilets), which are slightly better maintained.

Safety Delhi, like the rest of India, is relatively safe, though the city has seen an increase in crime. It's unwise for women to travel alone at night.

Taxis See "Getting Around," above.

Weather Delhi's summers are notoriously unbearable; October/November to February are the best times to go.

Yoga & Meditation **Sivananda Yoga Sevashram** (© **98/1132-8067;** www.yoga yogini.com), **Studio Abhyas** (© **011/2696-2757;** http://abhyastrust.org), **Sri Aurobindo Ashram** (© **011/2652-4807**), **Tushita Meditation Centre** (© **011/ 2651-3400;** www.tushita.info)—all offer short- and long-term classes.

THE TOP ATTRACTIONS

India's capital has more sights than any other city in India, but they are concentrated in three distinct areas—Old Delhi, New Delhi, and South Delhi (known as the **Qutb Minar Complex**)—which should be tackled as separate tours (or at a push, two could be grouped together). Most organized tours spend a half-day covering the top attractions in New Delhi, and another half-day exploring the 17th-century capital, Shahjahanabad. Commonly referred to as "Old Delhi," Shahjahanabad lies a mere 5km (3 miles) north of centrally located Connaught Place, the commercial heart of New Delhi, but it feels a

Museum Monday

Most of the important museums in Delhi close on Mondays; if you're at loose ends, there are a handful of hangouts for the culturally inclined, or simply curious. First up is the totally unique and utterly original **Sulabh International Museum of Toilets** (Sulabh Gram, Mahavir Enclave, Palam-Dabri Marg; beyond the airport ✆ **011/2503-1518;** Mon–Sat 10am–5pm, www.sulabhinternational. org), which takes visitors on a journey through everything "loo"-related, from Thomas Crapper's first flushable commode to present-day innovations in Indian sanitation technology. If you have an interest in Tibetan art (particularly Buddhist *thangka* paintings and religious objects), and staying at or shopping in south Delhi area, visit the **Tibetan House Museum** (Tibet House, 1 Institutional Area, Lodhi Rd.; ✆ **011/2461-1515;** Mon–Fri 9:30am–5:30pm).

few hundred years away (400 to be exact). If you do only one sightseeing excursion, make it here, for this is most authentically India, where imposing **Lal Qila (Red Fort)** and **Jama Masjid,** India's largest mosque, pay testament to the vision and power of Shah Jahan, and the chaos and pungent smells from the overcrowded and ancient streets are a heady reminder that you are far from home. Surrounding and immediately south of Connaught Place is New Delhi, built by British imperialist architects Baker and Lutyens. Its primary attractions are the architectural gems centered around **Rajpath** and **Rashtrapati Bhavan,** official residence of the president of India. Of Delhi's remaining cities, all of which are today deserted and in ruins, only the 12th-century **Qutb Minar,** a World Heritage Site monument built in Delhi's first city and surprisingly intact, is definitely worth inclusion in your itinerary.

Shahjahanabad (Old Delhi) ★★★

Still surrounded by crumbling city walls and three surviving gates, the vibrant, bustling Shahjahanabad, built over a period of 10 years by Emperor Shah Jahan, is very much a separate city—predominantly a labyrinth of tiny lanes crowded with rickshaws, and lined with 17th-century *havelis* (Indian mansions), their balustrades broken and once-ornate facades defaced with rusted signs and sprouting satellite dishes. Old Delhi is inhabited by a predominantly Muslim population whose lives revolve around work and the local mosque, much as it was a century ago.

The best way to explore the area is to catch a taxi or auto-rickshaw to Red Fort (see below), then set off within Shahjahanbad in a cycle-rickshaw (agree on Rs 100), or on foot if it's too congested. Head down the principal street, **Chandni Chowk,** which leads from the main entrance to Red Fort. Along this busy commercial street are mosques, a church, and a number of temples. First up, opposite the fort, is **Digambar Jain Temple,** the oldest of its kind in Delhi and surprisingly simple compared with other Jain temples, which are renowned for the intricacy of their carvings. Attached is a **bird hospital,** which smells less charming than it sounds. If you're pressed for time, skip these and proceed to vibrant **Gauri Shankar Temple** (look for the mounds of marigolds, sold to worshipers as they enter), which has an 800-year-old lingam. Or stop at **Sisganj Gurudwara ★,** an unassuming but superbly atmospheric and welcoming Sikh temple, which marks the spot where Guru Tegh Bahadur, the ninth Sikh guru, was beheaded by the fundamentalist Aurangzeb (Shah Jahan's intolerant son). You will be expected to hand over your shoes at a superefficient kiosk and wash your hands and feet at the cheap taps plumbed right at the temple entrance; on the way out you may be offered food—no harm in indulging, if not for the food, then to appreciate the generosity that permeates Sikh culture, and to experience the rare joy of receiving sustenance from a stranger, which can be both uplifting and humbling. Then, either turn left into Kinari Bazaar (see below) or head the length of Chandni Chowk to **Fatehpuri Masjid,** designed by one of Shah Jahan's wives. Take a detour to the right into Church Mission Marg and then left into **Khari Baoli**—reputed to be Asia's biggest spice market—the colors, textures, and aromas that literally spill out into the street are worth the side trip, but be careful with your belongings in these packed streets. Then double back down Chandni Chowk, turn right into jam-packed **Kinari Bazaar,** and stop to admire the cheap gold (we're talking mostly tinsel) and silver trinkets and accessories. Or keep going until the right turn into **Dariba Kalan,** "the jewelers' lane," where you can bargain hard for gorgeous baubles. Go south down Dariba Kalan to reach **Jama Masjid** (see below), India's largest mosque, keeping an eye out on the right for the tall spire of **Shiv Temple.** Having explored Jama Masjid, you can head west down **Chawri Bazaar** for brass and copper icons and other souvenirs, then up **Nai Sarak** (which specializes in the most magnificent stationery, some bound into diaries). Or head south to **Churiwali Galli,** the "lane of bangle-sellers," and make a final stop at **Karim's** to sample the authentic Mughlai cooking that has kept patrons coming back for over 100 years. A little farther along is **Sunehri Masjid,** recognizable by its three gilt domes from where the Persian invader Nadir Shah enjoyed a bird's-eye view as his men massacred some 3,000 of Shahjahanabad's citizens in 1739.

This done, you've pretty much covered Shahjahanabad's top attractions by rickshaw; the last remaining sights of interest that lie further south within the old city walls are the pretty **Zinat-ul Masjid (Daryaganj),** or "Cloud Mosque," built in 1710 by one of Aurangzeb's daughters, and nearby **Rajghat** (Mahatma Gandhi Rd.; daily sunrise–sunset; leave shoes outside with attendant for a small tip), where Mahatma Gandhi, "Father of the Nation," was cremated. There's not much to see besides the black granite plinth inscribed with his last words, "Hé Ram!" ("Hail God!"), but it's worth getting here at 5pm on Friday (the day of the week he was assassinated), when devotees gather to sing melancholic *bhajans*. Nearby, **Gandhi Memorial Museum** (© 011/2331-1793; Tues–Sun 9:30am–5:30pm) documents his life and last rites, which must have been immensely moving. Also within the old city walls is **Feroze Shah Kotla (Bahadur Shah Zafar Marg),** the ruins of the palace of the fifth city, Ferozabad. The principal attraction here is the pristine polished sandstone pillar from the 3rd century B.C. that rises from the palace's crumbling remains. One of many pillars left by the Mauryan emperor Ashoka throughout North India, it was moved from the Punjab and erected here in 1356. North of Red Fort is **St. James Church** (Lothian Rd. near Kashmiri Gate; daily 8am–noon and 2–5pm). Consecrated in 1836, Delhi's oldest church was built by Col. James Skinner—the son of a Scotsman and his Rajput wife, who became one of Delhi's most flamboyant 19th-century characters—to repay a promise made during battle. (*Note:* For good tours within the old city, we recommend **Tallis & Company**—see "Guided Tours" earlier.)

Jama Masjid ★   Commissioned by Shah Jahan in 1656, this mosque took 5,000 laborers 6 years to complete and is still the largest in Asia, accommodating up to 25,000 worshipers during holy festivals such as Id. Sadly, non-Muslims are not allowed in during prayers, but photographs (sold elsewhere) of the thousands of supplicant worshipers provide some idea of the atmosphere as you wander the huge expanse within. The central pool is for washing hands, face, and feet; to the west (facing Mecca) is the main prayer hall with the traditional *mihrab* for the prayer leader. You can ascend to the top of the southern minaret to enjoy fantastic views from Old Delhi to the distinctly different rooftops and high-rises of New Delhi—the climb is pretty stiff, but worth it. *Note:* If your knees or shoulders are bare, you'll have to rent a scarf or *lungi* (sarong or cloth) at the entrance to cover up.

Off Netaji Subhash Marg. Free admission; Rs 50 for minaret rooftop viewing; Rs 150 camera or video. Daily 8:30am–12:15pm and 1:45pm to half-hour before sunset; opens at 7am in summer. Closed during prayers 12:15–1:45pm. Shoes to be removed outside.

Lal Qila (Red Fort) ★   Built by Shah Jahan, the most prolific architect and builder of the Mughal empire, Lal Qila must have been a very modern departure from labyrinthine Agra Fort (which is older but a great deal better preserved and atmospheric). It was the seat of Mughal power from 1639 to 1857. Named after the red sandstone used in its construction, Red Fort covers an area of almost 2km (1¼ miles). Visitors enter via three-story **Lahore Gate,** one of six impressive gateways. You'll pass through **Chatta Chowk,** which has quaint shops selling cheap souvenirs (some rather nice handbags). You'll arrive at **Naqqar Khana,** where the emperor's musicians used to play. From here you look up into **Diwan-I-Am,** the 60-pillared "hall of public audience," from where Emperor Shah Jahan used to listen to his subjects' queries and complaints as he sat cross-legged upon the beautifully carved throne (an age-old custom that his despotic son, Aurangzeb, who cared little for his subjects, discontinued). Behind this lie **Rang Mahal,** the royal quarters of the wives and mistresses, and **Mumtaz Mahal,** probably used by a favored wife or by Princess Jahanara, who evoked such envy in her sister's heart (see "Agra" introduction, later in this chapter). Next up are **Khas Mahal,** which housed the emperor's personal quarters (he would greet his subjects across the Yamuna River from the balcony); gilded **Diwan-I-Khas,** where the emperor would hold court with his inner circle from the famous jewel-encrusted Peacock Throne (taken by Persian invader Nadir Shah in 1739 and still in Iran); and finally the **Hamams,** or royal baths, whose fountains of rose-scented water would give modern-day spas a run for their money. In front of the *hamams* is **Moti Masjid,** built by Aurangzeb exclusively for his own use—a far cry from the huge Jama Masjid his father built in order to celebrate the faith together with thousands of his subjects.

A few examples of beautiful carving, inlay, and gilding remain, particularly in Diwan-I-Khas, but after so many years of successive plunder it takes some contemplation (and a guide) to imagine just how plush and glorious the palaces and gardens must have been in their heyday; they were ruined when the British ripped up the gardens and built their ugly barracks (the fort is incidentally still a military stronghold, with much of it off-limits). Consider hiring a guide at the entrance, but negotiate the fee upfront and don't expect much by way of dialogue (guides often speak English by rote and don't understand queries); do expect to be hassled for more money. If you're staying in an upmarket hotel, arrange a guide through the concierge.

Chandni Chowk. ℂ **011/2327-7705.** Rs 250 entry; Rs 25 video; Rs 100–Rs 150 guide. Tues–Sun sunrise–sunset. Evening light show 7:30pm Nov–Jan, 8:30pm Feb–Apr, 9pm May–Aug; Rs 60; information ℂ **011/2327-4580.**

New Delhi

Almost all of New Delhi's attractions lie south of **Connaught Place,** which you will no doubt visit to make onward bookings, get cash, eat, or shop. Built on concentric circles surrounding a central park, the retail heart of New Delhi was designed by Robert Tor

Russell in the late 1920s. With its deep colonnaded verandas, gleaming banks, and host of burger joints and pizzerias, it's a far cry from Chandni Chowk but is still quite chaotic, crawling with touts and hucksters whose aim is to part you from your money as quickly and seductively as possible. From here, the closest attraction well worth visiting (unless you're moving on to Jaipur) is **Jantar Mantar ★** (daily sunrise–sunset), which lies on Sansad Marg, on the way to Rashtrapati Bhavan. It's one of five open-air observatories built in the 18th century by Maharaja Jai Singh II, the eccentric genius who built Jaipur. The sculptural qualities of the huge instruments he designed are worth a visit alone, but note that Jantar Mantar in Jaipur, built by the same king, is both bigger and better preserved (see chapter 11).

The easiest way to take in central New Delhi's imperial architecture—for many the chief attraction—is to drive to **India Gate,** built to commemorate those who died in World War I. There an eternal flame burns in memory of those who gave their lives in the 1971 Indo-Pakistan war, their names inscribed on the memorial. Sadly it's hardly worth pausing here—the last time we visited, the beautiful lawns were slushy, unkempt and littered courtesy the hundreds who come every day, and the boating facility disfigured with canvas advertisements—but set off on foot west along **Rajpath** (the 3.2km/2 mile boulevard once known as King's Way) to the beautifully ornate gates of **Rashtrapati Bhavan,** flanked by the two almost identical **Secretariat buildings** (see "New Delhi's Imperial Architecture," below). Having covered the architectural attractions of New Delhi, you can double back to **The National Museum** (see below) or catch a ride to the **National Gallery of Modern Art,** which lies near India Gate (Jaipur House; ✆ 011/2338-2835; Rs 150; Tues–Sun 10am–5pm). Farther west lies **The Crafts Museum** (see below). Although the National Gallery is one of India's largest museums of modern art, it's pretty staid fare and unlikely to thrill those used to such Western shrines as London's Tate or New York's Museum of Modern Art.

Other museums you may consider in the area, particularly if you have an interest in the last 100 years of India's history, are (all three are incidentally a short auto-rickshaw ride from each other, so easy to combine) as follow: Try the colonial bungalow where Gandhi stayed when he was in Delhi, and where he was assassinated; it's in many ways more atmospheric than the museum near Raj Ghat in Old Delhi. You can visit it now in its present guise as the **Eternal Gandhi Multimedia Museum** at **Gandhi Smriti and Darshan Samiti ★** (5 Tees January Marg; ✆ 011/3095-7269; www.eternalgandhi.org; Tues–Sun 10am–5pm, closed second Sat of the month). **Nehru Memorial Museum and Library** (Teen Murti Marg; ✆ 011/2301-6734; free admission; Tues–Sun 9:30am–5pm) was the grand home of India's own "Kennedy clan": Nehru was India's first prime minister, a role his daughter and grandson, Indira and Rajiv respectively, were also to play before both were assassinated. The mantle has now been passed on to Rajiv's Italian wife Sonia, who holds the reins tightly as the President of the currently ruling Congress Party. Although Indians share a love-hate relationship with her (many feel she doesn't have the right to become prime minister owing to her Italian origins), there is no denying the fact that she is one of the most well known and powerful women in politics. Her dimpled poster-boy son Rahul, although being groomed to become the PM eventually, is at present happy to concentrate on building up youth initiatives and raking controversies (considered as acts of immaturity or breaking conventions, depending on where you are standing), while his sister Priyanka prefers to play from behind the scenes and is considered by many as a young Indira. Those interested in contemporary Indian history may thus also wish to visit **Indira Gandhi Memorial Museum** (1 Safdarjung Rd.; ℭ **011/ 2301-0094;** free admission; Tues–Sun 9:30am–4:45pm). A huge force in postindependence India (see "India Past to Present," in chapter 2), Indira Gandhi was murdered here by her Sikh bodyguards. Among the displays (which provide a real sense of the woman) is her blood-soaked sari, as well as the clothes worn by her son Rajiv when he was killed in 1991.

The best temples to visit in central New Delhi are **Lakshmi Narayan Mandir** ★ (west of Connaught Place, on Mandir Marg; leave cameras and cellphones at counter outside), an ornate yet contemporary Hindu temple built by the wealthy industrialist B. D. Birla in 1938; and **Bangla Sahib Gurudwara** ★ (off Ashoka Rd.), Delhi's principal Sikh temple. If you aren't heading north to the Golden Temple at Amritsar (see chapter 13 for more on Sikhism), a visit to the *gurudwara* is highly recommended, if only to experience the warm and welcoming atmosphere that seems to pervade all Sikh places of worship— evident in details like the efficient shoe deposit, a scarf to cover your head (both free), genuinely devoted guides who expect no recompense (available at the entrance), devotional hymns (sung constantly sunrise–9pm), free food (served three times daily), and *prasad* (communion) offered as you leave—be warned that it can be oily and you won't give offense if you decline. The *gurudwara* is certainly an interesting contrast to Lakshmi Narayan Mandir; a visit to one of the first Hindu temples to open its doors to all castes (including "outcasts" like the foreign Britishers) makes you feel very much like a tourist, whereas the more embracing atmosphere of the *gurudwaras* has you feeling welcomed and humbled.

If all this sightseeing has you beat, you can retreat to **Lodi Gardens** (5km/3 miles south of Connaught Place), where green lawns surround the crumbling tombs of the 15th-century Sayyid and Lodi dynasties—the tombs are not well-preserved, but the green, shaded oasis may suffice as a break from the hectic traffic or shopping at nearby Khan Market. Early mornings are quite lovely and in case you want a bit more history to the gardens, we suggest you take a walk with **INTACH** (ℭ **011/2464-1304;** www. intach.org; Rs 50) who also organize walking tours in Hauz Khas, another delightful area to explore on foot, and ideal for early birds. The 18th-century **Safdarjang's Tomb** lies just south of Lodi Gardens, but more impressive by far is **Humayun's Tomb** (a short rickshaw ride west) and, across the street, **Hazrat Nizamuddin Aulia** (both discussed below).

Finally, for the special-interest traveler, you can view India's largest collection of rare stamps free of charge at the **National Philatelic Museum,** located at the post office at Dak Bhavan (Sansad Marg; enter at back of post office; Mon–Fri 9:30am–4:30pm, closed 12:30–2:30pm).

Humayun's Tomb ★★★ This tomb, built for the second Mughal emperor, launched a great Mughal architectural legacy—even the Taj, which was built by Humayun's great-grandson, was inspired by it. Though the Taj's beauty (and the money spent) eclipsed this magnificent example of the garden tomb, it's well worth a visit, even if your next step is to visit its progeny. Paid for by Humayun's "senior" wife, Haji Begum, and designed by the Persian (Iranian) architect Mirak Mirza Ghiyas, it's another grand testimony to love. Set in peaceful surrounds, the tomb features an artful combination of red sandstone and white marble, which plays with the wonderful symmetry and scale used by the makers of the Mughal empire. Though it doesn't have the fine detailing of the Taj, aspects such as the intricately carved stone trellis windows are lovely. If you're traveling on to Agra, it is interesting to see how the Mughals' prolonged stay in India started to influence design elements (the Persian finial that mounts the central marble dome was, for instance, later supplanted by the lotus). There are a number of outlying tombs, and if you want to do more than simply wander through the beautifully restored gardens and walkways and marvel at the sheer generosity of scale, this is again one place where the services of a guide are worthwhile. Hire one through your hotel or the central tourism office.

Lodi and Mathura Rd. (*C*) **011/2435-5275.** Rs 250; Rs 25 video. Daily sunrise–sunset.

The National Museum ★   Okay, so this museum boasts 150,000 pieces covering some 5 millennia, but it is frustratingly hard for the layperson to traverse these hallowed corridors, a number of which have displays with little or no information; best by far is to hire the audio tour available at the entrance. There are some gems here, like the **12th-century statue** of the cosmic dance of Lord Shiva (South Indian bronzes), which is almost as archetypal of India as the Taj; and a truly wonderful collection of **miniature paintings**—this is one area where you could easily spend a few hours. And if you have any interest in history, the sheer antiquity of many of the pieces will amaze you—here lies the country's finest collection of Indus Valley relics (ca. 2700 B.C.), as well as those garnered from central Asia's "Silk Route" but given that it's not artfully displayed, with no attempt to make history come alive, it takes time and some effort to appreciate the wealth of history that lies throughout the 30-odd galleries spread over three floors.

Corner of Janpath and Rajpath. (*C*) **011/2301-9272.** Entry Rs 300 (inclusive of audio-tour charges); camera fee Rs 300. Tues–Sun 10am–5pm.

New Delhi's Imperial Architecture ★★★   Nehru wrote that "New Delhi is the visible symbol of British power, with all its ostentation and wasteful extravagance," but no one with any design interest fails to be impressed by the sheer scale and beauty of these buildings and the subtle blending of Indian influence on an otherwise stripped-down Western classicism—a far cry from the ornate Indo-Saracenic style so deplored by chief architect Sir Edwin Lutyens. Lutyens, known for his racist views, in fact despised all Indian architecture (he conveniently convinced himself that the Taj was actually the work of an Italian designer), but he was forced to include some "native" elements in his designs. Clearly, at first glance the Lutyens buildings of Central Delhi are symbols of imperial power intended to utterly dwarf and humble the individual, yet the Indian influences, such as the neo-Buddhist dome, tiny helmetlike *chattris* (cenotaphs), and filigree stonework, add a great deal to their stately beauty. Once the home of the viceroy of India, **Rashtrapati Bhavan** is today the official residence of the president of India and is closed to the public (though the Mughal Gardens, spread over 5.2 magnificent hectares [13 acres] and among the best in India, are open to the public Feb 14–Mar 14). It's worth noting that this is the largest residence of any president on earth, with over 350 rooms (the White House has a mere 132). Do take note of the slender 44m (145 ft.) Jaipur Column near the entrance gates; donated by the Maharaja of Jaipur, it is topped by a bronze lotus and six-pointed glass star. The two Secretariat buildings, designed by Sir Herbert Baker, show a similar subtle blend of colonial and Mughal influences and today house the Ministry of Home Affairs and the Home and Finance ministries. Northeast, at the end of Sansad Marg, is Sansad Bhavan (Parliament House), also designed by Baker, from where the country is managed (or not, as Booker Prize–winner Arundhati Roy argues so succinctly in *The Algebra of Injustice*—a recommended but somewhat depressing read). Take a drive around the roads that lie just south of here (Krishna Menon Marg, for instance) to view the lovely bungalows, also designed by Lutyens, that line the tree-lined avenues.

The Crafts Museum ★ If you plan to shop for crafts in India, this serves as an excellent introduction to what's out there, though when it comes to the antiques, like the 200-year-old life-size Bhuta figures from Karnataka or the Charrake bowls from Kerala, picking up anything nearly as beautiful is akin to winning a lottery. Some 20,000 artifacts—some more art than craft—are housed in five separate galleries, showcasing the creativity that has thrived here for centuries, not to mention the numerous ways in which it's expressed, depending on where you travel. The **Crafts Museum Shop** is also worth your time, at the very least to again familiarize yourself with the best crafts and textiles, and there are live demonstrations by artisans.

Bhairon Rd., Pragati Maidan. © 011/2337-1641. Free admission. Tues–Sun 10am–5pm.

Hazrat Nizamuddin Aulia ★ Originally built in 1325, but added to during the following 2 centuries, the tomb of the saint Sheikh Nizamuddin Aulia (along with a few prominent others, including the favorite daughter of Shah Jahan) is one of the holiest Muslim pilgrimages in India. It is certainly one of Delhi's most fascinating attractions, not least because the only way to get here is to traverse the tiny, narrow medieval lanes of old Nizamuddin on foot. The entire experience will transport you back even further than a foray into Shahjahanabad. This is not for the fainthearted (or perhaps the recently arrived), however—the streets are claustrophobic, you will be hassled by hawkers (perhaps best to purchase some flowers as a sign of your good intentions upfront), and the smells are almost as assaulting as the hawkers who bar your way. Once there, you may be pressured into making a heftier donation than is necessary (Rs 50 is fair). This would in fact be a three-star attraction if it weren't for the sense that outsiders are not really welcome (though many report otherwise)—note that the main structure is a mosque, Jam-at Khana Masjid, off limits to women. Best to dress decorously (women should consider covering their heads), pick up some flowers along the way, get here on a Thursday evening when *qawwals* gather to sing the most spiritually evocative devotional songs, take a seat, and soak up the medieval atmosphere.

Nizamuddin. 6km (3¾ miles) south of Connaught Place. Donation expected.

South Delhi

Delhi's sprawling suburbs keep expanding southward, impervious of the remnants of the ancient cities they surround. Die-hard historians may feel impelled to visit the ruins of **Siri** (the second city), **Tughlaqabad** (the third), and **Jahanpanah** (the fourth), but the principal attraction here is the **Qutb Complex** (see below), built in the area that comprised the first city of Delhi. Located in Mehrauli Archaeological Park, it has a number of historic sites centered around the Dargah of Qutb Sahib, as well as a number of cafes and boutiques frequented by Delhi's well-heeled.

Nearby is **Hauz Khas** on the Delhi-Mehrauli road. Once a village, Haus Khas is now a gentrified upmarket suburb known more for its glossy boutiques and restaurants than for its 14th-century reservoir and ruins, including the **tomb of Feroze Shah Tughlaq** (Rs 100). If you happen to have a train fetish, you shouldn't miss **The National Railway Museum** (© 011/2688-1816; Rs 10; Tues–Sun 9:30am–7:30pm, closes 5pm in winter), said to be one of the world's most impressive—hardly surprising given India's huge network. You can ogle all kinds of saloon cars and locomotives, and even swoon at model trains and railway maps of yore. It is situated southwest of Lodi Gardens, in Chanakyapuri.

If you've traveled this far south, head a little east to look at the **Bahá'i House of Worship,** or "Lotus Temple," where 27 huge and beautiful marble "petals" create the

Delhi's Spiritual Disneyland

Already a landmark, Delhi's youngest attraction is the modern-era pilgrimage center **Akshardham** (Noida, © **011/2201-6688;** www.akshardham.com). This temple and cultural complex rises from the banks of the Yamuna River in east Delhi, surrounded by landscaped lawns and an air of civility. Supposedly, visitors come here to worship—largely in the main temple, splendid in white marble and pink sandstone, and borne on the shoulders of 149 life-size stone elephants. At a cost of $50 million, the modern architectural landmark took 5 years to complete, involving the efforts of some 11,000 artisans and craftsmen who toiled for an estimated 300 million worker hours to create the ornate pillars and domes, thousands of sculpted idols, and a 3.3m (11-ft.) gold-plated version of Swaminarayan. The whole effect is one of spiritual decadence with, in a tribute to Disney-style theme parks, visitors able to take a boat ride through key moments of Indian cultural and religious history. One can only speculate at the significance of the attached shopping complex and IMAX theater. Akshardam is open Tuesday to Sunday 9am to 6pm; temple entry is free, but there's a fee (Rs 125) for exhibitions and to see the ecclesiastical feature film on the life of Lord Satyanarayan.

lotus-shaped dome. Often likened to a miniversion of the Sydney Opera House, it's a beautiful contemporary temple, and invites people of all faiths for worship. It's sometimes described as a modern counterpoint to the Taj, but this is an injustice to the Taj, as the Lotus Temple lacks any detailing and has a drab interior (Kalkaji; © **011/2644 4029;** Apr–Oct Tues–Sun 9am–7pm, Nov–Mar Tues–Sun 9:30am–5:30pm).

Qutb Complex ★★★ Originally built by Quibuddin Aibak, first of the Delhi Sultanates who were to rule for some 4 centuries, the complex surrounds Qutb Minar, the sandstone Victory Tower that he started in 1193. The Minar was added to by his successor, Iltutmish (whose tomb lies in one corner); and the topmost stories, reaching 70m (230 ft.), were built in 1368 by Feroze Shah Tughlag. It is remarkably well preserved, and photographs don't really do the tower justice—not in scale, nor in the detail of its carving. The surrounding buildings show some of the earliest Islamic construction techniques used in India, as well as the first mingling of Islamic and Hindu decorative styles—Koranic texts are inscribed in the Minar and Alai Darwaza (old gateway), while Hindu motifs embellish the pillars of Quwwat-ul-Islam ("Might of Islam") mosque. The iron pillar in the courtyard, which remains amazingly rust-free, dates from the 4th century.

Aurobindo Marg, near Mehrauli. 15km (9 1/3 miles) south of Connaught Place. Rs 250; Rs 25 video. Daily sunrise–sunset.

WHERE TO STAY

The capital draws countless diplomats and businesspeople, which in turn has led to a thriving (and ridiculously pricey) five-star accommodations sector, meaning that you'll probably need to dig a little deeper in your pockets if you want a certain level of luxury—not a bad idea if this is your first stop in India. Although a five-star hotel may serve as a gentle introduction to India, most are bland reproductions of what you can expect anywhere in the world, and some are downright hideous despite the hefty price tags. While big luxury hotels are more numerous than we need to mention, there are a few very special options for travelers looking for affordability, style, and something out of the ordinary—we've reviewed them below, but here's a brief overview of our favorites. In the budget category, we've long acknowledged the pleasure of staying at **Master Guest House,** the best place by far to stay if you're watching your rupees and would like to live among charming Delhiites. Costing a little more, but so ultra stylish that they are worth every rupee, **Amarya Haveli** and **Amarya Gardens,** owned and operated by a pair of Frenchmen, are truly in a league of their own. We also like **Oberoi Maidens,** Delhi's oldest hotel; and for excellent value, **The Manor,** the city's first, although no longer the only, boutique-style option—all offer an alternative to the anonymous atmosphere of larger hotels. There's much parity in the very top-end of the market, with the exception of the **Aman New Delhi,** which opened early in 2009. First of the respected Aman group's "metro resorts" it represents a revolution in the Delhi hospitality industry; not only is the room count relatively low for a luxury Delhi hotel (just 31 rooms and eight suites) but the more established (and essentially business-oriented) hotels don't really compete with the Aman's genuine sanctuary feel—The Imperial, for example, despite it's sense of refinement and Old World elegance, has an ever-bustling, busy lobby. That said there's something to be said for being in walking distance from Connaught Place, and our hands-down recommendation after the (admittedly very pricey) Aman is still **The Imperial,** with its authentic colonial old-world atmosphere, friendly staff, and super restaurants; the only drawback is the temperamental approach to honoring reservations. The other top-end option that we applaud is **The Oberoi:** More of a chain-hotel feel than the one-off Imperial, but still the ultimate in luxury, **The Oberoi** has the most lavishly cozy rooms you could wish for, and unbeatable service standards, but you'll shell out for the privilege.

Of the big chains, **Hyatt Regency** offers predictable facilities and room standards but superb dining options as well as—depending on the day—good value rates. Another unadventurous big hotel option, which is a resounding favorite with foreigners (including Bill Clinton), is the **ITC Sheraton Hotel and Towers ★** (✆ **011/2611-2233;** www. welcomgroup.com; from $400 double). Its location in the diplomatic sector and the expensive rooms are major drawbacks, but foodies will enjoy easy access to Bukhara, widely considered the best restaurant in the country (see "Where to Dine," later). Note, too, that there is now a second Sheraton property in south Delhi (Sheraton New Delhi Hotel, District Centre, Saket; ✆ **011/4266-1122**), with typically sumptuous rooms starting at a far more affordable $300.

Note that if you're literally in transit, the **Radisson ★** (National Highway 8, New Delhi 110 037; ✆ **011/2677-9191;** fax 011/2677-9090; www.radisson.com) is your best bet near the airport. It's perched on the edge of a major highway, but guest rooms (from $300) are large and sumptuous, with contemporary furnishings and king-size beds. Ask for a pool- or garden-facing unit.

Although congestion (the Delhi-Gurgaon region has the highest density of vehicles in India) means it now takes a good half hour to 40 minutes to get to the airport from Delhi's satellite town Gurgaon (once considered a good choice "close" to the airport), the new highway should ease this to 15 minutes. Should business or pleasure draw you to stay in Gurgaon, we recommend the charming **Tikli Bottom ★** (✆ **124/276-6556;** www.tiklibottom.com; all-inclusive doubles Rs 12,000), a Lutyens-style farmhouse offering an atmosphere of complete relaxation. Alternatively there's the spanking new

Leela ★ which offers the usual ultraluxe rooms and facilities at a hefty price (© 124/ 477-1234; www.theleela.com/hotel-gurgaon.html; doubles from Rs 22,500) or the very modern, good value **Crowne Plaza** (© **011/4358-7088;** www.ichotelsgroup.com; doubles from Rs 10,400) which also has a superb Brazilian restaurant, Wildfire (reviewed later).

Note: The prices below are mostly given in rupees. Some are stated in U.S. dollars only, which is how many hotels targeting foreign markets quote their rates. Most of the city's upmarket hotels offer significant discounts on published rates depending on occupancy; so do check online and use the rates below (and above) only as guidelines.

New Delhi
Very Expensive
Aman New Delhi ★★★ Aman is hands-down the country's best (and most expensive) city hotel. You come here not just for the sensuous luxury, but for its array of personalized services—airport pickups in a souped up silver Ambassador; tours in reconditioned auto-rickshaws (with air-conditioning and stereos); fabulous day-long wedding rituals, and escorted train journeys to see the Taj Mahal. The exterior looks not unlike a neat Soviet-era administration block, but move inside to a cool-slick palace, inspired by Delhi's classic Mughal architecture. The biggest drawback is that you might not want to leave your room—elegantly stripped down and very pampering, with wall-to-ceiling windows framing views of Humayun's Tomb. In terms of size, accommodations put the rest of the city to shame, each with a private pool and shaded terrace from where you can watch hawks skillfully harassing pigeons. Spend the better part of a day luxuriating in the city's best spa; or book a session in the salon (and discover why staff all looks like a hair model).

Lodhi Rd., New Delhi 110 003. © **800/532-333** In the U.S., or 011/4363-3333. Fax 011/4363-3335. www. amanresorts.com. amannewdelhi@amanresorts.com. 39 units, 28 apt.-style "Lodhi" suites. High season (Oct–Apr) $750 Aman Room double, $1,400 Aman Suite, $1,250–$1,650 Lodhi Suite, $1,450–$2,400 Lodhi Pool Suite. May–Sept: $550 Aman Room double, $1,200 Aman Suite. Lodhi Suites and Lodhi Pool Suites, with 1, 2, or 3 bedrooms, priced from $1,250. Rates include airport or train station transfers. 10% service charge and taxes extra. AE, DC, MC, V. **Amenities:** 2 restaurants; library-lounge; cigar lounge; bar; airport transfers (free); highly specialized city tours; health club and spa (w/Ayurvedic, sports, Russian, and Thai treatments, and traditional Turkish *hammams*); Pilates studio; pool (outdoor, heated); room service; 3 squash courts; 3 tennis courts; yoga. *In room:* A/C, TV/DVD, butler service, hair dryer, minibar (free), music system, MP3 docking station, plunge pool, Wi-Fi (free).

The Imperial ★★★ This gracious establishment (built in 1931) is the best large hotel in Delhi—certainly for anyone wanting something more atmospheric than any chain, no matter how luxurious, can offer. Only at The Imperial can you recover from your jet lag in the elegance of colonial-era Delhi—without even setting foot out of the lobby. It's also incredibly convenient (only a short stroll to Connaught Place) yet tranquil, and has one of the deepest, largest pools in Delhi. Spacious guest rooms (no need for a suite; opt for an Imperial or Heritage Room) with wonderfully high ceilings are furnished in colonial-era elegance. However, it is the public areas, like the double-volume colonnaded veranda and grand 1911 bar, that are a sheer delight—huge, elegant, and everywhere a showcase of Delhi's imperial past. A huge collection of original art adorns every corridor (a veritable museum of 18th- and 19th-c. art, which you can explore with the resident curator). Silver-service breakfasts are among the best in the world, and Spice Route one of our favorite restaurants.

1 Janpath, New Delhi 110 001. ℂ **011/2334-1234** or 011/4150-1234. Fax 011/2334-2255. www.the imperialindia.com. luxury@theimperialindia.com. 231 units. Rs 22,500 Imperial double; Rs 27,500 Heritage double; Rs 32,000–Rs 2,00,000 suite; Rs 6,000 (above 12), Rs 3,000 (below 12) extra bed. AE, DC, MC, V. **Amenities:** 5 restaurants; 2 bars; pastry shop; airport transfer (Rs 2,600); art gallery babysitting; concierge; currency exchange; doctor-on-call; fitness center; heated pool; room service; valet. *In room:* A/C, TV, butler service (luxury suites only), DVD player (all except Imperial Rooms), fax machine (on request), hair dryer, minibar, Wi-Fi (Rs 300/hr., Rs 1,200/day).

The Oberoi ★★★   If you like being treated with the reverence of a celebrity, this is the place to stay—genuflecting staff is trained to make you feel like royalty, and every room comes with a butler; a typical characteristic of all the Oberoi hotels. Service aside, the hotel's location—east of the Lodi Gardens (near Humayun's Tomb) and surrounded by the green oasis of Delhi's golf course—makes for tranquillity, although, considering the heady buzz in the lobby and even in the popular coffee shop, **threesixty,** you need to be in your room or at the pool to really escape it all. The carpeted guest rooms are gorgeous and richly textured, bathrooms a little on the small side but impeccably decked out. The higher up your room, the better the view; odd-numbered rooms look towards Humayun's Tomb.

Dr. Zakir Hussain Marg, New Delhi 110 003. ℂ **011/2436-3030.** Fax 011/2436-0484. www.oberoihotels. com. reservations.tond@oberoihotels.com. 283 units. Rs 19,500 deluxe double; Rs 23,500 luxury double; Rs 28,500 premiere double; Rs 33,000 executive suite; Rs 45,000 special executive suite; Rs 59,000 deluxe suite; Rs 75,000 luxury and duplex suite; Rs 99,000 curzon suite; Rs 2,30,000 kohinoor suite. Taxes extra. AE, DC, MC, V. **Amenities:** 3 restaurants; bar; *enoteca* (wine bar); patisserie and delicatessen; airport transfer (free for premiere rooms and suites; Rs 3,250 for others); babysitting; concierge; doctor-on-call; fitness centre; Internet (Rs 450/hr.); indoor and outdoor heated pool; room service; spa; valet. *In room:* A/C, TV, butler service, DVD player, fax machine (except 1st floor), hair dryer, minibar, Wi-Fi (Rs 800/40 min.–24 hr.).

Shangri-La Hotel ★   Making good use of space and light, and less pretentious than some of the city's more established luxury hotels, this is a good choice if you're looking for a central location but don't want to shell out on The Imperial; it also has a gorgeous pan-Asian restaurant, **19 Oriental Avenue,** which is beautiful to look at, with two live kitchens serviced by hardworking kimono-clad waitresses. Most guest rooms enjoy great views of the city; the higher up you go, the more intriguing the city scene—ask for a "Parliament View" if you'd like to see a greener Delhi. Deluxe rooms start on the 12th floor; they're carpeted and dressed in earthy tones, and are very spacious compared to that of many other large city hotels. Horizon rooms are on higher (17th and 18th) floors and are priciest, but come with a host of amenities. Outdoor areas, although small, include a fabulous pool surrounded by trees.

19 Ashoka Rd., Connaught Place, New Delhi 110 001. ℂ **011/4119-1919.** Fax 011/4119-1988. www. shangri-la.com. slnd@shangri-la.com. 320 units. Rs 16,000 superior double; Rs 19,000 deluxe double; Rs 19,000 premiere double; Rs 22,000 Horizon superior double; Rs 22,000 Horizon premiere double; Rs 25,000–Rs 92,000 suite; Rs 2,500 extra bed. Taxes extra. AE, DC, MC, V. **Amenities:** 2 restaurants; bar; lobby lounge-bar; pastry shop; airport transfer (Rs 2,590); babysitting; doctor-on-call; health club; Internet (complimentary); indoor and outdoor Jacuzzis; Ayurvedic massage; heated outdoor pool; room service. *In room:* A/C, TV, hair dryer, minibar, Wi-Fi (complimentary).

Expensive
The Ambassador Hotel ★   Not far from Lodi Gardens and Humayun's Tomb, and practically next door to Khan Market, this hotel—operating since 1950—has an old-world ambience, with plenty of wood paneling and understated 21st-century luxuries like i-Pod docking stations. It's not particularly elegant, and you might find standard guest rooms small and cluttered, but if you're counting your rupees it offers relatively

good value in this price category and is perfectly acceptable if the other recommendations **435** are full. The superior guest room are worth the extra Rs 1,500 with French doors opening onto private balconies (not that there's all that much to see) and large naturally lit bathrooms. Buffet breakfasts are taken in the bright, laid-back **Yellow Brick Road** coffee shop, which has an outdoor section that can be lovely in the morning. It's less opulent and grandiose than some of the other upmarket hotels in town, with less formal but pleasant enough service.

Sujan Singh Park, Cornwallis Rd., New Delhi 110 003. © **011/2463-2600.** Fax 011/2463-8219. www. tajhotels.com. ambassador.delhi@tajhotels.com. 88 units. Rs 10,000 standard double; Rs 11,500 superior double; Rs 13,500 executive double; Rs 18,000 deluxe suite; Rs 1,000 extra bed. Taxes extra. AE, DC, MC, V. **Amenities:** 2 restaurants; bar; airport transfer (Rs 1,200); babysitting; currency exchange; doctor-on-call; Internet (Rs 552/hr., Rs 2,758/8 hr.); pool; room service; spa. *In room:* A/C, TV, minibar, MP-3 docking station on request, Wi-Fi (Rs 220/hr., Rs 661/day).

The Claridges ★ With over half a century behind it, this elegant old-fashioned hotel—in an upmarket residential neighborhood, convenient to many Central Delhi sights—may not offer the same posh luxury as the city's overrepresented Western chains, but provides good access to local life as its smart, down-to-earth restaurants and watering holes feature highly on the local social barometer. **Dhaba,** the Punjabi restaurant, serves a refined, hygienic version of the simple, tasty food found along North India's busy highways; **Sevilla** is the semialfresco Mediterranean restaurant under a canopy of trees and thatch; the attached vodka bar is sublime. Ongoing room renovations in recent years have been met with several steep jumps in price, and accommodations are a mixed bag, with rates charged according to the relative level of comfort and aesthetic appeal. The Claridges rooms in both wings have private balconies and a more sumptuous look than the deluxe category; club suites are aimed with business travelers in mind.

12 Aurangzeb Rd., New Delhi 110 011. © **011/4133-5133.** Fax 011/2301-0625. www.claridges.com. info@claridges.com. 137 units. Rs 11,500 deluxe double; Rs 13,000 Claridges Room double; Rs 16,000 Club double; Rs 25,000–Rs 45,000 suites; Rs 2,000 extra bed. Taxes extra. AE, DC, MC, V. **Amenities:** 4 restaurants; 2 bars; tea lounge; patisserie; airport transfer (Rs 2,200); babysitting; currency exchange; doctor-on-call; health club w/spa/sauna/steam; Internet (Rs 200/hr., Rs 700/day); outdoor pool; kiddies' pool; room service. *In room:* A/C, TV, DVD on request, hair dryer, minibar, scale, Wi-Fi (Rs 200/hr., 700/day).

The Park ★ The fabulous Park has injected some humor into the serious aspirations of Delhi's other five-star properties, with a chichi designer makeover that extends from the cool drama of the prettily festooned lobby, to the ultratrendy restaurants and bar, and right into the elegant guest rooms and intelligently designed bathroom. If you require a tub, book a "luxury premium" room, which is enormous. Because of the curved shape of the hotel, guest rooms vary in size somewhat: The largest are at the corners of each floor—it's worth requesting these. For indulgences, there's Aura—gym, spa, and saloon; and there's often a party in and around the funky pool, which not only has a bar but a net—so guests can play water volleyball—and a giant mirror ball to remind them they're on vacation! Our favorite chain hotel in its price range, with enough visual fabulousness to just about make up for the disconcertingly indifferent service levels.

15 Parliament St., New Delhi 110 001. © **011/2374-3000.** Fax 011/2373-4400. www.theparkhotels.com. resv.del@theparkhotels.com. 220 units. Rs 12,000 luxury double; Rs 14,000 premium double; Rs 18,000 residence double; Rs 30,000 deluxe suite; Rs 50,000 presidential suite. Rates include breakfast. Residence units, and suites, include airport transfers. Taxes extra. AE, DC, MC, V. **Amenities:** 3 restaurants; 2 bars; airport transfer (Rs 2,096); babysitting; doctor-on-call; health club; library of DVDs and CDs; massage; pool; room service; spa with sauna and steam; Wi-Fi (Rs 400/hr., Rs 800/day). *In room:* A/C, TV, DVD, hair dryer, Internet (Rs 400/hr., Rs 800/day), minibar, MP-3 docking station (only in Residence rooms and suites).

Taj Mahal Hotel ★   Among our top five-star hotel picks in the Capital, and as such offering hands-down best value in the superior room category, this opulent, slightly brash hotel has an exciting atmosphere, award-wining restaurants and a range of superefficient amenities. Its major drawing card is the high esteem in which it is held locally—this is one of the best places to watch the Delhi glitterati at play and work: Capped by *zardozi* domes, the lobby alone sees a huge variety of beautiful models and high-powered execs swishing by. Despite wonderful service and every amenity you could wish for, guest rooms are unexceptional, designed more for efficiency and all-around comfort than to keep you staring at the walls (or boxed in the little bathrooms). No matter: After a day's sightseeing, head for the pool, where you can watch as raptors cut their way through a darkening sky, or chill out in the spa before heading to **Rick's,** one of Delhi's best bars. (*Note:* With doubles starting from Rs 8,500 it may be the slightly cheaper option, but don't get bumped down to the **Taj Palace Hotel,** which attracts see-and-be-seen weddings, gigantic corporate functions, and other high-end social functions that impact negatively on service; the location in the Diplomatic Enclave is also a drawback.)

Number One Mansingh Rd., New Delhi 110 011. ✆ **011/2302-6162.** Fax 011/2302-6070. www.tajhotels. com. mahal.delhi@tajhotels.com. 294 units. Rs 11,500 superior rooms; Rs 18,500 deluxe double; Rs 20,500 Taj Luxury; Rs 23,000 Taj Club double; Rs 40,000–Rs 250,000 suite. Taj Club and Suites include one-way airport transfer, breakfast, valet, wine, chocolates, and cocktail hour. Taxes extra. AE, DC, MC, V. **Amenities:** 7 restaurants; bar; airport transfer (Rs 2,481); babysitting; concierge; currency exchange; doctor-on-call; DVD and CD library; health club, spa and gym; Internet (Rs 400/hr.); pool; 24-hr. room service; yoga. *In room:* A/C, TV, fax machine (all except superior), minibar, Wi-Fi (Rs 200/hr., Rs 600/day).

Moderate

Ahuja Residency ★   Situated adjacent to a park in Golf Links, one of the most expensive residential areas in Delhi, this family-run hotel offers reasonable comfort, a peaceful retreat from the city, and well-meaning service. The owners maintain standards and upgrade facilities regularly, so if you prefer a more intimate lodging experience and can't quite afford to stay at Amarya (or, more likely, can't get a reservation there) than Ahuja and Shanti are the next options you need to enquire into. Try to reserve no. 12, a slightly larger-than-average corner unit, or fork out on no. 11 converted to a suite but costing the same. You may find mattresses a trifle soft, but cool white linens make up for this. Guests tend to make a beeline for the lovely terrace overlooking the park and the neat little lawn out front. There's a quaint country-style dining room for homey Indian meals. The Ahuja family also offers serviced apartments and has another guesthouse in Defence Colony.

193 Golf Links, New Delhi 110 003. ✆ **011/2461-1027.** Fax 011/2464-9008. www.ahujaresidency.com. info@ahujaresidency.com. 12 units. Rs 5,738 double. Rates include taxes, breakfast. AE, DC, MC, V. **Amenities:** Dining room; airport transfer (Rs 750); doctor-on-call; Internet (Rs 50/hr.); limited room service; travel and transport assistance. *In room:* A/C, TV, minibar, Wi-Fi (complimentary).

Amarya Haveli & Amarya Gardens ★★★ (Value)   Finally—exclusive boutique-style lodgings that combine eye-catching style, useful amenities (including round-the-clock chefs), relatively salubrious locations, *and* reasonable rates. Located in Hauz Khas, **Amarya Haveli** has six handsome rooms, each inspired by a different region of India and done out in luxurious locally sourced fabrics (owners Alex and Mathieu are in the textile business)—it's a clever synthesis of traditional and contemporary elements, with a hefty injection of personality. Pricier, but with an even greater sense of exclusivity, **Amarya Gardens** is a little farther south in a masterfully transformed Defence Colony mansion: Rooms are big and airy, and there's a cheerful, tree-shaded garden terrace. The signature here is the extensive use of white, accented with bold colors, antiques, and fresh flowers. Sexy and characterful, the Amarya properties are a real find, and rates remain very fair considering their obvious popularity. Besides good looks and luxurious accommodations, the homey-yet-sophisticated atmosphere means that you can really find yourself warming up to what is often experienced as a chaotic, alienating city.

Haveli: P-5 Hauz Khas Enclave, near Safdarjung Dev. Area, New Delhi 110 016. ℭ **011/4175-9268.** Fax 011/4265-1106. 6 Units. Rs 6,900 double; Rs 2,000 extra bed. **Gardens:** C 179 Defence Colony, New Delhi 110 024. ℭ **011/4656-2735.** Fax 011/4656-2734. www.amaryagroup.com. amaryahaveli@hotmail.com. 4 units. Rs 8,900 deluxe double; Rs 9,900 master suite. Rs 2,500 extra bed. Rates include breakfast and taxes. AE, MC, V. **Amenities:** Restaurant; lounge; bar; airport transfers (Rs 850–Rs 1,350); room service. *In room:* A/C and fans, TV, Wi-Fi (free).

Hans Plaza Hotel The best reason to stay here is the location: conveniently located near (10-min. walk) Connaught Place. Staff members at this small hotel are also wonderfully friendly and enthusiastic, which is a major draw, particularly after surviving the dread induced by the building's hideous facade (the hotel occupies only the ground and upper floors of some sort of office block). Inside, things have been spruced up quite dramatically, with a modern makeover in shades of brown against white marble floors, but be aware that guest rooms vary quite a bit. Ask for an executive room on the 17th or 18th floor, and you'll have a decent wood-floor room with larger windows; deluxe doubles have better beds and furnishings. The rooftop restaurant and bar afford grand views of the city. However, at the current rates, we'd personally prefer to be at one of the classier options such as Amarya Haveli & Gardens or The Manor.

15 Barakhamba Rd., Connaught Place, New Delhi. ℭ **011/6615-0000.** Fax 011/6615-0000. www.hans hotels.com. 74 units. Rs 9,000 executive double; Rs 10,000 deluxe double; Rs 12,000 suite. Rates include breakfast. Taxes extra. AE, DC, MC, V. **Amenities:** 2 restaurants; bar; airport transfer (Rs 1,200); babysitting; currency exchange; doctor-on-call; Internet (Rs 700/hr.); room service. *In room:* A/C, TV, hair dryer, minibar, Wi-Fi (Rs 200/hr., Rs 675/day).

Hotel Palace Heights ⟨Value⟩ If you're in town with an urgent need to be in a very central location, and don't demand too much from your lodgings, this is a great value, and considering its location—in the very heart of Connaught Place and just a 2-minute walk to the Rajiv Chowk Metro station—a good find. It is not however by any means a palace, and the only sense of height you'll get is the view from either the restaurant or the rooftop terrace, from where you can watch the mayhem on the street below or the fairly ugly urban scene created by the surrounding Connaught Place buildings. Accommodations, which occupy a single floor, have been entirely refurbished in a modern, clean aesthetic: LCD TVs, small marble bathrooms with glass-walled showers, and fairly comfortable mattresses, all packaged in a neutral, pleasing palette. Windows, thankfully, are double glazed to keep out noise and have both blinds and curtains to keep out the light.

D 26/28, Connaught Place, New Delhi 110 001. ℭ **011/4358-2610,** -2620, or -2630. Fax 011/4358-2640. www.hotelpalaceheights.com. reservations@hotelpalaceheights.com. 14 units. Rs 6,000 double. Rate includes breakfast. Taxes extra. DC, MC, V. **Amenities:** Restaurant; bar; doctor-on-call; room service. *In room:* A/C, TV, cookies, hair dryer, minibar, Wi-Fi (complimentary).

The Manor ★★ ⟨Value⟩ If you favor intimate, boutique-style hotels, this is a preeminently classy option, head and shoulders above the Hans Plaza, but it is somewhat inconveniently situated in Friends Colony, a smart residential quarter in the southwestern part of New Delhi. As such it's a little cut off from the sights and shops, but the neighborhood provides a wonderful respite from the madness and traffic of the city, and if you're in transit or only here for a couple of nights you won't need to seek out dining options, as the little restaurant, **Indian Accent,** has an excellent reputation. Given the over-all elegance, facilities and gracious service (as well as a spirit of generosity typified with free airport transfer and Wi-Fi), and an intimate atmosphere unmatched by the larger city hotels, the standard rooms offer one of the best value deals in town.

77 Friends Colony (West), New Delhi 110 065. ✆ **011/2692-5151** or -7510. Fax 011/2692-2299. www. themanordelhi.com. info@themanordelhi.com. 12 units. Rs 7,500 standard double; Rs 9,500 superior room; Rs 12,750 junior suite; Rs 18,000 Manor suite. Rs 2,000 extra bed. Rates include breakfast, one-way airport transfer, and Wi-Fi. Taxes and service charge extra. AE, DC, MC, V. **Amenities:** Restaurant; bar; airport transfer (free one-way); concierge; doctor-on-call; room service. *In room:* A/C, TV, DVD (selection of movies available), minibar, Wi-Fi (complimentary).

Shanti Home ★ (Value Winner of the Best Bargain category in the 2009 Traveller's Choice Awards (though it's nowhere near as fine as either of the similarly priced, and comparatively luxurious Amarya properties), this addition to the despairingly small number of nonhotel options has fast become very popular, so book early. Hardly surprising: it's both an ideal transit option, offering excellent value and super efficient airport pickups, as well as a comfortable, reliable base in the city. Aside from the clean functional rooms, thematically styled by owners Rajat and Sanjana, the well-trained staff is knowledgeable about city sights and shops. There is a lovely terrace garden which doubles as a restaurant and plenty of lounges to read, watch TV, or chat with fellow guests. With easy availability of all manner of facilities, we're happy to overlook its slightly inconvenient location—half hour from the city center; the metro station is however, a mere hop away.

A1/300, Janakpuri, New Delhi 110 058. ✆ **011/4157-3366.** Fax 011/2561-9418. www.shantihome.com. 17 units. Rs 7,000 premium double; Rs 8,000 luxury double; Rs 1,000 extra bed. Rates include taxes and breakfast. MC, V. **Amenities:** 1 restaurant; bar; airport transfer (Rs 500); concierge; currency exchange; doctor-on-call; complimentary laptop in lounge; ayurvedic massage; room service; steam; TV in lounge. *In room:* A/C, minibar (on request); Wi-Fi (complimentary).

Inexpensive

Delhi Bed and Breakfast (Value This is an excellent homestay-style option if you don't mind being a little way out of the center. Besides a comfortable, homey bedroom (with fresh flowers, back-supporting foam mattresses, and plenty of cupboard space) and the option of regular home-cooked meals (served in a tiny family dining room), you'll have access to the advice, assistance, and lively repartee of your enthusiastic and hands-on host, Sheikh Pervez Hameed, who can hook you up with good guides, taxis, and all sorts of tours; his wife, Lubna, will even take you shopping. The nearby commercial center also has dozens of restaurants and bars. Bear in mind that you'll be in a fairly busy neighborhood: Traffic sounds are never far away. But you get to live like a pampered local: Have the family barber summoned for a trim or escape to a plant-dappled terrace and meditate on suburbia.

A-6, Friends Colony East, Delhi 110 065. ✆ **98-1105-7103.** www.delhibedandbreakfast.com. delhibed andbreakfast@gmail.com. 3 units (with showers). Rs 3,550 double; Rs 1,250 extra bed. Rate includes breakfast. No credit cards. **Amenities:** Dining room; airport transfer (Rs 650); cooking lessons; doctor-on-call; mobile phone hire; TV lounge. *In room:* A/C, Wi-Fi (complimentary).

Master Guest House ★★ (Value Staying here is your best opportunity to rub shoulders with sophisticated, down-to-earth, extremely knowledgeable Delhiites—Avnish and Urvashi Puri are the hands-on owners who've put their immense energy and creative panache into making this one of Delhi's most satisfying experiences. Don't expect hotel-like amenities, however, but rather a genuine opportunity to dip into local life. You'll stay in one of four immaculate guest rooms—each with comfortable bed, writing table, and carefully sourced artwork. Rooms share pristine, eco-conscious bathroom facilities; all rooms how have attached eco-conscious bathrooms, and the purification system means you'll shower in water that's clean enough to drink. Book at least one healing session with Urvashi, a reiki master, and then set off with Avnish on one of his wonderful "Hidden Delhi" tours; he'll show you a world seldom seen by visitors to Delhi, and he'll unravel Hinduism's spiritual origins in a profoundly logical way. Book several months in advance, or risk staying elsewhere.

R-500 New Rajinder Nagar, New Delhi 110 060. ℭ **011/2874-1089** or 011/6547-9947 or 011/2874-1914. www.masterbedandbreakfast.com. info@master-guesthouse.com. 4 units. Rs 3,500 double. Rate includes breakfast. No credit cards. **Amenities:** Dining room; airport transfers (pickup Rs 595–Rs 850; drop-off Rs 295 Rs 395); library; meditation; reiki; yoga. In room: A/C, heater, Wi-Fi (free).

South Delhi

Hyatt Regency ★ Like all the city's big, modern hotels, the exterior is forgettable, and the lobby, with its faint resemblance to a Hindu temple, feels a little dated, but it has some of the city's best dining options, supported by locals, which keeps it abuzz. Accommodations, styled with business travelers in mind, are constantly updated to keep with the times. They're not huge, but the parquet-wood floors, sleek furnishings, and queen-size beds with thick mattresses will certainly make you feel comfortable—ask for the pool-facing bay rooms, aside from the view, they're a fraction more spacious (but slightly more expensive). Hyatt Regency features the city's most authentic Italian restaurant (don't miss the pizzas here), the excellent China Kitchen (arguably the best Chinese restaurant in India), our favorite Japanese restaurant and the **Polo Bar,** rated one of the city's best after-dark hangouts.

Bhikaji Cama Place, Ring Rd., New Delhi 110 066. ℭ **011/2679-1234.** Fax 011/2679-1122. www.delhi. hyatt.com. 508 units. Rates change daily and can vary from Rs 10,000–Rs 25,000 depending on whether you opt for the Hyatt Guest Room, Pool View Room or the Regency Club Room. Taxes extra. AE, DC, MC, V. **Amenities:** 4 restaurants; bar; patisserie; babysitting; currency exchange; doctor-on-call; fitness club; outdoor pool; room service; 2 outdoor tennis courts. In room: A/C, TV, minibar, Wi-Fi (Rs 325/hr., Rs 925/day).

North Delhi

Oberoi Maidens ★★ This peaceful Georgian gem is a little out of the center of Delhi, but it has more character and charm than most of the big hotel competitors and is just a short stroll from the nearest Metro station, so getting into the city is a breeze. Operating since 1903, it retains much of its grand architectural ambience—all stained-glass windows, thick columns, stately arches, and deep corridors—hinting at what it might have been like when Lutyens stayed here while supervising the development of the Raj Bhavan. Of the standard (superior) rooms, no. 105 is a particularly good option, with a second, smaller bedroom, a large bathroom and plenty of natural light. Lovely grounds, with plenty of established trees and shrubs, and a period kidney-shaped pool add further serenity, only disrupted when parties and weddings are hosted here. Good news is that the Maidens is just a short stroll from the nearest Metro and convenient to city center.

7 Sham Nath Marg, Delhi 110 054. ℭ **011/2397-5464** or 1800/11-7070. Fax 011/2398-0771. www. maidenshotel.com. 56 units. Rs 11,500 superior double; Rs 13,500 premium; 17,500 deluxe suite; Rs 20,500 luxury suite; Rs 3,500 extra bed. Taxes extra. Check online for good off-season discounts. AE, DC, MC, V. **Amenities:** 2 restaurants; bar; airport transfer (Rs 2,000); babysitting; currency exchange; doctor-on-call; outdoor pool; room service; 2 tennis courts. In room: A/C, TV, DVD player (deluxe suites only), hair dryer, minibar, Wi-Fi (Rs 250/hr., Rs 1,000/day).

Five-Star Culinary Flagships
Where You Can't Go Wrong

The city's five-star hotels offer consistent, refined service, and unlike in most capitals, the (elite) locals dine at them. All listings (barring South Delhi's Hyatt and Crowne Plaza in Gurgaon) are in Central Delhi. Expect to pay a premium.

Bukhara ★★★ (✆ 011/2611-2233), the Indian restaurant at the ITC Maurya Sheraton (p. 432), has a busy display kitchen, where meat and vegetables hang from swordlike kebab spears and chefs slave to produce delicacies from a menu that hasn't changed in 30 years and continues to earn accolades as one of the world's finest Asian restaurants. Staff is for instance immensely proud that Bill Clinton apparently chose to stay at the hotel "because of our restaurant," and there's even a dish named in his honor. Start by ordering an assorted kebab platter and follow that up with any of the classic lamb *(raan)* dishes, best savored with thin butter *naans*. Finish off with a traditional rice-based *phirni* pudding or one of their amazing *kulfis* (ice cream). Next door to the Sheraton is the glitzy Taj Palace Hotel (p. 436), where the city's elite line up (sometimes literally) to get a table at **Masala Art** ★★★ (✆ 011/2611-0202), which makes a very conscious (usually successful) attempt to dazzle. The chefs turn cooking into performance art, putting on engaging food demonstrations at mealtimes; spectators eat whatever delicacies are produced. Of the daily a la carte specials, look for *achari jhinga* (prawns flavored with raw mango), and *galouti* kebabs prepared with finely minced lamb and 126 different herbs. Reinventing Indian cuisine is **Varq** ★★★, the new restaurant at Taj Mahal (p. 436). Absolutely sumptuous in design and cuisine, it soars higher than any of legendary Chef Hemant Oberoi's creations so far; a mix of contemporary meets classic, innovatively using Indian recipes with exotic ingredients—prawns and asparagus curry from Calicut, meat curry cooked in a *martabaan* (clay pot), sea bass, and diver's scallops—all seem to blend in effortlessly. Taj Palace also does old-school dining pretty well, so if you prefer a stiff, formal (and potentially very romantic) evening in the company of exquisite French cuisine, dress smart for **Orient Express** ★ (✆ 011/2611-0202), where you dine in a posh replica of a Pullman train carriage. Enjoy preboarding drinks on the "platform," as the bar area is called; your four-course journey is inspired by the countries through which the Orient Express passes on its Paris-to-Istanbul run, and is likely to include items such as Camembert soufflé with paprika sauce, pan-seared reef cod with raw papaya salad, and the extremely popular oven-roasted New Zealand rack of lamb, encrusted with herbs and almonds and served with lamb jus.

If you need a good excuse to swan through the lobby of The Imperial (p. 433), reserve a table at **The Spice Route** ★★★ (✆ 011/2334-1234), voted one of the top-10 restaurants in the world by *Condé Nast Traveler*. The decor alone is worth a visit—every nook and cranny is hand-painted by temple artists flown in from Kerala. The food takes you on a complex culinary journey, from the Malabar Coast to Sri Lanka, Malaysia to Indonesia, Thailand to Vietnam. Certainly, it has the best ever *tom kha kai* (classic Thai soup) and mouthwatering *chemeen thoren* (Kerala-style prawns).

There's a veritable war going on among supporters of Delhi's top Chinese restaurants. Many lean toward **Taipan** ★★★ ((℃) **011/2436-3030**) at The Oberoi (p. 434), where you can fill up on amazing *dim sum* (tiny dumplings filled with an assortment of tasty morsels, steamed, and served in bamboo baskets), best enjoyed at lunchtime with fantastic views over Delhi Golf Course. On par is the range of Oriental dishes served at the Shangri-La's (p. 434) beautiful **19 Oriental Avenue** ★★★ ((℃) **011/4119-1919**), where you can savor close to perfect Thai, Japanese, and Chinese cuisine. Thai chicken soup (flavored with galangal and lemon grass), Cantonese-style steamed red snapper (green spring onions and top-notch soy sauce bring out the flavor), and silky-smooth *teppanyaki* tofu steak are just a handful of recommendations from a diverse menu. There's also an exquisite sushi bar (arguably the finest in town). The Taj Mahal Hotel (p. 436) boasts the excellent **House of Ming** ★★★, which is gorgeously decorated and, thanks to a recent revolution in the kitchen, has emerged as a formidable culinary force focusing on Cantonese and Szechuan cooking; it now also offers delectable dim sum and seafood selections and has an enviable tea menu. But our current favorite is Hyatt Regency's (p. 439) **China Kitchen** ★★★ the restaurant that has become pretty much the talk of the town and understandably so—one bite of the fresh prawn dim sum and you know you've arrived! The setting is refined and the Peking duck reputed to be the best in the country with much drama attached to the way it is served; we sampled 25 different dishes and loved every one, so put your money here—it's a sure win.

The Hyatt is also incidentally where you'll find the best pizzas in town, at **La Piazza** ★ ((℃) **011/2679-1234**). Chef Wladimiro Gadioli dishes out authentic Italian cuisine; an extensive wine list includes superb vintages from around the world, though the prices may have you gagging into your glass. Excellent, authentic Spanish and Catalan dishes are served in classy, beautiful surroundings (with a supersexy tapas bar downstairs) at **Lodhi** ★★★ in the new Aman hotel (p. 433). While it's a big draw with Delhi's young, fun-loving crowd, it's also a great family venue. For a Spanish dish with a slightly locally twist, order the fish stew prepared with saffron, or the lamb *paletilla,* made with dried fruits.

Delhi's only Brazillian churrascaria, located at Crowne Plaza (Site 2, Sector 29, Gurgaon; (℃) **0124/4530-0000;** dinner only) is very good indeed. The sheer length and styling of the room at **Wildfire** ★★, ending with flaming urns on large pebbles, makes for great ambience (make a reservation for a table by the window where the flaming urns are), but it's the food that has meat-lovers coming back for more. After sampling their salad buffet, you're meant to sit tight and experience the *rodizio* style of service—various meats are brought to the table on skewers and sliced straight on to your plate. Brazillian chefs believe in not letting your plate sit empty until you raise your hands and beg them to stop.

Finally, if you simply want to sit back and relax with a good bottle of wine and a buffet choice of pretty much anything from anywhere around the world, The Oberoi's (p. 434) smart, contemporary **Threesixtydegrees** ★ ((℃) **011/2436-3030**) is open all day and somehow almost always buzzing with businessmen.

Delhi's dining scene is booming. Ask locals to name their favorite restaurant, and the only thing you can be sure of is that you won't get a predictable response—from fiercely criticizing Bukhara (Delhi's long-reigning restaurant champion) to praising some modest hole-in-the-wall, people are talking, and writing, about food. With the culinary revolution clearly in full swing, it's no longer necessary to hide out in hotel eateries for fear of contracting "Delhi belly." More likely, you'll experience a dent in your budget if you choose to eat in the hotels, and you'll miss out on a highly recommended opportunity to see where the city's innumerable foodies are feasting these days. To help you make the leap of faith, we're discussing the best five-star hotel restaurants in a separate box, any of whom are worth dining at, but we hope you'll find your way to at least one of the stand-alone choices we've reviewed below. For many more options (hundreds, in fact), you'd do worse than to consult the annual *Times Food Guide,* originally written by *Times of India* food critic Sabina Sehgal Saikia (who tragically lost her life in the Mumbai terrorist attack in 2008) but now in a transition phase, it's available at booksellers and magazine vendors (Rs 100).

Expensive

An irritating trend (at least for voyeurs) among the moneyed crowd is to eat at "members-only" restaurants. The most popular of these very hip joints is **Oriental Octopus** (Habitat World, India Habitat Centre, Lodhi Rd.; ✆ **011/2468-2222** or 011/5122-0000, ext. 2512), where you dine at curved, meandering tables shared by gorgeous designer-clad Delhiites—a million miles from the streets of Shahjahanabad. See if your concierge can arrange a reservation, or find a member and tag along. The food isn't bad either—start with Singaporean steamed spring rolls, and move on to Malaysian black-pepper prawns tossed in garlic and crushed pepper. It also has an interesting bargain-priced buffet spread.

Even more irritating (for restaurateurs at any rate) has been the city's clampdown on health and safety regulations, which saw the closure of numerous venues because of unsound architecture (a problem in some of the city's more ancient structures). In mid-2007, for example, the sublime and wonderful **Olive Bar and Kitchen** that was located in Mehrauli had been closed and is still awaiting an imminent comeback; in the meantime, you can visit **Olive Beach** (9, Sardar Patel Marg, Chanakyapuri; ✆ **011/4604-0404;** www.olivebarandkitchen.com), although we find it better for drinks than for what comes on your plate.

For superb Italian by one of Delhi's most celebrated restaurateurs, Ritu Dalmia (also responsible for London's Vama), try to get a table at **Diva** ★★ (M-8, M Block Market, Greater Kailash I; ✆ **011/2921-5673**), which has drawn countless accolades despite fever-pitch prices. You simply can't go wrong here; any of the seafood starters are recommended, and the lamb chops in red wine are superb. Also under her able hands is the pizzeria Café ★ at the Italian Cultural Centre (Nyaya Marg, Chanakyapuri; ✆ **011/2467-4575**), best done if you're in the embassy zone running around for official work or cultural screenings, as well as the brand new café **Latitude 28** ★ (✆ **011/2465-7175**) run by Goodearth (see "Shopping" later): with an international menu, this all-day dining focuses on unpretentious freshly prepared food. One could just have a simple panini and a juice, or go for something more wholesome like a pasta or lamb stew; there is also a huge array of organic salads for the health conscious.

Tip: We've arranged our restaurants according to pricing but it may be more useful to know where the closest recommendations are depending on where you're based, or find yourself while sightseeing or shopping; herewith some guidance: While in Old Delhi, dine at Chor Bizarre, Karims or Haldirams. If near Connaught Place, visit Veda, Ploof, United Coffee House, or Basil & Thyme. If still in Central Delhi, but near Chanakyapuri, Khan Market or Lodhi Road, dine at Crepes and More, Oriental Octopus, Olive Beach or Khan Chacha's. And when in South Delhi, dine at Diva, Oh Calcutta, Park Balluchi, Punjabi by Nature, Swagath, Sagar, Smokehouse Grill, It's Greek to Me, or Naivedyam.

Ploof ★ Finds SEAFOOD/ECLECTIC   This is not only an underpublicized Gandhi-clan hangout, but it's also where our dearest Delhiite friends take us when we're in town. It may not be the most fashionable eatery in town, but it's bright, comfortable, and reliable, and the seafood is always fresh. The biggest drawback here has to be deciding what to have: The menu is notoriously long-winded and draws such diverse inspiration that you'll be hard-pressed to order. Here's a suggestion: Start with the Fisherman's Basket (grilled baby octopus, prawns, and fish), then choose between the garlic-flavored grilled jumbo prawns, Singaporean chili crab, pepper-crusted Japanese bluefin tuna, Kerala-style fish curry, or even braised abalone. Or select the fish of the day and arrange for it to be simply chargrilled with lemon butter or stir-fried with basil leaves and lemon grass.

13 Main Market, Lodhi Colony. ℭ **011/2464-9026**. Reservations recommended. Main courses Rs 275–Rs 950; marketplace seafood priced by weight. 10% service charge. MC, V. Daily 11am–3:30pm and 7–11pm.

Shalom ★ LEBANESE/MEDITERRANEAN   Catering to a younger upmarket dining crowd, this is a smart, sexy spot in south Delhi (also with a new branch in South Delhi's Vasant Vihar). Smartly attired waitstaff, upbeat lounge music soundtrack, and soothing decor (hand-plastered walls, burnt-wood furniture) indicate you're in for a night of fun, starting perhaps with a cocktail like the cucumber sparkle (spiked with vodka) or the Shalom iced tea and then moving swiftly on to a meze platter. Or tuck into a decadent tapas selection that includes skewered fish in a lemon, paprika, and garlic sauce. For mains, the char grilled chicken breast with tangy mustard sauce or the grilled fish with orange chilly sauce are favorites. Vegetarians will love the Spanish corn crepes, and the spiced couscous. The decent wine list is dominated by Chilean and Argentinean vintages. Do not pass up the frozen lemon pie or the cinnamon ice cream when you're offered dessert. Another branch is at D-4, D Block Market, Vasant Vihar (ℭ **98-1869-8784**).

N-18, N Block Market, Greater Kailash I. ℭ 98-1014-8084. www.shalomexperience.com. Reservations highly recommended. Main courses Rs 425–Rs 1,395. 10% service charge. AE, MC, V. Daily 12:30–3:30pm and 7:30pm–1am.

Véda ★ NORTH INDIAN   Designed by iconic fashion guru Rohit Bal, this centrally located restaurant is a place to see and be seen. The interior space has a dreamlike elegance—a careful balance of baroque fantasy and contemporary appeal—that feels light-years away from the chaos of Connaught Place just outside. It's garnered plenty of accolades but these are more for its fashionable status than for the cuisine, which is nothing exceptional. Nevertheless, you could do worse than to order one of the seven-course tasting menus. Alternatively, try the lamb Véda special, an unusual combination of lamb on the bone and minced lamb, or have the highly recommended Parsi sea bass (*paatra ni machi*). Dishes are generally spiced to suit an international palate, so you'll need to ask if you want the heat turned up. Oh, and plan on serious contemplation of the wine offerings.

H 27, Outer Circle, Connaught Circus. ℭ **011/4151-3535** or 011/4151-3940/1. www.vedarestaurants. com. Reservations essential. Main courses Rs 250–Rs 775; tasting menus Rs 975–Rs 1,175. AE, MC, V. Daily noon–3:30pm and 8–11:30pm.

One Connaught Place institution you certainly shouldn't pass up is **United Coffee House ★**, which began 5 decades ago as a coffeehouse and is now also a multicuisine restaurant where you can sit for hours ogling the fantastic array of people who come here to feast, drink, strike deals, play cards, and pass the time. Interesting Art Deco interiors, lit by chandeliers, make this more about nostalgia than particularly inspiring cuisine, but the reasonable standard Indian food (meal for two should cost Rs 150–Rs 400), and prolonged two-for-one happy hours make this a favorite with locals and travelers alike. And, yes, the coffee is freshly brewed and brought to your table in a French press. Reserve for dinner, just in case (E-15, Inner Circle; 𝒞 **011/2341-1697** or -6075). **Crepes and More** (66, first floor, Khan Market; 𝒞 **98-1890-0005**) is one of the few stand-alone breakfast joints in the city (everything from yoghurt and muesli to dozens of choices in crepes and eggs) and perfect if you opt for an early morning walk in the near-by Lodhi Gardens or want to dine light while shopping in Khan Market. A popular lunchtime venue, **Basil and Thyme ★** (Santushti Shopping Complex, New Wellington Camp; 𝒞 **011/2467-3322**), serves healthy Eurocentric fare from the kitchen of octogenarian gourmand Bhicoo Manekshaw. The day's special and other healthy selections rarely fail to please, and the fabulous homemade cheesecakes and ice creams should be declared illegal. Combine it with your visit to the surrounding shopping complex, which is bound to work up your appetite; reserve ahead.

If you want a theme restaurant and are in the Gurgaon area, head for the Garden of Five Senses and grab a table at **Baujee ka Dhaba** (Saed Ul Ajab; 𝒞 **011/2953-5847;** http://baujeekadhaba.com), where folk art decorates the mud-effect walls, and even the waitstaff is in traditional garb. The food is distinctively Mughlai and Punjabi fare, rich and heavy, but unquestionably well made and delicious. Get the ever-popular *shammi* kebab or *dum pukht* chicken. Or just nibble on assorted kebabs while you enjoy a reasonably priced chilled beer. A fairly recent addition to a Delhi dining scene is **Oh! Calcutta ★** (E Block, International Trade Towers, Nehru Place; 𝒞 **011/2646-4180;** www.speciality. co.in), which is obsessed with just one thing: authentic, excellent Bengali cuisine. A visit here should be prefaced with a warning, though: Don't come for the decor, service, or even the slightest hint of romantic atmosphere. The only thing you get by way of entertainment is the opportunity to watch dozens of local middle-class families who are, like you, here for reliable, reasonably priced meals. And the food really is scrumptious, which takes the bite out of the surly demeanor of the waiters (who nevertheless make very competent recommendations, so bear with them).

Chor Bizarre ★ NORTH INDIAN/KASHMIRI   A fantasy of kitsch twisted into a unique space that is more irreverent museum than restaurant, Chor Bizarre (a pun on *chor bazaar,* literally "thieves' market") lives up to its name. It's packed with fascinating odds and ends (matchboxes, coins, chessboards, antique combs, ivory sandals, jewelry, chandeliers, a jukebox) and out-of-place furnishings (one table was previously a maharaja's bed, while a 1927 vintage Fiat has become the buffet-carrying "*Chaat* mobile"). This has to be one of India's most visually dynamic restaurants, a branch of which is now also open in London. Start with deep-fried lotus roots, prepared Kashmiri-style, and move on to *kakori kebab,* lamb marinated in 36 different spices and grilled in a tandoor, or cardamom-flavored lamb meatballs (*goshtaba*). Or order the Kashmiri *tarami* (thali), filled with treats and served from a traditional royal platter. (*Tip:* Avoid their extremely dull walking tour-cum-lunch package) com. Main courses Rs 155–Rs 365; Rs 495 *tarami*. AE, DC, MC, V. Daily noon–3:30pm and 7:30–11:30pm.

It's Greek to Me ★ GREEK   Whitewashed walls with cerulean blue windows and doors beckon you into India's first and only Greek restaurant. The food is authentic, the crowd is noisy as it would be in a typical Greek eatery, and you're even given plates to break—but only if you're disappointed with the meal. Three levels of decor to suit your mood—iron and wood on the lowest, low seating with dim lighting in the mezzanine, high chairs and a rocking atmosphere in the uppermost lounge-cum-bar. Start with *avgolemono* (typical Greek soup with eggs, lemon, and cream), followed by a dip platter (each excellent), or salads, and for the mains there are all the classics: *moussaka* (baked lamb mince, eggplant, and cheese), *spanokopita* (sautéed spinach with feta cheese in layers), or the excellent baked chicken *vasilikos* (seared chicken breast with scarmoza cheese, ham, and mushrooms). Round off with homemade fig ice cream.

B-6/4 Commercial Complex, Safdurjung Enclave. ℰ **011/4101-2240.** www.itsgreektome.com. Reservations highly recommended. Main courses Rs 400–Rs 600. AE, MC, V. Daily 12:30–3:30pm, 7pm–midnight; lounge closed Mon.

Park Balluchi ★★★ MUGHLAI/AFGHANI   Turbaned waiters in this award-winning restaurant serve an extensive and exciting range of kebabs and spicy tandoor items in a parklike atmosphere. Come for lunch and you may glimpse rabbits and peacocks, or one of the 300 deer that roam the park. The specialty at Balluchi is the *sangam seekh,* tantalizing combinations of two meats (chicken and mutton marinated in herbs); try the Afghani-style *murgh-potli*—tandoori-prepared chicken breast stuffed with minced mutton and served over a flaming sword. Other favorites include *raan sikandari,* roast leg of lamb marinated in herbs, spices, and rum and then grilled in the tandoor. Vegetarians should order *mewa paneer tukra,* paneer stuffed with raisins, sultanas, walnuts, and other nuts; preparation of this dish takes at least 12 hours. Be sure to get a side order of *peshawri naan,* bread cooked in the tandoor oven with poppy seeds and coriander leaves.

Deer Park, Hauz Khas Village. ℰ **011/2685-9369** or 011/2696-9829. Reservations for dinner and weekends essential. Main courses Rs 190–Rs 780. 5% service charge extra. AE, MC, V. Daily noon–11:45pm.

Punjabi By Nature ★ PUNJABI   This is one of Delhi's best-regarded Punjabi restaurants (now a reliable chain); at the Basant Lok venue there are two floors for diners, and a pub upstairs, all a mere 10 minutes' drive west of Haus Khas Village (or 15 min. from Safdarjung's tomb, the Hyatt Regency, or the Santushti Shopping Complex (see shopping below). Ask for a table by the atmospheric display kitchen. Try masala quail *(bataear masaledar)* or fresh *tandoori* pomfret, and take heed of the wine suggestions. The staff is particularly proud of the *raan-e-Punjab,* marinated whole leg of lamb cooked in the tandoor—you're served the tender meat as it literally falls off the bone. If you're adventurous, arrive for happy hour (4–8pm) and try the house specialty, a "golguppa" shot: a tiny *puri* (fried puffed bread) filled with spicy vodka, which you pop into your mouth whole.

11 Basant Lok, Vasant Vihar. ℰ **011/4151-6666** or -6667. www.punjabibynature.in. Main courses Rs 245–Rs 795. 10% service charge. AE, DC, MC, V. Daily 12:30pm–midnight.

Smokehouse Grill ★ MODERN EUROPEAN   All shades of wood, jute, and gorgeous lampshades make up most of what you can see behind and in-between the crowds that throng this happening spot. Retro nights on Friday's are insane with a guarantee that you won't be able to hear yourself think, but that's the point—you are meant to indulge freely and wildly in the award-winning cocktails at the buzzing bar and then make your way to the dining area and get smoked! The seared John Dory was delicious, the steak less so, but the salads and apple martinis more than made up for it not to mention the baked white chocolate and blueberry cheesecake! Look out for owner Riyaz Amlani's ultracool Kawasaki VN 2000 parked outside, which has become as synonymous with the restaurant as the tottering logo.

North Wing VIPPS Centre, LSC Masjid Moth, Greater Kailash II. © 011/4143-5530. www.smokehouse grill.in. Reservations required for dinner. Main courses Rs 380–Rs 1150 AE, MC, V. Daily 12:30–3pm, 7:30pm–midnight; bar open till 1am.

Swagath ★ SOUTH INDIAN   This might just be the best seafood restaurant in Delhi. Always busy, the place has a no-nonsense ambience over several floors in Defence Colony Market, a popular shopping destination in a relaxed residential area. The classic South Indian menu—Mangalorean, Maharashtran, Keralan, Malabari, and Chettinad cuisines—is a great testament to the diversity of Indian culinary influences. This is also the only place in town where you can sample "Bombay Duck": dried, crispy fish that makes a finger-licking starter. We also love the garlicky prawns, done in butter and pepper followed by the "special fish"; be sure to specify *"surmai,"* which is the less bony kingfish (*bangda*—mackerel—is the bonier alternative). If you're fond of Thai curries, you might like the taste of fish *gassi,* a Mangalorean-style dish with coconut gravy. *Tip:* If you're feeling adventurous, the little mobile vendor stationed near Swagath's entrance prepares excellent *paan.* Considered a digestive and a stimulant, these parcels of tobacco, betel nut, and other assorted ingredients (some even include low traces of opiate) may not be something you want to do regularly, but they're certainly a vital part of Indian street culture. Ask for one of the sweeter blends and remember to chew, not swallow!

14 Defence Colony Market. © 011/2433-7538. www.swagath.in. Reservations highly recommended. Main courses Rs 125–Rs 900. AE, MC, V. Daily 11am–11:30pm.

Inexpensive

Sagar is one of Delhi's favorite restaurant chains, serving reliable vegetarian South Indian food at reasonable prices till 11pm. Have one of the South Indian thali platters, and eat with your hands. End your meal with Madrasi filter coffee, or you can start your day the same way—the restaurant opens at 8am, which is the best time for traditional *idli* (South India's favorite breakfast dumplings) and chutneys. You'll battle to spend more than Rs 90 on food here. There's a good outlet at 18 Defence Colony Market (© 011/2433-3110; www.sagarratna.in), just 10 minutes from India Gate. When in Old Delhi, one must-see eatery is **Haldiram's ★** (1454/2, Chandini Chowk © 011/2883-3007; www.haldiram.com), always bustling with frenetic activity as locals flock to pick up the city's most legendary range of Indian sweets. Another legendary shop, worth a look in even if only to bask in the historic glow of a place that served both Nehru and Indira Gandhi (not to mention other Indian prime ministers), is a *paratha* shop recognizable by the sign reading **the power of pranthas—pt. gaya prasad shiv charan** (© 98-1126-3137), which you'll probably need your guide to help you seek out (it's at 34 Gali Pranthe Wail, Chandni Chowk). This shouldn't be too difficult, as the little eatery has been satisfying locals since 1872 and any guide worth his salt should know it. There are 20 different varieties of *paratha* available, and each comes with a thalilike plate filled with *sambals,* vegetables, lentils, and sauces to make a more substantial meal out of the popular street food. Grab a seat and join the Old Delhi locals.

Karim Hotel ★ MUGHLAI   In the heart of Old Delhi, not far from the Jama Masjid, Old Delhi most famous eatery dates from 1913, when it was opened by a chef who

---

> ## (Moments) Saucy Fingers
>
> One of our absolute favorite eating experiences in Delhi has got to be **Khan Chacha Kabab Corner** ★ ((C) **98-1067-1103;** Mon–Sat noon–10pm, Sun 4–10pm), a hole-in-the-wall kebab counter in Khan Market serving legendary mutton *seekh kababs,* wrapped in light *roomali rotis* (Rs 55), from a tiny kitchen manned by a squadron of brothers who've continued what their father started back in 1972. These delicious, juicy meat-filled rolls are prepared while you wait and served as a take-away snack; you can hang around and munch them on the spot, or smuggle a batch into your hotel room and sit down to a feast. *Be warned:* They're utterly addictive. Ask for onions and green chutney if you'd like to add a spicy edge, and be prepared for a deliciously decadent sauce to dribble down your chin. To get there, seek out the crowd of devotees that inevitably forms (at 75 Middle Lane); it's right next to The Kitchen, a pretentious and anonymous neon-lit cafe.

---

claimed to have hailed from a family of royal cooks who served, among other guests, the great Mughal emperor Akbar. Don't be put off by the informal setting; the food is very good. It's primarily a meat-eaters' hangout, with the real princely treats being the mutton *burra* kebabs. The butter-cooked chicken *(makhani murgh)* is also wonderful, as is the *badshahi badam pasanda,* mutton cooked with blended almonds and yogurt and fragrant spices. If you're really adventurous, you can also sample exotic fare such as spiced goat feet, or the advance-order *bakra* feast—lamb stuffed with chicken, rice, eggs, and dried fruit, a meal made for a dozen people (about Rs 5,500). No doubt about it. This is the real deal.

16 Gali Kababian, Jama Masjid (C) **011/2326-4981** or -9880. www.karimhoteldelhi.com. Main courses Rs 51–Rs 250. No credit cards. Daily 7am–midnight.

Naivedyam ★ SOUTH INDIAN VEGETARIAN Delhi has five branches of this fantastic, cramped, and always busy little South Indian restaurant; the one in Hauz Khas (marked by the Nandi statue facing the front entrance) is the original, atmospherically decorated with mirror-framed Tanjore paintings and pillars that have been beautifully carved and embossed. Start your meal with a spicy peppery lentil soup, called *rasam,* which is drunk as a curative and is something of an acquired taste. Thalis, or multicourse platters, are served at mealtime, and are a good way to sample a variety of tastes from the south. Alternatively, you can choose from a whole range of *dosas* (rice and lentil flour pancake; ask the waiter for some advice regarding which to order), always served with chutney (made from ground coconut and green chilies, sometimes with mint), and *sambar,* a souplike concoction of lentils, tamarind, and vegetables. Tea and coffee are served in the style typical of the south; no alcohol is served.

1 Hauz Khas Village. (C) **011/2696-0426.** Main courses Rs 60–Rs 200; thali Rs 125. AE, DC, MC, V. Daily 11am–11pm.

SHOPPING

The Delhi shopping experience is every bit as exciting as that found in Mumbai and Jaipur, but the sprawling size of the city makes it difficult to cover all in one day—best to concentrate on one area at a time. If this is your first port of call, try not to load your luggage too early with stuff to take home; best to arrange for it to be shipped directly—ask your hotel to help you arrange this. There are literally hundreds of courier companies in the city; either ask your hotel to take care of it, or catch a cab to the closest courier (again, staff at any of our recommended hotels can recommend where to go) and ship it off yourself—it costs surprisingly little and we have always (touch wood!) been greeted by the welcome sight of our much cherished parcels on our return.

It is probably a good idea to kick off your shopping expedition with a stop at Dilli Haat (reviewed below) to get a perspective of the range of regional arts and crafts, and approximate prices. And if something here really captures your heart, purchase it and have it shipped home, for it may not be available when you return. Note that most shops (and markets) are open from 10am to 7pm and are closed on Sunday, unless mentioned otherwise. Besides the areas described below, you can spend an entire day covering the old city of Shahjahanabad (see "The Top Attractions," earlier in this section). Finally, keep in mind that the recommended shops that follow are only a fraction of what's out there; if you know what you're looking for, it's best to inquire at both your hotel and the Janpath tourist office for alternatives.

Connaught Place If you want to get an idea of what lies ahead on your travels, visit a few of the 22 **State Government Emporiums** that line Baba Kharak Singh Marg; some recommended options are Himachal for blankets and shawls in particular (© 011/2336-3087); Tamil Nadu ("Poompuhar") for sandalwood objects (© 011/2336-3913); Uttar Pradesh ("Gangotri") for the stone-inlay work made famous by the Taj, as well as copper/brasswork and leather goods (© 011/2336-4723); **Kashmir Emporium** for superb carpets; and Orissa (Utkalika) for fabrics and traditional paintings (the latter off the beaten tourist track). If you're not moving on to Rajasthan, don't miss visiting both this and **Gurjari Emporium.** These State Government Emporiums (like **Central Cottage Industries Emporium** (www.cottageemporiumindia.com) on nearby Janpath) have fixed prices, so you are spared the incessant haggling you'll have to master elsewhere. One place where it's worth bargaining is **Tibetan Market** (on Janpath), where it is said you will pick up a better selection of items (from antique locks to silver jewelry) at better prices than you will anywhere in Tibet. Having walked its length, you will find yourself in Connaught Place, the retail heart of imperial Delhi, where hundreds of outlets vie for your rupees. Visit **Banaras House** for saris and the most beautiful fabrics on earth (N-13 Connaught Place, opposite Scindia House; © 011/2331-4751). Head to **Jain Super Store** (172 Palika Bazaar, Gate 6; © 011/2332-1031; www.jainperfumers.com) for perfumes, incense, and teas; it also has a store on Janpath called **Arihant Fragrances** (17 Main Market; © 011/2335-3949), which sells lovely silver jewelry alongside fabulous scented products. Stop at **Shaw Brothers** (Shop 8, Palika Bazaar; © 011/2332-9080; www.shaw-brothers.com) for pure, high-quality Kashmiri shawls and elegant Pashminas—even if you don't buy, this is pretty much a must-see (note that the main showroom is in Defence Colony; call © 011/4155-0858 for free transport if you're very serious about buying). For beautiful (and expensive) gemstones, gold jewelry, and bridalwear, try **Bholanath Brothers** (L-23 Connaught Circus; © 011/2341-8630) or nearby **Kapur di Hatti** (L-16; © 011/2341-7183), which also has Kundan jewelry. The most famous shop in Connaught Place is **Fabindia** (see review below), specializing in stylish ethnic Indian homewear and clothing for all ages, at unbelievably low prices. Along the same lines is **The Shop** (10, Regal Bldg., Parliament St.; © 011/2334-0971; www.theshop india.com), supplying textiles to all parts of the world from Bloomingdale's in the U.K. to Au printemps in France. Just a (s)hop away is one of the coolest hangouts in Delhi:

The People Tree ★. A studio-cum-store, it makes excellent use of a hole in the wall (read: crammed) location and revels in the creativity of its 2-decade-old existence. Funky T-shirts with tongue-in-cheek social and environmental messages are their claim to fame but you could easily spend a couple of hours (unbelievable for such a tiny space) browsing or simply enjoying the madness that meets the eye (8, Regal Bldg., Parliament St.; ℂ 011/2334-0699; www.peopletreeonline.com).

Khan Market & Sunder Nagar Market Sunder Nagar is considered the best market to trawl for authentic antiques, interesting secondhand goods, and unique artworks. Khan Market is good for books, music, and DVDs and increasingly for designer stores. Browse **Anokhi ★** (32 Khan Market; ℂ 011/2460-3423; www.anokhi.com), patronized by expats and locals alike for its highly fashionable blend of Western and Eastern-style clothing (see "Jaipur: Shopping" in chapter 11 for full review of the Anokhi headquarters). **The Neemrana Shop ★** (23-B, Khan Market; ℂ 011/4358-7183; www.neemranahotels.com) has a range of homewares, trinkets, and pretty souvenirs that make ideal gifts and usable memorabilia; you can buy Kama Ayurvedic toiletries, gorgeous pewter teapots, and simple and stylish light cotton garments, perfect for you to wear during your travels in India. Whatever you do, don't miss **Good Earth ★** (9 Khan Market; ℂ 011/2464-7175; www.goodearthindia.com)—it's filled with fabulous homewares, furniture, and accessories and the perfect place to pick up beautiful linens, silk cushions, fragranced candles, glass votives, or colorful tea sets; it now also has the wonderful Latitude 28 ★ on its second floor where you can enjoy Mediterranean fare to keep you going as you comb the stores in the area. There's also a branch at Santushti (see below). If you want to pick some beautiful jewelry, head to **Frazer and Haws** (Shop no.11, main market, Lodhi Colony; ℂ 011/2464-7818; www.frazerandhaws.com)—they also have some very tasteful home and personal accessories which will dig a deep hole in your pocket no doubt but well worth it.

South Delhi Seek out **Ravissant ★★★** (ℂ 011/2683-7278; www.cest ravissant. com) in New Friends Colony for beautiful contemporary pewter and silver houseware items (or visit the outlet conveniently located in The Oberoi hotel lobby). **Santushti Shopping Complex ★★** is an upscale collection of shops (predominantly boutiques) housed in landscaped gardens 15 minutes from the center. Shopping here is wonderfully hassle-free (and there's parking); pick up cigars at **Kastro's,** visit **Tulsi** for beautiful garments, and step into **Anokhi** for off-the-shelf cottonwear.

Even farther south (convenient to visit after viewing Qutb Minar) is trendy **Hauz Khas Village,** set against a 12th-century backdrop; and, slightly southeast (40 min. from the center), **Greater Kailash**—the latter shopping area (divided into M and N blocks) is the least atmospheric but has a large variety of shops that will delight the serious shopper. Hauz Khas is the place to seek out designer boutique outlets, like the legendary **Ritu Kumar** (34/42 Archana Shopping Complex; ℂ 011/2923-1612; www.ritukumar.com). Or head straight for **Ogaan** (H-2; ℂ 011/2696-7595)—the formalwear version of Anokhi, it's perfect for unusual Indo-West and contemporary Indian designer clothing, and stocks a number of well-known labels. **Natural Selection** (1 Hauz Khas; ℂ 011/2686-4574) is an excellent space to browse for larger items like antique furniture; the proprietors can make all shipping arrangements. Hauz Khas also has a number of fine restaurants (see "Where to Dine," earlier), although some have been shut down because of unsound ancient architecture. For wonderful tailor-made garments, make your way to **Kavita & Vanita Sawhney** (B-78 Greater Kailash I; ℂ 011/2923-1822).

Dilli Haat ★   This open area imitates a *haat* (rural marketplace), where 200 little stalls form a permanent open-air arts-and-crafts market. It's a unique shopping experience, and the most authentic and affordable in Delhi. Dilli Haat offers you the opportunity to buy directly from rural artisans and craftspeople who are allotted space rotationally for 2 weeks, making this a great place to browse the variety of crafts from all over India, whether you are traveling farther afield or not. From Bihar's *Madhubani* art to silver jewelry and furniture, as well as unusual gifts and souvenirs or colorful linens and other furnishings, the range is exhausting, the prices excellent and you can bargain further. If you are in Delhi in early December, be sure to check out the **Master Crafts Fair** (normally held Dec 1–15), where award-winning artists and craftspeople display and sell their work. Numerous food stalls serve food from all over India, but the hygiene is questionable, and there's more flogging of Coke and mineral water than anything else—opt for the fruit beers instead. It's open daily from 10am to 10:30pm

Aurobindo Marg, opposite INA Market. ℭ **011/2611-9055**. www.india-crafts.com. Entry Rs 15.

Fabindia ★ Value   If you've coveted Indian ethnic-chic at stores like the Conran Shop in London or New York, here's your chance to buy the fabrics and crafts at one-tenth the price. Fabindia sources its products from more than 7,500 craftspeople and artisans around India. Their distinctive use of handloom weaving techniques, natural dyes, and both vivid and earthy colors have made their products very desirable. Do bear in mind that these fabrics usually require gentle hand washing and drip-drying. Also, sizing and quality can be inconsistent, so it's best to try on any item of clothing before you buy. There are branch stores all over India as well as in Rome and Dubai. The Connaught Place store is open daily from 10am to 7pm; the Khan Market store is open Monday to Saturday from 10am to 7pm.

N-Block Market, Connaught Place: ℭ **011/4151-3371** or -3372. Greater Kailash Part I: ℭ **011/2923-2183** or -2184. Fabindia Craft Store: Central Hall, Khan Market. ℭ **011/4368-3100**. www.fabindia.com.

DELHI AFTER DARK

"The dawn breaks orange . . . The peacock sings . . . And Delhi still swings . . ." go the words to an uplifting dance track by one of Delhi's top ethno-electronic-music outfits, the MIDIval PunditZ. Despite the capital's reputation for early nights (stand-alone restaurants, bars and clubs within Delhi proper must close at midnight) and boring diplomatic gatherings, you won't want for a buzz these days. That said, bars and nightclubs in Delhi can be extremely popular for months, or even years, and then suddenly and inexplicably the crowds stop coming. All the establishments listed below have been popular for a significant period of time and are unlikely to turn into has-beens by the time you get there, but fads and trends guide people's movements.

The trick is to sniff out the latest fad or craze before it's died out; your best bet—and where you'll find the most extensive news about current events and entertainment—is the twice-monthly *Time Out New Delhi,* and also check out the score at www.delhi events.com. And, if contemporary music is your thing, do try to catch the PunditZ live.

MUSIC, DANCE & FILM   **Dances of India** is an organization that regularly stages classical and folk dance performances, showcasing styles from around the subcontinent; call ℭ **011/98-1012-5772** to find out what events are lined up. Call the **India Habitat Centre** (Lodhi Rd.; ℭ **011/2468-2001;** www.indiahabitat.org) for information on theater, film festivals, and other cultural events held almost nightly. Nearby is **India International Centre** (ℭ **011/2461-9431;** www.iicdelhi.nic.in), which also hosts a variety of cultural performances and film screenings (mostly in the cooler months of the year), as does **Kamani Auditorium** (1, Copernicus Marg; ✆ 011/4350-3351; www.kamani auditorium.org). Entry to most events is free or nominally priced. Like in other big cities, you will find **Max Muller Bhavan** (✆ 011/2332-9506; www.goethe.de), **Alliance Francaise** (✆ 011/4350-0200; www.alliancefr.org) and **Italian Cultural Institute** (✆ 011/2687-1901; www.iicnewdelhi.esteri.it) organizing regular film screenings among other activities. Other than the bigger newspapers like the Times of India and Hindustan Times, cultural events are listed at **www.delhievents.com**.

BARS & PUBS Cultural attractions aside, Delhi is in many ways most interesting at nighttime, when the "conspicuous consumers" to whom William Dalrymple refers in his *City of Djinns* head out and schmooze. Note however that, unless they're in hotels, most restaurants and bars (many of which double as both) close around midnight.

Fancying itself Delhi's most exclusive pub is **Dublin** (ITC Maurya; ✆ 011/2611-2233; www.welcomgroup.com), although with its Irish theme, we can't imagine why. It does have a dance floor, however, as well as the largest selection of single malts in Delhi; on Friday and Saturday regular DJs spin popular commercial tracks—a mix of fast-paced rhythms from hip-hop to '90s rock and even London bhangra. For a more genteel and upmarket atmosphere, head to **Rick's** ★ at the Taj Mahal Hotel (1 Mansingh Rd.; ✆ 011/2302-6162), where you can sip some of the best cocktails in Delhi while watching the city's fashionable set unwind. A DJ (Wed–Sat) plays retro music from 10:30pm onwards. Far more formal, and perhaps a tad demure, is **Club Bar** (The Oberoi, Dr. Zakir Hussain Marg; ✆ 011/2436-3030); relaxed and spacious, and good for cigar smokers, it's the sort of place where you'll overhear patrons discussing the latest business deals. **1911 Bar** in The Imperial (✆ 011/2334-1234), with its horseshoe-shaped bar, quilted leather Montana chairs, vintage portraits, and stained-glass roof, is an elegant place to enjoy an evening drink; despite the TV stuck on sports channels, it attracts a discriminating clientele that includes expats, celebs, and political bigwigs. All the rage among the jet-set crowd is **Aura** ★, the sublime vodka bar at the Claridges (✆ 011/4133-5133); schmoozing on the black leather armchairs here is greatly enhanced by the 72 varieties of vodka on offer.

Beyond the hotels, another popular watering hole and lounge is **Q'Ba** (E 42-43, Inner Circle, Connaught Place; ✆ 011/5151-2888; www.qba.co.in). It features a funky island bar on the lower level and dining upstairs—a good place to hang out with travel companions and swap stories; there are two terraces from which to admire the mayhem down below. After 8:30pm the DJ plays commercial music. Nearby is sister outfit, another restaurant-cum-bar, called @Live (K-12 Connaught Place, Outer Circle; ✆ 011/4356-0008), which dishes out—you guessed it—live music. Our old favorite **Turquoise Cottage** (first floor, Regent Sq., DLF City, Phase-II, Gurgaon; ✆ 0124/280-4070), may have shifted to Gurgaon, a satellite town closer to the airport but people still head out here because they loved the TC when it was in Delhi and it's still a great place for rock music. Thankfully you no longer walk into a haze of nicotine smoke (due to the national smoking ban that came into effect in 2008) and the decor is pleasant, with candlelit tables. If you prefer a venue that looks and feels a bit more local (we're talking Khajuraho-inspired erotic sculptures and wall-mounted Harappan seals), head to South Delhi's **Urban Pind** (N-4, N Block Market, Greater Kailash I; ✆ 011/395656; www.urban pind.com); you can sip Masala Martinis or cocktails infused with Indian spices while tapping your feet to commercial tracks spun by resident DJ Praveen. The crowd is as eclectic as the decor; although it's a rather sedate eatery by day, there's dance floor action at night. Another decent option for a night of unwinding is **Baci Bar** (23 Sundar Nagar Market; midway btw. Central and South Delhi; ℂ **011/4150-7445**), which is also an authentic Italian restaurant and joining the ranks is the new **Ikko** resto-bar/lounge (6/48, Malcha Marg, Chanakyapuri, east of Khan Market; ℂ **98-1109-4448**), which draws in those craving the "real stuff"—Russian vodka and vintage wines to go along with South Asian cuisine served with impeccable sophistication—you'll be sure to find the Delhi diplomat circle buzzing merrily.

NIGHTCLUBS   Delhi has its fair share of nightclubs, though most play standard commercial music. Because stand-alone bars and clubs are required by law to close at midnight, you'll find most of the late night carousing at hotels, or alternatively, witness the major after-hours exodus to Noida and Gurgaon (suburbs which are actually in different states), especially on weekends.

There's no getting around the megalithic popularity of ultrachic and trendy **Agni ★★★** (ℂ **011/2374-3000**). The Park's hugely popular (and undeniably sexy) bar—with a small dance floor for bhangra swingers—designed by London's Conran & Partners; it's worth popping into, not least for its funky decor, beanbags, and leather sofas, and nifty bar staff in designer gear by Rohit Bal. On weekends there's sure to be a crowd you won't be able to take your eyes off, although things shut down around 3am. If you want to party into the wee hours (5am), make your (rather long) way to **Elevate ★** (fifth floor, Centre Stage Mall, Noida, southeast of Delhi; ℂ **0120/436-4611** or 97-1100-0728; www.elevateindia.com), a spacious three-story club that plays a variety of sounds including commercial, R&B, and electronic music, with some trance/psychedelic stuff thrown in for good measure. Strictly for those who need to feel the music pulsate through their bodies, the club regularly has an international DJ playing the latest world trends— the 1-hour travel time from the heart of the city is the only drawback. With its black walls and pink lights, **Decibel** (Hotel Samrat, Kautilya Marg; ℂ **011/2611-0606**) in Chanakyapuri (east of Khan Market, easily accessed from anywhere in south or central Delhi) is another trendy nightclub with a large dance floor that draws a jet-setting crowd here to sip fine cocktails and dance away the calories to the fairly commercial music.

2 AGRA

200km (124 miles) SE of Delhi; 60km (37 miles) E of Bharatpur; 120km (75 miles) N of Gwalior

Agra is invariably included on every first-time visitor's itinerary, for who visits India without visiting the Taj? Home to three generations of one of the most dynamic dynasties in the medieval world, their talent and wealth immortalized in stone and marble, Agra is home to the finest examples of Mughal architecture in India, of which the Taj is simply the most famous. The beauty of these buildings will bowl you over, but knowing something of the dramatic history that played itself out on these stages (see "The Life & Times of the Mughal Emperors," below) makes the entire Agra experience come alive.

To soak up this fascinating history in the walls and rooms that resonated to Mughal voices, you should ideally set aside 2 full days here and hire the services of a good guide. And, if your budget can stretch that far, there's only one place to stay: the palatial Amarvilās, where every room has a view of the Taj.

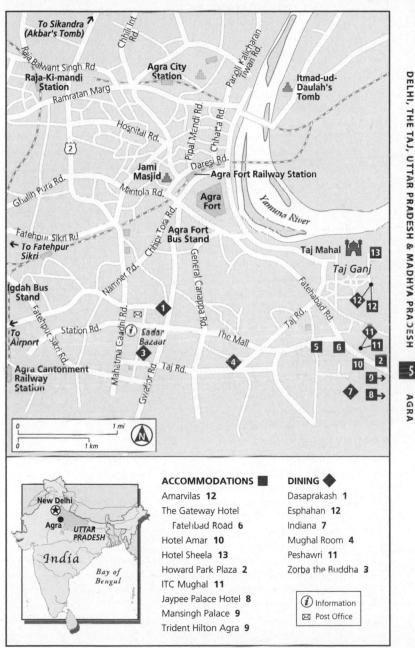

To Sikandra
(Akbar's Tomb)

Chhili Int.
Rd.

Raja Balwant Singh Rd.

Raja-Ki-mandi
Station

Ramratan Marg

Agra City
Station

Paroli Kalicharan
Tiwari Rd.

Itmad-ud-
Daulah's
Tomb

Hospital Rd.

Pipal Mandi Rd.

Chhata Rd.

Ghalib Pura Rd.

Jami
Masjid

Mantola Rd.

Daresi Rd.

Agra Fort Railway Station

Agra
Fort

Yamuna River

Fatehpur Sikri Rd.

To Fatehpur
Sikri

Namner Rd.

Chipi Tola Rd.

Agra Fort
Bus Stand

General Canappa Rd.

Taj Mahal

Taj Ganj

13

Fatehabad Rd.

12

12

Igdah Bus
Stand

Fatehpur Sikri Rd.

Station Rd.

Mahatma Gaadhi Rd.

Sadar
Bazaar

Gwalior Rd.

Taj Rd.

The Mall

Taj Rd.

1

3

4

Taj Rd.

5   6

11

11

10

2

9

To
Airport

Agra Cantonment
Railway
Station

7

8

0   1 mi
0   1 km

New Delhi

Agra

UTTAR
PRADESH

India

Bay of
Bengal

ACCOMMODATIONS ■

Amarvilas **12**
The Gateway Hotel
  Fatehbad Road **6**
Hotel Amar **10**
Hotel Sheela **13**
Howard Park Plaza **2**
ITC Mughal **11**
Jaypee Palace Hotel **8**
Mansingh Palace **9**
Trident Hilton Agra **9**

DINING ◆

Dasaprakash **1**
Esphahan **12**
Indiana **7**
Mughal Room **4**
Peshawri **11**
Zorba the Buddha **3**

ⓘ Information
✉ Post Office

The Life & Times of the Mughal Emperors

Babur, the first Mughal emperor—inspired by the Persians' belief that a cultured leader should re-create the Islamic ideal of a "garden of paradise" here on earth—built three gardens on the banks of the Yamuna. But Agra only took shape as a city under his grandson, Akbar, the third Mughal emperor. Son of the poet-astronomer-philosopher Humayun (whose tomb is in Delhi, described earlier in this chapter), Akbar moved the capital here in 1566. While Akbar was as versatile as his father, he was also a better statesman, revered for his religious tolerance and relatively understated lifestyle. He took the throne at age 13 and ruled for almost 50 years, when he consolidated the Mughal empire and wooed the Hindu "underlings" by abolishing taxes, banning the slaughter of cows, promoting Hindu warriors within his army, and taking a Rajput princess as his bride, who bore him a son, Jahangir. In gratitude for the appearance of an heir, Akbar built a brand-new city, **Fatehpur Sikri,** which lies 40km (25 miles) southwest and is today one of Agra's top attractions.

The grandeur of this statement of gratitude indicates that Akbar must have, at least at first, been a very indulgent father, though his joy must later have been tinged with disappointment, for at an age when he himself was ruling India, Jahangir (who was to be his only surviving son) was relishing his reputation as a womanizer and acquiring a deep affection for alcohol, opium, painting, and poetry. When Jahangir fell in love with **Nur Jahan,** his "light of the world," who was at the time married, Akbar opposed the alliance. But after her husband died (under mysterious circumstances, it must be said), Jahangir promised to give up "the pleasures of the world," so Akbar gave his consent. Jahangir had a coin minted in her honor, and when he was crowned emperor in Agra Fort in 1628, it was in fact the strong-willed and ambitious Nur Jahan who ruled the empire from behind the *jalis* (screens) for 16 years. She also built

ESSENTIALS

VISITOR INFORMATION   The **Government of India Tourist Office** is at 191 The Mall (© **0562/222-6368;** goitoagr@sancharnet.in; Mon–Fri 9am–5:30pm, Sat 9am–2pm). A 24-hour **Tourism Reception Centre** is at Cantonment Railway Station (© **0562/242-1204**). Not as much on the ball, the **U.P. Tourism Bureau** is at 64 Taj Rd. (© **0562/222-6431;** Mon–Sat 10am–5pm; closed second Sat of the month).

GETTING THERE & AWAY   By Road   Agra lies less than 4 hours away, on a good two-lane highway from Delhi. Many Delhi operators offer bus tours to Agra; see "Essentials" in the Delhi section, above. If you don't mind being part of a bus tour, a good option is to take a day trip from Delhi with **TCI** (see "Guided Tours" below); alternatively, hire a car and driver. Should you need to stop for refreshments, the **Country Inn** at Kosi, 99km (61 miles) from Delhi, is a good bet.

By Air   At press time, the only flights into Agra are charters; it is unknown whether commercials flights (suspended several years back) will ever resume.

a magnificent garden tomb, another of Agra's top attractions and affectionately referred to as the "mini-Taj", for her father. By the time Jahangir died in 1644, reputedly a drunkard, Akbar must have been turning in his tomb (yet another of Agra's top attractions).

It was Jahangir's third son, **Shah Jahan** (not incidentally born of Nur Jahan), who came to power—apparently after murdering his two elder brothers, their two children, and two male cousins. Known as the "architect" of the dynasty, the fifth Mughal emperor began renovating the Agra Fort at age 16, but achieved the apotheosis of Mughal design when he built the Taj Mahal for his beloved **Mumtaz** (the niece of Nur Jahan). Bored, he moved the capital to Delhi when he was 47, building an entirely new city from scratch, designing modern geometric palaces (including a separate royal apartment for his favored daughter, Jahanara Begum) and beautiful gardens within the new Red Fort. But he was to pay a bitter price for the favoritism he showed Jahanara and his son, **Dara Shikoh.** His pious third son, **Aurangzeb,** aided by **Roshanara Begum** (Jahanara's embittered younger sister), seized the throne by betraying and/or murdering most of their siblings. Aurangzeb, the last of the great Mughal emperors, became the most repressive ruler North India had yet seen, destroying Hindu temples and images throughout the region and banning the playing of music or any other form of indulgent pleasure. Known as much for his cruelty as his ambition, Aurangzeb allegedly poisoned his ally Roshanara when he caught her in an illicit liaison in her quarters at the Red Fort. Having imprisoned his father in Agra Fort, Aurangzeb sent him a platter upon which he garnished the head of his favorite son, Dara. According to legend he instructed his servant to present it with the words, "Your son sends you this to let you see that he does not forget you."

By Train The **Bhopal Shatabdi** leaves New Delhi at 6am daily, arriving at **Agra Cantonment Railway Station** (© **131** or 133 information, or 0562/242-0998 reservations) at 8am; it returns to Delhi at 11:05pm. Alternatively, you can catch the **Taj Express,** which leaves Delhi's Nizamuddin Station at 7:15am, returning to Delhi at 10:05pm (book the A/C Chair Car, which should run you just under Rs 300). The station has a prepaid taxi/auto-rickshaw service (Rs 50–Rs 150) to take you the 2km (1¼ miles) to downtown; you can also book a city sightseeing tour here. *Note:* Trains arriving from Rajasthan pull in at the Agra Fort Station. (If arriving from elsewhere, avoid inconveniently located Agra City Station.)

GETTING AROUND **By Taxi & Auto-Rickshaw** As is the case everywhere in India, make sure you negotiate your taxi or auto-rickshaw rate upfront (or use the prepaid facility). Hiring an air-conditioned car for 4 hours should run you around Rs 1,200, while a full day will cost upwards of Rs 2,000, depending on how far you want to go. Unless you're traveling to Sikandra or Fatehpur Sikri, an auto-rickshaw should suffice (avoid the shared auto-rickshaws, which although a fraction of the price are horribly claustrophobic with six others packed in like sardines). In an attempt to cut down on the air pollution that threatens the Taj, motorized transport is not allowed in the Taj Sanctuary area (2km/1¼-mile radius); walk or hire a cycle-rickshaw.

GUIDED TOURS   **Uttar Pradesh Tourism** operates city tours that cover all the major sights, departing from Agra Cantonment Station (it is timed to coincide with the arrival of the Taj Express); alternatively, you could ask them to pick you from your hotel provided it falls in the route taken for the tour. The tour usually starts at 10:15am, costs Rs 1,700, and covers the Taj, Agra Fort, and Fatehpur Sikri and includes all entrance fees, a guide, and transport by air-conditioned bus; book with the manager of Hotel Taj Khema (© **0562/233-0140;** tajkhema@up-tourism.com). A recommended private tour operator from Delhi is **TCI** (504-505, New Delhi House, Barakhama Rd.; © **011/2331-5834** through -5838; www.tcindia.com). The TCI bus departs Delhi at 6am and returns at 10am, covering Agra Fort and the Taj, and costs Rs 2,000 including breakfast and lunch (at Taj View Hotel) and excluding entry fees. Traveling around with a tour group is far from the ideal way to experience the mystery and magical allure of the Taj however, and you shouldn't miss out on the full spectrum of great Agra sights, ie visit more than just the Taj and Agra Fort. **Tallis & Company** (© **0124/400-4458;** www.tallisandco.com) specialize in customized tours to Agra (and Jaipur); prices vary depending on number of persons, type of vehicle and number of stops but their rates are very reasonable. If you're already in Agra on own steam, and just want a local guide, the intelligent and knowledgeable **Rajiv Rajawat** (© **98-3702-3601;** rajivrajawat@yahoo.com) is one of the best; book him before you even get to India, to ensure he is available on the days you'd like to use his services (Rs 2,000). Pitching himself more affordably is **Sudhir Agarwal** (© **94-1000-5896;** sudhir_agra@rediffmail.com), who charges Rs 1,200 for the day, from 8am through 5pm.

WHAT TO SEE & DO

Agra is today a large industrial city with a woeful infrastructure, but sightseeing is quite manageable given that there are five major attractions and very little else to keep you here. Ideally, you will see the **Taj** at dawn, then visit **Itmad-ud-Daulah's Tomb** and **Agra Fort,** and move on to **Fatehpur Sikri** the following dawn. Besides those sights listed below, you may also want to make time to visit beautiful **Jama Masjid,** built in 1648 by Jahanara Begum, Shah Jahan's favorite daughter, who clearly inherited some of his aesthetic sensibilities. It is in the heart of the medieval part of Agra, best approached by cycle- or auto-rickshaw; you can stop along the way to bargain for jewelry, fabrics, or carpets. The other sight worth swinging by is **Dayal Bagh Temple**—begun 97 years ago, it is still under construction and is being built by the progeny of the laborers who built the Taj. The families guard their traditional craft techniques like gold, passing them on only to the sons in the family. Other minor attractions are ill-kept and a disappointment after viewing those reviewed below. Note that Bharatpur, where Keoladeo Ghana National Park lies (see chapter 11), is only 54km (34 miles) from Agra, with a stop at Fatehpur Sikri along the way.

Taj Mahal ★★★   You expect to be disappointed when coming face to face with an icon that is almost an archetype, but nothing can really prepare you for the beauty of the Taj Mahal. Built by Shah Jahan as an eternal symbol of his love for his favorite wife, whom he called Mumtaz Mahal ("Jewel of the Palace"), it has immortalized him forever as one of the great architectural patrons of the world. It's not just the perfect symmetry,

> ## ⓘ Tips   Be the First to Arrive
>
> Get to the Taj entrance at dawn, before it opens, then rush—run if you must—straight to the cenotaph chamber (remember to remove your shoes before ascending the marble steps). If you manage to get there first, you will hear what might aptly be described as "the sound of infinity"—the vibration created by air moving through the huge ventilated dome. As soon as the first visitor walks in, jabbering away, it reverberates throughout the room, and the sacred moment is lost until closing time again.

the ethereal luminescence, the wonderful proportions, or the sheer scale (which is virtually impossible to imagine from staring at its oft-reproduced image), but the exquisite detailing covering every inch of marble that justifies it as a wonder of the world. What appears from afar to be perfectly proportioned white marble magnificence is in fact a massive bejeweled box, with *pietra dura* adorning the interior and exterior—said by some to be an Italian technique imported to Agra by Jahangir, but more likely to be a craft originating in Persia. These intricately carved floral bouquets are inlaid with precious stones: agate, jasper, malachite, turquoise, tiger's eye, lapis lazuli, coral, carnelian—every stone known to man, as well as different shades of marble, slate, and sandstone. Beautiful calligraphy, inlaid with black marble, is carefully increased in size as the eye moves higher, creating an optical illusion of perfectly balanced typography, with the letters the same size from whichever angle you look. Carved relief work, again usually of flowers, which symbolized paradise on earth for the Mughals, decorates much of the interior, while the delicacy of the filigree screens that surround the cenotaph, carved out of a single piece of marble, is simply astounding. The tomb is flanked by two mosques—one is a prerequisite, but the other is a "dummy" built only in the interests of symmetry; both buildings are worthy of examination in their own right. At the center of it all lies Mumtaz Mahal's cenotaph with the words HELP US OH LORD TO BEAR WHAT WE CANNOT BEAR; Shah Jahan's cenotaph was added later.

Work started in 1641, and the structure took 20,000 laborers 22 years to complete—legend has it that Shah Jahan cut off the hands of the architect (Persian-born Ustad Ahmad Lahori) and his laborers to ensure that they would never build another, but there is little to substantiate this sensational story.

The Taj changes color depending on the time of day, and many recommend that you witness this by visiting in the morning and evening; however, your ticket is valid for one entry only. Eat a hearty breakfast before you head out (no food is allowed past security), and stay the day, or come in the early morning.

Finally, to understand the symbolism of the Taj, as well as what has been lost since Shah Jahan's day (such as the plunder of the pearl-encrusted silks that covered Mumtaz's cenotaph), it's definitely worth hiring the services of a good (read: official), well-spoken guide. Besides **Rajiv Rajawat** and **Sudhir Agarwal** (for contact details, see above), you can consider arranging a reputable guide through your hotel.

If you're an absolute romantic, you might like to check with your hotel whether or not one of the **full moon Taj-viewing experiences** is likely to fall on one of the nights during your stay. Since early 2005, the Taj has been open for night viewing for 5 days each lunar cycle: the full moon night and the 2 nights before and after. These after-hours sessions happen between 8pm and midnight and are highly regulated (and certainly no substitute for daytime visits); try to time such a visit for around 10pm.

Note: The Taj is closed on Friday. Your Taj ticket also entitles you to a small discount at the other four major attractions (Agra Fort, Itmad-ud-Daulah, Sikandra, and Fatehpur Sikri), so keep it on hand and show it when paying to enter the others.

Taj Ganj. © **0562/233-0498.** Admission Rs 750, children under 15 free; Rs 50 limited video use. Sat–Thurs sunrise–sunset. Only water, camera, film, batteries, medicines, and other similar essentials are allowed. No food, sharp objects, tripods, or electronics—if you have any of these items, you can leave them at reception. Mobile phone use is a criminal offense.

Agra Fort ★★★   Built by Akbar (or rather, by his 4,000 workmen) on the west bank of the Yamuna, Agra Fort first took shape between 1565 and 1573, but each successive emperor was to add his imprint, and today the towering red-sandstone ramparts house a variety of palace apartments, representing the different building styles of Akbar and his grandson Shah Jahan. Akbar's son, Jahangir, installed a **"chain of justice"** (1605) by which any of his subjects could call on him, which provides some insight into the ruling qualities of the man many dismiss as a drunkard. Entrance is through impressive **Amar Singh Gate.** On your right-hand side you pass **Jahangiri Mahal,** the palace that housed the women of the court, dating to Akbar's reign (ca. 1570). In front is a stone pool with steps both inside and outside—legend says it was filled with rose petals during Nur Jahan's time, so that she could bathe in their scent. Much of the exterior (the jutting *jarokhas,* for example, and the domed *chattris*) and almost the entire interior were clearly built by Hindu workmen, who used Hindu building styles and decorative motifs—indicative of Akbar's all-embracing religious tolerance. Adjacent, facing **Anguri Bagh (Grape Garden,** where flowing water, flower beds, hidden lamps, and hanging jewels would have transformed it into a fantasy garden), is **Khas Mahal** (1636), built overlooking the cooling breezes of the Yamuna. You are now entering Shah Jahan's palaces, immediately recognizable by the extensive use of white marble. Historians also point out that here—unlike in Akbar's buildings, which feature straightforward Hindu elements next to Islamic—a subtle blend of Hindu and Persian elements resulted in a totally new style, referred to as the "Mughal style," with its classical purity. The Khas Mahal is flanked by two **Golden Pavilions** (a reference to the fact that they were once gilded): the bedrooms of the princesses Jahanara and Roshanara, before the latter plotted the downfall of her father and sister. On the left is **Mussaman Burj,** an octagonal tower open to the cooling breezes, which may have been the emperor's bedroom. Romantic accounts would have us believe that Shah Jahan, imprisoned by his son in this room, would gaze at the Taj Mahal until his death of a broken heart in 1666. However, evidence points to death by a massive dose of opium, complicated by the prolonged use of aphrodisiacs. Near the tower are the mirrored **Sheesh Mahal** and **Mina Masjid (Gem Mosque);** adjacent is **Diwan-i-Khas (Hall of Private Audience;** 1637), its marble columns inlaid with semi-precious stones in *pietra dura* floral patterns. In front of Diwan-i-Khas are two **thrones** (from where the emperor watched elephant fights below); facing these is **Machchhi Bhavan (Fish House),** once filled with the sounds of trickling water. Beyond lies **Diwan-i-Am (Hall of Public Audience),** the arcaded hall where the emperor would listen to the complaints of his subjects, seated on the Peacock Throne (see Lal Qila [Red Fort], in Delhi, earlier in this chapter). Note the insensitive placement of the tomb of John Russell Colvin, who died here during the Mutiny and was laid to rest in front of Diwan-I-Am. The ugly barracks to the north are also 19th-century British additions. From here on, most of the

buildings (except for **Nagina Masjid,** the private mosque of the ladies of the court) are
closed to the public, undergoing extensive excavation at press time.

Yamuna Kinara Rd. Admission Rs 300. Rs 50 discount with Taj ticket. Keep ticket until visit is over. Daily sunrise–sunset. **Note:** Avoid Fri, when the Taj is closed and entry is half-price for Indian visitors, making the place crowded.

Fatehpur Sikri ★★★   Built from scratch in 1571 by Akbar in honor of the Sufi saint Salim Chisti, who had predicted the birth of a son (see "The Dargah Sharif & Other Ajmer Gems" in chapter 11), this grand ghost city is carved entirely from red sandstone. It was only inhabited for 14 years, after which—some say because of water shortages—it was totally abandoned. It's a bizarre experience to wander through these magnificent, architecturally fascinating sandstone arches, courtyards, and buildings. (Try to get here right when it opens, the only time it's peaceful.) The buildings combine a fine sense of proportion—indicative of Akbar's Persian ancestry—with strong Hindu and Jain design elements, indicative again of his embracing attitude to the conquered and their faiths. Upon entering, you will see **Diwan-i-Khas,** thought to be a debating chamber, on the right. Facing it is **Ankh Michali,** thought to be the treasury, which has mythical Hindu creatures carved on its stone struts. To the left is large **Parcheesi Court,** where Parcheesi (from which games such as backgammon and ludo were subsequently derived) was played with live pieces: the ladies of the harem. It is said that Akbar learned much about the personalities of his court and enemies by watching how they played, won, and lost. Surrounding the court are, from the left, **Diwan-i-Am,** a large pavilion where public hearings were held; the **Turkish Sultana's House,** an ornate sandstone pavilion; and **Abdar Khana,** where drinking water and fruit were apparently stored. Walk between the two latter buildings to enter **Akbar's private quarters.** Facing **Anoop Talao**—the four-quartered pool—are the rooms in which he slept (note the ventilating shaft near his built-in bed) and his personal library with shelves carved into the walls. Also overlooking Parcheesi Court is **Panch Mahal,** the tallest pavilion, where Akbar's wives could watch the games and enjoy the breeze without being seen. Behind Panch Mahal are the female quarters, including **Maryam's House** and the **Haram Sara Complex.** The harem leads to **Jodha Bai's Palace,** a large courtyard surrounded by pavilions—note the green glazed roof tiles. To the east is **Birbal's House,** a two-story pavilion noted for its carvings; beyond lie the **servants' cells.** From here you exit to visit **Jama Masjid,** a mosque even more spectacular than the larger one Akbar's grandson built in Delhi. Set like a glittering pearl amid the towering red-sandstone bastions, punctuated by a grand gateway, is the white marble *dargah* (tomb) of Salim Chisti, which has some of the most beautiful carved screens in India. It attracts pilgrims from all over India, particularly (given the good fortune he brought Akbar) the childless, who make wishes while tying cotton threads onto the screens that surround the tomb.

Again, the services of a good guide are indispensable to a visit here (don't bother hiring one of the "official" guides at the entrance, however). Also note that if you are moving on to Rajasthan and plan to visit Bharatpur (for its bird sanctuary), Fatehpur Sikri can be visited en route.

37km (23 miles) west of Agra on the road to Bharatpur. No phone. Admission Rs 260 Daily sunrise–sunset.

Itmad-ud-Daulah's Tomb ★★★   Described as a mini-Taj, this is the tomb of Mirza Ghiyath Beg, who served under Akbar and fathered Nur Jahan, the powerful wife of Jahangir who helped promote her father to his position as Lord of the Treasury and enshrined him here in this "bejeweled marble box"—proof of her powerful hold on the purse strings. Also built of translucent white marble, it was the most innovative building of 17th-century India, and marked the transition from the heavy red sandstone so favored by previous Mughal emperors. It no doubt inspired Shah Jahan with its beautiful symmetry and detailing; the *pietra duras* are as delicate as embroidery, and the dense gilding and paintwork feature typical Persian motifs, such as the wine-vase and the dish and cup, much favored by Jahangir at the time. The scale may be far less grand than that of the Taj, but the polychrome geometric ornamentation is more obviously decorative, and given the beauty of the proportions and the intricacy of its inlays and mosaics, it's amazing how little traffic this tomb sees relative to the Taj. It definitely warrants a short visit, if only to get a sense of how almost generic opulence was to the Mughal court.

Eastern Bank of Yamuna (30 min. from Taj). Admission Rs 110. Rs 10 discount with Taj ticket. Daily sunrise–sunset.

Sikandra (Akbar's Tomb) ★   Someone once described the rise and fall of the Mughal empire as rulers who started "as titans and finished as jewelers." To this end, Akbar's tomb is a less-elegant version of the bejeweled tombs of his great-granddaughter (or his daughter-in-law's father), yet more ornate than that of his father Humayun (see "Delhi: The Top Attractions"). The perfect symmetry is typical of Persian architecture, and the scale is huge; the gateway alone, featuring more than 20 panels inlaid with intricate geometric patterning, will stop you in your tracks. Geometric patterning in fact dominates, with relatively few floral designs, as befits the last "titan" ruler. It's not surprising to hear that the tomb is believed to have been designed by Akbar; the detailing reflects the altogether more restrained lifestyle and masculine personality of this great ruler.

8km (5 miles) from Agra on NH 2. ✆ **0562/264-1230**. Admission Rs 110. Rs 10 discount with Taj ticket. Rs 25 video. Daily sunrise–sunset.

WHERE TO STAY

Given that it is one of the most-visited tourist destinations in the world, Agra's accommodations can be disappointing, no doubt a case of resting on the Taj's laurels. The big exception is **Amarvilas,** which—even if it means scrimping elsewhere—is worth every cent, not least for its proximity to the Taj and the matchless views.

Within the moderate price category, all located south and southwest (known as the Cantonment) of the Taj, there is incredible price parity; of these only the **Trident** offers good value. The best budget option, conveniently located within Tajganj (where the Taj is located), is the **Hotel Sheela,** reviewed below. (*Note:* Again we urge you to stay at one of the better properties; a bad hotel experience can really spoil the whole romanticism attached to the Taj. Check online for daily price variations, particularly for the Gateway and Trident hotels: You can sometimes get an ultralow bargain rate.).

Very Expensive

Amarvilās ★★★   It's one of the most talked-about hotels in the world and your experience visiting the Taj Mahal and Agra will be enhanced by a thoroughly worthwhile splurge at this extraordinary property. The lobby, bar, and lounge all offer the same surreal views of the Taj, but even those public spaces that don't offer a monument view are lovely, with large reflecting pools, colonnaded courts, terraced lawns, and pillowed pavilions. By day some of the exteriors look a little bland and in need of the detailing featured in the interior, but at night it's a pure *Arabian Nights* fantasy, when burning braziers provide a wonderful contrast to the fountains and trickling streams. The rooms are

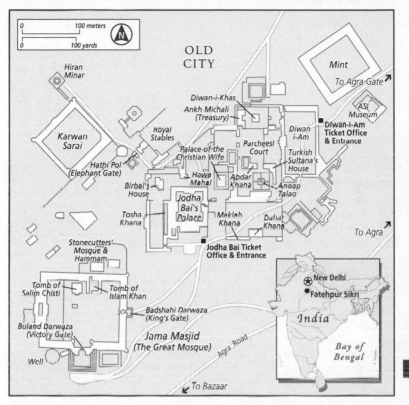

compact but extremely luxurious, showcasing the best-quality Indian craftsmanship available but with every modern amenity. The only significant choice you need make is whether or not to pay extra for a balcony (recommended!). While the hotel scores high points for its understated opulence, it's the silky smooth service that accompanies your encounter with the Taj that really makes a difference; be sure to make use of the courtesy golf cart rides to just within striking distance of the monument's East Gate.

Taj East Gate Rd., Taj Nagari Scheme, Agra 282 001. ℂ **0562/223-1515.** Fax 0562/223-1516. www.oberoi hotels.com. 102 units. Rs 30,500–Rs 40,000 premiere double; Rs 36,000–Rs 45,5000 premiere double with balcony; Rs 70,000–Rs 224,000 suite. Taxes extra. AE, DC, MC, V. **Amenities:** 2 restaurants; lounge; bar; airport transfer (Rs 1,268); cultural performances (Oct–Mar); doctor-on-call; drop-off at Taj; fitness center; Internet (Rs 220/hr., Rs 881/day); outdoor heated pool; room service; Banyan Tree spa. *In room:* A/C, TV, personal butler, DVD, hair dryer, minibar, MP-3 docking station (on request), Wi-Fi (Rs 220/hr., Rs 881/day).

Expensive

ITC Mughal ★★ Kids Before Amarvilās, this was billed the best lodging in town, winning awards for its design (supposedly emulating a Mughal palace), but it's always struck us as rather brash and very, very busy, with a distinct lack in service-to-price ratio. However, the renovations and refurbishing that took place during 2008 has given the

(Moments) Room with a View

It's been enjoyed by a global who's who: from Salman Rushdie to William Dalrymple, Will Smith to Meg Ryan, not to mention a host of world leaders but no matter what anyone tells you, there's little to beat the satisfaction of enjoying all-day views of the Taj from your bedroom at the Amarvilās hotel (p. 460)—just 600m (1,968 ft.) away. Every room has a beautiful view. You can literally sip a cappuccino in your king-size bed at dawn, watching the subtle color variations the monument undergoes as the sun rises; or you can order a cocktail on your private balcony at sunset, admiring the ethereal marble silhouette as staff light the burners that line the hotel's grand stepped terraces leading down to the central pool. The in-house spa also has views of the Taj—lying there, gazing at the dreamlike monument, you might just have to ask the masseuse to pinch you.

ITC a new lease, and it has now proudly taken its place as the second most popular lodging option in Agra, though we think the Trident offers better value. A major draw are the facilities for children, with nannies, an amusement park and tons of games to keep them occupied, so you can spend time soaking in some exotic therapy at the spa. **Kaya Kalp,** winning accolades galore including the prestigious Tatler's Best City Spa in 2008, reinforces what the Mughals introduced to India—space, green, and water—plenty of which is to be found in its sprawling 9,197 sq. m (99,000 sq. ft.) area. The use of the pomegranate as a constant motif comes courtesy the Mughal King Babar, who allegedly introduced it to India and not surprisingly, among its long list of therapies, the fruit features as an exotic and ultimate treatment. And yes, only in-house guests get to enjoy it.

194 Fatehabad Rd., Taj Ganj, Agra 282 001. (*) **0562/402-1700.** Fax 0562/233-1730. www.luxury collection.com/itcmughal. 269 units. Rs 16,000 Chamber of Emperors double, Rs 19,000 Mughal Chamber double, Rs 30,000 Deluxe Suite, Rs 35,000 Deluxe Suite (Taj facing); Rs 45,000 luxury suite; Rs 80,000 presidential suite. Taxes extra. AE, DC, MC, V. **Amenities:** 4 restaurants; bar; airport transfer (Rs 550); astrologer; babysitting; badminton; bank; billiards; boating; croquet; cultural performances; currency exchange; doctor-on-call; miniature golf; health club w/sauna; internet (Rs 600/hr.); jogging track; children's amusement park; outdoor pool; room service; spa; 2 tennis courts. *In room:* A/C, TV, minibar; MP-3 docking station (only in suites), Wi-Fi (Rs 600/hr.).

Jaypee Palace Hotel ★   This huge hotel and convention center has a host of facilities; again this will suit those traveling with kids: youngsters can lose themselves at Leisure Mall, which offers a bowling alley and virtual reality games (and other kinds of entertainment you probably never came to India for!). Despite being at the edge of town it tends to get very busy, which can prove a real nuisance. Nevertheless, the red-sandstone buildings (more reminiscent of a modern library than a palace) are wonderfully set on 10-hectare (25-acre) grounds with well-tended gardens, lovely walkways, fountains, and pergolas—you can even take a camel ride through the grounds. Unfortunately, the hotel's size and the rather brusque staff can make your stay here memorable for the wrong reasons: One revamped wing has given rise to so-called Palace Rooms: Escape to these spacious rooms with their semiprivate terraces to avoid the crowds; along with various in-room freebies, Palace Rooms also come with a free massage.

Fatehabad Rd., Agra 282 003. (C) **0562/233-0800.** Fax 0562/233-0850. www.jaypeehotels.com. 350 units. $250–$270 double; $315 palace room; $400–$2,600 suite. $38 extra bed. Taxes extra. Ask about discounts. AE, DC, MC, V. **Amenities:** 3 restaurants; bar; tea lounge, patisserie; disco; airport transfers (Rs 440); aerobics; babysitting; billards; bowling alley; children's play areas; currency exchange; doctor-on-call; jogging track; health club and spa; helipad; outdoor pool; putting greens; room service; squash; outdoor tennis; virtual reality games; Wi-Fi(Rs 150/hr., Rs750/day). *In room:* A/C, TV, hair dryer, minibar.

Moderate

If for some reason our reviewed recommendations below are full, note that you can get a reasonably good deal at the **Mansingh Palace** (Fatehabad Rd.; (C) **0562/233-1771;** www.mansinghhotels.com; doubles from Rs 8,000), where you'll have the option of getting a room from which you can (just) see the Taj. Styled as a faux fortress-palace, Mansingh Palace has similar amenities to the Taj-owned Gateway Hotel and Trident. For those on a more restricted budget, your best bet would be **Howard Park Plaza** (Fatehabad Rd.; (C) **0562/233-1870;** www.parkplaza.com), conveniently located near the Taj (15-min. walk). With doubles from Rs 5,000, this is good value for the host of amenities offered (including a pool).

The Gateway Hotel Fatehbad Road Agra ★

Don't be put off by the unattractive exterior of this, one of the first big tourist hotels to be built in Agra; what looks a bit like a 1970s apartment block offers a wide range of amenities and comfortable guest rooms, the best of which offer views of the monument you're in town to see—at a fraction of the cost of both ITC Mughal and Amarvilas (though in truth, there's no comparison in terms of design, luxury, or proximity). It's worth reserving a Taj-facing room (room 518 has the best view) but bear in mind that it's around 1km (½ mile) away. Generally, the deluxe rooms have more appeal, with marble floors and colorful throws and cushions, but they aren't that much different from the slightly smaller, cheaper superior rooms. With extensive landscaped lawns and a marble pool with its own swim-up bar, this is a fair place to come home to after the rush of sightseeing.

Fatehabad Rd., Taj Ganj, Agra 282 001. (C) **0562/223-2400** through -2418. Fax 0562/223 2420. www. tajhotels.com. 100 units. Rs 7,100 standard double; Rs 7,850 superior double; Rs 8,850 executive double Rs 19,000 executive suite; Rs 1,200 extra bed. Taxes extra. AE, DC, MC, V. **Amenities:** 2 restaurants; bar; airport transfer (Rs 750); astrologer; babysitting; cultural performances by arrangement; currency exchange; doctor-on-call; health club and spa; Internet (Rs 250/hr, Rs 750/day); outdoor pool; putting green; room service, outdoor tennis court. *In room:* A/C, TV, hair dryer, minibar.

Trident Agra ★ (Value)

This is our second favorite hotel in Agra, predominantly because of the service levels, which are a great deal slicker than anywhere else in this price category—hardly surprising given that Trident is part of the distinguished Oberoi group (of which Amarvilas is their Agra flagship). In a low-key attempt to emulate Agra's architectural heritage, this hotel uses the same red sandstone favored by the Mughal kings, but that's where the similarity ends. In fact, the moment you step into the lobby, you'll feel thoroughly located in the 21st century. Guest rooms use vibrant colors to inject energy into the otherwise ordinary spaces; the effect is refreshing, although hardly a stand-in for a bedside view of the Taj. Accommodations are arranged around a central garden, with manicured lawns, trimmed hedges, and a swimming pool; try to reserve a room facing this.

Taj Nagri Scheme, Fatehabad Rd., Agra 282 001. (C) **0562/233-5000.** Fax 0562/233-1827. www.trident hotels.com. 138 units. Rs 8,500 deluxe garden view double; Rs 9,200 deluxe pool-view double; Rs 14,500 suite; no extra beds. Actual rate varies daily. Taxes extra. A friendly child policy is offered. Rates include breakfast. AE, DC, MC, V. **Amenities:** Restaurant; bar; airport transfer (Rs 790); babysitting; doctor-on-call; Internet (Rs 200/hr., Rs 700/day); kids club; outdoor pool; room service; table tennis. *In room:* A/C, TV, minibar, Wi-Fi (Rs 200/hr., Rs 700/day).

If you're watching your rupees but want to be near the Taj, the Hotel Sheela (reviewed below) is less than 2 minutes' walk from the entrance; it's ideal for travelers who can put up with absolute basics. But our budget preference is for **Hotel Amar** (Tourist Complex Area, Fatehabad Rd.; ✆ **0562/233-1884** through -1889; www.hotelamar.com). Away from the main hype, but around a 10-minute walk from the Taj, it offers clean but basic rooms with en-suite bathrooms; amenities include a pool, and there's regular hot water. All the rooms may be noisy given the proximity of traffic: Be sure to insist on an upstairs room looking toward the pool, which is well maintained and sets the Amar apart from the other faceless options along busy Fatehabad Road. Doubles start at Rs 3,600. (It may be worth checking the Howard Park Plaza rates before booking anywhere else though, as they sometimes offer specials that beat even the budget lodgings—for contact details see above, under moderate options.)

Hotel Sheela ⊙ **Value**   The best (and only) reason to stay here is its proximity to the Taj Mahal. This peaceful ocher-colored complex offers very basic accommodations in a pleasant garden courtyard surrounded by trees. Guest rooms are very spartan, and bathrooms tiny (no hot water). Beds are firm with thin mattresses, but you're provided with bedding. Reserve well ahead for one of only two units that have A/C. Rooms are en-suite and are relatively clean but hot water is only available in winter. Cheaper guest rooms have fans and mosquito screens over the windows, and a few more rooms have aging air coolers. Service standards are generally in keeping with the ultralow tariffs; keep in mind that you will have to lug your luggage about 300m (984 ft.), as the hotel is now in the no-vehicle zone.

East Gate, Taj Ganj, Agra 282 001. ✆ **0562/233-1194.** www.hotelsheelaagra.com. 22 units. Rs 400–Rs 500 double; Rs 600 air-cooler double; Rs 800 A/C double. No credit cards. **Amenities:** Restaurant. *In room:* A/C (2 rooms), air cooler (some).

WHERE TO DINE

Dining (and nightlife) options are limited in Agra, with little stand-alone choice. Even if you're not staying at Amarvilas, **Esphahan** (reviewed below) is definitely worth a splurge. Among the dining options in the other big hotels, one of the finest remains **Peshawri** in the Mughal Sheraton, still a firm favorite among locals in the know, or **Mughal Room** in the Clarks Shiraz, where live *ghazals* (poetry readings) add to the experience, although needs a bit of an acquired taste.

If you want to get away from the hotels, you could do far worse than the delicious and satisfying dishes served at **Indiana** (✆ **0562/400-1192;** daily 7:30am–10:30pm), which is hardly an inspiring venue (behind Hotel Ratan Deep on Fatehabad Rd.), but will satisfy any hunger. Portions are rather large (you may even consider sharing some of the dishes between two people). The best dishes are North Indian specialties, although the habit of adding Western and Chinese items persists. If you don't mind something spicy, order *murg boti masal,* chicken in a wonderfully tasty gravy, or go for the spiced fish curry *(rasili machhli).* If you really can't decide, opt for a thali, a platter covering all the courses and including dessert or lassi.

You can get a satisfying, reasonably priced meal at **Zorba the Buddha** (E13 Shopping Arcade, Gopi Chand Shivare Rd., Sadar Bazaar; ✆ **0562/222-6091**), which serves excellent, nongreasy vegetarian food. This tiny eatery is extremely hygienic, reason enough to go. Go early to get a good table and order the light spinach *parathas,* any of the Indian fare, or even a salad—all quite passable, if a trifle bland. Vegetarians (or others avoiding meat) have another option: **Dasaprakash** (✆ **0562/246-3535**), located in the Meher

Theatre Complex at 1 Gwalior Rd., is the city's best-known South Indian restaurant.
Regular fare includes *sada dosa* (plain rice and lentil pancakes), *masala dosa* (pancake with
potato stuffing), *uttappams* (thicker pancakes), and *idlis* (steamed dumplings), all served
with coconut chutney and *sambar* (spiced *dal*). No alcohol is served. At some point, you
will hear of **Only** restaurant on Taj Road, mentioned in every guidebook on the planet,
but we find it avoidable.

Warning: Agra is renowned for moneymaking restaurant scams. Besides the fact that
guides, taxi drivers, and auto-rickshaw *wallas* earn commissions for taking you to certain
eateries, you need to be wary of getting caught up in more dangerous pursuits. Some
unsuspecting diners have been taken for a ride by unscrupulous restaurateurs working in
tandem with rickshaw-*wallas* and so-called doctors. Everyone involved might feign major
concern over your health, but you'll pay dearly for the experience. *Bottom line:* Be careful where you eat, and if you feel sudden illness coming on, don't rely on the restaurateur
to call a "doctor"—insist on being taken back to your hotel.

Esphahan ★★★ INDIAN Even if you aren't staying at Amarvilas, you should dine
at this exceptional restaurant—not only are the cuisine, service, and live Indian music
superb, but arriving at the flame-lit latter-day palace is one of Agra's most memorable
moments. (When you reserve, ask to have your predinner cocktail on the veranda so you
can watch the sunset hues color the Taj and the magnificent pool area below.) Start with
tandoori phool, stuffed cauliflower in a yogurt and star anise marinade; *tandoori* prawns
or the succulent chicken *tikka,* prepared in saffron and garlic. Highly recommended is
palak ke kofte (cheese dumplings in spinach gravy) and the *rogan gosht,* lamb braised in
kashmiri chilies—beware though as it is rather oily. There's also delicious Persian-style
quail. Alternatively, you could loosen your belt and make *room* for a filling thali (platter),
which affords the opportunity to sample a range of tastes. All in all, a most memorable
evening out, and the perfect place to celebrate seeing the Taj.

Amarvilas, Taj East Gate End. (*(*) **0562/223-1515** Reservations essential. Main courses Rs 550–Rs 1,250.
AE, DC, MC, V. Daily 7–10:30pm.

SHOPPING

Agra is famous for its marble and soft-stone inlay, as well as *zardori*-embroidered fabrics,
leather goods, brassware, carpets, and jewelry. However, it's hard work dealing with what is
probably the worst concentration of touts and scamsters in all India, so if you can, avoid
shopping here. Don't be fooled by Cottage Industries Exposition, which is not a branch of
the similarly named government-owned (Emporium) shops in other parts of the country.
This one is overpriced, and whatever is sold here can quite easily be obtained in Delhi at
half the price. If you absolutely must buy something to remind you of your visit here,
Subhash Emporium (18/1 Gwalior Rd.; (*) **0562/222-5828**; www.subhashemporium.
com) sells good-quality inlay work, souvenirs, and other gifts. Or make your way to one of
the *official* government emporiums for reasonably priced sources of local handicrafts.

3 VARANASI (BENARAS)

320km (198 miles) SE of Lucknow; 765km (474 miles) SE of Delhi

A crumbling maze of a city that rises from the *ghats* (steps) on the western banks of the
Ganges, Varanasi is in many senses the quintessential India. With an ancient history—
Mark Twain famously described it as "older than history, older than tradition, older even

than legend, and looks twice as old as all of them put together"—it is also one of the most sacred cities in the world today. Kashi, or "City of Light, where the eternal light of Shiva intersects the earth," as Varanasi is seen by devotees, is the holiest of Indian pilgrimages, home of Shiva, where the devout come to wash away their sins. It is also one of the holiest *tirthas* (literally a "crossing" or sacred place where mortals can cross over to the divine, or the gods and goddesses come to bathe on earth), where many return to die in the hope that they may achieve *moksha,* the salvation of the soul from the cycle of birth, death, and rebirth.

Named after the confluence of two rivers, Varuna and Asi, the city is centered on the *ghats* that line the waterfront, each honoring Shiva in the form of a *linga*—the rounded phalliclike shaft of stone found on every *ghat.* Cruise the waterfront at dawn and you will witness the most surreal scenes, when devotees come to bathe, meditate, and perform ancient rituals to greet the sun. Or even come at sunset, when *pundits* (priests) at Dasashwamedh Ghat perform *aarti* (prayer ritual) with complicated fire rituals, and pilgrims light candles to float along the sacred waters.

Earliest accounts of the city go back 8,000 years, and "the city of learning and burning," as it is affectionately referred to, has attracted pilgrims from time immemorial, not all of them Hindu—even Buddha visited here in 500 B.C. after he achieved enlightenment, sharing his wisdom at nearby Sarnath. Successive raids by Muslim invaders (the last of whom was the Mughal emperor Aurangzeb) led to the destruction of many of the original Hindu temples, which means that most of the buildings here date back no further than the 18th century. Yet the sense of ancient history is almost palpable. Getting lost in the impossibly cramped labyrinth, you are crowded by pilgrims purchasing flowers for *puja* (offering or prayer), grieving relatives bearing corpses, chanting priests sounding gongs, and sacred cows rooting in the rubbish—an experience you will never forget.

ESSENTIALS

VISITOR INFORMATION   The **India Tourism Office** is located at 15B The Mall, Cantonment (✆ **0542/250-1784;** Mon–Fri 9am–5pm, Sat 9am–2pm). A satellite information counter is open during flight arrivals. The **U. P. Tourist Office** is on Parade Kothi (✆ **0542/220-6638;** Mon–Sat 10am–5pm); a satellite counter is at the railway station (daily 9am–7pm).

GETTING THERE   By Road   Unless you have a lot of time on your hands, driving to Varanasi means spending too much time on a bumpy road with no interesting stops.

By Air   The airport is 23km (14 miles) from the Cantonment (Cantt.) area, where the large chain hotels are located, and 30km (19 miles) from the riverfront. The flight from Delhi lasts 75 minutes. Best to fly in with **Jet Airways** (reservations ✆ **0542/262-2026,** or airport 0542/262-2795 through -2797), who offer the most reliable and regular flights here, or—for the best-priced deal—with **SpiceJet** (www.spicejet.com), which at press time offered flights from Delhi for just over Rs 2,000 (check out their website or www.yatra.com for best deals from other destinations). A taxi should run you Rs 450 to the Cantonment, and Rs 500 to Assi Ghat; use the prepaid service and try to inspect the vehicle before jumping in. Ignore all attempts by drivers to get you to stay at hotels they recommend (or "own").

By Train   Varanasi is conveniently reached by overnight train from Delhi; the Swatantrata Express and Shiv Ganga Express take 12 to 13. Avoid the smelly and non-air-conditioned second class sleeper; the 2-tiered Second AC is generally the most comfortable but if you want to save pennies then even the 3-tiered Third AC should work. It

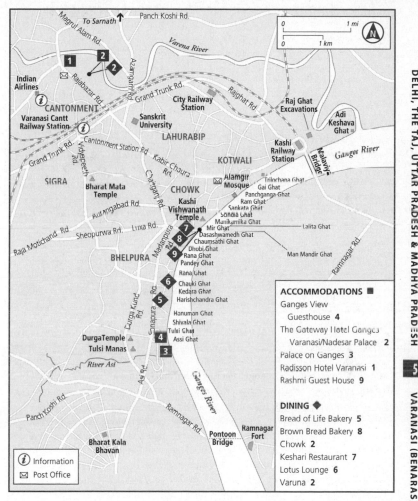

is also connected with a host of other cities and towns. For information, call © **1331**; for Varanasi Cantonment reservations, call © **0542/220-3475** or 0542/243-1740. Prepaid taxis are available from the station. Be sure to disembark at Varanasi Cantonment station.

Getting Around   By Auto-Rickshaw & Cycle-Rickshaw   The narrow and extremely crowded streets of the Old City and in and around Godaulia (also Gowdalia) are penetrable only by two-wheelers and very determined cycle-rickshaws. These are also useful—if sometimes bone-jarring—ways of getting from your hotel to the area near the *ghats* and other attractions. Once at (or near) the *ghats,* set off on foot. Note that cycle-rickshaws are notorious for not having functioning brakes; their technique of stopping is

ⓘ Tips Getting the Better of Transport Tricksters

Remember that Varanasi is a city of transport tricksters, and you have little chance of escaping at least one rickshaw-related con job. Ask your hotel what the current going rate is for any trip in either an auto- or a cycle-rickshaw, and bargain for the correct fare—the best technique is to quote your price and walk away disinterestedly. Be further warned that rickshaw-*wallas* will readily agree to take you somewhere without having the faintest idea where it is. Once you've been onboard for several minutes, you will suddenly be asked where you want to go and, more likely than not, you will end up at a shop where the driver expects to make a commission off your purchase. To avoid falling into this annoying and time-wasting trap, ensure that the driver can repeat the name of your destination (or the nearest prominent landmark), in recognizable English. In addition, avoid the shopping scam by using a bit of trickery yourself. To begin with, never use the word "shopping" with a rickshaw-*walla*. If you're heading to the shopping area in Godaulia, ask to be taken to Dasashwamedh Ghat, as if you plan to go there for a stroll. When you're almost there, you'll pass the Old City shopping area and Godaulia; stop your rickshaw and get off before you reach the *ghats,* or get to the *ghats* and take the 5-minute walk back into the market

to merely roll into the cycle-rickshaw in front; hold on and try not to be alarmed, although you must know that they're very uncomfortable, and tend to have you constantly sliding forward. To tour the environs you'll need to hire a car and driver; expect to pay at least Rs 800 for a half-day or Rs 1,500 for a full day.

GUIDED TOURS   We recommend that you explore the area with a personal guide, if only to know which temples you can enter or which street food to sample, and to avoid getting lost or conned. One of Varanasi's best guides is **Ajit Kumar Yadav** (ⓒ **0542/258-1052** or 94-1522-5994; ajitashay@yahoo.com; Rs 600 half-day for one to five persons or Rs 800 for a full day), an official, government-approved guide; he's often engaged for group tours during peak season, so book before you leave. Ajit is perfect for those looking for an understanding of the city that goes beyond its history, covering religious rituals and mythological stories as well. His knowledge of Hinduism and Buddhism (for Sarnath) is unmatched; most important, he never asks if you want to shop, unless you express a strong interest. **Shailesh Tripathi** (ⓒ **94-1528-7257**), an archaeology Ph.D. from Benares University, is another government-approved guide with a wealth of knowledge, as is **Devesh Agarwal** (ⓒ **98-3904-2347**); both charge Rs 700 for a half-day and Rs 1,200 for a full day. Alternatively, you can arrange both guide and car through your hotel, or contact the **India Tourism Office** (see "Visitor Information," above) to arrange for an approved guide and vehicle (ⓒ **0542/220-6638**). To hire a boat (with oarsman), head for Dasashwamedh; the price should be around Rs 100 per hour.

FESTIVALS   Varanasi is in many ways like a huge trippy trance party that started centuries ago and has kept on going, its revelers refusing to discard their costumes and come down to earth. So there's no real reason to time your visit with a festival—on the contrary,

Moments   Up in Flames

You need a pretty strong constitution to hang around Varanasi's burning *ghats* (**Harish Chandra** or **Manikarnika**) and watch a human corpse, wrapped in little more than a sheet, being cremated in public view. Bodies are burned around the clock at these famous open-air cremation sites, which draw a constant crowd of grievers, curious pilgrims, bug-eyed travelers, and confused cows. Only one particular Hindu caste group is allowed to touch the bodies or perform the cremation. After bathing the body one last time in the holy Ganges, they place it on wood piles, and cover it with more logs (ask your guide about the kinds of wood—teak, sandalwood, and so on—used and their significance) before being doused in a flammable paste, or ghee, and lightly coated with incense powder (the latter used to hide the smell of burning flesh) Then a male relative, usually the son (female relatives of the deceased, even wives, rarely if ever visit the cremation grounds), lights the pyre. No photography is allowed, and you should treat the mourners with the respect their grief deserves. Avoid touts offering to show you a cremation up close; not only do many drug addicts trying to part tourists from their cash hang around these areas, but gawking at an unknown person's funeral pyre from close quarters is considered fairly offensive. To get a quiet glimpse of a cremation ritual from a respectable distance, without causing any offense, take a boat ride down to Manikarnika Ghat.

any increase in numbers is worth avoiding. However, the huge **Dev Deepavali (Diwali)** festival is by all accounts a spectacle, held during the full moon in October/November. Almost every *ghat* and building is covered by glowing earthen lamps, and the river is aglitter with floating candles (but with about 100,000 pilgrims about, you may never even get to the river). Other auspicious occasions are **Mahashivratri** (Jan/Feb), **Holi** (Mar/Apr), **Ganga Dashehra** (May/June), and **Sri Krishna Janmashtami** (Sept/Nov).

WHAT TO SEE & DO

If you do only one thing in Varanasi, take a **boat cruise** past the *ghats* at dawn (see below); you can repeat this at sunset or, better still, head for **Dasashwamedh Ghat** to watch the **Ganga Fire Aarti.** For 45 minutes, young Brahmin priests perform age-old prayer rituals with conch shells and burning braziers accompanied by drummers, while children hawk candles for you to light and set adrift. Unfortunately, the recent addition of live musical prayer recitals through loudspeakers has somewhat robbed the original format of its mesmerizing effect and enigma.

Aside from these two must-sees, you should set aside some time to wander the ancient streets of the **Old City,** particularly those centered around **Kashi Vishwanath Temple** (see below)—but a few hours of picking your way past cow pats amid the incessant din of clanging temple gongs, not to mention striking out to view the 24-hour cremations at **Manikarnika Ghat,** are likely to have you craving peace and solitude. Hire a car and visit **Sarnath,** where Buddha first revealed his Eightfold Path, and where you can spend a few hours exploring the archaeological ruins, visit a modern Buddhist temple, and admire the beautiful Indo-Greek and Mathura styles of Buddhist art and sculpture at the museum. Alternatively, stay in Varanasi to explore the fascinating collection in the **Bharat Kala Bhavan Museum** at Benaras Hindu University. Both experiences are enriched by having a good guide with you.

Ramnagar Fort (Rs 12; Oct–Mar daily 8am–noon and 2–6pm, Apr–Sept daily 10am–5pm), the palace of the former Maharaja of Varanasi, is billed as another worthwhile attraction. Although the actual palace is beautiful in a run-down sort of way, and the location (the only Varanasi site on the east bank of the river) is lovely, the museum is filled with dusty, moth-eaten, decaying exhibits, such as the once-ornate *howdas* (elephant seats) that transported the royal family—fascinating in a way to see such beauty so discarded. Do stop for a glance at the palace's grand Durbar Hall, though it's hard to see through the filthy windows. The lack of care says much about the dedication of the current young maharaja. Although he is said to involve himself in local tourism, his name does not enjoy the reverence that the Maharajas of Rajasthan still evoke. Attempts at renovation continue, so check for improvements. Another of Varanasi's fascinating sights is **Bharat Mata,** or **Mother India Temple** (located just north of the Old City), worth highlighting if only because it is the incarnation of the spoken Hindu belief that the very land of India is sacred (ironic, given the pollution). Pilgrims walk around a large relief map of the subcontinent before Partition, featuring all its holy *tirthas,* mountains, and rivers.

Varanasi has produced some of India's most talented musicians (the great Ravi Shankar was born here; if you're unfamiliar with his genius, purchase without delay the CD *Chants of India,* produced by George Harrison—highly recommended). Ask your hotel what performances are being hosted while you are in town, or head for the **International Music Centre** in Ganesh Mahal on Wednesday and Saturday (check with your hotel for exact dates and times) for live Indian classical music performances by up-and-coming artists.

If you'd like to learn to play the **tabla** (set of two small drums) in Varanasi, which is renowned for its tabla merchants, head for **Triveni Music Centre** (D24/38 Pandey Ghat) and ask for Nandlal. Nandlal and his father also stage regular concerts at Triveni.

Yoga schools and teachers are plentiful in Varanasi; even your hotel will likely have a morning yoga session. If you're more serious, however, contact **Dr. Vagish Shastri** at his residence behind the Bread of Life Bakery (Vagyoga Chetanapitham, B3/131A, Shivala; ✆ **0542/227-5706;** vagyoga@hotmail.com) between 7 and 9am. He operates a range of courses in yoga as well as kundalini meditation and Sanskrit; as he's always on the move, it's worth contacting him well before you intend traveling to see if he will be resident while you are here.

Note: If you take a cycle-rickshaw for the evening *aarti* ceremony, you will encounter terrible pollution. Additionally, because the supply of electricity to Varanasi is erratic, most hotels and restaurants use diesel generators. Unfortunately, their exhaust pipes are often at face level, spewing diesel fumes into Varanasi's narrow streets as you walk or cycle by. Carry a cotton handkerchief/scarf with you, cover your nose and mouth with it, and breathe through the cotton to make your way through an otherwise suffocating environment.

Cruising the Ghats ★★★

Drifting along the Ganges, admiring the densely textured backdrop of 18th- and 19th-century temples and palaces that line the 84-odd bathing *ghats,* you will be confronted with one of the most spiritually uplifting or downright weird tableaus on the entire crazy

subcontinent: Down below, waist-deep pilgrims raise their arms in supplication, priests
meditate by staring directly into the rising sun or are frozen in complicated yoga positions, wrestlers limber up, and disinterested onlookers toss live rats from the towering
walls of the Old City, among other assorted goings-on. Note that you'll need to get here
between 4:30 and 6am (check sunrise times with your hotel, as well as the time it takes
to get to the *ghats*), so plan an early wake-up call. You should be able to hire a boat
anywhere along the *ghats,* but most people either catch one from **Assi Ghat,** the southernmost *ghat,* or—particularly if you're staying in the Cantonment area—from **Dasashwamedh** (literally "10-horse-sacrifice," referring to an ancient sacrificial rite performed
by Brahma). Situated roughly halfway, this is the most accessible and popular *ghat* and is
always crawling with pilgrims, hawkers, and priests surveying the scene from under
bamboo umbrellas. Boats operate at a fixed rate of Rs 100 per hour (one to four persons)—this hasn't changed in years. The following descriptions of the 100-odd *ghats*
assume that you will leave from here; note that it's worth traveling both north and south.
You can do another trip in the evening as the sun is setting, but don't travel too far—
boating is limited after sunset (except at the time of *aarti,* when you can sail up to watch
the ceremony from the water).

Heading North from Dasashwamedh Ghat From here, you pass **Man Mandir Ghat,**
which, along with the beautiful palace that overlooks it, was built by the Maharaja Man
Singh of Amber in 1600. Jai Singh, who built the Jantar Mantars, converted the palace
into an observatory in 1710. Hours are 7am to 5:30pm; entrance costs Rs 100. Next is
Mir Ghat, where the New Vishwanath Temple, Vishalakshi shrine, and Dharma Kupa
(where the Lord of Death relinquished his hold over those who die in Varanasi), are
found. North lies **Lalita Ghat,** with its distinctive Nepalese Temple, and beyond it is the
"burning" **Manikarnika Ghat,** the principal and favored *shamshan ghat* (cremation
ground) of Varanasi, where you can see funeral-pyre flames burning 24 hours, tended by
the *doms,* or "Untouchables"—touching the dead is considered polluting to all but these
low castes. Boats are requested to keep their distance as a sign of respect. On this *ghat* is
the venerated **Manikarnika Kund,** the world's first *tirtha,* said to have been dug out by
Vishnu, whose sweat filled it as he created the world as ordered by Shiva. Some say that
Shiva shivered in delight when he saw what Vishnu had created, dropping an earring into
the pool; others say that it was the earring of Sati, Shiva's dead wife, hence the name
Manikarnika: "jeweled earring." Between the Kund and the *ghat* is what is supposed to
be Vishnu's footprint. Adjacent is **Scindia Ghat,** with its distinctive, half-submerged
Shiva temple, toppled by weight; then **Ram Ghat** and **Panchganga Ghat** (said to be
empowered by the five mythical streams that flow here into the Ganges), and one of the
five *tirthas* at which pilgrims perform rituals. Behind the *ghat* glowers **Alamgir Mosque,**
built by Aurangzeb on a Hindu temple he destroyed; note also the almost submerged
cells where the Kashi pundits (priests) are freeze-framed in meditation poses. Proceed
from here to **Gai, Trilochana,** and **Raj** *ghats,* but it's best (if you still want to proceed
south) to turn back at Panchganga (or explore the north banks further on foot).

Heading South Passing **Chaumsathi Ghat,** where the temple houses images of Kali
and Durga; and **Dhobi Ghat,** alive with the sound of laundry workers rhythmically beating clothing that have been "cleansed" by the Ganges, you come to **Kedara Ghat,**
notable for its red-and-white-striped South Indian–style temple. Farther south lie **Har-
ishchandra Ghat,** Varanasi's second cremation *ghat* (though less popular because it also
houses an electric crematorium); and **Tulsi Ghat,** named in honor of Goswami Tulsidas,
a revered Hindu poet. Nearby is **Lolark Kund,** where childless women come to bathe

> ## (Fun Facts)   The Polluted Elixir of Life
>
> According to religious belief, the Ganges is *amrita,* elixir of life, "cleanser of sin," "eternal womb," and "purifier of souls." Even from a scientific point of view, the river once had an almost miraculous ability to purify itself—up to 100 years ago, microbes such as cholera could not survive in these sacred waters. Sadly, the Ganges is today one of the most polluted rivers in the world. This is mostly due to the chemical toxins dumped by industrial factories that line the river, but Varanasi's ancient sewers and a population with equally ancient attitudes toward waste disposal (including the dumping of an estimated 45,000 uncremated corpses annually) are problems the Uttar Pradesh Water Board struggles to overcome. Several eco-groups like the Sankat Mochan Foundation at Tulsi Ghat are working to alleviate the environmental degradation of the Ganges, but as you will find abundantly clear within an hour of being in Varanasi, much more needs to be done. Still, it may be something of a miracle that so many people perform their daily ablutions—with full-body immersions—in the waters and apparently suffer no harm; it's even a popular stunt with braver tourists.

and pray for progeny. The final stop (or the first, if your accommodations make a south-north journey more convenient) is **Assi Ghat,** a simple clay bank situated at the confluence of the Ganga and Assi rivers. From here you can walk to **Durga Temple,** which lies farther west from the *ghat.* *Note:* If you want to walk from Assi Ghat to Dasashwamedh, the trip will take a leisurely 60 to 90 minutes. Although the best time to walk or cruise the river is at sunrise or before sunset, you may wish to see the river in a completely different and relatively quiet "avatar," in which case take a late-afternoon stroll down the *ghats* in winter.

Bharat Kala Bhavan Museum ★   As is so often the case in India, this museum suffers from poor curatorship, with exhibits—which are marvelous—haphazardly displayed and poorly labeled. You may even have trouble persuading the guards to turn on all the lights and show you the rooms behind the screen—hence the need for a good guide. The miniature-painting collection is superb, as are many of the Hindu and Buddhist sculptures and Mughal artifacts, though again, without a guide there is no way to know, for instance, that the otherwise nondescript coin behind the glass was minted by the Mughal emperor Akbar—and in keeping with his legendary religious tolerance, it has a Hindu symbol printed on one side and an Islamic on the other. Set aside 2 hours to explore.

Benaras Hindu University. www.bhu.ac.in. Admission Rs 100; still camera free, video not allowed. July–Apr Mon–Sat 11am–4pm; May–June closes at 12:30pm.

Kashi Vishwanath Temple ★   Of the more than 2,000 temples in Varanasi, the most important is Kashi Vishwanath Temple, or "Golden Temple," dedicated to Lord Shiva, the presiding deity of the city. Because of repeated destruction by the invading sultans and later by Aurangzeb, the current Vishwanath is a relatively modern building: It was built in 1777 by the Maharani of Indore, and the *shikhara* (spire) and ceilings were plated with 820 kilograms (1,808 lb.) of gold, a gift from Maharaja Ranjit Singh, in 1839. Five major *aartis* are held daily, but the temple is always abuzz with worshipers.

Sadly, non-Hindus may not enter, but by taking a stroll through the Vishwanath Galli **473** (pronounced *Gul*-ley, meaning lane) that runs the length of it, you can get a glimpse of the interior, which exudes pungent smells and constant noise. For a small donation, you can climb to one of the second floors or rooftops of the shops that line the lane and get a good view. Note that adjacent is **Gyanvapi Mosque,** built by Aurangzeb on a Hindu temple site and heavily guarded to ensure that no trouble erupts. Ironically, this is also the starting point for many pilgrims on their quest to visit all the *tirthas* in a ritual journey, accompanied by a priest who recites the *sankalpa,* or "declaration of intent." Nearby is **Annapurna Temple,** dedicated to Shakti.

Vishwanath Galli. Temple is closed to non-Hindus; compound is accessible. No cameras or cellphones allowed within the Galli and temple compound.

A Side Trip to Sarnath

After gaining enlightenment, **Sarnath** ★ is where Buddha gave his first sermon some 2,500 years ago, and continued to return with followers. For many centuries after this, it was renowned as a Buddhist center of learning, housing some 3,000 monks, but successive Muslim invasions and later lootings destroyed the monasteries and much of the art. Today it still attracts many pilgrims, but—unless you're very familiar with Buddha's personal history or are an archaeologist—the site itself is nowhere near as inspiring as his teachings, and you're likely to experience it all as nothing more than a boring pile of bricks. The most impressive sight is **Dhamekh Stupa,** if only for its sheer age. Built around A.D. 500, with a massive girth, it still towers 31m (102 ft.) into the air and is said to mark the very spot where Buddha revealed his Eightfold Path leading to nirvana. The ruins of **Dharmarajika Stupa** lie immediately north of the entrance. Beyond is the **Ashokan Pillar**—the stupa is said to have been one of 28 built by Ashoka, the 3rd century B.C. Mauryan king and bloodthirsty warrior who was to become one of the most passionate converts to Buddhism. Beyond these are the ruins of monasteries. Across the road from the entrance to the main site is **Sarnath Archaeological Museum,** where you can view the four-headed lion that once topped the Ashoka Pillar; created in the 3rd century B.C., it's made from sandstone, polished to look like marble. The lion capital, with the wheel beneath representing Buddha's "wheel of dharma," is today a national emblem for India, found on all currency notes and official government documents. East of the Dhamek Stupa is **Mulagandha Kuti** (main temple), which houses an image of Buddha (ironically enough, against his wishes, images of Buddha abounded after his death). The walls contain frescoes pertaining to his life history—a good crash course for the novice if accompanied by a guide. You can also visit the peaceful **Tibetan Buddhist Monastery,** a lovely, bright space with display cases filled with hundreds of miniature Buddhas.

Sarnath is 10km (6¼ miles) north of Varanasi. Admission Rs 100. Daily 7am–6:30pm. Museum Rs 2; Sat–Thurs 10am–5pm; cameras not allowed (lockers provided). Mulagandha Kuti 4–11:30am and 1:30–8pm. Daily chanting Rs 5 for use of still camera, Rs 25 video; Nov–Feb 6pm, Mar–May 6:30pm, June–Oct 7pm. Tibetan Buddhist Monastery free admission; 5am–noon and 2–6:30pm.

WHERE TO STAY

In a general sense, you have two options: You can stay in one of the waterfront lodgings, most of which (with the exception of the two reviewed below) are very basic; or you can spend the night in the relative peace and comfort of the Cantonment area, where the most "luxurious" options are. Still, with the exception of our three choice picks, below, the Cantonment hotels tend to look very frayed, if not downright decaying. And the downside of staying in the Cantonment is that you feel very cut off from the real Varanasi, and require an earlier morning wake-up call to get to the *ghats;* for the sunset *aarti,* when the streets are often jammed, it may take 30 minutes (and a blood-curdling taxi or rickshaw ride) to get there, and you'll walk the last part. These issues can be solved by staying in a hotel on the Ganges, but this also means you have no chance of unwinding at a pool, eating meat, or drinking alcohol—still, if you manage to bag a river-facing room, you will have the delight of a waterfront view, with the surreal experience of Varanasi on your doorstep. *Note:* Staying in one of the budget hotels away from the *ghats* is inadvisable unless you're used to budget traveling; many have no windows, and the noise is incessant.

Cantonment

The Gateway Hotel Ganges Varanasi ★
The Gateway is located within an ugly 1970s monolith, but rooms have been renovated over the past few years to create a more contemporary ambience. Executive rooms are now stylishly furnished with comfy divans and plasma TVs, but the best rooms are the lovely, cozy suites (book no. 527, which occupies a top corner and is very spacious and gracious, with a huge bathroom). What distinguishes this old five-star stalwart are service and the vast array of amenities, as well as a real passion for the region; the hotel hires the best guides in the city, shopping tips are excellent, and the travel desk will arrange tours as far afield as Bodhgaya. It also has huge, sprawling grounds, a great pool, and two of the best restaurants in town (this does not mean that the meal will be the best you have in India, however).

Nadesar Palace, Varanasi 221 002. ℭ **0542/250-3001** through -3019. Fax 0542/250-1343. www.tajhotels. com. 130 units. Rs 8,500 standard double; Rs 9,500 executive double; Rs 11,500 executive suite; Rs 12,500 deluxe suite; Rs 1,200 extra bed. AE, MC, V. **Amenities:** 2 restaurants; bar; airport transfer (Rs 745); astrologer; badminton; doctor-on-call; golf (at Nadesar Palace); gym; outdoor pool; room service; spa (at Nadesar Palace); table tennis; tennis; yoga. *In room:* A/C, TV, minibar, Wi-Fi (Rs 200/hr., Rs 600/full day).

The Nadesar Palace ★★★
This 175-year old property, once the city residence of the Maharaja Singh and today a Taj-operated hotel, and our top hotel choice by far in the Cantonment, blends the luxury of two different eras: original 19th-century architectural detailing is augmented with Victorian claw-foot bathtubs and a mix of authentic and reproduction antiques, yet offers all the modern conveniences you'd expect from a hotel that opened in 2009. Rooms come dressed in muted colors, with four-poster beds draped in silks and hand-woven carpets; plenty of common areas to lounge in both upstairs and down in the veranda by the pool, which although tiny, is in keeping with the general facade. The grounds are as yet undeveloped (golf course in the making) but it's worth taking a ride on the Maharaja's 220-year old buggy, which clip-clops its way through the 16 hectares (40 acres), the proud coachman pointing to a myriad of trees planted decades ago.

Nadesar Palace Grounds, Varanasi 221 002. ℭ **0542/250-3001** through -3019. Fax 0542/250-1406. www. tajhotels.com. 10 units. Rs 20,000 palace rooms; Rs 30,000 historical suites; Rs 36,000 royal suites; Rs 1,250 extra bed; check website for best available rates. AE, MC, V. **Amenities:** Restaurant; airport transfer (Rs 745); buggy ride; doctor-on-call; golf; gym; outdoor pool; room service; spa; outdoor tennis. *In room:* A/C, TV, minibar, Wi-Fi (Rs 200/hr., Rs 600/day).

Radisson Hotel Varanasi ★ Ⓥalue
The most popular choice in Varanasi's cantonment offers ultracontemporary accommodations, reliable service, and the usual five-star Radisson amenities at a relatively affordable price—a good deal if you think being on the river will be too much. Guest rooms are large and comfortable, with thick drapes and

chocolate-brown furniture offset by pale walls. There's a full spa and a smallish pool with wooden deck chairs and its own bar; breakfasts are served in the bright sunflower themed coffee shop. The free railway station transfer is very convenient if you're arriving by overnight train from Delhi. The only drawback of this otherwise good chain hotel is that none of the rooms have views worth mentioning.

The Mall, Cantonment, Varanasi 221 002. C **0542/250-1515.** Fax 0542/250-1516. www.radisson.com. radvar@sify.com. 116 units. Rs 5,000 superior double; Rs 7,000 club room; Rs 9,000 suite; Rs 1,100 extra bed. Rates include breakfast; taxes extra. Check online for special deals. AE, DC, MC, V. **Amenities:** 2 restaurants; bar; lounge and pastry bar; airport transfer (Rs 715); babysitting; currency exchange; doctor-on-call; health club; Internet (Rs 300/hr., Rs 1,300/day); palmist; outdoor pool; room service; spa. *In room:* A/C, TV, hair dryer, minibar, Wi-Fi (complimentary).

Waterfront

Ganges View Guesthouse ★★ (Value) You're required to remove your shoes upon entering this lovely colonial lodge at the edge of the Ganges, and it's an appropriate gesture of respect given the effort that has turned the best budget guesthouse into such a comfortable haven. In fact, it's so popular with certain repeat guests (many of them artists and musicians) that you'd do well to book your room up to a year in advance. The gorgeous, simple guest rooms feature marble floors and French doors that open onto enclosed corridors filled with ornamental columns, charming objets de art, good art, antique furniture, and animal trophies. Book an upstairs room and specify clearly if you also want a waterfront view. Evening meals (which should be booked in advance) are traditional (vegetarian only) affairs taken in the pretty dining room, but the large, open-air upstairs terrace is a delightful spot for breakfast (additional charge), accompanied by excellent views of activity at the *ghats* down below.

B1/163 Assi Ghat, Varanasi 221 006. C **0542/231-3218.** Fax 0542/236-9695. hotelgangesview@yahoo. com. 14 units (with showers). Rs 2,500 downstairs double; Rs 3,500 upstairs double. Rates are discounted Apr–Sept. No credit cards. **Amenities:** Dining room; airport transfer (Rs 1,200); musical performances; room service. *In room:* A/C

Palace on Ganges ★ It's no palace, and it's not in the center of things, but for the waterfront this is a reasonably smart option. Guest rooms are small but attractive, with marble or parquet floors and rugs, king-size beds with hard foam mattresses, and some of the best amenities on the Ganges. Walls are decorated with artworks reflecting aspects of Indian heritage sites, and each room is a tribute to a different regional style. Bathrooms (showers only) are tiny. The heritage theme is carried throughout, with polished brown marble stairways, dark wood paneling, and intricately carved period furniture featuring inlaid decorative tiles. Although its location overlooking the Ganges is one of the selling points, you aren't guaranteed a river-view room (do request one, though longer stays enjoy first dibs), and views from the rooftop terrace restaurant (Jain food only) include an unpleasant garbage dump at the water's edge.

B-1/158 Assighat, Varanasi 221 001. C **0542/231-5050,** -4304, or -4305. Fax 0542/220-4898 or 0542/ 231-4306. www.palaceonganges.com. info@palaceonganges.com. 24 units (with showers). Rs 3,000 double; off season (May–July) Rs 2,000 double. Taxes extra. AE, MC, V. **Amenities:** 2 restaurants; doctor-on-call; room service. *In room:* A/C, TV, minibar.

A Palace on the River/Rashmi Guest House ★ Also strategically located by the banks of the river, this hotel/guesthouse is more expensive than Ganges View or Palace on Ganges but is highly popular for its exceptional, friendly staff—everyone loves Pappu, their in-house guide and perhaps Rashmi's biggest asset, along with their rooftop restaurant (stick to Indian food, which is consistently good). The atmosphere is great thanks to the hands-on attitude of host Rashmi and her family, and offers generous amentias like an efficient, free railway pick up (there's a charge however for drop off) and free Internet (don't opt for the massage, though; the room's a tad claustrophobic). For the best views (and it's definitely worth booking a river-facing view) try to book rooms on one of the top floors (third to fifth floor), though be warned, there is no elevator. Again, bathrooms are tiny.

D 16/28 A, Manmandir Ghat. ✆ **0542/2402778.** www.palaceonriver.com. 16 units (8 with showers, 8 with bathtubs). Rs 2,500 standard, Rs 6,000 river-facing deluxe. Taxes extra. MC, V. **Amenities:** Restaurant; airport transfer (Rs 750); doctor-on-call. *In room:* A/C, TV, fridge (only in deluxe rooms), heater (in winters), Wi-Fi (complimentary).

WHERE TO DINE

Varanasi is not known for its culinary finesse as far as the westerner's palate goes but Indians feel quite the contrary and eating here is almost as ritualistic as dipping oneself in the Ganga. Since many of these eats are catered essentially by street vendors or hole-in-the-wall establishments, we choose not to make any specific suggestions, keeping in mind the average Indian's strong immunity system. However, for the bold and adventurous, throw aside all caution and follow the crowds: in the mornings, you'll find the populace indulging enthusiastically (almost as if it's their first even though they do this on a daily basis) in what is called *alu kachori* (fried puff pastry or bread served with spicy potato curry). In the thick of the afternoon when all you want to do is faint, down a massive glass of *badaam thandai*—almond-flavored sweet milk. In the evening ask your hotel for guidance to the closest and best *chaat* shop where you can have just about anything on the menu—try the curd-based items as they mitigate the accompanying fiery chilies to some extent. After this, you can make a dash for any confectioner's shop which sells *rabari*—thickened sweet milk which you eat with a spoon instead of gulping it. And although you need to be bolder and more adventurous than normal for the next one, it is a trademark of a visit to Varanasi—the famous Banarasi *paan* (a leaf of a particular plant with a whole assortment of betel nuts and various other ingredients made in less than 20 sec.; insist they put no tobacco in it). On the safer side of the culinary fence, Varanasi's best and smartest restaurant is **Varuna** (✆ **0542/250-3001;** only dinner), in the Taj Ganges hotel, which features a vast menu of Indian specialties (illustrated with chilies to indicate those that are superstrength), a comfortable air-conditioned interior, and helpful service. For the works, served on a traditional Varanasi silver platter, order the Satvik Thali (Rs 500). This is very much a hotel restaurant, and you may not be in the Cantonment area at lunchtime. The Taj's **Chowk** restaurant does dinner buffet spreads that are popular with foreign tour groups, and at Rs 575, the buffets offer very good value. For a hygienic meal while exploring the Old City, your options are limited. Varanasi caters rather haphazardly to the budget Western traveler, with a split focus on affordability and cleanliness, presumably implied by the involvement of foreign management. If you want authentic Indian food, we recommend calling ahead to find out about the possibility of a meal at either Dolphin restaurant at **Rashmi Guest House** or **Ganges View Guesthouse** (see above) or head for the old stalwart Keshari (reviewed below). There's the rather iconic **Bread of Life Bakery & Restaurant** (B3/322 Shivala), established by James and Monika Hetherington, an American interior designer and a German flight attendant. The decor is very sterile (white-vinyl-top tables), and staff borders on comatose, but you can enjoy wholesome Western dishes and freshly baked breads and muffins knowing that you are making a positive contribution—all profits from the bakery and the silk shop above (which, incidentally, has a good selection of scarves and linen made by local weavers) go to local charities, including the Mother Teresa Hospice. Daily specials include steaming-hot vegetable moussaka, chickpea goulash, ratatouille, and warm Portuguese salad. Hot dishes take awhile to arrive, so you can be certain that everything is freshly prepared and, in a city known for food-related mishaps, that hygiene is a priority Sadly, there is talk of shutting, but nothing had been decided at press time. Another favorite is the **Brown Bread Bakery,** conveniently located on Dashaswamedh Ghat (D5/17, Tripura Bhairavi; ℂ 93-3546-5176 or 0542/240 3566). It's got a mouth-watering selection of breads, rolls, and pastries, as well as pizzas and a variety of Tibetan fare—this could save the day if you haven't taken to the city's traditional cuisine. You could also consider laid-back **Lotus Lounge** ★ (D14/27, Mansarowar Ghat; ℂ 98-3856-7717), an open-air eatery on the *ghats,* benefiting from a bird's-eye view of the Ganges. Perfect for all-day chilling (lounge on floor cushions or sit at tables set with candles at night), the space is lorded over by a serene-looking Buddha mural and oper-ated by an Indo-German couple, Martina and Atul, who vary the menu seasonally. Count on fresh ingredients and wide-ranging international choices: gazpacho (made with ginger), red Thai curry, impressive ravioli, and wonderful Tibetan-style *momos* (dump-lings). While meat is generally an absolute no-no anywhere near the river, here you can even order fresh chicken. It's open September through mid-May.

The Keshari Restaurant (**Value** INDIAN   A stern-looking, bespectacled clerk sits counting cash at the entrance of this busy, cramped restaurant (ideal if you're exploring the Old City) hidden away down a near-impossible-to-find back street (to get here, head down the lane opposite the La-Ra Hotel). Inside, wall-mounted fans and ancient cooling systems blast away while waiters dash between tables packed with locals, pilgrims, and bewildered foreigners. There's a huge selection of Indian, Chinese, and other dishes, all vegetarian, but we recommend you stick to the Indian fare, which includes an admirable assortment of curries, *biryanis, pulao,* and traditional breads—you could also opt for a thaali, which comes with an assortment of dishes. It also contains a list of command-ments for diners that includes AVOIDING COMBING OF HAIR and NOT WASHING HANDS IN UTENSILS! Lassis are all fantastic. It may not be particularly relaxing, but this is certainly a place to mingle with real Indians.

D14/8 Teri Neem, Godaulia (Off Dasashwamedh Rd., near Godaulia crossing). ℂ **0542/240-1472.** Main courses Rs 35–Rs 120; thalis Rs 55–Rs 125. No credit cards. Daily 9am–10:30pm.

SHOPPING

Varanasi is famous above all for its silk—every Indian bride wants a Benarasi silk sari in her trousseau, and around 3,000 kilograms (6,614 lb.) of silk are consumed by the weav-ing units daily. Wander through the Old City, or ask at your hotel or the tourist office for recommended wholesalers. **Resham India** (ℂ **0542/243-1673**), comes highly rec-ommended as does **Taj Estate** (ℂ **0542/245-2228**). Or head for **Ushnak Mal Mool Chand** (ℂ **0542/227-6253**), a recommended sari shop in Chowk. Another recom-mended stop is the contemporary, friendly **Open Hand Shop and Café** (B1/128-3, Dumraun Bagh Colony, Assi; ℂ **0542/236-9751;** www.openhandonline.com)—it pro-vides a respite from the cloying traditionality of the city, allowing you to browse through its varied selection of textiles, furnishings and accessories over some pretty decent coffee.

For an excellent selection of Indian fiction and books on philosophy and religion, not to mention good CDs, visit **Kashi Annapurna Book House** (B1/185B, Main Assi Ghat; ℂ **0542/231-5992**), a small enterprise near Ganges View Guesthouse.

Death as Road to Salvation?

Of all the *sadhus* (ascetics) and holy men you will see in Varanasi, perhaps the hardest to understand without brutal judgment are the Aghori sect and their rituals. You may spot the occasional Aghori at a *shamshan ghat* (cremation ground) in Varanasi, usually with matted hair and no clothing, or just covered in white ash, or at most wearing a funeral shroud. The skull he carries is his cranial eating and drinking bowl. Aghoris roam the cremation grounds, where they may smear themselves with the ash from the pyres and/or meditate sitting atop a corpse. It is alleged that as a once-in-a-lifetime act they sometimes also eat a piece of a corpse's flesh. While their rituals are extremely radical and even abhorrent to most, it's interesting to understand what underlies this behavior. Aghoris believe that acting contrary to the accepted norms and taboos of Brahmin ritual and belief is the necessary path to enlightenment. As a result, they eat meat, drink alcohol, and smoke intoxicants. By seeking to reverse all values entrenched within mainstream Hinduism, they choose to embrace all that a Brahmin considers impure. Close contact with the dead, they believe, is a way of focusing on their single-minded quest to live with reality. The funeral pyre is thus for the Aghoris a continual reminder that everyone has to die, and their obsession with death an attempt to live in intimate awareness of it.

4 KHAJURAHO ★★★

600km (372 miles) SE of Delhi; 415km (257 miles) SW of Varanasi; 395km (245 miles) SE of Agra

Legend has it that when the moon god saw the young maiden Hemavati bathing in a river, her beauty was such that he descended to earth to engage in a passionate affair. Before his return to the celestial realm, he swore she would bear a son who would one day erect a great temple to celebrate the beauty of their divine love. Thus the founder of the mighty Chandela dynasty, a robust clan of the warrior Rajputs, was born, and between A.D. 900 and 1100, the Chandela kings—who settled in remote Khajuraho, where they were clearly unhindered by the usual distractions of fighting off invading forces—built not one but 85 temples, almost all of them featuring exquisite sculptures of men and women joyfully engaging in the most intimate and erotic acts. The Chandelas held sway here until the start of the 13th century, when the Sultans of Delhi strengthened their hold over vast swaths of central North India. By the end of the 15th century, the temples were abandoned, hidden deep within thick jungle, until their accidental discovery by a British military adventurer in 1838. By this time, 7 centuries after the political decline of their Chandela creators, only around 24 of the original 85 temples were found. Today these UNESCO World Heritage Site monuments are famous for their erotic sculptures, images that—despite being transgressive by India's conservative contemporary standards—are almost as intimately associated with India as the Taj. But the temples also represent an outstanding synthesis of advanced architecture and refined sculpture, and their beauty means that a trip here should definitely be included in your North India itinerary, particularly if you plan to fly from Agra or Delhi to Varanasi.

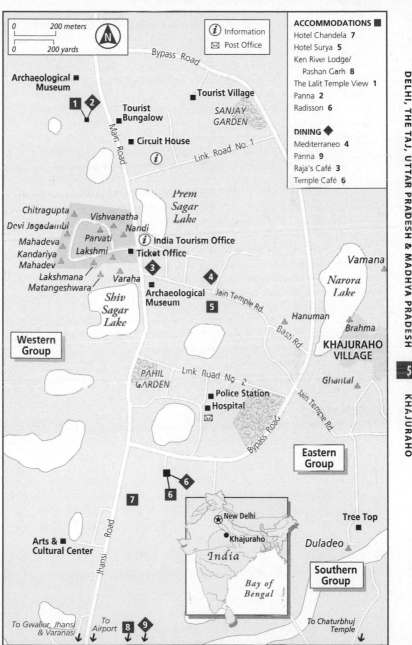

(Fun Facts   India's Ancient Sex Manual

Khajuraho's shops are filled with an endless variety of versions of the *Kama Sutra,* an ancient precursor of modern-day do-it-yourself sex manuals. With information about everything from "increasing the size of the male organ" to the benefits of "slaps and screams" and "bites and scratches," the ancient treatise on sensory pleasures—recorded by the scribe Vatsyayana from oral accounts sometime between the 1st and 6th century A.D.—remains the most famous Indian text in the world. The first English translation was published in 1883 by the Victorian adventurer Richard Burton, who adapted the text in order to dodge charges of obscenity; among other confusing details, he used the Sanskrit words *lingam* and *yoni* to denote the sexual organs. Meanwhile, the debate around the purpose of the erotic temple carvings continues: The most likely theory, and one accepted by many scholars, is that worshippers were meant to leave all sexual desires at the door. The temple is a representation of the life of an ordinary man; the erotics are concentrated on the lower levels of sculptures, and as you go higher, they turn from sexual to sensual and ultimately to sublime in a spiritual sense, in effect symbolizing man's walk towards the divine. Another interpretation is that the images are "manifestations of tantric practices," which is why these temples were known as Yogini temples, where images of exotic sexual positions possessed the power to ward off the evil eye. Yet another theory—this one considered total hokum by those in the know, and best discarded (along with the guide who might pander it) with contempt—suggests that the erotica served to educate young men who as boys lived in hermitages, obeying the Hindu law of being *"brahmacharis"* until they attained manhood when studying the sculptures—and the earthly passions they depicted—prepared them for the worldly role of husband.

ESSENTIALS

GETTING THERE & AWAY   By Air   It's most convenient to fly in on your way to or from Varanasi (a mere 35-min. hop), on **Jet Airways'** or Kingfisher. You can then continue on to Delhi or Mumbai, or Varanasi, the following day. Note that you should stay 2 nights if you really want to explore the temples thoroughly or visit the nearby Panna National Park. Daily Jet Airways flights leave Delhi at 10:40am and take off from Varanasi at 12:20pm, arriving in Khajuraho by 1pm. During the high season (winter), these are usually pretty full of package tour groups, so you'll need to book well in advance; by April, however, the planes are quite empty. Khajuraho's airport is 3km (2 miles) from the town center; taxis operate according to very strict fixed rates.

BY TRAIN & ROAD   Khajuraho finally has its very own railway station: Catch the **UP Sampark Kranti** which departs from Delhi (Nizamuddin) at 12:35pm and reaches Khajuraho the next day at 7:50am (only Tues, Fri, and Sun; make sure to book a 3 AC coach or you'll be delinked at an earlier station). On any other day, if you're traveling by train from Delhi or Chennai, you will disembark at Jhansi (175km/109 miles from Khajuraho). From New Delhi, catch the **Bhopal Shatabdi,** which leaves the capital's Nizamuddin Station at 6:15am and pulls in at Jhansi at 11:03am. From here, MPSRTC runs a bus service from Jhansi to Khajuraho, scheduled to meet the train from Delhi

---

| **Tips** | **Services Unlimited** |

As you wend your way around town, all sorts of men and boys will try to "adopt" you by starting up polite conversations—a pattern you will quickly recognize—before getting down to the business of offering their services for a range of possible needs: tour guides, transport, bicycle hire, shopping assistance, advice, or a tour of the local village school. All are moneymaking enterprises of which you should be wary; best to make it very clear that you have no intention of parting with your money, and leave it to your new friend to decide whether or not to stick around.

(around Rs 105—not recommended as the buses are in terrible condition), or you can catch a taxi (Rs 3,000) to Khajuraho (4 hr.). You can also rent a car and driver for a few days if you have plans to see more of the region—note that Orchha (20km/12 miles from Jhansi) is definitely worth a stop en route to Khajuraho (Orchha is discussed later in the chapter); try to spend the night if you have time. If you're traveling by train from Mumbai, Kolkata, or Varanasi, you will arrive at Satna, which is 117km (73 miles) or 3 hours from town. Note that it is possible to rent a vehicle and driver for the arduous overland journey onwards from Khajuraho to Bandhavgarh (discussed later); this should set you back a maximum of Rs 6,000 for a car with A/C, during peak season.

Note: We cannot overemphasize the appalling state of the roads in Madhya Pradesh. Avoid lengthy road trips, ensure sufficient stops, and don't travel at night. If you must, rent the services of a sturdy 4WD and driver, and check that your vehicle has at least one spare wheel. We highly recommend **Grey Hornbill** (© 94-2530-4970; greyhornbill tours@yahoo.co.in) for travel in this region.

VISITOR INFORMATION　M. P. Tourism (© 07686/27-4051; khajuraho@mptourism. com; Mon–Sat 10am–5pm, closed Sun and second and third Sat of the month) is in the Chandela Cultural Centre, Khajuraho. The more helpful **India Tourism office** (© 07686/27-2347; Mon–Fri 9:30am–6pm) is located opposite the Western Group of Temples. Note that the state tourism website, **www.mptourism.com**, as well as the unrelated **www.khajuraho-temples.com**, are both decent sources of information.

GETTING AROUND　By Taxi, Auto-Rickshaw & Cycle-Rickshaw　You will be flooded with offers to take you from Khajuraho's airport to your accommodations; in return, touts and drivers expect you to use their services for the duration of your stay, and will even continue to lurk outside your hotel. Make it clear that yours is a one-time fare, and stick to cycle-rickshaws and walking for the duration of your stay (average rickshaw costs are Rs 150 for a half-day trip including a stop at the Southern Group). To visit the Panna National Park, expect to pay Rs 900 for a taxi.

GUIDES　Guides charge Rs 600 for a group of one to five people for 4 hours. You can hire the services of a guide at **Raja Café** (opposite the Western Group of temples; see below). Alternatively, the MPSTDC offers a "Walkman Tour"—an audioguide tour purchased at the M. P. Tourism counter at the entrance to the Western Group; this costs Rs 50, but check that everything is in working order before you set out. Be warned that most guides in Khajuraho are just plain dreadful. They may be fine for pointing out details you might otherwise miss, but they regularly spout fundamentalist nonsense and

ⓘMoments   A Jolly Good Ride!

If you have the legs for it, hire a cycle from the hotel you're staying at or from outside the Western Group (Rs 30/hr). Despite the tourist influx, Khajuraho is still steeped in its traditional rural ways and as you cycle through the village, making your way to the Eastern and Southern temples, you'll enjoy a much more authentic and warmer interaction with the locals (versus those who lurk outside the main temples); for directions, you just have to say your destination and you'll be sent the right way. Kids are absolutely delightful and will run after you or just wave depending on how involved they are with their own game of (usually) cricket; wizened faces smile and nod as if they were expecting you all this time; and with enough goats and cows and chickens along the way, you are bound to feel like you're in a rural idyll—especially during sunset, when everything turns strangely quiet and magical, and with the wind in your hair and the smell of earth and clean air, you feel, for the briefest moment, that this is home.

provide the most unbelievable explanations for why erotica was carved on these temples (one classic explanation is that the scenes were created to tell people what "*not* to do"). An exception to the normal drivel is **Samson George** (ⓒ **98-9317-3280**), a lighthearted guy who provides savvy historical information, with explanations that separate fact from legend. If you're staying at one of the top-end hotels, ask them to arrange a guide.

FESTIVALS   The **Khajuraho Dance Festival** ★ is held between February 25 and March 2, when the temples are transformed into a magical backdrop for India's top classical dancers, who perform traditional Odissi, Kuchipudi, and Bharatnatyam dance forms, as well as contemporary Indian dance styles. For up-to-date information, visit **www.khajuraho-temples.com**. *Tip:* Hotels get packed during this time, so you may need to book months ahead.

EXPLORING KHAJURAHO'S TEMPLES

Known for the profusion of sculptural embellishments on both exterior and interior walls, Khajuraho's temples are also recognizable for the exaggerated vertical sweep in the majority of the temples, with a series of *shikharas* (spires) that grow successively higher. Serving as both metaphoric and literal "stairways to heaven," these *shikharas* are believed to be a visual echo of the soaring Himalayan mountains, abode of Lord Shiva. Most of the sculpted temples are elevated on large plinths (often also shared by four smaller corner shrines), and follow the same five-part design. After admiring the raised entrance area, you will enter a colonnaded hall that leads to a smaller vestibule and then an inner courtyard, around which is an enclosed sanctum. You can circumnavigate the sanctum (move around the temple in a clockwise direction, in the manner of the ritual *pradakshina*, with your right shoulder nearest the temple building) to view the beautifully rendered friezes of gods, nymphs, animals, and energetically twisting bodies locked together in acts of hot-blooded passion.

Originally spread across a large open area, unprotected by walls, the temples—most of them built from sandstone lugged on bullock carts from the banks of the River Ken 30km (19 miles) away—are today roughly divided into three sections according to geographic location: the Western, Eastern, and Southern groups. The most spectacular—and those most obviously dripping with erotic sculpture—are within the Western Group. The Eastern Group is located near the old village, and the Southern Group, which is the most missable, lies south of this. As none of the temples outside the Western Group are likely to evoke quite the same delighted reaction, see these first if you're pushed for time or tired; they're also conveniently located near the majority of hotels. Try to enter as soon as they open (sunrise), not only for the quality of light but to avoid the busloads of tourists who will almost certainly detract from the experience.

You can cover the Western Group in 2 hours. The baritone voice of Amitabh Bachchan, arguably India's most popular screen icon, narrates the fascinating history of Khajuraho for the 50-minute **sound-and-light show** held here each night at 6:30pm (1 hr. later in summer). Try to time your visit to the Eastern Group for about 3 or 4pm, so you can enjoy the sunset while you return either to the Western Group or to the imminently more peaceful Chaturbhuj Temple in the Southern Group.

Tip: Remember when setting out to explore the temples that you need to wear shoes that you can easily slip on and off before and after you enter a temple building—even if it is no longer in use.

Western Group ★★★

As you make your way around the complex in a clockwise direction, the first important structure you'll encounter is **Lakshmana Temple ★★★**, one of the three largest in Khajuraho. Built in commemoration of military victory and temporal power, it is thought to be one of the earliest Chandela temples, completed around A.D. 954, yet relatively intact. The structure is as high as it is long, and its raised platform is, like the entire temple, heavily decorated with a variety of sculptures that allude to the pleasures, pastimes, lifestyle, desires, and conquests of the Chandela dynasty. Here you will witness an astonishing diversity of scenes: horse-mounted hunters pursuing their prey, musicians providing lively entertainment for the court, couples drunk on love and liquor, female attendants fanning their king, elephants engaged in playful battle, soldiers on the march, and, of course, amorous couples keeping themselves occupied in the most literal of pleasures. Higher up, above bands of images of Shiva and Vishnu, are the voluptuous depictions of women engaged in worldly activity while draped in little more than jewelry and gossamer-like garments. Inside the temple, covered with more depictions of gorgeous women and deities in their various avatars and incarnations, light pours in through high balconies on each side of the structure, and shadows are cast seductively over the imaginatively carved walls. The main shrine was built to house the three-headed image of Vishnu-Vaikuntha, which features one human head and the head of two of Vishnu's avatars (incarnations), a lion and a boar.

Opposite the temple are two smaller structures, **Devi Mandap** and **Varaha Mandap ★**. The latter is an open sandstone pavilion on a high platform with 14 pillars supporting a high pyramidal roof with a flat ceiling carved with lovely lotus designs. A large stone sculpture of Varaha, the incarnation of Vishnu as the boar, dominates the space. Varaha's polished monolithic body is carved with hundreds of tiny Brahmanical gods and goddesses.

At the northeastern end of the Western Group complex, a number of magnificent temples are found in proximity to one another. Thought to have been built between A.D. 1017 and 1029, elegantly proportioned **Kandariya Mahadev Temple ★★★** is considered the finest temple in Khajuraho, with 872 statues adorning the interior and exterior. Within niches around the temple are images of Ganesh and the seven mother goddesses or *Sapta Matrikas.* Again, among the sculptures of Shiva and the other deities is a profusion of female figures engaged in daily activities made lovely by the sheer exuberance of the sculptural technique: A woman stretches, another plays with a ball, another admires her reflection in a mirror. You won't have to search too hard to find fascinating erotic panels; kissing, caressing couples are depicted with their bodies entwined in blissful union, while others, sometimes in groups of three or four, engage in more lascivious activities. To enter the temple building, you pass through the beautiful entrance *toran;* sculpted from a single piece of stone, this is a floral garland that stems from the mouths of *makaras,* ever-watchful mythical crocodiles, and is carried across the doorway by flying nymphs. Within the temple, walls are covered with exquisite carvings: Don't forget to look upward to appreciate the sculpted flower and leaf motifs of the ceilings. There's a Shiva lingam deep within the *garbha griha,* or "womb chamber"; devotees today place flowers on and around the lingam.

Next to Kandariya Mahadev Temple is small **Mahadev Shrine,** which features a sculpted figure of what is thought to be the emblem of the Chandela dynasty, a raging lion fighting with a kneeling figure. Alongside it is **Devi Jagadambi Temple ★**—note the graceful woman who stands half naked as she interrupts her bath, possibly to catch a glimpse of Shiva's wedding procession. The southern wall includes a panel with a woman climbing up her lover's stout, standing body so that she can kiss him passionately. Although originally dedicated to Vishnu, the temple now houses a large image of Devi Jagadambi, the goddess of the universe, also known as Kali, one of the avatars of Shiva's divine consort. In both this and nearby **Chitragupta Temple ★**, images of Parvati and Shiva in the throes of amorous passion are symbolic of the "cosmic union that makes the world go round." Chitragupta, which was poorly renovated by the Maharaja of Chattarpur, is dedicated to Surya, the sun god; the relief carving around the entrance is the temple's highlight. Within the temple is the figure of Surya riding his sun chariot across the eternal sky.

Back near the entrance of the complex stands the **Temple of Vishvanatha ★**, built in A.D. 1002 by King Dhanga, and notable for three female figures that decorate the building. One maiden plays the flute, her back sensuously exposed to the viewer, another cradles a baby, and the third has a parrot seated on her wrist. Opposite the main entrance is **Nandi Pavilion** (or *mandap*), in which one of the largest figures of Shiva's companion, Nandi the bull, can be found, sculpted from a single piece of stone.

Outside the walls of the Western Group complex, but right alongside the Lakshman Temple, is the still-functioning **Matangeshvar Temple.** It is here that the annual Maha-Shivratri Festival culminates when the Shiva-Parvati marriage ceremony is accompanied by latter-day wedding rituals, lasting through the entire night in a fantastic collaboration of myth and reality.

Planning a major upgrade and a move is the **Archaeological Museum,** at press time still situated across the road from the entrance to the Western Group. By the time you visit, the museum will have relocated to fancy new quarters just outside the town, adjacent to the Grand Temple View hotel. Hopefully, the modest collection of sculptures sampling various Khajuraho sites will be expanded and improved upon. The advantage of spending a few minutes here is that you get to see close-up details of carved figures that usually occur high up on the temple *shikharas.*

Main Rd., opposite the State Bank of India. Admission Rs 250 or pay $5 in foreign currency. Daily sunrise–sunset. English-language sound-and-light show Rs 300; Mar–June 7:30pm, Sept–Oct 7pm, Nov–Feb 6:30pm. Archaeological Museum Rs 10; Sat–Thurs 10am–5pm. No photography in the museum.

Homoeroticism in the Temple: India's Ancient Gay Rights

The Western group of temples comprise innumerable sculpted images of hetero-sexual coupling, usually involving buxom women in the company of lean, lithe men no doubt captivated by the physical beauty and impossibly supple bodies of their seductresses. Amid all these scenes of "mainstream" or "straight" desire, we've come across one carving that bucks the trend: At the **Jagadambi Temple,** search the left-hand side exterior wall along the third band of carvings rising up towards the main *sikhara;* discreetly positioned among the hetero couples is a nude man apparently fondling the erect member of a second naked younger man, who—in turn—caresses his lover's face. Centuries ago Indians were far more progressive on matters related to homosexuality, which is why many were gratified when the high court in Delhi recently overturned a 148-year-old law (dating from the British Raj) that criminalized consensual sex between homosex-uals. In a landmark judgment delivered in July 2009, the high court declared the statute to be "the antithesis of the right to equality," and ordered it to be repealed. No doubt the discreetly placed couple in Jagadambi would, were they mortal, be much relieved.

Eastern Group

The Eastern Group comprises both Hindu and Jain temples. The entrance to the Jain **Shantinath Temple** is guarded by a pair of mythical lions; inside, you are confronted by esoteric charts detailing some of the finer points of Jain philosophy. Photographs of important sculptures and Jain architecture line some of the walls, while the individual shrine entrances are carved with amorous, nonerotic couples and other figures. The main shrine contains a large sculpted image of a naked saint. Throughout the temple, devotees place grains of rice and nuts as tributes at the feet of the various saints.

Parsvanatha Temple ★ dates from the middle of the 10th century A.D. and is the finest and best preserved of Khajuraho's old Jain temples. Since Jainism promotes an ascetic doctrine, there are no erotic images here, but the sculptural decoration is rich nonetheless. In a large panel at the right side of the entrance are images of meditating and naked Jain saints *(tirthankaras),* while the temple exterior is covered in decorative sculptures of voluptuous maidens, embracing couples, and solo male figures representing various Hindu deities. This is a strong indication that the temple—which recalls the temples of the Western Group—was perhaps originally Hindu. In the same complex, **Adinath Temple** has been modified and reconstructed with plastered masonry and even concrete.

Moving north to the Hindu temples, you will pass **Ghantai Temple;** built in A.D. 1148, it is named for the pretty sculpted bells that adorn its pillars. Passing between Javari Temple and the granite and sandstone "Brahma" Temple (more likely to be dedi-cated to Shiva given the presence of a lingam), you come to the northernmost of the Eastern Group temples, the Hindu **Vamana Temple,** built between A.D. 1050 and 1075. Vamana is the short, plump, dwarf incarnation of Vishnu. The entrance to the inner sanctum of this temple is decorated with small erotic relief panels; within the sanctum you will see Vishnu in many forms, including the Buddha, believed to be one of his incarnations.

One of the last temples to be built, **Duladeo Temple** dates from the 12th century A.D. but has been subjected to later restoration. Standing on the banks of Khuddar Stream, facing east, the temple is dedicated to Shiva. Elaborately crowned and ornamented *apsaras,* flying *vidyadharas,* crocodile-mounted *ashtavasu* figures, and sculptures of over-ornamented and stereotypically endowed characters in relatively shallow relief decorate the interior. As at Parshvanath Temple, the walls of Duladeo feature a narrow band of sculptures that depict the celestial garland carriers and musicians in attendance at the wedding of Shiva and Parvati.

The unexceptional **Chaturbhuj Temple,** 3km (2 miles) south of Duladeo, sees very little traffic but has a remarkable sculpture of Vishnu and is a peaceful place at the best of times, not least at sunset. Nearby excavations continue to unearth new temple complexes, as Khajuraho keeps revealing more hidden gems.

AN EXCURSION TO PANNA NATIONAL PARK

A mere 27km (17 miles) from Khajuraho, Panna covers 542 sq. km (211 sq. miles) of dry deciduous forests, fed by the Ken River—jungles of teak, Indian ebony, and flame-of-the-forest trees alternate with wide-open grassy plains in what were once the hunting grounds of several royal families. Tragically, Panna has lost all its tigers (barring a recent introduction of a female tigress), but this is a good place to visit for birds and smaller animals including jungle cats (similar to the serval, it is distinguished by its long legs and uniform coat color, which ranges from sandy yellow to reddish brown) and beautiful *nilguy* (blue-bulls). With the lack of tigers, chances of spotting a leopard increase (as there is less competition for prey), but this really is matter of luck. Adjacent to the park is the ancient town of Panna, home to the largest diamond mines in Asia.

27km (17 miles) from Khajuraho. ✆ **07732/25-2135.** Bookings through Forest Department, located at the park entrance. Park fees: Rs 2,180 admission (includes vehicle entry and up to 4 persons); Rs 100 guide; still and video camera (free); Rs 600 per person tiger viewing on elephant back. Park open Oct 16–June 30, 6:30–10:30am and 3–5:30pm

WHERE TO STAY

If you're simply overnighting and here to see the temples, it's best to stay in the village, from where you can walk to the majority of temples—the Lalit Temple View is your best bet here. If you want to combine the temples with a safari, take a look at our recommended lodgings in Panna National Park, located approximately 45 minutes' drive from the temples; of these, Ken River Lodge is still a great option, offering a more adventurous, earthy experience but for the ultimate in safari chic, opt for the fabulous Pashan Garh: Panna's newest safari lodge is managed by the Taj and safari specialists &Beyond, the same team responsible for the exquisite Mahua Kothi and Banjaar Tola (see Bandhavgarh and Kanha accommodations, later in this chapter). *Note: Still* under discussion is the proposed creation of Khajuraho's first heritage accommodations, at the hitherto deserted 19th-century **Rajgarh Palace.** Situated some 25km (16 miles) from the village, at the foot of the Manijagarh Hills, this beautiful palace has exceptional views, and the end result is likely to be spectacular. You can get updated information about developments from the local tourism bureau.

In Khajuraho

During winter, groups of tourists pass fast and furious through this dusty and otherwise non-descript little town, and hotels (some with almost 100 rooms) fill up quickly, so it's

a good idea to plan ahead. A few self-billed "luxury" options are situated along Khajuraho's main road; if they're not included below, it's because they really aren't worth it. A
large strip of hotels and guesthouses is dedicated to backpackers; rooms vary considerably. Economy-minded travelers should head for **Hotel Surya** (Jain Temple Rd.;
© **07686/27-4145;** www.hotelsuryakhajuraho.com), the best budget hotel in town: Rs
750 to Rs 1,200 buys you a clean, spartan deluxe room with a fan, attached drench
shower, and a balcony, from where you can watch early risers practice yoga in the garden.
A bit more expensive are the "executive" rooms, distinguished by their relative newness
and their considerable size. Surya has a decent dining facility and bikes for hire, and
guests can take cooking classes.

Hotel Chandela ★ (Value) Located 1km (½ mile) from Khajuraho's main temple
complex, on the main road into town, this reliable low-rise Taj chain hotel has peaceful
gardens, comfortable accommodations, and staff that is willing to oblige. It won't win
any awards for design or innovation, but guest rooms are smart if not particularly luxurious—the rate is however good value, and this is our top Khajuraho choice if you don't
want to shell out for the Lalit. Ask for a ground-floor room that opens directly onto the
pool mezzanine with its lawns and palms; those nearest the lobby are best.

Airport Rd., Khajuraho 471 606. © **07686/27-2355** through -2364. Fax 07686/27-2365 or -2366. www.
tajhotels.com. chandela.khajuraho@tajhotels.com. 94 units. Rs 4,215 superior garden-facing double; Rs
5,015 superior pool-facing double; Rs 6,015 junior suite; Rs 7,515 deluxe suite. Rates include breakfast.
Taxes extra. AE, DC, MC, V. **Amenities:** 3 restaurants; bar; airport transfer (Rs 303); archery; badminton;
doctor-on call; fitness center; outdoor pool; pool table; room service; table tennis; outdoor tennis court.
In room: A/C, TV, hair dryer, minibar, Wi-Fi (Rs 221/hr., Rs 662/day).

The Lalit Temple View ★ Benefiting from a great location (just beyond the town
and 200m/656 ft. from the Western Group of temples, even the gym's treadmill has a
view of the main temples), The Lalit (named after Lalit Suri, the dynamic founder of
Bharat Hotels) is your best bet, with decor that can be described as contemporary Indian
chic—a reasonably pleasing integration of modern furnishings and passable replicas of
artful artifacts that tie the hotel in with the heritage town you've come to visit. Rooms
are comfortable and modern, with marble tile floors and pale sandstone walls offset by
colorful throws. Drapes and blinds hang over massive picture windows, the best of which
enjoy views of little lotus ponds outside (slightly more expensive executive suites face the
clover-shaped pool; the "garden-facing" units look toward the new archaeological
museum). Of all the distractions here, the beautiful spa is where you'll want to spend the
most time between temple-spotting.

Opposite Circuit House, Khajuraho 471 606. © **07686/27-2111** or -2333. Fax 07686/27-2123. www.the
lalit.com/Khajuraho. khajuraho@thelalit.com. 47 units. Rs 15,000 garden view double; Rs 17,000 temple
view; Rs 20,000 executive; Rs 35,000–Rs 65,000 suite. Special rates on request. Taxes extra. AE, DC, MC, V.
Amenities: Restaurant; bar; bicycles; billiards; children's playground; cultural performances; doctor-on-
call; fitness center; jogging track; outdoor pool; room service; spa; table tennis; yoga; sightseeing excursions; board games; Wi-Fi (Rs 225/hr., Rs 700/day). In room: A/C, TV, hair dryer, minibar.

Radisson ★ Guest rooms at the Radisson (also known as the Radisson Jass, the name
the Radisson inherited when they took the hotel over in 2005) are not the best in town,
but this is an elegant and relatively luxurious option worth considering, particularly if the
price is right on the particular day you are enquiring into. Bright white marble-floored
public spaces are decorated with attractive Indian artworks including a fine collection of
large Mughal paintings. Guest rooms have a plush contemporary look and are fairly spacious with private balconies and either garden, pool, or mountain views; those on the first

floor (reached via a twisting marble staircase with an impressive chandelier hanging from a domed ceiling) overlooking the lawn-fringed pool are best. Unusual for the Radisson, service standards have dropped and the staff can be quite surly.

By-Pass Rd., Khajuraho 471 606. ✆ **07686/27-2777.** Fax 07686/27-2345. www.radisson.com/khajurahoin. 90 units. Rs 5,600 super deluxe double; Rs 10,600 suite. Taxes extra. AE, DC, MC, V. **Amenities:** Restaurant; bar; airport transfer (Rs 250); babysitting with prior notice; billiards room; currency exchange; doctor-on-call; health club; outdoor pool; room service; outdoor tennis court. In room: A/C, TV, hair dryer, minibar, Wi-Fi (Rs 120/hr., Rs 600/day).

In Panna

Ken River Lodge ★★★ (Value) Close to the entrance to the Park, this 18-hectare (45-acre) "resort," located right on the river, is an ideal hideaway in a forest setting, where fishing enthusiasts can cast a line; experienced naturalists are among the best in the country and certainly transformed us into avid birders. Accommodations are in 10 cottages or in 10 mud-walled huts; unless you're with children, choose the latter. They have straw roofs, fireplaces, separate dressing areas, and big, simple attached bathrooms with occasional wildlife lurking in corners. Good food and a bar on a raised wooden platform contribute to the resort's appeal. Romantic dinners can be arranged on a tiny private island in the middle of the river or you could sit up at the machan at night and wait with bated breath. (Note that Ken can arrange a fabulous night safari nearby where you will have good chances of seeing not just plenty of wildlife, but animals at their calmest.)

Village Madla, District Panna 488 001. ✆ **07732/27-5235.** In Delhi contact Manav Khanduja (✆ 98102-53436). www.kenriverlodge.com. wildlifer@vsnl.net. 20 units (with showers). Rs 12,500 jungle plan double. No credit cards. **Amenities:** Restaurant; bar; airport transfer (Rs 700); boating; doctor-on-call; fishing; jeep safaris with naturalist; night safari. In room: Fans, water coolers (some units), no phone.

Pashan Garh ★★★ Although we would still rate Ken higher for the wildlife experience it offers, Pashan Garh is where you come if you want to really pamper yourself (and won't get a chance to visit any of the other Taj &Beyond safari ventures). Spread through 80 hectares (200 acres) of forested land, cottages of stone and brick resembling local architectural styles are exquisitely private (30m/98 ft. apart); inside the decor breathes luxury. A raised platform acts as a divan with a fireplace surrounded by large glass windows overlooking the jungle while a gazebo outside with a khujuraho motif running along its sides is perfect for an after-safari massage. Have a sun-downer on the common veranda before moving to the dining hall—a single long chunky wooden table—great if there are plenty of guests around it, but not so cozy when less busy. The pool offers a cool respite to sultry afternoons and you can also explore the woods on the property itself instead of doing an evening safari—note that it takes almost an hour to get to the gates of Panna national park, which means getting up at an unearthly 4:30am or leaving in blistering heat at 2:30pm.

Panna National Park, Amanganj Rd, District Panna 488 001. Info ✆ **94-2542-0801.** Reservations: ✆ **866/969-1825** in the U.S. and Canada; or **1800-111-825** or 022/6601-1825 in India. www.tajsafaris.com. tajsafaris@tajhotels.com. 12 units. Rs 32,000 per person per night. AE, MC, V. **Amenities:** Dining room; bar; butler; doctor-on-call; library; outdoor pool; jeep safaris w/naturalists. In room: A/C, flashlight, hair dryer.

WHERE TO DINE

If you're down with a case of culinary homesickness, you may find some comfort in the fact that Khajuraho is awash with eateries offering "multicuisine" menus; in fact, the term seems to be a favorite among staff in most of the top hotels. Unfortunately, the hotels are where you'll find the best dining options. These are headed up by the **Temple Café** at

the Radisson, and **Panna,** the multicuisine eatery at The Lalit Temple View (an altogether easier, and cheaper, option for lunch). If you don't mind something a little more
down home, sample the Italian fare offered at **Mediterraneo** (Jain Temple Rd., opposite
Surya Hotel; $\mathcal{C}$ **07686/27-2246;** no credit cards; daily 7:30am–10:30pm), an alfresco
rooftop restaurant with friendly staff and little pretense beyond the gigantic letters along
the side of the building exclaiming MEDITERRANEO CHEF TRAINED IN ROME. While this
bit of ambitious advertising is something of an exaggeration, Rama, the owner, *is* from
Rome, and he has personally trained all his staff. The menu offers a range of Italian
favorites, including wood-fired pizza (when available; Rs 150–Rs 275), pasta, and tasty
Roman-style chicken. Don't expect to be blown away, but you can be sure your meal will
be made with fresh ingredients, and there's real espresso. Another local hangout—conveniently situated across the road from the Western Group entrance—is **Raja Café Swiss
Restaurant** ($\mathcal{C}$ **07686/27-2307;** no credit cards), which has a rooftop terrace and a
ground level courtyard under a shady peepul tree. The only real advantage here is that
you get to enjoy excellent views of the Western Group (it's an ideal place for a beer after
you've visited the site); we're afraid that since the longstanding Swiss proprietor passed
away several years ago, the food has gone from unremarkable to just passable.

SHOPPING

Khajuraho can be a nightmare. In contrast with the tranquil village atmosphere, hawkers
and touts ooze from every corner and have record-setting persistence. You'll no doubt
develop a gut-wrenching dislike for the overstretched shopping areas in and around the
main square, where everyone seems to demand that you step into yet another handicrafts
shop to "just look, no buy." Do not enter any shop in Khajuraho with anyone other than
fellow travelers. If you make a purchase on your own, you'll save yourself around 20%,
which is the standard commission, borne by you, demanded by "agents" (taxi drivers,
guides, or someone who has "befriended" you) for their "service" of bringing foreign
business to local stores.

If you're looking to buy miniature artworks—perhaps an erotic interpretation inspired
by the temple carvings—consider stopping in at **Artist** (Surya Hotel Complex, Jain Temple
Rd.; $\mathcal{C}$ **07686/27-4145**), an appropriately named outlet for Pichhwai and Mughal paintings rendered by Dilip Singh and his two brothers, whose late father was a recipient of a
National Award for Art many years back. Their paintings vary in subject, size, and quality,
but the selection includes something to suit everyone's pocket. Miniatures on silk, fabric,
or paper start at a mere Rs 10, and go up to Rs 13,000; you can also commission a work if
there's something in particular that you want to take home with you.

5 BANDHAVGARH NATIONAL PARK ★★★

237km (147 miles) S of Khajuraho

Known as "Kipling Country," despite the fact that the writer never set foot here, the
nature reserves of Madhya Pradesh are archetypal India, with vast tracts of jungle, open
grassy plains, and, of course, tigers. Bandhavgarh National Park occupies 437 sq. km
(168 sq. miles), making it a great deal smaller than its more famous cousin, Kahna
National Park. But despite its relatively diminutive size, the park is home to some 50 to
70 tigers; around 25 of these are in the tourist zone, and at press time there are several
new litters on their way contributing to what is probably the highest density of tigers in

> ## (Fun Facts) The White Tiger of Rewa
>
> The last elusive white tiger ever to roam free was a Bandhavgarh cub that was snared by Martand Singh, who bred the animal in captivity in order to exploit its deviant genes and so produce a new "genus"—the "White Tiger of Rewa." Today, the only places you'll see white tigers are zoos.

any park on earth. Once the personal hunting grounds of local maharajas who almost wiped out the tiger population, Bandhavgarh continues to experience problems with wayward poachers, usually suppliers for China's lucrative traditional medicine industry. But, as locals will assure you, your chances of seeing a wild tiger (those at Ranthambhore are almost tame) are still unmatched anywhere else in India. Best of all, you will approach your predator on elephant-back, giving the entire experience a totally unreal air. Besides the sought-after tiger, the sanctuary is home to spotted deer, *sambar, nilgai* antelope, barking deer, shy *chinkara* (Indian gazelle), and wild boar; leopards and sloth bears are far more elusive. The varied topography includes dramatic cliffs that proved a natural location for the 14th-century **Bandhavgarh Fort.** If you give enough notice, you can arrange to visit the reserve's rock-cut caves, with inscriptions dating as far back as the 2nd century B.C.

ESSENTIALS

VISITOR INFORMATION   Entry to Bandhavgarh is via the tiny village of Tala, where a number of lodges and resorts, a handful of *dhabas* (snack shacks), and several souvenir stalls are the only distractions from park activities. Try to get any information you require in advance, but you can pretty much rely on your chosen lodge to make all local arrangements for you. Contact **M. P. Tourism** at the White Tiger Forest Lodge at Bandhavgarh (© 07627/26-5366; www.mptourism.com) or the **Project Tiger Field Director** in Umaria (© 07653/22-2214).

GETTING THERE   By Road   Set aside an entire day for road journeys from destinations within Madhya Pradesh; surfaces are terrible at best, consisting of little more than endless potholes linked by clusters of asphalt and islands of sand. The nearest town of tourist interest is Khajuraho—a rather bumpy 5-hour drive away and would cost you Rs 6,000—we suggest you opt for an Innova or Scorpio which are best suited for MP roads.

By Air   If you can afford it, take advantage of the helicopter trips from Delhi offered by several of the upmarket resorts in Bandhavgarh. If you decide to catch a commercial flight, Jabalpur is the nearest airport with most big cities connected to it. It is situated 165km (102 miles) away; the 4-hour onward taxi trip will cost upward of Rs 4,500.

By Train   Umaria, 45 minutes from Tala, is the nearest railhead. The best train from Delhi is the **Kalinga Utkal Express,** which leaves Nizamuddin Station at 12:50pm and arrives in Umaria the following day at 6:15am, a little too late for early entry to the park. Taxi rides to Tala cost around Rs 1,000; **Om Prakash Shukla** has a reliable service (© 94-2534-4226 or 94-2534-4227) and is used by most of the resorts. Other nearby railheads are Katni and Jabalpur (if you're coming from Mumbai).

WHEN TO GO   The park opens as early as October (depending on the monsoon situation), but sightings are best February through June, when the heat forces more animals to search for water. Although the park attracts smaller crowds than Corbett and Ranth-ambhore, avoid Bandhavgarh on weekends and the week before and after Diwali, Holi, and New Year's holidays, when the park is filled with queue-jumping VIPs and noisy families.

ORGANIZING YOUR BANDHAVGARH SAFARI

Regarding entry fees and permits, the best plan is to book accommodations that include *everything;* the resorts and lodges we've reviewed below will take care of all your safari arrangements. Get to the park first thing in the morning, when you will join the line of open-top jeeps and other 4WDs waiting at the entrance for the daily rush, which starts promptly at dawn. If you've hired a vehicle and driver privately, you will have to pay a small fee for the services of a park guide who will accompany you; this and other charges for entry permits, cameras, and such are all paid at the park entrance. Jeep safaris can cover a relatively large area within the park, but most sightings occur as a result of information shared among the various drivers and guides. Drivers must take a lottery-decided route to a central point where a token is collected; this token then allows access to the rest of the park. In particular, the token enables your jeep to join the queue for the much-anticipated elephant-back tiger-viewing experience. Elephant mounted *mahouts* head out early to search for tigers; once they locate them, they wait at the nearest road until the jeeps begin to congregate and word spreads, ensuring the arrival of other vehicle-driven visitors. Rs 600 buys you an elephant-back ride for an unnervingly close-up view of the tigers, usually encountered minding their own business deep within the sal forest. You then have around 3 minutes to capture the elusive cat on film before your elephant returns to the road to pick up new passengers.

Tip: Being at the rear of the queue of jeeps may involve some waiting, but *mahouts* usually allow the last elephant-trippers a few extra moments with the tigers. During the afternoon, the park offers more-substantial elephant safaris that are as much relaxing as they are a good opportunity to see more tigers in the wild, this time without feeling like you're part of a tourist conveyor belt.

With any luck, your guide will be as interested in showing you the terrain, which is rugged and beautiful, as he is in finding your tiger. He may point out other species such as the *chital,* blue bull antelope, and *sambar;* and the many bird species such as spotted black kites, crested serpent eagles, storks, ibises, hornbills, white-eyed buzzards, black vultures, golden-backed woodpeckers, kingfishers, and dove parakeets. If all else fails, there are plenty of black-faced langur monkeys and rhesus macaques ("red-bummed monkeys") to keep you amused.

Note: There is no doubt that seeing a tiger in the wilds is one of the most amazing experiences, but the manner in which all the jeeps gun for the poor animal is a little disconcerting. It is obvious that the inevitable "tip" is calling the shots and all ethical conduct generally takes a back seat. If you prefer to experience the park in a sensitive manner, then we advise you to go with Mahua Kothi (see below) or else make it clear to the guide and driver that you don't wish to partake in behavior that effectively "corners" these magnificent, critically endangered cats.

Park entrance is at Tala. Park fees: Rs 2,180 admission; Rs 1,500 vehicle entry; video and still photography is complimentary; Rs 600 tiger viewing on elephant per person (3–5 min.); Rs 25,000 for 1 person with an additional Rs 10,000 per person up to maximum 3 guests for a 6-hr. elephant ride; last-minute cancellations are allowed. Daily 6:15–10am and 3–6pm.

10

Note that rates quoted here are "Jungle Plan" packages, which include all meals and two safaris into the park as well as all entrance, guide, and vehicle fees, and that all are situated within striking distance of the entrance. Besides the thoroughly swish and sexy Mahua Kothi (reviewed below), there are two more options worth considering, and they won't break the bank in quite the same way. Located on the park's southern edge, **Tree House Hideaway** ★ (© 94-2583-8688; www.treehousehideaway.com; Rs 20,000 all-inclusive double) is a unique property with accommodation perched on top of five different kinds of trees. Contrary to what one would expect from a treehouse, the interiors are quite comfortable yet in keeping with the surroundings, although some guests have had a nightmarish time with rats (a problem the management can't really solve given that one is surrounded by a forest); on the bright side, you may also chance across (as we did) herds of wild boar, literally under your tree, grunting and rummaging in the dark—an authentic and slightly surreal experience for a city slicker. At press time, the owners were waiting to install a CCT camera by the side of a natural waterhole shared with the park boundary, so that guests can view any visiting wildlife while sitting in the lounge area; if only the staff and managers were more enthused and enterprising, this could become one of the best properties in Bandhavgarh.

An older sister property is the **King's Lodge** ★ (info © 07627/28-0536; reservations 011/2588-5709; www.kingslodge.in), which is also responsible for Ken River Lodge in Panna, near Khajuraho. Accommodations (most of which are raised off the ground on stilts) have large covered porches, mud-effect walls, and sliding doors that open to bedrooms with high A-frame ceilings; floors are stone tiled and there's plenty of wood, including entire branches and tree trunks used as part of the decor. They're smart and have working iron fireplaces, air-conditioning, and good, firm mattresses covered with white cotton linens; bathrooms have tubs and showers. The lodge also offers a good range of amenities, including a pool, and there's a mellow atmosphere enhanced by the breezy layout of the public spaces. Rates start at Rs 15,000 for two people on the Jungle Plan.

Mahua Kothi ★★★ Although luxury comes at a stiff price, this is easily the best all-round safari experience in Bandhavgarh, and arguably India. A groundbreaking collaboration between India's Taj luxury hotel chain and Africa's renowned high-end safari operator &Beyond, Mahua Kothi brought glamour and sex appeal to jungle lodgings as well as a hitherto unknown level of intelligent guiding and tiger tracking. The original homestead has been lavishly furnished and decorated to become a homey public space with an open-plan interior filled with memorabilia that suggests the collected history of several generations. Lunches are taken at the tremendous dining tables with fat tree-stump legs, and a deep, comfortable veranda is just the spot for postsafari gin and tonics. Then slink off to one of 12 gorgeous village-style *kutiyas*, or mud-walled suites: each harmoniously located within the forested setting. Mahua Kothi's naturalists, who are passionate about the outdoors and have been impeccably trained by &Beyond, have set a whole new standard in game tracking on the subcontinent.

Bandhavgarh National Park, Village Tala, District Umaria 484 661. Reservations: © **866/969-1825** in the U.S. and Canada, or **1800-111-825** or 022/6601-1825 in India. www.tajsafaris.com. tajsafaris@tajhotels. com. 12 units. Rs 32,000 per person per night all inclusive. AE, MC, V. **Amenities:** Dining room and various dining areas; bar; airport transfers (Rs 6,000); bicycles; butler; doctor-on-call; jeep safaris; Internet (complimentary); library; outdoor pool. *In room:* A/C, flashlight, hair dryer.

6 KANHA NATIONAL PARK ★★★

160km (99 miles) S of Jabalpur

A continuation of "Kipling Country," Kanha is in many ways the most beautiful and fascinating national park in the country, not only for its sizeable tiger population but the landscape that keeps changing as you traverse the 250 sq. km (98 sq. miles) open to tourists; thick wooded areas open into scrubland, which in turn dissolves into meadows, and all periodically interspersed with natural bodies of water and streams. Kanha was included into Project Tiger in 1973 and here, we can say with some relief, it has had positive results (currently India is battling under the ignominy of losing its tigers at an alarming rate to poachers due to insufficient infrastructure and conservation mismanagement). Another success story is that of the Barasingha—a handsome deer whose numbers had dwindled to 66 in 1970, but is now at 450 and climbing! Although sighting a tiger is not as easy here as in Bandhavgarh, the picturesque park is teeming with all kinds of birds and mammals which you will most definitely come across during the safari; even on the worst of days, finding langurs, chital and peacocks is guaranteed.

ESSENTIALS

VISITOR INFORMATION   There are two zones open to tourists—Mukki and Kanha. Given that you will most probably be staying at one of the Mukki resorts, it would make sense to cover Kanha in the morning when the Park is open for longer (6am–noon), and the close-by Mukki in the evening (3:30–6pm). As in most other national parks, it is best to let your resort make all the necessary arrangements by opting for the "jungle plan." Although they have their own in-house naturalists, to create employment, guides have been inducted into the forest department from the villages around Kanha—each has been given some training, binoculars, and a bird guidebook and it is compulsory to have one accompany you on the safari—this makes perfect sense as they are more aware of the animal movement and besides, the more eyes the better. You are advised to tip them at least Rs 50, a figure that would increase depending on how many of you there are and how happy you have been with his services.

GETTING THERE   By Air   Both Nagpur and Jabalpur have flights from Delhi, Mumbai, and Chennai. At press time, there were talks on for connecting all wildlife areas in MP by charter flights, arranged through some of the upmarket resorts.

By Train   Jabalpur and Nagpur are your closest rail connections. Your chosen resort will make the necessary travel arrangements for you. If you're coming from Bandhavgarh, there is an option of catching a train from Umaria (40 min. from Tala) to Jabalpur, although the timings aren't quite suitable; instead, you could do it the other way round and go from Jabalpur to Umaria by the early morning Narmada Express and thereafter by road to Bandhavgarh.

By Road   There are no shortcuts to getting to Kanha—nearest airports and railway stations are at Nagpur and Jabalpur (both take 4–5 hr. to Mukki). You could also drive from Bandhavgarh (6–7 hr. on something that calls itself a road). *Note:* There are no restroom facilities along the way so be prepared.

WHEN TO GO   The park opens by October, but the best time to visit would be February to April. After that the heat intensifies dramatically and although the animals may be forced to search for water and thus expose themselves, whether visitors can bear with the blazing sun is another matter.

ORGANIZING YOUR SAFARI

There is very little that differs in the system that is followed by the other Parks in Madhya Pradesh—refer to our section on Bandhavgarh for a detailed account of how it works. Once again, we must warn our readers that while the sighting of a tiger is extraordinary, you may feel squeamish, especially when tourist numbers are high, at the manner in which this magnificent animal is literally cornered. While authorities claim that the tiger is free to make its own path and remain sequestered from our ravenous gaze, in truth, given its tendency to mark its territory and use the same trails, it has little option but to run up against eager tourists twice a day. Perhaps if you were to clearly state the level to which you are willing to go, your naturalist would conduct the safari accordingly.

Park entrance is at Mukki or Kanha. Park fees: Rs 2,000 admission; Rs 600 elephant ride per person for 3–5 min. Daily 6:15–10am and 3–6pm; park closed July 1–Oct 15.

WHERE TO STAY

Kanha has some fairly upmarket and lovely accommodation choices in hand, with the latest Taj and &Beyond masterpiece—**Banjaar Tola** (reviewed below) taking first prize. **Singinawa** ★ (𝓒 98-1026-5781 or 0124/406-8852; www.singinawa.in; Rs 29,820 double) was a tad too formal for us, but that was to be expected given the pedigreed background that it revels in, a little too obsessively perhaps. Owned by Latika and Nanda Rana, part of the Nepal royal family and both of whom have studied tigers extensively, in partnership with Mike and Claire Gallery, it consists of 12 air-conditioned cottages and a massive central stone lodge where guests discuss their sightings over cocktails and dine on the massive wooden table, surrounded by fabulous photographs taken by Nanda. Food is catered to suit the first-timers palate but a little too dull and mismatched for those who crave Indian spices. Much of the 23 hectares (57 acres) has been left untouched—nice to explore, with a lovely pool to soak in after. Their vehicles are decidedly the most comfortable and, with eager naturalists as part of their team, you will undoubtedly have a wonderful wildlife experience. But really, our money's on Banjaar Tola. If you'd rather opt for something more informal and relaxed (not to mention less exorbitant), we recommend **Shergarh** (reviewed below). (PS: Keep a lookout for **Kanha Earth Lodge,** scheduled to open at the end of 2009 (www.kanhaearthlodge.com)— owned by the same group that operates Kings Lodge and Ken River Lodge, it's sure to be a good option.

Tip: If you decide to go by rail from Kanha via Umaria on your way to Bandhavgarh, then you will need to leave Kanha the evening before and stay overnight at Jabalpur in order to catch the early morning train. The only decent en route option is the **Narmada Jacksons** (𝓒 0761/400-1122; www.jacksons-hotel.com; doubles from Rs 2,500) but don't expect much—this is basic accommodation, just booked to facilitate your onward journey.

Banjaar Tola ★★★   We wish there were more stars to give this absolutely wonderful creation, another of the Taj-safari properties, this one spectacularly located on the River Banjaar. The two camps, each with just nine tents, lie along the riverside, across which are the woods; the massive half-moon shaped rooms lead out through large glass doors onto an outdoor deck with the most terrific view in Kanha (nos. 6–8 don't have views of the river). Decor is gorgeous but it is the bathrooms that have hydrohedonists in heaven—almost the same size as the room, and with equally gorgeous views. Food is

intelligently planned with light and healthy lunches of salads to keep you awake during
your evening ride followed by a heavier but exceptional choice of dishes during dinner.
Naturalists/guides are wonderful to interact with. Although staying here may land you
with a considerably lighter pocket, consider it as a treat of a lifetime.

Manji Tola Village, Baihar, Balaghat District 481116. (*C* **93-0365-1100**. Reservations: (*C* **866/969-1825**
in the U.S. and Canada; or 1800-111-825 or 022/6601-1825 in India. www.tajsafaris.com. tajsafaris@tajhotels.
com. 18 units. Rs 32,000 per person per night; special rates for off-season available along with special
discounts if you opt for more than one Taj Safari Lodge. AE, MC, V. **Amenities:** Dining room and various
dining areas; bar; airport transfers Rs 7,500; butler; cycles; doctor-on-call; Internet (complimentary); jeep
safaris; library; outdoor pool. *In room:* A/C, flashlight, hair dryer.

Shergarh ★ Also tented (although comparative to Banjaar Tola, very rustic), the
Shergarh tents offer comfortable and spacious en-suite tents, and air-coolers in summers
and *angithis* (lit coal) in winters. Each of the six units comes with a veranda (ask for the
tent next to the pond) where you can soak in the amazingly unpolluted night sky. Electricity may be erratic but there is a backup generator as well as oil lanterns—immediately
providing a more romantic ambience. The intimate living room/lobby doubles as a dining room; lunches can be served outdoors under a gorgeous mango tree. If the rigorous
routine of morning and evening safaris is too exhausting, owners Jehan and Katie can
organize cycling to the river, guided walks to a hilltop where you can take in a beautiful
sunset while sipping cocktails, or visits to the local market. The jeeps used for the safari
are not as comfortable as at the other lodges, but the price makes up for this.

Village Bahmni, Post Kareli, Tehsil Baihar, District Balaghat 481 111. (*C* **07637/22-6215** or 90-9818-7346.
www.shergarh.com. enquiries@shergarh.com. 6 units. Rs 10,500 per person on jungle plan. No credit
cards, traveler's checks and cash only; wire transfers in advance. **Amenities:** Dining room and various
dining areas; bar; airport transfer (Rs 6,800); cycling, Internet (complimentary); library; market trips, jeep
safaris; guided walks. *In room:* Air-coolers in summer, coal-fire in winter, flashlight.

---

7 ORCHHA ★★★

440km (273 miles) SE of Delhi; 238km (148 miles) S of Agra; 120km (74 miles) SE of Gwalior

Located on a rocky island on the Betwa River, the deserted royal citadel of Raja Rudra
Pratap is one of India's most fabulous Mughal heritage sites, yet Orchha (literally "hidden
place") is mercifully free of development, making this a wonderfully relaxing stop.
Founded in 1531, it was the capital of the Bundela kings until 1738. Today the weathered
temples, palaces, and cenotaphs are the royal quarters of emerald parakeets and black-faced
langurs, while traditional whitewashed, flat-roofed structures house the laid-back villagers.
Besides the palace complex, three beautiful temples are worth seeking out, as well as 14
graceful *chhatris* (cenotaphs) commemorating the Orchha rulers, built upstream along the
riverbank. Most of these sights can be covered in a day excursion on the way to Khajuraho,
but to get the most out of this surreally tranquil haven, spend at least 1 night here.

ESSENTIALS

VISITOR INFORMATION   The **MPSTDC Sheesh Mahal** (*C* **07680/25-2624**) acts
as an informal tourism office (see "Where to Stay," below). They will arrange day trips
and transfers.

GETTING THERE   The best way to get to Orchha is to catch a train to Jhansi, where
trains from Delhi, Mumbai, or Chennai pull in, carrying visitors on their way to Khajuraho (see "Khajuraho: Getting There & Away," earlier in this chapter). You can catch an

The Gems of Gwalior

If you've chosen to travel by rail or road from Agra, 118km (73 miles) north, to Khajuraho via Orchha, 120km (74 miles) south, set aside a day to explore Gwalior's fine sights. To see them all necessitates an overnight stay in the palace that is part of the attraction and one of central India's best heritage properties.

Looming over the three cities of modern Gwalior—Lashkar, Morar, and Gwalior—its 3km-long (2-mile) thick walls built atop steep cliff surfaces, **Gwalior Fort** ★ (Rs 100 entrance allows you into most sites, Rs 25 video; daily sunrise–sunset) is believed to date back to the 3rd century A.D. The oldest surviving Hindu fort in the Bundelkund, it changed hands repeatedly and was admired by all who invaded it—even the first Mughal emperor, Babur, who admired very little else of India, famously described it as "the pearl among the fortresses of Hind" (though he still allowed his army to desecrate the Jain rock-cut sculptures, viewed as you approach the Urwahi Gate). Within the ancient walls are a number of palaces, temples, step wells, and underground pools (best to hire a taxi, available at the entrance), but its most significant structure is the monumental **Man Mandir Palace,** built by Raja Man Singh of the Tomara dynasty in the 15th century. Ornamented with a variety of glazed tile patterns, this is considered one of the finest examples of pre-Mughal Hindu palace architecture in India. Now housing a rather good **Archaeological Museum** (Tues–Sun 10am–5pm), **Gujari Mahal** was also built by Man Singh, this time for his favorite wife, a queen of the Gujjar tribe; he famously fell in love with her after he witnessed her courageously separate two warring buffaloes.

The oldest temple in the fort is **Teli-ka Mandir,** or **Temple of the Caste of Oil Sellers,** dating from the 9th century. Built in the South Indian, or Dravidian, style, it was originally dedicated to Vishnu before apparently being used as a soda factory by the British when they occupied the fort in the 1800s. Just north of here is a large pool of water known as **Suraj Kund.** It was here that a divine hermit named Gwalipa, for whom the fort is named, is believed to have cured the fort's founder, King Suraj Sen, of leprosy. Other notable temples are late-11th-century **Sas Mandir (Temple of the Mother-in-law)** and **Bahu Mandir (Temple of the Daughter-in-law),** which form an elegant pair. Guides hired at the fort should cost Rs 300 for 2 hours; **Samar Singh** (✆ 98-2623-0564) is a reliable choice—his grandfather was the very first guide to work here.

The last rulers of Gwalior were the Scindia clan, and during the British era the Scindia Maharaja, Jiyaji Rao, was known to be one of the most decadent of the Rajput rulers. In 1875 he built the over-the-top 19th-century **Jai Vilas Palace** ★ for the express purpose of impressing the Prince of Wales. He filled it with treasures imported from Europe; in the Durbar Hall are the world's heaviest chandeliers, each weighing 3½ tons, which hang over the largest handmade carpet in Asia. In the dining room you can see the electric silver-and-crystal toy train the maharaja used to dispense drinks and cigars around the massive dinner table—apparently refusing to stop the train in front of those he disliked. Jai Vilas Palace (© **0751/232-1101;** Rs 200, Rs 30 camera; Thurs–Tues 10am–5pm) is still occupied by his descendants (if the flag is flying, royalty is in residence); there's also a torturous series of museum galleries filled with a mix of banal and unusual trifles. You might be shocked to see the collection of stuffed tigers and cheetahs labeled "Natural History Gallery."

Gwalior's has a long-standing tradition of musical excellence and innovation, and to this end **Sarod Ghar** ★ traces and showcases this legacy in the beautiful sandstone home of the Bagnash family. You might inquire about the **musical recitals** occasionally held in the museum's marble courtyard (© **0751/ 242-5607;** www.sarod.com; entry free; Tues–Sun 10am–1pm, 2–4pm); don't pass up the chance of hearing Amjad Ali Khan, an internationally recognized master. Or find out whether musicians are performing at the simple white memorial **Tomb of Miyan Tansen.** One of India's greatest musicians, Miyan Tansen was considered one of the *navratna* (nine gems) of Mughal Emperor Akbar's court. For recital information, contact **M. P. State Tourism Development Corporation** (© **0751/234-0370;** gwalior@mptourism.com; open 24 hr.).

The best place to overnight is the Taj's luxurious **Usha Kiran Palace Hotel** ★ (© **0751/244-4000;** www.tajhotels.com), located right next door to the Jai Vilas Palace. Scindia royalty once resided here, and this handsome heritage hotel, extensively renovated in 2005, retains an evocative old-world atmosphere. Most accommodations (with A/C, TV, and minibar) are arranged around a courtyard and are tastefully furnished, with high ceilings, pleasant sitting areas, and furniture that once belonged to the maharaja. Of the massive deluxe rooms, 201 and 202 offer the best value (Rs 12,000 double). A stay here is definitely a taste of luxury, particularly if you stay in one of the fabulous **villas** ★★★ added in 2006, which have private pools and smart designer interiors (from Rs 25,000). The hotel offers guests several royal experiences, notably at the gorgeous poolside spa; among the decadent offerings is a bathing ritual *(Mangal snana)* where you soak in a tub infused with rich traditional ingredients while live musicians play from behind a curtain. Around the hotel building, you'll discover broad passages, 51 differently designed sandstone trellises, ornate chandeliers, and an upstairs terrace affording views of Jai Vilas Palace and Gwalior Fort, ideal as a sundowner venue. If you do spend the night, you might want to watch the 45-minute sound-and-light show (Rs 150; tickets available at the fort; closed July–Sept 15) held at the fortress each night at 7:30pm November through February and 8:30pm March through October.

auto-rickshaw from Jhansi to Orchha (20km/12 miles) for about Rs 300. Alternatively, with time on your hands, you can hire a car and driver and travel by road from Agra, overnighting at Gwalior (see "The Gems of Gwalior," below).

EXPLORING ORCHHA'S FORGOTTEN MONUMENTS

The monuments of Orchha are fairly spread out, but close enough to be explored entirely on foot. You can spend a quick-paced morning poking through the ruins in which you're most interested, or take your time and spread your explorations over an entire day. A few of the sights require a ticket, which you can purchase from a booth at the front of the Raj Mahal (daily 9am–5pm); the Rs 250 ticket provides access to all the main monuments.

Visible as you enter the village, Orchha's fortified palace complex is approached by a multi-arched medieval bridge. Once over the bridge, you'll first encounter the earliest of the palaces, **Raj Mahal ★**, built during the 16th century by the deeply religious Raja Madhukar Shah, who befriended the Mughal Emperor Akbar, an alliance that was to serve the rulers of Orchha well. Look for the bold, colorful murals on walls and ceilings, and climb to the uppermost levels of the palace for a more complete view of the entire complex. A pathway leads to the two-story **Rai Praveen Mahal;** according to legend, it was built in the mid–17th century for a concubine who the then-ruling Raja loved to watch dance. Surrounded by lovely lawns, the palace includes a ground-level hall where performances were once held, and naturally cooled subterranean apartments. Deemed Orchha's finest palace, with delicate *chhatris* (dome-shaped cenotaphs) and ornate stone *jalis* (screens) along its outer walls, **Jahangir Mahal ★** is distinguished by its domed pavilions, fortified bastions, and ornamental gateway flanked by stone elephants holding bells in their trunk, perhaps to announce the entry of the man in whose honor the palace was built: Emperor Jahangir, Akbar's son (see "The Life & Times of the Mughal Emperors," earlier in the chapter). He is said to have promised to visit, but accounts vary as to whether he actually arrived. The sandstone exterior bears the remains of beautiful turquoise- and lapis lazuli–tiled embellishments, while interior walls are decorated with lovely carvings. **Sheesh Mahal,** now a hotel, is a section of the palace complex built by a local king as a country getaway some time after Orchha's decline. If you wander along the paths away from the palace complex (to your left after you cross the bridge), you'll find the ruins of a number of small, atmospheric temples amid fields belonging to local farmers.

With both Persian and Rajput architectural influences, seven-story **Chaturbhuj Mandir ★** looms hauntingly over Orchha village. Reached by a steep flight of steps, the 16th-century temple consists of an expansive vaulted assembly hall with impressive spires; make your way up the narrow spiral staircases for lovely views from the temple roof. Never used, the temple was supposed to have housed an image of Lord Rama brought from Ayodhya by the wife of Orchha's king. Upon arriving, she found the temple incomplete, so she temporarily installed the deity in her palace. When Chaturbhuj was finally completed, the god refused to be moved, so the queen's palace became **Ram Raja Mandir** (daily 8am–noon and 8–10pm; the *aarti/*devotional prayer is open to non-Hindus—ask for timings from your hotel). Today this is one of Orchha's main attractions for Hindus, despite its secular architecture.

Behind Ram Raja Mandir is a paved path that leads to **Lakshminarayan Mandir ★**, atop a low hill less than 1km (½ mile) from the village. The walk takes you past lovely flat-roofed houses that line part of the pathway. The 17th-century temple features interesting murals depicting military battles and religious myths. Although it's usually open to ticket-holders between 9am and 5pm, the temple is sometimes locked up, with no trace of the attendant.

After exploring the village and its trinket-filled stores, don't miss the 14 sandstone *chhatris,* or cenotaphs, along the Betwa River. Built as memorials to expired rulers of the Bundelkhand, they celebrate old alliances, mixing elements of Mughal architecture, such as the arches, and Hindu temple design, such as the *shikharas* (spires). You can get the most fantastic sunset with the *chhatris* in the background if you cross the bridge across the river.

WHERE TO STAY

Orchha is small, with few decent lodging options, all much the same; given that it is very popular be sure to book well in advance, particularly in winter when tour groups can arrive en masse. The best room in Orchha is the **Maharaja Suite ★** in the **Sheesh Mahal Hotel** (*©* 07680/25-2624 or 011/2336-6528; www.mptourism.com; Rs 4,990); alternatively the Maharani Suite, at Rs 3,990. An enormous room, with a domed ceiling over an assortment of paintings, cabinets, and fascinating Raj-era relics, the Maharaja suite has its own dining area and a wonderful terrace with magical views. Even the bathroom is huge, with a marble tub and polished stone flooring. Despite refurbishments, the rest of the hotel's guest rooms are quite ordinary, and, like most government-run establishments, the place is poorly managed, and the second-rate food is only to be consumed if you have no other option. Despite these shortcomings, the Sheesh Mahal—no doubt because of its heritage status—is usually booked up days in advance If you can't book either of these two suites consider the **Amarmahal Hotel ★** (*©* **07680/25-2102;** www. amarmahal.com doubles from Rs 3,150). Built in a style meant to imitate that of Bundelkhand royal architecture, this is the smartest modern option in Orchha—large spacious rooms with latticework on the ceilings and four-poster beds, spotless marble throughout the hotel, good views, lovely pool, plenty of green areas and marginally more intimate than Orchha Resort (though be warned, it too caters to group bookings). It's a tossup between Amarmahal Hotel and Bundelkhand Riverside, really: the benefit of staying at **Budelkhand Riverside** (*©* **07680/25-2612;** www.bundelkhandriverside.com; from Rs 3,400 double) is, as the name suggests, its location, literally hugging the Betwa river and giving splendid views (specially postmonsoon); it's the main reason to book here, so do ask for a room with a riverside view. The rooms were a tad run down when we last visited but it does have a charming sitting area on the roof, again with lovely views, and is particularly atmospheric in the evenings. It is however quite popular for local functions, which can reach unbearable volumes so do check with reservations if anything is happening here before confirming. Although also located on the Betwa river, The Orchha Resort (info *©* **07680/25-2222,** or 0562/222-5712 for reservations; www. orchharesort.com; Rs 2,550–Rs 4,950 double) does not have any views (unless one literally climbs the wall by the pool), but remains a popular choice particularly with European tour groups, with plenty of amenities. The resort is built in attractive pink sandstone, and includes 11 deluxe tents (pitched Oct–Apr 15) arranged around the tennis court; at Rs 2,250 double, these are best value. They're comfortably furnished and include all the regular amenities as well as en-suite toilets and showers and a small porch from where you have an incredible, close-up view of several impressive cenotaphs. Guest rooms in the main building are more expensive; they have marble floors, smallish bathrooms with tubs, and good-quality fabrics in shades of green and cream. Do beware of the slippery area around the pool when you go for a post-sightseeing dip. Owned by Jains, the restaurant is strictly vegetarian, but the food is fresh and appetizing.

8 BHOPAL & SANCHI

Bhopal is 744km (461 miles) S of Delhi; Sanchi is 46km (29 miles) NE of Bhopal

Despite its exciting marketplaces, grand old mosques, and lovely palaces, the capital of Madhya Pradesh is perhaps best known as site of the world's worst urban industrial disaster (see box below). But most foreign visitors find themselves in Bhopal in order to visit nearby Sanchi, a UNESCO World Heritage Site, and one of the most impressive Buddhist monuments in Asia. Architecturally unique and far from the beaten tourist track, the monuments and surrounding ruins are tranquil, free of hawkers and touts, and a worthwhile diversion from the more frequented destinations of Varanasi, Agra, Khajuraho, and Delhi.

If Bhopal's few monuments, its market, and the glorious Buddhist monuments at Sanchi leave you with time on your hands, head for the caves of **Bhimbetka,** where red-and-black prehistoric drawings recall the antics of ancient dancers and hunters, sticklike in the company of tigers and charging bulls.

ESSENTIALS

VISITOR INFORMATION For extensive information about any destination in Madhya Pradesh, as well as transport options, contact the **Madhya Pradesh State Tourism Development Corporation (MPSTDC)** at its Bhopal hotel, Palash Residency (45 Bungalows, New Market, T.T. Nagar; © **0755/255-3006;** www.mptourism.com). Sanchi is 46km (29 miles) from Bhopal, less than 2 hours by road. Regular train services from Bhopal pass through Sanchi.

GETTING THERE & AWAY As the state capital, Bhopal is well connected by air with numerous cities (including Delhi, Mumbai, Gwalior, and Indore). Bhopal is also on a main railway line, and frequent **trains** connect the city with Delhi, Agra, Gwalior, Jhansi (for Orchha), Mumbai, and Hyderabad.

GETTING AROUND Taxis and auto-rickshaws are easy to flag down.

GUIDED TOURS Mrs. Rekha Chopra, of **Radiant Travels** (243/B, First Floor, Krishna Palace, M. P. Nagar, Zone I; © **0755/254-0560** or 94-2530-3572) is not only an experienced tour guide, but introduces visitors to basic Indian cuisine with vegetarian meals at her home.

WHAT TO SEE & DO IN BHOPAL

No one spends much time in Bhopal itself, but the "City of Lakes" is not without its charms, and a handful of sights are worth setting time aside for. Note that most places are closed on Monday, and on Friday mosques are off-limits, unless you're Muslim.

A visit to the **Chowk (Bazaar),** in the heart of the Old City, can be a wonderful way to gain insight into the daily lives of Bhopal's warm, friendly citizens. Its ramshackle streets are lined with old havelis and atmospheric stalls; it's impossible not to get involved in the village vibe, where shopping, hard-core haggling, and gossiping occupy one's time. Shop around for embroidered velvet cushions, *tussar* silk, silver jewelry, and intricate beadwork. While you're in the Chowk, visit lovely **Jama Masjid;** built in 1837, it features gold-spiked minarets, distinguishing it from the "Pearl Mosque," or **Moti Masjid** (1860), farther south. Sporting three large white Mughal domes and two soaring minarets, **Taj-ul-Masjid ★**, one of India's largest mosques, was started at the end of the 19th century

The Bhopal Gas Tragedy

On the night of December 2, 1984, a tank at the Union Carbide pesticide manufacturing plant near Bhopal ruptured, leaking highly poisonous methyl isocyanate gas into the atmosphere. By the time it had dissipated, 1,600 people were dead—but final estimates are as high as 20,000. A claim of $6 billion in compensation was initially demanded by the government, but it settled out of court for $470 million. Adding insult to injury, the money, paid to the government, took 7 years and many more deaths before even a fraction of it reached the victims. More than 2 decades later, survivors continue to protest the haphazard and inadequate manner in which the families of the victims were compensated. Evidence suggests that the continuing effects of the gas disaster may have affected as many as 300,000 people afflicted with various cancers and birth defects. Effigies of the Union Carbide bosses are regularly burned at memorial protests (failing to reach more than the evening news), and many victims continue to go without aid or recourse from the law. Meanwhile, Union Carbide, having abandoned the factory, has started up elsewhere as Eveready Industries India Ltd.

by Bhopal's eighth ruler, the great queen Shah Jahan Begum, but was only completed in the 1970s.

Designed by the preeminent Indian architect, Charles Correa, the breezy, modern **Bharat Bhavan** ★ (Shamla Hills; © **0755/266-0353;** Rs 10, Fri free; Feb–Oct Tues–Sun 2–8pm, Nov–Jan Tues–Sun 1–7pm), overlooking Upper Lake, is one of the best cultural centers in the country, showcasing some wonderful contemporary and tribal art exhibitions.

If you're set on seeing a white tiger, **Van Vihar National Park** is the place to do it. Zoo conditions at this "safari-park" are better than elsewhere in India, but it's still a depressing place to see a wild animal (Zoo Rd.; Rs 100, vehicle entry Rs 30; Wed–Mon 7–11am and 3–5:30pm; carnivores are fed around 4pm).

EXPLORING THE BUDDHIST COMPLEX AT SANCHI ★★★

Now a deserted site resembling an *X-Files* set, the monuments of Sanchi have not only survived despite nearly 2,000 years of neglect, but the stupa at Sanchi is considered India's finest and most evocative example of ancient Buddhist architecture. The Mauryan emperor Ashoka—famous for converting to Buddhism during a personal spiritual crisis after massacring thousands during his military campaigns in Orissa—was responsible for laying the foundations in the 3rd century B.C. Set upon a squat hill affording lovely views of the surrounding countryside, the complex of *stupas* (fat, domelike monuments housing Buddhist relics), monasteries, and temples probably owes its location as much to the serenity of the site as it does to its proximity to the once-prosperous city of Vidisha, where Ashoka's devoted Buddhist wife, Mahadevi, lived. Located at the confluence of the Bes and the Betwa rivers and two important trade routes, the Buddhist complex elicited the patronage of Vidisha's wealthy merchant communities. Even during the invasions of the Hun, life at Sanchi appears to have gone undisturbed, and is believed to have continued until the 13th century A.D., when a resurgence of Hinduism and an increasingly militant Islamic movement led to a decline of Buddhism in India. The site was deserted for more than 500 years before its rediscovery—again by a British military adventurer-type—in 1818. Today, aside from the attractive complex of ruins, Sanchi is little more than a railway station, a few guesthouses, snack stands, a museum, a restaurant, and a shop.

During the excavation that has taken place over the last century, the ruins of around 55 temples, pillars, monasteries, stupas, and other structures have been unearthed. It appears that Sanchi is unique in that its monuments cover the gamut of Buddhist architectural structures—dating from the 3rd century B.C. to the 12th century A.D.

The star attraction is Ashoka's large hemispherical **stupa,** which rises from the ground like a massive stone-carved alien craft. Around the middle of the 2nd century B.C., a balustrade was erected around the stupa, and the mound was covered in stone by the rulers of the Sunga dynasty. Facing the cardinal directions and contributing to the mystical appearance of the main stupa are the four intricately carved gateways, erected around 25 B.C. under the later Satvahana rulers. These striking entranceways feature finely detailed panels depicting incidents from the life of the Buddha and tales from the *Jatakas.* Note that at that time, the depiction of the Buddha in human form had not yet emerged, so instead he is depicted symbolically, as a bodhi tree, lotus, wheel, pair of feet, or stupa.

The Sanchi monasteries consist of a central courtyard surrounded by cells that served as the sleeping quarters for the nuns or monks. Of these, the best is **Monastery 51,** which was first excavated in the 19th century.

WHERE TO STAY & DINE

Overlooking the Bada Talab or the big lake, **Noor-Us-Sabah** ★ has perhaps the most scenic location in town. Originally a palace constructed in 1920, it is now under the wing of the WelcomHeritage group; rooms are a mixed bag; make sure you ask for a lake-facing view. All basic amenities are offered including a pool; note there is no alcohol served (V.I.P Rd., Koh-Eh-Fiza. 🕐 **0755/422-3333;** www.noorussabahpalace.com; from Rs 4,700 double).

Jehan Numa Palace ★ ⓥalue Built in 1890 as a royal guesthouse, this handsome low-rise white colonial-era building is fronted by attractive lawns with fountains, hedges, and colorful bougainvilleas, and is the best option in Bhopal. The two original heritage suites (ask specifically for either "Bourbon" or "Goddard") are very swish, with huge bedrooms, poster-beds, Regency furniture, spacious bathrooms with separate tubs and showers, and private patios. "Regal" guest rooms are off verandas around a fountain courtyard; these are large, with French doors and high ceilings. Standard rooms are best avoided, as are the "cottage rooms." Colored with natural vegetable dyes, the eco-friendly linens are handmade by a local cottage industry, and walls are decorated with local handicrafts. Service is excellent. Facilities include the state's largest pool and a fitness center offering Ayurvedic massage.

157 Shamla Hill, Bhopal 462 013. 🕐 **0755/266-1100** through -1105. Fax 0755/266-1720. www.hotel jehanumapalace.com. 98 units. Rs 3,550 cottage double; Rs 4,850 standard double; Rs 5,550 Regal double; Rs 6,850 Imperial double; Rs 9,550 suite; Rs 12,000 Heritage Suite; Rs 1000 extra bed. Rates include breakfast. Taxes and 5% service charge extra. AE, DC, MC, V. **Amenities:** 3 restaurants; bar; club/pub; garden barbecue; patisserie; airport transfer (Rs 500); concierge; currency exchange; doctor-on-call; minigolf; health club; horseback riding; Internet (Rs 61/hr.); jogging track; children's playground; outdoor pool; pool table; room service; table tennis; tennis court. *In room:* A/C, TV, hair dryer, minibar, Wi-Fi (complimentary).

9 THE FORTRESS CITY OF MANDU ★★★

90km (56 miles) from Indore

Built at a cool height of over 600m (1,968 ft.) on the southwestern edge of the Malwa Plateau, with sweeping views of the Nimar Plains below, Mandu was once the largest fortified city on earth, and playpen to some of central India's most powerful rulers. Initially christened by the Malwa sultans as the "City of Joy," the medieval capital inspired its rulers to celebrate the most pleasurable of pastimes—one of Mandu's most famous palaces was built solely to house some 15,000 concubines, and it is said that the Mughal emperor Humayun was so mesmerized by Mandu's sanguine beauty that he developed an opium habit during his stay here. Today the exotic ghost city—still one of the most atmospheric destinations in India—draws but a handful of tourists, which makes the excursion here all the more rewarding. It's just 2 hours away from the industrial hub of Indore, yet Mandu, even more so than Orchha, is rural India at its best: a place of enduring beauty, both natural and man-made, with panoramic views. It's the perfect antidote to the well-traveled North India circuits. You can visit Mandu as a rather long day trip out of Indore, but for those willing to sacrifice luxury for serenity, it's worth spending a night or two here to revel in silence, fresh air, and wide-open space. Then again, you could stay in the lovely Ahilya fort-palace at nearby Maheshwar and combine serenity with luxury.

ESSENTIALS

GETTING THERE & AWAY   To visit Mandu, most people travel via Indore, which is connected to important regional centers by daily flights and regular train services. The airport (© **0731/262-0819** or -0758) is 8km (5 miles) out of the center. The train trip from Bhopal lasts 6 hours; the **Intercity Express** from Delhi takes 13 hours; and the **Avantika Express** from Mumbai takes 15 hours. A far more convenient option is to base yourself in the small town of Maheshwar, 56km (35 miles) from Mandu, and about 2 hours by road from Indore. To get to Mandu (or Maheshwar) from Indore, hire a taxi through **President Travels** (Hotel President, 163 R.N.T. Rd.; © **0731/252-8866**); you can arrange a pickup at the airport/station, and drive straight to Mandu (around Rs 2,500 for an A/C car); M. P. Tourism (see below) also arranges cars. If you're traveling on the cheap, there's a long, tiring bus trip to Mandu.

VISITOR INFORMATION   Madhya Pradesh Tourism has an office on the ground floor of Jhabua Tower, R.N.T. Road, in Indore (© **0731/252-8653;** mptourismind@airtelbroadband.in; Mon–Sat 10am–5pm, closed Sun and second and third Sat of the month). In Mandu, ask the manager at MPSTDC-run **Malwa Resort** (© **07292/26-3235**) for assistance.

GETTING AROUND   Indore has plenty of **taxis** and **auto-rickshaws;** ask the driver to use his meter. In Mandu, you can hire a **bicycle,** or ride on the back of a **motorcycle** with a local guide as your driver.

EXPLORING MANDU

After passing through the narrow gates of the fortress and continuing for some distance, you'll arrive in "downtown" Mandu (a collection of shops and stalls in the vicinity of the **Central Group** of monuments). As soon as you emerge from your car or bus, you'll no doubt be approached by a local guide who will offer his services. Even if your guide—and there are only a couple in Mandu—is not a certified expert, this is one place where it can be fun to have someone show you around and enrich your experience with a version of history that overdoes the myth, romance, and fantasy. Establish that he speaks passable English, and agree on a price upfront; expect to pay up to Rs 500 for the day. Monuments are open from 8am to 6pm.

If you don't plan to spend the night in Mandu, start your tour immediately with 15th-century **Jama Masjid** ★. Said to have been inspired by the mosque in Damascus, this colossal colonnaded structure bears some Hindu influences, such as the carvings of lotus flowers and decorative bells. Adjacent to the mosque is the **mausoleum of Hoshang Shah,** the first white marble tomb in India, said to have inspired those in Agra; it's ultimately missable. The **Royal Enclave** ★ (Rs 100; daily 8am–6pm) is dominated by enormous **Jahaz Mahal,** commonly known as the "ship palace." Built between two artificial lakes, it certainly was intended to be the ultimate stone pleasure cruiser, where the sultan Ghiyas Shah kept his 15,000 courtesans and an additional 1,000 Amazonians from Turkey and Abyssinia to guard them. Behind the ship palace is **Hindola Mahal;** its oddly sloping buttress walls have given it the nickname "Swing Palace."

Mandu's main road stretches southward, through open fields dotted with ruins and a few village houses, and continues into the **Rewa Kund** group of monuments, where the passionate romance between Maharaja Baz Bahadur, the last independent sultan of Malwa, and the beautiful Hindu shepherdess, Rupmati, is preserved in striking stone constructions. Apparently smitten by Rupmati's glorious singing voice, Baz built the **Rupmati Pavilion** ★ (Rs 100) so that she could see her village in the Narmada Valley below, but things went awry when the Mughal emperor Akbar came to hear of her legendary beauty and voice and wanted to take her home as a souvenir. After a fierce battle in which Baz was defeated, his beloved committed suicide. The view from the pavilion, which stands on the edge of a sheer precipice rising 365m (1,197 ft.) from the valley floor, is still sublime. On the way back from the pavilion, stop at **Baz Bahadur's Palace** (Rs 100), where the acoustics enjoyed by the musically inclined king remain quite astonishing, even if some of the restoration work is a bit ham-handed.

WHERE TO STAY & DINE

While there are basic lodgings in Mandu, we highly recommend a stay at Ahilya Fort (reviewed below), a fantastic destination in itself, situated on the Narmada River in the town of Maheshwar, some 91km (56 miles) from Indore. From either city, the journey to Mandu should take 2½ hours. If you arrive in Indore too late to move on to Mandu or Maheshwar, you'll easily find a room in one of the city's standard business hotels; the best of these is **Fortune Landmark** (✆ **0731/398-8444;** www.fortunehotels.com; from $90 double). The amenities and comforts here match those of any reasonable city hotel, and the surrounding lawns and gardens are lovely. If, however, you'd prefer a more personal experience, see if you can manage to stay at **Rashid Kothi** (22 Yeshwant Niwas Rd., Indore 452 003; ✆ **0731/254-5060;** ashanu@hotmail.com), a family home run by Anuradha Dubey and Arshad Rashid. Of the two rooms, one is a garden cottage; furnishings are comfortable and contain thoughtful touches that enhance the homely atmosphere. All meals (strictly vegetarian) are included in the room rate (Rs 5,500 single, Rs 10,000 double without air-conditioning).

If you decide to stay in Mandu itself, be prepared to rough it somewhat. Our first choice among the small selection of spartan lodgings is **Hotel Rupmati** (Mandu 454 010; ✆ **07292/26-3270**), a budget charmer with 12 simple rooms (from Rs 1,300 double). Close to the village bazaar on the edge of a cliff, the hotel enjoys great views.

Guest rooms are in a long stone building; all are large with whitewashed walls and a thin, rock-hard mattress with white linens and a blanket (most also have A/C and a TV for double the price). The view can be enjoyed from a small private balcony. Attention has been paid to the grounds, which feature a children's play area, and the cleanliness and tranquillity of the place make up for the budget facilities.

Ahilya Fort ★ A haven of tranquillity, the hassle-free sacred town of Maheshwar is home to one of the loveliest heritage properties in the state. The summer palace of Indore's Prince Richard Holkar (a whiz in the kitchen with a number of cookbooks to his name), the fort is a labyrinthine 18th-century palace, complete with maintained English flower gardens and evocative battlements of rough-hewn stone. Each guest room is a unique combination of colonial period furniture and personal touches, with smart attention to detail. Choose between a river-facing unit (the "royal" rooms have balconies overlooking the river) or one with a private courtyard, or ask to stay in one of two luxurious tents. Besides visiting Mandu (56km/35 miles away), you can explore the Maheshwar temple just next door or visit the local Holkar-resuscitated handloom center. Have dinner on the river under moonlight, or select a terrace, courtyard, or battlement to be your preferred dining spot; the refined meals are a real highlight.

Maheshwar 431 224. (C) **92-0390-5948.** www.ahillyafort.com. info@ahillyafort.com. Reservations in Delhi: (C) **011/4155-1575.** Fax 011/4155-1055. 14 units. Rs 10,700 standard and tent double (non-air-conditioned); Rs 13,700 superior double; Rs 15,700 royal double. Rates include all meals, soft drinks, Indian alcoholic beverages, laundry, boating, local sightseeing, and taxes. 2-night minimum stay. 50% discount mid-Apr through mid-Oct. MC, V. **Amenities:** Various dining areas; airport transfer (Rs 2,500; same price each way to Mandu); babysitting; boat trips; doctor-on-call; guided excursions; picnics; outdoor pool; TV and game room. *In room:* A/C (royal and superior rooms), air-cooler (standard rooms and tents), hair dryer on request, Wi-Fi (complimentary).

11

Rajasthan: Land of Princes

For many, Rajasthan is the very essence of India, with crenelated forts and impregnable palaces that rise like giant fairy-tale sets above dusty sun-scorched plains and shimmering lakes. India's second-largest state—similar in size to France—is largely covered by the ever-encroaching Thar Desert, but despite its aridity, Rajasthan was once remarkably prosperous: Traders from as far afield as Persia and China had to cross its dry plains to reach the southern ports of Gujarat, something the warrior princes of Rajasthan were quick to capitalize on. Today the principal attraction of Rajasthan—the postindependence name for Rajputana, literally "land of princes"—is the large variety of forts and palaces its aristocrats built throughout the centuries, in usually breathtaking sites, that makes it one of the most popular destinations in India. But Rajasthan offers so much more than Rajput warrior history, desert castles and culture—from tracking down tigers in the Ranthambhore jungle (arguably the most reliable place to spot wild tigers in Asia) to gaping at the world's most intricately carved marble temples on historic Mount Abu. Peopled by proud turbaned men and delicately boned women in saris of dazzling colors, the "land of princes" is rich with possibilities. It's also high on contrasts: You could bed down amid some of the most sumptuous luxury on earth and then spend the day roaming ancient villages, exploring medieval marketplaces.

You could plan to spend your entire trip to India in Rajasthan, which is within easy striking distance of Delhi (and the Taj Mahal) by train, plane, or road. Certainly you'll need at least a week to take in the major destinations, of which the lake city of Udaipur is the top highlight. If you are inclined to seek peace and tranquillity away from the larger more obvious attractions, then we recommend you amble from here along the ancient and undulating Aravalli Hills, which predate even the Himalayas, discovering its quaint, manageable villages and truly special hotels. Also vying for your time is the "blue city" of Jodhpur, which has the state's most impressive and best-preserved fort as well as the largest palace in India; the desert fort of Jaisalmer—the only fort in the world still inhabited by villagers; the tiny but increasingly commercial town of Pushkar, built around a sacred lake and host to the biggest camel *mela* (fair) in Asia; the painted *havelis* (historic homes or mansions) of the Shekhawati region, referred to as India's open-air gallery; the tiny Keoladeo "Ghana" National Park, which boasts the largest concentration and variety of bird life in Asia; the untainted, almost medieval atmosphere of little towns like Bundi; and the bumper-to-bumper shops and bazaars in Jaipur (the state and retail capital of Rajasthan). Shopping, in fact, is another of the state's chief attractions: Because of the liberal patronage of the wealthy Rajput princes, skilled artisans from all over the East settled here to adorn the aristocrats and their palaces. Today these same skills are on sale to the world's designers and travelers, and no one—from die-hard bargain-hunters to chichi fashionistas—leaves Rajasthan empty-handed. The question is how to choose from an unbelievable array of textiles, jewelry, paintings, rugs, pottery, diaries—even kitchen utensils—and then how to fit them into your bulging suitcase.

But perhaps the best reason to visit Rajasthan is to experience its unusual hotels: The state has at least 100 heritage properties—castles, palaces, forts, and ornate havelis—many of which are still home to India's oldest monarchies. This must be the only place in the world where, armed with a credit card, you can find yourself sleeping in a king's bed, having earlier dined with the aristocrat whose forebears built and quite often died for the castle walls that surround it. Known for their valor and honor, and later for their decadence (see "Once Were Warriors: The History of the Rajput," below), the Rajputs are superb hosts, and it is almost possible to believe that you, too, are of aristocratic blood, as a turbaned aide awaits your every wish while you marvel at the starry night from the bastion of your castle. Long live the king (and queen), for you are it.

1 PLANNING YOUR TRIP TO RAJASTHAN

Rajasthan has so much to see, with long travel distances between top sites, that a trip here requires careful planning (particularly if you hire a car and driver, which is the best way to tour the state). The following overview can help you plan your itinerary.

The three biggest cities in Rajasthan, all with airports, are **Jaipur,** the "Pink City"; **Jodhpur,** the "Blue City"; and **Udaipur,** the "White City." All are worthwhile destinations, not least because they offer easy access to great excursions. The tiny **Jaisalmer,** or "Golden City," is the most awkward to reach, and while some find it the highlight of their Rajasthan trip, others feel it isn't worth the schlep it takes to get there, given the state of its decaying fort and untrammeled development beneath it.

For most, the entry point is the state capital of Jaipur, near the eastern border, which is the third point (the others being nearby Delhi and Agra) of the much-traveled **Golden Triangle.** Should you choose to start your trip here, you are in fact well positioned to visit some of Rajasthan's top sites: Only a few hours from the city is **Ranthambhore National Park**—where you have good chances of spotting a wild tiger—and Bharatpur's **Keoladeo National Park,** a must-see for birders (though ultimately missable for most other folk), and literally on the way from Agra. Jaipur is also within driving distance of Shekhawati and its painted towns and is also the start of the beautiful Aravalli's that are home to some of our favorite specialty boutique hotels.

Other than its proximity to these sites, however, as well as the excellent rail and flight connections to the rest of India, the only good reason to dally in Jaipur itself is to indulge in some retail therapy. Most visitors planning to travel farther by car circle Rajasthan in a counterclockwise direction, starting off in Jaipur and traveling the rather circuitous route west to Jodhpur (with a short sojourn in Pushkar—particularly for younger travelers); then, from Jodhpur, you could make the 5½- to 6-hour drive west to Jaisalmer for a few nights before you return to Jodhpur. An alternative route to Jaisalmer, which means you don't have to travel both to and from Jodhpur, is to travel from Delhi through the Shekhawati region to Mandawa, known for its painted havelis, and from there on to Jaisalmer, before you travel east again to Jodhpur. (The other alternative is to skip Jaisalmer altogether, and if you're short on time this is what you should do. From Jodhpur you then travel south to Udaipur lingering en route in the charming lodgings (Mihir Garh and Rawla Narlai) surrounded by the Aravalli Hills and finally, head back north to

(Tips) An Aravalli Ramble

If you wish to try a largely city-free option that will encourage a more peaceful, activity based trip, far from the crowds and tourist groups then try the rustic beauty and pastoral tranquillity of the ancient Aravalli Hills and its folk and culture. It is possible to plan your itinerary accordingly and overnight at properties that are not diluted by the chaos, pressures, and noise of larger cities. Even the smaller towns, while charming, can sometimes break the hypnotic calm of an Aravalli countryside sojourn. You can choose a route with the appropriate properties, together with unique activities, that maintains the distinct charm of these villages and its people. A recommended route (southwest to northeast, Udaipur to Delhi, or vice versa), which tracks the Aravalli Range, would include the lakeside Deco heritage of Dungapur's Udai Bilas Palace. Then move on to Udaipur, where you can escape the crowds by staying a night at Devi Garh before moving on to the charming Rawla Narlai. Then you could take in the impressive Kumbhalgarh Fort and the Jain temples at Ranakpur (overnighting at HRH's Aodi). After that head northeast towards Bhilwara and the homely Shahpura Bagh (halfway between Udaipur and Jaipur) for a few days before the drive to Jaipur. After shopping and sightseeing in the Pink City spend a night at Samode Palace after seeing the Amber Fort, but be sure not to miss Amanbagh for a final few days of relaxation and pampering before the short trek to Delhi and home.

Jaipur, stopping en route at one of many lovely palace hotels (or at Shahpurah Bagh or Amanbagh) for a most relaxing end to your journey.

For someone with limited time (say, only enough to visit one of Rajasthan's cities), it's far better to fly direct to Udaipur—with great lodging options in all price brackets, this is arguably Rajasthan's most attractive city (though you should check the status of the lakes, which have gone dry for an entire season in recent years, before planning your entire trip around it). From Udaipur you can take a wonderful (but long) day trip to **Kumbhalgarh Reserve** to take in Ranakpur's exquisitely carved **Jain temples** and impressive **Kumbhalgarh Fort** before overnighting at **Devi Garh,** one of India's most stylish hotels or push a little further into the Aravalli countryside and spend a few days at Rawla Narlai,. Alternatively, you can head east from Udaipur pausing at Shaphura Bagh for serious downtime in an otherwise city-based itinerary, via the historic fort of **Chittaurgarh,** and then move on to **Ranthambhore National Park.** Or take the short trip directly south to the relatively undiscovered **palaces of Dungarpur,** or head much further out west to **Mount Abu,** the state's only hill station and sacred pilgrimage of the Jains, who come to visit the famous **Dilwara Temples.** Jodhpur and its majestic **Mehrangarh Fort** lie only 5 hours north of Udaipur by road, and you can break up the trip by overnighting at one of the recommended heritage properties along the way.

As mentioned, the state's other fascinating but endangered city is Jaisalmer, which is rather inconveniently situated on the far-flung western outreaches of Rajasthan's Thar Desert; to get there, you have to either set off from Jodhpur, or travel via the desert town of Bikaner (staying 30km outside at Gajner Palace)—both routes involve a lot of driving

RAJASTHAN: LAND OF PRINCES

11

PLANNING YOUR TRIP TO RAJASTHAN

Once Were Warriors: The History of the Rajput

Rajasthan's history is inextricably entwined with that of its self-proclaimed aristocracy: a warrior clan, calling themselves *Rajputs,* that emerged sometime during the 6th and 7th centuries. Given that no one too low in the social hierarchy could take the profession (like bearing arms) of a higher caste, this new clan, comprising both indigenous people and foreign invaders such as the Huns, held a special "rebirth" ceremony—purifying themselves with fire—at Mount Abu, where they assigned themselves a mythical descent from the sun and the moon. In calling themselves Rajputs (a corruption of the word *Raj Putra,* "sons of princes"), they officially segregated themselves from the rest of society. Proud and bloodthirsty, yet with a strict code of honor, they were to dominate the history of the region right up until independence, and are still treated with deference by their mostly loyal subjects.

The Rajputs offered their subjects protection in return for revenue, and together formed a kind of loose kinship in which each leader was entitled to unequal shares within the territory of his clan. The term they used for this collective sharing of power was "brotherhood," but predictably the clan did not remain a homogenous unit, and bitter internecine wars were fought. Besides these ongoing internal battles, the Hindu Rajputs had to defend their territory from repeated invasions by the Mughals and Marathas, but given the Rajputs' ferocity and unconquerable spirit, the most skillful invasion came in the form of diplomacy, when the great Mughal emperor Akbar married Jodhabai, daughter of Raja Bihar Mal, ruler of the Kachchwaha Rajputs (Jaipur region), who then bore him his first son, Jahangir.

Jahangir was to become the next Mughal emperor, and the bond between Mughal and Rajput was cemented when he in turn married another Kachchwaha princess (his mother's niece). A period of tremendous prosperity for the Kachchwaha clan followed, as their military prowess helped the Mughals conquer large swaths of India in return for booty. But many of the Rajput clans—particularly those of Mewar (in the Udaipur region)—were dismayed by what they saw as a capitulation to Mughal imperialism. In the end it was English diplomacy that truly tamed the maharajas. Rather than waste money and men going to war with the Rajput kings, the English offered them a treaty. This gave "the Britishers" control of Rajputana, but in return the empire recognized the royal status of the Rajputs and allowed them to keep most of the taxes extorted from their subjects and the many travelers who still plied the trade routes in the Thar Desert.

(Jodhpur is a 5½- to 6-hr. drive away; Bikaner a 6- to 7-hr. drive). You can opt to travel from Jodhpur to Jaisalmer by overnight train, but make sure to get a berth in the air-conditioned compartment of the Delhi-Jaisalmer Express (even though the desert nights can be bitterly cold, this is your best option until Jaisalmer's airport arrives) and carry a warm blanket.

This resulted in a period of unprecedented decadence for the Rajputs, who now spent their days hunting for tigers, playing polo, and flying to Europe to stock up on the latest Cartier jewels and Belgian crystal. Legends abound of their spectacular hedonism, but perhaps the most famous surround the Maharaja Jai Singh of Alwar (north of Jaipur), who wore black silk gloves when he shook hands with the English king and reputedly used elderly women and children as tiger bait. When Jai Singh visited the showrooms of Rolls-Royce in London, he was affronted when the salesman implied that he couldn't afford to purchase one of the sleek new models—he promptly purchased 10, shipped them home, tore their roofs off, and used them to collect garbage. The English tolerated his bizarre behavior until, after being thrown from his horse during a polo match, he doused the animal with fuel and set it alight. Having ignored previous reports of child molestation, the horse-loving British finally acted with outrage and exiled him from the state.

Above all, the Rajput maharajas expressed their newfound wealth and decadence by embarking on a frenzied building spree, spending vast fortunes on gilding and furnishing new palaces and forts. The building period reached its peak in Jodhpur, with the completion of the Umaid Bhawan Palace in the 1930s, at the time the largest private residence in the world.

When the Imperialists were finally forced to withdraw, the "special relationship" that existed between the Rajputs and the British was honored for another 3 decades—they were allowed to keep their titles and enjoyed a large government-funded "pension," but their loyalty to the British, even during the bloody 1857 uprisings, was to cost them in the long run.

In 1972 Prime Minister Indira Gandhi—sensibly, but no doubt in a bid to win popular votes—stripped the Rajputs of both stipends and titles. This left the former aristocracy almost destitute, unable to maintain either their lifestyles or their sprawling properties. While many sold their properties and retired to middle-class comfort in Delhi or Mumbai, others started opening their doors to paying guests like Jackie Kennedy and members of the English aristocracy, who came to recapture the romance of Raj-era India. By the dawn of a new millennium, these once-proud warriors had become first-rate hoteliers, offering people from all walks of life the opportunity to experience the princely lifestyle of Rajasthan.

You can fly between Rajasthan's major cities and hire a vehicle and driver from one of the recommended operators for the duration of your stay in each region, but the long-term hire of a car and driver is highly recommended—this is really the best way to tour Rajasthan because it means you can travel at your own pace, avoid public transport (or the daily grind of haggling with taxis), and get right off the beaten track. Rajasthan's potholed roads make for slow going, drivers have unknown rules (but clearly the big trucks and cows rule, no matter what the circumstances), and traveling by night is only for the suicidal—even day trips will have you closing your eyes in supplication to a higher being.

Many operators are reluctant to provide a breakdown of pricing, leaving you with the distinct feeling that you are being ripped off. To avoid this, get a per-kilometer rate for the specific kind of car you wish to hire, and the overnight supplement for the driver. For a trustworthy and reputable transport and logistics contact, who provides fluent English-speaking Tourist Licensed Drivers (with 3-year license reviews) at bona-fide rates, contact Indoarya (✆ **011/2651-1634;** indoarya@vsnl.net). At press time, an air-conditioned car (a standard small sedan such as a Tata Indigo) and driver in Jaipur cost about Rs 1,350 for a full day (8 hr.), up to 80km (50 miles), plus a negotiated fee for every hour after that. For out-of-town trips, expect to pay Rs 7.50 to Rs 10 per kilometer plus Rs 200 per night out. A romantic way to go is in an air-conditioned Ambassador, India's quaint homegrown brand of sedans, which provides you with a real sense of being in another world, not to mention another era. They can be unpredictable and are best used for city touring. The best organized travel company in Rajasthan is Tushita Travels Pty Ltd., and although Delhi based, they have a deep and extensive network of offices and agents throughout Rajasthan and can organize anything (✆ **011/2573-0256** or -2779; fax 011/ 2575-2745; www.tushita-india.com; tushind@vsnl.com). Tuhita has branches and expert agents in each of the main cities; rates may be a little pricier than you'll find elsewhere, but they're fixed, so there's no bargaining, and service and local knowledge is of an excellent standard.

Note: At press time, tax on Rajasthan hotel accommodations varied between 8% and 10% (depending on the city), although this does not apply to economy rooms; sales tax of 12.5% is charged on dining bills.

WHERE TO STAY & DINE EN ROUTE TO OR FROM DELHI

Instead of hightailing it to or from the capital, consider breaking up your journey and enjoying some of the marvelous luxury and architectural heritage available between Delhi and Jaipur.

Amanbagh ★★★   For its inspired location alone, this fabulous Amanresort property deserves three stars. Made almost entirely of pink sandstone by local stonemasons, the best and most expensive suites are the palatial pool pavilions. A light-filled entrance foyer leads directly through to your own emerald marble pool, a gorgeous, massive bedroom on one side and a spacious domed bath chamber on the other. For significantly fewer dollars, you can forgo a private pool (arguably eclipsed by the 33m/108 ft. marbled magnetic main pool), while still being thoroughly ensconced in luxury in one of the three categories of haveli suite (the elevated terrace units are best, up in the mango trees gazing directly at the hills; ask for one facing the canal rather than the pool). If you can bear to leave the premises, you can undertake a number of truly worthwhile activities: picnics into the countryside, hike to ancient Somsagar Lake, explore the haunted ruins at Bhangarh, visit the archaeological sites in the Paranagar area. Amanbagh's staff is enchanting: warm, discreet; dining is world-class.

Ajabgarh, Rajasthan. ✆ **01465/22-3333.** Fax 01465/22-3335. www.amanresorts.com. amanbagh@aman resorts.com. Reservations: Amanresorts Corporate Office ✆ **77/774-3500** in Colombo 24/7. Fax 011/ 237-2193. reservations@amanresorts.com. 40 Units. $1,250 pool pavilion; $850 terrace haveli; $700 garden haveli; $650 courtyard haveli. Rates exclude 10% service charge. AE, MC, V. **Amenities:** 2 restaurants;

bar; doctor-on-call; gym; Internet (complimentary); library; guided meditations; 2 heated pools; room **513**
service; safaris—horse, camel, jeep; spa; walks; yoga. *In room:* A/C, CD player, minibar, pool pavilion
rooms have private heated pool; Wi-Fi (complimentary).

2 JAIPUR

262km (162 miles) SW of Delhi; 232km (144 miles) W of Agra

After independence, Jaipur became the administrative and commercial capital of what
was known as Rajputana, a suitable conclusion to the dreams of its founder Maharaja
Sawai Jai Singh II, a man famed for his talents as a politician, mathematician, and
astronomer. At age 13 he ascended the throne of the Kachchwaha Rajputs, a clan that
had enjoyed tremendous prosperity and power as a result of their canny alliance, dating
from Humayun's reign, with the Mughal emperors. It was in fact the emperor Aurangzeb,
a fanatically pious Muslim, who—despite the fact that Jai Singh was a Hindu prince—
named him Sawai, meaning "one and a quarter," for his larger-than-life intellect and wit.
Having proved his prowess as a military tactician for Aurangzeb, increasing the emperor's
coffers substantially, Jai Singh felt it safe to move his capital from the claustrophobic hills
surrounding Amber to a dry lake in the valley below.

Begun in 1727 and completed in just 8 years, Jaipur was the first city in India to enjoy
rigorous town planning according to the principles laid down in "Shilpa Shastra," an
ancient Indian treatise on architecture. The city is protected by high walls, with wide,
straight avenues that divide it into nine sectors, or *chokris* (apparently reflecting the nine
divisions of the universe, resembling the Indian horoscope), each named after the com-
modity and caste who lived and practiced their specific skills here—the order and space
was at the time a total revolution in Indian cities. Although these market names still
provide some clue as to what was once found in the otherwise rather uniform rows of

(Fun Facts) Why Pink?

Jaipur is known as the Pink City, a highly idealized description of the terra-cotta-
colored lime plaster that coats the old part of the city's walls, buildings, and temples. The reasons for painting the town pink are unknown, but various theories
have been tossed about, from using pink to cut down glare, to Jai Singh II's
apparent devotion to Lord Shiva (whose favorite color is reputedly terra cotta).
Others believe Singh wanted to imitate the color of the sandstone used in the
forts and palaces of his Mughal emperor-friends. The most popular reason
(spread no doubt by "Britishers" during the Raj era) is that pink is the traditional
color of hospitality, and the city was freshly painted and paved with pink gravel
to warmly welcome Edward VII for his visit here in 1876. The city is painted pink
once every 10 years by the Municipal Corporation, and in 2000 the painting was
timed for a state visit, this time by former U.S. president Bill Clinton. A few streets
became off-limits to cars, but this is not the case anymore, and cars and rickshaws crowd areas such as Bapu Bazaar, which otherwise is one of the better
places to browse. If you are being driven around, especially at peak hour, it will
take a very long time to get to your destination.

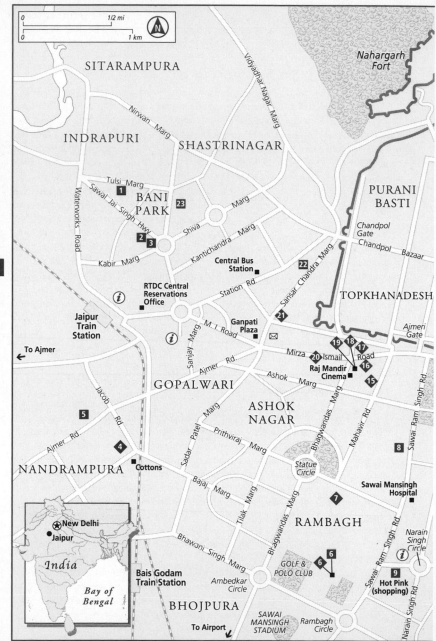

0   1/2 mi
0   1 km

SITARAMPURA

Nahargarh
Fort

Nirwan Marg

INDRAPURI

SHASTRINAGAR

Vidyadhar Nagar Marg

PURANI
BASTI

Tulsi Marg

1

BANI
PARK

23

Marg

Waterworks Road

Sawal Jai Singh Hwy

Shiva Marg

Chandpol
Gate

Chandpol Bazaar

2 3

Kantichandra Marg

Kabir Marg

Central Bus
Station

22

Sansar Chandra Marg

TOPKHANADESH

RTDC Central
Reservations
Office

Station Rd.

Ajmeri
Gate

Jaipur
Train
Station

Sanjay Marg

M.I. Road

Ganpati
Plaza

21

To Ajmer

Ajmer Rd.

Mirza Ismail Road

19 18 17

20

16

Raj Mandir
Cinema

15

GOPALWARI

Ashok Marg

Sawai Ram Singh Rd.

Jacob Rd.

Sadar Patel Marg

Prithviraj Marg

ASHOK
NAGAR

Bhagwandas Marg

Mahavir Rd.

5

Ajmer Rd.

Statue
Circle

8

4

Cottons

Bajaj Marg

NANDRAMPURA

Tilak Marg

Sawai Mansingh
Hospital

7

RAMBAGH

New Delhi
Jaipur

India

Bhawani Singh Marg

Bhagwandas Marg

Sawai Ram Singh Rd.

Narain
Singh
Circle

Bay of
Bengal

Bais Godam
Train Station

Ambedkar
Circle

GOLF &
POLO CLUB

6

6

9

Hot Pink
(shopping)

Narain Singh Rd.

BHOJPURA

To Airport

SAWAI
MANSINGH
STADIUM

Rambagh
Circle

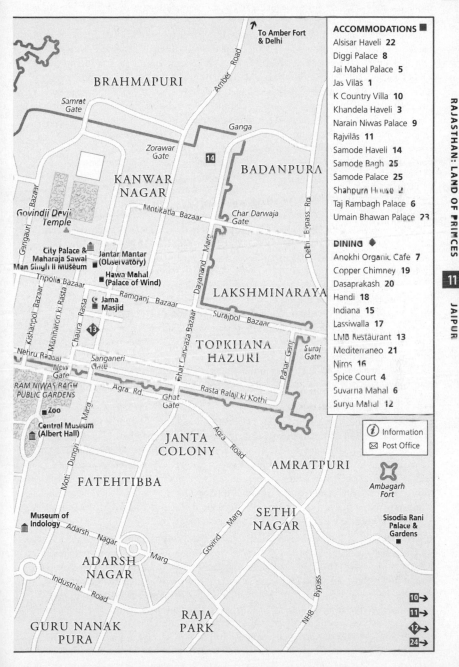

To Amber Fort & Delhi

BRAHMAPURI

Samrat Gate

Zorawar Gate

Ganga

14

BADANPURA

KANWAR NAGAR

Motikatla Bazaar

Char Darwaja Gate

Delhi Bypass Rd

Govindji Devji Temple

Gangauri Bazaar

City Palace & Maharaja Sawai Man Singh II Museum

Jantar Mantar (Observatory)

Hawa Mahal (Palace of Wind)

Tripolia Bazaar

Ramganj Bazaar

Dayanand Marg

LAKSHMINARAYA

Kishanpol Bazaar

Maniharon ki Rasta

Chaura Rasta

Jama Masjid

13

Surajpol Bazaar

Ghat Darwaza Bazaar

Pahar Ganj

Suraj Gate

Nehru Bazaar

New Gate

Sanganeri Gate

TOPKHANA HAZURI

RAM NIWAS BAGH PUBLIC GARDENS

Agra Rd.

Ghat Gate

Rasta Ralaji ki Kothi

Zoo

Central Museum (Albert Hall)

JANTA COLONY

Agra Road

AMRATPURI

Moti Dungri Marg

Ambagarh Fort

Museum of Indology

Adarsh Nagar

FATEHTIBBA

SETHI NAGAR

Sisodia Rani Palace & Gardens

Marg

Govind Marg

ADARSH NAGAR

Industrial Road

GURU NANAK PURA

RAJA PARK

NH8 Bypass

ℹ️ Information

✉️ Post Office

10→
11→
12→
24→

ACCOMMODATIONS ■
Alsisar Haveli **22**
Diggi Palace **8**
Jai Mahal Palace **5**
Jas Vilas **1**
K Country Villa **10**
Khandela Haveli **3**
Narain Niwas Palace **9**
Rajvilās **11**
Samode Haveli **14**
Samode Bagh **25**
Samode Palace **25**
Shahpura House **2**
Taj Rambagh Palace **6**
Umaid Bhawan Palace **23**

DINING ◆
Anokhi Organic Cafe **7**
Copper Chimney **19**
Dasaprakash **20**
Handi **18**
Indiana **15**
Lassiwalla **17**
LMB Restaurant **13**
Mediterraneo **21**
Niros **16**
Spice Court **4**
Suvarna Mahal **6**
Surya Mahal **12**

shops that line the streets, the overall significance of these historic divisions is today lost to the traveler on foot trying to negotiate the chaos of the filth-strewn streets and pushy traders.

Despite the romantic nickname the "Pink City," Jaipur is not one of Rajasthan's most attractive cities, which is why, after taking in the centrally located City Palace (where the principal sights are located), it's probably wise to concentrate on sites farther afield: **Amber Fort,** first royal residence of the Maharajas of Kachchwaha, lies 11km (7 miles) north; and popular **Samode Palace** is an hour's drive away. But if the heat has you beat and the very thought of traipsing through another fort or durbar hall leaves you feeling exhausted, check out the shopping recommendations. A central repository for the region's wonderful crafts, Jaipur is famous for its gems and jewelry, enamel- and brassware, blue pottery, embroidered leather footwear, rugs, tie-and-dye cotton fabrics, handblocked prints, fine *Kota doria* saris, and ready-made linens and home furnishings.

ESSENTIALS

VISITOR INFORMATION The **Rajasthan Tourism Development Corporation (RTDC)** information bureau is located on Platform 1 at the Jaipur Railway Station (© **0141/ 220-3531;** open 24 hr.). There's an RTDC **tourist help desk** at Hotel Swagatam (behind Sadar Thana; © **0141/220-2586** or 0141/220-3531; Mon–Sat 10am–5pm; closed second Sat of every month). The **Tourist Reception Centre** is located at the Government Hostel, Paryatan Bhawan (© **0141/511-0595** through -0598; same hours as station office; mainly for emergencies or problems) on M.I. Road, the main thoroughfare in Jaipur. You'll find the less helpful **Government of India Tourist Office** at the Khasa Kothi hotel (© **0141/237-2200;** Mon–Fri 9am–6pm, Sat 9am–2pm), or call their **24-hour help line,** © **1363,** for information or assistance in an emergency, or to organize a guide. For predeparture planning, check out the RTDC's website (www.rtdc.in), or contact cro@rtdc.in.

To find out about any events or festivals or current arts and entertainment listings, ask your concierge, or pick up a copy of the daily *Hindustan Times* or the *Jaipur Vision.*

Getting There & Away

BY AIR Both **Jet Airways** (© **0141/511-2222** through -2225) and **Indian Airlines** (© **0141/274-3500** or -3324) have daily flights between Jaipur and Delhi (40–60 min.), Jodhpur (45 min.), Udaipur (50 min.), and Mumbai (directly1½ hr.). Indian also flies to Kolkata (2 hr., 25 min. to 3 hr., 45 min.) four times a week. **Sanganer Airport** lies 15 minutes south of the center of town; most hotels are 30 minutes away. Use the prepaid taxi service for the most convenient trip into the city (unless your hotel provides a complimentary transfer); a taxi ride to the Old City should cost under Rs 300). It's a terribly grueling auto-rickshaw ride (but slightly cheaper at around Rs 200).

BY TRAIN The Jaipur Railway Station is located west of the Old City (reservations Mon–Sat 8am–2pm and 2:15–8pm, Sun 8am–2pm). You can reach Jaipur by train from just about anywhere. The Ajmer Shatabdi connects Jaipur with Delhi in 4½ hours (daily except Wed); from Agra the Marudhar Express (early morning, alternate days) takes about 5 hours, while the late-night Howrah Express (arriving midnight) takes 4 hours. You will be inundated with offers from rickshaw-*wallas* upon your arrival at Jaipur Station—to avoid this, go to the prepaid auto-rickshaw counter. Dial © **131** for railway inquiries, © **0141/220-4531** for recorded arrival and departure information, and © **135** for reservations. Reservations for foreign tourists are made at counter 8. To book a ticket, your easiest option is to get your hotel or a travel agent to do it for you. Either will charge a service fee of Rs 50 to Rs 100 per passenger.

BY BUS Buses arrive at the Inter-State Bus Terminal (called Sindhi Camp bus stand) on Station Road. For information, call ℭ **0141/220-7912** for regular buses; or ℭ **0141/ 220-4445** for deluxe buses. Deluxe Volvo coaches from Delhi will drop you off at Bikaner House, near India Gate. Departing from the same depot, you'll pay Rs 5,000 for a seat on an A/C deluxe bus to Delhi; these leave half-hourly between 6am and 12:30am. It's a 5½-hour trip.

BY CAR As is the case everywhere, you will need to hire a driver with your car. Book one with Indoarya at ℭ **011/2651-1634;** indoarya@vsnl.net. The Jaipur-Delhi National Highway no. 8 is a divided highway that should get you between the two cities in 4 hours, depending on traffic and what time you depart. The undivided highway between Agra and Jaipur through Fatehpur Sikri and Bharatpur is in reasonable condition, too. There's not much you can do about the driving habits of other drivers, but you can, and should, certainly say something if you feel yours is driving rashly.

Getting Around

Unprecedented commercial development in the state capital in recent years has not been accompanied by infrastructural change; rush-hour traffic is arguably worse here than anywhere else in the country, although there are plans afoot to address the crisis. Construction is underway for a Metro, which should be ready by the end of 2010, and new overpasses. The best way to get around the crowded city center is on foot or by rickshaw. A rickshaw should cost Rs 50 to Rs 100 per hour—always discuss the fare upfront before you get into the rickshaw. If you're in a bind and simply need a taxi right away, call **Pink City Taxi** (ℭ **0141/511-5100** or 0141/325-5500). More viable, however, is to hire an air-conditioned car and driver for use within the city for approximately 4 hours (40km/25 miles) at Rs 700; 8 hours (80km/50 miles) at Rs 1,200. If your intention is to hire a car and driver to tour Rajasthan at your own pace, contact Kaaljeet Singh of Indoarya at ℭ **011/2651-1634;** indoarya@vsnl.net, or you can try the government **RTDC Transport Unit** (ℭ **0141/220-0778**). For more information on hiring a car and driver from elsewhere, see chapter 3. If you like to support small local businesses, we suggest you contact Shankar Meena (ℭ **98-2939-6947**) of **Rama Tours & Travels** (Srinath Colony, Near Airport, Sanganer) to arrange a car of really excellent quality at standard rates. Chances are Shankar or his brother Ramavtar will be your driver, and although their English may not be all that great, service is good-natured, and you'll be doing your bit for local entrepreneurship. You can also contact **Hari Ram Choudhary** (ℭ **94-1444-2618**) for trips in the city or farther afield; he's been in the business for nearly 25 years and knows his way around. Another good local guide-driver is Jaideep Singh Sumal; call him at ℭ **98280-62625** or e-mail him at jaideepsumal@gmail.com.

GUIDED TOURS Official guides, who hang around outside attractions (and charge Rs 100) tend to have their commentary down pat, but their enthusiasm wanes as soon as they've been hired and a price has been settled upon; while they often can't engage in dialogue, they will convince you that the tour is going to last a lot longer than it needs to be. Don't take chances with these professional amateurs: Hire **Jaimini Shastri** (ℭ **93-1450-9684;** shastri_guide@yahoo.co.in; Rs 600 for the day), one of the most respected guides in Jaipur and well-versed in the city's history, culture, and arts and crafts. He can give you the best guided tour of Jantar Mantar, speaking at length on astronomy, astrology, and the observatory. Book him well in advance, and—if you are planning to

(Moments) Sunset over Jaipur ★★

See the pink city at its rosiest from Nahargarh Fort (or "Tiger Fort") when the sun sinks behind the Aravalli Hills. Then—as night falls—watch the city skyline turn into the twinkling jewels for which it is famed. Purpose built to protect Amber, the view from here is always a winner, but during the festival of Diwali in November, when firecrackers explode above the city, it's one you will never forget. The fort (Rs 40; 10:30am—6:30pm) itself is largely in ruins, but the great vantage point alone is worth the trip. An RTDC-run cafe serves drinks and snacks.

tour the whole state—consider booking him for the entire trip. Alternatively, organize a guide through your hotel, or contact **Rajasthan Travel** (© 0141/236-5408) or **Sita World Travel** (© 0141/237-3996 or 0141/510-2020); you will inevitably pay a higher rate if you use a middleman, but the official rate is Rs 600 per day.

Tip: Consider picking up a copy of Dharmendar Kanwar's *Jaipur—10 Easy Walks* (Rupa; Rs 295) either from your hotel or from the excellent new **Crossword** bookstore (First Floor, K. K. Sq., C 11, Prithvi Raj Marg; © 0141/237-9400), which will also deliver books to you.

City Layout

The major attractions and best bazaars lie within the walls of the Old City. Just south of the wall lies **Mirza Ismail (M.I.) Road**—running west to east, this major thoroughfare is where most of the primary retail outlets and a few good restaurants are located, and divides the city between the old (north) and new (south). The Old City is clearly distinguishable by its terra-cotta-colored walls and ramparts, and the new by its modern shops. Station Road, Sansar Chandra Marg, and Bhagwan Das Marg all intersect M.I. Road. Along these you will find all the services you need, from travel agents and moneychangers to ATMs, restaurants, and Internet cafes. Farther south (but still within walking distance), diagonally opposite both Ajmeri Gate and New Gate of the Old City, lie Albert Hall and the Museum of Indology.

Festivals

As is the case everywhere in India, Jaipur seems to celebrate something new every month, but the following are worth noting: In February during the **Harvest Festival (Basant Panchami)** the city celebrates a Kite Festival, when hundreds of colorful kites sail the blue Jaipur sky, especially around the City Palace area; there's also a competition and display. In March, when Holi celebrants throughout the country splash color on anything that moves, Jaipur celebrates an **Elephant Festival.** The massive pachyderms—dressed to the nines and decorated with paint—march through the city's streets to the City Palace, accompanied by loud drumbeats and chanting. The event sees a tug-of-war between the elephants and their *mahouts* (elephant trainers/caretakers), as well as men playing polo—on elephant-back, of course. Make sure you book accommodations in advance during this period.

The following month (Apr) is **Gangaur,** when the women of Rajasthan pray to the goddess Parvati (also known as Gangaur) for the longevity of their husbands or for husbands fair and kind. This culminates in a procession to Gangaur Temple by the symbolic Siva, accompanied by elephants, to take his bride home. **Teej** (July–Aug) sees Rajasthan's always colorfully clad women dressed in full regalia to celebrate the onset of the mon- soon, while **Diwali (Festival of Lights),** the Hindu New Year, is celebrated throughout India in November.

Tip: Although all festivals are meant to be fun celebrations, a few unruly young men may try to ruin it with their aggressive behavior, especially during Holi and Diwali. Ask your hotel where it is advisable to go, and make sure you have your own transport if you are going to watch the festivities; single women travelers are advised to go with a male companion, escort, or guide.

(*Fast Facts*) Jaipur

American Express Located on M.I. Road (✆ **0141/237-0117** or -0119) near Ganpati Plaza, the office is open daily 9am to 6pm.

Area Code For Jaipur, the area code is **0141.**

Banks You'll find several banks and ATMS on M.I. Road. The **Thomas Cook** office for foreign exchange is at Jaipur Tower (✆ **0141/236-0940;** Mon–Sat 9:30am–6pm). There's a Citibank ATM next to the General Post Office, HDFC Bank ATM on Ashok Marg, ICICI Bank ATM in Ganpati Plaza, and others within the Old City.

Climate Summers have a mean maximum temperature of 104°F (40°C) and a minimum of 75°F (24°C), while winters range between a mean maximum of 70°F (21°C) and minimum of 48°F (9°C). The best weather occurs October through February.

Directory Assistance For telephone numbers call ✆ **197.** The number ✆ **0141/274-4447** is a privately operated general information number (talking Yellow Pages) that you can call for directory inquiries or information on shopping, restaurants, and the like.

Emergencies Ambulance ✆ **102;** fire ✆ **101;** police ✆ **100.**

Hospitals **Santokba Durlabji Memorial Hospital** (✆ **0141/256-6251** to -6257) is located on Bhawani Singh Marg. **SMS Hospital** (✆ **0414/256-0291**) is on Sawai Ram Singh Road.

Newspapers & Books You can pick up an amazing selection of newspapers, magazines, and books from tiny, inconspicuous **Books Corner** on M.I. Road; *Jaipur Vision* is a local newspaper. Also look out for the Jaipur Time Out.

Police **Sindhi Camp Police Station** can be reached at ✆ **0141/220-6201.**

Post Office The GPO (✆ **0141/236-8740**) is on M.I. Road (Mon–Sat 10am–6pm).

Tourist Help Desk Call the **24-hour tourist help desk** (✆ **1364**) if you want to report a theft or register a tourism-related complaint. If you can't get through, you can call the help desk's Delhi office at ✆ **98-1157-3315.**

WHAT TO SEE & DO

The principal attraction of the Old City of Jaipur is its **City Palace** (see below), nearby **Jantar Mantar** (also described below), and much-photographed **Hawa Mahal (Palace of Wind).** Built by Maharaja Sawai Pratap Singh in 1799, Hawa Mahal (✆ **0141/261-8862;**

Rs 5 entry, Rs 30 camera, Rs 70 video; daily 9am–4:30pm) is principally a pyramid-shaped five-story honeycombed facade of 593 latticed-stone screened windows, known as *jarokhas,* behind which the ladies of the palace could view the city without being seen. You can walk along the corridors that line the windows, which are mostly one room thick, but the building's principal attraction is the facade, which is best viewed in the early morning from the street level (entrance from Tripolia Bazaar, Police HQ lane). Also within the city complex, opposite Chandra Mahal, is **Govindji Temple** (daily 5–11am and 6–8pm): The family temple of the Maharajas of Jaipiur and the most famous in the city it is dedicated to Lord Krishna, and installed here so that Jai Singh II could see his favorite deity from the Chandra Mahal. The Krishna image was brought here from Brindavan in the late 17th century; devotees are allowed only a glimpse of it seven times a day. You will notice that the temple is open sided and is more like a Mughal audience hall; the reason being that it was originally a palace pavilion but after Krishna appeared to Jai Singh in a dream here he honored the deity by converting it into a temple.

In the new part of the city lies **Ram Niwas Bagh,** the city garden, which houses a depressing zoo and aviary. At the heart of the garden lies the beautifully proportioned Albert Hall, which houses the **Central Museum** (© 0141/257-0099; Rs 35; daily 10am–4:30pm; cameras not allowed inside although from the top you'll pay another Rs 40). Designed by the prolific architect and past master of the hybrid Indo-Saracenic style of architecture, Swinton Jacob, this is of principal interest from an architectural point of view, and a slow circular turn around the building in a car will suffice for many. That's not to say that the exhibits are devoid of interest—the eclectic collection covers a wide range from musical instruments to bottled organs, and the tiny terra-cotta figures demonstrating myriad yoga positions are worth a look. A short drive due south lies the even stranger **Museum of Indology** (© 0141/260-7455; Rs 40, Rs 100 camera, Rs 500 video; Sat–Thurs 9:30am–4:30pm), where an incredible selection of objects—all collected in one lifetime by the writer Acharya Ram Charan Sharma "Vyakul"—has been crammed into countless dusty display cases in every nook and cranny of his house. Like a journey into the mind and thought processes of the collector himself, the collection is as eclectic as they come, including a map of India painted on a grain of rice, misprinted rupees, a 180-million-year-old fossil, a letter written by Jai Singh, and the Gayatri Mantra written on a single strand of hair. It's a great shame more money is not available to edit and present this collection professionally.

On M.I. Road, near the Panch Batti intersection (where you'll see a **statue of Sawai Jai Singh II**) is **Raj Mandir** (© 0141/237-9372 or 0141/236-4438)—one of the most over-the-top and famous cinemas in the country. This is the place to watch a Bollywood blockbuster, though you will need to book tickets in advance to avoid waiting in line for hours. If the film is a new release, book a day in advance (daily 10am–2pm and 3–6pm). If you don't want to sit through 3 hours of Hindi melodrama, request that the doorman let you in for a sneak peek; he may oblige for a small tip if the hall isn't packed. Or arrive a few hours before the film, purchase your ticket, and kill time over a coffee and a pastry across the street at Barista, while you browse books on Rajasthani art and architecture, magazines, and bestsellers.

CITY ESCAPES If the populous nature and heavy traffic of Jaipur gets to be too much, take a trip to **Amber Fort** (see below), which can be covered in a few hours. Do bear in mind, however, that even here the crush of people can be exhausting, particularly over weekends; try to get here as soon as it opens or buy a ticket just before the ticket office closes which still gives you ample time, and space, to walk around in the softer light. Time allowing, you may want to include a visit to **Jaigarh Fort** (Rs 55 City Palace entry ticket includes Jaigarh; daily 9am–4:30pm), whose walls snake high above Amber, creating a crenelated horizon. Built for defense purposes by Sawai Jai Singh II, it has a number of buildings, gardens, and reservoirs as well as the world's largest cannon on wheels (the massive Jaivana cannon needed 100kg of powder to fire a shot) and the only surviving medieval cannon foundry, but its principal attraction is the panoramic view across Amber. You can walk to Jaigarh from Amber, a steep 20-minute climb. The path begins just below the palace entrance and branches off the windy road used by the mahouts and their two tonners. You'll arrive at the Awani Gate, and inside on your left is the museum. You can also drive (Rs 450 return from Amber village); take the same road to get to Nahargarh, arriving at the entrance near the Jaivana cannon.

On the way to Amber you'll see the turnoff for the imposing hilltop fort of **Nahargarh** (see "Sunset over Jaipur," above). Also known as Tiger Fort, Nahargarh is the first of the three forts built by Maharaja Jai Sawai Singh of Jaipur in 1734 and commands great views over the city. Just below it is **Gaitor** (free admission, Rs 10 camera, Rs 20 video), a walled garden that houses the marble *chhatris*—erected over cremation platforms—of the Kachchwaha rulers. Needless to say, the most impressive one belongs to Jai Singh II. Farther along Amber Road you will see **Jal Mahal,** a lake palace originally built by Sawai Pratap Singh in 1799, who spent much of his childhood at Udaipur's Lake Palace. Sadly, Man Sagar Lake is dry from the protracted drought, stripping it of much of its romance. If it's romance you're after, take a leisurely drive to **Samode Palace** (see "Where to Stay," below; lunch Rs 500) where, after touring Diwan-i-Khas and Diwan-i-Am, you can enjoy tea in the lovely courtyard, where bold sparrows will attempt to nibble your cookies. Or enjoy a dip and a drink on their spectacular new roof terrace infinity pool, and stay for dinner in their brand-new Indian fusion restaurant.

TOP ATTRACTIONS

Amer (or Amber) Fort ★★   Amber was the capital of the Kachchawahs from 1037 to 1727, when Sawai Jai Singh II moved the capital to Jaipur. Technically more a palace than a fort, it is said to have gotten its name from the many inlaid jewels and gemstones in the decoration of the inner sanctums of the fort. The approach is through a narrow pass, and the fort, an imposing edifice that grew over a period of 2 centuries, starting from around 1000 B.C., is naturally fortified by the Aravalli Hills, making it an ideal stronghold. It's a stiff 20-minute climb to **Suraj Pol (Sun Gate)** unless you opt for an elephant ascent or a jeep ride (Rs 280 return including Rs 30 parking fee), beyond which lies a beautiful and spotless complex of palaces, halls, pavilions, gardens, and temples. Either travel by car or pretend you are of royal blood and ascend on elephant-back (Rs 600 and up) for one to four riders; if you want to take pictures of the elephants, they pose for you for around Rs 50. After entering Jaleb Chowk through Suraj Pol (more elephants take riders for a turn around the courtyard), dismount and take the flight of stairs up through **Singh Pol (Lion Gate)** to **Diwan-i-Am (Hall of Public Audience),** a raised platform with 27 colonnades. Opposite you'll see the ornately carved silver doors leading to **Shila Devi Temple,** which contains an image of the goddess Kali, the appropriate family deity for the warring Rajput Kachchwaha. Massive, three-story, intricately decorated **Ganesh Pol (Elephant Gate)** leads to the private apartments of the royal family, built around a Mughal-style garden courtyard. **Sheesh Mahal (Mirror Palace)**—covered in mirror mosaics and colored glass—would have been the private quarters of the maharaja and his maharani, literally transformed into a glittering jewel box in flickering candlelight; guides will point out the "magic flower" carved in marble at the base of one of the pillars around the mirror palace—recognizable by the two butterflies hovering around it, the flower can be seen to contain seven unique designs (a fish tail, a lotus, a hooded cobra, an elephant trunk, a lion's tail, a cob of corn, and a scorpion). Above is **Jas Mandir,** a hall of private audience, with floral glass inlays and alabaster relief work. Opposite, across the garden, is **Sukh Mahal (Pleasure Palace)**—note the perforations in the marble walls and channels where water was piped to cool the rooms. South lies the oldest part, the **Palace of Man Singh I.** If you want to explore the old town and its many temples, exit through Chand Pol, opposite Suraj Pol. *Note:* As is the case elsewhere, the press of bodies and noise levels can seriously detract from the experience—try to get here as soon as it opens to avoid the heat and crowds, and, if possible, avoid visiting on weekends, or better still, arrive just before the last ticket is sold where you will have more of a solitary ramble and great photo opportunities with the softer light

Tip: Perhaps the most novel way to see the palace, fort, and its environs is with Jaipur Balloon Safaris (© **0141/401192324;** www.skywaltz.com), a new venture that has European pilots and provides aerial views of the area (Rs 12,000 per person for two people to Rs 10,000 for four).

Amber, 11km (7 miles) north of Jaipur. © **0141/253-0293.** Rs 100, Rs 150 with camera, Rs 250 video. Free lockers to store cameras. Daily 8am–5:30pm.

City Palace ★★   Although the former ruling family still lives in the seven-story Chandra Mahal (Moon Palace) built by Sawai Jai Singh II, most of what you'll experience here is the poorly managed **Maharaja Sawai Man Singh II Museum** and an overwhelming number of overpriced shops (even here you won't be free of India's omnipresent hustling; most guides are keen observers of the commission system—you have been warned!). Depending on which entrance you use, the first courtyard is where you'll find **Mubarak Mahal (Welcome Palace),** a "reception center" constructed by Maharaja Sawai Madho Singh II, grandfather of the present maharaja. Mubarak houses the textiles and costume museum, where a narrative of ritual adornments and regal costumes provide insight into the tremendous wealth and status that the family enjoyed, as well as the extraordinarily high level of craftsmanship available to them over the centuries. These include embroidery so fine it looks like printwork, some of the best *bandhani odhnis* (tie-dye scarves/veils) to come out of Sanganer, Kashmiri shawls, gossamer muslin from Bangladesh, and silk saris from Varanasi. There's also insight into the lifestyles of Jaipur's royals in the form of a specialized polo and billiards outfit (note the boots) worn by the king. The **Armoury,** with a selection of exquisitely crafted yet truly vicious-looking daggers and swords, is housed in the adjacent palace. If Mughal history, with all its valor and intrigue, has caught your imagination, ask one of the red turbaned attendants to point out the items belonging to the emperors Akbar, Jahangir, and Shah Jahan. The next courtyard reveals the raised **Diwan-i-Khas (Hall of Private Audience),** built in sandstone and marble. Look for the sun emblems decorating the walls—like most Rajput princes, the Kachchwaha clan belonged to the warrior caste, who traced their origins back to the sun (see "Once Were Warriors: The History of the Rajput," earlier in this chapter). To the west is **Pritam Niwas Chowk (Peacock Courtyard),** with its four beautifully painted doorways—from here you can search for signs of life from the royal residence that towers above. Move on to **Diwan-i-Am (Hall of Public Audience),** which houses a simply fantastic collection of miniature paintings, carpets, manuscripts, and photographs. Unfortunately, the entire exhibition is poorly lit, and display cases make browsing very awkward, but do try to look for the self-portraits of eccentric and fashionably dressed Ram Singh II, who found expression for his vanity in a passion for photography. The

> ## (Fun Facts) I'll Take My Ganges Water to Go, Thanks
>
> Inside Diwan-i-Khas are two huge silver urns, each weighing 345 kilograms (760 lb.). According to the *Guinness Book of Records,* these are the largest silver objects in the world. The Maharaja Sawai Madho Singh II, a devout Hindu, had these made before attending the coronation of King Edward VII in England to ensure that he had a constant supply of Ganges water to drink and to purify himself from extended contact with the "outcastes."

Friends of the Museum section is a bazaar selling art and crafts by respected artisans; it's a good place to pick up a quality miniature painting or Kundan jewelry, although prices are blatantly inflated. During our last visit we were also horrified to notice that not a single woman artist was represented.

Chokri Shahad, Old City. Entrance through Atish Gate or Nakkar Gate. ℂ **0141/260-8055.** www.royal familyjaipur.com. Admission Rs 180 includes still camera; Rs 75 children aged 5–12; Rs 200 video. Daily 9am–5pm. Get here as soon as it opens or at least before 11am.

Jantar Mantar ★★ Living proof of the genius and passion of Sawai Jai Singh, this medieval observatory is the largest of its kind in the world, and the best preserved of Jai Singh's five observatories. There are 18 instruments in all, erected between 1728 and 1734—many of Jai Singh's own invention. The observatory looks more like a modern sculpture exhibition or sci-fi set—hard to believe these instruments were constructed in the 18th century and remain functional. Some are still used to forecast how hot the summer will be, when the monsoon will arrive, and how long it will last. Whether or not you understand how the instruments are read (and for this, you should try to avoid coming on an overcast day—almost all the instruments require sunlight to function), the sheer sculptural shapes of the stone and marble objects and the monumental sizes of many (like the 23m-high/75-ft. Samrat Yantra, which forecasts crop prospects based on "the declination and hour of the heavenly bodies") are worth the trip and make for great photographs (evidenced by the Indian visitors who like to pose atop many of them as if they were starring in some esoteric Bollywood blockbuster). After a major upgrade of the observatory in 2007, improvements now include more visitor-friendly explanations of how everything works; alternatively, hire a guide at the gate for Rs 100 to Rs 150, but you'll do far better booking **Jaimini Shastri** (see "Guided Tours," earlier in this chapter); be sure to book him well in advance. *Tip:* If you'd prefer a forecast of future events that are more focused on yourself, you could always call upon the renowned (and very important) **Dr. Vinod Shastri,** who practices palmistry, predictive dice-throwing *(ramal),* and computer-aided astrological predictions in an office just around the corner (Chandni Chowk, behind Tripolia Gate; ℂ **0141/261-3338).** A professor of astrology and palmistry at Rajasthan University, Dr. Shastri is available between noon and 7pm, but you should know that his asking fee ranges from Rs 600 to Rs 3,000 for a session lasting just 10 minutes.

Follow signs from city palace. ℂ **0141/261-0494.** Rs 10, Rs 50 still camera, Rs 100 video. Daily 9:30am–5pm.

WHERE TO STAY

Jaipur has a plethora of places to stay, from standard Holiday Inns to the usual back-packer hostels. But no one in their right mind comes to Rajasthan to overnight in a bland room in some nondescript hotel chain when you could be sleeping in the very room where a maharaja seduced his maharani, or in the royal apartments of the family guests—hence our focus on heritage hotels of which the following reviews represent the best in the city, in a variety of price categories. The exceptions to this are the good-value Shahpura House, K Country Villa—where you get to mingle with aristocratically connected locals—and the decadent Rajvilas, which not only imitates the heritage property concept, but in many ways improves upon it.

Very Expensive

An alternative in this pricy category that you may want to consider (if you like your bling) is the **Raj Palace** ★ (© **0141/263-4077;** fax 0141/263-0489; www.rajpalace. com; from Rs 22,000 for a Heritage Double, Rs 32,000 for a Heritage Suite, Rs 52,000 for a Prestige Suite, and right up to Rs 600,000 for the Presidential Suite) The oldest mansion in Jaipur (1727), it is well placed right next to the city gate through which this palatial Haveli has a private entrance and has plenty of interesting amenities including an in-house cinema. A member of The Small Luxury Hotels of the World, rooms are suitably posh (each of which has its own display cabinet of museum-worthy artifacts) in elegant buildings that look as though they were converted from palace to hotel by an Indian Gianni Versace. Yet, while there's gold, glitz, and glamour aplenty, we can't understand exactly how it is positioned, and where trite, piped classical music fit in with a look that's trying so hard to be bling.

Rajvilās ★★★ Rajvilās is one of those luxury hotels that is a destination in its own right, albeit along a rather industrial-looking road some distance from Jaipur's center. With a budget of $20 million, no expense was spared in showcasing the fine craftsmanship typical of the region to create and decorate what is ostensibly a traditional fortified Rajasthani palace. Although it may not have the history of an original heritage hotel, it more than makes up for this with a level of comfort and luxury that is only matched by the better-located but more historical Rambagh Palace. Set amid 13 hectares (32 acres) of orchards, formal gardens, and decorative pools, accommodations are separate from the main fort (which houses the public spaces) in clusters of rooms—between four and six around each central courtyard—and a few luxury tents. all luxuriously decorated in a colonial style offset by Rajasthani elements (fabrics, textiles, and miniatures). Dining enjoys a well-deserved reputation; service throughout is of the renowned exceptional Oberoi quality.

Goner Rd., Jaipur 303 012. © **800/5-OBEROI** [-623764] in the U.S. and Canada, or 0141/268-0101. Fax 0141/268-0202. www.oberoihotels.com. 71 units. Rs 30,000 premiere double; Rs 36,000 luxury tent; Rs 80,000 royal tent; Rs 1,50,000 luxury villa (with pool); Rs 2,200,000 Kohinoor villa. 10% Taxes extra. AE, DC, MC, V. **Amenities:** 2 restaurants; library/bar; airport transfers complimentary; babysitting; concierge; doctor-on-call; health club; helipad; 5-hole putting green; Internet (Rs 113 30 min.; Rs 225 60 min.; Rs 885 24 hr.); pool; room service; spa; 2 outdoor tennis courts; yoga. In room: A/C, TV, DVD player (complimentary access to CD and DVD library), minibar, villas have private pools, butler, sound system, Wi-Fi (30 min Rs 113; 60 min Rs 225; 24 hrs. Rs 885).

Taj Rambagh Palace ★★★ If you're hell-bent on experiencing the blue blood of heritage properties, Rambagh Palace is both the largest and most elegant option in Jaipur, with every amenity you could wish for, and was voted best hotel in the *Condé Nast Traveler*'s Readers Choice Award 2009. Converted into a hotel in 1957, it remains a favorite of Bollywood stars and socialites. It's where Jaipur royalty celebrates birthdays, and where the elite and Mayo princes gather to strike deals and cement friendships. A sense of grandeur accompanies every room (even in the simpler, more affordable luxury rooms), but if you want to feel as if you're actually living in a royal apartment, opt for a "palace" room (no. 317 is just fabulous). Dining at the swish **Suvarna Mahal** is a grand affair (see review later). The kid-friendly drinking and dining venue, **Steam,** which inhabits an old train carriage, is novel but seems very out of place in the grand environment with its pizza oven and dated tartan carriages.

Sawani Sing Rd., Jaipur 302 005. (C) **0141/221-1919.** Fax 0141/238-5098. www.tajhotels.com. rambagh. jaipur@tajhotels.com. 85 units. Rs 30,000 luxury double; Rs 40,000 palace double; Rs 83,000 historical suite; Rs 140,000 royal suite; Rs 195,000 grand royal suite. Taxes extra. AE, DC, MC, V. **Amenities:** 3 restaurants; bar; airport transfers (Rs 500 pickup, A/C); butler service; concierge; cultural performances; doctor on call; health club; golf on request; indoor and outdoor heated pools; room service; spa and outdoor Jacuzzi; squash court; tennis; table tennis. In room: A/C, TV, electric fireplace; some suites have Jacuzzi; minibar, Wi-Fi (30 mins Rs 125; 1 hour Rs 200; 2 hours Rs 300; 3 hours Rs 600).

Expensive

A couple of heritage properties deserve a mention in this category, and none more so than the **Jai Mahal Palace** ★★ (Jacob Rd., Civil Lines; (C) **0141/222-3636;** www.tajhotels. com; Rs 18,000 luxury double). The hotel is architecturally splendid, with buildings dating from 1745, and it's recently undergone a life-altering renovation that has made it even more comfortable and homely but somehow it cannot shake its tag as a local corporate hangout. The grounds are large and manicured, with a huge pool and tennis court. Guest rooms are bright, if a little compact, and dining venues funky (particularly the sultry, mauve **Cinnamon,** known as much for its cocktails as it is for its Indian cuisine), but it's neither as grand as Taj Rambagh nor as romantic or authentic as Samode or Alsisar havelis (both of which offer better value for money).

Samode Haveli ★★ This 200-year-old city mansion is well located (one of the few accommodations within the old walled city) and oozes authenticity, with higgledy-piggledy rooms of various sizes furnished in typical Rajasthani antiques and featuring pillars and cusped arches painted with traditional motifs, tiny colored-glass windows, marble floors, and deep alcoves for lounging. Accommodations all have newly renovated luxury bathrooms with tubs and separate showers; 106 has its own balcony and view of the courtyard. If you want to be close to the pool and garden book 116 through 120, which have porches and direct access. The most interesting rooms are those housed in the *zenana* (traditionally the part of the house where women were secluded), particularly the Sheesh Mahal Suite, in which every inch of wall and ceiling is covered in tiny glass mirrors or delicately executed miniature paintings—the effect in candlelight is not dissimilar to the celebrated Sheesh Mahal at nearby Amber Fort (though it's worth mentioning that some find the extralow ceilings and numerous pillars claustrophobic). *Note:* At press time, there were plans to introduce nine more guest rooms and a new restaurant in an adjoining but quite separate property on the other side of the lawns. These promise to be newly renovated in a more modern classical style and may provide some lift to the old haveli style,

Samode Haveli, Ganga Pol, Jaipur 302 992. (C) **0141/263-2407,** -2370, or -1942. Fax 0141/263-1397. www. samode.com. reservations@samode.com. 40 units. Low season (May 1–Sept 30) to high season (Oct 1– Apr 31): Rs 10,950 deluxe double; Rs 12,500 deluxe suite; Rs 15,000 Sheesh Mahal, Rs 13,500 Haveli suite; Rs 2,700 extra bed. Rates include breakfast; taxes extra. AE, MC, V. **Amenities:** Dining hall; bar; airport transfers; children's playground; doctor-on-call; fitness center; spa pool; steam room; Internet and Wi-Fi free. In room: A/C, fan, TV, minibar.

Moderate

Alsisar Haveli ★★ (Value) This is the most elegant, well-maintained heritage property in its price category in Jaipur, offering excellent value for money. Built in 1892 and still owned by the amiable Kachchwaha clan of Rajputs, it has all the traditional elements of Rajput architecture—scalloped arches and pretty cupolas, painted ceilings and colored glass windows, and a maze of corridors and stairs around and through inner courtyards. Rooms vary in size, but all are furnished with antiques. Ask for deluxe no. 110 set around the cool, inner courtyard with plants and birdsong or the wonderful suites (107, 108) off Sheesh Mahal. You can take tea around the pool, or retreat to the tables on the lawn for total peace. The lounge is beautifully furnished, but the dining hall sets the place apart. Unlike the oppressive rooms so typical of heritage properties (like Samode Haveli), Alsisar's is filled with light; the food (local Shekhawati fare) is tasty; breakfast will run you Rs 350, while lunch and dinner (both buffets) costs Rs 550 plus taxes.

Sansar Chandra Rd., Jaipur 302 001. ℭ **0141/236-8290** or -4685. Fax 0141/236-4652. www.alsisar.com. 37 units. Rs 3,900 double; Rs 4,550 deluxe suite; Rs 850 extra bed. Rates exclude taxes. AE, MC, V. **Amenities:** Restaurant; bar; doctor-on-call; Internet (Rs 100 per hour); Ayurvedic massage; pool; room service. *In room:* A/C, TV, Wi-Fi (Rs 100/hr.).

Narain Niwas Palace Like Alsisar, Narain Niwas provides you with an opportunity to live in a heritage property for relatively little money (though Alsisar still has the edge in terms of atmosphere, ambience, decor, and service). Built in 1928 by Gen. Amar Singh, the 3-hectare (7-acre) property is still a green oasis surrounded by the city, but some of the spaces have started to show signs of wear in recent years. Look out for the newly renovated rooms (nos. 51–57); individually furnished with antique beds and chairs, these feature pretty frescoes and block-print fabrics (on rather thin mattresses) and are close to the pool, opening onto a particularly lush part of the garden—an essential balm after tackling Jaipur's streets. Avoid the monstrously overpriced new "garden suites." Buffet-style meals are taken on the lawns or in the dark, claustrophobic dining hall, which, like the antiques-filled lounge, features scalloped arches decorated with frescoes.

Kanota Bagh, Narain Sing Rd., Jaipur 302 004. ℭ **0141/256-1291** or -3448. Fax 0141/256-1045. www. hotelnarainniwas.com. 31 units. Rs 4,200 standard double; Rs 5,500 suite; Rs 6,500 Kanota suite; Rs 9,500 garden suite; Rs 1,400 extra bed. Breakfast included; taxes extra. AE, MC, V. **Amenities:** Dining hall; bar; doctor-on-call; Internet (Rs 50/hr.); Ayurvedic massage; pool; room service; table tennis; yoga and meditation. *In room:* A/C, fan, TV in some, minibar, Wi-Fi (Rs 112/hr.).

Shahpura House ★ (Value) Located in the heart of a relaxed residential neighborhood, yet only 10 minutes (3km/1¾ miles) from the city, one of Jaipur's best-value hotels was built just half a century ago by a noble member of the Shekhawat's Shahpura clan (Shahpura is 65km/40 miles from Jaipur). It's still a family run affair and the aristocratic owner has dressed the place in what might be termed "haveli style," with decor that runs from framed black-and-white family photographs to elaborate chandeliers to detailed frescoes. Accommodations are very comfortable, with marble floors, antique furniture, block-print curtains, and beds covered with smart white linen. The cheaper deluxe rooms are more boxy, but if you can book no. 206, you'll have a spacious bathroom, large bed, and a window overlooking the pool. Of the decently priced suites, no. 306 has a balcony overlooking the pool.

Devi Marg, Bani Park, Jaipur 302 016. ℭ **0141/220-2292** or -2293. Fax 0141/220-1494. www.shahpurahouse. com. shahpurahous@usa.net. 32 units. Rs 3,500 deluxe double; Rs 4,500 suite; Rs 5,000 royal suite; Rs 800 extra bed. Taxes extra. AE, DC, MC, V. **Amenities:** Restaurant; bar; airport transfers (Rs 400 one-way);

Inexpensive

Another budget option—though nowhere as nice as Diggi Palace (below) **Umaid Bhawan** (C 0141/220-6426, 0141/231-6184, or 0141/220-1276; fax 0141/220-7445; www. umaidbhawan.com; email@umaidbhawan.com) is an old haveli in a residential street offering dark but clean rooms—all with A/C which have the usual antique furnishings and attached showers; ask to see a few as they are all different. It also has a nice pool out front. Deluxe Rooms go for Rs 1,500 but rather ask for a Royal Deluxe Room overlooking the pool (Rs 1,800) which comes with A/C and fan. Internet and Wi-Fi are Rs 60 per hour.

Diggi Palace ★ (Value) This is still the best budget option in Jaipur, where you get the opportunity to overnight in a rambling, 200-year-old haveli for a fraction of the rates charged elsewhere. The drawbacks of this budget-value haven are that it can be busy and it's a long walk from the Old City. The "palace"—which it is not—lies at the edge of a big open lawn and is within walking distance of Ram Niwas Gardens and the Central Museum. The leafy, well-established gardens filled with bird chatter and brand-new pool are a wonderful respite. Rooms vary in size, but all feature cool, clean white tiles and whitewashed walls; some have antique furniture offset with bright block-printed fabrics. Book an air-conditioned room set around a cool open courtyard to beat the heat—they're substantially larger and still great value; unit 108 is a gorgeous first-floor room with a large four-poster metal frame bed and big bathroom. Alternatively, book one of the quiet, cool cottage rooms, which have marble floors and bright block-print fabrics—these all have tubs *and* showers, and some have antique furniture; most significantly, they're away from the potentially noisy main building and overlook the garden. If you want access to a semiprivate veranda, ask for no. 209, a spacious "suite" with a large bathroom and shared balcony overlooking the courtyard. Meals are served in the spacious restaurant and on the open-air, first-floor veranda; dinner costs from Rs 150.

Tip: Over the past 3 years Diggi Palace has played host to the internationally recognized Jaipur Literary Festival, which takes place in January (21–25, 2010) and attracts famous authors such as Ian Mckewan, Salman Rushdie, William Dalrymple, and Kiran Desai. If you intend to stay over this exciting period, which coincides with the high season, be sure to book ahead.

Shivaji Marg, C-scheme, Sawai Ram Singh Hwy., Jaipur 302 004. C **0141/237-3091,** 0141/236-6120, or -6196. Fax 0141/230-359. www.hoteldiggipalace.com. 48 units. Rs 1,200 air-cooled double; Rs 2,000 A/C standard double; Rs 3,200 A/C deluxe; Rs 3,800 A/C suite. Rates include breakfast, taxes extra. AE, V. **Amenities:** Dining hall; bar; station (free) and airport transfers (Rs 400 one-way); doctor-on-call; room service; Internet (Rs 60 per hour); pool; *In room:* A/C in most, fan, TV in most, minibar in most.

Where to Stay Outside Jaipur

K Country Villa ★★ A top choice for anyone grown weary of hotel anonymity, this dressed-to-kill luxury home just outside Jaipur, personally run by impeccably debonair hosts, Ridhiraj ("Tony") Singh and his wife, Rithu, provides a fine introduction to aspirational Indian life. The plush accommodations, beautifully decorated by Rithu, are outfitted with top-quality fabrics, furnishings, and fittings (with some borderline kitsch thrown in for good measure) and artworks collected from across the country. You can stay in one of the large guest rooms in the main house or in one of the huge cottages a short distance away. Meals are taken in the company of your hosts, with predinner drinks in any of the different lounge spaces; conversations can be a real eye-opener. Various sight-seeing trips can be arranged (Rithu is the ideal source of lowdown shopping information), and you can go horseback riding or fishing if you'd like to take a break from polluted city life.

Near Malpura Hill, Kanota Irrigation Dam, Vill. Post—Sumel, Jaipur 303 012. © **98-2906-3897** or 98-2921-3897. Fax 0141/237-7531. www.kcountryvilla.com. kcountryvilla@mail.com. 7 units. Rs 9,000 luxury double; Rs 12,000 luxury deluxe double; Rs 17,000 premium cottage; Rs 1,200 extra bed. Rates include breakfast, dinner, and soft minibar; taxes extra. MC, V. **Amenities:** Dining room; bar; billiards table; bird-watching; currency exchange; cultural performances; doctor-on-call; horse riding; jeep safari; library; pool; Ayurvedic massage and yoga; transfers Rs 800 A/C car; room service. *In room:* A/C, TV, DVD; minibar, luxury deluxe room and cottages have Jacuzzi; cottages have massage chairs.

Samode Palace ★★   An hour's drive (45km/28 miles) from Jaipur, 400-year-old Samode Palace is popular, pretty, and newly renovated. The original palace suites are beautiful: huge, with loads of natural light and furnished with a mix of antiques and contemporary pieces but best value-for-money option is one of the rooms overlooking the lovely pool area—ask for one with a balcony and a renovated bathroom. If you have the cash, ask for the newly renovated Royal Suite 314, which is of Oberoi quality. Many visitors use this as a relaxing base to explore Jaipur, whose major attractions can be covered in a day trip, and it's also a good stepping-stone into the Shekhawati. The palace itself is worth exploring (especially for the gorgeous 250-year-old frescoes in Durbar Hall, or the even lovelier Sultan Mahal); other than this there's not much to see or do here besides sample the cuisine, relax at their beautiful new rooftop infinity pool, or sit in the corner Jacuzzi cantilevered out in space over the hills with Samode Fort casting a watchful eye over you.

Tip: An interesting and less expensive alternative to the palace (although not nearly as exclusive or characterful), lies 10 minutes away, at **Samode Bagh,** a large garden established by the royal family, in which 44 comfortable, closely spaced, air-conditioned tents with stone floors and permanent attached bathrooms are pitched. The tent walls feature beautiful Mughal-inspired patterns and are attractively furnished with carpets, standing lamps, and pretty wooden beds and chairs. The Bagh has its own pool and tennis courts, and all in all is an extremely peaceful getaway. The tents are situated a little too close to each other, and the dining tent can be claustrophobic when full—in which case ask about meals served on the spacious lawns.

Samode, Jaipur 303 806. © **01423/24-0023.** Reservations through Samode Haveli, Ganga Pol, Jaipur 302 992. © **0141/263-2407,** -2370, or -1068. Fax 0141/263-1397. www.samode.com. 43units (Palace); 44 units (Bagh). Low season (May 1–Sept 30) to high season (Oct 1–Apr 30): **Samode Palace** Rs 13,000 deluxe double; Rs 16,500 deluxe suite; Rs 30,000 royal suite (includes dinner); Rs 3,200 extra bed. **Samode Bagh** Rs 7,000 double; Rs 2,250 extra bed. Rates include breakfast; taxes extra during high season. AE, MC, V. **Amenities:** 2 restaurants; bar; Bagh includes badminton, bicycles, table tennis, tennis and volleyball; doctor-on-call; gym; Internet (free); 2 pools; room service; safari—camel and jeep. *In room:* A/C, TV, minibar.

WHERE TO DINE

All the hotels reviewed above have dining halls or restaurants that usually serve buffets or a la Carte featuring mediocre to good North Indian food and mediocre to inedible international ("Continental") options. If you're spending more than 1 night or looking for somewhere local to lunch, check out the following, but our advice is to eat at your hotel as the food in Jaipur is known not to be worth travelling for. Note that you'll find the largest concentration of restaurants along M.I. Road, which is also the main shopping drag outside the Old City. Two popular choices with tourists here, both close to the very famous Niro's, are the glass-fronted, air-conditioned, reliable **Copper Chimney** and on its left is the tandoor **Handi.** Also on M.I. Road is the famous **Dasaprakash** (© 0141/ 237-1313), which serves fresh pomegranate juice with which to enjoy excellent *dosas* (filled South Indian pancakes). When the heat gets to you, and you still have dozens more shops to visit, you may want to forgo a large lunch and opt for something healthy and light; for this, your prayers have been answered in the form of **Anokhi's organic deli** (see "Shopping," below). With daily specials and great, healthful salads, this is arguably the freshest fare in town.

Widely considered one of Jaipur's best, **Indiana** ★ (J2-34, Mahaveer Marg, behind Jai Club; © 0141/236-2061 or -2062) is a bit of a tourist trap, owned by a local graduate of Purdue University who harbors considerable fondness for his alma mater and has a keen eye for kitsch (watch how a tacky fountain issues an upward spray from the head of a stone god). Although locals are hardly ever seen here, the Indian fare is reasonable, and prices are only marginally inflated to cover the nightly "complimentary" open-air folk dance show (which can be a lot of fun, although it's very inauthentic—more like a floor show—and tellingly pitched at a dumbed-down foreign audience). Although service is abysmal, you can watch some of the kitchen action and appreciate the spectacle of *naan* and *roti* being prepared before making its way to your table. Although there's not much serious focus on Rajasthani cuisine, you can feast on thali (multicourse platter), or ask for regional specialties like *ker sangri* (spicy capers and desert beans) and *laal maas* (spicy meat curry), which aren't on the menu; main courses start at Rs 150, and a nonvegetarian thali is Rs 400. Another tourist-oriented place, with a firmer focus on food and a more stylish ambience, is **Spice Court** (Hari Bhawan, Achrol House, Jacob Rd., Civil Lines; © 0141/222-0202; www.spicecourtindia.com), which has a pretty all-encompassing menu but also offers regional Rajasthani specialties, served at tables designed like large display cabinets for spices and other dry food ingredients. It's also well located for shoppers, being right near **Cottons,** a great little place to pick up cool, summery garments.

If it's atmosphere you're after, not to mention a highly memorable visual experience, grab a late lunch and linger for a sundowner at the Rambagh Palace's **Verandah** overlooking the Rambagh's lawns where Rajasthani musicians and dancers serve as predinner entertainment. Or get there early evening, having reserved dinner at Rambagh Palace's swanky **Suvarna Mahal** (see below).

LMB (Laxmi Misthan Bhandar) ★★ INDIAN/VEGETARIAN/SWEET SHOP   If you're headed for Johari Bazaar to shop, make sure you stop at this renowned local hangout. Anyone with even half a sweet tooth shouldn't miss stepping out of the madness of the bazaar into this cool oasis—even if it's just to salivate over the huge selection of sweets beautifully (and hygienically) displayed behind glass counters in the sweet *(mithai)* shop section. Beyond the takeout area lies the large air-conditioned restaurant; it remains strictly vegetarian, and no onion or garlic (believed to inflame the senses) is used in food preparation; no alcohol is served either. Try the freshly prepared *samosas* or potato and cashew-nut *tikkis,* and wash them down with delicious *lassis* (yogurt drinks) or pomegranate juice. For an authentic, filling meal, order the Rajasthani thali, which begins with tangy *papad mangori* soup and includes traditional *ker sangri,* Rajasthani *kadhi* (dumplings in a yogurt sauce), five different vegetables, and three kinds of bread.

Johari Bazaar. © 0141/256-5844. Rs 80–Rs 350 AE, MC, V. Daily 8am–11pm. Snacks only 4–7pm.

Niros ★★ NORTH INDIAN/CHINESE   Although the name sounds terribly inauthentic, and the appalling covers of '80s pop songs are almost unbearable, this remains

> **Moments Lassi Heaven**
>
> Across the road from Niros is **Lassiwalla,** favored by locals as *the* place to experience a *lassi* (cold yogurt drink). Not only is the lassi (salty or sweet; sadly, no banana) exquisitely creamy, but the price (just Rs 20–Rs 30 for a large) includes the handmade terra-cotta mug it's served in—to be kept as a memento or (as the locals do) thrown away after use. You need to buy a token at the front and then join a second thronging mass at the side to exchange it for your rewarding drink. Imitators have sprung up next door, so make sure you go to the right one; the original *lassi-walla* is *always* busy, and a sign above the stall reads OLDEST SHOP IN JAIPUR and features an image of baby Krishna. The current owner is Ashok Agarwal (✆ **0141/237-6892**), grandson of Govind Narain, who started the stall decades ago. He serves nothing but *lassis* and is usually sold out by 4pm.

the favored haunt of extended bourgeois Indian families, visiting Bollywood celebs, and foreign travelers, all drawn by its reputation for excellent food. Well-situated on the shopping route, Niros does typical Rajasthani dishes. And, if your stomach is starting to curdle from the traditional (and liberal) use of ghee as a cooking medium, you'll be happy to know that Niros's chefs use only refined soybean oil. House specialties include *laal maas* (mutton cooked in spicy red gravy) and *reshmi* kebab (mutton marinated in traditional spices and chargrilled). The *korma* dishes are all prepared in a deliciously creamy cashew-nut-based sauce, while the ever-popular chicken *tikka masala* is spicier than usual. You certainly won't want for choice: The numbered menu runs right up to 286! Forego dessert and head across the street to Lassiwalla (see box below).

M.I. Rd. ✆ **0141/237-4493** or 0141/221-8520. www.nirosindia.com. Rs 85–Rs 500. AE, DC, MC, V. Daily 10am–11pm.

Surya Mahal ★★ INDIAN/INTERNATIONAL   This fine dining restaurant at Rajvilās vies with Survana Mahal as the most romantic place to have dinner in Jaipur. Lit by huge burning braziers, the courtyard features a raised platform where beautiful Rajasthani women give a short performance of their traditional dance (Sept 15–Mar only). Apart from the live entertainment—and there's always melodic musical accompaniment—cuisine is excellent. You can sample the tastes of the region with a Rajasthani thali (multicourse platter), or order the *laal maas* (lamb braised with Mathania chilies and yogurt, and smoked with cloves and garlic) or the *shammi kebab*, minced lamb flavored with mace and cardamom and then filled with hung yogurt. Or you can give the Indian dishes a break, and choose from roasted Chilean sea bass, or perfectly roasted Australian rack of lamb.

Rajvilās, Goner Rd., Jaipur. ✆ **0141/268-0101.** Reservations essential. Rs 700–Rs 1,850. AE, DC, MC, V. Daily noon–3pm and 7–10:30pm.

Suvarna Mahal ★★ INDIAN/CONTINENTAL   A must for any special occasion, this is one of those venues that turns the most ordinary night into a memorable one. A grand double-volume colonial dining room lies behind enormous doors that signal a night of opulence: the glow of four alabaster lamps is enhanced by huge gilded mirrors, walls are covered in rich gold fabric, and the ceiling is painted in Italian Renaissance style

While the menu changes regularly, you can ask your waiter for suggestions; food is very
good but it's the old-world ambience that makes this such a special place to dine.

Rambagh Palace (see "Where to Stay," above) (C) **0141/221-1919.** Rs 500–Rs 1,700. AE, MC, V. Daily 7–11pm.

SHOPPING

Only Mumbai or Delhi comes close to offering the array of goods found here, and foreign buyers for wholesale and retail outlets descend in droves to stock up on textiles, rugs, pottery, jewelry, shoes, miniature paintings, and ready-made clothing and housewares. It's a cornucopia here, and the pressure to buy is immense—not least because everyone seems to be a tout for someone (see "Understanding the Commission System," below). Finding your way around the Old City is relatively easy—the divisions based on what is produced still hold true, though you'll find much more besides. Following are a few rough guidelines.

For jewelry and gems, head for **Johari Bazaar** in the Old City—the gem center of Jaipur (look for Bhuramal Rajmal Surana). While you're there, pick up a cool pair of *jootis* (traditional camel-hide sandals) at **Shivam Nagara Palace** (Shop 11, Johari Bazaar; (C) 0141/257-1468). Alternatively, wander through **Chameliwala Market,** beyond Zarawar Singh Gate, on Amber Road, particularly if you're in search of silver, tribal, or ornamental jewelry. **Silver Mountain** ((C) 0141/237-7399) and **Maneeka** ((C) 0141/237-5913), both located at Chameliwala Market, are recommended.

Numerous factories and showrooms run the length of Amber Road, including those specializing in hand-blocked prints and antiques. And if you're looking to take home some of Jaipur's famous blue pottery, Amber Road is also where you'll find the largest concentration of outlets: **Jaipur Blue Pottery Art Centre** (near Jain Mandir, Amber Rd.; (C) 0141/263 5375) is a reliable place to pick up items like blue pottery vases, trays, coasters, and wall plates. If you're considering redecorating your home with a classy, upscale Indian look, definitely venture into **AKFD** (B-6/A-1 Prithviraj Rd., C-Scheme; (C) 0141/236-4863), a fantastic one-stop interior design store with beautiful creations by the hard-working owners and covetable items from across the country.

The cutting, polishing, and selling of gems and the making of silver jewelry take place in the predominantly Muslim area of Pahar Ganj in the **Surajpol Bazaar.** Jewelry designers from all over the world continue to nurture the superlative gem-cutting and -setting skills of these craftspeople, but here, as in Johari Bazaar, be aware that bargains are hard to come by—more often than not, you really do get what you pay for. If you're knowledgeable enough, shop for gems and jewelry in the bazaars, but for most, a trip to the shops listed below is recommended.

Fabric is another must-buy, as the finest quality silk, chiffon, and cotton are transformed through traditional block printing and tie-and-dye techniques into intricately patterned fabrics with vibrant contrasts and colors. The finest tie-dye process is known as *bandhani* (literally "to tie"): Tiny circles are made by tying the cloth with thread in a detailed design; the cloth is often sold with the thread still tied on (to be removed before first use) and is traditionally worn unironed, showing off the crinkly circles. **Bapu Bazaar** (around the corner from Johari Bazaar; closed Sun) is where you can bargain for a wide range of textiles and ready-made garments, as well as traditional camel-leather shoes (*jootis*) and bangles of glass and lacquer; it's also by far the most pleasant shopping street because it's pedestrianized. If you're looking for great inexpensive gifts, take a look at the tiny workshops producing beautiful bangles in **Maniharon Ka Rasta,** an alley off Tripolia Bazaar (closed Sun).

For block-print fabrics, a trip to Sanganer, a village 16km (10 miles) south of Jaipur, is a must—here printing takes place in the courtyard of almost every house. Famous as the birthplace of block-work (and home to the largest handmade-paper industry in India), this is where you'll find the most refined block-print work in the world. Visit **Shilpi Handicrafts** (© 0141/273-1106) or **Sakshi** (© 0141/273-1862) for fabrics, and **Salim Paper** (© 0141/273-0222) for a range of handmade paper you'll be loathe to write on! If you are really serious about picking up block-printed fabrics, make an appointment to visit the colorful workshop of **Surabhi Exports** (© 0141/237-2202), where creative powerhouse, Gitto, works with renowned interior designers to come up with looks that are unique and totally fabulous. Also visit **Anokhi** (reviewed below) for lovely block-print garments.

One of the most reliable shops for knickknacks is **Neelam Handicrafts** at the Arya Niwas (© 0141/237-2456 or 0141/510-6010). This little shop stocks maps, postcards, and books on India as well as some music CDs. It also has a small collection of silver jewelry, Indian teas, handmade paper, and souvenirs—all good quality and sold at a fixed marked price (a rarity in Jaipur); incidentally, they are half the price quoted at most other city shops.

Finally, if you'd like to find all the finest jewelry, designer wear, Pashminas, books, and selected homewares under one roof and aren't against traveling some distance out of town, consider undertaking the 90-minute drive to **Amanbagh,** in the Ajabgarh valley. This remote, beautifully situated resort has one of the finest boutiques we've encountered. Christina Patnaik (a Mexican who married locally) sources exceptional items from all over India, and some of the clothing and jewelry displayed here costs marginally less than what you'd find in Jaipur (only here you won't have to contend with heavy traffic, the commission system, or trying to figure out high quality from average items; everything at Amangagh is top-notch). There's some extraordinary jewelry (including chunky tribal ankle bracelets), and funky Indian twists on Western garments by sought-after Delhi-based designer Malini Ramani; check out her colorful miniskirts with mirror-work and detailed *sitara* (sequin) designs—gorgeous, if pricey, at around Rs 9,000. Pashmina shawls of the highest quality start at Rs 1,500.

Blue Pottery

Kripal Kumbh Singh Shekhawat ★★★   If you want to make sure you're purchasing top-quality blue glazed pottery, make an appointment to view the work of Jaipur's most famous ceramist, Kripal Singh, often credited with reviving this dying art. Made from ground blue quartz stone, glass, borax, and clay, and utilizing traditional designs, his work is nothing short of exquisite. Open 10am to 7pm. Closed Sundays. B-18A Shiv Marg, Bani Park. © 0141/220-1127.

Books

Books Corner ★   You could easily miss this corner shop, but even though it's tiny, it's chockablock with magazines and books. If you're looking for more information on India, coffee-table books on Rajasthan, or just a good paperback read, this has the best selection around, at the fairest prices. M.I. Rd. © 0141/236-6323.

Clothing & Housewares

Anokhi ★★   This company was created in the 1960s by a British designer who had items made here for export to the U.K. and elsewhere. The combination of Eastern and Western influences has resulted in flattering designs that have become hugely popular

| (Moments) **Bargaining Is Part of the Deal**

If you'd like to take home a couple of pairs of inexpensive leather sandals or sequined slippers, head for the string of shops beneath the Hawa Mahal on Tripolia Bazaar; you'll find mountains of shoes, as well as the opportunity to try your hand at bargaining. The trick is to go at it with gusto, enthusiasm, and, most important, good humor and a smile. To the shopkeeper, there is almost nothing worse than failing to make a sale. He expects you to challenge his offer (usually about five times any acceptable amount), so sets off by suggesting an outrageous amount (based on what you look like you can afford) at which you must shake your head despondently. Then (and you may well remember the famous bazaar bargaining scene from Monty Python's *The Life of Brian*) make an equally impossible counter-offer and you'll find yourself locked in a battle of psychological warfare that's more exciting than chess. After all, even when you've shaved several hundred rupees off the price, you'll have no idea what your prize is really worth. But you'll have something to wear to remind you of your very Indian interaction.

around the world. Anokhi is part of a growing design movement that taps into the skills of local craftspeople and gives those crafts a modern twist. Hand-blocked prints, handwoven fabrics, and natural dyes are the hallmark of Anokhi's products, which include gorgeous garments for men, women, and children, and a wide range of feminine home furnishings—anything from duvet and cushion covers to napkins. Prices are significantly higher than those in the bazaars, but the quality of design is in another league. After stuffing your shopping basket, eat a healthy lunch at the **Organic Cafe,** which serves daily specials, salads, desserts, and fresh juices. Open daily 9am to 6pm. 2nd Floor, C-11, K.K. Sq., Prithviraj Marg, C-Scheme, (✆) **0141/400-7244.** www.anokhi.com.

Gem Palace ★★★ When the maharajas of Rajasthan were suddenly deprived of their privy purses in 1972, many were forced to sell off the family jewels. Gem Palace, whose owners had been serving their needs for four generations, was a discreet place to do so. Today you can admire these priceless items, now owned by the Kasliwals and displayed in this beautiful store, along with antiques from the Mughal period. You can also view the craftspeople here creating new pieces, destined for the necks, wrists, and fingers of the privileged all over the world; its celebrity customers have included Princess Diana, Bill Clinton, and Paul McCartney. This is arguably the best and most exclusive jewelry shop in Jaipur, but it's not the place to pick up a bargain. Open 10:30am to 7:30pm. Closed Sundays. M.I. Rd. (✆) **0141/236-3061** or 0141/237-4175. www.gempalacejaipur.com.

Hot Pink ★★★ We love the small, cool, stylish space of this designer boutique in the garden of Narain Niwas Palace. Browse for beautiful garments, fashion accessories, and textiles from 25 hot Indian designers; look for gorgeously stylish clothing by Rajesh Pratap Singh or the almost avant-garde designs of Manish Arora (who's branded as "Fish Fry" internationally). The menswear is highly desirable too, and there are some fantastic, bright, daring cushion covers that you'll want to cram into your luggage. If you're particularly interested in Indian fashion, this is a great place to strike up conversation with western designers who base themselves here because of great local innovations (Thierry

Journo is the French in-house designer). Narain Niwas Palace, Marain Singh Rd. ℭ **0141/510-8932.** www.hotpinkindia.com.

JewelryAmrapali ★★   In 1980, two young entrepreneurs, Rajesh Ajmera and Rajiv Arora, saw a gap in the market and started adapting traditional jewelry styles to appeal to a broader international market. Conveniently situated near Panch Batti and the city gate that leads into Jauhri Bazaar, Amrapali is famous for its tribal silver jewelry, but the gold showroom also contains some rare examples of *kundan* jewelry, a technique in which each gem is set by pressing fine strips of highly purified gold around it. Depending on how much you spend, you may be able to negotiate a discount. Open 11am to 6pm. Closed Sundays. M.I. Rd. ℭ **0141/237-7940** or 0141/236-2768.

K. S. Durlabhji, Emerald House ★   When a new emerald mine was discovered in Rhodesia (now Zimbabwe) in the 1920s, Mr. M. S. Durlabhji got on the very next boat and traveled south. Once there, he took one look at the deep-green quality of the emeralds and purchased the entire consignment, then continued to purchase every stone until the mine ran dry. Today his son Yogendra has a collection of emerald jewelry that makes jewelers across the world green with envy, and their buyers include a who's who of the world's top jewelers: Van Cleef, Harry Winston, Tiffany, Cartier, and Boucheron, to name a few. Subhash Marg, C-Scheme. ℭ **0141/237-2318** or -6044.

3 THE NATIONAL PARKS

The two most famous parks in Rajasthan, both within easy striking distance of Jaipur, are **Bharatpur-Keoladeo Ghana National Park,** a 2,600-hectare (6,400-acre) tract of land that attracts the largest concentration and variety of birdlife in Asia; and **Ranthambhore National Park,** which enjoys an enviable reputation as the one area where you are virtually guaranteed to see a tiger. Also relatively close to Jaipur (110km/68 miles; 2 hr.) is **Sariska National Park** (see "Wanted: Tigers," below). The Sariska Palace Hotel, an aspiring luxury hotel built by the Machiavellian Maharaja Jay Singh of Alwar (see "Once Were Warriors: The History of the Rajput," earlier in this chapter) is a rather lovely French-Indo concoction (if you like your buildings to resemble over-the-top confections) furnished with many original pieces (rotting trophies included). Reports of service have been less than satisfactory, and it's really only worthwhile to pop in for tea if you're in the area. By contrast, Ranthambhore is far more beautiful and has at least three excellent accommodations as well as a fascinating conservation history.

BHARATPUR & THE KEOLADEO GHANA NATIONAL PARK

Referred to as the Eastern Gateway to Rajasthan, Bharatpur lies almost exactly halfway between Delhi (152km/94 miles) and Jaipur (176km/109 miles), and is a mere 55km (34 miles) from the Taj Mahal. The town itself holds no fascination, but a few kilometers south on National Highway 11 is Keoladeo "Ghana" National Park. Recognized by UNESCO as a World Heritage Site, the park is definitely worth visiting if you're a keen birder, but it's not a must-see for people who don't know the difference between a lark and a peacock.

A natural depression of land that was initially flooded by Maharaja Suraj Mal in 1726, the park abounds in large tracts of wetlands (covering more than a third of the terrain) as well as wood, scrub, and grasslands, a combination that attracts a large number of

Wanted: Tigers

Project Tiger was a conservation initiative launched by Indira Gandhi, the late Indian prime minister, in 1973. Sadly it's central mission—to not only halt but boost the fast declining number of Bengal tigers in India—has been a failure, as the program has failed to prevent India's tiger population from plummeting to 1,411 (census data from Feb 2008): down from 3,642 in 2002, and an estimated 40,000 a century ago. The decline is largely as a result of poaching, but sadly mismanagement has also played a role, as evidenced recently when the Wildlife Institute of India (WII) airlifted three Bengal tigers (two females and a male) by helicopter from Ranthambore reserve to nearby Sariska, which has been tigerless for the past 4 years. A method developed in South Africa by pioneer conservationist Ian Player, this is the first relocation of its kind in India, and part of the WII £93 million emergency plan to revive the flagging population. However, recent DNA samples taken from the three tigers (to see whether they needed to bring in tigers from other parts of the country) have indicated that all three tigers are likely siblings, thereby drastically reducing their chances of becoming successful long term breeding partners.

migratory birds that fly thousands of miles to find sanctuary here. It was not always so—for centuries, the area was the Maharaja of Bharatpur's private hunting reserve, and in 1902 it was inaugurated by Lord Curzon as an official duck-shoot reserve (some 20 species of duck are found here). In the most shameful incident in the park's history, Lord Linlithgow, then Viceroy of India, shot 4,273 birds in 1 day—the inscription of his record can still be read on a pillar near Keoladeo Temple. Thankfully, the park became a sanctuary in 1956 and was ultimately upgraded to national park status in 1982.

Today the park supports more than 375 bird species, including a large variety of herons, kingfishers, pelicans, storks, and ducks. It is the only known wintering region of the rare and endangered Siberian crane, which flies 8,050km (5,000 miles) to get here. The numbers are indeed staggering, and birds will fill your vision throughout your visit—particularly during the winter months (Oct–Feb), when the resident bird population swells to over half a million.

Essentials

VISITOR INFORMATION The **wildlife office** is located at the main gate on National Highway 11 (© **05644/22-2777**). Entry is Rs 200 per person, Rs 200 per video camera. To really get into the excitement of birding, you should borrow a copy of Sálim Ali's *The Book of Indian Birds* (OUP India), or Rajpul Singh's *Birds of Bharatpur,* and start ticking off those sightings! If you're staying at The Bagh (reviewed below), you'll find an excellent range of guides, including several copies of Krys Kazmierczak's *A Field Guide to the Birds of India.*

GETTING THERE Bharatpur is a 4½-hour drive from Delhi; it's 55km (34 miles) west of Agra and 175km (108 miles) east of Jaipur. If you travel by train from Delhi, it will take 2½ hours by the convenient Kota Janshatabdi; it takes a little over 2 hours for this train to link you with Sawai Madhopur (Ranthambhore National Park). From Agra, the Marudhar Express gets you here in just 55 minutes.

GETTING AROUND   Park hours are 6:30am to 5pm in winter, and 6am to 6pm in summer. You can set off **on foot** or rent your own **bicycle** near the entrance to the park (Rs 25 per hour; some rental shops ask that you leave your passport or a deposit of no more than Rs 500), but roads aren't great and you will often find yourself on foot, actually burdened by the bike, especially if you try to traverse the dirt tracks. You can explore certain areas by **boat** (Rs 100), though if the drought persists, these will continue to be out of operation. The best way to get around the park is with a **cycle-rickshaw** or **horse-drawn tonga** (Rs 100 per hour); many of the rickshaw-*wallas* have spent years trundling visitors around and now have a good knowledge of the birdlife as well as keen eyesight (though a less than satisfactory command of English). If you want them to double as guides, they will expect a tip (Rs 200 is fair, depending on how long you use them). Official guides (Rs 200 per hour) carrying binoculars are also available at the entrance to the park; in a rather unwieldy arrangement, they travel alongside on their bicycles. The park now offers battery-operated **minibus tours** and **electric auto-rickshaw** rides through the park; these are considerably quieter than you might imagine; a 90-minute ride costs Rs 250.

Where to Stay & Dine

The Bagh ★★★   The Bagh is a truly classy, good-value oasis, and a perfect base—not only from which to explore the bird sanctuary, but as an alternative to busy, overrun Agra. The resort layout emphasizes space, peace, and privacy, and once you step through the gate, you'll feel far away from everything. There are three separate residential complexes, each set a considerable distance from the other and each comprising various large suites set along wide verandas with crenellated archways, classic cane armchairs, and the odd fountain or two. Here, the absence of televisions and minibars only adds to the thrill of the setting; when you're not out spotting birds, entertain yourself by lounging at the pool, getting rubbed down with Ayurvedic oils at the spa, or simply wandering through the property.

Old Agra-Achnera Rd., Pakka Bagh Village, Bharatpur 321 001 (3.5km/2¹/₄ miles from town; 55km/34 miles from Agra). (© **05644/22-8333** or -5191. Fax 05644/22-58051. www.thebagh.com. thebagh@hotmail.com. 23 units. Rs 7,200 deluxe double; Rs 9,000 junior suite; Rs 13,750; Rs 2,200 extra bed. Taxes extra. AE, MC, V. **Amenities:** Restaurant; bar; coffee shop; guided tours and bird sanctuary guides; gym; library; pool; spa with Ayurvedic massage, Jacuzzi, sauna, and steam room; yoga. *In room:* A/C, fan.

RANTHAMBHORE NATIONAL PARK

Ranthambhore—for many decades the hunting preserve of the princes of Jaipur—covers a mere 40,000 hectares (98,800 acres) but offers a fascinating combination of crumbling monuments, living temples, wild beauty, and your best chance to spot a wild tiger. Set within a high, jagged escarpment, **Ranthambhore Fort** (save a few hours for a visit) has towered over the park's forests for nearly a thousand years and has witnessed many a bloody combat—even the Mughal emperor Akbar fought a battle for supremacy here in the 16th century. Inside the fort (open dawn–dusk at no cost) lie a number of ruined palaces, step wells, and a celebrated Ganesha temple visited every year in September by two million pilgrims who come to worship during the Lord Ganesha's birthday. But it is the forests, that lie shimmering in the gorges below, scattered with more ancient crumbling monuments, that attract the foreign pilgrims, who come during the winter months to catch a glimpse of the mighty Bengal tiger. Sightings are recorded fairly regularly—it is said that between 75% and 95% of all the photographs ever taken of a tiger in the wild have been taken in Ranthambhore. This has meant that the 26-odd tigers living here have

Free Range: The Trade in Tiger Parts

It is a fact that most of the poaching in India is driven by demand from China, the world's biggest market for tiger body parts, due to the fact that the use of tiger bone is common in prescriptions of traditional Chinese medicines. At the time of writing there is a de jure (although not in practice) ban on the internal trade in tiger body parts in China (imposed in 1993), although in 2009 there has been a surge in Indian tiger deaths with at least 68 killings. India has approximately 1,300 wild tigers, while China has only a few. Consequently, and in contradiction to its legislated ban, China sanctions the establishment of controversial tiger farms to harvest and supply the parts. There are around 4,000 tigers in such farms that clearly encourage consumer demand of the parts, which then spills over into the wild tiger sanctuaries. Much of the parts are smuggled through Nepal and Myanmar, but a fair amount also find their way through India. China recently announced there's a strong possibility they'll lift the ban and strangely they feel that the farms are not much of a concern for conservation; this thinking could be catastrophic for the tigers. China, as India, is a member of CITES (Convention on International Trade in Endangered Species), which has called for an end to the breeding of tigers for their parts. If such a ban is lifted it may be the beginning of the end of these tigers.

become totally habituated to human observation and are almost entirely indifferent to the sight and sound of vehicles and camera flashes.

The success of the park is due in no small measure to the efforts of Fateh Singh Rathore. A member of the princely family of Jodhpur, Rathore was made field director of Ranthambhore in 1972, the year tiger hunting was banned in India. Almost single-handedly, Rathore mapped and built the park's roads and persuaded 12 entire villages to move voluntarily, having arranged financial compensation and constructed new villages with modern facilities that included schools, wells, and electricity. He also used a powerful spiritual argument: It is the tiger that always accompanies the goddess and demon-slayer Durga (who embodies the power of good over evil), so it therefore deserves protection; however, its survival remains forever compromised in a habitat shared with humans (see "Free Range: The Trade in Tiger Parts" above).

Under Rathore's protection, the Ranthambhore tiger population increased from 13 to 40, and his dedicated study and photography of the subjects brought much of the tiger's beauty and plight into the international spotlight. But at no small cost—Rathore was awarded the WWF International Valour Award after a mob of villagers, angry at no longer having access to their ancestral lands for grazing and hunting, attacked him, shattering his kneecaps and fracturing his skull. On his release from the hospital, Rathore simply returned to the village and challenged them to do it again.

After a brief scare in the early 1990s, when poaching (apparently by the park's own wardens) almost halved the resident tiger population, numbers stabilized by the year 2000. Today, people like Rathore and Valmik Thapar, one of India's foremost campaigners for the protection of the tiger, are once again fighting a crucial battle against widespread poaching; they argue that the authorities set up for the protection of the reserve

Not Just a Pretty Face: Fascinating Tiger Tidbits

Unlike most cats, tigers have round pupils and are adept swimmers. Cubs are, however, born blind; it takes 1 to 2 weeks before they can see. When a tiger sticks its tongue out, curls its lips, and closes its eyes slightly (as if snarling), it's actually checking for scents in the air. This behavior is called the "Flehmen Response," wherein the tiger analyzes smells using sensory receptors in the roof of its mouth. Tigers are immensely powerful—strong enough to kill and drag an animal heavier than itself—and can eat over 30 kilograms (66 lb.) of meat in a single night. Females make better hunters, while the males are notoriously lazy—even when it comes to sex. When a female is in heat and makes a mating call, the male will often hide until the female seeks him out and foists herself upon him. Much like the human fingerprint, every tiger's pug markings (footprints) are totally unique. By the time hunting was banned in the 1970s, only 2,000 tigers were left out of an estimated population of 50,000 in the 19th century. Today some 6,000 survive throughout the world, of which between 2,000 and 3,000 are found in India.

are doing little. In fact, unofficial stories tell that Rathore was summarily banned form the park at one stage, having been too vocal against corrupt officials and their hopeless policies. But Rathore and Thapar were proven right; in mid-2005 an independent committee appointed to carry out a tiger census discovered that numbers in Ranthambhore had dwindled from 40 to 26, in spite of the presence of several new cubs. Some local tiger aficionados are more positive, however, and will remind you that by mid-2007 there had been a 2-year period without any poaching incidents; apparently there are now six cubs in the tourist zone and 12 in the entire reserve.

If you want to understand the tiger politics of the region, you will no doubt find yourself engaged in intense discussion at Sher Bagh and Ranthambhore Bagh, both good accommodations. Fateh Singh's daughter-in-law manages Sher Bagh, while his son Goverdhan, a doctor, runs the nearby charitable hospital for the welfare of local people; it's one of the best-run rural hospitals in India. They also run an excellent rural school (visitors are welcome to visit both the school and hospital)—all this based on the philosophy that unless one develops solutions in concert with local people, it won't be possible to save the tiger for posterity. With an estimated 90,000 humans and almost a million livestock living within a 5km (3-mile) radius of the park, the pressure on this island of wilderness remains immense, but its popularity and the efforts of many wildlife supporters will hopefully stand it in good stead. You can also go to the website of **Travel Operators For Tigers** (www.toftiger.org), a U.K.-based organization promoting responsible tiger tourism and tiger research.

While tiger sightings are relatively common, don't expect the experience to be necessarily a romantic one. It can be ruined by the presence of other vehicles, particularly the open-topped 20-seater Canters buses with whooping kids on board. Only a limited number of vehicles are allowed at any sighting, but this regulation is not always respected, hence the designation of different routes (see "Game Drive Formalities," below) to keep number densities spread throughout the park. Even if you don't spot a tiger (and be prepared for this eventuality), the sheer physical beauty of the park is worth experiencing—from lotus-filled lakes and dense jungle to craggy, boulder-strewn cliffs and golden grasslands. Other species worth looking for include caracal (a wildcat), crocodile, *nilgai* (large antelope resembling cattle), *chital* (spotted deer), black buck (delicate buck with spiraling horns), *chinkara* (a dainty gazelle), and sambar (their distinctive barking call often warns of the presence of a tiger nearby). The park also has leopards (notoriously shy), wild boars, and sloth bears, and is rich in birdlife—over 400 resident and migrant species.

Note, too, that park authorities are planning to introduce a small safari park that should provide impatient visitors who are hell-bent on spotting tiger with an almost zoo-like experience. If you're desperate, ask your host about this development.

Essentials

VISITOR INFORMATION   Ranthambhore National Park is closed July through September due to the monsoon. Unlike at Bharatpur, traffic and numbers are closely regulated. For general information, call the **Sawai Madhopur Tourist Centre** (Sawai Madhopur Railway Station; ℂ **07462/22-0808;** Mon–Sat 10am–1pm and 2–5pm).

GETTING THERE   The nearest airport is Jaipur's, which lies 180km (112 miles) away; it is just under a 4-hour drive. Alternatively, the sprawling village of Sawai Madhopur (10km/6¼ miles from the park gates) is well connected by rail to Jaipur (just over 2 hr.) and to Jodhpur (8 hr.), and is on the main line between Delhi (5½ hr.) and Mumbai. All accommodations listed will arrange pickups from the station.

GAME-DRIVE FORMALITIES   Only official vehicles with sanctioned drivers and guides are permitted to take visitors into the park. There are two types of vehicle: jeeps and Canter buses. The latter—ferrying up to 25 passengers—should be avoided, even though they're slightly cheaper. To ensure your place in a game-drive jeep, it's best to arrange well in advance through your hotel. Places on the 40 vehicles that are allowed into the park for each drive session are often booked up to 2 months in advance. For bookings in a jeep, call the **Project Tiger office** (ℂ **07462/22-0223;** Mon–Sat 5–7am and noon–2pm for advance booking). If you have no alternative, Canter buses can be booked a day in advance at the tourist reception center at RTDC's Hotel Vinayak. If you book with any of the accommodations recommended below, they will arrange all this for you (they also enjoy unofficial priority access to the park, and seem to be able to arrange entrance at short notice, although you shouldn't count on it). Please note, however, that you must let your host know when and how often you would like to go on a game drive as soon as possible—these officially need to be booked 60 days in advance. The price varies depending on where you stay; the official rate charged by the park is Rs 800 for a seat on a jeep (which includes park entry, but excludes a Rs 200 video fee), but you can also book through your lodge, essentially sparing you the bother of exchanging cash at the park entrance. For a wonderful introduction to the park, ask your host to find a copy of *The Ultimate Ranthambhore Guide* (Rs 175) by Sheena Sippy and Sanjna Kapoor, also sold at the park's gate.

Tip: Although the park's seven routes are assigned randomly, and you are normally not allowed to choose which route you would like to go on, you *can* request that your host try to have at least one game drive either near a body of water in the park or in an area where a tiger was spotted the day before. The best time to visit the park is between November and April (Jan–Apr is best for tiger sightings). The park closes during the monsoon season (July–Sept).

There are two game drives: The early morning drive (winter 7:30–10:30am; summer 6:30–9:30am) is often preferable to the afternoon drive (winter 3–5:30pm; summer 4–6:30pm), given that temperatures can make for muggy afternoons. However, you should pack something warm—it can get cold both early in the morning and once darkness approaches.

Routes (which drivers are pretty much forced to stick to) and guides are randomly allotted, which means you may be on a tight budget yet find yourself in a jeep with an excellent guide, watching a tiger bathe in the lotus lake that fronts the beautiful 250-year-old Jogi Mahal, while a hapless guest paying top dollar for the same trip trundles around with a monosyllabic guide with halitosis. Note that the overhaul of tourist entry procedures and rules are a constant topic for bureaucratic debate, and procedures may change on a whim at any time, so check ahead.

Where to Stay & Dine

Almost all the best options are on Ranthambhore Road, which flanks the park. If you're watching your budget, a good-value option is the tastefully rustic **Ranthambhore Bagh** (© **07462/22-1728,** or 011/2691-4417 or 94-1403-0221 reservations in Delhi; www.ranthambhorebagh.com), where you can book twin-bedded luxury tents for Rs 4,950 with all meals included; Rs 1,500 per person for a game drive by jeep. Located 5km (3 miles) from the park gate, accommodations here are simple but comfortable (it has slightly cheaper traditional walled rooms—with A/C—if the tents sound too rough (Rs 4,300), and the fixed-menu buffet meals are often served outdoors. Frequented by photographers and conservationists, this is a good place to meet and talk with wildlife enthusiasts. Another option worth highlighting is **Khemvillas ★★** (Khem Villas, VPO Sherpur Khiljipur, Dist. Sawai Madhopur, Rajasthan; © **094/1403-0262** or 074/6225-2099; khemvillas@anokhi.com), rated by *Condé Nast Traveler* on its Hot List Hotels 2007, this 4-hectare (10-acre) resort has a choice of premium, free-standing cottages (Rs 16,000), each with its own plunge pools and outdoor showers; rustic but comfortable tents (Rs 13,000), and four smart, airy modern bedrooms in the main building with views from the top floor (Rs 9,000). This is a great, authentic place to stay with a lot of soul, and if you want to be close to the park in understated luxury this is recommended.

Aman-i-Khás ★★★ A stay here is truly magical, utterly romantic, and certainly the most perfect integration of luxury and nature in Rajasthan. The superb and spacious air-conditioned (or heated) white tents are located a sensible distance away from one another, and featuring typical Aman touches of discreet luxury. Designed to echo the look of a traditional step well, the pool here is equally blissful—another perfectly idyllic spot to unwind between game drives. Each room is assigned a batman who is superbly efficient yet completely invisible unless you need him—screen windows open and close, beds are turned in, bathrobes replaced, all quite magically. Food is simply superb—fresh organic produce from the garden enhances refreshingly delicate flavors. At night, lanterns light the path from your room to the outdoor lounge, where a giant *uruli* (traditional bronze bowl) forms the central fireplace, and guests gather to enjoy the night sky, the ethereal calm, and the occasional call from the wild.

Ranthambhore Rd. (just beyond Sher Bagh), Sawai Madhopur. © **07462/25-2052** or -2224. Fax 07462/25-2178. Reservations, in Singapore: © **65/6887-3337.** Fax 65/6887-3338. www.amanresorts.com. reservations@amanresorts.com. 10 units. Oct–Apr only. $1,000 double. Minimum 2 (preferably 3) nights' stay required, arriving Mon or Thurs. Rate includes all meals and drinks; 10% tax and 10% service charge extra. Game drives $60 minimum per person. AE, MC, DC, V. **Amenities:** Dining tent; library/lounge; outdoor lounge w/fireplace; room service; spa tent. *In room:* A/C, cooler box.

Sher Bagh ★★ If you're looking for a more authentic safari experience, this intimate camp is a great choice. The irrepressible and charming owner, Jaisal Singh, is a superb host (when around), and a member of what could be described as Ranthambhore royalty. (He is Fateh Singh Rathore's godchild and practically grew up in the park between bouts of polo playing and hobnobbing with the rich and famous.) Accommodations comprise a semicircle of comfortable tents (originally designed for the Maharaja of Jodhpur's hunting expeditions), each with its own veranda and an en-suite bathroom. Tents are a little too close together and hot during the day (fans, but no air-conditioning), but there are a number of places to relax; the coolest is the first-floor bar/lounge area in the main building, which looks and feels a bit like a Spanish hacienda. Meals are a welcome relief from standard North Indian fare. At night, when the lanterns and torches are lit, the camp really comes into its own. Engaging in idle chatter while imbibing G&Ts, your feet in the sand and stars above, makes this one of the most relaxing experiences in North India.

Sherpur-Khiljipur, Sawai Madhopur 322 001. ℂ **07462/25-2120** or -2119. Reservations: ℂ 011/2374-3194 or -3195. Fax 011/2334-5429. www.sujanluxury.com or www.sherbagh.com. reservations@sujanluxury.com. 12 units. Rs 20,000 double. Rate includes all meals, morning and evening tea, and transfers. Taxes extra. MC, V. Closed Apr 15–Oct 1. **Amenities:** Dining tent; bar and jungle bar; hospital-on-call; massage; excursions room service; complimentary station transfer.

Vanyavilās ★★★ Set on 8 hectares (20 acres) of landscaped gardens, this superb resort retreat exemplifies the type of cosseted luxury of the Oberoi. Surrounded by a mud wall enclosing a wraparound garden the tent "rooms" are not as safari-like as those at Aman-i-Khás, and the overall outdoor setting not quite as back-to-nature, but they are nevertheless gorgeous, featuring huge canvas roofs shot through with gold sparkles, teak floors, solid walls hung with artwork, opulent Indo-colonial furnishings, and all the modern conveniences. Bathrooms are the size of most hotel rooms. The property does sprawl somewhat amid lotus ponds and lush bird-filled vegetation, forcing rather long walks (you can, of course, call for a golf cart), and, unlike Sher Bagh and Aman i Khas, the well manicured surroundings give you little sense of being near a wilderness. But the superb service, great dining, excellent spa, sparkling pool, and sheer opulence of the public spaces more than make up for this. Best of all is the opportunity to sit in on one of the regular lectures given by Fateh Singh Rathore, the man who put Ranthambhore on the map.

Ranthambhore Rd., Sawai Madhopur 322 001. ℂ **07462/22-3999.** Reservations: ℂ **800/6-OBEROI** [623764] in the U.S., or 1600/11-2030. www.oberoihotels.com. 25 units. Rs 36,500 double. Taxes extra. AE, DC, MC, V. **Amenities:** Restaurant; library bar; billiards room; chauffeur-driven cars; currency exchange; doctor-on-call; elephant safaris; fitness tent; game drives; Internet (charges as below); pool; complimentary station transfer; spa; observation tower; yoga. *In room:* A/C, TV, DVD/CD music system (including selection of CDs and DVDs), minibar, Wi-Fi (30 min Rs 113; 60 min Rs 225; 24 hrs. Rs 885).

Perfect Pit Stop Between Jaipur & Udaipur

Of the two recommendations below, our first choice is for Shahpura Bagh, not least because it gives you easy access to the nearby village which is still as yet unspoiled by tourism.

Deogarh Mahal ★ & Fort Seengh Sagar ★★ Comprising an ornate 17th-century fort-palace with domed turrets and balconies, Deogarh Palace towers over the village that shares (pronounced Devgarh) below. Rooms vary considerably (you are welcome to and should look around when you arrive, and choose one), and some are beautifully furnished, with little done to change the authenticity of the architecture (right down to the slightly erratic plumbing); others are looking dated. Book one of the six suites (there are three categories but ask for nos. 235, 250–251) and pretend that all you survey from your private balcony is yours. It is authentic (ask for the historical audio tour researched by William Dalrymple and proprietor historian Col. Randhir Singhji), but thanks to the town village temple's loudspeaker (which chimes on the half hour and extensively on the hour!) as well as regular group tours it is not as peaceful as nearby sister establishment, **Fort Seengh Sagar.** An island fortress set on a tranquil lake surrounded by palms, acacias, and rocky granite outcrops, this intimate, old hunting fort has been converted into a luxury villa with just four suites, each a rich amalgam of traditional Rajasthani furniture and modern elements. Each room has a private lake-view balcony; there's also a sublime public terrace where you can dine under the stars, and on winter nights a roaring fire vies with the stars for attention. Both palace and fort are personally managed by Col. Randhir Singhji, the Thakur of Deogarh, and his son VB, who will make you feel like a long-lost aristocrat. Note that Deogarh is ideal to stop at after or before you've visited the Ranakpur Temples and Kumbhalgarh Fort (see Excursions under Udaipur entry), en route to or from Jaipur (280km/174 miles away) or Jodhpur (170km/105 miles away).

Deogarh Madaria, District Rajsamand, Rajasthan 313 331. (℃ **02904/25-2777.** Fax 02904/25-2555. www. deogarhmahal.com. info@deogarhmahal.com. Deogarh: 60 units. Low season (Apr–Sept)/high season (Oct–Mar): Rs 7,000/Rs 8,050 deluxe double; Rs 9,000/Rs 10,350 deluxe suite; Rs 12,000/Rs 14,800 royal suite. Seenghh Sagar: 4 units. Rs 15,000 suite, with discounts on each additional suite; Rs 48,000 for all 4 suites. Taxes extra. AE, DC, MC, V. **Amenities:** 2 restaurants (1 rooftop); bar; coffee shop; lounge; babysitting; bicycles; doctor-on-call; gym; henna; horse riding; Internet (Rs 100/hr.); Jacuzzi; jeep safaris, library; Ayurvedic massage; movies; pool; kids' pool; snooker; table tennis. *In room:* A/C, TV (not in all the rooms), minibar (and at Seeghh Sagar).

Shahpura Bagh ★★★ (**Kids**) Located precisely midway between Jaipur and Udaipur, this is one of our favorite destinations, a place for calm contemplation and serious relaxation. Beautifully appointed and set in a lush, verdant, 18-hectare (45-acre) wooded estate, the buildings are pukka colonial-era, with a classic veranda lined by squat white pillars. Most guest rooms are vast, double-volume affairs with tall, arched windows that make for plenty of light, and large well-appointed bathrooms. The large man-made dam along the perimeter of the north and west boundaries of the property is a bird-watcher's paradise (with an island heronry) while the lush forested surrounds attract jungle cats and jackals. Aside from the immaculate accommodations, Shahpura Bagh has an incredibly homely atmosphere, because it is still the family's home and is run as such with home-cooked meals (prearrange for authentic Rajasthani cooking lessons) served at the family table (though arrangements can be made to decamp to various romantic spots around the property). Their expansive new infinity pool is one of the best in Rajasthan, presided over by a towering pepul tree and surrounded by peacocks and date palms. Packed lunches for picnic walks and cycle tours make it easy to spend the day exploring the lush surrounds or the quaint adjacent village.

Shahpura Bagh, District Bhilwara 311 404. (℃ **98-281-22012** or -22013. Fax 01484/22-2077. www.shahpura bagh.com. res@shahpurabagh.com. 10 units. Rs 10,500 double; Rs 14,500 royal suite; Rs 2,500 extra bed. Rates include breakfast and one jeep safari with nonalcoholic refreshments; taxes extra. 20% discount May–Sept. MC, V. **Amenities:** Dining room; bar; lounge; boating and canoeing; bicycles; doctor-on-call; Internet (free); library; room service; transfers by arrangement; TV lounge; yoga and meditation. *In room:* A/C, fan, WorldSpace radio, Broadband Internet complimentary in some rooms.

---

4 BUNDI

210km (130 miles) S of Jaipur; 279km (173 miles) SE of Udaipur; 438km (272 miles) SW of Agra

If you have a few extra days, then the small town of Bundi, established in 1241, is worth considering, not least to view the architectural magnificence of a palace and fort that clings to the cliff above the town. The lack of modernization (although arguably not a

benefit to its residents) and presence of temples, cenotaphs, and step wells, as well as its **543**
renowned school of miniature paintings (arguably the best-value paintings in Rajasthan)
are a further boon. Approached through a long, winding gorge, the town is protected by
the embracing Aravalli Hills, topped by Taragarh Fort (which interestingly has no
Mughal design influences), and eclipsed only by the new telecom tower ironically shaped
as a Mughal minaret. Its narrow streets, with tiny cupboardlike shops raised a yard or
more above street level to avoid the monsoon floods, are pretty much unchanged for
centuries, but the community has lost much of its naïve charm and cleanliness that so
delighted us when we first discovered it a decade ago. If you're looking for a more
untouched village experience, we recommend you visit the one near Shahpura Bagh.

Garh Palace ★★ (described by Rudyard Kipling as "the work of goblins" and one of
the few examples of pure Rajput style) is still Bundi's chief attraction and while the Palace's exterior is astounding, much of the interior is falling apart; nevertheless, entry to
some areas (with spectacular views of the blue-tinged town below) is allowed (entry Rs
60, Rs 50 camera, Rs 100 video; dawn–dusk) and makes for fascinating, hassle free
exploration. The labyrinthine network of rooms, chambers, balconies, and nooks and
crannies turns up a good number of surprises, including murals in various states of faded
elegance. Above the main part of the palace, you can also visit the arcaded **Chitra Shala**,
which is decorated with many of the fine murals in the miniature style the town is
famous for (free entry; dawn–dusk). Chitra Shala alone is worth the steep walk up to the
imposing gates, as are the views of the town—much of it painted the same blue seen in
the more famous "blue city" of Jodhpur. For an even better vantage point, keep ascending
the rough path that leads up to Taragarh (not necessarily to the top), for a great sense of
peace (you're unlikely to encounter anyone, bar the Hanuman langur monkeys and a
lone goat herder) and superb photo-ops of the town. Back down in town, take a few
minutes to visit **Raniji-ki-Baori** ★★ (the state's most impressive step well), which lies
in a small park in the center of town; it dates from the 17th century and features ornately
carved gates, pillars, and friezes.

Note: There is absolutely no need to waste time with the stuffy Moti Mahal Museum
of rotting taxidermied animals and Bundi family portraits.

Sights farther afield, like **Sukh Mahal,** a summer palace where Kipling wrote *Kim,* are
best explored with Haveli Braj Bhushanjee's picnic and sightseeing tour, or with the
expert guide Om Prakash Kuki. Closer to town (2km/1¼ miles) are the Royal Cenotaphs
(Shaar Bagh), which are way better than Jaisalmer's and reputed to be the best in India—
ask the caretaker for the key. This can also be arranged through Bundi Haveli.

ESSENTIALS

VISITOR INFORMATION   The **Tourist Information Bureau** (© 0747/244-3697;
Mon–Sat 10am–5pm, closed second Sat of the month and Sun) is located at Circuit
House, but the owners of the Haveli Braj Bhushanjee heritage hotel (see below) are a
mine of information, supplying you with maps, arranging transport, and ready with
advice on anything from how much to pay for a rickshaw to opening hours. For an expert
guide with true archeological and historical passion for all sights in and around Bundi
call Om Prakash Kuki (on his mobile © 982/840-4527 or arrange through Bundi
Haveli). You can usually change money at your guest house and there are several currency
traders in town; ATMs are in the southern part of the town.

GETTING THERE   You'll likely be arriving by car which is 37km (23 miles) from Kota
arriving by bus. If you're bussing it, it's only a short Rs 40 at most to the guesthouses.

The better option is rail now that the train stops in Bundi proper (20 minutes after the Kota stop) and is well connected to the rest of the state, including the main Delhi-to-Mumbai line, Jaipur, Sawai Madhopur, and Chittaurgarh. From the station it's a short Rs 50 rickshaw ride to your hotel. Kota is 130km (81 miles) by road from Sawai Madhopur and 175km (96 miles) from Chittaurgarh, so you can either visit it after you see Ranthambhore and/or Jaipur or combine it with a trip from Udaipur via Chittaurgarh. An A/C taxi to Bundi from Kota will run you Rs 600; a jeep costs Rs 550.

GETTING AROUND You can get around the town on foot with ease. Should you tire, auto-rickshaws traverse the narrow streets. If you book into Haveli Braj Bhushanjee or Bundi Haveli, the proprietors will arrange all your transport at very reasonable prices—yet another reason the hotel is so highly recommended. Expect to pay around Rs 1,200 for an air-conditioned taxi for the day.

WHERE TO STAY & DINE

Bundi Haveli Hotel ★★ This 250-year-old beautifully restored *haveli* literally opposite Naval Sagar, the town lake (and 3 min. from Haveli Braj Bhushanjee), is owned and managed by Salim and Lulu. Its loving renovation, clean lines, and whitewashed walls with splashes of fine, colorful detail are testament to their eye (and successful other business, Nazim Handicraft, based in Udaipur). Rooms are uncluttered and free of mismatching antiques and ageing bric-a-brac found so common with haveli-style decor. For a beautiful super deluxe room ask for no. 109, which has partial lake and fort views. Room 107 is large and spacious, while 110 and 104 are the Haveli Suites, where Mick Jagger reputedly spent a night. The restaurant serves both typical nonvegetarian and vegetarian dishes and can be taken downstairs in the open air courtyard or on the rooftop terrace accompanied by 360-degree views.

Bundi Haveli Hotel, 107 Balchand Parra, near Naval Sagar, Bundi 323 001. ℭ **747/244-6716**. Fax 0747/244-6046. www.hotelbundihaveli.com. info@hotelbundihaveli.com. 12 units. Rs 1,000 standard double (no A/C but with fans); Rs 2,000 super deluxe double; Rs 3,000 Haveli Suites. 10% taxes extra only on suites. MC, V. **Amenities:** Restaurant, roof dining; doctor-on-call; Internet (Rs 50/hr.); room service; *In room:* A/C (nonstandard room), fan, TV.

Haveli Braj Bhushanjee ★★ Situated on a narrow lane inside the walled city, just below the palace, this is an authentic and professionally run guesthouse in India, managed by the discreetly proud Braj Bhushanjee brothers (four of whose ancestors were prime ministers of Bundi State in the 19th c.). Many of the walls are covered with exceptional-quality murals (recently repainted by a local expert), and though each room is traditionally decorated, the choice of objects, fabrics, and carpets (all sourced from Bundi and surroundings) shows a great deal of thought and innate flair. Two brand new rooftop suites were being built at time of writing, promising the best views of the Fort and Palace; on top of these will arguably be the best terrace in Bundi, with a 360-degree view. No alcohol is served and meat is definitely not permitted on the premises but the home-cooked meals are of exceptional quality.

Below Fort, opposite Ayurvedic Hospital, Bundi 323 001. ℭ **0747/244-2322** or -2509. Fax 0747/244-2142. www.kiplingsbundi.com. 25 units. Rs 750 economy double; Rs 1,500 standard double; Rs 2,850 deluxe double; Rs 5,000 super deluxe double. Taxes extra. MC, V. **Amenities:** Dining hall; doctor-on-call; Internet (Rs 50/hr.); room service. *In room:* A/C, fan, TV, Wi-Fi (Rs 50/hr.).

5 SHEKHAWATI

200km (124 miles) SW of Delhi; 160km (99 miles) NW of Jaipur

Shekhawati, known as the open-air art gallery of Rajasthan, lies in the roughly triangular area between Delhi, Jaipur, and Bikaner, and encompasses the districts of Jhunjhunu, Sikar, and Churu. Its largely semidesert, wide open (uninhabited) spaces offer a peaceful respite from the cities, and its ubiquitous evergreen *kejri* trees create a far greener landscape than the Jaisalmer area. But the primary drawing card is its remarkable art collection—unusual for the unique painting styles and for the fact that the exhibition space consists of the exterior and interior walls of literally hundreds of havelis, temples, cenotaphs, wells, and forts in the region. The trend for decorating walls in this way was imported from the courts of Amber and Jaipur, where the Rajput princes in turn were inspired by the Mughal emperors' patronage of the miniature-mural art form. The Shekhawati's patronage was funded by duties imposed on merchandise carried across that section of the Spice Route that traversed their region (cleverly, the local barons here ensured that their duties were lower than those of the house of Jaipur, thereby diverting trade), or by raids across the borders, but patronage truly flourished during the British Raj, a period when the Shekhawati merchants, renowned for their business acumen, moved to the ports of Calcutta, Madras, and Bombay to capitalize on the growing trade in these new centers. There they made small fortunes and celebrated their wealth by adorning their mansions—an age-old urge, and the result here is a great deal more interesting than anything Martha Stewart might have suggested.

The demand was such that skilled artists could not paint fast enough. Even local masons tried their hand, injecting a wonderful naiveté and humor into many of the paintings. Subject matters vary tremendously, from mythological stories and epics such as the *Ramayana* and *Mahabharata* to local legends of battles and hunts and of course the ever-present erotica, nearly all of which has now been painted over; but perhaps the most amusing are copies of British photographs featuring hot-air balloons, "airships," trains, and cars—objects most of the painters had never set their eyes on but faithfully rendered according to the descriptions and prints supplied by their employers.

Today there are some 30 "painted towns" in the region, but the most essential to include in a first-time itinerary are **Ramgarh** (the town with the most painted buildings), **Nawalgarh** (second in number, but with a superior selection, some better preserved than Ramgarh's, particularly the restored Anandi Lal Poddar Haveli), **Fatehpur** (together with Jhunjhunu, this is Shekhawati's oldest town, featuring murals that predate any others in the region as well as the **Haveli Française;** see box below), and **Mandawa** (a quaint town with a number of beautiful painted buildings, and centrally located with the best accommodations in the area).

Armed with a good map (see "Visitor Information," below) and a car and driver, it is relatively easy to explore the surrounds on your own—not least because of the usual army of small kids eager to accompany you and point out the relevant sights. But to know more about the history of the buildings, the artisans, and the area, you may wish to hire the services of a guide through the hotels listed below. Most of the buildings are uninhabited and caretaker families usually look after the ones that are, with the real owners being in the big Indian cities of Kolkata and Delhi; and are accessible for a small fee (Rs 10/15–Rs 20/25 per haveli to the caretaker or watchman); negotiating payment (and whether you should offer to pay at all) is where a guide comes in handy. (Remember that,

Haveli Française

In 1999 French artist Nadine Le Prince bought a 19th-century haveli in Fatehpur and, with the help of Dinesh Dhabhai of Mandawa Haveli, spent the next year locating the right artisans, paints, and methods of restoring it. Now called **Haveli Nadine** (though locals call it *angrez ki haveli*—Englishwoman's haveli), it's been converted into a cultural center that's aimed at bringing together the art of Rajasthani with that of foreign artists, and preserving the art forms of Shekhawati. When rain and humidity damaged her newly restored haveli in 2003, Nadine waited for the walls to dry up, and began restoration work in earnest again. Serious art lovers should make an effort to stop here, particularly when an exhibition is on; you can discover Rajasthan through paintings or sculptures not available in any of the regular tourist centers. Either way, touring this gorgeous, painstakingly restored haveli is one way you can visualize what this region's art might have looked like in its heyday. It's generally open between 8am and 7pm each day, but call to check (© **01571/23-3024;** nadine.leprince@free.fr; Rs 100 admission).

as is the case in all temples, you may need to *remove your shoes* to enter the inhabited havelis; ask before you enter.) Although the region evokes real passion in some and has resulted in a number of excellent books, it must be said that many of the murals are mere shadows of their former selves, either defaced by human indifference—posters and graffiti mar many of the walls—or faded by the increased water supply to the region, the rise in the water table creating damper conditions (see box below).

Note that including this area in your itinerary can be tricky, unless you are intent on traveling the long, dusty haul through Bikaner (where overnighting is not advised) to Jaisalmer, or journeying directly from Delhi and then moving on to Jaipur or vice versa, both of which mean many hours spent on a bumpy, nerve-wracking road with virtually no scenery except the brightly colored boulder-laden trucks bearing down on you. You should know that the area has become a European tour groups' delight and seems to be oversold by French and Italian agents.

ESSENTIALS

VISITOR INFORMATION Jhunjhunu has a tourist office (© **015945/23-2909;** Mon–Sat 10am–5pm; closed Sun and second Sat of the month), but you'll have more success finding information and arranging a guide through your hotel. Ilay Cooper's illustrated *The Painted Towns of Shekhawati* (Prakash 2009, or Mapin Guides) is still the original bible, with a concise history of the region as well as a breakdown of towns, easy-to-follow maps, and listings of all the sites worth visiting. You can purchase a copy at Books Corner in Jaipur, at Mandawa Castle, or at Desert Resort. Another book worth considering is *Shekhawati: Rajasthan's Painted Homes* by Pankaj Rakesh and Karoki Lewis (Lustre Press Roli Books).

GETTING THERE Public transport is relatively limited, so the easiest way to explore the area is to hire a car and driver in Jaipur or Delhi, stop at a few towns along the way, and overnight at Mandawa or Nawalgarh. Or you could take a 2-day detour to Mandawa en route from Delhi to Jaipur (driving time Delhi-Mandawa 7 hr.; Mandawa-Jaipur 4 hr.) or vice versa; or if driving on to or from Jaisalmer overnight at Gajner Palace to break the monotony.

with ease. For a reputable local driver and guide contact Indoarya at ℂ **011/2651-1634;**
indoarya@vsnl.net. Once there, it is relatively easy to explore each area on foot with a
guide or by following Ilay Cooper's detailed, hand drawn maps in his instructional *The
Painted Towns of Shekhawati.*

DRIVING TOUR Travel from Jaipur (or Samode Palace) to Sikar, stopping to look at
the *havelis* (historic homes or mansions of wealthy merchants) in Nawalgarh. Have lunch
at Roop Niwas, and then set off for Mandawa and overnight there either at its labyrinthine Castle or the rustic, tranquil Desert Resort. For the best accommodation in the area
use Mandawa as your base and spend 2 nights. From here it is a short hop to Jhunjhunu,
Nawalgarh, and Alsisar. The following day, visit Fatehpur (see "Haveli Française," below)
and Lachhmangarh before heading south to Sikar and back down to Jaipur or onward to
Delhi.

WHERE TO STAY & DINE

If you're traveling here directly from Delhi, a highly recommended overnight stop is
Amanbagh (see "Where to Stay & Dine En Route To or From Delhi," earlier in this
chapter). Situated 3½ hours from Delhi on the far eastern outskirts of Shekhawati, it is
one of the best destination hotels in the country.

Castle Mandawa ★★ The castle is one of the most authentic heritage properties in
Rajasthan: A labyrinthine, well restored former abode of the Maharajah of Mandawa,
whose portraits and family pictures adorn the walls. Given the age of the property—it
dates from the 16th century—the conversion to modern hotel in the 1970's has been
remarkably sensitive, maintaining much of the original feel of the castle without sacrific-
ing comfort. (Bear in mind that this cannot be said of the most recently added wing,
which features boring, uniformly sized rooms with none of the authentic charm of the
original castle.) If you have a poor sense of direction, the journey from the veranda bar
to your room can be challenging, but really, getting lost and clambering up and down
the narrow staircases is half the fun. Rooms vary hugely, but generally you pay for what
you get; nos. 303, 304, 308, 313, 314, and 401 are particularly lovely; no. 215 is smaller
(standard) but also a good choice.

Mandawa, Jhunjhunu District, Shekhawati 333 704. ℂ **0141/237-4112** or -4130 reservations. Fax 0141/
237-2084 or 0141/510-6082. www.castlemandawa.com. reservation@castlemandawa.com. 70 units. Rs
4,000 standard double; Rs 6,000 deluxe cottage; Rs 10,000 suite. Breakfast Rs 350, lunch Rs 600, dinner Rs
650. Taxes extra. AE, MC, V. **Amenities:** Various dining areas; bar; badminton; billiard room; cultural performances; doctor-on-call; heritage walk; Internet (Rs 50 30 min., Rs 100 per hour); Ayurvedic massage;
pool table; pool; safaris—camel, horse, and jeep; spa; table tennis; vintage car rides. *In room:* A/C, minibar
(suites only).

Desert Resort Mandawa ★★★ (Kids) Surrounded by plains of *kejri* trees punctuated
with seasonal crops of millet and corn, and built in the style of a Rajasthani village, this is
unquestionably Shekhawati's most peaceful and luxurious option. Ethnic accommodations
consist primarily of circular mud-thatch huts, their organic shapes charmingly decorated
with tribal motifs; almost everything in and on each hut has been sourced from the Shekhawati region. Our recommendation is a room by the pool, which has an attached private
garden looking out over the fields You'll be hard-pressed to leave the pool, which is filled
with wonderfully soft, fresh spring water every second day from the borehole, is not chlo-
rinated, and is used to irrigate the crops below. As at Castle Mandawa, dinners are tasty

buffets using their organic locally grown produce accompanied by entertainment and served under the stars.

Mandawa, Jhunjhunu District, Shekhawati 333 704. Reservations: ℰ **0141/237-1194** or -4112. Fax 0141/ 237-2084 or 0141/510-6082. www.castlemandawa.com. desertresortmandawa@gmail.com. 60 units. Rs 4,000 standard double; Rs 6,000 deluxe cottage; Rs 10,000 suite. Breakfast Rs 350, lunch Rs 600, dinner Rs 650. Taxes extra. AE, MC, V. **Amenities:** Restaurant; bar; badminton; billiard room; children's play area; cultural performances; helipad; Internet (Rs 50 30 min., 100/hr.); in-house dairy pool; Ayurvedic massage; safaris—camel, horse, and jeep; table tennis;. *In room:* A/C, fan, minibar (suites only).

SHOPPING

Outside some havelis, caretakers sell Rajasthani puppets and postcards. You can see artisans and craftspeople at work in their shops in Mandawa, along Sonthaliya Gate and the bazaar. *Lac* bangles in bright natural colors make pretty gifts (from as little as Rs 15 each); if you find the sizes too small, have a pair custom-made while you wait. Another good buy is the camel-leather Rajasthani shoes *(jootis),* once a symbol of royalty. The shop at Mandawa's Desert Resort sells handicrafts in vivid colors, all produced by rural women of the region.

---

6 PUSHKAR

288km (179 miles) W of Jaipur

On the eastern edge of the vast Thar Desert, with a beautiful backdrop in the embracing arms of the Aravalli Hills, Pushkar is one of the most sacred—and atmospheric—towns in India. Legend has it that the holy lake at its center was created when Brahma dropped the petals of a lotus flower *(pushpa)* from his hand *(kar).* The tiny temple town that sprung up on the lake shores remains an important pilgrimage site for Hindus, its population swollen dramatically in recent years by the hippies who came for a few days and never left—a sore point for visitors who remember its untouched charm, and a real nuisance for first-time travelers who now discover a town steeped in commercial prospectors who thrive on making a quick buck, often at the expense of Pushkar's spiritual roots. Their presence has transformed the sleepy desert town into a semi-permanent trance party, however, with *bhang* (marijuana) lassis imbibed at the myriad tiny eateries, falafels on every menu, long-bearded rabbis on bicycles, boys perfectly dressed up like Shiva posing for photographs, and world music pumping from speakers that line the street bazaar that runs along the lake's northern edge. This street bazaar is the center of all activity in Pushkar and incidentally one of the best shopping experiences in Rajasthan, where you can pick up the most gorgeous throwaway gear, great secondhand books, and mountains of CDs at bargain prices.

Pushkar is something akin to Varanasi, only without the awful road traffic—it really is possible to explore the town entirely on foot, and outside the annual camel *mela.* It doesn't have the same claustrophobic crowds you find in Varanasi. What you will find exasperating, however, is the tremendous commercialization of just about everything—particularly "spirituality"—except without service standards to match. It takes about 45 minutes to walk around the holy lake and its 52 *ghats.* Built to represent each of the Rajput Maharajas who constructed their "holiday homes" on its banks, *ghats* are broad sets of stairs from where Hindu pilgrims take ritual baths to cleanse their souls. Note that you will need a "Pushkar Passport" to perambulate without harassment (see "Passport to Pushkar: Saying Your Prayers," below), that shoes need to be removed 9m (30 ft.) from

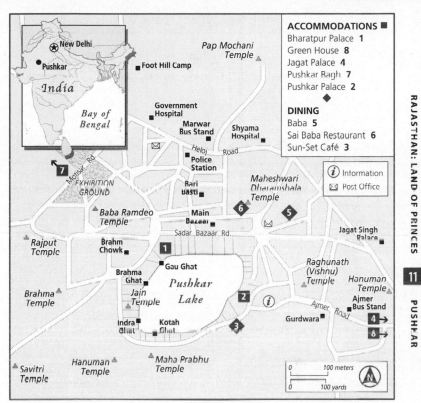

ACCOMMODATIONS ■
Bharatpur Palace **1**
Green House **8**
Jagat Palace **4**
Pushkar Bagh **7**
Pushkar Palace **2**
◆

DINING
Baba **5**
Sai Baba Restaurant **6**
Sun-Set Café **3**

ⓘ Information
✉ Post Office

RAJASTHAN: LAND OF PRINCES

11

PUSHKAR

the holy lake (bring cheap flip-flops if you're worried about losing them), and that photography of bathers is prohibited.

Surrounding the lake and encroaching on the hills that enhance the town's wonderful sense of remoteness are some 500 temples, of which the one dedicated to Brahma, said to be 2,000 years old, is the most famous, not least because it's one of only a handful in India dedicated to the Hindu Lord of Creation. The doors to the enshrined deity are shut between 1:30 and 3pm, but you can wander around the temple courtyard during these hours. The other two worth noting (but a stiff 50-min. climb to reach) are dedicated to his consorts: It is said that Brahma was cursed by his first wife, Savitri, when he briefly took up with another woman, Gayatri—to this day, the temple of Savitri sits sulking on a hill overlooking the temple town, while across the lake, on another hill, no doubt nervous of retribution, the Gayatri Temple keeps a lookout. Ideally, Savitri should be visited at sunset, while a visit to Gayatri should coincide with the beautiful sunrise. *Note:* The Vishnu temple, encountered as you enter town, is the only temple off-limits to non-Hindus, but photography is permitted from outside the temple gates.

Unless you're expecting authentic untouched India, Pushkar is a delight to visit any time of the year, with its laid-back, almost European atmosphere offset by the unique

(Finds) The Dargah Sharif & Other Ajmer Gems

Ajmer is not an attractive town, and most foreigners experience it only as a jumping-off point to the pilgrim town of Pushkar. However, it is worthwhile to plan your journey so that you can spend a few hours exploring Ajmer's fascinating sights (particularly the Dargah, one of the most spiritually resonant destinations in India) before you head the short 11km (7 miles) over a mountain pass to the laid-back atmosphere of Pushkar and its superior selection of accommodations.

Founded in the 7th century and strategically located within striking distance of the Mewar (Udaipur) and Marwar (Jodhpur) dynasties, as well as encompassing most of the major trade routes, Ajmer has played a pivotal role in the affairs of Rajasthan over the years. The Mughal emperors realized that only by holding this city could they increase their power base in Rajasthan. This is principally why the great Mughal emperor Akbar courted the loyalty of the nearby Amber/Jaipur court, marrying one of its daughters. But Ajmer was important on an emotional and spiritual level too, for only by gaining a foothold in Ajmer could Akbar ensure a safe passage for Muslim pilgrims to **Dargah Sharif (Khwaja Moin-ud-Din Chisti's Dargah).** The great Sufi saint Khwaja Moin-ud-Din Chisti, "protector of the poor," was buried here in 1235.

Said to possess the ability to grant the wishes and desires of all those who visit it, the **Dargah Sharif ★** is the most sacred Islamic shrine in India, and a pilgrimage here is considered second in importance only to a visit to Mecca. After a living member of the Sufi sect, Sheikh Salim Chisti, blessed Akbar with the prophecy of a much-longed-for son (Emperor Jahangir, father of Shah Jahan, builder of the Taj), Emperor Akbar himself made the pilgrimage many times, traveling on foot from distant Fatehpur Sikri and presenting the shrine with cauldrons (near the entrance) large enough to cook food for 5,000 people. It was not only Akbar and his offspring who made the pilgrimage—even the Hindu Rajputs came to pay homage to "the divine soul" that lies within.

Today the shrine still attracts hundreds of pilgrims every day, swelling to thousands during special occasions such as Urs Mela (Oct/Nov), the anniversary of Akbar's death. Leaving your shoes at the entrance (Rs 10/at exit), you pass through imposing **Nizam Gate** and smaller **Shahjahani Gate;** to the right is **Akbar's mosque,** and opposite is the equally imposing **Buland Darwaza.** Climb the steps to take a peek into the **two huge cauldrons** (3m/10 ft. round) that flank the gates—they come into their own at Urs when they are filled to the brim with a rice dish that is then distributed to the poor. To the right is **Mehfil Khana,** built in 1888 by the Nizam of Hyderabad. From here you enter another gateway into the courtyard, where you will find another mosque on the right, this one built by Shah Jahan in his characteristic white marble. You'll also see the great **Chisti's Tomb**—the small building topped by a marble dome and enclosed by marble lattice screens. In front of the tomb, the *qawwali* singers are seated, every day repeating the same beautiful haunting melodies (praising the saint) that have been sung for centuries. Everywhere, people abase themselves and sing, their eyes closed, hands spread wide on the floor or clutching their chests, while others feverishly pray and knot bits of fabrics to the latticework of the tomb or shower it with flowers. The scene is moving, the sense of faith palpable and, unlike the Dargah in Delhi, the atmosphere welcoming (though it's best to be discreet: no insensitive clicking of cameras or loud talking). Entry is free, but donations, paid to the office in the main courtyard, are welcome and are directly distributed to the poor. Entered off Dargah Bazaar, the Dargah is open daily, from 4 or 5am to 9 or 10pm (except during prayer times) depending on the season.

Having laid claim to Ajmer through a diplomatic marriage, Akbar built a red-sandstone fort he called **Daulat Khana (Abode of Riches)** in 1572. This was later renamed the Magazine by the British, who maintained a large garrison here, having also realized Ajmer's strategic importance. In 1908 it was again transformed, this time into the largely missable **Rajputana Museum** (small fee; Sat–Thurs 10am–4:30pm). The fort is significant mostly from a historical perspective, for it is here in 1660 that the British got a toehold in India when Sir Thomas Roe, representative of the British East India Company, met Emperor Jahangir and gained his permission to establish the first British factory at Surat.

The British also established a number of first-rate educational institutions, particularly **Mayo College** ★, known as the Eton of the East. Originally designed to educate only the sons of the aristocracy, it opened its doors in 1875 to princes arriving on elephant-back, followed by retinues of 1,000 servants. The school is worth visiting, even just to view the building from the road; it's a superb example of Indo-Saracenic architecture, with much symbolic detailing. The sun and the moon, for instance (featured on the college hall roof and on the school coat of arms), signify the mythical descent of the maharajas (see "Once Were Warriors: The History of the Rajput," earlier in this chapter). To enter the school, you will need to get the principal's permission (with a bit of patience, this can be arranged through the gate attendant).

Another Ajmer attraction definitely worth seeing is **Svarna Nagari Hall** ★ behind the Jain Nasiyan Temple in Anok Chowk. It's a totally unassuming building from the outside, but ascend the stairs to the second floor and you gaze down upon a fantasy world; a breathtaking display that fills the double-volume hall with tiny gilded figures celebrating scenes from Jain mythology. Sadly, no guide is available to explain what it all means, but the workmanship and sheer scale of the display are spellbinding.

(Tips) **Passport to Pushkar: Saying Your Prayers**

Hard proof of Pushkar's pushiness lies in the passport control as you enter the town—many foreigners (mostly Israeli hippies, hence the inclusion of falafels and pitas on the menu of even the most traditional Brahmin eatery) have come to experience its idyllic location and quaint, laid-back vibe and have never left, marrying locals and starting small businesses. As a result, there is now a moratorium on the length of time you can stay—a maximum of 3 months. So even though this measure is not always enforced, have your passport on hand as you enter. For those who wish to walk onto the *ghats* lining the lake, you'll need an entirely different kind of passport: Brahmin priests will bully you into performing *puja*—prayers that involve a scattering of flowers into the lake—after which you will be expected to make a hefty donation (inquire at your hotel for the going rate or you will almost certainly be ripped off). The priest will then tie a thin red thread around your wrist, which you can brandish at the next Brahmin priest who will almost certainly approach you, but who will quickly retreat upon seeing your "passport." To experience Pushkar from a pilgrim's perspective, and not as a disenchanted tourist, try to gain a closer insight into what makes this an important place for Hindu pilgrims, and gain your wrist thread without being ripped off, call on **Giriraj** (© **94-1430-0053**; *puja* fee Rs 150), a local priest who is also a licensed guide. His English isn't perfect, but he can throw some light on the history and background of the area, and help out with practical information; he charges Rs 350 a half day, and Rs 500 a full day.

aromas of India and tons of tiny shops, temples, Brahmin eateries, and operators offering camel- and horseback safaris into the surrounding desert (camels are about Rs 250 per hour, Rs 700 full day; horses are Rs 450 per hour). But the town is most famous for its annual *mela*—the largest camel fair in Asia. Attracting an estimated 200,000 rural traders, red-turbaned Rabari and Bhil tribal folk, pilgrims, and tourists, the *mela* stretches tiny Pushkar into sprawling villages of temporary campsites—interspersed with food stalls and open-air theaters—created solely to house, feed, and entertain the swollen population that flocks to the specially built amphitheater on the outskirts of the town to watch the races and attend the auctions. Like most desert destinations, however, it is at night that the atmosphere takes on an unreal intimacy, as pilgrims and tourists get to know each other around the many campfires, and Rajasthani dancers and traditional folk singers create a timeless backdrop. The Pushkar *mela* takes place in the Hindu month of Kartik, over the waxing and waning of the full moon that occurs in late October or in November.

On the evening of the full *mela* moon, as the desert sun sets behind the low-slung hills (a spectacular sight at the best of times), temple bells and drums call the devout to *puja*, and hundreds of pilgrims wade into the lake—believed to miraculously cleanse the soul—before lighting clay lamps and setting them afloat on its holy waters, the twinkling lights a surreal reflection of the desert night sky. If you're lucky enough to have booked a room at Pushkar Palace, you can watch this ancient ritual from a deck chair on the terrace (it can be quite a scramble to get a view from the *ghats* themselves)—a wonderful sight and one of those mystic moments that make a trip to India among the most <u>553</u> memorable of your life.

ESSENTIALS

VISITOR INFORMATION   Pushkar doesn't have its own tourist office. The rather useless **RTDC office** is located at the very mediocre RTDC Hotel Sarovar ((℃ **0145/277-2040**), and is open daily from 9am to 5pm.

GETTING THERE   Pushkar lies about 3 hours west of Jaipur; a deluxe bus here costs about Rs 125. Udaipur is 300km (186 miles) away by bus (Rs 300); Jodhpur 215km (133 miles; Rs 265); and Jaisalmer 550km (341 miles; Rs 1,050). Pushkar lies 145km (90 miles) from the closet airport, which is at Jaipur and is 400km (248 miles) from Delhi (Rs 500 by bus)

GETTING AROUND   Pushkar is easily explored on foot. There is no public transport system (and only a limited number of cycle- or auto-rickshaws) in town. If you prefer not to walk, the only option is to hire a small private taxi that costs in the region of Rs 800 to Rs 1,000.

WHERE TO STAY

You really want to get a room overlooking the sacred lake—despite the early-morning and evening chanting calls to *puja* and blaring temple music, it's by far the most atmospheric location in Pushkar. Of the surprisingly limited options that offer direct lake views, Pushkar Palace (reviewed below) is the only luxurious option; for the rest you'll have to rough it (we're talking basic furnishings—a plastic chair and bed and the possibility of sharing a bathroom and toilet).

Far and away the best budget option in town is **Inn Seventh Heaven** (**Value** (next to Mali ka Mandir; (℃ **0145/510-5455**; www.inn-seventh-heaven.com; Rs 600–Rs 4,000), located in a 100-year-old haveli with rooms (with names like "Hilly Billy" and "Rapunzel") around a fountain and garden courtyard. Anoop, the enterprising young owner, has ensured that rooms are clean and dressed with some sense of style; despite its location (away from the lake), it has a pleasant, informal, homey feel, and the great second-floor restaurant does satisfying Indian food. If you plan well in advance, you can bag the most recently added room, "Asana," also the most expensive, but it's bright and situated on the roof, where there's a good view. It has antique furniture and four-poster beds (as do some of the other rooms).

Green House ★★   The newest (2009), most luxurious option in Pushkar is located just 7.5km (4½ miles) outside town, on the Kishenpura-Tilora Road. Touted as a "most luxurious eco-boutique resort," its 20 luxury tents are arranged around manicured lawns with indigenous *ardoo* trees and a lovely pool. While the word "eco" should be entirely removed ("green house" refers to the two huge plastic tunnels dedicated to raising a multicolored variety of exotic Dutch rose, and the restaurant and bar, housed in a similar uninsulated plastic, are blasted with A/C during meal times), the other descriptors do indeed hold. The tents are beautifully decorated with comfy beds and crisp new cotton linen; travertine bathrooms have walk in glass-encased rain showers and most of the tents have outdoor wooden decks from where you can watch the sun set and the moon rise over the Aravalli hills reflected in the pool before you.

The Greenhouse Resort, Kishanpur Rd., Village Tilora, Pushkar, Rajasthan 305022. (℃ **0145/230-0079** or 0145/322-6137. Fax 0145/277-3704. www.thegreenhouseresort.com. reservation@thegreenhouseresort. com. 20 tents (8 superior, 8 premier, 4 suites). Winter rates Rs 6,700–Rs 7,700 superior and premier (only bathrooms have walls); Rs 9,700 suites (which have walls). Includes breakfast and taxes. Pushkar mela rates: Rs 13,000 double superior; Rs 15,000 double premier tent and suite. Taxes extra. AE, MC, V. **Amenities:** Restaurant; bar; billiard table; cultural performances; Internet (Rs 100/hr.); Ayurvedic massage; pool; safaris—camel, horse, and jeep; table tennis. *In room:* A/C, TV, cable, hair dryer (on request), minibar (suites only).

Pushkar Palace ★★ (Value) This pretty but dated 400-year-old palace—its thick white walls reflected in the holy waters of the lake—is the best place to stay in Pushkar itself but Green House is the more luxe. The best rooms are the suites below the terrace (nos. 101 and 102)—these are the closest to the lake, with windows that provide serene (or surreal, depending on the time of day) views directly onto it; do bear in mind, however, that such proximity to the lake also means picking up most sounds. In the deluxe category, the corner rooms (nos. 209, 309, and 409), despite being significantly smaller but comfortably furnished, have the best views—you can literally lie in bed and watch the sunsets. Even if you don't have a room with the best of views (most are set behind the open-air corridors that link the rooms), you can enjoy it all from the terrace, where waiters are on hand to provide the necessary liquid refreshments (be aware that, as elsewhere in Pushkar, no alcohol is allowed). (Pushkar Palace also arranges a **Royal Desert Camp** during the *mela:* 351 tents with attached bathrooms and four dining tents).

Tip: The Palace has a sister establishment, the three star **Jagat Palace,** built on the outskirts of town. The same rates apply for an experience that's somewhat isolated and disconnected from Pushkar, but with the added incentive of a pool. Many of the public interior spaces are gloomy, the soulless atmosphere clearly designed to deal with large groups of package tourists. That said, it's probably the most luxurious hotel option if Pushkar Palace and Green House are full, though you'll need a car or taxi for the 5-minute drive to town; if you want to walk, it's a 15-minute trek along a dusty main road.

Pushkar 305 022, Rajasthan. ☏ **0145/277-2001** or -2402. Fax 0145/277-2226 or -2952. www.hotelpushkar palace.com. hppalace@datainfosys.net. Pushkar Palace: 48 units. Jagat Palace: 85 units. Rs 3,450 super deluxe double; Rs 1,100 extra bed. Taxes extra. All meals extra. AE, DC, MC, V. **Amenities:** 2 restaurants (only vegetarian); doctor-on-call; room service; camel/horse safaris. Jagat has 2 restaurants, pool at Jagat Palace only, Ayurvedic massage. *In room:* A/C, fan, TV, minibar.

WHERE TO DINE

Dining options are plentiful but far from spectacular, catering largely to budget travelers more concerned with imbibing marijuana than partaking of quality cuisine; if you're staying at Seventh Heaven or Pushkar Palace, you'd be well advised to make full use of their dining facilities. However, if you're up for a culinary adventure of the backpacking kind, you'll find numerous strange and unusual places around the lake, many of them proud of their multifarious global cuisines, all fairly Indianized. Do be aware that you won't find meat, eggs, or alcohol served anywhere near the sacred lake of Pushkar.

Sai Baba Haveli Restaurant is a favorite with young foreign tourists and aging hippies—it serves gratifying baked goods and decent (egg-less) croissants (although their idea of espresso is simply stronger-than-usual coffee). We're sure most people come here because of the liberal attitude toward smoking intoxicants, which tends to happen in the garden, lorded over by a statue of Sai Baba ("the living god") himself; on Saturday nights, festivities include a desert gypsy (Kalbeliya) dance program and party. There's also a rooftop restaurant. **Prems Venkatesh,** a basic eatery overseen by a Brahmin who cooks his delicious chapatis with vegetables of the day and *dal* over a wood-burning fire, is widely considered the best in town for cheap Indian food; ask anyone to direct you there, but don't expect it to be sparkling clean.

Beware: Please take special care with belongings and chatting to strangers as over the past few years there have been numerous incidents involving drug dealing and the attendant sexual harassment cases—all involving the notorious *bhang* or marijuana, and no doubt other drugs too. The *Bhang* (or "special") *lassi* is served at numerous outlets around Pushkar; these seem innocent, and invariably taste sweet, but the narcotic after-effects take awhile to set in and will have you losing all sense of reality (and direction). Be sure you know your way back to your hotel.

SHOPPING

The main thoroughfare, **Sadar Bazaar,** is just over 1km (a half-mile) long, and is lined with tiny shops selling ridiculously cheap (though usually low-quality) clothing, jewelry, leather sandals, excellent music (anything from Hindu temple to Hindi pop to global trance), and the best selection of books in Rajasthan. This is definitely the place to come with empty bags—its almost cheaper to stock up on a new wardrobe here than pay hotel laundry fees, and you can pick up a huge selection of Indian music to listen to back home and make you long to return.

7 UDAIPUR

405km (251 miles) SW of Jaipur; 260km (161 miles) S of Jodhpur

The "City of Sunrise," often described as the most romantic city in India, was built around four man-made lakes, the placid blue waters reflecting ethereal white palaces and temples, beyond which shimmer the distant Aravalli Hills, apparently the oldest range in the world, predating even the Himalayas. Udaipur has a real sense of space and peace, and the city is mercifully free of the kind of intense hucksterism that so marks the Indian street experience. This may have something to do with its proud Hindu history, for the city is not only known for its gracious palaces, temperate climate, and beautiful views, but for maintaining a fierce independence from even the most powerful outside influences. It fought bloody wars to repel Turkish, Afghan, Tartar, and Mongol invaders and rejected allegiances with the Mughals, only to acquiesce in 1818, when the state grudgingly came under British political control.

Capital of the legendary Sisodias of Mewar, believed to be direct descendants of the Sun (an insignia you'll see everywhere), Udaipur was built on the shores of Lake Pichola by Udai Singh II in 1559, who returned here after the third and final sacking of the previous Mewar stronghold, Chittaurgarh (see "Top Excursions," later in this chapter). Udai Singh's son, Pratap, kept the Mughal invaders at bay for a further 25 years and is said to have been so disgusted by Man Singh and the Jaipur raja's obsequious relations with the Mughals that, after one historic meeting, he had the ground where Man Singh had walked washed with Ganges water in order to purify it. Maharana Fateh Singh was also the only Rajput prince who refused to attend the Delhi Durbar held for King George V in 1911, despite the fact that the British had acknowledged him as the head of the princely states of Rajputana.

Much of Udaipur, particularly the old part located on the shores of Lake Pichola, is where you'll find the city's most striking landmarks—the towering **City Palace** and **Lake Palace**—and it still feels remarkably like a 16th-century Rajput stronghold, with the benevolent Maharana still treated like a reigning king by his devoted and loyal subjects. You can witness this firsthand by attending the temple at nearby Eklingji on a Monday evening, when the Maharana—the 76th ruler of one of the world's oldest surviving dynasties—often joins his subjects to pay his respects to Shiva.

Try to spend at least 3 to 4 days in Udaipur, whether you spend them aimlessly wandering its mazelike lanes, taking a slow cruise on Pichola Lake, exploring the giant medieval fortress and palaces that rise from its shores, or setting off to see the intricately carved Jain temples of Ranakpur and the ancient fort of Kumbhalgarh—or whether you do nothing but loll on a comfortable divan from a hanging Jarokha overlooking the lake. You'll find the City of Sunrise the most relaxing part of your sojourn in Rajasthan, in fact so much so that many end their Indian sojourn with a few days reflecting in its tranquil waters.

ESSENTIALS

VISITOR INFORMATION   Rajasthan Tourism Development Corporation (RTDC), though inconveniently located in the Tourist Office at Fateh Memorial in Suraj Pol (✆ **0294/241-1535;** Mon–Sat 10am–5pm), can arrange accommodations, licensed guides, maps, and brochures. You can also call the RTDC Hotel Kajri at ✆ **0294/241-0501** through -0503 for tourist information and assistance. Satellite tourist offices can be found at the airport (✆ **0294/265-5433;** open at flight times) and at the railway station, which was scheduled to reopen once new train services begin (see "Getting There: By Train/Bus," below).

The most convenient place to draw money against your credit card/ATM card is near the Jagdish Temple (City Palace Rd.). There is also an ICICI Bank next to the Jet Airways office (Madhuban), an SBI ATM next to Indian Airlines (Delhi Gate), and several others near Town Hall, Bapu Bazaar. There are two convenient LKP foreign exchange offices on Lake Palace Road (next to Rang Niwas Palace Hotel) and near Jagdish Temple. A useful private hospital is **American International Hospital** on Kothi Baugh, Bhatt Ji Ki (✆ **0294/242-8701** through -8704).

GETTING THERE   By Air   **Dabok Airport** is 25km (16 miles) from Udaipur. As always, **Jet Airways** is the preferable option (✆ **0294/256-1105-60**), connecting the city with Delhi, Mumbai (both 1 hr., 15 min.), and Jaipur (45 min.). **Indian Airlines** (✆ **0294/265-5453** airport, 0294/241-0999 Delhi Gate) covers the same routes, as well as Jodhpur. A regular non-air-conditioned taxi into town should cost about Rs 300). **Travel Plan** (details below) offers air-conditioned taxis from the airport to the city for Rs 400

By Train/Bus   The **Mewar Express** departs Delhi's Nizamuddin station at 6:35pm and arrives at Udaipur City station at 6:10am the following morning; significant stops en route are Bharatpur, Sawai Madhopur (for Ranthambhore), and Chittaurgaur. There's an evening train from Jaipur, departing 9:40pm, which arrives at 7:10am the following morning. From Ahmedabad there is the Ahmedabad Express departing at 7:45pm arriving at 4:20am and the Fast Passenger departing 9:20am arriving at 8:55pm. There are deluxe bus connections from Jaipur, Jodhpur, and Ahmedabad (roads are in fairly good condition). In the unlikely event that you've opted for a bus, you will most likely be dropped off just north of the City Railway Station.

GETTING AROUND   Due to the narrow, winding alleyways of the Old City, the best way to get around the main tourist sights (the area surrounding the City Palace) is on foot, but if you want to spend a rather satisfying day taking in all the sights in the city, consider renting a **moped** or **bicycle** from **Heera Cycle Store & Tours & Travels** (inside Hotel Badi Haveli, 86 Gangaur Ghat Rd., easy walking distance from Jagdish Temple; ✆ **0294/513-0625;** copy of passport and driver's license required; daily 7:30am–9pm)

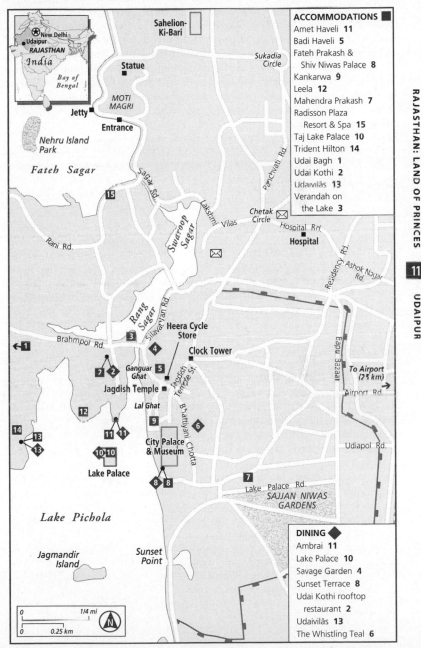

ACCOMMODATIONS ■
Amet Haveli **11**
Badi Haveli **5**
Fateh Prakash &
 Shiv Niwas Palace **8**
Kankarwa **9**
Leela **12**
Mahendra Prakash **7**
Radisson Plaza
 Resort & Spa **15**
Taj Lake Palace **10**
Trident Hilton **14**
Udai Bagh **1**
Udai Kothi **2**
Udaivilās **13**
Verandah on
 the Lake **3**

DINING ◆
Ambrai **11**
Lake Palace **10**
Savage Garden **4**
Sunset Terrace **8**
Udai Kothi rooftop
 restaurant **2**
Udaivilās **13**
The Whistling Teal **6**

For journeys farther afield, hiring a car with driver is probably the only way to go; you will certainly need one for the recommended trips described below. To hire one for the day, or for a self-planned tour in Rajasthan, call **Travel Plan** (© **0294/252-4688** or -242/1902; fax 0294/241-0213) and ask for Mr. Mahipul Sigh (or try him at © **098/2905-9319;** mahipul@travelplanraj.com). Mr. Singh will provide experienced qualified and licensed guides in all languages for Rs 660 for half day and Rs 800 for full day. Or call Gajraj Singh, a bright young man who is passionate about his city and is well educated in its history and culture and speaks perfect English (mobile © **098/28509651;** gajraj_punawat@yahoo.co.in). Alternatively, the efficient Ramesh Dashora, proprietor of **Parul Tours and Travel,** opposite Jagat Niwas Hotel, at 32 Lal Ghat (© **0294/242-1697;** info@rajasthantravelbycab.com); Ramesh offers English-speaking guides (Rs 1,000/day), plus A/C Ambassadors (or Indicas) for Rs 1,500 for a full day; this includes 250km (155 miles) with each additional kilometer costing around Rs 6, and there's an overnight fee of Rs 150. More substantial vehicles will push prices up considerably. You can even reserve a car online (www.rajasthantravelbycab.com).

FESTIVALS   Udaipur's biggest festivals are the **Mewar Festival,** held every March or April, and the **Holi Festival,** held every March. October's Ashwa Poojan is another celebration worth inquiring about (your hotel should be able to advise you on exact dates and where best to experience the festivities). The **Gangaur Festival** is celebrated with special zeal by the women of Udaipur (end of Mar to Apr). During this festival, unmarried women pray to the goddess Gauri (manifestation of Parvati, Shiva's wife) for a good husband, while the married pray for the well-being of their husbands and a happy married life. Women decorate their hands and feet with *mehendi* (tattoos of henna paste) and carry colorful images of Gauri and terra-cotta lamps on their heads as they dance and sing songs in street processions. At the end of the festival they break these lamp-pots and celebrate with a feast. Festivities last 18 days and include many colorful processions and a fireworks display.

WHAT TO SEE & DO

To make Udaipur's intriguing and valorous history really come alive, consider taking on the services of a qualified guide in the city, which can be requested through your hotel or by contacting one of the recommended local operators (see above).

If your idea of a vacation is lying by a pool with a good book, only visits to the City and Lake palaces (see "Top Attractions," below) need top your list of things to do in Udaipur proper. The city is the ideal base for a number of day trips, however. The most highly recommended is a round-trip through Kumbhalgarh Wildlife Sanctuary and Fort, taking in the temples of Ranakpur along the way, and possibly stopping at Eklingji on the way back (see "Top Excursions," below). The lovely, scenic drive passes picture-postcard rural hamlets and fields of mustard, scattered with boys tending cattle and women clad in bright saris tilling the soil.

For those interested in seeing more of the city, the following day tour—to be tailored to your needs—provides an overview of the top sights in and around Udaipur. Start your day by exploring the City Palace, which usually towers over the city's raison d'être, Lake Pichola. Two more palaces can be seen on what would be the islands of Jag Niwas and Jag Mandir (see "Top Attractions," below). Exit through Tripolia Gate to explore the Old City of Udaipur, which sprawls north of the palace. **Jagdish Temple ★**, the largest in Udaipur, is its chief attraction. Despite some lovely exterior carvings (including hidden erotic pieces your guide will point out), the temple itself is rather ordinary (if you've seen a number of them elsewhere, that is), but its attraction lies in its massive popularity. The temple has seen a constant stream of people who come to worship Lord Jagannath, an aspect of Vishnu (the black stone image enshrined within), since it first opened its doors in 1652. *Aarti* takes place at around 10am, 7:30pm, and 10pm—try to time your visit for when the *bhajans* (prayer-songs) make for a most atmospheric experience. (Remove your shoes before entering, and an attendant will look after them for a small tip; no photography inside.) The bronze half-man, half-bird statue of Garuda outside is the vehicle of Vishnu. From Jagdish Temple you can wander the mazelike streets of old Udaipur, admiring the whitewashed havelis and popping into tiny shops before reaching the clock tower that marks the northern edge. Near the lake edge, at Gangaur Ghat, you can visit the **Bagore-ki-Haveli Museum** (© 0294/242 2567), a restored royal haveli with plenty of idiosyncratic design detail that's now part of a museum and cultural center; it's best visited on evenings for the nightly music and dance performances. If you haven't picked up a bicycle from **Heera Cycle Store** (86 Gangaur Ghat Rd., near Jagdish Temple), catch a taxi from here (or have your driver waiting) to **Bharatiya Lok Kala Museum** (Panch Vati Rd.; entry Rs 35, Rs 20/50 camera; daily 9am–6pm), Udaipur's unofficial "Puppet Museum" (Rajasthan being the birthplace of this favored Indian storytelling medium), where you can watch a good show, staged almost hourly throughout the day. The best is held each evening at 6pm (Rs 30 with traditional folk dances added on (though note that most hotels have a puppet show as part of their evening's entertainment including the rooftop at Jagat Niwas). The folk museum also contains models, instruments, and photographs documenting other local traditions and crafts, but for this you're better off visiting **Shilpgram** (© 0294/241-9023; www.shilpgram.org). This extremely faux rural arts-and-crafts "village" is located 3km (2 miles) out of town; follow the road that runs along the north of Fateh Sagar Lake; daily 11am to 7pm, folk dances 11am and 7pm; admission is just Rs 25 but you'll pay for extras such as camel rides and the use of cameras. Created to "promote and preserve the traditional architecture, music, and crafts of the tribal village of western India," Shilpgram has a distinctly artificial feel but interesting cultural performances; you can also ride a camel and browse for tribal knickknacks that the "traditionally" attired craftspeople will be only too delighted to finally off-load. If you're in a particularly touristy mood, you can dress up in a traditional Rajasthani outfit and have your picture taken. Beware that it is very touristy and in season can become extremely crowded. Along the way, stop for a brief wander through **Saheliyon-ki-Bari (Garden of the Maids of Honour)** north of Bharatiya Lok Kala Museum—turn left at Sukadia Circle. It's open daily 8am to 7:30pm (small admission fee). Created by Sangram Singh in the 18th century for the ladies of his household (some say to re-create the monsoon climate for his sickly daughter), this is billed as Udaipur's finest garden, but it suffers from neglect, with none of the fountains operating. Still, it's a peaceful place, and the array of established indigenous trees may interest keen botanists. If the monsoon has been good and lake levels in Udaipur have risen, from Saheliyon-ki-Bari make your way to nearby **Fateh Sagar Lake,** along a scenic winding road, passing **Moti Magri** on your left, atop which is the statue of Maharana Pratap and his beloved horse, Chetak (largely missable, but the views from here are lovely). Fateh Sagar, the large lake that lies north of Lake Pichola, has a small island garden of its own, the rather neglected **Nehru Park.** Make sure you stop off for a drink or lunch at Raaj Bagh (© 0294/243-1700), a delightful garden restaurant serving regional cuisine overlooking the lake, which serves inexpensive, quality food by efficient staff. It also has a small vintage car collection (note the Corgi scooter) and ice cold drinks.

An excellent place to view the sunset is **Sajjan Garh (Monsoon Palace),** built by the Maharana Sajjan Singh as an observatory in the late 19th century. You can enter the palace building by tipping the guard (though it's a restricted security area). Head to one of the alcoves from where views of the surrounding mountains are breathtaking. Then rush down to have a sundowner nearby at the new Fateh Garh with its award-winning (*Condé Nast Traveler* Best Pools July 2009) infinity pool (see "Where to Stay," below) and commanding views towards Lake Pichola and the city. If this sounds like one stop too many after a rather exhausting day, head straight for one of the rooftop or garden restaurants in the city (Ambrai at **Amet Haveli,** or the rooftop at **Jagat Niwas** Palace); get a table on the **Sunset Terrace** (near the Dovecoat lobby of the Fateh Prakash hotel); or sit on the marbled "deck" at the Lake Palace, where you can relax with a drink as the sun sinks behind the distant jagged outline of the Aravalli Hills, and the flautist conjures up the moon.

TOP ATTRACTIONS

City Palace and Museum ★★★ For full effect, the staggering, monumental City Palace complex is best viewed from either of the islands on Lake Pichola; the palace's cream-colored stone walls tower some 30m (98 ft.) above its mirrorlike reflection in the lake and stretch almost 250m (820 ft.) across its eastern shore. The 300-year-old complex actually comprises 11 palaces (or *mahals*) built by its successive maharanas, making it by far the largest palace complex in Rajasthan. Purchase the useful guidebook at the entrance (or hire the services of a guide through your hotel; those who hang around the ticket office charge on average Rs 300 for a 2-hr. tour) to help you maneuver the sprawling museum, much of it connected by a maze of rather claustrophobic tunnel-like stairways designed to confuse and slow down potential invaders. (This is why it's essential to get here as soon as the palace doors open—finding yourself trapped between busloads of jeering families who mysteriously come to regular standstills in these airless passages is sheer purgatory.) The entire palace is a delight, but highlights include the large peacock mosaics in the 17th-century **Mor (Peacock) Chowk;** mirror-encrusted **Moti Mahal;** the glass and porcelain figures of **Manak (Ruby) Mahal,** which has a central garden; the collection of miniatures featuring Krishna legends in **Krishna Vilas** (dedicated to a 16-year-old princess who committed suicide here); exquisite Zenana Mahal (Palace of the Queens); and the Chinese and Dutch ceramics of **Chini Mahal.** When the lake levels are normal, the cusped windows provide superb views of the serene waters of Pichola Lake, on which white-marble Lake Palace appears to float. The last two palaces built, both now open to visitors wishing to overnight or dine, are the grand but rather staid **Shiv Niwas** and gorgeous **Fateh Prakash.** The latter can be visited for high tea (a rather dull affair) to view the Durbar Hall's royal portrait gallery, with its massive chandeliers and Venetian mirrors, and to see the Crystal Gallery, which has a huge collection of rare cut-crystal furniture and ornaments imported by Maharana Sajjan Singh from England in 1877. (For more on these palaces, see "Where to Stay" and "Where to Dine," later in this section.) Vintage-car lovers should ask about the tour of the Mewar family's Classic Car Collection. Set aside 3 hours to do the palace justice. (Water and soft drinks are available at a small stand inside the palace complex.)

City Palace. ✆ **0294/241-9021.** Rs 50 Jagdish Temple end, Rs 75 via Hotel Fateh Prakash; Rs 200 any camera. Daily 9:30am–4:30pm. Crystal Gallery Rs 500; daily 10am–1pm and 3–8pm; no photography.

Lake Pichola & Lake Palace ★★★ Most beautiful at sunrise and sunset, Lake Pichola reflects what seems to be a picture-perfect inversion of the many whitewashed and cream buildings that rise majestically from its shores and islands, known locally as Jag Niwas and Jag Mandir. Jag Niwas island is entirely covered by the Lake Palace, built by the maharana in 1740 as a summer idyll and today perhaps the most romantic—certainly the most photographed—hotel in India. What you will see if the lake remains parched is a magnificent palace that should be floating on water but instead sits on a vast, dry lake bed. A little farther south is the slightly larger Jag Mandir, upon which domed Gul Mahal stands. Famous as the star location in the movie *Octopussy*, it has also been a place of refuge: first for the young prince Shah Jahan who—in a typical Mughal ascension—was plotting to overthrow his father, Jahangir (incidentally, Udaipuris believe that Gul Mahal is what later inspired Jahan to build Taj Mahal); and later for European women and children, whom Maharana Swaroop Singh protected during the Mutiny. You can catch a boat to Jag Mandir from the City Palace (Bansi Ghat) jetty, but once you have alighted, there's not much to do but purchase overpriced refreshments and take some snaps; the trip around the lake includes a visit to Sunset Terrace (near Dovecoat Wing) or the Lake Palace Hotel. If you haven't booked a room at the hotel, make sure you come for dinner—the views alone are worth it, and the opulent and elegant setting is sublime (see "Where to Stay" and "Where to Dine," later in this section).

To make a table reservation at Lake Palace, call (✆) **0294/252-7961.** To charter a boat (Rs 3,000/hr.), or book a seat on one (Rs 300), call (✆) **92-1473-2149;** launches are from Lal Ghat and there are prices to suit all budgets and trips.

TOP EXCURSIONS IN & AROUND UDAIPUR

A number of recommended excursions from Udaipur can either be tackled as round-trips or as stopovers on your way elsewhere in the state. The first option is the easiest, a half-day excursion (at most) that takes in some of the most important temples in Udaipur. The second option—which you can combine with the first for a rather grueling but very satisfying round-trip—takes you to the awesome Jain temples at Ranakpur through Kumbhalgarh Wildlife Sanctuary, past wonderful pastoral scenes that haven't changed since medieval times, to view magnificent Kumbhalgarh Fort. From here you can either head northwest for Jodhpur or double back to Udaipur, possibly taking in the temples at Nathdwara, Nagda, and Eklingji. (If you're pressed for time, leave out Nathdwara—beyond the superb examples of *pichhwai* paintings, there's not much to see, as non-Hindus may not enter the temple.) To plan this as a round-trip, you will need to hire a driver familiar with the distances and terrain, and overnight along the way (see the listing for Kumbhalgarh Fort, below).

The third option is another long full-day trip, this time with the sole purpose of viewing Chittaurgarh, site of the most legendary Mewar battles. From here you can return to Udaipur or push on east to the little town of Bundi (see earlier in this chapter), and from there proceed to Jaipur or Ranthambhore National Park. For those interested in an off-the-beaten-track experience to the south, the fourth option, relatively undiscovered Dungarpur Palace, is well worth the time, not least for Deco fans who will relish overnighting in the family manse—Udai Bilas Palace, a living Deco museum—before returning to Udaipur. If Ranakpur's temples have whet your appetite for more, a fifth option, an excursion to the west ascending the Aravalli Hills to Mount Abu, the only hill station in Rajasthan and home to Dilwara—the most famous Jain temples in India—can also be tackled from Udaipur, though the distances will necessitate an overnight stay. Details of distances for all excursions are given below.

An excursion to an attraction that is not described in detail below, but which may interest birders or those in search of more peace, is **Jaisamand Lake,** the second-largest man-made lake in Asia, created in 1691 by Maharana Jai Singh and, thankfully, still containing water. Located a little over an hour away from Udaipur, it has a number of marble pavilions but is more famous for the many aquatic birds that have found a home in what is now **Jaisamand Wildlife Sanctuary.**

Day Trip 1: A Half-Day Temple Excursion

Eklingji & Nagda Temples ★★   Housing a manifestation of Shiva, the god who guards the fortunes of the rulers of Mewar, Eklingji is a lovely marble complex made up of 108 temples, the first of which was built in A.D. 734 by Bappa Rawal, legendary founder of the Sisodia clan, who ruled the Mewar kingdom for hundreds of years. The entire complex, most of it rebuilt in the 15th century, has a wonderfully uplifting atmosphere, particularly during prayer times (see below), and never more so than on the Monday evenings when the Maharana of Udaipur is in town and comes to pay his respects here, walking among his subjects as a mere mortal despite the attendant bowing and scraping. The four-faced black lingam (phallic symbol) apparently marks the spot where Bappa Rawal (that's him riding the peacock) was given the title Darwan ("servant") of Eklingji by his guru; outside, facing Shiva, is Nandi, Shiva's vehicle. Wander around the temple complex and you'll find a number of carvings from the *Kama Sutra;* your explorations won't exceed 30 minutes but the crush at the gate on festival times can be daunting. Deserted **Nagda,** which lies 2km (1¼ miles) north, is a far cry from this vibrant place of worship. All that survives of the site of the ancient capital of Mewar, which dates back to A.D. 626, are the ruins of the **Saas Bahu,** a 10th-century Vaishnavite twin temple (*Saas* meaning "mother-in-law" and *Bahu* "daughter-in-law") and the remains of Adbhutji Temple. Regrettably, the temples have been vandalized over the years and look much the worse for wear—unless you're of the archaeological bent, skip them if you're pushed for time despite it being a supremely peaceful place set among lush fields and a picturesque lotus pond.

22km (14 miles) north of Udaipur (30–40-min. drive one-way). Eklingji daily 4:15–6:45am, 10:30am–1:30pm, and 5:15–7:45pm. Prayer times: 15-min. *Aartis* are performed at 5:30am, 8:15am, 9:15am, 3:30pm, 4:30pm, 5pm, and 6:30pm; a 45-min. *aarti* is performed at 11:30am.

Nathdwara ★   Said to be the second-richest temple in India, Nathdwara's **Shri Nathji Temple,** home to a 600-year-old black marble statue of Lord Krishna, is one of the most important pilgrimage sites in India, attracting thousands, particularly during the festivals of Diwali, Holi, and Janmashthami. According to legend, in 1669 as the statue was being carried from Mathura to protect it from the destructive blows of the pious Mughal emperor Aurangzeb, it fell off the wagon at this site; the carriers (no doubt pretty exhausted) took this as a sign and built the temple around the statue. That said, the interior is closed to non-Hindus, so many of you won't even get a glimpse of the statue. The main reason to visit is to view what many believe are the finest examples of *pichhwai* paintings that adorn the interior and exterior of the temple. Hand-spun cloth painted with vibrant scenes depicting Krishna's life, these were originally created to teach illiterate low castes (who in the past were also barred from entering the sacred inner sanctum). You can purchase your own *pichhwai* paintings in the local bazaar, or look for more examples in Udaipur. Note that this is also a center for traditional *meenakari* (enamel) work.

48km (30 miles) from Udaipur (1-hr. drive one-way).

Ranakpur Temples ★★★   If you visit only one temple complex in Rajasthan, it should be Jain. Those at Ranakpur offer the finest examples of the complex and sustained levels of craftsmanship the Jains are renowned for, comparable in every way to the more famous Dilwara Temples at Mount Abu. If anything, a visit here is preferable—despite being a great deal more accessible, the area is infinitely more peaceful, with less traffic. Known for their asceticism and religious fervor (Jains are not only strict vegetarians, but the most orthodox among them walk with care to ensure no hapless insect should die underfoot due to their carelessness, and wear permanent masks to protect even the tiniest bug from the possibility of being ingested), the Jains put all their passion (and not inconsiderable wealth) into the creation of ornately carved temples. The Ranakpur Temples are jaw-droppingly beautiful, with exquisitely detailed relief carvings (and strangely, a few pieces of tinfoil) covering every inch of pillar, wall, and ceiling. The main triple-volume Chaumukha Temple, built from 1446 and dedicated to Adinatha Rishabdeva, the first Jain *tirthankara*, or "Enlightened One," is surrounded by 66 subsidiary shrines; inside are 1,444 intricately carved pillars—not one of them the same. (Incidentally, the land was donated to the Jains by Rana Kumbha, the warrior who built 32 forts, of which Kumbhalgarh is the most famous.) Note that no leather items (including belts and handbags) are allowed on the premises, no photography of the statues or enshrined deities is allowed (general temple pictures are permitted), and you are requested to dress conservatively (legs and shoulders must be covered; you can rent garments at the ticket desk should you require). Jain customs also strictly forbid menstruating women from entering. *Note:* There are no good accommodations in the immediate vicinity, so it is best to push on to the peaceful and welcoming HRH **Aodhi Hotel,** near Kumbhalgarh Fort (see below). Or, if you're on your way to Jodhpur, try **Rawla Narlai** or **Deogarh Mahal** (see "A Special Spot Between Udaipur & Jaipur/Jodhpur," later in this section). If you want to grab an early lunch of authentic Jain food, make your way to the canteen-style eatery near the main temple, which operates between 11:30am and 1pm; if you're visiting late, perhaps stay for an early dinner, served from 5pm until sunset (5:45pm in winter, and around 7pm in summer).

Tip: Two kilometers (1¼ miles) north of Ranakpur, you will pass **Tribal Dhurrie Udyog,** a traditional *dhurrie* (carpet) "shop" (© **0294/241-7833**), where you can pick up a beautifully crafted 4×6m (13×20-ft.) carpet for around $75—a great deal cheaper than what you'll pay in the cities.

65km (40 miles) from Udaipur (2½-hr. drive one-way). Rs 50 camera. Long pants needed. Summer 11:30am–5pm; winter noon–5pm. For information, contact office manager Prema Ramji © **02934/28-5019.**

Kumbhalgarh Fort ★★★   Built in the 15th century by Rana Kumbha, this mountain fortress is, together with Jodhpur's Mehrangarh Fort, one of the most impressive sights Rajasthan has to offer. Take one look at the impenetrable walls (said to be the second largest man-made object visible from space),that snake for 36km (22 miles) along 13 mountain peaks, and you know that this is one of the most inaccessible fortifications ever built by humans. It was in fact only captured once, when the Mughal emperor Akbar had its water supply poisoned. This is also where the infant Udai Singh, who was spirited here by his nanny while Chittaurgarh (see below) was being sacked, spent his formative years. The wall, the second longest in the world, culminates in a fairy-tale fort within which lie the **Palace of Rana Kumbha** and **Badal Mahal** (or **Palace of Clouds,** so named because it literally is in the clouds during the monsoon months). The fort is situated deep within Kumbhalgarh Wildlife Sanctuary, and the drive there—through tiny villages and pastoral countryside—is one of the great highlights of a trip to Rajasthan and a great contrast to the crowded cities. Kumbhalgarh is considered the most important fort after Chittaurgarh, but its relative accessibility and the charm of the drive make this the preferable option. That said, while the sheer size and initial spectacle of the fort stays with you, be warned that the climb to the palaces is steep and stiff, and the buildings themselves are pretty lifeless (there's hardly anything left to suggest anything of the life and times of the people who once occupied these lofty chambers). The real reward for your physical exertion will be the unforgettable views of the surrounding valleys—let your imagination soar and you may just be able to hear the sounds of war.

To have adequate time to explore the fort, or to take in Eklingji on the return journey, it's worth overnighting near the fort. The closest and best choice is the charming **Aodhi Hotel,** a former royal hunting lodge now owned by the Udaipur king's hotel chain HRH (© **02954/24-2341** through -2346; www.hrhindia.com; Rs 6,000 deluxe double, Rs 8,000 deluxe suite). Built of the local packed granite stone and rock, it mimics a hillside fortress, complete with cannons and crenellated walls and elevated thatched towers high up in the tree canopy where you can dine by candlelight. Accommodations are spacious and reasonably neat (each with A/C, TV, and big, thick, comfortable new beds) and overlook a large blue pool and a pretty alfresco dining area. Room nos. 4, 5, 10, 11, and 23 enjoy good views, but you'll no doubt find yourself sharing the hotel with groups during the winter season. Even if you don't stay here, consider stopping for a meal (the Indian food is excellent) and a special drink at the bar—ask for a glass of *kesar kastari,* a unique heritage liqueur made with saffron and 20 other herbal ingredients. *Note:* There is now an evening **sound-and-light show** at the fort; it starts at 7pm, which means you almost *have* to be a guest at Aodhi if you want to see it.

90km (56 miles) from Udaipur (2-hr. drive one-way; 1 hr. from Ranakpur Temples). Admission $2.45 (£1.25). Sunrise–sunset.

Day Trip 3: A History of Valor

Chittaurgarh (Chittor) ★★ Chittaurgarh is 3 hours (115km/71 miles) from Udaipur and covers 280 hectares (700 acres), making it a rather long day trip (it takes around 2 hr. to explore), but it's well worth it if you're armed with information and a good imagination (both of which can be supplied by a good guide; ask your hotel for recommendations). Thrusting 180m (590 ft.) into the sky, the fort houses a number of monuments and memorials, but with much of it in ruins, its primary importance lies in its evocative history. The fort has witnessed some of the bloodiest battles in history, and songs recording the valor and sacrifice of its inhabitants are still sung today.

Built in the 7th century, it remained the capital of Mewar until 1568, when the capital shifted to Udaipur. During this time Chittaurgarh was ravaged three times, but the story of the first sacking that took place in 1303 during the reign of Rana Ratan Singh is perhaps the most romantic (see "Battling for a Glimpse of Beauty," below).

Chittaurgarh returned to Rajput rule in 1326 and the Mewar enjoyed 2 centuries of prosperity before it was again laid siege to, this time by Sultan Bahadur Shah of Gujarat. To save the life of the Rajput heir Udai Singh, his nursemaid Panna Dai sacrificed her own infant son, leaving him as a decoy for the murderous sultan and spiriting the tiny heir away to Kumbhalgarh Fort. The women and children of Chittaurgarh committed *jauhar* (mass ritual suicide) while their men died in battle.

When, at the age of 13, Udai was reinstated at Chittaurgarh, he searched in earnest for a new site for the capital, building Udaipur on the shores of Lake Pichola. Eight years later, the Mughal emperor Akbar, trying to contain the arrogance of Udai Singh—who

Battling for a Glimpse of Beauty

It is said that the rapacious sultan Allauddin Khilji laid siege to the fort because he had become obsessed with tales of the legendary beauty of the Maharana (or Rana) Ratan Singh's queen, Rani Padmini. He promised to withdraw, provided Singh allow him an opportunity to lay eyes on her—an outrageous demand considering that a strange man's gaze was tantamount to the defilement of a Rajput royal woman. But in the spirit of compromise, Singh reluctantly agreed to present him with her reflection in the lotus pond that lay below the palace's women's quarters. The sultan used this opportunity to betray the king, ambushing and capturing him on his departure. The next day a bereft Padmini sent word to the sultan that she would give herself to him in return for her husband and the withdrawal of his troops. She then descended through the seven *pols* (gates), surrounded by what appeared to be her maids-of-honor—Singh's troops, disguised as women. Singh was rescued from the sultan's camp, but the ensuing battle cost the lives of some 7,000 of Singh's men—a crippling loss. When it was clear that the Rajputs would be defeated, the funeral pyres were lit, and Padmini and 13,000 women and children committed *jauhar*, flinging themselves onto the flames, after which the last of Singh's men went to meet certain death below the ramparts.

poured such contempt on Jai (of Jaipur) Singh's collaboration with the emperor—attacked Chittaurgarh. This time 30,000 Rajput lives were lost, and the women and children again flung themselves on the flames rather than be captured by the Muslims. Chittaurgarh was given back to the Rajputs in 1616, much of it in ruins, but by this time the royal family was comfortably ensconced in Udaipur, and the fort was never lived in again.

The fort is approached through seven massive *pols*, or gates—look for the *chhatri* (cenotaph) of the chivalrous Jaimal and his cousin Kala near Bhairon Pol. Jaimal was seriously wounded defending Chittaur against Emperor Akbar but he refused to give up and was carried back into battle on the shoulders of Kala, where both were slain. At Ram Pol is a **memorial to Phatta** who, at 16, having lost his father in battle and witnessed the deaths of his sword-wielding mother and young wife on the battlefield, led his saffron-robed men to certain death while the women of the fort yet again ended their lives by committing *jauhar*.

As you enter the final *pol*, you will see **Shingara Chauri Mandir,** a typically adorned Jain temple, and the crumbling **15th-century palace** built by Rana Kumbha up ahead. Under the palace lies a series of cellars where Padmini reputedly committed *jauhar* (see box). Rana Kumbha was one of the Mewar's most powerful rulers: In addition to the palace, he built nearby **Khumba Shyam Temple,** dedicated to Varah (an incarnation of Vishnu), as well as **Meera Temple,** dedicated to the poet and princess Meera, whose devotion to Krishna reputedly saved her from being poisoned. (Incidentally, Krishna is usually depicted as blue as a result of the poison he consumed, thereby saving the world.) Within the cenotaph in front of the temple is a **carved figure** of five human bodies with one head—in a rare overture to tolerance, this supposedly demonstrates caste equality. Farther south lies Kumbha's **Vijay Stambh (Tower of Victory)**—a lavishly ornamented tower built by Maharana Kumbha to commemorate his victory over the combined forces of Malwa and Gujarat.

Other sites of interest are **Padmini's Palace,** where the sultan Allauddin Khilji gazed upon Padmini's reflection in the lotus pond; **Kirti Stambh,** a 12th-century tower ornamented with figures, dedicated to the first Jain *tirthankara;* **Fateh Prakash Palace,** built for the maharana during the 1920s and housing a dry archaeological museum (small fee; Sat–Thurs 10am–4:30pm); and **Kalika Mata Temple,** originally built as a Sun Temple by Bappa Rawal in the 8th century but rebuilt during the 14th century and dedicated to Kali, goddess of power and valor. Some of the best views are from **Gaumukh (Cow's Mouth) Reservoir,** so-called because the spring water trickles through a stone carving of a cow's mouth.

Note: You can get here by train from Udaipur, but it's a late-night trip, departing at 9:40pm and arriving 2 hours later, so you would have to overnight, and perhaps consider moving on to Jaipur the following evening (on the same connecting train). Accommodations in Chittor are limited, with no luxury options. If you *have* to overnight, the best option is **Pratap Palace** (© **01472/24-0099;** Rs 1,500–Rs 4,500 double); the priciest rooms have A/C units with tubs in the attached bathrooms.

115km (71 miles) from Udaipur (3-hr. drive one-way). No admission charge.

Day Trip 4: Undiscovered Palaces & Deco Delight

Note: If you've come through the hardships of Gujarat over the Araveli Hills and into Rajasthan and are not quite ready for the throngs of Udaipur, then a night or two at Dungarpurs' Udai Bilas Palace is highly recommended. Play lawn tennis, soak in the Jacuzzi, row on the lake, or simply bird-watch from the infinity pool with a gin and tonic in one hand and binoculars in the other. Dungarpur is a peaceful and welcoming town with extraordinary history and the oldest palace in India, and is an easy must-do side trip.

Dungarpur's Palaces ★★★ (Finds) It's hard for anyone flipping through Angelika Taschen's book *Indian Style* to refrain from gasping when they come to the pages recording the magnificent apartments of 13th-century **Juna Mahal.** The palace—one of three, and the only one not too dangerous to visit—commands a sweeping view of Dunparpur and the Araveli Hills. A seven-story fortresslike structure that appears to spring forth from its rocky surrounds it doesn't look like much from the outside, but inside, it houses one of the world's most interesting "art galleries": Every wall and column is covered with beautiful, intricate frescoes—tiny paintings; mosaics with glass, mirror, and tiles; or artfully used porcelain plates embedded into the walls. And don't forget to look above you: On one ceiling panel, gorgeous images of Krishna depict the playful god getting up to all kinds of shenanigans. In one of the massive downstairs reception rooms, the entire floor is covered with huge decaying Persian carpets. Yet even though it houses a treasure trove of art and design, the palace is far from being a tourist attraction: There are very few visitors and not a single hawker in sight, only the toothless old retainer whose trembling hands hold the keys while he waits for you to drink it all in before he opens another, even more stunning room. Perhaps it is precisely this—viewing such beauty in absolute solitude—that makes the experience so special, but the artworks are considered to be of the very best in Rajasthan. Don't miss (you're unlikely to, as long as the old man is around to leer at your reaction) the collection of miniature paintings depicting scenes from the *Kama Sutra;* locked away behind cupboard doors in the Maharaja's Suite on the top floor so as not to corrupt his subjects, it's a veritable A to Z of erotic possibilities, including some near-impossible feats (definitely bring a flashlight).

Although Dungarpur is slightly less than a 2-hour drive from Udaipur, you will surely want to consider combining the tour with a stay at nearby **Udai Bilas Palace** ★★ (© **02964/23-0808** or 93-1465-3967; www.udaibilaspalace.com; 22 units; doubles from Rs 5,100, suites Rs 6,300, grand suites Rs 8,000, Art Deco suite Rs 11,000, Maharawal suite Rs 15,000), which has a magical lakeside setting and offers no hardship except if you choose to row your own boat that is. This, too, is a wonderful experience, particularly if you are looking for some privacy far from the madding crowd, have an interest in the Deco period, relish a sense of nostalgia, or are a keen bird-watcher. Built on the shores of the pretty Gaibsagar Lake, it's excellent for birders all year-round.

Dungarpur Is 120km (75 miles) south of Udaipur (a 2-hr. drive one-way), and 175km (109 miles) from Ahmedabad, Gujarat. Admission: Rs 150

WHERE TO STAY

Sadly, there is always the remote possibility that the fabulous Lake Pichola will succumb to climatic pressure and finally dry up. We strongly urge you to call ahead and check on the status of the lake waters to make an informed lodging choice; we'd hate for you to fork out a load of cash for a special lake-facing room, only to end up staring at a parched lake bed. For instance, without a view you can rule out the Fateh Prakash and Lake Palace and consider instead a room at Udaivilas or the new Fateh Garh, or one of the other more reasonably priced options such as Jagat Niwas, then head off to spend a night at Devi Garh, or stay at Fort Seengh Sagar or Shahpura Bagh en route to Jaipur, or Rawla Narlai en route to Jodhpur. Assuming that the lake is full of water, then it is definitely worth booking into a hotel or haveli with a view of the lake, which is magical; accommodations on the eastern shore are best for sunsets, but this is also the best time to be on one of the islands: the Lake Palace itself, or on Jag Mandir.

Aside from the top recommendations below, it may be worth looking into the **Trident** (© **1600/11-2122** or 0294/243-2200; www.tridenthotels.com). It's a large, mellow, purpose-built hotel set behind Udaivilas with plenty of amenities and facilities but set some way from the lake among the tranquil Aravalli Hills, about a 25-minute drive from town. Ranging from Rs 10,000 to Rs 14,000 per double (check online for daily rates and deals), this comfortable, reputable option offers relatively good value (pool-facing rooms, which also have views towards the hills, are best) and will suit the less-adventurous traveler, but it's a bit soulless for our taste, and far from the action. Similarly the new five-star **Radisson Plaza Resort and Spa, Udaipur** (© **294/305-2600** or 1800/1800-333; fax 294/305-2666; www.radisson.com/udaipur; reservations@radissonplazaudaipur.com), while predictably robust with its service and decor, can also be a bit bland compared to the options below and is also some way from the city and Lake Picola.

Lake Pichola

Lake Palace Hotel ★★★ Just looking at this much photographed 18th-century island palace is enough to make you want to start planning a trip to India; and it certainly lives up to its promise, from the experience of being ferried there by boat, to being gently serenaded at dusk by the flautist, or being treated like royalty in the beautiful bar. Both standard and deluxe rooms feature wood paneling and murals, lovely marble bathrooms, well-crafted furniture, opulent fabrics, and blissful Egyptian cotton linens. Best of all, everywhere you look—be it from the 263-year-old mango-tree-shaded pool, your room, or the restaurant—you have picture-perfect views: the statuesque City Palace walls and crenelated rooftops to the east, the whitewashed havelis and temples of the Old City lining the shores of the lake to the north, the Aravalli Hills to the west, or Jag Mandir to

> **(Moments)** **Floating Bliss**
>
> A must-do romantic experience is to book an early evening treatment on the Lake Palaces floating spa boat, and emerge totally destressed moored in the middle of the lake, to the image of the sun setting over the Aravalli hills and the lights of the palace reflected in the water.

the south. The huge and opulent suites (of which nos. 116 and 117 housed the queen and the king, respectively) were thankfully left more or less as inherited from the royal family and have a timeless grandeur that the City Palace hotels could only wish for. Note that the luxury rooms with City Palace views tend to be smaller than those facing the hills, which are like miniature suites (albeit with cramped bathrooms), and be very careful to insist on a room with a view over the lake—a few deluxe units overlook the lily pond in the internal courtyard.

P.O. Box 5, Udaipur 313 001. © **0294/252-8800.** Fax 0294/252-7975. www.tajhotels.com. 85 units. Rs 34,650 luxury double; Rs 40,000 palace double; Rs 140,000 royal suite; Rs 192,500 grand royal suite. Taxes extra. AE, DC, MC, V. **Amenities:** 2 restaurants; bar; astrologer; babysitting; boat trips; currency exchange; doctor-on-call; 2 outdoor Jacuzzis; minigym; pool; reading room; room service; spa; 24-hr. water taxi. *In room:* A/C, TV, DVD/CD player, personal butler, minibar, Wi-Fi (30 min Rs 125; 1 hour Rs 200; 3 hrs. Rs 600).

Eastern Shores of Lake Pichola

Fateh Prakash & Shiv Niwas Palaces   The last two palaces built within the City Palace walls are now both hotels, but unless you want to overnight in what feels like a wealthy old aunt's large but stuffy apartment, there's only one section worth considering: the relatively new **Dovecoat Wing** in Fateh Prakash. Almost all the rooms in this wing, which stretches along the shoreline, have the most wonderful views of the lake and its palace, as well as views beyond the distant Aravalli Hills (perfect at both sunset and dawn); room nos. 511 and 617 even have little sitting rooms that jut over the water. By contrast, Fateh Prakash's much pricier "Regal Suites," while a great deal larger, are overdressed, overcarpeted, and old-fashioned—these definitely need sprucing up. Crescent-shaped Shiv Niwas Palace, built around the pool courtyard, is positioned farther south, and without the lovely Lake Palace floating before you, its views are a great deal less magical. And that's *if* you get a lake view. Service will almost certainly try your patience. Overall we recommend you look elsewhere.

City Palace Complex, Udaipur 313 001. © **0294/252-8016** or -8019. Fax 0294/252-8006. www.hrhindia. com. Fateh Prakash 28 units. Shiv Niwas 31 units. **Fateh Prakash:** Rs 24,000 dovecote doubles and regal suites. **Shiv Niwas:** Rs 15,000 palace double (no views); Rs 36,000 terrace suite (nos. 15 and 16 lake-facing); Rs 44,000 royal suite (nos. 5, 6, 7, and 18 lake-facing); Rs 80,000 imperial suite (no. 17 lake-facing). AE, MC, V. **Amenities** (shared by hotels): 3 restaurants; billiards; doctor-on-call; Internet (Rs 150/hr.); massage; pool; spa; squash. *In room:* A/C, TV, minibar.

Jagat Niwas ★★ (Value)   This 17th-century haveli literally rises from the waters of Lake Pichola and is the best in its price category. Approached through a narrow street that runs into the entrance, it is essentially a cluster of buildings around a central courtyard. Rooms vary considerably, with only suites and deluxe rooms providing lake views—of these, no. 102 (super deluxe) and nos. 101, 110, and 116 (suites), are particularly pleasing options, and the latter is the most romantic. Note that deluxe rooms with lake views are generally much smaller than those without. Ceilings often feature colored glass

baubles typical of Rajasthani havelis; walls have painted murals; fabrics are traditional
Rajasthani block prints; and many rooms have alcoves with mattresses. The best part of
the hotel is the wonderful covered terrace that overlooks the lake and hosts evening
shows. But if you want a pool, Udai Kothi (see below) is a better option.

23–25 Lal Ghat, Udaipur 313 001. (℧ **0294/242-0133** or -2860. Fax 0294/241-8512. www.jagatniwaspalace.
com. mail@jagatniwaspalace.com. 29 units. Rs 1,550 standard double; Rs 2,150 regular deluxe double; Rs
2,550 lake-facing deluxe double; Rs 3,650 super deluxe double; Rs 5,999 suite; Rs 750 extra bed. Taxes
extra. AF, MC, V. **Amenities:** Restaurant; bar; currency exchange; doctor-on-call; horseback riding; Internet (Rs 150/hr.); room service; safaris. In room: A/C, TV.

Western Shores of Lake Pichola

A real gem, situated in the nearby countryside on a hilltop alongside the otherworldly
Monsoon Palace, the regal Fateh Garh ★★ ((℧ **0294/3290228;** www.fatehgarh.in; resv@
fatehgarh.in) is the place to stay if you want to be far from the crowds of Udaipur, yet
close enough (20 min.) to buzz in and out without compromising on understated luxury.
A new property (opened Nov 2008), which has already featured in *Condé Nast Traveler's*
Hot List and Worlds Sexiest Pools (May, Aug 2009), it commands sweeping views east
towards Lake Pichola. Constructed with found objects and antique architectural pieces
and restored on the principle of Vastu (Indian Feng Shui), and owned and managed by
the Jitendra Singh Rathore family (of HRH fame), it cuts a symmetrical, almost roman
presence into the countryside but is softened by the use of airy verandah's, local stone and
sustainable power. With 48 rooms in total including 10 suites, the ones to go for are the
corner suites which are a steal at Rs 20,000 (standard rooms are Rs 14,000, rooms 9 and
10 have their own plunge pool and terrace). If you don't decide to stay the night then the
least you should do is come for a sundowner and a swim in the infinity pool, and linger
for dinner at one of the two restaurants.

Amet Haveli ★ (Value Located on the shores of Lake Pichola, with views of Jag Niwas
directly opposite, this pretty 350-year-old haveli has enough charm to have found its way
into glossy books, but it's rather basic for anyone wanting lots of amenities. Nevertheless,
all accommodations face the lake, and if you book suite no. 16, or 7, a corner unit with
a large mattressed *jarokha* that juts over the water, you'll have lovely views of the City and
Lake palaces, which you can even see from your king-size bed. Freshly whitewashed, with
simple furnishings, the room is airy and light, and very good value. Suite no. 8 is almost
twice as large—a bright, marble-floored space with antique furnishings—but the views
are not nearly as spectacular. The five new upstairs guest rooms are completely modern
additions. Despite the standard menu, the **Ambrai** restaurant has a good reputation for
its tandoori dishes, and its lakeside setting makes it an ideal sunset spot under shady
mango trees.

Outside Chandpole, Udaipur 313 001. (℧ **0294/243-1085** or -4009. Fax 0294/252-2447. regiudr@datainfo
sys.net. 15 units. Rs 4,000 double; Rs 5,000 suite; Rs 500 extra bed. Taxes extra. AE, MC, V. **Amenities:**
Restaurant; bar; doctor-on-call; Internet (Rs 50/hr.); pool. In room: A/C, fan, TV.

The Leela Palace Kempinski Udaipur ★★
The Disneyfication of the pristine
heritage landscape of Udaipur continues with the opening (May 2009) of this world-class
hotel. Attempting to borrow from both the Taj Lake Palace and the somewhat corporate
Oberoi, yet with neither the sense of history or location, it must start as a third choice.
That said, once you are resigned to its failed exterior design and step inside, the magic
begins to take hold. Rooms are arguably the plushest in Rajasthan in the sense that they
are brand-new, with the latest technology, and extremely well thought out; even the

standard category rooms have everything you'd expect from a five-star suite. The destination fine Indian dining at the rooftop lakeside Sheesh Mahal is a grand affair, and The Dining Room has an amazing walk-in global wine collection to match its worldly cuisine (chef Karim Hassene brings his Michelin two-star restaurant experience from Paris). In fact one cannot help gawk at the exquisite lighting, the ornate *thekri* work and tasteful adornment of Indian artifacts throughout—never gaudy, oppressive, or trying too hard.

The Leela Palace Kempinski, Udaipur, P.O. Box 125, Lake Pichola, Udaipur 313001, India. ℂ **294/670-1234.** Fax 294/670-1212. www.theleela.com. reservations.udaipur@theleela.com. 80 units. Lakeview room Rs 13,500 per night; heritage view room Rs 15, 500. Taxes extra. Rates include breakfast and return airport transfer. AE, DC, MC, V. **Amenities:** 2 restaurants; lounge/bar; babysitting; butler service; boating; concierge; doctor-on-call; Internet; limousine transfer from airport on request; 2 pools; room service; spa (with Ayurvedic treatments); water taxis. *In room:* A/C, TV, DVD/CD library, minibar, iPod docking station, Wi-Fi (Rs 150/hr.).

Udai Kothi ★ ⓥalue   The fragrant scent of marigold fills the air at this laid-back hotel built by entrepreneurial Vishwa Vijay Singh and decorated by his keen-eyed shopaholic wife. Together, they've created a relatively authentic replica of a traditional haveli. It may not be as well located (with regards to top attractions) as Jagat Niwas or Amet Haveli, but it's an easy stroll to the Old City, with Udaipur's only rooftop pool, situated on a trellised terrace where meals are served—the views at night are breathtaking. Accommodations are comfortable, with canopied beds, block-print fabrics, frescoes, and individually sourced pieces. Ask for a lake-facing room on the third floor for the best views. Underscoring the immense popularity of this unassuming place, there are plans to double the size of the property with new pools, new suites, an additional restaurant, and a launch for budget-conscious jet-setters who enjoy arriving by boat.

Udai Kothi, Udaipur 313 001. ℂ **0294/243-2810** or -2812. Fax 0294/243-0412. www.udaikothi.com. 32 units. Rs 5,000 standard double; Rs 6,000 deluxe double; Rs 7,000 suite; Rs 1,500 extra bed. Taxes extra. MC, V. **Amenities:** 2 restaurants; bar; airport transfers Rs 500; boating; bookshop; cultural performances; doctor-on-call; garden; health club; Internet (free); Jacuzzi; pool; roof terrace; room service; traditional performances. *In room:* A/C, TV.

Udaivilas ★★★   You'd be forgiven for relinquishing all sightseeing responsibilities and simply giving in to your inner indolence at this highly relaxing resort, much lauded in various glossy magazines and influential travel sites. If you're a first-time visitor to Udaipur, you'll want to reserve a lake-view room (which automatically has access—from your own personal porch—to a semiprivate infinity pool that forms a veritable moat along the length of the accommodations wing); this is the best way of ensuring round-the-clock visual access to the city's favorite sights. Otherwise, book a cheaper room and plan on spending your days at the spa pool (the main resort pool, designed like a monumental step-well, is lovely but lacks views). As in all Oberois hotels, the staff and service levels are exceptional, all look absolutely beautiful and they are engaging, sincere and intuitive, and cuisine is superb.

Haridasji Ki Magri, Udaipur 313 001. ℂ 0294/243-3300. Oberoi hotels: ℂ 800/562-3764. Fax 0294/243-3200. www.oberoihotels.com. 87 units. Rs 30,500 premiere double; Rs 36,500 premiere lake-view double; Rs 170, 000 luxury suite with private pool; Rs 240,000 Kohinoor suite with private pool. Taxes extra. AE, DC, MC, V. Amenities: 2 restaurants; lounge/bar; babysitting; boating; butler service; CD/DVD library; doctor-on-call; limousine transfer from airport complimentary on request; 2 pools; room service; Banyan Spa (with Ayurvedic treatments); Wi-Fi (30 min. for Rs 113; 60 min. for Rs 225; 24 hours for Rs 885); adjacent wildlife conservatory. In room: A/C, TV, DVD/CD, Internet, minibar, semi-private pools (some); suites have private pools.

Reviewed below is the famous Devi Garh, which we feel is slipping somewhat from its revered pedestal but hopefully will soon be back on track. It's a short distance from Udaipur (26km/16 miles or 45 min.) along a winding, scenic road with fields of corn, sugarcane and mustard seed, and hotel staff will arrange camel or horse safaris, jeep treks, or chauffeured tours of Udaipur, Eklingji, Nagda, Nathdwara, Kumbhalgarh Fort, and Ranakpur. If it doesn't suit your budget, or if you'd prefer to be within even easier striking distance of the city, you'll be pleased to learn that the owners of popular Udai Kothi have come up with a marvelous little property just 6km (3¾ miles) from Lake Pichola. Surrounded by dramatic hilly landscape, **Udai Bagh** ★ (see Udai Kothi, above; www. udaibagh.com) is a serene country retreat with a big pool and just seven luxury tents; there are plans in the not-too-distant future for an upmarket destination spa with additional rooms (from Rs 8,500 double), to be designed by Nimesh Patel, who had his hand in Udaivilas. The air-conditioned en-suite tents—outfitted with clay tile floors, block-print-fabric ceilings, and metal frame beds (reserve no. 1 if you want a double bed) have lovely wooden furniture and piles of magazines and books to keep you entertained (there's also a TV, minibar, Wi-Fi, and room service if reading doesn't suffice). Bathrooms have big, smart showers, and there's a little porch with seats out front (it's not very private, but you won't be sharing the property with too many people). Udai Bagh is also just Rs 8,500 double, with breakfast. There's no restaurant, but a butler brings you whatever you want, and there's a free shuttle service to and from Udaipur—just 10 minutes away.

Devi Garh ★★   This is an unparalleled masterpiece in design, marrying the towering exterior of an original 18th-century Rajput palace (which remains totally unchanged) with a re-invented minimalist contemporary interior, in which almost everything, from the bed and sofa bases, sunken bathtubs to ashtrays and vases, is carved out of white marble. Little wonder that it's become a popular Bollywood and VIP wedding location and reaped numerous international awards. But we were distressed during our last visit to find an overall sense of neglect and arrogance, including small but essential things such as old towels, uncomfortable pillows, insufficient water pressure, a heated pool in the middle of summer, general staff disenchantment, and dated bathrooms—at the price, inexcusable. Designwise the hotel is still stupendous and we hope that management issues will be ironed out to make this highly acclaimed hotel (by, among others, *Condé Nast Traveler Gold List and RCA 2009, Vogue, Wallpaper*) once again one of our favorites. (Write and let us know if in your experience it does!)

Devi Garh, Delwara Village 313 001. ⓒ **02953/28-9211.** In Delhi: 011/2335-4554 or 011/2375-5540. www.deviresorts.com. devigarh@deviresorts.com. 49 units. Low season (Apr–Sept)/high season (Oct–Mar): Rs 37,000/Rs 45,000 garden suite; Rs 57,000/Rs 73,000 palace suite; Rs 77,000/Rs 93,000 Aravalli suite; Rs 117,000/Rs 133,000 Devi Garh suite; Rs 2,000 extra bed. Taxes extra; certain ultra peak-season supplements apply. AE, DC, MC, V. Meals extra: Breakfast Rs 650/725, lunch Rs 1,300/1,500, and dinner Rs 1,500/1,700. Special venue meals extra lunch Rs 1,000, dinner Rs 2,000. **Amenities:** Restaurant; bar; astrologer; babysitting; cycling; doctor-on-call; health club/gym; horse/camel riding; Internet free; kite flying; library; pool; pool table; room service; spa; table tennis; tennis court; village walks. *In room:* A/C, TV, DVD/CD, minibar, free Wi-Fi.

WHERE TO DINE

When it comes to Udaipur's fine-dining experiences, don't miss an evening at the **Lake Palace Hotel,** where you can watch beautiful young Rajasthani Banjari women twirl to a hypnotic drumbeat (while behind them are sublime views of the City Palace turning pink). This waterside dance routine is usually followed by a more elaborate performance in an open-air courtyard alongside the fabulous bar where you can order a cocktail and enjoy canapés served by the splendid waitstaff. After the show, head to one of the hotel's very smart restaurants; be prepared to shell out considerably for the privilege of dining in one of the most special spots in India, especially the unforgettable rooftop terrace in winter, and make sure to book in advance (*C* **0294/252-8800**)—you'll need a reservation in order to get ferried to the hotel in the first place.

If you're gathering memorable (and pricey) dining experiences and don't mind journeying to the far western shore of Lake Pichola, you could check out the alfresco dining at **Udaivilas** (*C* **0294/243-3300**); be warned that although most dishes are excellent, the food is not the best we've had in the state (the signature *laal maas,* for example, tasted watered down, and even the *naan* bread was unexpectedly doughy). Nevertheless, a meal here might give you the chance to explore the hotel's spectacular architecture and landscaped gardens, and service is on a par with that at the Lake Palace, which you can see here from your table.

If you really feel deserving of excellent cuisine and don't mind traveling out of town to a gorgeous country scene, set aside time for a midday tour to **Devi Garh** ★★ (see details above), one of the classiest hotels in India. The food is exquisite (and expectedly pricey), and if you are here for a midday sojourn, you can admire the brilliant restoration of the castle and perhaps explore the little village after you've dined. The menu is limited, but if you want to know where Udaipur's informed movers and shakers take their out-of-town guests for a special treat, this is an ideal venue. Reservations are essential.

A more casual but bland dining experience is the **Sunset Terrace** at the Fateh Prakash Palace. This is the perfect place to watch the sunset, and when the sun finally disappears behind the Aravalli Hills, the ambience just gets more romantic as candles are lit and the Lake Palace, which floats in the foreground, glows like an ocean liner on the lake. That said, the food—which ranges from toasted sandwiches (adequate) to tandoori (overcooked)—is very much a letdown. Far better fare and more comfortable seating are to be had at nearby **Jagat Niwas** (see details above). Unlike almost everywhere else in town, this restaurant terrace is open to the cooling breezes but covered by a roof, which provides some escape from the midday heat, rather go one level up to the very top: It has comfortable mattressed alcoves with bolsters where you can curl up with a book or appreciate the sublime views of the lake. This is the kind of place where you could spend an entire afternoon relaxing; in fact, one guest, who wasn't even staying in the hotel, did exactly that every day for the duration of his stay in Udaipur. Service is slow but friendly (some of the waiters have been here 18 years), and the food is good. Stick to the Indian dishes, either the vegetarian (*paneer matar masala,* Indian cheese simmered in a thick gravy with peas and tomatoes; or *paneer do pyaja,* cheese cooked with onion, tomato, and chilies) or local dishes like fish a la Jagat (slices of the local freshwater fish from Jaisamand Lake, caught daily, cooked in a lemon sauce, and served with fries) or chicken lababdar in a cashew tomato gravy, signature lamb Lal Maas, Afghani *murgh malai tikka* (creamy chicken kebabs). Main courses cost between Rs 85 and Rs 350.

Two other dining options are worth considering, both with lake views. **Ambrai,** at the Amet Haveli (details above), serves decent enough tandoori dishes (and some Indo-Chinese and "Continental" as well). The place has a mellow ambience created by the warm light from candlelit tables, and wrought-iron chairs in the pleasant sprawling garden right on the edge of Lake Pichola. It is also great for a lunchtime beer, where you can watch the locals water bombing one another from the nearby ghat and an elephant munching beside them. **Udai Kothi's** rooftop restaurant is also a lovely spot at night

(especially with the terrace pool lit up), with good service. Choose a small alcove by the
pool—with mirrored dome, cushions, candlelight, and a good butter chicken, this could
be one of the most memorable meals you have in India.

Set in the garden courtyard of Jhadol Haveli, **The Whistling Teal** (103 Bhatiyani
Chohatta; 🕿 **0294/242-2067** or 094-1416-3727) is one of the most romantic dining
spots in Udaipur. Despite its lack of lake views, it's a relative oasis. You can saddle up
(literally) to the bar (seats are made of horse saddles), or chill out with a hookah (sheesha)
pipe, sampling different flavored tobaccos. There are various seating areas, either on the
lawn or under canopies, and you can sample an array of traditional Rajasthani dishes.
The royal Jhadol family also organizes some of the most intriguing visits to rural areas,
where you get to come to grips with the customs of the tribal Bhil people. For more
information, visit **www.jhadol.com**.

Finally, if you're after something light, healthy, and affordable, particularly for lunch,
consider the ironically named **Savage Garden** (22 Inside Chandpole; 🕿 **0294/242-
5440**), set over several floors of a pleasant building with cascading bougainvilleas and a
towering banana tree in its blue-walled courtyard. Besides some standard Indian fare, you
can order toned-down, simplified versions of traditional cuisine, such as "spinach mutton," served with boiled potatoes (*boiled*, not fried!), or grilled fish with mash, and even
an unusual vegetarian "Kela curry": slices of banana in an onion-curd sauce, seasoned
with fragrant spices from the south. There are basic, healthy salads and a few pasta dishes,
not to mention a delicious mulligatawny soup. You'll pay Rs 80 to Rs 250 for a main
course.

SHOPPING

Udaipur has a number of attractive handicrafts. You're probably best off purchasing them
directly from small factories whose touts will beg you to visit, but beware that the commission system can add significantly to the price, so don't buy the first beautiful thing
you see. The main shopping streets run from the City Palace along Jagdish Temple Street
to the clock tower and beyond to Hathi Pol. Good areas are Suraj Pol, Bapu Bazaar,
Chetak, and Ashwini markets. **Rajasthali** (Chetak Circle; beware similarly named stores
elsewhere), the government-run handicraft shop, is a good place to both pick up basic
handicrafts and gauge fair prices. **Mangalam** (Sukhadia Circle; 🕿 **0294/256-0259**) is
best for textiles, handicrafts, *dhurries,* and a variety of products.

If you'd like to contribute to local communities, visit the city showroom of **Sadhna**
(Jagdish Temple Rd.; 🕿 **0294/241-7454;** www.sadhna.org) where you can browse hand-
stitched garments, homewares, and linens. A purchase here means contributing to the
income of 500 rural and tribal women who are involved in this enterprise. If you're looking for silver, a great place to start is **Boutique Jagat Nikhar** at the Jagat Niwas hotel (see
details above); here, Mr. Harish Arora offers advice on silver items, and his excellent collection comes with fixed prices. Udaipur is considered a good place to purchase miniature
paintings (it has its unique style, but if you're looking for a bargain, you're better off
purchasing in off-the-beaten-track towns, like Bundi) and *pichhwai* paintings—wall
hangings painted on cloth or silk, often featuring scenes from Krishna's life, that originated in Nathdwara; see "Top Excursions," earlier in this chapter. Alternatively, you
could pick up some of these at the **City Palace Museum shop;** the prices are higher but
well worth the quality.

Further along the City Palace Road and on the same street as Jagdish Temple, is
Ganesh Handicraft Emporium (🕿 **294/252-3647**), which occupies one of Udaipur's
oldest, most beautifully renovated havelis. With its cool marble floors, courtyards and

ancient carved wooden guajarati doorframes it works perfectly as a store to browse through its uncongested and spacious rooms. The experienced and hassle-free owner brothers will offer you chai or cold water and will leave you to your own devices to wander around their 350-year-old living museum. They specialize in Rajasthani, Guajarati, Central and South Indian and Kutchi textiles.

Other goods worth keeping an eye out for are puppets and wooden folk toys, enamel or Meenakari work, *dhurries* (rugs), tie-dye and block-printed fabrics, embroidered bags and clothing, and silver jewelry. As is always the case, consider carefully before you buy (cheaper is not always better and often means the object is a poor imitation), and try to bargain. Plenty of places will try to sell you paintings, but if you're looking for top quality (or at least want to understand the difference), you'll need to visit the artist **Kamal Sharma** (15A, New Colony, Kalaji-Goraji; © 0294/242-3451 or 98-2904-0851). A four-time national award winner, Sharma works on paper, marble, and silk. Nearer the City Palace, you can visit **Shreenath** (City Palace Rd.), where a father-and-son team has been in business for years and conducts considerable export trade; ask to view the more elaborate (and expensive) paintings in the back room, bearing in mind that quality is determined by the intricacy of the brush strokes, which (at first) really need to be viewed under a magnifying glass. You'll soon develop a knack for spotting finer paintings at a glance. For a really kitschy souvenir, you can even commission a traditional miniature with your own face in the scene; just bring a photograph!

To view traditional Udaipur (and Gujarati) embroidery, visit **Jagdish Emporium** on City Palace Road; but note that a far superior and more affordable outlet, **Rama Art Gallery** (Haridas ji ki Magri; © 0294/512-0771), is located near Udaivilās and the Trident. For beautiful beaded bags, head for **Chandpole Road,** where you will also find a number of jewelry stores.

A Special Spot Between Udaipur & Jodhpur

If you are traveling by car from Udaipur, Jodhpur signals the start of the flat, semiarid landscape that leads north-west towards the Thar Desert, and we recommend that you spend a few nights unwinding in the lusher more characterful landscape of the Aravalli Hills, and here there is no better place than Rawla Narlai.

The Rawla Narlai ★★★ Ⓥalue A stylish 17th-century hunting retreat of the Maharaja of Jodhpur, located in the heart of the semi–arid, granite-boulder strewn Aravalli Hills halfway between Udaipur and Jodhpur (an ideal and well-priced overnight stop after you visit the Jain temples of Ranakpur which are less than an hr. away, and/or Kumbhalgarh Fort), the lovely Rawla Narlai is an excellent-value destination, providing good food, good taste and undivided attention to the individual needs of guests. It's also a destination in its own right, one completely free of touts, shops, and pushers; your dapper, congenial host, "Tikka," who has been in the hospitality trade for 42 years, will gladly provide a guide to take you on a relaxed walk through the village, and personally accompany you on sundowner and bird-watching visits to the lake, local temples or the beautiful 7th century *baoli* (step well, still using both its old and new water drawing methods). Or you could go riding on beautiful Marwari horses. Follow these activities with cocktails in the idyllic garden or courtyard accompanied by a devotional sitar singer (jogi), a neck and shoulder rub, and a delectable, romantic, candlelit rooftop dinner.

140km (87 miles) from Udaipur (via Ranakpur 125km/78 miles); 160km (99 miles) from Jodhpur. Reservations through Ajit Bhawan, Near Circuit House, Jodhpur 342 006. © 0291/251-0410, -1410, or -0610. Fax 0291/251-0674. www.narlai.com. reservations@ajitbhawan.com. 25 units. Rs 8,000 standard double; Rs 9,000 deluxe double; Rs 10,000 luxury tents around pool; Rs 15,000 luxury room double; Rs 2,000 extra bed. Taxes extra. AE, MC, V. **Amenities:** Restaurant and rooftop dining; babysitting; bird-watching; camel safaris; currency exchange; doctor-on-call; excursions; horse riding; Internet (complimentary); pool; rock climbing; transfers. *In room:* A/C, fan.

8 JODHPUR

336km (208 miles) E of Jaipur; 260km (161 miles) NW of Udaipur; 295km (183 miles) SE of Jaisalmer

Founded in 1459 by Rao Jodhaji, chief of the Rathore Rajputs who ruled over Marwar, "land of death," Jodhpur was to become one of Rajputana's wealthiest cities, capitalizing on its central position on the Delhi-Gujarat trade route and protected by one of the most impenetrable forts in history. Today it is the state's second-largest city, much of it a sprawling, polluted metropolis, but within the old walls—where every building is painted the same light blue hue, earning Jodhpur the nickname "Blue City"—you'll find a teeming maze of narrow medieval streets and bazaars, where life appears much as it has for centuries. Towering above is **Mehrangarh (Majestic) Fort,** its impenetrable walls rising like sheer cliffs from the rocky outcrop on which it is built. From its crenelated ramparts you enjoy postcard views of the ancient blue city below and, in the distance, the grand silhouette of **Umaid Bhawan Palace,** residence of the current Maharaja and award winning (*Condé Nast Traveler* 2009 Hotel of the Year) heritage hotel. Within the fort is a typical Rajput palace that today houses one of the state's best-presented museums, artfully displaying the accumulated accouterments of the royal house of Rathore in the beautifully preserved royal apartments.

The labyrinthine Old City is a more visually exciting experience than Jaipur, but besides exploring these medieval streets and visiting Mehrangarh Fort and Umaid Bhawan Palace, there's not much to hold you here for more than a day or two—most people use Jodhpur as a jumping-off point to Jaisalmer or as an overnight stop before traveling on to Jaipur or Udaipur.

ESSENTIALS

VISITOR INFORMATION The tourist reception center is located in the **RTDC Ghoomar Tourist Bungalow,** on High Court Road (**(** **0291/254-5083** or 254-4010; Mon–Sat 10am–5pm; closed second Sat of the month). Your own hotel's reception will assist with reservations for sightseeing and day tours. The tourist **help line** number is **(** **1364** (Mon–Sat 9am–5pm). Convenient places to withdraw cash against your credit card are the HDFC or ICICI ATM at Ratanada Chauraha, **UTI Bank** (near Kwality Inn, Chandra Hotel), or **Bank of Baroda** (Sojati Gate).

GETTING THERE Traveling by car from Udaipur takes approximately 5½ hours with no stops; the journey from Jaipur takes about 6½ to 7 hours. However, Jodhpur is very well connected by rail and air. As always, try to book flights with the more professional **Jet Airways** (**(** **0291/510-3333** or -2222 city office, 0291/251-5551 or -5552 airport), though you'll have to use **Indian Airlines** (**(** **0291/251-0757** or -0758 city office, 0291/251-2617 airport) if you want to fly to Udaipur. Jodhpur's **airport** (**(** **0291/251-2934**) lies 4km (2½ miles) south of the city. Expect to pay about Rs 270 for a taxi into town; this will be less if you use the prepaid taxi service. Jodhpur's main **train station** (**(** 131 or 132) is on Station Road, just south of the Old City walls. The overnight Mandor Express links the city to Delhi in 12½ hours; the Jaipur Intercity Express gets you here from Jaipur in 5 hours. There are two daily trains from Jaisalmer (6 hr.), early morning and late at night. At press time, train services to/from Udaipur were still suspended until the completion of the new railway line.

GETTING AROUND   Rickshaws are the most useful way to get around the Old City (a 15-min. ride should cost around Rs 50), but you'll need to hire a taxi if you plan to visit the outlying attractions. To hire a car and driver for the day (or longer—for instance, for a round-trip to Jaisalmer or to Udaipur), contact Kawaljeet Singh on **Rajasthan Tours** (*©* **0291/251-2428** or -2932; www.rajasthantouronline.com). For local travel needs call Dilip Singh at Travel Plan at *©* **0291/251-2354** (jodhpur@travelplanraj.com; A-1 Sir Pratap Colony, Airport Rd.), who can arrange excellent guides (ask for Kalyan Singh) and everything from tailored packages to drivers and onward travel.

FESTIVALS   **Diwali,** the Hindu New Year celebration that takes place in October/November, is celebrated all over India, but the "Festival of Lights" is particularly exciting when viewed from the lawns of Umaid Bhawan Palace. At the grand bash held by Maharaja Gaj Singh II, you can experience firsthand the deep reverence with which the former ruler of Jodhpur and Marwar is still treated—everyone wants to kiss the hem and touch the hand of their beloved father figure. The 2-day **Marwar Festival,** held during the full moon in October, is also worth attending, particularly to see the fire dance held on the Osian dunes. Celebrations include classical folk music concerts, puppet shows, camel polo, and even turban-tying contests. The end of the festivities is heralded with the **fire dance,** when men jump over burning wood to the rhythm of drums and chants. Sometimes dancers perform on top of red-hot coals, moving in an almost trancelike state to percussion beats.

WHAT TO SEE & DO

Having visited the fort and Umaid Bhawan Palace, there's no reason to overextend yourself, especially given the dusty heat. If you're here for a few days you may opt to include a trip to **Mandore,** which lies 9km (5½ miles) north of the Old City. The previous capital of Marwar (not to be confused with Mewar, the princely state of Udaipur), Mandore has as its principal attractions today gardens (in dire need of attention) in which lie the templelike cenotaphs built to honor the Rathore rulers before final rites were moved to Jaswant Thada (see Mehrangarh Fort & Museum, below). The largest and grandest of the red-sandstone structures was also the last to be built here; it commemorates the life of Maharaja Dhiraj Ajit Singh, who died in 1763. Beyond, in a totally separate section (pious to the end), is a group of smaller cenotaphs, built to commemorate the female counterparts. Opposite the weird but ultimately missable museum is the **Hall of Heroes,** a collection of 18th-century deities and Rajput heroes carved out of a rock wall. If you haven't tired of temples by now, you can move on to visit the Hindu and Jain temples at **Osian,** 65km (40 miles) north of Jodhpur. You first come across the **Vishnu** and **Harihara temples,** which were built between the 8th and 9th centuries, but more impressive (or at least still alive with worship) are **Sacchiya Mata** (12th c.) and **Mahavira Jain temples** (8th and 10th c.). See Ranakpur Temples, earlier in this chapter, for rules on entering a Jain temple. Virtually every hotel and agent in town arranges **village safaris,** in which you are taken into the arid surrounds to make contact with the rural Bishnoi people, sample their food, and learn about their traditional remedies and crafts; expect to pay from Rs 1,500 for two people for a 5-hour trip that should include some wildlife sightings. If you're curious, ask your operator or hotel if you can also see a traditional opium tea drinking ceremony, which forms part of the daily rituals of village life. You can arrange these safaris through Travel Plan or the RTDC at the tourist office (see "Visitor

Information," above), but you'll save yourself much effort by asking your hotel to make all arrangements.

Mehrangarh Fort & Museum ★★★ "The work of angels, fairies and giants . . . he who walks through it loses sense of being among buildings; it as though he walked through mountain gorges . . ." wrote Rudyard Kipling in 1899. Little has changed since then, and for many this looming 15th-century edifice to Rajput valor is still Rajasthan's most impressive fort, with walls that soar like sheer cliffs 120m (400 ft.) high, literally dwarfing the city at its base, and a proud history of never having fallen to its many invaders. Before you start exploring the fort, pick up an audioguide (free with entry fee; passport or driver's license required as deposit). This is in fact one of the best audioguides you will get at a tourist site in India, with sound effects and commentaries from former rulers of Jodhpur recorded on an MP3 player in seven languages. It contains additional information on subjects like the caste system, the maharajas, miniature paintings, and more. If you prefer a more interactive tour, where you do not have to stand around in listening groups and can ask questions, then hire a local guide (there are few better than Kalyan Singh (see Visitor Information above). Do not hire one at the fort entrance, most of whom consider the audioguide useless and will ultimately steer you toward some ill-considered shopping in order to reap a commission (you have been warned). There is an elevator, but rather choose to walk past cannon-pockmarked and *sati*-daubed **Loha Gate** (the maharajas' wives would traditionally immortalize their lives by leaving handprints on the fort walls before tossing themselves on the flames to join their deceased husbands). Once at the top, you enjoy not only the most spectacular view, but you enter one of India's finest museums, with a rich collection of palanquins, royal cradles, miniature paintings, musical instruments, costumes, furniture, and armor. Every room is worth exploring (allow at least 2 hr.), but among the highlights are ladies intricately carved Zennana (note the overhangs on the outside of the *jarokhas* to protect the sandstone latticework from the rain) the gorgeous **royal chamber** where the Maharaja entertained his 30-plus wives (we're not even counting concubines; look out for the large wall mirrors in which his wives could get glimpses of his antics from their quarters); **Moti Mahal,** featuring the throne on which every Marwar Maharaja has been crowned; and **Phool Mahal,** the "dancing hall" with its pure gold ceiling as well as The Armoury with its fascinating collection of carved swords and daggers. A massive **silk and velvet tent,** taken from Emperor Shah Jahan in Delhi, is a vivid illustration of the superlative wealth and decadent pomp with which the Rathore rulers lived. After visiting the courtyard of **Chamunda (Sun Goddess) Temple** (remember to remove your shoes), take the road that leads to the left to view what is apparently among the rarest collections of cannons in India—again, the view alone is worth it. There is a very good museum shop (look for the exquisite silk and chiffon fabrics made by award-winning Tyeb Khan) and a restaurant where you can catch your breath.

On the road that leads to and from the fort, you will notice **Jaswant Thada,** a white marble cenotaph (built in the same marble as the Taj) built to commemorate the life of Maharaja Jaswant Singh II, who died in 1899, and where the last rites of the Jodhpur rulers have been held since then. It's a pretty and relaxing place and worth the short stop off for its respite after the crush of the fort and its great views. If you finish with the fort before sunset, descend to the cobbled streets of **Sadar Market,** where the sights and aromas of India's ancient and narrow streets—packed with cows, people, goats, carts, and chickens, and remarkably untouristed—may leave you wondering whether you've wandered onto the set of a movie about medieval times. If it all gets too claustrophobic, hire

---

(Fun Facts   Eighteenth-Century Tree Huggers

Traveling on the road to or from Jodhpur, you will no doubt come across black buck, a delicate antelope with spiraling horns, and Khejri, the tough, desert-surviving trees that provide shelter and sustenance for the desert tribes and the black buck. Both animal and tree are sacred to the Bishnoi tribes, so much so that when an 18th-century Jodhpur ruler sent his army out to clear Khejri trees to make way for a new road, the Bishnoi women clung to the trees in protest—363 women died with their arms wrapped around their beloved Khejris before the Jodhpur king intervened. You can still visit the Bishnoi on "village safaris" offered by just about every hotel and guesthouse in town.

---

a rickshaw in which to sit in relative comfort and watch the passing parade or escape to the nearby Pal Haveli for a rooftop drink. All in all, this will be one of your most satisfying outings in Rajasthan. (*Note:* Try and tour the fort in the morning in summer [out of season] and in the evening in winter.)

The Fort, Jodhpur. © **0291/254-8790.** Mehrangarh Fort: Rs 250 includes camera fee and audioguide; Rs 200 video; Rs 15 elevator. Apr–Sept 8:30am–5:30pm; Oct–Mar 9am–5pm. Jaswant Thada: Rs 20; Rs 25 camera; Rs 50 video. Daily 8:30am–5:30pm.

Umaid Bhawan Palace ★★★   This splendid palace is as much a top attraction as far and away the best place to stay in Jodhpur (see below). Situated on another raised outcrop, and commanding the south eastern horizon, with broad views and manicured grounds creating an almost rural ambience, it was built by Maharaja Umaid Singh (the current Maharaja's Gaj Singh's father who now occupies a third of the palace with his family) as a large scale poverty-relief exercise to aid his drought-stricken subjects with employment. With 347 rooms, including a cinema, it was at the time the largest private residence in the world—a vivid reminder of the decadence the Rajput rulers enjoyed during the British Raj. Designed by Henry Lanchester, a great admirer of Lutyens (the man who designed the great New Delhi buildings), it was commenced in 1929, took 3,000 laborers 15 years to complete, and remains one of the best examples of the Indo-Saracenic Art Deco style, topped with a massive dome which rises 56m (184 ft.) high, beyond which the buildings are perfectly symmetrical. Its original Art Deco furniture and fittings were en route from Maples in London and were sunk by a German U-boat during the height of WW2 but the ever-resourceful Maharaja instead utilized the services of a Polish refugee, Stefan Norblin, who completed the interiors true to the grand Art Deco theme. After the spectacle of the 32m (105-ft.) central dome in the Palm Court (where you really need to pause and let your eyes drink it all in), you'll want to spend some time exploring the various public spaces (decorated in Art Deco furniture and fittings), swanning up and down the sweeping marble staircases, and heading down to the spa and hypnotic indoor pool—which will transport you to back to the 1940s with its bold blue zodiac-sign mosaics.

Guests are taken on a personal tour of the entire palace (excluding the private residence of the royal family); ask if you can see the Maharaja and Maharani suites, which have not been renovated but represent another opportunity to peek back in time. After your tour, stop to sip a coffee at The Pillars, from where you enjoy a spellbinding view of the fort in the distance (note that nonguests are technically required to pay a cover charge even when dining at The Pillars, though this will be deducted from your bill). There is also a museum that features photographs of the construction and a model of the building, as well as items collected by the maharaja's ancestors.

Umaid Bhawan Palace, Jodhpur. (C) 0291/251-0101. Admission to hotel restaurants Rs 2,000 payable at reception, and deductible from your dining bill. Museum: Rs 50. Daily 9am–5pm.

WHERE TO STAY & DINE

If you want to experience the medieval spirit of daily life within the Old City (and catch the early morning market vibe), your best bets are the quaint Pal Haveli or at the other end of the price range the mod, expensive boutique hotel Raas (both reviewed below).

If you'd prefer to escape the chaos of the Old City, head for the outskirts, to the newer part of town (20 min. from the fort) where there are a number of well-run, respectable guesthouses and hotels, of which we like Ratan Villas, Devi Bhawan and Ajit Bhawan (in ascending order of price, all reviewed below). Aside from these there is the reliable **Taj Hari Mahal** ★ (5 Residency Rd.; (C) 0291/243-9700; www.tajhotels.com; from Rs 14,000 for a well-appointed superior pool-facing room), a smart, spacious hotel built in the style of a Marwari palace. Aimed predominantly at the wealthy business market, this will suit those who want to be cocooned in a bland modern hotel with professional service but at the expense of character; if you can afford it, you'll be far better off at the Taj-managed Umaid Bhawan Palace (reviewed below).

Jodhpur is not renowned for its restaurants; you're pretty much limited to dining in hotels. Even if you're not overnighting at Umaid Bhawan, spend a few hours at **The Pillars,** the hotel's informal cafe restaurant where you sit at the base of a cavernous colonnaded veranda that steps down to the palace lawns—get there before the sun goes down to watch the almost surreal changing hues of the sky over the fort, have a drink or two, and then head down the marbled corridor to Risala and sample a selection of their delicious kebabs and signature Lal Maans.

Widely regarded as the best tourist restaurant in town, with a great nighttime atmosphere (make sure they're serving in the garden), **On the Rocks** (next to Ajit Bhawan; (C) 0291/510-2701 or -7880) is famous for its barbecue dishes—skewers of spicy vegetables, *paneer,* or meat tenderized in a yogurt-based marinade and cooked over an open fire. For a more leisurely dinner, with decent Indian food and enchanting views of the Fort, head to **Indique,** the rooftop restaurant at Pal Haveli.

Ajit Bhawan ★★ (Kids) This recently renovated resort-style hotel is a hugely popular place, and some may prefer its more laid-back, down-home atmosphere to Umaid's plush palace. It's also significantly cheaper and has a wonderful outdoor pool and a good restaurant. Built at the turn of the century for Maharaj Ajit Singh (younger brother of the Maharaja Umaid Singh), it incorporates crenelated castlelike walls and traditional Hindustani elements, as well a variety of rooms depending on budget and mood: from the luxury thatched "Bishnoi" stone cottages, with their own little garden and patios, to a selection of gorgeous luxury tents, to slick executive rooms. Decor is the work of Raghavendra Rathore, the owner's son and one of the country's most celebrated designers. (Car enthusiasts may dig the fleet of 10 vintage cars on offer—the oldest Buicks and Fords date from 1928.)

Near Circuit House, Jodhpur 342 006. (C) 0291/251-1410. Fax 0291/251-0674. www.ajitbhawan.com. 54 units. Rs 9,000 deluxe double; Rs 10,000 executive double; Rs 15,000 luxury double; Rs 30,000 suite. Rs 2,000 extra bed. Breakfast included. Taxes extra. AE, DC, MC, V. **Amenities:** Restaurant; pool; airport transfers from Rs 400; currency exchange; vintage cars for hire; doctor-on-call; evening folk dancing;

health club; Internet (Rs 100/hr.); room service; safaris—horse, camel, and village; spa. *In room:* A/C, TV, minibar, Wi-Fi in some rooms (Rs 100/hr.).

Devi Bhawan ★★ (Value) This low-slung sandstone residence is a great surprise—a bungalow with free-standing cottages set within a lush, tranquil garden with pool, personal service, and offering unbelievable value. Ask for an air-conditioned semideluxe (bungalow) room (particularly no. 10), or spend a little extra on deluxe unit no. 11, or try booking one of the new rooms (nos. 17–21) in the new pool facing block. All the rooms are clean and neat with simple, casually stylish furnishings—there's not a hint of plastic anywhere. Completely overhauled in 2007, with the added advantage of air-conditioning, the restaurant spills out onto a neat little lawn surrounded by greenery; you can (and should) dine here. All in all, a very comfortable, relaxing, good-value option, and once seduced by the pool, you may just find yourself extending your stay in Jodhpur.

1 Defence Lab. Rd., Ratanada Circle, Jodhpur 342 011. © **0291/251-1067** or 98-2803-5359. Fax 0291/ 251-2215. www.devibhawan.com. devibhawan@sify.com. 18 units. Rs 1,200 standard/garden double; Rs 1,500 semi-deluxe/bungalow double; Rs 1,800 deluxe double. 10% luxury tax on rooms over Rs 1,200. MC, V. **Amenities:** Restaurant; bar/lounge; doctor-on-call; Internet access (Rs 60/hr.); pool; Wi-Fi free. *In room:* A/C (most rooms), fan, TV.

Pal Haveli ★ This heritage haveli is *the* place to stay if you want to be in the real heart of the bustling (and admittedly noisy) town (especially if you want to get those early morning shots of the empty medieval market place); it also has wonderful views of the Fort towering directly in front of it. Once you enter—via a steeply sloped ramp and through massive traditional doors—you can shut out the world. Rooms are a mixed bag so have a look: All are spacious and decorated to enhance the ambience of an earlier era; beds are comfortable, and bathrooms are exquisitely clean. You have a choice of either lake-facing, fort-facing, or heritage room; those arranged around the fountain courtyard tend to be quieter, with a more sophisticated look but rooms 101, 102 (gran's rooms), 103, 107, and 121 are wonderfully renovated. Meals at the alfresco rooftop restaurant, **Indique,** are accompanied by views of the fort, palace, and lake.

Gulab Sagar, Jodhpur 342 001. © **0291/329-3328,** 0291/263-8344, or 09350408034. www.palhaveli. com. info@palhaveli.com. 21 units. Rs 3,000 standard double; Rs 4,000 heritage double; Rs 6,000 suite; Rs 8,000 Historical Suite; Rs 500 extra bed. Taxes extra. MC, V. **Amenities:** 2 restaurants; airport transfers from Rs 400; bar; billiards room; complimentary station pickup; doctor-on-call; room service; village safaris; Internet and Wi-Fi free. *In room:* A/C, TV, minibar.

Ratan Vilas ★ (Value) Built in 1920 by current owner Brij Raj Singh's grandfather, this haveli has been painstakingly restored, preserving its traditional character while adding modern comforts—which makes it an excellent option in this price category. Air-conditioned rooms are simple, naturally lit and tastefully styled with antique furniture (which Brij Raj collects) and traditional hand-block-printed curtains and bed sheets (book deluxe room no. 101, 102, or 104, or bag one of the slightly larger units in the new wing). It's a homey place with old family photographs and souvenirs adorning the walls—no five-star amenities, of course, but the food has home-cooked freshness, service is prompt and personalized, and you can even ask to step into the kitchen for a demonstration of traditional Rajasthani cooking. Sun-worshipers can take advantage of the sun-deck chairs on the terrace and veranda,

Loco Shed Rd., Ratanada, Jodhpur 342 001. ©/fax **0291/261-4418.** www.ratanvilas.com. info@ratanvilas. com. 21 units. Rs 900 non-A/C double; Rs 1,200 A/C double; Rs 2,000 deluxe double; Rs 2,650 superior double; Rs 500 extra bed. Taxes extra. MC, V. **Amenities:** Dining hall; bar; complimentary pickup; currency exchange; doctor-on-call; Internet (Rs 100/hr.); village jeep safari. *In room:* A/C, TV.

Umaid Bhawan Palace ★★★   Far and away the grandest lodging in Jodhpur, this is also one of the proudest pieces of architecture in the state (see "What to See & Do," above). Its formidable sense of grandeur is augmented by the galley of turbaned staff who will make you feel like royalty. It has every amenity; even an in-house cinema, which you can reserve (ask the concierge to recommend a big-budget Bollywood DVD). The quality of rooms varies according to what you're able to spend; this is a good place to indulge if you can afford one of the historical suites—these grand spaces are packed with gorgeous period furniture, lovely artworks, and every possible amenity. Alternatively, ask for a room with a private terrace. Wherever you stay you can wander the vast lawn where Liz Hurley staged her much-publicized wedding to her Indian beau, Arun Nayar, then head for the outdoor pool—a tranquil spot to unwind at the end of the day and, with cocktail in hand, watch the fort light up as the sun descends.

Umaid Bhawan Palace, Jodhpur 342 006. (℃) **0291/251-0101.** Fax 0291/251-0100. www.tajhotels.com. 75 units. Rs 40,000 palace double; Rs 83,000 historical suite; Rs 140,000 royal suite; Rs 300,000 grand royal suite—Maharaja; Rs 500,000 grand presidential suite Maharani. Taxes extra. AE, DC, MC, V. **Amenities:** 3 restaurants; bar; smoking lounge/reading room; airport transfers from Rs 500; billiards room; cinema; concierge; doctor-on-call; DVD library; gym; health club; Internet (as below); outdoor pool; indoor pool; room service; spa; marble squash court; tennis. *In room:* A/C, TV, CD/DVD player, hair dryer, minibar, personal butler, WI-FI (30 mins Rs 125; 1 hour Rs 200; 2 hours Rs 300; 3 hours Rs 600).

Outskirts of Jodhpur

Mihir Garh ★★★   As you canter through the Thar Desert on your Marwari horse you start to make out the crenellated ramparts of the regal and perfectly proportioned Mihir Garh, "Fortress of the Sun," home—hopefully for more than a day. Like a mirage that rises from the surrounding savanna, this natural mud fort, finished with Jaisalmer desert sand, is surrounded by the space and peacefulness that only the desert brings. Catching the breeze blowing off the plains and surrounded by natural vegetation of indigenous trees, shrubs and local crops, the nine well-appointed suites, all with plunge pools or Jacuzzis, and with spacious bathrooms (bathtubs and walk-in showers) command sweeping views over the savanna and are exquisitely decorated with a nod to the local vernacular. Private terraces extrude tastefully where you can watch the sunset, practice yoga, dine privately or sleep under the stars. This is a special place, and one that demands at least 2 full nights to drink it all in, participate in the unique activities, and experience the beauty, peace, and culture of the local Marwari in their natural surroundings.

Mihir Garh (℃) **02936/268531.** Fax 02936/268331. www.mihirgarh.com. Rs 24,000 suite. Rates include all meals and drinks excluding imported liquor and champagne and includes village safari. Taxes extra. AE, MC, V. **Amenities:** Restaurant; bar; bird-watching by bicycle or horse; concierge; cooking demonstrations and classes; currency exchange; doctor-on-call; Internet (Rs 150/hr.); royal picnic lunch; pool; room service and in-room dining; safaris—jeep, horse, and camel (Mihir Garh hosts an annual horse show, showcasing the Marwari horses); spa; village safaris; yoga. *In room:* A/C, Jacuzzi or plunge pools and fireplaces in all rooms.

Rohet Garh ★★ (ⓥ̲alue)   Professionally run by its aristocratic owner, Sidharth Singh, Rohet Garh may be a tad far from Jodhpur, but the rural peace is intoxicating—peacocks lazily strut on the lawns and pose on the rooftops, while the adjacent village makes for great exploration without the hassle of wandering the streets of the city. It also has a lovely pool in the central courtyard, from which you can access the dining room, serving good-quality Rajasthani food (try the barbecued meats and dal makhani). Rooms, as is always the case with heritage properties, vary dramatically (ask to see what's available when you arrive), but all are relatively spacious, featuring frescoes and Rajasthani antiques in bright, minimalist arrangements. Book the most recently renovated rooms

The Liquid Lifeline

The environment of western Rajasthan is harsh, semidesert and receives very little rainfall. The region is infamous for its fragile and inhospitable eco-system characterized by sandy soils, scarce surface water, depleted groundwater supplies, sparse vegetation cover, low humidity and high transpiration. Drought is a common recurrence and has occurred for 43 out of the last 50 years. Its largely rural inhabitants depend on an agro-pastoral economy and operate in great uncertainty regarding rainfall and subsistence. The Indira Gandhi canal, one of the biggest projects in India was introduced to address this need in March 1958 and was finally completed in 1986. Commencing from the Harika Barrage, a few miles below the confluence of the Sutlej and Beas rivers in Punjab State, the canal runs south southwest in Punjab and Haryana and retracts most of Rajasthan for a total of 650km (404 miles). The canal has provided a guarantee of water from the Himalayas and while it is a life-giver that has changed the face of the Thar Desert and has checked its encroachment, it has consequently changed much of the conservation culture and farming methods in the area. This presumptuousness has also extended to the hospitality industry, so much so that the new 150-plus roomed hotels in Jaisalmer all have large bathtubs in the bathrooms with TV's. Vote with your feet and at all times use water sparingly.

(nos. 6 and 7) though these are around the pool, so are not that private (for more privacy, ask for no. 15 or 30). Room 27 is especially large, with a big shower and a huge carved bed, and has (along with other lake-view suites) a lovely window seats for lazing about with a good book. A couple of the rooms have direct views into the stables, where there are 12 Marwar steeds. Outings include visits to traditional Bishnoi villages; if you have the time, ask about the miniature paintings workshops or sign up for a cooking class.

Note: Also available for travelers with a greater sense of adventure are six luxury tents (Rs 11,500 double, including all meals, evening tea, and village safari), pitched in the desert, 17km (11 miles) away. The tents are a great extension of the activities available at Rohet, and if you are doing the village safari on horseback and stopping for a royal picnic lunch at a small lake you should consider completing your day out in the countryside and stay the night. The campsite offers deep tranquillity, and phenomenal stargazing (though Madonna and her entourage, who stayed for 2 nights, have since left!)

Rohet Garh, Vill P.O. Rohet, District Pali, Rajasthan 306 401. (C) **02936/268-231** or reservations in Jodhpur 0291/243-1161. Fax 0291/264-9368. www.rohetgarh.com. 34 units. Rs 5,000 deluxe double; Rs 7,000 suite. Taxes extra. AE, MC, V. **Amenities:** Restaurant; bar/lounge; bird-watching by bicycle; cooking demonstrations; currency exchange; doctor-on-call; health club; Internet (Rs 150/hr.); pool; room service; safaris—jeep, horse, and camel. *In room:* A/C, fan.

SHOPPING

Jodhpur is famous for its antiques dealers, most lining the road that runs between Ajit Bhawan and Umaid Bhawan. These can be prohibitively pricey, however, particularly when you factor in freight prices. Jodhpur is also good for tie-dye fabrics. The best bazaars are around Sojati Gate, Tripolia, Khanda Falsa, and Lakhara—the latter special- izes in colorful *lac* bangles, which make great gifts. If you're looking for more serious jewelry, head for Station Road. Traditional Jodhpur coats and riding breeches are now only made to order; ask your hotel to recommend a tailor. *Tip:* Beware of making any purchases in or around the fort, particularly if you are encouraged to do so by the local guides; not only will you be paying inflated prices for anything you buy, but guides are paid a hefty commission to get you to part with your cash.

9 JAISALMER

285km (177 miles) W of Jodhpur; 333km (206 miles) SW of Bikaner

Jaisalmer was founded by Rao Jaisal in 1156 as a substitute for his more vulnerable capital at Lodurva, making it the oldest "living" fortified city in Rajasthan. For many, a visit here is the start of an enduring romance. Located in the heart of the Thar Desert on the far western border of India (55km/34 miles from Pakistan), it was strategically positioned on one of the central Asian trade routes, and fortunes were made by the Rajputs and Jain merchants who levied enormous taxes on caravans laden with silks, opium and spices, particularly during the 14th and 16th centuries. In the 18th century, some merchants, wanting to expand their homes, moved out of the fort to settle on the plateau below. Much as in the Shekhawati region, the wealth generated by their taxes was used to decorate the havelis of these wealthy Jain businessmen. Where frescoes satisfied the Shekhawats, here power was expressed by the construction of mansions whose soft sandstone facades were embellished with intricate, almost lacelike carvings. These oft-photographed sandstone mansions are indeed breathtakingly beautiful, but it is Sonar Killa, literally "Golden Fort," that makes it worth traveling this far west. It may not be as impressive or as clean as Jodhpur's Mehrangarh Fort, but its charm lies in the fact that this is the world's only inhabited medieval fort, its families living in homes they have colonized for more than 800 years. Unfortunately this charm is being eroded by the unchecked proliferation of hotels—with close to 40 at the last count.

Built entirely from yellow sandstone, the fort rises like a giant sand castle from its desert environs, with great views from the overhanging cannon ramparts; stare down on the city and desert vista, and you get a sense of how forts such as these once served the most basic of needs: protection against invaders from the plateau below. Sadly within you will find a place that has been commercialized—its alleys lined with goods for sale and buzzing with traffic (tuk-tuks, hawkers, and tourists), excessive pollution (no bins or sewage infrastructure, and watch out for the cow dung), yet still with an awesome sense of timelessness (bar the motorcycles and persistent salesmanship). It takes no more than a few hours to tour the fort, including stops to visit the Jain and Hindu temples. And if you want to ride a camel into the sunset, Jaisalmer is one of the places to do it, as is Bikaner. So plan to spend 2 or more nights here, not least because it takes so long to get here (until the new airport is finished, that is) but also to acclimatize to the desert pace and climate, and seek out the essence of this border town.

ESSENTIALS
VISITOR INFORMATION You'll find the **RTDC tourist office** near Gadi Sagar Pol (© 02922/25-2406; Mon–Sat 10am–6pm; closed second Sat of every month and Sun).

GETTING THERE At press time, Jaisalmer's new airport was expected to open late 2010, finally making it possible to fly to India's easternmost city directly from Delhi. Until flights commence, the nearest airport is at Jodhpur (a 5½-hr. drive; about 2 hr. longer in a bus—not recommended). *Tip:* The best place to stop for lunch or a snack on this route is **Manvar Desert Resort** (near Shergarh; © **02928/266-137;** www.manvar. com), which serves a mean chicken *pakora.* It takes 6 to 7 hours to get from Bikaner to Jaisalmer by road (and there is now a train too which leaves at 10:45pm from Bikaner and arrives in Jaisalmer at 6am). The train journey from Jodhpur takes 5½ hours (on the overnight Jodhpur-Jaisalmer Express), arriving at the station 2km (1¼ miles) east of town. Avoid the touts soliciting riders by asking your hotel to arrange a transfer. From Delhi, take the Delhi-Jaisalmer Express from Delhi's Sarai Rohilla Station; it departs at 5:25pm, arriving in Jaisalmer at 11am the next day. From Jaislamer to Delhi the daily train leaves at 5:15pm and arrives at 11am in Delhi.

GETTING AROUND Both inside and outside the fort, the town is small enough to explore on foot; for journeys farther afield you will need to hire an auto-rickshaw (at the station or Gadsisar Tank) or taxi (Sam Dunes). For the latter, you'll probably take an all-inclusive trip with your hotel, almost all of which offer safaris of various duration; or contact Mr. I. V. Singh from Travel Plan at © **02992/252759** or on his mobile at 09928022496 (jaisalmer@travelplanraj.com). Mr. Singh has over 20 years of local travel experience and can arrange unique travel experiences. For Sam and Khuri camel safaris contact Harish Bhai at **K.K. Travels** (© **02992/253-087;** kktravels_2000@yahoo.com). You'll also find taxis around Suraj Pol or through one of several travel agencies at the entrance to the fort.

FESTIVALS The **Desert Festival** held at the end of January or in February (incidentally, the best time of the year to visit Jaisalmer—in 2010 it will be held Jan 28–30) is the highlight of the year, when dance shows, turban-tying competitions, and camel races are held below the fort, cheered on by colorful crowds who are as much a part of the spectacle as the entertainment. While its relative inaccessibility keeps tourist numbers down, during the festival the town is packed.

WHAT TO SEE & DO

Jaisalmer's main attraction is its yellow sandstone **fort,** whose 9m (30-ft.) walls grow in a roughly triangular shape, springing from Trikuta (Triangular) Hill, on which it is built, and buttressed by 99 bastions. Within you will find a number of elaborately carved havelis overlooking the narrow streets, but the best examples of Jaisalmer's unique **havelis** are situated in the town below. Hordes of tourists end the afternoon by taking a trip out to Sam Dunes or Khuhri to watch the **setting desert sun** from the back of a camel; with a little planning, however, you can enjoy a totally unique **dune-and-camel experience** that will have you falling in love with the desert (see "Camel Safari," below, for our recommendation). If you're more sedentary, head for **Saffron,** the rooftop terrace at the Nachana Haveli, for a view of the fort, which starts to glow as the sky darkens; you'll also witness all manner of daily life on the town's rooftops.

Other attractions are **Gadsisar Tank,** excavated by the Maharaja Gadsi Singh in 1367, which has a few temples and a *chhattri* (cenotaph) overlooking it, but is principally worth visiting to access the nearby **Folklore Museum.** The private museum contains some interesting exhibits, particularly the handcrafted items (look for the mobile temple, and the depiction of the tragic love story of Princess Moomal and King Mahendra, which, incidentally, is told in detail on the Palace Museum audio tour). Exhibits are not well labeled, however; if the proprietor, Mr. Sharma, is not on hand, a guide could prove use- ful here. The small entrance fee is not always charged, but do leave a donation; hours are 8am to noon and 3 to 6pm daily. A shop at the end of the museum sells reasonably priced postcards (and overpriced books).

The best way to experience Jaisalmer's desert surrounds is on a **camel safari** (see below), many of which include the following places of interest. **Amar Sagar** is a small settlement with a palace and a restored Jain temple built around the shores of a lake that lies 5km (3 miles) northwest of Jaisalmer. **Barra Bagh,** which lies 6km (3¾ miles) north of town, is a collection of old and recent cenotaphs to Jaisalmer's Rajput rulers, set paradoxically between two wind farms. Note the decrease in size of the recent structures (daily 6am—8pm Rs 50, cameras Rs 50). Another 10km (6¼ miles) north lies **Lodurva,** the capital of the Bhatti Rajputs from the 8th to 12th century, until it was devastated by Mohammed Ghori before Jaisalmer was built. The main attractions here are more restored Jain temples, with the usual fine carvings (daily 8am–6pm; Rs 20, camera Rs 50, video Rs 100). The entrance to **Thar Desert National Park** lies about an hour (45km/28 miles) from Jaisalmer, near Khuri. Wildlife you are likely to encounter include deer, desert fox, black buck, and the rare long-necked bird known as the Great Indian Bustard.

Tip: For the best views (and photographs) of the fort, the sprawling town below and the encroaching desert, make your way to Shuli Dungari on the northern side of the Fort. From here you can see the desert sun setting into the vast arid plains and have unencumbered views of the fort unspoiled by power lines and mobile network towers (which have been erected with scant regard for the town's profile) while the locals go about their business, kids fly kites and play on swings, and dinner is prepared.

Exploring the Golden Fort

Some 1,000 people still live in the tiny village inside **Sonar Killa,** or Golden Fort, which has twisting lanes so narrow they can be blocked by a single cow (be warned that these animals *know* that they have the right of way, so step aside, and watch their waste products too). Exploring the fort is easily done in a morning—you access the fort through Gopa Chowk, ascending the battle-scarred ramparts to enter the main courtyard, overlooked by seven-story Raja Mahal, or Maharaja's Palace, which now operates as the **Fort Palace Museum & Heritage Centre** ★★★ (© 02992/25-2981). Thanks to a brilliant audioguide tour, the palace has become one of the most alluring tourist attractions in the state, packed with information that not only brings to life the history of this unique place, but waxes vividly about the aristocrats who built and frequently defended it. It also does an excellent job of shedding light on intriguing aspects of regional culture. Set aside around 2 hours for the tour; admission is Rs 250 and includes the audioguide as well as still camera use (video is Rs 150)

After the palace, the other great reason to visit the fort is to check out the panoramas of the city below and the distant desert vistas (although a number of exquisite bird's-eye views are afforded throughout the palace tour) from various perspectives. There are a number of interesting vantage points (a few are specifically marked), but do be aware that buskers may try to take advantage of you by starting up a tune and then insisting on a donation. Search for the many strategic cannon points which are peppered around the periphery or head straight for the pretty **Jain temples,** which lie west (just ask for directions) The best among these (Rishabnath and Sambhavnath) are open only to non-Jains after 11am. Entry is Rs 30 and you'll pay Rs 50 to take a camera in, double that for video. No leather is allowed within the temple, and menstruating women are restricted from entering. Constructed between the 14th and 16th centuries, these temples are typical of

> **(Fun Facts) Buying a Sense of Place**
>
> The beautiful carvings and latticework on the *havelis* are a source of pride and a show of wealth for the local owners and neighborhoods, as well as being tourist attractions in their own right. Some, however, find their way into modern hotels as stand-alone pieces in spare, cathedral-like lobbies hoping to import some heritage into their ill-designed structures. This is technically illegal but does occur and is likely to increase given the rise in local construction, demand for rooms and unique, authentic design attractions which cannot be easily or cost-efficiently replicated. If you spot some of these "relocations," have a polite word with the GM of the relevant hotel and ask about its provenance.

Jain craftsmanship, with every wall and pillar as well as the ceiling covered with the most intricate relief carvings, and large statues representing the Jain *tirthankaras,* or "Enlightened Ones"—note that you cannot enter the caged sanctuaries in which these sculptures sit, or touch or photograph them. A small library has a collection of rare manuscripts, books, and miniature paintings. Take a breather at **Toap Khana (Place of Cannon)** for the views, then head north, turning right at some stage to find **Laxminath Temple** (again, just ask). Although the Jain temples are worth a visit to see the intricacy of the carvings, it is the Hindu temple that pulsates with energy, particularly if you get here when worshipers chant their *bhajans,* devotional songs (about 10:30am and at several other times during the day; check with your hotel). From here it's a short walk back to the main courtyard.

(Note that cars are not allowed to drive up or down the fort, so you'll need to use an auto-rickshaw or simply take the pleasant walk up its winding cobblestone streets.)

The Jaisalmer Havelis

Haveli refers to a traditional, ornate Rajasthani "mansion," with one or more internal courtyards. Steps lead up to an ornate door through which you enter a central courtyard, around which the family apartments are arranged. The facades of the Jaisalmer havelis, built as elsewhere by the town's wealthy merchants, are unsurpassed for the delicacy of their relief carvings, filigreed windows, and lacelike screens and *jarokhas* (small projecting balconies). A testament to the softness of the sandstone but even more to the skill of the *silavats,* Jaisalmer's community of stonemasons, these beautiful facades, some of which date back more than 300 years, have been perfectly preserved, thanks largely to the hot, dry climate. You will find them dotted all over town, but the most impressive are Patwon ki Haveli, Salim Singh ki Haveli, and Nathmalji ki Haveli. **Patwon ki Haveli** (Rs 50) actually comprises five ornate houses built by the wealthy Patwon for his five sons between 1800 and 1860. The houses are connected from within (though some are privately owned and not open to the public) and have flat-topped roofs. Inside one of the houses is the **Basant Art Emporium,** where you can pick up truly exquisite handicrafts—but certainly not at bargain prices—collected by the owner from the desert tribes. Patwon ki Haveli is open daily between 10am and 5pm (8:30am–7pm in summer); admission is Rs 50 (cameras extra). South of this, near the fort entrance, is **Salim Singh ki Haveli,** built by a particularly mean-spirited and greedy prime minister who extorted the hell out of the Rajput's kings' subjects, and even squeezed the royal family by providing huge loans and then charging exorbitant interest rates. It was apparently once two stories 587higher, but legend has it that the Rajput king blew away the top floors in a fit of pique, and Salim Singh was later stabbed to death. It's not necessary that you enter, and it's not always open (though times advertised are 8am–6pm, up to 7pm in summer). You can't enter **Nathmalji ki Haveli,** but it's still worth swinging by to play "spot the difference" with the beautiful facade. The right and left wings look identical at first glance, but they were separately carved by two brothers—the numerous tiny differences can take hours to discover (this is where a guide comes in handy!). It's on the road to Malka Pol (just ask for directions). Note that many of the havelis now house overpriced handicraft shops; you will have to bargain hard to get the prices down.

Camel Safari

Spending some time in the desert on camelback is touted as one of Jaisalmer's must-do activities and almost every hotel and innumerable agents offer camel trips in various locations. Don't book one just outside of town, where there are no dunes but a semi-desert rocky terrain surrounded by wind farm turbines and mobile network base stations. Hardcore travelers may opt to spend a night or even two "camping" out in the desert (some outfitters have semipermanent camps, with en-suite tents), trekking to sites of interest during the day and enjoy meals around bonfires under the stars (pack warm sleepwear for this) but most people choose to spend only a few hours in the desert, usually watching the sun set from **Sam Dunes,** about an hour from town by car. Keep in mind that the popularity of these short trips means you will more than likely be surrounded by noisy travelers in areas that are looking increasingly degraded—with discarded bottles and cigarette packages, and kids cajoling you to buy warm colas and make "donations." The whole experience can be unbearable if you value solitude and want a unique experience that doesn't feel like an overhyped tourist trap. If the idea of a communally enjoyed sunset doesn't ruin the romance for you, you can take a camel ride at sunset from Khuhri, which lies almost 2 hours away by car. The latter is obviously less popular, so it's not as busy, but it is no longer the unspoiled experience it was 15 years ago.

Should you wish to saddle up with the masses, the most reliable camel safari agent is **Royal Desert Safaris** (Nachana Haveli; ℂ **02992/252-538;** rsafari@sancharnet.in). Expect an all-inclusive late-afternoon camel ride, with dinner and jeep transfers, to cost Rs 1,050 per head. The camel ride without food and transfers is Rs 250; also offered are overnight packages for camping out in the desert in Swiss cottages (Rs 4,500 double, including rides, entertainment, and meals). Alternatively you can drive out yourself and negotiate directly with one of the camel drivers who line the road with camels—the state of the saddle is a good indication of which one to choose. In any case, your backside is likely to start aching after a while—the best part of the ride might be getting out of the saddle and strolling over a dune or two; or, if you're feeling adventurous, ask your camel-*wallah* to climb up behind you and take you for a canter.

If you'd rather escape the tedium of done-to-death camel safaris, contact **Shakti Singh** of Nachana Haveli (see "Where to Stay," below); he'll arrange a unique, tailor-made, and totally private **desert experience** ★★ that will combine a camel safari with visits to remote villages, perhaps a meal on the dunes, and a delightfully intimate knowledge of the environment. Shakti, the unassuming son of a maharaja, lived in the desert for 2 years getting to grips with a way of life most sophisticated urbanites could hardly conceive. He's knowledgeable about the flora and fauna that you come across as you traverse the dunes; although young and modest, he knows the region better than the multitude of "professionals" offering camel safaris.

RAJASTHAN: LAND OF PRINCES

JAISALMER

Jaisalmer offers three general choices: Stay inside the fort, stay in the town that sprawls at its base, or head out into the desert and stay at one of the "resorts" or tented camps a few minutes' drive from the town itself, built where there is space for such luxuries as swimming pools and gardens. The best of the latter are Rang Mahal (closest to town), Jaisalmer Gateway Hotel, and Fort Rajwada (all reviewed below). Choices in the town are a mixed bag, but if you're looking for historic ambience, good food and great atmosphere, nothing beats **Nachana Haveli.** As for staying inside the fort, there is now such a strong argument against it that we cannot in good faith recommend it. The increase in water usage (mostly due to tourist traffic), which relies on medieval drainage systems, has started to literally pulp the ancient sandstone fort, and clearly the best way to preserve it is to avoid staying in the fort itself (please see box below). And our top overall pick? The new Serai, located deep in the desert, where you can feel the sand between your toes. (An excellent value desert alternative is Moolraj Sagr which has 18 water-cooled tented suites, set in lush gardens with its own *baoli;* © **03014/207070;** www.jodhanaheritage.com; Rs 12,500 double, plus 10% taxes, including all meals.)

Sand Castle in Peril

The oldest living fort in history is literally crumbling and as a result has been listed on the World Monument Fund's Most Endangered Sites. The ancient bantonite sandstone structure is exhibiting very real signs of an imminent collapse—with its external walls saturated with dark wet stains, seepage from lack of drainage systems and a direct result of tourism activity inside the fort itself (excessive water and sewerage use); one can already see areas which have crumbled and are undergoing repair work. In 1998 six people died when an exterior wall collapsed, which was followed by a number of its bastions in 2000 and 2001. Once merely a small village consisting of a handful of tiny dwellings and home to only the fort inhabitants, lack of regulation and legislation, and demand, has seen unchecked development with close to 40 hotels crammed into the tiny historic space. And it's not only the structure that is being destroyed: the ambience and history is now covered with rank commercialism—rows of fabric and textiles cover the beautiful sandstone walls, Thai fishermen's pants and signs for Tibetan restaurants fill the winding, cobbled alleyways, discarded plastic bottles and litter accumulate in every corner, while you are constantly requested to "just look." The *pols* are lined with reclining touts and the families who live in the fort, most who do not have associated business interests with it, are becoming increasingly irate with the situation. In fact more and more of the young families have decided to make their homes outside the fort due to cultural pressures, lack of space, and the inability to continue their lives undiluted by tourism. This is not the Jaisalmer to which people have traveled from all over the world, and then across the Thar Desert to find; nor is it the one that will provide its inhabitants with a sustainable income or historical legacy. Its beautiful honeycombed fort, the nectar of this desert flower city, is in danger of being ruined on every level (structural, experiential, and cultural) and it is for this reason that we have *not* included any accommodation or restaurant reviews inside the fort, choosing rather to focus on the ample range of lodgings and dining outside this ancient endangered sandcastle.

An international campaign, Jaisalmer in Jeopardy (JiJ), has been established to facilitate repair and maintenance work for the fort. It has upgraded homes, implemented drainage and sewage infrastructure among other fortifying work. For the past 10 years, and at the time of writing, the authorities have made regular assessments and have that the best solution in the interests of preservation would be to shut down the hotels and restrict tourism activities. Of course when people's livelihoods are affected it is a political football and a sensitive and emotional subject.

If you'd like to contribute in any way contact JiJ (℃ **020/352-4336;** www.jaisalmer-in-jeopardy.org).

The Gateway Hotel, Rawalkot, Jaisalmer ★★ Ⓥalue A smaller (only 31 units) and arguably quieter and more peaceful option than the next-door Fort Rajwada, this Taj property, geared more for the independent traveler than groups, is wonderfully laid out with natural stone and a sense of scale and proportion that makes its neighbor appear cumbersome and unwieldy. The attractive dining room serves signature *Laal Maas* and *Bajra and Sogra,* and opens out onto a lovely courtyard that includes a perfect pool which has a stunning view of the fort in the distance. In fact, this is the best pool in Jaisalmer and is for residents only. The rooms are a bit affected for a new Gateway property.

Jodhpur-Jaisalmer Rd., Jaisalmer 345 001, Rajasthan. ℃ **0299/225-1874** or -252-638. Fax 0299/225-0444. www.thegatewayhotels.com. gateway.jaisalmer@tajhotels.com. 32 units. Rs 6,500 suite; Rs 800 extra bed. Taxes extra. AE, DC, MC, V. **Amenities:** Restaurant; bar; babysitting; doctor-on-call; pool; room service. *In room:* A/C, TV.

Nachana Haveli ★★ Ⓥalue This is by far the best heritage option in the city, and particularly good if you're young at heart and want to hang with Jaisalmer's friendly and hip elite. Almost 3 centuries old, this atmospheric mansion (next door to the royal palace) has seen better days, but it has real character and charm, with 13 individually styled rooms (we like room nos. 111 and 107; and no. 112 is quite lovely). The family run hotel is the brainchild of Vikram, the globe trotting son of the Maharaja of Nachana and cousin of Jaisalmer's own king. He's a bit of a collector, so all spaces are decorated with eclectic paraphernalia; the vaulted ground-floor lounge, in particular, feels like a motley family museum. Vikram's younger brother, Shakti, arranges unique desert experiences for you, provided you give him sufficient warning (see "Camel Safari," above) while their beautiful sister Divya will pick out something perfect for you from her boutique. At press time, Vikram was planning an underground lounge bar and rooftop pool, both welcome prospects. *Note:* As with most hotels, rates are increased by Rs 1,000 during the Desert Festival. Saffron rooftop restaurant serves typical Rajasthani cuisine from an open kitchen specializing in a variety of tandoori kebabs and their signature organic *lal maas.*

Hotel Nachana Haveli Goverdhan Chowk, Jaislamer 345001 ℃ **02992/25- 2110,** -5565. Fax 02992/25-1910. www.nachanahaveli.com. nachana_haveli@yahoo.com. 12 units. Rs 3,000 deluxe double; Rs 4,000 suite, Rs 700 extra bed. Rates include all meals and drinks except imported liquor and champagne and includes village safari. Taxes extra. AE, MC, V. **Amenities:** Restaurant; rooftop dining; bar; bird-watching; concierge; currency exchange; doctor-on-call; Internet free; room service; safaris, jeep, horse, and camel. *In room:* A/C, fan, Wi-Fi in some (free).

Rang Mahal ★★ Ⓥalue The newest property in Jaisalmer and arguably the fanciest, and offering relatively good value, this modern, mediaeval styled hotel has ambitiously developed over 150 rooms in anticipation of the new airport. Set around beautiful gardens and a large, clean pool the rooms are the most luxurious in Jaisalmer (ask for a pool facing deluxe or suite) and even come with flatscreen TVs in the marbled bathrooms. It has a pool bar, a billiard table, and its comfortable a la carte restaurant (the dining hall is rather large and faceless) serves reliable local and Continental fare. For those looking for modern brand-new comforts, and it being closer to town than the two options below, and with eager-to-please management and really good rooms, our vote is split between this and the Gateway above.

5, Hotel Complex, Sam Rd., Jaisalmer. ℂ **02992/25-0907,** -0908, 3943, 3944, or -1485. Fax 02992/25-1305. www.hotelrangmahal.com. info@hotelrangmahal.com. 150 units. Rs 3,500 standard double; Rs 5,000 deluxe room; Rs 8,100 royal room and tower suite; Rs 14,000 royal suite; Rs 1,000 extra bed. Meals extra: breakfast Rs 300, lunch Rs 550, dinner Rs 650. Taxes extra. AE, DC, MC, V. **Amenities:** 2 restaurants; bar; sunset bar; billiards room; currency exchange; doctor-on-call; health club; Ayurvedic massage; pool; room service. In room: A/C, TV, minibar.

The Serai ★★★   In the heart of the Thar Desert (40km/25 miles outside Jaisalmer) on a secluded 40-hectare (100-acre) estate lies the latest Sujan resort: a luxury camping safari-style experience. The resort is built using Jaisalmer stone, and incorporates local colors such as indigo and madder, local dhurries and urns and is set against white canvas and the stark desert, which makes for a seductive contrast. However it is the elevated infinity pool built along the lines of a traditional step well or *baoli* that really blows you away, and offers the perfect vantage point for you to survey the beautiful, stark desert surrounds. The main tent has a well-proportioned reception area and the dining tent includes a lounge bar and library—very comfortable with leather chairs and dhurries. The tents are all very spacious and beautifully appointed; a pity they're a little too close together. An organic garden provides fresh produce for the kitchen and the food ranges from traditional Rajasthani dishes to European cold soups. If you find the energy to step out of the pool or pry yourself away from your luxury tent some of the activities include village trips, sundowner trips to the dunes and, of course, Jaisalmer fort.

Bherwa, Chandan, District Jaisalmer, Rajasthan. Info ℂ **011/2374-3194.** Reservations and corporate office: 58-59 Regal Bldg., Parliament St., New Delhi 110 001. ℂ **011/4606-7608,** fax 011/4165-5052. www.sujanluxury.com. 21 units. Rs 25,000 tented suite; Rs 35,000 luxury tented suite; Rs 50,000 royal tented suite. Rates include breakfast and taxes. Transfers and excursions are not included and must be booked in advance. AE, DC, MC, V. **Amenities:** Restaurant; bar; babysitting; doctor-on-call; library; pool; room service; safaris—desert, sightseeing, camel rides, jeep rides, sundowners on sand dunes, village excursions. In room: A/C, TV, minibar.

WHERE TO DINE

Eateries within the fort are entirely not worth the effort or the environmental damage (see box), so you'd do better to head into town.

Desert Boy's Dhani ★ ECLECTIC/VEGETARIAN   Just below the fort, this atmospheric restaurant has a lovely outdoor section; you can sit in the garden courtyard or get closer to the ground on thin mattresses at one of the low tables, where lazy reclining is definitely encouraged. The nostalgic strains of old Hindi film music sets the mood, and at night the garden is lit up with candles, creating a romantic atmosphere; from November through January, traditional dance performances are held from 9 to 11pm. The specialty here is tasty vegetarian dishes (including thin-crust pizzas smothered with cheese from the Punjab), and you really should consider Desert Boy's specialty, *kair sanagari,* a delicious yogurt-based concoction made with capers and a local desert-dwelling string bean that's purported to have antibiotic properties. If that doesn't appeal, another Jaisalmer specialty is *govind gatta,* chickpea-flavored balls stuffed with dried fruit and served with yogurt spiced with turmeric, coriander, and chili. Finish off with a *kaju dakh* milkshake, made with cashews and raisins.

Near Nagar Palika. ℂ **02992/25-4336.** Main courses Rs 100–Rs 200. No credit cards. Daily 9am–11pm.

The Trio ★★★ RAJASTHANI/ECLECTIC   This unassuming eatery, with its open walls and thin cotton flaps providing a welcome breeze (not to mention views of the town and the Maharaja's palace), is Jaisalmer's top restaurant and one of the best in Rajasthan.

It's not just that the food is delicious, but the chef brings a few interesting variations to signature Rajasthani dishes—a relief to one who has exhausted the almost standardized North Indian menu. The *murgh-e-subz*—succulent, boneless strips of chicken stir-fried with shredded vegetables—is one not to miss. If you want to reward your taste buds, order the very tasty mutton *nabori*, a somewhat creamy Thar Desert specialty; be warned, however, there's enough garlic in it to scare camels away. If you have a hearty appetite, the tandoor thali is tops: two chicken dishes, vegetable kebab, mint sauce, and *naan*. Sensitive stomachs can opt for the *kadhi pakora*, fried graham-flour dumplings dunked in yogurt sauce, or *bharwan aloo* (potatoes stuffed with mint paste and simmered in gravy). Wash all of it down with the coldest beers and Cokes in the state.

Gandhi Chowk, Mandir Palace (near the Amar Sagar Gate). (*f* **02992/25-2733**. Main courses Rs 80–Rs 250. MC, V. Daily 11am–10:30pm.

Saffron ★★★ RAJASTHANI One of the best night dining views of the fort, with its uplit buttresses, Nachana Haveli's rooftop terrace serves authentic Rajasthani cuisine in pleasant surrounds (accompanied by local musicians) under the stars or under a shaded canopy (lunch). They also have a small, elevated private terrace at the back that you can request for a special romantic rendezvous. Start with the barbeque/tandoori kebabs (a trio of chicken, lamb, and fish) and move on to their signature organic free range *lal maas* and smooth, creamy (but with a bite) *dal makhani*. For something lighter go for the delicious local lake fish that can be either grilled or served in a mild, piquant curry and the vegetarian *seekh* or *harabahra* kebabs. Shakti will gladly share his impressive and deep knowledge of the local history, flora, and fauna, while Vikram, the elder brother, is a whiskey connoisseur and will gladly take you on a tasting tour of the local blended malts—be sure to eat first, and have a room downstairs before commencing this journey!

Nachana Haveli (Govardhan Chowk). (*f* **02992/25-2110**. nachana_haveli@yahoo.com. Main courses Rs 60–Rs 180. MC, V. Daily 11am–10:30pm.

SHOPPING

Don't miss the **Jaisalmer Art Palace** (near Patwon ki Haveli) for unique local Shoda family (migrants from Pakistan), Sindi and Megwar embroidery, and local *dhurries*. Just around the corner on the square is the **Barmer Embroidery House** (near Patwon ki Haveli); it's owned by Abhimanyu Rathi, legendary for his fine eye for antique textiles. Designers have been known to cross the Thar just to plunder his exquisite selection. Jaisalmer is also famous for its wool products, particularly *dhurries* (rugs), as well as its fine hand embroidery, which turns average skirts and tops into real conversation pieces. Because the town is so easily explored, the best shopping experience is to set aside a morning and wander around, comparing prices before making your selection. Start by exploring the main **Bhatia Market** (begins at the entrance to the fort) and follow your nose. Note that **Rangoli** has a large collection of embroidered garments, particularly for children, and is a fixed-rate shop (you don't have to bargain), which can be quite a relief. You'll find it opposite the Bank of Baroda, in Gandhi Chowk.

Kanu Swami (*f* **98/2909-7319**) is a skillful miniaturist who produces original and beautiful paintings, typically of birds and trees; you'll see evidence of his affinity for nature in the near-microscopic detail that figures into his work. Not satisfied with portraits of trees featuring well over 4,000 individual leaves, he continues to attempt record-breaking images that have the quality of computer-generated graphic artworks but are executed with an artist's touch. If you'd like to take home a painting that combines

A Scarce Resource

The very late, rather weak—and for some—absent monsoon rains of 2009 have been cause for alarm and panic in a country that 2 years ago endured a severe drought, especially when 70% of the nation is rural and relies substantially on subsistence farming and agriculture. Alongside shocking stats (Paddy Cultivation Area Shrinks by 20%; Distress Cattle Sale Rampant in Jhabua), full-page ads in the daily papers with appeals to save water and advertised rates of relief have become commonplace. State governments publicize compensation rates and also to appease panicked constituents. For example, in Haryana, compensation is set at Rs 2,700 per acre for wheat, paddy, and cotton and Rs 2,100 for other crops in case the damage to the standing crops is 51% and above. Other states have promulgated public works programs offering remuneration for up to 100 days of community service. Besides this construction of new water canals, repair of old canals and deeper wells are being sunk ensuring equitable distribution of water throughout the state. Such is the concern that one state qualified its tasks as "being carried out in the entire state on war footing." That's not to say that farmers are not doing their bit. Many have formed arrangements where they collectively irrigate a designated area and share the spoils, ensuring that at least they have some guarantee of success.

traditional skills with a contemporary look, spend some time surveying Kanu's work; you'll spend a mere Rs 800 for a beautifully crafted artwork that's taken 2 full days to complete. Kanu's workshop-cum-outlet is adjacent to the entrance of 8 July Restaurant (opposite the palace entrance).

For more upmarket designer selections, stop at **Killa Boutique** (Gandhi Chowk), run by Luca Borella of Killa Bhawan, where you can pick up stylish fashion accessories, scarves, and Western outfits made of Indian fabrics and prints.

12

Gujarat: India's Eclectic Wild West

Gujuratis, renowned worldwide for their business sense, are at the helm of some of the most successful business outfits in India, and enjoy the highest GDP per capita in the country. Home to Hindus, Jains, Parsis, and Muslims, as well as the colorful seminomadic tribes that inhabit the immense salt flats of Kutch, the state of Gujarat has seen its image as industrial powerhouse somewhat tarnished by occasional spates of politically fueled communal violence, and as a consequence its popularity as a travel destination has dropped off. Despite this, Gujarat's atmosphere remains very peaceful, and traveling through this state will expose you to a vast, varied, and dramatic Indian landscape unlike any other. It is also a haven for some of the most interesting craftwork in India, and while you may encounter some of the work typical of the state in other big cities you will pay a fraction for the handiwork you unearth here. If this is your interest, a visit to the villages of Kutch and its Ranns, where you can also personally interact with the humble artisans producing these astonishing crafts and textiles, is essential.

What makes the Gujarati experience all the more pleasurable is the fact that it is so wonderfully free of the touts and tourists who increasingly plague India's more well-traveled trails. The downside is that tourism and particularly road infrastructure is still pretty basic, and Gujarat is probably best suited to the intrepid traveler who has plenty of time on his or her hands, and does not need a wellness spa or butler service attached to their hotel. Scattered around the state there are new resorts and some ageing palaces that have been converted into heritage hotels but be warned: none compare even remotely with the luxury and standard of service found in neighboring Rajasthan. Getting around is also extremely arduous—you can attempt to cover the state's top attractions in around 8 days with a good driver and reliable vehicle, but given the distances and the poor state of the roads, we recommend you set aside at least 10 to 12 days (and think twice if you happen to have a weak back). For some, Gujarat's highlights, while interesting and unique, may arguably not merit the distance and effort taken to visit them. But for those special interest travelers, particularly those on a third or fourth visit to India, who have become slightly disillusioned by the immense growth in tourism and the all-pervasive Western influence on once traditional ways of life, a trip to Gujarat will be just the ticket to restore your sense of wonder.

1 AHMEDABAD

Once part of the expansive Mughal empire, Ahmedabad (also known as Amdavad) is Gujarat's largest city, with a population of around six million extending along the banks of the Sabarmati River, and is best used as a platform to enter or exit Gujarat, or as a base from which to explore the state. As is typical of India's modern cities, Ahmedabad is an intriguing blend of medieval and contemporary history, with a big-city atmosphere seemingly indifferent to its ancient walled heart, with step wells, temples, bazaars, and *pols* (as the charming old city neighborhoods and residential areas are known). While not a university town per se, the city also has some of the best tertiary educational institutions in India, including the Institute of Fashion Design which clearly draws on its history as a textile hub. It's an industrial powerhouse yet the frenetic pace and chaos belies an informal and carefree attitude, and it appears to have (at least to a Westerner) none of the snootiness and social pressures of Mumbai.

It's got none of the heady sex appeal of Mumbai, and the first-time visitor may experience it as unpleasant and noisy, its history all but obscured by pollution, and its culture too urbanized. But stick around and you'll find a city with its soul still intact, and refreshingly indifferent to the tourism that has transformed the more popular Indian states.

A fascinating window to Gujarati traditional culture and history, its industrious inhabitants play host to over 40% of India's pharmaceuticals and textile businesses, and is a vital component of most other commercial and industrial enterprises. This would come as no surprise to it's tolerant and progressive founder Ahmed Shah, who in 1411, inherited the Sultanate of Gujarat and judiciously relocated it from Patan to its current position on the ancient site of Ashaval and Karnawati, and named it after himself: the suffix "abad" means to prosper. Ahmed attracted traders, skilled artisans, and established a formidable merchant class. Although its fortunes waxed and waned on the back of famines and political unrest, prosper it certainly did, and in the late 19th century the city again rose to prominence as a huge textile centre similarly exporting valuable textiles. Congruously, while Gandhi was revitalizing and restructuring small-scale textile industry, its fame came from its role as a home to Gandhi's famous ashram, which became synonymous with the Indian Freedom Movement. The last textile mills closed in the early 1970s and the economic hardship that followed most likely played a part in the communal and religious conflict in 2002.

ESSENTIALS

VISITOR INFORMATION   Confusingly, you'll find the main tourism office across the river from the main tourist attractions, on the west bank of the Sabarmati, in HK House, just off Ashram Road, 1km (½ mile) north of Nehru Bridge. (Mon–Sat 10:30am–1:30pm and 2–6pm, closed second and fourth Sat of the month; (C) **079/2658-9172;** www.gujarattourism.com). For more detailed advice on planning we highly recommend you contact the Gujarat specialists **North West Safaris,** whose operations manager Anil Bhagia and owner, the experienced travel writer Anil Mulchandani, will tailor make your trip (North West Safaris 113 Kamdhenu Complex, across from Sahjanand College, Panjarpole Cross Roads, Ambawadi, Ahmedabad; (C) **079/26302019** or 26308031; fax 26300962; mobile 098240 72075; www.northwestsafaris.com).

GETTING AROUND   Taxis and metered auto-rickshaws are ubiquitous and you can generally negotiate a day rate dependent on what you want to cover and for exactly how long. Ask your hotel to arrange or step out into the road and bargain. The Municipal Transport Service runs city bus tours from the bus stand at Lal Darwaja (9am–1pm, 1:30–5:30pm; Rs 60)

GETTING THERE & AWAY   The easiest way to get here is to fly; check www.yatra.com for best prices. To and from the airport by prepaid taxi is Rs 250–Rs 300 and by autorickshaw is Rs 150. Alternatively, catch a train. If traveling from or to Mumbai, you will

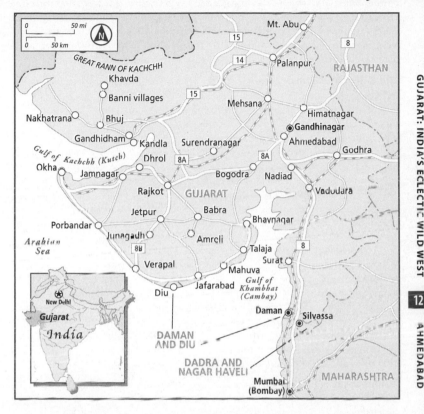

need to book the Gujarat Mail 8 hours 40 minutes, or Shatabdi Express (7 hr., 5 min.). To Delhi take the Ashram Express departing Ahmedabad at 5:45pm and arriving in Delhi 16½ hours later. To Udaipur take the Udaipur City Express, which departs Ahmedabad at 11:05pm and takes 8 hours and 35 minutes. To Jodhpur hop on the Ranakpur Express at 12:25pm arriving at 9:45am the following day. If you are heading out to Kutch, the Nagari Express departs Ahmedabad at 11:25pm on a journey of 7 hours and 35 minutes.

WHAT TO SEE & DO IN THE CITY

If you have time to do only one thing in Ahmedabad, step back in time with the city's **Heritage Walk ★★★**, which takes you through the historic heart and soul of the old city and unveils the true nature of its people and the way they used to, and still do, live. The guided walk (© **079/2539-1811;** daily at 8am for 2½ hrs; Rs 50) is preceded by a short but informative slide show, before leaving from Temple Swaminarayan and covering about 3km (2 miles), through the labyrinthine alleyways and old carved wooden residences which are so much a part of the fabric of the city, and ending at Jama Masjid (see below). It provides excellent photographic opportunities, especially of its picturesque *pols* (the self- contained neighborhoods defined by trade, not religion). The ornate architecture, community wells, secret passages, old wooden gates and doors, and the many chabaturas for housing and feeding birds provide a true sense of wonder of how a bygone era can still infuse life in the city today. Note that the Municipality also runs city bus tours for areas not covered by the walk (© **079/2550-7739;** 9am–1pm and 1:30–5:30pm; Rs 60; depart from the bus stand at Lal Darwaja).

The Calico Museum of Textiles ★★★   This museum is another compulsory history lesson and offers an unrivaled insight into the warp and weft of the history and culture of a city as told through the woven thread. It is without doubt the finest collection of textiles and local indigenous crafts in the country, if not in the world, and is a prerequisite for anyone wanting an understanding of the diversity and depth of the value and skill of the craftsmen and women who produce these fine textiles. The museum, set in lush grounds with koi ponds and a 200-year-old relocated Burmese teak *haveli,* is a welcome respite from the road and rail traffic outside its large wooden gates. Appropriately gifted by a wealthy textile merchant, the museum fully occupies his aged mansion and fills up room after musty room with exquisite garb and craftsmanship. The tours explain the rich history of textiles in India, and showcases garments made for the British and Portuguese, the Indian royal family (including royal tents) as well as religious vehicles. It's a startling array of styles of weaving and design including embroideries, tie-dye, block printing as well as the technical explanations of different stitching methods and the respective needles or looms used in this fascinating profession. The tours are free, and the morning tour (daily 10:30am–12:30pm) displays the vast range of textiles in its wooden galleries; the afternoon also take in the collection of Indian deities and the textile galleries (2:45–4:45pm). In the off-season it is collapsed into one long morning tour. Do call to check and book. *Note:* Take water and dress lightly as the rooms can be rather stuffy.

Sarahai Foundation, 3km (2 miles) north of Delhi Gate, across from Shahibagh underbridge. © **079/ 2786 8172.** Admission free. Daily 10:30am–12:30pm, no entry after 11am, and 2:45–4:45pm.

Jama Masjid ★   At the end of the Heritage Walk you will arrive at the Jama Masjid, completed in 1424 by Ahmed Shah with the material of demolished Jain and Hindu temples. Set aside some time to study its 260 intricate pillars (legend has it they are impossible to count exactly as one always arrives at a different number) of which no two are the same. You will also notice the two stunted minarets that were destroyed in the 1957 earthquake and the similarities to the beautiful Fatehpur Sikri complex (near Agra), which this predates and inspired. The Tomb of Ahmed Shah stands just outside the Jama Masjid's east gate and includes the cenotaphs of his son and grandson. Across the road and in poor condition is his queen's tomb. *Note:* No shorts or short dresses or bare shoulders. Women are not permitted into the central chamber. Avoid Friday when it is at its busiest!

MG Rd (close to Teen Darwaja). Open 24 hr.

Sabarmati Gandhi Ashram ★★★   Peacefully located on the river's west bank, this renowned ashram was Gandhi's base and headquarters from 1917—1930 during his protracted and resolved fight for Indian independence. It was also from this very site that he set out on his famous salt march to Dandi on the Gulf of Cambay in protest against the British control of the essential mineral. His frugal quarters are well preserved, including his belongings (spectacles, sandals and some utensils) and there is an excellent record of his life and times in chronological context, as well as excerpts from his speeches, political missives and autobiography. The testimonials from famous peers and colleagues are both humbling and inspiring and one leaves feeling a real sense of awe at this great man who said, "My life is my message." There is also an excellent bookshop where you can buy his works and some Gandhi memorabilia (we incidentally recommend *The Life of Mahatma Gandhi* by Louis Fischer, one of the most readable biographies on Gandhi).

Northern end of Ashram Rd. (℃ 079/2755 7277. Free admission. Daily 8:30am–6:30pm.

EXCURSIONS FURTHER AFIELD

Shatrunjaya, Palitana ★★   The holy Jain mount of Shatrunjaya is located alongside the small, insipid town of Palitana which is not worth a stop over by any means. But with over 900 beautiful temples in relatively good shape (some in mint condition, always being worked on through donations from wealthy businessmen) this is a must-visit if you have an interest in temple architecture, are relatively fit, and like sweeping views—here of the surrounding countryside, the Gulf of Cambay to the south, Bhavnagar to the north, and the Shatrunjaya mountains and river flowing through the verdant hills behind. Records prove that the hill was a tirtha (the Jain's first tirthankara, Adinath, achieved enlightenment here) as far back as the 5th century, however due to the Muslim raids the existing temples date from the 16th century. It is a special place and one that requires silence and meditation along its beautiful path and up into its pious, labyrinthine temples. The climb takes between 1 and 2 hours and is utterly rewarding, but if you feel you really cannot manage it, you can hire a *dholi* (four pole bearers with a seat). Be sure to take lots of water and a hat, as there are no shops or services atop.

There is a small museum located 400m (1,312 ft.) before the start of the temple steps displaying some Jain religious artifacts.

Daily 6:30am–7:45pm, museum hours daily 8am–noon and 4–8:30pm. Museum entry Rs10. Photography fee Rs 100.

Rani-ki-Vav Baoli, Patan ★★   The old Gujarati capital Anhilawada Patan, 2km (1 mile) northwest of today's dusty town, served several Rajput dynasties and the Solankis between the 8th and 12th centuries before being taken by the Mughals. In 1411 it began to fall into decline when Ahmed Shah moved his capital to Ahmedabad and today few signs of this history remain except for Patan's beautiful and well-restored Rani-ki-Vav baoli (step well), which is certainly worth the 130km (81-mile) day trip or stopover to/ from Ahmedabad en route to Dasada, Kutch. Built in 1050 for the Solanki queen Udaimati, it is the oldest and finest in Gujarat, and has been brought to life through its excellent restoration in the 1980s. Prior to that it had been almost completely hidden and protected by silt, with only its top exposed. Its carvings are exquisite and the various incarnations of Vishnu are something to behold. After gaping at these well-preserved sandstone beauties take a short drive into Patan town to wander the quaint old quarters' streets of wooden havelis and to look at its famous export (especially to royalty) Patola silk saris, with bright, distinctive patterns, some of which fetch up to Rs 70,000 and can take upward of 6 months to create.

Daily 8am–6pm. Rs 100.

Modhera ★★★   The stunning Sun Temple, located 102km (63 miles) northwest of Ahmedabad, was built by King Bhimdev I in 1026, and is perhaps the state's highlight in religious architecture, and well worth a visit en route to Dasada, or even a day's outing from Ahmedabad together with Patan (above). In tribute to its solar deity it was designed in the Solanki style so as to capture the dawn sunlight on the image of Surya, the sun god, during the equinoxes. Set in lush peaceful grounds one approaches first to the Surya Kund, a beautifully proportioned rectangular baoli (step well) containing over 100 shrines to Ganesh, Vishnu, and Shiva. There is a wonderful view from the side that looks directly on to the Main Hall and the Shrine's pillared pavilions and one can immediately appreciate the perfect proportions of this intricate, modest complex. Up close the carved detail is especially elaborate and the 52 pillars depict scenes from the Mahabaratha and Ramayana with erotic beauties seeming to pose for your camera. Look out for the interior display of the 12 representations of Surya's different monthly expressions and note the damage where the temple was ruined by the Muslim ruler Mahmud of Ghazni (who effected similar damage to Rani-ki-Vav at Patan).

Daily 8am–6pm. Rs 100.

WHERE TO STAY

House of Mangaldas Girdhardas (House of MG) ★★ The only option with any real character, this is by far our top pick in Ahmedabad, though it is in a noisy location. Built in the 1920s by Seth Mangaldas Girdhardas, this was the wealthy industrialist and textile merchant's family home, and is today as much family heirloom (still owned and run by the family) as quirky boutique hotel. While noisy, it is certainly convenient (very central), and the service is friendly, rooms are spacious (a tad schizophrenic in terms of decor), and the restaurant one of the best in the city (see "Where to Dine," below). It really is the only place to stay in Ahmedabad, and with free airport transfers, and incidental Wi-Fi costs, offers good value (though we do not approve of the 9am check-out time; if this doesn't suit your itinerary, bargain upfront that you can leave later at no charge, or you have to cough up). Be sure to ask for a Deluxe Room at the back (nos. 1, 2, 3, 5, 6, 7) or a quiet Grand Deluxe Suite (nos. 14, 15, 16) to escape the racket of the road. All the rooms are large but if you are craving space then try The Mangaldas Suite (Rs 12,990) on the top floor.

House of Mangaldas Heritage Hotel. Dr. Tankaria Rd., across from Sidi Sayyid's Mosque, Lal Darwaja. ⓒ **079/2550 6946.** Fax 079/2550 6535. www.houseofmg.com. 11 units. Mangaldas Suite Rs 12,990; Rs 9,990 Grand Deluxe Suite double; Rs 6,490 Grand Deluxe Room double; Rs 4,990 Deluxe Room. Rates include breakfast. Taxes extra. AE, DC, MC, V. **Amenities:** 2 restaurants; airport transfers (free); gym; Internet Rs100/24 hr.; DVD and book library; indoor pool; room service. *In room:* A/C, TV, DVD-MP3, iPod, minibar, Wi-Fi (Rs100/day).

The Taj Gateway Ummed Ahmedabad ★ Located 1.6km (1 mile) from the airport and less than 6.4km (4 miles) from the CBD, this Gateway Hotel is the most peaceful option in Ahmedabad, with upmarket, corporate-style accommodation within easy striking distance of the chaos of the city. Designwise it's not going to win any awards but rooms are cool, clean, and spacious, room service is efficient, and the large pool a boon. Only 15 minutes from the city center (assuming moderate traffic) it is understandably popular with business travelers, but it has none of the character and history of the House of MG, and it's a great deal more expensive. The four deluxe suites are fabulous but a pool-facing double will more than do.

International Airport Circle, Hansol, Ahmedabad 382 475, Gujarat, India. ⓒ **079/6666 1234** or 1800/111-TAJ [825]. Fax 079/6666 4444. www.tajhotels.com. gateway.ahmedabad@tajhotels.com. Rs 10,000 Garden view room, Rs 10,500 Superior Pool View Room, Rs 18,500 Executive Suite, Rs 25,000 Deluxe Suite (6% tax extra; for best rates and deals check online). AE, DC, MC, V. **Amenities:** 2 restaurants; airport transfers from Rs 400; babysitting; gym; pool; room service. *In room:* A/C, TV, DVD player, minibar, Wi-Fi (Rs225/hr.).

> ## (Tips) **Veg Out for Under $1**
>
> One of the highlights of traveling to Gujarat is sampling the local cuisine, which differs from the richer Rajasthani fare, and the Gujarati's are rightfully proud of—a tasty, slightly sweet style of vegetarian cooking. Order at least one Gujarati thali, the state staple, which is a simple platter of a number of seasonal vegetarian dishes. These may include bindi (okra), aloo (potato), bhaigan (brinjal) or dhobi (cauliflower) or a mix of all of these with side dishes of dhal, pickles, atchar (spicy) and chutneys (sweet) accompanied by a variety of breads (chappati's, naan). It is customary at lunch or/and dinner to scoff one of these reasonably priced (usually around Rs 100) "all you can eat" meals with your right hand, washed down with a chilled glass of buttermilk and followed by a cleansing cup of cardamom spiced masala chai. For one of the most simple, no-frills, authentic vegetarian dining experiences in Gujarat, head for **Gopi Dining Hall** on Pritamrai Road (© **079/657 6388**). Staff here has been efficiently and graciously serving its loyal patrons some of the tastiest, freshest Gujarati and Kathiawadi thalis in Gujarat at ridiculously low prices (Rs 40–Rs 75) for years; as a result it's a hot spot for locals and Westerners alike (which means you may need to wait for a short while).

WHERE TO DINE

Agashiye ★★ GUJARATI Set on the rooftop terrace of the House of Mangaldas Hotel, this is one of the best restaurants in Gujarat for both traditional Gujarat, Indian, and Continental fare, and at night is a great spot to escape from the chaos of the streets. Chill out on the cushions and await what will definitely be a delicious meal—prices are high by local standards but venue alone is well worth the few dollars more. If money is an issue simply eat downstairs at the Green House, which is just as good, but far noisier, serving extensive lunchtime meals outside including tasty, local flavored ice creams (try the rose or litchi).

House of Mangaldas Heritage Hotel. Dr. Tankaria Rd., across from Sidi Sayyid's Mosque, Lal Darwaja. © **079/2550-6946.** www.houseofmg.com. Main courses Rs 200–Rs 300. AF, DC, MC, V. Daily 11am–11pm.

Vishala ★ GUJARATI Apparently unable to get a permit for a restaurant, the owner of Vishala cunningly constructed a small traditional village-style open-air restaurant, set in lush grounds, and included a home for his personal Utensil Museum, with thousands of unique and fascinating artifacts from stirrups, nut crackers and pots to bellows, chapati carriers, and dowry boxes (look out for a pot that is over 1,000 years old!). The food is excellent and serves all-you-can-eat traditional vegetarian thalis on long wooden tables while you are seated on the floor. We recommend you make an evening of it and arrive early to tour the museum and then take in the post-prandial entertainment of traditional dance and music, and delicious ice cream.

On the southern edge of town across from Vasana Tol Naka. © **079/26602422.** Lunch from Rs120; dinners from Rs 200. No credit cards. Daily 11am–3pm and 8–11pm.

2 KUTCH / KUCHCHH / KACHCHH

Bounded on its north and east by marshy salt flats and desert scrub known as the Greater and Little Ranns, and on the southwest by the Gulf of Kutch and the Arabian Sea, the province of Kutch is a distinct realm in every sense, and the most worthwhile expedition in Gujarat. Arguably closer to Pakistan and its pre-Partition Sind populace, the landscapes alone are beautiful if you like arid, barren, bleak vistas: Northern Kutch or the **Banni** area is semidesert with no perennial rivers and dry, acacia thorn scrub—in stark contrast is the color used and displayed by its local tribes who rely on livestock and the sale of their distinctive handicraft and art. With some research and preparation (read Judy Frater's excellent book **Threads of Identity,** Mapin Publishing, 1995; see box below) meeting and trading with the local inhabitants could very well be the most memorable and inspiring part of your visit to India.

Note: You will need a permit to visit the villages north of Bhuj and although this is easy to arrange, and is free, it takes a little time and patience. Take an extra photograph and a copy of your passport and visa (including the originals) and present yourself to the District Superintendents Office (11am–2pm, 3–6pm Mon–Sat), complete the form naming the villages you need to visit, get it stamped, and be on your way.

BHUJ & ENVIRONS

The dusty, baking-hot capital of Kutch is slowly being reconstructed after the devastating 2001 earthquake that killed over 10% of the city's 150,000 people. To be honest, it's a pit, and really only good to get your permit to visit the villages, or to purchase crafts and textiles (if you have not already done so from the creators themselves up in the Rann for half the price). With no sites or attractive accommodations you'd be far better placed closer to the ethnic villages—the real reason you are in Kutch. If you really have to sleep here, there is only one option worth considering: the new Hotel Ilark (© **02832/258999;** www.hotelilark.com; super deluxe rooms Rs 3,500) on Station Road, recently built by a wealthy businessman in the construction industry and by far the best place in town.

The easiest way to get to Bhuj is to fly. Jet Airways have daily flights to and from Mumbai. You can book at their offices near Bank of Baroda on Station Road © **02832/ 253671**) or at the airport (© **02832/244101**). You can also take a train directly to or from Ahmedabad: catch the 9116 Nagari Express, which departs 10:30pm and arrives 5:15am, or the 9032 Kutch Express (departs 8pm arrives 2:45am), before continuing on to Mumbai (11:45am). (No one is advised to take buses here; as stated you will need your own driver and vehicle.)

A raised, newly resurfaced tar road leads north of Bhuj to the Banni Villages and the craft hubs of **Hodka, Dhordo,** and **Khavda,** where decorated mud thatch-roofed huts *(liponkan)* form the stop-off for your meeting with traditional Rabari and Ahir cultures, and an opportunity to inspect their handiwork and wares. These tiny clay villages are all gathered close together (about 40 min. or so apart) and depending on where you are based, either at Shaam-e- Sarhand or Infinity Resort, it will take you not less than 2 hours to reach the closest village. Our advice is therefore to set out very early and reach the farthest village of Khavda first, then work back down to your base. *Tip:* Ask your hosts to provide a packed lunch or at least some snacks and take plenty of chilled water, preferably in an ice chest.

Ludia is another good stop to meet the locals and inspect the work, and is your second visit after Khavda if working back down. Take your time doing this and be patient. The

(Tips) Rare Gifts North of Bhuj

Working out of Sumrasar Sheikh, 25km (16 miles) north of Bhuj, the **Kala Raksha Trust** (10am–2pm, 3–6pm; © **02808/277238**; www.kala-raksha.org) is an authentic and successful grassroots social initiative dedicated to the preservation of traditional arts. The trust has a small museum displaying works by over 800 artists from seven different communities and can arrange visits to villages to meet with the artists. There are some magnificent pieces on sale, of which a substantial proportion goes to the artists who also help price the works. Aside from learning about the various crafts and styles, you can ask to be taken for a village tour where you can observe the women meticulously plying their craft in embroidery, dyeing and patchwork techniques. Another excellent local cooperative is Shrujan, in Bhujodi, 12km (7½ miles) north of Bhuj, which also works with a network of 80-plus villages and has some excellent pieces. If your interest extends beyond the ordinary, contact Judy Frater while in Bhuj. She is a specialist in textiles on the local ethnic tribal cultures and communities, has lived with and studied them for many years and is author of the informative book *Threads of Identity, Embroidery and Adornment of the Nomadic Rabaris* (Mapin Publishing, 1995). She can be contacted at Judy@kala-raksha.org for specialist tours or can be arranged by Mr. Malik at Rann Riders.

traditional dress is arresting and their *cholis* (backless blouses) will have you literally asking for the shirts off their backs. The mood is relaxed and there is very little pressure to buy, so take your time and do not be shy to have a good look at all the work. It may seem like a lot of effort to unpack but try to see it as an education and there is no reason not to have a healthy interaction without buying. We did however encounter a certain surliness when we didn't buy from a woman in Hodka, who apparently is famous in Paris with the French media. Beautiful embroidery can be found at **Bhirendiara,** just a 20-minute drive south of Ludia, and stop at the famous NGO **Kala Raksha** (see box below; © **02808/277238**; www.kala-raksha.org) that provides a fixed-price outlet, small museum, and workshop.

Covering 4,851 sq. km (1,873 sq. miles), the Little Rann, to the east of The Greater Rann is a vast, salt-encrusted desert plain that becomes a marsh during the monsoon rains. It is home to nine nomadic communities—the **Mir, Kharapat Rabhari's, Bharawads, Bajania, Kholi, Patels, Padhars, Jats, and Wadi's** (the latter incidentally known as snake charmers)—as well as the endangered wild ass, a petite tan and chestnut relative of the horse that consistently bucks the locals' repeated attempts at cross breeding (and refuses to pose for pictures!).

WHERE TO STAY & DINE

Less than 32km (20 miles) north of Bhuj, **Hodka** is an obligatory stop and the **Shaame-Sarhand Rural Resort** (© **02832/654124;** www.hodka.in), a successful sustainable eco-tourism project run by the local **Halepotra** tribe, is located here. It is indeed rural, offering rustic accommodation in mud huts or *bhungas* (Rs 2,500), or six luxury tents with private bathrooms (Rs 4,000), which are far more comfortable, although if you'd like to live as the locals do, then try a night in a *bhunga*. While it is very basic, this "Sunset at the Border" is an authentic homegrown project that is run by the people for the people and will give you not only the proximity you need to the local villages but also the insight to witness the daily lives of a local Kutchi community at work. The most comfortable place for an overnight stay in this area, although a little off the beaten track, is the **Infinity Rann of Kutch Resort** (© 02835/273431/2; www.campsofindia.com; kutch@campsofindia.com) located at Chari Fulay, **Nakhatrana,** 60km (37 miles) from Bhuj. With 16 luxury, A/C, tented en-suite cottages set around a green lawn and a large blue pool, it is an ideal base for comfortable accommodation into the Banni area of the Greater Rann.

The only place to stay and the real reason for visiting the Little Rann is the eco-friendly **Rann Riders ★★**, based just outside the charming little village of **Dasada** and a stone's throw from the **Little Rann.** The passionate and erudite owner, Mr. Muzahid Malik, a veritable mine of information on the area, together with his helpful and welcoming team, will attend to your every need. With the amazing activities and outings available (such as overnighting in the Little Rann on a camel cart), your experience here will be memorable. The pretty resort contains 22 deluxe suites in cottages resembling the *kooba* houses of the **Bajania** community of Dasada, and the *bhunga* houses of the **Kutchi Rabari's.** Moreover, they are all designed using locals materials and labor, tastefully decorated and set amid a lush flowering indigenous garden with a newly renovated infinity pool. Gardens produce organic food (grown out back) and the kitchen serves good local and Continental cuisine. Mr. Malik's family has deep local roots, a committed passion for the area, and a real understanding of international tourism and its demands—all rare commodities in Gujarat.

13

Higher Altitudes, Higher Powers: Amritsar, Himachal Pradesh & Ladakh

The ancient Sanskrit poet Kaldisa called the Himalayas "the measuring rod of the world"—in size and scale and splendor there is little on earth that compares in magnitude to the high altitude ranges that shelter these far northern reaches of India. Proclaimed by ancient Indian texts as *Devbhumi*—"Land of the Gods"—and believed to be the earthly home of the mighty Lord Shiva, the beautiful, far-flung **Himachal Pradesh** has an almost palpable presence of divinity. Bordered by Tibet to the east, Jammu and Kashmir to the north, and the Punjab to the west, the landlocked state is one of great topographic diversity, from vast bleak tracts of rust-colored high-altitude Trans-Himalayan desert to dense green deodar forests, apple orchards, cultivated terraces, and, everywhere you look, sublime snowcapped mountains. This is also where you'll find the largest concentration of Buddhists, their atmospheric *gompas* (monasteries) a total contrast to the pageantry of Hindu temples.

Shimla, the state capital, is easily accessed from Delhi by train, preferably via the Punjabi town of **Amritsar,** where the shimmering **Golden Temple** of the Sikhs takes the honors as India's best cultural attraction. Shimla shouldn't hold you longer than it takes to get ready to tackle one of the greatest road adventures in Asia—negotiating the ledges, landslides, and hairpin bends of the **Hindustan-Tibet Road** through the remote valleys of Kinnaur, Spiti, and Lahaul. Hidden from the world for most of the year by a cloak of thick, impenetrable snow, these easternmost districts emerge from their wintry slumber to reveal white-capped Himalayan mountains, lush green meadow-valleys dappled with flowers, and Tibetan Buddhist *gompas*, of which **Tabo,** a World Heritage Site, is one of the most spiritually significant destinations in India. Due to limited accessibility (some areas only opened to visitors quite recently and a few sections near the Chinese border require a special permit) and the impassability of the roads, the region—despite an upturn in tourist numbers in the last few years—remains the least visited and most exhilarating part of Himachal Pradesh. You should set aside at least 4 to 5 days to explore the area—stay longer if you want to visit more of its high altitude villages—before landing in **Manali,** a town somewhat enlivened (some say ruined) by its designated role as Himachal Pradesh's "hippie hot spot" and favorite Indian honeymoon destination. You can either set off on a trek from this popular adventure center, or head west (via Mandi) to the tea-carpeted hills of the westernmost **Kangra Valley** and the hill station of **Dharamsala**—seat of the Tibetan government-in-exile and home to the Dalai Lama.

Another option, but only in summer, is to head north to the lunar landscapes of **Ladakh.** Although Jammu and Kashmir, India's northernmost state, is a no-go area for many travelers, Ladakh, the western J&K province on the border of Tibet, is the exception. It sits astride the Ladakh and Zanskar mountains, surrounded by two of the world's highest ranges—the Greater Himalayas and the mighty Karakoram—and nothing will prepare you for the breathtaking, stark beauty of the landscape. Jagged peaks, rocky uplands, and vast barren plateaus are the dominant features of this harsh, dry land swept by dust devils and dotted with Buddhist *gompas,* large whitewashed *chortens* (pawn-shaped commemorative cairns), and chest-high *mani* walls made from stacks of engraved stones. Aptly nicknamed "Little Tibet," this is India at its remote best. Only visited for the few months of summer when the roads are passable, the communities outside of **Leh** (capital of Ladakh) and Padum (capital of Zanskar) remain literally frozen in time, with small Buddhist communities—such as those you'll find in far-flung **Lamayuru** or the spectacular **Nubra Valley**—living as they have for centuries, miraculously unhassled by outside influences, and with much spiritual and natural beauty to behold. Spend at least 5 days here (adjusting to the high altitude takes time), then fly out to Delhi and rejoin the 21st century.

1 STAYING ACTIVE

Himachal Pradesh and Ladakh are exceptional destinations for adventurous travelers. The area has a phenomenal array of trekking routes, and numerous tour operators offer anything from gentle strolls to walks lasting several days—including trips to serious rock faces for seasoned climbers. Besides the scenery, a visit here is an ideal opportunity to meet people more or less untouched by the modern world—outside of a handful of towns, much of the population in this region is rural and dependent on agriculture. It is also home to some of the world's last nomadic people. Manali is a popular starting point for treks into the lush Kullu and Parvati valleys, while **Dharamsala** is a good base from which to explore the Dhauladhar mountain range, and the Kangra Valley below is best seen while soaring through the air dangling from a paraglider. In Ladakh, myriad trekking expeditions out of **Leh** visit the many fascinating Buddhist monasteries along the way to higher altitudes and spectacular valleys, and the **Indus** and **Zanskar rivers** are excellent for white-water rafting. Treks in the **Spiti Valley,** some of which continue on to Ladakh, are among the most rewarding and, because of the altitude in both regions, quite challenging.

Note that most of the companies listed below are happy to arrange a variety of adventure activities almost anywhere in the Himalayas, including Sikkim (discussed in chapter 15), Bhutan and Nepal.

One of the best all-round companies is **Mercury Himalayan Explorations ★★★** (www.himalayanadventure.com), which does everything from ski trips to Indus and Zanskar river rafting, and works in conjunction with Mercury Travels, a subsidiary of the excellent Oberoi hotel chain. Mercury pioneered many of the adventure routes that are now among the most popular in the Himalayas.

Aquaterra Adventures ★★★ (*C* **011/2921-2641** or -2760; www.treknraft.com) is another well-established outfit and one of the best Indian adventure operators, specializing in trekking and rafting expeditions, and working with highly experienced and

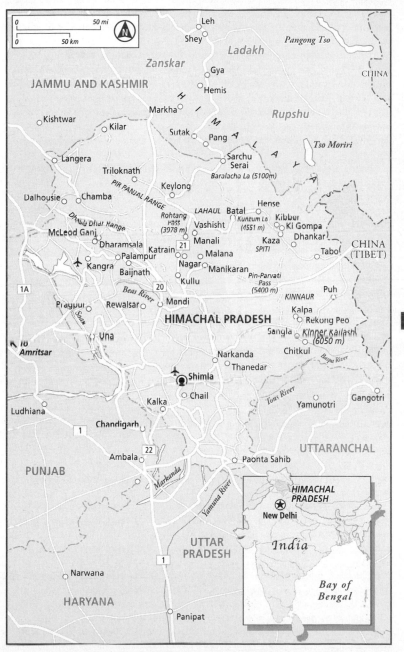

knowledgeable guides who come from the Himalayas and know the region extremely well. Operating since 1995, Aquaterra strives to cover routes that don't see other groups. They also offer climbing trips, and will customize their tours and treks to suit your personal interests and abilities. You can also combine trekking and rafting trips or opt for a unique bicycle camping expedition.

Another highly recommended operator is **Project Himalaya** ★★★ (© 977/98-0214-9789 in Kathmandu; www.project-himalaya.com; info@project-himalaya.com), a Kathmandu-based company run by the professional, dynamic trio of Jamie McGuinness, Joel Schone, and Kim Bannister. Joel and Kim lead the Ladakh treks, which run 20 to 24 days; the adventurous should definitely consider taking their exploratory trek to uncommon regions that you won't find on a map. This is an outfit that does things differently, with small groups, highly personalized service, and a real concern for local support staff.

Banjara Camps & Retreats ★★ (www.banjaracamps.com) operates a number of Trans-Himalayan jeep safaris, which generally start in Delhi and explore different parts of Himachal and Ladakh. Comfortable accommodations (some in beautifully situated deluxe campsites) and good meals accompany you along the way, and you can even customize your safari. Banjara also gets our thumbs up for their excellent treks throughout this region; they offer a range of experiences, with differing degrees of difficulty and all your basic needs expertly taken care of. Banjara also offers a strenuous 15-day cycling tour in Himachal that covers 803km (498 miles), including the mighty Kunzum Pass (4,590m/15,055 ft.). Accommodations are in a mix of small hotels, guesthouses and camp sites.

You can satisfy your cowboy fantasies on the Himalayan horse trails offered by **Dusty Trail Adventures** ★★ (Basement, Valley View Annexe, below Swatch Showroom, The Mall, Manali; © 94-5910-8691; http://dustytrail.in). Nitin Gupta, an inimitable mountain guide and horseman, puts together multiday, high-altitude horse-riding trails through Ladakh, Zanskar, Kullu, and Spiti; day rides are also possible if you're short on time. Everything—food, camping, and transfers—can be included in your package (roughly Rs 50,000 per person for a 10-day trail, with return transport to Delhi).

Rimo Expeditions ★ (www.rimoexpeditions.com) are considered to be at the top of their game and offer, among other treks, the famous "Chadar" winter trek, which involves traversing the frozen Zanskar River during the harsh months when it is totally frozen over. They can also lead you over a number of high mountain passes—a favorite, if you've got the time, is the month-long Zanskar Classic, which goes all the way to the superbly located Lamayuru monastery, passing through myriad medieval villages and incredible scenery along the way.

Shepherds Realms Camps & Adventures ★ (C-8/8115, Shepherd's House, Vasant Kunj, New Delhi; © 011/2649-2849 or 98-1871-2970; www.asiasafari.com), run by an ex-army captain, specializes in custom-made motorcycle and 4X4 safaris through Ladakh, as well as Tibet, Nepal, and Bhutan, along with other adventure activities in these regions.

Besides organizing trekking in Himachal and Ladakh, **Himalayan Journeys The Adventure Company** (The Mall, Manali; © 01902/25-4397; www.himalayanjourneys india.com) arranges ski courses, jeep safaris, river-rafting expeditions, mountain-biking tours, and, for well-heeled adventurers, luxury heli-skiing packages.

With 32 years in the business, Naushad Kaludi of **Antrek Tour and Travels** ★★ (1, Rambagh, The Mall, Manali; © 01902/25-2292 or 98-1602-2292; www.antrek.co.in)

offers a professional and very reliable service and specializes in putting together combination tours that include several days of trekking plus a few days of jeep safari; you can mix and match your journey to suit particular tastes and interest, and ask for a mix of camping and hotels or guesthouses; Antrek will provide dome tents, sleeping bags, a guide, a cook, an assistant, ponies and porters, as well as the vehicle and driver, and all meals and beverages—on average you'll be looking at spending 50€ to 70€ per person per day for a private two-person trip. Antrek can also provide all the ground services for mountain bike tours, and a range of specialty excursions, from trout fishing to climbing with proper equipment and serious guides.

A highly recommended alternative for exploring Himachal's remote and sensationally beautiful Spiti Valley is **Ecosphere** ★★ (✆ 94 1886 0099 or 98-9949-2417, www.spitiecosphere.com), a social enterprise that has pioneered homestays and community participation in the tourism industry by working at the grassroots level. Led by the dynamic Ishita Khanna, this is responsible tourism at its best and the income generated goes towards various conservation and development projects besides creating employment. Other than the fact that you will be directly interacting and aiding the rural communities, it is a wonderful opportunity to see the spectacular Spiti countryside and experience the perfect blend of jeep safaris and hiking, with the occasional yak to ride as well.

For details on more active vacations in this region see the individual sections on Manali, Dharamsala, and Leh later in this chapter.

---

2 AMRITSAR & THE GOLDEN TEMPLE

410km (254 miles) NW of Delhi

Amritsar (pronounced Um-*rit*-sir) has been the capital of the Sikh religion since the 16th century. Located in the northwestern state of Punjab, a wealthy and prosperous region and home to the majority of India's Sikhs, Amritsar is also the unlikely site of India's most dazzling temple. A shimmering monument in marble, bronze, and gold leaf, and a vivid architectural celebration of Sikhism's devotion (a faith that actively preaches unity and equality among all religions), **The Golden Temple** is both fascinating and spiritually invigorating, combining sheer physical beauty with a truly sacred atmosphere. The way in which its devotees worship is enough to hold your attention—and your heart—completely captive.

ESSENTIALS

VISITOR INFORMATION The best place to get information about the Golden Temple and the Sikh faith is at the temple's own **Information Office** (✆ 0183/255-3954; Apr–June daily 7:30am–7:30pm, July–Mar daily 8am–7pm). The Punjab government's **tourist office** (✆ 0183/240-2452; http://punjabgovt.nic.in; Mon–Sat 9am–5pm) is at the Palace Hotel, opposite the railway station, but you'll get a better introduction to the city from someone at your hotel or guesthouse.

GETTING THERE & AWAY You can fly from Delhi with **Kingfisher** (✆ 1800-233-3131), **Jet Airways** (Main Market, Ranjit's Ave. Shopping Complex; ✆ 0183/250-8003) or **Indian Airlines** (39A Court Rd.; ✆ 0183/221-3392, -3393, or -3141; Mon–Sat 10am–5pm), but the best way to get here is on the Shatabdi Express or the

> **Fun Facts   The Five "K's": How to Spot a Sikh**
>
> Most Sikh men wear turbans wrapped around their heads and sport full beards, making them highly distinctively recognizable in all parts of the world. However, there are five other symbols—known as the five K's (*kakkar* in Punjabi)—worn by Sikh men to indicate that they are part of Guru Gobind Singh's sacred Khalsa brotherhood, which unites all Sikhs and are said to be emblems of purity and courage. Traditionally, a Sikh man does not cut his hair or shave his beard; ask him why and he'll tell you that one of the tenets of Sikhism is to avoid interfering with nature. This unshorn hair is known as the *kesh,* and is kept neat with a wooden comb known as the *kangha.* As a symbol of dignity and power, he carries a saber or sword, known as the *kirpan,* at all times—usually these days it's a small, symbolic sword, and you'll also see some Sikh women carrying them. You won't see it, but a Sikh man wears loose underpants known as the *kachera* said to symbolize modesty. Finally, look on his right wrist: The *karra* is a traditional bangle of iron or steel that indicates fearlessness and strength; pick one up as a reminder of your visit—there are thousands for sale at any of the many stalls and shops directly outside The Golden Temple.

overnight Golden Temple Mail from Delhi—it is far more economical and quite a comfortable option. Taxis, auto-rickshaws, and bicycle-rickshaws are always available at the station to take you to your hotel, whereas if you fly, you'll be at the mercy of the overpriced prepaid taxi counter, with charges into the city starting at around Rs 700. You'll want to avoid spending time tracking down tickets, so either book your return or onward journey in advance, or have your hotel handle your reservation. If you're stuck, there is a computerized train reservation facility located at the Golden Temple complex.

GETTING AROUND   Note that any of the accommodation options reviewed below will make all your transport and sightseeing arrangements for you. A half-day sightseeing trip (4 hr.) costs Rs 800 to Rs 1,200, and a full 8 hours will be Rs 1,100 to Rs 2,000, depending on the quality of the vehicle. Should you want a guide, you'll need to add another Rs 750 to Rs 1,200. Auto-rickshaws are useful within Amritsar itself, especially since the roads are so terribly congested, but they're too slow for trips to Wagah border, for which you should arrange a car, and perhaps share it with fellow guests. If you're looking for a friendly, reliable auto-rickshaw *wallah,* try giving Bunty a ring on © 94-6352-2971. Cycle-rickshaws are popular, but if you're in a hurry, don't want to deal with the glaring sun, or need to cover more than a few miles, opt for a car or auto-rickshaw instead.

THE TOP ATTRACTIONS

The Golden Temple ★★★ (Moments   Prepare to be humbled by the most tangibly spiritual place in the country, one that, in its status as a living monument, even has the edge on the Taj Mahal. Arrive with a few good hours set aside and get lost in its magical beauty. Leave your shoes at the free facility near the entrance, cover your head (bandanas are provided, or you can purchase a "Golden Temple" souvenir bandana from a vendor), and wash your feet by wading through the shallow pool before entering. The most sacred part of the complex is **Hari Mandir Sahib (Divine Temple)** or **Darbar Sahib (Court of the Lord),** which you'll instantly recognize as the marble-and-gold sanctuary at the center of a large body of water within the temple complex. The name "Golden Temple" comes from this gold-plated building, which features copper cupolas and white marble walls encrusted with precious stones arranged in decorative floral patterns that show strong Islamic influence. Four *chattris* flank the structure, which is decorated inside and out with verses from the *Granth Sahib* (the Sikh Holy Book). Construction of the temple began in 1574, with ongoing restoration and embellishment over the years, including the addition in the 19th century of 100 kilograms (220 lb.) of gold to cover the inverted lotus-shaped dome.

To reach the temple, follow the *parikrama* (walkway), which circumscribes the sacred water tank—known as **Amrit Sarovar,** or the Pool of Nectar—in a clockwise direction. You'll need to cross a marble causeway, **Guru's Bridge,** which symbolizes the journey of the soul after death, in order to reach the *bangaldar* pavilion on which the temple stands. Access to the bridge is through marvelous **Darshani Deorhi,** a gateway marked by magnificent silver doors. Here, you will join the many devotees who, especially early and late in the day, pass through the temple to pay their respects (and give a donation) to their Holy Book. Within Hari Mandir, the scene—which is almost constantly being televised for Sikh viewers around India—is fascinating. Beneath a canopy studded with jewels, scriptures from the Holy Book are sung, while a crowd of fervent yet solemn devotees immerse themselves in the moment. A *chauri,* or whisk, is repeatedly waved dramatically in the air above the Book, while new musicians and singers continually join the ensemble after another participant has paid his respects. Like an organic human machine, lines of Sikhs pay their respects by touching their foreheads to the temple floor and walls, continuing in a clockwise direction at a moderate pace. After the long, sometimes crushing, wait in the nonstop queue on the causeway, finally being among such gracious devotion will fill you with a sense of inner calm. Once you've passed through Hari Mandir, either climb the narrow stairwells and take your time to drink in the atmosphere or head back along Guru's Bridge. It is along this bridge that the *Granth Sahib* is carried between Hari Mandir and **Akal Takht** (see "Spiritual Weightlifting," below), the seat of the Sikh parliament, built in 1609 and located directly across from Hari Mandir.

Don't miss **Guru-ka-Langar,** a community kitchen where each day around 35,000 people are fed by temple volunteers. In an act that symbolizes the Sikh belief in equality of all people, irrespective of caste or creed, everyone is welcomed and invited to join the communal breaking of bread—a simple and unlimited meal of chapatis (wheat bread) and *dal* (lentils) is served. Simply raise your hands palm-up in order to receive more chapati; the servers will continue dishing *dal* until you've had your fill. Before or after you join in for a meal, make a point of going behind the scenes to witness the extraordinary activities in the various industrial-size **temple kitchens** that prepare the food. There are three distinct sections. In one kitchen, *chapattis* are prepared by automated machines on a conveyor belt system that's as fascinating to observe as the unit where they're made by hand—you're even welcome to join in. Somewhat more medieval is where gigantic cauldrons of *dal* are cooked over burners and stirred with paddle-size ladles. In the **Central Sikh Museum** at the main entrance, galleries display images and remembrances of Sikh gurus, warriors, and saints; note that it includes some graphic portraits of gurus being tortured and executed in terrifying ways.

Unlike in many other temples in India, here you feel genuinely welcome and not at all pressured to take out your wallet. In fact, the local Sikhs are so proud of their religion, culture, history, and temple that you will almost certainly be offered enthusiastic conversation and valuable information by one of the regular devotees—in return for nothing

| Moments | **Spiritual Weight Lifting** |

The best time to visit The Golden Temple is during *Palki Sahib* ★★★, or the **night ceremony,** during which the *Granth Sahib* is carried from the main shrine in Hari Mandir to the sanctum, where it rests for a few hours until the opening ceremony the following morning. Any man can take part in this ceremony by joining one of the queues that form behind and ahead of the heavy palanquin on which the Holy Book is moved. Several devotees simultaneously help support each arm of the palanquin, giving each person a few seconds to take part in the auspicious event. As though it were being transported along a human conveyor belt, one person from each side moves away from the palanquin and is replaced by a new shoulder from each of the lines; in this way, everyone gets at least one chance to participate, and you can join the end of the line again and again until your shoulder refuses to cooperate.

more than your attention. The welcoming information office to the left of the main gate gives helpful advice and information, as well as free guides and booklets on Sikhism (see our "India in Depth" chapter, p. 17, for a brief summary). Guest quarters are also available for visitors (for a nominal fee), and at least 400 simple rooms are provided free of charge to pilgrims (and you do not need to be Sikh to stay here—the atmosphere will be very welcoming).

For further information, contact the **Temple Manager** (✆ **0183/255-3953,** -3957, or -3958; fax 0183/ 255-3919), or call the **Information Office** (✆ **0183/255-3954**). Daily 7:30am–7:30pm in summer and 8am–7pm in winter. Activity at the temple goes on till late, and even when the last ceremonies of the evening have been concluded, volunteers get to work by cleaning or preparing for the next day. The main gate never closes, and the Hari Mandir is open according to hours determined by the lunar cycle— some 20 hr. in summer and 18 hr. in winter. In summer, the closing ceremony takes place at 11pm and the sanctum is reopened at 2am; winter times are usually 9:30pm and 3am. Best to call and check, although your hotel or guesthouse will know all the details, too.

Flag Ceremony at Wagah Border ★★ | Moments | Direct from the Monty Python Ministry of Silly Walks, this early evening border closing ceremony has grown into one of the most spectacularly bizarre attractions in all of India. A thrillingly pompous display of military bravado, it attracts countless Indian tourists every day, and is some of the most delightfully fun modern-day events you'll ever get around to witnessing in India. It's an intricately choreographed high-kicking, toe-stepping, quick-marching ceremony wherein the Indian and Pakistani flags are lowered on either side of the only border that remains open between the two more-often-than-not hostile countries. As the event has grown into a full-blown spectator sport, organizers have added an emcee and laid on many more grandstands (and security measures) to ensure that each show is a mighty success, not to mention ego-stoking celebration of all things "Indian"—when we last visited, part of the warm-up included children dancing passionately to *Jai Ho,* the hit tune from *Slumdog Millionaire,* while whistle-blowing soldiers try their darndest to keep the crowd seated. A number of officers from each team put on a raised-eyebrow performance to the satisfaction of the cheering, chanting crowds, and the atmosphere is nothing short of electric. The pointless exercise ends with the furious slamming of the border gates, at which time each side's flag is urgently carried to a room for overnight safekeeping. For anyone interested in

Bloody History of the Holy Temple

In 1984, the Sikh fundamentalist Sant Bhindranwale and his followers armed themselves and occupied The Golden Temple as part of a campaign for a separate Sikh state, which they wanted to call Khalistan. Acting on Prime Minister Indira Gandhi's orders, the Indian Army attacked, killing Bhindranwale and others and causing serious damage to the temple. Sikh honor was avenged when Indira Gandhi was later assassinated by two of her Sikh bodyguards, which in turn led to a massacre in which thousands of Sikhs lost their lives. The Sikh community refused to allow the central government to repair the damage to the temple, instead undertaking the work themselves. Although most of the cracks and crevices have been repaired, the incident has not been forgotten, and you will find many people in Amritsar keen to explain the Sikh side of the story.

unbridled nationalist pride, the Flag Ceremony is an unforgettable outing (only half an hour from Amritsar). Arrive well ahead of the crowds in order to get a close-up seat—the grimaces of the mighty military men in their rooster caps add to the fun, and you'll get a better look at the Pakistani delegation. Foreigners are entitled to occupy one of the better-situated grandstands (bring your passport, just in case someone wants to check), but there are even better "VIP" seats for which you can arrange access through political connections (or, if you're a guest there, from the manager of the Ista hotel).

Wagah is at the border between India and Pakistan, 32km (20 miles) from Amritsar. You need to arrive at the border at least 30 min. before the ceremony commences (around 6pm). No bags of any sort are permitted into the border area—leave them in your room or you'll waste time trying to find a locker facility. Bring your passport to speed up your entry to the "special seating" area reserved for guests and foreigners. Round-trip taxi Rs 950–Rs 1,500; Rs 450 by auto-rickshaw.

WHERE TO STAY

Amritsar is undergoing a revolution. There's news of all kinds of business hotels going up, and the Punjab's first five-star hotel, **Ista Amritsar** (reviewed below), opened in early 2009. Of the fairly decent midrange hotels, your best option is the **Ritz Plaza Hotel** (45 The Mall; © **0183/256-2836** through -2839; www.ritzhotel.in), which has comfortable rooms, a pool, and all the standard facilities for around Rs 4,400 double (including breakfast). But if you'd prefer a more personal environment, the two guesthouse options below offer not only value for money, but a more memorable experience.

Ista Amritsar ★★ Marking a big step up for the dusty border town, Amritsar's first five-star hotel offers no-nonsense luxury, and there are plenty of diversions here to keep you entertained between visits to the Temple. Although its location at the edge of town (it feels a bit like a dull suburb) leaves a lot to be desired, the hotel compensates with state of the art facilities—the best pool in town, an extensive spa (with a range of therapies, from Thai massage and aromatherapy to crystal healing and Ayurveda), an authentic Thai and Chinese restaurant, and a sexy little bar off the flash designer lobby. Rooms are sleek and contemporary, with solid, elegant furnishings. Even if it's clearly aimed at an elite business clientele, it's cushioning enough to have all-round appeal. Shuttles run you to the Golden Temple and staff can organize VIP seating privileges at the Wagah border

Not Quite the City of the Future: Stopover in Chandigarh

More than merely a useful stopover en route to Amritsar or Shimla, the entirely planned city of **Chandigarh** is celebrated as a daring experiment in modernist urban design. It's the creation of Le Corbusier, the father of modernism, whose grid-plan "living organism" design was a response to Nehru's dream to build, in his words, "a new town symbolic of the freedom of India, unfettered by the traditions of the past, an expression of the nation's faith in the future." When Punjab was divided after Partition, Lahore went to Pakistan, leaving the state without a capital; Chandigarh—a groundbreaking experiment, built from scratch during the 1950s—was envisioned as the new headquarters. When Punjab was once again divided into smaller states, the city became a Union Territory serving as the administrative capital for both Punjab and Haryana. Le Corbusier is largely responsible for designing the mesh of rectangular units, or "sectors," into which the city is divided. Characterized by broad boulevards, large landscaped parks with abundant trees, and quadrants of tidy, self-sufficient neighborhoods made up of buildings with louvered screens *(brise-soleil)*, exposed brickwork, boulder stone masonry, and unfinished concrete surfaces, Le Corbusier's city doesn't quite function as the living organism it's intended to be. Urban decay and waste have crept in, and the sheer scale of the city—much of which is given over to civic administration—lends it a slightly ghostly, alienating atmosphere (especially on weekends). With the city layout designed to keep residences away from main roads, and the rigid grid system ensuring plenty of space between buildings, the city lacks the frenetic buzz that's synonymous with urban centers around the country. Chandigarh ends up feeling very un-Indian, something of a shock if you've just arrived from a metro like Delhi. But architecture buffs will find Le Corbusier's structural contributions intriguing. If you're particularly interested, start with a visit to the **Architecture Museum** (Sector 10), where the story behind the city is revealed through a dated display of archive materials which includes original design sketches, plans, and newspaper articles. The museum forms part of a larger Cultural Complex, where you might want to explore the **Art Gallery** (Tues–Sun 9:30am–5pm) which includes Modernist works. To get a sense of the scope of Le Corbusier's project, you really need to drive around the city and evaluate a selection of the buildings (even Nehru admitted not liking them all). If you don't want to shell out on a taxi, you could use the city's **Hop on Hop off Bus,** which stops at key points around the city (half-day ticket Rs 50). The main architectural attractions include the **Capitol Complex ★★** (Sector 1), where the geometrical concrete buildings of the **Legislative Assembly, High Court,** and **Secretariat** represent structural innovation. At the southern end of the complex piazza, the **Vidhan Sabha (Legislative Assembly)** building is capped by a startling cupola, a pyramidal tower, and a cuboid tower, while within the portico is a bright **Cubist mural** by Le Corbusier himself. Also within the complex is the **Open Hand Monument,** a giant metal hand standing 26m (85 ft.) high that is able to rotate in the wind. Symbolizing the give-and-take of ideas, the hand has become the city's official emblem. Technically, tours of the complex start from the reception area, but these half-hourly episodes don't always materialize; check with someone from the **Chandigarh Industrial & Tourism Development Corporation (CITCO;** (C) **0172/270-4761** or -4356) in advance.

Known as a garden city, Chandigarh prides itself on having the largest **Rose Garden** in Asia (it's in Sector 16, but a real let-down) Chandigarh's real highlight—and in fact reason enough to make a detour to the city—is the breathtakingly alternative **Rock Garden of Nek Chand** ★★★ (Sector 1, adjacent the Capitol Complex; Rs 10 adults; 9am–6pm), a surreal fantasyland created by "outsider artist" Nek Chand—a former road inspector—from rocks, concrete, and urban rubbish. Set on 8 hectares (20 acres) of wooded landscape, the "garden" comprises a series of mazelike archways, tunnels, pavilions, waterfalls, and bridges, with passages leading from one open-air gallery to another. Each gallery is occupied by unusual characters, figures, and creatures fashioned from an unbelievable array of materials Chand started collecting in 1958; almost half a century later, the garden continues to grow. Unfortunately, the garden's fame has grown exponentially, too, so it's advisable to arrive early in order to avoid the crowds that descend, especially on weekends.

Chandigarh can be visited en route between Amritsar and Shimla, or directly from Delhi by train. The best connections between Delhi and Chandigarh are several daily Shatabdi Express trains or the Himalayan Queen. From Amritsar, choose the Paschim Express, a section of which also links Chandigarh with Kalka, starting point for the "toy train" to Shimla, a slow but memorable way of getting to the famed Raj-era hill station. The **railway station** ((C) **0172/270-8573,** 0172/264-1651, 131, or 132) is in Sector 17, around 8km (5 miles) from the city center. For railway inquiries, call the **city reservation center** ((C) **0172/270-8573;** Mon–Sat 8am–8pm, Sun 8am–2pm). There are also daily flights from the capital; the airport is 12km (7½ miles) from the city. **Chandigarh Tourism** ((C) **0172/270-3839**) has offices at the airport and at the railway station.

Unless you're hell-bent on racing on to your nest destination, there's no reason not to book into the **Taj Chandigarh** ★★ (Block No. 9, Sector 17-A; (C) **0172/661-3000;** www.tajhotels.com), which is the city's smartest hotel by a long stretch. Although it's geared towards business folk (not to mention numerous VIPs and politicos in town on "official" business), there's a fine pool and plush rooms to come home to after trying to make sense of Le Corbusier's vision. Doubles cost Rs 11,000, but you should be able to score a "rate of the day" deal; at the same time, book a table for dinner at **Black Lotus** ★★, the in-house Chinese restaurant. If you'd prefer Indian food, ask the concierge to point you in the direction of **Pal Dhaba**—famous for its mutton—in Section 28; alternatively, head to **Swagath,** which is particularly good with seafood.

ceremony. And as for the service, well, we haven't heard *"Namaskar"* repeated so enthusiastically by so many different people in a long time.

Adj. Alpha One City Centre, MBM Farms, Main G.T. Rd., Amritsar 143 001. ℂ **0183/270-8888.** Fax 0183/270-9999. www.istahotels.com. 248 units. Rs 6,000–Rs 8,000 premium double, Rs 7,000–Rs 9,000 deluxe double, Rs 7,500–Rs 10,000 luxury double, Rs 11,000–Rs 18,000 deluxe suite, Rs 18,000–Rs 25,000 presidential suite. AE, MC, V. **Amenities:** 2 restaurants; lounge-bar, delicatessen; airport transfers (Rs 1,070–Rs 1,666); large outdoor pool with Jacuzzi; room service; health club and spa; yoga. *In room:* A/C, TV/DVD, hair dryer, Internet (Rs 1,000/day), minibar.

Mrs. Bhandari's Guesthouse ★ (Value)

Legendary Mrs. Bhandari passed away in 2007, but her famous guesthouse flourishes under her ever-hospitable daughter, Ratan. The late-Raj family estate packs in large gardens, a pool, and its own team of curious water buffalo; these provide milk as well as the essential ingredient (fresh dung) for homemade fire "briquettes." Accommodations vary in size and location, arranged in and around the ivy-covered family home. Most rooms resemble "chummeries," the bachelor quarters assigned to Raj officials of junior rank with an attached room for their Indian servant. Modest though they are, interiors have nostalgic charm, with high ceilings, Art Deco tiles, and eclectic period furnishings and decor that underscore the homey touch. Bathrooms feature drench showers or old-fashioned tubs with original piping. The kitchen genie prepares home-cooked dishes from a small menu, and staff will help you plan an itinerary, organizing any transport and temple visits you require. It's not faultless, but service and management are hands-on and well meaning.

No. 10, Cantonment, Amritsar 143 001. ℂ **0183/222-8509.** Fax 0183/222-2390. http://bhandari_guesthouse. tripod.com. bgha10@gmail.com. 16 units. Rs 1,600 double, Rs 1,900 double with A/C and heater; Rs 300 extra bed. Camping Rs 170 per person with own equipment. MC, V (3% surcharge). **Amenities:** Restaurant; beer fridge; TV lounge; airport transfers (Rs 550–Rs 850); camping facilities; children's play area; Internet (broadband) (Rs 40/hr.); large outdoor pool (open Mar–Nov); limited room service. *In room:* A/C, heater, fireplace (extra charge).

Ranjit's Svaasa ★★★

After the hustle and bustle of Amritsar's traffic-choked streets, returning to this pretty, professionally run boutique hotel is sheer bliss. The owners have transformed a 250-year-old colonial redbrick mansion into a haven of small town refinement, carving out a tiny, sensuous spa and developing a selection of appealing suites, each with heaps of character—antiques, artworks, and thoughtful touches (like organic towels and jute slippers)—that make the place stand out as the most intimate and special place to stay in Amritsar. Rooms are furnished with colonial-era furniture (including four-poster beds) and open onto a cool balcony overlooking a landscaped garden. Pleasant accommodations aside, the focus here is on serving delicious, healthy, organic food and pampering you at the spa: we wouldn't dare leave without having at least one of the authentic Ayurvedic treatments; before visiting the Golden Temple, detoxify your system with a lime and ginger aromatherapy session. There's no longer a pool (Amritsar is bitterly cold in winter anyway), but with its comfortable lounges and nooks, you need not even notice.

47A The Mall, Amritsar 143 001. ℂ **0183/256-6618** or 0183/329-8840. Fax 0183/500-3728. www.svaasa. com. spa@svaasa.com. 17 units, most with shower only. Rs 6,000 Rai Bahadur double; Rs 8,000 Svaasa Suite double; Rs 10,000 Ratnavali Suite double; Rs 16,000–Rs 18,000 Presidential Suite (2–4 guests); Rs 1,500 extra bed. Rates exclude 4% tax. MC, V. **Amenities:** Restaurant, TV lounge; airport transfers (Rs 850); Ayurvedic spa; small library; organic health shop; room service; Wi-Fi (in lounge and lobby; free); yoga and meditation. *In room:* A/C, TV (in some), DVD (in Presidential suite), fridge (in some), hair dryer.

That the people of Amritsar live to eat is obvious from the scores of *dhabas*, Punjabi-style "fast-food" joints serving tasty and filling thalis (multicourse platters), that showcase various traditional dishes everywhere. This is the land of *desi-ghee* (clarified butter) and butter, added to almost every dish: Those watching their weight or unable to consume rich, heavy food should take it easy on the Indian fare here. But if you're up for the adventure, this is a culinary exploration like few others in India, where for as little as Rs 50 you'll be served a sizable spread that you eat with your fingers, dipping piping-hot *parathas* (fried flatbread) into *maa ki dal, channa,* and other concoctions arranged in little heaps on your platter.

If you're looking for a clean, glitzy restaurant that serves a wide range of dishes, then the one just about everybody in town will steer you to, is **Crystal** ★ (Crystal Chowk, Queens Rd.; ⓒ **0183/222-5555** or -9999), which is the most famous restaurant in Amritsar. It may not win any awards for atmosphere, and service is atrocious (especially on weekends and after 8:30pm when the place is usually packed), but it's the most popular "upmarket" restaurant in town. The menu is eclectic, with the standard array of Chinese and Continental dishes thrown in, but we suggest you stick to what they're really good at: North Indian specialties like the delicious *malai tikka*. Although it doesn't yet have quite the same legacy, another contender worth considering is **Astoria:** Tucked into a posh colony and run by young Navneet Singh, Astoria also offers an extensive menu and great value for money (38 District Shopping Centre, Ranjit Ave., G.T. Rd.; ⓒ **0183/250-5722**).

Smart options aside, what Amritsar is known for are its traditional *dhabas*, simple eateries where food-mad Punjabis happily look beyond the less-salubrious surrounds in favor of a lip-smacking meal. Chief among these is **Kesar da Dhaba** ★★ in Bazaar Passian, where, for close to 100 years, superb vegetarian curries have created countless devotees. For Amritsari fish—here, fabulous batter-fried sole from the Beas River, flavored with lovage (a thymelike spice)—you must go to **Makhan Fish House** (Lawrence Rd.), another famous *dhaba*, where things are eternally simple and cheap. Another stalwart serving delectable fish and chicken is **Bharawan da Dhaba** ★ (ⓒ **0183/253-2575**), which also does simple, delicious *paratha*, and *dal* is dished; wash your meal down with one of their utterly decadent *lassis*. **Surjit's Chicken House** (Lawrence Rd.) is the spot if you're looking for a sit-down meal of delicious butter chicken and *kulchas* or *lachedar parathas*.

Finally, if aesthetics matter to you, the smartest restaurant in town is **Thai Chi** ★ at the Ista hotel (G.T. Rd.; ⓒ **0183/270-8888**), where you can get authentic, surprisingly good-value Thai and Chinese dishes served in chic surroundings. Everything's made to your specifications, so you can ask chef Mani to tone down the spices if you prefer (incidentally, anything with silken tofu is highly recommended, as is the Szechuan-style bean curd). If you're not staying in the hotel, have after-dinner drinks at the **Lotus Lounge** (just off the lobby) which has become a favorite haunt for wealthy nonresident Punjabis out to pay tribute to their holy temple.

3 SHIMLA

107km (66 miles) NE of Chandigarh; 360km (223 miles) N of Delhi

In the days when Shimla inspired scenes from Rudyard Kipling's *Kim*, it was a popular pickup center for lusty British officers and flirtatious maidens keen to create a stir among the scandalmongers who gathered along The Mall during the summers. Shimla enjoys a proud history as the preferred mountain escape retreat from the unbearable summer heat of the plains (or "downstairs," as many Himachalis refer to their low-altitude neighbors)—a cool spot in which to sink into a life of idle gossip, romantic conquests, and military brown-nosing. Today, this romantic image has been somewhat ruined by unchecked urbanization and reckless construction. Development has now been curbed, but the clogged roads and ugly concrete tenements that cling to the mountainsides beneath Shimla detract significantly from the town's former glory.

Sprawling over seven hills fringed by dense forest and magnificent mountains, Shimla is a useful starting point from which to explore more untouched parts of Himachal, and the town's timbered cottages and wood-gabled buildings retain a degree of charm, but if you're expecting a quiet hill station, you may be disappointed. The Mall, a promenade on the southern slopes of the ridge, remains a pedestrian preserve, thronged by tourists and local Anglophiles who tend to echo the social mannerisms of the Raj at its most British. Below the ridge, however, an overwhelmingly Indian conglomeration of buildings constitutes the bazaar, and a sweep of modern dwellings has the distinctly untidy appearance of unplanned urban sprawl. Shimla is, however, in close proximity to a number of lesser-known hill resort getaways: Naldehra, Narkanda, Kufri, Mashobra, and Chadwick Falls are all destinations offering relative peace and quiet as well as scenic splendor guaranteed to capture your imagination. And for those seeking adventure and remote beauty, Shimla is a useful confluence of roads leading west to the Kangra Valley; north to Kullu, Lahaul, and Ladakh; and east into the valleys of Kinnaur and Spiti.

ESSENTIALS

GETTING THERE & AWAY **By Road** All of the more reputable hotels (see "Where to Stay & Dine," below) will arrange transfers from practically any starting point in India, should you wish to arrive in chauffeured style. From Delhi, you'll take National Highway 1 (Grand Trunk Rd.) north to Ambala (in Haryana) and then continue on a fierce and beautiful journey along a hillside road that snakes all the way up to Shimla. You can also drive directly from Chandigarh, following National Highway 21 south until you join the main Delhi-Shimla road.

By Air Daily flights connect Shimla with Delhi (1 hr.); try Kingfisher for the best service and price. Weather can interfere with flights in and out of Shimla's **Jubbar Hatti Airport,** 23km (14 miles) from the city (taxi into town around Rs 650). Some flights also continue on to Kullu's **Bhuntar Airport,** which serves northern Himachal Pradesh.

By Train The most romantic way to get to Shimla, the **Himalayan Queen** runs from New Delhi to Kalka (640m/2,099 ft. above sea level), where the train switches to a narrow-gauge track and continues on to Shimla (2,060m/6,757 ft.). Traveling at an average speed of 25 to 30kmph (15–19 mph), the "toy train" journey will consume nearly a full day of your itinerary. It's 96km (60 miles) of travel through some 100 tunnels, numerous bridges, and sharp curves, taking in picturesque views of green forests and meadows, capsicum fields, and red-roofed chalets; the historic train was given UNESCO World Heritage status in 2008. The train back to Kalka departs Shimla at 10:35am, arriving in time for you to make the onward connection to Delhi, where you'll arrive before midnight. Check out www.indianrail.gov.in (see p. 59 for more information). *Note:* During the high season (May–June, Dec/Jan), it's difficult to secure tickets without at least several days' advance booking, so do so through the Internet or an agency.

VISITOR INFORMATION Check out the website of the **Himachal Pradesh Tourism Development Corporation** (HPTDC; ✆ **0177/265-4589;** www.himachaltourism.nic. in) if you really must, and you can even pop into their office for what feels like a sharp, unenthusiastic slap in the face. Much better to simply ask at your hotel or guesthouse for help—they'll be more likely to (a) respond, and (b) recommend interesting and decent places to stay elsewhere in Himachal. Be extremely wary of advice suggesting you should stay at one of the HPTDC-run establishments, which generally offer some of the most appalling lodgings and service in the country.

GETTING AROUND **On Foot** Central Shimla is free of traffic, which means that you'll spend a lot of your time exploring on foot. You'll need some degree of stamina to deal with the numerous steep inclines, and as much patience dealing with the constant mob of fellow pedestrians, especially during the summer. A two-stage elevator, **The Lift,** operating between 8am and 10pm, connects The Mall with Cart Road; ticket prices are nominal.

By Car Shimla has a number of restricted and sealed roads, and farther routes are no-go zones for heavier vehicles. Should you arrive in town by train, you can find a taxi (or even the odd auto-rickshaw), which will drop you at your hotel—although you may be surprised at the route necessary to get around "no traffic" zones. Day trips (see "Excursions Around Shimla," below) will generally require a taxi or jeep—but the prices can fluctuate wildly. Get advice from your hotel on hiring a car and driver at reasonable rates. For prepaid taxi trips, contact the government-run service at ✆ **0177/265-8892,** or **Vishal Himachal Taxi Operator Union** at ✆ **0177/265-7645.**

GUIDED TOURS & TRAVEL AGENTS For intelligent, entertaining, and exclusive **tours of Shimla** itself, your best bet is to make contact with noted local historian Raaja Bhasin, author of *Simla: The Summer Capital of British India.* Raaja conducts interesting and tailor-made walks around Shimla and will provide you with fond memories of the town and an acute understanding of its juicy history. E-mail or call Raaja in advance to make sure he's available (✆ **0177/265-3194;** www.raajabhasin.com; mail@raajabhasin. com). Tours normally start from your hotel and run from 10am to 5pm for a charge of $170 (for two people this includes lunch, for larger groups evening tea). In 2010, Raaja plans to start doing **customized Himachaltrips** around the entire state, arranging everything from transport to accommodation, and including some of the very best insights into Himachali life.

Government-operated tours are annoying, claustrophobic excursions, best avoided unless you're on a tight budget. The office of the **Himachal Pradesh Tourism Development Corporation** (HPTDC; ✆ **0177/265-2561** or -8302; www.hptdc.nic.in; Apr 15–July 15 and Sept 15–Jan 1 daily 9am–8pm, rest of year daily 9am–6pm) is along The Mall, near Scandal Point.

The Mall has an abundance of **travel agencies;** you may need to approach one of them to arrange transport, tours, and trekking around the state. Be warned, however, that we've been increasingly disenchanted with the service provided out of Shimla, so you might want to contact one of the operators recommended in other parts of this chapter and have them collect you in Shimla (or Delhi if you prefer). One agent you can approach is **Band Box** (9 The Mall; ✆ **98-1606-1160** or 0177/265-8157), although because it's a small business (and operates from the back of a clothing store) you don't always find someone in the office.

(*Fast Facts* Shimla

Ambulance Dial ℂ **0177/280-4648** or 0177/265-2102.

ATMs, Banks & Currency Exchange The Mall has outlets of HDFC, City Banks, ICICI Bank, and UTI Bank. You can change cash and traveler's checks, and organize cash advances on certain credit cards Monday to Saturday 8am to 8pm. In an emergency, guests at the Cecil and Wildflower Hall can also draw money against their credit cards for a small percentage.

Hospital For around-the-clock service, call **Tara Hospital** (ℂ **0177/280-3275**).

Police There's a police office (ℂ **0177/281-2344**) adjacent to the Town Hall, on The Mall. It's closed on Sunday.

Post Office The **General Post Office** (Mon–Sat 10am–6pm) is located just above Scandal Corner.

WHAT TO SEE & DO

Shimla's main promenade is **The Mall,** a pedestrian avenue stretching across the length of the city from Gopal Mandir in the west to the suburb of Chhota Shimla, roughly south of the town center. Along this stretch, crumbling remnants of the British Raj abound, but it's hard not to be startled by the attendant concrete sprawl. Above The Mall is **The Ridge,** a wide-open esplanade watched over by a statue of Gandhi to the east, where the nearby Gothic **Christchurch** is one of Shimla's most imposing structures, situated adjacent the faux-Tudor half-timbered **library.** Note the fresco around the chancel window, designed by Lockwood Kipling, Rudyard's father.

Also on The Mall are the **Telegraph Office,** an interesting example of stone ashlar work completed in 1922 and, to its right, the old **Railway Booking Office,** a sadly decaying building frequently overrun by obnoxious monkeys. Marking the area where The Ridge joins with The Mall, **Scandal Point** continues to be a popular social hangout, supposedly taking its name from an unconfirmed scandal involving the elopement of a handsome Patiala prince with the daughter of a British commander-in-chief. Beyond the fire station, after the dressed stone building housing the Municipal Offices, is the **Gaiety Theatre,** originally the Town Hall. Renowned for its excellent acoustics, the Gaiety has seen some notable personalities grace its planks, including Lord Robert Baden-Powell and novelist M. M. Kaye, once—not all with great success; a fashionable piece of gossip tells how Rudyard Kipling was booed off the stage. The neo-gothic theater reopened in July 2009 after a mammoth 5-year restoration, and will presumably become a social hub once again.

A short walk east of The Ridge will take you to the start of a rather strenuous but worthwhile hike to the summit of **Jakhu Hill** ★, which, at an altitude of 2,445m (8,020 ft.), is Shimla's highest point and affords excellent views of the city and surrounding valleys. You need to trudge up a steep 1.5km (1-mile) path, commencing at The Ridge and culminating at Shimla's highest point, to get to the **Hanuman Temple** on Jakhu's summit. Try to make it to the top in time for sunrise or sunset, either of which is glorious. The little temple is dedicated to Hinduism's popular monkey god (who is said to have rested on Jakhu Hill on his return from a mission in the Himalayas). Today his brazen descendants continue to patrol the path, so beware of carrying food or doing *anything* likely to provoke them. After you sound the bell at the temple entrance, enter to discover a curious concoction of serious Hindu faith and jovial Christmas pomp suggested by the tinsel and streamer decorations; the priest will happily give you a blessing.

To the west of the city, beyond the Cecil hotel, is the vast six-story Scottish baronial mansion formerly known as **Viceregal Lodge** (Observatory Hill; Tues–Sun 9am–1pm and 2–5pm). The admission fee of Rs 50 includes a guide but be warned that if you turn up when it's busy, the tour will feel unpleasantly oversubscribed so try to arrive early in the day. Built in 1888 at the behest of the British viceroy in an approximation of the Elizabethan style, the lodge is Shimla's single greatest architectural testament to the influence of the British Raj, and its luxuriant woodwork and lovely views attract numerous visitors. Even in 1888 it had electric light and an indoor tennis court, both rare for the times. The building was the summer residence of all viceroys until 1947, when India was granted independence and the building renamed Rashtrapati Niwas, a retreat for the president of India. The first president of India thought it should be put to better use, however, and in 1964 it was inhabited by the Indian Institute of Advanced Study, an academic foundation still housed here. It has a museum of photographs and other artifacts that highlight the important events that took place in Shimla during the preindependence days.

If you want to get beyond the usual tourist experience and steer clear of the crowds, head down one of the stairways leading down into the hodgepodge warren of narrow streets and back alleys that constitute Shimla's **bazaar,** right below The Mall. After the touristy buzz, it feels a bit like stepping into another world with tiny eating houses, shops selling everyday goods, miniature temples, and dodgy travel agents crammed tightly together and bustling with activity.

EXCURSIONS AROUND SHIMLA

A mere 12km (7½ miles; 30 min.) from Shimla, the forested village of **Mashobra** is great for scenic walks but is best visited as an excuse to step into one of India's loveliest hotels, **Wildflower Hall** (see "Where to Stay & Dine," below), for high tea or lunch. From the village, you can attempt a trek to the area's highest peak—Shali—which reaches 3,200m (10,496 ft.), or take the 2km (1¼-mile) pedestrian track to the "sacred grove" of Sipur, where you'll find the charming, indigenous-style temple dedicated to the local deity, Seep. Because they are considered the personal property of Seep, no trees may be cut here; the locals are so superstitious that they pat themselves down before leaving to ensure no fallen cedar needles have accidentally dropped on them. A further 45 minutes beyond Mashobra is the popular picnicking resort of **Naldehra** (23km/14 miles from Shimla), which has an extraordinary 9-hole golf course designed by Lord Curzon (British viceroy of India, 1899–1905). Golfing on the world's highest course is best arranged through your hotel in Shimla, or you can opt to stay at one of the local "resorts"—**The Châlets Naldehra** (© **0177/274-7715** or 98-1606-2007; www.chaletsnaldehra.com; from Rs 6,500 double, without tax) has a pleasing alpine feel, with clean, comfortable, Scandinavian prefab wood cabins. Staff will arrange golf, river rafting, horseback-riding, fishing, and a range of hikes. The hot sulfur springs of **Tattapani** lie 28km (17 miles) farther away.

Chail (2,150m/7,000 ft.), 2 hours from Shimla, can be visited as a day trip out of the capital (or a relaxing, peaceful accommodations alternative; see below). Chail grew out of a romantic scandal, when Bhupinder Singh, the dashing Maharajah of Patiala, eloped with (or abducted, depending on who's telling the story) the daughter of Lord Kitchener. Predictably, the Maharajah was forced to return the daughter and was banned from ever again entering the Raj's summer capital. Enraged, the Raja combed the neighboring hills in search of a location from where he could literally look down on the town that had snubbed him. Chail was the answer to his ego-driven quest, and there he set about establishing his own "summer capital," building a lavish Georgian palace, as well as the highest cricket pitch in the world (2,444m/7,800 ft.). Sadly, the once-elegant palace has been converted into a poorly managed government-owned hotel (✆ 01792/24-8141 through -8143).

WHERE TO STAY

A destination in its own right, the Oberoi's **Wildflower Hall** (reviewed below) in Mashobra (around 30 min. from Shimla) is by far your best option, but if the rates exceed your budget, nothing can beat the homey Raj-era experience of **Chapslee,** run by the aristocratic Reggie Kapurthala (see below). If this is not available, you could try **Clarke's** (The Mall; ✆ 0177/265-1010 through -1015; www.clarkessimla.com), a small, modest, Oberoi-owned hotel, interesting in some respects because it was the hotel on which the Oberoi empire was built. Today it's a bit of a throwback to another era, with perfectly comfortable (if ordinary) accommodations (doubles from Rs 8,500 including all meals) and service that—in the words of one of the managers—only begins when you walk through the front door. Once inside, there's enough personality and historic ambience to help you enjoy your stay, but not enough that you'll end up wasting your time indoors. For more character, but comparatively lackluster accommodations, you could bed down at **Woodville Palace,** a converted Gothic pile built in the late 1930s—while it's filled with period relics, it lacks both the personal charm of Chapslee and the professionalism of Clarke's. It's also looking terribly run-down (Raj Bhavan Rd.; ✆ 0177/262-3919; www.woodvillepalacehotel.com; doubles with all meals from Rs 7,370 and up, excluding 10% tax; ask for a room in the new block; suites cost twice as much). Nevertheless, its location in the posh Raj Bhavan area is superb, surrounded as it is by large gardens—a luxury in Shimla. It also has some fantastic furniture and antiques, some of it unfortunately languishing dispiritedly in corners, along with great photographic displays that provide an interesting insight into the lives of Indian royalty. If, however, you want a full-service luxury hotel in Shimla itself, the **Cecil** is the top choice (reviewed below); it's only competition—but without any historical ambience—is the **Radisson Hotel Shimla** (Good wood Estate, Lower Bharari; ✆ 0177/265-9012; www.radisson.com), which takes full advantage of the views from an unbeautiful block that juts out from the side of the hill. Rooms are characteristically modern and sleek, but you'll surely miss the ambience of the heritage properties. The best rates—from around Rs 5,525 double—are available online.

Another interesting option, especially if you're traveling with family and prefer a degree of independence, is **Violet Hill** (✆ 98-1544-2233), a gorgeous three-bedroom self-contained cottage in verdant Mashobra. It costs Rs 15,000 per night with the promise of fine home-style meals (breakfast Rs 200, lunch and dinner Rs 400) and ever-splendid scenery amid immaculate gardens with bikes on hand to explore the surrounding forest terrain. Also in Mashobra, an even better deal, but perhaps not quite as pretty, is **Forest Hill Villas** (✆ 011/4053-3992; www.foresthillvillas.com), a massive three-story cottage with room for up to 10 guests (in three bedrooms and the attic; Rs 10,000 per night). You have to cook for yourself, and there's a decent kitchen for you to do so—kindly supplied with basic provisions, including vegetables and milk.

Or, if you prefer things ultramodern, check out the outrageously beautiful and upmarket **Clairmont Mashobra** ★★ (www.clairmont-mashobra.com), which opened in 2009—ensconced in utter luxury with the finest contemporary design details, you'll have the pleasure of enjoying utterly matchless views across Mashobra's thick forest—and **621**

Cecil ★★★ (**Kids**) Open since 1884, the Cecil has hosted the likes of Mahatma Gandhi and continues to draw political bigwigs, celebrities, and vacationing families, kids in tow. It was rebuilt in the Gothic style of Shimla's most elegant Raj monuments, and the interiors are luxurious with plenty of wood paneling, leather, and opulent furniture. Guest rooms follow through with old fashioned good taste and a sophisticated period ambience that's typical of the Oberoi's classic design ethos; the much-larger premiere rooms have walk-in closets and a large bathroom with separate tub and shower. Request a south-facing room (nos. 411–415 are best) with spectacular views of the Shimla Valley foothills. While you're being pampered in the spa, kids have their own entertainment hub, with everything from a doll's house to video games, and staff doesn't seem to mind them playing in the public areas, too (if you want a quiet, romantic getaway, head for Wildflower Hall). This is a less intimate, personal experience than Chapslee, but exceptional nonetheless.

Chaura Maidan, Shimla 171 004. (✆) **0177/280-4848** or **1600/11-2030** toll-free reservations in India. Fax 0177/281-1024. www.oberoihotels.com. reservations@oberoigroup.com. 75 units (most with tub. 8 with shower only). Rs 14,850 deluxe double; Rs 17,050 premier double; Rs 27,500 deluxe suite; Rs 33,000 luxury suite. 10% tax extra. Book online for best rate of the day and multiday specials. AE, DC, MC, V. **Amenities:** Restaurant; lounge bar, garden lounge; airport transfers (Rs 1,800 plus tax); babysitting; billiards room; children's activity center; health club and spa; library; heated indoor pool; room service. In room: A/C, central heating, TV/DVD, hair dryer, minibar, Wi-Fi (Rs 300/hr.; Rs 800/24 hr.).

Chapslee ★★ Chapslee remains the quintessential creaky-floorboards Shimla homestead, its Raj-era aura hardly dented by modern conveniences or the slightly fraying Art Deco wallpaper and faded tapestries. Owned and lovingly managed by Ratanjit "Reggie" Singh, the regal grandson of Raja Charanjit Singh of Kapurthala, this charming home is the most authentically old-world lodging in town. Originally built in 1835 as the summer residence of a British family, the house received an Edwardian face-lift in 1896 with teak paneling (part of the same consignment used for the Viceregal Lodge), wood parquet floors, and a dramatic staircase. Be sure to request either of the two upstairs suites; the original master bedrooms in each afford lovely valley views (glorious at sunset), a massive brass four-poster bed, and delicate ornamentation, as well as a vast bathroom with a raised tub, an enormous shower, a bidet, and its own fireplace. Chapslee's kitchen prepares British-influenced dishes, as well as delectable tandoori chicken and mouthwatering *shami* kebabs, all served by hard-working white-gloved attendants as you dine with your aristocratic host.

Lakkar Bazaar, Shimla 171 001. (✆) **0177/280-2542.** Fax 0177/265-8663. www.chapslee.com. chapslee@vsnl.com. 6 units. Rs 12,500–Rs 15,500 double; add 50% per extra person. Rates include breakfast, dinner, taxes, and service charges. MC, V. **Amenities:** Dining room, lounge; card room; croquet; Internet (for e-mail checking); library; tennis court. In room: Fireplace. no phone.

Wildflower Hall ★★★ Smack-dab in the middle of magnificent deodar cedar forests, atop its own hill 300m (1,000 ft.) above Shimla, surrounded by swirling mist and snowy peaks, this remake of the fire-gutted mountain retreat of Lord Kitchener is the ideal setting for a beautifully eerie alpine fantasy. Affording show-stopping views of some of the most scenic mountains and valleys in India, this opulent resort offers lovely service and top-notch facilities—it's romantic, but sedate, and you'll need to head outdoors to make the most of your time here (difficult, perhaps, since rooms are so cosseting). There are many adventure activities to put you in touch with the great outdoors, whether on

AMRITSAR, HIMACHAL PRADESH & LADAKH

13

SHIMLA

Hole up in a Himalayan fortress

Shimla itself is not a particularly relaxing town, and unless you're sequestered in one of the smart hotels, or able to splash out on the peaceable surrounds on offer at Wildflower Hall, it really doesn't make too much sense to stick around. If you've got a car and driver, another fine option is **Nalagarh ★★** (© **01795/22-3179,** -3009, or -3667; www.nalagarh.in), a glorious white-and-blue palatial fort a few hours north of Shimla and one of the finest heritage properties in the state. Built in 1421, Nalagarh, surrounded by sprawling lawns, offers a degree of eccentricity coupled with enough period character that will ensure you don't forget your stay. In terms of getting a feel for Himachal's great outdoors, it's a huge improvement on staying in Shimla itself, plus there's the advantage of a gorgeous pool and Ayurvedic spa; staff arranges excursions to see local handicrafts being made or to look at havelis in nearby villages. Standard doubles cost Rs 2,700, and suites run Rs 3,000 to Rs 6,500; meals are extra.

foot, on horseback, or rafting the waters of the Sutlej. And for more laidback pastimes, book at least one session at the spa. Besides traditional Ayurvedic treatments, therapists offer a series of tantalizing touch therapies, Hungarian body wrap treatments, and combination rituals; after being thoroughly pampered head for the outdoor Jacuzzi, perched on the lip of a vast mountain wilderness.

Chharabra, Shimla 171 012. © **1800/11-2030** toll-free reservations in India, or 0177/264-8585. Fax 0177/ 264-8686. www.oberoihotels.com. reservations@wildflowerhall.com. 85 units. Rs 22,500 premier double, Rs 24,500 premier mountain view double, Rs 40,500 deluxe suite, Rs 60,500 Lord Kitchener Suite. Rates exclude 10% tax. AE, DC, MC, V. No children under 12. **Amenities:** 2 restaurants, bar, lounge; airport transfers (Rs 2,500 plus tax); archery; bikes and mountain-biking trails; billiards room; card room; concierge; croquet; DVD library; golf (at Naldehra); health club and spa; hiking trails; horseback riding; ice-skating rink (mid-Dec to mid-Mar); outdoor Jacuzzi; library; heated indoor pool; rafting; room service; tennis court (summer); yoga & meditation. *In room:* A/C, TV/DVD, butler, hair dryer, minibar, Wi-Fi (Rs 200/ hr.; Rs 800/day).

WHERE TO DINE

Shimla has no dearth of dining options, but the town definitely suffers from a lack of quality specialty venues—most places tend to spread their bets in their attempt to satisfy the tastes of tourists, most of whom come from India's cities. Of these bland, mostly anonymous joints, your best bet is probably **Baljee's** (26 The Mall; © 0177/265-2313), where there's plenty of choice (stick to the Indian dishes, though, unless you're dead-set on a substandard burger or uninteresting Chinese), and the mix of diners provides decent entertainment. If you want to have a taste of a local specialty, then don't miss the *aloo sabzi* and *poori* (potato curry with deep-fried pancakelike bread) at **Mehar Chand** (Lower Bazaar; © 0177/265-3402), which also sells Indian sweets. But, honestly, the only place in Shimla where you'll find consistently spectacular and authentic Himachal specialties is at **The Restaurant** at the Cecil hotel (reviewed above)—the *baluchi raan* (tandoor roasted lamb leg flavored with mace, cardamom, and saffron) in particular is excellent, and there are eight different Himachali specialty dishes available per day.

Finally, **high tea** at Wildflower Hall is legendary—sample the local infusions along with traditional Irish tea brack bread—a baked reminder of the Raj, speckled with raisins and sultanas, steeped in Darjeeling tea, and served with unsalted butter and lemon curd.

cravings—everything, from traditional *Chaa gosht* (a Himachali preparation of baby lamb in yogurt) to delicious ravioli and risotto, is prepared with a masterful hand.

4 KINNAUR, SPITI & LAHAUL ★★★

The arid, dust-covered, snowcapped slopes in the Indo-Tibetan regions of Kinnaur, Spiti, and Lahaul are the stuff adventurers' dreams are made of, offering sublime mountainscapes, twisting roads, and fascinating Tibetan Buddhist communities with atmospheric *gompas* (monasteries). Negotiating the rough, drop-off ledges of the **Hindustan-Tibet Road** (bizarrely enough, known as "National Highway" 22) is an action-packed art in itself, and the impossible road is made all the more unnerving when buses, trucks, and jeeps headed in the opposite direction seem to appear out of nowhere. Although the spectacular scenery is undoubtedly the highlight of any trip through Kinnaur and Spiti, there are also marvelous monuments, including some of the world's most intriguing Buddhist complexes (such as the World Heritage Site of **Tabo Monastery** in Spiti), as well as high-altitude villages that seem to cling to the sides of mountains or balance on the edges of sharp cliffs.

ESSENTIALS

VISITOR INFORMATION Pick up information from the **tourism office in Shimla** (or Manali if you're doing the trip in reverse), and make detailed inquiries regarding accessibility and weather developments. Ajay Sud, an ex-army captain and adventurer who together with Rajesh Ojha founded **Banjara Camps,** is one of the best sources of information, tips, and assistance in the Kinnaur region. He's also a very experienced trekker and can give great advice and suggestions for treks throughout the Himalayas. He and the equally helpful Rajesh take turns manning the Sangla camp; best to reach either through the **head office** (1A Hauz Khas Village, New Delhi 110 016; *©* **011/2686-1397;** fax 011/2685-5152; www.banjaracamps.com).

If you'd like to have a more interactive vacation, staying with (and getting to know) local folk, contact **Ecosphere** (Ishita Khanna; *©* **98-99492417** or 01906/22-2724; www.spitiecosphere.com). Ecosphere has pioneered homestays and grassroots community participation in the Spiti region and can help put together a really memorable trip. If you're a hiker, **Aquaterra Adventures** (www.aquaterra.in), one of India's leading adventure travel specialists, runs "homestay trails"—fantastic hiking holidays through the rugged terrain with accommodations arranged in local village homes rather than tented camps—thereby providing a glimpse into the lifestyle and culture of this region. Aquaterra also organizes a yearly descent of the Spiti-Pin rivers from Kiato to Sumdo.

GETTING AROUND Ultra-budget-conscious travelers undertake the journey on what seems like a wing and a prayer in state buses that rely on luck as much as faith to reach their destination, while born-to-be-wild adventurers do it on the back of a motorbike—sign up with Capt. Raaj Kumar of **Shepherds Realms** (see "Staying Active" above). For the rest, we highly recommend renting a jeep and driver—the heftier the jeep (a Toyota Qualis or a Mahindra Scorpio), the better your chances of actually enjoying the adventure. Most of the villages can be explored on foot, and the region lends itself to trekking (see "Staying Active," earlier in this chapter). For one-stop shopping, we recommend you utilize the services of Banjara Camps (see "Visitor Information," above), which offers

> **Tips** **You Can't Eat Plastic**
>
> Obtaining cash against credit cards can be problematic in more remote parts of Himachal Pradesh (such as Kinnaur and Spiti) and anywhere in Ladakh outside Leh. Make sure you draw cash (easiest at ATMs) in the tourist hubs of Shimla, Dharamsala, and Manali before heading into the mountains.

most of the best lodging options in the area and can arrange your entire jeep safari. Based in Tabo, **Phuntsok Dhuondup** (© 94-1857-6181 or 01906/22-3452; www.spitivalley.com) is a reliable driver—a former Buddhist monk, he has many interesting stories to tell along the way.

INNER LINE PERMITS Foreigners may not travel through the zone closest to the Tibetan border without first obtaining an **Inner Line Permit** from one of several government offices in Himachal. It's a fairly easy, if laborious and potentially frustrating, process (taking anywhere from 3 hr. to a whole day); although you can have a travel agent in Shimla handle this for you (you will need your passport, three passport-size photographs, and two copies of both the main page of your passport and your visa), we strongly recommend that you apply in Reckong Peo, where one agent at the so-called **Tourist Information Centre** (Mr. Bhagwan Negi; © 94-1811-9617) handles all applications and does so with the least possible amount of fuss. The permit, arranged here, will cost Rs 150 and does not require any photos; permits are usually issued at 11am and 3pm (Mon–Sat only). Fill in your application and you'll be asked to report back before being led to the Deputy Commissioner's Building for a personal appearance and photograph which will be printed directly onto the permit. It takes a few hours, but use the time to check out the views from the village of Kalpa, a few miles above Reckong Peo. Another way of dealing with the slow pace is to apply and then collect your papers the following day after overnighting in beautiful Kalpa nearby. It's a good idea to phone ahead to ensure that the **SDM office** (© 01786/222-253; Mon–Sat 10am–5pm) is definitely open on the day you plan to apply.

THE JOURNEY: KINNAUR & SPITI IN 7 DAYS

This itinerary is designed for a slightly more leisurely journey through the Kinnaur and Spiti valleys than you may have time for. This is not an area to be covered in a hurry—rather extend your vacation, or you'll spend most of your trip regretting that you have to return at all. If you're pressed for time, you could probably shave off a day or two, but you're likely to be shell-shocked by the end of it if you don't. If you're really short on time, but want to see the Spiti Valley and take in a couple of its Buddhist villages and monasteries, you can forgo the trip through Kinnaur and instead make your way into Spiti from Manali; the trip from Manali to Kaza (the main hub in Spiti) takes a full day. If you're journeying this way and don't intend continuing beyond Tabo, you won't need to procure an Inner Line Permit; however, if you are doing the following trip in its entirety in reverse, you can get the necessary documents in Kaza (any travel agent should be able to assist).

Day 1 & 2: Shimla to Sangla

Heading east out of Shimla, "National Highway" 22 takes you to **Narkanda** (2,708m/ 8,882 ft.), a ski resort (Jan–Mar) where you can take in excellent views from Hatu Peak.

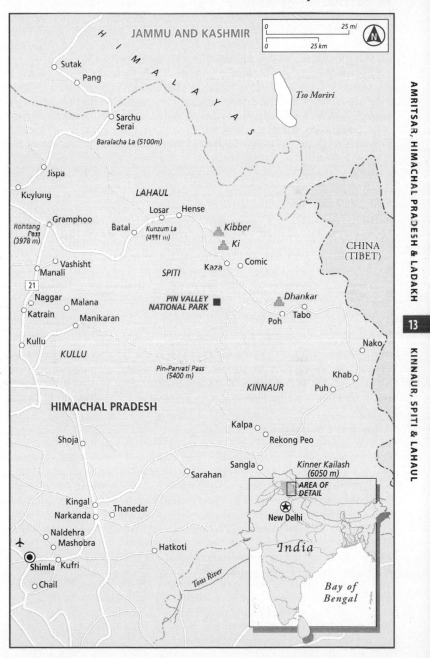

Then continue north past the commercial town of **Rampur,** a former princely capital. The road descends towards the raging Sutlej River, following its contours until you come upon the dusty village of **Jeori.** From here, a twisting, hairpin-heavy climb leads to the charming village of **Sarahan** (2,165m/7,101 ft., 6 hr. from Shimla), which enjoys spectacular views of the snowcapped peaks across the river. Trapped in time, Sarahan is the site of the famous pagoda-style **Bhimakali Temple** (see box on p. 630).

Once you've satisfied your curiosity at the temple, follow the same road back down to Jeori. About 3km (2 miles) ahead of Karchham (Baspa-Sutlej Junction), take a U-turn to come back to Karcham and then follow the steep dirt tracks (the road from Karcham to Sangla is fairly wide now, and two small cars/jeeps can comfortably pass by each other) of the **Sangla Valley** ★★★, through which the raging Baspa River flows. You won't find any flashy accommodations, but comfortable **Banjara Sangla Valley Camp & Retreat** ★★, 8km (5 miles) beyond Sangla, is an excellent place to spend a night or two, and serves as the perfect base from which to explore the remote hamlet of **Chitkul** ★★ (3,450m/11,316 ft.). Tents are set up in a gorgeous open meadow (wildflowers in full bloom July–Oct) alongside the Baspa River, beneath towering Khargala Peak. Besides the well-established camp, there are now also a handful of spacious, immaculate rooms in a low-rise building built overlooking the river near the campsite. A night in one of the Swiss tents (with attached showers that dispense hot water at the flick of a switch) costs Rs 5,500 double, including all meals and taxes, while the Retreat rooms are Rs 6,000. Make use of the opportunity to pick the brains of Banjara founders Ajay or Rajesh (one of whom is generally in camp) for details of the best treks in the area. Both are wonderful hosts (as is Sonu, the camp manager), with plenty of ideas for what you can do (besides lying in one of the inviting hammocks overlooking the river). Evening mealtimes kick off with predinner drinks and snacks around the bonfire, which can be quite sociable; besides the standard buffet, there's an optional barbeque, and there's nothing stopping you from picking up fresh fish from a local farm (the area is known for trout fishing) and asking the kitchen team to grill it for you. The setting is scintillating, and you'll regret not spending 2 nights, especially after the exhausting full-day drive spent getting here; and if you do have trouble getting here—or get caught up or delayed—call ✆ **98-1811-9871** or 98-1695-9904 for assistance.

If You Have More Time

To break up the journey, you can add an extra day or two right at the start with a side-trip to the apple-growing slopes at **Thanedar.** From Narkanda, a 16km (10-mile) detour off the main highway brings you to the vast orchards, heavy with fruit in summer, and best visited in August/September during the apple harvest. Set in the midst of this sea of apple trees is the modern, whitewashed **Banjara Orchard Retreat,** its pleasant rooms decked with thick, colorful throws and attached bathrooms. It's a very comfortable place to kick back and relax and enjoy astonishingly beautiful sunsets. Prakash Thakur, host and owner of this small retreat, is also the resident expert on local history and culture, and you can request a guide to take you for an innervating 3-hour trek through the shady forest. Evenings are spent around a bonfire, where Prakash serves up anecdotes, *paneer*-on-a-toothpick, and spicy chicken snacks before an Indian buffet is laid out. Taste the homemade apple juice, chutneys, and other concoctions Prakash makes from the orchard fruit. Doubles cost Rs 4,400 including all meals, but the log cabins (Rs 5,500 double) are much more private and, unlike the modern rooms and suites, don't feel as if they belong in a city suburb. Book in advance through www.banjaracamps.com.

| (Fun Facts **The Apple of His Eye**

Samuel Stokes, an American who settled here in the early 1900s, is credited with bringing over and planting the region's first apple trees. He aligned himself with the freedom movement and was highly regarded by a number of important leaders in the struggle for independence. Today, thanks to Stokes's apple industry, the region claims to have the highest per capita income in Southeast Asia. His daughter, Vidya Stokes, is in her mid-80s and is the MP for Thanedar—a member of India's ruling Congress Party; she's also the leader of the opposition in BJP-led Himachal Pradesh.

From Thanedar you can either backtrack to Narkanda or continue farther on the Narkanda-Thanedar road which meets the highway at Bithal, 21km (13 miles) from the retreat.

Another overnight option along the way to Sangla (and in many ways, a more interesting choice), is **Sarahan,** especially good if you have any desire to witness the early morning ceremonies (not always guaranteed) at the Bhimakali Temple. Traditionally, just about the only half-decent place to stay has been the half-baked government-run **Hotel Shrikhand** (© 01782/27-4234; www.hptdc.nic.in), a concrete monstrosity with an out-of-this-world setting and low rates (the disgusting, viewless cheap room goes for Rs 500, while slightly better doubles with balconies are Rs 1,400). You'll be able to console yourself over the state of the room thanks to the incredible views, but for the best room deal, book a deluxe room in the cottage (Rs 1,500), which gets you a spacious, high-ceilinged room in a separate block with a fireplace, television, and enclosed porch/sitting room. The hotel has a really slack restaurant, but it's probably the most hygienic place in town. Far better, though, if you want to stay in Sarahan, is to forgo the cliff-edge views and rather try **The Wild Side Retreat** ★ (© 94-1800-0056 or 98-1720-0002; www.wildside.in), situated a few miles back down the road to Jeori. Occupying a restored traditional teakwood building set among the apple orchards, the 10 rooms (renovated in 2009) here are simple, but neat, and are suite-sized; far and away your best option anywhere near Sarahan—certainly they're the cleanest and best-maintained. There's also a cozy lounge and terrace restaurant. A night for two, with all meals costs Rs 4,400, and your host can supply guides for local treks (Rs 300 per day). The owners are committed to eco-friendly principles and organize treks and overnight camping in the nearby wildlife sanctuaries, as well as multiday high-altitude treks in the western Himalayas.

From Sarahan, the onward journey to Sangla should take around 3–4 hr.

Day 3 & 4: Sangla to Spiti Valley

From Sangla, head off early back to "National Highway" 22 to continue east towards Kinnaur's main town of **Recong Peo** (2,670m/8,758 ft.), where you must complete the paperwork for your Inner Line Permit, which will allow you to enter and pass through the zone closest to the Tibetan border (see "Inner Line Permits," above). If you arrive early enough (10am is a good bet) to have your Permit processed by lunchtime, you'll be able to press on to Spiti the same day (although it's a tricky 6-hr. drive). Most people choose to let the bureaucratic wheels run while spending the night in the village of **Kalpa** ★★ (2,960m/9,709 ft.), well worth a visit for its crisp, clear air and view across the valley of the majestic Kinner-Kailash massif; it's a 20-minute drive up the mountain above Recong Peo. **Hotel Kinner Villa** (ⓒ 01786/22-6006; www.kinnervilla.freehostia.com; doubles Rs 1,300–Rs 1,600 plus 10% tax) is the best place to stay (well at least service is a notch better given that it is privately run), with simple, clean, and comfortable accommodations (although bathrooms are basic and tiny). Rooms 201 and 208 have the most exquisite views; 101, 104, 202, and 207 aren't bad, either. When the hotel is quiet, you'll have to book meals in advance (call manager Anil Purohit, ⓒ 94-1844-1036, if you're arriving late or to have him keep the best room for you); a newly-installed generator kicks in during Kalpa's interminable power failures. Also affording good views are rooms at the **Tourist Complex** of Kinner Kailash, an HPTDC (state-run) hotel (ⓒ 01786/22-6159). Double rooms (without meals) start from Rs 1,700, but you still have to put up with dire service.

Set out from Kalpa/Recong Peo either the moment you have your permit, or—if you've decided to stay in Kalpa for the night—early the following day; once you pass the first Inner Line checkpoint (in 2009 this was at Spillo, but in 2010 may shift 9km/5½ miles east, to Dubling), you will notice dramatic changes in the landscape, as fir trees give way to rock and stone sloping up toward distant summits and down into the raging River Sutlej. The journey through Inner Line territory takes you past the off-limits turnoff for 5,500m-high (18,040-ft.) Shipki-La Pass, which heads into China. **Nako Lake ★** and its pretty village lie farther along (it's the ideal spot to stretch your legs, and there are a few tented camps and other guesthouses where you could overnight if you have the time). Beyond the turnoff for Nako, the road attains its most sinister aspect as you enter the notorious section known as the Malling Slide, heavily punctuated with precipitous drops—an ideal place to strengthen your faith in the divine. However, the bypass to Malling via Nako has been operational for some time now—though not "fault" free, there is every chance that you will get through here; this road meets the highway again at Chango. Upon reaching the final Inner Line checkpoint at Sumdo—some 115km (71 miles) from Recong Peo and 363km (225 miles) from Shimla—the road heads northwest into the alien landscapes of Spiti.

Day 4, 5 & 6: The Spiti Valley

Some 6 hours from Recong Peo, the Buddhist village of **Tabo** (365km/226 miles from Shimla) is the most frequented stop in Spiti, and for good reason. With a population of around 400, this Buddhist settlement, situated at 3,050m (10,004 ft.) in lower Spiti, is centered around its celebrated 1,000-year-old monastic complex (see box on p. 631). It's the oldest continuously functioning Buddhist monastery in India and said to be the place where the present Dalai Lama will "retire." A serene village of flat-roofed houses topped by thatch packed with branches, mud, and grass, Tabo has as its obvious focus its monastery, or "doctrinal enclave." This consists of nine temple buildings, chambers for monks and nuns, 23 snow-white *chortens,* and piles of stones, each inscribed with scripture. We recommend you stay at **Dewachen Retreats** (ⓒ 01906/22-3301, 94-1836-3999, or 98-1709-1312; rajinertabo@yahooo.com; open May–Oct), certainly the cleanest guesthouse in the village. There are eight double rooms (Rs 4,000 including all meals; 10% tax extra), most of which have views over Tabo's cultivated fields, and one viewless family suite (Rs 7,000 for four people). Rooms are fairly basic, but very neat and clean, with tiled bathrooms, wardrobe space, reading lights, thick duvets, and hot water bottles just in case. The manager will organize guides for sightseeing and can arrange various kinds of excursions and adventure activities in the Valley. Many visitors traveling on a tight budget (or in town to do research at the monastery library) stay at the monastery guesthouse (℃ **01906/23-3313** or -3315), which is indeed cheap (Rs 300–Rs 550), but when we last stayed here found the rooms extremely dirty, with dodgy plumbing in the attached and the shared bathrooms. The Tibetan food at the guesthouse restaurant, on the other hand, is good. Another fine place to stop for a meal is the **Kunzum Top Restaurant** (℃ **94-1850-3966**), where you can sit in the sun-drenched garden courtyard, or head inside for one of the low tables. Here it's possible to sample authentic Spitian cuisine (as humble as this may be), so try the slightly nutty-tasting *tsampa* porridge, made using the locally grown roasted barley flour; you can also ask them to make you a *tsampa* pancake. If you're here for dinner, order the Spiti *thali;* it comes with butter tea, *timok* (a type of steamed bread), potato with glass noodles, and cheese. Cheap, delicious *momos* are also served. Restaurant proprietor Sonam Tsering (sonam_nadaan8@yahoo.co.in) organizes traditional music gatherings here in the winter, and also offers advice on local activities, trekking and homestay opportunities throughout Spiti and Kinnaur.

Not far from Tabo is the village of **Dhankar,** which hugs the side of a hill and offers breathtaking glimpses of the surrounding mountains and valley below—a visit to the precariously perched monastery is one of Spiti's most exciting highlights (see box on p. 630). Visit Dhankar on your way from Tabo, and then continue on to the town of **Kaza** (47km/29 miles from Tabo). As the administrative headquarters of Spiti, Kaza offers little excitement (although the new **Sakya Tenggyu Monastery,** inaugurated in July 2009, is very beautiful), but serves as the lodging, transport and market hub for the entire region. It's a useful base from which to visit the beautiful, fortresslike *gompa* of **Ki** and the high-altitude villages of **Kibber** and **Comic** (see box on p. 630). Kaza is also useful for treks through the **Pin Valley,** a national park inhabited by endangered snow leopard and Siberian ibex, as well as rare birds such as the Himalayan snow cock, snow partridge and Tibet snow finch.

Plan on spending at least 2 nights here at **Kaza Retreat,** another inn operated by the Banjara group (www.banjaracamps.com; doubles Rs 4,400 including all meals). The building is a bit of an eyesore at the edge of town, but accommodations are the best for miles—fairly spacious, comfortable, clean, and with attached bathrooms (and round-the-clock hot water). A great option if you'd rather not stay in Kaza (which has a problem with dogs howling all through the night), is **Spiti Sarai** (℃ **01906/22-2670** or 94-1843-9247; loteykaza@yahoo.co.in), which sits on a large plot a few miles north of Kaza, and has double rooms from Rs 2,200 including all meals. You can book through their office (Spiti Holiday Adventures) in Kaza's Main bazaar, or Waymark Adventures in New Delhi (℃ **011/2891-5686** or 98-1130-1228; waymark@vsnl.com).

Day 7: The Final Stretch

North of Spiti is **Lahaul**. Linked to the rest of Himachal by the Rohtang Pass, dotted with villages of flat-roofed houses, fluttering prayer flags, and whitewashed *chortens,* Lahaul is cut off from the world by heavy snow for 8 months of the year. This mountainous region attracts adventurers to its Buddhist monasteries, mountain passes, spectacular glaciers, and high-altitude lakes. Visitors traveling by road to Leh in Ladakh, farther north, pass through Lahaul.

Moving on from Kaza, you can either head for Manali (it'll take a full day) to catch your breath, or travel directly to Leh. The latter is a 2-day trip; the best (at least the only half-decent) place to stay along the way is the **Hotel Ibex** (www.hotelibexjispa.com; Rs 2,400 double with dinner and breakfast).

A Guide to the Top Temples, Gompas & Villages in Spiti & Kinnaur

BEST FOR HINDU MYSTIQUE: Bhimakali Temple ★ Chanting and music blast from the temple loudspeakers very early each morning and again in the evenings, transforming Sarahan village into a place that literally resonates with spirituality. Combining Hindu and Buddhist architectural elements, the main section of the temple comprises two pagoda-style pitched slate-roof towers. Built from layers of interlaced stone and timber, the towers rise from a courtyard around which are living quarters and a small museum with a collection of weapons and other unusual ritual objects and relics. Had you visited the temple 200 years ago, you might have witnessed one of the annual human sacrifices that kept the gods satisfied; today, animals suffice. The tower on the right was damaged in an earthquake a century ago, and the presiding deity was relocated to the tower on the left. Climb the stairs to get to the main shrine with its family of idols. Bhimakali is the main deity, while Durga, Ganesha, and even Buddha are all in attendance. The priests don't speak English, but it's worth taking part in the small *puja* (prayer) ceremony, so bring your rupees and buy some religious paraphernalia outside the temple. Morning and evening prayers are scheduled but don't always take place.

BEST CLIFF-EDGE FORTRESS: Dhankar Monastery ★★★ Overlooking the confluence of three valleys, *Dhankar* means "fort" or "palace on the rock," and one glimpse of Dhankar Tashi Choling Monastery tells you what a brilliant protective stronghold it must have been. Precariously perched on a hill jutting out from a sharp mountainside, this was once the castle of the Nono, the ruler of Spiti, and the architecture reflects a keen defensive strategy. Entry to the temple is nerve-wracking; access steps and uppermost rooftops drop away to perilously steep rocky slopes, and if you climb higher, beyond the temple, you discover an entire community that has chosen to live on what feels like the edge of the world. Legend has it that Ladhaki invaders posing a threat to the monastery were invited for a feast. As was customary, a strong local brew was served, and once inebriated, the guests were rolled down the steep precipice by the hosts—no need, however, to regard the butter tea offered by the monks with suspicion! Today, Dhankar is a repository of Bhoti-scripted Buddhist scriptures, and there's a small museum of unusual artifacts in the room next to the entrance. Precarious as it looks, built on what look like massive stalactites carved by wind and glacial erosion, Dhankar has survived for 1,300 years. Which is kind of good to know as you wonder around its rather spooky, gravity-defying ledges.

HIGHEST-ALTITUDE VILLAGES: Kibber & Comic ★★★ Just north of Kaza, a road veers off the main highway and zigzags its way up a steep mountainside. At the end of this stretch is Kibber, perched on a rocky spur at an altitude of 4,205m (13,792 ft.). Surrounded by limestone rocks and cliffs, the remote and isolated village offers stunning views of the barren valley below. There's even a handful of very basic guesthouses should you require accommodations. Until just a few years back, Kibber enjoyed a reputation as the highest permanent settlement with electricity and accessibility by motor road, but then Comic (4,600m/15,088 ft.) was connected and the record books changed; you can hike from Kaza to Comic (where you can visit the interesting Tenggyu Komic Monastery overlooking the peaceful village) in around 3¹/₂ hours, passing through some phenomenal scenery, and the views changing constantly as you quickly ascend to high altitudes fairly. Incidentally, as roadworks continue, there may soon be another village or two that usurp Comic's title.

BIGGEST: Ki Gompa ★★★ Between Kibber and Kaza is Spiti's largest monastery, Ki Gompa, which is about 700 years old. Home to a large community of lamas (of the Gelugpa sect), Ki Gompa is well accustomed to receiving visitors; the monk on duty will brew you a welcoming cup of tea and show you around the different prayer rooms and assembly halls filled with holy relics. The most exciting time to visit is late June or early July, when a festival involving *chaam* dancing and the ceremonial burning of butter sculptures draws large numbers of pilgrims.

MOST HOLY: Tabo Gompa ★★★ The sanctity of this World Heritage Site is topped only by Tholing monastery in Tibet. Don't arrive expecting some cathedral-like masterpiece; the monastery (© **01906/22-333** or -3315; www.tabo monastery.com) is a rustic center that is more spiritually than architecturally engaging. A high mud wall surrounds the compound, and the pale mud-covered low-rise monastery buildings suggest nothing of the exquisite wall paintings and stucco statues within. You'll need a flashlight to properly appreciate many of the frescoes and other artworks that adorn the various dark, ancient spaces; only narrow shafts of natural light from small skylights illuminate the frescoed walls, saturated with rich colors and an incongruous variety of scenes. There's a distinctly surreal, often nightmarish quality to the work—gruesome torture scenes compete with images of meditative contemplation and spiritual discovery.

At the core of the complex is the **Temple of Enlightened Gods (Tsug Lha-khang),** which includes the **Assembly Hall** (or *du-khang*) housing a 2m-high (6¹/₂-ft.) white stucco image of Vairocana, one of the five spiritual sons of the primordial, self-creative Buddha, or Adibuddha. Below this are two images of the great translator and teacher Rin-Chan-Sang-Po, who is believed to have founded Tabo in A.D. 996. Thirty-three other life-size stucco deities surrounded by stylized flaming circles are bracketed along the walls. Directly behind the assembly hall is the **sanctum,** with five bodhisattvas of the Good Age and beautifully rendered Indian-style frescoes depicting the life of the Buddha. Monks are initiated in the smaller **Mystic Mandala Temple (dKyil-hKhor-khang),** situated behind the main temples. At the northern edge of the complex is the **Temple of Dromton (Brom-ston Lha-khang),** entered via a small portico and long passage. Only enter the **Mahakala Vajra-Bhairava Temple (Gon-Khang)** once you've performed a protective meditation—it's filled with fierce deities that inspire its nickname, "the temple of horrors." Just outside the complex are several contemporary monastic buildings, including an atmospheric guesthouse run by the monks. Above Tabo, across the highway, a group of caves on a sheer cliff-face was once used as monastic dwellings. (*Note:* No photography is allowed inside the monastery.)

5 MANALI & THE VALLEY OF THE GODS

Manali is 280km (174 miles) N of Shimla

Central Himachal's fertile valleys—centered around the towns of Mandi, Kullu, and Manali—are watered by the Beas River, and are famous for a variety of fruits, excellent treks, and what is considered—by the stoned hippies of Manali, at least—the finest marijuana in the world. Fear not: Narcotics and stoners have little to do with the region's wide renown as the undisputed "Valley of the Gods."

The drive from Shimla to Manali—starting point for the spectacular road journey to Leh and a number of adventure activities—is around 280km (174 miles) and can be done in a day. The route is scenic, especially in July and August, when the heavy monsoon rains cause the river to swell and waterfalls to cascade spectacularly. Time allowing, it's a good idea to spend the night en route in the scruffy town of Mandi, where you can use the atmospheric Raj Mahal palace hotel as a base for a visit to the nearby hill hamlet of **Rewalsar ★**. A fascinating confluence of Buddhist, Sikh, and Hindu spirituality, the village is centered around a small black lake that teems with fish (supposedly holy) and beautifully reflects the soaring mountain ranges above. Sacred to all three religions, the lake's banks sport lively Buddhist *gompas,* an important Sikh *gurudwara* (place of worship), and a Hindu temple.

Farther north (about 70km/43 miles), in the heart of the Valley of the Gods, is the unattractive town of **Kullu,** famous for its sheer volume of Hindu temples and the Dussehra Festival (usually in Oct), which attracts substantial crowds and hundreds of valley gods to take part in the annual festivities: 7 days of jubilant processions, music, dancing, and markets. Unless you stop specifically to catch any festival action or want to visit the "first and biggest angora farm in Asia," there's no real reason to linger in Kullu.

Bhuntar, not too far south of Kullu, is the turnoff point for drives to Jari, Kasol, and the therapeutic hot springs of **Manikaran,** which is the main jumping-off point for a variety of treks to less-visited villages. **Khirganga,** farther east, is the site of even more thermal water springs, while isolated **Malana,** to the north, is an anthropologist's dream and—if the experts in Amsterdam are to be believed—home of the world's top-rated *ganja,* the infamous Malana Gold. Adventures to any of these remote areas should not be undertaken without the help of a recognized guide—not only is getting lost a strong possibility, but there have been reports of what are believed to be drug-related crimes, including the assault and "disappearance'" of travelers (some 250 tourists have mysteriously vanished over the years).

ESSENTIALS

GETTING THERE & AROUND   It's possible to avoid Shimla entirely by flying directly to **Bhuntar Airport** 10km (6¼ miles) south of Kullu. In Manali, taxis and auto-rickshaws charge ridiculously inflated rates that fluctuate seasonally and according to the whim of the near-militant local taxi union. Hire a car for the duration of your stay; if you've used a car and driver to get to Manali, you might consider planning ahead to retain the service for any further travel, bearing in mind that a sturdy vehicle with off-road capabilities and a driver who knows the terrain will be essential if you plan on getting to Ladakh or the regions east of the Beas River.

⚠ **Warning!**   **Avoid the Rush**

The low-level but ongoing threat of war in Kashmir has meant that Manali's popularity has soared over the last decade. Visitors who once would have gone to Kashmir for the snow and possibility of skiing now swamp Manali during the Indian high season, which stretches from April until the rains hit in early July, and then again from September to November. Manali's charms have been all but eroded by this tourist explosion, which sets off a soulless cash-rally that seems to involve every proprietor, merchant, and taxi-tour operator in town; hotel tariffs also soar during this period. **Bottom line:** Try to avoid this usually peaceful town during these months.

VISITOR INFORMATION & TRAVEL AGENTS   For information about the Kullu and Parvati valleys, visit **Himachal Pradesh Tourism** (© **01902/22-2349;** www.himachal tourism.nic.in) in Kullu, near the Maidan. In Manali, the **Tourist Information Centre** (The Mall, Manali; © **01902/25-2175;** Mon–Sat 10am–1pm and 1:30 5pm) can give you a pile of booklets on destinations throughout the state (most of these are also available from the office in Shimla). Alternatively, try the **HPTDC** office (© **01902/25-2360**). An ad-saturated tourist map of Manali is available for Rs 15, and more detailed books and booklets are available for purchase. **Matkon Travels** (© **01902/25-3738** or 98-1600-3738) can also help you with domestic flights and deluxe bus bookings.

ADVENTURE & TREKKING SPECIALISTS   If you have questions about what's possible in and around Manali, make contact with the **Himalayan Institute of Adventure Sports** (Roshan Thakur; © **98-1601-6554**); you should be able to get assistance organizing reputable and reliable guides for sightseeing, trekking, rafting, paragliding, and skiing—at the very least they'll point you in the right direction. If you arrive in Manali with no prearranged outdoor activities, you can contact two places. **Himalayan Outdoor Centre** (en route to Rohtang Rd., 1.5km/1 mile from Manali; © **01902/25-2581** or 98-1600-3035) offers a wide range of adventure activities, including rafting on the Beas River, skiing (Apr to mid-May), snowboarding, treks, jeep safaris, and tandem paragliding. You can also approach **Antrek** (p. 606), the oldest agency in Manali, and the one we recommend for organized treks.

MANALI

Yes, it's set amid dense pine forests and shadowed by snowy peaks, but Manali's reputation as a spectacular Himalayan resort is much exaggerated. The primary reason to be here is to set off for Leh in Ladakh, a 2-day drive away, or to participate in the many treks or adventure sports, including heli-skiing.

Manali comprises several neighborhoods, each with a distinct personality. North of the Manalsu Nala River is **Old Manali,** with its historic stone buildings; to the west is the pleasant village of **Dhungri;** while messy **Model Town** is a motley collection of concrete buildings tucked behind the main bazaar area, concentrated around The Mall. East of the Beas River, a few kilometers north of Manali is **Vashisht,** a village known for its hot springs and laid-back atmosphere. Unfortunately, Vashisht has lost much of its charm, thanks to an influx of long-stay budget tourists; a dunk in the communal hot-water bath of the local temple is hardly reason enough to visit.

The most peaceful area is **Dhungri Village** (around 2km/1¼ miles from the bazaar), where you can stroll through deodar forests or visit a 450-year-old temple where animal sacrifice is still practiced. On the outskirts of the neighborhood, the multitiered wooden pagoda-style **Hadimba Devi Temple ★**, built in 1553, is Manali's oldest and most interesting shrine, dedicated to the demon goddess Hadimba (an incarnation of Kali). Look around for the sheltered sacrificial stone used for blood rituals during important ceremonies; the central hollow is where the blood from a slain buffalo or goat drains into Hadimba's mouth.

Another good walk takes you through Old Manali (center of cheap backpackers' accommodations), the temple dedicated to Manu, and beyond to silent hillside paths where you'll encounter village women passing the day over idle gossip while their men unhurriedly herd goats and cows toward greener pastures at higher altitudes. Most visitors pay a visit to Manali's two more modern Buddhist *gompas* in the town's Tibetan quarter south of the bazaar. **Gadhan Thekchhokling gompa** was built in 1969, and is recognizable by its yellow, pagoda-style roof; memorial notices outside draw attention to the extermination of Tibetans in China.

Just 24km (15 miles) short of Manali is **Naggar,** which like Manali is slowly being wrecked by unchecked construction and tourism. Visit the **Nicholas Roerich Museum** (© 01902/24-8290 or -8590; Tues–Sun 10am–1pm and 1:30–6pm), where the famous Russian artist lived from 1923 until he died in 1947. In this small but well-maintained museum, paintings and books by the prolific artist and philosopher are on display. In this stunning location, it's easy to see why Roerich and his wife, Helena, were so inspired by their surroundings (though not everyone feels the same about his artworks). Also part of the estate is the **Urusvati Himalayan Folk Art Museum** (Tues–Sun 10am–6pm), created for the preservation of folk art and craft.

WHERE TO STAY

For those keen on outdoor pursuits like paragliding in summer and skiing in winter, you can skip the towns completely and head directly for **Solang Valley Resort** (© 01902/25-6132;** www.solangvalleyresorts.com; doubles from Rs 6,500), situated only 0.5km (0.3 miles) from the beautiful Solang Valley (about 45 min. from Manali town). Accommodations—in a small cluster of buildings that look like an unfortunate attempt to imitate a Swiss suburb—are very comfortable.

Mandi & Kullu

If you're traveling by road from Shimla direct to either Manali or Dharamsala, it's a good idea to take a break en route. In Mandi, 70km (43 miles) south of Kullu, **Raj Mahal** (© 01905/22-2401,** -3434 or 98-1602-1126; www.rajmahalpalace.com), a creaky-floorboards "palace," is recommended for its serious time-warp character. Book one of the four enormous Royal Suites (Rs 4,400 double), which showcase an assortment of kitsch furnishings and objets d'art (in one room a stuffed leopard grimaces on a table with rifles for legs!). Generally, the service at Raj Mahal is quite awful, and the ancient plumbing acts up at times, but as a place to lay your head for a night and as a base for visiting nearby Rewalsar, it's adequate. If you're after a more typical hotel experience, head on to **Apple Valley Resort** (© 01902/26-0001 or -0006; www.applevalleyresorts. co.in), just short of Kullu town. Set on the banks of the Beas River, the luridly decorated country-style cabins with ivy-covered walls and stone chimneys are Rs 4,780 double, with all meals; insist on a cabin with a view. However, far better than either of these slightly institutional places is Banjara's new, magnificently situated **Sojha Retreat** ★★ (www.banjaracamps.com) way off the beaten track (and a good 117km/73 miles, or 4 hr., short of Manali). Getting there requires quite a detour, heading first in the direction of Kinnaur before heading north of the Jalori Pass (3,223m/10,571 ft.), but its sublime mountain setting makes it a destination in its own right, with great walks (you can trek to Raghupur Fort or Serolser Lake) and excellent trout fishing in the nearby Tirthan River. A night in one of the 10 big pine rooms with attached bathrooms costs Rs 4,400 double, including all meals and taxes.

Manali

For the most atmospheric room in town, you're best off in an original lodge apartment at **Jimmy Johnson Lodge** (aka Johnson Hotel, but not to be confused with the adjacent Johnson's Lodge) or at **Negi's Hotel Mayflower;** even better for a peaceful stay farther away from the main bazaar, is **Casa Bella Vista,** which has an inkling of small town glamour about it (all three are reviewed below). Alternatively, one of the most comfortable places in the vicinity of Manali is **Span Resorts,** which enjoys a superb riverside location (also reviewed below). If none of the following recommendations are available, Manali's **Private Hoteliers' Information Centre** (The Mall, near the taxi stand) is well established and can assist you in finding suitably priced accommodations if you haven't prebooked. Note that during the busy season (mid-Apr to early July) you will have difficulty finding any decent guest accommodations in Manali (not necessarily a bad thing, considering how packed it gets).

Casa Bella Vista ★★   As close as Manali is ever likely to come to a boutique-style lodge, this collection of two large self-contained cottages and two double rooms offers a very comfortable stay with accommodations that are clean, neat, and fairly new. Girimer and his Spanish wife, Marta, spent 3 years building this place and finally opened in 2007; they've had the foresight to pick a relatively peaceful location (some distance away from the center, but still with in easy walking distance of the town's main market and the more bohemian vibe of Old Manali), and have left lots of space so it doesn't feel cluttered, nor is it likely to become oversubscribed. Part of the setup includes an outdoor cafe with an open-air wood-burning pizza oven—it's a really relaxing place to enjoy a beer and a simple meal (although you may feel sorry for the waiter running up and down the stairs to the kitchen). Already, it's attracting its fair share of wealthy, sophisticated Indian families come to unwind on the lawn or browse at the small women's boutique that adjoins the restaurant and library area. *Note:* In 2010, the couple will be opening a new guesthouse at the end of the same road.

Log Hut Rd., Manali 175 131. *Ⓒ* **01902/25-1985** or 98-1669-9663. www.casabellavistamanali.com. 2 cottages and 2 rooms. Rs 3,500 deluxe double, Rs 11,100 cottage (3 bedrooms; 6 people); Rs 900 extra person over 12; Rs 500 extra child 5–12. Rates exclude 10% tax. MC, V. **Amenities:** Restaurant; beer served; badminton; children's playground; Wi-Fi (in restaurant; free). *In room:* TV, DVD (in cottage), fireplace (in cottage), heater, kitchen (in cottage).

Jimmy Johnson Lodge ★   Set among lovely lawns, this "lodge" was the first inhabited property in New Manali, and it offers a choice of vintage or modern accommodations not too far from the thick of things. Now run by Piya, the cosmopolitan granddaughter of the man who built the original stone lodge apartments, Johnson's may be relatively close to the bazaar, but it remains a tranquil spot with lovely views. If you opt for one of the slate, stone, and wood guest rooms in the upper complex, ask for a corner unit—these are larger and have extra windows from which to enjoy the mountain scenes. If you'd prefer an old-fashioned experience, the three huge ivy-covered stone-walled balconied suites ("cottages") in the original building are atmospheric curiosities, with aging furnishings, original fittings, and loads of space. Wood-beam ceilings, screened windows, and small, homey kitchens add to the ambience. Ask for cottage II, which is the neatest and quietest, although a bit pricier than the rest. A real highlight here is the presence of Manali's chicest dining option.

Circuit House Rd., Manali 175 131. ✆ **01902/25-3023,** -3764, or 98-1627-3023. Fax 01902/24-5123. www. johnsonhotel.in. johnsonshotel@gmail.com. 18 units, all with shower only. In season Rs 2,250 standard double, Rs 2,500 deluxe double, Rs 5,000–Rs 5,625 cottage (sleeps 4). Rates discounted in off season. Rates exclude 10% tax. MC, V (credit cards payments have a 2^1/$_2$% surcharge). **Amenities:** Restaurant (The Johnson's Café; see "Where to Dine," below), bar; airport transfers (drop only; Rs 1,500); room service. *In room:* TV, fan or heater on request.

Negi's Hotel Mayflower ★★ **Kids**   In a town overflowing with characterless hotels, this handsome, unpretentious, and comfortable option comes as quite a relief. Rooms are massive, with wooden floors and paneling, rocking chairs by the fireplace, tasteful lamps with rice-paper shades, desks in cozy corners, warm sitting areas, and spotless bathrooms (with bathtubs) overlooking the pine forests—what more could you possibly want? Even the standard double rooms have enough room for a few children. Best of all is the veranda that runs the length of the facade, furnished with wicker chairs to lounge around in while sipping cups of lemon tea. The extremely reserved proprietor keeps a low profile, but thankfully not in the kitchen—his Irish stew, roast lamb, caramel custard with stewed apricots, and bread and butter pudding are legendary. Manager Dharamendra looks after each of his guests with real care and can help with planning a detailed itinerary.

Club House Rd., Manali 175 131. ✆ **01902/25-2104** or -0256. Fax 01902/25-3923. www.negismayflower. com. reservation@mayflowermanali.com. 19 units. Rs 2,200 double, Rs 2,500 suite; Rs 350 extra bed. Rates exclude 10% tax. MC, V. **Amenities:** 2 restaurants (1 in the garden); airport transfers (Rs 900–Rs 2,000); room service. *In room:* TV, fireplace (in some), heater.

Span Resorts ★   A riverside location, 15km (9⅓ miles) from the center of Manali, makes this resort a peaceful respite from the crowds, enhanced by the generous range of amenities and outdoor activities on offer. Accommodations are in stone-and-wood cottages shaped like stars and spread around well-maintained grounds; they're comfortable and offer a fair degree of privacy. Riverside units, with wooden floors, are the best. There isn't a heck of a lot of space, but each cottage has a fireplace and a covered porch from which to appreciate the relaxed setting and mountain views. There is plenty to keep you occupied during the snowy season, including what may be the best-stocked bar in the state.

Kullu-Manali Hwy., P.O. Katrain 175 129. Info ✆ **01902/24-0138** or -0538. Fax 01902/24-0140. www.span resorts.com. spanres@del3.vsnl.net.in. Reservations: Vijaya (1st Floor), 17 Barakhamba Rd., New Delhi 110 001. ✆ **011/2331-1434.** Fax 011/2335-3148. 30 units. Rs 6,300 standard double, Rs 6,800 deluxe double, Rs 7,800 elite double. Rates include breakfast; 10% tax extra. 25% discount in off season. AE, DC, MC, V. **Amenities:** 2 restaurants, card room, bar; badminton; basketball; billiards; children's park; croquet; darts; fishing; heath club; library; minigolf; outdoor pool; room service; tennis; table tennis. *In room:* A/C, TV, minibar.

WHERE TO DINE

Cool cafe-style joints are all the rage in Manali—especially in the backpacker-haunted quarter of **Old Manali,** where you can sit for hours, chilling out to the pleasant vibrations of good music, decent coffee, and a generally laidback crowd; the best of these is **The Lazy Dog Café** (reviewed below). Bear in mind that most of these joints don't take credit cards (they're usually only open in the summer months, Apr–Oct, so operate cash businesses), and on the odd occasion you might be forced to put up with ill-mannered dope-smoking groups. Although you'll just as easily find a crowd of very sociable, mindful types.

If you're prepared to travel a bit to track down good Tibetan cuisine, ask your driver to head for **Phunsok,** a family run eatery on the riverbank 2.5km (1½ miles) from Manali toward Solang (it's on the left-hand side just ahead of the turn to Vashisht). Food is freshly cooked so don't expect it to arrive in any hurry; seating is outdoors, and you can enjoy the scenery while you wait. For fine Tibetan fare (and a very warm, sociable vibe) closer to town, stop by Old Manali's **Yangkhor Garden** (© **01902/25-4160** or 98-0525-7981), presided over by a jolly Tibetan mother figure named Kumsamg. It's a seasonal restaurant (which shifts to Goan in the winter) and feels bit like a fifties diner, with red vinyl sofa benches, a TV in the corner, classic rock tunes, and an intimate lounge atmosphere—not to mention a photo of the Dalai lama peering down at you from one wall. The ceiling is strung with bags of water said to scare away the flies—and it seems to work. Kumsamg's menu is a mixed and multifangled one; Italian, Indian, and even Chinese items are available, but stick to the Tibetan dishes, and ask Kumsamg to help you understand the difference between *thukpa, tingmo, thanthuk, and fingsha;* if you can't decide, ask for a plate of steaming *momos* (dumplings).

Manali's best Indian restaurant is **Mayur** (Mission Rd.; © **01902/25-2316**), located in the main bazaar, just off The Mall. Kangra Valley–born Rajesh Sud has been in the restaurant business since 1970 and opened this Manali institution back in 1978. Try the *murgh tikka masala* (barbecued chicken with spices) or the fresh, locally caught wild trout, prepared in the tandoor oven with a subtle blend of yogurt and aromatic spice.

For authentic Italian (including reasonably good coffee), **Il Forno ★** (© **98-1692-2481**), housed in a century-old house in Dunghri en route to the Hadimba Temple, is your most authentic option, although it's only open for dinner. Roberta Angelone, who is from Naples, returns to Manali each year to create memorable fresh-made pastas (ask if the ravioli is available) and real-deal pizzas. If you couldn't be bothered to hike up to Il Forno, then head for **Johnson's Café** (see below).

Johnson's Café ★ ECLECTIC   Adjoining the famous Jimmy Johnson Lodge, this cozy, informal venue enjoys a lively atmosphere and pretty garden in which to enjoy views of the mountain surrounds (pity, though, about the plastic chairs on the lawn). Besides its Italian offerings (which seem pretty much standard in Manali), Johnson's serves plenty of Indian standards and specializes in fresh, locally caught trout, and it's a fine place to have coffee and breakfast while you plan the day's trek. There's now a cool bar (with some groovy mocktails, too), and plenty of small touches designed to give this country inn a more contemporary ambience.

Jimmy Johnson Lodge, The Mall, Manali. © **01902/24-3764.** Main courses Rs 60–Rs 360. MC, V (credit card payments have 2½% surcharge). Summer Mon–Sat 7am–11:30pm.

The Lazy Dog Lounge ★ (Moments) INTERNATIONAL/LIGHT FARE   Cool finally arrived in Manali in July 2008 with the opening of this lovely cafe-style eatery and bar that's probably more about atmosphere than food, but what the heck. By day, grab a seat on the rocky terrace hanging over the river—the setting is extraordinary, and the soundtrack of water cascading over the boulder-strewn river bed beneath you is quite overwhelming and utterly calming. Look up and there are looming mountains and towering trees, and below are fishermen casting a line. Started by two drifters who met at an ashram, this is a good place for travelers to hang out—there's a wide variety of dishes

Up in Smoke with the Boom Shiva Hippies

With the apple-market slump causing rising local unemployment in recent years, the appeal of **marijuana,** Himachal Pradesh's naturally occurring crop, has become all too obvious. High on the knowledge of the availability of cheap and easy-to-come-by dope, backpackers and hippies have flocked to the region for decades. But over the last 8 years, some pockets of Himachal (such as Old Manali, Kasol, and Dharamsala) have become flooded with Israeli tourists, 20-somethings cutting loose after completing their mandatory 3-year stint in the army. The attraction here is of course drugs, with about 1,600 hectares (4,000 acres) of Himachal reportedly under cannabis cultivation. The arrival of so many young Israelis has changed the tourism industry as well, with restaurants now serving *falafel,* *baba ghanouj,* and *laban* (yogurt), and a surprising number of signs and menus in Hebrew. There's serious smoke rising at full-moon rave parties where Boom Shiva (read: hashish) can be found in abundance and young Israelis inhale with "full power." Excessive indulgence has now motivated the Israeli government to sponsor a home in Old Manali to rescue drug-addicted youngsters, as well as Kfar Izum (Balance Village) on the Mediterranean coast to rehabilitate youth who are sending their futures up in smoke in Himachal.

from around the world (Chinese, Japanese, Korean and Thai options included), all-day breakfasts (try the burrito stuffed with egg, spinach, and mushroom, and served with your choice of fruit juice or lassi), free Wi-Fi, sheesha hookahs, and all-round good vibes. Grilled rainbow trout—fresh from the river—is usually available, and there are Indian *thalis,* as well as traditional favorites such as butter chicken and chicken curry, and plenty of vegetarian choices. Service is rather middling, and the coffee wasn't up to scratch, but we like it nonetheless.

Old Manali, P.O. Tehsil Manali. ✆ **01902/25-4277.** www.thelazydog.in. Most meals Rs 80–Rs 200. No credit cards. Apr–Oct Mon–Sat 10:30am–11:30pm; Sun 1:30–11:30pm.

6 DHARAMSALA & THE KANGRA VALLEY ★★★

Dharamsala is 253km (157 miles) W of Manali

Tenzin Gyatso, the 14th Dalai Lama, chose Dharamsala as the capital-in-exile of the Tibetan people after fleeing Chinese oppression in 1959, and whether it's the endless spinning of Buddhist prayer wheels, the magnificence of the surrounding mountains, or simply the divine presence of His Holiness, the Tibetan enclave at Dharamsala draws seekers of spiritual enlightenment from all over the world.

Admittedly, a visit to Everyman's spiritual center of the universe seems like the ultimate New Age cliché, but the town and its environs have much more to recommend than the fervent chanting of *Om mani padme hum* ("Hail to the jewel in the lotus"). The natural beauty of Dharamsala's snow-tipped mountains and mist-soaked valleys compares favorably with that of any of Himachal's best-loved resort towns, and for those not single-mindedly wrapped up in a quest for spiritual fine-tuning with Buddhist lectures and meditation courses, this is an ideal base for walks and treks into the Dhauladhar range. It's also a good place to simply experience a toned-down India at a more leisurely pace.

The hillside town stretches along a spur of the Dhauladhar mountain range and is divided into two very distinct parts—Lower Dharamsala and **McLeod Ganj** (often called Little Lhasa). Only the latter is worth considering as a place to stay and explore; it's an intriguingly cosmopolitan mix of brightly robed Buddhist monks in their Oakleys and Crocs (with thick woolen socks), traditionally attired Tibetan women reciting holy mantras, and spiritual tourists in search of enlightenment. It's also become increasingly popular with Israeli travelers who tend to install themselves in the concrete village of Bhagsu, a short drive from the main bazaar; many long-stay visitors now congregate here and participate in myriad courses and workshops, from reiki to jewelry making, and there are scores of teachers, healers, and artists offering their services. A former British hill station rocked by an earthquake in the early 1900s, McLeod Ganj today harbors several institutes and organizations dedicated to raising funds for the Tibetan people and promoting and preserving Buddhist culture. Among these is the government-in-exile's administration complex, or *Gangchen Kyishong*, where you'll find the fascinating **Library of Tibetan Works and Archives.**

Higher up the mountain, above McLeod Ganj and Bhagsu, is the more salubrious, uncrowded area of **Dharamkot**—more country village than suburb—where it's possible to escape the activity along McLeod Ganj's **Temple Road,** always lined with Tibetan vendors and a nonstop shuffle of people from all over the world. Dharamkot is the starting point for many excellent hikes into the Dhauladhar mountains that loom over Dharamsala, and in the uppermost part of the village, far, far from the maddening crowd is **Eagles Nest,** Himachal's coziest, loveliest guesthouse.

North of Dharamsala are spectacular mountain-hugging drives to the remote towns of Dalhousie and Chamba, while farther south you can visit (and stay in) the charming heritage village of **Pragpur** and explore the tea-covered valleys around historical Taragarh Palace Hotel, not far from the scruffy town of **Palampur.**

ESSENTIALS

VISITOR INFORMATION There's a **Tourist Information Office** (*✆* 01892/22-1205 or -1232; Mon–Sat 10am–1:30pm and 2–5pm) in McLeod Ganj, but you'll be hardpressed to squeeze anything worthwhile out of the lackluster staff; you'd do better to make inquiries at your hotel. *CONTACT* is a free monthly newsletter distributed in and around McLeod Ganj (www.contactmag.org). Although its primary aim is to promote Buddhist issues, it also carries up-to-date information and advertisements regarding cultural events and activities likely to be of interest to foreign visitors. If you are here for massage, meditation, alternative healing, yoga, or Tibetan cooking classes, this publication will point you in the right direction. Online sources of information include **www. dharamsalanet.com**, and the politically orientated **www.tibet.org**.

AUDIENCES WITH HH THE DALAI LAMA & HH THE KARMAPA If your main reason for visiting Dharamsala is to attend a **public teaching by His Holiness the Dalai Lama,** you had better plan well ahead, first by checking out his schedule on www.tibet.com, and then by making the necessary arrangements through the Branch Security Office (Bhagsu Rd.; *✆* 01892/22-1560) when you arrive; a **private audience** will require you to write to His Holiness many months before you get here, and, unless you're Richard Gere, you'll need to make a very strong case for meeting him (Office of His Holiness the Dalai Lama, P.O. Mcleod Ganj, Dharamsala 176 219, India; *✆* 01892/22-1343 or

-1879; fax 01892/22-1813; ohhdl@dalailama.com). When attending one of his teachings, be sure to bring a cushion, an FM radio with headphones, a cup (for tea), sun protection, your passport (and a few extra passport photos, just in case), and as little else as possible (for security reasons). A **public audience with His Holiness the Karmapa** is easier to guarantee—he usually gives a public lecture, and a blessing to all who attend, at 2:30pm on Wednesdays and Saturdays at his monastery in Sidhpur. You don't need to make an appointment, but can contact Lama Phuntsok (✆ **94-1829-4401** or 01892/23-6637) for details, or to arrange a **private audience,** for which you should call at least 5 days in advance.

GETTING THERE & AROUND　It's possible to **drive** from Shimla or Chandigarh to Dharamsala, and there are two great overnight options along the way—choose between **Taragarh Palace,** outside Palampur, or **The Judge's Court,** in Pragpur (see later in this chapter). The most pleasant way to get to the Kangra Valley directly from Delhi is by **train** (driving by car takes almost 12 hr.). The overnight Jammu Mail from Delhi allows you to rest up before hiring a car for the scenic 3-hour road trip from Panthankot to Dharamsala (80km/50 miles). Another option is to **fly**—Kingfisher operates daily to **Kangra Airport** in Gaggal, 15km (9⅓ miles) from Dharamsala. In Dharamsala, you will find it easy to get either a taxi or auto-rickshaw. (Auto-rickshaws are incredibly impractical for getting up to McLeod Ganj, however, because of the engine-killing gradient of the town.) **Ways Tours & Travels** (Temple Rd., McLeod Ganj; ✆ **01892/22-1910** or -1988; www.waystours.com; waystour@gmail.com) hires out cars with drivers for local sightseeing, and the friendly Mr. Gupta can help with all your travel arrangements as well as organize individually packaged tours throughout the region. (You can also contact Ways in New Delhi, at House no. 45, New Tibetan Camp, Majnu-Ka-Tilla; call ✆ **011/2381-3254** or 98-1128-9552.) A chauffeured round trip from McLeod Ganj to Pragpur or Palampur, with a guide, should cost around Rs 3,000. If you just want to hire a reliable taxi driver to take you just anywhere in Himachal (or on a tour of specific sights), call **Jagmohan Attri** (✆ **98-1639-4043**); he operates out of Pragpur in the Kangra Valley and is not only great company, but full of unusual insights about the region and its people.

TREKKING & ADVENTURE SPORTS　If you love the outdoors, it would be unthinkable not to trek in the magnificent Dhauladhar Range, and there are some impressive hikes whether you have limited time or are prepared to spend a few days exploring. You could start by approaching the **Mountaineering Institute** (Dharamkot Rd.; ✆ **01892/22-1787**) for maps and information on the myriad trekking possibilities, or to join one of their outings. However, the best mountaineer in the region is **John Hughes** (✆ **98-0547-2037**), who is probably the only person you should trust completely to take you into the mountains on more challenging treks and climbs. He won't allow you to go up if you're not properly prepared or don't have the right shoes, for example. If you're serious about getting into the mountains, contact him ahead of your visit.

　　Warning: Every year, a number of gung-ho, unprepared trekkers head off into the Dhauladhars and don't come back. Don't underestimate these mountains, and be aware that nightfall comes suddenly, along with potentially freezing conditions. Do not hike alone and always inform someone of your intended route. If you get injured in these mountains, there's little chance of being found, and the lammergeiers (vultures, aka "bone breakers") that nest here will finish you off without a trace.

　　Paragliding has become huge in the Kangra Valley, and the region's expert is **Bruce Mills** (✆ **98-0567-8478;** bruce@paranirvana.com), a New Zealand–born flyer who will

set you up with a tandem flight that will leave you breathless for all the right reasons.
Bruce has been flying in Himachal Pradesh since 1989 and launches from Billing; he
charges Rs 3,000 for a half-hour flight, which can be extended if the weather is right and
you're particularly interested. Bruce can also fly-guide paraglider pilots who want to be
shown around a bit before they head off on their own.

THE TOP ATTRACTIONS

Church of St. John in the Wilderness ★   Ten minutes of downhill walking from
McLeod Ganj brings you to the Church of St. John in the Wilderness, surrounded by
deodar cedars. It's a neo-Gothic stone construction, with its original Belgian stained glass
intact in spite of a severe earthquake in 1905 that leveled the rest of town. Buried in the
grassy adjoining graveyard is British Viceroy Lord Elgin (whose somewhat infamous
father was responsible for the controversial Elgin Marbles).

Daily 10am–5pm.

Norbulingka Institute ★★★   If you're interested in getting a firsthand under-
standing of the techniques (and unbelievable patience) required to produce authentic
Tibetan arts and crafts, the institute is a good starting point. Set in well tended grounds
some 40 minutes from Dharamsala, it comprises workshops, training centers, a temple,
a guesthouse, a cafe, and a doll museum. You can contact the management in advance to
organize a tour through the facilities, where you can witness the creation of colorful
tantric *thangkas* (embroidered wall hangings), paintings, metalware, furniture, and traditional garments. You can also sign up for Tibetan language lessons, particularly useful if
you intend spending time here to work as a volunteer, or wish to explore Buddhism in
more depth. The beautiful **Seat of Happiness Temple ★★** features astounding murals,
including impressions of all 14 Dalai Lamas and 1,173 images of the Buddha, which
decorate the 13m-high (43-ft.) temple hall. The gilded copper Buddha Sakyamuni was
crafted by Norbulingka's master statue-maker, Pemba Dorje, and is one of the largest of
its kind outside Tibet; the arch behind the statue is decorated with sculpted clay images.
Head for the richly ornamented temple rooftop for magnificent views of the surrounding
landscape. The Institute's **Losel Doll Museum ★★** features diorama-style displays of
miniature figures (Tibetan dolls) in traditional costumes and historical regalia.

P.O. Sidhpur. (℉ **01892/24-6402** or -6405. www.norbulingka.org. Free admission; doll museum Rs 20.
Daily 9am–5:30pm.

Thekchen Chöling Temple Complex ★★   Life in McLeod Ganj revolves around
this Buddhist temple complex, linked to the off-limits private residence of the Dalai
Lama. A good example of Buddhism's spiritual and artistic traditions, the complex comprises **Namgyal Monastery** and **Tsuglakhang Temple,** both worth a visit if you're keen
to get a sense of active lamaistic practice. In the outside courtyard, you'll often witness
monks debating or meditatively preparing colorful sand *mandalas,* diagrams that symbol-
ize the universe and are used in the ritual of spiritual empowerment known as the
kalachakra ceremony, after which the meticulous designs are destroyed. The *gompa*
houses various cultural relics brought from Lhasa during the Cultural Revolution,
including a 1,500-year-old idol of Guru Padmasambhav, and a life-size image of Avalokiteshvara, of whom the Dalai Lama is believed to be an incarnation. Public appearances
by the Dalai Lama occur from time to time; consult the local authorities for information
(and see "Essentials," above). The complex courtyard is the venue for an all-day festival
of traditional dance held in honor of His Holiness's birthday on July 6, although the

Dalai Lama is not always in attendance on this auspicious day. It's worthwhile to take a break from the prayer wheels and settle in at the tiny, laid-back Nyamgal Café in the temple complex (see "Where to Dine," below) which serves as a vocational training opportunity for young Tibetans. Snag the window-side table for beautiful views over the valley below.

Temple Rd. The temple closes at 8pm.

Tibetan Institute for Performing Arts (TIPA)   One hour from McLeod Ganj is TIPA, one of the first institutes set up by the Dalai Lama when he settled in McLeod Ganj, for the study and preservation of traditional Tibetan opera, dance, and music. Tibetan opera *(Lhamo)* performances can be long (some last 6 hr.) and are best experienced during the annual 9-day-long Shoton Opera Festival held in February and March (usually held in Dharamsala, but sometimes in other Tibetan settlement areas). Many other performances are held throughout the year as well, and interested visitors are welcome to watch classes. Ask at your hotel, check bulletin boards in local cafes for announcements, or go to the website for details.

Dharamkot Rd. 🕾 **01892/22-1478.** www.tibetanarts.org.

The Tibet Museum ★   If you'd like to learn more about the plight of the Tibetan people, then step into this sophisticated but rather depressing installation that provides a historical overview of the situation in Tibet. *A Long Look Homeward,* the main exhibition, consists of two parts. The downstairs display highlights the atrocities that have been carried out against millions of Tibetans during the Chinese occupation. Although events are detailed primarily through textual displays, the collection of data is emotionally challenging. Upstairs, the exhibition focuses more on Tibetan history. Particularly moving is the "testimony corner," where visitors can record the names of loved ones whose deaths are a result of the occupation. Lectures, presentations, and video screenings are presented in the small lecture hall; visit **www.thetibetmuseum.org** if you're interested in upcoming events.

Near the main temple and Namgyal Monastery Gate. Admission Rs 5. Tues–Sun 10am–6pm.

WHERE TO STAY

In McLeod Ganj, the best place to stay is the Norbulingka Institute–run **Chonor House,** not least for its dining. If you have a yearning to live in a forest surrounded by nature's bounty, another good option is **Glenmoor Cottages.** (Both options are reviewed below.) For those who prefer a more secluded stay, head out to **Dharamkot,** a small borough just above McLeod Ganj with stupendous views of the Dhauladhar mountains and Kangra Valley. **Hotel Dev Cottage** (🕾 **01892/22-1558;** www.devcottage.com) has pleasant rooms with large windows, balconies, and lovely views, for Rs 2,200 double including tax. However, if you're here to get a sense of just how dreamy and miraculous this part of Himachal really is—enjoying in equal measure the finest views of snow-tipped mountains, a valley spread far beneath your feet, and a warm, homey environment you won't easily find anywhere else in the state—look no further than **Eagles' Nest.** It's also reviewed below, but be warned that it's strictly for those of us who relish getting away from it all, so mall rats can skip it.

If the recommended places in McLeod Ganj and Dharamkot are full, the two best options in Dharamsala are White Haven Estate and **Grace Hotel,** a 200-year-old haveli converted into a heritage hotel. Although its approach isn't too inspiring (through the congested clutter of the main street into a narrow over-concretized lane), the views of the valley from the other side are splendid. The house is built in the traditional hill style, with narrow galleries, 200-year-old deodar tree pillars, alcoves, balconies and terraces, wooden latticed screens and doors, antique brass locks, and some beautiful pieces of furniture—it may not be very polished or sophisticated but it certainly is atmospheric (558 Old Chari Rd., Kotwali Bazaar, Dharamsala; (*) 01892/22-3265; www.welcomheritagegracehotel. com; Rs 3,800 double).

Another option far from town but worth considering is **Norling Guesthouse** (at the Norbulingka Institute; (*) 01892/26-4606; guesthouse@norbulingka.org), which has eight charming, artist-decorated rooms (Rs 1,400 double, excluding tax) and a couple of very impressive suites (Rs 2,300 double), all with attached modern bathrooms. Vegetarian meals can be served in your room, or in the Institute's very pleasant **Norling Café**, and the manager organizes reliable Tibetan drivers and luxury vehicles.

Cheryton Cottage (Value) For a clean, well-maintained good-value budget stay, consider this small family run guesthouse near enough the center of McLeod Ganj, but far from the hustle and bustle and inevitable noise. The rooms are spartan 1970s throwbacks dressed in bold colors (of the four units, the aptly named "Blue" and "Pink" have views). Above the guesthouse is an entire apartment (one double bedroom with attached bathroom, living room with TV, equipped kitchenette including a gas cooker, and balcony) which can be rented on a daily basis or taken for a month at a time (at a very generous rate; gas and electricity is charged extra, but the apartment is serviced 6 days a week). Oenophiles take note: Owner Cheryl Templeton was the first woman in India to produce wine, and she started the first winery in the Kangra district a few years ago; ask if you can sample her vintages, made from grapes, ginger, and blackcurrants, using old Italian family recipes.

Jogibara Rd., McLead Ganj, Dharamsala 176 219. (*) 01892/22-1993 or 94-1802-2858. tcheryl_89@ yahoo.com. 5 units, including 1 apt., all with shower only. Rs 700 double; Rs 1,500 apt. (or Rs 21,000 per month). Rates include tax. MC, V. Minimum 2-night stay. **Amenities:** Cafe; winery. *In room:* TV, kitchenette (in apt.), no phone.

Chonor House ★★★ (Value) A stone's throw away from the main *gompa*, and filled with genuine character and beautiful decor, this is the best option in McLeod Ganj. Each room was designed and decorated by artists from the Norbulingka Institute, based around Tibetan cultural themes. There are three categories of rooms, each offering different amenities: Some have balconies, some have tubs, and some (like the magnificent "Voyage at Sea" room) are simply enormous. "Nomad" features strikingly painted yaks, goats, and traveling tribespeople and also has a lovely balcony from which you have a direct view of the *gompa*. Indeed, you need hardly step outside the front door to get a good feel for Tibetan art and culture—this is a treasure chest of style and meticulous attention to details most Westerners probably don't think about. *Note:* Tibetan hospitality at its very best can, of course, do nothing to stop the chorus of barking hounds that seems to be the typical prelude—or interruption—to a good night's sleep.

Thekchen Choling Rd. (road ends at Pema Thang, walk the last 50m/164 ft.), P.O. McLeod Ganj, Dharamsala 176 219. (*) 01892/22-1468 or -1006. Fax 01892/22-0815. www.norbulingka.org. chonorhs@norbulingka. org. 11 units. Rs 2,200–Rs 2,850 double, Rs 3,300 suite; add 25% for extra bed. 10% tax extra. MC, V. **Amenities:** Restaurant; TV lounge; airport transfers (Rs 850); cybercafe; library; room service. *In room:* A/C (planned for 2010), heater, Wi-Fi (Rs 80/day).

Glenmoor Cottages ★★ Literally hidden from the world in the midst of a hillside forest, 1km (½ mile) beyond McLeod Ganj, these private cottages are perfect if you want

Meditation in the Mountains

Frazzled young executives from the plains looking to destress and recharge their batteries head for Dharamsala to attend meditation programs at **Osho Nisarga** (Shilla, PO Pantehar, Dharamsala 176 057; ✆ **01892/27-5592**, -5730, 94-1803-7370, or 94-1803-7373), a retreat offering a spiritual vacation aligned with the philosophies of the 20th-century guru Bagwan Rajneesh (aka Osho; see p. 175). The center is part ashram, part getaway, where you're encouraged to get in touch with yourself through a program of meditation (including dance meditation), group therapy, and discussion—on top of that, you're fed healthy vegetarian meals made with organic ingredients. The retreat is superbly designed and works especially well in the context of the beautiful forested surroundings; spread over 2.5 hectares (6 acres), it's bordered by orchards, dense pine forest, and mountain streams. Best of all, you needn't forgo any of the comforts you traditionally expect on a vacation, and you'll leave feeling refreshed, rejuvenated, and having experienced a moment of clarity that will hopefully stay with you the rest of your life—or at least until you hit rush hour traffic again. The Zen-themed accommodations are in a choice of interesting buildings, from the Greek-styled three-story Matreiya House with its pyramidal bedroom, to a number of luxury cottages with smart marble bathrooms and an emphasis on tranquillity. If you're not staying at the center, you can only visit with prior appointment from 10am to 1pm and from 3 to 5pm. The organizers won't be thrilled to have you unless you show at least some interest in Osho's work—at the very least, read some of his books before coming. While you're here you can attend daily dynamic meditation at 6:30am, kundalini and dance meditation, and evening meetings of the Osho White Robe Brotherhood; the center also hosts regular silent retreats and a variety of workshops and special events. Find out more through the website as you'll need to pick a program before asking about costs; www.oshonisarga.com. **Note:** This Osho retreat is not connected with the Osho Meditation Resort in Pune, but is a result of a split in the global Osho brand that happened after his death; folks here are a little less interested in attracting "beginners."

to be left to your own devices. Remote and peaceful (you feel as if you're a thousand miles from anything), Glenmoor is owned and run by the mild-mannered Ajai Singh, whose parents bought the tree-covered Om Bhawan estate in the 1940s. Ajai—who is filled with elegantly told tales of behind-the-scenes McLeod Ganj—built the simple stone cottages around the original colonial-era manor house. Perfect hideaways, the cottages are done out in rustic country style with pine interiors and private verandas from which to appreciate the infinite peace and quiet (save for the ceaseless chorus of cicadas). Upper cottages are larger—but the smaller lower cottages have loads of space, too. If you don't feel like walking into town, order ahead to arrange home-cooked Indian meals or simple continental breakfasts in the small dining room above the manor house—or have them delivered to your cottage.

Above Mall Rd., Upper Dharamsala 176 219. ℂ **01892/22-1010.** Fax 01892/22-1021. www.glenmoor cottages.com. info@glenmoorcottages.com. 6 units. Rs 4,300 upper cottage, Rs 3,200 lower cottage, Rs 1,800 double room; add 25% for extra bed. Rates exclude 10% tax. MC, V. **Amenities:** Dining room; airport transfers (Rs 850); room service. *In room:* TV, fridge, heater, Wi-Fi (Rs 60/hr.).

Hotel Eagle's Nest ★★★ (Finds) You'll arrive on the back of a mountain horse and instantly fall in love with our favorite Himachal hideaway. Bo and Sheila traded London's music industry for the tranquillity of the hills high above Dharamsala, transforming this old mission station into a gorgeous guesthouse. From high up here, the mayhem of McLeod Ganj seems light-years away and yet it's a mere half-hour walk down the mountain. Rooms, on two levels around a homey dining room/library, have been personally designed, each one a different style (pick between Moghal, Tibetan, Modern, Himachali, or simply ask for the most spectacular view). Nothing feels even remotely hotel like, and yet little luxuries are laid on to make you feel like a special guest. Your hosts are particularly endearing—Bo doles out dry, robust wit, and Sheila lavishes you with warmth, and they both make you feel like you're part of the family; you can join in activities in the kitchen, either watching over the chef's shoulder, or having a go at making momos; one member of staff is a qualified Ayurvedic masseuse. Despite having all the comforts of home, the property is in a mountain wilderness with abundant fauna—langur monkeys hang out on the lawn (with the guesthouse horses), and there are pinemartins, porcupines, barking deer, leopard, Himalayan black bear, and plenty of birdlife in the vicinity. Sheer bliss.

Upper Dharamkot, McLeod Ganj, Dharamsala 176 219. ℂ **01892/22-1920,** -0793, -0794, or 92-1840-2822. www.hoteleaglesnest.com. info@hoteleaglesnest.com. 7 units. Summer & winter Rs 4,000–Rs 7,000 double; Off-season (Jan 5–Feb 15 & Jul–Aug) Rs 4,000–Rs 5,000. Rates include breakfast and porterage; Rs 400 lunch, Rs 600 dinner. MC, V. **Amenities:** Dining room, TV/DVD lounge; airport transfers (Rs 1,200); badminton; croquet; horseback riding; Internet (in study; free); small outdoor heated pool/Jacuzzi. *In room* Central heating, fireplace (in some), no phone.

Pema Thang ★ (Value) Prayer flags flutter between the trees outside this small, congenial guesthouse that has distinguished itself as one of the more auspicious budget options in McLeod Ganj. Ask for a room on the top floor—though all overlook the valley the view improves as you go up (along with a small hike in price); and there are balconies up here from which to take it all in. Things are decidedly modest and simple; rooms are clean with reasonably comfortable beds, and the restaurant prepares delicious vegetarian dishes, including authentic Tibetan fare. Away from the noise of the central square and yet only a stone's throw from it, this very likable place is aided along by good vibrations from the friendly management team, always ready to lend a helping hand.

Hotel Bhagsu Rd., McLeod Ganj, Dharamsala 176 219. ℂ **01892/22-1871** or 92-1840-2718. www. pemathang.net. 15 units. Rs 825–Rs 1,155 double. No credit cards. **Amenities:** Restaurant; small library; room service; yoga. *In room:* Heating (Rs 150–Rs 200/day), TV (in some), Wi-Fi (8am–10:30pm; Rs 150/day).

WHERE TO DINE

As with many of the towns popular with tourists, McLeod Ganj is disproportionately restaurant-heavy. There's also a huge emphasis on vegetarian dining, thanks to the presence of the Dalai Lama. By far the best place to eat is Chonor House, which specializes in Tibetan cuisine (see below). Other Tibetan restaurants worth highlighting are **Green Restaurant** (Bhagsunag Rd.; ℂ **01892/22-1200**), which uses only organic produce, and the newly opened **Tibet Kitchen** on Jogibara Road, very close to the town square. Also on Jogibara, look for the lovely **Tibetan women selling homemade vegetable** *momos* out on the street just outside the Norling Café—they're extremely cheap, piping hot, and

A Taste of Tibet

Confused by what's available in the Tibetan restaurants of the Indian Himalayan region? Here's a guide: *Gyathuk* is a traditional egg noodle soup, typically prepared with tofu and black-and-white mushrooms. *Thenthuk* is a broth made with handmade noodles. *Pishi* is another name for wontons, often served in a vegetable broth with Tibetan tofu. You'll find Tibetan tofu and dumplings swimming in your *mothuk,* another traditional Tibetan broth. *Shabaklab* or *shabalay* is the Tibetan version of a pie, typically accompanied by broth. *Momos* are Tibetan dumplings, filled with cheese, vegetables, or meat. *Shabri* are seasoned meat or vegetable balls. *Bobi* are Tibetan spring rolls, filled with glass noodles, tofu, and mixed vegetables. Most Tibetan dishes can be served with vegetables, chicken, mutton, or even pork. *Bod-jha* is the staple Tibetan tea, copious quantities of which are consumed by Tibetans everywhere, and by almost no one else. It tastes nothing like any tea you've ever had—besides tea and milk, it contains salt and butter.

delicious. You can ask for them either steamed or fried, and eat them right there on the small bench provided, watching the world go by as you debate whether or not to order a second helping. You won't regret it if you do, but be cautious with the hot sauce.

A personal favorite, though, is the **Namgyal Café ★★** (Namgyal Monastery; ✆ 98-1615-0562; daily 10am–9:30pm) in the same complex as the Tsuglakhang or Main Temple. It's a wonderfully vibey haunt, where cool young Tibetans serve various tasty dishes and indulgences amid a tidy collection of books, plastic flowers, and hip jazzy lounge tunes. Market fresh ingredients are used to prepare traditional Tibetan *thukpa,* scrumptious salads, and exquisite thin-crust pizzas (which really have been improving over the past few years—look for the daily specials). Try the tofu stroganoff or *tsampa* (roasted flour) crepes; if you're not feeling too experimental, stick to noodles, *momos,* or you can try out the international vegetarian dishes ranging from Indonesian *gado-gado* to Cuban *arroz a la cubana.* There's no alcohol, but this is a great place to try Tibetan herbal tea or a refreshing *lassi.* They also serve butter tea and some great cakes to go with it.

While Tibetan fare would appear to be the way to go, you'll pretty much find something for everyone—from falafels to focaccia, *momos* (dumplings) to tempura. At least four German bakeries and as many pizzerias also cater to the large number of foreigners who come to McLeod Ganj. There's even a nifty grub-'n'-pub-style restaurant called **Mc'Llo** (at the top of Temple Rd.; ✆ 01892/22-1280), an extremely popular hangout for travelers that prides itself on having once entertained Pierce Brosnan (celebrity culture having few geographical boundaries). If you want Japanese, **Lung Ta** is an intimate diner with meat-free dishes that includes a small floor-seating area with traditional low tables (Jogibara Rd.; ✆ 01892/22-0689). Daily set meals feature a curious mix of Japanese vegetarian dishes; all meals a real steal at under Rs 100.

For Italian, head to **Nick's Italian Kitchen** (in the Kunga Guesthouse, Bhagsu Rd., McLeod Ganj; ✆ 01892/22-1180), which is something of a local institution, as much for the surprisingly good meals as for the views from its massive terrace. Gnocchi, cannelloni, and ravioli are prepared fresh every morning. The eggplant, spinach, and cheese lasagnas are star attractions, as is the aptly named "Pizza Everything." Nick's has the edge,

---

Tips **"The Dalai Lama Speaks Here & Richard Gere Slept There"**

One of the best people to speak to if you're eager to organize an audience with His Holiness is the spirited owner of Nick's Italian Kitchen, Tenzin. His father worked as security officer for the Dalai Lama from the age of 18, and Tenzin remains a proud and committed follower of the Dalai Lama. He also organizes occasional talks on Tibet and Buddhism at the restaurant, and is overflowing with personal theories about the local community and the diplomatic situation with the Chinese government. Staunch Richard Gere fans traveling on a limited budget can try to get the extremely popular Gere Suite at the seriously laid-back **Kunga Guesthouse** (© 98-1602-1180), above the restaurant; Gere was the first guest when it opened on January 24, 1996. Rooms here are basic, but have attached bathrooms, hot showers, and double beds for Rs 300; Rs 500 gets you one with a balcony, and Rs 600 gets you the Gere unit.

---

but if you're passing **The Pizzeria** (past Tushita into Dharamkot village—ask anyone), you'll find simple, tasty pizzas prepared by a local *Gaddi* family, apparently taught how to make wood-fire pizzas by a visiting Italian.

Chonor House ★★★ TIBETAN McLeod Ganj's best guesthouse also offers its most impressive dining. The menu is a veritable encyclopedia of Tibetan dishes, many of them borderline addictive. Share a plate of *momos* to start—these butter dumplings are steamed to perfection and filled with tasty fresh white cheese. Or experiment with the excellent *bobi*, which allows you to build your own Tibetan spring rolls, a fun alternative to the greasy version popular in Chinese takeout joints. You can build all night, using thinly grilled bread wraps, seasoned glass noodles, mixed vegetables, tofu, and Basmati rice. Or have the *bobi* as a starter, after which you can try the delicious fried *pishi* (wontons), deliciously seasoned *shabri* (meat or vegetable balls in garlic sauce), or steaming mutton-filled *shabalay* (bread pie). For the health conscious there are scrumptious, fresh salads, but you'll probably be more tempted by the utterly decadent selection of cakes on display.

Chonor House, Thekchen Choling Rd., McLeod Ganj. © **01892/22-1468.** Main courses Rs 65–Rs 175. MC, V. Daily 7am–10pm.

SHOPPING

McLeod Ganj is full of shops selling curios, books, or trekking gear—and you'll see lots of unlikely combinations like "laundry and bakery." You can buy reasonably priced Tibetan rugs and handicrafts from the **Tibetan Handicraft Centre** (near McLeod Ganj Post Office, Jogibara Rd.; © **01892/22-1415**), but a far more memorable experience is to hike through the forest to the **Tibetan Children's Village Handicraft Centre** (© **01892/ 22-1592;** www.tvc.org.in); it's a pleasant half-hour walk north of McLeod Ganj, near Dal Lake. Back in town, **Stitches of Tibet** (Temple Rd.; © **01892/22-1198** or -1527) is an enterprise that trains local women in handicraft production. Their shop stocks the completed handicrafts as well as Tibetan clothing. If you want to buy a traditional Tibetan *thangka* (painted or embroidered banner or wall decoration), the **Norbulingka Institute** is where this art is preserved and taught; they also take orders. Shop at the institute or at Chonor House, knowing that your purchase will actually contribute to the development of Tibetan craftsmanship. For beautiful women's wear, including gowns and kimonos in fabulous fabrics, stop at **Eternal Creation** (4 Temple Rd.; www.eternal creation.com), which stocks only its own brand, produced in Dharamsala under fair trade conditions in a project that aims to give opportunities to local people and refugees. Another interesting boutique is **Tamana** (Jogiwara Rd.; ✆ **98-1614-1192** or 01892/22-21921) with clothing created by a French designer who works locally with predyed South Indian fabrics to create some fascinating women's and children's wear.

For books, visit **Namgyal Bookstore** in the temple complex; its excellent collection focuses primarily on Tibetan culture and Buddhism, but it has a good number of beautiful publications on Himachal Pradesh and other Himalayan regions as well. Also filled with an interesting assortment of books on the history, culture, and art of the region is **Youtse Book Shop** (Mount View Complex, Temple Rd.).

If you'd like to pick up handcrafted mementos and support a good cause, stop by the **Rogpa Shop & Café** (Jogiwara Rd., McLeod Gang; ✆ **98-1665-9549;** www.rogpa.com), run by a charitable trust that creates opportunities for unemployed Tibetans as well as encouraging entrepreneurs and artists. A number of local Tibetan organizations sell their merchandise here, and you can pick up handmade paper, Tibetan crafts, and designs from the "Made in Exile" label that aims to promote global awareness about the Tibetan cause. You can also donate clothing for resale, or volunteer by working in the shop or helping at Rogpa's Baby Care Centre.

Tip: If you're looking for cash, an SBI (State Bank of India) ATM is located on the main street of McLeod Ganj; be warned, however, that there's inevitably a queue, 20-strong, waiting to use it. At press time there were two other ATMs on the verge of opening, but we'd still strongly advise that you draw cash before landing in McLeod Ganj where so much of the shopping is cash only. Consider stopping at the ICICI or HDFC machines that operate in lower Dharamsala on your way up. For changing or transferring foreign exchange, you can use Thomas Cook (next to SBI) or any of the Western Union outlets.

THE KANGRA VALLEY

If you have the time and want to veer slightly off the beaten track, definitely head southeast of Dharamsala toward the gently undulating tea-covered hills of Kangra Valley. Although it lacks any particular charms of its own, **Palampur** is a popular starting point for Kangra Valley. Nearby is **Tashijong Monastery,** a colorful *gompa* established in the years after the Dalai Lama made his home in Dharamsala. The neighboring town of Baijnath is the site of the beautiful **Saivite Vaidyanath Temple complex ★★** (Baijnath Main Rd.; daily 5am–9pm in summer and 6am–8pm in winter), one of the more interesting and best-preserved Hindu shrines in Himachal Pradesh, dating from the early 13th century. Surrounded by a wall decorated by fine carvings, the main temple enshrines a squat Shiva lingam protected by a five-headed metallic cobra; devotees usually cover the lingam with flowers and other offerings. A half-hour drive in the other direction will take you to **Andretta Pottery and Craft Society** (✆ **01894/25-4243;** www.andrettapottery. com), where the extremely passionate Jugal Kishore will be happy to explain the objectives behind this training school—modest accommodation is available for those who feel like attending short-term classes.

Pragpur ★★★ (6 hr. from Shimla; 7 hr. from Manali; 2½ hr. from Palampur) is a time-trapped village with mud-plastered, slate-roofed houses, elegant *havelis* (mansions), Italianate buildings, and narrow cobblestone roads. Designated India's first official "Heritage Village," this tiny hamlet was founded as a memorial to a brave warrior princess who

(Tips) Digs for the Time Traveler

If you want to stay in the heart of a pretty, well-preserved medieval village, look into the availability of one of the two semidetached 17th-century houses in Pragpur's highly atmospheric **Kuthiala Courtyard.** They're operated as annexes to the lovely Judge's Court hotel, and can be rented for short or long stays: Accommodations are fairly basic, giving you a truly hands-on insight into more or less how these villagers live. Marble floors are offset by mud-themed walls, an ancient gas-powered kitchen, and big bedrooms with tiny shuttered windows. And when you leave the house, you get to experience life along the narrow lanes and cobbled walkways, meeting and perhaps befriending neighbors—an experience you'll never get from a hotel populated by other foreigners. While this is an authentic experience don't expect any luxuries beyond the normal conveniences of a home trapped in another age; when you need a bit of pampering, though, you can trundle off to the restaurant at Judge's Court and enjoy kid glove service before scurrying back to your village nest. See our review of Judge's Court, below, for contact details.

led a resistance against invaders in the 17th century. Pragpur is wonderful to explore, a veritable warren of tiny lanes and old, atmospheric buildings. Sadly, though, some of the luster has begun to disappear since the village first landed on the map; among other bad planning decisions, some idiotic council allowed a ghastly telecommunication tower to be constructed in one part of town (right at the edge of the Judge's Court, in fact), which dramatically detracts from the "heritage" concept. Nevertheless, you still get a very good out of time feel here, and the surrounding landscape offers opportunities for nature walks, cycling, bird-watching, and fishing. Upper Pragpur is known for its home-weaving industry, so this is the place to look for good deals on local crafts. Best of all, you get to spend the night in Pragpur's beautiful **Judge's Court,** one of Himachal's most enchanting hotels (reviewed below). Near Pragpur is the strangely named **Pong Lake,** officially known as Maharana Pratap Sagar—a reservoir that attracts local and migratory birds, mostly from Siberia (best time to visit: Oct/Nov–Mar/Apr). Some 1,300 hundred species of birds are found in the Indian subcontinent, of which more than 500 species are present in Kangra—if you're interested it's worth picking up a copy of the *Birds of Kangra* by Jan Willem den Besten, a very comprehensive book on the extensive birdlife of this region.

Where to Stay

Taragarh Palace (reviewed below), Palampur's famous heritage hotel has now become something of a sprawling resort catering to groups; if you'd prefer to be in the midst of a tea plantation, rather than encountering busloads of tourists, consider holing up at the family run **Country Cottage** (Chandpur Tea Estate; © 01894/23-0647; www.country cottageindia.com; Rs 2,800–Rs 4,000 double), set in the cantonment area of Palampur amid a 20 hectare (50-acre) organic tea garden. It's a simple, unpretentious, low-key operation with just a handful of cottages and the emphasis firmly on appreciating your surroundings rather than on exciting accommodations. At press time, two brand-new cottages were due to open, and these (more expensive) units with the best location will be the ones to book. The owner is a veritable font of information (on tea, among other things—with a couple of days he'll even let you make your own), and puts together all kinds of interesting excursions, including an innovative anthropological tour that investigates various tribes in the Kangra Valley; he'll also point you towards some wonderful local treks and organize mahaseer fishing expeditions. Besides staring out into the gardens and trying different teas, there's not very much to do *at* the cottages—definitely bring books.

The Judge's Court ★★   This atmospheric Indo-European haveli, architecturally detailed with domes, galleries, terraces, and porticoes, is filled with the sort of tranquil charm that whisks guests straight back into a bygone age. Set on a magnificent property with orchards of mango, litchi, plum, persimmon, and citrus-fruit trees, the main manor house was built in 1918 by a descendant of Pragpur's founders as a gift for his son, a well-known judge of the Punjab High Court. Laboriously restored, the hotel offers a variety of accommodations, including the swish new "Residency" wing at the back of the property. Best to go for one of the spookily romantic heritage suites, each with it's own special charm—fireplaces, plush armchairs, original antiques, and chunky furniture throughout. Between exploring the village and tucking into extravagant multicourse meals, try to spend some time chatting with the owner, Vijay Lal—his spirited conversation is always a highlight of our time in the Kangra Valley.

Heritage Village Pragpur, Tehsil Dehra, District Kangra 177 107. Info 𝄞 **01970/24-5035** or -5335. Reservations: 3/44, Shanti Niketan, New Delhi 110 021. 𝄞 **011/2411-4135.** Fax 011/2411-5970. www.judges court.com. 17 units, plus 3 self-contained apts. in the village. Rs 4,500 deluxe double, Rs 5,200 Residency double, Rs 6,000 heritage suite; Rs 1,000 extra bed. Rates exclude 10% tax. Breakfast Rs 250, lunch Rs 350, dinner Rs 450. MC, V. **Amenities:** Restaurant; 3 lounges; bar service; cultural performances; small pool. *In room:* A/C and fans, TV (in most), fireplace (in most), fridge, heater, no phone.

Taragarh Palace Hotel ★   Once known as Al Hilal (The Land of the Crescent Moon), this Art Deco mansion (now described as the Heritage Wing) was built in the 1930s as the summer resort of the Nawab of Bahawalpur until he fled to Pakistan after Partition. One of the least-visited destinations in the heart of the scenic and serene Kangra Valley, Taragarh is enveloped in thick vegetation, moss-covered walls, and gorgeous grounds. Before the addition of the bland Palace Wing (frankly, a very unsympathetic appendage, in style an appalling imitation of the original), Taragarh was the ideal setting for a brooding Agatha Christie whodunit, the mansion is all high ceilings, broad staircases, chandeliers, and long passages lined with family portraits, Buddhist *thangkas,* and animal skins. Book the characterful Maharajah, Maharani, or Princess suites—smart, spacious, and elegantly decorated with authentic period touches entirely absent from the rather dull double rooms, which are more reminiscent of small English country-hotel rooms (with musty carpets) than royal retiring quarters. Traditional Indian, Kashmiri, and local dishes are served in the wood-paneled dining room with a gorgeous old copper *bukhari* almost hidden in the fireplace.

P.O. Taragarh, District Kangra 176 081. Info 𝄞 **01894/24-2034** or -3077. www.taragarh.com. Reservations: 15 Institutional Area, Lodhi Rd., New Delhi 110 003. 𝄞 **011/2464-3046** or 011/2469-2317. Fax 011/ 2465-6491. reservations@taragarh.com. 26 units, most with shower only. Rs 4,500 heritage double, Rs 5,500 superior deluxe double, Rs 6,100 heritage suite; add 25% for extra bed. 10% tax extra. MC, V. **Amenities:** Restaurant, lounge, bar; airport transfers (Rs 2,500); badminton; children's park; cybercafe; health club and spa; horseback riding; Internet (broadband in business center; Rs 100/hr.); large outdoor pool (Apr–Oct); limited room service; table tennis; tennis court; yoga. *In room* A/C (in suites), TV, DVD (in suites), hair dryer, heater, minibar (in suites).

Leh is 475km (295 miles) from Manali

The region of Ladakh, in the state of Jammu and Kashmir, has often been described as a moonscape, a desolate high-altitude desert kingdom of mysticism and mystery. It is all of these, and more, a thoroughly awe-inspiring world of harsh reality, with few luxuries. Local lives are centered around Buddhism, yaks, and survival, and more recently on the small tourism industry that sprouts in the relatively warmer months of the year (July–Sept).

Leh, Ladakh's capital city, is little touched by rain, but the extreme cold during the long winter season means that this remote region remains isolated for much of the year. Come June, however, when the tourists begin to trickle (and then pour) into Leh, the sober, somber slumber of this remote high-altitude town lifts along with the temperatures. Situated in a fertile valley at the foot of Namgyal Tsemo peak, 8km (5 miles) northeast of the Indus River, Leh is deeply reliant on this short, intense tourist season. From June to September the surrounding barren mountains and distant snowcapped peaks are the perfect natural backdrop for the verdant fields and avenues of trees that cluster around the whitewashed, flat-roofed buildings.

Developed as a market for traders from across the North India belt, Leh was an important stop for travelers traversing the challenging caravan routes to Yarkand and Kashgar. The Silk Road brought Buddhist travelers, and today the population remains predominantly Buddhist. You can spend up to a week exploring the town and the numerous Buddhist monuments within a 2- or 3-hour drive of Leh; far better, though, to head off to more remote (and less touristed) monasteries, such as **Lamayuru.** If you plan properly, you can head over the **Khardung-La** (the highest motorable pass on earth) into the spectacular **Nubra Valley** to discover more remote and time-trapped villages and monasteries, set against extraordinary slopes. Adventure-seekers can get caught up in river-rafting on the Zanskar and Indus, high-level mountain-climbing, or treks into remote, barren wilderness regions, which can easily extend your stay by an additional week, or more. The more laid-back traveler will be rewarded by awe-inspiring excursions to high-altitude lakes such as **Pangong Tso** and **Tso Moriri.**

ESSENTIALS

GETTING THERE   By Air   If you'd rather save time and get to Leh without the arduous cliff-hanging road journey, both **Kingfisher** and **Jet Airways** (Dreamland Complex, Main Bazaar; ℰ **01982/25-0444;** Mon–Sat 10am–5pm, Sun 10am–3pm) offer daily flights between New Delhi and Leh's Bakula Rinpoche Airport in the summer; you'll be touching down at Asia's highest commercial airport (3,600m/11,808 ft.). The disadvantage of flying in is that you may need to spend up to 48 hours acclimatizing anyway, whereas the road journey gently puts you through your paces. Flying out of Leh is definitely a good idea; reserve a window seat. Indian Airlines also flies to Leh, but these flights are often booked up by military personnel.

By Road   Typically, you require two rather tiring days in a Jeep (or bus) to get from Manali to Leh. But for those seeking an adventurous road trip coupled with exquisite, endlessly changing scenery, the journey—by off-road vehicle or bus—is highly recommended; see "The Ride of your Life: Negotiating the Manali-Leh Highway," below.

The Ride of your Life: Negotiating the Manali-Leh Highway

Nearly 475km (295 miles) of tricky roads, mountain passes, and exceptional roller-coaster scenery separates Leh from Manali. For most of the year, this spectacular stretch of road is closed to traffic, covered by thick snow. Even when the road is officially open in late June and early July, the danger of unexpected snowfall looms, bringing with it various risks associated with getting stuck in the middle of vast unpopulated areas with only freezing cold nights for company. Once summer has set in, a variety of makeshift *dhabas* and *chai* stalls are gathered in minicolonies along the way. You'll need your passport for a string of checkpoints, the first of which is just beyond the Rohtang Pass at the head of the Kullu Valley. Beyond this, you enter **Lahaul,** a vast Trans-Himalayan landscape dotted with flat-roofed, whitewashed houses built from sun-dried bricks. **Sarchu,** a motley collection of tented camps, is where you'll probably bed down for the night; you'll be too cold to complain about the limited facilities. You reach the world's second-highest motorable road at the summit of the Tanglang-La Pass (5,241m/17,190 ft.); here you will find a small multifaith shrine adorned by images of gurus, deities, and religious icons. Beyond the pass, exquisite mountains in a host of unbelievable colors compete with charming villages for your attention.

Your cheapest viable option is an ostensibly "luxury" bus operated by **HPTDC** (© **0177/265-2651;** www.hptdc.nic.in; July–Sept 15). For Rs 1,600 you get an ass-numbing 2-day trip (starting at a civilized 11am) with spartan tented accommodations and dinner en route at **Keylong;** you arrive in Leh at 7pm the following evening. Occasional stops for *chai* and photographs are obligatory, but bring plenty of refreshments. Bottled water is particularly important because dehydration is one of the symptoms of altitude sickness. Garlic in any form also apparently helps. Jeeps and minivan taxis are pricier but represent relative luxury and the opportunity to explore villages and off-road sites along the way. Hiring your own vehicle and driver is an even better way to go—it costs Rs 12,000 for the whole vehicle divided by the number of passengers. If you've hired your own vehicle, overnight at **Hotel Ibex** in Jispa, beyond Keylong (© **01900/23-3203;** www.hotelibexjispa.com; Rs 2,400 double with dinner and breakfast). Don't even consider the 1-day minibus trips that leave Manali at 2am in the morning and arrive in Leh around 9pm; not only will your nerves, gut, and body be frazzled by the end of it, but you'll miss out on the awesome scenery at the start and end of the trip. Very popular these days are motorbike safaris that make the journey from Manali to Leh; an experienced operator is Capt. Raaj Kumar of **Shepherds Realms, Camps & Adventures,** who also offers 14- to 21-day tailor-made safaris (© **98-1871-2970;** www. asiasafari.com; shepherdsrealms@gmail.com) that take in wider explorations of Ladakh once you're there.

⚠️ Warning! Altitude Sickness

Arriving by air into Leh makes most people feel slightly knocked out, with headaches, loss of appetite, drowsiness, and disturbed sleep—all early signs of altitude sickness. It's necessary to stay put and drink lots of fluids for 48 hours to acclimatize before venturing higher into the mountains. Monitor your body and health, and don't ignore worsening symptoms, which could lead to a pulmonary or cerebral edema. In Leh you can get 24-hour medical help for altitude sickness at **Sonam Norbu Memorial (SNM) Hospital** (✆ **01982/25-2012**).

VISITOR INFORMATION   Leh has a Tourist Information Center, but you are advised not to waste your time there. Speak to your hotel manager or any of the many tour operators who offer various services throughout Ladakh. You could also check out www. leh.nic.in. If you're interested in learning more about Ladakhi culture and Buddhism, you can contact **Open Ladakh** (www.openladakh.com), which offers basic courses in Buddhist philosophy, not to mention "alternative" cultural and adventure tours through the region.

GETTING AROUND By Car   Thanks to a strong military presence in the region, Ladakh's roads are excellent and the network of accessible destinations extensive. Although Leh has but one auto-rickshaw, it has as many as 1,500 taxis, with fixed rates to practically any place in the state, or beyond. For taxi rates and bookings, call the **Leh Taxi Stand** (✆ **01982/25-2723**). If you want to explore extensively, your best bet is to share a jeep (booked only through a travel agency) with fellow travelers interested in visiting similar destinations; most agencies will even advertise shared jeeps on your behalf. Mr. Tundup Dorje, a prolific writer, is the owner of **Overland Escape** (Raku Complex, Fort Rd., Leh; ✆ **01982/25-0858;** www.overlandescape.com), the agent used by most hotels, and considered the most reliable in town; try him first. *Note:* You cannot rent a vehicle outside Leh if you want to tour within Ladakh.

GUIDED TOURS & ADVENTURE & TREKKING COMPANIES   It's easy to plan your own outings and give the instructions to your jeep or taxi driver. If you want to deal with an outfitter, refer to the "Staying Active" section earlier in this chapter. If you are very keen on receiving expert information as you explore monasteries and other sights, then a licensed operator may be useful; use one of our recommendations, or ask your hotel to put you in touch with the right people. For a tour that includes good accommodations in pleasantly converted rooms in traditional village family homes, see "Village Homestays, Boutique-Style," on p. 658.

   Overland Escape (see above) should be your first stop for all kinds of adventure activities or tours through Ladakh. Also recommended is **Yama Adventures** (✆ **01982/ 25-0833** or 94-1917-8763; www.yamatreks.com), a small Ladakhi-owned company with a good track record; owner Rinchen Namgial (✆ **99-0698-7782**) has previously worked with teams from the Smithsonian Institute and *National Geographic*, and puts together jeep safaris, relatively easy treks (such as the 8- to 10-day Markha Valley hike), and also more thrill-oriented experiences such as climbing the Stok glacier. **Banjara Camps,** although based in Delhi, is also highly recommended, and is the only outfit to use the services of a qualified geologist (Delhi office: ✆ **011/2686-1397,** 011/2685-5153, or 98-1064-5455; www.banjaracamps.com). For more leisure-oriented travelers,

Walking on Water & Other Adventures for Serious Trekkers

One of the crazier (or more adventurous) treks is the arduous 16-day **Chadar Trek** ★★★ along the Zanskar River, sufficiently semifrozen to support your weight for 2 months of the year. For 4 days (one-way) you trek on slippery ice and occasionally climb around open water on this ancient trade route; at night, outside temperatures plummet to a bone-chilling 3.8°F (–15°C). By day (when it's a mere 23.8°F/–4°C or so) the challenges are many, but the setting is awesome and there's always the chance of meeting local Zanskaris. One of the best operators offering this trek is **Project Himalaya** ★★★ (© 977/98-0214-9789 in Kathmandu; www.project-himalaya.com; info@project-himalaya.com), a Kathmandu-based company with good ethics and a somewhat unformulaic approach to its routes. Also taking in parts of Zanskar is the **Markha Valley Trek** (10–12 days)—considered one of the most exhilarating and varied on earth—undertaken by **Himalayan River Runners** (www.hrrindia.com) You cross two Himalayan passes at altitudes over 4,500m (14,760 ft.) and descend into the Zanskar Valley before finishing the in upper parts of the Markha, surrounded by jagged peaks. **Banjara** offers an 8-day version that follows the riverbed more closely and includes one very high pass. Bajara also offers a 2-week trek that culminates at **Lamayuru,** one of the most enchanting monasteries in Ladakh, and reached by way of some truly intense scenery. If you're wanting to climb the Stok Glacier (traversing altitudes over 4,800m/16,000 ft.), contact Rinchen Namgial at **Yama Adventures** (www.yamatreks.com), who will make all the necessary arrangements (and get the special license required). Also ask about **treks to Pangong Tso and Tso Moriri;** again see "Staying Active," earlier in this chapter, for more adventure companies.

Banjara also conducts jeep safaris of Ladakh. In Leh itself, **Rimo Expeditions** (Hotel Kanglhachen Complex, opposite the Police Station; © 01982/25-3257 or -3348; www.rimoexpeditions.com) is a reliable outfit that undertakes a multitude of adventure-oriented multiday excursions. The company also arranges less hectic trekking expeditions, as well as jeep and yak safaris, and skiing, mountain biking, and challenging mountaineering packages for serious climbers. English-speaking mountain guides are provided, as well as all equipment, porters, cooks, and other staff.

WHAT TO SEE & DO IN LEH

Leh's wide street **bazaar** runs east-west. Together with the labyrinth of adjoining side streets and alleys, the bazaar is the center of business and shopping—particularly for visitors who find the plethora of antiques shops irresistible. Locals tend to visit the alternative market nearer the Leh **polo ground,** east of the center. For a truly exotic and atmospheric experience, visit the **Old Village** ★, a disorganized cluster of cobblestone streets, ancient homes, and low-vaulted tunnels. It's well worth an exploratory jaunt, during which you should sample the freshly baked breads sold by local bakers. Walking northwest of the city (beyond the **Women's Alliance of Ladakh** headquarters, where you can shop for traditional Ladakhi handicrafts), you will quickly discover a **rural farm community.** Gone are the shops and eager sellers—here you'll find only fields of green sprinkled with bright yellow blossoms, gentle streams trickling past squat stone walls, and

(Moments) The Great Ladakhi Gatherings

If you're hoping to coincide your visit to Ladakh with a special event, there's always the increasingly commercial 2-day **Hemis Tsechu,** a colorful festival with *chaam* dances, temple music, and a number of sacred rituals seemingly put on for the enjoyment of the heaving crowd. Sadly, the authenticity of the festival has been seriously compromised as this region grows in popularity and Hemis is mobbed by tourists and stall-keepers out to make a quick buck. An exciting new, nonreligious alternative festival is the **Ladakh Confluence** ★★★ (http://the confluence.in), which premiered in 2009, and is set to become a highlight on India's event circuit. Held for 4 days in July or August (check the website for this year's exact dates), the festival is a celebration of music, art, nature and culture that promises some outstanding performances, as well as many workshops showcasing everything from Ladakhi dance and drumming to meditation and storytelling; there's a film lounge, outdoor cafe, nomadic camping site where traditional crafts are demonstrated, food stalls, and a number of chill-out spaces. While Hemis is a religious festival blown out of proportion, the Confluence aims to get people thinking about the environment and rethinking their relationship with cultural tradition. Even so, the lineup of events includes a momo-eating competition and plenty of pure entertainment. It's held on the banks of the Indus River just outside Choglomsar, some 8km (5 miles) from Leh; in 2009, entry cost Rs 5,000 for a 4-day adult pass, or Rs 1,500 for a day ticket. For a more authentic and spiritually meaningful festival experience, make a date for the annual **Lamayuru festival** ★★★ held between late June and early July. Tourists are few, but villagers from miles around don their best traditional finery and make the pilgrimage on foot to join in some of the most enchanting Buddhist celebrations still happening today.

small Ladakhi houses with little vegetable gardens; these days, there are also an ever-increasing number of guesthouses and hotels, though. To the west are the cobbled streets of the popular **Changspa** neighborhood, characterized by the number of guesthouses, restaurants, and laid-back marijuana-smoking travelers who seem to come here to hang out with each other. To the west of Changspa lies **Shanti Stupa,** a Buddhist monument most easily reached by motorable road. Inaugurated by the Dalai Lama in the 1980s, the large white *stupa* (commemorative cairn) was conceived as part of a Japanese-inspired peace movement to spread Buddhism throughout the world. From the vast courtyard at the base of the stupa you can enjoy matchless **panoramic views** ★★★ of Leh and the rugged beauty of the surrounding mountains, which seem to stretch on forever. Looming over Leh from the side of Tsemo Hill is the nine-storey **Leh Palace** ★★ (Rs 100; sunrise–sunset), reached by following any number of pathways through the old quarter that stretches out behind the **Jama Masjid** in the northeastern corner of the main bazaar area. Built mainly of stone and wood with mud bricks and mud mortar, construction began in 1553 under Tsewang Namgyal, the founder of the Hyamgal Dynasty; it's designed as a miniature version of Llasa's Potala Palace, but has long languished in a state of disrepair, but reconstruction and restoration are well under way and will no doubt continue for some years. There's still quite a bit to investigate, including an atmospheric temple inside the palace, and the views from its balconies and windows are magnificent. A stiff climb farther up the hill will bring you to the **Namgyal Tsemo Gompa,** where the dangerous-looking ramparts invite cautious exploration; there's a small temple hidden away right at the top and at some point a young monk might just jump out of nowhere asking you to buy a Rs 20 ticket. Again, the views are simply awesome—take your time and mind your step.

Back in the main part of town, make a point of finding the **fruit and vegetable market,** entered via an unmarked entrance opposite the Hotel Ga-Ldan Continental on Zangsti

WHERE TO STAY IN & AROUND LEH

With tourism the single most important industry in town, Leh is inundated with accommodations, most of them offering very good value, often with a homey, welcoming atmosphere rather than five-star luxury. Remember that virtually all these places are closed for most of the year during a prolonged harsh winter, so it doesn't really pay to have heaps of facilities that are only operative for a few months. Besides, you're here to see the dramatic Ladakhi landscape and discover its unique culture and Buddhist heritage, so forgive occasionally basic conditions, especially when it comes to bathrooms which, for the most part, are merely adequate (check into the glitzy Grand Dragon if you demand more). Try to be understanding about hot water facilities (which may be restricted to certain hours), and consider the fragility of the environment and the fact that running water is in fact a very scarce resource.

We've long enjoyed the out-of-the-way setting of the welcoming **Shambha-La Hotel,** and this, together with family run **Omasila** (both reviewed below) remains our top choices.

There is no tax in Ladakh, but most hotels do charge an additional 10% service charge which will be added to your bill; most hotels have meal plans in addition to the standard bed and breakfast options for which we've provided rates below. It's definitely worth venturing beyond your hotel and trying some of the restaurants in town, though, so rather avoid signing up for all-inclusive meal packages. The same does not apply once you step outside Leh, when finding a reliable place to eat can be quite challenging.

The Grand Dragon (Overrated) Ladakh's first and only full-on hotel, complete with elevator, business-style rooms and the best bathrooms for hundreds of miles, is sadly afflicted by incompetence. Full marks for getting the mattresses and linens right (not to mention plasma TVs), some interesting artworks and providing great views, but it's a tactless luxury. The hulking block of concrete may echo local architecture, but it's ultimately an eyesore that belongs in a big city, not at the gateway to a high-altitude paradise, and we couldn't help feeling a little guilty (and ripped off) for staying at what feels like an attempt to turn Leh into Las Vegas. Add to that lost bookings, absent manager, absent travel desk, forgotten wake-up call, Leh's rudest reception clerk, and big-ego prices, it amounts to a place that we won't be returning to in a hurry.

Old Rd., Sheynam, Leh 194 101. (C) **01982/25-0786,** -5866, or -5266. Fax 01982/25-5266. www.thegrand dragonladakh.com. 53 units. Rs 6,500 deluxe double, Rs 9,000 Royal suite, Rs 10,000 Maharaja suite; Rs 1,000 extra person, Rs 500 child aged 5–10 without extra bed. Rates include breakfast; 10% service charge extra. MC, V. **Amenities:** 2 restaurants; lounge; airport transfers (Rs 300); room service. *In room:* TV, central heating, hair dryer.

Hotel Dragon ★ (Value) Owned by Ghulam and Mohiuddin Mustafa since 1974, this is Ladakh's oldest hotel and remains one of the best places to stay in Leh—we definitely prefer it to its enormous new sibling, The Grand Dragon (reviewed above), down the road. This place is just so much cozier, more intimate, and better-managed, even if it's a lot more basic. Each floor of the squat, Ladakhi-style building has its own terrace, and you can catch fantastic 360-degree views of Leh from the rooftop. Upstairs, room nos. 131 through 133 are more spacious than the other, typically small doubles, and the suites are well worth the extra rupees. At night, when a campfire is lit, the small garden courtyard becomes an ideal spot in which to wind down the day. Good Ladakhi and Tibetan meals are served in the traditionally-styled dining room, decorated with gorgeous paintings by Ghulam Mustafa.

Old Rd., Leh 194 101. ⓒ **01982/25-2139,** -2720, -1227, or -0786. Fax 01982/25-2720. www.travelladakh. com. 30 units. Rs 2,421 standard double, Rs 2,842 suite; add 40% for extra bed. Rates include breakfast; 10% service charge extra. MC, V. **Amenities:** Dining hall; airport transfers (Rs 150); musical performances on request; limited room service. *In room:* TV.

The Mogol Hotel ★ In the popular backpacker hangout quarter of Changspa, The Mogol is (like Omasila) a delight to find, offering sweet, neat little rooms with tiled bathrooms and curtained-off showers that ensure the entire bathroom doesn't get wet when you wash. In your room you'll find a desk, some decent cane furniture, and narrow beds; the good-value suite has a much smarter look. There's not much of a garden, but the rooftop sitting area is a decent place to relax. Most importantly, owners Rahul and Karen Kalon are extremely helpful and will help arrange your entire trip—they also own the lovely **Silk Route Cottages** in the Nubra Valley (p. 664). One drawback is the constant hum of a nearby generator when the power goes out.

Changspa, Leh 194 101. ⓒ **99-9009-4107,** 94 1965 7333, or 99-9911-9435. www.hotelmogol.com. info@hotelmogol.com or hotelmogol@rediff.com. 18 units, all with shower only. Rs 2,550 standard double, Rs 2,800 deluxe double, Rs 3,900 suite; add 40% for extra bed. Rates include breakfast; 10% service charge extra. MC, V. **Amenities:** Restaurant; airport transfers (Rs 150). *In room:* TV.

Omasila ★★ Ⓥalue This family run hotel occupies a cluster of pleasant Ladakhi-style buildings that conceal spectacular views that you don't see when approaching from busy, overbuilt Changspa Lane. In summer the mountains surrounding Leh provide the perfect backdrop for magnificent sweeps of colorful flora perfectly visible from each room in the hotel. Fresh vegetables, apricots, and apples are grown in an adjoining garden (much of this ends up on the table for lunch or dinner), and the stream alongside is a natural aural tonic during laid-back afternoons on cane chairs on the sun-drenched terrace. The extremely good-value suites—including no. 21, where Brad Pitt stayed in 2006—offer the best comfort, with a faintly Tibetan aesthetic; six newer suites have tubs and modern fittings (book 18 or 19 for views). (Omasila, with its gas-regulated heating system, is one of the few hotels to remain open throughout the year.)

Karzoo-Changspa, Leh 194 101. ⓒ **01982/25-2119,** -1178, or -0207. www.omasila.com. 40 units (including 6 with tubs). Rs 1,800–Rs 2,000 standard double, Rs 2,300–Rs 2,500 deluxe double, Rs 3,100–Rs 3,900 suite. Rates include breakfast. MC, V. **Amenities:** Restaurant; TV lounge; Internet (in cybercafe; Rs 50/hr.); oxygen facilities, room service. *In room:* TV, central heating.

Poplar Eco Resort ★ Ⓕinds Set amid a virtual jungle of apple, apricot, walnut, and poplar trees that were planted here when the hotel was built, this is a really lovely low-key find tucked away near the edge of town. Separated from the adjacent farmland by just a low wall, this collection of simple little cottages linked by concrete pathways that snake their way through the overgrown garden (you may need to duck and dive a bit as you head to your room) is a lovely change from the heavily touristed places that are just up

13

(Moments) Village Homestays, Boutique-Style

The smartest way to see Ladakh is with the innovative and stylish Himalayan specialists, **Shakti** ★★★ (℃ **0124/456-3899;** www.shaktihimalaya.com), which runs all-inclusive personalized airport-to-airport trips (minimum 5 days) that give you a genuine feel for the region. Supported by your very own team of English-speaking guides, porters, a cook, and a driver, you'll get to overnight in unspoiled villages where you become VIP guests in renovated upstairs rooms in traditional family homes. It's a novel approach to the homestay experience, where you needn't forgo basic luxuries such as a decent mattress or comforting linens—Shakti used Ladakhi craftsmen to upgrade parts of traditional family homes, resulting in slick-but-cozy spaces that are infinitely more suitable for travelers unaccustomed to the cold, harsh and basic conditions that are the norm for most Ladakhis. So instead of rough mats and a pile of blankets, you get a plump bed, chic duvets, and your very own wood-burning fireplace—chances are you'll have a wonderful view through lots of windows, too. Besides getting an inside look at traditional Ladakhi life (increasingly absent from Leh, which has become very much a tourist town jam-packed with guesthouses and hotels and little room left for authentic culture), Shakti relies on guides, chefs, and chauffeured vehicles to get you where you need to be—not to mention amazing treks, rafting experiences, and plenty of interaction in the villages and insights at the monasteries. A week-long package costs $6,092 for two people traveling together (this includes all transport within Ladakh, accommodation, all meals, drinks, personnel, and taxes; children pay approximately half).

If, on the other hand, you don't mind abstaining from many of your basic home comforts, you could always investigate an entirely authentic experience with **Himalayan Homestays** (www.himalayan-homestays.com). Rooms will be basic but clean, and have some lighting (either candle or solar-powered), and meals will be the genuine article, prepared hygienically using mostly local ingredients and served with the family. The organization now has 44 homestays in 11 villages around Leh region and a farther nine homestays in Zanskar. You'll pay just Rs 800 double with all meals (Rs 450 single) with meals. You can book through Maitreya Tours (DB2, Zangsti, Leh; ℃ **01982/25-0060,** -1466, 94-1917-6036, or 96-9738-7083; www.spiritualhimalaya.com).

the road but feel quite distant once you're here. The hotel offers neat, clean accommodations with basic furnishings and beds covered with clean white linens and block-printed Indian throws. And, from the lush, wild garden, superb views of Khardung-La and the Stok mountain range; jump into a hammock or one of the cane chairs scattered around the property and meditate on the beauty of it all.

Shenam Fort Rd., Leh 194 101. ℃ **01982/25-3518** or 94-1917-8468. www.poplar-ecoresrt.com. poplarecoresort@yahoo.co.uk. 20 units. Rs 2,310 double; Rs 921 extra bed. Rates include breakfast. No credit cards. **Amenities:** Dining hall, TV lounge; airport transfers (Rs 150); Wi-Fi (in lobby; free for e-mail checking); yoga (Aug–Sept). *In room:* No phone.

Shambha-La Hotel ★ Owned by Ladakh's former tourism minister, who lives here with his Tibetan wife, Shambha-La offers straightforward but dignified accommodations in a flat-roofed Ladakhi-style lodge with fluttering prayer flags and comfortable hammocks in the neat garden. Public areas—including a colorful Tibetan lounge area—are attractive, and the views from the upstairs terrace are mesmerizing. Standard guest rooms are far from lavish, but they're cozy and you get a warm bed, and the executive and penthouse rooms are actually quite smart. Power outages can be a serious problem this far from the town center, so have your hot shower early, just in case. A hotel jeep is on hand to drop you in town whenever you require a lift, and the helpful manager is a mine of useful information.

Skara, Leh 194 101. ✆ **01982/25-1100**, 2607, or -3500. Fax 01982/25-1100. www.hotelshambhala.com. ladakh@hotelshambhala.com. Reservations: A-10/5 Ground Floor, DLF Phase I, Gurgaon, Haryana. ✆ **0124/428-6665**, 98-103-5145, or 94-1917-7900. 26 units. Rs 3,000 deluxe double, Rs 4,000 executive double, Rs 5,200 penthouse; Rs 1,300 extra bed. Rates include breakfast; 10% service charge extra. AE, MC, V. **Amenities:** Restaurant, TV lounge; free airport transfers; billiards; small library. *In room:* TV, central heating.

WHERE TO DINE IN LEH

For the best Tibetan dishes in Leh, dinner at **The Tibetan Kitchen** is recommended; for the most relaxing meal, anytime of the day, don't miss the **Penguin Garden Restaurant** (both are reviewed below). In the Main Street Bazaar, you might be forgiven for not even noticing the reliable **Himalaya Café** (✆ **01982/25-0144**; Rs 45–Rs 150; no credit cards), where Tibetan and Chinese dishes are served in the Ladakhi version of a dimly lit bistro—one of the few eating establishments in Leh where you'll experience some sort of atmosphere. In the Main Street Bazaar, **Cafe Amdo** has brilliant *thupka*—the local staple, a soup noodle mixed with veggies, succulent meat, and a round of hot, delicious sauces that'll clear your sinuses. And **Dreamland** on Fort Road is another popular all-day restaurant with a varied menu, including Kashmiri dishes.

One of the coolest newcomers (and there have been many additions to Leh's fly-by-night restaurant scene) in Changspa, is **Jeevan Restaurant** and, above it, the rooftop **Café Jeevan**. The restaurant is swish and slightly more formal, while the canopied open-air place upstairs is a better bet during the day. The menu is predictably overladen with options—from Italian and Israeli to Indian and Chinese—and it's definitely not catering to locals, but it's a pleasant enough spot to unwind (they play fresh lounge tracks, have a library to browse, and offer laptops to surf the internet).

Penguin Garden Restaurant & German Bakery ★★ ECLECTIC/LIGHT FARE

For a spacious, outdoorsy cafe experience, head to this laid-back hangout—it's almost impossible to imagine the peace, quiet and twittering birds you'll discover in this garden oasis where nostalgic Western music plays from speakers that decorate the apple trees that form a natural canopy above. Aside from being the most relaxed place in town, it's a good place to try a few simple-but-special items. For starters, there's always a large chunk of yak cheese displayed alongside the chocolate walnut cake, doughnuts, and croissants—at lunchtime, a yak cheese sandwich really fills the gap; it's also the only place in town you'll find avocado *lassi*, or a made-to-order watermelon ginger juice (simply delicious). The menu covers mostly Tibetan, India and Italian dishes, but you can also get basic comfort foods like chicken burgers, quiches, and even vegetable stroganoff. Healthy breakfasts, salads, and tandoor-grilled trout are also served.

Fort Rd. ✆ **94-1917-8630** or 99-0699-9896. www.penguinrestaurant.co.nr. Main courses Rs 55–Rs 170. No credit cards. June–Sept daily 7am–10:30pm.

The Tibetan Kitchen ★★ (Value) TIBETAN   Tibetan fare is *de rigueur* in Leh, and after more than a decade, the town's best restaurant does not disappoint, even if the new venue is a bit characterless and they've added Indian and Chinese dishes to the otherwise authentic menu. Preorder (1 day ahead) the traditional Tibetan hot pot, or *gyako,* suitable for four hungry diners. A brass pot with a communal broth is heated at the table, while salads, *papads,* fine noodles, rice, and mutton (or vegetables) are served in abundance for you to cook at will. Note that the restaurant has only one pot, so be sure to book well ahead. If you'd prefer to have your food cooked for you by skilled Tibetan and Nepalese chefs, there's plenty more to choose from, starting with the steamed cheese *momos,* so order a plate while you consider the rest of your options. You can try wonton *pishi* soup, a traditional Tibetan salad (avocado, tomato, and mint), or delicious *shabalay* (a freshly baked meat- or vegetable-filled bun).

Opposite Hotel Tso-Kar, Fort Rd. ℭ **96-2296-9578.** Main courses Rs 80–Rs 230; Tibetan hot pot for 4 Rs 1,400–Rs 1,800. 10% service charge. No credit cards. Daily 11am–10:30pm.

SHOPPING IN LEH

Eternal Creation (first floor, Raku Complex, Fort Rd.; ℭ **96-2296-9570;** www.eternal creation.com) is a fair-trade boutique with colorful and beautiful garments for women, children, and babies. Designed in Australia, but with workshops in Dharamsala providing employment for 80 people (Tibetans, Nepalis and Indians), this is as close as it comes to dressing up for a good cause. Fabrics are generally bright and big-patterned, well suited to the summery dresses and gorgeous kimonos; the silk-bordered shawls and accessories are also great buys.

You could spend a whole lot of your time in Leh dodging overbearing Kashmiri salesmen hawking everything from carpets to gold jewelry. Occasionally their hard-sell tactics are enough to send you screaming into the mountains. Operating with a completely different set of ethics is **L'Araba Fenice** (Zangsti Rd.; ℭ **01982/25-4516** or 94-1921-9341) where the mild-mannered George Sher Ali (who also came here from Kashmir many years ago) sells a wide assortment of Rajasthani miniature paintings executed on silk and paper. Besides the usual subjects, he also commissions special Ladakh-influenced scenes and unusual designs that may include gorgeous white yaks or a snow leopard, painted from photographs by artists who have never stepped foot in the Himalayas. Look for the shop (one of the few in Leh without a merchant looming in the doorway) at the edge of the main bazaar and set aside some time to listen to George explaining the intricate process of miniature painting. For books, look no further than the well-stocked **Ladakh Book Shop** (Main Bazaar, near State Bank of India; ℭ **01982/25-6464** or 98-6811-1112) which carries trekking maps, books on spirituality, coffee table glossies, local guidebooks, and everything in between, including plenty of good Indian literature.

Do also make a point of dropping by the **Ladags Apricot Store** (LBA Shopping Complex, Zangsti; ℭ **01982/25-1222** or 94-1917-7529), an eco-friendly shop specializing in organic products grown by Ladakhi farmers. Dried apricots are a must, and they also sell apricot nut kernels (which are known to have cancer-fighting properties) as well as *yos,* a traditional Ladakhi snack food made with roasted barley—it's a perfect accompaniment on a long drive.

EXPLORING LADAKH

While exploration of Ladakh's Buddhist *gompas* are likely to consume a large part of your time here, bear in mind that the region has other wonders worth witnessing—not least, its matchless scenery. Unless you have a specific interest, don't feel compelled to see every monastery, or you'll likely reach saturation point before you've crossed them all off your list. And don't give in to the urge to race between the Buddhist sites—half the pleasure in visiting lies in taking time to chat with the monks, or share a cup of butter tea with villagers. And, often, simply witnessing the landscape around you will make your heart soar. Note that entrance to most of the gompas requires the purchase of a ticket; most cost Rs 20, while more famous ones, like Alchi, are Rs 50.

The Road to Lamayuru ★★★

There are enough Buddhist *gompas* within easy reach of Leh to keep enthusiasts busy for several days. North along the road to Srinagar are **Phyang Gompa** ★★ (16km/10 miles from Leh), and 15th-century **Spituk Gompa** ★★ (8km/5 miles from Leh), which sits atop a lone rocky hill, crazily poised above Leh's airport. If you've a craving to see more remote, extraordinary Buddhist settlements, and are prepared to spend some time on the road, though, it's worth undertaking the scintillating journey to Lamayuru. En route are three more of Ladakh's most alluring monastic sites, the most famous of which is Alchi (along the left bank of the Indus around 70km/43 miles northwest of Leh, a short way off the Srinagar-Leh Rd.). On the way to Alchi, stop at **Basgo** ★★, where a hillside citadel consists of several Buddhist temples attached to a ruined castle. A two-story-high golden statue of the future Buddha is housed in the Maitreya Temple, which has fantastic murals of fierce divinities that were the guardian deities of the royal family once resident here.

One of the oldest monasteries in the region, **Alchi** ★★★ (8am–1pm and 2–6pm) dates from the 11th century, and is unique for the influence of Kashmiri art versus the pure Tibetan styles prevalent in most other monasteries. Situated in a quiet hamlet with a handful of souvenir and snack stalls and an increasing number of guesthouses and a camping ground, Alchi is centered around its inactive five-temple *gompa* complex, administered by the Yellow-Hat Gelugpa monks of Likir Monastery 30km (19 miles) across the river. You'll need a flashlight to explore the temple interiors, which are covered with vibrant, colorful, detailed murals and wooden figures. A courtyard leads to the *dukhang*, or assembly hall, where the statue of Avalokiteshvara is believed to be of pure gold. In the temple *(Sumtsek)*, you can spend forever studying the trumpet-blowing angelic figures and trying to make sense of the tantric poses assumed by a host of elegant nudes. Sadly, Alchi's popularity, has started to detract somewhat from the experience here; the wonderful Vairocana Temple, for example, has become a sales outlet with cheap booklets and postcards for sale—somewhat off-putting when you're trying to understand the epic tales told in panels painted on the walls.

Likir ★★★, in fact, may not be as famous as Alchi, but to our minds makes a far more enjoyable visit (with far fewer tourists), and can be seen either on the way to Alchi, or on your return from Lamayuru. Said to occupy an area once inhabited by fairies (the name "Lu-khyil" means "circled by water spirits,") Likir was founded by a meditation master, Lama Duwag Chosje, after the 5th King of Ladakh gave him the land in 1065. The monks here are especially friendly and laid-back—try to spend some time chatting with them as they unlock the various temples and prayer rooms for you. The monastery also includes a small **museum** (Rs 20); among the unusual items is a 400-year-old bulletproof iron jacket (or *thaap*) displayed alongside a 900-year-old shield *(fak-fali)* and equally ancient quiver *(sakdhu)*, suggesting an incredible history of conflict in the region that's generally associated with peace.

If you decide to venture all the way into Zanskar (and, truly, you should), you will come across what is perhaps the most fantastical monastery of all. About 4 hours from

Leh, en route to Kargil, **Lamayuru ★★★** is not only interesting as a hub of spirituality but enjoys such a unique and unusual cliff-side setting that it's sometimes difficult to imagine that you haven't left the planet entirely. A monk will admit you to the prayer rooms; in the Du-khang, be sure to look for the gap in the wall that reveals part of the cave where the tantric master Naropa meditated in the 10th century. Below the monastery, the dusty village spills down the steep mountain, defying the onslaught of modernity. You can pick your way through the raggedy clusters of time-battered medieval houses and look up to find yourself peering directly into the underside of the temple's terraces. A peaceful, palpably remote settlement (now linked to the world by a brand-new tarmac road) where the arrival of a bus or truck is still greeted with some excitement, Lamayuru has a few small places to stay (the best of which is noted below), and we'd suggest you overnight here rather than rushing off to rejoin the crowds in Leh

Where to Stay

Capital of Ladakh during the 15th century, the village of Tingmosgang—80km (50 miles) west of Leh on the Likkir-Kheltsi trekking route—doesn't see too much action these days, but does have one of Ladakh's better village accommodation options. **Namra Hotel** (© **01982/22-9033** or 94-1917-8324; namrahotel@gmail.com) has clean and comfortable rooms with warm beds, attached bathrooms and hot water, and there are great Himalayan views; the hotel also has a traditional Ladakhi kitchen. It's off the well-trodden tourist path, but makes an excellent alternative base from which to explore Lamayuru, Alchi, Basgo, and Likkir—Tingmosgang Palace is a 15-minute walk from here, and you're within easy reach of Leh, too.

In Lamayuru, the best place to stay is the relatively new **Hotel Moonland** (© **94-1988-8508,** 01982/22-4551, or 01892/22-4576; Morup_moonland@rediffmail.com; open May 25–Sept). It's a pleasant family run affair with simple rooms (most with attached bathrooms and hot showers) in a cluster of small Ladakhi-style buildings arranged around a little vegetable garden a short distance from the main village, but within striking (and viewing) distance of the monastery. Ask for one of the new upstairs rooms (due to open in early 2010), which will have the best view. The owner, Morup Dorje, is a Lamayuru local and can make arrangements for treks out to nearby villages; he charges Rs 1,500 for a double room including all meals (around Rs 800 without food) which feature vegetables that his ancient, traditionally attired mother grows here.

Gompas & Palaces South of Leh ★★

Venturing south of Leh along the same road that goes all the way to Manali, you can take in a number of monasteries, and one or two Ladakhi palaces. Located across from Choglamsar on the opposite side of the Indus, **Stok Palace ★★** (Rs 25; May–Oct daily 8am–7pm) is the only inhabited palace in Ladakh, home to the 74th generation of the Namgyal dynasty. The land-holding rights of Stok were granted to the royal family by General Zorawar Singh in 1834 when he deposed Tshe-spal-Namgyal, the *Gyalpo* (king) of Ladakh. It's an imposing complex, with around 80 rooms, only a few of which are still used by the current widowed *Gyalmo* (queen), who is sometimes in residence with her immediate family. Several rooms are taken up by the modest museum housed in one section. Museum highlights include a vast *thangka* collection, weapons, jewels, and, of special note, the queen's *perak,* a turquoise-studded headdress. The ghostly Buddhist shrine is an experience not to be missed.

Fifteen kilometers (9 miles) from Leh, **Shey Palace and Monastery ★★** (May–Oct daily 8am–7pm) is worthwhile for the *gompa,* but the palace is little more than crumbling ruins. **Thikse Gompa** ★★★ (daily 6am–6pm) located 25km (16 miles) south of Leh, is a striking 12-story edifice with tapering walls that sits atop a craggy peak. From here you get magnificent views of the valley, strewn with whitewashed stupas. Note that 6am morning prayers at Thikse are worth rising early to witness (but it's quite popular with tourists so don't expect to see it alone).

Hidden from the world on a remote verdant hillock, **Hemis Gompa** ★★★ (45km/28 miles from Leh) is considered the wealthiest Ladakhi monastery, its atmospheric prayer and assembly halls rich with ancient relics and ritual symbols. During the summer season in June and July, the monastery comes alive for the annual **Hemis Tsechu,** a (now very commercial) festival commemorating Guru Padmasambhava's birth. Masked dancing by the lamas and ritual dramas are played out in the courtyard, and the locals sell Ladakhi handicrafts and jewelry; unfortunately, hordes of hawkers also trudge in from all over the country to push their wares, somewhat diminishing the visibility of local people. Every 12 years, a magnificent embroidered silk *thangka* (tantric wall hanging) is displayed to the public; the next such unveiling takes place in June 2016, when the Year of the Monkey comes around again. On your daylong trip into **Hemis National Park,** you may—with luck—come across brown bear, ibex, or (if the stars are truly aligned in your favor) the extremely elusive snow leopard. The popular Markha Valley trek also traverses this park.

The Nubra Valley ★★★

Today, a 5-hour jeep drive over the world's highest motorable pass, **Khardung-La** (5,514m/18,380 ft.), leads you to northern Ladakh's lush **Nubra Valley** ★★★, a fertile region with more incredible *gompas* and some of the most extraordinary mountain scenery in the Himalayas. For centuries, the journey into Nubra was part of the legendary Silk Route used by caravans of traders dealing in gold, silk, hashish, and carpets, carried between the Punjab and various regions within central Asia—the Route breathed its final gasp in the 1930s when communism in China and Partition in India put an end to the traditional silk trade. Deep within the breathtaking Karakoram mountain range, the twin-tiered valley combines terrific desert-scapes and fertile fields watered by the Siachen and Shayok rivers—sand dunes and oases lie side by side. Predictably, the valley is dotted with peaceful, pleasant, sparsely populated villages—while "bucolic," "idyllic," and countless other clichéd travel adjectives might describe these hamlets (like most of Ladakh's villages), there's a surprising lack of sentimentality, most probably because of the harsh conditions that manifest for most of the year. These are hardier people than most Westerners could imagine and meeting them in this little-explored landscape really adds to the sense of escape; set off on foot or rent a bike and take time to explore. Tourist literature (and out-of-the-loop travel agents) also punt the famed hot sulfur springs (at Panamik) and rides on double-humped camels as reasons to visit, but these are misguided attempts to spoil your vacation. Nubra's real pleasures are of the untouristy sort. Wander through its humble villages and hike into the looming, craggy mountains to discover shrines and fluttering prayer flags, and the sense of a being in a remote, forgotten world will take your breathe away. To visit, you need to arrange an Inner Line Permit in Leh (do it through any travel agent or through your hotel), and technically you must be traveling in a group of at least four people. Hire a jeep with driver (count on spending Rs 8,000 for 3 days, unless you share the vehicle with others), and set off early in the day. If you have more time and really want to get under the skin of this cut-off region, consider a multiday hike—Banjara offers an 11-day Nubra Valley trek with camping along the way (see "Staying Active," earlier in this chapter).

There are also two special monasteries worth highlighting here and the first is strikingly photogenic **Diskit Gompa** ★★★, now marked by a newly created gigantic golden Buddha posing on the hilltop nearest the road. Reached via a maze of stairways, Diskit is populated by some very friendly, charming monks, many of whom have studied extensively and are happy to share their knowledge and insights with interested visitors. In the **Protector's Room** you'll see some very severe stucco figures, most with their faces covered (these are revealed only during the festival held here in Oct), as well as myriad *thangkas* and tantric drawings—it's like stepping into a frozen moment in a Tibetan opera. At the front of the temple, a white-faced demon holds in his hands the skull and hand of a Mongolian warlord who came here some 350 years ago; ask the monk on duty to tell you the full story.

Along the other arm of the Valley, en route to Panamik, the **Samstanling Monastery** ★★ just above the pleasant village of Sumur may feel a little too modern and pagoda-like to strike you as an authentic stop, but the murals inside the assembly hall *(dukhang)* are exquisite, and the monastery has one very special surprise. This is where you can meet and receive a blessing from the recently discovered reincarnation of the great visionary lama Bakula Rinpoche. Barely 3½ years old in July 2009, the young boy spends much of his time placing lengths of sacred thread on those who come to visit him (a small donation is appreciated). His private nursery, where he is also receiving training for the many life tasks that lie ahead of him, is just below the monastery's parking area. It's an enchanting, if little understood, encounter with an auspicious, enlightened soul.

Where to Stay

The best places to stay are in and around Sumur en route to Panamik, near the Samstanling Monastery; here there are three comfortable options, including **Hotel Yarab Tso** (℄ **01980/22-3544** or 94-1934-2231; reservations in Leh: Mamosthong High Adventure Travels; ℄ **01982/25-2480** or 99-0698-6047; Rs 3,212 double, including all meals and service charge) just outside the village of Tegar (close to Sumur), along the Nubra River. It offers clean accommodations with attached Western bathrooms and a fairly lovely setting (rooms 105, 107, and 110 are best for views); the sitting room is particularly lovely, and feels just like a Ladakhi family lounge. In mid-2009, the owner was promising an imminent makeover of all the rooms (which have been feeling a bit run-down for some time now), so you can expect proper mattresses and fresh linens. Nearby, the newer (and somewhat more professional) option is **Hotel Rimo** (℄ **94-1934-0747;** hotelrimonubra@rediffmail.com) at the edge of Tegar village. It has more of a hotel feel to it and (besides being a very nasty-looking bit of construction), is unfortunately slap bang against the main road (which, of course, doesn't see too much traffic). Bedrooms have attached bathrooms and rather better mattresses than most places, not to mention proper linens. Bookings can be made through Rimo Expeditions (details above); ask for a corner unit (which has more windows and better views) and expect to pay Rs 2,900 for a double room with all meals (Rs 1,200 without food).

A good deal better than both of these, and with more than a glimmer of charm, would be to stay at **Silk Route Bamboo Cottages** ★, in a lush section of Sumur Village. They offer 14 cozy en suite cottages and five "Swiss" tents (a plush version of the basic canvas tent: spacious, carpeted, with good beds and bedding). A double room costs Rs 3,300 (plus 10% service charge) with all meals included (Rs 2,200 for just the room). Like most half-decent places in the Valley, it's geared up for tour groups, so best to secure your

(Moments) Rafting in Ladakh

Without doubt, Zanskar offers one of the most exhilarating and challenging white-water rafting journeys in India. Beginning on the Stod River in Zanskar—"the land of white copper"—the multiday river adventure descends through rapids of Class IV and V, passes incredibly desolate, scenic gorges and stupendous cliffs down the Zanskar River, and ends on the Indus, near Alchi Monastery. The adventure takes a minimum of 12 days round-trip from Leh and is best attempted as part of an organized expedition. **Aquaterra Adventures** (© **011/2921-2641** or -2760; www.treknraft.com) is possibly the best choice for discerning travelers looking to raft the Indus or Zanskar rivers, and the very professional **Mercury Himalayan Explorations** (www.himalayanadventure. com) does a number of all-inclusive trips that combine several days of rafting with sightseeing and general exploration. If you're looking for something less hairy, there are tamer options close to Leh: a half-day rafting trip from Nimoo to Alchi that's got some adrenaline packed in, a 3-hour gentle rafting trip from Hemis to Choglamsar where your guide does most of the paddling work with well-practiced efficiency, or a 4-hour trip from Phey to Nimoo that packs in a bit of both. Enquire about daily trips through **Rimo Expeditions** (www.rimoexpeditions.com) which also does 12-night trips down the Zanskar Gorge. For a slightly more gentle river-riding experience, upmarket **Shakti** (© **0124/456-3899;** www.shaktihimalaya.com) offers a 3-day rafting trip in the Nubra Valley, with nights spent in above-ordinary camp sites.

cottage in advance—they're bookable through The Mogol Hotel in Leh (© **99-9009-4107,** 94-1965-7333, or 99-9911-9435; www.hotelmogol.com; info@hotelmogol.com or hotelmogol@rediff.com).

Ladakh's Jewel-Like Lakes ★★★

East of Leh are two stunning high-altitude lakes that can be visited on a 2- to 3-day jeep safari. The only way to visit these lakes, close to the sensitive border with Tibet, is to book though an agent who can organize everything, including travel, guides, basic accommodations in tents or a village, and special permits. **Pangong Tso ★★** is a huge lake, a large chunk of which lies across the border in China (*Note:* There are practically no accommodations at the lake itself, so many prefer to return the same day—start, say by 5am for the 5- to 6-hr. one-way drive and return after a 3- to 4-hr. stay; back by late evening); farther south, surrounded by some of Ladakh's highest peaks, is **Tso Moriri ★★★** —"mountain lake"—where the colors of the water are as lovely as the birds you'll spot. On the shores of the lake, you'll often see herds of wild ass—or kiang—grazing, and cheeky-looking marmots (yellow furry creatures resembling beavers) perch upon the rocks. Nestled in a valley of nomads, the lake is a summer migration stop for bar-headed geese (or *nangpa*), not to mention the Khampa, among the original people of Ladakh. Korzok village, on the northern tip of Tso Moriri, is the only place that has basic accommodation, in tents and guesthouses.

Uttarakhand: Sacred Source of the Ganges

For devout Hindus, a trip into the Himalayan ranges of Uttarakhand—source of the sacred **Ganges**—is no mere journey, but a *yatra,* or spiritual pilgrimage. For the city-smothered traveler, it's balm for the soul, particularly the less commercial Kumaon region. This relatively untouched area sees far less tourist traffic than the more hyped neighboring Himachal Pradesh, yet is in many ways more accessible, with plenty of wonderful places to stay.

Comprising the territories of Garhwal (west) and Kumaon (east), tiny Uttarakhand was carved from Uttar Pradesh in 2000, when it was named Uttaranchal; 7 years later it adopted the name bestowed upon it in the ancient Hindu scriptures, the Puranas: Uttarakhand. Besides Hindu pilgrims and adventurous trekkers and river rafters, Garhwal attracts New Age

Westerners who flock to the ashrams of **Rishikesh** on the banks of the holy river Ganges, and to nearby **Ananda-in-the-Himalayas,** one of the top spa destinations in the world. For visitors looking for a gentle road trip, the picturesque lower-altitude **hill stations of the Kumaon** offer glorious views of snowcapped mountains and a chance to spot tigers in one of the country's best-known wildlife sanctuaries, **Corbett National Park,** which vies with Rajasthan's Ranthambore National Park in terms of accessibility (264km/164 miles from Delhi; 6–7 hr. by road or rail). With the addition of **Shakti's** fabulous village walks through Kumaon and stunning accommodation perched high on a tableland, Uttarakhand can now comfortably vie for attention along with other top Himalayan destinations in India.

1 GARHWAL

Sacred source of the Ganges, the western part of Uttarakhand is where Hindu devotees come on mountain *yatras* (pilgrimages) to Badrinath, Kedarnath, Gangotri, and Yamunotri. Westerners tend to head straight for **Rishikesh,** said to be the "birthplace" of yoga, and made famous by the Beatles, who visited what was then a peaceful village back in the 1960s. As a result, scores of garish concrete ashrams and temples line the banks of the Ganges here, drawing thousands of visitors seeking their own yogis and tantric enlightenment, as well as hippies and backpackers keen to contemplate life, the universe, and everything through an edifying cloud of hash smoke. Up in the hills, with staggering views of the vast Doon Valley and western Garhwal's Himalayan peaks, **Mussoorie** is the quintessential Raj-era hill station, but it gets crowded and detestable in summer (and on weekends), packed with honeymooning and vacationing domestic tourists who send the decibel level skyrocketing. In winter, however, much of its near-haunted charm returns.

ESSENTIALS

GETTING THERE & AWAY **By Air** Dehra Dun's **Jolly Grant Airport** is a 55-minute flight from Delhi; the most reliable airline flying into Jolly Grant is **Kingfisher Airlines** (© **1800-309-3030;** www.flykingfisher.com). From there, catch a taxi to either Mussoorie or Rishikesh, or have your hotel pick you up; transfer rates are included in reviews where possible.

By Train Mussoorie: **Dehra Dun** is the terminus of the Northern Railway, and is the jumping-off point for Mussoorie. For Rishikesh, **Haridwar** is the more convenient terminal, 30 minutes away by taxi; Haridwar itself is now worth staying in for a possible night or two—see box below.

There are several good connections between Delhi, the capital, and both Dehra Dun and Haridwar, including the **Dehra Dun Shatabdi** and the **Dehra Dun Janshatabdi** (Mon–Sat), which both stop at Haridwar. An overnight alternative is the **Mussoorie Express.**

Trekking Through the Land of the Gods

Below are some of the best treks in Uttarakhand. You should definitely engage the services of a guide for any of the routes, and bring clothes and footwear to withstand extreme weather conditions. Note that certain treks in Garhwal require a **permit;** your trekking company can arrange this as well as equipment should you require any. We have recommended trekking companies below; for more assistance, contact the local tourism office (see "Visitor Information," under Garhwal below).

Garhwal   From Uttarkashi, a short drive takes you to Kalyani, which is the starting point for one of Garhwal's most popular treks—to fabulous **Dodital ★**, a striking lake surrounded by fantastic alpine forests. A relatively easy trek lasting 3 days, the 23km (14-mile) route takes you through the Asi Ganga River valley.

Several treks of varying levels of difficulty start out from **Gangotri** (at an altitude of 3,000m/10,000 ft.), a small pilgrim town at the confluence of the Bhagirathi and Kedar Ganga rivers, in the shadow of Mount Sudarshan (6,500m/21,325 ft.), some 98km (60 miles) from Uttarkashi. One popular trek from Gangotri goes along **Kedar Ganga Valley,** to **Kedartal,** a gorgeous lake surrounded by mountain peaks. But arguably the most beautiful Garhwal trek is the 26km (16-mile) hike that takes you along a gradual ascent from Gangotri, along the Bhagirathi, to **Gaumukh ★**, which is where the river has its source in the Gangotri Glacier—here the water gushes out from a small amphitheater carved out of the 15- to 20m (50–65-ft.) ice walls. En route, you pass through scenic alpine forests near Chirbasa, following an ancient pilgrimage route; a panorama of snowcapped peaks accompanies you throughout. At night, you camp on the banks of the embryonic Ganges, known here as the **Bhagirathi.**

By Road   The drive from Delhi to Rishikesh (250km/155 miles) takes between 5 and 6 hours. Regular buses leave Delhi for Haridwar/Rishikesh. If you're at Corbett, the drive to Rishikesh takes around 4 hours. Mussoorie is 280km (173 miles) from Delhi, including a final 33km (20 miles) from Dehra Dun, along a steeply ascending series of troublesome hairpin bends; plenty of luxury buses ply the route (best bus option is Volvo; expect to pay around Rs 450).

VISITOR INFORMATION   In Mussoorie, the **Tourist Bureau** (✆ **0135/263-2682;** Mon–Sat 10am–5pm, closed second Sat of the month) is located near the ropeway, on the Mall. **Dehra Dun's** GMVN office is at 74/1 Rajpur Rd. (✆ **0135/274-8478,** -6817, or -9308). In Rishikesh, visit the **Garhwal Mandal Vikas Nigam (GMVN) Tourist Information Centre** (Railway Station, Haridwar; ✆ **01334/224-240** or 01334/228-686; www.gmvnl.com; same hours as above); you can contact the same office for rafting (Nov–May) and other adventure inquiries.

GETTING AROUND   Hire a car and driver for the duration of your visit, unless you plan on trekking. Note that in Mussoorie, the taxi union frowns upon outside taxis.

Beyond Gaumukh, you can cross the glacier to reach the high-altitude meadows of **Tapovan** ★★★ and **Nandanvan;** note that the route to Tapovan varies with the constant downward movement of the glacier. You can schedule the full trek to last anywhere between 6 and 9 days; longer if you wish to explore the meadows and glaciers at the foot of Hinduism's center of the universe, **Mount Meru.** Another short and fabulous option is the **Chopta/Tungnath** ★★★ hike which can be done in a relaxed 5 days, including travel time to/from Delhi. The high altitude meadows are breathtaking and with the quaint temple at Tungnath, a walk to the Chandrashila Pass and camping without any concrete around, this is a great option.

There are a number of reputable operators organizing treks in Garhwal but our number one choice is **Aquaterra Adventures India** ★★★ (((© 011/2921-2641 or -2760; www.treknraft.com), not least for their highly professional and reliable service. Other good options are **Himalayan Eco Adventure** ((© **01389/222-446** or -252; based in Joshimath) and **Garhwal Himalayan Explorations** ((© **0135/244-2267** or -2667; www.thegarhwalhimalayas.com; based in Rishikesh).

Kumaon   One of the best-known and simplest routes in the Kumaon is the **Pindari Glacier Trek** ★★, a fairly moderate trek that lasts up to 8 or 9 days and can easily be combined with a sojourn in or near Corbett National Park. A shorter trek takes you on a 20km (12-mile) climb through **Valley of Flowers National Park** ★★, high up in the Himalayas. Between June and September, hundreds of species of flowers—many of them rare alpine varieties—cover the valley floor, through which the Pushpawati River flows. We recommend Nainital's **Parbat Tours** ((© **05942/23-5656**) for organized treks in the Kumaon.

MUSSOORIE
278km (172 miles) NE of Delhi; 35km (22 miles) N of Dehra Dun; 67km (42 miles) NW of Rishikesh

Smaller than Shimla and some 450m (1,500 ft.) lower, this hill station enjoys a more spectacular setting but has rather gone to seed, its regal colonial mansions marred by peeling plaster and overgrown hedges. It was once a favorite summer refuge of the Raj, but these days the strutting sahibs and memsahibs have been replaced by hordes of visitors escaping Delhi's blistering summer heat (which is when Mussoorie is best avoided). Until recently, Mussoorie's historical ambience was also overwhelmed by unchecked urban development; the government has now intervened (a little late, it must be said).

Unlike Shimla, Mussoorie in its glory days was pleasantly free of administrators, with plenty of nocturnal cavorting between young men and the wives of the hardworking bureaucrats who had remained back in the plains—it is said that a bell was rung just before dawn at the famous **Savoy Hotel** (once host to royalty and the likes of Rudyard Kipling and Arthur Conan Doyle; now sadly closed and looking near collapse) to encourage impious lovers to get back to their own beds.

The town's lifeline is the **Mall,** a stretch of pedestrian road that links its two centers, Library Bazaar and Kulri Bazaar. During peak time, the mall is not only jam packed with domestic tourists out to have a good time come what may, even if that means pushing and shoving, but also (and quite irritatingly), cars amidst the crowds. Despite moving at a snail's pace, these drivers will honk incessantly, and no number of admonishing looks will bring respite. While beauty may be entirely lacking from walking the Mall, it is an amusing and interesting pastime to observe all shades and manner of tourists: grown men sporting cowboy hats and shooting air balloons, tattooed hipsters and scantily clad diva wannabes shivering in the name of vanity, and children pushing each other up steep inclines in prams. You can walk the entire length of the ridge, from the bandstand at the western end of the Mall to the old churches and cemeteries at the quieter end of Kulri. Above the town is **Gun Hill,** from where the British punctually fired their noonday guns. Today, visitors reach the summit by means of a ropeway; you could also walk up (1/2 hr.) or rent horses for a 15-minute ride from the central police station. Along Mussoorie's upper ridge, **Camel's Back Road** is another fine place for a stroll. Farther east of Kulri Bazaar is **Landour,** which is quieter and better-preserved than touristy Mussoorie, primarily because the rich and famous of near-by Delhi have their summer homes here. Even though there are no hotels in the area, it is lovely and worth walking through (1-hr. walk from the main Mall). You could start with **Lal Tibba,** where the lookout point provides sensational views of the Himalayas depending on the weather, as well as the litter that has sadly begun to make its way up the mountainside, with tourists happy to add colorful packets of chips to the otherwise gorgeous scene. Farther still is **Sisters' Bazaar,** a wooded area named for the nurses who attended to convalescing soldiers, and where you can explore an empty colonial mansion, said to be haunted. Speaking of which, the **Graveyard** with tombs dating back more than 200 years is a great atmospheric place to explore. You will probably find it padlocked but the caretaker lives inside—you just have to shout out and request him to open up in exchange for a small token of appreciation! Make sure to have him show you the ancient cypress planted by the Duke of Edinburgh in 1870 which has withstood storms, changes in power, dwindling soil, and numerous visitors whose stab at immortality has left their names etched in the yielding bark and rampaging tourists looking for bark to etch their names on. And when you're done with diving into the past, walk on to explore **Woodstock**—no this is not an Indian

---

White-Water Adventures

If you'd like to raft the Ganges or the border-hugging Kali River, either sign up for a 1-day experience or set aside several days for the adventure, allowing time for transfers and a variety of rapids, gorges, and the occasional shallow waterfall. **Aquaterra Adventures India** ★★★ (② 011/2921-2641 or -2760; www.trekn raft.com) ranks as one of India's top adventure outfits and is our pick for most activities in the region. Also worth checking out are **Outdoor Adventures India** ★★ (② 98-1018-4360 or 98-1051-3571; www.outdooradventuresindia.com); and **Mercury Himalayan Explorations** ★★ (② 011/2334-0033 or 2334-6209; www.himalayanadventure.com). All provide overnight eco-friendly camping on the Ganges River beach, reasonably good food and most important, professionally trained guides who are adept at negotiating rivers and organizing rescue in the unlikely event that something goes wrong.

Finds **An Office in the Clouds ★★★**

There are few places within the Mussoorie district which can still be said to retain their charm and one of them, believe it or not, happens to be what was once a workplace—**Everest House,** or the office of George Everest, the first surveyor-general of India after whom Mt. Everest is named. Thankfully, most tourists don't go there because it involves a fair amount of walking, but the trail is lovely, winding through sudden meadows, abandoned roads made for ferrying timber, Nepali hamlets and finally leading to an open tabletop with the outer shell of the office, the grandness of which one can imagine going by the arched gate. The only sound you hear is of the Tibetan flags fluttering incessantly in the chilly breeze. This has to be the most wonderfully located office in the world! (For directions, consult the tourism office next to the cable-car starting point.)

version of the festival but one of the earliest international schools which is popular even today with the diplomatic crowd.

Where to Stay & Dine

Set on the outskirts of town, **Claridges Nabha Residence ★** (© 0135/263-1426, -1427, or 011/2301-0211; fax 011/4133-5133; www.claridges-hotels.com; doubles from $250, breakfast and dinner included; ask about off-season discounts) is Mussoorie's best option, though not in the same class as its Delhi namesake. It is located on a serene and lovely estate (ca. 1845), once used by the Maharajah of Nabha for his summer escapades, and surrounded by cedar forest, where langur monkeys perform acrobatic feats watched by visitors lounging on the terrace—a welcome break from the buzz of Mussoorie. Accommodations are large and comfortable but fittings (particularly in bathrooms) looking a little tired; the best are room nos. 110 through 115, which enjoy attractive forest views (no. 114 is the biggest room). The hotel conducts courtesy pick-ups from the Mall (about 10 min. away) throughout the day. If this old charmer is full, or you'd rather be in the heart of town, consider **Park Plaza Sylverton** (www.parkplaza.com; from Rs 7,000 double), a good and very popular option with Delhites—located right on the Mall, it does offer some of the best Doon Valley views (ask for a room with one), but we prefer the more characterful stately mansion **Kasmanda Palace Hotel** (© 0135/263-2424 or -3949; www.welcomheritagehotels.com; doubles from Rs 4,000; you can negotiate a 20% discount on a double room in low season). The well-preserved former holiday palace of the Maharajah of Kasmanda, it's packed with antiques, animal skins, and hunting trophies, including an elephant's-foot piano stool. Ask for rooms with views of the Doon Valley, but be warned that you'll have to put up with stuffed animal heads mounted on the walls and a liberal use of gaudy floral fabrics; service can also be very laid-back. On the budget front, there are tons of choices, of which **Padmani Nivas** (Library, The Mall. © 0135/2631093; www.hotelpadmininivas.com; doubles from Rs 1,300) is arguably the best—almost next to the Mall, it screens off most of the chaos with its cocoon of greenery and has great views with one side overlooking the valley; food (vegetarian only) is also good.

Tips Soul Searching: Top Ashrams

Most genuine spiritual retreats shy from any kind of media attention, which while understandable means that it is hard for the newcomer to differentiate between the great masters and masters of fraud. All over India, and in Rishikesh particularly, ashrams have increasingly begun to cater to Western aspirations for spirituality, doling out a mere part of the magnificent ancient Indian concept of Yoga, namely, the physical exercises known as *yogasanas*. Combine these with deep-breathing techniques and meditation and you have a package ready to be delivered, but it's worth noting that this is far from completing a journey (and not considered as even necessary by the serious adherent) along the spiritual path. It can nevertheless become a useful stepping-stone for the first-timer. Rishikesh offers all manner of courses, schools, ashrams, and holy men—other than contributing to general bewilderment, some of these are highly suspect, and you should only sign up with an organization or person who comes personally recommended by someone you trust. Or choose from the following; while by no means comprehensive, these Rishikesh ashrams are safe, solid options.

The Divine Life Society (© 0135/243-0040; http://sivanandaonline.org) although the most "true" to the ideal following the great master Sivananda, sadly offers yoga courses only to men. Also for serious students (open to all genders), the **Yoga Niketan Ashram** (© 0135/243-0227; www.yoganiketan ashram.org) is an excellent place to learn, but demands serious commitment as it follows a rather strict disciplined schedule, with sessions as early as 4:30 in the morning. More relaxed but a tad commercial, the **Anand Prakash Yoga Ashram** (© 0135/244-2344; www.anandprakashashram.com), offers its share of courses to both learn and teach, while the **Parmarth Ashram** (© 0135/244-0088; www.parmarth.com), will woo you with its lovely *arti* in the evenings (attracting hordes of visiting tourists; see box) and courses that have obviously been fine-tuned to suit the average Westerner—the latter is the most expensive and, driven by serious marketing strategies, in many ways the most user-friendly. All options offer courses ranging from 2 weeks to several months and offer in-house staying arrangements with meals.

Note: The summer months (Apr–June) and October are extremely popular with domestic tourists, and hotels everywhere in the hills tend to cave under the strain of rampant business, and what would otherwise be a quiet environ can turn into a nightmare for those looking for a peaceful retreat.

RISHIKESH
238km (148 miles) NE of Delhi

The Beatles, who came here during the 1960s to visit Maharishi Mahesh Yogi (a visit that inspired much of *Sgt. Pepper*), put Rishikesh on the map, and today the town is full of ashrams and yoga schools catering to Westerners who want to fine-tune their spiritual tool kits. *Sadhus* (holy men) in red and saffron robes, hippies in tie-dyed cheesecloth, and

(Moments) **The Real Happy Clappies ★★★**

All the elements of a good, heady get-together conspire to make Rishikesh's evening **Ganga Aarti** a truly special, spiritually intoxicating experience. Arrive early at the *ghat* in front of Parmarth Niketan Ashram (leave your shoes at the counter first) and spend time watching the crowds flood in, while orange-robed boys from the ashram usher in VIPs. The whole service, at the edge of the river, is centered on a gigantic white statue of Shiva, who sits cross-legged and serene behind a central flame, around which the holy fire ceremony, or *yagna*, is performed. A concoction of herbs mixed with ghee (clarified butter) is offered to the fire, accompanied by the chanting of mantras (prayers), said to purify the area where *aarti* is being performed and to call up the holy vibrations. Try to get a seat as close as possible to the fire ceremony, preferably at a raised elevation so you can clearly watch the intricate rites as well as the crowds.

But things are only just getting started. At an appropriate moment, as the sun starts to set, the ashram's high guru, His Highness Pujya Swami Chidanand Saraswatiji, descends the broad steps leading down to river's edge; he arrives like some highly venerated celebrity (which he is), all flowing robes and long, shaggy hair on his head and face. He'll join in the rites around the fire, and then, taking his place at the microphone, launch into some of the most stirring singing you'll hear in India, performed with calm and grace. In a beautiful, sublime moment, shot through with an urgent spiritual charge, the crowd, whether sitting or standing, will spontaneously sway and clap in rhythm to the swami's crystal voice and gentle aura, the movement occasionally building to a passionate frenzy. You are very likely to lose yourself in a moment of bliss, and feel your heart soar as you offer thanks to the life-giving waters of the Ganges. After he has sung, Swami Chidanand philosophizes in Hindi for a while, the kindness in his voice more telling than the words themselves. And then, in a blink, he'll disappear up the steps and into the ashram, guarded by an entourage of supplicants. Be prepared to devote around 2 hours to the whole experience, and then pick up the CD, *Songs for the Soul* (Rs 325), featuring the very hymns that have just touched your heart.

14

backpackers with plenty of time (and plenty of First World credit) gather on the banks of the Ganga to talk about the evils of the West and the failure of capitalism. By day, it's a spiritual Disneyland, where the commercial excesses of packaged meditation hang heavily about the concrete ashrams, bedecked with gaudy statues of Vishnu and Shiva. The place to concentrate your time is around the Lakhsman Jhula area, where there are plenty of simple eateries and stores selling all kinds of devotional paraphernalia; books and CDs in particular are worth browsing for. To get to the far side of the Ganga, where the most interesting *ghats*, ashrams, and people are concentrated, you'll need to cross the suspension bridge on foot. Here you can undertake any and every sort of self-improvement course, from yoga and reiki to cooking and music. A visit here in time for the sunset **Ganga Aarti** on the *ghat* of the Parmarth Niketan Ashram is highly recommended (see

"The Real Happy Clappies," below)—to the accompaniment of hypnotic prayers and harmonious singing, Rishikesh undergoes a magical transformation, reminding all that this really is a spiritual retreat.

Where to Stay & Dine

In a town full of ashrams and *sadhus*, you might very well expect Rishikesh luxury to involve a bed of sharpened nails. Fortunately, you can indulge in the unadulterated luxury of one of the country's finest (indeed internationally renowned) spa resorts: **Ananda-in-the-Himalayas** (reviewed below), located just outside Rishikesh itself. But for the most unusual and truly lovely place to stay, don't miss **The Glasshouse on the Ganges** (reviewed below), which enjoys a remarkable location slap-bang on the edge of the great Ganga; if you book the right room, you can hear the waters roaring by from the comfort of your four-poster bed; in terms of value and location it gets our top recommendation but bear in mind it is about an hour from Rishikesh, and won't suit those looking for a hotel with action. Also well situated on the river, about 19km (12 miles) from Rishikesh is **Himalayan Hideaway ★** (© 011/2685-2602; www.hhindia.com), a lodge owned by the couple who run the Himalayan River Runners outfit (their riverside camp is 2km/1¼ miles away). Accommodations are in stone cottages set in a forest near the Ganges (an 8-min. walk); all have air-conditioning and decent bathrooms (shower only) done out in stone and tile. Select a river-view room (Rs 4,900 double), gorge on delicious meals, go rafting, or while away the hours watching the river; trips to Rishikesh for sightseeing and the evening Ganga Aarti are easily arranged. If you really want to be near the action (and the noise), the most acceptable choice is **Hotel The Great Ganga** (Muni-ki-Reti, Rishikesh 249 201; © 0135/244-2243; www.thegreatganga.com; doubles from Rs 2,790), which is fine if you just need a clean place to sleep and don't plan on hanging around during the day. Some of the rooms have little terraces that overlook the Ganges, but be aware that you'll be picking up a lot of traffic noise. Accommodations have marble floors, kitschy fabrics, and very firm mattresses, and the small tiled bathrooms have aging tubs. Do not even consider the suites, which are in a shabby apartment block next door.

Ananda-in-the-Himalayas ★★★ At this destination spa, voted one of the best in the world, high-class pampering is the order of the day. The resort's immaculate, palatial reception rooms are in the restored Viceregal Palace, while a short distance away is a characterless block, although with well-furnished and comfortable rooms, each with a balcony and a terrific view of the Rishikesh Valley. In between lie fabulously landscaped grounds and water features, several villas, each with a private pool, and the Wellness Center offering an overwhelming choice of relaxing, soothing, and restorative treatments provided by a lineup of excellent therapists from all over the world. From the moment you wake (to a steaming cup of honey, lemon, and ginger tea) until you retire to a bath (for which a candle is lit to heat fragrant essential oils) and bed (warmed by a hot-water bottle), you'll feel extremely nurtured. There are also talks on spirituality, treks, yoga sessions, and escorted excursions to Rishikesh for the evening Ganga Aarti.

The Palace Estate, Narendra Nagar, Tehri Garhwal 249 175. © **01378/22-7500.** Fax 01378/22-7550 or 01378/22-7555. www.anandaspa.com. 78 units. $345 deluxe palace-view double; $405 deluxe valley-view double; $550–$860 suite; $980 1-bedroom villa with pool; $1,375 2-bedroom with pool. AE, MC, V. **Amenities:** Restaurant; airport transfer (Rs 2,400; free w/spa packages, suites and villas); in-house doctor; 6-hole golf course; daily health and relaxation program; Internet (complimentary); jogging track; library; temperature controlled pool; room service; safaris; spa; squash court; trekking; white-water rafting. *In room:* A/C, TV, DVD player; hair dryer, minibar, pool (only in villas), Wi-Fi (complimentary).

Saying Goodbye to the Ganga at the Gateway to God

Not exactly the lesser-known neighbor, **Haridwar** (*Dwar* of *Hari*, or "Gateway to God") is even holier than Rishikesh—according to Hindu mythology, this is one of the four sacred sites where a drop of the nectar of immortality (*amrita*) accidentally fell (at a point referred to as Brahmakund) while being carried by the mythical bird Garuda (the other three sites are Nasik, Allahabad and Ujjain). This is also the point where the Ganga river leaves the hills to enter the plains. Most time-bound tourists give this sacred site a miss and while it is by no means a necessary stop, it does have a unique atmosphere, with literally hundreds of devotees gathering daily at *har-ki-pauri* for the evening *arti* (6:30pm). Unfortunately a tad commercial, you will be approached by seemingly innocent priests and touts who will first seat you comfortably and then ask for donations "if possible"—make your intentions to refuse clear beforehand. The ceremony isn't as elaborate as the one in Varanasi or as hypnotic as Rishikesh but it's interesting to observe the frenzied crowd, many of whom have traveled for days for this moment of devotion. That apart, the walk to *har-ki-pauri*, through narrow streets lined with all manner of fascinating shops (food like *rabri*—sweetened milk cooked for hours; copperware; traditional white and brown ceramic *martabans* or jars) and a trip to the many temples to see benignly smiling Gods dressed in loud gaudy colors can make for an interesting day or two. Thankfully, there is also now a fairly decent option to stay: **Haveli Hari Ganga** ★ (Pilibhit House, 2 Ramghat, Haridwar; ✆ **01334-265207;** www.leisurehotels.in; doubles from $100 with breakfast) is a traditional old mansion with airy courtyards, a private mini-*ghat* (steps leading into the river) and a temple with a morning and evening *arti*. Rooms are quirky—palace architecture broken by ill-fitting modern amenities, well-sprung mattresses on concrete platforms, original tiles, alcoves and niches; the best rooms have a terrace facing the river—delightful to watch seagulls pass by every few minutes while the Ganga glides past languidly.

The Glasshouse on the Ganges ★★ (Value) Spectacularly situated on the banks of the Ganges, 23km (14 miles) north of Rishikesh, this former garden retreat of the Maharajahs of Tehri Garhwal is thrillingly close to the sacred river; there's even a little "beach" where you can swim in the clean, refreshing waters. Accommodations are divided into two categories: the main block, fronted by a pillared veranda with relaxing planter's chairs, or in cottages in the lush gardens of hammock-strung trees and tropical plants (sadly the grounds have grown slightly shabby over the years). The best room (book well in advance!) is Gangeshwari (on the top floor of one of the cottages)—with fantastic views from the terrace, and a sunken tub built right into the rock; there's also a working fireplace. Alternatively, ask for Jamuna, where simple antique furnishings, a working fireplace, and soft white linen provide superb comfort. Of the cheaper (much smaller) rooms, ask for Gomti or the unit above it. Service standards are not the greatest. Also bear in mind that alcohol is not available.

23rd Milestone, Rishikesh-Badrinath Rd., Village and P.O. Gular-Dogi, Tehri-Garhwal District 249 303. ℘ **01378/26-9218.** Reservations: 13 Main Market, New Delhi 110 013. ℘ **011/2435-6145** or 011/4182-5001. Fax 011/2435-1112. www.neemranahotels.com. 15 units. Rs 3,000–Rs 6,000 standard and "grand" doubles and triples; Rs 4,000 triple suite; Rs 6,000 luxury triple suite; Rs 8,000 Gangeshwari suite. Rs 800 extra bed; taxes extra. AE, MC, V. **Amenities:** Restaurant; dining terrace; airport transfer (Rs 2,200, 2 days notice); doctor-on-call, Ayurvedic spa; yoga. *In room:* A/C, TV in some, no phone in some.

---

2 KUMAON

It's not hard to fathom why the British Raj claimed this eastern pocket of Himalayan India from Nepal in 1815. Free of the hustle and bustle of urban India and blessed with a gentle, laid-back quality, the Kumaon, studded with gorgeous lakes, not all of which are overcrowded with construction, is great for viewing breathtaking scenery, breathing in restorative oxygen-rich air, taking wonderful walks, and seeing decaying reminders of the British preoccupation with transforming remote villages into proper English towns. Prominent among these are **Nainital** and **Ranikhet.** Both are surrounded by pine forests and are good spots for taking a break; the latter is prettier and arguably the most evocative former British hill station in India. However, with the opening of Fisherman's Lodge at Bhimtal (30km/19 miles from Nainital), we recommend giving Nainital a miss altogether, and heading straight for this restorative retreat. Kumaon is great road-trip country: A good route is to spend a couple of nights at Fisherman's Lodge, possibly overnighting at Mukteshwar next, before setting off for Binsar or Almora—this is untouched Kumaon, with superb places to rest your head: other than the two stalwarts listed, there is the absolutely fabulous 360° at Leti, perhaps the most exclusive mountain resort in the country. Next, either head east to Ranikhet or return back south to Naukuchiatal (or Jilling) for your next stop, ending your journey at Corbett National Park. Wherever you overnight, the road journeys between these destinations are the real joy of the Kumaon; when you're this close to gorgeous Himalayan mountain ranges, you simply cannot escape breathtaking views.

ESSENTIALS

GETTING THERE & AROUND   There are many trains heading out of both Delhi and Lucknow towards Kathgodam, 35km (22 miles) from Nainital. The overnight Ranikhet Express leaves Old Delhi at 10:45pm and arrives at 6:05am. There are always taxis (from Rs 500) and share-taxis available (from Rs 50 a seat), or you can have your hotel pick you up from the station. There are also overnight private deluxe buses (pick the Volvo; departure 9.30pm with 7:30am arrival; Rs 700 return) from Delhi to Nainital. Ranikhet is an additional 60km (37 miles) from Nainital, or a 3½-hour journey from the Kathgodam railway station. Once you've found your bearings, hire a car (preferably a four-wheel-drive) and driver for the duration of your stay in Uttarakhand. You can expect to pay around Rs 14 per kilometer, plus an additional fee per day and a reasonable contribution (Rs 250) towards the driver's overnight expenses.

VISITOR INFORMATION   While in Delhi, you can visit the **KMVN Tourist Information Office** (103 Indraprakash Bldg., 21 Barakhamba Rd.; ℘ **011/4151-9366;** fax 011/2331-9835; www.kmvn.org). In Nainital, the KMVN is at Oak Park House (℘ **05942/23-6356).**

A ROAD TRIP THROUGH KUMAON

Your first stop, Nainital, is set around the ebony-emerald **Naini Tal (Lake)**—according to Hindu mythology, one of the eyes of Shiva's wife, Sati. **Naina Devi Temple** is said to be the precise spot where Sati's eye fell when her body parts were scattered throughout the country in a bid to stop Shiva's "dance of cosmic destruction," which began when he discovered that Sati had immolated herself, an act provoked by her father's incessant insults of Shiva. High above the town, at 2,235m (7,450 ft.), is the aptly named **Snow View**, a hilltop area from where you can see Nanda Devi, India's second-highest peak. Make use of the Aerial Express ropeway; round-trips (daily 10am–5pm) cost Rs 100. You can overnight here, but Nainital is as ghastly as most of Himachal's towns, so we recommend you choose between the smaller Bhimtal or the picturesque **Naukuchiatal (Nine-Cornered Lake)**—both are under 30km (19 miles) away from Nainital, and there are recommended places in Where to Stay below. According to local folklore, when you get to a point where you can see all nine corners of the lake, make a wish and it will come true. This is certainly the case if you're looking for picture-perfect serenity, solitude, and enchanting trails, filled with wildflowers. Even if you don't opt to overnight here, make time for a day trip and take a leisurely ride or a swim in the lake. Alternatively, head north from Nainital to remote and lovely **Mukteshwar** some 50km (30 miles) away.

On a ridge some 2,254m (7,513 ft.) above sea level, where you are surrounded by little more than dramatic views of the Himalayas, conifer forests, fruit orchards, and fresh, clean air, Mukteshwar enjoys one of the most charming settings in the Kumaon. At the edge of town, atop a cliff, is century-old **Mukteshwar Temple**, dedicated to Lord Shiva. On the same hill is an ashram administered by a hermit whose disciples come from around the world. Behind the temple, a rocky cliff juts out of the hillside at Chauthi Jaali; take an early morning walk here for stunning views.

Then set off for Binsar for the best view in motorable Kumaon. Here, in another of the region's most untouched areas, you can watch the sunrise over Nepal and the sun set on Garhwal. Time allowing, visit the **Jageshwar Temple** complex, and explore **Binsar Sanctuary** (Rs 100 per head, Rs 50 per car) for glimpses of Himalayan wildlife. Overnight at **Kalmatia Sangam,** in Almora (66km/41 miles from Nainital). Although there is little evidence that Almora, with its ramshackle display of concrete and tin, has a 500-year-old history, the town (34km/21 miles southwest of Binsar) does nevertheless attract westerners with its history of spiritual gurus and induction into the hippie circuit. The new or main town is avoidable but do walk through the old town where you will find interesting remnants of local architecture on both sides of a cobbled road; also look out for typical local products like copperware (**Anokhi Lal Hari Kishan,** Karkhana

---

Stinging Scarves

Hemp bags and shawls—once all the rage—are now passé; the new "in," manufactured by local Kumaonis, are stoles made from the stinging nettle. The plant is converted into fiber, and the resulting hand-woven stoles are stylish, soft, and ultra-luxurious; and no, they don't itch. Initiated by a women's cooperative, you can take a fascinating tour of the **Panchachuli** factory (Pataldevi Industrial Area; *℘* **05962/23-6817;** www.panchachuli.com) which also has a shop attached. Or, if time is of essence, then head for the outlet in Almora market (Mall road; *℘* **05962/23-0968;** from Rs 2,000).

> ## (Tips) Flower Power
>
> En route from Naukuchiatal to Bhowali, make sure you stop at **Fruitage,** which sells apple chutney, apricot halves, and a refreshing rhododendron squash. Some species of rhododendron are believed to have medicinal qualities that cool you down (ideal on a hot day). In addition, the plant's extracts (or honey produced from its nectar) are thought to alleviate cardiac problems, high blood pressure, and asthma. Connoisseurs of honey should also stop at the sleepy state-run **apiary** in Jeolikot, 17km (11 miles) from Nainital, famous for its pure wildflower honey. Sample unique, naturally occurring honey varieties like mustard, litchi, and eucalyptus.

Bazaar; (✆ **94-1131-7500**) and stinging nettle (see "Stinging Scarves" box). Alternatively, you could simply sign up for the wonderful 2- to 3-day village walks organized by Shakti (see where to stay below), ending at their gorgeous resort in Leti, after which Corbett would be the ideal end point.

If it is a choice between Nainital and Ranikhet (don't have to cross Nainital to get to Ranikhet) then head straight for Ranikhet—surrounded by slopes draped with forests of thick pine and deodar and impeccable views of Nanda Devi. It exudes the ambience of a haunted English Gothic township, forever waiting for a cloak of thick mist and the echoes of a long-lost era to descend.

Whether you arrive from Nainital (60km/37 miles away) or Binsar, you'll first encounter the typically Indian **Sadar Bazaar,** an unappealing town center that is entirely avoidable. Take the turnoff for the **Mall,** and head into the peaceful Cantonment area. Ranikhet is occupied by the army's Kumaon Regiment, which maintains a strict code that seems to have had a positive impact on the Sleepy Hollow serenity evident here. You'll encounter an abundance of flagstone colonial buildings topped by tin roofs, many used by the military and in fairly attractive condition, surrounded by hedges and greenery. **Lower Mall Road,** as you head farther south, is good for walks, with only ancient trees for company. Continue on, past 14th-century **Jhula Devi Temple,** and 10km (6¼ miles) south you'll come upon the state-run **Chaubatia Orchards,** a great place (though best avoided May–June) for a picnic (ask your hotel to pack one).

From here it's an easy drive to Corbett.

WHERE TO STAY & DINE

The Kumaon Hills are dotted with laid-back, atmospheric accommodations that offer guests either a laid-back but relatively luxurious guest house experience such as Fisherman's Lodge or the more intimate experience of a homestay: an opportunity to mingle with Indian families who live in the hills—a wonderful reprieve from overcrowded tourist hubs, and a chance to really help the local communities as well. Note, though, that because these are not hotels, hot water in the bathrooms often comes via a geyser, which must be switched on when required (or in buckets carried into your bathroom). Room service is limited, and food cannot be rustled up in minutes, on demand. Other than the options listed below, take a look at Himalayan Lodges (✆ **98-1170-4651;** www. himalayanlodges.com); the company has a good selection of comfortable homestay type properties throughout the region aimed at the more budget conscious traveler.

Out of season, a good place to stay in Nainital is the **Palace Belvedere** ★ (📞 05942/23-7434; www.welcomheritagehotels.com). Built in 1897, this former summer palace offers a casual historic ambience with personal, attentive service. Book a lake-facing room (from Rs 6,400 double), which has an enclosed porch-cum-study (no. 19 is particularly large) from where the view of the sun rising over Nainital Lake is simply exquisite; bathrooms also have views of the lake. Other than this, consider **The Naini Retreat** (📞 05942/23-5105 or -5108; www.leisurehotels.in). The gabled bluestone summer retreat of the Maharajah of Pilibhit, situated above Naini Lake, retains much of its charm. Standard ("deluxe") rooms are neat but a tad cramped (book nos. 304–311; doubles from $150), so it's best to reserve one of three "garden" units ($210), which share a common balcony, or opt for a lake-facing room ($230). Avoid staying there in the peak season when ghastly outdoor live music all but kills any illusion of being in a retreat. If you are on a budget a comfortable and interesting option is **Balrampur House** (📞 05942/23-6236 or -9902; www.balrampurhotels.com; doubles from Rs 3,166), once the summer home of the Maharaja of Balrampur and now a heritage hotel run by his descendant Jayendra Pratap Singh.

Nainital offers many accommodations, but a visit during peak season is likely to be accompanied by crowds, noise, and irritation. Duck the crowds by opting for one of the following fully reviewed options, or for one of two recommendations at Naukuchiatal: **Déjà-vu** (reservations through Corbett Trails, New Delhi; 📞 011/4282-8232; www.naukuchiatal.com; Rs 2,000 per person per night) is a small, cozy, two-bedroom stand-alone cottage overlooking the lake. It comes with cable TV, DVD and music system, as well as housekeeping attendants and a cook who will prepare meals on demand; you just need to pay for ingredients. Be prepared for frequent power cuts although there is a backup inverter. For more hotel-style amenities (albeit in a concrete and stone block with plenty of face-brick and mortar), **The Lake Resort** (📞 05942/24-7183 or -7184; www.lakeresort.in; from Rs 2,400 double) is a newer hotel whose sprawling grounds hug Naukuchiatal Lake. Every room has a view of the lake; ask for the pricier log hut with wooden floors and a bathtub for two. Room nos. 1, 5, and 12 have lounge areas and fine views, but bathrooms are small. But, should you opt to overnight at Bhimtal, Fisherman's Lodge is the perfect choice.

The Cottage (Value) This 100-year-old house set in a 3-hectare (8-acre) orchard has herringbone-patterned wood floors, ivy-covered stone walls, and a sloping red tiled roof—all of which give it a distinctly English appearance and old-world charm, offset by the carved Kumaoni door and window frames. Each room has a private patio with wonderful views of lush green mountains. The Middle Room (where floral drapes decorating the ceiling are a tad kitschy) is the best in the house; the Blue Room is great for more privacy and better views, but a little too blue. The bed heights in the various guest rooms have been thoughtfully adjusted to give guests the best possible views. Simple, tasty meals are served in the homey living room/dining area.

Jeolikot, District Nainital 263 002. 📞 **05942/22-4013.** Fax 05942/22-4182 www.thecottagejeolikot.com. 5 units (with en-suite showers). Rs 3,500 double. Rates include breakfast, dinner, tea, and coffee. No credit cards. **Amenities:** Dining room; railway transfer (Rs 500); badminton; doctor-on-call; room service for snacks; trekking. *In room:* Air cooler.

Emily Lodge ★ (Finds) This colonial-era bungalow is the nicest homestay in Nainital. Gracious hosts Siddharth Singh and his family have a homey cottage well away from the main mall, decorated in subdued floral drapes and country-home decor. Figures of elephants and birds stenciled on the walls give the place a lively ambience in spite of the hunting-lodge atmosphere created by the old teak wood furniture, deer horns, swords, and rifles adorning the walls. Warm and comfortable, the living room has an old fireplace that's lighted at mealtimes in cold weather; it's also where wholesome home-cooked meals are served. Rooms are clean and bathrooms spacious. Jim Corbett's house (Gurney House) is just a stone's throw away, and if you are lucky the caretaker might let you in.

Ayarpata Hill, near Sherwood College, Nainital 263 002. ℂ **05942/23-5857** or 99-1702-1129; http://emilylodgenainital.com. 4 units (with en-suite showers). Rs 2,000–Rs 2,800 double; extra bed Rs 400. Rates include breakfast, tea/coffee. No credit cards. **Amenities:** Dining hall; railway transfers (Rs 500); board games; bonfire on request; doctor-on-call.

Fishermen's Lodge ★★ (Kids) Rated as the best Specialty Lodging in Bhimtal by Tripadvisor and among the top 10 boutique destinations in India by local travel magazine Outlook Traveller, Fishermen's Lodge basks in the warm comfort that is generated by a place that feels like one's own home. Owners Bunty and Bindu have invested real effort into creating a tasteful, relaxing lodge, and impeccably trained staff. Rooms are spacious with wonderfully simple, classy interiors; the piece de resistance is the common deck overlooking the lake—having sundowners here to the accompaniment of a fabulous repertoire of nostalgic music tunes is a highlight (guests are allowed to carry their own alcohol as there is no liquor license at the Lodge). All the activities—hikes, angling, cycling—allow you to rake up an appetite for the delicious meals served by the affable Suman who will be happy to send you off with some of his culinary secrets.

Mandir Marg, Bhimtal 263 136. ℂ **0594/224-7052** or 94-1110-7852; www.thefishermenslodge.com. Reservations: ℂ **99-1016-2244.** 12 units. Rs 8,000 double; Rs 6,000 single; additional bed (above 12 years old) Rs 2,000. Rates include breakfast, high tea and dinner. AE, MC, V. **Amenities:** Dining hall; railway transfers (Rs 500); angling; cycling; doctor-on-call; hiking. *In room:* Fan, fridge, heater, Wi-Fi (complimentary).

Jilling Estate ★ For a real outback experience in a magnificent setting, just 17km (11 miles) from Nainital, Jilling Estate is your best choice—though not for the faint-hearted or unfit. Access to this huge estate, where arch-conservationist Steve Lall, his wife, Parvati, and daughter Nandini live a couple of miles from the nearest drivable road, is only by foot or horseback; and you'll have to lug yourself up this distance just to get through the front door. All four cottages are completely private—you won't run into your neighbors even by chance. Facilities are rustic but extremely quaint; each room has an eclectic collection of books, and hot water for your bucket bath is heated on wooden fires by an attendant assigned to your room. Evenings are spent around a bonfire with the Lalls and their friendly mutts. Steve may even encourage you to go for a completely private hike in the woods of his estate, in the buff. Or let Parvati teach you how to milk cows.

P.O. Padampuri, District Nainital 263 136. ℂ **97-5875-5704.** Reservations: Neelam Rai Singh, Beckon Tours Pvt. Ltd., G22 1st floor, Lajpat Nagar Part 1, New Delhi 110 024. ℂ **011/2981-3546** or -1796. Fax 011/2981-4259. www.jilling.net. 4 units (bucket showers only). $90 double. Rate includes all meals; taxes extra. No credit cards. **Amenities:** Campfire; camping; picnic baskets; room service; table tennis; trekking.

Mountain Quail Camp & Tented Lodge ★ The drive to this out-of-the-way mountainside resort provides jaw-dropping views back down over the town and lake, as well as intoxicating vistas of the Himalayan range—particularly gorgeous just after sunrise, when a striking color palette whips over mountain peaks. The hill-hugging half-hour journey brings you to a remote, exquisitely peaceful site with deluxe tents and a lodge in a clearing between forested hills and terraced farmland. Opt for the tented accommodations, half of which have attached bathrooms with basin, shower (with hot water), and Western toilet. The resort is ideal for scenic walks, bird-watching, and easy treks, and even more perfect for doing nothing. Be warned that this is a popular place for groups (notably youngsters) engaged in outdoor team-building events; you might want to check that you're not sharing the place with noisy, city-slicking teenagers.

Pangot 263 001. © **94-1267-9723.** Fax 05942/23-5493. Reservations: Blaze a Trail Adventures. © **98-3707-7537.** www.blazeatrailadventures.com. 10 tents, 3 lodge units (with showers). $90 tent double; $120 lodge double. Rates include all meals. No credit cards. **Amenities:** Restaurant; railway transfers (Rs 1,200); mountain biking; doctor-on-call; fishing; horse safaris; jeep safaris; river rafting; rock climbing; trekking.

Mountain Trail

This is the best place to overnight if you want to stay in Mukteshwar itself. Mountain Trail is well-maintained and is on a terraced slope with a lovely rose garden and direct views of the Himalayas. Accommodations are large, neat, and simple. Ask for a deluxe double room; each has high-pitched ceilings, enclosed porch with exquisite views, large tiled shower, and fridge. All rooms are comfortable and spotless, and the pleasant restaurant has a working fireplace. There's no bar or room service, but most other facilities are available, and there's a game room with table tennis and a small library. The resort also runs a *chocolaterie*, where delicious center-filled chocolates are made with ingredients imported from Belgium.

P.O. Sargakhet, Mukteshwar 263 132. © **05942/28-6040** or -6240. www.mountaintrail.com. Reservations: Mountain Trail Holidays, 224 Vardhaman Plaza, 9 Local Shopping Centre, I.P. Extension, Delhi 110 092. © **011/2272-0675** or -0677. 12 units (with showers). Rs 3,000 double; Rs 4,500 4-bed family room. During high season (May–June) full-board packages only, from Rs 3,500 double. AE, MC, V. **Amenities:** Restaurant; railway transfers (Rs 800); adventure activities; doctor-on-call; game room; library; river rafting; room service; TV lounge; yoga and meditation in summer.

The Ramgarh Bungalows ★★

For a restful, soul-calming sojourn in atmospheric colonial accommodations that aren't quite hotels and are definitely not homestays, Neemrana's Ramgarh Bungalows is hard to match. Featuring deep verandas, bay windows, fireplaces, and dainty gardens bordered by chestnut trees. The Writers' Bungalow was built in 1860, while the Old Bungalow dates from 1830; both have been given a bright, homey atmosphere with floral fabrics. Two additional bungalows, the Vista Bungalow and the Rose Cottage, were added more recently, all dressed in the same 19th-century English ambience; the Rose Cottage is perfect if you desire exclusivity and privacy: It comprises one luxury suite with a sleeping room for one couple and three children, and has a great private terrace. Many of the various and varied rooms and suites sleep three or four, making them ideal for families. Ramgarh is 24km (15 miles) from Mukteshwar; because of the remote location you must make travel arrangements and reservations in advance.

Ramgarh (Malla), Kumaon Hills, Nainital District 263 137. © **05942/28-1156** or -1137. Reservations: Neemrana Hotels Pvt. Ltd., A-58 Nizamuddin E., New Delhi 110 013. © **011/2461-6145,** -8962, or -5214. Fax 011/2462-1112. www.neemranahotels.com. 11 units (with showers). Rs 1,500–Rs 4,500 Old Bungalow; Rs 3,750–Rs 5,000 Writers' Bungalow; Rs 2,400–Rs 3,500 Vista Bungalow; Rs 4,750–Rs 6,000 Rose Cottage; Rs 3,000–Rs 6,000 Ashok Vatika. Rates vary according to season. Taxes extra. AE, MC, V accepted at main office. **Amenities:** Restaurant; airport transfer (Rs 2,500 from Pantnagar); doctor-on-call; Internet (Rs 100/hr); river rafting; trekking; yoga.

Sitla Estate ★ Kids

This is a wonderful place to unwind, spot rare birds, and explore the Kumaon forests. Facilities are a bit rustic but the stunning views of Himalayan peaks from your window more than make up for it. Deluxe rooms are lovely, with bay windows that allow you to sip tea and enjoy the sunrise from your bed. Vikram Maira, the genial owner-host, can suggest the best trails to take through dense forests, but just walking around the 16 hectares (39 acres) of orchards and organic gardens is a cleansing experience. Since Vikram is the head chef, spontaneous local counselor, and organizer of treks, river rafting, and jeep safaris, make sure you plan your next day with him the night before. And yes, he does cook up lip-smacking meals—his mulberry crumble is legendary. With farm animals and ponies around, there's plenty to keep kids occupied.

P.O. Mukteshwar, District Nainital 263 138. ℂ 05942/28-6330 or -6030. www.sitlaestate.net. 7 units (with showers). Rs 4,000 regular double; Rs 4,700 deluxe double; Rs 5,500 suite. Rates include all meals, tea, and coffee. Taxes extra. No credit cards. **Amenities:** Dining hall; railway transfers (Rs 900 to/from Kathgodam); adventure activities/rafting; doctor-on-call; picnic lunch. *In room:* Sawdust heater.

Binsar & Almora Surrounds

Best option near Almora is the wonderful Kalmatia Sangam (reviewed below), on the road to Kasardevi Temple. Nature lovers on a strict budget might want to look at the **Forest Resthouse.** Located high on the hill within Binsar Wildlife Sanctuary, it's characterized by long, musty rooms, high ceilings, old-fashioned furnishings, a lack of electricity, and reasonable room rates (Rs 1,400/night). The rest house is looked after by a *chowkidar* (caretaker), who may even prepare meals for you if you bring your own supplies. Book a room through the DFO, **Almora Forest Office** (ℂ **05947/25-1489;** http://almora.nic.in). Also near Almora, within a forest, the **Deodars** (Papparsalle; ℂ **05962/23-3025;** rwheeler@rediffmail.com) is a family run lodging offering one of the best budget options, with just three guest rooms in an old stone cottage; solitude is guaranteed for just Rs 4,000 double, including all meals. Guest rooms have fireplaces, and one unit has a bathtub.

Our top pick for the region is however the unbeatable **360° at Leti** (reviewed below), which although still a good deal farther than Almora (5 hr. by road), is an absolute must—but it doesn't come cheap.

Kalmatia Sangam ★★   You won't find fancy amenities in any of the resort's nine cottage rooms, but each oozes charm and most feature lovely views. Eagle's Nest is the largest of the rooms, with the best mountain views and overlooking the brightly lit valley at night. (Note the two "category 3" cottages are rather inconveniently located and come with no views.) Food is good and wholesome; alcohol is not available but you're free to bring your own. Though you can wander around on your own, owners Geeta and Dieter Reeb also conduct fascinating guided walks—including a great village walk, which allows guests to observe the local architecture and interact with locals. Everything about Kalmatia is geared toward de-stressing, so if walking isn't your thing, get yourself a glass of rhododendron squash and retire to the library, or book a treatment with the resident reflexologist. For the higher price (compared with other Kumaon properties), you are assured utmost privacy, personalized attention, and serenity.

Kalimat Estate, Post Bag 002, Almora 263 601. ℂ/fax 05962/23-1572. www.kalmatia-sangam.com. Reservations: Kalmatia Sangam Travels Pvt. Ltd., c/o Triage Overseas, Mr. Basu or Mr. Khanduri, B-11, Gulmohar Park, New Delhi 110 049. 9 units. Rs 6,900 category 3 double; Rs 9,300 category 2 double; Rs 11,000 category 1 double. Rs 3,200 extra bed. These rates include breakfast; all-meal inclusive packages available. MC, V. Full advance payment required for reservation confirmation. **Amenities:** Restaurant; railway transfer (Rs 2,250); aromatherapy; Ayurvedic diet advice; bonfire; doctor-on-call; library; picnic lunches; reflexology; room service; guided walks; yoga. *In room:* Fan, wood-burning stove.

360° at Leti ★★★   A heady mix of local culture, pure Himalayan air and plenty of exercise, not to mention added incentives like eco-conscious and sustainable tourism (which got them the Highly Commended tag by Virgin Holidays Responsible Tourism Awards), make the Shakti Tours offering in Kumaon one of a kind. Walks start from Almora, with three villages on offer. Accompanied by an English-speaking escort, guide and porter (inducted from local villages), you wind your way through hamlets, terraced fields and forests, leading eventually to a spruced-up village house, comfortable but not robbed of its traditional feel. The walks are a prelude to a 3-hour trudge (those with vertigo will need support and preferably horse blinkers!) which leads to 360°—where what greets you is quiet, tasteful simplicity, understated luxury, and views, views, views! Four stone cottages built with Burmese teak and double-paned glass overlook strategic points of the deep plunging valleys and the distant glaciers. Rooms come with wood-burning stoves, Pashmina shawls made by local women, "snoozer" mattresses, superbly located desks, which will compel you to write your first novel, and porches with a pit for a fire, ideal for evening drinks or even dinner under the stars. But for all good things, there is a heavy price to pay, which ensures the exclusivity that this little mountain-top paradise offers.

Shakti Uttaranchal Tours Pvt Ltd, Near Kalimath Estate, Kasardevi, Almora 263601. (⌀ 124/456-3899. www.shaktihimalaya.com. Reservations (no walk-ins allowed): Shakti Uttaranchal Tours Pvt Ltd, 903-904, Vatika City Point, Sector 25, MG Road, Gurgaon 122002; info@shaktihimalaya.com. Village Walks: $1,034 per person for 3 nights. 360° Leti (4 units): $1,755 per person for a minimum 3-night stay. Discounts available for children under 16 and groups of 4-6. Rates for both include private guides, porterage, meals/drinks, room, hiking, laundry, tips. For Village Walks, transfers to/from railway station included. For 360° Leti, transfers from Almora region included. **Amenities:** Dining, bar, bonfire; library; picnic lunches; guided walks; yoga and meditation by prior arrangement. In room: Wood-burning stove.

Ranikhet

This area hasn't really taken off like the rest of Kumaon in terms of accommodation standards—for luxury you'll need to head to Nainital or Rishikesh, but lodgings are by and large adequate in a simple sort of way. An attractive alternative to the hotel reviewed below is **Chevron Rosemount** ((⌀ 05966/22-1391; www.chevronhotels.com), a century-old, two-story colonial bungalow in a forest clearing that's showing its age but in a charmingly dilapidated way. In particular, reserve room no. 202, the Nirvana Suite ★ (Rs 5,000): Unwind on the armchairs, chaise longue, or large comfortable bed; the large bathroom has plenty of natural light. There's tremendous scope for birders in the ravines surrounding the property, and on a clear day you can see the lovely Trisuli range. Another option worth considering is **Holm Farm,** the first bungalow in Ranikhet, with suites from Rs 4,000, and even cheaper Swiss huts. This is ideal for those looking for relaxed, old-world atmosphere—though when the place is full, you'll find tents pitched outside for guests ((⌀ 05966/22-0891 or 97-5939-5520; www.holmfarmranikhet.com); there are also indoor and outdoor activities for children.

West View Hotel ★   This stone brick colonial mansion—an atmospheric relic of the Raj set in a lovely garden is the most comfortable option in Ranikhet, offering spacious accommodations with carpeted bedrooms, old dark wooden furniture, upholstered arm-chairs, hard mattresses on big beds, and massive bathrooms with drench showers and natural light. Deluxe guest rooms have working stone fireplaces, half-canopied two-poster beds, and floral blinds and bed frills. Ask for the best room in the house, no. 21, not least for the view. Suites feature four-poster beds and separate lounges—great if you're traveling with kids but deluxe category is spacious enough. The public lounge is quaint and old-fashioned; the homey dining room with log fire has wallpapered walls decorated with blue-patterned porcelain plates. Note that hot water is only available mornings and evenings. The outdoor cafe is a pleasant spot at which to relax after traipsing around the hills nearby.

Mall Rd., Ranikhet 263 645. 𝒞 **05966/22-0261** or -1075. Fax 05966/22-0396. www.westviewhotel.com. westviewhotel@gmail.com. Reservations: 115, Pushpanjali, New Delhi 110 092. 𝒞 **011/2237-3389.** Fax 011/2237-2996. 18 units (with showers). Rs 3,111 deluxe double; Rs 4,500 luxury suite; Rs 5,111 family suite. Children 5–12 pay 25%. Rates include breakfast and dinner. Taxes extra. Check for off-season discounts. No credit cards. **Amenities:** Restaurant, coffee shop; railway transfer (Rs 1,200); badminton; doctor-on-call; rock climbing; room service table tennis. *In room:* TV.

3 CORBETT NATIONAL PARK ★★★

264km (164 miles) NE of Delhi; 436km (270 miles) NW of Lucknow

Covering 1,319 sq. km (509 sq. miles), Corbett became India's first national park on August 8, 1936, when it was declared a reserve; 37 years later Project Tiger, a government undertaking aimed at saving India's dwindling tiger population, was launched here in 1973. Today the biggest draw of the park remains the possibility of spotting a tiger in the wild but despite the fact that 140 or so tigers reside here, sightings are not to be taken for granted, and your chances of an encounter are far better at Ranthambore (Rajasthan) and Bandavgarh (Madhya Pradesh). The advantage of Corbett, however, is that you can overnight in the park, and it's a relatively affordable option. It's also the closest and easiest park to get to from Delhi. Staying here also means you place less pressure on those increasingly popular parks (if you equate a real vacation with the most luxurious safari lodgings, you'll be far better off at either the much lauded Aman or Oberoi properties adjoining Ranthambore, or the gorgeous Taj safari lodges near Bandavgarh).

Corbett National Park's landscape consists of *Sal* forests and bamboo trees, with an abundance of other wildlife, including leopards, wild elephants, boars, black bears, sambar, four-horned antelope *(chausingha),* monkeys, and, among the reptile population, pythons and the endangered gharial crocodile. Corbett's many water bodies are a birder's delight, with more than 400 species recorded. Inside the park, you can hole up in a

The Hunter-Turned-Conservationist

Born in Nainital, Jim Corbett was a reformed hunter who, like so many of the world's conservationists, spent his formative years hunting large animals for pleasure, killing his first leopard at the age of 8. During the 1920s, he gave up killing as a hobby but regularly shot man-eating tigers or cats believed to be threats to humans, but with an increasing sense of loss. (To get yourself in the mood for a visit to the park he helped create, pick up a collection of Corbett's fearsome hunting tales or a copy of his first book, *Man-Eaters of the Kumaon,* which recounts how he hunted and killed the Champawat tigress that was responsible for the death of 434 people.) When the reformed hunter finally passed away in Kenya in 1955, the park he helped establish was renamed in his honor.

Sightings from the Saddle

Saddle up for a 3-day (or 6-day) horse safari in the reserve forest bordering Corbett National Park. **Corbett Horse Safari** takes you out on thoroughbred horses retired from Mumbai's racetracks across the Kosi River, up and down ridges and mountains, through thick forests of *sal* and elephant and tiger country to Kaladungi, where Jim Corbett lived. Trips are professionally led, and horses have accompanying *syces* (stable-hands). Riders overnight in spartan 19th-century forest rest houses (or tents) along the way. The whole experience is a step back in time. Call ℂ **98-1110-9596** or 98-7187-8671; or go to www.corbettriverside.com. Customized trips with accommodation and all meals cost approximately Rs 6,000 per person, per day. Or saddle up for 3 hours for Rs 500.

watchtower near a waterhole for hours. Areas outside the park, especially along the Kosi River, are almost as good.

VISITING THE PARK

Corbett is open from November 15 through June 15, much of it closed when the monsoon causes rivers to flood their banks. Sightings are best between March and June. Access to the park is via the town of Ramnagar, where the **Park Office** (opposite the Ramnagar bus stand; ℂ **97-1925-1997;** www.jimcorbettnationalpark.com; Dec–May daily 8:15am–noon and 1–4pm, June–Nov daily 10am–noon and 1–5pm) processes and issues the required permits, and handles all park-managed accommodations as well as jeep safaris. There are direct trains from Delhi to Ramnagar; driving takes 6 to 8 hours (about 300km/186 miles).

Corbett is divided into four mutually exclusive tourist zones, and you can visit only one zone at a time. If you do not have your own vehicle, hire one in Ramnagar or at Dhangari Gate for around Rs 700 to Rs 900 (jeep and fuel). It's best to undertake jeep safaris early in the morning; each zone has a separate fee: for half-day excursions entry/vehicle/guide fee for **Bijrani** and **Dhikala** is Rs 200/100/250, **Jhirna** is Rs 100/75/250, and **Durga Devi** is Rs 100/75/250; full-day fees are double throughout. You also have the option to go for a 6-hour safari in the government-run 18-seater minibus (Rs 1,200). The park is open daily 7am to 5pm in winter, and 6am to 6pm when the days are longer. You are not permitted to enter the park less than 30 minutes before the sun descends, and nighttime driving within Corbett is not allowed. Don't make the mistake of arriving in Ramnagar too late in the day; you will have to fill out forms, pay for permits and accommodations, and still get to the gate 30 minutes before sunset. Corbett is extremely popular and likely to be fully booked, so don't arrive unprepared.

Perhaps the most visually attractive area of the park is **Jhirna,** which is the only section that does not close during the monsoon season (June 15–Nov 15). Try to visit **Ramganga Reservoir,** where endangered gharial crocodiles bask on the banks and a sign warning against swimming proclaims that SURVIVORS WILL BE PROSECUTED. Surrounded by vast elephant grassland savannas, **Dhikala** has the greatest selection of accommodations, and substitutes solitude for access to facilities like restaurants and even film screenings. Dhikala is reached via **Dhangarhi Gate** (16km/10 miles north of Ramnagar), and is only accessible to visitors with accommodations reserved inside this zone; entry to Dhikala costs Rs 450 per person for 3 nights, plus Rs 150 for a car or Jeep and Rs 250 for the guide (4 hr.).

Tip: If you want to plan a flexible itinerary, you'll need your own vehicle from Delhi or you can hire a vehicle (preferably a jeep) with driver once you arrive; otherwise all accommodations will arrange pickups from Ramnagar Station. If you don't plan on staying in the park, it's far easier (particularly if you're staying at one of the resorts below) to have your hotel management make all your safari arrangements; the bureaucracy and form-filling that go along with acquiring the necessary permits can be exasperating.

WHERE TO STAY & DINE
Inside the Park

Although overnighting at one of the official park lodges has many advantages (particularly for your budget), comfort and service are not among them, and you're best off at Hideaway Lodge (reviewed below). The popular and often crowded **Dikhala** camp is one of the few places (others are Gairal and Bijrani) where you can get food in the park; it has two vegetarian restaurants (non-vegetarian food and alcohol are forbidden in the park and at park lodges, with the exception of Hideaway River Lodge). Dikhala's accommodations include cabins and three-bed "hutments" with attached bathrooms, and dorms that sleep 12 and are serviced by a separate washroom. **Forest bungalows (rest houses)** are scattered throughout the reserve and are best booked at least 1 month in advance; they offer seclusion and complete privacy, but—as with all of the rest houses outside Dikhala—you'll have to bring your own supplies. (Don't leave food lying around—there are reports of elephants ripping out the screen windows of forest rest houses to get to the provisions inside.) One of the best bungalows is at **Gairal,** near the Ramganga River and close to a hide bank. **Kandha Resthouse** is set on the highest point within the park. If you're up for a little more style, ask about **lodges** once used by British hunters; these have such unexpected luxuries as attached bathrooms, fireplaces, and carpets. For reservations at any of these camps, contact the Director, Corbett Reserve Reception Centre, Ramnagar 244 715 (© **05947/25-1489;** fax 05947/25-1376; www.corbettnationalpark.in). At Dhikala, rates range from Rs 200 per person for a log-hut dorm to Rs 1,400 for a room in a cabin, and up to Rs 2,000 or Rs 2,800 for a room in a more private forest bungalow. Rooms in various other rest houses throughout the park cost between Rs 800 and Rs 2,800. Credit cards are not accepted.

Outside the Park

Nature lovers who don't necessarily require top-notch hotel amenities will love the rustic but terrific **Camp Forktail Creek ★★** (© **05947/28-7804;** www.campforktailcreek. com), run by a young, enthusiastic couple, Ritish Suri and Minakshi Pandey. Accommodations are in safari tents, with elevated wooden floors and attached toilets, or in mud huts with thatched roofs and verandas. Customized walks, safaris, and birding and angling trips include the services of a resident naturalist or tracker. A double at Rs 4,400 includes all meals, cold drinks, and escorted walks; no credit cards. Half- or full-day game drives are offered, and you can also opt for a camping trip into the forest reserve or multiday elephant safaris. Delicious buffet-style meals are served in "The Thatch"; lit by lanterns at night (there is no electricity), it houses a collection of some 700 books for guests to peruse.

Corbett Hideaway ★★ The Hideaway is essentially your best located choice (the other options are all some distance from the gates); other than this it is slightly cheaper than Ramganga (and certainly very affordable option relative to Ranthambore and Madhya Pradesh's best!). Pebbled pathways interweave with pretty gardens and cozy mustard-colored cottages in a mango orchard. The older, "jungle-themed" cottages have thatched pitched ceilings, stone-tile flooring, comfortable beds, and separate sitting areas with fireplaces. A lovely place to relax is the thatched-roof bar; there's also a well-stocked library with a selection of Jim Corbett's books to get you in the mood for tiger-spotting. If you don't feel like lazing you can go river rafting on the Kosi River, or check out the resort's resident herd of water buffalo. The evening's entertainment features Kumaoni folk dancing, a wildlife movie, or a rather uninspiring slide show.

Zero Garjia, Dhikuli 224 715. © 05947/28-4132 or -4134. Fax 05947/28-4133. www.leisurehotels.in. 52 cottages. $170 deluxe double; $210 superior double; $250 suite; $280 family (room only). Taxes extra. AE, MC, V. **Amenities:** 2 restaurants, bar; railway transfer (Rs 650); archery; badminton; billiards; bird-watching; cultural performances; doctor-on-call; fishing; Ayurvedic massage; pool; kids' pool; river rafting; safaris; table tennis; nature walks. *In room:* A/C.

Corbett Ramganga Resort ★★ Not only tiger-spotters but die-hard anglers head here in hope of bagging India's ultimate big-game fishing trophy: the mighty *mahseer.* This decade-old resort, on the banks of the Ramganga River, is not as attractive as its riverfront neighbor Solluna, but it draws an interesting mix of people, many here only to fish—the world record *mahseer* was bagged just 500m (1,600 ft.) from the Corbett Resort. Of the two options available, we prefer the tented accommodations to the concrete cottages—each large, air-cooled, army-style structure is encased in a thatch shell, with a tiny dressing room and a small shower room attached; mattresses here are also more comfortable. At night, guests—mostly moneyed Indians and diplomats—gather around a bonfire and share rum-induced fishing tales; in the background, the gurgling Ramganga reminds you that you're miles away from the city. (*Note:* It can take almost an hour to get to the Park from here.)

Village Jhamaria, P.O. Sankar, Marchula. Info © 93/1051 0582. Reservations: Surbhi Adventures, No. 5, C-1 Lane, Sainik Farms, Khanpur Gate, New Delhi 110 062. © 011/3298-9876. Fax 011/2955-1428. www.ramganga.com. 30 units. Rs 6,000 air-cooled safari tent double; Rs 7,250 air-conditioned double; Rs 8,250 super deluxe double; Rs 10,000 suite. Rs 2,000 extra bed. Rates include all meals, bed tea. Taxes extra; separate summer/winter package rates available. AE, DC, MC, V. **Amenities:** Restaurant, bar; railway transfer (Rs 800); adventure activities for groups only; badminton; cycling; doctor-on-call; fishing; pool; children's pool; room service; river-rafting; night safaris; outdoor tennis court. *In room:* A/C (tents are air-cooled only), heater, suites have kitchenettes.

The Hideaway River Lodge ★★ If you want a back-to-basics authentic safari, with a little more luxury than Camp Forktail, Hideaway River Lodge is the place to book. Besides offering pleasing digs and the best meals you'll find in the area (not to mention the only alcohol!), the lodge is located right on the Ramganga River and spread out over 1.2 hectares (3 acres) on the periphery of the park—at night animal calls are unnervingly loud and thrilling. Accommodations are in en-suite tents (specify of you want a double bed); while all tents have a private veranda, the deluxe category has a clear view of the river which makes it worth the extra buck. There is no electricity and hot water is only available in the mornings and evenings, but this should not be a major drawback. Besides the regular safari activities (in a jeep or on an elephant), the lodge also offers fishing, and the location is ideal for birders; there's also a natural pool where you can laze away the hotter parts of the day or alternatively accompany the mahouts to bathe the elephants.

Zero Garjia, Dhikuli 224 715. ℭ **05947/28-4132** or -4134. www.leisurehotels.in; www.corbetthideaway. com. Reservations: 011/4652-0000. 10 Units (bucket bath only): $450 deluxe double, $500 superior double (direct river view); rates include meals, transfers from Corbett Hideaway, entrance fees, tea and coffee, two safaris/day, naturalist, angling, and all taxes. AE, MC, V. *In room:* flashlight, hot-water bottle.

Infinity Resorts ★★   Another option catering essentially to the domestic tourist market, activities at this pleasant riverside hotel center around a huge enclosed octagonal building with a terrace and indoor bonfire; this is where meals are served, wildlife movies are shown, and cultural performances are held. The deluxe guest rooms are worth paying a little more for; they lead off open corridors on the floor above the standard units. They're spacious (though not particularly tasteful), and each one has a large terrace with a river view. From your room, you can hear the river and enjoy great bird-watching. The setting is peaceful, perhaps more so than at Corbett Hideaway, with a relaxing swimming pool area, riverside pond filled with *mahseer* and hammocks strung up between the mango trees and rhododendrons.

P.O. Dhikuli, Ramnagar 244 715. ℭ **05947/25-1279** or -1280. Fax 05947/25-1280. www.infinityresorts. com. Reservations: C-32 Sushant Lok, Phase-I, Gurgaon 122 002. ℭ **0124/4655-800** or 0124/4655-801. Fax 0124/4655-804. 32 units. Oct 1–June 30: $400 luxury double. Rates include all meals and taxes. AE, DC, MC, V. **Amenities:** Restaurant, bar; railway transfer (Rs 600); billiards; cultural events; fishing; health club; medical center; pool; pool table; room service; jeep safaris, nature walks; wildlife film shows. *In room:* A/C, heater.

The Solluna Resort ★★   Not as well known as neighbor Corbett Ramganga, this 10-hectare (25-acre) resort has better accommodations: gorgeous cottages (with bay window seats, furnished verandahs and a skylight that allows you to watch the stars from your bed) surrounded by expansive lawns and mango and cherry trees. However, it's not as convivial as popular Corbett Ramganga—a problem related to marketing rather than any innate flaw, but gregarious types be warned. If you like your solitude, head for the lovely elevated viewing terrace with comfortable wicker chairs—great for lazing and drinking in the natural spectacle all around you. At night, pathways glow from the light of storm lanterns, and a bonfire is lit for a communal chinwag. Alcohol isn't available, but you're welcome to bring your own. (With 27 more units under construction, it may be worth checking how far renovations are before booking here.)

Marchula 244 715. ℭ **98-1003-0262** reservations. Fax 011/2362-7738. www.sollunaresort.com. 23 units. Rs 6,300 double; Rs 1,800 extra person. 2 children under 7 stay free in parent's room. Rates include breakfast. Discounts available from mid-June to mid-Nov. Taxes extra. No credit cards. **Amenities:** Restaurant, 24-hr. coffee shop; railway transfer (Rs 800); bird-watching; doctor-on-call; fishing; pool; room service; safaris; minitheater. *In room:* A/C, fridge, heater.

15

Kolkata (Calcutta) & East India

The image most people have of Calcutta is one of abject poverty and misery—the residual effect of the many years the media focused on Mother Teresa's good works. Despite this unfortunate perception, Kolkata (as the Communist-ruled West Bengal Capital became known in 2001) attracts its fair share of visitors, many of whom are pleasantly surprised by the seductive charms of this intoxicating city.

Believed to be the ethereal abode of the goddess Kali, who embodies *shakti*—fortitude and strength—it is home to a joyous, cerebral, and sophisticated community; some of the best Raj-era architecture in India; many of the country's best artists; a thriving film industry; and a host of superb restaurants.

Kolkata is also the natural starting point for a trip to the Himalayan mountains of the North, where you can drink in the crystal-clear air of **Darjeeling,** India's most famous hill station, imbibing the "champagne of teas" before picking up a permit to hike the tiny state of **Sikkim.** One of the least-explored regions of India, Sikkim is a world apart, surrounded by jagged peaks and home to snow-fed lakes, remote Buddhist monasteries, yak-herding Tibetans, high-altitude forests, and some 4,000 varieties of wildflowers (including 600 varieties of orchid).

South of West Bengal, in the coastal state of Orissa—often called the "soul of India"—you can join the pilgrims who gather by the thousands to pay homage to the Lord of the Universe, who resides at the seaside town of Puri. Within easy striking distance from here is Konark's **Sun Temple,** a World Heritage Site, a testament to the technical and artistic brilliance of Orissa in the 13th century, and unreservedly one of India's top attractions.

To cover all three eastern states, you will need a minimum of 9 days, ideally flying directly to Bhubaneswar, capital of Orissa, to visit Puri and Konark, then heading northward to West Bengal to visit the capital, Kolkata, and the state's idyllic hill station, Darjeeling. End your tour in laidback Sikkim before flying back to Delhi from nearby Bagdogra Airport. Set aside extra time for trekking in Sikkim or a tribal tour in Orissa.

1 KOLKATA

1,310km (812 miles) SE of Delhi

Once the proud capital of the British Raj, Kolkata is deeply evocative of an era and sensibility lost in time. Established as the trading post for the East India Company on the banks of the Hooghly River by Job Charnock in 1690, it grew to be the biggest colonial trade center in Asia, earning it the name "Jewel of the East." With its splendid Victorian buildings, ornamental pools, stone-paved footpaths, figured lampposts, and sweeping esplanade, it was entirely European in its architecture and sensibility, and the burgeoning city became the stomping ground of a new breed of sahibs and memsahibs who wore their white skins and British manners as though they were royal insignias. But

The Dance of Destruction

For Hindus, India is a holy land, with thousands of *tirthas*—celestial "crossover" points where mortals can access the world of the gods. Legend has it that these were created after Lord Shiva's wife, Sati, jumped into a fire in an act of shame because her father, Raja Daksha, had neglected to invite Shiva to an important ritual. Unable to bear the loss, the grief-struck Shiva—carrying Sati's body—began to pace India in a *tandava nritya*, or "dance of destruction." Terrified that his fury and pain would destroy the universe, Brahma, Vishnu, and Shani dispersed her body across the vast plains and peaks of India, and wherever a body part fell, this became a *tirtha*. Many of these are important pilgrimage sites Hindu believers must visit at least once in their lifetime, such as those at Varanasi (see chapter 10). One of Sati's toes also fell in a dense forest in southwest Bengal. Today, this site—now **Kalighat Temple**—is one of India's most important pilgrimage centers, where the goddess is worshipped as Kali. The toe is supposedly housed in a chamber of the temple. Every year in June, as part of a secretive ritual, the toe is bathed.

Kolkata was effectively built on a disease-breeding swamp—the marshy delta of the Ganges and Brahmaputra rivers—and this, combined with the heat, humidity, and the Bengalis' prominence in the struggle for independence, finally persuaded the British to transfer the capital. In 1911 they left for Delhi, leaving Calcutta to rot.

Today, much of the city's architectural heritage stands crumbling and in ruins, its monumental colonial structures not nearly as well maintained as those of Mumbai. Moss and grime cover tattered buildings that should be celebrated as the city's finest—the collapsing masonry, peeling paint, and sun-scorched woodwork testaments to the indifference of time. Unable to stem the long-term industrial and commercial decline of the city, or the flood of refugees that have continually arrived from Bangladesh since the first days of Partition, the Communist ruling parties (CPI and CPIM) struggle to adequately provide for the city's 14 million inhabitants. The second-largest city on the subcontinent (after Mumbai), it is packed to capacity, politically beleaguered, and an entrepôt of India's social woes.

Yet its proud citizens, who speak rapturously of its benefits over the other big Indian metropolises, fiercely tout the charms of Kolkata. In fact, meeting Bengalis is one of the best aspects of traveling here—Kolkata is the self-proclaimed capital of India's intellectuals, home to three Nobel Prize laureates (including the revered Rabindranath Tagore, who became Asia's first Nobel laureate in 1913) and an Oscar-winning film director (Satyajit Ray). Warm, helpful, and imbued with a great sense of humor (not to mention a famously keen appreciation for dining), the Bengalis live by the maxim that "what Bengal does today, India will do tomorrow," and engaging in lively discussion on the benefits or drawbacks of Communism, or on the original recipe for *sandesh* (milk-based sweets, a Bengali specialty), is likely to be one of your more memorable experiences in India.

In some ways, the city is as frightening as you might fear, a degraded mess where squalor, filth, and the ubiquitous *bustees* (slums) can overwhelm the senses. If you're in India to enjoy the country's softer side, don't tarry here. Head for the Himalayan mountainscapes of Sikkim or Darjeeling, or the temples and beaches of Orissa, farther south. But if you delight in eclectic city culture, spend at least 2 or 3 nights in this thrilling city.

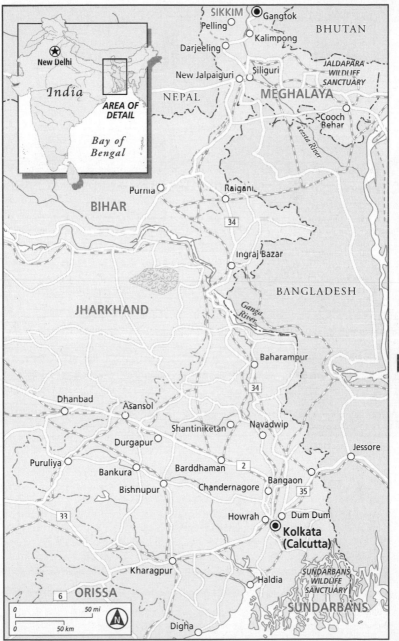

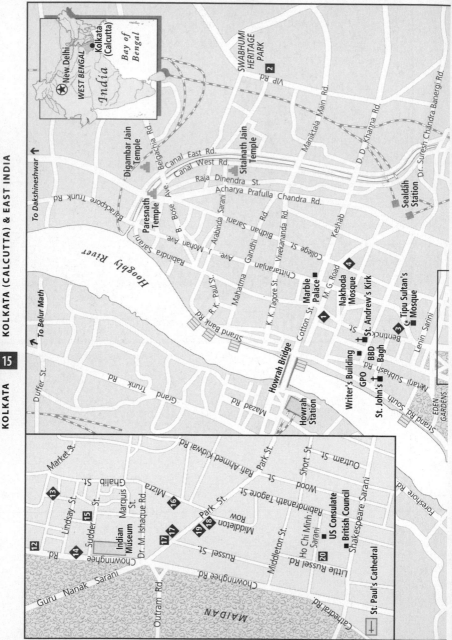

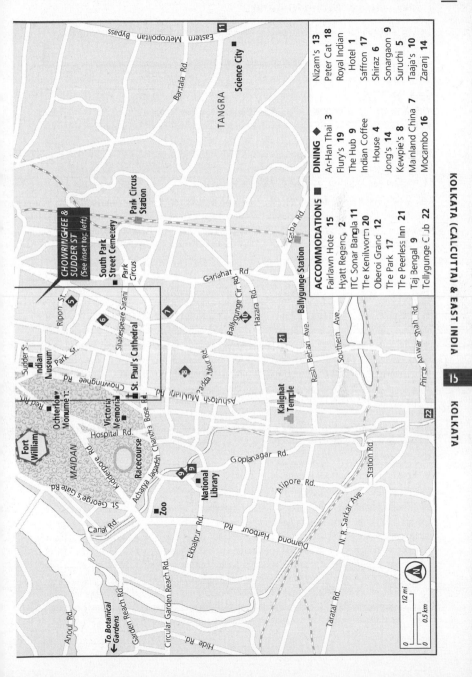

ACCOMMODATIONS ■

Fairlawn Hote **15**
Hyatt Regency **2**
ITC Sonar Bangla **11**
The Kenilworth **20**
Oberoi Grand **12**
The Park **17**
The Peerless Inn **21**
Taj Bengal **9**
Tollygunge Club **22**

DINING ◆

Ar-Han Thai **3**
Flury's **19**
The Hub **9**
Indian Coffee
House **4**
Jong's **14**
Kewpie's **8**
Mainland China **7**
Mocambo **16**

Nizam's **13**
Peter Cat **18**
Royal Indian
Hotel **1**
Saffron **17**
Shiraz **6**
Sonargaon **9**
Suruchi **5**
Taaja's **10**
Zaranj **14**

> **Tips** **Sorry, Wrong Number . . .**
>
> Dial 🕾 **1952** for a recorded message (in English) if the number you're dialing has been changed.

ESSENTIALS

VISITOR INFORMATION   The **West Bengal Tourism Centre** (3/2 B.B.D. Bagh E.; 🕾 **033/2248-8271** or -8272; www.wbtourism.com; Mon–Sat 10am–6pm) is good for up-to-date information and you can also arrange city tours here. Visit the **India Tourism Kolkata** (MSE Bldg., 4 Shakespeare Sarani; 🕾 **033/2282-5813,** -1475, or -7731) for (limited) information on the entire subcontinent. *Cal Calling* is a monthly catalog of events and general information (🕾 **98-3185-6097**).

GETTING THERE & AWAY   **By Air**   Kolkata is served by domestic flights from most major destinations in India. The websites www.yatra.com (🕾 **98-7180-0800**) and www.ezeego1.co.in (🕾 **1800-22-0177**) are reliable airline reservation sites with both online and phone facility. Netaji Subhash Chandra Bose International Airport, formerly Dum Dum Airport (🕾 **033/2511-6026** or -8299; www.calcuttaairport.com) is 15km (9⅓ miles) northeast. You can exchange currency and get tourist information from two separate booths here. Use the prepaid taxi stand; the 40-minute trip into town should cost Rs 500.

By Train   Kolkata's **Howrah Junction** (🕾 **033/2660-2518**), just south of Howrah Bridge, connects the city with most other parts of the country. It's made up of the adjoining Old and New Howrah stations. You should purchase tickets through your hotel or a travel agent, but there is a section specifically for foreigners in the main **reservations office** (daily 10am–5pm). For general inquiries, call 🕾 **1310;** for prerecorded information, call 🕾 **1331.** Trains to destinations farther east and to the northern areas of West Bengal often depart from **Sealdah Station** (Bepin Behari Ganguly St.; 🕾 **033/2350-3535** or -3537); check your ticket to confirm which station you need to be at. Also arrive with time to spare so that you can navigate through the crowds and find out about any changes to the schedule. You can also log on to **www.indianrail.gov.in** for information (see chapter 3).

By Road   Don't consider getting to or from Kolkata by motor vehicle (either driving yourself or by bus); otherwise you'll waste a great deal of your vacation time.

GETTING AROUND   **By Taxi & Auto-Rickshaw**   The full-to-capacity streets of Kolkata can be the very devil to get around, but a jaunt in a hired Ambassador is a good way to experience the city. Taxi drivers here are notoriously keen on ripping you off, even after you've negotiated a fare. Ask your hotel concierge for an approximate idea of the fare for your route, check that the meter is reset, and make sure that the driver knows where you're going (use a street map to ensure you aren't taken on a detour). You can hire a good car and driver through **Avis** (The Oberoi Grand; 🕾 **033/2217-0147**) or through **Orix** (6, Royd St.; 🕾 **033/2227 -5531**). See "Car Rentals" under "Fast Facts: Kolkata," below. Note that rickshaws are outlawed from entering many of the city's major streets.

The Tollywood Oscar Achiever

Kolkata has its own film industry, known throughout the Bengali world as Tollywood. In fact, it was this city that gave birth to India's finest filmmaker, **Satyajit Ray,** who died in 1992—the same year he received a Lifetime Achievement Oscar. While Bollywood was churning out dazzling choreographic daydreams, Ray made classic films that filled art-house cinemas around the world.

The Metro   India's first underground railway was started in Calcutta in 1984; it currently connects Tollygunge in the south with Dum Dum Station in the north. It's a reliable, clean, and surprisingly uncrowded transport option (except for peak office hours), and tickets are cheap (Rs 4–Rs 8). The Metro operates Monday through Saturday from 7am to 9:45pm, and on Sunday from 3 to 9:45pm. For information, contact the **Metro Rail Bhavan** (33/1 Jawaharlal Nehru Rd.; ✆ 033/2226-7280 or -1054).

By Bus or Tram   To experience India at its most confusing, claustrophobic, and unpredictable, by all means hop aboard one of Kolkata's battered buses or road-clogging trams. If you're looking for a joyride, take a tram around Victoria Memorial.

On Foot   If you don't mind breaking a sweat and rubbing shoulders with the *aam janta* (common man), Kolkata is quite a walkable city, at least in parts, with its pavements lined end to end with makeshift shacks selling practically anything that is sellable! Early morning is the best time to get out and stroll through the streets; it's still relatively quiet, and the air is cooler and less choked by pollution. Pick up a cup of tea from the *chaiwallas* who serve their sweet brew in tiny unfired clay cups—India's answer to the polystyrene cup, these are simply discarded after use. A great way to get acquainted with Kolkata is to pick up a copy of *Ten Walks in Calcutta* by Prosenjit Das Gupta (Hermes Inc.) from a bookstore (see "Shopping," later).

GUIDED TOURS   The guide services of the following two men are worth booking before you arrive. **Shanti Bhattacharjee** is a retired history teacher with a profound knowledge of his city, who provides in-depth tours of Kolkata (✆ 033/2350-1576 or 98-3024-2803). He charges Rs 1,500 per day irrespective of the number of people (all entrance and transport costs to be paid by tourists). Other than organizing festivals, **Action Research in Conservation of Heritage** ★★ conducts excellent heritage walks (usually on Sun) of northern Kolkata and Dalhousie Square (✆ 033/2359-6303 or 033/2337-5757; www.centrearch.org; Rs 350 per person). Alternatively, you could get in touch with **Husna-Tara Prakash** ★★ (✆ 033/2288-5630), the charming owner of the amazing Glenburn Tea Estate (reviewed later) who, along with an expert team of guides, conducts walks throughout the city—the rates are far higher than others mentioned here but inclusive of an air-conditioned vehicle, breakfast, entry fees and little personal touches that make it worthwhile. **The Tourism Centre** (3/2 B.B.D. Bagh E.; ✆ 033/2248-8271 or -8272) conducts two different daily sightseeing tours of the city; these inevitably involve a great deal of bus travel and little sightseeing. In the same center, the **West Bengal Tourist Development Corporation** (✆ 033/2243-7260) organizes short and long-distance tours of the state and selected destinations around the country.

⦗*Fast Facts*⦘ **Kolkata**

Airlines **Jet Airways:** ℂ 033/3989-3333. **Kingfisher Airlines:** ℂ 1800-1800-101. **Air Sahara:** ℂ 1600-22-3020. **Indian Airlines:** ℂ 033/2511-9720.

Ambulance **Bellevue Clinic,** 9 Loudon St. (ℂ **93318-41265** or 98318-21850) has a 24-hour ambulance service.

American Express The office is located at 21 Old Court House St., near Raj Bhavan (ℂ **033/2222-3001** or -3026). Open Monday to Friday 10am to 2pm and Saturday 10am to noon.

Area Code The area code for **Kolkata** is **033.**

ATMs There are plenty of 24-hour ATMs: **Citibank** (Kanak Bldg., 41 J.L. Nehru [Chowringhee] Rd.; ℂ 033/2283-2484), **UTI Bank** (7 Shakespeare Sarani; ℂ 033/2282-2933), **HDFC Bank** (Stephen House, 4 B.B.D. Bagh E.; ℂ 033/2210-7546), **Standard Chartered Grindlays Bank** (41 J.L. Nehru [Chowringhee] Rd.; ℂ 033/2242-8888), and **HSBC Bank** (8 Netaji Subhash Rd., 31 B.B.D. Bagh; ℂ 033/2243-8585).

Banks Most banks are open Monday to Friday 10am to 2 or 3pm, and Saturday 10am to noon.

Car Rentals Contact **Car-Cab** (2, Manook Lane, off Ezra St., Kolkata 1; ℂ **033/2235-3535**), Rs 90/hour for a maximum of 50km (31 miles). **Avis Rent-A-Car** is at The Oberoi Grand (15 Jawaharlal Nehru Rd.; ℂ **033/2249-2323,** ext. 6325 or 6335).

Consulates **United States:** 5/1 Ho Chi Minh Sarani; ℂ **033/2282-3611;** Monday to Friday 8am to 1pm and 2 to 5pm. **United Kingdom:** 1A Ho Chi Minh Sarani; ℂ **033/2288-5172;** Monday to Friday 8:30am to 1pm and 1:30 to 4pm. **Canada:** Duncan House, 31 N.S. Rd.; ℂ **033/2230-8515;** Monday to Friday 9:30am to 1pm.

Currency Exchange **Thomas Cook** is at 19B Shakespeare Sarani, first floor (ℂ **033/2283-0473** or -0475); hours are Monday to Saturday 9:30am to 6pm.

Drugstores Twenty-four-hour chemists include **AMRI Apollo Hospital Pharmacy** (P4 Gariahat Rd., Block A-29; ℂ **033/2461-2626,** ext. 606), **Dhanwantary** (48A/1 Diamond Harbour Rd.; ℂ **033/2449-3204**), **Jeevan Deep** (1-14B Hazra Rd.; ℂ **033/2455-0926**), and **Life Care** (1/2A Hazra Rd.; ℂ **033/2475-4628**).

Emergencies For fire brigade, dial ℂ **101** or 033/2244-0101.

Hospitals **Belle Vue Clinic** (9 U.N. Brahmachari St.; ℂ **033/2287-2321,** -6921, -6925, or -7473) also has a blood bank. There are English-speaking doctors at the 24-hour **B.M. Birla Heart Research Center** (1/1A National Library Ave.; ℂ **033/2456-7001** to -7009).

Newspapers & Magazines Peruse the pages of *The Statesman,* one of India's oldest English dailies, for information about special events. Kolkata's other very popular paper is *The Telegraph,* which has a metro section that lists local events.

Police Dial ℂ **100** or **033/2250-5000** through -5004. Police headquarters are in Lal Bazaar (ℂ **033/2214-3230** or -3024).

Post Office B.B.D. Bagh; Monday to Saturday 8am to 8:30pm and Sunday 8am to 3:30pm.

Finds Tigers in the Sundarbans: India's Best-Kept Secret

One of the most enigmatic national parks in India, the **Sundarbans** is the largest delta in the world, with saline mud flats and thick mangrove forests teeming with wildlife, of which the Royal Bengal tiger is the most exotic inhabitant. Spanning around 4,264 sq. km (1,663 sq. miles) in India and an even larger area in neighboring Bangladesh, and surrounded by the Ganga, Brahmaputra, and Meghna rivers, it was declared a World Heritage Site by UNESCO in 1987 but remains one of the least developed parks in Asia, as access is only via water. Although there are affordable government ferries (West Bengal Tourism Development Corporation; © **033/2248-7302**) offering overnight trips, it is a bit of a slog just to get to the ferry itself, as it involves several switches between cabs and smaller boats, and accommodation is below par. However, for the enthusiastic, **Vivada Inland Waterways** (© **033/2463-1990**; www.vivada.com; waterways@vivada.com), offers comfortable accommodation in boats, as well as relatively easy access; packages vary, but be prepared to shell out in the region of $735 to $885 for a 4-day luxury cruise, and of course with no guarantee to sighting anything bigger than a Kingfisher. The **Sunderban Tiger Camp** (© **033/3293-5749**; www. sunderbantigercamp.com) offers a cheaper alternative with its range of river-side accommodation (huts, tents, cottages, A/C cottages; non-A/C doubles from Rs 2,750) set in the midst of gardens teeming with waddling ducks and geese. While the watchtowers and museum are in a sorry state, the cruise along the silent mangroves is quite lovely.

ORIENTATION

Kolkata is a huge, sprawling city, divided into **north** and **south**, both spread along the eastern bank of the Hooghly River, which divides it from the vast suburb of **Howrah**, located on the western bank. Howrah is where you'll be deposited if you arrive by train; the main station is close to the Howrah Bridge, which connects with the city proper. Just east and south of Howrah Bridge are Kolkata's commercial and tourist hubs, centered around **B.B.D. Bagh,** still known by its colonial name, Dalhousie Square, and the long stretch of road once known as **Chowringhee** (now Jawaharlal Nehru Rd.) that runs southward, alongside the Maidan, Kolkata's vast urban park. Many visitors base themselves around Chowringhee; nearby Sudder Street teems with budget accommodations, while Park Street has plenty of boutiques and fine restaurants.

To the northeast is the rapidly expanding business district of **Salt Lake City,** which has few historical sites but is steadily developing a reputation for its upscale business hotels and high-tech entertainment facilities. It's the closest district to the airport.

WHAT TO SEE & DO

You need at least 2 full days to cover Kolkata. Spend the first day exploring central and south Kolkata, and the second visiting sites in the north, for which you should hire a car and driver.

Day 1 (Central & South Kolkata)

Start by catching a taxi south to the city's most famous temple, **Kalighat Kali** (p. 699). After this, visit Mother Teresa's **Nirmal Hriday** home for the destitute and dying, right

Cruising Down the Ganges

Great mountains spawn great rivers. No surprise then that from mighty Himalayas flow two of the world's longest, the Ganges and the Brahmaputra. Meeting in Bengal, a province now split between India and Bangladesh, their combined flow enters the sea through the world's largest delta. The Ganges in particular has always been the highway of empires—Hindu, Buddhist, Moghul, and British—and a cruise along it and the Hugli (its westernmost branch through the delta) is a journey through history. Regular steamer services ended before World War II, but now **Assam Bengal Navigation** ★★ is running cruises of 1 to 2 weeks both along the Hugli from Kolkata through rural Bengal and, from 2010 onwards, along the Ganges proper as far as Patna, with its associations ranging from the Buddha's life on earth to the East India Company's opium trade. Cruises also take in the scene of Robert Clive's victory at Plassey, the medieval ruins of Gaur, and Murshidabad, the capital of the Nawabs of Bengal. The ships are intimate (no more than 24 guests), air-conditioned and comfortable, with knowledgeable guides on board to elucidate the complexities of the region's long history ($350 per person per night).

next door (see "The Miracle of Mother Teresa & the 'Pure Hearts,'" on p. 700). Or, if you're a bookworm, check out the **National Library** in the 300-year-old former summer residence of Prince Azim-us-Shan, the grandson of Emperor Aurangzeb. The library has a catalog of over 2 million books. Our recommendation is to enjoy the relaxing, tranquil atmosphere of **South Park Street Cemetery** (p. 700) before you head into the chaos of central Kolkata. If you're hungry, nearby **Suruchi** (89 Elliot Rd., near Mallik Bazaar; ✆ 033/2229-1763; no credit cards; open Mon–Sat 10am–5:45pm, Sun 10am–2:45pm) is an authentic Bengali restaurant, with a no-frills, homegrown atmosphere.

You can save time by using a vehicle to move on to central Kolkata, or enjoy the walk along Park Street to **Chowringhee Road,** taking in the upmarket shops and boutiques and perhaps stopping at **Flury's** (✆ 033/2229-7664; credit cards accepted; daily 7:30am–10pm) for tea and a sandwich. Now officially known as "Jawaharlal Nehru Road," Chowringhee is Kolkata's main drag, with less human excrement along its sidewalks than almost anywhere else in the city. It is lined with colonial Victoriana—including the monumental **Indian Museum** (see below) and that pinnacle of Calcutta's society life, **The Oberoi Grand.** Continue north along Chowringhee into the heart of the city, where you can explore the roads around **B.B.D. Bagh** (see below).

When you've had your fill of life on the sidewalks, make your way south again, along Government Place East. You'll soon find yourself in the green expanse that is the **Maidan**—one of the largest city-center parks in the world—where the Ochterlony Monument, or **Shahid Minar (Martyr's Tower),** is worth noting. Walking west through the Maidan will bring you to **Eden Gardens,** India's most famous cricket stadium, while much farther south is the imperious **Victoria Memorial** (see below). Buy a ticket and venture in if you are keen to broaden your knowledge of the city's history. But don't feel guilty if you just want to lie on the lawn and watch Bengalis socializing. Otherwise, brave the traffic and catch a cab to Howrah to explore the 18th-century **Indian Botanical Gardens** (Shibpur; ✆ 033/2668-0554; Rs 50; closes 1 hr. before sunset), said to house

the largest banyan tree on earth. Scientists, when they are available (usually after
11:30am), will act as guides at no charge.

Top Attractions

B.B.D. Bagh ★★★ For those interested in colonial architecture, this part of central
Kolkata makes for very worthwhile exploration on foot. Once called Dalhousie Square,
B.B.D. refers to the names of three Indian freedom fighters (Benoy, Badal, and Dinesh)
who shot a British police inspector-general in 1930. At the center of the square *(bagh)* is
Lal Dighi Tank, where locals wade and bathe in the dodgy-looking, spring-fed water.
Most impressive of the surrounding monuments is the **Writers' Building,** the office of
the West Bengal government, which stretches along B.B.D. Bagh North Road; it was
built to house the British bachelors imported to serve the East India Company. Across
the road is the early-19th-century **St. Andrew's Kirk,** recognizable by its tall white
steeple. At the other end of B.B.D. Bagh North is the **General Post Office,** with a
monumental rotunda; it's thought to be the site of the notorious Black Hole of Calcutta
incident (see p. 25). Southwest of the tank is the St. Martin-in-the-Fields–inspired **St.
John's Church** (✆ **033/2243-6098;** Rs 10; daily 9am–6pm) and, within the grounds,
the tomb of Calcutta's founding father, Job Charnock. East of B.B.D. Bagh, to the south
of Lal Bazaar, you'll find numerous tea merchants, where teas from Darjeeling, the
Dooars, and Assam are packed and exported. **Nilhat House,** located behind the Old
Mission Church, is the oldest tea auction house in India—join the action on Monday
and Tuesday mornings.

Central Kolkata, south of Howrah Bridge, and north of Jawaharlal Nehru Rd.

Indian Museum ★★★ Containing things beautiful, unusual, and ancient, the
museum is known to locals as *Jadu Ghar,* the House of Magic. The oldest institution of
its kind in the Asia-Pacific region, it holds the country's largest repository of artifacts
(over 100,000 exhibits). Among the dinosaur and mammoth skeletons and the
4,000-year-old Egyptian mummy are extraordinary Indian cultural items, including
Shah Jahan's emerald goblet, and an urn said to contain the Buddha's ashes. Don't miss
the cultural anthropology section—accompanied by good explanations—if you are interested in India's many tribal groups. The textiles-and-decorative-arts gallery is most
impressive. It can be difficult to find, however—ask for assistance.

27 Jawaharlal Nehru Rd., at the corner of Sudder St. ✆ **033/2286-1699.** Rs 150. Tues–Sun 10am–4pm.

Kalighat Kali Temple ★★ Violent, vengeful Kali is the patron goddess of Kolkata,
and this temple complex—believed to be the site where the toe of Shiva's wife fell when
her body was scattered across the earth by the gods anxious to stop Lord Shiva's dance of
destruction (see "The Dance of Destruction," p. 690)—is a major pilgrimage center,
drawing some 20,000 visitors each day. If you're a non-Hindu, you cannot enter the
inner sanctum, sticky with the rotted remains of fresh flowers offered by devotees every
day, but it's worth your while to explore the courtyards and the various stalls selling flowers, fruit, and religious paraphernalia. If you're uneasy about the idea of animal sacrifice,
avoid the enclosure to the south of the temple where at least one goat is offered to Kali
every day (a ritual that allegedly replaced the ancient practice of human sacrifice). Be
equally wary of the so-called priests—temple "guides" who usher you into the complex
and conduct a whirlwind tour of the facilities, only to present you with a donation book
that records the radically generous donations of other foreigners.

Kalighat Rd., Kalighat. Free admission. Daily 5am–1:30pm and 3–10pm (Tues, Sat–Sun, and festival days
are terribly crowded with mile-long lines of devotees; Wed and Thurs are least congested).

The Miracle of Mother Teresa & the "Pure Hearts"

Mother Teresa's **Missionaries of Charity (MOC)** is now headed by Sister Nirmala, a converted Brahmin. There are some 3,500 MOC sisters around the world, working in 569 centers in 120 countries, but their selfless efforts are not without controversy. Even during Mother Teresa's time, tales of pecuniary troubles and controversies over the way in which the poor and dying were being treated (and converted) beleaguered the MOC. There have always been plenty of cynics, despite the Vatican's confirmation of Mother Teresa's "miraculous" healing of a young woman's malignant tumor (the woman claims to have been cured after seeing Mother Teresa in her dreams), a move that has irritated rationalists and the medical profession. Still, in Kolkata alone, more than 50,000 destitute sick and dying are looked after by the blue-and-white-sari-wearing nuns of the MOC, a demonstration of selflessness that you might deem miraculous in itself. Adjacent to the Kali Temple is "Pure Heart," or **Nirmal Hriday** (251 Kalighat Rd.; ✆ **033/2464-4223;** Fri–Wed 8–11:30am and 3–5:30pm), the very first MOC center. **Mother House** (54 A.J.C. Bose Rd.; ✆ **033/2249-7115;** same hours as Nirmal Hriday) is the MOC headquarters, where Mother Teresa is buried. Nearby is **Nirmal Shishu Bhawan** (78 A.J.C. Bose Rd.; same hours as Nirmal Hriday), where some 250 orphans are cared for.

South Park Street Cemetery ★★ This is Kolkata's most famous cemetery, where monumental gravestones and lichen- and moss-covered tombstones to large numbers of ill-fated Brits buried on Indian soil provide a tranquil retreat. A really atmospheric place to wander around, the cemetery contains headstones that bear unlikely epitaphs like MAJ. GEN. C. GREEN DIED 51TH OF JULY.

Park St. and southeast end of Cemetery Rd. Free admission. Daily 7:30am–4:30pm.

Victoria Memorial ★ Conceived of by Lord Curzon as a monument to his queen 4 years after her death, this domed structure is Kolkata's most recognizable landmark. It's billed as one of the city's top attractions, but with portraits of fairly boring-looking individuals filling many of the walls, it's more likely to excite Rajophiles. There are 25 galleries in the central hall, and about 3,500 articles relating to the Raj on display, including the queen's rosewood piano. Exhibits are not restricted to Raj-artifacts; the black marble throne that belonged to Siraj-ud-Daulah is impressive, as is a gigantic painting of a Jaipur royal procession, said to be one of the largest paintings in Asia.

Queen's Way. ✆ **033/2223-1890,** or -1891. www.victoriamemorial-cal.org. Rs 150. Tues–Sun 10am–4:30pm; closed on public holidays. Sound-and-light show: winter Tues–Sun 7:15pm (in English); summer 7:45pm (in English); Rs 20.

Day 2 (North Kolkata)

Early in the morning, head toward **Howrah Bridge,** where you can witness people bathing at the *ghats* (steps leading down to the Hooghly River) or the pandemonium at the colorful **flower market** (you need to arrive before 7am). There you can sip *chai* and watch the stall holders deftly thread marigold garlands for the gods and bridal headgear

The **Indian Coffee House** (15 Bankin Chatterjee St., first floor; ℂ **033/2241-4869;** Mon–Sat 9am–9pm, Sun 9am–12:30pm and 5–9pm), where the Young Bengal Movement started, is the quintessential College Street haunt. This is where M. N. Roy, founder of the Communist Party of India (as well as the Mexican Communist Party), Satyajit Ray, Nobel Laureate Dr. Amartya Sen, and a host of other famous personalities discussed the future of India over platefuls of fish fingers and coffee. A lone photograph of Rabindranath Tagore looks across a vast former 1930s dance hall with sagging ceiling fans and scattered tables around which men, young and old, demonstratively argue the issues of the day. Surly waiters plod around rather aimlessly, so be patient while waiting for your greasy *pakora* and a strong Coorg. Meals are not the reason to come, but it's a good place to strike up a conversation over a cup of coffee. For an even more animated and authentic interaction with locals, head for the **Calcutta races** (www.rctconline.com); ask any waiter or at your hotel about the next event. All walks of life are to be seen here, many in their finest glad rags. As everyone celebrates the chance to escape their dharma, the atmosphere is electric

from tuberoses and dahlias. Crossing over Howrah Bridge, head toward the **Belur Math Shrine** (see below). From here you can either incorporate a short stop at popular **Dakshineshwar Temple** (across Vivekananda Bridge; ℂ **033/2564-5222;** daily 6:45am–12:30pm and 3:30–8:30pm), or take a look at the potters' village at **Kumartuli** (N. Chitpur Rd.), a warren of alleys where clay deities and images of Mother Teresa are produced by the thousands. If you prefer to slow the pace, however, skip these and head south to beautiful **Paresnath Temple** (see below)—not as famous as the Kali temple, but certainly Kolkata's prettiest, and north Kolkata's star attraction. From here, you can head east to shop and eat at **Swabhumi Heritage Plaza,** a mall with 2.4 hectares (6 acres) of shopping, dining, and entertainment diversions; or head south to **Rabindra Bharati University Museum** (ℂ **033/2269-5241;** Rs 50; Tues–Sun 10:30am–4:30pm; no photography) to visit the **Rabindranath Tagore House Museum.** Born to a wealthy entrepreneurial family in 1861, Tagore remains Bengal's best-loved artist and intellectual, and his home is filled with artworks and collectibles (closed Sun, and open only until 1:30pm on Sat). Move on to the nearby **Marble Palace** (see below).

By now, you may be in serious need of sustenance, which you'll find in the vicinity of the enormous **Nakhoda,** Calcutta's largest mosque (Rabindra Sarani and M.G. Rd.). The mosque is closed to non-Muslims during prayers, but is set within a busy bazaar area where Muslim trades people sell all sorts of goods, as well as a range of breads, sweetmeats, and snacks. Alternatively, enjoy a cheap, substantial Kolkata-Mughlai meal at the century-old **Royal Indian Hotel** (147 Rabindra Sarani; ℂ **033/2268-1073;** daily 9am–11:30pm). Browse through the thousands of bookstalls along **College Street,** and finish with coffee at the **Indian Coffee House** (see below).

Top Attractions
Belur Math Shrine ★★   The headquarters of the international Ramakrishna Order, Belur Math combines the architectural elements of a church, a mosque, and a temple, symbolically embodying the teachings of the monk and seer Sri Ramakrishna Paramahansa.

(Moments) Durga Puja—Not Just Another Festival

Indians celebrate all year long throughout the country, but the grande dame of festivals is the **Durga Puja** ★★ (signifying the return of the goddess to her parents' home), the most sacred festival for the Bengalis. Though it is celebrated with much pomp all over northeastern India, Kolkata does it best, and if you're traveling here in September or October you simply have to include Kolkata in your itinerary. Literally every family is involved, not just in their own celebrations, but also as participants of the collective neighborhood presentation of Goddess Durga. *Pandals,* a kind of marquee used to shelter the idol, abound in the city, and have over the last decade become a commercial enterprise, with lucrative cash prizes for the most impressive—this has led to some highly innovative designs, where the raw materials include everything from bamboo and cloth to futuristic high-tech gizmos. The mode of transport for Durga is declared by the pundits just before the festival commences, and for many orthodox Bengalis, it is a sign of what awaits them in the coming year—for instance, an elephant could mean prosperity, while a boat may signify natural disasters. The festivities last for 4 days, with dances and frenzied drumming, lots of food, and endless bouts of shopping—it is mayhem on a grand scale and well worth experiencing. On the last day, idols (ranging from 1 inch to grandiose figures of over 9m/30 ft.) are immersed in the Hoogly, which carries many a prayer into deeper realms.

It was established in 1897, and the ashes of Sri Ramakrishna were placed here by his most prominent disciple, Swami Vivekananda, who also set up the Order. The location is lovely: Smaller shrines line the riverbank, and devotees and seekers of spiritual peace roam the grounds. Within the immaculate main shrine, activity is enlivened by evening *aarti* (musical prayers).

Belur Rd., Howrah. (℃ **033/2654-5700.** Daily 6:30–11:30am and 3:30–6pm; prayer *(aarti)* time: 5:30pm.

College Street ★   This stretch of road, deep in the heart of the university quarter, is famous for its 5,000 or so secondhand bookstalls, and for the renowned Presidency College, where India's greatest filmmaker, Satyajit Ray, studied. Many of the booksellers here are semi-literate, but remarkably, each is able to recall the titles and prices of thousands of academic and technical books, the volumes typically piled feet high. Look for the bust commemorating the father of Bengali prose literature, the reformer and philanthropist Pandit Iswar Chandra Vidyasagar, who also introduced a ban on forced marriages.

Bidhan Sarani, N. Kolkata.

Marble Palace ★★   Up a back street, in what was once known as Black Town, stands a vast mansion—a wonder to behold—sporting a plush Romanesque veneer that incorporates at least 90 different varieties of marble. Built in 1835 by the wealthy *zamindar* (landowner) Raja Rajendra Mullick Bahadur, this palatial family home has seen better days, and is now the center of a bitter feud between relatives, some of whom have been accused of sneaking off with the more valuable displays. But several works attributed to Titian and Renoir remain, while Venetian chandeliers, Ming vases, Egyptian statuary, as well as paintings, sculptures, furniture, and antique vases accumulated from 90 countries crowd the enormous, dimly lit rooms that open off deep verandas around an inner courtyard.

(Finds) Santiniketan: Where the World Makes a Home in a Single Nest

Known as the intellectual capital of India, Bengal has given birth to plenty of big personalities, but the one every Indian is most familiar with is the Nobel laureate Rabindranath Tagore. His collected works are easily available in any bookshop or library but the literary domain was not the only one he contributed to. Visit his creation **Viswa Bharati University** (which means communion of the world with India) at Santiniketan, 160km (99 miles) from Kolkata, where you will find a unique setting for imparting education, with classes held in the open; much the same way as the ancient Indian school system *(gurukul)*. Education takes on a different meaning here and with prior appointment, you can spend time amid students and teachers to learn more. If you decide to stay overnight, you could opt for one of the four guesthouses on campus (contact PRO) or try the simple but charming **Hotel Chhuti Holiday resort** (© 033/3293-4545; www.chhutiresort.com) or **Hotel Camellia** (© 03463/54-778; www.camelliagroup.org). (*Note:* Nearby, the exquisite terra-cotta temples of **Kalna** are an added incentive to make the trip.) Santiniketan, Birbhum, West Bengal 731 235. (© 03463/26-2751, or PRO 03463/ 26-2626; www.visva-bharati.ac.in. Closed on Wednesday.

Get there soon, since the feuding of the Mullicks makes it uncertain which prized item might next disappear. Admission is free, but you need a pass from the India Tourism Kolkata Office; if you arrive without one, the guard will let you in for a small fee (although this simply adds to the culture of corruption in India). A guide (at times, a young boy trying to make pocket money) is sent with you but it's pretty much a sham—insist on someone knowledgeable. In the same compound, you'll find a small garden and an animal enclosure.

46 Muktaram Basu St., off Chittaranjan Ave. © 033/2269-3310. Free admission but you need a pass from the India Tourism Kolkata Office. Tues–Wed and Fri–Sun 10am–4pm.

Paresnath Temple ★★ Jain temples are generally the most beautifully adorned in India, and Paresnath, dedicated to Sithalnath—one of the 24 perfect souls *(tirthankaras)* of the Jain religion—is no exception. Built in 1867 by a jeweler whose love of intricate designs, mirrors, and colored glass is evident everywhere, it boasts lavishly adorned patterned marble, beautiful European chandeliers, and stained-glass windows. A quiet garden is dotted with silver statues, and the temple houses an eternal flame that's apparently never gone out.

Badridas Temple St. Free admission. Daily 6am–noon and 3–7pm.

WHERE TO STAY

Decent budget rooms are all but nonexistent in Kolkata, and quality mid-range accommodations are also hard to find. That said, for rooms under Rs 5,000 you have two good options, both downtown in the busy Chowringhee area. **Fairlawn Hotel** is a famous option (see below) but **Middleton Inn,** a neat 21-room business hotel at 10 Middleton St. (© 033/2265-0449 through -0451) may suit you more. The Inn's dull entrance belies the scrupulously clean deluxe air-conditioned doubles that go for just Rs 4,400, including breakfast. Service in general is crisp and courteous, and though there's no

KOLKATA (CALCUTTA) & EAST INDIA

15

KOLKATA

restaurant, they have 24-hour room service. If neither of these options is available and you don't have the budget for one of the higher-end properties below, you could consider either of the following two: **The Peerless Inn** (✆ **033/4400-3900;** www.peerlesshotels. com) or **The Kenilworth** (✆ **033/2282-3939;** www.kenilworthhotels.com); both are well located (a few hops in case you want a slice of nightlife at The Park or shop in the New Market area) and in the same range of doubles from Rs 10,000, but the former is by far more popular with visitors, perhaps due to the friendly service that it's come to be known for. Note however, that they are rather bland and useful purely in a functional way.

Fairlawn Hotel (Value) This aged family run institution, still managed by 86-year-old Mrs. Smith, remains popular with people who are not too finicky about service, and are quite prepared to trade modern furnishings and fittings for character and quirkiness (not to mention great location and rates). News clippings, hotel awards, and copious family and celebrity photographs cover the walls, while old wicker chairs, vases, decorative plates, and even Buddhas and Ganeshas are used to create a homey atmosphere. Guest rooms (book nos. 16–21) are cozy, if simply furnished. In the kitchen, a wood- and coal-fire stove is used to prepare wholesome home-style meals from a menu that changes daily, but meal times are strict. Service standards have lagged significantly of late, and the heritage property is really showing signs of wear and tear, so please don't overnight here if you prefer pristine accommodations and don't mind bland, functional places (such as the Middleton Inn; see above).

13/A Sudder S., Kolkata 700 016. ✆ **033/2252-1510** or -8767. Fax 033/2252-1835. www.fairlawnhotel. com. 18 units. Rs 2,600 double with breakfast; extra bed Rs 1,000. 20% discount Apr–Sept. AE, MC, V. **Amenities:** Restaurant; bar; small library; room service. *In room:* A/C, TV, fridge (in some).

Hyatt Regency ★★ (Value) If it's a design-conscious luxury-cum-business hotel near the airport you're after, book yourself into the Hyatt, right next door to Swabhumi Heritage Park in the rapidly expanding business district of Salt Lake City, a good 45 minutes away from the tourist hub. Stylish rooms (174 of which are nonsmoking) have warm teak-wood floors, sunken baths, panoramic floor-to-ceiling windows, and walk-in closets. The large pool is backed by tall trees, while inside, a trendy cigar lounge appears suspended in midair. It's a schlep getting into the city from here, but if you're more or less in transit, with just a day to spare in Kolkata, this is a very good option, particularly if the rate drops to $150 double, which it does at certain times—check the website for the latest "Rate of the Day" tariff.

JA-1, Sector III, Salt Lake City, Kolkata 700 098. ✆ **033/2335-1234.** Fax 033/2335-1235. www.kolkata. regency.hyatt.com. Toll-free reservations from within India: ✆ 1-800/228-001. 233 units. There is no fixed tariff with the Hyatt working on a "Rate of the Day" system fluctuating between $150–$400 double, depending on the month; check the website or call reservations. AE, DC, MC, V. **Amenities:** 3 restaurants; bar; pool bar; airport transfer (Rs 1,124); bakery; babysitting; concierge; doctor-on-call; fitness center and spa; outdoor pool (adult and child); room service; squash; outdoor tennis; valet service; Wi-Fi (Rs 250/hr., Rs 900/day). *In room:* A/C, TV, hair dryer, Internet (Rs 250/hr).

ITC Sonar, A Luxury Collection Hotel, Kolkata ★★ If you want to stay far from the congested heart of Kolkata, like large open spaces, and want the pampering of a good spa, this "business resort" hotel offers just that. (If, however, you want the added benefits of having the sights on your doorstep and prefer not to deal with endless taxi rip-offs, The Oberoi Grand and The Park are better.) The ITC looks from the outside like the quintessential grotesque concrete structure rising from open marshland; once inside, you'll find a soporific escape. Courtyards and lily ponds separate accommodations blocks; the rooms to ask for are the ITC One rooms, with bathrooms which overlook natural light courts and the Olympic-sized pool and spa are welcome respites after a day trudging Kolkata's streets. Schedule a meal at **Dum Pukht** or **Peshawri** to get a taste of Awadhi or North West Frontier cuisine, respectively. And for those keen to travel responsibly, it's worth knowing that ITC Sonar Kolkata takes its role in reducing the hospitality sector's carbon footprint very seriously: The first hotel in the world to successfully register for Clean Development Mechanism Project under UNFCCC, it is also committed to environmental practices as per ISO 14001 Management System & British Safety Council Environmental Practices.

1 JBS Haldane Ave., opposite Science City (Eastern Metropolitan Bypass), Kolkata 700 046. 𝓒 **033/2345-4545.** Fax 033/2345-4555. www.starwoodhotels.com. 238 units. $450 Executive Club double; $550 The Towers double; $650 ITC One double; $850 junior suite; $1,400 queen suite; $2,150 presidential suite. Rates include breakfast. Taxes extra. Check online for specials for stays of 2 nights or more. AE, DC, MC, V. **Amenities:** 5 restaurants; bar; lounges; nightclub; airport transfers (Rs 1,700); babysitting; chip and putt golf course; health club; Internet (complimentary); jogging track; pastry shop; Olympic-sized outdoor pool; kids pool; room service; spa; outdoor tennis courts. *In room:* A/C, TV, minibar, Wi-Fi (Rs 300/30 min., Rs 600/full day).

The Oberoi Grand ★★★ This quintessential Kolkata monument is the city's top accommodations and one of the best hotels in India. Elegant, with regal old-world charm, its guest rooms draw ambassadors, diplomats, heads of state, and royalty (although the Hollywood party crowd heads for The Park). Deluxe suites, elegant and never too opulent, come with balconies, wooden floors, and Victorian furniture. Premier guest rooms (city or garden view) are marvelous; if you want a private balcony, book a room on the third floor. In the central courtyard, amid palms and gnarled frangipani trees, you can sip gin and tonics around the best pool in town. Or opt for the smoky ambience of the **Chowringhee bar.** Despite being cheek-by-jowl with one of the most chaotic streets, not a honk can be heard, courtesy of the old thick stone walls. The **Spa,** operating under the banner of famous Banyan Tree, is exclusively for guests and reason enough to stay here.

15 Jawaharlal Nehru Rd., Kolkata 700 013. 𝓒 **033/2249-2323.** Fax 033/2249-1217. www.oberoihotels. com. 209 units. Double: Rs 20,500 deluxe; Rs 23,500 luxury; Rs 25, 500 premier; Rs 35,000–Rs 65,000 suite; taxes extra. Premier room and suite rates include breakfast and airport transfers. Check website for online discounts. AE, DC, MC, V. **Amenities:** 2 restaurants; bar; airport transfer (Rs 2,200); babysitting; doctor-on-call; health club and spa; outdoor pool; room service. *In room:* A/C, TV, DVD player, hair dryer, minibar, MP3 docking station, Wi-Fi (Rs 20/min., Rs 800/day).

The Park ★★★ A five-star property, this chic boutique hotel is in the best downtown location, with proximity to both the business and the entertainment hubs of the city. But the real reason many choose to stay here is the on-tap party: Like so many Park properties, this hotel has four top "after dark" destinations under one roof—a pub, a nightclub, a cocktail bar, and a poolside alfresco bar lounge (see "Kolkata After Dark," later), providing easy access to the city's hippest, most happening nightlife. Guest rooms are small, but they're neat, functional, and bright, with bold color combinations and a very spacey look, specially in the Premier Luxury category. If you're in town for a while, book a Residence Room and you get a private lounge, a slightly larger bedroom with walk-in dressing room, stylish furniture, a thick mattress on a queen-size bed, a floor butler, and a Jacuzzi in the bathroom.

17 Park St., Kolkata 700 016. 𝓒 **033/2249-9000.** Fax 033/2249-7343 or -4000. www.theparkhotels.com. 149 units. $250 deluxe double; $350 luxury double; $450 The Residence suite double; $500 Presidential suite. $25 extra bed. AE, DC, MC, V. **Amenities:** 4 restaurants; pub; disco; airport transfers (free with suites at the Residence, Rs 1,450 for others); butler service; currency exchange; doctor-on-call; golf on request;

health club; outdoor pool. *In room:* A/C, TV, DVD, hair dryer, Jacuzzi (Residence rooms), minibar, Wi-Fi (Rs 200/hour, Rs 600/day).

Taj Bengal ★★ Popular with businesspeople, this is a good choice if you want to stay south of the city, enjoy views of the Maidan, and dine in-house—Taj Bengal boasts some of Kolkata's most impressive restaurants, under the aegis of the highly experienced chef Sujan Mukherjee. Besides **Sonargaon** and **The Hub**, it houses one of India's best Chinese restaurants, **Chinoiserie** (all reviewed below). Quieter rooms face the pool, or you can ask for a room with a view of the Victoria Memorial. Club Rooms (top floor) have added space (thanks to a window alcove), personal butler service, and access to posh lounges and exclusive restaurants (with strict dress codes) where the city's elite plot and play. The "gentlemen's club" ambience in the residents' lounge goes down well with a game of pool, a book from the small library, or time at the Internet bar.

34B Belvedere Rd., Alipore, Kolkata 700 027. ✆ **033/2223-3939.** Fax 033/2223-1766 or -8805. www.taj hotels.com. calcutta@tajhotels.com. 229 units. Rs 19,500 deluxe double; Rs 21,000 luxury double; Rs 24,000 Taj Club; Rs 30,000 executive suite; Rs 45,000 luxury suite; Rs 80,000 presidential suite; Rs 1,000 extra bed. Rates include breakfast. Rates up to 50% lower Apr–Sept. AE, DC, MC, V. **Amenities:** 3 restaurants; bar; tea lounge; airport transfers (Rs 1,875; free with suites); concierge; currency exchange; in-house doctor; health club; pool; room service. *In room:* A/C, TV, hair dryer, minibar, Wi-Fi (Rs 200/hr., Rs 600/day).

The Tollygunge Club ★★ (Moments) Far from the stereotypical hotel experience, this former home of a British Planter, and subsequently the exiled family of the late Tipoo Sultan of Mysore, has been voted one of the top 20 clubs in the world, and is the most unusual place to stay in Kolkata. Lush grounds abound with exotic bird and plant life, and even a family of hyenas which sing for the guests at twilight every day. Add to that the sporting facilities, affordable alcohol, great dining options (legendary steak kebab and chicken masala-toast) and old-world charm. Service is laid back and rooms are comfortable but not plush—opt for the suites facing the golf course, or the cottages (very large double rooms with a separate sitting area). A great oasis with quirky fellow guests but it's a 30-minute drive from the city center and note that collared shirts for men and proper footwear are required in the more formal areas.

120, Deshapran Sasmal Rd., Kolkata 700 033. ✆ **033/2417-6022.** www.thetollygungeclub.com. Reservations: Glenburn (✆ **033/2288-5630** or 98-3007-0213). 66 units (with showers). Rs 5,000 single or double, including breakfast and taxes. MC, V. **Amenities:** 3 restaurants; 4 bars; lounge; billiards; bridge room; doctor-on-call; 18-hole golf course; health club; horse riding; Internet (Rs 33/30 min); ice-cream parlor; outdoor/indoor/heated pool; room service; outdoor tennis; ayurvedic spa; squash. *In room:* A/C, TV, fridge.

Vedic Village ★ For those yearning for a taste of the famous vigorous and oily massage, the Vedic Village is a boon. Located just 20 minutes from the airport and about an hour from the city, it is a collection of thoughtfully landscaped villas, suites, studios, and farmhouses—the interiors for most are a little bland but the deluxe lake villas and earth villas are quite decent with extremely spacious bathrooms. Local materials like bamboo and grass coexist with state of the art massage chairs; a lovely lake acts as a centerpiece, while cabbages grow boisterously amid blooming flowers. The lotus-shaped pool is their pride but we found it lacked privacy, specially since there are eight conference rooms in the area. The USP is decidedly the medical spa—it is the only one of its kind hereabouts and offers long-term naturopathy and Ayurvedic therapies as well as cosmetic and relaxing treatments—ideal for a quick stopover before taking your flight back home.

PS Rajarhat PO Bagu, Shikharpur, Rajarhat, Kolkata 700 135. ✆ **03216/27-2760** or 98308-20445. Fax 033/2287-1311. www.thevedicvillage.com. 200 units. Rs 5,000 studio; Rs 6,000 deluxe resort bungalow

12,000 deluxe villa; rates include breakfast for 2 persons and taxes. AE, DC, MC, V. **Amenities:** 2 restaurants; bar; airport transfer (Rs 850); doctor-on-call; health club and spa; outdoor pool; room service. *In room:* A/C, TV, Internet (Rs 50/30 min.), massage chairs in villas, minibar.

WHERE TO DINE

Bengalis are known for their fine palates and love of dining out, and a wide range of cuisines are theirs to choose from. Make sure to sample **Kolkata-Mughlai food**—blending the best of the Bengali *Nawabs'* cuisine with influences from the Deccan, Awadh, and North India—at least once. **Nizam's,** which has been given a makeover recently (1 Corporation Place, just behind The Oberoi Grand), claims to be the place where the *kathi* kebab roll (kebabs wrapped in a *paratha*—fried bread) was invented. The food is legendary, and the prices unbeatable but don't expect any sophistication in service or ambience. Another popular Bengali-Muslim joint is **Shiraz** (56 Park St., at the intersection of Park St. and A.J.C. Bose Rd.; ☎ 033/2287-7702 or 033/2280-5006). Go to the first floor for air-conditioned comfort, or up to the rooftop. The extensive menu includes numerous exotic-sounding Kolkata-Mughlai items, as well as a range of kebabs.

If you're in the vicinity of Nakhoda Mosque, try the **Royal Indian Hotel** (147 Rabindra Sarani; ☎ 033/2268-1073), which opened in 1905 and is the oldest restaurant of its kind. On Thursday or Sunday, you can order *murgh mussalam* (chicken); mutton *chanps tikiya* (chops) is another specialty (available on all days except Thurs).

Chinese cuisine is popular with Kolkatans—**Mainland China** ★ (Uniworth House, 3A Gurusadary Rd.; ☎ 033/2283-7964 through -7969; www.mainlandchinaindia.com) is one of the most popular, but serves typical Indian-Chinese: a tomato base, and heavy emphasis on chilies. Good choices include Peking-style lamb cooked in black pepper sauce, Hunan-style prawns, and Szechuan chili crab.

Park Street, one of the city's busiest hubs, is lined cheek-by-jowl with restaurants and stalls serving all kinds of interesting food. **Peter Cat** (18A Park St.; ☎ 033/2229-8841 or 033/2217-2942), set in a pleasant colonial bungalow, serves an outstanding *chelo kebab* platter (Rs 148), skewered meat kebabs on a bed of flavored rice. This is a popular after-work watering hole, though service is often shoddy. Avoid it at lunchtime on weekdays when it's packed with local office-goers. Also on Park Street is **Mocambo** (25B Park St.; ☎ 033/2229-0095 or 033/2217-5372), which serves decent Western fare (try the tasty deviled crabs and sizzlers (steak or kebab and vegetable platters).

For Bengali cuisine, try **Oh Calcutta** ★★ (10/3 Elgin Rd., fourth floor, Forum Mall; ☎ 033/2283-7162; www.speciality.co.in) and ask for specials like *dab chingri* (prawns in coconut gravy), *kakra chingri bhapa* (crabmeat and minced prawn cooked with mustard sauce, wrapped in banana leaf, and steamed), or Anglo-Indian fare like the Railway Mutton Curry; nothing fancy about the decor but its popularity is evident. If you don't mind sitting in cramped surroundings, **Bhojohari Manna** (☎ 033/2440-1933) is where you get the most authentic Bengali fare at dirt-cheap prices. There are four branches; best to give a call and ask which one is closest to you.

Anyone with a sweet tooth is headed for heaven: *Mishti doi* (yogurt with caramelized sugar) is a must-try, as are Bengali staples like *sandesh* (cottage cheese with jaggery), *chanar payesh* (cottage cheese or milk with nuts and raisins), *ledikeni* (said to be named after Lady Canning, who was a great admirer of this sweet!), *rossogolla* (spongy balls of cottage cheese dipped in sugar syrup), and *khir kadom,* more delicately sweetened than the *gulab jamuns* (sweet milk-and-dough balls) and *halwas* (semolina desserts) of the north, and available all over the city. Shop where sweet gourmands do, at the most

(Moments) **Fast Food, Kolkata Style ★★★**

At almost any time of the day you'll see expectant customers standing outside the various *kathi* roll booths all over the city. They're waiting for one of Kolkata's favorite lunchtime snacks, a *paratha* (thick *chapati,* or fried bread) filled with spiced chicken, mutton, egg, potato, or *paneer* (Indian cheese) topped off with *chaat* masala, onion, and lemon juice—simply delicious. The hygiene at many of these places is often suspect, so look for a stall with lots of customers. (Try **Kusum** at 21 Park St., the one outside Oxford Book Store; or another stall next to Peter Cat.) Order the double-side egg mutton roll. *Puchkas* (deep-fried hollow balls made of wheat, filled with mashed and spiced potato along with tangy mint), omelet bread (where the bread is cooked inside the egg!), and *jhalmuri* (a truly delicious mix of a dozen snack items, served dry or with onions, tomatoes, and spicy chutneys), are also favorites with the local people and a must-have if you really want a taste of Kolkatan life.

popular **K.C. Das** (11A Planet East, Dharamtala; ✆ **033/2248-5920;** www.kcdas.co. in). You could also try **Ganguram** (11 C.R. Ave.; ✆ **033/2236-5502;** www.ganguram. com), **Gokul** (1 A.J.C. Bose Rd.), **Mithai** (48B Syed Amir Ali Ave.), and **Bhim Chandra Nag** (5, Nirmal Chandra St.; ✆ **033/2212-0465**).

Baan Thai ★★★ THAI   The Oberoi's Baan Thai is one of those rare places where you are assured of real authenticity, with chefs Thida and Prayong earning many accolades in the last 3 years. Start with *kai rue koong hor bai toey* (marinated chicken or prawn morsels wrapped in pandana leaf, deep fried, and served with soy sesame dip) or the *som tam esan* (tangy salad of young papaya, peanut, and tomato dressed with lemon juice and palm). Follow this with the best *tom yam soup* in the country. For the mains, traditional flat rice noodles goes great with spicy green curry, *pla kapong/phet samros* (deep-fried *bekti* [fish]/duck in spicy sweet and sour sauce), *patani* (stir-fried lamb with ginger), or *kai takrai* (traditional stir-fried chicken)—all winners. You must order a most refreshing Chendol Ice (pineapple juice and coconut milk). The ambience is nicer in the evening, but if it's purely the cuisine you're after, any time is a good time.

The Oberoi Grand, 15 Jawaharlal Nehru Rd., Kolkata. ✆ **033/2249-2323.** Fax 033/2249-1217. www. oberoihotels.com. Average meal for 2 Rs 2,000. AE, DC, MC, V. Daily 12:30–2:30pm and 7:30–11:30pm.

Chinoiserie ★★★ CHINESE   The finest Chinese restaurant in Kolkata dishes out delicious Szechuan and Cantonese cuisine. Centered around a beautiful raindrop chandelier, with private corners for business lunches and romantic dinners, cloth paintings done by an artist from Shantiniketan, photographs of ancient Chinese artifacts, and, bizarrcly, a blues and soul soundtrack—Chinoiserie breaks all stereotypes. If the menu proves bewildering, turn to chef Lian for guidance, but be warned: He is passionate about almost everything! Our recommendation would be to start with crispy duck with pancakes and sweet bean sauce or the delicious banana fish roll. Amazingly light golden-fried prawns are accompanied by Lian's special green sauce. For the main course try stir-fried chicken with pickled chilies, braised Chinese cabbage with ginger, and fish with oyster sauce. End with white fungus (which, contrary to its name, is delicious) or tofu with coconut—and pair the meal with cups of Chinese tea. Unlike in most other Chinese restaurants, the emphasis here is on flavor, which comes across in everything you eat.

Taj Bengal, 34B Belvedere Rd., Alipore. ℭ **033/2223-3939.** www.tajhotels.com. Average meal for 2 Rs 2,000. AE, DC, MC, V. Daily 12:30–2:45pm and 7:30–11:45pm.

Fire and Ice ★ ITALIAN   When Annamaria started out selling tomato sauce to hotels it probably never crossed her mind that a decade later she would be serving her brand of simple, authentic Italian in two restaurants (in India and Nepal). Fire and Ice is excellent value for money and the spacious restaurant an unpretentious haven, with exposed brick walls, photographs of Hollywood and Bollywood classics, and an open kitchen where you can see Annamaria puttering around, making sure the pizzas are just right. The *antipasta misto* and penne pesto are highly recommended, as is the Fire of Bengal pizza. Make sure you save space for the delicious homemade apple pie served with imported vanilla ice cream. The evenings are great here specially since they got their liquor license, but it's also a lovely place to hang out during the day over a cup of excellent coffee or iced tea.

Kanak Bldg., 41, J.L. Nehru Rd., opposite Jeevan Deep Bldg. ℭ **033/2288-4073.** www.fireandicepizzeria. com. Meal for 2 Rs 500. AE, DC, MC, V. Daily 11am–midnight.

The Hub ★★ ECLECTIC   A highlight here is the "food theater" experience, during which guests can watch a five-course meal being prepared, and then dig into the results. Start with the intriguing souplike concoction called *porcini cappuccino* (porcini mushrooms, white wine, pepper, cream, and butter), followed by the pan-fried *bhetki* (fish) with grilled vegetables, white wine, and garlic bisque sauce; leave enough space to end with the scrumptious mud pie with banana caramel ice cream. You could also opt to save a visit for its fabulous Sunday brunch.

Taj Bengal, 34B Belvedere Rd., Allpore. ℭ **033/2223-3939.** www.tajhotels.com. Main courses Rs 450–Rs 1,500; buffet Rs 800. Food theater Rs 425–Rs 850. Sun brunch Rs 1,395. AE, DC, MC, V. Open 24 hr.

Kewpie's BENGALI   Popular with local celebrities and bigwig visitors to the city, this tiny family kitchen has been well marketed but is not necessarily the most authentic (for that you're better off visiting **Suruchi,** ideally combined with a visit to South Park Cemetery). The menu changes daily, but the highlight is Kewpie's thali (multicourse platter)—various fish, vegetable, and meat items (or strictly vegetarian items), served with different breads.

2 Elgin Lane, off Heysham Rd., behind Netaji Bhavan. ℭ **033/2486-1600** or -9929. Nonvegetarian thali Rs 415 per person. MC, V. Tues–Sun 12:30–3pm and 7:30–11pm.

Saffron ★★★ CONTEMPORARY INDIAN/FUSION   Saffron's executive chef Rajiv Khullar has transformed the menu to showcase local Bengali cuisine as well as a host of Pan-Indian specialties, all cooked strictly using Indian methods, but often with ingredients from around the world. The *daab chingri,* prawns simmered in coconut milk gravy, is a real treat, as is the *jhalfarezi masala duck. Shahtoosh kebab,* a chicken filet marinated with pistachio and cooked in a tandoor is guaranteed to melt in your mouth and is one of the restaurant's signature dishes. Or try the more traditional saffron-infused *kucchi gosht biryani* or chicken Chettinad. Vegetarians are also well catered to. Leave space for creative desserts like *mishthi doi mousse* (traditional Bengali sweet curd made into mousse) and *notun gurer rasmalai ice cream*—they even have a sampler if you share the same weakness as the Bengalis for sweets.

The Park hotel, 17 Park St. ℭ **033/2249-9000.** www.theparkhotels.com. Main courses Rs 355–Rs 795. AE, DC, MC, V. Daily 12:45–2:45pm and 7:30–11:45pm (last orders).

Sonargaon ★★ BENGALI/NORTH INDIAN Exposed stone masonry, a well, whitewashed walls, wooden tables, tribal wall hangings, a separate fish-market kitchen (where guests can watch their fish being cooked), and enormous storm lanterns set the atmosphere for this upmarket take on village-style North Indian and Bengali dining. Order a large glass of the most delicious *ganne ka ras* (fresh sugar cane juice) to go along with a traditional Bengali thali (multicourse meal; it's not on the menu, but you can order it in advance), served on a silver platter, and give yourself plenty of time to recover; diners tend to leave with full stomachs. For an excellent starter, get the melt-in-your-mouth *kakori kebab* (tender minced mutton kebab blended with rose petals, cardamom, saffron, and secret spices), introduced by Sonargaon to Kolkata 15 years ago. Leave space for *rossogolla payesh*, a Bengali dessert made from *paneer* (cheese) and thickened sweet milk or the innovative *Baileys kulfi* (frozen thick ice-cream-like milk dessert flavored with Baileys Irish Cream).

Taj Bengal, 34B Belvedere Rd., Alipore. ℂ 033/2223-3939; www.tajhotels.com. Main courses Rs 395–Rs 800. AE, DC, MC, V. Daily 12:30–2:45pm and 7:30–11:45pm.

Zaranj ★★ NORTHWEST FRONTIER Named for a hamlet in Afghanistan, this upmarket restaurant is one of the city's most opulent dining options, where miniature waterfalls and plush seating provide a warm, luxurious atmosphere. The **Raphael Lounge** is an ideal spot to kick off the evening in style, with its fine selection of imported wines and champagnes. Affable manager Protik Dey will help you pick fare to suit your taste buds, but if you like lamb, his hands-down recommendation is the Zaranj *raan*. Other popular dishes include *macchli masala* kebabs (*bhetki* fish mixed with the chef's secret spices), tandoori prawns *(jhinga)*, and *dahi ka* kebab, prepared in the display kitchen behind a wall of glass. For dinner, be sure to reserve in advance, or you'll be watching the city's movers and groovers feasting while you wait.

26 Jawaharlal Nehru Rd. ℂ 033/2249-5572, -9744, -0369, or -0370. Reservations essential. Main courses Rs 200–Rs 525. AE, DC, MC, V. Daily 12:30–3pm and 7:30–11pm; closed at lunchtime on Tues.

Zen House ★★ ASIAN This is the second notable offering from The Park: Bangkok-born master chef Nut Kunlert serves Asian specialties like lemon-grass fish, barbecued prawns, double-fried pork in chili garlic or excellent duck in hoisin sauce with the delicious green tea tiramisu as a perfect ending. The ambience is informal with a very active open kitchen that dishes out a whole lot of aroma and orchestrated sizzle and pop of culinary creation.

The Park hotel, 17 Park St. ℂ 033/2249-9000. www.theparkhotels.com. Main courses Rs 350–Rs 995. AE, DC, MC, V. Daily (except Mon) 7:30–11:45pm (last orders); additional lunch on Sun 12:45–2:45pm.

SHOPPING

Kolkata is also renowned for its fashion designers. Look for garments by the promising local **Sabyasachi Mukherjee,** who is taking Kolkata's fashion industry to new heights (there's an outlet at 37/1C Hazra Rd.; ℂ 033/2285-2381). Another name to reckon with is Anamika Khanna, recognized for her flamboyant fashions for both men and women. If time is short, drop in at **85 Landsdowne Road** (ℂ 033/2486-2136), a one-stop shop stocking all the major Indian labels like the two mentioned before along with others like Kiran Uttam Ghosh and Ritu Kumar. However, if you're looking for something very ethnic and traditional, you should head to **Shamlu Dudeja's** workshop (4/1 Alipore Park Rd. near Taj Bengal; ℂ 98-3002-6288; call for appointment). With a team of rural women (SHE-Self-Help Enterprise), Shamlu has successfully revived the art of

Kantha embroidery, making it into a much sought-after craft both locally and abroad. Smaller but also worth visiting are **Women's Friendly Society** (29 Park Lane; ✆ 033/2229-5285) and **Good Companions** (13 C, Russell St.; ✆ 033/3292-9612) for hand-embroidered linen from the villages of West Bengal—both can be done when you head out to explore the New Market or if you are staying at The Oberoi or Peerless Inn. In fact, a few steps from here will also get you to the government-operated **Central Cottage Industries Emporium** in Chowringhee (7 Jawaharlal Nehru Rd.; ✆ 033/2228-4139 or -3205) where you can pick up a wide range of Indian curios, along with everything from saris to silk carpets. But the place to visit if you are madly interested in textiles is Darshan Shah's brainchild **Weaver's Studio** (5-1 Anil Moitra Rd., Ballygunge Place; from Garihat road, take a left at the Industrial Training Institute; ✆ 033/2440-8937; www.weaversstudio.com). Other than a fabulous resource center for all kinds of Indian textiles, thousands of hand-printing wooden blocks and books, you can also watch the intricate processes of weaving, printing and natural dyeing, which makes the final shopping aspect very special, if not altogether enlightened (*note:* You can only visit the factory by appointment). If scouting around The Park, visit **Bengal Home Industries** (11 Camac St.; ✆ 033/2282-1562) or **Sasha** (27 Mirza Ghalib St.; ✆ 033/2252-1586) for Bengali handicrafts, In the same area, hop into **Dolly's Collection of Earthcraft** (18J Park St., next to Petercat) for natural products—a hole in the wall but with some simple and sweet items like mats made out of banana fiber or tiny terracotta turtles with cocky grins. You can pick up a wide range of Indian curios, along with handlooms and handicrafts, from **Dakshinapan** (2 Garihat Rd.), an open-air shopping complex (on the same lines as Dilli Haat in Delhi). It's a great place to browse, and while there, you absolutely must pop into the 20-year-old **Dolly's Tea Shop** (G62, Dakshinapan), which has become an institution by itself. Other than having a cuppa, you can also purchase excellent quality tea and as Dolly herself will tell you, "India has the best tea in the world, so why look elsewhere?" **Hugli** (Hastings Court, 96 Garden Reach Rd.; ✆ 033/2489-2104) and **Khazana** at the Taj Bengal hotel are two good options for handicrafts as well; although the prices are high, quality is excellent. If you feel you can lug some heavier stuff back home, drop in at **Minnoli** (Karnani Estate, Unit G-I 209, AJC Bose Rd.; ✆ 033/2289-1307), where owner Sharad Narula shows his obvious passion for antique furniture. Proud of a collection that includes everything from silver spoons dating from the first World War to 60-year old glass lamps, Minnoli encapsulates the very spirit of Kolkata.

Inevitably, Kolkata is also home to one of India's best bookstores, **Oxford Bookstore** (17 Park St., Kolkata; ✆ 033/2229-7662 or 033/2217-5266; www.oxfordbookstore.com), which carries a good range of local and imported periodicals, books on India and Kolkata, and fiction. Another shop worth investigating is **Family Book Shop** (1A Park St.; ✆ 033/2229-3486 or 033/3290-6003); it's tiny but has an interesting upstairs section. You can also try **Crossword** on Elgin Road or **Starmark** on Lord Sinha Road.

KOLKATA AFTER DARK
Drinking & Partying
Kolkata is officially dry on Thursday, but this doesn't affect the upscale hotels. Local laws supposedly prohibit the sale of alcohol after 10:30pm, so if you're up for an all-nighter, be sure to ask the exact time for last rounds at any bar you visit. In the budget-oriented Sudder Street precinct, the open-air bar at the **Fairlawn Hotel** (13/A Sudder St.; ✆ 033/2252-1510) is an atmospheric place for sundowners and early-evening drinks. **The Park**

(© **033/2249-9000;** www.theparkhotels.com) is *the* place to hang out after hours—**Someplace Else** ★ rocks all night long with live bands belting out alternative rock, salsa, blues and jazz every night of the week. Together with vibrantly hued **Tantra** ★★ (strictly for couples and room guests; Rs 500 on weekends per couple), which has the largest dance floor in the city, it attracts the city's hippest crowd. The '60s-styled and -themed cocktail bar **Roxie's** ★★ (entry is free if staying at The Park hotel or on recommendation by an existing guest) is worth trying to get an invite to, if not for the decor (rough and classy with exposed red bricks), then definitely for the music that darts between the '50s, '60s, and '70s, enjoyed best with what the bar prides itself on—"mood cocktails." If this wasn't already enough, The Park also has **Aqua,** a poolside alfresco lounge. Wooden loungers and deck beds, suspended timber deck, hot tub, and cool pool—Aqua has it all. Known earlier as Cinnamon, the **Marrakesh Lounge** (24 Park St.; © **033/2227-4974**) and **Virgose,** at the Hotel Hindustan International (235/1ACJ Bose Rd.; © **033/2283-0505;** www.hhihotels.com), are also popular, especially with those who want to stray far from the bustling crowds that throng in and around The Park.

Live Performance

Theater, music, dance, and poetry recitals all thrive here. Check out the listings in the "Bulletin Board" section of *The Times of India.* Upscale hotels also carry the useful monthly booklets *City Info* and *Cal Calling.* **Rabindra Sadan** concert hall (A.J.C. Bose Rd. and Cathedral Rd.; © **033/2223-9936** or -9917) hosts regular theater and musical events, as well as dance-drama performances and local-flavored Bengali poetry evenings. Cultural events also take place at the **Academy of Fine Arts** (2 Cathedral Rd.; © **033/2223-4302**). The **British Council** (5 Shakespeare Sarani; © **033/2242-5478;** www.britishcouncil.org) often offers plays and performances in English. Bengali and English dramas are performed at **Kala Mandir** (48 Shakespeare Sarani; © **033/2287-9086**). For musical programs, contact **Sisir Mancha** (1/1 A.J.C. Bose Rd.; © **033/2223-5317**). Indo-German productions are occasionally held at **Max Mueller Bhavan** (8 Pramathesh Barua Sarani; © **033/2486-6398;** www.goethe.de).

Cinema, Galleries & Exhibitions

Considered the art capital of India, Kolkata hosts a huge number of art exhibitions. Scan the newspapers for information about what's on while you're in town. Or check out the **Birla Academy of Art and Culture** (108–109 Southern Ave.; © **033/2466-6802;** www.birlaart.com) or the **Centre for International Modern Art** (Sunny Towers, 43 Ashutosh Chowdhari Ave.; © **033/2485-8717;** www.cimaartindia.com; Tues–Sat 11am–7pm, Mon 3–7pm, closed Sun). The **Academy of Fine Arts** (2 Cathedral Rd.; © **033/2223-4302**) has art galleries (daily 3–8pm) and a museum (Tues–Sun noon–6:30pm; admission Rs 5), where you can see works by Rabindranath Tagore.

While most Malls have multiplexes, the best cinema complex in the city is **Nandan** (1/1 A.J.C. Bose Rd.; © **033/2223-1210** or -0970), with excellent screens and a fantastic sound system. Nandan also regularly hosts art-film screenings and retrospectives (the annual Kolkata Film Festival takes place in Oct/Nov; www.kff.in). There are a number of stand-alone cinemas in Chowringhee where you can watch movies in the company of feverishly excitable Indian audiences.

The tropical state that flourished during the 13th century on India's central eastern seaboard, Orissa is famous for its temples, which draw thousands of pilgrims here throughout the year, predominantly to **Jagannath Temple** in the coastal town of **Puri,** to worship Vishnu in his avatar as the Lord of the Universe. Architecturally, the **Sun Temple** at **Konark** is of even greater significance, with its massive stone-carved chariot adorned with sculptures, rising to carry Surya, the sun god, to the heavens. Even Orissa's capital, **Bhubaneswar** (the third point of Orissa's Golden Triangle), is more important for its enormous collection of Hindu temples—at one time 7,000—than it is as an administrative or industrial center.

Orissa remains largely tribal, with many villages still off-limits to outsiders, but the state is also well-known for its "Tribal Tourism." For the anthropologically inclined, this offers you a chance to get way off the beaten track and meet people who live on the fringes of civilization. The state is also a good place to pick up crafts, particularly textiles and paintings—even when tending to the rice paddies, the women of Orissa are dressed in glamorous saris. Cottage textile industries are the mainstays for entire villages, which produce beautiful *ikat* (patterned) textiles, palm-leaf paintings, and bright *patachitra* (cloth) paintings (the best-known of Orissa's handicrafts). *Note:* Although Orissa has long, golden beaches that curve around the Bay of Bengal, the infrastructure here is limited and the sea can be treacherous; beach lovers are best off heading for Kerala or Goa.

BHUBANESWAR

485km (300 miles) SW of Kolkata

Orissa's capital emerged in the 7th century as a center of prolific and accomplished temple building, and by the 11th century the city of Bhubaneswar (derived from Shiva's incarnation as Tribhubaneswar, Lord of the Three Worlds) had become a significant religious hub, with an estimated 7,000 temples. Of these, only several hundred remain, but those that survive reveal the evolution of the Nagara style into an architectural form unique to Orissa. You won't need to stay here more than a day—Konark's Sun Temple, one of India's top attractions, is just under an hour's drive away.

Essentials

VISITOR INFORMATION You can try the **Government of Orissa Tourist Office** (5 Jaydev Nagar; © **0674/243-2022;** Mon–Sat 10am–5pm, closed on the second Sat of each month) for information about the region.

GETTING THERE   By Air Bhubaneswar is connected to most of the main cities in India: **Kingfisher** (© **180-0209-3030;** www.flykingfisher.com) and **Jetlite** (© **1800-22-3020;** www.jetlite.com) have direct flights to Kolkata (55 min.); to Delhi (2 hr.) **Indian Airlines** (© **1800-180-1407;** www.indianairlines.in), Jetlite, Kingfisher, **Indigo** (© 1800-180-3838; http://book.goindigo.in); and to Mumbai (3 hr.) you can use Indian Airlines and Kingfisher. There are connections to and from several destinations in South India, including Chennai and Hyderabad. **Bhubaneswar's Biju Patnaik Airport** is about 4km (2½ miles) from the center, in the southwest. The airport has a tourist information counter, as well as a taxi service; though this is not a prepaid service, transfers into the city should cost no more than Rs 200.

By Train The best train from Delhi is the **Rajdhani Express,** but the trip is lengthy—25 hours—and departures are only 2 days per week; other trains may take 30 to 42 hours. From Kolkata, the **Howrah-Puri Express** is the most convenient (it's overnight); however, the quickest is the **Faluknama Express** (under 7 hr.). Puri is 1½ hours from Bhubaneswar, and there is regular train service between the two cities. For inquiries and reservations, your best bet is to see a travel agent or to visit the train reservation office personally (see chapter 3).

By Road If you want to drive or bus it here from Kolkata (500km/310 miles away), count on spending 13 hours propped up in your seat.

GETTING AROUND **By Taxi & Auto-Rickshaw** Auto-rickshaws in Bhubaneswar are unusually comfortable and well maintained. Drivers are genuinely helpful, if sometimes unable to understand you. Taxis from Bhubaneswar to Puri or Konark are readily available; for taxi excursions, be clear about the duration of your journey, and the sights you wish to cover. Hiring a car and driver is a good way to save time. Try **Mercury Travels** at the Trident Hilton (Nayapalli; ✆ **0674/230-1010,** ext. 49), or **Swosti Travels** (103 Janpath; ✆ **0674/253-5773** or -5771)—each of which handles flights, car rentals, and tours of the state. Inexpensive full-day coach tours of the city and the entire Golden Triangle region are administered by the **O.T.D.C. Head Office** (✆ **0674/243-2382;** www.orissa-tourism.com), but these are targeted at domestic visitors.

Tip: **Heritage Tours** (www.heritagetoursorissa.com) is a reputable outfit with years of experience. Located at the entrance of the Mayfair Beach Resort in Puri, it specializes in "Lifestyle Tours" (including learning trips on such subjects as yoga, Odissi dance, Ayurveda, stone carving, and sand sculpting) as well as rural and tribal excursions. Besides organizing every aspect of trips lasting anything from 1 to 20 days, Heritage Tours also deals with ticketing and transportation matters.

Bhubaneswar's Top Attractions

In the heart of Bhubaneswar's Old Town, the most important temples—almost all Shaivite—are clustered around **Bindusagar Lake,** a holy reservoir believed to hold water from each and every holy river and lake in India. Of the 7,000 temples that are said to have once surrounded the tank, only around 500 remain. Traditionally, pilgrims perform their ablutions in the lake before heading into the temples to perform *puja* (a ritual of respect, such as prayer). The best are easily visited in a morning (more than three or four is overkill), leaving you time to explore some of the outlying sights during the afternoon.

The best of the city's Nagara-style temples (7th c. and 12th c. A.D.) are testament to both a radical resurgence of Hinduism and Buddhist defeat—frequently represented in temple sculptures by the image of a lion lunging for an elephant. With the exception of wonderful **Rajarani Temple** (see below), all of those worth visiting are living temples. The best are magnificently carved **Mukteshwar Temple**—the 10th-century "Gem of Orissan Architecture," where a squat, cobra-protected lingam stands in the sanctum sanctorum—and **Lingaraj Temple;** although the complex is off-limits to non-Hindus, you can admire it from a well-known vantage point, a raised platform built by the British, where you'll be harassed by a hood with a phony register of donations from other foreigners (ignore his advances and mention the police). If you have time, make a stop at the well-preserved 7th-century **Parasurameswar Temple (Brahmeswar),** for its lavish carvings, including a number of amorous couples. For something more "exotic," visit **Vaital Temple** ★ and view its creepy tantric carvings; you'll need a flashlight to see the images of humans being put to death while the goddess Chamunda looks on.

Chilka Lake ★★ A unique ecosystem of marine, brackish, and fresh water, this Wetlands of International Importance is a haven for migratory birds: Come in October and the 1,100 sq. km (429 sq. miles) of Asia's largest brackish water lake resound with the delightful cacophony of thousands of birds. Besides birdlife, the lake has pods of dolphins and a central island with an important Hindu temple dedicated to Goddess Kalijai. There isn't much infrastructure around, so best to keep it as a day trip, preferably from Puri. Contact the Orissa tourism office (© **0674/243-2382;** www.orissa-tourism. com) for help in planning your trip.

Best time to visit: Oct–Mar.

Dhauli ★ The glistening, white-domed **Shanti Stupa (Peace Pagoda)** at the top of Dhauli Hill is visible from the main road as you head toward this site, where historic Ashokan rock edicts are carved. Guarded by pale yellow Ashokan lions, the Kalinga World Peace Pagoda is a celebration of Ashoka's decision, 2,300 years ago, to renounce violence and war and embrace Buddhism—a decision made in the wake of his massacre against the Kalinga people, then rulers of Orissa. A plaque here notes that Ashoka built 84,000 *stupas* (commemorative cairns), some as far away as Greece.

Free admission. Daily 5am–8pm.

Museum of Tribal Art and Artifacts ★ Everything connected with the life of Orissa's tribal people is on display in the exhibition rooms at this newly built museum decorated with primitive murals. Traditional costumes, jewelry, household appliances, and hunting equipment such as bows and arrows, axes, and traps for birds and fish indicate the ways of life of the tribal peoples of Orissa.

Near C.R.P. Sq., NH 5. © **0674/256-1635** or -3649. Free admission. Tues–Sun 10am–5pm; closed 2nd Sat of each month.

Orissa State Museum ★ This collection convincingly explains the religious context of Hindu sculptures, but you may be more fascinated by the erotic friezes that date back as far as the 7th century A.D. Upstairs, the **Manuscript Gallery** includes early examples of the type of work you'll encounter in some Orissan crafts villages. Along with a collection of musical instruments, a number of dioramas depict different Orissan tribes. Next door is a collection of *patachitra* (cloth) paintings dealing primarily with the Jagannath cult and tales from the *Ramayana*.

Lewis Rd., near Kalpana Sq. © **0674/243-1597.** Rs 50. Tues–Sun 10am–5pm.

Rajarani Temple ★★ Surrounded by open space and paddy fields, this 11th-century temple—maintained by the Archaeological Survey of India—glimmers in the light of day, built as it was using a superior-quality burgundy-gold sandstone. Unusual for Orissan temples, the tower *(shikhara)* features miniature versions of itself. Sculptural representations of lotus flowers with the guardians of the eight cardinal directions are a standout feature of the temple walls, which also feature delightful female figures engaged in mundane (but beautiful) daily activities.

Tankapani Rd. Rs 220. Daily 6am–6pm.

Udaygiri and Khandagiri caves ★ Barely 7km (4⅓ miles) from the chaos of Bhubaneswar, the twin caves of Udaygiri and Khandagiri were once home to aspiring Jain monks. They were built in the 1st century B.C. by King Kharevala, and each complex numbers roughly 15 to 18 caves. Of the two, Udaygiri is more interesting, with caves filled with ornate carvings—look for caves 1, 3, 5, 9, 10, and 14; Khandagiri's cave no.

3 is also rich in carvings. If you go in the evening, the atmosphere gets a little more interesting, with monkeys gamboling from one cave to another and the odd lone *sadhu* playing his flute. The caves bathed in golden light around sunset look very beautiful and serene despite the tourist influx. (For those academically interested in other cave sites, the **Lalitgiri, Udaigiri,** and **Ratnagiri** trio are located 100km (62 miles) from Bhubanswar and contain Buddhist excavations, sculptures and stupas. Note that these are entirely lacking in nearby infrastructure.)

Small entry fee. Daily 8am–6pm.

Where to Stay

Mayfair Lagoon ★   Not as luxe or delightfully serene as the Trident, the Mayfair is nevertheless hugely popular with the international corporate world and Indian tourists. Cottages and villas with plush interiors and views of the lagoon are set amid gardens, and facilities like the only spa in the city as well as the pub **10 Downing Street** does pull in the crowd. While you would be better off staying clear of Lemon Grass, their Thai/Chinese offering, you could opt for typical Oriya cuisine at **Kanika** or dine in the open-air **Nakli Dhaba:** an imitation of a typical roadside eatery in India that serves the night highway traffic, there's even a faux gas pump and truck.

8-B Jaydev Vihar, Bhubaneswar 751 013. ✆ **0674/236-0101.** Fax 0674/236-0236. www.mayfairhotels. com. 102 units. Rs 8,000 executive cottage/club room; Rs 14,000 deluxe cottage/club suite; Rs 28,000 villa; Rs 1,500 extra bed. Check website for online specials. AE, DC, MC, V. **Amenities:** 4 restaurants; 2 bars; airport transfer (Rs 800); babysitting; butler service; concierge; currency exchange; doctor-on-call; outdoor pool; room service; spa. *In room:* A/C, TV, DVD player; hair dryer, Jacuzzi and a lake-view deck (only villas), minibar, Wi-Fi (Rs 331/hr., Rs 899/day).

Trident Hilton ★★   Situated some distance out of the city center, this classy low-rise hotel is surrounded by 5.6 hectares (14 acres) of exquisite lawns, mango groves, and rock gardens. Drawing businesspeople, travelers, and even the English cricket team, this is Bhubaneswar's most fabulous, and expensive, hotel. Stepping inside the lobby is like entering a temple, sans the usual chaos brought by thronging worshipers. The space has been carefully designed with stone columns, beautiful brickwork, and trellised railings enhanced by concealed lighting and spectacular brass-bell lighting features. Mythical lions perch above, looking down on guests as they arrive, and in the evenings, live Indian music is featured. Guest rooms are smart, stylish, and well laid out. Bird-watchers should ask for a room facing the rose garden. The kitchen will prepare a picnic basket for you should you be heading out on a long day of temple-exploring.

C.B.-1, Nayapalli, Bhubaneswar 751 013. ✆ **0674/230-1010.** Fax 0674/230-1302. www.tridenthotels.com. 62 units. Rs 11,000 deluxe room; Rs 14,000 junior suite; Rs 18,000 executive suite; Rs 22,500 presidential suite. Check website for online specials. AE, DC, MC, V. **Amenities:** Restaurant; bar; airport transfer (Rs 729); babysitting; badminton court; doctor-on-call; jogging track; pool; room service; 2 floodlit tennis courts. *In room:* A/C, TV, DVD player (in suites), hair dryer, minibar, Wi-Fi (Rs 200/hr., Rs 700/day).

Where to Dine

Ignore the seedy neighborhood and dour look of the lodge where this upstairs eatery, **Venus Inn** (217 Bapuji Nagar; ✆ **0674/253-1908**), is and you'll find a good location for a quick South Indian *dosa*. Soft Hindi music fills the neat, clean interior as you dine on butter paper *masala dosa* (crepe-thin filled pancake), the onion *rawa masala dosa,* a *dosa* stuffed full of potato, or an *uttapam* (thicker pancake) with coconut. For the best chicken in town, **Cook's Kitchen** (260 Bapuji Nagar; ✆ **0674/253-0025**) is the place to be—chicken *tikka* butter masala is for those who can handle their spices. Order an

Orissan thali at Swosti Plaza's **Chandan** ★ (© **0674/230-1936** through -1939; www. swostiplaza.com), where waiters can talk you through the evening's selection while old Hindi film music provides prerecorded entertainment. The menu changes daily, but a typical selection might include fragrant dry Oriya mutton *(mangsha kasha)*; Rohu fish (beware of the fine bones) cooked in a mustard sauce *(sorisa machha)*; traditionally prepared mixed vegetables *(santula)*; and soft *paneer* (Indian cheese) cooked under charcoal and then caramelized *(chhena poda)*—all served with breads and condiments on a brass platter.

Hare Krishna ★ VEGETARIAN   You won't find garlic or onion (Hare Krishna culinary no-nos) in the vegetarian dishes served at this surreally decorated restaurant reached via a series of Art Deco linoleum steps. The food is rich and flavorful, so don't overorder. Lord Krishna's favorite is apparently Govinda's Pasanda, a *paneer* (Indian cheese) based dish that's heavy on the spices and includes cashew nuts, tomato, and fresh vegetables. Also spicy, but with an added hint of sour, is Chaitanya's Pasanda, made with *paneer* as well. We can heartily recommend Nanda Moharaja's *palak paneer*, which makes good use of mineral-rich spinach and is accompanied by thick, warm, fresh *naan*. The steaming-hot vegetable *biryani* is known as Bhaktivinod's Delight, and it's good.

1st floor, Lalchand Market, Jan Path. (© **0674/253-4188.** www.harekrishna.com. Main courses Rs 50–Rs 125. No credit cards. Daily 11am–3pm and 7–10:15pm.

Shopping

Sixteen kilometers (10 miles) north of Puri, **Raghurajpur Crafts Village,** a quaint rural village of thatched-roof houses, offers a variety of traditional Oriya crafts. Craftspeople will meet you as you emerge from your taxi or auto-rickshaw and lead you to their homes, which double as production centers for specific art forms. Along with a cup of *chai*, you'll be given a thorough account of the creative process. *Patachitra* paintings, the best-known of Orissa's handicrafts, fetch up to Rs 15,000 and are created on a cloth canvas, using a brush made from mouse hair. Vibrant colors are used to create extraordinarily detailed depictions of mythological events—most of these revolve around the life of Krishna. Also impressive are traditional palm-leaf drawings made with an iron pen. These are typically presented as a concertina-style fold-up poster made from palm fronds and featuring concealed erotic images and Sanskrit inscriptions. Those who want to watch artisans at work can spend time at the **Pattachitra Centre Handicraft Museum** (© **0675/224-508;** daily 9am–7pm; www.pattachitracentre.com). *Note:* Although prices are reasonable, they are slightly inflated, and you shouldn't feel pressured to buy something you don't want. You can also try and get these at any of the **Utkalika** showrooms present in all the cities within the state. Although Sambalpur is the right place to pick up tons of gorgeous *ikkat* (traditional weaves from the region), if you can't manage going to this small town (77km/48 miles from Bhubaneswar), drop in at any **State Emporium** (Priyadarshini, V.I.P. Rd., Puri; © **06752/22-9982;** or Western Tower Market Bldg., Bhubaneswar; © **0674/253-2140**). Both the delicate **silver filigree work** *(tarakasi)* as well as crude **brass and metal work** crafted by tribal folk using traditional casting methods *(dhokra)* are extremely popular not just in India but abroad as well. While they are sold with almost a 200% markup internationally, in Orissa you will get them at far more reasonable rates. If you are traveling to Konark by road, you will come across a sudden splash of color spilling on to the blue tar—welcome to **Pipli,** a tiny village where almost everyone is involved in appliqué work. The street is lined with shops on both sides selling massive umbrellas, cushion covers, bedspreads, wall hangings, and lampshades, all in bright colors and bold patterns. Every shop has a couple of tailors (often the owners themselves are on the machines), and it's fascinating to watch them at work. Finally large scale village fairs and *haats* (markets) held periodically (Ekamra haat Nov–Dec; Bali Yatra Jan) in Bhubaneswar as well as neighboring Cuttack, are simply delightful in atmosphere and the range of goods is bewildering. Ask the OTDC for further information if you want to time your visit with these.

EXPLORING PURI & THE SUN TEMPLE AT KONARK

Puri is 65km (40 miles) S of Bhubaneswar; Konark is 35km (22 miles) NE of Puri

Puri is considered one of the four holiest places in India, home to magnificent 15th-century **Sri Jagannath Temple,** where pilgrims throng to be absolved of past sins by the Lord of the Universe. But given that this is off-limits to non-Hindus, the real highlight lies farther up the coast, in the mellow town of Konark, site of the legendary 13th-century **Sun Temple.**

Sri Jagannath Temple ★　Topped by Vishnu's wheel and flag, the 64m (210-ft.) *shikhara* (spire) of Jagannath Temple dominates Puri's skyline, and it's possible to circumambulate the entire complex by wandering through the market streets around the periphery walls. However, for non-Hindus, the best view of this mighty Kalinga temple is from the balcony of **Raghunandan Library,** across the street. From here, you not only get a glimpse of the tremendously active temple life, but you'll be privy to the colorful activity around the souvenir stalls that spread around the temple in every direction. From this viewing point, both the size of the temple and the sheer numbers of swarming people are impressive; the temple buildings themselves are filthy with mildew. Incidentally, you will find images of Lord Jagannath and his siblings everywhere in this part of India. Pitch-black with squat physiques and exaggerated features, they could well have been inspiration for the animation technique used by the creators of *South Park:* The crude, flat-featured, raccoon-eyed faces have thin red curling grins. You will be asked to sign a register on your way out with a column for donations with suspiciously high figures (for instance, two zeros added after Rs 20); in all fairness, make a donation, but don't get conned.

Raghunandan Library is open daily 7am–noon and 4–8pm. All rickshaw drivers can show you the way.

Sun Temple ★★★　Visualized as the gigantic chariot of Surya, the sun god, emerging from the ocean, the Sun Temple at Konark was built (though not completed) at the zenith of Orissan architectural development, at the edge of a 483km (300-mile) beach. Guarded by stone elephants and mythical lions, the immense structure was carved from rock so as to look like an enormous war chariot (originally drawn by seven galloping horses), with detailed sculpted scenes of everyday facets of life. Even the spokes of the 24 giant wheels that adorn the base of the temple are intricately carved. The temple was at some point submerged by sand; when the ocean retreated just over a century ago, the temple that had been lost to the world was uncovered and excavated by the British, who consequently tried to carry away as much of it as they could but failed given the extraordinary dimensions of Indian sculpture. The entire complex is surrounded by a periphery wall. To first get an idea of the enormity of the project, circumnavigate the temple by slowly skirting this outer wall. The sanctum has collapsed inward, so it is no longer possible to enter the temple building, but you can clamber over most of the exterior for close-up views of the various scenes of love and war, trade and commerce, sports and mythical figures, and of course the four depictions of Surya in each of the directions. Among the friezes are those depicting amorous dalliances between entwined couples—these provide stiff competition for the world-renowned sculpted erotica at Khajuraho—including spokes with miniature examples of the erotic carvings found all over the rest of the temple.

The earlier you arrive, the better your chances of enjoying this World Heritage Site in peace. Definitely avoid visiting the temple on the weekend, when day-tripping local visitors swarm to Konark as part of a high-paced pilgrimage around Orissa's golden circuit.

If you're here during the first week of December, you may be able to catch the 5-day **Konark Dance Festival ★★★**, which offers performances by some of the country's most sought-after dancers. The monument forms a remarkable backdrop to traditional dance styles accompanied by music played on classical Indian instruments.

Konark, 64km (40 miles) southeast of Bhubaneswar; 35km (21 miles) northeast of Puri. Rs 205. Sunrise-sunset. For information on the Konark Dance Festival, contact O.T.D.C. in Bhubaneswar (© 0674/243-2382; www.panthanivas.com).

Where to Stay

Small, intimate, peaceful, and close to the beach, **Z Hotel**—the former seaside residence of the Raja of Serampore—is the best budget lodging in the state, offering huge, simply furnished guest rooms with sea views. Reserve room no. 25, 26, or 27 (© 06752/22-2554; www.zhotelindia.com; doubles from Rs 700; no credit cards) well in advance to secure an upstairs unit with attached bathroom (drench shower only). Don't miss the beach view from the rooftop which, unfortunately, also reveals Puri's unchecked development. Alternatively, try **Toshali Sands,** en route to Konark (© 06752/25-0571 through -0574; www.toshalisands.com; doubles from Rs 4,500). Though it's never going to win any design awards, this is the closest acceptable accommodations to the Sun Temple. A beach lies nearby, and the restaurant's not bad. "Villa" units are the best choices, they feature small sitting rooms, porches, shared kitchenettes, and big bathrooms with tubs. In Puri itself, the one reviewed below is the only one actually located on the beach itself while all the others are either away or across the road. Of these, **The Hans Coco Palms** (© 06752/230-038; www.hanshotels.com) is the best pick with the usual facilities at hand, making it convenient, functional but entirely devoid of the "ah" factor.

Mayfair Beach Resort This is the best place to stay in the vicinity of the Sun Temple by a long shot, popular with middle-class Indian families who come to strut their stuff on the wide expanse of beach, a short walk from the resort. However, service can be pretty surly. Disinterested staff members wear bright Hawaiian shirts, and the entrance and lobby areas are equally colorful, playing off the Jagannath Temple theme. The rough-hewn red-brick resort makes the most of its limited space, its gardens profuse with lovely trees, potted plants, and stone statues of various deities. Unless you can afford the presidential suite, book a garden cottage; it has a small sitting area, a semiprivate veranda, and a small shower room. Beyond the crow-infested pool, a nice stretch of beach is watched by the resort's lifeguards, although hawkers still ply their trades. If the early checkout doesn't suit you, the management should be able to help.

Chakratirtha Rd., Puri 752 002. © 06752/22-7800 through -7809. Fax 06752/22-4242. www.mayfairhotels.com. 34 units. Rs 6,000 deluxe room/cottage; Rs 9,000 premier suite. Rs 1,000 extra person. Ask about discounts. AE, MC, V. **Amenities:** 2 restaurants; 2 bars; airport transfers (Rs 2,500); currency exchange; doctor-on-call; indoor games; health club with steam and Jacuzzi; outdoor pool; pool table; room service; table tennis. In room: A/C, TV, minibar, Wi-Fi (Rs 331/hr., Rs 899/day).

Where to Dine

Besides **Mayfair's Aquarium & Veranda** (© 06752/22-7800; www.mayfairhotels.com), where you can sample Orissan seafood specialties (*chingudi tarkari,* prawns prepared in a traditional Orissan gravy, is delicious), you can dine at **Wild Grass** (V.I.P. Rd.; C **06752/ 22-9293;** daily 11am–11pm), a self-consciously eco-friendly open-air restaurant set in a lush garden with stone and slate pathways and tables arranged in various nooks at different levels. Come for the delightful ambience, but don't expect the most spectacular food or service. One of the highlights here is an Orissan thali, but it must be ordered at least 2 hours in advance (well worth it). Grilled *brinjal* (eggplant, known as *baigan poda*) is another favorite; or try tandoori prawns, *nargisi* fish kebab, or prawn *malai* curry. For dessert, try the local cheesecake, *chhena poda*. **Restaurant Peace** is an utterly laid-back cafe-style eatery with plastic chairs under thatched roofing; it opens early and serves the best bowl of muesli in India. A genuinely huge portion of fresh fruit, mixed nuts, curd, and honey is a perfect way to start the day (C.T. Rd.; C **06752/22-6642;** no credit cards; daily 7am–11pm).

Tribal Tours in Orissa

Venturing into Orissa's tribal heartland is a true off-the-beaten-track adventure, allowing you to meet people with social, cultural, and agricultural practices that have remained unchanged for centuries. Many of Orissa's tribal people are still hunter-gatherers, and are physically distinct from any other ethnic group on the subcontinent. Opportunities for travelers to interact with members of these unique societies are generally limited to weekly markets held at various tribal centers. Visitors with an especially strong interest in anthropology can arrange to spend a night or two in a traditional village, but expect plenty of walking—and forget any modern conveniences. You may, however, want to consider the fact that you will be visiting one of India's poorest regions. Also check whether any of the spoils of your tourist venture are actually reaching these village folk. Visitors have reported that some tribal tours are exploitative, making a freak-show/spectacle of the poor. In Puri, your best option for a responsibly organized tribal tour is **Heritage Tours** (p. 714); to ensure that a suitable trip is planned around your specific interests, e-mail the highly knowledgeable Bubu in advance (C **06752/22-3656** or 94-3702-3656; www.heritagetours orissa.com). A typical tribal tour for two persons will cost in the vicinity of $70 to $100 per person per day, for a minimum of 6 or 7 days. The fee factors in the services of a guide, an Ambassador car and driver, food, and (ultra-basic) accommodations.

3 DARJEELING

500km (310 miles) N of Kolkata

Darjeeling, "Land of the Celestial Thunderbolt," was given to the British as a "gift" from the once-independent kingdom of Sikkim. Lying in the Himalayan foothills and entirely surrounded by snowcapped vistas, Darjeeling soon became the favorite summer resort of the British Raj during the heyday of Calcutta—when Mark Twain visited, he exclaimed it was "the one land that all men desire to see, and having seen once by even a glimpse would not give that glimpse for the shows of the rest of the world combined." Today, the incredible view of the world's third-highest mountain, Mount Kanchenjunga (8,220m/27,400 ft.), is undoubtedly Darjeeling's best-loved attraction, though the town has also acquired a global reputation for producing the "champagne of teas," and retains some of its haunting Gothic Victorian ambience. Most visitors are here to pick up a permit and get acclimatized for hikes through the mountainous state of Sikkim. It's worth noting that if you want a sleepy colonial hill-station environment, with splendid flower-filled walks, this is not it. Head instead for nearby **Kalimpong,** which offers a number of charming old-world accommodations.

Two nights in Darjeeling should be more than enough, particularly if you're moving on to other Himalayan foothill towns. As with most hill stations, Darjeeling involves a considerable amount of climbing, and you'll do well to avoid the ugly mess of lower Darjeeling, which is typically congested, with suspicious odors, confusing back alleys, and a jumble of paths and stairways. Stick to The Mall and Chowrasta (crossroads) in upper Darjeeling, where life proceeds at a polite pace, and you can enjoy leisurely walks, stopping for a cup of tea or to browse shops stuffed full of trinkets and artifacts.

Note: There has been a fair amount of political turmoil off late with the Nepali residents clamoring for Darjeeling to become a separate state called Gorkhaland; quite unfortunately and with little foresight, the politics has directly affected tourists so it is advisable to find out what the mood is like prior to making bookings. The travel agents and operators recommended in this book can advise you; alternatively check with your embassy or state tourism department (see the planning chapter).

ESSENTIALS

VISITOR INFORMATION Darjeeling's **Tourist Information Centre** (The Mall, (℃) 0354/225-5351 or -4214; www.wbtourism.com/darjeeling; June to mid-Mar Mon–Sat 10am–4:30pm, mid-Mar to May daily 9am–7pm) is helpful and will give you a free map of the area.

ACQUIRING YOUR SIKKIM PERMIT IN DARJEELING *Be warned:* Getting your Sikkim permit is a laborious process that will last at least an hour. Take your passport to the **District Magistrate's Office** (off Hill Cart Rd.; Mon–Fri 10am–1pm and 2:30–4:30pm). Fill in a permit application form (remember to have it stamped), then go to the **Foreigners' Registration Office** (Laden La Rd.; (℃) 0354/225-4203; daily 10am–7pm), where a policeman will endorse your form. Finally, head back to the District Magistrate's Office, making sure you arrive before closing time, and your passport will be stamped and the permit issued free of charge. Valid for 15 days, it states clearly which areas you may enter. (Permits are also available from the Ministry of Home Affairs in New Delhi or from Indian consulates abroad.)

GETTING THERE **By Road** Darjeeling is 80km (50 miles) from Siliguri, which is the nearest main transit point. Buses from Darjeeling usually leave from the Bazaar bus stand on Hill Cart Road. Darjeeling is connected by road with Siliguri, Bagdogra, Gangtok, and Kathmandu across the Nepali border. Kalimpong is 2½ hours from Bagdogra as well as Darjeeling.

By Air The nearest airport is at Bagdogra (near Siliguri), 90km (56 miles) away. **Jet Airways** ((℃) 033/3989-3333; www.jetairways.com) and **Spicejet** ((℃) 1800-180-3333; www.spicejet.com) have flights to Bagdogra from Kolkata (1 hr.) and Delhi (2 hr.). If you decide to fly to or from Assam, there are 50-minute flights available from **Go-Air** ((℃) 1800-222-111; www.goair.in). A taxi ride from Bagdogra to Darjeeling should take 3½ hours and cost about Rs 2,000 to Rs 2,500. From Siliguri, catch the **toy train** (8 hr.; see below) or a **taxi** (2–3 hr.; Rs 1,000) to get to Darjeeling.

By Train From Kolkata (Sealdah Station), the best option is the overnight Darjeeling Mail, which is supposed to arrive at the New Jalpaiguri railway station (scheduled arrival 8:40am) in time to connect with the Darjeeling Himalayan Railway's famous **toy train.** The toy train departs at 9am for the scenic 8-hour journey (see "The Most Spectacular

(Moments) The Most Spectacular Train Journey

A polite voice at New Jalpaiguri railway station frequently announces that "the train is running 30 minutes late, the inconvenience caused is deeply regretted." It's a small price to pay for what must be one of the slowest, most spectacular train journeys in the world. Since July 4, 1881, Darjeeling's aptly named **toy trains**— including the world's oldest functioning steam locomotive—have puffed and wheezed their ways between the hill station and the plains. In December 1999, the railway became India's 22nd World Heritage Site, only the second railway in the world to be so recognized on the list. The trip between New Jalpaiguri and Darjeeling covers a mere 87km (54 miles) but takes almost an entire day to transport passengers up 2,055m (6,850 ft.). En route, with rhododendron slopes, rolling hills, and Kanchenjunga in almost constant view, you pass through villages with names like Margaret's Hope, and puff past the front doors of homes that range from shacks to quaint red-tiled cottages surrounded by potted flowers. You also traverse a total of 498 bridges and 153 unmanned level crossings. The final stop before Darjeeling is **Ghum (Ghoom),** the second-highest railway station in the world. For details, see "Getting There: By Train," above, or **www.dhr.in.**

Train Journey," below). Or you can hire a taxi or share a jeep (readily available), directly from the station, for the 3-hour, 88km (54-mile) journey to Darjeeling. Although the toy train runs daily, bad weather may disrupt services. If you intend to catch the toy train out of Darjeeling at the end of your stay, and wish to travel in first class (Rs 247), you must book your ticket in advance at the counter at New Jalpaiguri Station. You can reserve other tickets for major trains out of New Jalpaiguri at the Darjeeling railway station daily between 8am and 2pm.

GETTING AROUND It's best to explore Darjeeling on foot, and if you need to haul luggage, ask for a porter and pay him well. Taxis are overpriced and unnecessary (with the exception of excursions to places some distance from the town). For local sightseeing tours or even jeep trips to Gangtok and other mid-distance destinations, contact the helpful **Darjeeling Transport Corporation** (30 Laden La Rd., opposite Apsara Hotel). It's open from 8am until 8pm and can advise you on alternatives if they're unable to accommodate you.

TREKKING & ADVENTURE ACTIVITIES Darjeeling is a good base for various "acclimatization treks" at lower altitudes than those you're going to come up against if you intend to trek in Sikkim. For sightseeing as well as trekking tours around Darjeeling and western Sikkim **Gurudongma Tours and Treks** (② 90-0269-2611 or 94-3406-2100; www.gurudongma.com) comes highly recommended. For white-water rafting, contact **D.G.H.C. Tourism** (Silver Fir Bldg., The Mall; ② 0354/225-5351). A well-established tour and travel agency in Sikkim, with a branch in Darjeeling, is **Himali Travel Specialists** (30 D.B Giri Rd., Darjeeling; ② 0354/225-2741 or 98-3204-5091; somgff@rediffmail.com).

Darjeeling is the type of place where you might easily find yourself wanting to do very little other than drink in the restorative climate and tea. There are over 70 different tea plantations in the area, and a typical tour demonstrates everything from harvesting to how different varieties of tea are sorted and prepared for export around the globe. For the finest selection of organic and nonorganic teas—20 to 30 plantations are represented— pay a visit to **Nathmulls** (✆ **0354/225-6437**; www.nathmulltea.com; Mon–Sat 9am– 7pm), a family business that's been selling tea since 1931. Better still, stay at the Glenburn Tea Estate (reviewed below). For a good vantage point, climb **Observatory Hill,** held sacred by Hindus and Buddhists. A Kali shrine is guarded by foul-tempered monkeys that play on the colorful Buddhist prayer flags strung between the pine trees.

Darjeeling has a sizable Tibetan presence and a number of Buddhist monasteries you can visit. Set against the backdrop of Kanchenjunga, colorful **Bhutia Busty Gompa,** near Chowrasta, is famous for the contents of its upstairs Buddhist library—one of the texts kept there is the original *Tibetan Book of the Dead.* On Tenzing Norgay Road, you may be able to buy Tibetan and Sikkimese handicrafts at **Aloobari Monastery.**

An hour's walk from town is **Padmaja Naidu Zoological Park,** where you can give the animals a miss and head straight for the secluded **Snow Leopard and Red Panda Breeding Programme,** the only successful breeding program of these endangered species in the world. Sit patiently and watch snow leopards in their cages or a red panda in the trees, or chat with Kiran Motane, the program's dedicated zoologist.

A Glorious Sunrise

Watching the sun rise from **Tiger Hill,** near the sleepy town of Ghoom, is one of the best things to do in the area (11km/7 miles from Darjeeling; private taxi costs Rs 800 round-trip): The sight of the first rays of dawn carving a dramatic, golden silhouette around the not-too-distant eastern Himalayan peaks is brilliant. Occasionally, Mount Everest is also visible, just 225km (140 miles) away. Come armed with spare film and warm clothing— at an altitude of 2,550m (8,160 ft.), predawn Tiger Hill is bone-jarringly cold, and if you want to join the crowds who flock here each morning, you have to be up before dawn. The entry fee is Rs 5, but you can pay a little extra for VIP treatment inside a special observation tower (Rs 40), where heating is accompanied by soothing Darjeeling tea. On the way back, visit **Ghoom (Liga Choling) Gompa;** possibly the best-known Buddhist monastery around Darjeeling, it was founded in the late 1800s and enshrines a 5m-high (16-ft.) clay statue of the Maitreya Buddha. In the early morning light, the colorfully painted figures over the facade and rooftops—intended to scare away evil spirits—are radiant. Along the exterior walls are prayer wheels that are spun in order to send countless prayers to the heavens, while inside, butter lamps are lit in offering to the deity.

WHERE TO STAY

Darjeeling is a great place to experience real colonial coziness, with several charming heritage hotels. In this category our preference is for **Mayfair Hill,** but **Windamere Hotel** (✆ **0354/225-4041** or -4042; www.windamerehotel.com; doubles from Rs 8,550), originally a Victorian boardinghouse for English tea-planters on Observatory Hill, has atmospheric public spaces (though the list of do's and don'ts put a slight damper on the holiday). Its huge heritage rooms come with immense charm, but the hotel is showing signs of wear and tear (as you'd expect from a place built in 1889), as does the service. Another heritage property (and better bet) is **The Elgin Hotel** (✆ **0354/225-7226** or -7227; www.elginhotels.com; doubles from Rs 5,800; includes all meals). With the air of a country manor, the hotel is frequented by an upmarket foreign crowd looking to relive the splendor of the British Raj. Like that of Windamere, its public spaces are filled with old-world charm—old-fashioned sofas, deep armchairs, fireplaces, and beautiful rugs—but some of the rooms aren't quite as grand (some odd color combinations, too), and the bathrooms are small. The best views are from room nos. 21 to 23, 31 to 33, and 51 to 53.

If daily walks are what you're looking for, then **Kurseong** (an hour below Darjeeling) offers some nice hikes. The town is ramshackle but fortunately the best place to stay is tucked away from it. Choc-a-bloc with quirky antiques, wooden floors, frayed rugs, inexplicable teddy bears, a few dusty corners and a lot of atmosphere what with a Volkswagen perched on the awning, **Cochrane Place** (✆ **99-3203-5660;** www.imperialchai. com) is great to stay at but not for more than 2 days because the food is below average and given that the restaurant is the best the town has, you should be on your way pretty soon—walk a lot, stick to the momos and enjoy our favorite Batasia suite which comes with an attic or take a pick from the deluxe rooms (Rs 4,380–Rs 5,870; all meals included). Finally, if you want to be assured of absolute peace and quiet, head for the nearby hill station of Kalimpong.

Dekeling Hotel ★ ⓥalue   Some of the cedar-paneled guest rooms at this charming hotel (best choice for tight budgets) have the best views in town. Spotlessly clean and simple, this is the place to go for Tibetan hospitality (run by the wonderfully warm Norbu and Sangay Dekeva) rather than Raj-style sophistication. An old iron chimney heater keeps the lounge/library (stone tile floors, Tibetan sofas, *thangkas,* Tibetan paintings) cozy and warm; it's a wonderful place to kick back with a book, watched by the family dog, Doma. Guest rooms are basic, and although the bathrooms are a little small (with shower only), they're immaculately clean. On cold nights, a hot-water bottle is usually tucked into your bed. On the attic floor, room no. 3 has a 180-degree view that takes in Darjeeling town and Mount Kachenchunga in all its snowcapped magnificence. For security reasons, the hotel, located high above Dekevas Restaurant, is locked up at 11pm; inform the management by 9pm if you expect to be late.

51 Gandhi Rd., Darjeeling 734 101. ✆ 0354/225-3298 or -4159. Fax 0354/225-3298. www.dekeling.com. 22 units. Rs 1,000 back-facing double; Rs 1,250 standard and attic double; Rs 1,600 deluxe double. Rs 250 extra bed. Discounts of up to 50% off season (July 1–Sept 14 and Jan 15–Mar 14). AE, MC, V. **Amenities:** Restaurant; library; room service; Wi-Fi (Rs 60/hr.). *In room:* TV, electric heater on request, hot water.

Dekeling Resort ★ ⓥalue   This little guesthouse (resort is an ill-chosen descriptor) is the best value-for-money deal in town. A stiff, athletic climb leads you to "Hawke's Nest," the colonial bungalow with a commanding location high above the town, now redubbed Dekeling Resort. Prayer flags flutter around this 120-year-old green-roofed, bay-windowed, two-leveled, all-suite cottage offering simple comfort, effortless charm, and complete privacy. There's a small, one-table dining room where breakfasts and home-cooked meals are served; or you can be served in bed, which the obliging staff of two will arrange. Ask for a double bed in an upstairs room; accommodations there are huge and charming, with wood floors, carved antique dressers, Tibetan rugs, pale floral fabrics, and lovely fireplaces. Bathrooms have large drench showers and plenty of natural light. This is a true haven if you don't mind the 20-minute walk to The Mall.

2 A.J.C. Bose Rd., Darjeeling 734 101. ✆ 0354/225-3092 or -3347. Fax 0354/225-3298. www.dekeling. com. 4 units (with showers). Rs 2,900 double without meals; Rs 4,350 double with meals. Up to 40% discount off season. AE, MC, V. **Amenities:** Dining room; library; lounge; room service. *In room:* TV, fireplace.

The Glenburn Tea Estate ★★★   Homestays are aplenty in India, as are tea gardens and luxurious resorts, but a combination of all three is very rare. The creative offspring of the dynamic Husna-Tara Prakash, Glenburn centers around the 100-year-old Burra Bungalow and Water Lily Bungalow, each with separate sitting rooms and fire place, and a traditional common dining room where multicourse meals are served in true planter's style. Each of the rooms is unique and makes delightful use of space, light, and color. Add to that the gorgeous views of the Kanchenjunga that can be had from the sit-outs and verandas, and you can see why we think Glenburn is a little chunk of heaven. Trails wind through pockets of forest or slopes of tea all the way from 1,110m (3,700 ft.) to the banks of the rivers Rungeet and Rung Dung, across which lies the neighboring state of Sikkim. Picnics are served by liveried bearers on portable tables complete with a tablecloth, delicate crockery, and a vase of fresh flowers—all that is lacking is a chandelier. *Note:* Guests have an option to enjoy the day or even stay overnight at the Glenburn Lodge by the river, without giving up their room at the Bungalow—the two rooms here are simple but charming, especially at night when bathed in the orange glow of hurricane lamps (no electricity) with only the burbling of the river for music.

City Office: Kanak Bldg., 41, Chowringhee Rd., Kolkata 700 071. Darlene Khan ☏ **033/2288-5630** or -1805; Husna-Tara Prakash ☏ 98-3007-0213. Fax 033/2288-3581. www.glenburnteaestate.com. U.K. ☏ +44 (0)1295/758-150. www.mahoutuk.com. 8 units: Rs 18,000 double; Rs 12,000 single; Rs 6,000 extra person; Rs 2,500 child 3–15. Children under 3 stay free in parent's room. Entire estate rental: Rs 1,300,000 per night. 10% discount for stays of 4 nights or more. Off-season discounts mid June to mid Sept. Complimentary tea, coffee, mineral water, fresh juice, and soft drinks; day trips to Darjeeling town/Kalimpong. MC, V. **Amenities:** Dining; fishing; library; board games; massage and reflexology; guide/naturalist; river rafting; shop; vehicle at disposal. *In room:* Electric blankets, fireplace (except Rose and Kanchenjunga suites), fresh fruit and flowers, heater, hot water bottles.

Mayfair Hill Resort ★ Once the summer palace of the Maharajah of Nazargunj, this class act has warmer staff and better ambience than popular New Elgin, and the views are far superior. Two copper elephants guard the entrance of the main building, and a signboard informs guests of daily weather conditions. It's set in a lovely garden with potted plants, sculpted deities, and its own temple. The partially wood-paneled guest rooms—in ivy-covered buildings, which feel more like cozy cottages—are a tad feminine (floral fabrics, predominantly pink) but lovely, featuring Tibetan rugs, fireplaces, fine wooden furnishings, bay windows with seats, and entrance/dressing rooms. They receive plenty of natural light and enjoy superb views of the town, the mountains, and the valley below. The tiled, well-spaced bathrooms have good shelving and vintage-style freestanding wooden towel racks. Guests are allowed use of sports facilities at the Darjeeling Gymkhana Club.

Opposite Governor's House, The Mall, Darjeeling 734 101. ☏ **0354/225-6376** or -6476. Fax 0354/225-2674. www.mayfairhotels.com. 44 units. Rs 9,000 deluxe double. Rs 2,500 extra bed. Rates include all meals. MC, V. **Amenities:** Restaurant; bar; babysitting; billiards; currency exchange; doctor-on-call; health club and tennis privileges; ice-skating; library; pool table; squash; tea-leaf shop; travel assistance. *In room:* TV, DVD player, fireplace, hair dryer, heater.

WHERE TO DINE

The following recommendations are all within walking distance of each other; ask for directions before you set out. For Tibetan food, **Dekevas Restaurant** (☏ **0354/225-4159;** no credit cards) has some delicious favorites, including *momos* (dumplings) and wonton soup, with a choice of chicken, pork, or vegetable as a base. Try a delicious *shabalay,* Tibetan pie filled with mince, onion, and spring onion; spice it up with a hint of chili sauce. Also sample the awesome *tsampa*—roasted barley served with cheese, butter, and a glass of milk. For those extracold days, it has a selection of soups. Also available are Chinese dishes, pizzas, and burgers. Adjacent is the no-frills matchbox-size **Kunga,** where the beef or pork *thenthuk* (flat noodles) soup is excellent. At **Lemon Grass** (also known as The Park), you can order from the Thai or Indian menu—the Indian tandoori chicken is a standout (✆ **0354/225-5270;** no credit cards). Part of a three-floor food center, with a delicatessen and Internet cafe one floor below and an American diner at the basement level, **Glenary's** has been serving guests since 1935. Although staff may boast about the Continental cuisine, the best options are Indian—try *mahi tikka* (spicy fish tandoori) or *bhuna gosht,* a mutton curry cooked with ginger, garlic, and masala in its own juices (✆ **0354/225-7554**). A new addition in the basement, the **Buzz** acts as a pub, dishing out great music and hosting live bands in the evenings from Thursday to Sunday. **Joey's Pub** (✆ **0354/225-8216;** no credit cards) is your quintessential bar, and that just about sums up Darj's nightlife. Spectacular views of Mount Kachenjunga make **Keventer's Snack Bar** (1 Nehru Rd.; ✆ **0354/225-6542** or -4026) something of a Darjeeling institution, even if the food is nothing to write home about. Sit upstairs on the terrace for breakfast served by disaffected waiters. Darjeeling also boasts an **Inox multiplex** and **Rink Mall** where you can have a good cuppa at the tea lounge or Café Coffee Day. Finally, for Nepali cuisine (a must if you're in the region), there's no better place than **Penangs** (just opposite the Rink Mall on the first floor of a shabby building), where you should order the traditional Nepali thali (multicourse platter) and *momos* (dumplings).

4 SIKKIM

Sikkim's original inhabitants are the Lepchas, also called Rongtub (literally "the dearest people of Mother Earth"), who call their land *Ney Mayal Lyang,* or "heaven." And how! Crammed in between Tibet, Nepal, Bhutan, and West Bengal, this tiny, mountainous state is as pristine a pocket of India as you are likely to encounter, with some 4,000 varieties of wildflowers (including 600 varieties of orchids), snow-fed lakes, high-altitude mountain forests, and hidden Buddhist monasteries. Some travelers come simply to enjoy the refreshing views and clean air, but most are here to tackle the fantastic treks through western Sikkim, exploring remote valleys and villages of yak-herding Tibetans. Ideally, you should spend a day or two in the state capital, **Gangtok,** to organize permits and transport/trekking arrangements, then head to **Pelling** before undertaking a demanding high-altitude trek for several days. Or you can skip Gangtok and either hire a jeep that goes directly from Siliguri (near the railway station at New Jalpaiguri) to Pelling, or travel from Bagdogra, the nearest airport; both are about 6 hours away by road. If you want to avoid serious trekking and enjoy easier hikes, you can opt for **Tendong Hill** or **Menam Hill,** which can be accessed via Namchi and Rawangla in South Sikkim. There is relatively very little to offer in terms of accommodation in these areas, but the scenery of endless terraced paddy fields with dense forests higher up is worth the visit—this is also home to the famous Temi Tea Garden. Remoter still and even more gorgeous is **North Sikkim,** with some spectacular drives—the Chungthang-to-Lachung stretch is riddled with waterfalls, while Lachung to Yumthang ascends 1,000m (3,280 ft.) in just 25km (16 miles), cruising through the Singba Rhododendron Reserve, which in spring is a riot of colors. If you've come this far, make sure you dip your weary bones in the hot sulfur springs at Yumthang. (*Note:* North Sikkim is accessible only via a tour agency—the government does not want to overburden the natural resources with an uncontrolled tourist influx.)

ESSENTIALS
PERMITS   In addition to the standard visa, foreign visitors must be in possession of an **Inner Line Permit** (see "Acquiring your Sikkim Permit in Darjeeling," earlier in this

chapter). This, together with your passport, must be carried at all times. If you wish to travel north of Gangtok or Pelling, you will require an additional endorsement or **Protected Area Permit** from Sikkim Tourism in Gangtok.

VISITOR INFORMATION   **Sikkim Tourism** (Mahatma Gandhi Marg; ✆ **03592/22-1634;** www.sikkimindia.com) is open Monday to Saturday, May through August, 10am to 4pm; March through April and September through October daily 9am to 7pm. The center has a computerized touch-screen kiosk that will provide more-or-less up-to-date tourist information (when it's working). This is where you can book highly recommended scenic helicopter rides. The office downstairs is where you must have your Sikkim permit endorsed if you intend to visit certain restricted areas in the state. There's also an **Information Counter** (✆ **0353/269-8030** daily 10am–2:30pm) at Bagdogra Airport.

GETTING THERE   **Bagdogra** in neighboring West Bengal is the closest airport, and is served by flights from major cities like Kolkata, Mumbai and Delhi (refer to "Getting There" in the section on Darjeeling). From Bagdogra, Sikkim Helicopter Service runs daily 30-minute flights to Gangtok for around Rs 1,700, well worth it just for the views. Alternatively, taxis (4 hr.; Rs 2,500) and buses are available. Shared jeep services are also available from Darjeeling, Siliguri, and Kalimpong, all in West Bengal. These are highly affordable; book more than one seat for yourself, preferably the two front seats for the best views. If you're coming from Kathmandu, fly to **Bhadrapur** in east Nepal, and head to Gangtok via Kakarbhitta (on the Nepalese-Indian border) and Siliguri in West Bengal.

GETTING AROUND SIKKIM   Unless you pick up a helicopter from Bagdogra Airport, you will travel in Sikkim by road. Use either a private or shared jeep. Although roads are open throughout the year, bear in mind that all of Sikkim is mountainous and routes inevitably take far longer than they appear on maps. The shared taxi and jeep services from Gangtok to Pelling (Rs 175) that depart twice a day at 7am and 12:30pm are served by **Nam Nam taxi stand;** book your seat in advance. Again, book both front seats, for the views, and also because drivers tend to pack way more people into the car than you'd have imagined possible. Sikkim's roads invariably traverse steep mountains and deep valleys, so travel can be exhausting (the journey to Pelling, via Ravangla, takes 5 hr.), but the scenery is spectacular. Alternatively, you could break journey at the delightful Yangsum Farm (reviewed later) at Rinchenpong (1½ hr. from Pelling). Within **Gangtok,** you're best off doing most of your wandering on foot; because of one-way roads, taxis are frequently required to skirt much of the city. To get to the Tibetology Institute and to Rumtek Monastery, you'll have to use a taxi.

GUIDED TOURS & TRAVEL AGENTS   For all kinds of adventure tourist activities as well as tour arrangements, contact Jimmy Singh of **Gurudongma Tours and Treks** (✆ **90-0269-2611** or 94-3406-2100; www.gurudongma.com). **Blue Sky Tours & Travel** (Tourism Building, Mahatma Gandhi Marg; ✆ **03592/20-5113;** www.blue-sky-tours. com) specializes in jeep tours of northern Sikkim. They can also help you with local sightseeing, and offer a 2-day Monastery Tour that takes in several Buddhist monasteries in the state. Like all tour operators in Gangtok, their rates depend on the number of riders.

For trekking arrangements, try **Sikkim Tours & Travels** (Church Rd.; ✆ **03592/20-2188;** www.sikkimtours.com). **Tashila Tours & Travels** (✆ **03592/20-2978;** www.tashila. com) undertakes a range of services, including trekking, rafting, and specialist tours. **Siniolchu Tours and Travels** (✆ **03592/20-5569** or 94-3402-4572; info@ourhimalayas. com; Mon–Sat 9am–1pm and 2–8pm) is reliable. Headquartered in Gangtok, it undertakes a wide range of spectacular treks and tours in various regions of Sikkim and beyond.

Most treks cost in the vicinity of $80 per person per day, and include tents, food, porters, yaks, and guides.

GANGTOK & ENVIRONS

Sikkim's capital sits at an altitude of 1,780m (5,800 ft.), straddling a high ridge where houses and concrete blocks spill down the hillside; below is the Ranipul River. With only 29,000 inhabitants, it's relatively laid-back and generally free from the malaise that stalks India's many overpopulated towns and cities. For visitors, the most noble of Gangtok's charms is its proximity to marvelous mountain vistas; the town itself is threatened by unchecked construction. A base for visitors who come to organize treks or wind down after a high-altitude experience, it's pleasant to roam around but certainly not packed with attractions. The town's most significant drawing card is the **Namgyal Institute of Tibetology** ★ (admission Rs 10; Mon–Sat 10am–4pm), which houses a collection of Tibetan, Sanskrit, and Lepcha manuscripts, as well as statues, Buddhist icons, masks, scrolls, musical instruments, jewelry, incense burners, and beautiful *thangkas* (painted or embroidered tapestry wall hangings).

Nearby, **Do-Drul Chorten** is a fine example of a whitewashed Buddhist stupa, encircled by prayer wheels. **Enchey Monastery** is a Tibetan Buddhist lamasery worth visiting, and the **Flower Exhibition Centre** (Rs 5 adults, Rs 5 camera), near White Hall, attracts orchid buffs. In the manner of traditional hill kingdom forts and castles, Sikkim's royalty once resided within the yellow tin-roofed palace in the uppermost reaches of the town. From here, the Chogyal and his family enjoyed the best views in Gangtok. Sadly, the Chogyal palace is off-limits to visitors. When the British turned up, they installed their very own "White Hall" alongside the palace and, despite initial bickering, soon got round to several decades of contented socializing. A good morning excursion (8am–noon) is to the stunning high-altitude **Changu Lake** ★★. This is barely 18km (11 miles) from the Indo-Chinese border post **Nathu-La,** which has only recently been opened up for trade. It is extremely cold here, even in the summer, so come prepared. Permits are a must for all travelers, and the 90-minute return journey will cost Rs 650 per person in a shared taxi.

Rumtek Monastery ★★   The region's top attraction lies 24km (15 miles) from Gangtok. Rigpe Dorjee, the "supreme head" of one of Tibetan Buddhism's four major sects—the Kagyu, or "Black Hat" order—revived it in 1959 after the Chinese invaded Tibet. Regarded as the richest Buddhist monastic center in India, Rumtek houses some of the world's rarest and most unique religious artifacts; its design is said to replicate that of the original Kagyu headquarters in Tibet. Try to get here during prayer times, when the red-carpeted benches are occupied by the Vajra chant and disciplinary master, who leads the chanting of prayers. The venerated part of the complex is the **Golden Stupa,** a 4m-high (13-ft.) *chorten* in which the mortal remains of the 16th Gyalwa Karmapa (founder of the Black Hat order; see box below) are enshrined. Gold-plated and embedded with jewels, turquoise, and coral, the stupa is kept in a locked shrine room, which must be specially unlocked for visitors. Ask a monk to help you track down the keeper of the key. (*Note:* If you come in Feb, you will be able to witness the fascinating annual mask dance and other ceremonies that take place in all the monasteries in the region, all celebrating the Tibetan New Year.) For more information, go to www.rumtek.org.

Where to Stay & Dine

If you're traveling on a budget, **Mintokling Guest House** (© 03592/20-4226; www.mintokling.com; doubles Rs 1,500–Rs 1,800; all credit cards except AE) is a Sikkimese home with fairly spacious, clean guest rooms; our favorite is no. 304. The owner is a fantastic source of information on Sikkimese history, especially if you're interested in the political lowdown; his mother was the niece of the last king of Sikkim.

Sikkim's smartest hotel, **Nor-Khill** (see below), also hosts one of the better restaurants, **Shangri-La** (✆ **03592/20-5637**). Splurge on an all-inclusive full-course Sikkimese meal, which you will have to order beforehand. Find out if the stir-fried fiddlehead ferns or the popular *sisnu* (a dish made from stinging nettle) are available, and do try their juicy chicken/pork *momos* (Tibetan dumplings). Book a table at the window. Nor-Khill also has the best pub in town, the cozy **Dragon Bar. Snowlion** (✆ **03592/20-1024** or 20-3710; all credit cards accepted) is equally good for Tibetan fare, including chicken *sha-dre* (rice noodles with a curry sauce) and *sumei*, or open *momos*. Adventurous diners can sample traditional *dre-thuk*, a thick, porridgelike rice soup topped with a mountain of finely grated cheese. It serves delicious, body-warming beverages—try the hot toddy with brandy, rum, and cloves, or the hot whiskey lemonade. **Little Italy** (SNOT) Complex, Deorali; ✆ **03592/28-1980**) rustles up good pizzas and pastas and plays great music, with a live band on the weekends (bar attached). **Bakers Café** (M.G. Marg; ✆ **03592/22-0195**) is also a good place to hang out over coffee and freshly baked cakes and croissants.

The Hidden Forest Retreat ★★ Offering an authentic homestay experience, this is a fabulous alternative to the hotels in Gangtok. It's owned by a family that admits it's a little crazy because their plants come first before all else. Spending a few days here, surrounded by the 30-year-old nursery, taking in lots of fresh air and mountain views and being overfed by the lovely Kesang, is a rare pleasure. With 12 rooms, it's a small, personal affair—interiors are similar with colorful Sikkimese *tenthis* (low stools) and *choktsis* (low tables), pinewood floors and ceilings, and dimly lit but clean bathrooms. Spend the evening on the patio with wind chimes for company, and warm up with *chang* (a local alcoholic beverage made with millet) served in a beautiful container fashioned out of old wood and silver.

The Hidden Forest Retreat, Sinchey Busty, Gangtok 737 101. (✆)/fax **03592/20-5197** or 94-7498-1367 www.hiddenforestretreat.org. 12 units (with shower). Rs 2,150 single; Rs 3,000 double. Rs 700 extra bed. Rates include all meals. No credit cards at press time but may soon accept MC, V; please check. **Amenities:** Dining; doctor-on-call; heater; television.

Netuk House ★★ (Value) Buddhist prayer flags flutter above this gorgeously situated and well-run family guesthouse with real Sikkimese flavor. The warm Denzong family, who are always pleased to introduce guests to local culture, owns it. All accommodations are unique; four guest rooms are in the main house and six are in the colorful annex, with its traditional rainbow-hued Sikkimese-style facade. Guest rooms are simple but lovely, and have good, comfortable mattresses covered in crisp white linen. Carefully prepared traditional four-course Sikkimese meals are served in the dining room; there is a charming Sikkimese-style living room with an attached bar.

Tibet Rd., Gangtok 737 101. (✆ **03592/20-6778** or 94-7435-2975. netukhouse@gmail.com. 12 units (with shower). Rs 4,150 double, Rs 2,450 single, Rs 1,455 extra person; Rs 725 children 8–12; Rs 375 children 4–7; free for children under 4; taxes extra. Rates include all meals. No credit cards. **Amenities:** Restaurant; bar; doctor-on-call; TV lounge.

Nor-Khill ★★★ This stylish hotel, once the royal guesthouse of the former king, offers the priciest and most luxurious accommodations in the state of Sikkim, fronted by a lovely lawn (sadly, overlooking Gangtok's sports stadium). The renovated deluxe units resemble suites, with a large bedroom area extending off a comfortable and beautiful living area; views are excellent. Huge floral or dragon-motif rugs cover the wood tile floors, and the furnishings and fittings are carved and painted Sikkimese-style. Beds are a little narrow and slightly soft, but have lovely fabrics and scatter cushions. Bathrooms are spacious, with tubs and natural light. Standard doubles are spacious and equally beautiful; reserve room no. 43 or 44, which are large and well-positioned. The room rate includes all meals, served as a set-menu in the formal **Shangri-La Restaurant.**

Paljor Stadium Rd., Gangtok 737 101. ℂ **03592/20-5637** or 0359/22-0064. Fax 03592/20-5639. Reservations: 5 Park Row, 47 Park St., Kolkata 700 016. ℂ 033/2226-9878. Fax 033/2246-6388. www.elginhotels. com. 25 units. Rs 5,900 single; Rs 6,200 standard double. Rs 2,450 extra bed. Rates include all meals. AE, MC, V. **Amenities:** Restaurant; bar; airport transfer (Rs 2,200); babysitting; currency exchange; doctor-on-call; room service. *In room:* TV, heater.

Near Rumtek

There are plenty of small guesthouses in the area, but the biggest and best would be **Martam Village Resort** (reviewed below) and the **Bamboo Resort** (ℂ **03592/25-2516;** www.sikkim.ch/bamboo-resort.html; Rs 4,200 double) set amid paddy fields. The rooms are small but clean; some come with balconies. Each has its own color scheme according to Feng Shui principles—frankly, the red and blue is a trifle overpowering. Another option is the **Teen Talay Eco-Garden Resort** (ℂ **98-3201-4867;** Rs 3,100 double)—more a homestay, it is run by an affable family who go out of their way to make guests feel comfortable, even throwing in *tabla* lessons for free. Sadly, the **Shambhala Mountain Resort,** located right next to the monastery, has become quite seedy and is to be avoided.

Martam Village Resort ★ Ⓥ Value   Although it covers barely an acre, this lovely resort (a bit of a misnomer) is an excellent place to stay for several reasons. Just half an hour from Rumtek, it is one of the few places where you get fantastic views, not of Kanchenjunga for once, but of the lower hills, their terraced fields of mustard, corn, and paddy creating a ripple effect: brown in winters and green and golden in the summers. Awakened by boisterous roosters, guests are taken for short or long walks through villages and forests full of giant bamboo and wild orchids by the enthusiastic Pema, who will point out the many varieties of natural herbs used for everything from toothaches and antiseptics to writing ink and paper. Facilities in the 14 thatched cottages are basic—rooms spartan, doddering heaters, bathrooms just okay, cuisine unimaginative—but the atmosphere all around more than makes up for these small inconveniences.

Gangkha, Martam, East Sikkim. ℂ **03592/20-3314.** info@sikkim-martam-resort.com. 14 units (with showers). Rs 3,300 full-board double; Rs 2,500 single. Extra bed Rs 1,200. No credit cards. **Amenities:** Restaurant; bar; currency exchange. *In room:* Hot water, room heater, no phone.

PELLING & ENVIRONS

Traditionally a stopover for trekkers headed for Yoksum, Dzongri, and similar high-altitude spots in western Sikkim, Pelling has begun to establish itself as a tourist destination in its own right, and as a result, concrete lodges have sprung up indiscriminately to cash in on the passing trade. Nevertheless, the surrounding scenery is spectacular, and the sunrise behind snow-clad Khangchendzonga will leave you breathless. Besides hiking or rafting, the top attractions are the nearby monasteries. From Pelling, a pleasant 30-minute walk along the main road toward Geyzing will lead you to one of Sikkim's oldest and most revered monasteries, **Pemayangtse** ★ (entry Rs 5; daily 7am–4pm), situated at 2,085m (6,672 ft.) in a cliff-top forest clearing. Set up as a monastery for *Ta-Sang*, or

Himalayan Brew

Chang, made from fermented millet, is the brew of choice in Sikkim. It's usually served in a wooden tumbler (a *tomba*) with a bamboo straw and should look like a small mountain of chestnut-colored caviar sprinkled with a few grains of rice. Believed to aid sleep, it supposedly never causes hangovers. Many Western travelers would disagree. The locals advise you to not gulp it but let it sit as long as possible in the *tomba,* thereby allowing it to get stronger.

"pure monks" of the Nyingmapa order, Pemayangtse was established in 1705 by Lhatsun Chempo, one of the lamas who performed the consecration ritual of Sikkim's first king. Its prized treasure is a 7m tall (22 ft.) wooden depiction of Guru Rimpoche's *Sang-tok-palri,* or "heavenly palace," encased in glass in the monastery's upper room. Note that it's worth trying to contact Yapo S. Yongda, who resides here—he's a fascinating source of information on Sikkimese history.

Southeast of Pemayangtse (30-min walk), on a lower hillock, are the ruins of the late-17th-century **Rabdentse Palace** ★, from where you can see **Tashiding Monastery** ★★, one of the most idyllic, peaceful, and sublime monasteries in India. Hire a jeep from Pelling to get here (Rs 1,400 round-trip). A mere glance at Tashiding's **Thongwa Rangdol,** Sikkim's most venerated *chorten,* will (if Buddhist legends are to be believed) absolve you of all your sins. Also of special significance is the *bhumpa,* a copper vase that contains the holy water used each year during the *Bhumchu* festival, when a sacred ritual reveals Sikkim's fate for the upcoming year. It's a somewhat stiff 50-minute hike in the opposite direction to hilltop **Sanga Choling Monastery** ★—but it's worth it, for the most panoramic views around. Constructed in 1697, this is believed to be the second-oldest Buddhist monastery in Sikkim. Go when morning or evening prayers are held. For more information on the region, call the Tourism Information Office at © **94-3463-0876.** There is, however, one more optional stopover for those with more time to explore—2 hours south of Pelling is the small town of Rinchenpong—worth including just so you can overnight at **Yangsum Farm** (reviewed below).

Where to Stay & Dine

With basics like electricity and water in short supply, don't expect luxury in Pelling. The town is spilling over with tour and travel agents, many of whom are quite suspect in their dealings—single women travelers would do well to be cautious and use only accredited travel agents, based preferably in Gangtok. Aside from Norbu, the best place to stay is newly opened **The Mount Pandim** ★, set atop a hill, with the most terrific views of the mighty Kanchenjunga, and a 10-minute amble distance from the Pemayangtse Monastery (and 30 min. from the Rabdentse Ruins). The hotel had only just opened at press time, but guest rooms and facilities are in keeping with the Elgin chain of hotels: comfortable and positively luxurious when compared with your other options. Try to reserve deluxe room no. 203 (© **03595/25-0756** or -0273; www.elginhotels.com; doubles Rs 5,100, include all meals). If you're keen on the homestay experience, your best bet is the delightful Yangsum, a working farm reviewed below, near the village of Rinchenpong. If you want to be based in Pelling itself (and you're watching your rupees), a good budget option is **Hotel Phamrong** (Upper Pelling; © **03595/25-8218** or -0660; www.sikkim hotelphamrong.com; doubles from Rs 1,400–Rs 2,850), which have large en-suite rooms

KOLKATA (CALCUTTA) & EAST INDIA

15

SIKKIM

> ## (Finds) Walking the Eastern Himalayas: Discovering Rural Life on Foot
>
> While the tougher mountain trails have always lured serious trekkers to Sikkim, ambling through local villages and getting a taste of traditional life and culture along with the stunning terrain and views, with the mighty Kanchenjunga for company, wasn't commonly found on the agenda until now. **Shakti** has changed all that with its foray into the eastern Himalayas (© **0124/456-3899;** www.shakti himalaya.com; info@shaktihimalaya.com; Oct–Apr except Jan). Village Walks are $1,356 per person on twin-share basis for 4 night/5-day experience, and rates include transfers to/from Bagdogra airport, private guides, porterage, meals/drinks, room, and service charge for staff. The 4-day walks are designed to suit even the unfit—5 to 6 hours of walking (can be adjusted to suit your needs) lead you to a new village each day, where a local house has been refurbished sensibly and sensitively to suit western travelers without robbing its authenticity. The families are a delight to interact with, meals prepared by the Shakti chef are simple and delicious, and the accompanying staff and guide well versed in giving you an insight into this enigmatic part of the country. For more on Shatki, see p. 658.

that generally come with fantastic views. Don't expect luxury, but the sunrises are brilliant. Pelling's best dining is at the Norbu Ghang Resort (see below), but the restaurant at tiny **Garuda** guest lodge (next door to Hotel Phamrong) serves a solid selection, including Tibetan and Sikkimese specialties.

Norbu Ghang Resort ★   Norbu Ghang (which means "Jewel on the Hilltop") has the most tasteful accommodations in western Sikkim (the Mount Pandim has the edge with its glorious views, but it's located outside of town, which may not suit you if you're just here to arrange trekking). The resort is built on four levels over a 2-hectare (5-acre) stretch of flower-speckled terraced hillside. The corrugated-roof cottages are fairly decent in size. All the best rooms and cottages have views of mighty Khangchendzonga (book cottage no. 601, 801, or 804). You can also opt for the cozy Denzong suite, with its atticlike feel, where even the tiny windows are excusable. The resort also has Pelling's best restaurant, serving traditional Sikkimese cuisine.

Pelling 737 113. © **03595/25-8245,** -8272, or -0566. Fax 03595/25-8271. Reservations: C.N.Ghosh © **98-3048-7119.** www.sikkiminfo.net/norbughang. 30 units. Rs 3,100 deluxe double; Rs 3,600 super deluxe double; Rs 4,400 Denzong Suite. Rs 1000 extra bed. MC, V. **Amenities:** Restaurant; bar; currency exchange; doctor-on-call; Internet (on request); room service; travel assistance. *In room:* TV, heater.

Yangsum Farm ★ (Finds)   With an idyllic location, surrounded by fields and edge-to-edge mountain ranges, Yangsum Farm is a real find. Owner-run by Thendup Tashi and Pema, this is a working farm: The resident rooster and watchdog geese ensure that everyone is up at the crack of dawn to welcome the early morning rays and contemplate another relaxing day. You'll spend your time soaking in views, or getting fat on Sikkimese cuisine. (Growing everything from mandarin, plums, pears, and peaches to spinach, radish, cauliflower, and cardamom, this is one place you won't be going hungry.) Burn it all off with long, lovely walks around the countryside, coming across monasteries, ancient *lepcha* houses, and fog-filled forests (not to mention a leech or two). Of the four rooms, the heritage and the mud cottage are the best—spacious with curtains fashioned out of

(Moments) Wildlife Safari by Boat

The Brahmaputra flows for some 644km (400 miles) through Assam, and a river cruise is the best way to visit this little-known region in comfort. There is hardly any traffic on the river, just the occasional country boat taking fishermen to their traps. Otherwise you'll find total solitude, rare indeed in India. The two 12-double-cabin riverboats of **Assam Bengal Navigation** ★★ (www.assam bengalnavigation.com; assambengal@aol.com) are comfortable without being pretentious. Rooms are all air-conditioned, the en-suite bathrooms are workman-like, and the furnishings, which make use of local weaving, rattan, and bamboo, are simple and unfussy. Each boat has a saloon and bar with glass doors looking out on a small foredeck and the river ahead, while upper sun decks are furnished with sun loungers and generous seating. ABN's cruises range in length from 4 to 14 nights and cost from $350 per person per night. Most days the boat stops for a visit on land, whether to a wildlife park, tea garden, temple, or tribal village. A fleet of jeeps is used to take guests on longer excursions, but be warned, Assam's road surfaces leave a lot to be desired. Transfers are included in the tariff. Pickups can be done at either of the two airports in Dibrugarh or Guwahati, both of which are connected to Delhi and Kolkata.

silks, *thangkas* on walls, and tiny balconies overlooking the fields with the range in the backdrop.

Yangsum Farm, P.O. Rinchenpong, West Sikkim 737 111. ℂ **94-3417-9029**. www.yangsumfarm.com. 4 units (with showers). $81 premier heritage double with balcony and mountain views; $75 double; price includes all meals; $60 singles. No credit cards. **Amenities:** Doctor-on-call; hot water. *In room:* Heater, no phone.

TREKS THROUGH WESTERN SIKKIM ★★★

Treks around western Sikkim are justifiably popular, not least because of the spectacular views afforded throughout, but they are challenging. If you want something relatively short and undemanding, the 4-day trek from Pelling to Tashiding and back is ideal, covering both cultural sights and majestic scenery. Far more challenging, and requiring more time and extra stamina, are the high-altitude treks to **Dzongri** (3,861m/12,870 ft.; 6 days) and **Goeche La** (4,740m/15,800 ft.; 9–10 days). There are also other treks to Singalila and Versay in the west, Greenlake in the north, and Kedi and Teenjure in the east. Trekking here is only allowed with a recognized trekking operator in Gangtok; a daily fee of $50 to $75 will include guides, porters, yaks, tents, and food. March through May, the fabulous—and less strenuous—5-day **Rhododendron Trek** through the exotic forests of the Singalila Range, near the border with Nepal, become possible. For trek operators, see "Essentials: Guided Tours & Travel Agents," earlier. (**Note:** Due to the damp climate and vegetation, Western Sikkim is notorious for its leeches; local tech-niques of applying limestone chalk or tobacco help but aren't foolproof.)

EXPLORING THE WILDS OF ASSAM ★★★

To most, Assam means tea, and indeed some 20% of the world's tea is grown here. But Assam's remote location (best reached by plane from Kolkata or Bagdogra, flying into Guwahati, after which you need to travel by road, with the closest park approximately 4 hr. away) has meant that it remains one of India's best-kept secrets, despite boasting two out of India's five World Heritage environmental sites—Manas and Kaziranga. In **Manas,** apart from a small and extremely basic but superbly located **Forest Rest House** at Mothanguri (contact the Field Director, Manas Tiger Reserve; © **03666/233-413**), deep in the park, the only place to stay is the **Bansbari Lodge** (www.assambengalnavigation.com; assambengal@aol.com), right beside the park entrance. The 16 fan-cooled rooms are spacious and have small balconies. The lodge arranges performances of Bodo tribal dancing. *Be warned:* The access road to the park from the National Highway is in dire need of attention. The more popular **Kaziranga** is among the top five places to see wildlife in India. This marshy plain beside the Brahmaputra was turned into a wildlife sanctuary by Lord Curzon, Viceroy of India, in 1908. At that time there were only a handful of rhinos left; now around 1,800 graze the park; they constitute the vast majority of the world population of the Asian one-horned rhinoceros. Also present here are wild elephant, buffalo, swamp deer, hog deer, sambar, wild boar, as well as the densest tiger population in India. But don't get your hopes up—tiger in Kaziranga are harder to spot than almost anywhere else, thanks to the lush vegetation. The best way to get close to the rhinos is atop an elephant: Every morning cavalcades of 20 or so elephants head out rhino tracking—and visitors are seldom disappointed. If you aren't staying on board one of Assam Bengal Navigation's river cruise ships (see box below), a good alternative would be their **Diphlu River Lodge** ★ (www.diphluriverlodge.com) with thatched cottages on stilts looking across the water into the park itself—from the machan at night you can watch rhino graze on the far bank. The cottages are air-conditioned, and marvelously spacious. Otherwise **Wild Grass** (© **03776/226-2011;** www.oldassam.com) offers a good standard of comfort and is close to the entrance to Kaziranga's Central Range.

16

Fast Facts

FAST FACTS: INDIA

AREA CODES The international telephone access code for India is **91.** Area codes for principal cities and towns are listed in the "Fast Facts" sections in each chapter. All numbers listed in this guide include the local area code (which you would dial from another Indian town or city); this is separated from the actual telephone number by a forward slash (/).

BUSINESS HOURS Banks are usually open weekdays from 10am to 2pm and Saturday from 10am to noon, though banks in larger cities have much longer hours (9:30am–5pm on weekdays, and until 2pm on Sat). Most museums are closed Monday; the Taj Mahal is closed on Friday, along with all other Muslim sites. Hours of retail outlets vary, but many close on Sunday.

DRINKING LAWS Attitudes toward alcohol vary considerably. In Gujarat, prohibition is in force and liquor can only be obtained from the permit rooms of luxury hotels, a concession made principally for foreigners and out-of-state businesspeople. In most other non-Muslim areas, alcohol is freely available and exceedingly popular. In top hotels, you'll find a full range of imported liquor, available to those who can afford the extravagance. In most cities you will encounter "country liquor" bars and insalubrious liquor "dens"; and somewhere on your travels you may be offered local bootlegged stuff—all of which you're advised to stay clear of. In a few of the southern states, notably Kerala and Tamil Nadu, stringent alcohol laws are in place: Liquor is found in many hotels and restaurants (but not all, since liquor licenses can be difficult to obtain), but outside these licensed premises, alcohol may only be sold by government-owned outlets (where you'll often see queues forming from early in the morning)—part of an attempt to prevent the sale of dangerous illicit concoctions that have in the past caused death and blindness.

The **legal drinking age** differs from state to state, and ranges from 18 to 25; in Mumbai, for example, wine and beer may be consumed from the age of 21, but you must be 25 to drink spirits. Foreigners are unlikely to be questioned about their age in the context of alcohol consumption. Laws concerning alcohol use change regularly, often in response to serious concerns around abuse. It's best to drink modestly and restrict drinking to places where it is obviously permitted. Certain religious sites place restrictions on intoxication or even alcohol use, so best to be on your toes if you don't mean to cause offence.

DRIVING RULES See "Getting There and Getting Around," p. 52.

ELECTRICITY 220–240 volts AC.

EMBASSIES & CONSULATES Embassies of major English-speaking countries are listed in the "Fast Facts" section for Delhi; see chapter 10. For quick reference, here are some embassy numbers: **Australia** ⓒ **011/4139-9900; Canada** ⓒ **011/4178-2000; New Zealand** ⓒ **011/2688-3170;** and the **U.K.** ⓒ **011/2419-2100.** The U.S. State Department encourages American citizens visiting India to register at the **U.S. Embassy** in New Delhi (Shantipath, Chanakyapuri; 🕻 **011/2419-8000;** fax 011/2419-0017; http://newdelhi.us embassy.gov) or at one of the U.S. consulates in India. The U.S. Consulate General in Mumbai is located at Lincoln House, 78 Bhulabhai Desai Rd., 400 026 (🕻 **022/ 2363-3611;** fax 022/2363-0350; http:// mumbai.usconsulate.gov). The U.S. Consulate General in Kolkata is at 5/1 Ho Chi Minh Sarani, 700 071 (🕻 **033/3984-2400;** fax 033/2282-2335; http://kolkata. usconsulate.gov). The U.S. Consulate General in Chennai is at 220 Anna Salai, Gemini Circle, 600 006 (🕻 **044/2857-4000;** fax 044/2811-2020; http://chennai. usconsulate.gov).

EMERGENCIES Refer to "Fast Facts" sections in individual chapters for police, ambulance, and emergency contact numbers.

HOLIDAYS Expect to find a different schedule of public holidays for each state. There are, additionally, just four national public holidays: January 26 is Republic Day, August 15 is Independence Day, October 2 is Gandhi's Birthday, and December 25 is Christmas Day. Expect a host of religious holidays and festivals (see the "Calendar of Events" in the Planning Chapter) which may or may not cause businesses or other places of interest to close for the day (or perhaps for a few hours).

INSURANCE While the cost of quality medical care in India is nowhere near as expensive as it is in the West, you're advised to get yourself covered for any major medical emergency. A basic consultation with a specialist doctor costs between Rs 300 and Rs 1,000, so that's not your real insurance concern. Should you need hospitalization, major medical assistance, or medical evacuation, travel medical insurance will help ease the process and cover all expenses. *Note:* Try to get "cash-free" insurance for major medical expenses, and carry a list of facilities where this is possible; otherwise you will have to pay first and get reimbursed later—which is the norm in most of India. For travel overseas, most U.S. health plans (including Medicare and Medicaid) do not provide coverage, and the ones that do often require you to pay for services upfront and reimburse you only after you return home.

It's a good idea to get insurance for any specific valuable items (such as laptops and cameras), and to also cover any luggage that you intend checking in on flights. Most airlines require that you report delayed, damaged, or lost baggage within 4 hours of arrival. Though airlines are required to deliver luggage, once found, directly to your house or destination free of charge, in India they cannot do so because Customs rules require that you clear your bags through Customs personally. Once your lost bags have arrived, you will have to make a trip to the airport to claim them.

For information on traveler's insurance, trip-cancellation insurance, and medical insurance while traveling please visit www. frommers.com/planning.

INTERNET ACCESS Today even small towns have decent Internet connectivity, although coverage may be more limited in remote places such as Ladakh, where the Internet must be accessed via satellite connection. Business centers at luxury hotels often charge exorbitant rates; there's often Internet connection for 10% of the cost just around the corner. Although they're not always fantastic in terms of connection speed (or cleanliness), cybercafes are a roaring trade and usually cheap, albeit frustratingly slow. Keep an eye out for **Sify iway** (www.iway.com) and **Reliance Webworld** (www.rcom.co.in) Internet centers, both offering much faster broadband connections than average stand-alone establishments. Sify, for instance, has some 2,500 Internet browsing centers around the country, half of which also offer Internet telephone services. Log on to their website to find a list of centers in a particular city. If you're planning on being in India for an extended period, or rely heavily on Internet access while traveling, consider investing in a data card that allows you to connect to the Internet through your laptop while on the road: **Reliance Netconnect** (www.rcom.co.in) is one of a number of mobile phone service providers that also offers wireless Internet connectivity by means of a USB modem.

LANGUAGE You shouldn't have to battle too much if you speak English with a clear accent. Don't assume, however, that everyone in India understands or speaks English (or Hindi for that matter). Also don't feel affronted when you run into locals who seem to smile in acknowledgment, only to reveal much later that they haven't the foggiest notion what you're talking about; they are simply trying to make you feel more at home. Hindi is widely spoken throughout North India, while all the states are divided linguistically. For example, Tamil is spoken in Tamil Nadu, Kannada in Karnataka, Telugu in Andhra Pradesh, Malayalam in Kerala, Gujarati in Gujarat, and Konkani in Goa; and there are literally hundreds of local dialects. You'll also come across a lot of what is often called Hinglish, where local terms (in Hindi) are mixed with English phrases. This usage is becoming increasingly widespread. You'll notice it immediately in advertising billboards and on television shows, but also in general conversation.

LEGAL AID The local strategy for dealing with most potentially sticky encounters with the police or traffic department is to offer a bribe *(baksheesh)*. Should you find yourself in any legal tangle, it's best to immediately contact your local consular representative and seek their advice.

MAIL Buy stamps for letters and postcards from your hotel, and have your concierge post them for you. International postage is extremely affordable, and the Indian postal service is generally efficient. However, sending a package or parcel abroad involves a tedious process of wrapping it in cloth and sealing it with string and wax (again, ask your concierge); you'll also have to complete a Customs declaration form. All this may cost you a great deal of time at the post office (9am–5pm). Also, bear in mind that surface mail runs the risk of spending months in the system, or of never arriving at all. You can spare yourself a great deal of torment by having a local or international courier company deliver packages (including shopping that can't fit into your case!); it's relatively inexpensive and there are literally dozens of these companies in every town (again, ask your concierge or host).

NEWSPAPERS & MAGAZINES Major English dailies include *The Hindu* (www. hindu.com), *The Indian Express* (www. expressindia.com), *The Times of India* (http://timesofindia.indiatimes.com), and *Hindustan Times* (www.hindustantimes. com), as well as Kolkata's *The Statesman* (www.thestatesman.net) and *The Telegraph* (www.telegraphindia.com). These make for interesting reading and will keep you up to date on local and international events. You may find that much of the writing assumes a great deal on your part, however. If you haven't been following certain stories for some time, the latest update may be impossible to fathom. *The Economic Times* and *Mint* provide the most detailed business news. Each week you can pick up fresh issues of *The Week, India Today, Outlook,* and *Frontline* (which provide quite venomous analyses of the nation's social, political, and economic situations). These are available at newsstands and railway stations and not only help you pass travel time but add immensely to your understanding of India. If you're looking for general travel features, the monthly *Outlook Traveller* (www.outlooktraveller.com) features colorful articles from an Indian perspective. In Mumbai and Delhi, the twice-monthly *Time Out* is indispensable if you're looking for what's hot and happening.

PASSPORTS See www.frommers.com/planning for information on how to obtain a passport.

For other information, please contact the following agencies:

For Residents of Australia Contact the **Australian Passport Information Service** at ☎ **131-232,** or visit the government website at www.passports.gov.au.

For Residents of Canada Contact the central **Passport Office,** Department of Foreign Affairs and International Trade, Ottawa, ON K1A 0G3 (☎ **800/567-6868;** www.ppt.gc.ca).

For Residents of Ireland Contact the **Passport Office,** Setanta Centre, Molesworth Street, Dublin 2 (☎ **01/671-1633;** www.irlgov.ie/iveagh).

For Residents of New Zealand Contact the **Passports Office** at ☎ **0800/225-050** in New Zealand or 04/474-8100, or log on to www.passports.govt.nz.

For Residents of the United Kingdom Visit your nearest passport office, major post office, or travel agency or contact the **United Kingdom Passport Service** at ☎ **0870/521-0410** or search its website at www.ukpa.gov.uk.

For Residents of the United States To find your regional passport office, either check the U.S. State Department website or call the **National Passport Information Center** toll-free number (☎ **877/487-2778**) for automated information.

POLICE Emergency and police contact numbers are listed in "Fast Facts" sections for major cities.

SMOKING Whatever curbs the government has tried to place on cigarette usage, there are still relatively slim signs of society giving in to concerns about the hazards of smoking. Things are improving, though, and whereas just a few years ago it seemed as though just about every male in India smoked something, there's a marked drive towards health and social consciousness—this is probably more evident among the upper echelons of society and in cities where people are more regularly exposed to forward-thinking advertising campaigns. On the other hand, the cities are also where high-cool is sometimes defined by cigar toking, so it's ultimately up to the lawmakers to change attitudes. Where they have made changes, they've been pretty thorough: Shimla (in Himachal Pradesh) theoretically forbids smoking in any public place, including on the streets; Chandigarh (the Union Territory from where the Punjab government operates) has been working towards similarly far-reaching legislation; and in Trivandrum (Kerala's capital), smoking in restaurants and public places is banned (and the rule is being enforced). Smoking is also forbidden on all trains, so if someone is smoking on your train, you are well within your rights to ask them to stop. Most luxury hotels have introduced nonsmoking rooms; if you don't smoke, request one when you book your reservation.

TAXES The tax on hotel accommodations varies from state to state, and sometimes by city; it may be anywhere between 5% and 12.5%, and may differ within the same hotel according to the level of luxury and comfort you're experiencing. On the other hand, in regions like Ladakh, there is no taxation. Additional taxes on restaurant food and alcohol also vary from state to state. Imported liquors attract a similarly disagreeable sin tax, making local brands far more attractive than their quality might suggest. In Tamil Nadu, for example, a whopping 73.5% tax is levied on imported liquor. Restaurant bills often include additional charges (such as a service tax) that usually account for between 10% and 15% of the total cost of your meal.

TELEPHONES Phone numbers in India change at the drop of a hat, and businesses are slow in updating contact information, including websites.

To call India:

1. Dial the international access code: 011 (from the U.S. and Canada); 00 (from the U.K., Ireland, or New Zealand); or 0011 (from Australia).
2. Dial the country code: 91.
3. Dial the city code (these are provided in the relevant chapters), omitting the first zero.
4. Dial the telephone number.

Note: To call a cellphone number in India, follow up to step 2 above and then dial the 10-digit cellphone number, which should begin with "9."

Making calls within India: Hotel telephone costs are exorbitant, even when you make a domestic long-distance call. All over India, you'll see yellow ISD/STD signs indicating a privately operated "International Subscriber Dialing" and "Standard Trunk Dialing" facility; these are very reasonably priced. To call a mobile phone number that is not in the city in which you are based, dial "0" before the 10-digit number. Note that the Indian toll-free numbers (1/800) cannot be dialed from cellphones and land lines that don't belong to the MTNL or BSNL networks.

Making calls from cellphones: When making calls from cellphones, you'll need to punch in the full area code of the city and telephone number irrespective of where you are calling from (even for local calls). To call a cellphone number within a city, just dial the 10-digit cellphone number; to call a cellphone outside your city, add a "0" before the number.

To make international calls: Dial 00 and then the country code (U.S. or Canada 1, U.K. 44, Ireland 353, Australia 61, New Zealand 64). Next, dial the area code and number. For example, if you want to call the British Embassy in Washington, D.C., dial ℭ 00-1-202-588-7800.

For directory assistance: Dial ℭ 197 if you're looking for a local number within India, and dial ℭ 183 for long-distance numbers within India. Don't hold your breath for accurate or up-to-date assistance, and speak slowly and clearly.

For operator assistance: If the phone you're using is not an International Subscriber Dialing (ISD) facility, you'll need operator assistance and must dial ℭ 186. Using an ISD facility without the need for an operator will save you a great deal of time. **Toll-free numbers:** To call a 1-800 number in the U.S. from India, first contact the international operator through the Direct Access service. For a call to the U.S., call ℭ 000-117 (AT&T Direct Access), which gives you an AT&T operator, through whom you can make your toll-free or collect call. Note, however, that these Direct Access calls cannot be made from everywhere; to ensure you won't be charged for the call, check with your hotel before dialing.

TIME Despite India's vastness, the entire country operates according to the same time zone, 5½ hours ahead of Greenwich Mean Time. That's 9½ hours ahead of Eastern Standard Time (New York) or 10½ when daylight saving time comes into effect in the U.S. *Note:* You may find your sense of time threatened while you're in India; the rule of thumb is *don't panic.* Remember that there's no point in getting worked up about delayed trains and such. In fact, when you arrive on time or ahead of schedule, be thankful. Use "wasted time" to chat with locals.

TIPPING Tipping in India is an industry unto itself, and it's a relief to find yourself in an environment like the Oberoi, where individual tipping is not encouraged, for this very reason. Bear in mind that many of the people who serve you are possibly living on the bread line, and your monetary contribution will be greatly appreciated; handing over a Rs 10 or Rs 20 note will hardly dent your pocket.

Obviously it's not worthwhile to tip someone who hasn't eased your journey, but do reward those drivers, guides, and hotel staff who go out of their way to make your stay an enjoyable one. A driver or guide who's been with you an entire day will be most grateful for an extra Rs 200 to Rs 300.

Tipping is but one strain of India's all-pervasive *baksheesh* system, which is apparently an accepted means of distributing wealth to the lower echelons of society. As a foreigner, you will be regarded as wealthy, and your endless charity is almost expected by those who are less fortunate. It's therefore an excellent idea to always keep a stash of Rs 10 notes in an easy-to-access pocket, so that you can hand cash to the person who has just carried your bags or given you an unsolicited tour or looked after your shoes (the list is endless), and is now hanging around hopefully. Occasionally, someone will bluntly demand *baksheesh,* which is the same term that may be used by beggars, religious mendicants, and barefoot children looking for a handout. You are not obliged to pay anything, of course, but your conscience and irritation level will probably sway you either way. *Tip:* In Hindu temples, priests will happily encourage you to hand over huge sums of cash, often insisting that the money is for the poor. Be wary of such scams, and bear in mind that many temple officials have grown wealthy on charity intended for the poor.

TOILETS Use only toilets in your hotel, in reputable restaurants, shopping malls, airports, and other modern-looking institutional buildings. Tales of toilet horror stories may be exaggerated to some extent, but there's no point exposing yourself to potential shock. If you do feel compelled to use a "local" or traditional toilet, be prepared by carrying toilet paper, as its use is not the norm among the vast majority of the population. However, toilet paper is a major contribution to environmental devastation and, by all accounts, the use of water rather than paper (which often cannot be flushed down the system) is more hygienic and environmentally friendly. If you're unsure of toilet etiquette in any place, simply ask.

VISAS See the planning chapter.

VISITOR INFORMATION India Tourism is going all out to seduce international visitors, and has fairly extensive representation around the globe. Access its **website** (www.incredibleindia.org) for general information, but be aware that some pages may be out of date or permanently under construction. The websites do offer links to all of India's regional tourism departments, some of which provide fantastic coverage of what's on offer.

India Tourism offices may be found worldwide as follows. In the **U.S.:** 3550 Wilshire Blvd., Room 204, Los Angeles, CA 90010, ✆ **213/380-8855;** and Suite 1808, 1270 Avenue of the Americas, New York, NY 10020, ✆ **212/586-4901.** In the **U.K.:** 7 Cork St., London W1X 3LN; ✆ **020/7437-3677.** In **Canada:** 60 Bloor St. (W), Suite 1003, Toronto, Ontario M4W 3B8; ✆ **416/962-3787.** In **Australia:** Level 5, 135 King St., Glasshouse Shopping Complex, Sydney, NSW 2000; ✆ **2/9221-9555.**

You can access up-to-the-minute news and stories through the websites of some of the country's largest English dailies, including **http://timesofindia.indiatimes. com, www.hindustantimes.com, www. expressindia.com,** and **www.hindu.com,** as well as Mumbai-based **www.dnaindia. com.** For up-to-date news from the two premier English-language 24/7 news channels, and updates on Bollywood movies, visit **www.ndtv.com** or **http://ibnlive.in. com;** for travel-related information and features, visit **www.outlooktraveller.com.**

WATER Refer to the section on "Health" in the planning chapter for full details on the dangers of using tap water in India.

INDEX

See also Accommodations index, below.